Twenty Questions
An Introduction to Philosophy

Twenty Questions
An Introduction to Philosophy

G. Lee Bowie
Mount Holyoke College

Meredith W. Michaels
Hampshire College

Robert C. Solomon
University of Texas at Austin

Under the general editorship of Robert J. Fogelin
Dartmouth College

HBJ **Harcourt Brace Jovanovich, Publishers**

San Diego   New York   Chicago   Austin   Washington, D.C.
London   Sydney   Tokyo   Toronto

Preface

This book is the product of many years of teaching successful introductory philosophy courses. By "successful courses" we mean courses that engage and sustain the students' attention in genuine philosophical activity. We have tried to re-create here some of the elements that have made for success in the classroom.

First, we have included a large number of "classic" philosophical texts, both old and new. Philosophy builds heavily on its own tradition, and the introductory student profits from joining in that tradition. However, philosophers are not the only people who address philosophical questions. The student will also find here pieces on philosophical themes written by scientists, novelists, journalists, political activists, poets, religious figures, economists, and others. We are, along with Socrates, convinced that philosophical questions permeate so-called ordinary life. Students benefit from, and appreciate, the philosophical reflections of those outside the philosophical profession.

Second, in assembling the selections we have kept in mind that while most traditional philosophers are white males, many students are not. Students need to know that people like them sometimes do philosophy. We have made sure that women writers and issues are well represented throughout the book; we have also made an effort to include works of nonwhite writers.

We have arranged the selections in each chapter in a way that creates a natural philosophical conversation from the beginning of the chapter to the end. In many cases this order is antichronological. For example, in the chapter on death, the article by Thomas Nagel precedes the one by Plato because Nagel poses some questions that Plato can be seen as responding to. Instructors will certainly want to take liberties with our arrangements and create "conversations" that are different from the ones we envisaged. Other instructors may wish to gather material from several chapters into groupings that are quite different from what we thought natural. We believe that the design of the book allows a fairly full range for the expression of idiosyncrasy.

Because we have been so concerned to include historical and contemporary material from both philosophical and nontraditional sources, this is a large book. Consequently, there is enormous flexibility in the design of a course that uses this book. One could diverge from the intention of the authors and teach a course entirely from historical materials. A course could focus on women writers. A course might be constructed very traditionally, or it might achieve eccentricity of truly epic proportions. There is no substitute in the classroom for the instructor's enthusiasm for the material; to make that enthusiasm possible, we have offered a broad range of options.

Because this book draws from such a range of sources, it has been in the process of revision since it began. This process will continue, and for the book to be improved by use, we hope that instructors will pass on to us their complaints, their praise, and especially their suggestions.

A number of people have helped us enormously with the creation of this book. Early on, we received important help from Phyllis Green, Sarah Heegaard, and Beth Ryan. As the project got going, Anna May Dion, Colleen Nolan, and especially Maura Colbert were instrumental in researching and preparing the manuscript. Kathleen Higgins was helpful both in conceiving and in carrying out the plan for the book. Grace Rose graciously loaned us some sources that were particularly difficult to find. Gail Davidson was extraordinarily helpful in the selection of the artwork, on which Lee Badger and Reid Badger also gave some selective but critical advice. We would also like to thank Kisor Kuman Chakrabarti, Winona State University, and William C. Gay, University of North Carolina at Charlotte, for their reviews of the book.

A number of people whom we worked with at Harcourt Brace Jovanovich nurtured and developed this project. Bill McLane liked the initial idea and was willing to nurse it along. Cindy Robinson worked unstintingly on the artwork and Eleanor Garner on the permissions. Kathy Walker read every word at least twice. Her combination of competence and congeniality made the production of the book not only possible but also pleasurable. Our thanks also to Cheryl Solheid, Designer; Dee Salisbury, Production Editor; and Lynn Edwards, Production Manager. Finally, we want to thank our thousands of former students; both their enthusiastic responses and their blank looks have made this book far better than it otherwise might have been.

G. L. B.
M. W. M.
R. C. S.

Contents

Part
TWO

Science, Mind, and Nature

3
What Does Science Tell Me About the World?   /   72

4
Which Should I Believe: Darwin or Genesis?   /   124

5
How Is My Mind Connected to My Body?   /   169

Part

THREE

Thinking and Knowing

6

What Do I Know? / 206

7

How Does My Brain Think? / 242

8

Does Language Make Me Think the Way I Do? / 283

Part
FOUR

The Dilemmas of Personhood

9
Who Am I? / 326

10
How Are My Emotions Important to Me? / 364

11
How Should I Feel about Abortion? / 400

Part
FIVE

Living a Good Life

Part

SIX

Justice and Responsibility

18
Am I Free to Choose What I Do? / 672

19
What Do I Justly Deserve? / 706

20
How Should I Make Money? / 738

Twenty Questions

An Introduction to Philosophy

Introduction

At certain times in your life, you have undoubtedly stumbled across a peculiar sort of question, a question for which you haven't got a straightforward answer, a question that provokes head-scratching or that leaves you feeling slightly out of sorts. Suppose that you are sitting outdoors with a friend on a beautiful spring day. Both of you are looking up at the sky. "Isn't the sky amazingly blue today?" remarks your friend. "Yes," you respond, but just as you answer, a problem occurs to you. *How do you know that you and your friend are seeing the same color?* Well, your friend is seeing blue, and you are seeing blue, so doesn't that settle it? Not really, for now you can push the question further. Even if you both use the word 'blue' to *describe* what you see, it's still possible that what you see is not what your friend sees. At this point you may begin to get a headache (and not from looking at the sky) and turn your attention to a more manageable question, such as "Is it time for lunch?" Indeed, one of the characteristics of the peculiar question about the color of the sky (the "Color Question") is precisely that it seems so unmanageable. How would one go about trying to answer a question such as that?

All of us have well-developed strategies for answering most questions. If you want to know whether it is time for lunch, you check your watch. If you haven't got a watch, you ask someone who does. If nobody around has a watch, you call the operator, find a sundial, or decide that no matter what the actual time is, you'll follow the dictates of your stomach. (This last point shows that we also have a sense of when to give up.) But in the case of the Color Question, it is simply not clear what strategy you ought to adopt in attempting to answer it. It's tempting to give up before you even begin.

If the Color Question isn't one that has crossed your mind, perhaps you'll find this one more familiar. Imagine that you have spent the day chasing down various pieces of paper that are required for you to register for your classes. After standing in one line for twenty minutes, you are told that you belong in another line. After filling out four green cards, it turns out that you were supposed to fill out yellow cards. After gathering all your course books at the bookstore, you discover that they don't accept checks. After waiting for your chance to order a sandwich, you are informed that there is no more bread. After carefully choosing your courses, your advisor tells you that three of them are closed. Returning home, you think to yourself, "What a useless day. What was the purpose of standing in all those lines? Nothing works out. I'm like a rat in a maze, running crazily around chasing its tail. In fact, *what is the point, the purpose of life? What does it all mean?*" Most of the time, we just

1

do what we do, content to believe that the purpose in buttering the bread is simply to make it taste better. We don't then ask, *but what is the point in making it taste better?* But sometimes, when we are particularly frustrated or defeated in our attempts to perform ordinary activities, those activities appear in a different light. They appear futile, disconnected from the particular purposes they are designed to serve. Since they fail to achieve their immediate purposes, it is not surprising that the purposes themselves begin to look futile, utterly lacking in meaning. That is when the "Life Question" is likely to strike.

If the Color Question appears unmanageable, then the Life Question, being the biggest question of all, seems even less likely to yield to our ordinary strategies. Where would you begin to answer it? How would you know that you were making progress toward an answer? How would you know whether you had arrived at an answer? Perhaps the strangest thing about these peculiar questions is that they are clearly important and fundamental questions, even *profound* questions, and yet it is equally clear that people are expected to lead their lives without answering them, indeed, without giving them more than a passing glance.

There are some people, however, who take these and other questions like them very seriously. Socrates, one of the earliest Western philosophers, said, "The unexamined life is not worth living." As we all know, to examine something is to look at it very carefully. Of course, we can't look at life in the same way we look at a virus under a microscope. In the case of life itself, there is more to it than meets the eye. The process of examination, then, involves thinking about different aspects of life, focusing now on the color of the sky and later, for example, on the existence of God or the importance of truthtelling. Socrates is suggesting that there is something wrong with a life that does not subject itself to scrutiny, at least from time to time. While his claim doesn't provide an answer to the questions we've been considering, it does suggest that we forge on in our attempt to answer them. That is precisely what he did, and what philosophers since then have done.

There are as many ways of thinking about these questions as there are philosophers. What unifies philosophers as a group, and philosophy as a field of study, is the belief that these questions deserve systematic attention. As a result, philosophy is a discipline that seeks to provide strategies for answering these questions, for seeing how they are related to one another and to our more ordinary beliefs and values. For example, if you believe that there is a god, then your answer to the Life Question might be quite different from that of a person who doesn't.

There is no one strategy that appeals to every philosopher. Different strategies yield different answers and different answers inevitably lead to new questions. Some philosophers think that some questions, the Life Question being a good example, are so general and vague as to be meaningless. In fact, a favorite strategy of some philosophers is to show that something that looks like a question really isn't. It is like going to the doctor, only to discover that your symptoms are psychosomatic. You thought that you were sick, but you really aren't. Or, if you are sick, your illness is not at all what you thought it was. Other philosophers believe that most philosophical questions are really about language. They might try to answer the Color Question by urging us to consider the way in which we use words such as 'blue.' If you and your friend always use the word in the same way, then there is no further interesting fact about whether what the two of you see is the same or not.

As you read through this book and discuss the issues it raises in class, you will begin to discover that you have certain philosophical inclinations. You will find the strategies of some philosophers congenial or persuasive. You will undoubtedly find, too, that some of them seem to you to miss the point, or to avoid it by distracting us with another issue. Sometimes, you will simply find that the question being considered isn't terribly pressing to you at the moment. People have philosophical preferences just as they have preferences for other things. Some people, for example, are particularly interested in ethical questions (see Chapters 13, 15, 19, and 20) because such questions are closely connected to choices that all of us have to make every day. Although these ethical choices may not be very serious, even the decision of whether or not to skip class has ethical consequences!

Other people are drawn to questions that never explicitly arise in the course of ordinary experience (except when they're doing philosophy), but which nevertheless underlie and inform our ways of thinking about that experience. You can get through the day without having to question whether your mind is something over and above your brain (Chapters 5 and 7). You can't, however, get through the day without there being some relationship between your mind and your brain. Philosophy permits you to think seriously and systematically about the nature of that relationship.

As you may have noticed, Socrates' claim about the importance of looking at the "inside" of life is itself a philosophical claim. After you have had a chance to do some philosophical thinking, you will be able to decide whether you think that he was right. You might even develop some good reasons for thinking that he was wrong. If so, Socrates would have been proud of you. Showing that a great philosopher is mistaken can be an enormously gratifying experience.

Some Advice about Studying Philosophy and Using This Book

Philosophy is notoriously difficult. Philosophers use an array of unfamiliar concepts and don't always do a good job of letting us know what they mean by those concepts. Also, in their attempt to be logical and rigorous, they sometimes leave out such things as examples, cases, and stories that might help us to judge whether or not we are following their reasoning. Nevertheless, when you read philosophy, always begin by trying to understand a philosopher on his or her own terms. Remember that no matter how strange what you are reading appears to be, it was written by an ordinary human being with a mind roughly like your own. You simply need to accustom yourself to seeing the world from the perspective of another person whose central concerns, at least initially, appear to be very different from your own. Once you've climbed inside the head of a philosopher, it is much easier to see the world in his or her particular way. Doing so doesn't mean that you will like what you see, nor does it involve adopting that way of seeing as your own, but it does give you a better chance of being able to understand and evaluate what you read.

To help you make that first step into a philosopher's world, this book presents a bit of biographical information at the beginning of each essay or story. Be sure to read it before you plunge into the text. Remember, if someone lived from 1596 to 1650, then he is not going to be worried about nuclear war, nor will he have heard of robots or the Equal Rights Amendment. It may well be, however, that what he does have to say will help you to understand the philosophical issues raised by these and other phenomena of the world in which you live.

In addition to the biographical information provided for each author, each section of this book has an introduction that is designed to give you both an idea of the questions that section explores and some sense of what each author included in that section is trying to accomplish. Since these introductions attempt to situate philosophical questions in a setting that is familiar to you, it is a good idea to read them carefully before you read the selections themselves. Remember, too, that rereading the introductions may help you to reorient yourself if you begin to get lost midway through a difficult essay.

Finally, you will notice that not every selection in this book is written by a philosopher. It also contains fiction, scientific writing, newspaper articles, and essays from popular magazines. By setting strictly philosophical writing in a more familiar context, this book allows you to see the ways in which philosophy creeps into ordinary life. It also allows you to see that people other than philosophers are capable of great philosophical insight (and sometimes are more fun to read!).

Long after you've finished this course, you may find yourself reading an article in the newspaper and saying "Hmmm . . . I wonder what Plato would say about this." Philosophy is everywhere, once you learn how to recognize it. An introductory philosophy course is designed to show you how to do just that.

Part
ONE

Religion and the Meaning of Life

1

How Do I Know that God Exists?

Your most important philosophical belief, the one that provides the framework for almost all of your other beliefs and that determines so much of your attitude toward life, is your belief (or lack of belief) in a Supreme Being, an Almighty God who not only created the universe but still watches over it with affection and concern. To believe in God is to never feel alone or abandoned. It is a ground for lifelong optimism, the confidence that "everything will turn out for the best." It is to have a basic explanation for the way things are, especially the existence of the universe. Not to believe in God is to give up this sense of security, to lose that ground for optimism, and for some people, this opens the way to metaphysical despair and a sense of cosmic loneliness. It is to leave the question, Why is there something rather than nothing? without an answer. Science might explain how things are and even how they got that way, but not even the best science can make a crack in the ultimate metaphysical question, Why does the universe exist at all?

Belief in God, however, is not so much an ultimate explanation as it is an inspiration. It has inspired some of the most beautiful poetry, art, and music and some of the greatest human achievements, as well as some of the bloodiest civil wars and most complex philosophies. Different societies seem to believe in God in different ways and they believe different things about Him. They may even believe in different Gods. Protracted wars have been fought over such technical theological questions as whether God, the Son, and the Holy Ghost are in fact one or three. The Old and New Testaments present significantly different portraits of God: as a wrathful and jealous God in the former and as a thoroughly merciful and loving God in the latter. The God of the Old Testament destroys cities, has disobedient messengers swallowed by whales, and tests the faith of His believers by making them suffer (as in the story of Job). The God of the New Testament sacrifices his only son for your salvation. How are disputes about the true nature of God to be settled? How do you know what to believe in? How do you know that God exists?

The problem is that belief in God does not seem to rest on any particular foundation. Most likely, you were raised with that belief, taught it as a child, and encouraged in it as you grew to maturity. You were taken to church and naturally came to assume that the deity to which everyone referred, and to whom you yourself had often prayed, existed. But what is the evidence for that belief? How can you prove that your natural assumption is justified? A few people have actually had God speak to them, but they are few and far between and are not always the most reliable witnesses. One popular proof of God's existence is the fact that the Bible tells us, over and over again, about God. But the problem is that appealing to the Bible as evidence of God's existence presupposes just that sort of belief that is at issue, a logical fallacy often called "begging the question." Believing in God and believing that the Bible is the revealed word of God are two aspects of one and the same belief, and one cannot be used to prove the other.

You may have "felt" God's presence, but feelings, too, must be justified, for sometimes they can be misleading. Sometimes you sense danger when there is no danger, and in the same way it is possible to have a religious feeling without that proving that the feeling refers to anything outside of you. Indeed, the very nature of God, according to many theorists and theologians, is such that He "transcends" the world and is outside of our experience. God cannot be seen or sensed as such and that is why it is necessary to *believe in* Him. If He could simply be presented to us, like a statue or a missing person, such a powerful notion of belief would not be necessary.

A different way of putting the same point is to say that believing in God is a matter of *faith* and not a matter of knowledge. But many believers have refused to accept the idea that this most important belief is not part of our knowledge in the strongest sense. How can our most important belief not also be the best known? Accordingly, much of the history of theology has been devoted to the project of *proving* God's existence. The idea is not to replace faith or undermine the need to believe, but to supplement faith and belief with a demonstration that they are indeed justified and based on knowledge of the most secure kind.

Numerous such arguments or proofs have been presented throughout the history of philosophy, but the three most popular arguments for God's existence are the **ontological, cosmological**, and **teleological** proofs. The ontological argument, originated by Saint Anselm in the twelfth century, is a deductive proof that proceeds from the premise that God is (by definition) the being greater than whom none other can be conceived, with the conclusion that God therefore *must* exist. The cosmological argument has appeared in many versions, and Saint Thomas Aquinas presents several of them in his famous "Five Ways" (of proving God's existence). What they all share is the inference from the existence of some imperfect, merely contingent being (for example, ourselves) to the existence of a necessary being, namely God.

The teleological argument is different in that it begins with a very complex and detailed observation: the marvelous complexity and harmony of the world. You have possibly had such an awe-filled experience, for instance, when observing the wonderful array of exotic fish in an aquarium. You may have even said at the time that the variety of life is a miraculous thing and evidence of God's great creativity. This is the essence of the teleological argument, the hypothesis that such a complex, varied, and workable world could not be the product of chance but must have been the creation of an intelligent, powerful creator, namely God. An analogy, suggested in a classic work by William Paley, is this: walking along a deserted beach, you find a watch in the sand. Now, it is barely possible, but highly unlikely, that the wind and surf had pounded together pieces of sand until they happened to take the form of this intricate piece of machinery. It is much more likely, however, that the watch was made by a watchmaker and dropped in the sand by some passerby whom you have not seen. So too, it may be imaginable that the world as we know it came into existence quite by accident, but it seems much more plausible to assume that it was intelligently created by God.

These three arguments have met with considerable criticism, often from critics who are themselves devout. The ontological proof has been revised and updated many times using the most sophisticated techniques available in logic. The cosmological proof also gets revised with each new development in cosmology. Old inferences are discarded and new, improved steps take their place. The teleological argument was often lampooned as soon as it appeared, for example, by the German aphorist Lichtenberg, who sarcastically commented that it certainly was convenient that God put slits in cats' skin right where their eyes were, and by Voltaire, who noted in his novel *Candide* that it was good of God to give us noses, for otherwise, how would we wear spectacles? The most protracted and devastating criticism of the teleological argument, however, was offered by David Hume in his *Dialogues on Natural Religion,* which were so blasphemous that he dared not publish them in his own lifetime.

There have been many believers and philosophers, however, who rejected the entire project of trying to prove that God exists. They see nothing wrong with insisting that belief in God is a matter of faith and not knowledge. Indeed, they insist that the importance of belief in God rests on exactly that, for if we could really prove God's existence, faith would be superfluous. Perhaps the most single powerful argument of this sort appeared in the mid-nineteenth century in the works of Soren Kierkegaard, a Danish philosopher who was extremely devout but also rejected the modernization of religion. In this century, the American philosopher William James also argued that what was important about religious belief was not so much its contribution to knowledge as its role in making our lives happy and fulfilled. And finally, many contemporary philosophers insist that belief in God is not the sort of belief that can be proven or disproven, but that is no argument against it. Belief in God may be sufficiently important in our lives that questions of proof are secondary.

Saint Anselm
The Ontological Argument

Saint Anselm *(1033–1109), Archbishop of Canterbury, was one of the main opponents of the then antiintellectualism of the church. He is best known for his* Monologion *and his* Proslogion, *in which the ontological argument is developed.*

Truly there is a God, although the fool hath said in his heart, There is no God.

*A*nd so, Lord, do thou, who dost give understanding to faith, give me, so far as thou knowest it to be profitable, to understand that thou art as we believe; and that thou art that which we believe. And, indeed, we believe that thou art a being than which nothing greater can be conceived. Or is there no such nature, since the fool hath said in his heart, there is no God? (Psalms xiv. 1). But, at any rate, this very fool, when he hears of this being of which I speak— a being than which nothing greater can be conceived—understands what he hears, and what he understands is in his understanding; although he does not understand it to exist.

For, it is one thing for an object to be in the understanding, and another to understand that the object exists. When a painter first conceives of what he will afterwards perform, he has it in his understanding, but he does not yet understand it to be, because he has not yet performed it. But after he has made the painting, he both has it in his understanding, and he understands that it exists, because he has made it.

Hence, even the fool is convinced that something exists in the understanding, at least, than which nothing greater can be conceived. For, when he hears of this, he understands it. And whatever is understood, exists in the understanding. And assuredly that, than which nothing greater can be conceived, cannot exist in the understanding alone. For, suppose it exists in the understanding alone: then it can be conceived to exist in reality; which is greater.

Therefore, if that, than which nothing greater can be conceived, exists in the understanding alone, the very being, than which nothing greater can be conceived, is one, than which a greater can be conceived. But obviously this is impossible. Hence, there is no doubt that there exists a being, than which nothing greater can be conceived, and it exists both in the understanding and in reality.

> God cannot be conceived not to exist.—God is that, than which nothing greater can be conceived.—That which can be conceived not to exist is not God.

And it assuredly exists so truly, that it cannot be conceived not to exist. For, it is possible to conceive of a being which cannot be conceived not to exist; and this is greater than one which can be conceived not to exist. Hence, if that, than which nothing greater can be conceived, can be conceived not to exist, it is not that, than which nothing greater can be conceived. But this is an irreconcilable contradiction. There is, then, so truly a being than which nothing greater can be conceived to exist, that it cannot even be conceived not to exist; and this being thou art, O Lord, our God.

So truly, therefore, dost thou exist, O Lord, my God, that thou canst not be conceived not to exist; and rightly. For, if a mind could conceive of a being better than thee, the creature would rise above the Creator; and this is most absurd. And, indeed, whatever else there is, except thee alone, can be conceived not to exist. To thee alone, therefore, it belongs to exist more truly than all other beings, and hence in a higher degree than all others. For, whatever else exists does not exist so truly, and hence in a less degree it belongs to it to exist. Why, then, has the fool said in his heart, there is no God (Psalms xiv. 1), since it is so evident, to a rational mind, that thou dost exist in the highest degree of all? Why, except that he is dull and a fool?

> How the fool has said in his heart what cannot be conceived.—A thing may be conceived in two ways: (1) when the word signifying it is conceived; (2) when the thing itself is understood. As far as the word goes, God can be conceived not to exist; in reality he cannot.

But how has the fool said in his heart what he could not conceive; or how is it that he could not conceive what he said in his heart? since it is the same to say in the heart, and to conceive.

But, if really, nay, since really, he both conceived, because he said in his heart; and did not say in his heart, because he could not conceive; there is more than one way in which a thing is said in the heart or conceived. For, in one sense, an object is conceived, when the word signifying it is conceived; and in another, when the very entity, which the object is, is understood.

In the former sense, then, God can be conceived not to exist; but in the latter, not at all. For no one who understands what fire and water are can conceive fire to be water, in accordance with the nature of the facts themselves, although this is possible according to the words. So, then, no one who understands what God is can conceive that God does not exist; although he says these words in his heart, either without any, or with some foreign, signification. For, God is that than which a greater cannot be conceived. And he who thoroughly understands this, assuredly understands that this being so truly exists, that not even in concept can it be non-existent. Therefore, he who understands that God so exists, cannot conceive that he does not exist.

I thank thee, gracious Lord, I thank thee; because what I formerly believed by thy bounty, I now so understand by thine illumination, that if I were unwilling to believe that thou dost exist, I should not be able not to understand this to be true.

Saint Thomas Aquinas
Whether God Exists

Saint Thomas Aquinas *(1225–1274) was the architect of the most comprehensive theological structure of the Roman Catholic Church, the* Summa Theologica. *It has long been recognized as the "official" statement of orthodox Christian beliefs by many theologians. Aquinas borrowed many of his arguments from Aristotle, as can be seen in his "five ways" of demonstrating God's existence.*

Ojection 1. It seems that God does not exist; because if one of two contraries be infinite, the other would be altogether destroyed. But the word "God" means that He is infinite goodness. If, therefore, God existed, there would be no evil discoverable; but there is evil in the world. Therefore God does not exist.

Obj. 2. Further, it is superfluous to suppose that, what can be accounted for by a few principles has been produced by many. But it seems that everything that appears in the world can be accounted for by other principles, supposing God did not exist. For all natural things can be reduced to one principle, which is nature; and all things that happen intentionally can be reduced to one principle, which is human reason, or will. Therefore there is no need to suppose God's existence.

On the contrary, It is said in the person of God: *I am Who am* (Exod. iii. 14).

I answer that, The existence of God can be proved in five ways.

The first and more manifest way is the argument from motion. It is certain and evident to our senses that some things are in motion. Whatever is in motion is moved by another, for nothing can be in motion except it have a potentiality for that towards which it is being moved; whereas a thing moves inasmuch as it is in act. By "motion" we mean nothing else than the reduction of something from a state of potentiality into a state of actuality. Nothing, however, can be reduced from a state of potentiality into a state of actuality unless by something already in a state of actuality. Thus, that which is actually hot as fire, makes wood, which is potentially hot, to be actually hot, and thereby moves and changes it. It is not possible that the same thing should be at once in a state of actuality and potentiality from the same point of view, but only from different points of view. What is actually hot cannot simultaneously be only potentially hot; still, it is simultaneously potentially cold. It is therefore impossible that from the same point of view and in the same way anything should be both moved and mover, or that it should move itself. Therefore, whatever is in motion must be put in motion by another. If that by which it is put in motion be itself put in motion, then this also must needs be put in motion by another, and that by another again. This cannot go on to infinity, because then there would be no first mover, and, consequently, no other mover—seeing that subsequent movers only move inasmuch as they are put in motion by the first mover; as the staff only moves because it is put in motion by the hand. Therefore it is necessary to arrive at a First Mover, put in motion by no other; and this everyone understands to be God.

The second way is from the formality of efficient causation. In the world of sense we find there is an order of efficient causation. There is no case known (neither is it, indeed, possible) in which a thing is found to be the efficient cause of itself; for so it would be prior to itself, which is impossible. In efficient causes it is not possible to go on to infinity, because in all efficient causes following in order the first is the cause of the intermediate cause, and the intermediate is the cause of the ultimate cause, whether the intermediate cause be several, or one only. To take away the cause is to take away the effect. Therefore, if there be no first cause among efficient causes, there will be no ultimate cause, nor any intermediate. If in efficient causes it is possible to go on to infinity, there will be no first efficient cause, neither will there be an ultimate effect, nor any intermediate efficient causes; all of which is plainly false. Therefore it is necessary to put forward a First Efficient Cause, to which everyone gives the name of God.

The third way is taken from possibility and necessity, and runs thus: We find in nature things that could either exist or not exist, since they are found to be generated, and then to corrupt; and, consequently, they can exist, and then not exist. It is impossible for these always to exist, for that which can one day cease to exist must at some time have not existed. Therefore, if everything could cease to exist, then at one time there could have been nothing in existence. If this were true, even now there would be nothing in existence, because that which does not exist only begins to exist by something already existing. Therefore, if at one time nothing was in existence, it would have been impossible for anything to have begun to exist; and thus even now nothing would be in existence—which is absurd. Therefore, not all beings are merely possible, but there must exist something the existence of which is necessary. Every necessary thing either has its necessity caused by another, or not. It is impossible to go on to infinity in necessary things which have their necessity caused by another, as has been already proved in regard to efficient causes. Therefore we cannot but postulate the existence of some being having of itself its own necessity, and not receiving it from another, but rather causing in others their necessity. This all men speak of as God.

The fourth way is taken from the gradation to be found in things. Among beings there are some more and some less good, true, noble, and the like. But "more" and "less" are predicated of different things, according as they resemble in their different ways something which is in the degree of "most," as a thing is said to be hotter according as it more nearly resembles that which is hottest; so that there is something which is truest, something best, something noblest, and, consequently, something which is uttermost being; for the truer things are, the more truly they exist. What is most complete in any genus is the cause of all in that genus; as fire, which is the most complete form of heat, is the cause whereby all things are made hot. Therefore there must also be something which is to all beings the cause of their being, goodness, and every other perfection; and this we call God.

The fifth way is taken from the governance of the world; for we see that things which lack intelligence, such as natural bodies, act for some purpose, which fact is evident from their acting always, or nearly always, in the same way, so as to obtain the best result. Hence it is plain that not fortuitously, but designedly, do they achieve their purpose. Whatever lacks intelligence cannot fulfil some purpose, unless it be directed by some being endowed with intelligence and knowledge; as the arrow is shot to its mark by the archer. Therefore some intelligent being exists by whom all natural things are ordained towards a definite purpose; and this being we call God.

*Reply Obj.*1. As Augustine says: *Since God is wholly good, He would not allow any evil to exist in His works, unless His omnipotence and goodness were such as to bring good even out of evil.* This is part of the infinite goodness of God, that He should allow evil to exist, and out of it produce good.

Reply Obj. 2. Since nature works out its determinate end under the direction of a higher agent, whatever is done by nature must needs be traced back to God, as to its first cause. So also whatever is done designedly must also be traced back to some higher cause other than human reason or will, for these can suffer change and are defective; whereas things capable of motion and of defect must be traced back to an immovable and self-necessary first principle.

William Paley

The Teleological Argument

William Paley (1743–1805) was an English theologian and moral philosopher. He believed that the miracles on which Christianity is based are genuine. He regarded the parts of nature as mechanisms that form the basis of the argument from design, which he developed in his Natural Theology.

STATE OF THE ARGUMENT

*I*n crossing a heath, suppose I pitched my foot against a *stone,* and were asked how the stone came to be there, I might possibly answer, that for any thing I knew to the contrary it had lain there for ever; nor would it, perhaps, be very easy to show the absurdity of this answer. But suppose I had found a *watch* upon the ground, and it should be inquired how the watch happened to be in that place, I should hardly think of the answer which I had before given, that for any thing I knew the watch might have always been there. Yet why should not this answer serve for the watch as well as for the stone; why is it not as admissible in the second case as in the first? For this reason, and for no other, namely, that when we come to inspect the watch, we perceive—what we could not discover in the stone—that its several parts are framed and put together for a purpose, *e.g.* that they are so formed and adjusted as to produce motion, and that motion so regulated as to point out the hour of the day; that if the different parts had been differently shaped from what they are, or placed after any other manner or in any other order than that in which they are placed, either no motion at all would have been carried on in the machine, or none which would have answered the use that is now served by it. To reckon up a few of the plainest of these parts and of their offices, all tending to one result: We see a cylindrical box containing a coiled elastic spring, which, by its endeavor to relax itself, turns round the box. We next observe a flexible chain—artificially wrought for the sake of flexure—communicating the action of the spring from the box to the fusee. We then find a series of wheels, the teeth of which catch in and apply to each other, conducting the motion from the fusee to the balance and from the balance to the pointer, and at the same time, by the size and shape of those wheels, so regulating that motion as to terminate in causing an index, by an equable and measured progression, to pass over a given space in a given time. We take notice that the wheels are made of brass, in order to keep them from rust; the springs of steel, no other metal being so elastic; that over the face of the watch there is placed a glass, a material employed in no other part of the work, but in the room of which, if there had been any other than a transparent substance, the hour could not be seen without opening the case. This mechanism being observed—it requires indeed an examination of the instrument, and perhaps some previous knowledge of the subject, to perceive and understand it; but being once, as we have said, observed and understood, the inference we think is inevitable, that the watch must have had a maker—that there must have existed, at some time and at some place or other, an artificer or artificers who formed it for the purpose which we find it actually to answer, who comprehended its construction and designed its use.

I. Nor would it, I apprehend, weaken the conclusion, that we had never seen a watch made—that we had never known an artist capable of making one—that we were altogether incapable of executing such a piece of workmanship ourselves, or of understanding in what manner it was performed; all this being no more than what is true of some exquisite remains of ancient art, of some lost arts, and, to the generality of mankind, of the more curious productions of modern manufacture. Does one man in a million know how oval frames are turned? Ignorance of this kind exalts our opinion of the unseen and unknown artist's skill, if he be unseen and unknown, but raises no doubt in our minds of the existence and agency of such an artist, at some former time and in some place or other. Nor can I perceive that it varies at all the inference, whether the question arise concerning a human agent or concerning an agent of a different species, or an agent possessing in some respects a different nature.

II. Neither, secondly, would it invalidate our conclusion, that the watch sometimes went wrong, or that it seldom went exactly right. The purpose of the machinery, the design, and the designer might be evident, and in the case supposed, would be evident in whatever way we accounted for the irregularity of the movement, or whether we could account for it or not. It is not necessary that a machine be perfect, in order to show with what design it was made: still less necessary, where the only question is whether it were made with any design at all.

III. Nor, thirdly, would it bring any uncertainty into the argument, if there were a few parts of the watch, concerning which we could not discover or had not yet discovered in what manner they conduced to the general effect; or even some parts, concerning which we could not ascertain whether they conduced to that effect in any manner whatever. For, as to the first branch of the case, if by the loss, or disorder, or decay of the parts in question, the movement of the watch were found in fact to be stopped, or disturbed, or retarded, no doubt would remain in our minds as to the utility or intention of these parts, although we should be unable to investigate the manner according to which, or the connection by which, the ultimate effect depended upon their action or assistance; and the more complex the machine, the more likely is this obscurity to arise. Then, as to the second thing supposed, namely, that there were parts which might be spared without prejudice to the movement of the watch, and that we had proved this by experiment, these superfluous parts, even if we were completely assured that they were such, would not vacate the reasoning which we had instituted concerning other parts. The indication of contrivance remained, with respect to them, nearly as it was before.

IV. Nor, fourthly, would any man in his senses think the existence of the watch with its various machinery accounted for, by being told that it was one out of possible combinations of material forms; that whatever he had found in the place where he found the watch, must have contained some internal configuration or other; and that this configuration might be the structure now exhibited, namely, of the works of a watch, as well as a different structure.

V. Nor, fifthly, would it yield his inquiry more satisfaction, to be answered that there existed in things a principle of order, which had disposed the parts of the watch into their present form and situation. He never knew a watch made by the principle of order; nor can he even form to himself an idea of what is meant by a principle of order, distinct from the intelligence of the watchmaker.

VI. Sixthly, he would be surprised to hear that the mechanism of the watch was no proof of contrivance, only a motive to induce the mind to think so.

VII. And not less surprised to be informed, that the watch in his hand was nothing more than the result of the laws of *metallic* nature. It is a perversion of language to assign any law as the efficient, operative cause of any thing. A law presupposes an agent; for it is only the mode according to which an agent proceeds: it implies a power; for it is the order according to which that power acts. Without this agent, without this power, which are both distinct from itself, the *law* does nothing, is nothing. The expression, "the law of metallic nature," may sound strange and harsh to a philosophic ear; but it seems quite as justifiable as some others which are more familiar to him, such as "the law of vegetable nature," "the law of animal nature," or, indeed, as "the law of nature" in general, when assigned as the cause of phenomena, in exclusion of agency and power, or when it is substituted into the place of these.

VIII. Neither, lastly, would our observer be driven out of his conclusion or from his confidence in its truth, by being told that he knew nothing at all about the matter. He knows enough for his argument; he knows the utility of the end; he knows the subserviency and adaptation of the means to the end. These points being known, his ignorance of other points, his doubts concerning other points, affect not the certainty of his reasoning. The consciousness of knowing little need not beget a distrust of that which he does know. . . .

APPLICATION OF THE ARGUMENT

Every indication of contrivance, every manifestation of design which existed in the watch, exists in the works of nature, with the difference on the side of nature of being greater and more, and that in a degree which exceeds all computation. I mean, that the contrivances of nature surpass the contrivances of art, in the complexity, subtilty, and curiosity of the mechanism; and still more, if possible, do they go beyond them in number and variety; yet, in a multitude of cases, are not less evidently mechanical, not less evidently contrivances, not less evidently accommodated to their end or suited to their office, than are the most perfect productions of human ingenuity. . . .

David Hume

Why Does God Let People Suffer?

David Hume (1711–1776), *a Scottish philosopher, was refused professorships at the leading universities for his "heresies." Nevertheless, he is regarded as the outstanding genius of British philosophy. In addition to writing a number of influential books, among them* A Treatise of Human Nature, An Inquiry Concerning the Principles of Morals, *and* Dialogues on Natural Religion, *Hume was a much sought-after guest in London, Edinburgh, and Paris.*

*I*n short, I repeat the Question: Is the World, consider'd in general, and as it appears to us in this Life, different from what a Man or such a Limited Being would, *beforehand,* expect from a very powerful, wise, and benevolent Deity? It must be strange Prejudice to assert the contrary. And from thence I conclude, that, however consistent the World may be, allowing certain Suppositions and Conjectures, with the Idea of such a Deity, it can never afford us an Inference concerning his Existence. The Consistence is not absolutely deny'd, only the Inference. Conjectures, especially where Infinity is excluded from the divine Attributes, may, perhaps, be sufficient to prove a Consistence; but can never be foundations for any Inference.

There seem to be *four* Circumstances, on which depend all, or the greatest Part of the Ills, that molest sensible Creatures; and it is not impossible but all these Circumstances may be necessary and unavoidable. We know so little beyond common Life, or even of common Life, that, with regard to the Oeconomy of a Universe, there is no Conjecture, however wild, which may not be just; nor any one, however plausible, which may not be erroneous. All that belongs to human Understanding, in this deep Ignorance and Obscurity, is to be sceptical, or at least cautious; and not to admit of any Hypothesis, whatever; much less, of any which is supported by no Appearance of Probability. Now this I assert to be the Case with regard to all the Causes of Evil, and the Circumstances, on which it depends. None of them appear to human Reason, in the least degree, necessary or unavoidable; nor can we suppose them such, without the utmost Licence of Imagination.

The *first* Circumstance, which introduces Evil, is that Contrivance or Oeconomy of the animal Creation, by which Pains, as well as Pleasures, are employ'd to excite all Creatures to Action, and make them vigilant in the great Work of Self-preservation. Now Pleasure alone, in its various Degrees, seems to human Understanding sufficient for this Purpose. All Animals might be constantly in a State of Enjoyment; but when urg'd by any of the Necessities of Nature, such as Thirst, Hunger, Wearyness; instead of Pain, they might feel a Diminution of Pleasure, by which they might be prompted to seek that Object, which is necessary to their Subsistence. Men pursue Pleasure as eagerly as they avoid Pain; at least, might have been so constituted. It seems, therefore, plainly possible to carry on the Business of Life without any Pain. Why then is any Animal ever render'd susceptible of such a Sensation? If Animals can be free from it an hour, they might enjoy a perpetual Exemption from it; and it requir'd as particular a Contrivance of their Organs to produce that Feeling, as to endow them with Sight, Hearing, or any of the Senses. Shall we conjecture, that such a Contrivance was necessary, without any Appearance of Reason? And shall we build on that Conjecture as on the most certain Truth?

But a Capacity of Pain wou'd not alone produce Pain, were it not for the *second* Circumstance, *viz,* the conducting of the World by general Laws; and this seems no wise necessary to a very perfect Being. It is true; if every thing were conducted by particular Volitions, the Course of Nature wou'd be perpetually broken, and no man cou'd employ his Reason in the Conduct of Life. But might not other particular Volitions remedy this Inconvenience? In short, might not the Deity exterminate all Ill, wherever it were to be found; and produce all Good, without any Preparation or long Progress of Causes and Effects?

Besides, we must consider, that, according to the present Oeconomy of the World, the Course of Nature, tho' suppos'd exactly regular, yet to us appears not so, and many Events are uncertain, and many dissappoint our Expectations. Health and Sickness, Calm and Tempest, with an infinite Number of other Accidents, whose Causes are unknown and variable, have a great Influence both on the Fortunes of particular Persons and on the Prosperity of public Societies: And indeed all human Life, in a manner, depends on such Accidents. A Being, therefore, who knows the secret Springs of the Universe, might easily, by particular Volitions, turn all these Accidents to the Good of Mankind, and render the whole World happy, without discovering himself in any Operation. A Fleet, whose Purposes were Salutary to Society, might always meet with a fair Wind: Good Princes enjoy sound Health and long Life: Persons, born to Power and Authority, be fram'd with good Tempers and virtuous Dispositions. A few such Events as these, regularly and wisely conducted, wou'd change the Face of the World ; and yet wou'd no more seem to disturb the Course of Nature or confound human Conduct, than the present Oeconomy of things, where the Causes are secret, and variable, and compounded. Some small Touches, given to *Caligula's* Brain in his Infancy, might have converted him into a *Trajan*: One Wave, a little higher than the rest, by burying *Caesar* and his Fortune in the bottom of the Ocean, might have restor'd Liberty to a considerable Part of Mankind. There may, for aught we know, be good Reasons, why Providence interposes not in this Manner; but they are unknown to us: And tho' the mere Supposition, that such Reasons exist, may be sufficient to *save* the Conclusion concerning the divine Attributes, yet surely it can never be sufficient to *establish* that Conclusion.

If every thing in the Universe be conducted by general Laws, and if Animals be render'd susceptible of Pain, it scarcely seems possible but some Ill must arise in the various Shocks of Matter, and the various Concurrence and Opposition of general Laws: But this Ill wou'd be very rare, were it not for the *third* Circumstance which I propos'd to mention, *viz*, the great Frugality, with which all Powers and Faculties are distributed to every particular Being. So well adjusted are the Organs and Capacities of all Animals, and so well fitted to their Preservation, that, as far as History or Tradition reaches, there appears not to be any single Species, which has yet been extinguish'd in the Universe. Every Animal has the requisite Endowments; but these Endowments are bestow'd with so scrupulous an Oeconomy, that any considerable Diminution must entirely destroy the Creature. Wherever one Power is encreas'd, there is a proportional Abatement in the others. Animals, which excell in Swiftness, are commonly defective in Force. Those, which possess both, are either imperfect in some of their Senses, or are oppressed with the most craving Wants. The human Species, whose chief Excellency is Reason and Sagacity, is of all others the most necessitous, and the most deficient in bodily Advantages; without Cloaths, without Arms, without Food, without Lodging, without any Convenience of Life, except what they owe to their own Skill and Industry. In short, Nature seems to have form'd an exact Calculation of the Necessities of her Creatures; and like a *rigid Master,* has afforded them little more Powers or Endowments, than what are strictly sufficient to supply those Necessities. An *indulgent Parent* wou'd have bestow'd a large Stock, in order to guard against Accidents, and secure the Happiness and Welfare of the Creature, in the most unfortunate Concurrence of Circumstances. Every Course of Life wou'd not have been so surrounded with Precipices, that the least Departure from the true Path, by Mistake or Necessity, must involve us in Misery and Ruin. Some Reserve, some Fund wou'd have been provided to ensure Happiness; nor wou'd the Powers and the Necessities have been adjusted with so rigid an Oeconomy. The Author of Nature is inconceivably powerful: His Force is suppos'd great, if not altogether inexhaustible: Nor is there any Reason, as far as we can judge, to make him observe this strict Frugality in his Dealings with his Creatures. It wou'd have been better, were his Power extremely limited, to have created fewer Animals, and to have endowed these with more Faculties for their Happiness and Preservation. A Builder is never esteem'd prudent, who undertakes a Plan, beyond what his Stock will enable him to finish.

In order to cure most of the Ills of human Life, I require not that Man should have the Wings of the Eagle, the Swiftness of the Stag, the Force of the Ox, the Arms of the Lion, the Scales of the Crocodile or Rhinoceros; much less do I demand the Sagacity of an Angel or Cherubim. I am contented to take an Encrease in one single Power or Faculty of his Soul. Let him be endow'd with a greater Propensity to Industry and Labor; a more vigorous Spring and Activity of Mind; a more constant Bent to Business and Application. Let the whole Species possess naturally an equal Diligence with that which many Individuals are able to attain by Habit and Reflection; and the most beneficial Consequences, without any Allay of Ill, is the most immediate and necessary Result of this Endowment. Almost all the moral, as well as natural Evils of human Life arise from Idleness; and were our Species, by the original Constitution of their Frame, exempt from this Vice or Infirmity, the perfect Cultivation of Land, the Improvement of Arts and Manufactures, the exact Execution of every Office and Duty, immediately follow; and Men at once may fully reach that State of Society, which is so imperfectly attain'd by the best regulated Government. But as Industry is a Power, and the most valuable of any, Nature seems determin'd, suitably to her usual Maxims, to bestow it on men with a very sparing hand; and rather to punish him severely for his Deficiency in it, than to reward him for his Attainments. She has so contriv'd his Frame, that nothing but the most violent Necessity can oblige him to labor, and she employs all his other Wants to overcome, at least in part, the Want of Diligence, and to endow him with some Share of a Faculty, of which she has thought fit naturally to bereave him. Here our Demands may be allow'd very humble, and therefore the more reasonable. If we requir'd the Endowments of superior Penetration and Judgment, of a more delicate Taste of Beauty, of a nicer Sensibility to Benevolence and Friendship; we might be told, that we impiously pretend to break the Order of Nature, that we want to exalt Ourselves into a higher Rank of Being, that the Presents which we require, not being suitable to our State and Condition, wou'd only be pernicious to us. But it is hard; I dare to repeat it, it is hard, that being plac'd in a World so full of Wants and Necessities; where almost every Being and Element is either our Foe or refuses us their Assistance; we shou'd also have our own Temper to struggle with, and shou'd be depriv'd of that Faculty, which can alone fence against these multiply'd Evils.

The *fourth* Circumstance, whence arises the Misery and Ill of the Universe, is the inaccurate Workmanship of all the Springs and Principles of the great Machine of Nature. It must be acknowledg'd, that there are few Parts of the Universe, which seem not to serve some Purpose, and whose Removal wou'd not produce a visible Defect and Disorder in the Whole. The Parts hang all together; nor can one be touch'd without affecting the rest, in a greater or less degree. But at the same time, it must be observ'd, that none of these Parts or Principles, however useful, are so accurately adjusted, as to keep precisely within those Bounds, in which their Utility consists; but they are, all of them, apt, on every Occasion, to run into the one Extreme or the other. One wou'd imagine, that this grand Production had not receiv'd the last hand of the Maker; so little finish'd is every part, and so coarse are the Strokes, with which it is executed. Thus, the Winds are requisite to convey the Vapours along the Surface of the Globe, and to assist Men in Navigation: But how oft, rising up to Tempests and Hurricanes, do they become pernicious? Rains are necessary to nourish all the Plants and Animals of the Earth: But how often are they defective? how often excessive? Heat is requisite to all Life and Vegetation; but is not always found in the due Proportion. On the Mixture and Secretion of the Humours and Juices of the Body depend the Health and Prosperity of the Animal: But the Parts perform not regularly their proper Function. What more useful than all the Passions of the Mind, Ambition, Vanity, Love, Anger? But how oft do they break their Bounds, and cause the greatest Convulsions in Society? There is nothing so advantageous in the Universe, but what frequently becomes pernicious, by its Excess or Defect; nor has Nature guarded, with the requisite Accuracy, against all Disorder or Confusion. The Irregularity is never, perhaps, so great as to destroy any Species; but is often sufficient to involve the Individuals in Ruin and Misery.

On the Concurrence, then of these *four* Circumstances does all, or the greatest Part of natural Evil depend. Were all living Creatures incapable of Pain, or were the World administer'd by particular Volitions, Evil never cou'd have found Access into the Universe: And were Animals endow'd with a large Stock of Powers and Faculties, beyond what strict Necessity requires; or were the several Springs and Principles of the Universe so accurately fram'd as to preserve always the just Temperament and Medium; there must have been very little Ill in comparison of what we feel at present. What then shall we pronounce on this Occasion? Shall we say, that these Circumstances are not necessary, and that they might easily have been alter'd in the Contrivance of the Universe? This Decision seems too presumptuous for Creatures, so blind and ignorant. Let us be more modest in our Conclusions. Let us allow, that, if the Goodness of the Deity (I mean a Goodness like the human) cou'd be establish'd on any tolerable Reasons *a priori*, these Phænomena, however untoward, wou'd not be sufficient to subvert that Principle; but might easily, in some unknown manner, be reconcilable to it. But let us still assert, that as this Goodness is not antecedently establish'd, but must be inferr'd from the Phænomena, there can be no Grounds for such an Inference, while there are so many Ills in the Universe, and while these Ills might so easily have been remedy'd, as far as human Understanding can be allow'd to judge on such a Subject. I am Sceptic enough to allow, that the bad Appearances, notwithstanding all my Reasonings, may be compatible with such Attributes as you suppose: But surely they can never prove these Attributes. Such a Conclusion cannot result from Scepticism; but must arise from the Phænomena, and from our Confidence in the Reasonings, which we deduce from these Phænomena.

Look round this Universe. What an immense Profusion of Beings, animated and organiz'd, sensible and active! You admire this prodigious Variety and Fecundity. But inspect a little more narrowly these living Existences, the only Beings worth regarding. How hostile and destructive to each other! How insufficient all of them for their own Happiness! How contemptible or odious to the Spectator! The whole presents nothing but the Idea of a blind Nature, impregnated by a great vivifying Principle, and pouring forth from her Lap, without Discernment or parental Care, her maim'd and abortive Children.

Here the *Manichæn* System occurs as a proper Hypothesis to solve the Difficulty: And no doubt, in some respects, it is very specious, and has more Probability than the common Hypothesis, by giving a plausible Account of the strange Mixture of Good and Ill, which appears in Life. But if we consider, on the other hand, the perfect Uniformity and Agreement of the Parts of the Universe, we shall not discover in it any Marks of the Combat of a malevolent with a benevolent Being. There is indeed an Opposition of Pains and Pleasures in the Feelings of sensible Creatures: But are not all the Operations of Nature carry'd on by an Opposition of Principles, of Hot and Cold, Moist and Dry, Light and Heavy? The true Conclusion is, that the original Source of all things is entirely indifferent to all these Principles, and has no more Regard to Good above Ill than to Heat above Cold, or to Drought above Moisture, or to Light above Heavy.

There may *four* Hypotheses be fram'd concerning the first Causes of the Universe; *that* they are endow'd with perfect Goodness, *that* they have perfect Malice, *that* they are opposite and have both Goodness and Malice, *that* they have neither Goodness nor Malice. Mixt Phænomena can never prove the two former unmixt Principles. And the Uniformity and Steadiness of general Laws seem to oppose the third. The fourth, therefore, seems by far the most probable.

Fyodor Dostoevsky

Rebellion

Fyodor Dostoevsky *(1821–1881) was one of the greatest creative artists of the nineteenth century. He was born in Russia, where he lived most of his life. Opposed to the oppressive practices of the government, he was imprisoned for a time in Siberia. His belief in the fundamental evil of human nature permeates his novels, the most famous of which are* The Brothers Karamozov *and* Crime and Punishment.

I meant to speak of the suffering of mankind generally, but we had better confine ourselves to the sufferings of the children. That reduces the scope of my argument to a tenth of what it would be. Still we'd better keep to the children, though it does weaken my case. But, in the first place, children can be loved even at close quarters, even when they are dirty, even when they are ugly (I fancy, though, children never are ugly). The second reason why I won't speak of grown-up people is that, besides being disgusting and unworthy of love, they have a compensation—they've eaten the apple and know good and evil, and they have become 'like gods.' They go on eating it still. But the children haven't eaten anything, and are so far innocent. Are you fond of children, Alyosha? I know you are, and you will understand why I prefer to speak of them. If they, too, suffer horribly on earth, they must suffer for their fathers' sins, they must be punished for their fathers, who have eaten the apple; but that reasoning is of the other world and is incomprehensible for the heart of man here on earth. The innocent must not suffer for another's sins, and especially such innocents! . . .

. . . Do you understand that, friend and brother, you pious and humble novice? Do you understand why this infamy must be and is permitted? Without it, I am told, man could not have existed on earth, for he could not have known good and evil. Why should he know that diabolical good and evil when it costs so much? Why, the whole world of knowledge is not worth that child's prayer to 'dear, kind God'! I say nothing of the sufferings of grown-up people, they have eaten the apple, damn them, and the devil take them all! But these little ones! I am making you suffer, Alyosha, you are not yourself. I'll leave off if you like."

"Never mind. I want to suffer too," muttered Alyosha.

"One picture, only one more, because it's so curious, so characteristic, and I have only just read it in some collection of Russian antiquities. I've forgotten the name. I must look it up. It was in the darkest days of serfdom at the beginning of the century, and long live the Liberator of the People! There was in those days a general of aristocratic connections, the owner of great estates, one of those men—somewhat exceptional, I believe, even then—who, retiring from the service into a life of leisure, are convinced that they've earned absolute power over the lives of their subjects. There were such men then. So our general, settled on his property of two thousand souls, lives in pomp, and domineers over his poor neighbours as though they were dependents and buffoons. He has kennels of hundreds of hounds and nearly a hundred dog-boys—all mounted, and in uniform. One day a serf boy, a little child of eight, threw a stone in play and hurt the paw of the general's favourite hound. 'Why is my favourite dog lame?' He is told that the boy threw a stone that hurt the dog's paw. 'So you did it.' The general looked the child up and down. 'Take him.' He was taken—taken from his mother and kept shut up all night. Early that morning the general comes out on horseback, with the hounds, his dependents, dog-boys, and huntsmen, all mounted around him in full hunting parade. The servants are summoned for their edification, and in front of them all stands the mother of the child. The child is brought from the lock-up. It's a gloomy cold, foggy autumn day, a capital day for hunting. The general orders the child to be undressed; the child is stripped naked. He shivers, numb with terror, not daring to cry. . . . 'Make him run,' commands the general. 'Run! run!' shout the dog-boys. The boy runs. . . . 'At him!' yells the general, and he sets the whole pack of hounds on the child. The hounds catch him, and tear him to pieces before his mother's eyes! . . . I believe the general was afterwards declared incapable of administering his estates. Well—what did he deserve? To be shot? To be shot for the satisfaction of our moral feelings? Speak, Alyosha!"

"To be shot," murmured Alyosha, lifting his eyes to Ivan with a pale, twisted smile.

"Bravo!" cried Ivan delighted. "If even you say so . . . You're a pretty monk! So there is a little devil sitting in your heart, Alyosha Karamazov!"

"What I said was absurd, but—"

"That's just the point that 'but'!" cried Ivan. "Let me tell you, novice, that the absurd is only too necessary on earth. The world stands on absurdities, and perhaps nothing would have come to pass in it without them. We know what we know!" . . .

Ivan for a minute was silent, his face became all at once very sad.

"Listen! I took the case of children only to make my case clearer. Of the other tears of humanity with which the earth is soaked from its crust to its centre, I will say nothing. I have narrowed my subject on purpose. I am a bug, and I recognise in all humility that I cannot understand why the world is arranged as it is. Men are themselves to blame, I suppose; they were given paradise, they wanted freedom, and stole fire from heaven, though they knew they would become unhappy, so there is no need to pity them. With my pitiful, earthly, Euclidian understanding, all I know is that there is suffering and that there are none guilty; that cause follows effect, simply and directly; that everything flows and finds its level—but that's only Euclidian nonsense, I know that, and I can't consent to live by it! What comfort is it to me that there are none guilty and that cause follows effect simply and directly, and that I know it—I must have justice, or I will destroy myself. And not justice in some remote infinite time and space, but here on earth, and that I could see myself. I have believed in it. I want to see it, and if I am dead by then, let me rise again, for if it all happens without me, it will be too unfair. Surely I haven't suffered, simply that I, my crimes and my sufferings, may manure the soil of the future harmony for somebody else. I want to see with my own eyes the hind lie down with the lion and the victim rise up and embrace his murderer. I want to be there when every one suddenly understands what it has all been for. All the religions of the world are built on this longing, and I am a believer. But then there are the children, and what am I to do about them? That's a question I can't answer. For the hundredth time I repeat, there are numbers of questions, but I've only taken the children, because in their case what I mean is so unanswerably clear. Listen! If all must suffer to pay for the eternal harmony, what have children to do with it, tell me, please? It's beyond all comprehension why they should suffer, and why they should pay for the harmony. Why should they, too, furnish material to enrich the soil for the harmony of the future? I understand solidarity in sin among men. I understand solidarity in retribution, too; but there can be no such solidarity with children. And if it is really true that they must share responsibility for all their fathers' crimes, such a truth is not of this world and is beyond my comprehension. Some jester will say, perhaps, that the child would have grown up and have sinned, but you see he didn't grow up, he was torn to pieces by the dogs, at eight years old. Oh, Alyosha, I am not blaspheming! I understand, of course, what an upheaval of the universe it will be, when everything in heaven and earth blends in one hymn of praise and everything that lives and has lived cries aloud: 'Thou art just, O Lord, for Thy ways are revealed.' When the mother embraces the fiend who threw her child to the dogs, and all three cry aloud with tears, 'Thou art just, O Lord!' then, of course, the crown of knowledge will be reached and all will be made clear. But what pulls me up here is that I can't accept that harmony. And while I am on earth, I make haste to take my own measures. You see, Alyosha, perhaps it really may happen that if I live to that moment, or rise again to see it, I, too, perhaps, may cry aloud with the rest, looking at the mother embracing the child's torturer, 'Thou art just, O Lord!' but I don't want to cry aloud then. While there is still time, I hasten to protect myself and so I renounce the higher harmony altogether. It's not worth the tears of that one tortured child who beat itself on the breast with its little fist and prayed in its stinking outhouse, with its unexpiated tears to 'dear, kind God'! It's not worth it, because those tears are unatoned for. They must be atoned for, or there can be no harmony. But how? How are you going to atone for them? Is it possible? By their being avenged? But what do I care for avenging them? What do I care for a hell for oppressors? What good can hell do, since those children have already been tortured? And what becomes of harmony, if there is hell? I want to forgive. I want to embrace. I don't want more suffering. And if the sufferings of children go to swell the sum of sufferings which was necessary to pay for truth, then I protest that the truth is not worth such a price. I don't want the mother to embrace the oppressor who threw her son to the dogs! She dare not forgive him! Let her forgive him for herself, if she will, let her forgive the torturer for the immeasurable suffering of her mother's heart. But the sufferings of her tortured child she has no right to forgive; she dare not forgive the torturer, even if the child were to forgive him! And if that is so, if they dare not forgive, what becomes of harmony? Is there in the whole world a being who would have the right to forgive and could forgive? I don't want harmony. From love for humanity I don't want it. I would rather be left with the unavenged suffering. I would rather remain with my unavenged suffering and unsatisfied indignation, *even if I were wrong*. Besides, too high a price is asked for harmony; it's beyond our means to pay so much to enter on it. And so I hasten to give back my entrance ticket, and if I am an honest man I am bound to give it back as soon as possible. And that I am doing. It's not God that I don't accept, Alyosha, only I most respectfully return Him the ticket."

"That's rebellion," murmured Alyosha, looking down.

"Rebellion? I am sorry you call it that," said Ivan earnestly. "One can hardly live in rebellion, and I want to live. Tell me yourself, I challenge you—answer. Imagine that you are creating a fabric of human destiny with the object of making men happy in the end, giving them peace and rest at last, but that it was essential and inevitable to torture to death only one tiny creature—that baby beating its breast with its fist, for instance—and to found that edifice on its unavenged tears, would you consent to be the architect on those conditions? Tell me, and tell the truth."

"No, I wouldn't consent," said Alyosha softly.

Søren Kierkegaard

The Leap of Faith
and the Limits of Reason

Søren Kierkegaard (1813–1855) *was a Danish philosopher and theologian. Generally recognized as the father of existentialism and religious irrationalism, he believed that each individual must choose his own way of life. Christianity is one such choice.*

*B*ut what is this unknown something with which the Reason collides when inspired by its paradoxical passion, with the result of unsettling even man's knowledge of himself? It is the Unknown. It is not a human being, in so far as we know what man is; nor is it any other known thing. So let us call this unknown something: *God*. It is nothing more than a name we assign to it. The idea of demonstrating that this unknown something (God) exists, could scarcely suggest itself to the Reason. For if God does not exist it would of course be impossible to prove it; and if he does exist it would be folly to attempt it. For at the very outset, in beginning my proof, I will have presupposed it, not as doubtful but as certain (a presupposition is never doubtful, for the very reason that it is a presupposition), since otherwise I would not begin, readily understanding that the whole would be impossible if he did not exist. But if when I speak of proving God's existence I mean that I propose to prove that the Unknown, which exists, is God, then I express myself unfortunately. For in that case I do not prove anything, least of all an existence, but merely develop the content of a conception. Generally speaking, it is a difficult matter to prove that anything exists; and what is still worse for the intrepid souls who undertake the venture, the difficulty is such that fame scarcely awaits those who concern themselves with it. The entire demonstration always turns into something very different from what it assumes to be, and becomes an additional development of the consequences that flow from my having assumed that the object in question exists. Thus I always reason from existence, not toward existence, whether I move in the sphere of palpable sensible fact or in the realm of thought. I do not for example prove that a stone exists, but that some existing thing is a stone. The procedure in a court of justice does not prove that a criminal exists, but that the accused, whose existence is given, is a criminal. Whether we call existence an *accessorium* or the eternal *prius,* it is never subject to demonstration. Let us take ample time for consideration. We have no such reason for haste as have those who from concern for themselves or for God or for some other thing, must make haste to get its existence demonstrated. Under such circumstances there may indeed be need for haste, especially if the prover sincerely seeks to appreciate the danger that he himself, or the thing in question, may be non-existent unless the proof is finished; and does not surreptitiously entertain the thought that it exists whether he succeeds in proving it or not.

If it were proposed to prove Napoleon's existence from Napoleon's deeds, would it not be a most curious proceeding? His existence does indeed explain his deeds, but the deeds do not prove *his* existence, unless I have already understood the word "his" so as thereby to have assumed his existence. But Napoleon is only an individual, and in so far there exists no absolute relationship between him and his deeds; some other person might have performed the same deeds. Perhaps this is the reason why I cannot pass from the deeds to existence. If I call these deeds the deeds of Napoleon the proof becomes superfluous, since I have already named him; if I ignore this, I can never prove from the deeds that they are Napoleon's, but only in a purely ideal manner that such deeds are the deeds of a great general, and so forth. But between God and his works there exists an absolute relationship; God is not a name but a concept. Is this perhaps the reason that his *essentia involvit existentiam?* The works of God are such that only God can perform them. Just so, but where then are the works of God? The works from which I would deduce his existence are not immediately given. The wisdom of God in nature, his goodness, his wisdom in the governance of the world—are all these manifest, perhaps, upon the very face of things? Are we not here confronted with the most terrible temptations to doubt, and is it not impossible finally to dispose of all these doubts? But from such an order of things I will surely not attempt to prove God's existence; and even if I began I would never finish, and would in addition have to live constantly in suspense, lest something so terrible should suddenly happen that my bit of proof would be demolished. From what works then do I propose to derive the proof? From the works as apprehended through an ideal interpretation, i.e., such as they do not immediately reveal themselves. But in that case it is not from the works that I prove God's existence. I merely develop the ideality I have presupposed, and because of my confidence in *this* I make so bold as to defy all objections, even those that have not yet been made. In beginning my proof I presuppose the ideal interpretation, and also that I will be successful in carrying it through; but what else is this but to presuppose that God exists, so that I really begin by virtue of confidence in him?

And how does God's existence emerge from the proof? Does it follow straightway, without any breach of continuity? Or have we not here an analogy to the behaviour of these toys, the little Cartesian dolls? As soon as I let go of the doll it stands on its head. As soon as I let it go—I must therefore let it go. So also with the proof for God's existence. As long as I keep my hold on the proof, i.e., continue to demonstrate, the existence does not come out, if for no other reason than that I am engaged in proving it; but when I let the proof go, the existence is there. But this act of letting go is surely also something; it is indeed a contribution of mine. Must not this also be taken into the account, this little moment, brief as it may be— it need not be long, for it is a *leap.* However brief this moment, if only an instantaneous now, this "now" must be included in the reckoning. If anyone wishes to have it ignored, I will use it to tell a little anecdote, in order to show that it really does exist. Chrysippus was experimenting with a sorites to see if he could not bring about a break in its quality, either progressively or retrogressively. But Carneades could not get it in his head when the new quality actually emerged. Then Chrysippus told him to try making a little pause in the reckoning, and so—so it would be easier to understand. Carneades replied: With the greatest pleasure, please do not hesitate on my account; you may not only pause, but even lie down to sleep, and it will help you just as little; for when you awake we will begin again where you left off. Just so; it boots as little to try to get rid of something by sleeping as to try to come into the possession of something in the same manner.

Whoever therefore attempts to demonstrate the existence of God (except in the sense of clarifying the concept, and without the *reservatio finalis* noted above, that the existence emerges from the demonstration by a leap) proves in lieu thereof something else, something which at times perhaps does not need a proof, and in any case needs none better; for the fool says in his heart that there is no God, but whoever says in his heart or to men: Wait just a little and I will prove it—what a rare man of wisdom is he! If in the moment of beginning his proof it is not absolutely undetermined whether God exists or not, he does not prove it; and if it is thus undetermined in the beginning he will never come to begin, partly from fear of failure, since God perhaps does not exist, and partly because he has nothing with which to begin.—A project of this kind would scarcely have been undertaken by the ancients. Socrates at least, who is credited with having put forth the physico-teleological proof for God's existence, did not go about it in any such manner. He always presupposes God's existence, and under this presupposition seeks to interpenetrate nature with the idea of purpose. Had he been asked why he pursued this method, he would doubtless have explained that he lacked the courage to venture out upon so perilous a voyage of discovery without having made sure of God's existence behind him. At the word of God he casts his net as if to catch the idea of purpose; for nature herself finds many means of frightening the inquirer, and distracts him by many a digression.

The paradoxical passion of the Reason thus comes repeatedly into collision with the Unknown, which does indeed exist, but is unknown, and in so far does not exist. The Reason cannot advance beyond this point, and yet it cannot refrain in its paradoxicalness from arriving at this limit and occupying itself therewith. It will not serve to dismiss its relation to it simply by asserting that the Unknown does not exist, since this itself involves a relationship. But what then is the Unknown, since the designation of it as God merely signifies for us that it is unknown? To say that it is the Unknown because it cannot be known, and even if it were capable of being known, it could not be expressed, does not satisfy the demands of passion, though it correctly interprets the Unknown as a limit; but a limit is precisely a torment for passion, though it also serves as an incitement. And yet the Reason can come no further, whether it risks an issue *via negationis* or *via eminentia*.

What then is the Unknown? It is the limit to which the Reason repeatedly comes, and in so far, substituting a static form of conception for the dynamic, it is the different, the absolutely different. But because it is absolutely different, there is no mark by which it could be distinguished. When qualified as absolutely different it seems on the verge of disclosure, but this is not the case; for the Reason cannot even conceive an absolute unlikeness. The Reason cannot negate itself absolutely, but uses itself for the purpose, and thus conceives only such an unlikeness within itself as it can conceive by means of itself; it cannot absolutely transcend itself, and hence conceives only such a superiority over itself as it can conceive by means of itself. Unless the Unknown (God) remains a mere limiting conception, the single idea of difference will be thrown into a state of confusion, and become many ideas of many differences. The Unknown is then in a condition of dispersion (διασπορά), and the Reason may choose at pleasure from what is at hand and the imagination may suggest (the monstrous, the ludicrous, etc.).

But it is impossible to hold fast to a difference of this nature. Every time this is done it is essentially an arbitrary act, and deepest down in the heart of piety lurks the mad caprice which knows that it has itself produced its God. If no specific determination of difference can be held fast, because there is no distinguishing mark, like and unlike finally become identified with one another, thus sharing the fate of all such dialectical opposites. The unlikeness clings to the Reason and confounds it, so that the Reason no longer knows itself and quite consistently confuses itself with the unlikeness. On this point paganism has been sufficiently prolific in fantastic inventions. As for the last named supposition, the self-irony of the Reason, I shall attempt to delineate it merely by a stroke or two, without raising any question of its being historical. There lives an individual whose appearance is precisely like that of other men; he grows up to manhood like others, he marries, he has an occupation by which he earns his livelihood, and he makes provision for the future as befits a man. For though it may be beautiful to live like the birds of the air, it is not lawful, and may lead to the sorriest of consequences: either starvation if one has enough persistence, or dependence on the bounty of others. This man is also God. How do I know? I cannot know it, for in order to know it I would have to know God, and the nature of the difference between God and man; and this I cannot know, because the Reason has reduced it to likeness with that from which it was unlike. Thus God becomes the most terrible of deceivers, because the Reason has deceived itself. The Reason has brought God as near as possible, and yet he is as far away as ever.

William James
The Will to Believe

William James (1842–1910) *was one of the greatest American philosophers. He graduated from Harvard with a medical degree but decided to teach (at Harvard) rather than practice medicine. A founder of modern pragmatism, he also established himself as one of the fathers of modern psychology with his* Principles of Psychology.

I have long defended to my own students the lawfulness of voluntarily adopted faith; but as soon as they have got well imbued with the logical spirit, they have as a rule refused to admit my contention to be lawful philosophically, even though in point of fact they were personally all the time chock-full of some faith or other themselves. I am all the while, however, so profoundly convinced that my own position is correct, that your invitation has seemed to me a good occasion to make my statements more clear. Perhaps your minds will be more open than those with which I have hitherto had to deal. I will be as little technical as I can, though I must begin by setting up some technical distinctions that will help us in the end.

Let us give the name of *hypothesis* to anything that may be proposed to our belief; and just as the electricians speak of live and dead wires, let us speak of any hypothesis as either *live* or *dead*. A live hypothesis is one which appeals as a real possibility to him to whom it is proposed. If I ask you to believe in the Mahdi, the notion makes no electric connection with your nature,—it refuses to scintillate with any credibility at all. As an hypothesis it is completely dead. To an Arab, however (even if he be not one of the Mahdi's followers), the hypothesis is among the mind's possibilities: it is alive. This shows that deadness and liveness in an hypothesis are not intrinsic properties, but relations to the individual thinker. They are measured by his willingness to act. The maximum of liveness in an hypothesis means willingness to act irrevocably. Practically, that means belief; but there is some believing tendency wherever there is willingness to act at all.

Next, let us call the decision between two hypotheses an *option*. Options may be of several kinds. They may be—1, *living* or *dead*; 2, *forced* or *avoidable*; 3, *momentous* or *trivial*; and for our purposes we may call an option a *genuine* option when it is of the forced, living, and momentous kind.

1. A living option is one in which both hypotheses are live ones. If I say to you: "Be a theosophist or be a Mohammedan," it is probably a dead option, because for you neither hypothesis is likely to be alive. But if I say, "Be an agnostic or be a Christian," it is otherwise: trained as you are, each hypothesis makes some appeal, however small, to your belief.

2. Next, if I say to you: "Choose between going out with your umbrella or without it," I do not offer you a genuine option, for it is not forced. You can easily avoid it by not going out at all. Similarly, if I say, "Either love me or hate me," "Either call my theory true or call it false," your option is avoidable. You may remain indifferent to me, neither loving nor hating, and you may decline to offer any judgment as to my theory. But if I say, "Either accept this truth or go without it," I put on you a forced option, for there is no standing place outside of the alternative. Every dilemma based on a complete logical disjunction, with no possibility of not choosing, is an option of this forced kind. . . .

The thesis I defend is, briefly stated, this: *Our passional nature not only lawfully may, but must, decide an option between propositions, whenever it is a genuine option that cannot by its nature be decided on intellectual grounds; for to say, under such circumstances, "Do not decide, but leave the question open," is itself a passional decision,—just like deciding yes or no,—and is attended with the same risk of losing the truth.* . . .

Wherever the option between losing truth and gaining it is not momentous, we can throw the chance of *gaining truth* away, and at any rate save ourselves from any chance of *believing falsehood,* by not making up our minds at all till objective evidence has come. In scientific questions, this is almost always the case; and even in human affairs in general, the need of acting is seldom so urgent that a false belief to act on is better than no belief at all. Law courts, indeed, have to decide on the best evidence attainable for the moment, because a judge's duty is to make law as well as to ascertain it, and (as a learned judge once said to me) few cases are worth spending much time over: the great thing is to have them decided on *any* acceptable principle, and got out of the way. But in our dealings with objective nature we obviously are recorders, not makers, of the truth; and decisions for the mere sake of deciding promptly and getting on to the next business would be wholly out of place. Throughout the breadth of physical nature facts are what they are quite independently of us, and seldom is there any such hurry about them that the risks of being duped by believing a premature theory need be faced. The questions here are always trivial options, the hypothesis are hardly living (at any rate not living for us spectators), the choice between believing truth or falsehood is seldom forced. The attitude of sceptical balance is therefore the absolutely wise one if we would escape mistakes. What difference, indeed, does it make to most of us whether we have or have not a theory of the Röntgen rays, whether we believe or not in mind-stuff, or have a conviction about the causality of conscious states? It makes no difference. Such options are not forced on us. On every account it is better not to make them, but still keep weighing reasons *pro et contra* with an indifferent hand. . . .

But now, it will be said, these . . . cases, . . . have nothing to do with great cosmical matters, like the question of religious faith. Let us then pass on to that. Religions differ so much in their accidents that in discussing the religious question we must make it very generic and broad. What then do we now mean by the religious hypothesis? Science says things are; morality says some things are better than other things; and religion says essentially two things.

First, she says that the best things are the more eternal things, the overlapping things, the things in the universe that throw the last stone, so to speak, and say the final word. "Perfection is eternal,"—this phrase of Charles Secrétan seems a good way of putting this first affirmation of religion, an affirmation which obviously cannot yet be verified scientifically at all.

The second affirmation of religion is that we are better off even now if we believe her first affirmation to be true.

Now, let us consider what the logical elements of this situation are *in case the religious hypothesis in both its branches be really true.* (Of course, we must admit that possibility at the outset. If we are to discuss the question at all, it must involve a living option. If for any of you religion be a hypothesis that cannot, by any living possibility be true, then you need go no farther. I speak to the 'saving remnant' alone.) So proceeding, we see, first that religion offers itself as a *momentous* option. We are supposed to gain, even now, by our belief, and to lose by our nonbelief, a certain vital good. Secondly, religion is a *forced* option, so far as that good goes. We cannot escape the issue by remaining sceptical and waiting for more light, because, although we do avoid error in that way *if religion be untrue,* we lose the good, *if it be true,* just as certainly as if we positively chose to disbelieve. It is as if a man should hesitate indefinitely to ask a certain woman to marry him because he was not perfectly sure that she would prove an angel after he brought her home. Would he not cut himself off from that particular angel-possibility as decisively as if he went and married some one else? Scepticism, then, is not avoidance of option; it is option of a certain particular kind of risk. *Better risk loss of truth than chance of error,*—that is your faith-vetoer's exact position. He is actively playing his stake as much as the believer is; he is backing the field against the religious hypothesis, just as the believer is backing the religious hypothesis against the field. To preach scepticism to us as a duty until 'sufficient evidence' for religion be found, is tantamount therefore to telling us, when in presence of the religious hypothesis, that to yield to our fear of its being error is wiser and better than to yield to our hope that it may be true. It is not intellect against all passions, then; it is only intellect with one passion laying down its law. And by what, forsooth, is the supreme wisdom of this passion warranted? Dupery for dupery, what proof is there that dupery through hope is so much worse than dupery through fear? I, for one, can see no proof; and I simply refuse obedience to the scientist's command to imitate his kind of option, in a case where my own stake is important enough to give me the right to choose my own form of risk. If religion be true and the evidence for it be still insufficient, I do not wish, by putting your extinguisher upon my nature (which feels to me as if it had after all some business in this matter), to forfeit my sole chance in life of getting upon the winning side,— that chance depending, of course, on my willingness to run the risk of acting as if my passional need of taking the world religiously might be prophetic and right.

All this is on the supposition that it really may be prophetic and right, and that, even to us who are discussing the matter, religion is a live hypothesis which may be true. Now, to most of us religion comes in a still further way that makes a veto on our active faith even more illogical. The more perfect and more eternal aspect of the universe is represented in our religions as having personal form. The universe is no longer a mere *It* to us, but a *Thou,* if we are religious; and any relation that may be possible from person to person might be possible here. For instance, although in one sense we are passive portions of the universe, in another we show a curious autonomy, as if we were small active centres on our own account. We feel, too, as if the appeal of religion to us were made to our own active good-will, as if evidence might be forever withheld from us unless we met the hypothesis half-way. To take a trivial illustration: just as a man who in a company of gentlemen made no advances, asked a warrant for every concession, and believed no one's word without proof, would cut himself off by such churlishness from all the social rewards that a more trusting spirit would earn,—so here, one who should shut himself up in snarling logicality and try to make the gods extort his recognition willy-nilly, or not get it at all, might cut himself off forever from his only opportunity of making the gods' aquaintance. This feeling, forced on us we know not whence, that by obstinately believing that there are gods (although not to do so would be so easy both for our logic and our life) we are doing the universe the deepest service we can, seems part of the living essence of the religious hypothesis. If the hypothesis *were* true in all its parts, including this one, then pure intellectualism, with its veto on our making willing advances, would be an absurdity; and some participation of our sympathetic nature would be logically required. I, therefore, for one, cannot see my way to accepting the agnostic rules for truth-seeking, or wilfully agree to keep my willing nature out of the game. I cannot do so for this plain reason, that *a rule of thinking which would absolutely prevent me from acknowledging certain kinds of truth if those kinds of truth were really there, would be an irrational rule.* That for me is the long and short of the formal logic of the situation, no matter what the kinds of truth might materially be.

I confess I do not see how this logic can be escaped. But sad experience makes me fear that some of you may still shrink from radically saying with me, *in abstracto,* that we have the right to believe at our own risk any hypothesis that is live enough to tempt our will. I suspect, however, that if this is so, it is because you have got away from the abstract logical point of view altogether, and are thinking (perhaps without realizing it) of some particular religious hypothesis which for you is dead. The freedom to 'believe what we will' you apply to the case of some patent superstition; and the faith you think of is the faith defined by the schoolboy when he said, "Faith is when you believe something that you know ain't true." I can only repeat that this is misapprehension. *In concreto,* the freedom to believe can only cover living options which the intellect of the individual cannot by itself resolve; and living options never seem absurdities to him who has them to consider. When I look at the religious question as it really puts itself to concrete men, and when I think of all the possibilities which both practically and theoretically it involves, then this command that we shall put a stopper on our heart, instincts, and courage, and *wait*—acting of course meanwhile more or less as if religion were *not* true—till doomsday, or till such time as our intellect and senses working together may have raked in evidence enough,—this command, I say, seems to me the queerest idol ever manufactured in the philosophic cave. Were we scholastic absolutists, there might be more excuse. If we had an infallible intellect with its objective certitudes, we might feel ourselves disloyal to such a perfect organ of knowledge in not trusting to it exclusively, in not waiting for its releasing word. But if we are empiricists, if we believe that no bell in us tolls to let us know for certain when truth is in our grasp, then it seems a piece of idle fanasticality to preach so solemnly our duty of waiting for the bell. Indeed we *may* wait if we will.—I hope you do not think that I am denying that,—but if we do so, we do so at our peril as much as if we believed. In either case we *act,* taking our life in our hands. No one of us ought to issue vetoes to the other, nor should we bandy words of abuse. We ought, on the contrary, delicately and profoundly to respect one another's mental freedom: then only shall we bring about the intellectual republic; then only shall we have that spirit of inner tolerance without which all our outer tolerance is soulless, and which is empiricism's glory; then only shall we live and let live, in speculative as well as in practical things.

Anthony Flew, R. M. Hare, Basil Mitchell

Theology and Falsification

Anthony Flew *teaches philosophy at the University of Reading in England. He has written many books and articles, among them* Hume's Philosophy of Belief *and* The Politics of Procrustes. **R. M. Hare** *taught philosophy at Oxford for many years and now teaches at the University of Florida. An influential moral philosopher, his books include* The Language of Morals, Moral Thinking, *and* Plato. **Basil Mitchell** *teaches philosophy of religion at Oxford. His works include* Law, Morality and Religion in Secular Society *and* Law, Belief and Morality: Religious and Secular.

*L*et us begin with a parable. It is a parable developed from a tale told by John Wisdom in his haunting and revelatory article 'Gods.' Once upon a time two explorers came upon a clearing in the jungle. In the clearing were growing many flowers and many weeds. One explorer says, 'Some gardener must tend this plot.' The other disagrees, 'There is no gardener.' So they pitch their tents and set a watch. No gardener is ever seen. 'But perhaps he is an invisible gardener.' So they set up a barbed-wire fence. They electrify it. They patrol with bloodhounds. (For they remember how H. G. Wells's *The Invisible Man* could be both smelt and touched though he could not be seen.) But no shrieks ever suggest that some intruder has received a shock. No movements of the wire ever betray an invisible climber. The blood-hounds never give cry. Yet still the Believer is not convinced. 'But there is a gardener, invisible, intangible, insensible to electric shocks, a gardener who has no scent and makes no sound, a gardener who comes secretly to look after the garden which he loves.' At last the Sceptic despairs, 'But what remains of your original assertion? Just how does what you call an invisible, intangible, eternally elusive gardener differ from an imaginary gardener or even from no gardener at all?'

In this parable we can see how what starts as an assertion, that something exists or that there is some analogy between certain complexes of phenomena, may be reduced step by step to an altogether different status, to an expression perhaps of a 'picture preference.' The Sceptic says there is no gardener. The Believer says there is a gardener (but invisible, etc.). One man talks about sexual behaviour. Another man prefers to talk of Aphrodite (but knows that there is not really a superhuman person additional to, and somehow responsible for, all sexual phenomena). The process of qualification may be checked at any point before the original assertion is completely withdrawn and something of that first assertion will remain (Tautology). Mr. Wells's invisible man could not, admittedly, be seen, but in all other respects he was a man like the rest of us. But though the process of qualification may be, and of course usually is, checked in time, it is not always judiciously so halted. Someone may dissipate his assertion completely without noticing that he has done so. A fine brash hypothesis may thus be killed by inches, the death by a thousand qualifications.

And in this, it seems to me, lies the peculiar danger, the endemic evil, of theological utterance. Take such utterances as 'God has a plan,' 'God created the world,' 'God loves us as a father loves his children.' They look at first sight very much like assertions, vast cosmological assertions. Of course, this is no sure sign that they either are, or are intended to be, assertions. But let us confine ourselves to the cases where those who utter such sentences intend them to express assertions. (Merely remarking parenthetically that those who intend or interpret such utterances as crypto-commands, expressions of wishes, disguised ejaculations, concealed ethics, or as anything else but assertions, are unlikely to succeed in making them either properly orthodox or practically effective.)

Now to assert that such and such is the case is necessarily equivalent to denying that such and such is not the case. Suppose then that we are in doubt as to what someone who gives vent to an utterance is asserting, or suppose that, more radically, we are sceptical as to whether he is really asserting anything at all, one way of trying to understand (or perhaps it will be to expose) his utterance is to attempt to find what he would regard as counting against, or as being incompatible with, its truth. For if the utterance is indeed an assertion, it will necessarily be equivalent to a denial of the negation of that assertion. And anything which would count against the assertion, or which would induce the speaker to withdraw it and to admit that it had been mistaken, must be part of (or the whole of) the meaning of the negation of that assertion. And to know the meaning of the negation of an assertion, is as near as makes no matter, to know the meaning of that assertion. And if there is nothing which a putative assertion denies then there is nothing which it asserts either: and so it is not really an assertion. When the Sceptic in the parable asked the Believer, 'Just how does what you call an invisible, intangible, eternally elusive gardener differ from an imaginary gardener or even from no gardener at all?' he was suggesting that the Believer's earlier statement had been so eroded by qualification that it was no longer an assertion at all.

Now it often seems to people who are not religious as if there was no conceivable event or series of events the occurrence of which would be admitted by sophisticated religious people to be a sufficient reason for conceding 'there wasn't a God after all' or 'God does not really love us then.' Someone tells us that God loves us as a father loves his children. We are reassured. But then we see a child dying of inoperable cancer of the throat. His earthly father is driven frantic in his efforts to help, but his Heavenly Father reveals no obvious sign of concern. Some qualification is made—God's love is 'not merely human love' or it is 'an unscrutable love,' perhaps—and we realize that such sufferings are quite compatible with the truth of the assertion that 'God loves us as a father (but, of course, . . .).' We are reassured again. But then perhaps we ask: what is this assurance of God's (appropriately qualified) love worth, what is this apparant guarantee really a guarantee against? Just what would have to happen not merely (morally and wrongly) to tempt but also (logically and rightly) to entitle us to say 'God does not love us' or even 'God does not exist'? I therefore put to the succeeding symposiasts the simple central questions, 'What would have to occur or to have occurred to constitute for you a disproof of the love of, or the existence of, God?'

I wish to make it clear that I shall not try to defend Christianity in particular, but religion in general—not because I do not believe in Christianity, but because you cannot understand what Christianity is, until you have understood what religion is.

I must begin by confessing that, on the ground marked out by Flew, he seems to me to be completely victorious. I therefore shift my ground by relating another parable. A certain lunatic is convinced that all dons want to murder him. His friends introduce him to all the mildest and most respectable dons that they can find, and after each of them has retired, they say, 'You see, he doesn't really want to murder you; he spoke to you in the most cordial manner; surely you are convinced now?' But the lunatic replies, 'Yes, but that was only his diabolical cunning; he's really plotting against me the whole time, like the rest of them; I know it I tell you.' However many kindly dons are produced, the reaction is still the same.

Now we say that such a person is deluded. But what is he deluded about? About the truth or falsity of an assertion? Let us apply Flew's test to him. There is no behaviour of dons that can be enacted which he will accept as counting against his theory; and therefore his theory, on this test, asserts nothing. But it does not follow that there is no difference between what he thinks about dons and what most of us think about them—otherwise we should not call him a lunatic and ourselves sane, and dons would have no reason to feel uneasy about his presence in Oxford.

Let us call that in which we differ from the lunatic, our respective *bliks*. He has an insane *blik* about dons; we have a sane one. It is important to realize that we have a sane one, not no *blik* at all; for there must be two sides to any argument—if he has a wrong *blik*, then those who are right about dons must have a right one. Flew has shown that a *blik* does not consist in an assertion or system of them; but nevertheless it is very important to have the right *blik*.

Let us try to imagine what it would be like to have different *bliks* about other things than dons. When I am driving my car, it sometimes occurs to me to wonder whether my movements of the steering-wheel will always continue to be followed by corresponding alterations in the direction of the car. I have never had a steering failure, though I have had skids, which must be similar. Moreover, I know enough about how the steering of my car is made, to know the sort of thing that would have to go wrong for the steering to fail—steel joints would have to part, or steel rods break, or something—but how do I know that this won't happen? The truth is, I don't know; I just have a *blik* about steel and its properties, so that normally I trust the steering of my car; but I find it not at all difficult to imagine what it would be like to lose this *blik* and acquire the opposite one. People would say I was silly about steel; but there would be no mistaking the reality of the difference between our respective *bliks*— for example, I should never go in a motorcar. Yet I should hesitate to say that the difference between us was the difference between contradictory assertions. No amount of safe arrivals or bench-tests will remove my *blik* and restore the normal one; for my *blik* is compatible with any finite number of such tests.

It was Hume who taught us that our whole commerce with the world depends upon our *blik* about the world; and that difference between *bliks* about the world cannot be settled by observation of what happens in the world. That was why, having performed the interesting experiment of doubting the ordinary man's *blik* about the world, and showing that no proof could be given to make us adopt one *blik* rather than another, he turned to backgammon to take his mind off the problem. It seems, indeed, to be impossible even to formulate as an assertion the normal *blik* about the world which makes me put my confidence in the future reliability of steel joints, in the continued ability of the road to support my car, and not gape beneath it revealing nothing below; in the general non-homicidal tendencies of dons; in my own continued well-being (in some sense of that word that I may not now fully understand) if I continue to do what is right according to my lights; in the general likelihood of people like Hitler coming to a bad end. But perhaps a formulation less inadequate than most is to be found in the Psalms: 'The earth is weak and all the inhabitants thereof: I bear up the pillars of it.'

The mistake of the position which Flew selects for attack is to regard this kind of talk as some sort of *explanation,* as scientists are accustomed to use the word. As such, it would obviously be ludicrous. We no longer believe in God as an Atlas—*nous n'avons pas besoin de cette hypothèse.* But it is nevertheless true to say that, as Hume saw, without a *blik* there can be no explanation; for it is by our *bliks* that we decide what is and what is not an explanation. Suppose we believe that everything that happened, happened by pure chance. This would not of course be an assertion; for it is compatible with anything happening or not happening, and so, incidentally, is its contradictory. But if we had this belief, we should not be able to explain or predict or plan anything. Thus, although we should not be *asserting* anything different from those of a more normal belief, there would be a great difference between us; and this is the sort of difference that there is between those who really believe in God and those who really disbelieve in him.

The word 'really' is important, and may excite suspicion. I put it in, because when people have had a good Christian upbringing, as have most of those who now profess not to believe in any sort of religion, it is very hard to discover what they really believe. The reason why they find it so easy to think that they are not religious, is that they have never got into the frame of mind of one who suffers from the doubts to which religion is the answer. Not for them the terrors of the primitive jungle. Having abandoned some of the more picturesque fringes of religion, they think that they have abandoned the whole thing—whereas in fact they still have got, and could not live without, a religion of a comfortably substantial, albeit highly sophisticated, kind, which differs from that of many 'religious people' in little more than this, that 'religious people' like to sing Psalms about theirs—a very natural and proper thing to do. But nevertheless there may be a big difference lying behind—the difference between two people who, though side by side, are walking in different directions. I do not know in what direction Flew is walking; perhaps he does not know either. But we have had some examples recently of various ways in which one can walk away from Christianity, and there are any number of possibilities. After all, man has not changed biologically since primitive times; it is his religion that has changed, and it can easily change again. And if you do not think that such changes make a difference, get acquainted with some Sikhs and some Mussulmans of the same Punjabi stock; you will find them quite different sorts of people.

There is an important difference between Flew's parable and my own which we have not yet noticed. The explorers do not *mind* about their garden; they discuss it with interest, but not with concern. But my lunatic, poor fellow, minds about dons; and I mind about the steering of my car; it often has people in it that I care for. It is because I mind very much about what goes on in the garden in which I find myself, that I am unable to share the explorers' detachment.

Flew's article is searching and perceptive, but there is, I think, something odd about his conduct of the theologian's case. The theologian surely would not deny that the fact of pain counts against the assertion that God loves men. This very incompatibility generates the most intractable of theological problems—the problem of evil. So the theologian *does* recognize the fact of pain as counting against Christian doctrine. But it is true that he will not allow it—or anything—to count decisively against it; for he is committed by his faith to trust in God. His attitude is not that of the detached observer, but of the believer.

Perhaps this can be brought out by yet another parable. In time of war in an occupied country, a member of the resistance meets one night a stranger who deeply impresses him. They spend the night together in conversation. The Stranger tells the partisan that he himself is on the side of the resistance—indeed that he is in command of it, and urges the partisan to have faith in him no matter what happens. The partisan is utterly convinced at that meeting of the Stranger's sincerity and constancy and undertakes to trust him.

They never meet in conditions of intimacy again. But sometimes the Stranger is seen helping members of the resistance, and the partisan is grateful and says to his friends, 'He is on our side.'

Sometimes he is seen in the uniform of the police handing over patriots to the occupying power. On these occasions his friends murmur against him; but the partisan still says, 'He is on our side.' He still believes that, in spite of appearances, the Stranger did not deceive him. Sometimes he asks the Stranger for help and receives it. He is then thankful. Sometimes he asks and does not receive it. Then he says, 'The Stranger knows best.' Sometimes his friends, in exasperation, say 'Well, what *would* he have to do for you to admit that you were wrong and that he is not on our side?' But the partisan refuses to answer. He will not consent to put the Stranger to the test. And sometimes his friends complain, 'Well, if *that's* what you mean by his being on our side, the sooner he goes over to the other side the better.'

The partisan of the parable does not allow anything to count decisively against the proposition 'The Stranger is on our side.' This is because he has committed himself to trust the Stranger. But he of course recognizes that the Stranger's ambiguous behaviour *does* count against what he believes about him. It is precisely this situation which constitutes the trial of his faith.

When the partisan asks for help and doesn't get it, what can he do? He can (a) conclude that the Stranger is not on our side or; (b) maintain that he is on our side, but that he has reasons for withholding help.

The first he will refuse to do. How long can he uphold the second position without its becoming just silly?

I don't think one can say in advance. It will depend on the nature of the impression created by the Stranger in the first place. It will depend, too, on the manner in which he takes the Stranger's behavior. If he blandly dismisses it as of no consequence, as having no bearing upon his belief, it will be assumed that he is thoughtless or insane. And it quite obviously won't do for him to say easily, 'Oh, when used of the Stranger the phrase "is on our side" *means* ambiguous behaviour of this sort.' In that case he would be like the religious man who says blandly of a terrible disaster, 'It is God's will.' No, he will only be regarded as sane and reasonable in his belief, if he experiences in himself the full force of the conflict.

It is here that my parable differs from Hare's. The partisan admits that many things may and do count against his belief: whereas Hare's lunatic who has a *blik* about dons doesn't admit that anything counts against his *blik*. Nothing *can* count against *bliks*. Also the partisan has a reason for having in the first instance committed himself, viz, the character of the Stranger; whereas the lunatic has no reason for his *blik* about dons—because, of course, you can't have reasons for *bliks*.

This means that I agree with Flew that theological utterances must be assertions. The partisan is making an assertion when he says, 'The Stranger is on our side.'

Do I want to say that the partisan's belief about the Stranger is, in any sense, an explanation? I think I do. It explains and makes sense of the Stranger's behaviour: it helps to explain also the resistance movement in the context of which he appears. In each case it differs from the interpretation which the others put upon the same facts.

'God loves men' resembles 'the Stranger is on our side' (and many other significant statements, e.g. historical ones) in not being conclusively falsifiable. They can both be treated in at least three different ways: (1) As provisional hypotheses to be discarded if experience tells against them; (2) As significant articles of faith; (3) As vacuous formulae (expressing, perhaps, a desire for reassurance) to which experience makes no difference and which make no difference to life.

The Christian, once he has committed himself, is precluded by his faith from taking up the first attitude: 'Thou shalt not tempt the Lord thy God.' He is in constant danger, as Flew has observed, of slipping into the third. But he need not; and, if he does, it is a failure in faith as well as in logic. The challenge, it will be remembered, ran like this. Some theological utterances seem to, and are intended to, provide explanations or express assertions. Now an assertion, to be an assertion at all, must claim that things stand thus and thus; *and not otherwise*. Similarly an explanation, to be an explanation at all, must explain why this particular thing occurs; *and not something else*. Those last clauses are crucial. And yet sophisticated religious people—or so it seemed to me—are apt to overlook this, and tend to refuse to allow, not merely that anything actually does occur, but that anything conceivably could occur, which would count against their theological assertions and explanations. But in so far as they do this their supposed explanations are actually bogus, and their seeming assertions are really vacuous.

Mitchell's response to this challenge is admirably direct, straightforward, and understanding. He agrees 'that theological utterances must be assertions.' He agrees that if they are to be assertions, there must be something that would count against their truth. He agrees, too, that believers are in constant danger of transforming their would-be assertions into 'vacuous formulae.' But he takes me to task for an oddity in my 'conduct of the theologian's case. The theologian surely would not deny that the fact of pain counts against the assertion that God loves men. This very incompatibility generates the most intractable of theological problems, the problem of evil.' I think he is right. I should have made a distinction between two very different ways of dealing with what looks like evidence against the love of God: the way I stressed was the expedient of qualifying the original assertion; the way the theologian usually takes, at first, is to admit that it looks bad but to insist that there is—there must be—some explanation which will show that, in spite of appearances, there really is a God who loves us. His difficulty, it seems to me, is that he has given God attributes which rule out all possible saving explanations. In Mitchell's parable of the Stranger it is easy for the believer to find plausible excuses for ambiguous behaviour: for the Stranger is a man. But suppose the Stranger is God. We cannot say that he would like to help but cannot: God is omnipotent. We cannot say that he would help if he only knew: God is omniscient. We cannot say that he is not responsible for the wickedness of others: God creates those others. Indeed an omnipotent, omniscient God must be an accessory before (and during) the fact to every human misdeed; as well as being responsible for every non-moral defect in the universe. So, though I entirely concede that Mitchell was absolutely right to insist against me that the theologian's first move is to look for an *explanation,* I still think that in the end, if relentlessly pursued, he will have to resort to the avoiding action of *qualification.* And there lies the danger of that death by a thousand qualifications, which would, I agree, constitute 'a failure in faith as well as in logic.'

Hare's approach is fresh and bold. He confesses that 'on the ground marked out by Flew, he seems to me to be completely victorious.' He therefore introduces the concept of *blik.* But while I think that there is room for some such concept in philosophy, and that philosophers should be grateful to Hare for his invention, I nevertheless want to insist that any attempt to analyse Christian religious utterances as expressions or affirmations of a *blik* rather than as (at least would-be) assertions about the cosmos is fundamentally misguided. *First,* because thus interpreted they would be entirely unorthodox. If Hare's religion really is a *blik,* involving no cosmological assertions about the nature and activities of a supposed personal creator, then surely he is not a Christian at all? *Second,* because thus interpreted, they could scarcely do the job they do. If they were not even intended as assertions then many religious activities would become fraudulent, or merely silly. If 'You ought *because* it is God's will' asserts no more than 'You ought,' then the person who prefers the former phraseology is not really giving a reason, but a fraudulent substitute for one, a dialectical dud cheque. . . . Religious utterances may indeed express false or even bogus assertions: but I simply do not believe that they are not both intended and interpreted to be or at any rate to presuppose assertions, at least in the context of religious practice; whatever shifts may be demanded, in another context, by the exigencies of theological apologetic.

2

Does Religion Give My Life Meaning?

What do you believe in? What gives your life meaning? It is true that most of your days are filled with things to do, people to see, assignments to be completed, promises to be kept, and special events to be looked forward to and then enjoyed. But what does all of this add up to? What makes it significant? Why does it make a difference whether or not you do anything? Indeed, why does it even make a difference whether you are alive or not? These are the questions that are often summarized under the heading "the meaning of life," and they are among the oldest and most important questions in philosophy.

Religion is as old as these questions, and the various religions of the world are, in part, answers to these questions. The primary function of religion is to give our lives meaning, to show us how we fit into the world and God's plan. But there are many religions and conceptions of religion, and they explain life's meaning in very different ways. Judaism and Christianity insist that life has meaning because there is an Almighty God who created us and looks over us. There are, however, other ways of making sense of our existence, and some of them do not involve a being such as the Judeo-Christian God at all.

How does religion give meaning to life? Steven Cahn suggests that it is a combination of theory and practice, rituals, prayers, metaphysical beliefs, and moral commitments. But, he argues, it is not necessary that such theories and practices be part of an established traditional religion, nor is it necessary for a person who is religious to believe in a single supreme being or an afterlife—two fundamental tenets of Christianity but relative rarities among the various religions of the world. There are great religions in the East, as old as Judaism and Christianity, which explain the meaning of life without appealing to any conception of God like our own. And any number of "spiritual attitudes" to life exist that are not part of any particular religion. Religion may make life meaningful, but no particular religion does so exclusively, and many if not all of the ingredients of a meaningful life—rituals, moral commitments, metaphysical beliefs, and even prayers (to whom or what?)—might also be part of someone's strictly secular life. What is essential is that a person's life involves some sensibility that goes beyond the ordinary and everyday concerns of life, and it is this sense of "beyond" that gives life meaning.

Some of the great thinkers have suggested that what is central to religion is not so much belief in a particular deity, but rather a transformation of one's self, a rising "above" ordinary, everyday concerns and appreciating the nature of the cosmos as a whole. Believing in God is one way to do this, but there are other techniques and ways of viewing the world that make such "awakening" or "transcendence" possible. Zen Buddhism, for example, elaborates an all-encompassing attitude toward life and world that uses meditation and other forms of personal discipline to develop a religiously meaningful view of the world. There are "many paths to the same summit" writes Ramakrishna. It would be a mistake to think that there is only one religion or one way to make life meaningful. But then, neither can one simply embrace all religions at once, for it is the particularity of the "path" that makes meaningfulness possible. A Christian should be a Christian, a Hindu a Hindu, but this does not mean that there is or should be any conflict between them.

But then, it has also been argued that religion does not provide meaning to life at all; it rather gives us a distraction *from* life and a set of excuses for not taking life's problems seriously. So conceived, religion may *take away* rather than contribute to life's meaning. So thought Sigmund Freud, who saw religion as a carry-over from childish dependency and the need for security, and Bertrand Russell, who saw in the history of Christianity a horrifying story of protracted violence and intolerance. Mary Daly has a different objection to the Judeo-Christian tradition: it assumes without argument that God is male and consequently elevates male and demeans female characteristics. She accordingly recommends nothing less than a feminist revolution in religion, not just recognizing women as equals in a "patriarchal" universe (a contradiction, she says), but rather involving a reconception of the very nature of religion.

Finally, it may be that life has no meaning and that the attempts of all religions to provide that meaning is just denial and refusal to accept the facts. Albert Camus argues that this is the sensibility of the current age, that life is really "absurd" and religion cannot undo that single, overwhelming truth.

Steven M. Cahn

Religion Reconsidered

Steven M. Cahn *is a professor of philosophy and Dean of the City University of New York. He teaches and publishes in the philosophy of religion and education.*

Most of us suppose that all religions are akin to the one we happen to know best. But this assumption can be misleading. For example, many Christians believe that all religions place heavy emphasis on an afterlife, although, in fact, the central concern of Judaism is life in this world, not the next. Similarly, many Christians and Jews are convinced that a person who is religious must affirm the existence of a supernatural God. They are surprised to learn that religions such as Jainism or Theravada Buddhism deny the existence of a Supreme Creator of the world.

But how can there be a non-supernatural religion? To numerous theists as well as atheists the concept appears contradictory. I propose to show, however, that nothing in the theory or practice of religion—not ritual, not prayer, not metaphysical belief, not moral commitment—necessitates a commitment to traditional theism. In other words, one may be religious while rejecting supernaturalism.

Let us begin with the concept of ritual. A ritual is a prescribed symbolic action. In the case of religion, the ritual is prescribed by the religious organization, and the act symbolizes some aspect of religious belief. Those who find the beliefs of supernaturalistic religion unreasonable or the activities of the organization unacceptable may come to consider any ritual irrational. But, although particular rituals may be based on irrational beliefs, nothing is inherently irrational about ritual.

Consider the simple act of two people shaking hands when they meet. This act is a ritual, prescribed by our society and symbolic of the individuals' mutual respect. There is nothing irrational about this act. Of course, if people shook hands in order to ward off evil demons, then shaking hands would be irrational. But this is not the reason people shake hands. The ritual has no connection with God or demons but indicates the attitude one person has toward another.

It might be assumed that the ritual of handshaking escapes irrationality only because the ritual is not prescribed by any specific organization and is not part of an elaborate ceremony. But to see that this assumption is false, consider the graduation ceremony at a college. The graduates and faculty all wear peculiar hats and robes, and the participants stand and sit at appropriate times throughout the ceremony. However, there is nothing irrational about this ceremony. Indeed, the ceremonies of graduation day, far from being irrational, are symbolic of commitment to the process of education and the life of reason.

At first glance it may appear that rituals are comparatively insignificant features of our lives, but the more one considers the matter, the more it becomes apparent that rituals are a pervasive and treasured aspect of human experience. Who would want to eliminate the festivities associated with holidays such as Independence Day or Thanksgiving? What would college football be without songs, cheers, flags, and the innumerable other symbolic features surrounding the game? And those who disdain popular rituals typically proceed to establish their own distinctive ones, ranging from characteristic habits of dress to the use of drugs, all symbolic of a rejection of traditional mores.

Religious persons, like all others, search for an appropriate means of emphasizing their commitment to a group or its values. Rituals provide such a means. It is true that supernaturalistic religion has often infused its rituals with superstition, but nonreligious rituals can be equally as superstitious as religious ones. For example, most Americans view the Fourth of July as an occasion on which they can express pride in their country's heritage. With this purpose in mind, the holiday is one of great significance. However, if it were thought that the singing of the fourth verse of "The Star-Spangled Banner" four times on the Fourth of July would protect our country against future disasters, then the original meaning of the holiday would soon be lost in a maze of superstition.

A naturalistic (i.e. non-supernaturalistic) religion need not utilize ritual in such a superstitious manner, for it does not employ rituals in order to please a benevolent deity or appease an angry one. Rather, naturalistic religion views ritual, as Jack Cohen has put it, as "the enhancement of life through the dramatization of great ideals." If a group places great stress on justice or freedom, why should it not utilize ritual in order to emphasize these goals? Such a use of ritual serves to solidify the group and to strengthen its devotion to its expressed purposes. And these purposes are strengthened all the more if the ritual in question has the force of tradition, having been performed by many generations who have belonged to the same group and have struggled to achieve the same goals. Ritual so conceived is not a form of superstition; rather, it is a reasonable means of strengthening religious commitment and is as useful to naturalistic religion as it is to supernaturalistic religion.

Having considered the role of ritual in a naturalistic religion, let us next turn to the concept of prayer. It might be thought that naturalistic religion could have no use for prayer, since prayer is supposedly addressed to a supernatural being, and proponents of naturalistic religion do not believe in the existence of such a being. But this objection oversimplifies the concept of prayer, focusing attention on one type of prayer while neglecting an equally important but different sort of prayer.

Supernaturalistic religion makes extensive use of petitionary prayer, prayer that petitions a supernatural being for various favors. These may range all the way from the personal happiness of the petitioner to the general welfare of all society. But since petitionary prayer rests upon the assumption that a supernatural being exists, it is clear that such prayer has no place in a naturalistic religion.

However, not all prayers are prayers of petition. There are also prayers of meditation. These prayers are not directed to any supernatural being and are not requests for the granting of favors. Rather, these prayers provide the opportunity for persons to rethink their ultimate commitments and rededicate themselves to live up to their ideals. Such prayers may take the form of silent devotion or may involve oral repetition of certain central texts. Just as Americans repeat the Pledge of Allegiance and reread the Gettysburg Address, so adherents of naturalistic religion repeat the statements of their ideals and reread the documents that embody their traditional beliefs.

It is true that supernaturalistic religions, to the extent that they utilize prayers of meditation, tend to treat these prayers irrationally, by supposing that if the prayers are not uttered a precise number of times under certain specified conditions, then the prayers lose all value. But there is no need to view prayer in this way. Rather, as Julian Huxley wrote, prayer "permits the bringing before the mind of a world of thought which in most people must inevitably be absent during the occupations of ordinary life: . . . it is the means by which the mind may fix itself upon this or that noble or beautiful or awe-inspiring idea, and so grow to it and come to realize it more fully."

Such a use of prayer may be enhanced by song, instrumental music, and various types of symbolism. These elements, fused together, provide the means for adherents of naturalistic religion to engage in religious services akin to those engaged in by adherents of supernaturalistic religion. The difference between the two services is that those who attend the latter come to relate themselves to God, while those who attend the former come to relate themselves to their fellow human beings and to the world in which we live.

We have so far discussed how ritual and prayer can be utilized in naturalistic religion, but to adopt a religious perspective also involves metaphysical beliefs and moral commitments. Can these be maintained without recourse to supernaturalism?

If we use the term *metaphysics* in its usual sense, to refer to the systematic study of the most basic features of existence, then it is clear that a metaphysical system may be either supernaturalistic or naturalistic. The views of Plato, Descartes, and Leibniz are representative of a supernaturalistic theory; the views of Aristotle, Spinoza, and Dewey are representative of a naturalistic theory.

Spinoza's *Ethics,* for example, one of the greatest metaphysical works ever written, explicitly rejects the view that there exists any being apart from Nature itself. Spinoza identifies God with Nature as a whole, and urges that the good life consists in coming to understand Nature. In his words, "our salvation, or blessedness, or freedom consists in a constant and eternal love toward God . . ." Spinoza's concept of God, however, is explicitly not the supernaturalistic concept of God, and Spinoza's metaphysical system thus exemplifies not only a naturalistic metaphysics but also the possibility of reinterpreting the concept of God within a naturalistic framework.

But can those who do not believe in a supernaturalistic God commit themselves to moral principles, or is the acceptance of moral principles dependent upon acceptance of supernaturalism? It is sometimes assumed that those who reject a supernaturalistic God are necessarily immoral, for their denial of the existence of such a God leaves them free to act without fear of Divine punishment. This assumption, however, is seriously in error.

The refutation of the view that morality must rest upon belief in a supernatural God was provided more than two thousand years ago by Socrates in Plato's *Euthyphro* dialogue. Socrates asked the following question: Are actions right because God says they are right, or does God say actions are right because they are right? This question is not a verbal trick; on the contrary, it poses a serious dilemma for those who believe in a supernatural deity. Socrates was inquiring whether actions are right due to God's fiat or whether God is Himself subject to moral standards. If actions are right due to God's command, then anything God commands is right, even if He should command torture or murder. But if one accepts this view, then it makes no sense to say that God Himself is good, for since the good is whatever God commands, to say that God commands rightly is simply to say that He commands as He commands, which is a tautology. This approach makes a mockery of morality, for might does not make right, even if the might is the infinite might of God. To act morally is not to act out of fear of punishment; it is not to act as one is commanded to act. Rather, it is to act as one ought to act. And how one ought to act is not dependent upon anyone's power, even if the power be Divine.

Thus, actions are not right because God commands them; on the contrary, God commands them because they are right. But in that case, what is right is independent of what God commands, for what He commands must conform with an independent standard in order to be right. Since one could act in accordance with this independent standard without believing in the existence of a supernatural God, it follows that morality does not rest upon supernaturalism. Consequently, naturalists can be highly moral (as well as immoral) persons, and supernaturalists can be highly immoral (as well as moral) persons. This conclusion should come as no surprise to anyone who has contrasted the life of Buddha, an atheist, with the life of the monk Torquemada.

We have now seen that naturalistic religion is a genuine possibility, since it is reasonable for individuals to perform rituals, utter prayers, accept metaphysical beliefs, and commit themselves to moral principles without believing in supernaturalism. Indeed, one can even do so while maintaining allegiance to Christianity or Judaism. Consider, for example, those Christians who accept the "Death of God" or those Jews who adhere to Reconstructionist Judaism.

Such options are philosophically respectable. Whether to choose any of them is for each reader to decide.

Ramakrishna

Many Paths to the Same Summit

Ramakrishna (1836–1886) *is perhaps the best known Hindu saint of modern times. He had his first experience of spiritual ecstasy at age seven. He worshipped Rama, Krishna, Shiva, Kali, Allah, and Jesus.*

God has made different religions to suit different aspirants, times, and countries. All doctrines are only so many paths; but a path is by no means God Himself. Indeed, one can reach God if one follows any of the paths with wholehearted devotion. One may eat a cake with icing either straight or sidewise. It will taste sweet either way.

As one and the same material, water, is called by different names by different peoples, one calling it water, another eau, a third aqua, and another pani, so the one Everlasting-Intelligent-Bliss is invoked by some as God, by some as Allah, by some as Jehovah, and by others as Brahman.

As one can ascend to the top of a house by means of a ladder or a bamboo or a staircase or a rope, so diverse are the ways and means to approach God, and every religion in the world shows one of these ways.

As the young wife in a family shows her love and respect to her father-in-law, mother-in-law, and every other member of the family, and at the same time loves her husband more than these; similarly, being firm in thy devotion to the deity of thy own choice, do not despise other deities, but honour them all.

Bow down and worship where others kneel, for where so many have been paying the tribute of adoration the kind Lord must manifest himself, for he is all mercy.

The devotee who has seen God in one aspect only, knows him in that aspect alone. But he who has seen him in manifold aspects is alone in a position to say, 'All these forms are of one God and God is multiform.' He is formless and with form, and many are his forms which no one knows.

The Saviour is the messenger of God. He is like the viceroy of a mighty monarch. As when there is some disturbance in a far-off province, the king sends his viceroy to quell it, so wherever there is a decline of religion in any part of the world, God sends his Saviour there. It is one and the same Saviour that, having plunged into the ocean of life, rises up in one place and is known as Krishna (the leading Hindu incarnation of God), and diving down again rises in another place and is known as Christ.

Every man should follow his own religion. A Christian should follow Christianity, a Mohammedan should follow Mohammedanism, and so on. For the Hindus, the ancient path, the path of the Aryan sages, is the best.

People partition off their lands by means of boundaries, but no one can partition off the all-embracing sky overhead. The indivisible sky surrounds all and includes all. So common man in ignorance says, 'My religion is the only one, my religion is the best.' But when his heart is illumined by true knowledge, he knows that above all these wars of sects and sectarians presides the one indivisible, eternal, all-knowing bliss.

As a mother, in nursing her sick children, gives rice and curry to one, and sago arrowroot to another, and bread and butter to a third, so the Lord has laid out different paths for different men suitable to their natures.

Dispute not. As you rest firmly on your own faith and opinion, allow others also the equal liberty to stand by their own faiths and opinions. By mere disputation you will never succeed in convincing another of his error. When the grace of God descends on him, each one will understand his own mistakes.

There was a man who worshipped Shiva but hated all other deities. One day Shiva appeared to him and said, 'I shall never by pleased with thee so long as thou hatest the other gods.' But the man was inexorable. After a few days Shiva again appeared to him and said, 'I shall never be pleased with thee so long as thou hatest.' The man kept silent. After a few days Shiva again appeared to him. This time one side of his body was that of Shiva, and the other side that of Vishnu. The man was half pleased and half displeased. He laid his offerings on the side representing Shiva, and did not offer anything to the side representing Vishnu. Then Shiva said, 'Thy bigotry is unconquerable. I, by assuming this dual aspect, tried to convince thee that all gods and goddesses are but various aspects of the one Absolute Brahman.'

Sigmund Freud
The Religious World View

Sigmund Freud (1856–1939), *the founder of pyschoanalysis, lived most of his life in Vienna. A physician by training, Freud sought to explain the existence and nature of mental phenomena. His clinical and theoretical work in this area was supplemented by numerous reflections on cultural and social matters. Virtually nothing escaped his fierce intelligence.*

If we are to give an account of the grandiose nature of religion, we must bear in mind what it undertakes to do for human beings. It gives them information about the origin and coming into existence of the universe, it assures them of its protection and of ultimate happiness in the ups and downs of life and it directs their thoughts and actions by precepts which it lays down with its whole authority. Thus it fulfills three functions. With the first of them it satisfies the human thirst for knowledge; it does the same thing that science attempts to do with *its* means, and at that point enters into rivalry with it. It is to its second function that it no doubt owes the greatest part of its influence. Science can be no match for it when it soothes the fear that men feel of the dangers and vicissitudes of life, when it assures them of a happy ending and offers them comfort in unhappiness. It is true that science can teach us how to avoid certain dangers and that there are some sufferings which it can successfully combat; it would be most unjust to deny that it is a powerful helper to men; but there are many situations in which it must leave a man to his suffering and can only advise him to submit to it. In its third function, in which it issues precepts and lays down prohibitions and restrictions, religion is furthest away from science. For science is content to investigate and to establish facts, though it is true that from its applications rules and advice are derived on the conduct of life. In some circumstances these are the same as those offered by religion, but, when this is so, the reasons for them are different.

The convergence between these three aspects of religion is not entirely clear. What has an explanation of the origin of the universe to do with the inculcation of certain particular ethical precepts? The assurances of protection and happiness are more intimately linked with the ethical requirements. They are the reward for fulfilling these commands; only those who obey them may count upon these benefits, punishment awaits the disobedient. Incidentally, something similar is true of science. Those who disregard its lessons, so it tells us, expose themselves to injury.

The remarkable combination in religion of instruction, consolation and requirements can only be understood if it is subjected to a genetic analysis. This may be approached from the most striking point of the aggregate, from its instruction on the origin of the universe; for why, we may ask, should a cosmogony be a regular component of religious systems? The doctrine is, then, that the universe was created by a being resembling a man, but magnified in every respect, in power, wisdom, and the strength of his passions—an idealized super-man. Animals as creators of the universe point to the influence of totemism, upon which we shall have a few words at least to say presently. It is an interesting fact that this creator is always only a single being, even when there are believed to be many gods. It is interesting, too, that the creator is usually a man, though there is far from being a lack of indications of female deities; and some mythologies actually make the creation begin with a male god getting rid of a female deity, who is degraded into being a monster. Here the most interesting problems of detail open out; but we must hurry on. Our further path is made easy to recognize, for this god-creator is undisguisedly called 'father'. Psycho-analysis infers that he really is the father, with all the magnificence in which he once appeared to the small child. A religious man pictures the creation of the universe just as he pictures his own origin.

This being so, it is easy to explain how it is that consoling assurances and strict ethical demands are combined with a cosmogony. For the same person to whom the child owed his existence, the father (or more correctly, no doubt, the parental agency compounded of the father and mother), also protected and watched over him in his feeble and helpless state, exposed as he was to all the dangers lying in wait in the external world; under his father's protection he felt safe. When a human being has himself grown up, he knows, to be sure, that he is in possession of greater strength, but his insight into the perils of life has also grown greater, and he rightly concludes that fundamentally he still remains just as helpless and unprotected as he was in his childhood, that faced by the world he is still a child. Even now, therefore, he cannot do without the protection which he enjoyed as a child. But he has long since recognized, too, that his father is a being of narrowly restricted power, and not equipped with every excellence. He therefore harks back to the mnemic image of the father whom in his childhood he so greatly overvalued. He exalts the image into a deity and makes it into something contemporary and real. The effective strength of this mnemic image and the persistence of his need for protection jointly sustain his belief in God.

The third main item in the religious programme, the ethical demand, also fits into this childhood situation with ease. I may remind you of Kant's famous pronouncement in which he names, in a single breath, the starry heavens and the moral law within us. However strange this juxtaposition may sound—for what have the heavenly bodies to do with the question of whether one human creature loves another or kills him?—it nevertheless touches on a great psychological truth. The same father (or parental agency) which gave the child life and guarded him against its perils, taught him as well what he might do and what he must leave undone, instructed him that he must adapt himself to certain restrictions on his instinctual wishes, and made him understand what regard he was expected to have for his parents and brothers and sisters, if he wanted to become a tolerated and welcome member of the family circle and later on of larger associations. The child is brought up to a knowledge of his social duties by a system of loving rewards and punishments, he is taught that his security in life depends on his parents (and afterwards other people) loving him and on their being able to believe that he loves them. All these relations are afterwards introduced by men unaltered into their religion. Their parents' prohibitions and demands persist within them as a moral conscience. With the help of this same system of rewards and punishments, God rules the world of men. The amount of protection and happy satisfaction assigned to an individual depends on his fulfilment of the ethical demands; his love of God and his consciousness of being loved by God are the foundations of the security with which he is armed against the dangers of the external world and of his human environment. Finally, in prayer he has assured himself a direct influence on the divine will and with it a share in the divine omnipotence. . . .

The scientific spirit, . . . has begun, in the course of time, to treat religion as a human affair and to submit it to a critical examination. Religion was not able to stand up to this. What first gave rise to suspicion and scepticism were its tales of miracles, for they contradicted everything that had been taught by sober observation and betrayed too clearly the influence of the activity of the human imagination. After this its doctrines explaining the origin of the universe met with rejection, for they gave evidence of an ignorance which bore the stamp of ancient times and to which, thanks to their increased familiarity with the laws of nature, people knew they were superior. The idea that the universe came into existence through acts of copulation or creation analogous to the origin of individual people had ceased to be the most obvious and self-evident hypothesis since the distinction between animate creatures with a mind and an inanimate Nature had impressed itself on human thought—a distinction which made it impossible to retain belief in the original animism. Nor must we overlook the influence of the comparative study of different religious systems and the impression of their mutual exclusiveness and intolerance.

Strengthened by these preliminary exercises, the scientific spirit gained enough courage at last to venture on an examination of the most important and emotionally valuable elements of the religious *Weltanschauung*. People may always have seen, though it was long before they dared to say so openly, that the pronouncements of religion promising men protection and happiness if they would only fulfil certain ethical requirements had also shown themselves unworthy of belief. It seems not to be the case that there is a Power in the universe which watches over the well-being of individuals with parental care and brings all their affairs to a happy ending. On the contrary, the destinies of mankind can be brought into harmony neither with the hypothesis of a Universal Benevolence nor with the partly contradictory one of a

Universal Justice. Earthquakes, tidal waves, conflagrations, make no distinction between the virtuous and pious and the scoundrel or unbeliever. Even where what is in question is not inanimate Nature but where an individual's fate depends on his relations to other people, it is by no means the rule that virtue is rewarded and that evil finds its punishment. Often enough the violent, cunning or ruthless man seizes the envied good things of the world and the pious man goes away empty. Obscure, unfeeling and unloving powers determine men's fate; the system of rewards and punishments which religion ascribes to the government of the universe seems not to exist. Here once again is a reason for dropping a portion of the animistic theory which had been rescued from animism by religion.

The last contribution to the criticism of the religious *Weltanschauung* was effected by psycho-analysis, by showing how religion originated from the helplessness of children and by tracing its contents to the survival into maturity of the wishes and needs of childhood. This did not precisely mean a contradiction of religion, but it was nevertheless a necessary rounding-off of our knowledge about it, and in one respect at least it was a contradiction, for religion itself lays claim to a divine origin. And, to be sure, it is not wrong in this, provided that our interpretation of God is accepted.

In summary, therefore, the judgement of science on the religious *Weltanschauung* is this. While the different religions wrangle with one another as to which of them is in possession of the truth, our view is that the question of the truth of religious beliefs may be left altogether on one side. Religion is an attempt to master the sensory world in which we are situated by means of the wishful world which we have developed within us as a result of biological and psychological necessities. But religion cannot achieve this. Its doctrines bear the imprint of the times in which they arose, the ignorant times of the childhood of humanity. Its consolations deserve no trust. Experience teaches us that the world is no nursery. The ethical demands on which religion seeks to lay stress need, rather, to be given another basis; for they are indispensable to human society and it is dangerous to link obedience to them with religious faith. If we attempt to assign the place of religion in the evolution of mankind, it appears not as a permanent acquisition but as a counterpart to the neurosis which individual civilized men have to go through in their passage from childhood to maturity. . . .

The struggle of the scientific spirit against the religious *Weltanschauung* is, as you know, not at an end: it is still going on to-day under our eyes. Though as a rule psycho-analysis makes little use of the weapon of controversy, I will not hold back from looking into this dispute. In doing so I may perhaps throw some further light on our attitude to *Weltanschauungen*. You will see how easily some of the arguments brought forward by the supporters of religion can be answered, though it is true that others may evade refutation.

The first objection we meet with is to the effect that it is an impertinence on the part of science to make religion a subject for its investigations, for religion is something sublime, superior to any operation of the human intellect, something which may not be approached with hair-splitting criticisms. In other words, science is not qualified to judge religion: it is quite serviceable and estimable otherwise, so long as it keeps to its own sphere. But religion is not its sphere, and it has no business there. If we do not let ourselves be put off by this brusque repulse and enquire further what is the basis of this claim to a position exceptional among all human concerns, the reply we receive (if we are thought worthy of any reply) is that religion cannot be measured by human measurements, for it is of divine origin and was given us as a revelation by a Spirit which the human spirit cannot comprehend. One would have thought that there was nothing easier than the refutation of this argument: it is a clear case of *petitio principii*, of 'begging the question'—I know of no good German equivalent expression. The actual question raised is whether there *is* a divine spirit and a revelation by it; and the matter is certainly not decided by saying that this question cannot be asked, since the deity may not be put in question. The position here is what it occasionally is during the work of analysis. If a usually sensible patient rejects some particular suggestion on specially foolish grounds, this logical weakness is evidence of the existence of a specially strong motive for the denial—a motive which can only be of an affective nature, an emotional tie.

We may also be given another answer, in which a motive of this kind is openly admitted: religion may not be critically examined because it is the highest, most precious, and most sublime thing that the human spirit has produced, because it gives expression to the deepest feelings and alone makes the world tolerable and life worthy of men. We need not reply by disputing this estimate of religion but by drawing attention to another matter. What we do is to emphasize the fact that what is in question is not in the least an invasion of the field of religion by the scientific spirit, but on the contrary an invasion by religion of the sphere of scientific thought. Whatever may be the value and importance of religion, it has no right in any way to restrict thought—no right, therefore, to exclude itself from having thought applied to it.

Scientific thinking does not differ in its nature from the normal activity of thought, which all of us, believers and unbelievers, employ in looking after our affairs in ordinary life. It has only developed certain features: it takes an interest in things even if they have no immediate, tangible use; it is concerned carefully to avoid individual factors and affective influences; it examines more strictly the trustworthiness of the sense-perceptions on which it bases its conclusions; it provides itself with new perceptions which cannot be obtained by everyday means and it isolates the determinants of these new experiences in experiments which are deliberately varied. Its endeavour is to arrive at correspondence with reality—that is to say, with what exists outside us and independently of us and, as experience has taught us, is decisive for the fulfilment or disappointment of our wishes. This correspondence with the real external world we call 'truth'. It remains the aim of scientific work even if we leave the practical value of that work out of account. When, therefore, religion asserts that it can take the place of science, that, because it is beneficent and elevating, it must also be true, that is in fact an invasion which must be repulsed in the most general interest. It is asking a great deal of a person who has learnt to conduct his ordinary affairs in accordance with the rules of experience and with a regard to reality, to suggest that he shall hand over the care of what are precisely his most intimate interests to an agency which claims as its privilege freedom from the precepts of rational thinking. And as regards the protection which religion promises its believers, I think none of us would be so much as prepared to enter a motor-car if its driver announced that he drove, unperturbed by traffic regulations, in accordance with the impulses of his soaring imagination. . . .

Our best hope for the future is that intellect—the scientific spirit, reason—may in process of time establish a dictatorship in the mental life of man. The nature of reason is a guarantee that afterwards it will not fail to give man's emotional impulses and what is deter-mined by them the position they deserve. But the common compulsion exercised by such a dominance of reason will prove to be the strongest uniting bond among men and lead the way to further unions. Whatever, like religion's prohibition against thought, opposes such a development, is a danger for the future of mankind.

It may then be asked why religion does not put an end to this dispute which is so hopeless for it by frankly declaring: 'It is a fact that I cannot give you what is commonly called "truth"; if you want that, you must keep to science. But what I have to offer you is something incomparably more beautiful, more consoling and more uplifting than anything you could get from science. And because of that, I say to you that it is true in another, higher sense.' It is easy to find the answer to this. Religion cannot make this admission because it would involve its forfeiting all its influence on the mass of mankind. The ordinary man only knows one kind of truth, in the ordinary sense of the word. He cannot imagine what a higher or a highest truth may be. Truth seems to him no more capable of comparative degrees than death; and he cannot join in the leap from the beautiful to the true. Perhaps you will think as I do that he is right in this.

Bertrand Russell

Why I Am Not a Christian

Bertrand Russell *(1872–1970) was one of the greatest philosophers of this century. He wrote an enormous number of philosophical books and articles, from* Principia Mathematica *(with Alfred North Whitehead) to some notorious polemics in favor of "free love" and atheism. Like Hume, he was too controversial for most universities, and a famous court case prevented him from teaching at City College of New York. He did, however, win the Nobel Prize for Literature in 1950. At the age of 89, he was jailed for protesting against nuclear arms. The selection here was delivered as a public lecture.*

As your Chairman has told you, the subject about which I am going to speak to you tonight is "Why I Am Not a Christian." Perhaps it would be as well, first of all, to try to make out what one means by the word *Christian*. It is used these days in a very loose sense by a great many people. Some people mean no more by it than a person who attempts to live a good life. In that sense I suppose there would be Christians in all sects and creeds; but I do not think that that is the proper sense of the word, if only because it would imply that all the people who are not Christians—all the Buddhists, Confucians, Mohammedans, and so on— are not trying to live a good life. I do not mean by a Christian any person who tries to live decently according to his lights. I think that you must have a certain amount of definite belief before you have a right to call yourself a Christian. The word does not have quite such a full-blooded meaning now as it had in the times of St. Augustine and St. Thomas Aquinas. In those days, if a man said that he was a Christian it was known what he meant. You accepted a whole collection of creeds which were set out with great precision, and every single syllable of those creeds you believed with the whole strength of your convictions.

WHAT IS A CHRISTIAN?

Nowadays it is not quite that. We have to be a little more vague in our meaning of Christianity. I think, however, that there are two different items which are quite essential to anybody calling himself a Christian. The first is one of a dogmatic nature—namely, that you must believe in God and immortality. If you do not believe in those two things, I do not think that you can properly call yourself a Christian. Then, further than that, as the name implies, you must have some kind of belief about Christ. The Mohammedans, for instance, also believe in God and in immortality, and yet they would not call themselves Christians. I think you must have at the very lowest the belief that Christ was, if not divine, at least the best and wisest of men. If you are not going to believe that much about Christ, I do not think you have any right to call yourself a Christian. Of course, there is another sense, which you find in *Whitaker's Almanack* and in geography books, where the population of the world is said to be divided into Christians, Mohammedans, Buddhists, fetish worshipers, and so on; and in that sense we are all Christians. The geography books count us all in, but that is a purely geographical sense, which I suppose we can ignore. Therefore I take it that when I tell you why I am not a Christian I have to tell you two different things: first, why I do not believe in God and in immortality; and, secondly, why I do not think that Christ was the best and wisest of men, although I grant him a very high degree of moral goodness.

But for the successful efforts of unbelievers in the past, I could not take so elastic a definition of Christianity as that. As I said before, in olden days it had a much more full-blooded sense. For instance, it included the belief in hell. Belief in eternal hell-fire was an essential item of Christian belief until pretty recent times. In this country, as you know, it ceased to be an essential item because of a decision of the Privy Council, and from that decision the Archbishop of Canterbury and the Archbishop of York dissented; but in this country our religion is settled by Act of Parliament, and therefore the Privy Council was able to override their Graces and hell was no longer necessary to a Christian. Consequently I shall not insist that a Christian must believe in hell.

THE EXISTENCE OF GOD

To come to this question of the existence of God: it is a large and serious question, and if I were to attempt to deal with it in any adequate manner I should have to keep you here until Kingdom Come, so that you will have to excuse me if I deal with it in a somewhat summary fashion. You know, of course, that the Catholic Church has laid it down as a dogma that the existence of God can be proved by the unaided reason. That is a somewhat curious dogma, but it is one of their dogmas. They had to introduce it because at one time the freethinkers adopted the habit of saying that there were such and such arguments which mere reason might urge against the existence of God, but of course they knew as a matter of faith that God did exist. The arguments and the reasons were set out at great length, and the Catholic Church felt that they must stop it. Therefore they laid it down that the existence of God can be proved by the unaided reason and they had to set up what they considered were arguments to prove it. There are, of course, a number of them, but I shall take only a few.

THE FIRST-CAUSE ARGUMENT

Perhaps the simplest and easiest to understand is the argument of the First Cause. (It is maintained that everything we see in this world has a cause, and as you go back in the chain of causes further and further you must come to a First Cause, and to that First Cause you give the name of God.) That argument, I suppose, does not carry very much weight nowadays, because, in the first place, cause is not quite what it used to be. The philosophers and the men of science have got going on cause, and it has not anything like the vitality it used to have; but, apart from that, you can see that the argument that there must be a First Cause is one that cannot have any validity. I may say that when I was a young man and was debating these questions very seriously in my mind, I for a long time accepted the argument of the First Cause, until one day, at the age of eighteen, I read John Stuart Mill's Autobiography, and I there found this sentence: "My father taught me that the question 'Who made me?' cannot be answered, since it immediately suggests the further question 'Who made God?' " That very simple sentence showed me, as I still think, the fallacy in the argument of the First Cause. If everything must have a cause, then God must have a cause. If there can be anything without a cause, it may just as well be the world as God, so that there cannot be any validity in that argument. It is exactly of the same nature as the Hindu's view, that the world rested upon an elephant and the elephant rested upon a tortoise; and when they said, "How about the tortoise?" the Indian said, "Suppose we change the subject." The argument is really no better than that. There is no reason why the world could not have come into being without a cause; nor, on the other hand, is there any reason why it should not have always existed. There is no reason to suppose that the world had a beginning at all. The idea that things must have a beginning is really due to the poverty of our imagination. Therefore, perhaps, I need not waste any more time upon the argument about the First Cause.

THE NATURAL-LAW ARGUMENT

Then there is a very common argument from natural law. That was a favorite argument all through the eighteenth century, especially under the influence of Sir Isaac Newton and his cosmogony. People observed the planets going around the sun according to the law of gravitation, and they thought that God had given a behest to these planets to move in that particular fashion, and that was why they did so. That was, of course, a convenient and simple explanation that saved them the trouble of looking any further for explanations of the law of gravitation. Nowadays we explain the law of gravitation in a somewhat complicated fashion that Einstein has introduced. I do not propose to give you a lecture on the law of gravitation, as interpreted by Einstein, because that again would take some time; at any rate, you no longer have the sort of natural law that you had in the Newtonian system, where, for some reason that nobody could understand, nature behaved in a uniform fashion. We now find that a great many things we thought were natural laws are really human conventions. You know that even in the remotest depths of stellar space there are still three feet to a yard. That is, no doubt, a very remarkable fact, but you would hardly call it a law of nature. And a great many things that have been regarded as laws of nature are of that kind. On the other hand, where you can get down to any knowledge of what atoms actually do, you will find they are much less subject to law than people thought, and that the laws at which you arrive are statistical averages of just the sort that would emerge from chance. There is, as we all know, a law that if you throw dice you will get double sixes only about once in thirty-six times, and we do not regard that as evidence that the fall of the dice is regulated by design; on the contrary, if the double sixes came every time we should think that there was design. The laws of nature are of that sort as regards a great many of them. They are statistical averages such as would emerge from the laws of chance; and that makes this whole business of natural law much less impressive than it formerly was. Quite apart from that, which represents the momentary state of science that may change tomorrow, the whole idea that natural laws imply a lawgiver is due to a confusion between natural and human laws. Human laws are behests commanding you to behave a certain way, in which way you may choose to behave, or you may choose not to behave; but natural laws are a description of how things do in fact behave, and being a mere description of what they in fact do, you cannot argue that there must be somebody who told them to do that, because even supposing that there were, you are then faced with the question "Why did God issue just those natural laws and no others?" If you say that he did it simply from his own good pleasure, and without any reason, you then find that there is something which is not subject to law, and so your train of natural law is interrupted. If you say, as more orthodox theologians do, that in all the laws which God issues he had a reason for giving those laws rather than others—the reason, of course, being to create the best universe, although you would never think it to look at it—if there were a reason for the laws which God gave, then God himself was subject to law, and therefore you do not get any advantage by introducing God as an intermediary. You have really a law outside and anterior to the divine edicts, and God does not serve your purpose, because he is not the ultimate lawgiver. In short, this whole argument about natural law no longer has anything like the strength that it used to have. I am traveling on in time in my review of the arguments. The arguments that are used for the existence of God change their character as time goes on. They were at first hard intellectual arguments embodying certain quite definite fallacies. As we come to modern times they become less respectable intellectually and more and more affected by a kind of moralizing vagueness.

THE ARGUMENT FROM DESIGN

The next step in this process brings us to the argument from design. You all know the argument from design: everything in the world is made just so that we can manage to live in the world, and if the world was ever so little different, we could not manage to live in it. That is the argument from design. It sometimes takes a rather curious form; for instance, it is argued that rabbits have white tails in order to be easy to shoot. I do not know how rabbits would view that application. It is an easy argument to parody. You all know Voltaire's remark, that obviously the nose was designed to be such as to fit spectacles. That sort of parody has turned out to be not nearly so wide of the mark as it might have seemed in the eighteenth century, because since the time of Darwin we understand much better why living creatures are adapted to their environment. It is not that their environment was made to be suitable to them but that they grew to be suitable to it, and that is the basis of adaptation. There is no evidence of design about it.

When you come to look into this argument from design, it is a most astonishing thing that people can believe that this world, with all the things that are in it, with all its defects, should be the best that omnipotence and omniscience have been able to produce in millions of years. I really cannot believe it. Do you think that, if you were granted omnipotence and omniscience and millions of years in which to perfect your world, you could produce nothing better than the Ku Klux Klan or the Fascists? Moreover, if you accept the ordinary laws of science, you have to suppose that human life and life in general on this planet will die out in due course: it is a stage in the decay of the solar system; at a certain stage of decay you get the sort of conditions of temperature and so forth which are suitable to protoplasm, and there is life for a short time in the life of the whole solar system. You see in the moon the sort of thing to which the earth is tending—something dead, cold, and lifeless.

I am told that that sort of view is depressing, and people will sometimes tell you that if they believed that, they would not be able to go on living. Do not believe it; it is all nonsense. Nobody really worries much about what is going to happen millions of years hence. Even if they think they are worrying much about that, they are really deceiving themselves. They are worried about something much more mundane, or it may merely be a bad digestion; but nobody is really seriously rendered unhappy by the thought of something that is going to happen to this world millions and millions of years hence. Therefore, although it is of course a gloomy view to suppose that life will die out—at least I suppose we may say so, although sometimes when I contemplate the things that people do with their lives I think it is almost a consolation—it is not such as to render life miserable. It merely makes you turn your attention to other things.

. . . Of course I know that the sort of intellectual arguments that I have been talking to you about are not what really moves people. What really moves people to believe in God is not any intellectual argument at all. Most people believe in God because they have been taught from early infancy to do it, and that is the main reason.

Then I think that the next most powerful reason is the wish for safety, a sort of feeling that there is a big brother who will look after you. That plays a very profound part in influencing people's desire for a belief in God.

THE CHARACTER OF CHRIST

I now want to say a few words upon a topic which I often think is not quite sufficiently dealt with by Rationalists, and that is the question whether Christ was the best and the wisest of men. It is generally taken for granted that we should all agree that that was so. I do not myself. I think that there are a good many points upon which I agree with Christ a great deal more than the professing Christians do. I do not know that I could go with Him all the way, but I could go with Him much further than most professing Christians can. You will remember that He said, "Resist not evil: but whosoever shall smite thee on thy right cheek, turn to him the other also." That is not a new precept or a new principle. It was used by Lao-tse and Buddha some 500 or 600 years before Christ, but it is not a principle which as a matter of fact Christians accept. I have no doubt that the present Prime Minister [Stanley Baldwin], for instance, is a most sincere Christian, but I should not advise any of you to go and smite him on one cheek. I think you might find that he thought this text was intended in a figurative sense.

Then there is another point which I consider excellent. You will remember that Christ said, "Judge not lest ye be judged." That principle I do not think you would find was popular in the law courts of Christian countries. I have known in my time quite a number of judges who were very earnest Christians, and none of them felt that they were acting contrary to Christian principles in what they did. Then Christ says, "Give to him that asketh of thee, and from him that would borrow of thee turn not thou away." That is a very good principle. Your Chairman has reminded you that we are not here to talk politics, but I cannot help observing that the last general election was fought on the question of how desirable it was to turn away from him that would borrow of thee, so that one must assume that the Liberals and Conservatives of this country are composed of people who do not agree with the teaching of Christ, because they certainly did very emphatically turn away on that occasion.

Then there is one other maxim of Christ which I think has a great deal in it, but I do not find that it is very popular among some of our Christian friends. He says, "If thou wilt be perfect, go and sell that which thou hast, and give to the poor." That is a very excellent maxim, but, as I say, it is not much practiced. All these, I think, are good maxims, although they are a little difficult to live up to. I do not profess to live up to them myself; but then, after all, it is not quite the same thing as for a Christian.

DEFECTS IN CHRIST'S TEACHING

Having granted the excellence of these maxims, I come to certain points in which I do not believe that one can grant either the superlative wisdom or the superlative goodness of Christ as depicted in the Gospels; and here I may say that one is not concerned with the historical question. Historically it is quite doubtful whether Christ ever existed at all, and if He did we do not know anything about Him, so that I am not concerned with the historical question, which is a very difficult one. I am concerned with Christ as He appears in the Gospels, taking the Gospel narrative as it stands, and there one does find some things that do not seem to be very wise. For one thing, He certainly thought that His second coming would occur in clouds of glory before the death of all the people who were living at that time. There are a great many texts that prove that. He says, for instance, "Ye shall not have gone over the cities of Israel till the Son of Man be come." Then He says, "There are some standing here which shall not taste death till the Son of Man comes into His kingdom"; and there are a lot of places where it is quite clear that He believed that His second coming would happen during the lifetime of many then living. That was the belief of His earlier followers, and it was the basis of a good deal of His moral teaching. When He said, "Take no thought for the morrow," and things of that sort, it was very largely because He thought that the second coming was going to be very soon, and that all ordinary mundane affairs did not count. I have, as a matter of fact, known some Christians who did believe that the second coming was imminent. I knew a parson who frightened his congregation terribly by telling them that the second coming was very imminent indeed, but they were much consoled when they found that he was planting trees in his garden. The early Christians did really believe it, and they did abstain from such things as planting trees in their gardens, because they did accept from Christ the belief that the second coming was imminent. In that respect, clearly He was not so wise as some other people have been, and He was certainly not superlatively wise.

THE MORAL PROBLEM

Then you come to moral questions. There is one very serious defect to my mind in Christ's moral character, and that is that He believed in hell. I do not myself feel that any person who is really profoundly humane can believe in everlasting punishment. Christ certainly as depicted in the Gospels did believe in everlasting punishment, and one does find repeatedly a vindictive fury against those people who would not listen to His preaching—an attitude which is not uncommon with preachers, but which does somewhat detract from superlative excellence. You do not, for instance find that attitude in Socrates. You find him quite bland and urbane toward the people who would not listen to him; and it is, to my mind, far more worthy of a sage to take that line than to take the line of indignation. You probably all remember the sort of things that Socrates was saying when he was dying, and the sort of things that he generally did say to people who did not agree with him.

You will find that in the Gospels Christ said, "Ye serpents, ye generation of vipers, how can ye escape the damnation of hell." That was said to people who did not like His preaching. It is not really to my mind quite the best tone, and there are a great many of these things about hell. There is, of course, the familiar text about the sin against the Holy Ghost: "Whosoever speaketh against the Holy Ghost it shall not be forgiven him neither in this World nor in the world to come." That text has caused an unspeakable amount of misery in the world, for all sorts of people have imagined that they have committed the sin against the Holy Ghost, and thought that it would not be forgiven them either in this world or in the world to come. I really do not think that a person with a proper degree of kindliness in his nature would have put fears and terrors of that sort into the world.

Then Christ says, "The Son of Man shall send forth His angels, and they shall gather out of His kingdom all things that offend, and them which do iniquity, and shall cast them into a furnace of fire; there shall be wailing and gnashing of teeth"; and He goes on about the wailing and gnashing of teeth. It comes in one verse after another, and it is quite manifest to the reader that there is a certain pleasure in contemplating wailing and gnashing of teeth, or else it would not occur so often. Then you all, of course, remember about the sheep and the goats; how at the second coming He is going to divide the sheep from the goats, and He is going to say to the goats, "Depart from me, ye cursed, into everlasting fire." He continues, "And these shall go away into everlasting fire." Then He says again, "If thy hand offend thee, cut it off; it is better for thee to enter into life maimed, than having two hands to go into hell, into the fire that never shall be quenched; where the worm dieth not and the fire is not quenched." He repeats that again and again also. I must say that I think all this doctrine, that hell-fire is a punishment for sin, is a doctrine of cruelty. It is a doctrine that put cruelty into the world and gave the world generations of cruel torture; and the Christ of the Gospels, if you could take Him as His chroniclers represent Him, would certainly have to be considered partly responsible for that.

There are other things of less importance. There is the instance of the Gadarene swine, where it certainly was not very kind to the pigs to put the devils into them and make them rush down the hill to the sea. You must remember that He was omnipotent, and He could have made the devils simply go away; but He chose to send them into the pigs. Then there is the curious story of the fig tree, which always rather puzzled me. You remember what happened about the fig tree. "He was hungry; and seeing a fig tree afar off having leaves, He came if haply He might find anything thereon; and when He came to it He found nothing but leaves, for the time of figs was not yet. And Jesus answered and said unto it: 'No man eat fruit of thee hereafter for ever' . . . and Peter . . . saith unto Him: 'Master, behold the fig tree which thou cursedst is withered away.' " This a very curious story, because it was not the right time of year for figs, and you really could not blame the tree. I cannot myself feel that either in the matter of wisdom or in the matter of virtue Christ stands quite as high as some other people known to history. I think I should put Buddha and Socrates above Him in those respects.

THE EMOTIONAL FACTOR

As I said before, I do not think that the real reason why people accept religion has anything to do with argumentation. They accept religion on emotional grounds. One is often told that it is a very wrong thing to attack religion, because religion makes men virtuous. So I am told; I have not noticed it. You know, of course, the parody of that argument in Samuel Butler's book, *Erewhon Revisited*. You will remember that in *Erewhon* there is a certain Higgs who arrives in a remote country, and after spending some time there he escapes from that country in a balloon. Twenty years later he comes back to that country and finds a new religion in which he is worshiped under the name of the "Sun Child," and it is said that he ascended into heaven. He finds that the Feast of the Ascension is about to be celebrated, and he hears Professors Hanky and Panky say to each other that they never set eyes on the man Higgs, and they hope they never will; but they are the high priests of the religion of the Sun Child. He is very indignant, and he comes up to them, and he says, "I am going to expose all this humbug and tell the people of Erewhon that it was only I, the man Higgs, and I went up in a balloon." He was told, "You must not do that, because all the morals of this country are bound round this myth, and if they once know that you did not ascend into heaven they will all become wicked"; and so he is persuaded of that and he goes quietly away.

That is the idea—that we should all be wicked if we did not hold to the Christian religion. It seems to me that the people who have held to it have been for the most part extremely wicked. You find this curious fact, that the more intense has been the religion of any period and the more profound has been the dogmatic belief, the greater has been the cruelty and the worse has been the state of affairs. In the so-called ages of faith, when men really did believe the Christian religion in all its completeness, there was the Inquisition, with its tortures; there were millions of unfortunate women burned as witches; and there was every kind of cruelty practiced upon all sorts of people in the name of religion.

You find as you look around the world that every single bit of progress in humane feeling, every improvement in the criminal law, every step toward the diminution of war, every step toward better treatment of the colored races, or every mitigation of slavery, every moral progress that there has been in the world, has been consistently opposed by the organized churches of the world. I say quite deliberately that the Christian religion, as organized in its churches, has been and still is the principal enemy of moral progress in the world.

HOW THE CHURCHES HAVE RETARDED PROGRESS

You may think that I am going too far when I say that that is still so. I do not think that I am. Take one fact. You will bear with me if I mention it. It is not a pleasant fact, but the churches compel one to mention facts that are not pleasant. Supposing that in this world that we live in today an inexperienced girl is married to a syphilitic man; in that case the Catholic Church says, "This is an indissoluble sacrament. You must endure celibacy or stay together. And if you stay together, you must not use birth control to prevent the birth of syphilitic children." Nobody whose natural sympathies have not been warped by dogma, or whose moral nature was not absolutely dead to all sense of suffering, could maintain that it is right and proper that that state of things should continue.

That is only an example. There are a great many ways in which, at the present moment, the church, by its insistence upon what it chooses to call morality, inflicts upon all sorts of people undeserved and unnecessary suffering. And of course, as we know, it is in its major part an opponent still of progress and of improvement in all the ways that diminish suffering in the world, because it has chosen to label as morality a certain narrow set of rules of conduct which have nothing to do with human happiness; and when you say that this or that ought to be done because it would make for human happiness, they think that has nothing to do with the matter at all. "What has human happiness to do with morals? The object of morals is not to make people happy."

FEAR, THE FOUNDATION OF RELIGION

Religion is based, I think, primarily and mainly upon fear. It is partly the terror of the unknown and partly, as I have said, the wish to feel that you have a kind of elder brother who will stand by you in all your troubles and disputes. Fear is the basis of the whole thing—fear of the mysterious, fear of defeat, fear of death. Fear is the parent of cruelty, and therefore it is no wonder if cruelty and religion have gone hand in hand. It is because fear is at the basis of those two things. In this world we can now begin a little to understand things, and a little to master them by help of science, which has forced its way step by step against the Christian religion, against the churches, and against the opposition of all the old precepts. Science can help us to get over this craven fear in which mankind has lived for so many generations. Science can teach us, and I think our own hearts can teach us, no longer to look around for imaginary supports, no longer to invent allies in the sky, but rather to look to our own efforts here below to make this world a fit place to live in, instead of the sort of place that the churches in all these centuries have made it.

WHAT WE MUST DO

We want to stand upon our own feet and look fair and square at the world—its good facts, its bad facts, its beauties, and its ugliness; see the world as it is and be not afraid of it. Conquer the world by intelligence and not merely by being slavishly subdued by the terror that comes from it. The whole conception of God is a conception derived from the ancient Oriental despotisms. It is a conception quite unworthy of free men. When you hear people in church debasing themselves and saying that they are miserable sinners, and all the rest of it, it seems contemptible and not worthy of self-respecting human beings. We ought to stand up and look the world frankly in the face. We ought to make the best we can of the world, and if it is not so good as we wish, after all it will still be better than what these others have made of it in all these ages. A good world needs knowledge, kindliness, and courage; it does not need a regretful hankering after the past or a fettering of the free intelligence by the words uttered long ago by ignorant men. It needs a fearless outlook and a free intelligence. It needs hope for the future, not looking back all the time toward a past that is dead, which we trust will be far surpassed by the future that our intelligence can create.

James Baldwin

Sunday in the Ghetto

James Baldwin, *born in New York City in 1924, is the son of a revivalist minister. Much of his work has aimed at unraveling the repressive myths of white society and providing a voice for estranged black people in America. His most famous works include* Go Tell It on the Mountain, *which is the source of this excerpt,* Notes of a Native Son, *and* The Fire Next Time.

*O*n Sunday mornings and Sunday nights the church was always full; on special Sundays it was full all day. The Grimes family arrived in a body, always a little late, usually in the middle of Sunday school, which began at nine o'clock. This lateness was always their mother's fault— at least in the eyes of their father; she could not seem to get herself and the children ready on time, ever, and sometimes she actually remained behind, not to appear until the morning service. Whey they all arrived together, they separated upon entering the doors, father and mother going to sit in the Adult Class, which was taught by Sister McCandless, Sarah going to the Infant's Class, John and Roy sitting in the Intermediate, which was taught by Brother Elisha.

When he was young, John had paid no attention in Sunday school, and always forgot the golden text, which earned him the wrath of his father. Around the time of his fourteenth birthday, with all the pressures of church and home uniting to drive him to the altar, he strove to appear more serious and therefore less conspicuous. But he was distracted by his new teacher, Elisha, who was the pastor's nephew and who had but lately arrived from Georgia. He was not much older than John, only seventeen, and he was already saved and was a preacher. John stared at Elisha all during the lesson, admiring the timbre of Elisha's voice, much deeper and manlier than his own, admiring the leanness, and grace, and strength, and darkness of Elisha in his Sunday suit, wondering if he would ever be holy as Elisha was holy. But he did not follow the lesson, and when, sometimes, Elisha paused to ask John a question, John was ashamed and confused, feeling the palms of his hands become wet and his heart pound like a hammer. Elisha would smile and reprimand him gently, and the lesson would go on.

Roy never knew his Sunday school lesson either, but it was different with Roy—no one really expected of Roy what was expected of John. Everyone was always praying that the Lord would change Roy's heart, but it was John who was expected to be good, to be a good example.

When Sunday school service ended there was a short pause before morning service began. In this pause, if it was good weather, the old folks might step outside a moment to talk among themselves. The sisters would almost always be dressed in white from crown to toe. The small children, on this day, in this place, and oppressed by their elders, tried hard to play without seeming to be disrespectful of God's house. But sometimes, nervous or perverse, they shouted, or threw hymn-books, or began to cry, putting their parents, men or women of God, under the necessity of proving—by harsh means or tender—who, in a sanctified household, ruled. The older children, like John or Roy, might wander down the avenue, but not too far. Their father never let John and Roy out of his sight, for Roy had often disappeared between Sunday school and morning service and had not come back all day.

The Sunday morning service began when Brother Elisha sat down at the piano and raised a song. This moment and this music had been with John, so it seemed, since he had first drawn breath. It seemed that there had never been a time when he had not known this moment of waiting while the packed church paused—the sisters in white, heads raised, the brothers in blue, heads back; the white caps of the women seeming to glow in the charged air like crowns, the kinky, gleaming heads of the men seeming to be lifted up—and the rustling and the whispering ceased and the children were quiet; perhaps someone coughed, or the sound of a car horn, or a curse from the streets came in; then Elisha hit the keys, beginning at once to sing, and everybody joined him, clapping their hands, and rising, and beating the tambourines.

The song might be: *Down at the cross where my Saviour died!*

Or: *Jesus, I'll never forget how you set me free!*

Or: *Lord, hold my hand while I run this race!*

They sang with all the strength that was in them, and clapped their hands for joy. There had never been a time when John had not sat watching the saints rejoice with terror in his heart, and wonder. Their singing caused him to believe in the presence of the Lord; indeed, it was no longer a question of belief, because they made that presence real. He did not feel it himself, the joy they felt, yet he could not doubt that it was, for them, the very bread of life—could not doubt it, that is, until it was too late to doubt. Something happened to their faces and their voices, the rhythm of their bodies, and to the air they breathed; it was as though wherever they might be became the upper room, and the Holy Ghost were riding on the air. His father's face, always awful, became more awful now; his father's daily anger was transformed into prophetic wrath. His mother, her eyes raised to heaven, hands arced before her, moving, made real for John that patience, that endurance, that long suffering, which he had read of in the Bible and found so hard to imagine.

On Sunday mornings the women all seemed patient, all the men seemed mighty. While John watched, the Power struck someone, a man or woman; they cried out, a long, wordless crying, and, arms outstretched like wings, they began the Shout. Someone moved a chair a little to give them room, the rhythm paused, the singing stopped, only the pounding feet and the clapping hands were heard; then another cry, another dancer; then the tambourines began again, and the voices rose again, and the music swept on again, like fire, or flood, or judgment. Then the church seemed to swell with the Power it held, and, like a planet rocking in space, the temple rocked with the Power of God. John watched, watched the faces, and the weightless bodies, and listened to the timeless cries. One day, so everyone said, this Power would possess him; he would sing and cry as they did now, and dance before his King. He watched young Ella Mae Washington, the seventeen-year-old granddaughter of Praying Mother Washington, as she began to dance. And then Elisha danced.

At one moment, head thrown back, eyes closed, sweat standing on his brow, he sat at the piano, singing and playing; and then, like a great, black cat in trouble in the jungle, he stiffened and trembled, and cried out. *Jesus, Jesus, oh Lord Jesus!* He struck on the piano one last, wild note, and threw up his hands, palms upward, stretched wide apart. The tambourines raced to fill the vacuum left by his silent piano, and his cry drew answering cries. Then he was on his feet, turning, blind, his face congested, contorted with this rage, and the muscles leaping and swelling in his long, dark neck. It seemed that he could not breathe, that his body could not contain this passion, that he would be, before their eyes, dispersed into the waiting air. His hands, rigid to the very fingertips, moved outward and back against his hips, his sightless eyes looked upward, and he began to dance. Then his hands closed into fists, and his head snapped downward, his sweat loosening the grease that slicked down his hair; and the rhythm of all the others quickened to match Elisha's rhythm; his thighs moved terribly against the cloth of his suit, his heels beat on the floor, and his fists moved beside his body as though he were beating his own drum. And so, for a while, in the center of the dancers, head down, fists beating, on, on, unbearably, until it seemed the walls of the church would fall for very sound; and then, in a moment, with a cry, head up, arms high in the air, sweat pouring from his forehead, and all his body dancing as though it would never stop. Sometimes he did not stop until he fell—until he dropped like some animal felled by a hammer—moaning, on his face. And then a great moaning filled the church.

There was sin among them. One Sunday, when regular service was over, Father James had uncovered sin in the congregation of the righteous. He had uncovered Elisha and Ella Mae. They had been "walking disorderly"; they were in danger of straying from the truth. And as Father James spoke of the sin that he knew they had not committed yet, of the unripe fig plucked too early from the tree—to set the children's teeth on edge—John felt himself grow dizzy in his seat and could not look at Elisha where he stood, beside Ella Mae, before the altar. Elisha hung his head as Father James spoke, and the congregation murmured. And Ella Mae was not so beautiful now as she was when she was singing and testifying, but looked like a sullen, ordinary girl. Her full lips were loose and her eyes were black—with shame, or rage, or both. Her grandmother, who had raised her, sat watching quietly, with folded hands. She was one of the pillars of the church, a powerful evangelist and very widely known. She said nothing in Ella Mae's defense, for she must have felt, as the congregation felt, that Father James was only exercising his clear and painful duty; he was responsible, after all, for Elisha, as Praying Mother Washington was responsible for Ella Mae. It was not an easy thing, said Father James, to be the pastor of a flock. It might look easy to just sit up there in the pulpit night after night, year in, year out, but let them remember the awful responsibility placed on his shoulders by almighty God—let them remember that God would ask an accounting of him one day for every soul in his flock. Let them remember this when they thought he was hard, let them remember that the Word was hard, that the way of holiness was a hard way. There was no room in God's army for the coward heart, no crown awaiting him who put mother, or father, sister, or brother, sweetheart, or friend above God's will. Let the church cry amen to this! And they cried: "Amen! Amen!"

The Lord had led him, said Father James, looking down on the boy and girl before him, to give them a public warning before it was too late. For he knew them to be sincere young people, dedicated to the service of the Lord—it was only that, since they were young, they did not know the pitfalls Satan laid for the unwary. He knew that sin was not in their minds—not yet; yet sin was in the flesh; and should they continue with their walking out alone together, their secrets and laughter, and touching of hands, they would surely sin a sin beyond all forgiveness. And John wondered what Elisha was thinking—Elisha, who was tall and handsome, who played basketball, and who had been saved at the age of eleven in the improbable fields down south. *Had* he sinned? Had he been tempted? And the girl beside him, whose white robes now seemed the merest, thinnest covering for the nakedness of breasts and insistent thighs—what was her face like when she was alone with Elisha, with no singing, when they were not surrounded by the saints? He was afraid to think of it, yet he could think of nothing else; and the fever of which they stood accused began also to rage in him.

After this Sunday Elisha and Ella Mae no longer met each other each day after school, no longer spent Saturday afternoons wandering through Central Park, or lying on the beach. All that was over for them. If they came together again it would be in wedlock. They would have children and raise them in the church.

This was what was meant by a holy life, this was what the way of the cross demanded. It was somehow on that Sunday, a Sunday shortly before his birthday, that John first realized that this was the life awaiting him—realized it consciously, as something no longer far off, but imminent, coming closer day by day.

Daisetz Suzuki

The Awakening of a New Consciousness in Zen

Daisetz Suzuki *(1870–1966) was the leading expositor of Zen Buddhism in the West. He translated the* Tao Te Ching, *the principal Buddhist text, into English.*

My position in regard to "the awakening of a new consciousness," summarily stated, is as follows:

The phrasing, "the awakening of a new consciousness" as it appears in the title of this paper, is not a happy one, because what is awakened in the Zen experience is not a "new" consciousness, but an "old" one which has been dormant ever since our loss of "innocence," to use the Biblical term. The awakening is really the re-discovery or the excavation of a long-lost treasure.

There is in every one of us, though varied in depth and strength, an eternal longing for "something" which transcends a world of inequalities. This is a somewhat vague statement containing expressions not altogether happy. "To transcend" suggests "going beyond," "being away from," that is, a separation, a dualism. I have, however, no desire to hint that the "something" stands away from the world in which we find ourselves. And then "inequalities" may sound too political. When I chose the term I had in mind the Buddhist word *asama* which contrasts with *sama*, "equal" or "same." We may replace it by such words as "differentiation" or "individualisation" or "conditionality." I just want to point out the fact that as soon as we recognise this world to be subject to constant changes we somehow begin to feel dissatisfied with it and desire for something which is permanent, free, above sorrow, and of eternal value.

This longing is essentially religious and each religion has its own way of designating it according to its tradition. Christians may call it longing for the Kingdom of Heaven or renouncing the world for the sake of divine love or praying to be saved from eternal damnation. Buddhists may call it seeking for emancipation or freedom. Indians may understand it as wishing to discover the real self.

Whatever expressions they may use, they all show a certain feeling of discontent with the situation in which they find themselves. They may not yet know exactly how to formulate this feeling and conceptually represent it either to themselves or to others.

I specified this obscure feeling as a longing for something. In this, it may be said, I have already a preconceived idea by assuming the existence of a something for which there is a longing on our part. Instead of saying this, it might have been better to identify the feeling of dissatisfaction with such modern feelings as fear or anxiety or a sense of insecurity. But the naming is not so important. As long as the mind is upset and cannot enjoy any state of equilibrium or perfect equanimity, this is a sense of insecurity or discontent. We feel as if we were in the air and trying to find a place for landing.

But we do not know exactly where this place for landing is. The objective is an altogether unknown quantity. It can nowhere be located and the fact adds a great deal to our sense of insecurity. We must somewhere and somehow find the landing.

Two ways are open: outward and inward. The outward one may be called intellectual and objective, but the inward one cannot be called subjective or affective or conative. The "inward" is misleading, though it is difficult to designate it in any other way. For all designations are on the plane of intellection. But as we must name it somehow, let us be content for a while to call it "inward" in contrast to "outward."

Let me give you this caution here: as long as the inward way is to be understood in opposition to the outward way,—though to do otherwise is impossible because of the human inability to go beyond language as the means of communication—the inward way after all turns to be an outward way. The really inward way is when no contrast exists between the inward and the outward. This is a logical contradiction. But the full meaning of it will I hope become clearer when I finish this paper.

The essential characteristic of the outward way consists in its never-ending procession, either forward or backward, but mostly in a circular movement, and always retaining the opposition of two terms, subject and object. There is thus no finality in the outward way, hence the sense of insecurity, though security does not necessarily mean "standing still," "not moving anywhere," or "attached to something."

The inward way is the reverse of the outward way. Instead of going out endlessly and dissipating and exhausting itself, the mind turns inwardly to see what is there behind all this endless procession of things. It does not stop the movement in order to examine what is there. If it does, the movement ceases to be a movement; it turns into something else. This is what the intellect does while the inward way refuses to do so. As soon as there is any kind of bifurcation, the outward way asserts itself and the inward way no longer exists. The inward way consists in taking things as they are, in catching them in their is-ness or suchness. I would not say, "in their oneness" or "in their wholeness." These are the terms belonging to the outward way. Even to say "is-ness" or "suchness" or "thusness" or in Japanese "*sono-mama*" or in Chinese "*chi-mo*," is not, strictly speaking, the inward way. "To be" is an abstract term. It is much better to lift a finger and say nothing *about* it. The inward way in its orthodoxy generally avoids appealing to language though it never shuns it.

The inward way occasionally uses the term "one" or "all," but in this case "one" means "one that is never one," and "all" means "all that is never all." The "one" will be "a one ever becoming one" and never a closed-up "one." The "all" will be "an all ever becoming all" and never a closed-up "all." This means that in the inward way the one is an absolute one, that one is all and all is one, and further that when "the ten thousand things" are reduced to an absolute oneness which is an absolute nothingness, we have the inward way perfecting itself.

Buddhism, especially Zen Buddhism as it developed in China, is rich in expressions belonging to the inward way. In fact, it is Zen that has effected, for the first time, a deep excavation into the mine of the inward way. To illustrate my point read the following—I give just one instance:

Suigan at the end of the summer session made this declaration: "I have been talking, east and west, all this summer for my Brotherhood. See if my eye-brows are still growing."

One of his disciples said, "How finely they are growing!"

Another said, "One who commits a theft feels uneasy in his heart."

A third one without saying anything simply uttered "Kwan!"

It goes without saying that all these utterances of the disciples as well as of the master give us a glimpse into the scene revealed only to the inward way. They are all expressions directly bursting out of an abyss of absolute nothingness. . . .

When Buddhists make reference to God, God must not be taken in the Biblical sense. When I talk about God's giving an order to light, which is recorded in the Genesis, I allude to it with the desire that our Christian readers may come to a better understanding of the Buddhist idea of the inward way. What follows, therefore, is to be understood in this spirit.

The Biblical God is recorded as having given his Name to Moses at Mount Sinai as "I am that I am." I do not of course know much about Christian or Jewish theology, but this "name," whatever its original Hebrew meaning of the word may be, seems to me of such significance that we must not put it aside as not essential to the interpretation of God-idea in the development of Christian thought. The Biblical God is always intensely personal and concretely intimate, and how did he ever come to declare himself under such a highly metaphysical designation as he did to Moses? "A highly metaphysical designation," however, is from the outward way of looking at things, while from the inward way "I am that I am" is just as "spontaneous" as the fish swimming about in the mountain stream or the fowl of the air flying across the sky. God's is-ness is my is-ness and also the cat's is-ness sleeping on her mistress' lap. This is reflected in Christ's declaration that "I am before Abraham was." In this is-ness which is not to be assumed under the category of metaphysical abstractions, I feel like recognising the fundamental oneness of all the religious experiences.

The spontaneity of is-ness, to go back to the first part of this paper, is what is revealed in the "eternal longing" for something which has vanished from the domain of the outward way of intellectualisation. . . . While in the world, we find ourselves too engrossed in the business of "knowing" which started when we left the garden of "innocence." We all now want "to know," "to think," "to choose," "to decide," "To be responsible," etc., with everything that follows from exercising what we call "freedom."

"Freedom" is really the term to be found in the inward way only and not in the outward way. But somehow a confusion has come into our mind and we find ourselves madly running after things which can never be attained in the domain of the outward way. The feeling of insecurity then grows out of this mad pursuit, because we are no more able to be in "the spontaneity of is-ness."

We can now see that "The awakening of a new consciousness" is not quite a happy expression. The longing is for something we have lost and not for an unknown quantity of which we have not the remotest possible idea. In fact, there is no unknown quantity in the world into which we have come to pass our time. The longing of any sort implies our previous knowledge of it, though we may be altogether ignorant of its presence in our consciousness. . . . The real object can never be taken hold of until we come back to the abode which we inadvertently quitted. "The awakening of a new consciousness" is therefore the finding ourselves back in our original abode where we lived even before our birth. This experience of home-coming and therefore of the feeling of perfect security is evinced everywhere in religious literature.

The feeling of perfect security means the security of freedom and the securing of freedom is no other than "the awakening of a new consciousness." Ordinarily, we talk of freedom too readily, mostly in the political sense, and also in the moral sense. But as long as we remain in the outward way of seeing things, we can never understand what freedom is. All forms of freedom we generally talk of are far from being freedom in its deepest sense. Most people are sadly mistaken in this respect. . . .

We humans have the very bad habit of giving a name to a certain object with a certain number of attributes and think this name exhausts the object thus designated, whereas the object itself has no idea of remaining within the limit prescribed by the name. The object lives, grows, expands, and often changes into something else than the one imprisoned within the name. We who have given the name to it imagine that the object thus named for ever remains the same, because for the practical purposes of life or for the sake of what we call logic it is convenient to retain the name all the time regardless of whatever changes that have taken place and might take place in it. We become a slave to a system of nomenclature we ourselves have invented.

This applies perfectly to our consciousness. We have given the name "consciousness" to a certain group of psychological phenomena and another name "unconscious" to another group. We keep them strictly separated one from the other. A confusion will upset our thought-structure. This means that what is named "conscious" cannot be "unconscious" and vice versa. But in point of fact human psychology is a living fact and refuses to observe an arbitrary system of grouping. The conscious wants to be unconscious and the unconscious conscious. But human thinking cannot allow such a contradiction: the unconscious must remain unconscious and the conscious conscious; no such things as the unconscious conscious or the conscious unconscious must take place, because they cannot take place in the nature of things, logicians would say. If they are to happen, a time-agent must come in and make consciousness rise out of the unconscious.

But Zen's way of viewing or evaluating things differs from the outward way of intellection. Zen would not object to the possibility of an "unconscious conscious" or a "conscious unconscious." Therefore, not the awakening of a new consciousness but consciousness coming to its own unconscious.

Language is used to give a name to everything, and when an object gets a name, we begin to think that the name is the thing and adjust ourselves to a new situation which is our own creation. So much confusion arises from it. If there is one thing Zen does for modern people, it will be to awaken them from this self-imposed thralldom. A Zen master would take up a staff, and, producing it before the audience declare, "I do not call it a staff. What would you call it?" Another master would say, "Here is a staff. It has transformed itself into a dragon, and the dragon has swallowed up the whole universe. Where do you get all these mountains, lakes, and the great earth?" When I got for the first time acquainted with Zen I thought this was a logical quibble, but I now realise that there is something here far more serious, far more real, and far more significant, which can be reached only by following the inward way.

Mary Daly
The Leap Beyond
Patriarchal Religion

Mary Daly, *who teaches at Boston College, is a leading feminist philosopher and theologian. She is the author of a number of influential books, among them* Beyond God the Father: Toward a Philosophy of Women's Liberation, Gyn/Ecology, *and* Pure Lust.

PROLEGOMENA

1. There exists a planetary sexual caste system, essentially the same in Saudi Arabia and in New York, differing only in degree.
2. This system is masked by sex role segregation, by the dual identity of women, by ideologies and myths.
3. Among the primary loci of sexist conditioning is grammar.
4. The "methods" of the various "fields" are not adequate to express feminist thought. Methodolatry requires that women perform Methodicide, an act of intellectual bravery.
5. All of the major world religions function to legitimate patriarchy. This is true also of the popular cults such as the Krishna movement and the Jesus Freaks.

6. The myths and symbols of Christianity are essentially sexist. Since "God" is male, the male is God. God the Father legitimates all earthly God-fathers, including Vito Corleone, Pope Paul, President Gerald Ford, the God-fathers of medicine (e.g. the American Medical Association), of science (e.g. NASA), of the media, of psychiatry, of education, and of all the -ologies.

7. The myth of feminine evil, expressed in the story of the Fall, is reinforced by the myth of salvation/redemption by a single human being of the male sex. The idea of a unique divine incarnation in a male, the God-man of the "hypostatic union," is inherently sexist and oppressive. Christolatry is idolatry.

8. A significant and growing cognitive minority of women, radical feminists, are breaking out from under the sacred shelter of patriarchal religious myths.

9. This breaking out, facing anomy when the meaning structures of patriarchy are seen through and rejected, is a communal, political event. It is a revelatory event, a creative, political ontophany.

10. The bonding of the growing cognitive minority of women who are radical feminists, commonly called *sisterhood,* involves a process of new naming, in which words are wrenched out of their old semantic context and heard in a new semantic context. For example, the "sisterhoods" of patriarchy, such as religious congregations of women, were really mini-brotherhoods. *Sisterhood* heard with new ears is bonding for women's own liberation.

11. There is an inherent dynamic in the women's revolution in Judeo-Christian society which is Antichurch, whether or not feminists specifically concern ourselves with churches. This is so because the Judeo-Christian tradition legitimates patriarchy— the prevailing power structure and prevailing world view—which the women's revolution leaves behind.

12. The women's revolution is not only Antichurch. It is a postchristian spiritual revolution.

13. The ethos of Judeo-Christian culture is dominated by The Most Unholy Trinity: Rape, Genocide, and War. It is rapism which spawns racism. It is gynocide which spawns genocide, for sexism (rapism) is fundamental socialization to objectify "the other."

14. The women's revolution is concerned with transvaluation of values, beyond the ethics dominated by The Most Unholy Trinity.

15. The women's revolution is not merely about equality within a patriarchal society (a contradiction in terms). It is about *power* and redefining power.

16. Since Christian myths are inherently sexist, and since the women's revolution is not about "equality" but about power, there is an intrinsic dynamic in the feminist movement which goes beyond efforts to reform Christian churches. Such efforts eventually come to be recognized as comparable to a Black person's trying to reform the Ku Klux Klan.

17. Within patriarchy, power is generally understood as power *over* people, the environment, things. In the rising consciousness of women, power is experienced as *power of presence* to ourselves and to each other, as we affirm our own being against and beyond the alienated identity (non-being) bestowed upon us within patriarchy. This is experienced as *power of absence* by those who would objectify women as "the other," as magnifying mirrors.

18. The presence of women to ourselves which is *absence* to the oppressor is the essential dynamic opening up the women's revolution to human liberation. It is an invitation to men to confront non-being and hence affirm their be-ing.

19. It is unlikely that many men will accept this invitation willingly, or even be able to hear it, since they have profound vested (though self-destructive) interest in the present social arrangements.

20. The women's movement is a new mode of relating to the self, to each other, to men, to the environment—in a word—to the cosmos. It is self-affirming, refusing objectification of the self and of the other.
21. Entrance into new feminist time/space, which is moving time/space located on the boundaries of patriarchal institutions, is active participation in ultimate reality, which is de-reified, recognized as Verb, as intransitive Verb with no object to block its dynamism.
22. Entrance into radical feminist consciousness involves recognition that all male-dominated "revolutions," which do not reject the universally oppressive reality which is patriarchy, are in reality only reforms. They are "revolutions" only in the sense that they are spinnings of the wheels of the same senescent system.
23. Entrance into radical feminist consciousness implies an awareness that the women's revolution is the "final cause" (pun intended) in the radical sense that it is the cause which can move the other causes. It is the catalyst which can bring about real change, since it is the rising up of the universally and primordially objectified "Other," discrediting the myths which legitimate rapism. Rapism is by extension the objectification and destruction of all "others" and inherently tends to the destruction of the human species and of all life on this planet.

Radical feminism, the becoming of women, is very much an Otherworld Journey. It is both discovery and creation of a world other than patriarchy. Some observation reveals that patriarchy is "everywhere." Even outer space and the future have been colonized. As a rule, even the more imaginative science fiction writers (seemingly the most foretelling futurists) cannot/will not create a space and time in which women get far beyond the role of space stewardess. Nor does this situation exist simply "outside" women's minds, securely fastened into institutions which we can physically leave behind. Rather, it is also internalized, festering inside women's heads, even feminist heads.

The journey of women *becoming*, then, involves exorcism of the internalized Godfather, in his various manifestations (His name is legion). It involves dangerous encounters with these demons. Within the Christian tradition, particularly in medieval times, evil spirits have some-times been associated with the Seven Deadly Sins, both as personifications and as causes. A "standard" and prevalent listing of the Sins is, of course, the following: pride, avarice, anger, lust, gluttony, envy, and sloth. I am contending that these have all been radically misnamed, that is, inadequately and even perversely "understood" within Christianity. These concepts have been used to victimize the oppressed, particularly women. They are particularized expres-sions of the overall use of "evil" to victimize women. The feminist journey involves confron-tations with the demonic distortions of evil.

Why has it seemed "appropriate" in this culture that a popular book and film (*The Exorcist*) center around a Jesuit who "exorcises" a girl-child who is "possessed"? Why is there no book or film about a woman who exorcises a Jesuit? Within a culture possessed by the myth of feminine evil, the naming, describing, and theorizing about good and evil has con-stituted a web of deception, a Maya. The journey of women becoming is breaking through this web—a Fall into free space. It is reassuming the role of subject, as opposed to object, and naming good and evil on the basis of our own intuitive intellection. . . .

THE QUALITATIVE LEAP

Creative, living, political hope for movement beyond the gynocidal reign of the Fathers will be fulfilled only if women continue to make qualitative leaps in living our transcendence. A short-circuited hope of transcendence has caused many to remain inside churches, and patriarchal religion sometimes has seemed to satisfy the hunger for transcendence. The problem has been that both the hunger and the satisfaction generated within such religions have to a great extent alienated women from our deepest aspirations. Spinning in vicious circles of false needs and false consciousness, women caught on the patriarchal wheel have not been able to experience women's own experience.

I suggest that what is required is *ludic cerebration,* the free play of intuition in our own space, giving rise to thinking that is vigorous, informed, multi-dimensional, independent, creative, tough. *Ludic cerebration* is thinking out of experience. I do not mean the experience of dredging out All That Was Wrong with Mother, or of instant intimacy in group encounters, or of waiting at the doctoral dispensary, or of self-lobotomization in order to publish, perish, and then be promoted. I mean the experience of being. *Be-ing* is the verb that says the dimensions of depth in all verbs, such as intuiting, reasoning, loving, imaging, making, acting, as well as the couraging, hoping, and playing that are always there when one is really living.

It may be that some new things happen within patriarchy, but one thing essentially stays the same: women are always marginal beings. From this vantage point of the margin it is possible to look at what is between the margins with the lucidity of The Compleat Outsider. To change metaphors: the systems within the System do not appear so radically different from each other to those excluded by all. Hope for a qualitative leap lies in *us* by reason of that deviance from the "norm" which was first imposed but which can also be *chosen* on our own terms. This means that there has to be a shift from "acceptable" female deviance (characterized by triviality, diffuseness, dependence upon others for self-definition, low self-esteem, powerlessness) to deviance which may be unacceptable to others but which is acceptable to the self and *is* self-acceptance.

For women concerned with philosophical/theological questions, it seems to me, this implies the necessity of some sort of choice. One either tries to avoid "acceptable" deviance ("normal" female idiocy) by becoming accepted as a male-identified professional, or else one tries to make the qualitative leap toward self-acceptable deviance as ludic cerebrator, questioner of everything, madwoman, and witch.

I do mean witch. The heretic who rejects the idols of patriarchy is the blasphemous creatrix of her own thoughts. She is finding her life and intends not to lose it. The witch that smolders within within every woman who cared and dared enough to become a philosophically/spiritually questing feminist in the first place seems to be crying out these days: "Light my fire!" The qualitative leap, the light of those flames of spiritual imagination and cerebral fantasy can be a new dawn. . . .

WANTED: "GOD" OR "THE GODDESS"?

Feminist consciousness is experienced by a significant number of women as ontological becoming, that is, being. This process requires existential courage, courage to be and to *see,* which is both revolutionary and revelatory, revealing our participation in ultimate reality as Verb, as intransitive Verb.

The question obviously arises of the need for anthropomorphic symbols for this reality. There is no inherent contradiction between speaking of ultimate reality as Verb and speaking of this as personal. The Verb is more personal than a mere static noun. However, if we choose to *image* the Verb in anthropomorphic symbols, we can run into a problematic phenomenon which sociologist Henri Desroche calls "crossing." "Crossing" refers to a notable tendency among oppressed groups to attempt to change or adapt the ideological tools of the oppressor, so that they can be used *against* him and *for* the oppressed. The problem here is the fact that the functioning of "crossing" does not generally move far enough outside the ideological framework it seeks to undermine. . . .

Some women religious leaders within Western culture in modern times have performed something like a "crossing" operation, notably such figures as Mary Baker Eddy and Ann Lee, in stressing the "maternal" aspect of the divinity. The result has been mixed. Eddy's "Father-Mother God" is, after all, the Christian God. Nor does Ann Lee really move completely outside the Christian framework. . . . But it is . . . necessary to note that their theologies lack explicit relevance to the concrete problems of the oppression of women. Intellection and spirituality remain cut off from creative political movement. In earlier periods also there were women within the Christian tradition who tried to "cross" the Christian all-male God and Christ to some degree. An outstanding example was Juliana of Norwich, an English recluse and mystic who lived in the last half of the fourteenth century. Juliana's "God" and "Jesus" were—if language conveys anything—hermaphroditic constructs, with the primary identity clearly male. While there are many levels on which I could analyze Juliana's words about "our beloved Mother, Jesus (who) feeds us with himself," suffice it to say here that this hermaphroditic image is somewhat less than attractive. The "androgynous" God and Jesus present problems analogous to and related to those problems which occur in connection with the use of the term "androgyny" to describe the direction of women's becoming. There is something like a "liberation of the woman within" the (primarily male) God and Jesus . . . .

One fact that stands out here is that these were women whose imaginations were still partially controlled by Christian myth. My contention is that they were caught in a contradiction. . . . I am saying that there is a profound contradiction between the inherent logic of radical feminism and the inherent logic of the Christian symbol system. . . .

Both the reformers and those who leave Judaism and Christianity behind are contributing and will contribute in different ways to the process of the becoming of women. The point here is not to place value judgments upon individual persons and their efforts—and there are heroic efforts at all points of the feminist spectrum. Rather, it is to disclose an inherent logic in feminism. The courage which some women have in affirming this logic comes in part from having been on the feminist journey for quite awhile. Encouragement comes also from knowing increasing numbers of women who have chosen the route of the logical conclusion. Some of these women have "graduated" from Christianity or religious Judaism, and some have never even been associated closely with church or synagogue, but have discovered spiritual and mythic depths in the women's movement itself. What we share is a sense of becoming in cosmic process, which I prefer to call the Verb, Be-ing, and which some would still call "God."

For some feminists concerned with the spiritual depth of the movement, the word "God" is becoming increasingly problematic, however. This by no means indicates a movement in the direction of "atheism" or "agnosticism" or "secularism," as these terms are usually understood. Rather, the problem arises precisely because of the spiritual and mythic quality perceived in feminist process itself. Some use expressions such as "power of being." Some reluctantly still use the word "God" while earnestly trying to divest the term of its patriarchal associations, attempting to think perhaps of the "God of the philosophers" rather than the overtly masculist and oppressive "God of the theologians." But the problem becomes increasingly troublesome, the more the "God" of the various Western philosophers is subjected to feminist analysis. "He"—"Jahweh" still often hovers behind the abstractions, stunting our own thought, giving us a sense of contrived doublethink. The word "God" just may be inherently oppressive.

Indeed, the word "Goddess" has also been problematic, but for different reasons. Some have been worried about the problem of "crossing." However, that difficulty appears more and more as a pseudo-difficulty when it is recognized that "crossing" is likely to occur only when one is trying to work *within* a sexist tradition. For example, Christian women who in their "feminist liturgies" experiment with referring to "God" as "she" and to the Trinity as "The Mother, the Daughter, and the Holy Spirit," are still working within all the boundaries of the same symbolic framework and the same power structure. Significantly, their services are at the same place and time as "the usual," and are regarded by most of the constituency of the churches as occasional variations of "business as usual."

As women who are outside the Christian church inform ourselves of evidence supporting the existence of ancient matriarchy and of evidence indicating that the Gods of patriarchy are indeed contrived, pale derivatives and reversals of the Great Goddess of an earlier period, the fear of mere "crossing" appears less appropriate and perhaps even absurd. There is also less credibility allowable to the notion that "Goddess" would function like "God" in reverse, that is, to legitimate an oppressive "female-dominated" society, if one is inclined to look seriously at evidence that matriarchal society was not structured like patriarchy, that it was non-hierarchical. . . .

Clearly, it would be inappropriate and arrogant to try to "explain" or "interpret" this experience of another person. I can only comment that many women I know are finding power of being within the self, rather than in "internalized" father images. As a philosopher, my preference has been for abstractions. Indeed I have always been annoyed and rather embarrassed by "anthropomorphic" symbols, preferring terms such as "ground and power of being" (Tillich), "beyond subjectivity and objectivity" (James), "the Encompassing" (Jaspers), or the commonly used "Ultimate Reality," or "cosmic process." More recently I have used the expression "Intransitive Verb." Despite this philosophical inclination, and also because of it, I find it impossible to ignore the realm of symbols, or to fail to recognize that many women are experiencing and participating in a remythologizing process, which is a new dawn.

It is necessary to add a few remarks about the functioning of the confusing and complex "Mary" symbol within Christianity. Through it, the power of the Great Goddess symbol is enchained, captured, used, cannibalized, tokenized, domesticated, tranquillized. In spite of this, I think that many women and at least some men, when they have heard of or imaged the "Mother of God," have, by something like a selective perception process, screened out the standardized, lobotomized, dull, derivative and dwarfed Christian reflections of a more ancient symbol; they have perceived something that might more accurately be described as the Great Goddess, and which, in human terms, can be translated into "the strong woman who can relate because she can stand alone." A woman of Jewish background commented that "Mother of God" had always seemed strange and contradictory to her. Not having been programmed to "know" about the distinctions between the "divine" and the "human" nature of "Christ," or to "know" that the "Mother of God" is less than God, this woman had been able to hear the expression with the ears of an extraenvironmental listener. It sounded, she said, something like "infinite plus one." When this symbolic nonsense is recognized, it is more plausible simply to *think* "infinite," and to *image* something like "Great Mother," or "Goddess."

It may appear that the suffix "-ess" presents a problem, when one considers other usages of that suffix, for example, in "poetess," or in "authoress." In these cases, there is a tone of depreciation, a suggestion that women poets and authors are in a separate and "inferior" category to be judged by different standards than their male counterparts. However, the suffix does not always function in this "diminishing" way. For example, there appear to be no "diminutive" overtones suggested by the word "actress." So also it seems that the term "Goddess"—or "The Goddess"—is *not only non-diminutive,* but very strong. Indeed, it calls before the mind images of a powerful and ancient tradition before, behind, and beyond Christianity. These are multi-dimensional images of women's present and future becoming/be-ing.

H. L. Mencken

Memorial Service

H. L. Mencken *(1880–1956) was a journalist and critic. A pungent satirist of American life, he also published a famous book,* The American Language, *which brought together American, rather than English, idioms and expressions.*

WHERE is the graveyard of dead gods? What lingering mourner waters their mounds? There was a time when Jupiter was the king of the gods, and any man who doubted his puissance was *ipso facto* a barbarian and an ignoramus. But where in all the world is there a man who worships Jupiter today? And what of Huitzilopochtli? In one year—and it is no more than five hundred years ago—50,000 youths and maidens were slain in sacrifice to him. Today, if he is remembered at all, it is only by some vagrant savage in the depths of the Mexican forest. Huitzilopochtli, like many other gods, had no human father; his mother was a virtuous widow; he was born of an apparently innocent flirtation that she carried on with the sun. When he frowned, his father, the sun, stood still. When he roared with rage, earthquakes engulfed whole cities. When he thirsted he was watered with 10,000 gallons of human blood. But today Huitzilopochtli is as magnificently forgotten as Allen G. Thurman. Once the peer of Allah, Buddha and Wotan, he is now the peer of Richmond P. Hobson, Alton B. Parker, Adelina Patti, General Weyler and Tom Sharkey.

Speaking of Huitzilopochtli recalls his brother Tezcatilpoca. Tezcatilpoca was almost as powerful: he consumed 25,000 virgins a year. Lead me to his tomb: I would weep, and hang a *couronne des perles*. But who knows where it is? Or where the grave of Quitzalcoatl is? Or Xiehtecutli? Or Centeotl, that sweet one? Or Tlazolteotl, the goddess of love? Or Mictlan? Or Xipe? Or all the host of Tzitzimitles? Where are their bones? Where is the willow on which they hung their harps? In what forlorn and unheard-of Hell do they await the resurrection morn? Who enjoys their residuary estates? Or that of Dis, whom Caesar found to be the chief god of the Celts? Or that of Tarves, the bull? Or that of Moccos, the pig? Or that of Epona, the mare? Or that of Mullo, the celestial jackass? There was a time when the Irish revered all these gods, but today even the drunkest Irishman laughs at them.

But they have company in oblivion: the Hell of dead gods is as crowded as the Presbyterian Hell for babies. Damona is there, and Esus, and Drunemeton, and Silvana, and Dervones, and Adsalluta, and Deva, and Belisama, and Uxellimus, and Borvo, and Grannos, and Mogons. All mighty gods in their day, worshipped by millions, full of demands and impositions, able to bind and loose—all gods of the first class. Men labored for generations to build vast temples to them—temples with stones as large as hay-wagons. The business of interpreting their whims occupied thousands of priests, bishops, archbishops. To doubt them was to die, usually at the stake. Armies took to the field to defend them against infidels: villages were burned, women and children were butchered, cattle were driven off. Yet in the end they all withered and died, and today there is none so poor to do them reverence.

What has become of Sutekh, once high god of the whole Nile Valley? What has become of:

Resheph	Isis	Dagon
Anath	Ptah	Yau
Ashtoreth	Baal	Amon-Re
Nebo	Astarte	Osiris
Melek	Hadad	Molech?
Ahijah		

All these were once gods of the highest eminence. Many of them are mentioned with fear and trembling in the Old Testament. They ranked, five or six thousand years ago, with Yahweh Himself; the worst of them stood far higher than Thor. Yet they have all gone down the chute, and with them the following:

Arianrod	Beltis	Vesta
Morrigu	Nusku	Zer-panitu
Govannon	Aa	Merodach
Gunfled	Sin	Elum
Dagda	Apsu	Marduk
Ogyrvan	Elali	Nin
Dea Dia	Mami	Persephone
Iuno Lucina	Zaraqu	Istar
Saturn	Zagaga	Lagas
Furrina	Nuada Argetlam	Nirig
Cronos	Tagd	Nebo
Engurra	Goibniu	En-Mersi
Belus	Odin	Assur
Ubilulu	Ogma	Beltu
U-dimmer-an-kia	Marzin	Kuski-banda
U-sab-sib	Mars	Nin-azu
U-Mersi	Diana of Ephesus	Qarradu
Tammuz	Robigus	Ueras
Venus	Pluto	

Ask the rector to lend you any good book on comparative religion: you will find them all listed. They were gods of the highest dignity—gods of civilized peoples—worshipped and believed in by millions. All were omnipotent, omniscient and immortal. And all are dead.

Albert Camus
The Absurd

Albert Camus *(1913–1960), a leading French intellectual, was a political activist and an associate of Jean-Paul Sartre. Awarded the Nobel Prize for Literature in 1957, Camus' philosophical concerns were often expressed in fiction. The Myth of Sisyphus focuses on the issue of suicide which, according to him, is the only philosophical problem.*

$\mathbf{L}$ike great works, deep feelings always mean more than they are conscious of saying. The regularity of an impulse or a repulsion in a soul is encountered again in habits of doing or thinking, is reproduced in consequences of which the soul itself knows nothing. Great feelings take with them their own universe, splendid or abject. They light up with their passion an exclusive world in which they recognize their climate. There is a universe of jealousy, of ambition, of selfishness, or of generosity. A universe—in other words, a metaphysic and an attitude of mind. What is true of already specialized feelings will be even more so of emotions basically as indeterminate, simultaneously as vague and as "definite," as remote and as "present" as those furnished us by beauty or aroused by absurdity.

At any streetcorner the feeling of absurdity can strike any man in the face. As it is, in its distressing nudity, in its light without effulgence, it is elusive. But that very difficulty deserves reflection. It is probably true that a man remains forever unknown to us and that there is in him something irreducible that escapes us. But *practically* I know men and recognize them by their behavior, by the totality of their deeds, by the consequences caused in life by their presence. Likewise, all those irrational feelings which offer no purchase to analysis. I can define them *practically*, appreciate them *practically*, by gathering together the sum of their consequences in the domain of the intelligence, by seizing and noting all their aspects, by outlining their universe. It is certain that apparently, though I have seen the same actor a hundred times, I shall not for that reason know him any better personally. Yet if I add up the heroes he has personified and if I say that I know him a little better at the hundredth character counted off, this will be felt to contain an element of truth. For this apparent paradox is also an apologue. There is a moral to it. It teaches that a man defines himself by his make-believe as well as by his sincere impulses. There is thus a lower key of feelings, inaccessible in the heart but partially disclosed by the acts they imply and the attitudes of mind they assume. It is clear that in this way I am defining a method. But it is also evident that that method is one of analysis and not of knowledge. For methods imply metaphysics; unconsciously they disclose conclusions that they often claim not to know yet. Similarly, the last pages of a book are already contained in the first pages. Such a link is inevitable. The method defined here acknowledges the feeling that all true knowledge is impossible. Solely appearances can be enumerated and the climate make itself felt.

Perhaps we shall be able to overtake that elusive feeling of absurdity in the different but closely related worlds of intelligence, of the art of living, or of art itself. The climate of absurdity is in the beginning. The end is the absurd universe and that attitude of mind which lights the world with its true colors to bring out the privileged and implacable visage which that attitude has discerned in it.

All great deeds and all great thoughts have a ridiculous beginning. Great works are often born on a street corner or in a restaurant's revolving door. So it is with absurdity. The absurd world more than others derives its nobility from that abject birth. In certain situations, replying "nothing" when asked what one is thinking about may be pretense in a man. Those who are loved are well aware of this. But if that reply is sincere, if it symbolizes that odd state of soul in which the void becomes eloquent, in which the chain of daily gestures is broken, in which the heart vainly seeks the link that will connect it again, then it is as it were the first sign of absurdity.

It happens that the stage sets collapse. Rising, streetcar, four hours in the office or the factory, meal, streetcar, four hours of work, meal, sleep, and Monday Tuesday Wednesday Thursday Friday and Saturday according to the same rhythm—this path is easily followed most of the time. But one day the "why" arises and everything begins in that weariness tinged with amazement. "Begins"—this is important. Weariness comes at the end of the acts of a mechanical life, but at the same time it inaugurates the impulse of consciousness. It awakens consciousness and provokes what follows. What follows is the gradual return into the chain or it is the definitive awakening. At the end of the awakening comes, in time, the consequence: suicide or recovery. In itself weariness has something sickening about it. Here, I must conclude that it is good. For everything begins with consciousness and nothing is worth anything except through it. There is nothing original about these remarks. But they are obvious; that is enough for a while, during a sketchy reconnaissance in the origins of the absurd. Mere "anxiety," as Heidegger says, is at the source of everything.

Likewise and during every day of an unillustrious life, time carries us. But a moment always comes when we have to carry it. We live on the future: "tomorrow," "later on," "when you have made your way," "you will understand when you are old enough." Such irrelevancies are wonderful, for, after all, it's a matter of dying. Yet a day comes when a man notices or says that he is thirty. Thus he asserts his youth. But simultaneously he situates himself in relation to time. He takes his place in it. He admits that he stands at a certain point on a curve that he acknowledges having to travel to its end. He belongs to time, and by the horror that seizes him, he recognizes his worst enemy. Tomorrow, he was longing for tomorrow, whereas everything in him ought to reject it. That revolt of the flesh is the absurd. . . .

That revolt gives life its value. Spread out over the whole length of a life, it restores its majesty to that life. To a man devoid of blinders, there is no finer sight than that of the intelligence at grips with a reality that transcends it. The sight of human pride is unequaled. No disparagement is of any use. That discipline that the mind imposes on itself, that will conjured up out of nothing, that face-to-face struggle have something exceptional about them. To impoverish that reality whose inhumanity constitutes man's majesty is tantamount to impoverishing him himself. I understand then why the doctrines that explain everything to me also debilitate me at the same time. They relieve me of the weight of my own life, and yet I must carry it alone. At this juncture, I cannot conceive that a skeptical metaphysics can be joined to an ethics of renunciation.

Consciousness and revolt, these rejections are the contrary of renunciation. Everything that is indomitable and passionate in a human heart quickens them, on the contrary, with its own life. It is essential to die unreconciled and not of one's own free will. Suicide is a repudiation. The absurd man can only drain everything to the bitter end, and deplete himself. The absurd is his extreme tension, which he maintains constantly by solitary effort, for he knows that in that consciousness and in that day-to-day revolt he gives proof of his only truth, which is defiance. . . .

But what does life mean in such a universe? Nothing else for the moment but indifference to the future and a desire to use up everything that is given. Belief in the meaning of life always implies a scale of values, a choice, our preferences. Belief in the absurd, according to our definitions, teaches the contrary. But this is worth examining.

Knowing whether or not one can live *without appeal* is all that interests me. I do not want to get out of my depth. This aspect of life being given me, can I adapt myself to it? Now, faced with this particular concern, belief in the absurd is tantamount to substituting the quantity of experiences for the quality. If I convince myself that this life has no other aspect than that of the absurd, if I feel that its whole equilibrium depends on that perpetual opposition between my conscious revolt and the darkness in which it struggles, if I admit that my freedom has no meaning except in relation to its limited fate, then I must say that what counts is not the best living but the most living. It is not up to me to wonder if this is vulgar or revolting, elegant or deplorable. Once and for all, value judgments are discarded here in favor of factual judgments. I have merely to draw the conclusions from what I can see and to risk nothing that is hypothetical. Supposing that living in this way were not honorable, then true propriety would command me to be dishonorable.

The most living; in the broadest sense, that rule means nothing. It calls for definition. It seems to begin with the fact that the notion of quantity has not been sufficiently explored. For it can account for a large share of human experience. A man's rule of conduct and his scale of values have no meaning except through the quantity and variety of experiences he has been in a position to accumulate. Now, the conditions of modern life impose on the majority of men the same quantity of experiences and consequently the same profound experience. To be sure, there must also be taken into consideration the individual's spontaneous contribution, the "given" element in him. But I cannot judge of that, and let me repeat that my rule here is to get along with the immediate evidence. I see, then, that the individual character of a common code of ethics lies not so much in the ideal importance of its basic principles as in the norm of an experience that it is possible to measure. To stretch a point somewhat, the Greeks had the code of their leisure just as we have the code of our eight-hour day. But already many men among the most tragic cause us to foresee that a longer experience changes this table of values. They make us imagine that adventurer of the everyday who through mere quantity of experiences would break all records (I am purposely using this sports expression) and would thus win his own code of ethics. Yet let's avoid romanticism and just ask ourselves what such an attitude may mean to a man with a mind made up to take up his bet and to observe strictly what he takes to be the rules of the game.

Breaking all the records is first and foremost being faced with the world as often as possible. How can that be done without contradictions and without playing on words? For on the one hand the absurd teaches that all experiences are unimportant, and on the other it urges toward the greatest quantity of experiences. How, then, can one fail to do as so many of those men I was speaking of earlier—choose the form of life that brings us the most possible of that human matter, thereby introducing a scale of values that on the other hand one claims to reject?

But again it is the absurd and its contradictory life that teaches us. For the mistake is thinking that that quantity of experiences depends on the circumstances of our life when it depends solely on us. Here we have to be over-simple. To two men living the same number of years, the world always provides the same sum of experiences. It is up to us to be conscious of them. Being aware of one's life, one's revolt, one's freedom, and to the maximum, is living, and to the maximum. Where lucidity dominates, the scale of values becomes useless. Let's be even more simple. Let us say that the sole obstacle, the sole deficiency to be made good, is constituted by premature death. Thus it is that no depth, no emotion, no passion, and no sacrifice could render equal in the eyes of the absurd man (even if he wished it so) a conscious life of forty years and a lucidity spread over sixty years. Madness and death are his irreparables. Man does not choose. The absurd and the extra life it involves *therefore do not depend on man's will,* but on its contrary, which is death. Weighing words carefully, it is altogether a question of luck. One just has to be able to consent to this. There will never be any substitute for twenty years of life and experience.

By what is an odd inconsistency in such an alert race, the Greeks claimed that those who died young were beloved of the gods. And that is true only if you are willing to believe that entering the ridiculous world of the gods is forever losing the purest of joys, which is feeling, and feeling on this earth. The present and the succession of presents before a constantly conscious soul is the ideal of the absurd man. But the word "ideal" rings false in this connection. It is not even his vocation, but merely the third consequence of his reasoning. Having started from an anguished awareness of the inhuman, the meditation on the absurd returns at the end of its itinerary to the very heart of the passionate flames of human revolt. . . .

The preceding merely defines a way of thinking. But the point is to live.

Part
TWO

Science, Mind, and Nature

3

What Does Science Tell Me about the World?

*H*ave you ever noticed that in your biology and chemistry classes you may get multiple choice exams, but in your English lit or philosophy classes you are more likely to get essay exams or paper assignments? Why is that? You may think that science deals in facts and that subjects such as philosophy and literature deal with opinions and interpretations. For example, it is a fact that common table salt is composed of sodium and chlorine, whereas it is simply a matter of opinion whether there is free will. You would probably have a hard time writing an entire five page paper on the chemical composition of table salt. And even if you think that it is a matter of fact whether there is life after death, you would be offended by a question on a philosophy exam that said, "True or false: There is life after death."

But in spite of this prevailing conception of science as being concerned only with facts, not opinions, science as it is actually practiced seems to be full of opinion and interpretation. It may surprise you to learn that scientists often disagree, not only about which of several scientific theories best explains what has been observed, but even about whether or not something has *been* observed. Moreover, the development of scientific theories is very seldom a process of first observing a lot of facts and then making straightforward generalizations from these observations. In this chapter, Richard Feynman, a Nobel Prize winner in physics, emphasizes the importance of imagination and guessing in science. As an example of imaginative guesswork in science, let's think about quarks. Most scientists believe that all matter is composed of curious particles (which don't really behave like particles) called quarks. The existence of quarks was first hypothesized in 1963. But no scientist has ever seen a quark, nor even a *trace* of a quark. So why do they believe that quarks exist? They believe it because some ingenious scientists *invented* quarks, noticing that if quarks did exist, they could explain some other puzzling things. This turned out to be a good guess: if you believe that there are quarks, you can explain a lot. Now most scientists do believe that quarks exist. But the only evidence for the existence of quarks is that if you invent them, there are many other complicated things that become simpler and can therefore be explained. Many other things in science were "invented" in this way before they were "discovered"—gravity, molecules, genes, and the planet Neptune, to name a few. Does it still sound to you as though science deals only with facts?

Hard as it may be to believe, the institution of science is a relatively new feature of Western civilization. In the seventeenth and eighteenth centuries, what is now called 'science' fell under the category of 'natural philosophy'. The modern use of the term 'science' dates from the nineteenth century, which was also the first century in which a person could make a living by being a scientist. (It was also the century in which the term 'scientist' was coined.) So although the study of nature is as old as recorded history, people have not always turned exclusively to scientists with questions about the workings of nature. In earlier times people also turned to storytellers, writers, artists, religious figures, and philosophers with such questions.

But in our contemporary culture, science has achieved a particularly exalted position. It seems to us that science deals with hard facts, whereas other subjects deal with mere opinions. We have come to believe that science is objective and verifiable. We think that science has a method ("The Scientific Method") for arriving at the "Absolute Truth."

But what is the scientific method, and how does it differ from the methods of literature, history, or philosophy? For that matter, is there really a scientific method? How can we be so sure that what science tells us is true? During the early part of the twentieth century, a group of philosophers and scientists known as the Vienna Circle (they were working in Vienna) tried to place both philosophy and science (and with them, psychology, economics, and other fields) on a more secure base. They tried to show how we could connect all knowledge securely to the pure observation of uninterpreted facts. Anything that could not be secured in this way they claimed was meaningless. (See Chapter 6 for more about this view.) The philosophy of science that grew out of the Vienna Circle has come to be known as the "received view," and is now the classic account of how science works. It is articulated clearly by Carl Hempel in his selection in this chapter.

The received view is often called "the hypothetico-deductive model" or "the deductive-nomological model." ('Nomological' means 'having to do with the laws of nature'.) It tries to show science to be an orderly process that moves from observation of facts to the confirmation of theories that explain those facts. It tries to explain what you may have had in mind a few paragraphs back if you thought that science, but not literature, deals with the facts.

The received view has been criticized, by both scientists and philosophers, for not reflecting the way that scientists actually work. Interestingly, the idea that to learn about how science works, we should pay attention to the way that actual scientists work, is a fairly new idea in this century. The now classic statement of this idea is Thomas Kuhn's *The Structure of Scientific Revolutions*, part of which is reprinted in this chapter. Kuhn argues that the progress of science is not purely logical and hence it cannot be isolated from its own historical context. Instead, it is conditioned by forces within the scientific community that he characterizes in deliberate political terms (for example, 'revolution').

Evelyn Fox Keller goes at least one step further than Kuhn. She argues that both our present concept and our practice of science are determined by unrecognized value assumptions. She claims further that the values assumed are masculine values and that their effect has been to create science as a male province. If, as she says, existing science is male science, then we are faced with the intriguing question of what female science would be.

The selection by Moulton and Robinson investigates the issue of fraud in science. You may be disturbed to learn that many of the greatest figures in the history of science are now accused of cheating—some of them of fiddling with the results of their observations and some of never having made the observations that they reported. Were these people really dishonest? Or is our picture of how scientists are supposed to work (and thus of how science is supposed to work) somehow wrong? If you were writing a lab report and treated your data the same way that Galileo, Newton, or Mendel seem to have treated theirs, you would be accused of cheating. Should we say the same of them? Or is what you do in your science labs somehow not what real science does?

Finally, a number of the selections give us some different perspectives on what science and scientists are really like. Susan Griffin begins the chapter with a cynical piece suggesting that perhaps we take scientists (and science) too seriously. Lewis

Thomas presents quite a different outlook with his glowing description of how wonderful it is to be a scientist. It might be interesting for you to compare his idyllic picture with Griffin's and with the idea of fraud in science. Richard Feynman gives us a feeling for how theoretical scientists think about the world. In particular, he talks about the process of guessing that was discussed at the beginning of this introduction. You might think about where the guesses come from and what makes some guesses seem better than others, in light of Kuhn's and Keller's remarks about psychological and cultural influences on scientific theory.

Finally, Gary Zukav ends the chapter on a mystical note. Much of current physics seems bizarre, even to people who understand it. Physicists talk about matter being made up of things that are sometimes particles and sometimes not particles but waves. They talk about particles that go from point A to point B without ever being anywhere in between, or without even existing in between. They talk about particles that travel backward in time and that can therefore change the past. Zukav argues that what seems so bizarre to Western minds would seem understandable from the viewpoint of Zen Buddhism, a major Oriental religion and philosophy. (See Chapter 2 for more about Zen.) In claiming that science is pointing us to a "higher dimension of human experience," he is trying to bring scientific and religious points of view closer together. If he is right in thinking that ultimately we must turn to religion to understand science, does that mean that religion actually deals with matters of fact?

Susan Griffin

Gravity

Susan Griffin *has published numerous feminist works, including a book of poetry, a play, a book of essays, and three nonfiction books including* Women and Nature, *from which this selection is drawn. Born in 1943, she lives in Berkeley, California.*

> Sooner or later the uniformly moving body will collide with the wall of the elevator destroying the uniform motion. Sooner or later, the whole elevator will collide with the earth destroying the observers and their experiments.
>
> ALBERT EINSTEIN and LEOPOLD INFELD,
> *The Evolution of Physics*

> . . . it is always possible to be "oriented" in a world that has a sacred history, a world in which every prominent feature is associated with a mythical event.
>
> MIRCEA ELIADE, "A Mythical Geography"

*T*he scientists are in a box. There are no windows. Nothing tells them which is right side up. The walls are empty. The ceiling and the floor are the same. They are standing in a perfect cube. Every surface is a square. This they measure and prove with their rulers. The scientists prove by experiment what is the nature of this world. One drops his handkerchief into space. It does not fall to the ground. It rests where the scientist's hand left it. Over time the handkerchief still does not move. This experiment is repeated with another scientist's eyeglasses. The scientist's eyeglasses do not move from where he has placed them in space. This experiment is repeated with different objects. First they push the eyeglasses, lending them motion, then the handkerchief, a pen, a piece of paper, and then their ruler. Each object moves continuously across space until it collides with the opposite wall. The scientists are delighted. They discover they are living in a perfect inertial system. Every body continues in a state of rest or motion. They will continue resting infinitely. They are delighted with this perfection. But gradually one scientist allows a question to enter his mind. It occurs to him that they do not know if they are at rest in an inertial system or if they are moving at a continuous rate of acceleration. Perhaps in a vacuum. Perhaps, and now the scientist feels a sense of disquiet, perhaps they are in a field of gravity, and *are* therefore accelerating continuously. He realizes that they do not know for certain where they are, nor where they are going, if they are going. He decides to break through the cube. Suddenly air rushes in. (They were suffocating, he realizes.) Through the hole he has made he sees the face of the earth coming closer and closer.

"Do you suppose that what we thought was true is not true?" he says with alarm. "We are falling," he admits, "down." Headfirst, the scientists dive from their cube. "I know where we are now," the doubting scientist shouts. "We are in a field of gravity." "And we are no longer falling at the same rate," another observes, "because of the resistance of the air." "Air!" another scientist sighs. "We are certainly not at rest now," the scientists assent. "We *are* moving," they agree.

"We know where we are now relative to the earth," they pronounce.

"And we know where we are going," another adds quickly.

"To the earth," they whisper.

"Where we were born," one says.

"And we know what will happen next," all of the scientists choir back. "We will all of us die."

Carl G. Hempel
The Deductive–Nomological Model of Science

Carl G. Hempel *is one of the most influential proponents of what is now regarded as the classic view of explanation in science. Much contemporary work in philosophy of science constitutes a reaction to his view. He was for many years a professor of philosophy at Princeton University. He wrote* Aspects of Scientific Explanation *and* Philosophy of Natural Science.

EXPLANATIONS

As was known at Galileo's time, and probably much earlier, a simple suction pump, which draws water from a well by means of a piston that can be raised in the pump barrel, will lift water no higher than about 34 feet above the surface of the well. Galileo was intrigued by this limitation and suggested an explanation for it, which was, however, unsound. After

Galileo's death, his pupil Torricelli advanced a new answer. He argued that the earth is surrounded by a sea of air, which, by reason of its weight exerts pressure upon the surface below, and that this pressure upon the surface of the well forces water up the pump barrel when the piston is raised. The maximum length of 34 feet for the water column in the barrel thus reflects simply the total pressure of the atmosphere upon the surface of the well.

It is evidently impossible to determine by direct inspection or observation whether this account is correct, and Torricelli tested it indirectly. He reasoned that *if* his conjecture were true, *then* the pressure of the atmosphere should also be capable of supporting a proportionately shorter column of mercury; indeed, since the specific gravity of mercury is about 14 times that of water, the length of the mercury column should be about 34/14 feet, or slightly less than 2½ feet. He checked this test implication by means of an ingeniously simple device, which was, in effect, the mercury barometer. The well of water is replaced by an open vessel containing mercury; the barrel of the suction pump is replaced by a glass tube sealed off at one end. The tube is completely filled with mercury and closed by placing the thumb tightly over the open end. It is then inverted, the open end is submerged in the mercury well, and the thumb is withdrawn; whereupon the mercury column in the tube drops until its length is about 30 inches—just as predicted by Torricelli's hypothesis.

A further test implication of that hypothesis was noted by Pascal, who reasoned that if the mercury in Torricelli's barometer is counterbalanced by the pressure of the air above the open mercury well, then its length should decrease with increasing altitude, since the weight of the air overhead becomes smaller. At Pascal's request, this implication was checked by his brother-in-law, Périer, who measured the length of the mercury column in the Torricelli barometer at the foot of the Puy-de-Dôme, a mountain some 4,800 feet high, and then carefully carried the apparatus to the top and repeated the measurement there while a control barometer was left at the bottom under the supervision of an assistant. Périer found the mercury column at the top of the mountain more than three inches shorter than at the bottom, whereas the length of the column in the control barometer had remained unchanged throughout the day. . . .

Consider . . . Périer's finding in the Puy-de-Dôme experiment, that the length of the mercury column in a Torricelli barometer decreased with increasing altitude. Torricelli's and Pascal's ideas on atmospheric pressure provided an explanation for this phenomenon; somewhat pedantically, it can be spelled out as follows:

(a) At any location, the pressure that the mercury column in the closed branch of the Torricelli apparatus exerts upon the mercury below equals the pressure exerted on the surface of the mercury in the open vessel by the column of air above it.

(b) The pressures exerted by the columns of mercury and of air are proportional to their weights; and the shorter the columns, the smaller their weights.

(c) As Périer carried the apparatus to the top of the mountain, the column of air above the open vessel became steadily shorter.

(d) (Therefore,) the mercury column in the closed vessel grew steadily shorter during the ascent.

Thus formulated, the explanation is an argument to the effect that the phenomenon to be explained, as described by the sentence (d), is just what is to be expected in view of the explanatory facts cited in (a), (b), and (c); and that, indeed, (d) follows deductively from the explanatory statements. The latter are of two kinds; (a) and (b) have the character of general laws expressing uniform empirical connections; whereas (c) describes certain particular facts. Thus, the shortening of the mercury column is here explained by showing that it occurred in accordance with certain laws of nature, as a result of certain particular circumstances. The explanation fits the phenomenon to be explained into a pattern of uniformities and shows that its occurrence was to be expected, given the specified laws and the pertinent particular circumstances.

The phenomenon to be accounted for by an explanation will henceforth also be referred to as the *explanandum phenomenon;* the sentence describing it, as the *explanandum sentence.* When the context shows which is meant, either of them will simply be called the explanandum. The sentences specifying the explanatory information—(*a*), (*b*), (*c*) in our example— will be called the *explanans sentences;* jointly they will be said to form the *explanans.*

As a second example, consider the explanation of a characteristic of image formation by reflection in a spherical mirror; namely, that generally $1/u + 1/v = 2/r$, where u and v are the distances of object-point and image-point from the mirror, and r is the mirror's radius of curvature. In geometrical optics, this uniformity is explained with the help of the basic law of reflection in a plane mirror, by treating the reflection of a beam of light at any one point of a spherical mirror as a case of reflection in a plane tangential to the spherical surface. The resulting explanation can be formulated as a deductive argument whose conclusion is the explanandum sentence, and whose premisses include the basic laws of reflection and of rectilinear propagation, as well as the statement that the surface of the mirror forms a segment of a sphere. . . .

The explanations just considered may be conceived, then, as deductive arguments whose conclusion is the explanandum sentence, E, and whose premiss-set, the explanans, consists of general laws, $L_1, L_2, \ldots, L_r$ and of other statements, $C_1, C_2, \ldots, C_k$, which make assertions about particular facts. The form of such arguments, which thus constitute one type of scientific explanation, can be represented by the following schema:

$$(\text{D-N}) \qquad \left. \begin{array}{c} L_1, L_2, \ldots, L_r \\ \underline{C_1, C_2, \ldots, C_k} \end{array} \right\} \text{Explanans sentences}$$
$$E \qquad \text{Explanandum sentence}$$

Explanatory accounts of this kind will be called explanations by deductive subsumption under general laws, or *deductive-nomological explanations.* (The root of the term 'nomological' is the Greek word 'nomos', for law.) The laws invoked in a scientific explanation will also be called *covering laws* for the explanandum phenomenon, and the explanatory argument will be said to subsume the explanandum under those laws.

The explanandum phenomenon in a deductive-nomological explanation may be an event occurring at a particular place and time, such as the outcome of Périer's experiment. Or it may be some regularity found in nature, such as certain characteristics generally displayed by rainbows; or a uniformity expressed by an empirical law such as Galileo's or Kepler's laws. Deductive explanations of such uniformities will then invoke laws of broader scope, such as the laws of reflection and refraction, or Newton's laws of motion and of gravitation. As this use of Newton's laws illustrates, empirical laws are often explained by means of theoretical principles that refer to structures and processes underlying the uniformities in question. . . .

Some scientific explanations conform to the pattern (D-N) quite closely. This is so, particularly, when certain quantitative features of a phenomenon are explained by mathematical derivation from covering general laws, as in the case of reflection in spherical and paraboloidal mirrors. Or take the celebrated explanation, propounded by Leverrier (and independently by Adams), of peculiar irregularities in the motion of the planet Uranus, which on the current Newtonian theory could not be accounted for by the gravitational attraction of the other planets then known. Leverrier conjectured that they resulted from the gravitational pull of an as yet undetected outer planet, and he computed the position, mass, and other characteristics which that planet would have to possess to account in quantitative detail for the observed irregularities. His explanation was strikingly confirmed by the discovery, at the predicted location, of a new planet, Neptune, which had the quantitative characteristics attributed to it by Leverrier. Here again, the explanation has the character of a deductive argument whose premises include general laws—specifically, Newton's laws of gravitation and of motion—as well as statements specifying various quantitative particulars about the disturbing planet.

Not infrequently, however, deductive-nomological explanations are stated in an elliptical form: they omit mention of certain assumptions that are presupposed by the explanation but are simply taken for granted in the given context. Such explanations are sometimes expressed in the form 'E because C', where E is the event to be explained and C is some antecedent or concomitant event or state of affairs. Take, for example, the statement: 'The slush on the sidewalk remained liquid during the frost because it had been sprinkled with salt'. This explanation does not explicitly mention any laws, but it tacitly presupposes at least one: that the freezing point of water is lowered whenever salt is dissolved in it. Indeed, it is precisely by virtue of this law that the sprinkling of salt acquires the explanatory, and specifically causative, role that the elliptical because-statement ascribes to it. That statement, incidentally, is elliptical also in other respects; for example, it tacitly takes for granted, and leaves unmentioned, certain assumptions about the prevailing physical conditions, such as the temperature's not dropping to a very low point. And if nomic and other assumptions thus omitted are added to the statement that salt had been sprinkled on the slush, we obtain the premises for a deductive-nomological explanation of the fact that the slush remained liquid. . . .

As the preceding examples illustrate, corresponding general laws are always presupposed by an explanatory statement to the effect that a particular event of a certain kind G (e.g., expansion of a gas under constant pressure; flow of a current in a wire loop) was *caused* by an event of another kind, F (e.g., heating of the gas; motion of the loop across a magnetic field). To see this, we need not enter into the complex ramifications of the notion of cause; it suffices to note that the general maxim "Same cause, same effect", when applied to such explanatory statements, yields the implied claim that whenever an event of kind F occurs, it is accompanied by an event of kind G.

To say that an explanation rests on general laws is not to say that its discovery required the discovery of the laws. The crucial new insight achieved by an explanation will sometimes lie in the discovery of some particular fact (e.g., the presence of an undetected outer planet; infectious matter adhering to the hands of examining physicians) which, by virtue of antecedently accepted general laws, accounts for the explanandum phenomenon. In other cases, such as that of the lines in the hydrogen spectrum, the explanatory achievement does lie in the discovery of a covering law (Balmer's) and eventually of an explanatory theory (such as Bohr's); in yet other cases, the major accomplishment of an explanation may lie in showing that, and exactly how, the explanandum phenomenon can be accounted for by reference to laws and data about particular facts that are already available: this is illustrated by the explanatory derivation of the reflection laws for spherical and paraboloidal mirrors from the basic law of geometrical optics in conjunction with statements about the geometrical characteristics of the mirrors.

An explanatory problem does not by itself determine what kind of discovery is required for its solution. Thus, Leverrier discovered deviations from the theoretically expected course also in the motion of the planet Mercury; and as in the case of Uranus, he tried to explain these as resulting from the gravitational pull of an as yet undetected planet, Vulcan, which would have to be a very dense and very small object between the sun and Mercury. But no such planet was found, and a satisfactory explanation was provided only much later by the general theory of relativity, which accounted for the irregularities not by reference to some disturbing particular factor, but by means of a new system of laws. . . .

THEORIES

Theories are usually introduced when previous study of a class of phenomena has revealed a system of uniformities that can be expressed in the form of empirical laws. Theories then seek to explain those regularities and, generally, to afford a deeper and more accurate understanding of the phenomena in question. To this end, a theory construes those phenomena as manifestations of entities and processes that lie behind or beneath them, as it were. These are assumed to be governed by characteristic theoretical laws, or theoretical principles, by means of which the theory then explains the empirical uniformities that have been previously discovered, and usually also predicts "new" regularities of similar kinds. Let us consider some examples.

The Ptolemaic and Copernican systems sought to account for the observed, "apparent", motions of the heavenly bodies by means of suitable assumptions about the structure of the astronomical universe and the "actual" motions of the celestial objects. The corpuscular and the wave theories of light offered accounts of the nature of light in terms of certain underlying processes; and they explained the previously established uniformities expressed by the laws of rectilinear propagation, reflection, refraction, and diffraction as resulting from the basic laws to which the underlying processes were assumed to conform. Thus, the refraction of a beam of light passing from air into glass was explained in Huyghens' wave theory as resulting from a slowing of the light waves in the denser medium. By contrast, Newton's particle theory attributed optical refraction to a stronger attraction exerted upon the optical particles by the denser medium. Incidentally, this construal implies not only the observed bending of a beam of light: when combined with the other basic assumptions of Newton's theory, it also implies that the particles of light will be accelerated upon entering a denser medium, rather than decelerated, as the wave theory predicts. These conflicting implications were tested nearly two hundred years later by Foucault in the experiment . . . whose outcome bore out the relevant implication of the wave theory.

To mention one more example, the kinetic theory of gases offers explanations for a wide variety of empirically established regularities by construing them as macroscopic manifestations of statistical regularities in the underlying molecular and atomic phenomena.

The basic entities and processes posited by a theory, and the laws assumed to govern them, must be specified with appropriate clarity and precision; otherwise, the theory cannot serve its scientific purpose. This important point is illustrated by the neovitalistic conception of biological phenomena. Living systems, as is well known, display a variety of striking features that seem to be distinctly purposive or teleological in character. Among them are the regeneration of lost limbs in some species; the development, in other species, of normal organisms from embryos that are damaged or even cut into several pieces in an early stage of their growth; and the remarkable coordination of the many processes in a developing organism which, as though following a common plan, lead to the formation of a mature individual. According to neovitalism, such phenomena do not occur in nonliving systems and cannot be explained by means of the concepts and laws of physics and chemistry alone; rather, they are manifestations of underlying teleological agencies of a nonphysical kind, referred to as entelechies or vital forces. Their specific mode of action is usually assumed not to violate the principles of physics and chemistry, but to direct the organic processes, within the range of possibilities left open by the physico-chemical laws, in such a way that, even in the presence of disturbing factors, embryos develop into normal individuals, and adult organisms are maintained in, or returned to, a properly functioning state.

This conception may well seem to offer us a deeper understanding of the remarkable biological phenomena in question; it may give us a sense of being more familiar, more "at home" with them. But understanding in this sense is not what is wanted in science, and a conceptual system that conveys insight into the phenomena in this intuitive sense does not for that reason alone qualify as a scientific theory. The assumptions made by a scientific theory about underlying processes must be definite enough to permit the derivation of specific implications concerning the phenomena that the theory is to explain. The neovitalistic doctrine fails on this account. It does not indicate under what circumstances entelechies will go into action and, specifically, in what way they will direct biological processes: no particular aspect of embryonic development, for example, can be inferred from the doctrine, nor does it enable us to predict what biological responses will occur under specified experimental conditions. Hence, when a new striking type of "organic directiveness" is encountered, all that the neo-vitalist doctrine enables us to do is to make the *post factum* pronouncement: "There is another manifestation of vital forces!"; it offers us no grounds for saying: "On the basis of the theoretical assumptions, this is just what was to be expected—the theory explains it!"

This inadequacy of the neovitalistic doctrine does not stem from the circumstance that entelechies are conceived as nonmaterial agencies, which cannot be seen or felt. This becomes clear when we contrast it with the explanation of the regularities of planetary and lunar motions by means of the Newtonian theory. Both accounts invoke nonmaterial agencies: one of them vital forces; the other, gravitational ones. But Newton's theory includes specific assumptions, expressed in the law of gravitation and the laws of motion, which determine (a) what gravi-tational forces each of a set of physical bodies of given masses and positions will exert upon the others, and (b) what changes in their velocities and, consequently, in their locations will be brought about by those forces. It is this characteristic that gives the theory its power to explain previously observed uniformities and also to yield predictions and retrodictions. Thus, the theory was used by Halley to predict that a comet he had observed in 1682 would return in 1759, and to identify it retrodictively with comets whose appearances had been recorded on six previous occasions going back to the year 1066. The theory also played a spectacular explanatory and predictive role in the discovery of the planet Neptune, on the basis of irregularities in the orbit of Uranus; and subsequently in the discovery, on the basis of irreg-ularities in Neptune's orbit, of the planet Pluto.

Broadly speaking, then, the formulation of a theory will require the specification of two kinds of principles; let us call them internal principles and bridge principles for short. The former will characterize the basic entities and processes invoked by the theory and the laws to which they are assumed to conform. The latter will indicate how the processes envisaged by the theory are related to empirical phenomena with which we are already acquainted, and which the theory may then explain, predict, or retrodict. Let us consider some examples.

In the kinetic theory of gases, the internal principles are those that characterize the "microphenomena" at the molecular level, whereas the bridge principles connect certain aspects of the microphenomena with corresponding "macroscopic" features of a gas. . . .

Without bridge principles, . . . a theory would have no explanatory power. Without bridge principles, we may add, it would also be incapable of test. For the internal principles of a theory are concerned with the peculiar entities and processes assumed by the theory (such as the jumps of electrons from one atomic energy level to another in Bohr's theory), and they will therefore be expressed largely in terms of characteristic "theoretical concepts", which refer to those entities and processes. But the implications that permit a test of those theoretical principles will have to be expressed in terms of things and occurrences with which we are antecedently acquainted, which we already know how to observe, to measure, and to describe. In other words, while the internal principles of a theory are couched in its charac-teristic *theoretical terms* ('nucleus', 'orbital electron', 'energy level', 'electron jump'), the test implications must be formulated in terms (such as 'hydrogen vapor', 'emission spectrum', 'wavelength associated with a spectral line') which are "antecedently understood", as we might say, terms that have been introduced prior to the theory and can be used independently of it. Let us refer to them as *antecedently available* or *pretheoretical terms*. The derivation of such test implications from the internal principles of the theory evidently requires further premises that establish connections between the two sets of concepts; and this, as the preceding examples show, is accomplished by appropriate bridge principles (connecting, for example, the energy released in an electron jump with the wavelength of the light that is emitted as a result). Without bridge principles, the internal principles of a theory would yield no test implications, and the requirement of testability would be violated.

Testability-in-principle and explanatory import, though crucially important, are nevertheless only minimal necessary conditions that a scientific theory must satisfy; a system that meets these requirements may yet afford little illumination and may lack scientific interest. . . .

In a field of inquiry in which some measure of understanding has already been achieved by the establishment of empirical laws, a good theory will deepen as well as broaden that understanding. First, such a theory offers a systematically unified account of quite diverse phenomena. It traces all of them back to the same underlying processes and presents the various empirical uniformities they exhibit as manifestations of one and the same basic laws. We noted earlier the great diversity of empirical regularities (such as those shown by free fall; the simple pendulum; the motions of the moon, the planets, comets, double stars, and artificial satellites; the tides, and so forth) that are accounted for by the basic principles of Newton's theory of gravitation and of motion. In similar fashion, the kinetic theory of gases exhibits a wide variety of empirical uniformities as manifestations of certain basic probabilistic uniformities in the random motions of the molecules. And Bohr's theory of the hydrogen atom accounts not only for the uniformity expressed by Balmer's formula, which refers to just one series of lines in the spectrum of hydrogen, but equally for analogous empirical laws representing the wavelengths of other series of lines in the same spectrum, including several series whose member lines lie in the invisible infrared or ultraviolet parts of the spectrum.

A theory will usually deepen our understanding also in a different way, namely by showing that the previously formulated empirical laws that it is meant to explain do not hold strictly and unexceptionally, but only approximately and within a certain limited range of application. Thus, Newton's theoretical account of planetary motion shows that Kepler's laws hold only approximately, and it explains why this is so: the Newtonian principles imply that the orbit of a planet moving about the sun under its gravitational influence alone would indeed be an ellipse, but that the gravitational pull exerted on it by other planets leads to departures from a strictly elliptical path. The theory gives a quantitative account of the resulting perturbations in terms of the masses and spatial distribution of the disturbing objects. Similarly, Newton's theory accounts for Galileo's law of free fall as simply one special manifestation of the basic laws for motion under gravitational attraction; but in so doing, it shows also that the law (even if applied to free fall in a vacuum) holds only approximately. One of the reasons is that in Galileo's formula the acceleration of free fall appears as a constant (twice the factor 16 in the formula '$s = 16t^2$'), whereas on Newton's inverse-square law of gravitational attraction, the force acting upon the falling body increases as its distance from the center of the earth decreases; hence, by virtue of Newton's second law of motion, its acceleration, too, increases in the course of the fall. Analogous remarks apply to the laws of geometrical optics as viewed from the vantage point of wave-theoretical optics. For example, even in a homogeneous medium, light does not move strictly in straight lines; it can bend around corners. And the laws of geometrical optics for reflection in curved mirrors and for image-formation by lenses hold only approximately and within certain limits.

It might therefore be tempting to say that theories often do not explain previously established laws, but refute them. But this would give a distorted picture of the insight afforded by a theory. After all a theory does not simply refute the earlier empirical generalizations in its field; rather, it shows that within a certain limited range defined by qualifying conditions, the generalizations hold true in fairly close approximation. The limited range for Kepler's laws includes those cases in which the masses of the disturbing additional planets are small compared with that of the sun, or their distances from the given planet are large compared with its distance from the sun. Similarly, the theory shows that Galileo's law holds approximately for free fall over short distances.

Finally, a good theory will also broaden our knowledge and understanding by predicting and explaining phenomena that were not known when the theory was formulated. Thus, Torricelli's conception of a sea of air led to Pascal's prediction that the column of a mercury barometer would shorten with increasing height above sea level. Einstein's general theory of relativity not only accounted for the known slow rotation of the orbit of Mercury, but also predicted the bending of light in a gravitational field, a forecast subsequently borne out by astronomical measurements. Maxwell's theory of electromagnetism implied the existence of electromagnetic waves and predicted important characteristics of their propagation. Those implications, too, were later confirmed by the experimental work of Heinrich Hertz, and they provided the basis for the technology of radio transmission, among other applications.

Such striking predictive successes will of course greatly strengthen our confidence in a theory that already has given us a systematically unified explanation—and often also a correction—of previously established laws. The insight that such a theory gives us is much deeper than that afforded by empirical laws; and it is widely held, therefore, that a scientifically adequate explanation of a class of empirical phenomena can be achieved only by means of an appropriate theory. Indeed, it seems to be a remarkable fact that even if we limited ourselves to a study of the more or less directly observable or measurable aspects of our world and tried to explain these . . . by means of laws couched in terms of observables, our efforts would have only limited success. For the laws that are formulated at the observational level generally turn out to hold only approximately and within a limited range; whereas by theoretical recourse to entities and events under the familiar surface, a much more comprehensive and exact account can be achieved. It is intriguing to speculate whether simpler worlds are conceivable where all phenomena are at the observable surface, so to speak; where there occur perhaps only changes of color and of shape, within a finite range of possibilities, and strictly in accordance with some simple laws of universal form.

Lewis Thomas

The Wonderful Pursuit of Science

Lewis Thomas *is a physician and an educator. He received his M.D. at Harvard, and is President Emeritus of the Sloan–Kettering Cancer Center. He is author of many books, including* Lives of a Cell, *from which this excerpt is taken, and* Late Night Thoughts on Listening to Mahler's Ninth Symphony.

*T*he essential wildness of science as a manifestation of human behavior is not generally perceived. As we extract new things of value from it, we also keep discovering parts of the activity that seem in need of better control, more efficiency, less unpredictability. We'd like to pay less for it and get our money's worth on some more orderly, businesslike schedule. The Washington planners are trying to be helpful in this, and there are new programs for the centralized organization of science all over the place, especially in the biomedical field.

It needs thinking about. There is an almost ungovernable, biologic mechanism at work in scientific behavior at its best, and this should not be overlooked.

The difficulties are more conspicuous when the problems are very hard and complicated and the facts not yet in. Solutions cannot be arrived at for problems of this sort until the science has been lifted through a preliminary, turbulent zone of outright astonishment. Therefore, what must be planned for, in the laboratories engaged in the work, is the totally unforeseeable. If it is centrally organized, the system must be designed primarily for the elicitation of disbelief and the celebration of surprise.

Moreover, the whole scientific enterprise must be arranged so that the separate imaginations in different human minds can be pooled, and this is more a kind of game than a systematic business. It is in the abrupt, unaccountable aggregation of random notions, intuitions, known in science as good ideas, that the high points are made.

The most mysterious aspect of difficult science is the way it is done. Not the routine, not just the fitting together of things that no one had guessed at fitting, not the making of connections; these are merely the workaday details, the methods of operating. They are interesting, but not as fascinating as the central mystery, which is that we do it at all, and that we do it under such compulsion.

I don't know of any other human occupation, even including what I have seen of art, in which the people engaged in it are so caught up, so totally preoccupied, so driven beyond their strength and resources.

Scientists at work have the look of creatures following genetic instructions; they seem to be under the influence of a deeply placed human instinct. They are, despite their efforts at dignity, rather like young animals engaged in savage play. When they are near to an answer their hair stands on end, they sweat, they are awash in their own adrenalin. To grab the answer, and grab it first, is for them a more powerful drive than feeding or breeding or protecting themselves against the elements.

It sometimes looks like a lonely activity, but it is as much the opposite of lonely as human behavior can be. There is nothing so social, so communal, so interdependent. An active field of science is like an immense intellectual anthill; the individual almost vanishes into the mass of minds tumbling over each other, carrying information from place to place, passing it around at the speed of light.

There are special kinds of information that seem to be chemotactic. As soon as a trace is released, receptors at the back of the neck are caused to tremble, there is a massive convergence of motile minds flying upwind on a gradient of surprise, crowding around the source. It is an infiltration of intellects, an inflammation.

There is nothing to touch the spectacle. In the midst of what seems a collective derangement of minds in total disorder, with bits of information being scattered about, torn to shreds, disintegrated, reconstituted, engulfed, in a kind of activity that seems as random and agitated as that of bees in a disturbed part of the hive, there suddenly emerges, with the purity of a slow phrase of music, a single new piece of truth about nature.

In short, it works. It is the most powerful and productive of the things human beings have learned to do together in many centuries, more effective than farming, or hunting and fishing, or building cathedrals, or making money.

It is instinctive behavior, in my view, and I do not understand how it works. It cannot be prearranged in any precise way; the minds cannot be lined up in tidy rows and given directions from printed sheets. You cannot get it done by instructing each mind to make this or that piece, for central committees to fit with the pieces made by other instructed minds. It does not work this way.

What it needs is for the air to be made right. If you want a bee to make honey, you do not issue protocols on solar navigation or carbohydrate chemistry, you put him together with other bees (and you'd better do this quickly, for solitary bees do not stay alive) and you do what you can to arrange the general environment around the hive. If the air is right, the science will come in its own season, like pure honey.

There is something like aggression in the activity, but it differs from other forms of aggressive behavior in having no sort of destruction as the objective. While it is going on, it looks and feels like aggression: get at it, uncover it, bring it out, grab it, it's mine! It is like a primitive running hunt, but there is nothing at the end of it to be injured. More probably, the end is a sigh. But then, if the air is right and the science is going well, the sigh is immediately interrupted, there is a yawping new question, and the wild, tumbling activity begins once more, out of control all over again.

Thomas Kuhn

The Structure of Scientific Revolutions

Thomas Kuhn *is a professor of philosophy at M.I.T. In 1962 he revolutionized the philosophy of science with publication of his book,* The Structure of Scientific Revolutions, *from which this selection is taken. In that book he challenged the classic view (represented by Hempel) by suggesting that we look at science as a social enterprise, rather than as a purely logical enterprise.*

In this essay, 'normal science' means research firmly based upon one or more past scientific achievements, achievements that some particular scientific community acknowledges for a time as supplying the foundation for its further practice. Today such achievements are recounted, though seldom in their original form, by science textbooks, elementary and advanced. These textbooks expound the body of accepted theory, illustrate many or all of its successful applications, and compare these applications with exemplary observations and experiments. Before such books became popular early in the nineteenth century (and until even more recently in the newly matured sciences), many of the famous classics of science fulfilled a similar function. Aristotle's *Physica*, Ptolemy's *Almagest*, Newton's *Principia* and *Opticks*, Franklin's *Electricity*, Lavoisier's *Chemistry*, and Lyell's *Geology*—these and many other works served for a time implicitly to define the legitimate problems and methods of a research field for succeeding generations of practitioners. They were able to do so because they shared two essential characteristics. Their achievement was sufficiently unprecedented to attract an enduring group of adherents away from competing modes of scientific activity. Simultaneously, it was sufficiently open-ended to leave all sorts of problems for the redefined group of practitioners to resolve.

Achievements that share these two characteristics I shall henceforth refer to as 'paradigms,' a term that relates closely to 'normal science.' By choosing it, I mean to suggest that some accepted examples of actual scientific practice—examples which include law, theory, application, and instrumentation together—provide models from which spring particular coherent traditions of scientific research. These are the traditions which the historian describes under such rubrics as 'Ptolemaic astronomy' (or 'Copernican'), 'Aristotelian dynamics' (or 'Newtonian'), 'corpuscular optics' (or 'wave optics'), and so on. The study of paradigms, including many that are far more specialized than those named illustratively above, is what mainly prepares the student for membership in the particular scientific community with which he will later practice. Because he there joins men who learned the bases of their field from the same concrete models, his subsequent practice will seldom evoke overt disagreement over fundamentals. Men whose research is based on shared paradigms are committed to the same rules and standards for scientific practice. That commitment and the apparent consensus it produces are prerequisites for normal science, i.e., for the genesis and continuation of a particular research tradition. . . .

Normal science . . . is a highly cumulative enterprise, eminently successful in its aim, the steady extension of the scope and precision of scientific knowledge. In all these respects it fits with great precision the most usual image of scientific work. Yet one standard product of the scientific enterprise is missing. Normal science does not aim at novelties of fact or theory and, when successful, finds none. New and unsuspected phenomena are, however, repeatedly uncovered by scientific research, and radical new theories have again and again been invented by scientists. History even suggests that the scientific enterprise has developed a uniquely powerful technique for producing surprises of this sort. If this characteristic of science is to be reconciled with what has already been said, then research under a paradigm must be a particularly effective way of inducing paradigm change. That is what fundamental novelties of fact and theory do. Produced inadvertently by a game played under one set of rules, their assimilation requires the elaboration of another set. After they have become parts of science, the enterprise, at least of those specialists in whose particular field the novelties lie, is never quite the same again.

We must now ask how changes of this sort can come about, considering first discoveries, or novelties of fact, and then inventions, or novelties of theory. That distinction between discovery and invention or between fact and theory will, however, immediately prove to be exceedingly artificial. Its artificiality is an important clue to several of this essay's main theses. Examining selected discoveries in the rest of this section, we shall quickly find that they are not isolated events but extended episodes with a regularly recurrent structure. Discovery commences with the awareness of anomaly, i.e., with the recognition that nature has somehow violated the paradigm-induced expectations that govern normal science. It then continues with a more or less extended exploration of the area of anomaly. And it closes only when the paradigm theory has been adjusted so that the anomalous has become the expected. Assimilating a new sort of fact demands a more than additive adjustment of theory, and until that adjustment is completed—until the scientist has learned to see nature in a different way—the new fact is not quite a scientific fact at all.

To see how closely factual and theoretical novelty are intertwined in scientific discovery examine a particularly famous example, the discovery of oxygen. At least three different men have a legitimate claim to it, and several other chemists must, in the early 1770's, have had enriched air in a laboratory vessel without knowing it. The progress of normal science, in this case of pneumatic chemistry, prepared the way to a breakthrough quite thoroughly. The earliest of the claimants to prepare a relatively pure sample of the gas was the Swedish apothecary, C. W. Scheele. We may, however, ignore his work since it was not published until oxygen's discovery had repeatedly been announced elsewhere and thus had no effect upon the historical pattern that most concerns us here. The second in time to establish a claim was the British scientist and divine, Joseph Priestley, who collected the gas released by heated red oxide of mercury as one item in a prolonged normal investigation of the "airs" evolved by a large number of solid substances. In 1774 he identified the gas thus produced as nitrous oxide and in 1775, led by further tests, as common air with less than its usual quantity of phlogiston. The third claimant, Lavoisier, started the work that led him to oxygen after Priestley's experiments of 1774 and possibly as the result of a hint from Priestley. Early in 1775 Lavoisier reported that the gas obtained by heating the red oxide of mercury was "air itself entire without alteration [except that] . . . it comes out more pure, more respirable." By 1777, probably with the assistance of a second hint from Priestley, Lavoisier had concluded that the gas was a distinct species, one of the two main constituents of the atmosphere, a conclusion that Priestley was never able to accept.

This pattern of discovery raises a question that can be asked about every novel phenomenon that has ever entered the consciousness of scientists. Was it Priestley or Lavoisier, if either, who first discovered oxygen? In any case, when was oxygen discovered? In that form the question could be asked even if only one claimant had existed. As a ruling about priority and date, an answer does not at all concern us. Nevertheless, an attempt to produce one will illuminate the nature of discovery, because there is no answer of the kind that is sought. Discovery is not the sort of process about which the question is appropriately asked. The fact that it is asked—the priority for oxygen has repeatedly been contested since the 1780's—is a symptom of something askew in the image of science that gives discovery so fundamental a role. Look once more at our example. Priestley's claim to the discovery of oxygen is based upon his priority in isolating a gas that was later recognized as a distinct species. But Priestley's sample was not pure, and, if holding impure oxygen in one's hand is to discover it, that had been done by everyone who ever bottled atmospheric air. Besides, if Priestley was the discoverer, when was the discovery made? In 1774 he thought he had obtained nitrous oxide, a species he already knew; in 1775 he saw the gas as dephlogisticated air, which is still not oxygen or even, for phlogistic chemists, a quite unexpected sort of gas. Lavoisier's claim may be stronger, but it presents the same problems. If we refuse the palm to Priestley, we cannot award it to Lavoisier for the work of 1775 which led him to identify the gas as the "air itself entire." Presumably we wait for the work of 1776 and 1777 which led Lavoisier to see not merely the gas but what the gas was. Yet even this award could be questioned, for in 1777 and to the end of his life Lavoisier insisted that oxygen was an atomic "principle of acidity" and that oxygen gas was formed only when that "principle" united with caloric, the matter of heat. Shall we therefore say that oxygen had not yet been discovered in 1777? Some may be tempted to do so. But the principle of acidity was not banished from chemistry until after 1810, and caloric lingered until the 1860's. Oxygen had become a standard chemical substance before either of those dates.

Clearly we need a new vocabulary and concepts for analyzing events like the discovery of oxygen. Though undoubtedly correct, the sentence, "Oxygen was discovered," misleads by suggesting that discovering something is a single simple act assimilable to our usual (and also questionable) concept of seeing. That is why we so readily assume that discovering, like seeing or touching, should be unequivocally attributable to an individual and to a moment in time. But the latter attribution is always impossible, and the former often is as well. Ignoring Scheele, we can safely say that oxygen had not been discovered before 1774, and we would probably also say that it had been discovered by 1777 or shortly thereafter. But within those limits or others like them, any attempt to date the discovery must inevitably be arbitrary because discovering a new sort of phenomenon is necessarily a complex event, one which involves recognizing both *that* something is and *what* it is. Note, for example, that if oxygen were dephlogisticated air for us, we should insist without hesitation that Priestley had discovered it, though we would still not know quite when. But if both observation and conceptualization, fact and assimilation to theory, are inseparably linked in discovery, then discovery is a process and must take time. Only when all the relevant conceptual categories are prepared in advance, in which case the phenomenon would not be of a new sort, can discovering *that* and discovering *what* occur effortlessly, together, and in an instant.

Grant now that discovery involves an extended, though not necessarily long, process of conceptual assimilation. Can we also say that it involves a change in paradigm? To that question, no general answer can yet be given, but in this case at least, the answer must be yes. What Lavoisier announced in his papers from 1777 on was not so much the discovery of oxygen as the oxygen theory of combustion. That theory was the keystone for a reformulation of chemistry so vast that it is usually called the chemical revolution. Indeed, if the discovery of oxygen had not been an intimate part of the emergence of a new paradigm for chemistry, the question of priority from which we began would never have seemed so important. In this case as in others, the value placed upon a new phenomenon and thus upon its discoverer varies with our estimate of the extent to which the phenomenon violated paradigm-induced anticipations. Notice, however, since it will be important later, that the discovery of oxygen was not by itself the cause of the change in chemical theory. Long before he played any part in the discovery of the new gas, Lavoisier was convinced both that something was wrong with the phlogiston theory and that burning bodies absorbed some part of the atmosphere. That much he had recorded in a sealed note deposited with the Secretary of the French Academy in 1772. What the work on oxygen did was to give much additional form and structure to Lavoisier's earlier sense that something was amiss. It told him a thing he was already prepared to discover—the nature of the substance that combustion removes from the atmosphere. That advance awareness of difficulties must be a significant part of what enabled Lavoisier to see in experiments like Priestley's a gas that Priestley had been unable to see there himself. Conversely, the fact that a major paradigm revision was needed to see what Lavoisier saw must be the principal reason why Priestley was, to the end of his long life, unable to see it. . . .

To a greater or lesser extent (corresponding to the continuum from the shocking to the anticipated result), the characteristics common to the . . . example above are characteristic of all discoveries from which new sorts of phenomena emerge. Those characteristics include: the previous awareness of anomaly, the gradual and simultaneous emergence of both observational and conceptual recognition, and the consequent change of paradigm categories and procedures often accompanied by resistance. There is even evidence that these same characteristics are built into the nature of the perceptual process itself. In a psychological experiment that deserves to be far better known outside the trade, Bruner and Postman asked experimental subjects to identify on short and controlled exposure a series of playing cards. Many of the cards were normal, but some were made anomalous, e.g., a red six of spades and a black four of hearts. Each experimental run was constituted by the display of a single card to a single subject in a series of gradually increased exposures. After each exposure the subject was asked what he had seen, and the run was terminated by two successive correct identifications.

Even on the shortest exposures many subjects identified most of the cards, and after a small increase all the subjects identified them all. For the normal cards these identifications were usually correct, but the anomalous cards were almost always identified, without apparent hesitation or puzzlement, as normal. The black four of hearts might, for example, be identified as the four of either spades or hearts. Without any awareness of trouble, it was immediately fitted to one of the conceptual categories prepared by prior experience. One would not even like to say that the subjects had seen something different from what they identified. With a further increase of exposure to the anomalous cards, subjects did begin to hesitate and to display awareness of anomaly. Exposed, for example, to the red six of spades, some would say: That's the six of spades, but there's something wrong with it—the black has a red border. Further increase of exposure resulted in still more hesitation and confusion until finally, and sometimes quite suddenly, most subjects would produce the correct identification without hesitation. Moreover, after doing this with two or three of the anomalous cards, they would have little further difficulty with the others. A few subjects, however, were never able to make the requisite adjustment of their categories. Even at forty times the average exposure required to recognize normal cards for what they were, more than 10 percent of the anomalous cards were not correctly identified. And the subjects who then failed often experienced acute personal distress. One of them exclaimed: "I can't make the suit out, whatever it is. It didn't even look like a card that time. I don't know what color it is now or whether it's a spade or a heart. I'm not even sure now what a spade looks like. My God!" In the next section we shall occasionally see scientists behaving this way too.

Either as a metaphor or because it reflects the nature of the mind, that psychological experiment provides a wonderfully simple and cogent schema for the process of scientific discovery. In science, as in the playing card experiment, novelty emerges only with difficulty, manifested by resistance, against a background provided by expectation. Initially, only the anticipated and usual are experienced even under circumstances where anomaly is later to be observed. Further acquaintance, however, does result in awareness of something wrong or does relate the effect to something that has gone wrong before. That awareness of anomaly opens a period in which conceptual categories are adjusted until the initially anomalous has become the anticipated. At this point the discovery has been completed. I have already urged that that process or one very much like it is involved in the emergence of all fundamental scientific novelties. Let me now point out that, recognizing the process, we can at last begin to see why normal science, a pursuit not directed to novelties and tending at first to suppress them, should nevertheless be so effective in causing them to arise.

In the development of any science, the first received paradigm is usually felt to account quite successfully for most of the observations and experiments easily accessible to that science's practitioners. Further development, therefore, ordinarily calls for the construction of elaborate equipment, the development of an esoteric vocabulary and skills, and a refinement of concepts that increasingly lessens their resemblance to their usual common-sense prototypes. That professionalization leads, on the one hand, to an immense restriction of the scientist's vision and to a considerable resistance to paradigm change. The science has become increasingly rigid. On the other hand, within those areas to which the paradigm directs the attention of the group, normal science leads to a detail of information and to a precision of the observation-theory match that could be achieved in no other way. Furthermore, that detail and precision-of-match have a value that transcends their not always very high intrinsic interest. Without the special apparatus that is constructed mainly for anticipated functions, the results that lead ultimately to novelty could not occur. And even when the apparatus exists, novelty ordinarily emerges only for the man who, knowing *with precision* what he should expect, is able to recognize that something has gone wrong. Anomaly appears only against the background provided by the paradigm. The more precise and far-reaching that paradigm is, the more sensitive an indicator it provides of anomaly and hence of an occasion for paradigm change. In the normal mode of discovery, even resistance to change has a use that will be explored more fully in the next section. By ensuring that the paradigm will not be too easily surrendered, resistance guarantees that scientists will not be lightly distracted and that the anomalies that lead to paradigm change will penetrate existing knowledge to the core. The very fact that a significant scientific novelty so often emerges simultaneously from several laboratories is an index both to the strongly traditional nature of normal science and to the completeness with which that traditional pursuit prepares the way for its own change. . . .

If awareness of anomaly plays a role in the emergence of new sorts of phenomena, it should surprise no one that a similar but more profound awareness is prerequisite to all acceptable changes of theory. On this point historical evidence is, I think, entirely unequivocal. The state of Ptolemaic astronomy was a scandal before Copernicus' announcement. Galileo's contributions to the study of motion depended closely upon difficulties discovered in Aristotle's theory by scholastic critics. Newton's new theory of light and color originated in the discovery that none of the existing pre-paradigm theories would account for the length of the spectrum, and the wave theory that replaced Newton's was announced in the midst of growing concern about anomalies in the relation of diffraction and polarization effects to Newton's theory. Thermodynamics was born from the collision of two existing nineteenth-century physical theories, and quantum mechanics from a variety of difficulties surrounding black-body radiation, specific heats, and the photoelectric effect. Furthermore, in all these cases except that of Newton the awareness of anomaly had lasted so long and penetrated so deep that one can appropriately describe the fields affected by it as in a state of growing crisis. Because it demands large-scale paradigm destruction and major shifts in the problems and techniques of normal science, the emergence of new theories is generally preceded by a period of pronounced professional insecurity. As one might expect, that insecurity is generated by the persistent failure of the puzzles of normal science to come out as they should. Failure of existing rules is the prelude to a search for new ones. . . .

Philosophers of science have repeatedly demonstrated that more than one theoretical construction can always be placed upon a given collection of data. History of science indicates that, particularly in the early developmental stages of a new paradigm, it is not even very difficult to invent such alternates. But that invention of alternates is just what scientists seldom undertake except during the pre-paradigm stage of their science's development and at very special occasions during its subsequent evolution. So long as the tools a paradigm supplies continue to prove capable of solving the problems it defines, science moves fastest and penetrates most deeply through confident employment of those tools. The reason is clear. As in manufacture so in science—retooling is an extravagance to be reserved for the occasion that demands it. The significance of crises is the indication they provide that an occasion for retooling has arrived. . . .

How, then, do scientists respond to the awareness of an anomaly in the fit between theory and nature? What has just been said indicates that even a discrepancy unaccountably larger than that experienced in other applications of the theory need not draw any very profound response. There are always some discrepancies. Even the most stubborn ones usually respond at last to normal practice. Very often scientists are willing to wait, particularly if there are many problems available in other parts of the field. . . . [D]uring the sixty years after Newton's original computation, the predicted motion of the moon's perigee remained only half of that observed. As Europe's best mathematical physicists continued to wrestle unsuccessfully with the well-known discrepancy, there were occasional proposals for a modification of Newton's inverse square law. But no one took these proposals very seriously, and in practice this patience with a major anomaly proved justified. Clairaut in 1750 was able to show that only the mathematics of the application had been wrong and that Newtonian theory could stand as before. Even in cases where no mere mistake seems quite possible (perhaps because the mathematics involved is simpler or of a familiar and elsewhere successful sort), persistent and recognized anomaly does not always induce crisis. No one seriously questioned Newtonian theory because of the long-recognized discrepancies between predictions from that theory and both the speed of sound and the motion of Mercury. The first discrepancy was ultimately and quite unexpectedly resolved by experiments on heat undertaken for a very different purpose; the second vanished with the general theory of relativity after a crisis that it had had no role in creating. Apparently neither had seemed sufficiently fundamental to evoke the malaise that goes with crisis. They could be recognized as counterinstances and still be set aside for later work.

It follows that if an anomaly is to evoke crisis, it must usually be more than just an anomaly. There are always difficulties somewhere in the paradigm-nature fit; most of them are set right sooner or later, often by processes that could not have been foreseen. The scientist who pauses to examine every anomaly he notes will seldom get significant work done. We therefore have to ask what it is that makes an anomaly seem worth concerted scrutiny, and to that question there is probably no fully general answer. The cases we have already examined are characteristic but scarcely prescriptive. Sometimes an anomaly will clearly call into question explicit and fundamental generalizations of the paradigm, as the problem of ether drag did for those who accepted Maxwell's theory. Or, as in the Copernican revolution, an anomaly without apparent fundamental import may evoke crisis if the applications that it inhibits have a particular practical importance, in this case for calendar design and astrology. Or, as in eighteenth-century chemistry, the development of normal science may transform an anomaly that had previously been only a vexation into a source of crisis: the problem of weight relations had a very different status after the evolution of pneumatic-chemical techniques. Presumably there are still other circumstances that can make an anomaly particularly pressing, and ordinarily several of these will combine. We have already noted, for example, that one source of the crisis that confronted Copernicus was the mere length of time during which astronomers had wrestled unsuccessfully with the reduction of the residual discrepancies in Ptolemy's system.

When, for these reasons or others like them, an anomaly comes to seem more than just another puzzle of normal science, the transition to crisis and to extraordinary science has begun. The anomaly itself now comes to be more generally recognized as such by the profession. More and more attention is devoted to it by more and more of the field's most eminent men. If it still continues to resist, as it usually does not, many of them may come to view its resolution as *the* subject matter of their discipline. For them the field will no longer look quite the same as it had earlier. Part of its different appearance results simply from the new fixation point of scientific scrutiny. An even more important source of change is the divergent nature of the numerous partial solutions that concerted attention to the problem has made available. The early attacks upon the resistant problem will have followed the paradigm rules quite closely. But with continuing resistance, more and more of the attacks upon it will have involved some minor or not so minor articulation of the paradigm, no two of them quite alike, each partially successful, but none sufficiently so to be accepted as paradigm by the group. Through this proliferation of divergent articulations (more and more frequently they will come to be described as *ad hoc* adjustments), the rules of normal science become increasingly blurred. Though there still is a paradigm, few practitioners prove to be entirely agreed about what it is. Even formerly standard solutions of solved problems are called in question. . . .

Confronted with anomaly or with crisis, scientists take a different attitude toward existing paradigms, and the nature of their research changes accordingly. The proliferation of competing articulations, the willingness to try anything, the expression of explicit discontent, the recourse to philosophy and to debate over fundamentals, all these are symptoms of a transition from normal to extraordinary research. It is upon their existence more than upon that of revolutions that the notion of normal science depends. . . .

In learning a paradigm the scientist acquires theory, methods, and standards together, usually in an inextricable mixture. Therefore, when paradigms change, there are usually significant shifts in the criteria determining the legitimacy both of problems and of proposed solutions.

That observation returns us to the point from which this section began, for it provides our first explicit indication of why the choice between competing paradigms regularly raises questions that cannot be resolved by the criteria of normal science. To the extent, as significant as it is incomplete, that two scientific schools disagree about what is a problem and what a solution, they will inevitably talk through each other when debating the relative merits of their respective paradigms. In the partially circular arguments that regularly result, each paradigm will be shown to satisfy more or less the criteria that it dictates for itself and to fall short of a few of those dictated by its opponent. There are other reasons, too, for the incompleteness of logical contact that consistently characterizes paradigm debates. For example, since no paradigm ever solves all the problems it defines and since no two paradigms leave all the same problems unsolved, paradigm debates always involve the question: Which problems is it more significant to have solved? Like the issue of competing standards, that question of values can be answered only in terms of criteria that lie outside of normal science altogether, and it is that recourse to external criteria that most obviously makes paradigm debates revolutionary.

Evelyn Fox Keller
Gender and Science

Evelyn Fox Keller *was trained as a biologist and wrote a biography of the Nobel Prize winning biologist Barbara McClintock. She has been a pioneer in bringing feminist perspectives to the study of science. She is a professor of mathematics and humanities at Northeastern University.*

INTRODUCTION

> The requirements of . . . correctness in practical judgments and objectivity in theoretical knowledge . . . belong as it were in their form and their claims to humanity in general, but in their actual historical configuration they are masculine throughout. Supposing that we describe these things, viewed as absolute ideas, by the single word 'objective', we then find that in the history of our race the equation objective = masculine is a valid one (George Simmel).

In articulating the commonplace, Simmel steps outside of the convention of academic discourse. The historically pervasive association between masculine and objective, more specifically between masculine and scientific, is a topic which academic critics resist taking seriously. Why is that? Is it not odd that an association so familiar and so deeply entrenched is a topic only for informal discourse, literary allusion, and popular criticism? How is it that formal criticism in the philosophy and sociology of science has failed to see here a topic requiring analysis? The virtual silence of at least the nonfeminist academic community on this subject suggests that the association of masculinity with scientific thought has the status of a myth which either cannot or should not be examined seriously. It has simultaneously the air of being "self-evident" and "nonsensical"—the former by virtue of existing in the realm of common knowledge (i.e., everyone knows it), and the latter by virtue of lying outside the realm of formal knowledge, indeed conflicting with our image of science as emotionally and sexually neutral. Taken seriously, it would suggest that, were more women to engage in science, a different science might emerge. Such an idea, although sometimes expressed by non-scientists, clashes openly with the formal view of science as being uniquely determined by its own logical and empirical methodology.

The survival of mythlike beliefs in our thinking about science, the very archetype of antimyth, ought, it would seem, to invite our curiosity and demand investigation. Unexamined myths, wherever they survive, have a subterranean potency; they affect our thinking in ways we are not aware of, and to the extent that we lack awareness, our capacity to resist their influence is undermined. The presence of the mythical in science seems particularly inappropriate. What is it doing there? From where does it come? And how does it influence our conceptions of science, of objectivity, or, for that matter, of gender?

These are the questions I wish to address, but before doing so it is necessary to clarify and elaborate the system of beliefs in which science acquires a gender—which amount to a "genderization" of science. Let me make clear at the outset that the issue which requires discussion is *not,* or at least not simply, the relative absence of women in science. While it is true that most scientists have been, and continue to be, men, the make-up of the scientific population hardly accounts, by itself, for the attribution of masculinity to science as an intellectual domain. Most culturally validated intellectual and creative endeavors have, after all, historically been the domain of men. Few of these endeavors, however, bear so unmistakably the connotation of masculine in the very nature of the activity. To both scientists and their public, scientific thought is male thought, in ways that painting and writing—also performed largely by men—have never been. As Simmel observed, objectivity itself is an ideal which has a long history of identification with masculine. The fact that the scientific population is, even now, a population that is overwhelmingly male, is itself a consequence rather than a cause of the attribution of masculinity to scientific thought. What requires discussion is a *belief* rather than a reality, although the ways in which reality is shaped by our beliefs are manifold, and also need articulating.

How does this belief manifest itself? It used to be commonplace to hear scientists, teachers, and parents assert quite baldly that women cannot, should not, be scientists, that they lack the strength, rigor, and clarity of mind for an occupation that properly belongs to men. Now that the women's movement has made offensive such naked assertions, open acknowledgment of the continuing belief in the instrinsic masculinity of scientific thought has become less fashionable. It continues, however, to find daily expression in the language and metaphors we use to describe science. When we dub the objective sciences "hard" as opposed to the softer, i.e., more subjective, branches of knowledge, we implicitly invoke a sexual metaphor, in which "hard" is of course masculine and "soft," feminine. Quite generally, facts are "hard," feelings "soft." "Feminization" has become synonymous with sentimentalization. A woman thinking scientifically or objectively is thinking "like a man"; conversely, a man pursuing a nonrational, nonscientific argument is arguing "like a woman."

The linguistic rooting of this stereotype is not lost among children, who remain perhaps the most outspoken and least self-conscious about its expression. From strikingly early ages, even in the presence of astereotypic role models, children have learned to identify mathematics and science as male. "Science," my five-year-old son declared, confidently bypassing the fact that his mother was a scientist, "is for men!" The identification between scientific thought and masculinity is so deeply embedded in the culture at large that children have little difficulty internalizing that identification. They grow up not only expecting scientists to be men, but also perceiving scientists as more "masculine" than other male professionals, than, for example, those in the arts. Numerous studies of masculinity and femininity in the professions confirm this observation, with the "harder" sciences as well as the "harder" branches of any profession consistently characterized as more masculine.

In one particularly interesting study of attitudes prevalent among English schoolboys, a somewhat different but critically related dimension of the cultural stereotype emerges. Hudson observes that scientists are perceived as not only more masculine than are artists, but simultaneously as less sexual. He writes:

> The arts are associated with sexual pleasure, the sciences with sexual restraint. The arts man is seen as having a good-looking, well-dressed wife with whom he enjoys a warm sexual relation; the scientist as having a wife who is dowdy and dull,

and in whom he has no physical interest. Yet the scientist is seen as masculine, the arts specialist as slightly feminine.

In this passage we see the genderization of science linked with another, also widely perceived image of science as antithetical to Eros. These images are not unrelated, and it is important to bear their juxtaposition in mind as we attempt to understand their sources and functions. What is at issue here is the kind of images and metaphor with which science is surrounded. If we can take the use of metaphor seriously, while managing to keep clearly in mind that it is metaphor and language which are being discussed, then we can attempt to understand the influences they might exert—how the use of language and metaphor can become hardened into a kind of reality. One way is through the internalization of these images by scientists themselves, and I will discuss more explicitly how this can happen later in the paper. As a first step, however, the imagery itself needs to be explored further.

If we agree to pursue the implications of attributing gender to the scientific mind, then we might be led to ask, with what or with whom is the sexual metaphor completed? And, further, what is the nature of the act with which this now desexualized union is consummated? The answer to the first question is immediate. The complement of the scientific mind is, of course, Nature—viewed so ubiquitously as female. "Let us establish a chaste and lawful marriage between Mind and Nature" wrote Bacon, thereby providing the prescription for the birth of the new science. This prescription has endured to the present day—in it are to be found important clues for an understanding of the posture of the virgin groom, of his relation toward his bride, and of the ways in which he defines his mission. The metaphoric marriage of which science is the offspring sets the scientific project squarely in the midst of our unmistakably patriarchal tradition. Small wonder, then, that the goals of science are so persistently described in terms of "conquering" and "mastering" nature. Bacon articulated this more clearly than today's self-consciousness could perhaps permit when he urged: "I am come in very truth leading you to Nature with all her children to bind her to your service and make her your slave." . . .

Having divided the world into two parts—the knower (mind) and the knowable (nature)— scientific ideology goes on to prescribe a very specific relation between the two. It prescribes the interactions which can consummate this union, that is, which can lead to knowledge. Not only are mind and nature assigned gender, but in characterizing scientific and objective thought as masculine, the very activity by which the knower can acquire knowledge is also genderized. The relation specified between knower and known is one of distance and separation. It is that between a subject and object radically divided, which is to say no worldly relation. Simply put, nature is objectified. The "chaste and lawful marriage" is consummated through reason rather than feeling, and "observation" rather than "immediate" sensory experience. The modes of intercourse are defined so as to insure emotional and physical inviolability. Concurrent with the division of the world into subject and object is, accordingly, a division of the forms of knowledge into "objective" and "subjective." The scientific mind is set apart from what is to be known, i.e., from nature, and its autonomy is guaranteed (or so it has been traditionally assumed) by setting apart its modes of knowing from those in which that dichotomy is threatened. In this process, the characterization of both the scientific mind and its modes of access to knowledge as masculine is indeed significant. Masculine here connotes, as it so often does, autonomy, separation, and distance. It connotes a radical rejection of any commingling of subject and object, which are, it now appears, quite consistently identified as male and female.

What is the real significance of this system of beliefs, whose structure now reveals a quite intricate admixture of metaphysics, cognitive style, and sexual metaphor? If we reject the position, as I believe we must, that the associations between scientific and masculine are simply "true"—that they reflect a biological difference between male and female brains—then how are we to account for our adherence to them? Whatever intellectual or personality characteristics may be affected by sexual hormones, it has become abundantly clear that our ideas about the differences between the sexes far exceed what can be traced to mere biology; that once formed these ideas take on a life of their own—a life sustained by powerful cultural and psychological forces. Even the brief discussion offered above makes it evident that, in attributing gender to an intellectual posture, in sexualizing a thought process, we inevitably invoke the large world of affect. The task of explaining the associations between masculine and scientific thus becomes, short of reverting to an untenable biological reductionism, the task of understanding the emotional substructure that links our experience of gender with our cognitive experience.

The nature of the problem suggests that, in seeking an explanation of the origins and endurance of this mythology, we look to the processes by which the capacity for scientific thought develops, and the ways in which those processes are intertwined with emotional and sexual development. By so doing, it becomes possible to acquire deeper insight into the structure and perhaps even the functions of the mythology we seek to elucidate. The route I wish to take proceeds along ground laid by psychoanalysts and cognitive psychologists, along a course shaped by the particular questions I have posed. What emerges is a scenario supported by the insights these workers have attained, and held together, it is to be hoped, by its own logical and intuitive coherence.

THE DEVELOPMENT OF OBJECTIVITY

The crucial insight which underlies much of this discussion—an insight for which we are indebted to both Freud and Piaget—is that the capacity for objectivity, for delineating subject from object, is *not* inborn, although the potential for it into doubt is. Rather, the ability to perceive reality "objectively" is acquired as an inextricable part of the long and painful process by which the child's sense of self is formed. In the deepest sense, it is a function of the child's capacity for distinguishing self from not-self, "me" from "not-me." The consolidation of this capacity is perhaps the major achievement of childhood development.

After half a century's clinical observations of children and adults the developmental picture which emerges is as follows. In the early world of the infant, experiences of thoughts, feelings, events, images, and perceptions are continuous. Boundaries have not yet been drawn to distinguish the child's internal from external environment; nor has order or structure been imposed on either. The external environment, consisting primarily of the mother during this early period, is experienced as an extension of the child. It is only through the assimilation of cumulative experiences of pleasure and pain, of gratification and disappointment, that the child slowly learns to distinguish between self and other, between image and percept, between subject and object. The growing ability to distinguish his or her self from the environment allows for the recognition of a world of external objects—a world subject to ever finer discrimination and delineation. It permits the recognition of an external reality to which the child can relate—at first magically, and ultimately objectively. In the course of time, the inanimate becomes released from the animate, objects from their perspective, and events from wishes; the child becomes capable of objective thought and perception. The process by which this development occurs proceeds through sequential and characteristic stages of cognitive growth, stages which have been extensively documented and described by Piaget and his co-workers.

The background of this development is fraught with intense emotional conflict. The primary object which the infant carves out of the matrix of his/her experiences is an emotional object, namely the mother. And along with the emergence of the mother as a separate being comes the child's painful recognition of his/her own separate existence. Anxiety is unleashed, and longing is born. The child (infant) discovers his dependency and need—and a primitive form of love. Out of the demarcation between self and mother arises a longing to undo that differentiation—an urge to re-establish the original unity. At the same time, there is also growing pleasure in autonomy, which itself comes to feel threatened by the lure of an earlier state. The process of emotional delineation proceeds in fits and starts, propelled and inhibited by conflicting impulses, desires, and fears. The parallel process of cognitive delineation must be negotiated against the background of these conflicts. As objects acquire a separate identity, they remain for a long time tied to the self by a network of magical ties. The disentanglement of self from world, and of thoughts from things, requires relinquishing the magical bonds which have kept them connected. It requires giving up the belief in the omnipotence—now of the child, now of the mother—that perpetuates those bonds and learning to tolerate the limits and separateness of both. It requires enduring the loss of a wish-dominated existence in exchange for the rewards of living "in reality." In doing so, the child moves from the egocentricity of a self-dominated contiguous world to the recognition of a world outside and independent of himself—a world in which objects can take on a "life" of their own.

The recognition of the independent reality of both self and other is a necessary pre-condition both for science and for love. It may not, however, be sufficient—for either. Certainly the capacity for love, for empathy, for artistic creativity requires more than a simple dichotomy between subject and object. Autonomy too sharply defined, reality too rigidly defined, cannot encompass the emotional and creative experiences which give life its fullest and richest depth. Autonomy must be conceived of more dynamically and reality more flexibly if they are to allow for the ebb and flow of love and play. Emotional growth does not end with the mere acceptance of one's own separateness; perhaps it is fair to say that it begins there. Out of a condition of emotional and cognitive union with the mother, the child gradually gains enough confidence in the enduring reality of both him/herself and the environment to tolerate their separateness and mutual independence. A sense of self becomes delineated—in opposition, as it were, to the mother. Ultimately, however, both sense of self and of other become sufficiently secure to permit momentary relaxation of the boundary between—without, that is, threatening the loss of either. One has acquired confidence in the enduring survival of both self and other as vitally autonomous. Out of the recognition and acceptance of one's aloneness in the world, it becomes possible to transcend one's isolation, to truly love another.

The final step—of reintroducing ambiguity into one's relation to the world—is a difficult one. It evokes deep anxieties and fears stemming from old conflicts and older desires. The ground of one's selfhood was not easily won, and experiences which appear to threaten the loss of that ground can be seen as acutely dangerous. Milner, in seeking to understand the essense of what makes a drawing "alive," and conversely, the inhibitions which impede artistic expression, has written with rare perspicacity and eloquence about the dangers and anxieties attendant upon opening ourselves to the creative perception so critical for a successful drawing. But unless we can, the world of art is foreclosed to us. Neither love nor art can survive the exclusion of a dialogue between dream and reality, between inside and outside, between subject and object.

Our understanding of psychic autonomy, and along with it, of emotional maturity, owes a great deal to the work of the English psychoanalyst Winnicott. Of particular importance here is Winnicott's concept of the transitional object—an object intermediate between self and other (as, for example, the baby's blanket). It is called a transitional object insofar as it facilitates the transition from the stage of magical union with the mother to autonomy, the transition from belief in omnipotence to an acceptance of the limitations of everyday reality. Gradually, it is given up, not so much forgotten as relegated to limbo. By this I mean that in health the transitional object does not "go inside" nor does the feeling about it necessarily undergo repression . . . It loses meaning, and this is because the transitional phenomena have become diffused, have become spread out over the whole intermediate territory between "inner psychic reality" and "the external world as perceived by two persons in common," that is to say, over the whole cultural field.

Emotional maturity, then, implies a sense of reality which is neither cut off from, nor at the mercy of, fantasy; it requires a sufficiently secure sense of autonomy to allow for that vital element of ambiguity at the interface between subject and object. In the words of Loewald, "Perhaps the so-called fully developed, the mature ego is not one that has become fixated at the presumably highest or latest stage of development, having left the others behind it, but is an ego that integrates its reality in such a way that the earlier and deeper levels of ego-reality integration remain alive as dynamic sources of higher organization."

While most of us will recognize the inadequacy of a static conception of autonomy as an emotional ideal, it is easy to fall into the trap of regarding it as an appropriate ideal for cognitive development. That is, cognitive maturity is frequently identified with a posture in which objective reality is perceived and defined as radically divided from the subjective. Our inclination to accept this posture as a model for cognitive maturity is undoubtedly influenced by the definition of objectivity we have inherited from classical science—a definition rooted in the premise that the subject can and should be totally removed from our description of the object. Though that definition has proved unquestionably efficacious in the past, contemporary developments in both philosophy and physics have demonstrated its epistemological inadequacy. They have made it necessary for us to look beyond the classical dichotomy to a more dynamic conception of reality, and a more sophisticated epistemology to support it.

If scientists have exhibited a reluctance to do so, as I think they have, that reluctance should be examined in the light of what we already know about the relation between cognitive and emotional development. Elsewhere I have attempted to show the persistence of demonstrably inappropriate classical ideas even in contemporary physics, where the most dramatic evidence for the failure of classical ideas has come from. There I try to establish some of the consequences of this persistence, and to account for the tenacity of such ideas. In brief, I argue that the adherence to an outmoded, dichotomous conception of objectivity might be viewed as a defense against anxiety about autonomy of exactly the same kind as we find interfering with the capacity for love and creativity. When even physics reveals "transitional phenomena"—phenomena, that is, about which it cannot be determined whether they belong to the observer or the observed—then it becomes essential to question the adequacy of traditional "realist" modes for cognitive maturity as well as for reality. Our very definition of reality requires constant refinement as we continue in the effort to wean our perceptions from our wishes, our fears, and our anxieties; insofar as our conception of cognitive maturity is dictated by our definition of reality, that conception requires corresponding refinement.

THE DEVELOPMENT OF GENDER

What, the reader may ask, has all this to do with gender? Though the discussion has led us on a sizable detour, the implicit argument which relates it to the genderization of science should already be clear. Before articulating the argument explicitly, however, we need an account of the development of gender identity and gender identifications in the context of the developmental picture I have presented thus far.

Perhaps the single most important determinant of our conceptions of male and female is provided by our perceptions of and experiences with our parents. While the developmental processes described above are equally relevant for children of both sexes, their implications for the two sexes are bound to differ. The basic and fundamental fact that it is, for most of us, our mothers who provide the emotional context out of which we forget the discrimination between self and other inevitably leads to a skewing of our perceptions of gender. As long as our earliest and most compelling experiences of merging have their origin in the mother-child relation, it appears to be inevitable that that experience will tend to be identified with "mother," while delineation and separation are experienced as a negation of "mother," as "not-mother." In the extrication of self from other, the mother, beginning as the first and most primitive subject, emerges, by a process of effective and affective negation, as the first object. The very processes (both cognitive and emotional) which remind us of that first bond become colored by their association with the woman who is, and forever remains, the archetypal female. Correspondingly, those of delineation and objectification are colored by their origins in the process of separation *from* mother; they become marked, as it were, as "not-mother." The mother becomes an object, and the child a subject, by a process which becomes itself an expression of opposition to and negation of "mother."

While there is an entire world which exists beyond the mother, in the family constel-lation with which we are most familiar, it is primarily the father (or the father figure) toward whom the child turns for protection from the fear of re-engulfment, from the anxieties and fears of disintegration of a still very fragile ego. It is the father who comes to stand for individuation and differentiation—for objective reality itself; who indeed can represent the "real" world by virtue of being *in* it.

For Freud, reality becomes personified by the father during the oedipal conflict; it is the father who, as the representative of external reality harshly intrudes on the child's (i.e., boy's) early romance with the mother—offering his protection and future fraternity as the reward for the child's acceptance of the "reality principle." Since Freud, however, it has become increasingly well understood that the rudiments of both gender and reality are established long before the oedipal period, and that reality becomes personified by the father as soon as the early maternal bond comes to be experienced as threatening engulfment, or loss of ego boundaries. . . . Thus it is that, for all of us—male and female alike—our earliest experiences incline us to associate the affective and cognitive posture of objectification with masculine, while all processes which involve a blurring of the boundary between subject and object tend to be associated with the feminine.

The crucial question of course is: What happens to these early associations? While the patterns which give rise to them may be quasi-universal (though strongest, no doubt, in our own form of nuclear family), the conditions which sustain them are not. It is perhaps at this point that specific cultural forces intrude most prominently. In a culture which validates subsequent adult experiences that transcend the subject-object divide, as we find for example in art, love, and religion, these early identifications can be counteracted—provided, that is, that such experiences are validated as essentially human rather than as "feminine" experience. However, in a culture such as ours, where primary validation is accorded to a science which has been premised on a radical dichotomy between subject and object, and where all other experiences are accorded secondary, "feminine" status, the early identifications can hardly fail to persist. The genderization of science—as an enterprise, as an intellectual domain, as a world view—simultaneously reflects and perpetuates associations made in an earlier, presci-entific era. If true, then an adherence to an objectivist epistemology, in which truth is measured by its distance from the subjective, has to be re-examined when it emerges that, by this definition, truth itself has become genderized. . . .

. . . it is important to recognize that, although children of both sexes must learn equally to distinguish self from other, and have essentially the same need for autonomy, to the extent that boys rest their very sexual identity on an opposition to what is both experienced and defined as feminine, the development of their gender identity is likely to accentuate the process of separation. As boys, they must undergo a twofold "disidentification from mother"—first for the establishment of a self-identity, and second for the consolidation of a male gender identity. Further impetus is added to this process by the external cultural pressure on the young boy to establish a stereotypic masculinity, now culturally as well as privately connoting independence and autonomy. The cultural definitions of masculine as what can never appear feminine, and of autonomy as what can never be relaxed, conspire to reinforce the child's earliest associations of female with the pleasures and dangers of merging, and male with both the comfort and the loneliness of separateness. The boy's internal anxiety about both self and gender is here echoed by the cultural anxiety; together they can lead to postures of exaggerated and rigidified autonomy and masculinity which can—indeed which may be designed to— defend against that anxiety and the longing which generates it. Many psychoanalysts have come to believe that, because of the boy's need to switch his identification from the mother to the father, his sense of gender identity tends always to be more fragile than the girl's. Her sense of self-identity may, however, be comparatively more vulnerable. It has been suggested that the girl's development of a sense of separateness may be to some degree hampered by her ongoing identification with her mother. Although she too must disentangle herself from the early experience of oneness, she continues to look toward her mother as a model for her gender identity. Whatever vicissitudes her relation to her mother may suffer during subsequent development, a strong identification based on common gender is likely to persist—her need for "disidentification" is not so radical. Cultural forces may further complicate her development of autonomy by stressing dependency and subjectivity as feminine characteristics. To the extent that such traits become internalized, they can be passed on through the generations by leading to an accentuation of the symbiotic bond between mother and daughter.

It would seem, then, appropriate to suggest that one possible outcome of these processes is that boys may be more inclined toward excessive and girls toward inadequate delineation— growing into men who have difficulty loving and women who retreat from science. What I am suggesting, then, and indeed trying to describe, is a network of interactions between gender development, a belief system which equates objectivity with masculinity, and a set of cultural values which simultaneously elevates what is defined as scientific and what is defined as masculine. The structure of this network is such as to perpetuate and exacerbate distortions in *any* of its parts—including the acquisition of gender identity.

THE DEVELOPMENT OF SCIENTISTS

Whatever differences between the sexes such a network might, however, generate—and, as I said earlier, the existence of such differences remains ultimately an empirical question— they are in any case certain to be overshadowed by the inevitably large variations that exist within both the male and female populations. Not all men become scientists, and we must ask whether a science which advertises itself as revealing a reality in which subject and object are unmistakably distinct does not offer special comfort to those who, as individuals (be they male or female), retain particular anxiety about the loss of autonomy. In short, if we can take the argument presented thus far seriously, then we must follow it through yet another step. Would not a characterization of science which appears to gratify particular emotional needs give rise to a self-selection of scientists—a self-selection which would, in turn, lead to a perpetuation of that characterization? Without attempting a detailed discussion of either the appropriateness of the imagery with which science is advertised, or of the personality char- acteristics which such imagery might select for, it seems reasonable to suggest that such a selection mechanism ought inevitably to operate. The persistence of the characterization of science as masculine, as objectivist, as autonomous of psychological as well as of social and political forces would then be encouraged, through such selection, by the kinds of emotional satisfaction it provides.

If so, the question which then arises is whether, statistically, scientists do indeed tend to be more anxious about their affective as well as cognitive autonomy than nonscientists. Although it is certainly part of the popular image of scientists that they do, the actual measurement of personality differences between scientists and nonscientists has proved to be extremely difficult; it is as difficult, and subject to as much disagreement, as the measurement of personality differences between the sexes. One obvious difficulty arises out of the ambiguity of the term scientist, and the enormous heterogeneity of the scientific population. Apart from the vast differences among individuals, characteristics vary across time, nationality, discipline, and, even, with degree of eminence. The Einsteins of history fail, virtually by definition, to conform to more general patterns either of personality or of intellect. Nevertheless, certain themes, however difficult they may be to pin down, continually re-emerge with enough prominence to warrant consideration. These are the themes, or stereotypes, on which I have concentrated throughout this paper, and though they can neither exhaustively nor even accurately describe science or scientists as a whole—as stereotypes never can—they do acquire some corroboration from the (admittedly problematic) literature on the "scientific personality." It seems worth noting, therefore, several features which seem to emerge from a number of efforts to describe the personality characteristics which tend to distinguish scientists from nonscientists.

I have already referred to the fact that scientists, particularly physical scientists, score unusually high on "masculinity" tests, meaning only that, on the average, their responses differ greatly from those of women. At the same time, studies report that they tend overwhelmingly to have been loners as children, to be low in social interests and skills, indeed to avoid interpersonal contact. McClelland's subsequent studies confirm these impressions. He writes, "And it is a fact, as Anne Roe reports, that young scientists are typically not very interested in girls, date for the first time late in college, marry the first girl they date, and thereafter appear to show a rather low level of heterosexual drive" (by which he presumably means sexual, thereby confirming, incidentally, the popular image of scientists as "asexual" which I discussed earlier). One of McClelland's particularly interesting findings was that 90% of a group of eminent scientists see, in the "mother-son" picture routinely given as part of the Thematic Apperception Test, "the mother and son going their separate ways"—a relatively infrequent response to this picture in the general population. It conforms, however, with the more general observation (emerging from biographical material) of a distant relation to the mother, frequently coupled with "open or covert attitudes of derogation."

Though these remarks are admittedly sketchy, and by no means constitute a review of the field, they do suggest a personality profile which seems admirably suited to an occupation seen as simultaneously masculine and asexual. Bacon's image of a "chaste and lawful marriage" becomes remarkably apt insofar as it allows the scientist both autonomy and mastery in his marriage to a bride kept at safe, "objectified" remove.

CONCLUSION

It is impossible to conclude a discussion of the genderization of science without making some brief comments on its social implications. The linking of scientific and objective with masculine brings in its wake a host of secondary consequences which, however self-evident, may nevertheless need articulating. Not only does our characterization of science thereby become colored by the biases of patriarchy and sexism, but simultaneously our evaluation of masculine and feminine becomes affected by the prestige of science. A circular process of mutual reinforcement is established in which what is called scientific receives extra validation from the cultural preference for what is called masculine, and, conversely, what is called feminine— be it a branch of knowledge, a way of thinking, or a woman herself—becomes further devalued by its exclusion from the special social and intellectual value placed on science and the model science provides for all intellectual endeavors. This circularity not only operates on the level of ideology, but is assisted by the ways in which the developmental processes, both for science and for the child, internalize ideological influences. For each, pressures from the other operate, in the ways I have attempted to describe, to create distortions and perpetuate caricatures.

Neither in emphasizing the self-sustaining nature of these beliefs, nor in relating them to early childhood experience, do I wish to suggest that they are inevitable. On the contrary, by examining their dynamics I mean to emphasize the existence of alternative possibilities. The disengagement of our thinking about science from our notions of what is masculine could lead to a freeing of both from some of the rigidities to which they have been bound, with profound ramifications for both. Not only, for example, might science become more accessible to women, but, far more importantly, our very conception of "objective" could be freed from inappropriate constraints. As we begin to understand the ways in which science itself has been influenced by its unconscious mythology, we can begin to perceive the possibilities for a science not bound by such mythology.

How might such a disengagement come about? To the extent that my analysis rests on the crucial importance of the gender of the primary parent, changing patterns of parenting could be of special importance. But other developments might be of equal importance. Changes in the ethos that sustains our beliefs about science and gender could also come about from the current pressure, largely politically inspired, to re-examine the traditionally assumed neutrality of science, from philosophical exploration of the boundaries or limitations of scientific inquiry, and even, perhaps especially, from events within science itself. Both within and without science, the need to question old dogma has been pressing. Of particular interest among recent developments *within* science is the growing interest among physicists in a process description of reality—a move inspired by, perhaps even necessitated by, quantum mechanics. In these descriptions object reality acquires a dynamic character, akin to the more fluid concept of autonomy emerging from psychoanalysis. Bohr himself perspicaciously provided us with a considerably happier image than Bacon's—one more apt even for the future of physics— when he chose for his coat of arms the yin-yang symbol, over which reads the inscription: *Contraria Sunt Complementa.*

Where, finally, has this analysis taken us? In attempting to explore the significance of the sexual metaphor in our thinking about science, I have offered an explanation of its origins, its functions, and some of its consequences. Necessarily, many questions remain, and it is perhaps appropriate, by way of concluding, to articulate some of them. I have not, for example, more than touched on the social and political dynamics of the genderization of science. This is a crucial dimension which remains in need of further exploration. It has seemed to me, however, that central aspects of this problem belong in the psychological domain, and further, that this is the domain which tends to be least accounted for in most discussions of scientific thought.

Within the particular model of affective and cognitive development I have invoked, much remains to be understood about the interconnections between cognition and affect. Though I have, throughout, assumed an intimate relation between the two, it is evident that a fuller and more detailed conception is necessary.

Finally, the speculations I offer raise numerous questions of historical and psychological fact. I have already indicated some of the relevant empirical questions in the psychology of personality which bear on my analysis. Other questions of a more historical nature ought also to be mentioned. How, e.g., have conceptions of objectivity changed with time, and to what extent have these conceptions been linked with similar sexual metaphors in other, prescientific eras, or, for that matter, in other, less technological cultures? Clearly, much remains to be investigated; perhaps the present article can serve to provoke others to help pursue these questions.

Richard Feynman
Seeking New Laws of Nature

Richard Feynman *is a professor of physics at California Institute of Technology. In 1945 he was declared mentally deficient for service in the U.S. Army. In 1965 he won the Nobel prize in physics. He is also well known for his abilities with the bongo drums.*

What I want to talk about in this lecture is not, strictly speaking, the character of physical law. One might imagine at least that one is talking about nature when one is talking about the character of physical law; but I do not want to talk about nature, but rather about how we stand relative to nature now. I want to tell you . . . what there is to guess, and how one goes about guessing. Someone suggested that it would be ideal if, as I went along, I would slowly explain how to guess a law, and then end by creating a new law for you. I do not know whether I shall be able to do that. . . .

In general we look for a new law by the following process. First we guess it. Then we compute the consequences of the guess to see what would be implied if this law that we guessed is right. Then we compare the result of the computation to nature, with experiment or experience, compare it directly with observation, to see if it works. If it disagrees with experiment it is wrong. In that simple statement is the key to science. It does not make any difference how beautiful your guess is. It does not make any difference how smart you are, who made the guess, or what his name is—if it disagrees with experiment it is wrong. That is all there is to it. It is true that one has to check a little to make sure that it is wrong, because whoever did the experiment may have reported incorrectly, or there may have been some feature in the experiment that was not noticed, some dirt or something; or the man who computed the consequences, even though it may have been the one who made the guesses, could have made some mistake in the analysis. These are obvious remarks, so when I say if it disagrees with experiment it is wrong, I mean after the experiment has been checked, the calculations have been checked, and the thing has been rubbed back and forth a few times to make sure that the consequences are logical consequences from the guess, and that in fact it disagrees with a very carefully checked experiment.

This will give you a somewhat wrong impression of science. It suggests that we keep on guessing possibilities and comparing them with experiment, and this is to put experiment into a rather weak position. In fact experimenters have a certain individual character. They like to do experiments even if nobody has guessed yet, and they very often do their experiments in a region in which people know the theorist has not made any guesses. For instance, we may know a great many laws, but do not know whether they really work at high energy, because it is just a good guess that they work at high energy. Experimenters have tried experiments at higher energy, and in fact every once in a while experiment produces trouble;

that is, it produces a discovery that one of the things we thought right is wrong. In this way experiment can produce unexpected results, and that starts us guessing again. One instance of an unexpected result is the mu meson and its neutrino, which was not guessed by anybody at all before it was discovered, and even today nobody yet has any method of guessing by which this would be a natural result.

You can see, of course, that with this method we can attempt to disprove any definite theory. If we have a definite theory, a real guess, from which we can conveniently compute consequences which can be compared with experiment, then in principle we can get rid of any theory. There is always the possibility of proving any definite theory wrong; but notice that we can never prove it right. Suppose that you invent a good guess, calculate the consequences, and discover every time that the consequences you have calculated agree with experiment. The theory is then right? No, it is simply not proved wrong. In the future you could compute a wider range of consequences, there could be a wider range of experiments, and you might then discover that the thing is wrong. That is why laws like Newton's laws for the motion of planets last such a long time. He guessed the law of gravitation, calculated all kinds of consequences for the system and so on, compared them with experiment—and it took several hundred years before the slight error of the motion of Mercury was observed. During all that time the theory had not been proved wrong, and could be taken temporarily to be right. But it could never be proved right, because tomorrow's experiment might succeed in proving wrong what you thought was right. We never are definitely right, we can only be sure we are wrong. However, it is rather remarkable how we can have some ideas which will last so long.

One of the ways of stopping science would be only to do experiments in the region where you know the law. But experimenters search most diligently, and with the greatest effort, in exactly those places where it seems most likely that we can prove our theories wrong. In other words we are trying to prove ourselves wrong as quickly as possible, because only in that way can we find progress. For example, today among ordinary low energy phenomena we do not know where to look for trouble, we think everything is all right, and so there is no particular big programme looking for trouble in nuclear reactions, or in super-conductivity. In these lectures I am concentrating on discovering fundamental laws. The whole range of physics, which is interesting, includes also an understanding at another level of these phenomena like super-conductivity and nuclear reactions, in terms of the fundamental laws. But I am talking now about discovering trouble, something wrong with the fundamental laws, and since among low energy phenomena nobody knows where to look, all the experiments today in this field of finding out a new law, are of high energy.

Another thing I must point out is that you cannot prove a vague theory wrong. If the guess that you make is poorly expressed and rather vague, and the method that you use for figuring out the consequences is a little vague—you are not sure, and you say, 'I think everything's right because it's all due to so and so, and such and such do this and that more or less, and I can sort of explain how this works . . . ,' then you see that this theory is good, because it cannot be proved wrong! Also if the process of computing the consequences is indefinite, then with a little skill any experimental results can be made to look like the expected consequences. You are probably familiar with that in other fields. 'A' hates his mother. The reason is, of course, because she did not caress him or love him enough when he was a child. But if you investigate you find out that as a matter of fact she did love him very much, and everything was all right. Well then, it was because she was over-indulgent when he was a child! By having a vague theory it is possible to get either result. The cure for this one is the following. If it were possible to state exactly, ahead of time, how much love is not enough, and how much love is over-indulgent, then there would be a perfectly legitimate theory against which you could make tests. It is usually said when this is pointed out, 'When you are dealing with psychological matters things can't be defined so precisely'. Yes, but then you cannot claim to know anything about it.

You will be horrified to hear that we have examples in physics of exactly the same kind. We have these approximate symmetries, which work something like this. You have an approximate symmetry, so you calculate a set of consequences supposing it to be perfect. When compared with experiment, it does not agree. Of course—the symmetry you are supposed to expect is approximate, so if the agreement is pretty good you say, 'Nice!', while if the agreement is very poor you say, 'Well, this particular thing must be especially sensitive to the failure of the symmetry'. Now you may laugh, but we have to make progress in that way. When a subject is first new, and these particles are new to us, this jockeying around, this 'feeling' way of guessing at the results, is the beginning of any science. The same thing is true of the symmetry proposition in physics as is true of psychology, so do not laugh too hard. It is necessary in the beginning to be very careful. It is easy to fall into the deep end by this kind of vague theory. It is hard to prove it wrong, and it takes a certain skill and experience not to walk off the plank in the game. . . .

Because I am a theoretical physicist, and more delighted with this end of the problem, I want now to concentrate on how you make the guesses.

As I said before, it is not of any importance where the guess comes from; it is only important that it should agree with experiment, and that it should be as definite as possible. 'Then', you say, 'that is very simple. You set up a machine, a great computing machine, which has a random wheel in it that makes a succession of guesses, and each time it guesses a hypothesis about how nature should work it computes immediately the consequences, and makes a comparison with a list of experimental results it has at the other end'. In other words, guessing is a dumb man's job. Actually it is quite the opposite, and I will try to explain why.

The first problem is how to start. You say, 'Well I'd start off with all the known principles'. But all the principles that are known are inconsistent with each other, so something has to be removed. We get a lot of letters from people insisting that we ought to make holes in our guesses. You see, you make a hole, to make room for a new guess. Somebody says, 'You know, you people always say that space is continuous. How do you know when you get to a small enough dimension that there really are enough points in between, that it isn't just a lot of dots separated by little distances?' Or they say, 'You know those quantum mechanical amplitudes you told me about, they're so complicated and absurd, what makes you think those are right? Maybe they aren't right'. Such remarks are obvious and are perfectly clear to anybody who is working on this problem. It does not do any good to point this out. The problem is not only what might be wrong but what, precisely, might be substituted in place of it. In the case of the continuous space, suppose the precise proposition is that space really consists of a series of dots, and that the space between them does not mean anything, and that the dots are in a cubic array. Then we can prove immediately that this is wrong. It does not work. The problem is not just to say something might be wrong, but to replace it by something—and that is not so easy. As soon as any really definite idea is substituted it becomes almost immediately apparent that it does not work.

The second difficulty is that there is an infinite number of possibilities of these simple types. It is something like this. You are sitting working very hard, you have worked for a long time trying to open a safe. Then some Joe comes along who knows nothing about what you are doing, except that you are trying to open the safe. He says 'Why don't you try the combination 10:20:30?' Because you are busy, you have tried a lot of things, maybe you have already tried 10:20:30. Maybe you know already that the middle number is 32 not 20. Maybe you know as a matter of fact that it is a five digit combination. . . . So please do not send me any letters trying to tell me how the thing is going to work. I read them—I always read them to make sure that I have not already thought of what is suggested—but it takes too long to answer them, because they are usually in the class 'try 10:20:30'. As usual, nature's imagination far surpasses our own, as we have seen from the other theories which are subtle and deep. To get such a subtle and deep guess is not so easy. One must be really clever to guess, and it is not possible to do it blindly by machine.

I want to discuss now the art of guessing nature's laws. It is an art. How is it done? One way you might suggest is to look at history to see how the other guys did it. So we look at history.

We must start with Newton. He had a situation where he had incomplete knowledge, and he was able to guess the laws by putting together ideas which were all relatively close to experiment; there was not a great distance between the observations and the tests. That was the first way, but today it does not work so well.

The next guy who did something great was Maxwell, who obtained the laws of electricity and magnetism. What he did was this. He put together all the laws of electricity, due to Faraday and other people who came before him, and he looked at them and realized that they were mathematically inconsistent. In order to straighten it out he had to add one term to an equation. He did this by inventing for himself a model of idler wheels and gears and so on in space. He found what the new law was—but nobody paid much attention because they did not believe in the idler wheels. We do not believe in the idler wheels today, but the equations that he obtained were correct. So the logic may be wrong but the answer is right.

In the case of relativity the discovery was completely different. There was an accumulation of paradoxes; the known laws gave inconsistent results. This was a new kind of thinking, a thinking in terms of discussing the possible symmetries of laws. It was especially difficult, because for the first time it was realized how long something like Newton's laws could seem right, and still ultimately be wrong. Also it was difficult to accept that ordinary ideas of time and space, which seemed so instinctive, could be wrong.

Quantum mechanics was discovered in two independent ways—which is a lesson. There again, and even more so, an enormous number of paradoxes were discovered experimentally, things that absolutely could not be explained in any way by what was known. It was not that the knowledge was incomplete, but that the knowledge was too complete. Your prediction was that this should happen—it did not. The two different routes were one by Schrödinger, who guessed the equation, the other by Heisenberg, who argued that you must analyse what is measurable. These two different philosophical methods led to the same discovery in the end.

More recently, the discovery of the laws of the weak decay I spoke of, when a neutron disintegrates into a proton, an electron and an anti-neutrino—which are still only partly known—add up to a somewhat different situation. This time it was a case of incomplete knowledge, and only the equation was guessed. The special difficulty this time was that the experiments were all wrong. How can you guess the right answer if, when you calculate the result, it disagrees with experiment? You need courage to say the experiments must be wrong. I will explain where that courage comes from later.

Today we have no paradoxes—maybe. We have this infinity that comes in when we put all the laws together, but the people sweeping the dirt under the rug are so clever that one sometimes thinks this is not a serious paradox. Again, the fact that we have found all these particles does not tell us anything except that our knowledge is incomplete. I am sure that history does not repeat itself in physics, as you can tell from looking at the examples I have given. The reason is this. Any schemes—such as 'think of symmetry laws', or 'put the information in mathematical form', or 'guess equations'—are known to everybody now, and they are all tried all the time. When you are stuck, the answer cannot be one of these, because you will have tried these right away. There must be another way next time. Each time we get into this log-jam of too much trouble, too many problems, it is because the methods that we are using are just like the ones we have used before. The next scheme, the new discovery, is going to be made in a completely different way. So history does not help us much. . . .

It is not unscientific to make a guess, although many people who are not in science think it is. Some years ago I had a conversation with a layman about flying saucers—because I am scientific I know all about flying saucers! I said 'I don't think there are flying saucers'. So my antagonist said, 'Is it impossible that there are flying saucers? Can you prove that it's impossible?' 'No', I said, 'I can't prove it's impossible. It's just very unlikely'. At that he said, 'You are very unscientific. If you can't prove it impossible then how can you say that it's unlikely?' But that is the way that is scientific. It is scientific only to say what is more likely and what is less likely, and not to be proving all the time the possible and impossible. To define what I mean, I might have said to him, 'Listen, I mean that from my knowledge of the world that I see around me, I think that it is much more likely that the reports of flying saucers are the results of the known irrational characteristics of terrestrial intelligence than of the unknown rational efforts of extra-terrestrial intelligence'. It is just more likely, that is all. It is a good guess. And we always try to guess the most likely explanation, keeping in the back of the mind the fact that if it does not work we must discuss the other possibilities. . . .

That reminds me of another point, that the philosophy or ideas around a theory may change enormously when there are very tiny changes in the theory. For instance, Newton's ideas about space and time agreed with experiment very well, but in order to get the correct motion of the orbit of Mercury, which was a tiny, tiny difference, the difference in the character of the theory needed was enormous. The reason is that Newton's laws were so simple and so perfect, and they produced definite results. In order to get something that would produce a slightly different result it had to be completely different. In stating a new law you cannot make imperfections on a perfect thing; you have to have another perfect thing. So the difference in philosophical ideas between Newton's and Einstein's theories of gravitation are enormous.

What are these philosophies? They are really tricky ways to compute consequences quickly. A philosophy, which is sometimes called an understanding of the law, is simply a way that a person holds the laws in his mind in order to guess quickly at consequences. Some people have said, and it is true in cases like Maxwell's equations, 'Never mind the philosophy, never mind anything of this kind, just guess the equations. The problem is only to compute the answers so that they agree with experiment, and it is not necessary to have a philosophy, or argument, or words, about the equation'. That is good in the sense that if you only guess the equation you are not prejudicing yourself, and you will guess better. On the other hand, maybe the philosophy helps you to guess. It is very hard to say.

For those people who insist that the only thing that is important is that the theory agrees with experiment, I would like to imagine a discussion between a Mayan astronomer and his student. The Mayans were able to calculate with great precision predictions, for example, for eclipses and for the position of the moon in the sky, the position of Venus, etc. It was all done by arithmetic. They counted a certain number and subtracted some numbers, and so on. There was no discussion of what the moon was. There was no discussion even of the idea that it went around. They just calculated the time when there would be an eclipse, or when the moon would rise at the full, and so on. Suppose that a young man went to the astronomer and said, 'I have an idea. Maybe those things are going around, and there are balls of something like rocks out there, and we could calculate how they move in a completely different way from just calculating what time they appear in the sky'. 'Yes', says the astronomer, 'and how accurately can you predict eclipses?' He says, 'I haven't developed the thing very far yet'. Then says the astronomer, 'Well, we can calculate eclipses more accurately than you can with your model, so you must not pay any attention to your idea because obviously the mathematical scheme is better'. There is a very strong tendency, when someone comes up with an idea and says, 'Let's suppose that the world is this way', for people to say to him,

'What would you get for the answer to such and such a problem?' And he says, 'I haven't developed it far enough'. And they say, 'Well, we have already developed it much further, and we can get the answers very accurately'. So it is a problem whether or not to worry about philosophies behind ideas.

Another way of working, of course, is to guess new principles. In Einstein's theory of gravitation he guessed, on top of all the other principles, the principle that corresponded to the idea that the forces are always proportional to the masses. He guessed the principle that if you are in an accelerating car you cannot distinguish that from being in a gravitational field, and by adding that principle to all the other principles, he was able to deduce the correct laws of gravitation.

That outlines a number of possible ways of guessing. I would now like to come to some other points about the final result. First of all, when we are all finished, and we have a mathematical theory by which we can compute consequences, what can we do? It really is an amazing thing. In order to figure out what an atom is going to do in a given situation we make up rules with marks on paper, carry them into a machine which has switches that open and close in some complicated way, and the result will tell us what the atom is going to do! If the way that these switches open and close were some kind of model of the atom, if we thought that the atom had switches in it, then I would say that I understood more or less what is going on. I find it quite amazing that it is possible to predict what will happen by mathematics, which is simply following rules which really have nothing to do with what is going on in the original thing. The closing and opening of switches in a computer is quite different from what is happening in nature.

One of the most important things in this 'guess—compute consequences—compare with experiment' business is to know when you are right. It is possible to know when you are right way ahead of checking all the consequences. You can recognize truth by its beauty and simplicity. It is always easy when you have made a guess, and done two or three little calculations to make sure that it is not obviously wrong, to know that it is right. When you get it right, it is obvious that it is right—at least if you have any experience—because usually what happens is that more comes out than goes in. Your guess is, in fact, that something is very simple. If you cannot see immediately that it is wrong, and it is simpler than it was before, then it is right. The inexperienced, and crackpots, and people like that, make guesses that are simple, but you can immediately see that they are wrong, so that does not count. Others, the inexperienced students, make guesses that are very complicated, and it sort of looks as if it is all right, but I know it is not true because the truth always turns out to be simpler than you thought. What we need is imagination, but imagination in a terrible strait-jacket. We have to find a new view of the world that has to agree with everything that is known, but disagree in its predictions somewhere, otherwise it is not interesting. And in that disagreement it must agree with nature. If you can find any other view of the world which agrees over the entire range where things have already been observed, but disagrees somewhere else, you have made a great discovery. It is very nearly impossible, but not quite, to find any theory which agrees with experiments over the entire range in which all theories have been checked, and yet gives different consequences in some other range, even a theory whose different consequences do not turn out to agree with nature. A new idea is extremely difficult to think of. It takes a fantastic imagination.

What of the future of this adventure? What will happen ultimately? We are going along guessing the laws; how many laws are we going to have to guess? I do not know. Some of my colleagues say that this fundamental aspect of our science will go on; but I think there will certainly not be perpetual novelty, say for a thousand years. This thing cannot keep on going so that we are always going to discover more and more new laws. If we do, it will become boring that there are so many levels one underneath the other. It seems to me that what can happen in the future is either that all the laws become known—that is, if you had enough laws you could compute consequences and they would always agree with experiment, which would be the end of the line—or it may happen that the experiments get harder and harder to make, more and more expensive, so you get 99.9 per cent of the phenomena, but there is always some phenomenon which has just been discovered, which is very hard to measure, and which disagrees; and as soon as you have the explanation of that one there is always another one, and it gets slower and slower and more and more uninteresting. That is another way it may end. But I think it has to end in one way or another.

We are very lucky to live in an age in which we are still making discoveries. It is like the discovery of America—you only discover it once. The age in which we live is the age in which we are discovering the fundamental laws of nature, and that day will never come again. It is very exciting, it is marvellous, but this excitement will have to go. Of course in the future there will be other interests. There will be the interest of the connection of one level of phenomena to another—phenomena in biology and so on, or, if you are talking about exploration, exploring other planets, but there will not still be the same things that we are doing now.

Another thing that will happen is that ultimately, if it turns out that all is known, or it gets very dull, the vigorous philosophy and the careful attention to all these things that I have been talking about will gradually disappear. The philosophers who are always on the outside making stupid remarks will be able to close in, because we cannot push them away by saying, 'If you were right we would be able to guess all the rest of the laws', because when the laws are all there they will have an explanation for them. For instance, there are always explanations about why the world is three-dimensional. Well, there is only one world, and it is hard to tell if that explanation is right or not, so that if everything were known there would be some explanation about why those were the right laws. But that explanation would be in a frame that we cannot criticize by arguing that that type of reasoning will not permit us to go further. There will be a degeneration of ideas, just like the degeneration that great explorers feel is occurring when tourists begin moving in on a territory.

In this age people are experiencing a delight, the tremendous delight that you get when you guess how nature will work in a new situation never seen before. From experiments and information in a certain range you can guess what is going to happen in a region where no one has ever explored before. It is a little different from regular exploration in that there are enough clues on the land discovered to guess what the land that has not been discovered is going to look like. These guesses, incidentally, are often very different from what you have already seen—they take a lot of thought.

What is it about nature that lets this happen, that it is possible to guess from one part what the rest is going to do? That is an unscientific question: I do not know how to answer it, and therefore I am going to give an unscientific answer. I think it is because nature has a simplicity and therefore a great beauty.

Janice Moulton
George M. Robinson
Cheating for Truth

Janice Moulton *has taught philosophy at the University of North Carolina, Smith College, and elsewhere. She writes in philosophy of mind, philosophy of language, philosophy of science, and feminist philosophy. She collaborated with George M.*

Robinson, her husband, on this paper and on books in linguistics and academic ethics. George M. Robinson teaches linguistics at Smith College.

When scholars read another scholar's research paper, they assume that many aspects of the report can be depended upon—that the data are accurate and complete, that observations are factual not fictional, and that, to the extent that there are no errors in reasoning, the conclusions can be relied on. The decision to commit time, effort, and money to a research project is based on the previous work in the field. It is a sacred principle of research ethics that one must never knowingly introduce false or misleading information that could subvert or stunt the growth of knowledge.

In recent years some of the most famous and influential scientists in history have been accused of research fraud. Ptolemy, Galileo, Newton, Darwin, Dalton, Mendel, and Freud have been indicted with shocking evidence. If these accusations are sound, it makes the sanctity of the scientific method seem to be a naive myth, setting standards that are ignored or distorted in practice. Leaders of scientific revolutions, like expedient political revolutionaries, may have used improper means to promote what today are seen as valuable ends.

. . . it is unrealistic and misguided to believe that scientists are impartial and that science consists only of logical reasoning. . . . [T]here are many other pressures on scientists, some of which lead them to ignore the rules of science and commit fraud. . . . [S]cientists are not impartial. We would go further and say that they need to be more than partial, even enthusiastic advocates of their theories. They have to present their results and theories as convincingly as possible. To do otherwise would be a disservice to themselves and to science. But partiality by itself does not necessarily lead to fraud. When the ground rules of science are broken it is either a mistake or fraud. Only when the rules are deliberately broken, do we call it fraud.

However, we believe that the ground rules of science are not well-defined, that they mutate, and that they cannot eliminate many methods of scientific research and argument that to a later methodology might appear to be fraudulent. We are going to argue that what counts as legitimate scientific reasoning changes as science changes, so that what may be considered fraud in one era or in one field may be acceptable scientific practice in another field or another time. The rules that tell scientists what they can and cannot do, the safeguards of the scientific method, are not constant. Nor is it the case that the ground rules of science change only for the better. While some practices of the past can now be ruled improper, new methods of scientific investigation and new forms of argument are being continuously introduced. Judgments about the propriety of a technique or argument form usually come well after the innovation has been tried out. Essential to the open-ended nature of scientific research, is that no finite rule system could ever cover all forms of investigation and argument. There will never be a rule system that can eliminate every means of research or argument that at some later time might be condemned.

In what follows we will summarize the indictments against some of the heroes of science. There is ample evidence that they violated *current* research standards. But we will argue that the reasoning required of scientists today differs from that required several hundred years ago or even 50 years ago.

One way of trying to lessen their moral culpability is to point out that these scientists believed completely in the truth of their doctrines; they were not trying to deceive anybody about their theories or their conclusions. Nearly everybody accused of scientific fraud ardently believed their own claims. They also ardently wanted others to accept the truth as they knew it. In fact, with all the accusations of research fraud, it is rare to find a case where false information was *deliberately* introduced in order to mislead. One exception is the "Piltdown Man," an archeological fraud in which modern parts were added to an ancient skull to suggest the existence of a human "missing link." This is one of the few clear examples where the perpetrators deliberately tried to undermine research. Until the hoax was discovered, many archeologists accepted the finding and changed their views of human evolution.

Although scholars who violate the principles of research honesty do not expect their conclusions to subvert the course of science, they do subvert the canons of scholarly evidence. Supporting evidence is fabricated, contradictory evidence distorted or suppressed. Scholarly evidence is evaluated according to high standards, especially in science. The rules governing research are conservative: it is considered worse to introduce something false than to fail to find a truth. Stringent criteria are used to prevent the introduction of a false path into the search for knowledge. There is always the possibility of an error, but standards of evidence are designed to keep the risks very small. Researchers who violate these standards are secretly taking much higher risks. They promote conclusions from inferior evidence while disguising the quality of that evidence. If the gamble pays off and their claim stands, the researcher will get the credit for introducing it.

While there are standards for scholarly *evidence,* albeit fluid ones, there are no standards for scholarly *conviction,* the belief that one is on the right track. Nor, as Michael Polanyi and others have pointed out, could there be well-defined standards. Intuition and esthetics are at least as important to scholarly conviction as those aspects of judgment that can be formalized. But this is what causes the problem of research fraud. Scholars become convinced of a position and want to share their conviction. They are unable to replicate for others the informal reasoning, the intuition and esthetic feelings that lead them to their conviction. When the formal evidence required to convince others falls short of accepted standards, they are tempted to invent or doctor evidence to make up the difference. . . . Note that it is not the drawing of conclusions from sparse evidence that is forbidden, only the *claim* that the evidence is stronger than it actually is. Nor is it considered wrong to use informal means to recruit other scholars to one's own position. Researchers, like other people, are allowed to state their beliefs and to use what prestige, authority and charisma they can muster to convince others, as long as they do not make false claims about their evidence.

Yet it is fairly clear that several famous scholars misrepresented data or its relationship to theory. If they were working today, their actions would be condemned as unethical because they broke the ground rules of science. They did things that every scientist today knows should not be done. But do we really want to say that these scientists committed fraud? Did they deliberately try to deceive? Did they suffer from self-deception? Or did they merely support their positions in ways that are no longer acceptable? We are going to suggest that these scientists of the past who are accused of fraud by modern critics may have been engaged in reasoning and presentation that was acceptable, and perhaps even required for their times. Our alternative explanation would preserve the reputations of the scientific greats, but at the expense of some cherished assumptions about the nature of scientific research. . . .

Galileo: Galileo was an early advocate of the value of observation and experiment. But he was accused of reporting experiments that he did not actually do. If we think of observation and experiment as basic to modern science and give Galileo credit for their introduction, his hypocritical behavior was especially sleazy. It looks as though he knew better, advised others to do the right thing, and then secretly violated his own advice.

Galileo has been defended by historians of science who have conducted some of Galileo's experiments to show that they indeed do produce the results Galileo claimed, but which his critics said were impossible. Still, even his defenders acknowledge that Galileo did not conduct all the experiments he described. Perhaps he was not as big a fraud as some have supposed, but, by today's standards, a fraud nonetheless.

Isaac Newton: Newton has been accused of freely reworking numerical data in order to make them look better. Newton strongly advocated measurement and the presentation of mathematical relationships of data to theory. But it looks like he achieved mathematical harmony using fabricated data, selected only the results that would improve his calculations and ignored others, and changed numbers (or advised his assistant to change them) in order to make the theory look good.

The effect of Newton's work is enormous. Millions of scientists have based their work on his theories. They measured and remeasured all sorts of phenomena, proposed extensions and applications of his theories, and continued to produce scientific achievements with increased accuracy of measurement and emphasis on mathematical relationships. Yet Isaac Newton himself played fast and loose with data in order to present a strong case for his theories. In Newton's defense it was suggested that perhaps he intended some of the fudged data to be *theoretical* and not *observational* support for his theories. But there is apparently no historic evidence for this alternative and considerable evidence that he was selecting the numbers in order to make it appear that his theory correctly described the physical world.

Dalton: Dalton's work on the chemical atomic theory is studied by historians to figure out how he arrived at his simple and brilliant theory. His idea that elements combine in simple proportions was not always easy to see from experimental results. For example, Dalton reported that "oxygen joins to nitrous gas sometimes 1.7 to 1, and at other times 3.4 to 1." The 1.7 to 1 ratio was known, but of the 3.4 to 1 ratio, the science historian Nash reports:

> This is a difficult ratio to come by, so much so that Partington has expressed doubt that Dalton achieved it until *after* he had a chemical atomic theory to guide him in "rounding off" his raw data. . . . It is . . . possible, but only *occasionally* possible, to get directly from experiment the ratio 3.4 to 1 cited by Dalton.

While Dalton is not so directly accused of fraud by his historians, he seems to have been engaged in the same sleight-of-hand as his distinguished predecessors. He picked out only the data that fit his theory and ignored the rest.

Gregor Mendel: The father of modern genetics has also been accused of fraud, adding his name to the list of great but suspected scientists. Mendel did his genetic experiments on pea plants. In these experiments, the texture of different types of peas had to be distinguished visually. It turns out that it is not so easy to distinguish pea types; some of the peas would have been accidentally misclassified. These errors should have shown up in his results, so that they would vary from what his theory predicted. But *none* of his results show this error. They all were all much too close to the predicted proportions to be realistic. Obviously, someone fiddled with the data. Perhaps they threw out some of the samples that did not work, perhaps adjusted the numbers. Fisher, the statistician who blew the whistle on Mendel, says:

> . . . It remains a possibility among others that Mendel was deceived by some assistant who knew too well what was expected. This possibility is supported by independent evidence that the data of most, if not all, of the experiments have been falsified so as to agree closely with Mendel's expectations.

However, if almost all of Mendel's data has been falsified in this way, it is even more likely that it was Mendel himself who was involved, the very person who supervised all the years of research. If the cheating had not been so systematic, then perhaps we might think that an overeager assistant, anxious to please and unacquainted with proper methodology, doctored some of the results. But the same absence of error occurs throughout. At best, Mendel must have been aware that his assistants were altering the data.

No one is denying that . . . Galileo, Newton, Mendel, and the others had pretty good theories. But the arguments and data they used to support their theories are suspicious. We might expect politicians, lawyers, and advertising agencies to leave out important information in order to convince us of what they want us to believe. They have a recognized agenda of self-interest. But we expect more of *scientific* reasoning. We think it should be different, in the service of truth, not self-interest, more exacting, less open to manipulation or carelessness, and therefore, less likely to admit shoddy arguments, less likely to be wrong. If scientists are selling their theories with the same half-truths that drug and cosmetic houses use, then we should not be surprised by accusations of fraud. Unethical scholars behave like crusading district attorneys who take shortcuts with evidence in order to ensure a conviction for someone they are convinced is guilty. But there are laws that try to prevent the introduction of improper evidence at a trial and there is an expectation that the legitimacy of evidence in a trial will be challenged. In contrast, it is much easier for an unscrupulous scientist to falsify data or hide disconfirming evidence. And, more important, the accepted methods of reporting data and the methods of explanation will vary from time to time and from field to field. No set of rules can anticipate and define the boundaries of the domain of acceptable means to support a scientific position. When methodology changes, the domain of acceptable support changes too.

To illustrate, consider the reasoning used in philosophy. If any field *ought* to be guided by logical reasoning, it is philosophy. But, as we know, brilliant philosophers in history have invented and advocated dubious arguments and original but invalid argument forms. In fact, it is still not always clear exactly what reasoning was used by Descartes, Aristotle, or Kant. Scientific reasoning is no less complex.

We can look at a classic philosophy of science paper written in 1949 by Hempel and Oppenheim. It argued that all scientific reasoning, and all scientific explanation, was basically of one kind. This paper was very influential in persuading philosophers and scientists that there was one Scientific Method and that it was governed by logic. We can use this paper as an illustration that what counts as proper reasoning and good evidence changes over time. Their conclusion was defended by referring to a few examples. These examples were not actual case studies from science, but were invented by Hempel and Oppenheim to illustrate ideal scientific explanations. Their paper was persuasive at the time. But now the methodology in much of philosophy of science has changed. We now expect examples to be ones that scientists actually have used. Someone might assume that Hempel and Oppenheim were either ignorant or unethical. Either they did not see how unrealistic their examples were, or they tried to deceive readers by using clear illustrations that fit their model but did not characterize real scientific explanations.

We can consider how they might have behaved unethically. Well, they might have *tried* to find examples in the history of science that fit their claim and failed to come up with any. So they sat down and worked out *imaginary* examples that did fit their claims, knowing full well that such examples were not typical of real science. But there is no evidence that they were being dishonest. Hempel and Oppenheim chose clarity and simplicity at the expense of realism. Because reasoning in philosophy is quite varied and complex, and because the methodology in any field changes, they used the best reasoning of their time to explain their thesis. We want to argue that reasoning in science is no different. And just as reasoning that was once acceptable in philosophy changes and becomes less acceptable, so reasoning in science also changes.

Some of the things that seem fraudulent now in science were not considered wrong even as recently as 50 years ago. Consider the act of throwing out data that contradict an experimental hypothesis after the study has been conducted. This is like trying to test the hypothesis that a particular roulette wheel is biased toward red, but only recording those spins when reds are appearing. Today, researchers believe that this is both methodologically unsound and, if concealed, ethically unsound.

It may seem that the unsoundness of this practice has always been evident, at least to any serious scientist. But this is not the case. In early psychology, the perception of psychological phenomena such as visual illusions was thought to be a skill, something to be developed and practiced. If one could not see a purported illusion, that did not mean that there was no illusion. Rather it meant that one was not trying hard enough or was not perceptually skilled. Quite reasonably, clinical psychology continues to consider the skill of the psychologist an important factor in the practice of psychology. In contrast, research on visual perception has changed from the introspection of perceiving to the study of the mechanisms of normal vision. So to count as a visual illusion for the purposes of psychological research, we now expect that nearly everyone will be able to see it. . . .

We should recognize that the methodology requiring unsuccessful cases to be included in the results is even today not practiced by many fields. Clinical psychology, sociology, and some areas of linguistics, for example, report the results of case studies. The cases reported are the interesting ones, the ones that illustrate an effect. Uninteresting cases are not reported. Of course, if a case *exactly* the same occurred without the same result, such a case should be reported. But it is very unlikely that two case studies would be exactly the same in all but one respect. In many fields, theories are based on one or a few cases without being subjected to rigorous statistical tests. This is not thought fraudulent because the methodology of the field and the nature of the theorizing do not lend themselves to statistical tests.

Now let us reconsider the accusations of cheating made about some of the great scientists. Most of them were accused of not presenting all the data, of giving us only the best cases, those that best supported their theories. In modern perspective, they committed the sin of claiming their evidence was stronger than it actually was. But our modern expectations about data reporting are shaped by modern conventions. It is possible that the main problem was not fraud but a different research methodology. It is noteworthy that those accused of fraud farthest back in history were at the forefront of physics. As that science developed, we find that the accusations of fraud fall on those who were at the forefront of chemistry in 1803, and then of biology in 1860. The less mature the science, the less developed and universal its methodology, the more likely it is that a scientist may do something that later is considered specious. Both methodology and the canons of scholarly evidence have changed over the years.

In earlier times, experiments and data were used as *demonstrations* of and *arguments* for theories as well as *tests* of theories. The individual scholar decided whether the results of an experiment supported the theory, and if it did, the results were offered as a demonstration of the truth of the theory. Just as the description of a theory was presented in as clear and convincing a way as possible, so also were the results of any experiments. This meant that the data could be "cleaned up" just as a theoretical equation or graph is cleaned up to appear in its most elegant form.

We know that the evidence required to support a conclusion has varied considerably through the history of science. For example, statistical methods have become much more sophisticated. The double-blind experiment is a recent innovation. Evidence required now might not have been required in earlier times. It is possible that confusion and self-deception, rather than deliberate fraud accounted for some of these errors in the past. As scientific methodology becomes more sophisticated it also becomes more complex. While complexity can be used to hide deliberate deception, it also makes it more likely that researchers get confused and make errors. When the errors go *against* what the scientist expects, they are very likely to be scrutinized. However, when an error produces a result the scientist *expects* to find, the data and analysis are not likely to be scrutinized as carefully. With inconsistent results, the committed scientist is more likely to search harder for weaknesses in those parts that do *not* fit the cherished hypothesis. Thus errors consistent with theory are more likely to slip by than those contradicting the theory. While sophisticated analyses greatly increase the sources of information that can be used to test scientific hypotheses, the number and complexity of the steps between data and conclusion also increases. In a recent study of previously published research papers in psychology, 25 percent of them contained such faulty statistical analyses that the conclusions drawn were not valid. Seventy percent had at least one error in the analysis. Error in scientific reporting seems to be much more frequent than we have supposed.

Should the great scientists of the past have known better anyhow? Maybe they should have realized that they were morally bound to produce the kind of evidence that was not actually required by the scientific community at the time, but which they might have known *ought* to have been required. In particular, shouldn't Galileo, who was such an ardent advocate of experimental verification, have known better than to report results of experiments that were never performed? Newton advocated precise mathematical description as essential for a theory. Shouldn't he have known better than to fudge numbers to fit his equations? . . .

Galileo was accused both by his contemporaries and more recently by Alexandre Koyre of not conducting experiments whose results he reported. It is likely that he did perform some of the experiments, but perhaps not all. He certainly did not report all his experiments in enough detail to allow others to replicate them. Can we suppose he knew better? Were the benefits of replication obvious to one of the first proponents of empirical methods for science? Perhaps Galileo's best defense is Koyre's own conduct in one of his criticisms. Galileo described an experiment in detail, in which a layer of water slowly traveled through a layer of wine to form a clear layer on the bottom. Koyre treated this with sarcasm, claiming that either Galileo made this up or we would have to believe that the properties of wine had radically changed, for obviously the two liquids would mix. In making this criticism, Koyre was guilty of just what he accused Galileo of. For Koyre did not do the experiment either! Koyre *assumed* that he knew what the results of Galileo's experiment would be without bothering to do the experiment himself. Someone else, MacLachlan, *did* do the experiment and showed that it came out exactly as Galileo said, a testimony to Galileo's experimental care and careful description of the results. And, although MacLachlan was too kind to point this out, Koyre is also an example that even those who believe that the Scientific Method requires everything to be experimentally confirmed, may think themselves exempt from that requirement whenever they feel certain of the outcome.

Newton has been accused not only of selecting some data and ignoring others, but of deliberately altering numbers and calculations in order to make his theory look good. Newton was a pioneer in advocating quantitative measurements and calculations for science. If the implications of this position had been all worked out, then we could be clear that Newton cheated. Newton was using the calculations so as to best support his theory. He wanted to show that his theory accounted for a wide range of phenomena. And he wanted to show this quantitatively. The trouble was that there were only very rough measurements of many of the phenomena he wanted to use as evidence. So, in order to use measurements at all, he had to choose some values from among conflicting rough ones, and he naturally chose the ones that best supported his theory. There were many criteria he could have used to select among conflicting measurements. His judgment of which to weigh more strongly was affected by his theoretical expectation. Since he also wanted to convince other people of the benefits of mathematical description, he wanted to provide exact calculations to show how wonderful were the benefits of using mathematics in science. With hindsight and a different methodology, a critic, Westfall, has shown that some of Newton's reasoning is not acceptable today. But at the time, with the new emphasis on mathematics as well as the defense of a new theory, Newton's reasoning was probably not only well-intentioned, but was not a violation of the methodology of his day.

It is obvious that Newton was not being impartial in selecting data to support his theories. What does it mean that Newton selected the data that made his theory look good and ignored other data? Newton wrote letters expressing concern about presenting his theory in the best possible light. Westfall uses these letters as evidence that Newton was deliberately cheating when he selected only the numbers that would support his theory. Westfall's assumption is shared by many—that scientists should present evidence impartially and not be primarily motivated by "public relations."

But this view is not only unrealistic, it presents a false picture of what a scientist ought to do. If scientists are really committed to what they are doing and want it to be accepted, it is counterproductive to fail to defend the theory with every permissible means. Commitment, with its accompanying dedication, is necessary for the development of science. This is especially true during those periods when new theories are born and are fighting to displace established paradigms. What new theories need are committed, enthusiastic, eager partisans who are willing to support [them], defend [them], and continue to work on [them] despite discouragement and opposition. When a new theory is proposed, before it has become accepted and entrenched, it is most subject to criticism, attack, challenge. If one really believes in a new theory and wants it to become accepted, it is very difficult to undermine one's own position. It is only mythical uncommitted scientists who can argue against their own position as resourcefully as they argue for it. The scientist needs to present the best possible case for the theory. Once the advocacy model of scientific explanation is acknowledged, scientists give their opponents the responsibility for revealing opposing evidence. A committed advocate will tend to leave out information that would discourage others from accepting the theory.

Presenting a theory to colleagues and presenting a theory to students have much in common. A teacher often simplifies and leaves out details that are confusing and make it harder for students to learn. A scholar who is convinced of the truth of a theory tends to do the same when arguing for its support among colleagues. A colleague who does not already agree with the scholar, needs to be "taught" to accept the position.

Even an advocate of impartiality would agree that scientists should not reveal all information that would damage their positions. One shouldn't say, for example, "While I believe this theory, I often have doubts about my own abilities and competence." This may be true, but it is no way to convince people. If revealed, one's lack of self-confidence may very well be a fact that would hurt the acceptance of one's theories, but one should not add that fact to one's other observations. Fortunately, the methodologies of most fields do not require scientists to report their inner feelings. That is left to poets and artists.

The methodologies of many sciences do require that scientists report some information that might damage their own position. Researchers have to describe their experiments carefully and give the details of data analysis. A scientist with clear evidence against an hypothesis is ethically bound to reveal it. But methodologies are merely ground rules designed to eliminate obvious abuses. They can never rule out all means of persuasion that might win acceptance for a theory. In almost no case would the evidence alone convince anyone. It is up to the defender of the theory to show its advantages, to draw convincing analogies, to explain its importance. As people like Hesse and Polanyi remind us, scientific reasoning often uses clever analogies, invented illustrations, case studies and anecdotes that defy statistical analysis. The rigid journal format (described by Broad and Wade) requires that the experimental details be separated from the theoretical conclusions. But they cannot isolate the persuasive elements of a report, since in some cases it is the facility with which technical details are presented that gives a report its air of authority so that conjectures in the conclusion section will be more readily accepted. Scientists with a new viewpoint may circumvent the rigid journal format and instead write an engaging book. Some will go to the lay public to get enthusiasm for a new view and only later begin to report details in scholarly journals. Such people are sometimes openly scorned but secretly envied. Others may rely on intellectual charisma, using scholarly lectures and a collection of committed graduate students to spread the word.

And even within the strictest methodology designed to prevent scientists from cutting corners, there will be a large undefined area between outright fraud and dedicated pursuit of the truth. We have drawn some parallels between legal ethics and research ethics. Where the two diverge is in the balance between advocacy and doubt. A lawyer who has evidence against a client is still bound to provide the best defense possible. At most, and this is very rare, the lawyer may withdraw as defense attorney. A scientist with clear evidence against an hypothesis, as defined by the current methodology, is ethically bound to reveal it. But a committed scientist is unlikely to see snags and setbacks as counterevidence. Such problems are seen as mere rough edges and loose ends. Scientists are also obligated to report if they have done the same experiment before and failed to obtain significant results. But it is easy to convince oneself that failures of previous experiments are attributable to methodological flaws. Naturally one varies the conditions of a failed experiment in the hopes of getting it to work the next time.

In the current methodology of many fields, a researcher is expected to report some experimental variations from theoretical predictions. Modern statistical analyses allow researchers to report some data points that deviate greatly from what the theory predicts and still have the overall results support the theory. Since variations are expected, data that are too neat are suspect. Reporting deviations even increases the credibility of a paper. This understanding of statistical variation is relatively recent. But there is no methodology or ethical code requiring that *every* doubt or problem be exposed. Current methodologies allow both committed and unethical scientists to hide weaknesses in their results as least as easily as earlier methodologies did. Although genuine counterevidence ought to be reported, commitment makes it hard to distinguish counterevidence from unresolved loose ends.

It is possible that early scientists accused of fraud really did commit acts they knew were wrong. They may have cheated in the service of what they believed to be a higher good, but on this view, they cheated nonetheless. In science, unlike the practice of law, there are no set procedures for detecting fraudulent evidence and no automatic disposition to suspect that evidence may be fraudulent. There is no mechanism in science for checking whether reported research has really been carried out, or whether data have been altered. The reasoning in a research paper can be questioned—other researchers may try to find an alternative explanation for the data reported—but the actual data is very rarely questioned. If an ill-gotten result turns out to be incorrect, later research may find it out. But if an ill-gotten result turns out to be correct, the cheating is very unlikely to be discovered.

But the assumption of fraud makes the solution look too easy. If deliberate cheating were the only problem, then stricter regulations and careful policing might turn science into the ideal we like to imagine it. However, we hope we have shown that what looks from our modern perspective like blatant fraud might have been acceptable procedure in other times. As our understanding of proper methodology changes, our beliefs about what is proper and improper changes as well. To this extent, research ethics is determined by research methodology. As long as there is scientific change, research methodology will be flexible and open ended and there will be no way to rule out scientific reasoning and scientific behavior that might some day be considered fraudulent.

Gary Zukav
Zen and Physics

Gary Zukav *attended Harvard University and is the author of* The Dancing Wu-Li Masters *in which he describes some of the anomalies of modern physics and argues that they can be better understood through Eastern modes of thought.*

*C*lassical science starts with the assumption of separate parts which together constitute physical reality. Since its inception, it has concerned itself with how these separate parts are related.

Newton's great work showed that the earth, the moon and the planets are governed by the same laws as falling apples. The French mathematician, Descartes, invented a way of drawing pictures of relationships between different measurements of time and distance. This process (analytic geometry) is a wonderul tool for organizing a wealth of scattered data into one meaningful pattern. Herein lies the strength of western science. It brings huge tracts of apparently unrelated experience into a rational framework of simple concepts like the laws of motion. The starting point of this process is a mental attitude which initially perceives the physical world as fragmented and different experiences as logically unrelated. Newtonian science is the effort to find the relationships between pre-existing "separate parts."

Quantum mechanics is based upon the opposite epistemological assumption. Thus, there are profound differences between Newtonian mechanics and quantum theory.

The most fundamental difference between Newtonian physics and quantum mechanics is the fact that quantum mechanics is based upon *observations* ("measurements"). Without a measurement of some kind, quantum mechanics is mute. Quantum mechanics says nothing about what happens between measurements. In Heisenberg's words: "The term 'happens' is restricted to the observation." This is very important, for it constitutes a philosophy of science unlike any before it.

We commonly say, for example, that we detect an electron at point A and then at point B, but strictly speaking, this is incorrect. According to quantum mechanics, there was no electron which traveled from point A to point B. There are only the measurements that we made at point A and at point B.

Quantum theory not only is closely bound to philosophy, but also—and this is becoming increasingly apparent—to theories of perception. As early as 1932, von Neumann explored this relation in his "Theory of Measurement." (Exactly when does the wave function associated with a particle collapse? When the particle strikes a photographic plate? When the photographic plate is developed? When the light rays from the developed photographic plate strike our retina? When the nerve impulses from the retina reach our brain?).

Bohr's principle of complementarity also addresses the underlying relation of physics to consciousness. The experimenter's choice of experiment determines which mutually exclusive aspect of the same phenomenon (wave or particle) will manifest itself. Likewise, Heisenberg's uncertainty principle demonstrates that we cannot observe a phenomenon without changing it. The physical properties which we observe in the "external" world are enmeshed in our own perceptions not only psychologically, but ontologically as well.

The second most fundamental difference between Newtonian physics and quantum theory is that Newtonian physics predicts events and quantum mechanics predicts the probability of events. According to quantum mechanics, the only determinable relation between events is statistical—that is, a matter of probability.

David Bohm, Professor of Physics at Birkbeck College, University of London, proposes that quantum physics is, in fact, based upon a perception of a new order. According to Bohm, "We must turn physics around. Instead of starting with parts and showing how they work together (the Cartesian order) we start with the whole."

Bohm's theory is compatible with Bell's theorem. Bell's theorem implies that the apparently "separate parts" of the universe could be intimately connected at a deep and fundamental level. Bohm asserts that the most fundamental level is an *unbroken wholeness* which is, in his words, "that-which-is." All things, including space, time and matter are forms of that-which-is. There is an order which is enfolded into the very process of the universe, but that enfolded order may not be readily apparent.

For example, imagine a large hollow cylinder into which is placed a small cylinder. The space between the smaller cylinder and the larger cylinder is filled with a clear viscous liquid like glycerine (such a device actually exists).

Now suppose that we deposit a small droplet of ink on the surface of the glycerine. Because of the nature of the glycerine, the ink drop remains intact, a well-defined black spot floating on a clear liquid.

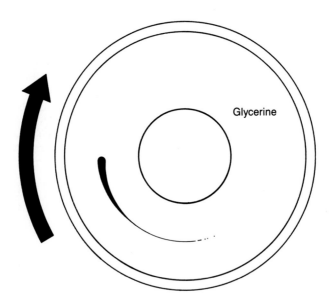

Glycerine

If we begin to rotate one of the cylinders, say in a clockwise direction, the drop of ink spreads out in the opposite direction, making a line which grows thinner and thinner until it disappears altogether. The ink droplet now is enfolded completely into the glycerine, *but it is still there.* When we rotate the cylinder in the opposite direction, the ink droplet reappears. A fine line appears which grows thicker and thicker and then collects into a single point.

If we continue the counterclockwise motion of the cylinder, the same thing happens, but in reverse. We can repeat this process as often as we like. Each time the ink spot becomes a fine line and disappears into the glycerine only to reappear again when the motion of the glycerine is reversed.

If it requires one complete revolution of the cylinder clockwise to make the droplet disappear completely, one complete revolution of the cylinder counterclockwise will make it reappear in its original shape and location. The number of revolutions required to make the droplet disappear or reappear is the enfolded order. Bohm calls this enfolded order the "implicate order," which means the same thing.

Suppose that we deposit a drop of ink on the surface of the glycerine, revolve the cylinder clockwise until the drop disappears (one revolution), add a second drop of ink to the glycerine, continue to revolve the cylinder in the same direction until *it* disappears (one more revolution), and then add a third drop of ink to the glycerine and revolve the cylinder one more revolution until the third drop also disappears. Now we have three ink drops enfolded into the glycerine. None of them are visible, but we know where each of them is in the implicate order.

When we revolve the cylinder in the opposite direction, one drop of ink (the third) appears after one revolution, another drop of ink (the second) appears after the next revolution, and another drop of ink (the first) appears after the third revolution. This is the unfolded, or "explicate," order. The three ink droplets appear to be unrelated in the explicate (unfolded) order, but we know that they *are* related in the implicate (enfolded) order.

If we consider the condensation of ink droplets in this experiment as "particles," we have Bohm's hypothesis of apparently random subatomic phenomena. "Particles" may appear in different places yet be connected in the implicate order. In Bohm's words, "Particles may be discontiguous in space (the explicate order) but contiguous in the implicate order."

"Matter is a form of the implicate order as a vortex is a form of the water—it is not reducible to smaller particles." Like "matter" and everything else, particles are forms of the implicate order. If this is difficult to grasp, it is because our minds demand to know. "What is the 'implicate order' the implicate order of?"

The "implicate order" is the implicate order of that-which-is. However, that-which-is is the implicate order. This world view is so different from the one that we are using that, as Bohm points out, "Description is totally incompatible with what we want to say." Description is incompatible with what we want to say because our thinking is based upon an ancient Greek mode of thought. According to this mode of thought, only Being *is*. Therefore, Non-being *is not*. This way of thinking gives us a practical tool for dealing with the world, but it doesn't describe what happens. Actually, Non-being also *is*. Both Being and Non-being are that-which-is. *Everything,* even "emptiness," is that-which-is. There is nothing which is not that-which-is.

This way of looking at reality raises the question of the consciousness of the observer. Our minds demand to know. "What is the 'implicate order' the implicate order of?" because our culture has taught us to perceive only the explicate order (the Cartesian view). "Things" to us are intrinsically separate.

Bohm's physics require, in his words, a new "instrument of thought." A new instrument of thought such as is needed to understand Bohm's physics, however, would radically alter the consciousness of the observer, reorientating it toward a perception of the "unbroken wholeness" of which everything is a form.

However, such a perception would not cause an inability to see the explicate order. Bohm's physics contains an element of relativity parallel to that of Einstein's theories. The implicate or explicate nature of order (or order of nature) depends upon the perspective of the viewer. The problem is that our present viewpoint is limited to the perspective of the explicate order. From the perspective of the implicate order the apparently "separate elements" of the explicate order are intimately related. Even the phrases, "elements" and "intimately related" imply a Cartesian separateness which does not exist. At the fundamental level of that-which-is, the "separate elements" which are "intimately related in the implicate order" *are* the implicate order.

The requirement for a new instrument of thought upon which to base Bohm's physics may not be as much of an obstacle as it first appears. There already exists an instrument of thought based upon an "unbroken wholeness." Furthermore, there exist a number of sophisticated psychologies, distilled from two thousand years of practice and introspection, whose sole purpose is to develop this thought instrument.

These psychologies are what we commonly call "Eastern religions." "Eastern religions" differ considerably among themselves. It would be a mistake to equate Hinduism, for example, with Buddhism, even though they are more like each other than either one of them is like a religion of the West. Nonetheless, all eastern religions (psychologies) are compatible in a very fundamental way with Bohm's physics and philosophy. All of them are based upon the experience of a pure, undifferentiated reality which is that-which-is.

While it would be naive to overstate the similarities between Bohm's physics and eastern philosophies, it would be foolish to ignore them. Consider, for example, the following sentences:

> The word "reality" is derived from the roots "thing" (*res*) and "think" (*revi*). "Reality" means "everything you can think about." This is not "that-which-is." No idea can capture "truth" in the sense of that-which-is.

The ultimate perception does not originate in the brain or any material structure, although a material structure is necessary to manifest it. The subtle mechanism of knowing the truth does not originate in the brain.

> There is a similarity between thought and matter. All matter, including ourselves, is determined by "information." "Information" is what determines space and time.

Taken out of context, there is no absolute way of knowing whether these statements were made by Professor Bohm or a Tibetan Buddhist. In fact, these sentences were excerpted from different parts of two *physics* lectures that Professor Bohm gave at Berkeley in April, 1977. The first lecture was given on the campus to physics students. The second lecture was given in the Lawrence Berkeley Laboratory to a group of professional physicists. Most of these statements were taken from the *second* lecture, the one given to the advanced physicists.

It is ironic that while Bohm's theories are received with some skepticism by most professional physicists, they would find an immediately sympathetic reception among the thousands of people in our culture who have turned their backs on science in their own quest for the ultimate nature of reality.

If Bohm's physics, or one similar to it, should become the main thrust of physics in the future, the dances of East and West could blend in exquisite harmony. Physics curricula of the twenty-first century could include classes in meditation.

The function of eastern religions (psychologies) is to allow the mind to escape the confines of the symbolic. According to this view, *everything* is a symbol, not only words and concepts, but also people and things. Beyond the confines of the symbolic lies that which is, pure awareness, the experience of the "suchness" of reality.

Nonetheless, every eastern religion resorts to the use of symbols to escape the realm of the symbolic. Some disciplines use symbols more than others, but all of them use symbols in one form or another. Therefore, the question arises, if pure awareness is considered distinct from the content of awareness, in what ways specifically does the content of awareness affect the realization of pure awareness? What types of content prompt the mind to leap forward. What enables it to activate the self-fulfilling capability to transcend itself.

It is very difficult to answer this question. Any answer is only a point of view. A point of view itself is limiting. To "understand" something is to give up some other way of conceiving it. This is another way of saying that the mind deals in forms of limitation. Nonetheless, there *is* a relationship between the content of awareness and the ability of the mind to transcend itself.

"Reality" is what we take to be true. What we take to be true is what we believe. What we believe is based upon our perceptions. What we perceive depends upon what we look for. What we look for depends upon what we think. What we think depends upon what we perceive. What we perceive determines what we believe. What we believe determines what we take to be true. What we take to be true is our reality.

The central focus of this process, initially at any rate, is "What we think." We at least can say that allegiance to a symbol of openness (Christ, Buddha, Krishna, "the infinite diversity of nature," etc.) seems to open the mind and that an open mind is often the first step in the process of enlightenment.

The psychological gestalt of physics has shifted radically in the last century to one of extreme openness. In the middle 1800s, Newtonian mechanics was at its zenith. There seemed to be no phenomenon which could not be explained in terms of mechanical models. All mechanical models were subject to long-established principles. The chairman of the physics department at Harvard discouraged graduate study because so few important matters remained unsolved.

In a speech to the Royal Institution in 1900, Lord Kelvin reflected that there were only two "clouds" on the horizon of physics, the problem of black-body radiation and the Michelson-Morley experiment. There was no doubt, said Kelvin, that they soon would be gone. He was wrong. Kelvin's two "clouds" signaled the end of the era that began with Galileo and Newton. The problem of black-body radiation led to Planck's discovery of the quantum of action. Within thirty years the entirety of Newtonian physics became a special limiting case of the newly developing quantum theory. The Michelson-Morley experiment foreshadowed Einstein's famous theories of relativity. By 1927, the foundations of the new physics, quantum mechanics and relativity, were in place.

In contrast to Kelvin's time, the allegiance of physicists today is to a symbol of extreme openness. Isidor Rabi, Nobel Prize winner and Chairman Emeritus of the Physics Department at Columbia University, wrote in 1975:

> I don't think that physics will ever have an end. I think that the novelty of nature is such that its variety will be infinite—not just in changing forms but in the profundity of insight and the newness of ideas. . .

Stapp wrote in 1971:

> . . . human inquiry can continue indefinitely to yield important new truths.

The "What we think" of physicists today is that the physics of nature, like human experience itself, is infinitely diverse.

Eastern religions have nothing to say about physics, but they have a great deal to say about human experience. In Hindu mythology, Kali, the Divine Mother, is the symbol for the infinite diversity of experience. Kali represents the entire physical plane. She is the drama, tragedy, humor, and sorrow of life. She is the brother, father, sister, mother, lover, and friend. She is the fiend, monster, beast, and brute. She is the sun and the ocean. She is the grass and the dew. She is our sense of accomplishment and our sense of doing worthwhile. Our thrill of discovery is a pendant on her bracelet. Our gratification is a spot of color on her cheek. Our sense of importance is the bell on her toe.

This full and seductive, terrible and wonderful earth mother *always* has something to offer. Hindus know the impossibility of seducing her or conquering her and the futility of loving her or hating her; so they do the only thing that they can do. They simply honor her.

In a particular story, Kali, the Divine Mother, is Sita, the wife of God. Ram is God. Ram, Sita, and Laksaman, who is Ram's brother, are walking along a jungle trail. The path is so narrow that most of the time Laksaman can see only Sita, who walks between him and Ram. Every so often, however, the path turns in such a way that Laksaman can see his brother, God.

These powerful metaphors have application to the developing drama of physics. Although most physicists have little patience (professionally) with metaphors, physics itself has become a powerful metaphor. Twentieth-century physics is the story of a journey from intellectual entrenchment to intellectual openness, despite the conservative prove-it-to-me nature of individual physicists. The realization that the discoveries of physics *never* will end has brought physicists, as well as those who have followed the story of physics, to an extremely fertile plateau. This realization invites the intellect to leap forward, although at great risk to its present hegemony.

The Wu Li Masters know that physicists are doing more than "discovering the endless diversity of nature." They are dancing with Kali, the Divine Mother of Hindu mythology.

Buddhism is both a philosophy and a practice. Buddhist philosophy is rich and profound. Buddhist practice is called *Tantra*. *Tantra* is the Sanskrit word meaning "to weave." There is little that can be said about *Tantra*. It must be done.

Buddhist philosophy reached its ultimate development in the second century A.D. No one has been able to improve much on it since then. The distinction between Buddhist philosophy and *Tantra* is well defined. Buddhist philosophy can be intellectualized. *Tantra* cannot. Buddhist philosophy is a function of the rational mind. *Tantra* transcends rationality. The most profound thinkers of the Indian civilization discovered that words and concepts could take them only so far. Beyond that point came the actual doing of a practice, the experience of which was ineffable. This did not prevent them from progressively refining the practice into an extremely effective and sophisticated set of techniques, but it did prevent them from being able to describe the experiences which these techniques produce.

The practice of *Tantra* does not mean the end of rational thought. It means the integration of thought based on symbols into larger spectrums of awareness. (Enlightened people still remember their zip codes.)

The development of Buddhism in India shows that a profound and penetrating intellectual quest into the ultimate nature of reality can culminate in, or at least set the stage for, a quantum leap beyond rationality. In fact, on an individual level, this is one of the roads to enlightenment. Tibetan Buddhism calls it the Path without Form, or the Practice of Mind. The Path without Form is prescribed for people of intellectual temperament. The science of physics is following a similar path.

The development of physics in the twentieth century already has transformed the consciousness of those involved with it. The study of complementarity, the uncertainty principle, quantum field theory, and the Copenhagen Interpretation of Quantum Mechanics produces insights into the nature of reality very similar to those produced by the study of eastern philosophy. The profound physicists of this century increasingly have become aware that they are confronting the ineffable.

Max Planck, the father of quantum mechanics, wrote:

Science . . . means unresting endeavor and continually progressing development toward an aim which the poetic intuition may apprehend, but which the intellect can never fully grasp.

We are approaching the end of science. "The end of science" does not mean the end of the "unresting endeavor and continually progressing development" of more and more comprehensive and useful physical theories. (Enlightened physicists remember their zip codes, too.) The "end of science" means the coming of western civilization, in its own time and in its own way, into the higher dimensions of human experience.

Professor G. F. Chew, Chairman of the Physics Department at Berkeley, remarked, in reference to a theory of particle physics:

> Our current struggle [with current aspects of advanced physics] may thus be only a foretaste of a completely new form of human intellectual endeavor, one that will not only lie outside physics but will not even be describable as "scientific."

We need not make a pilgrimage to India or Tibet. There is much to learn there, but here at home, in the most inconceivable of places, amidst the particle accelerators and computers, our own Path without Form is emerging.

4

Which Should I Believe: Darwin or Genesis?

In July 1925, a young teacher named John Scopes was brought to trial in Dayton, Tennessee, in one of the most celebrated court cases of the century. Assisting the prosecution was William Jennings Bryan, who had run for the presidency in 1896 and who is still regarded by many as the greatest orator in this country's history. Defending Scopes was Clarence Darrow, the most famous criminal lawyer of his generation. Reporters swarmed from all over the country to the small Southern town, and the trial soon became the showcase for a national debate. What was at issue was not a shocking murder or a scandalous political crime, but whether or not Scopes would be permitted to teach Charles Darwin's theory of evolution in the Tennessee public schools.

It will surprise many of you to learn that the debate over teaching evolutionary theory in the public schools has been going on for so long. Philosophers have been interested in the controversy for a number of reasons. It raises issues about the nature of science and about the relationship between science and religion. It also forces us to think about the responsibilities of public education.

Many religions have accounts of creation. You are probably already familiar with at least one of the creation accounts in the Bible. In some religions in India, the sky, the air, and the earth were understood as gods created by Aditi, a female goddess. In the Hindu religion, Brahma created himself along with other gods and men; he placed a golden egg into the ocean, and out of the egg hatched Brahma himself, who then divided into two to create the heavens and the earth. Religious liberals often take such accounts as metaphorical, or even as mythical. But a literal reading of scriptural or other accounts of creation will usually be incompatible with Darwin's evolutionary account. This incompatibility has fueled a continuing controversy between religious conservatives who are committed to a literal reading of creation stories and those committed to evolutionary theory. To understand this controversy, we must first see why scientists are so wedded to evolutionary accounts.

Nature seems to embody purpose. Animals have two eyes because two is the minimum number to enable them to see depth, and therefore to judge distance. Giraffes' long necks enable them to eat the leaves from the tall trees in their natural habitat. The delicate balance of hormones in your body enables it to adjust to changes in your environment, in everything from digestion to reproduction, and helps you to get around in the world. How could such delicate and complicated mechanisms arise by mere chance?

Evolutionary theory offers the following kind of explanation. Among members of an animal population, there will be small individual differences. (The mechanisms of genetic mutation were not known in Darwin's time, but they obviously provide an explanation of how such differences can arise.) Some of these differences will be advantageous to the organism, either because it will be better equipped to survive and reproduce or because its social structure will be better equipped (as with bees). Other differences will make either the individual organism or the social structure less likely to survive and reproduce. The differences that are advantageous will be genetically transmitted more often because the organisms that have those differences will survive and reproduce more; the differences that are not advantageous will be transmitted less often. Over the course of millions of years, species will therefore evolve in the direction of increasing adaptation to their environment. In the simplest cases, giraffes with longer necks will eat better, and hence reproduce more often, than short-necked giraffes; consequently, giraffes as a species will gradually become longer necked. In a more complicated way, the same account explains the origin of two eyes instead of one, and of complex hormonal and metabolic pathways to deal with complicated interactions between an organism and its environment. The result of all of this theorizing is that the *purpose* in nature gets explained without supposing that there is a creator who is arranging for his (or her) purpose to be met.

Evolutionary theory is not the only theory that works in this way. There are countless others. For example, in a "properly working" free capitalistic market, just the right amount of copper will be mined to serve the needs of the population. Nobody in the government needs to decide how much copper to mine; indeed, if anybody tries to, they will almost certainly do worse than if nobody thinks about it. It is as though there is an "invisible hand" guiding the individual decisions that people make for it to turn out that just the right amount of copper is produced. But market theory explains how the free market and the so-called law of supply and demand brings this about without guidance or control by any outside force.

Even though such explanations allow us to avoid the assumption of outside forces, such as God, they do not require us to do so. Economists can consistently believe that God directs the day-to-day workings of the market; undoubtedly some do. Similarly, some biologists believe that God directs the day-to-day workings of evolution. Others believe that at creation, God set in motion the initial laws of nature, including the mechanisms of evolution, and left them to run by themselves for all of time. Others do not believe in God at all. Evolutionary theory does not require that we choose between these kinds of alternatives. The conflict enters when we look at the details of some religious creation accounts.

For example, the creation stories from Genesis that are in this chapter both describe the creation all at once of fully developed species. Moreover, they describe this creation in a time frame of several thousand years, rather than the many millions of years required by the Darwinian account of creation. It is not the religious viewpoint in general that is incompatible with the evolutionary point of view, but rather the details of particular literal interpretations of religious doctrines.

One focus for the tension between these frameworks is in the teaching in school (usually high school) of accounts of creation. Many conservative religious figures who take creation accounts literally, nevertheless believe that it is on the basis of *faith*, not evidence, that they are to be accepted. Other **scientific creationists** believe that the literal Biblical account of creation is backed by scientific evidence and that the creationist account should thus be taught in science classes as an alternative to the evolutionary account. This has sparked a brisk debate on what exactly counts as science and what doesn't. Some of that debate is reproduced in this chapter.

The book of Genesis contains the Judeo-Christian creation accounts that most of the current controversy centers around. Notice that in Chapters 1 and 2 of Genesis there are actually *two* stories of creation that differ from one another, particularly in the order of creation that is given. Thus, it is inaccurate to speak simply of *the* Biblical account. Rather one must speak of the account of Chapter 1 or the account of Chapter 2.

About the middle of the nineteenth century, several biologists arrived independently at the notion of an evolutionary theory to explain the origin of biological adaptation. Darwin became the best known of these. Between 1831 and 1836 he traveled around the world on the ship "The Beagle"; in the course of that voyage he made many of the observations that gave a richness of detail to his theoretical account. In 1859 he published *The Origin of the Species*, the book that launched evolutionary theory. Later, in 1871, *The Descent of Man* was published. In it he responded to a number of critics, revised his views on a number of points, and expanded his account to talk in greater detail about the origin of humans. The selection here is from that book.

Because the U.S. Constitution establishes a clear separation between religion and government, the courts have prohibited the teaching of religious views in public schools. But many advocates of a literal reading of the Biblical account have argued not on religious, but on scientific grounds. They claim that evolutionary theory is itself bad science and that an unbiased, truly scientific look at the evidence will favor creationist views. Among their charges are that evolutionary theory is circular and not subject to the experimental method, that it stands against God and hence itself embodies a religious viewpoint, that it violates well-accepted scientific doctrine, and that it is not as well supported as creationism by the fossil record. Duane Gish, perhaps the primary contemporary spokesperson for creationist science, wrote the article included in this chapter, in which all of these claims are spelled out and defended.

In their articles, both Philip Kitcher and Arthur Caplan respond to Gish's charges. Kitcher discusses in detail the issue of the fossil record and some of the details of the empirical claims of creationist science. Caplan addresses the issue of whether evolutionary theory is scientific. Between them they discuss most of the charges that Gish raises against evolutionary theory.

Finally, Isaac Asimov takes a strong stance against creationism, accusing it of being a force for ignorance and against intellectual progress. The dialogue between him, Caplan, and Kitcher on the one hand, and Gish on the other, raises important questions about the extent to which scientific points of view are privileged in our culture and about the extent to which we understand the difference between science and nonscience.

The Bible

Genesis

The book of Genesis is the opening book of the Old Testament of **The Bible**. *The word 'genesis' means* beginning. *Most religious scholars believe that the accounts recorded in Genesis were compiled by a number of different people.*

CHAPTER 1

IN the beginning God created the heaven and the earth.

2 And the earth was without form, and void; and darkness *was* upon the face of the deep. And the Spirit of God moved upon the face of the waters.

3 And God said, Let there be light: and there was light.

4 And God saw the light, that *it was* good: and God divided the light from the darkness.

5 And God called the light Day, and the darkness he called Night. And the evening and the morning were the first day.

6 And God said, Let there be a firmament in the midst of the waters, and let it divide the waters from the waters.

7 And God made the firmament, and divided the waters which *were* under the firmament from the waters which *were* above the firmament: and it was so.

8 And God called the firmament Heaven. And the evening and the morning were the second day.

9 And God said, Let the waters under the heaven be gathered together unto one place, and let the dry *land* appear: and it was so.

10 And God called the dry *land* Earth; and the gathering together of the waters called he Seas: and God saw that *it was* good.

11 And God said, Let the earth bring forth grass, the herb yielding seed, *and* the fruit tree yielding fruit after his kind, whose seed *is* in itself, upon the earth: and it was so.

12 And the earth brought forth grass, *and* herb yielding seed after his kind, and the tree yielding fruit, whose seed *was* in itself, after his kind: and God saw that *it was* good.

13 And the evening and the morning were the third day.

14 And God said, Let there be lights in the firmament of the heaven to divide the day from the night; and let them be for signs, and for seasons, and for days, and years:

15 And let them be for lights in the firmament of the heaven to give light upon the earth: and it was so.

16 And God made two great lights; the greater light to rule the day, and the lesser light to rule the night: *he made* the stars also.

17 And God set them in the firmament of the heaven to give light upon the earth,

18 And to rule over the day and over the night, and to divide the light from the darkness: and God saw that *it was* good.

19 And the evening and the morning were the fourth day.

20 And God said, Let the waters bring forth abundantly the moving creature that hath life, and fowl *that* may fly above the earth in the open firmament of heaven.

21 And God created great whales, and every living creature that moveth, which the waters brought forth abundantly, after their kind, and every winged fowl after his kind: and God saw that *it was* good.

22 And God blessed them, saying, Be fruitful, and multiply, and fill the waters in the seas, and let fowl multiply in the earth.

23 And the evening and the morning were the fifth day.

24 And God said, Let the earth bring forth the living creature after his kind, cattle, and creeping thing, and beast of the earth after his kind: and it was so.

25 And God made the beast of the earth after his kind, and cattle after their kind, and every thing that creepeth upon the earth after his kind: and God saw that *it was* good.

26 And God said, Let us make man in our image, after our likeness: and let them have dominion over the fish of the sea, and over the fowl of the air, and over the cattle, and over all the earth, and over every creeping thing that creepeth upon the earth.

27 So God created man in his *own* image, in the image of God created he him; male and female created he them.

28 And God blessed them, and God said unto them, Be fruitful, and multiply, and replenish the earth, and subdue it: and have dominion over the fish of the sea, and over the fowl of the air, and over every living thing that moveth upon the earth.

29 And God said, Behold, I have given you every herb bearing seed, which *is* upon the face of all the earth, and every tree, in the which *is* the fruit of a tree yielding seed; to you it shall be for meat.

30 And to every beast of the earth, and to every fowl of the air, and to every thing that creepeth upon the earth, wherein *there is* life, *I have given* every green herb for meat: and it was so.

31 And God saw every thing that he had made, and, behold, *it was* very good. And the evening and the morning were the sixth day.

CHAPTER 2

THUS the heavens and the earth were finished, and all the host of them.

2 And on the seventh day God ended his work which he had made; and he rested on the seventh day from all his work which he had made.

3 And God blessed the seventh day, and sanctified it: because that in it he had rested from all his work which God created and made.

4 These *are* the generations of the heavens and of the earth when they were created, in the day that the LORD God made the earth and the heavens,

5 And every plant of the field before it was in the earth, and every herb of the field before it grew: for the LORD God had not caused it to rain upon the earth, and *there was* not a man to till the ground.

6 But there went up a mist from the earth, and watered the whole face of the ground.

7 And the LORD God formed man *of* the dust of the ground, and breathed into his nostrils the breath of life; and man became a living soul.

8 And the LORD God planted a garden eastward in Eden; and there he put the man whom he had formed.

9 And out of the ground made the LORD God to grow every tree that is pleasant to sight, and good for food; the tree of life also in the midst of the garden, and the tree of knowledge of good and evil.

10 And a river went out of Eden to water the garden; and from thence it was parted, and became into four heads.

11 The name of the first *is* Pí-son: that *is*

it which compasseth the whole land of Hav́-i-lah, where *there is* gold;

12 And the gold of that land *is* good: there *is* bdellium and the onyx stone.

13 And the name of the second river *is* Gí-hon: the same *is* it that compasseth the whole land of E-thi-ó-pi-a.

14 And the name of the third river *is* Hid́-de-kel: that *is* it which goeth toward the east of Assyria. And the fourth river *is* Eu-phrá-tes.

15 And the LORD God took the man, and put him into the garden of Eden to dress it and to keep it.

16 And the LORD God commanded the man, saying, Of every tree of the garden thou mayest freely eat:

17 But of the tree of the knowledge of good and evil, thou shalt not eat of it: for in the day that thou eatest thereof thou shalt surely die.

18 And the LORD God said, *It is* not good that the man should be alone; I will make him an help meet for him.

19 And out of the ground the LORD God formed every beast of the field, and every fowl of the air; and brought *them* unto Adam to see what he would call them: and whatsoever Adam called every living creature, that *was* the name thereof.

20 And Adam gave names to all cattle, and to the fowl of the air, and to every beast of the field; but for Adam there was not found an help meet for him.

21 And the LORD God caused a deep sleep to fall upon Adam, and he slept: and he took one of his ribs, and closed up the flesh instead thereof;

22 And the rib which the LORD God had taken from man, made he a woman, and brought her unto the man.

23 And Adam said, This *is* now bone of my bones, and flesh of my flesh: she shall be called Woman, because she was taken out of Man.

24 Therefore shall a man leave his father and his mother, and shall cleave unto his wife: and they shall be one flesh.

25 And they were both naked, the man and his wife, and were not ashamed.

Charles Darwin
The Descent of Man

Charles Darwin (1809–1882) *was an English naturalist whose theory of evolution formed the basis for modern evolutionary theory. He suffered most of his life from poor health; he was a reclusive man who shied away from the controversy that raged even then over the conflict between evolutionary theory and some religious doctrines.*

Natural Selection.—We have now seen that man is variable in body and mind; and that the variations are induced, either directly or indirectly, by the same general causes, and obey the same general laws, as with the lower animals. Man has spread widely over the face of the earth, and must have been exposed, during his incessant migrations, to the most diversified conditions. The inhabitants of Tierra del Fuego, the Cape of Good Hope, and Tasmania in the one hemisphere, and of the Arctic regions in the other, must have passed through many climates, and changed their habits many times, before they reached their present homes. The early progenitors of man must also have tended, like all other animals, to have increased beyond their means of subsistence; they must, therefore, occasionally have been exposed to a struggle for existence, and consequently to the rigid law of natural selection. Beneficial variations of all kinds will thus, either occasionally or habitually, have been preserved and injurious ones eliminated. I do not refer to strongly marked deviations of structure, which occur only at long intervals of time, but to mere individual differences. We know, for instance, that the muscles of our hands and feet, which determine our powers of movement, are liable, like those of the lower animals, to incessant variability. If then the progenitors of man inhabiting any district, especially one undergoing some change in its conditions, were divided into two equal bodies, the one-half which included all the individuals best adapted by their powers of movement for gaining subsistence, or for defending themselves, would on an average survive in greater numbers, and procreate more offspring than the other and less well endowed half.

Man in the rudest state in which he now exists is the most dominant animal that has ever appeared on this earth. He has spread more widely than any other highly organized form: and all others have yielded before him. He manifestly owes this immense superiority to his intellectual faculties, to his social habits, which lead him to aid and defend his fellows, and to his corporeal structure. The supreme importance of these characters has been proved by the final arbitrament of the battle for life. Through his powers of intellect, articulate language has been evolved; and on this his wonderful advancement has mainly depended. As Mr. Chauncey Wright remarks: "a psychological analysis of the faculty of language shows, that even the smallest proficiency in it might require more brain power than the greatest proficiency in any other direction." He has invented and is able to use various weapons, tools, traps, etc., with which he defends himself, kills or catches prey, and otherwise obtains food. He has made rafts or canoes for fishing or crossing over to neighboring fertile islands. He has discovered the art of making fire, by which hard and stringy roots can be rendered digestible, and poisonous roots or herbs innocuous. This discovery of fire, probably the greatest ever made by man, excepting language, dates from before the dawn of history. These several inventions, by which man in the rudest state has become so pre-eminent, are the direct results of the development of his powers of observation, memory, curiosity, imagination, and reason. I cannot, therefore, understand how it is that Mr. Wallace maintains, that "natural selection could only have endowed the savage with a brain a little superior to that of an ape."

Although the intellectual powers and social habits of man are of paramount importance to him, we must not underrate the importance of his bodily structure, to which subject the remainder of this chapter will be devoted; . . .

If it be an advantage to man to stand firmly on his feet and to have his hands and arms free, of which, from his pre-eminent success in the battle of life, there can be no doubt, then I can see no reason why it should not have been advantageous to the progenitors of man to have become more and more erect or bipedal. They would thus have been better able to defend themselves with stones or clubs, to attack their prey, or otherwise to obtain food. The best built individuals would in the long run have succeeded best and survived in larger numbers. If the gorilla and a few allied forms had become extinct, it might have been argued, with great force and apparent truth, that an animal could not have been gradually converted from a quadruped into a biped, as all the individuals in an intermediate condition would have been miserably ill-fitted for progression. But we know (and this is well worthy of reflection) that the anthropomorphous apes are now actually in an intermediate condition; and no one doubts that they are on the whole well adapted for their conditions of life. Thus the gorilla runs with a sidelong shambling gait, but more commonly progresses by resting on its bent hands. The long-armed apes occasionally use their arms like crutches, swinging their bodies forward between them, and some kinds of Hylobates, without having been taught, can walk or run upright with tolerable quickness; yet they move awkwardly and much less securely than man. We see, in short, in existing monkeys a manner of progression intermediate between that of a quadruped and a biped; but, as an unprejudiced judge insists, the anthropomorphous apes approach in structure more nearly to the bipedal than to the quadrupedal type.

As the progenitors of man became more and more erect, with their hands and arms more and more modified for prehension and other purposes, with their feet and legs at the same time transformed for firm support and progression, endless other changes of structure would have become necessary. The pelvis would have to be broadened, the spine peculiarly curved, and the head fixed in an altered position, all of which changes have been attained by man. . . .

The free use of the arms and hands, partly the cause and partly the result of man's erect position, appears to have led in an indirect manner to other modifications of structure. The early male forefathers of man were, as previously stated, probably furnished with great canine teeth; but as they gradually acquired the habit of using stones, clubs, or other weapons for fighting with their enemies or rivals they would use their jaws and teeth less and less. In this case the jaws, together with the teeth, would become reduced in size, as we may feel almost sure from innumerable analogous cases. In a future chapter we shall meet with a closely parallel case in the reduction or complete disappearance of the canine teeth in male ruminants, apparently in relation with the development of their horns; and in horses in relation to their habits of fighting with their incisor teeth and hoofs. . . .

Another most conspicuous difference between man and the lower animals is the naked-ness of his skin. Whales and porpoises (Cetacea), dugongs (Sirenia) and the hippopotamus are naked; and this may be advantageous to them for gliding through the water; nor would it be injurious to them from the loss of warmth, as the species which inhabit the colder regions are protected by a thick layer of blubber, serving the same purposes as the fur of seals and otters. Elephants and rhinoceroses are almost hairless; and as certain extinct species, which formerly lived under an Arctic climate, were covered with long wool or hair, it would almost appear as if the existing species of both genera had lost their hairy covering from exposure to heat. This appears the more probable, as the elephants in India which live on elevated and cool districts are more hairy than those on the lowlands. May we then infer that man became divested of hair from having aboriginally inhabited some tropical land? That the hair is chiefly retained in the male sex on the chest and face, and in both sexes at the junction of all four limbs with the trunk, favors this inference—on the assumption that the hair was lost before man became erect; for the parts which now retain most hair would then have been most protected from the heat of the sun. The crown of the head, however, offers a curious exception, for at all times it must have been one of the most exposed parts, yet is thickly clothed with hair. The fact, however, that the other members of the order of Primates, to which man belongs, although inhabiting various hot regions, are well clothed with hair, generally thickest on the upper surface, is opposed to the supposition that man became naked through the action of the sun. Mr. Belt believes that within the tropics it is an advantage to man to be destitute of hair, as he is thus enabled to free himself of the multitude of ticks (acari) and other parasites, with which he is often infested, and which sometimes cause ulceration. But whether this evil is of sufficient magnitude to have led to the denudation of his body through natural selection, may be doubted, since none of the many quadrupeds inhabiting the tropics have, as far as I know, acquired any specialized means of relief. The view which seems to me the most probable is that man, or rather primarily woman, became divested of hair for ornamental purposes, as we shall see under Sexual Selection; and, according to this belief, it is not surprising that man should differ so greatly in hairiness from all other Primates, for characters, gained through sexual selection, often differ to an extraordinary degree in closely related forms. . . .

I have now endeavored to show that some of the most distinctive characters of man have in all probability been acquired, either directly, or more commonly indirectly, through natural selection. We should bear in mind that modifications in structure or constitution which do not serve to adapt an organism to its habits of life, to the food which it consumes, or passively to the surrounding conditions, cannot have been thus acquired. We must not, however, be too confident in deciding what modifications are of service to each being; we should remember how little we know about the use of many parts, or what changes in the blood or tissues may serve to fit an organism for a new climate or new kinds of food. Nor must we forget the principle of correlation, by which, as Isidore Geoffroy has shown in the case of man, many strange deviations of structure are tied together. Independently of correlation, a change in one part often leads, through the increased or decreased use of other parts, to other changes of a quite unexpected nature. It is also well to reflect on such facts, as the wonderful growth of galls on plants caused by the poison of an insect, and on the remarkable changes of color in the plumage of parrots when fed on certain fishes, or inoculated with the poison of toads; for we can thus see that the fluids of the system, if altered for some special purpose, might induce other changes. We should especially bear in mind that modifications acquired and continually used during past ages for some useful purpose, would probably become firmly fixed, and might be long inherited.

Thus a large yet undefined extension may safely be given to the direct and indirect results of natural selection; but I now admit, after reading the essay by Nägeli on plants, and the remarks by various authors with respect to animals, more especially those recently made by Prof. Broca, that in the earlier editions of my "Origin of Species" I perhaps attributed too much to the action of natural selection or the survival of the fittest. I have altered the fifth edition of the "Origin" so as to confine my remarks to adaptive changes of structure; but I am convinced, from the light gained during even the last few years, that very many structures which now appear to us as useless, will hereafter be proved to be useful, and will therefore come within the range of natural selection. Nevertheless, I did not formerly consider sufficiently the existence of structures, which, as far as we can at present judge, are neither beneficial nor injurious; and this I believe to be one of the greatest oversights as yet detected in my work. I may be permitted to say, as some excuse, that I had two distinct objects in view; firstly, to show that species had not been separately created, and secondly, that natural selection had been the chief agent of change, though largely aided by the inherited effects of habit, and slightly by the direct action of the surrounding conditions. I was not, however, able to annul the influence of my former belief, then almost universal, that each species had been purposely created; and this led to my tacit assumption that every detail of structure, excepting rudiments, was of some special though unrecognized, service. Any one with this assumption in his mind would naturally extend too far the action of natural selection, either during past or present times. Some of those who admit the principle of evolution, but reject natural selection, seem to forget, when criticising my book, that I had the above two objects in view; hence, if I have erred in giving to natural selection great power, which I am very far from admitting, or in having exaggerated its power, which is in itself probable, I have at least, as I hope, done good service in aiding to overthrow the dogma of separate creations. . . .

Conclusion.—In this chapter we have seen that as man at the present day is liable, like every other animal, to multiform individual differences or slight variations, so no doubt were the early progenitors of man; the variations being formerly induced by the same general causes, and governed by the same general and complex laws as at present. As all animals tend to multiply beyond their means of subsistence, so it must have been with the progenitors of man; and this would inevitably lead to a struggle for existence and to natural selection. The latter process would be greatly aided by the inherited effects of the increased use of parts, and these two processes would incessantly react on each other. It appears, also, as we shall hereafter see, that various unimportant characters have been acquired by man through sexual selection. An unexplained residuum of change must be left to the assumed uniform action of those unknown agencies, which occasionally induce strongly marked and abrupt deviations of structure in our domestic productions.

Judging from the habits of savages and of the greater number of the Quadrumana, primeval men, and even their ape-like progenitors, probably lived in society. With strictly social animals, natural selection sometimes acts on the individual, through the preservation of variations which are beneficial to the community. A community which includes a large number of well-endowed individuals increases in number, and is victorious over other less favored ones; even although each separate member gains no advantage over the others of the same community. Associated insects have thus acquired many remarkable structures, which are of little or no service to the individual, such as the pollen-collecting apparatus, or the sting of the worker-bee, or the great jaws of soldier-ants. With the higher social animals, I am not aware that any structure has been modified solely for the good of the community, though some are of secondary service to it. For instance, the horns of ruminants and the great canine teeth of baboons appear to have been acquired by the males as weapons for sexual strife, but they are used in defense of the herd or troop. In regard to certain mental powers the case, as we shall see in the fifth chapter, is wholly different; for these faculties have been chiefly, or even exclusively, gained for the benefit of the community, and the individuals thereof have at the same time gained an advantage indirectly.

It has often been objected to such views as the foregoing, that man is one of the most helpless and defenseless creatures in the world; and that during his early and less well developed condition he would have been still more helpless. The Duke of Argyll, for instance, insists that "the human frame has diverged from the structure of brutes in the direction of greater physical helplessness and weakness. That is to say, it is a divergence which of all others it is most impossible to ascribe to mere natural selection." He adduces the naked and unprotected state of the body, the absence of great teeth or claws for defense, the small strength and speed of man, and his slight power of discovering food or of avoiding danger by smell. To these deficiencies there might be added one still more serious, namely, that he cannot climb quickly and so escape from enemies. The loss of hair would not have been a great injury to the inhabitants of a warm country. For we know that the unclothed Fuegians can exist under a wretched climate. When we compare the defenseless state of man with that of apes we must remember that the great canine teeth with which the latter are provided are possessed in their full development by the males alone, and are chiefly used by them for fighting with their rivals; yet the females, which are not thus provided, manage to survive.

In regard to bodily size or strength, we do not know whether man is descended from some small species, like the chimpanzee, or from one as powerful as the gorilla; and, therefore, we cannot say whether man has become larger and stronger, or smaller and weaker than his ancestors. We should, however, bear in mind that an animal possessing great size, strength, and ferocity, and which, like the gorilla, could defend itself from all enemies, would not perhaps have become social: and this would most effectually have checked the acquirement of the higher mental qualities, such as sympathy and the love of his fellows. Hence it might have been an immense advantage to man to have sprung from some comparatively weak creature.

The small strength and speed of man, his want of natural weapons, etc., are more than counterbalanced, firstly, by his intellectual powers, through which he has formed for himself weapons, tools, etc., though still remaining in a barbarous state, and secondly, by his social qualities which lead him to give and receive aid from his fellow-men. No country in the world abounds in a greater degree with dangerous beasts than Southern Africa; no country presents more fearful physical hardships than the Arctic regions; yet one of the puniest of races, that of the Bushmen, maintains itself in Southern Africa, as do the dwarfed Esquimaux in the Arctic regions. The ancestors of man were, no doubt, inferior in intellect, and probably in social disposition to the lowest existing savages; but it is quite conceivable that they might have existed, or even flourished, if they had advanced in intellect, while gradually losing their brute-like powers, such as that of climbing trees, etc. But these ancestors would not have been exposed to any special danger, even if far more helpless and defenseless than any existing savages, had they inhabited some warm continent or large island, such as Australia, New Guinea, or Borneo, which is now the home of the orang. And natural selection arising from the competition of tribe with tribe in some such large area as one of these, together with the inherited effects of habit, would, under favorable conditions, have sufficed to raise man to his present high position in the organic scale.

Duane T. Gish

Creationist Science and Education

Duane T. Gish *received his Ph.D. in biochemistry from the University of California. He has been a National Institute of Health Fellow and has held a number of research positions. He is currently Associate Director of the Institute for Creation Research, founded by Henry Morris, in El Cajon, California.*

It is commonly believed that the theory of evolution is the only scientific explanation of origins and that the theory of special creation is based solely on religious beliefs. It is further widely accepted that the theory of evolution is supported by such a vast body of scientific evidence, while encountering so few contradictions, that evolution should be accepted as an established fact. As a consequence, it is maintained by many educators that the theory of evolution should be included in science textbooks as the sole explanation for origins but that the theory of special creation, if taught at all, must be restricted to social science courses.

As a matter of fact, neither evolution nor creation qualifies as a scientific theory. Furthermore, it is become increasingly apparent that there are a number of irresolvable contradictions between evolution theory and the facts of science, and that the mechanism postulated for the evolutionary process could account for no more than trivial changes.

It would be well at this point to define what we mean by creation and evolution. By *Creation* we are referring to the theory that the universe and all life forms came into existence by the direct creative acts of a Creator external to and independent of the natural universe. It is postulated that the basic plant and animal kinds were separately created, and that any variation or speciation that has occurred since creation has been limited within the circumscribed boundaries of these created kinds. It is further postulated that the earth has suffered at least one great world-wide catastrophic event or flood which would account for the mass death, destruction, and extinction found on such a monumental scale in geological deposits.

By *Evolution* we are referring to the General Theory of Evolution. This is the theory that all living things have arisen by naturalistic, mechanistic processes from a single primeval cell, which in turn had arisen by similar processes from a dead, inanimate world. This evolutionary process is postulated to have occurred over a period of many hundreds of millions of years. It is further postulated that all major geological formations can be explained by present processes acting essentially at present rates without resort to any world-wide catastrophe(s).

Creation has not been observed by human witnesses. Since creation would have involved unique, unrepeatable historical events, creation is not subject to the experimental method. Furthermore, creation as a theory is non-falsifiable. That is, it is impossible to conceive an experiment that could disprove the possibility of creation. Creation thus does not fulfill the criteria of a scientific theory. That does not say anything about its ultimate validity, of course. Furthermore, creation theory can be used to correlate and explain data, particularly that available from the fossil record, and is thus subject to test in the same manner that other alleged historical events are subject to test—by comparison with historical evidence.

Evolution theory also fails to meet the criteria of a scientific theory. Evolution has never been witnessed by human observers; evolution is not subject to the experimental method; and as formulated by present-day evolutionists, it has become non-falsifiable.

It is obvious that no one has ever witnessed the type of evolutionary changes postulated by the general theory of evolution. No one, for example, witnessed the origin of the universe or the origin of life. No one has ever seen a fish evolve into an amphibian, nor has anyone observed an ape evolve into a man. No one, as a matter of fact, has ever witnessed a significant evolutionary change of any kind.

The example of the peppered moth in England has been cited by such authorities as H. B. D. Kettlewell and Sir Gavin de Beer as the most striking evolutionary change ever witnessed by man. Prior to the industrial revolution in England, the peppered moth, *Biston betularia*, consisted predominantly of a light-colored variety, with a dark-colored form comprising a small minority of the population. This was so because predators (birds) could more easily detect the dark-colored variety as these moths rested during the day on light-colored tree trunks and lichen-covered rocks. With the on-set of the industrial revolution and resultant air pollution, the tree trunks and rocks became progressively darker. As a consequence, the dark-colored variety of moths became more and more difficult to detect, while the light-colored variety ultimately became an easy prey. Birds, therefore, began eating more light-colored than dark-colored moths, and today over 95% of the peppered moths in the industrial areas of England are of the darker-colored variety.

Although, as noted above, this shift in populations of peppered moths has been described as the most striking example of evolution ever observed by man, it is obvious that no significant evolutionary change of any kind has occurred among these peppered moths, certainly not the type required to substantiate the general theory of evolution. For however the populations may have shifted in their proportions of the light and dark forms, all of the moths remained from beginning to end peppered moths, *Biston betularia*. It seems evident, then, that if this example is the most striking example of evolution witnessed by man, no real evolution of any kind has even been observed.

The world-famous evolutionist, Theodosius Dobzhansky, while endeavoring to proclaim his faith in evolution, admitted that no real evolutionary change has ever been observed by man when he said, ". . . the occurrence of the evolution of life in the history of the earth is established about as well as events *not witnessed by human observers can be*." It can be said with certainty, then, that evolution in the present world has never been observed. It remains as far outside the pale of human observation as the origin of the universe or the origin of life. Evolution has been *postulated* but *never observed*.

Since evolution cannot be observed, it is not amenable to the methods of experimental science. This has been acknowledged by Dobzhansky when he stated, "These evolutionary happenings are unique, unrepeatable, and irreversible. It is as impossible to turn a land vertibrate into a fish as it is to effect the reverse transformation. The applicability of the experimental method to the study of such unique historical processes is severely restricted before all else by the time intervals involved, which far exceed the lifetime of any human experimenter. And yet it is just such *impossibility* that is demanded by antievolutionists when they ask for 'proofs' of evolution which they would magnanimously accept as satisfactory."

Please note that Dobzhansky has said that the applicability of the experimental method to the study of evolution is an impossibility! It is obvious, then, that evolution fails to qualify as a scientific theory, for it is certain that a theory that cannot be subjected to experimental test is not a scientific theory.

Furthermore, modern evolution theory has become so plastic, it is non-falsifiable. It can be used to prove anything and everything. Thus, Murray Eden, a professor at Massachusetts Institute of Technology and an evolutionist, has said, with reference to the falsifiability of evolution theory, "This cannot be done in evolution, taking it in its broad sense, and this is really all I meant when I called it tautologous in the first place. It can, indeed, explain anything. You may be ingenious or not in proposing a mechanism which looks plausible to human beings and mechanisms which are consistent with other mechanisms which you have discovered, but it is still an unfalsifiable theory."

Paul Ehrlich and L. C. Birch, biologists at Stanford University and the University of Sidney, respectively, have said, "Our theory of evolution has become . . . one which cannot be refuted by any possible observations. Every conceivable observation can be fitted into it. It is thus 'outside of empirical science' but not necessarily false. No one can think of ways in which to test it. Ideas, either without basis or based on a few laboratory experiments carried out in extremely simplified systems, have attained currency far beyond their validity. They have become part of an evolutionary dogma accepted by most of us as part of our training."

Some evolutionists have been candid enough to admit that evolution is really no more scientific than is creation. In an article in which he states his conviction that the modern neo-Darwinian theory of evolution is based on axioms, Harris says ". . . the axiomatic nature of the neo-Darwinian theory places the debate between evolutionists and creationists in a new perspective. Evolutionists have often challenged creationists to provide experimental proof that species have been fashioned *de novo*. Creationists have often demanded that evolutionists show how chance mutations can lead to adaptability, or to explain why natural selection allows apparently detrimental organs to persist. We may now recognize that either challenge is fair. If the neo-Darwinian theory is axiomatic, it is not valid for creationists to demand proof of the axioms, and it is not valid for evolutionists to dismiss special creation as unproved so long as it is stated as an axiom."

In his introduction to a 1971 edition of Charles Darwin's *Origin of Species*, Matthews states, "In accepting evolution as a fact, how many biologists pause to reflect that science is built upon theories that have been proved by experiment to be correct, or remember that the theory of animal evolution has never been thus proved? . . . The fact of evolution is the backbone of biology, and biology is thus in the peculiar position of being a science founded on an unproved theory—is it then a science or a faith? Belief in the theory of evolution is thus exactly parallel to belief in creation—both are concepts which believers know to be true but neither, up to the present, has been capable of proof."

It can be seen from the above discussion, taken from the scientific literature published by leading evolutionary authorities, that evolution has never been observed and is outside the limits of experimental science. Evolution theory is, therefore, no more scientific than creation theory. That does not make it necessarily false, and it can be tested in the same way that creation theory can be tested—by its ability to correlate and explain historical data, that is, the fossil record. Furthermore, since evolution is supposed to have occurred by processes still operating today, the theory must not contradict natural laws.

Evolutionists protest, of course, that these weaknesses of evolution as a theory are not necessarily due to weaknesses of the theory, per se, but are inherent in the very nature of the evolutionary process. It is claimed that the evolutionary process is so slow that it simply cannot be observed during the lifetime of a human experimenter, or, as a matter of fact, during the combined observations of all recorded human experience. Thus, as noted above, Dobzhansky is incensed that creationists should demand that evolution be subjected to the experimental method before any consideration could be given to evolution as an established process.

It must be emphasized, however, that it is for precisely this reason that evolutionists insist that creation must be excluded from science textbooks or, for that matter, from the whole realm of science, as a viable alternative to evolution. They insist that creation must be excluded from possible consideration as a scientific explanation for origins because creation theory cannot be tested by the experimental method. It is evident, however, that this is a characteristic that it shares in common with evolution theory. Thus, if creation must be excluded from science texts and discussions, then evolution must likewise be excluded.

Evolutionists insist that, in any case, the teaching of the creation model would constitute the teaching of religion because creation requires a Creator. The teaching about the creation model and the scientific evidence supporting it, however, can be done without reference to any religious literature. Furthermore, belief in evolution is as intrinsically religious as is belief in creation.

If creation must be excluded from science in general and from science textbooks and science classrooms in particular because it involves the supernatural, it is obvious that theistic evolution must be excluded for exactly the same reason. Thus the only theory that can be taught according to this reasoning, and in fact, the only theory that is being taught in almost all public schools and universities and in the texts they use, is a purely mechanistic, natural-istic, and thus atheistic, theory of evolution. But atheism, the antithesis of theism, is itself a religious belief.

The late Sir Julian Huxley, British evolutionist and biologist, has said that "Gods are peripheral phenomena produced by evolution." What Huxley meant was that the idea of God merely evolved as man evolved from lower animals. Huxley desired to establish a humanistic religion based on evolution. Humanism has been defined as "the belief that man shapes his own destiny. It is a constructive philosophy, a *non-theistic religion*, a way of life." This same publication quotes Huxley as saying, "I use the word 'Humanist' to mean someone who believes that man is just as much a natural phenomenon as an animal or plant; that his body, mind, and soul were not supernaturally created but are products of *evolution*, and that he is not under the control or guidance of any supernatural being or beings, but has to rely on himself and his own powers." The inseparable link between this non-theistic humanistic religion and belief in evolution is evident.

George Gaylord Simpson, Professor of Vertebrate Paleontology at Harvard University until his retirement and one of the world's best-known evolutionists, has said that the Christian faith, which he calls the "higher superstition" (in contrast to the "lower superstition" of pagan tribes of South America and Africa) is intellectually unacceptable. Simpson concludes his book, *Life of the Past*, with what Sir Julian Huxley has called "a splendid assertion of evolutionist view of man." "Man," Simpson writes, "stands alone in the universe, a unique product of a long, unconscious, impersonal, material process with unique understanding and potentialities. These he owes to no one but himself, and it is to himself that he is responsible. He is not the creature of uncontrollable and undeterminable forces, but his own master. He can and must decide and manage his own destiny."

Thus, according to Simpson, man is alone in the Universe (there is no God), he is the result of an impersonal, unconscious process (no one directed his origin or creation), and he is his own master and must manage his own destiny (there is no God to determine man's destiny). That, according to Simpson and Huxley, is the evolutionist's view of man. That this is the philosophy held by most biologists has been recently emphasized by Dobzhansky. In his review of Monod's book, *Chance and Necessity*, Dobzhansky said, "He has stated with admirable clarity, and eloquence often verging on pathos, the mechanistic materialist philosophy shared by most of the present 'establishment' in the biological sciences."

No doubt a majority of the scientific community embraces the mechanistic materialistic philosophy of Simpson, Huxley, and Monod. Many of these men are highly intelligent, and they have woven the fabric of evolution theory in an ingenious fashion. They have then combined this evolution theory with humanistic philosophy and have clothed the whole with the term "science." The product, a non-theistic religion, with evolutionary philosophy as its creed under the guise of "science," is being taught in most public schools, colleges and universities of the United States. It has become our unofficial state-sanctioned religion.

Furthermore, a growing number of scientists are becoming convinced that there are basic contradictions between evolution theory and empirical scientific data as well as known scientific laws. On the other hand, these scientists believe special creation provides an excellent model for explaining the correlating data related to origins which is free of such contradictions. Even some evolutionists are beginning to realize that the formulations of modern evolution theory are really incapable of explaining anything and that an adequate scientific theory of evolution, if ever attainable, must await the discovery of as yet unknown natural laws.

The core of modern evolution theory, known as the neo-Darwinian theory of evolution, or the modern synthetic theory, is the hypothesis that the evolutionary process has occurred through natural selection of random mutational changes in the genetic material, selection being in accordance with alterations in the environment. Natural selection, itself, is not a chance process, but the material it must act on, mutant genes, is produced by random, chance processes.

It is an astounding fact that while at the time Darwin popularized it, the concept of natural selection seemed to explain so much, today there is a growing realization that the presently accepted concept of natural selection really explains nothing. It is a mere tautology, that is, it involves circular reasoning.

In modern theory, natural selection is defined in terms of differential reproduction. In fact, according to Lewontin, differential reproduction *is* natural selection. When it is asked, what survives, the answer is, the fittest. But when it is asked, what are the fittest, the answer is, those that survive! Natural selection thus collapses into a tautology, devoid of explanatory value. It is not possible to explain *why* some varieties live to reproduce more offspring—it is only known that they do.

In discussing Richard Levins' concept of fitness set analysis, Hamilton stated, "This criticism amounts to restating what I think is the admission of most evolutionists, that we do not yet know what natural selection maximizes." Now if evolutionists do not know what natural selection maximizes, they do not know what natural selection selects.

In a review of the thinking in French scientific circles, it was stated, "Even if they do not publicly take a definite stand, almost all French specialists hold today strong mental reservations as to the validity of natural selection." Creationists maintain that indeed natural selection could not result in increased complexity or convert a plant or animal into another basic kind. It can only act to eliminate the unfit.

Macbeth has recently published an especially incisive criticism of evolution theory and of the concept of natural selection as used by evolutionists. He points out that although evolutionists have abandoned classical Darwinism, the modern synthetic theory they have proposed as a substitute is equally inadequate to explain progressive change as the result of natural selection, and, as a matter of fact, they cannot even define natural selection in non-tautological terms. Inadequacies of the present theory and failure of the fossil record to substantiate predictions based on the theory leave macro-evolution, and even micro-evolution, intractable mysteries according to Macbeth. Macbeth suggests that no theory at all may be preferable to the present theory of evolution.

Using Macbeth's work as the starting point for his own investigation of modern evolution theory, Bethell, a graduate of Oxford with a major in philosophy, has expressed his complete dissatisfaction with the present formulations of evolution theory and natural selection from the viewpoint of the philosophy of science. Both Macbeth and Bethell present excellent reviews of the thinking of leading evolutionists concerning the relationship of natural selection to evolution theory. While both are highly critical, neither profess to be creationists.

According to modern evolutionary theory, ultimately all of evolution is due to mutations. Mutations are random changes in the genes or chromosomes which are highly ordered structures. Any process that occurs by random chance events is subject to the laws of probability.

It is possible to estimate mutation rates. It is also possible to estimate how many favorable mutations would be required to bring about certain evolutionary changes. Assuming that these mutations are produced in a random, chance manner, as is true in the neo-Darwinian interpretation of evolution, it is possible to calculate how long such an evolutionary process would have required to convert an amoeba into a man. When this is done, according to a group of mathematicians, all of whom are evolutionists, the answer turns out to be billions of times longer than the assumed five billion years of earth history!

One of these mathematicians, Murray Eden, stated, "It is our contention that if 'random' is given a serious and crucial interpretation from a probabilistic point of view, the randomness postulate is highly implausible and that an *adequate scientific theory of evolution must await the discovery and elucidation of new natural laws—physical, physico-chemical, and biological.*" What Eden and these mathematicians are saying is that the modern neo-Darwinian theory of evolution is totally inadequate to explain more than trivial change and thus we simply have no basis at present for attempting to explain how evolution may have occurred. As a matter of fact, based on the assumption that the evolutionary process was dependent upon random chance processes, we can simply state that evolution would have been impossible.

Furthermore, evolution theory contradicts one of the most firmly established laws known to science, the Second Law of Thermodynamics. The obvious contradiction between evolution and the Second Law of Thermodynamics becomes evident when we compare the definition of this Law and its consequences by several scientists (all of whom, as far as we know, accept evolutionary philosophy) with the definition of evolution by Sir Julian Huxley, biologist and one of the best-known spokesmen for evolution theory.

> There is a general natural tendency of all observed systems to go from order to disorder, reflecting dissipation of energy available for future transformations—the law of increasing entropy.
>
> All real processes go with an increase of entropy. The entropy also measures the randomness, or lack of orderliness of the system: the greater the randomness, the greater the entropy.
>
> Another way of stating the second law then is: 'The universe is constantly getting more disorderly!' Viewed that way, we can see the second law all about us. We have to work hard to straighten a room, but left to itself it becomes a mess again very quickly and very easily. Even if we never enter it, it becomes dusty and musty. How difficult to maintain houses, and machinery, and our own bodies in perfect working order: how easy to let them deteriorate. In fact, all we have to do is nothing, and everything deteriorates, collapses, breaks down, wears out, all by itself—and that is what the second law is all about.

Now compare these definitions or consequences of the Second Law of Thermodynamics to the theory of evolution as defined by Huxley:

> Evolution in the extended sense can be defined as a directional and essentially irreversible process occurring in time, which in its course gives rise to an increase of variety and an increasingly high level of organization in its products. Our present knowledge indeed forces us to the view that the whole of reality is evolution—a single process of self-transformation.

There is a natural tendency, then, for all observed natural systems to go from order to disorder, towards increasing randomness. This is true throughout the entire known universe, both at the micro and macro levels. This tendency is so invariant that it has never been observed to fail. It is a natural law—the Second Law of Thermodynamics.

On the other hand, according to the general theory of evolution, as defined by Huxley, there is a general tendency of natural systems to go from disorder to order, towards an ever higher and higher level of complexity. This tendency supposedly operates in every corner of the universe, both at the micro and macro levels. As a consequence, it is believed, particles have evolved into people.

It is difficult to understand how a discerning person could fail to see the basic contradiction between these two processes. It seems apparent that both cannot be true, but no modern scientist would dare challenge the validity of the Second Law of Thermodynamics.

The usual, but exceedingly naive, answer given by evolutionists to this dilemma is that the Second Law of Thermodynamics applies only to closed systems. If the system is open to an external source of energy, it is asserted, complexity can be generated and maintained within this system at the expense of the energy supplied to it from the outside.

Thus, our solar system is an open system, and energy is supplied to the earth from the sun. The decrease in entropy, or increase in order, on the earth during the evolutionary process, it is said, has been more than compensated by the increase in entropy, or decrease in order, on the sun. The overall result has been a net decrease in order, so the Second Law of Thermodynamics has not been violated, we are told.

An open system and an adequate external source of energy are necessary *but not sufficient* conditions, however, for order to be generated and maintained, since raw, undirected, uncontrolled energy is destructive, not constructive. For example, without the protective layer of ozone in the upper atmosphere which absorbs most of the ultraviolet light coming from the sun, life on earth would be impossible. Bacterial cells exposed to such radiation die within seconds. This is because ultraviolet light, or irradiation of any kind, breaks chemical bonds and thus randomizes and destroys the highly complex structures found in biologically active macromolecules, such as proteins and DNA. Biological activity of these vitally important molecules is destroyed and death rapidly follows.

That much more than merely an external energy source is required to form complex molecules and systems from simpler ones is evident from the following statement by Simpson and Beck: ". . . the simple expenditure of energy is not sufficient to develop and maintain order. A bull in a china shop performs work, but he neither creates nor maintains organization. The work needed is *particular* work; it must follow specifications; it requires information on how to proceed."

Thus a green plant, utilizing the highly complex photosynthetic system it possesses, can trap light energy from the sun and convert this light energy into chemical energy. A series of other complex systems within the green plant allows the utilization of this energy to build up complex molecules and systems from simple starting material. Of equal importance is the fact that the green plant possesses a system for directing, maintaining, and replicating these complex energy conversion mechanisms—an incredibly complex genetic system. Without the genetic system, no specifications on how to proceed would exist, chaos would result, and life would be impossible.

For complexity to be generated within a system, then, four conditions must be met:

1. The system must be an open system.
2. An adequate external energy source must be available.
3. The system must possess energy conversion mechanisms.
4. A control mechanism must exist within the system for directing, maintaining, and replicating these energy conversion mechanisms.

The seemingly irresolvable dilemma, from an evolutionary point of view, is, how such complex energy conversion mechanisms and genetic systems arose in the *absence* of such systems, when there is a general natural tendency to go from order to disorder, a tendency so universal it can be stated as a natural law, the Second Law of Thermodynamics. Simply stated, machines are required to build machines, and something or somebody must operate the machinery.

The creationist thus opposes the wholly unscientific evolutionary hypothesis that the natural universe with all of its incredible complexity, was capable of generating itself, and maintains that there must exist, external to the natural universe, a Creator, or supernatural Agent, who was responsible for introducing, or creating, the high degree of order found within this natural universe. While creationism is extra-scientific, it is not anti-scientific, as is the evolutionary hypothesis which contradicts one of the most well-established laws of science.

Finally, but of utmost significance, is the fact that the fossil record is actually hostile to the evolution model, but conforms remarkably well to predictions based on the creation model. Complex forms of life appear abruptly in the fossil record in the so-called Cambrian sedimentary deposits or rocks. Although these animals, which include such highly complex and diverse forms of life as brachiopods, trilobites, worms, jellyfish, sponges, sea urchins, and sea cucumbers, as well as other crustaceans and molluscs, supposedly required about two to three billion years to evolve, not a single ancestor for any of these animals can be found anywhere on the face of the earth. George Gaylord Simpson has characterized the absence of Precambrian fossils as "the major mystery of the history of life." This fact of the fossil record, incomprehensible in the light of the evolution model, is exactly as predicted on the basis of the creation model.

The remainder of the fossil record reveals a remarkable absence of the many transitional forms demanded by the theory of evolution. Gaps between all higher categories of plants and animals, which creationists believe constituted the created kinds, are systematic. For example, Simpson has admitted tht "Gaps among known orders, classes, and phyla are systematic and almost always large." Richard B. Goldschmidt, well-known geneticist and a rabid evolutionist, acknowledged that "practically all orders or families known appear suddenly and without any apparent transitions." E. J. H. Corner, Cambridge University botanist and an evolutionist, stated, ". . . I still think, to the unprejudiced, the fossil record of plants is in favor of special creation."

Recently, the well-known evolutionary paleontologist, David B. Kitts, stated, "Despite the bright promise that paleontology provides a means of 'seeing' evolution, it has presented some nasty difficulties for evolutionists the most notorious of which is the presence of 'gaps' in the fossil record. *Evolution requires intermediate forms between species and paleontology does not provide them. . . .*"

Lord Solly Zuckerman, for many years the head of the Department of Anatomy at the University of Birmingham, was first knighted and then later raised to the peerage as recognition of his distinguished career as a research scientist. After over 15 years of research on the subject, with a team that rarely included less than four scientists, Lord Zuckerman concluded that *Australopithecus* did not walk upright, he was not intermediate between ape and man, but that he was merely an anthropoid ape. *Australopithecus* (Louis Leakey's "Nutcracker Man," and Donald Johanson's "Lucy") is an extinct ape-like creature that almost all evolutionists believe walked erect and showed many characteristics intermediate between ape and man. Lord Zuckerman, although not a creationist, believes there is very little, if any, science in the search for man's fossil ancestry. Lord Zuckerman states his conviction, based on a life-time of investigation, that if man has evolved from an ape-like creature he did so without leaving any trace of the transformation in the fossil record. This directly contradicts the popular idea that paleontologists have found numerous evidences of ape-like ancestors for man, but rather suggests they have found none at all.

The explosive appearance of highly complex forms of life in Cambrian and other rocks with the absence of required ancestors, and the abrupt appearance of each major plant and animal kind without apparent transitional forms are the facts of greatest importance derivable from a study of the fossil record. These facts are highly contradictory to predictions based on the evolution model, but are just as predicted on the basis of the creation model of origins.

The facts described above are some of the reasons why creationists maintain that, on the basis of available scientific evidence, the creation model is not only a viable alternative to the evolution model, but is actually a far superior model. Furthermore, after more than a century of effort to establish Darwinian evolution, even some evolutionists are beginning to express doubts. This is evidently true, for example, of Pierre P. Grassé, one of the most distinguished of French scientists. In his review of Grassé's book, *L'Evolution du Vivant*, Dobzhansky states, "The book of Pierre P. Grassé is a frontal attack on all kinds of 'Darwinism.' Its purpose is 'to destroy the myth of evolution as a simple, understood, and explained phenomenon,' and to show that evolution is a mystery about which little is, and perhaps can be, known. Now, one can disagree with Grassé but not ignore him. He is the most distinguished of French zoologists, the editor of the 28 volumes of 'Traite de Zoologie,' author of numerous original investigations, and ex-president of the Academie des Sciences. His knowledge of the living world is encyclopedic. . . ." In the closing sentence of his review, Dobzhansky says, "The sentence with which Grassé ends his book is disturbing: 'It is possible that in this domain biology, impotent, yields the floor to metaphysics.' " Grassé thus closes his book with the statement that biology is powerless to explain the origin of living things and that it may possibly have to yield to metaphysics (supernatural creation of some kind).

In his Presidential Address to the Linnaean Society of London, "A Little on Lung-fishes," Errol White said, "But whatever ideas authorities may have on the subject, the lung-fishes, like every other major group of fishes I know, have their origin firmly based in *nothing*. . . ." He then said, "I have often said how little I should like to have to prove organic evolution in a court of law." He closed his address by saying, "We still do not know the mechanics of evolution in spite of the over-confident claims in some quarters, nor are we likely to make further progress in this by the classical methods of paleontology or biology: and we shall certainly not advance matters by jumping up and down shrilling 'Darwin is God and I, So-and-so, am his prophet'—the recent researches of workers like Dean and Hinshelwood (1964) already suggest the possibility of incipient cracks in the seemingly monolithic walls of the Neo-Darwinian Jericho." White thus seems to be suggesting that the modern neo-Darwinian theory of evolution is in danger of crashing down just as did the walls of Jericho!

Thus, today we have a most astounding situation. Evolution has never been observed by human witnesses. Evolution cannot be subjected to the experimental method. The most sacred tenet of Darwinism—natural selection—in modern formulation is incapable of explaining anything. Furthermore, even some evolutionists are conceding that the mechanism of evolution proposed by evolutionary biologists could account for no more than trivial change in the time believed to have been available, and that an adequate scientific theory of evolution, based on present knowledge, seems impossible. Finally, the major features of the fossil record accord in an amazing fashion with the predictions based on special creation, but contradict the most fundamental predictions generated by the theory of evolution. And yet the demand is unceasing that evolution theory be accepted as the only scientific explanation for origins, even as an established fact, while excluding creation as a mere religious concept!

This rigid indoctrination in evolutionary dogma, with the exclusion of the competing concept of special creation, results in young people being indoctrinated in a non-theistic, naturalistic, humanistic religious philosophy in the guise of science. Science is perverted, academic freedom is denied, the educational process suffers, and constitutional guarantees of religious freedom are violated.

This unhealthy situation could be corrected by presenting students with the two competing models for origins, the creation model and the evolution model, with all supporting evidence for each model. This would permit an evaluation of the students of the strengths and weaknesses of each model. This is the course true education should pursue rather than following the present process of brainwashing students in evolutionary philosophy.

Philip Kitcher

Against Creationism

Philip Kitcher *teaches philosophy at the University of California, San Diego. In addition to a book on sociobiology, he is author of* Abusing Science, *the book on evolutionary theory from which this selection is excerpted.*

Before turning to "scientific" Creationism itself—that is, the theory peddled by the Institute for Creation Research and advertised by the Moral Majority—it is important to distinguish two other forms that a belief in special creation might take. The central idea of strict Creationism is that all kinds of organisms presently existing, and perhaps some more, were formed on the earth in a single event. Some people hold this view purely as an article of religious faith, making no claim that it is a part of science supported by scientific evidence. Such people accept strict Creationism because its central doctrine follows from two other beliefs that they hold: (i) The Bible is to be read literally; (ii) When the Bible is read literally, it says that all kinds of organisms were formed on the earth in a single event. I disagree with this view, because I do not believe it is possible, let alone reasonable, to read the Bible literally. (Nor do I think that Christians and Jews are compelled, as sincere believers, to read the Bible literally.) However, I have no intention of criticizing Creationism insofar as it is held as an explicitly religious belief, a belief that is recognized as running counter to the scientific evidence.

There is another way to be a Creationist. One might offer Creationism as a scientific theory: Life did not evolve over millions of years; rather all forms were created at one time by a particular Creator. Although pure versions of Creationism were no longer in vogue among scientists by the end of the eighteenth century, they had flourished earlier (in the writings of Thomas Burnet, William Whiston, and others). Moreover, *variants* of Creationism were supported by a number of eminent nineteenth-century scientists—William Buckland, Adam Sedgwick, and Louis Agassiz, for example. These Creationists trusted that their theories would accord with the Bible, interpreted in what they saw as a correct way. However, that fact does not affect the scientific status of those theories. Even postulating an unobserved Creator need be no more unscientific than postulating unobservable particles. What matters is the character of the proposals and the ways in which they are articulated and defended. The great scientific Creationists of the eighteenth and nineteenth centuries offered problem-solving strategies for many of the questions addressed by evolutionary theory. They struggled hard to explain the observed distribution of fossils. Sedgwick, Buckland, and others practiced genuine science. They stuck their necks out and volunteered information about the catastrophes that they invoked to explain biological and geological findings. Because their theories offered definite proposals, those theories were refutable. Indeed, the theories actually achieved refutation. In 1831, in his presidential address to the Geological Society, Adam Sedgwick publicly announced that his own variant of Creationism had been refuted:

> Having been myself a believer, and, to the best of my power, a propagator of what I now regard as a philosophic heresy . . . I think it right, as one of my last acts before I quit this Chair, thus publicly to read my recantation.
>
> We ought, indeed, to have paused before we first adopted the diluvian theory, and referred all our old superficial gravel to the action of the Mosaic Flood. For of man, and the works of his hands, we have not yet found a single trace among the remnants of a former world entombed in these ancient deposits. In classing together distant unknown formations under one name; in giving them a simultaneous origin, and in determining their date, not by the organic remains we had discovered, but by those we expected hypothetically hereafter to discover, in them; we have given one more example of the passion with which the mind fastens upon general conclusions, and of the readiness with which it leaves the consideration of unconnected truths. . . .

Since they want Creationism taught in public schools, contemporary Creationists cannot present their view as based on religious faith. On the other hand, the doctrine is too dear to be subjected to the possibility of outright defeat. What is wanted, then, is a version of Creationism that is not vulnerable to refutation, but that appears to enjoy the objective status that can only be conferred by evidential support. This is an impossible demand. A theory cannot drink at the well of evidential support without running the risk of being poisoned by future data. What emerges from the conflict of goals is the pseudoscience promulgated by the Institute for Creation Research. It is vaguely suggested that the central Creationist idea could be used to solve some problems. But the details are never given, the links to nature never forged. Oddly, "scientific" Creationism fails to be a science not because of what it says (or, in its "public school" editions, very carefully omits) about a Divine Creator, but because of what it does not say abut the natural world. The theory has no infrastructure, no ways of articulating its vague central idea, so that specific features of living forms can receive detailed explanations.

Despite my best efforts, I have found only two problem-solving strategies in the writing of "scientific" Creationists. Most of the literature is negative. . . . The positive proposals of Creation "science" are remarkably skimpy. Even *Scientific Creationism* (the work that is intended to enable teachers to present the "creation model") spends far more pages attacking evolutionary theory than in developing the Creationist account. Nevertheless, there are passages where a positive doctrine seems to flicker among the criticisms. Similarly, the much earlier book *The Genesis Flood* (Whitcomb and Morris 1961), mixes attempts at constructing Creation "science" with its explicit Biblical interpretation. Because of the uniformly negative character of most other Creationist writings, my evaluation of the positive theory presented by "scientific" Creationists will be based primarily on these two works. The two problem-solving strategies of "scientific" Creationism are the attempt to use Flood Geology to answer questions about the ordering of fossils and an appeal to a mix of "design" and historical narrative to account for the properties, relationships, and distributions of organisms. I shall document my remarks about pseudoscience by taking a closer look at how these explanatory vehicles operate.

ROOM AT THE TOP FOR THE UPWARDLY MOBILE?

Creationists recognize that the fossil record is ordered. All over the earth we find a regular succession of organisms through the rock strata. At the lowest levels, we find only small marine invertebrates. As we move up, other groups of animals are encountered: Fish join the marine invertebrates; then come the amphibians, reptiles, and, finally, the mammals and birds. Of course, within each of these groups there is also an order. The first reptiles diversify, giving rise at later times to several different groups, some of which, like the dinosaurs, die out, while others of which, like the snakes, turtles, lizards, and crocodilians, persist to the present. Even without evolutionary assumptions, it is possible to offer a simple explanation of this order. The different strata all contain remains of the distinctive organisms that were alive at the time at which those strata were deposited, and the order reflects the fact that different groups of animals have existed at different times. In other words, the animals who have inhabited the earth were not all contemporaries.

Although this simple explanation makes no commitment to the *evolution* of organisms, Creationists cannot accept it. For they believe that all the animals that have ever existed were formed in one original event of Creation. Nor can they abandon this belief without forswearing the theological payoff of their "science." So how are they to explain the order of the fossil record? Some antievolutionists of the late nineteenth century ascended to new levels of ad hoc explanation with two transparent ruses: (i) The Devil placed the fossils in the rocks to deceive us; (ii) God put the fossils there to test us. Contemporary Creationists are more subtle. They invoke the Flood. They hypothesize a worldwide, cataclysmic deluge, which destroyed virtually all the animals of the earth and deposited almost all the fossil-bearing rocks, thereby producing the fossil record.

Here is an outline of their major ideas. The primeval earth was a very pleasant place, consisting of land masses divided by "narrow seas." It was surrounded by a canopy of water vapor, producing a "greenhouse effect.' In the Flood, water came from two directions; primitive waters inside the earth burst through the crust, and, at the same time, the vapor canopy was broken up to cause torrential rain. Some humans and animals escaped in boats (including, presumably, Noah, his family, and a pair of [land] animals of every kind). Others, less lucky, were drowned or destroyed, and some of them were engulfed by mud and other debris that were later deposited as sediments. (The latter animals are the ones that became fossilized.) Finally, the Flood came to an end, partly as the result of evaporation, partly because mountains erupted, producing basins in which the residual waters were entrapped. At this point, the remaining animals dispersed, bred, multiplied, and spread themselves over the new earth.

The attempt to explain geological formations by reference to the Flood is not new. Contemporary Creationists are heirs to a long tradition, begun by Thomas Burnet (whose *Sacred Theory of the Earth* was published in 1681). The idea of invoking a *single* cataclysm (and a single period of Creation) had been abandoned by the wiser geologists by the end of the eighteenth century, at which time the enterprise appeared hopeless. Nineteenth-century Catastrophists—Cuvier, Buckland, Sedgwick, and their followers—preferred to think of Noah's Flood as the last in a series of catastrophes. But "scientific" Creationists will have none of these newfangled compromises. So their account is vexed by all the questions that arose for their illustrious predecessors—as well as other questions inspired by the discoveries of the past 150 years. Here are just a few. How exactly did the land reemerge? (In traditional terms, how was "the pond drained"?) Did *all* kinds of land animals go on Noah's ship? If so, why are there so many kinds that are unrecorded in ""post-Deluge" strata? How were the domestic economies managed during the voyage of the Ark? Obviously, the *mechanisms* of the whole episode could stand considerably more description. Creationists sometimes admit the point; Morris exhorts teachers to prepare geology students who can help with the task of working out the details. However, neither he nor any other Creationist I have read seems to have any definite conception of where or how to begin this Herculean task. . . .

To see why Flood Geology deserves an obituary, let us watch it in action. The most ambitious attempt at detailed problem solving is presented by Henry Morris. Morris is very emphatic that flood Geology accounts for the order of the fossils. After announcing fourteen "obvious predictions" of his story, he concludes, "Now there is no question that all of the above predictions from the cataclysmic model are explicitly confirmed in the geologic column. The general order from simple to complex in the fossil record in the geologic column, considered by evolutionists to be the main proof of evolution, is thus likewise predicted by the rival model, only with more precision and detail. But it is the exceptions that are inimical to the evolution model." Bold words. Before we take up the large claims made for Flood Geology, let us consider the swipes at the evolutionary account. First, the "general order from simple to complex" in the fossil record is not considered "the main proof" of evolution. Evolutionary theory rests on its ability to subsume a vast number of diverse phenomena—including the *details* of biogeography, adaptive characteristics, relationships among organisms, and the sequence of fossils—under a single type of historical reasoning. To say that "the general order from simple to complex" in the fossil record is the primary evidence for evolution is like saying that the fact that most bodies tend to fall is the primary evidence for Newtonian theory. Second, those "inimical exceptions" are our old friends the overthrusts, the cave drawings— and, of course, Paluxy. As I have already pointed out, these are not genuine problems for evolutionary theory.

How exactly does Morris propose to "predict" the order of the fossils from his model? Let us look at some of his "predictions" and their justifications:

> 3. In general, animals living at the lowest elevations would tend to be buried at the lowest elevations, and so on, with elevations in the strata thus representing elevations of habitat or ecological zones.
> 4. Marine invertebrates would normally be found in the bottom rocks of any local geologic column, since they live on the sea bottom.

5. Marine vertebrates (fishes) would be found in higher rocks than the bottom-dwelling invertebrates. They live at higher elevations and also could escape burial longer.

6. Amphibians and reptiles would tend to be found at still higher elevations, in the commingled sediments at the interface between land and water. . . .

9. In the marine strata where invertebrates were fossilized, these would tend locally to be sorted hydrodynamically into assemblages of similar size and shape. Furthermore, as the turbulently upwelling waters and sediments settled back down, the simpler animals, more nearly spherical or streamlined in shape, would tend to settle out first because of lower hydraulic drag. Thus each kind of marine invertebrate would tend to appear in its simplest form at the lowest elevation, and so on.

10. Mammals and birds would be found in general at higher elevations than reptiles and amphibians, both because of their habitat and because of their greater mobility. However, few birds would be found at all, only occasional exhausted birds being trapped and buried in sediments.

It is hard to know where to start. Morris appears to have three possible explanatory factors: (1) *habitat* (lower dwelling animals were deposited first), (2) *hydraulic characteristics* (the order of deposition depends on the animal's resistance to the downward waters), (3) *mobility* (more mobile animals will be deposited later). The passages I have quoted juggle these three methods so as to obtain the desired results.

Now, for all the extravagant claims about "prediction" with "more precision and detail," the account Morris offers is extremely vague. Puzzles begin to appear in large numbers when we start to consider the details of the fossil record. Why are bottom-dwelling marine invertebrates found at *all* levels of the strata? Why are some very delicate marine invertebrates, which would have been likely to sink more slowly, found at the very lowest levels? Why are all the "modern" fishes (the *teleostean* fishes, which, on the standard account, emerged only in the age of dinosaurs and became spectacularly successful as the reign of the dinosaurs came to its end) found only in Morris's "late Flood" deposits? Why do these particular fishes not occur, as other fishes do, at lower levels? Why are whales and dolphins only found at high levels, while marine reptiles of similar size are found only much lower? Why do lumbering creatures like ground sloths appear only in Morris's post-Flood deposits, while much more agile mammals (such as the ancestors of contemporary carnivores and ungulates) appear much lower? Why are the *flying* reptiles found "in the commingled sediments at the interface between land and water"? Why were not *most* of the birds "exhausted," since perching places would have been hard to find in the raging Deluge? The sequence of questions could go on and on.

Morris does not consider the particularities. So the idea that we get *more* detail from his account is simply bluster. In fact, given that the problems raised for evolutionary theory are spurious—the "inimical exceptions" do not present any difficulty—the question we must ask is whether Flood Geology can *emulate* the ability of evolutionary theory to explain the fossil record. There are two ways in which Creationists might elaborate their proposals. One would be to acknowledge that the account so far given is programmatic and incomplete and to face up to the task of working out the details. The second would be to deny that there are residual questions for "scientific" Creationism to answer.

In the spirit of Morris's exhortation to young paleontologists, Creationists might concede that Flood Geology is only a "sketch." However, it is hardly a matter of adding a bit of detail to the main lines of the account. Problems are everywhere, solutions nowhere. What were the mechanics of the Flood? How were the animals preserved? Why are the details of the fossil ordering as we find them to be? It is reasonable to wonder what Flood Geology does have going for it that inspires people to work further on it. Wonderment increases when we realize that Creationists have abandoned the position of the most enlightened nineteenth-century Catastrophists. . . .

Here is a different "theory sketch" about the history of life on earth. For a very long time, the earth has been a laboratory for clever aliens who live in outer space. Periodically, they have "seeded" our planet with living organisms. In the beginning, they were only able to produce rather simple terrestrial organisms. So they started off with some marine invertebrates. After a while, they came for a visit to see how things were going. At this time, a dreadful thing happened. Something about the alien spacecraft caused a cataclysm on the earth; volcanoes erupted, there were massive earthquakes, enormous tidal waves, and so forth. Perhaps the spacecraft emitted some peculiar type of radiation that triggered all these unfortunate events. In any case, all the first crop of organisms was destroyed and buried in the cataclysm. The whole experiment was spoiled. However, since they understood the moral of Kipling's "If," the aliens decided to try again. Their technology had now improved, and they were able to manufacture more complicated animals. Some of those that had not performed well on the first round were dropped from the cast. The experiment went very well again— until they came to take another look. Once again, their presence led to disaster, and they were forced to start over from scratch. So it has gone for a number of trials. (How many would you like?) The aliens are very persevering. They still have not figured out what it is about their presence that makes the earth go into convulsions. But their technology is clearly improving by leaps and bounds. After all, last time they made us.

My brief acquaintance with the "theory sketch" of the last paragraph has not yet led to a deep attachment. (It took me about ten minutes to make it up.) So I shall not exhort others to join me in working out the details. However, I do want to suggest that, *from a scientific point of view*, my silly proposal is no worse than Morris's Flood Geology. It would not be difficult to mimic the "fourteen predictions." ("What evolutionists call *trends* are really the aliens' progress in fine tuning already workable designs." Notice, too, that my theory, like Morris's vague account of Flood Geology, has plenty of "wiggle room.") The point of the comparison should be obvious. There is utterly no reason to take either my proposal or Flood Geology seriously—or to exhort promising students to waste their careers in the pursuit of such obvious folly.

The second way in which the Creationists can respond to questions about the details is even worse. Instead of taking the problems of detail seriously, they can contend that we can never know how the Flood worked. All that can be done is to lay down some general considerations, which hold "as a rule," and suggest that, given some unknowable distribution of upwelling waters, torrential rains, and trapped animals, everything sorted out as it did. So, for example, the questions I have raised about teleostean fishes, whales, flying reptiles, and giant sloths can just be ducked. These are "the exceptional cases."

Some passages suggest that, when push comes to shove, Morris and his fellow Creationists will slide in this direction:

> 14. All the above predictions would be expected statistically but, because of the cataclysmic nature of the phenomena, would also admit of many exceptions in every case. In other words, the cataclysmic model predicts the general order and character of the deposits but also allows for occasional exceptions.
>
> In other localities, and perhaps somewhat later in the period of the rising waters of the Flood, in general, land animals and plants would be expected to be caught in the sediments and buried; and this, of course, is exactly what the strata show. Of course, this would be only a general rule and there would be many exceptions, as currents would be intermingling from all directions, particularly as the lands became increasingly submerged and more and more amphibians, reptiles and mammals were overtaken by the waters.

The remarkable point about these passages is not the *number* of qualifying phrases, but their *variable strength*. Are there "many exceptions in every case" or are the exceptions "occasional"? I do not know what Morris or Whitcomb intends. Yet one thing is clear. Such passages can be used to maintain that the anomalies I have mentioned are not genuine problems for Flood Geology. Morris and Whitcomb have carefully provided an all-purpose escape clause. So while (alleged) exceptions are "inimical" to evolutionary theory—they would mean refutation—exceptions, even hordes of exceptions, in no way weaken the case for Creation "science." For Creation "scientists" data has only one function; it is a potential source of problems for evolution. Counterexamples to the "theory" of Creation "science" do not count.

To see how severe the anomalies are, let us look at one example in more detail. Fossils of teleostean fishes (this class comprises just about all contemporary types from sardines to swordfish) are found only from late Triassic times (roughly 200 million years ago), and they show increasing abundance in the fossil record. Now recall that a leading principle of Flood Geology is that "animals living at the lowest elevations would tend to be buried at the lowest elevations." Overlooking such niceties as the fact that some teleosteans are deep-sea fish, let us ask what accounts for their success in resisting the Flood. Were they hydraulically special, less "streamlined" than other fish? No, as a group, there is more variation of shape *within* the teleosteans than there is between teleosteans and the groups of fish that were buried beneath them. So, perhaps the answer is that they found room at the top because they were upwardly mobile? But this explanation loses its attractiveness when we realize that the teleosts "range from speedy swimmers to slow swimmers to almost sedentary forms, from dwellers in the open ocean to bottom-living types to lake and river fishes." Yet all these lucky teleostean fishes managed to resist the flood waters for a long time, while large numbers of speedy fish are buried beneath them.

By considering this one example, I hope to have explained what lies behind my charge that Flood Geology faces serious anomalies. But my principal purpose is to illustrate the impotence of the idea that worrisome details can be written off as "exceptional cases." Were *all* the teleosts exceptional? Was there no single unlucky sardine, salmon, or swordfish who was buried in the early deposits? Is it enough to remind ourselves that there are bound to be exceptions "because of the cataclysmic nature of the phenomena"? The case of the teleosts is only one among many. Ground sloths, flying reptiles, whales, trilobites, and a host of other creatures prove similarly embarrassing. . . .

Writing in 1961, Whitcomb and Morris made it clear what their last resort would be if the difficult questions began to threaten: "It is because the Bible itself teaches us these things that we are fully justified in appealing to *the power of God*, whether or not He used means amenable to our scientific understanding, for the gathering of two of every kind of animal into the Ark and for the care and preservation of those animals in the Ark during the 371 days of the Flood." Today, "scientific" Creationists have pledged themselves to argue on the scientific evidence. So this last refuge is—officially, at least—out of bounds.

The second major biological problem-solving strategy offered by Creationism attempts to answer questions about adaptation, relationships among organisms, and biogeographical distribution. . . .

The basic idea is straightforward. When we recognize a characteristic of an organism as unmodified, the Creationist explanation of its presence will be to show how the feature manifests the Creator's design. The account of similarities among distinct "basic kinds" will identify the similar needs of organisms of those distinct kinds. Here are some sample "explanations." Bats have wings because the Creator endowed them with wings, and He did so because they need to fly. Chimps and humans have similar hemoglobins (and other biological molecules) because the Creator gave them similar molecules from the start, and He did so because their physiological requirements are similar. Some (perfectly palatable) butterflies mimic unpalatable butterflies of the same region because the Creator saw that they had to have some defense against predators. To each according to his need.

If one wants to believe in Creationism, the picture can easily lull critical faculties. Yet, if we think about it, it is bizarre. Surely we should not imagine the Creator contemplating a wingless bat, recognizing that it would be defective, and so equipping it with the wings it needs. Rather, if we take the idea of a single creative event seriously, we must view it as the origination of an entire system of kinds of organisms, *whose needs themselves arise in large measure from the character of the system*. Why were bats created at all? Why were any defenses against predation needed? Why did the Creator form this system of organisms, with their interrelated needs, needs that are met in such diverse and complicated ways?

Invocation of the word "design," or the passing reference to the satisfaction of "need," explains nothing. The needs are not given in advance of the design of structures to accommodate them, but are themselves encompassed in the design. Nor do we achieve any understanding of the adaptations and relationships of organisms until we see, at least in outline, what the Grand Plan of Creation might have been. This point has been clear at least since the seventeenth century. At the beginning of the *Discourse on Metaphysics*, Leibniz gave a beautiful exposition of it. He recognized that unless there are independent criteria of design, then praise of the Creator's design is worthless: "In saying, therefore, that things are not good according to any standard of goodness, but simply by the will of God, it seems to me that one destroys, without realizing it, all the love of God and all his glory; for why praise him for what he has done, if he would be equally praiseworthy in doing the contrary?" For Leibniz, to invoke "design" without saying what counts as good design is not only vacuous but blasphemous. Later in the same work, Leibniz developed the theme with a striking analogy. *Any* world can be conceived as regular ("designed") just as *any* array of points can be joined by a curve with some algebraic formula.

Why are contemporary Creationists silent about the Design? Because things did not go so well for their predecessors who tried to show how each kind of organism had been separately created with a special design. They found it hard to reconcile the observed features of some organisms with the attributes of the Creator. Contemporary Creationists have learned from these heroic—but fruitless—efforts.

So we encounter the strategy exemplified by Morris: Talk generally about design, pattern, purpose, and beauty in nature. There are many examples of adaptations that can be used—the wings of bats or "the amazing circulatory system," for example. But what happens if we press some more difficult cases? Well, if there seems to be no design or purpose to a feature (and if its presence cannot be understood as a modification of ancestral characters), one can always point out that some parts of the Creator's plan may be too vast for human understanding. *We* do not see what the design is, but there *is* design, nonetheless.

Since no plan of design has been specified, Creationists have available another all-purpose escape clause. But it is precisely this feature of Creation "science" that impugns its scientific credentials. To mumble that "the ways of the Creator are many and mysterious" may excuse one from identifying design in unlikely places. It is not to do science.

To provide scientific explanations, a Creationist would have to identify the plan implemented in the Creation. The trouble is that there are countless examples of properties of organisms that are hard to integrate into a coherent theory of design. There are two main types of difficulty, stemming from the frequent tinkerings of evolution and the equally common nastiness of nature. Let us begin with evolutionary tinkering. Structures already present are modified to answer to the organism's current needs. The result may be clumsy and inefficient, but it gets the job done. A beautiful example is the case of the Panda's thumb. Although they belong to the order Carnivora, giant pandas subsist on a diet of bamboo. In adapting to this diet they needed a means to grasp the shoots. Like other carnivores, they lack an opposable thumb. Instead, a bone in the wrist has become extended to serve as part of a device for grasping. It does not work well. Any competent engineer who wanted to design a giant panda could have done better. But it works well enough.

It is easy to multiply examples. Orchids have evolved complicated structures that discourage self-fertilization. These baroque contraptions are readily understood if we understand them as built out of the means available. Ruminants have acquired very complicated stomachs and a special digestive routine. These characteristics have enabled them to break down the cellulose layers that encase valuable proteins in many grasses. Their inner life could have been so much simpler had they been given the right enzymes from the start.

The second class of cases covers those in which, to put it bluntly, nature's ways are rather repulsive. There is nothing intrinsically beautiful about the scavenging of vultures, the copulatory behavior of the female praying mantis (who tries to bite off the head of the "lucky" male), or the ways in which some insects paralyze their prey. Let me describe one example in more detail. Some animals practice *coprophagy*. They produce feces that they eat. Rabbits, for example, devour their morning droppings. From an evolutionary perspective, the phenomenon is understood. Rabbits have solved the problem of breaking down cellulose by secreting bacteria toward the end of their intestinal tracts. Since the cellulose breakdown occurs at the end of the tract, much valuable protein and many valuable bacteria are liable to be lost in the feces. Hence the morning feces are eaten, the protein is metabolized, and the supply of bacteria is kept up. Creationists ought to find such phenomena puzzling. Surely an all-powerful, all-loving Creator, who *separately designed* each kind of living thing, could have found some less repugnant (and, I might add, more efficient) way to get the job done. (These examples are, of course, far less problematic for those who believe simply that the Creator set the universe in motion billions of years ago and that contemporary organisms are the latest product of the laws and conditions instituted in that original creative event.)

So far, I have concentrated on Creationist resources for answering questions about the characteristics of organisms and the similarities and differences among kinds of organisms. Let us now take a brief look at Creationist biogeography. Discussions of the distribution of animals are not extensive, but the following passage lays down the ground rules of the enterprise: "If the Flood was geographically universal, then all the air-breathers of the animal kingdom which were not in the Ark perished; and present-day animal distribution must be explained on the basis of migrations from the mountains of Ararat." One's first response is surely to ask: Why only one Ark? Why Ararat? (Why not New Jersey?) Of course, we know the answers to these questions. But what *scientific* evidence is there for supposing that there was just one vehicle for preserving land animals during the Deluge and that the subsequent radiation began from Mount Ararat? Creationists tie their hands behind their backs when they approach problems of biogeography with such gratuitous assumptions. There are obvious difficulties posed by the existence of peculiar groups of animals in particular places. The most striking example is the presence of marsupials as the dominant mammals of Australia. Given that all the land animals reemerged at the same place at the same time, why did Australia become a stronghold for marsupial mammals?

Whitcomb and Morris consider precisely this question. Much of their discussion is directed against claims made by one of their evangelical rivals, a geologist who advocated only a "local flood." However, they do indicate the main lines of their answer. In essence, they propose to accelerate the migration of organisms described in a standard evolutionary account. Here is the standard explanation of how the marsupials came to dominate Australia.

One central hypothesis is *placental chauvinism*: Marsupials are competitively inferior to the recent eutherian (placental) mammals. This hypothesis is confirmed by evidence of the consequences of introducing eutherian competitors into marsupial populations. It is usually suggested that the marsupials arose in North America about 130 million years ago and that they were able to compete successfully with the *early* eutherian mammals. The marsupials radiated extensively, established themselves in South America, and crossed over to Australia by way of Antarctica. (Australia, Antarctica, and South America become separated about 70 million years ago.) Their eutherian contemporaries did not reach Australia, so that the marsupials were able to diversify and attain their modern forms without competition from eutherians. Other marsupial strongholds (for example, South America) became vulnerable when new continental connections (the Isthmus of Panama) made it possible for the highly successful *recent* eutherians to invade. But Australia was sufficiently isolated, and a rich marsupial fauna developed there.

What Creationists propose to do is to squash something like this sequence of events into less than 100 centuries. Here, then, is the scenario. Noah's Ark lands on Mount Ararat. Out come the animals. They begin to compete for resources. Because they are inferior competitors, the poor marsupials are forced to disperse ever more widely. Spreading southward, they eventually manage to reach Australia. By the time the placentals have given chase, the land connection with Australia is severed. The marsupials are safe in their stronghold.

This is an exciting story, worthy of the best cowboy tradition. The trouble is that it has the marsupials arising in the wrong place, going by the wrong route, and competing with the wrong animals. Apart from that, the pace is just a bit too quick. If Creationists are going to explain fossil findings that, by their own lights, are post-Flood, they had better suppose that the marsupials reached Australia by travelling through Europe, North America, and South America. If they are going to insist that *contemporary* kinds of eutherian mammals emerged from the Ark, then they will have to explain why competition was not so severe that the marsupials were completely vanquished. Waiving these difficulties, let us consider the rate of the migration. When we think of marsupials, we naturally think of kangaroos—so we have the vision of successive generations of kangaroos hopping toward Australia. But kangaroos are relatively speedy. Some marsupials—wombats, koalas, and marsupial moles, for example—move very slowly. Koalas are sedentary animals, and it is difficult to coax them out of the eucalyptus trees on which they feed. Wombats, like marsupial moles, construct elaborate burrows, in which they spend their time and carry on their social relations. The idea of *any* of these animals engaging in a hectic dash around the globe is patently absurd. (On the evolutionary account, of course, they are all descendants of ancestral marsupials who had millions of years to reach their destination.)

Next we must face the question of why all the lucky refugees were *marsupials*. Surely, large numbers of animals would have found it prudent to disperse widely from the Ark. Why is it that the marsupials, almost *alone* among the mammals, were able to find the land connection to Australia and scurry across before other mammals in need of *Lebensraum* could catch up with them? And what about the conveniently disappearing land connection itself? Creationists seem to assume very rapid movements of land masses. Unlike orthodox geologists, who have independent evidence for slow separation of the continents, they maintain that, in a matter of centuries, a land connection that would support a full-scale exodus of marsupials presented an insuperable barrier to the pursuing eutherians. Indeed, if the marsupials were really *driven* across by eutherian competition, then we would expect the competition to be snapping at their heels—otherwise would not the wombat have stopped to dig a burrow, the koala have settled in a convenient tree? In that case, the bridge would have to be cut *very* quickly.

Once again, when the Creationist story is pressed for details, anomalies appear in droves. . . . What constraints govern hypotheses about past land connections? Since the Creationists have foresworn the apparatus of modern geology, their claims about the past relations of land masses seem invulnerable to independent checks. No worries about mechanisms for rapid land subsidence need perturb them, for they may always appeal to the after effects of the great cataclysm. Anything goes.

When Whitcomb and Morris wrote *The Genesis Flood* in 1961, Creationist strategy was somewhat different from that currently in vogue. Those were halcyon days, when Creationists did not mind admitting their reliance on unfathomable supernatural mechanisms. Perhaps they even hoped that a version of Creationism, explicitly based on the Genesis account, might find its place in science education. The following passage is far less guarded than more recent statements:

> The more we study the fascinating story of animal distribution around the earth, the more convinced we have become that this vast river of variegated life forms, moving ever outward from the Asiatic mainland, across the continents and seas, has not been a chance and haphazard phenomenon. Instead, *we see the hand of God guiding and directing these creatures in ways that man, with all his ingenuity, has never been able to fathom*, in order that the great commission to the postdiluvian animal kingdom might be carried out, and "that they may breed abundantly in the earth, and be fruitful, and multiply upon the earth" (Gen. 8 : 17).

There is the all-purpose escape clause. If the way in which the animals might have managed to leave the Ark and distribute themselves around the globe boggles your mind, do not tax yourself. They were guided, directed in ways that we are not able to understand.

Morris's subsequent writings take a different line about biogeographical questions. The subject is not discussed. Hence it is impossible to be sure that current Creationists would involve the actions of the Creator to help out when the going gets tough. Nevertheless, this is one more instance of the phenomenon that we have seen repeatedly. The alleged rival to evolutionary theory provides no definite problem-solving strategies that can be applied to give detailed answers to specific questions. . . .

Creation "science" is spurious science. To treat it as science we would have to overlook its intolerable vagueness. We would have to abandon large parts of well-established sciences (physics, chemistry, and geology, as well as evolutionary biology, are all candidates for revision). We would have to trade careful technical procedures for blind guesses, unified theories for motley collections of special techniques. Exceptional cases, whose careful pursuit has so often led to important turnings in the history of science, would be dismissed with a wave of the hand. Nor would there be any gains. There is not a single scientific question to which Creationism provides its own detailed problem solution. In short, Creationism could take a place among the sciences only if the substance and methods of contemporary science were mutilated to make room for a scientifically worthless doctrine. What price Creationism?

Arthur L. Caplan

Is Evolutionary Theory Scientific?

Arthur L. Caplan *is the Director of the Hastings Institute, a research institute for biomedical ethics. He has also done work in philosophy of science and in sociobiology.*

INTRODUCTION

If there is one philosophical spectre that has haunted Darwinian evolutionary theory—from the bilious initial assessments of various theologians and theologically minded scientists that greeted the publication of the *Origin of Species* in 1859, down to the present-day caterwauls and polemics of pseudoscientific creationists and fundamentalists at school board meetings, legislative hearings, and public rallies—it is the charge that Darwinian evolutionary theory is not really scientific. During the 125 years since Darwin's famous abstract of his book first went to press, the theory he propounded has been variously disparaged as wrong, satanic, untestable, ridden with ideology, and tautologous. Occasionally those offering such criticisms have deigned to advance a view concerning the nature of science such that the alleged scientific failings of Darwinism might be plainly revealed. More frequently, however, critics of Darwinian evolutionary theory have been content to blast away at the theory's supposed failings qua legitimate science while leaving the bases for their assorted charges unstated and, thus, irrefutable. There is no doubt that in the battle of rhetoric over matters of methodology the critics of Darwinism have fared somewhat better than its defenders.

If evolutionary theory in its contemporary guise—the so-called modern synthetic theory of evolution is to be promulgated by teachers in the public schools to hordes of innocent and, supposedly, gullible and malleable minds, then surely, generations of critics have argued, the theory must pass the rigorous conceptual muster accorded all theories in science. Since few parties among the disputants have given any serious consideration to what these rigorous conceptual standards might be, the critics seem to have Darwinists over a methodological barrel. Unless the proponents of Darwinism are able to say what distinguishes science from nonscience, they will find it difficult to defend the inclusion of the modern synthetic theory of evolution as science in textbooks, classrooms, or even grant applications. Since the proponents of Darwinism are usually biologists or social scientists, and not philosophers or historians of science, they are often quite ill-prepared to articulate the kinds of conceptual criteria and methodological attributes demanded by the critics. That many of the *critics* have no clue as to the properties distinguishing science from nonscience, much less nonsense, is not to the point. The inability of Darwinists to persuasively describe and defend their theory as scientific has, over the years, done much to discredit the theory in the eyes both of other scholars within the academy and among the general public.

IS DARWINIAN THEORY CIRCULAR?

Probably the most serious charge that has been leveled at the Darwinian theory of evolution is that the theory is a tautology. What critics contend by invoking this term is that Darwinian evolutionary theory is circular and, thus, lacks empirical content. The most favored target for this particular charge is the old saw that evolutionary theory ultimately explains evolution as resulting from a "natural selection of the fittest." The fittest, according to this analysis of the empirical content of the theory, are defined solely in terms of those organisms who do, as a matter of fact, survive. The circular or tautological character of evolutionary theory, either *sensu* Darwin or in its contemporary form, is said to be evident from the fact that the key explanatory device utilized in the theory—natural selection—is, by definitional sleight of hand, made synonymous with both fitness and survival. If those creatures observed to survive on earth today do so because they are fit, and if the only way available for assessing their fitness is their survival, then natural selection, the explanatory lynchpin of all Darwinian evolutionary accounts, is nothing but an elaborate semantic obfuscation—a kind of conceptual shell game where the shells are natural selection, fitness, and survival.

The charge of tautology, if true, would be a devastating indictment of the claim that evolutionary theory is acceptable as science. Whatever else scientific theories or scientific propositions may be, they surely must possess some empirical content. Tautologies have no such content. If evolutionary theory did actually utilize a truism to explain the phenomena of evolution in the organic world, there would be little reason for attending to it seriously as an explanatory account, much less for teaching it to children and college freshmen.

However, the claim that evolutionary theory rests on the necessarily tautologous definition of natural selection is an utter straw man. The easiest way to see the total emptiness of this criticism is to examine exactly what the theory of evolution *claims* in attempting to explain the facts of evolution. By examining the version of evolutionary theory propounded by Darwin in his *Origin of Species* and its subsequent refinement and modification by later researchers in evolutionary biology, it is possible to see both the nontautological character of Darwinian theory and the truly scientific character of Darwinian explanations. . . .

DARWIN'S EXPLANATORY SCHEMA

Critics of Darwinian evolutionary theories have been manifestly schizophrenic over the years in their assessments of scientific efforts to explain the facts and patterns of evolution. On the one hand, some critics insist that evolutionary theories are not testable, and that the bog of circularity manifested by all the talk of fitness, survival, selection, and adaptation makes all discussion of tests, falsification, and verification absurd. On the other hand, other critics have been concerned to note that Darwinian evolutionary theories are simply not equal to the task of explaining the data of nature. No theory, in their opinion, can adequately explain the exquisite perfection of the human eye for seeing, or the delicate symbiotic relationships that exist between many creatures. Darwinian theories are, in the eyes of its critics, caught in a methodological bind between a rock and a very hard place—too circular and opaque to be tested, and yet too inadequate and simple-minded to be powerful enough to account for the facts. Fortunately neither of the horns of this supposed dilemma is very pointed because, as the historical development of evolutionary theory plainly shows, Darwinian theories have been both testable and quite powerful.

In order to see the amenability of Darwinian theories to test and proof, it is necessary that some attention be given over to the content of the theory. Nowhere in any of the writings of Darwin or his scientific legatees is anything even vaguely reminiscent of a truism or tautology advanced as a theory of evolution. It is true that the explanation of evolution (as fact and process) in terms of the "survival of the fittest" is tautological when the fittest are defined as "those that survive." Unfortunately, those who have over the decades railed against this hapless emasculation have never noticed that it bears no relationship whatsoever to any theory Darwin or subsequent generations of evolutionists ever propounded.

Darwin's *Origin of Species* is as good a place as any to locate the gist of Darwinian evolutionary theory. In this book Darwin begins by noting three facts: First, the process of evolution is nonrandom. This is exemplified by the limited nature of organic variation in all parts of the globe, relative to what might be empirically possible. Second and third, by utilizing certain time-tested breeding tricks and techniques, some human beings have been able both to duplicate the fact of evolution and to extend the constraints on variation to be found in nature. Surely, Darwin argues, if pigeon fanciers and sheep farmers have been able to produce systematic changes in the behavior and appearance of domestic animals, then analogous mechanisms may have been at work in producing the ordered pattern of changes to be found in the natural world.

In addition to these facts, Darwin offers a number of other observations about life on earth. A key observation is that there ought to be many more organisms alive on the planet than there in fact are. Organisms, Darwin remarks, from rabbits to humans have tremendous reproductive capacities. Even the elephant, which Darwin cites as an example of one of the slowest breeding of all known creatures, is, in principle, capable of reproducing 19 million of its own kind in a period of no more than 750 years. Given the breeding inclinations and mighty reproductive capacities of insects, marine life, and many mammals, the entire earth ought to be full to the hilt with creatures. Yet this is not so. Moreover, Darwin notes, it is a matter of empirical fact that some varieties of creature are more abundant than others in patterns that do not always correlate with their reproductive abilities.

Darwin's hunch, fueled by his reading of Malthus on the dismal course of human history, is that limits on the gross numbers of creatures that can occupy the planet are set by the type and quantity of resources available for their use in various parts of the globe. These observations led Darwin, in the early chapters of the *Origin*, to propose a theoretical explanation for the empirically observable patterns of variation in the quantity and kinds of life on earth. His analysis runs as follows:

The Argument for a Struggle for Existence

Empirically verified principles—

(P1) *Principle of Reproduction:*   Nearly all organisms possess both the capacity and the drive to reproduce themselves at rapid rates.

(P2) *Principle of Dependence:*   All organisms depend on natural resources such as air, water, and energy for life.

To these principles Darwin adds three factual observations:

Factual observations—

(F1) There are a limited number of places on the earth where natural resources exist.

(F2) The locations where natural resources can be found fluctuate over time.

(F3) A good deal of variation exists in the form and behavior of organisms.

Darwin then argues that the facts he has cited, when combined with the principles he had discerned to be operative in nature, lead directly to two important conclusions:

Logically necessary conclusions derived from principles and facts—

(C1) There must obtain a competition or a "struggle for existence" among organisms for natural resources.

(C2) The struggle for existence is a possible source for the patterns of quantity and variation found among the organisms dwelling on the earth.

The struggle for existence, so beloved of critics of evolutionary theory as the quintessential tautology, is not a tautology at all. Rather, competition or struggle is a logical consequence of certain principles and facts. Darwin argues that, if it is true that organisms can reproduce quickly and that resources are finite, struggle and competition are inevitable. This conclusion is generated from premises that say nothing about fitness, selection, or adaptation. The struggle for existence is as contingent a fact as one could ever hope for—diminish reproductive capacity or increase resources, and the struggle for existence disappears!

But Darwin knew that there were more puzzling uniformities in nature than the regulation of animal numbers. Some organisms simply fare better than others in certain habitats. Some organisms have fared so poorly, in fact, that all that remains of them are their bones!

Darwin observed the great variety that exists among organisms and asked what the effect of such variation would be in the context of a struggle for existence. Furthermore, he observed a "strong tendency" for organisms to produce offspring that closely resemble their parents. If, Darwin reasoned, some traits or behaviors were more advantageous than others in terms of obtaining resources; and if it were true that organisms tended to pass along similar traits and behaviors to their offspring; then, in the context of a struggle for existence for scarce resources, a natural selection would occur tending to produce animals and plants with the traits and behaviors most likely to be advantageous in obtaining those scarce resources.

Schematically, the second part of Darwin's theory of evolution can be summarized as follows:

The Argument for Natural Selection

Empirically verified principles—

(P1) Certain traits and behaviors will allow organisms that possess them to obtain more resources than organisms that do not.

(P2) Organisms tend to reproduce similar organisms.

(P3) Organisms possessing advantageous traits and behaviors will tend to have higher survival and, thus, reproductive success than organisms possessing less advantageous traits and behaviors.

Factual observations—

(F1) A struggle for existence exists in nature.

(F2) A great deal of variation exists in the traits and behaviors possessed by organisms.

(F3) Some traits and behaviors, when assessed relative to other traits and behaviors, can be classified as advantageous, neutral, or disadvantageous in securing scarce natural resources.

Logically necessary conclusion deducible from principles and facts—

(C1) There will be a natural selection among the variegated traits and behaviors of organisms tending to favor an increase in organisms possessing the most advantageous traits and behaviors relative to those possessed by other organisms.

Natural selection, to put the matter succinctly, is a logical consequence of the combination of a struggle for existence with certain principles of inheritance and variation. This schematization of Darwin's theory, as presented in the *Origin*, makes plain the relationship between the struggle for existence and natural selection. The concepts are not related via definitional fiat, as hordes of critics have erroneously maintained; rather, natural selection is the logical consequence of the struggle for existence when supplemented with other valid principles and facts. Thus, while it is true that a relationship does exist between the struggle for existence and natural selection, it is not of the circular sort so dear to the hearts of pseudoscientific creationists and other methodologically befuddled critics of Darwinian theory.

Darwin used this two-part theory to explain the innumerable facts and peculiar uniformities in nature. He argued against his fellow creationists, catastrophists, and Lamarckians that natural selection was the key causal mechanism driving the evolutionary process. One need not posit disasters of a Divine or natural sort to explain the fact that the number of animals and plants is not as large as it could be: The struggle for existence is a sufficient natural check on animal numbers. And one need not resort to Lamarckian influences in hereditary or Divine design to explain the regularities and patterns of variation found in nature, past or present. The interaction of a tendency toward reproductive constancy with differences in the utility of organic traits and behaviors in securing resources will produce a natural selection among organisms in which some organisms will fare better in the struggle for existence than will others.

Darwin's theory was, in its own time, recognized by many scientists as far preferable to its theoretical competitors—creationism, catastrophism, and Lamarckianism. All of Darwin's principles and alleged facts were susceptible to empirical verification and test. Indeed, the bulk of the *Origin of Species* is given over to just such an enterprise. The theoretical alternatives to Darwin's theory, by contrast, were truly untestable (as in the case of Biblical creationism), or relied on a steady stream of *ad hoc* events: catastrophes, upheavals, fortuitous environment/heredity interactions, and so on.

Nevertheless, despite the fact that Darwin's theory of evolution had far more empirical support than its available rivals, there were many problems and puzzles confronting the first version of the theory. Not the least of these was the question of how new variations could appear in nature once selection began to occur. Advantageous traits and behaviors would be favored, but once organisms lacking these had been eliminated, evolution would and should have come to a grinding halt. Moreover, as Darwin himself noted, some organisms existed that did not reproduce at all, such as neuter insects and sterile hybrids. How could Darwin's theory, resting on principles of inheritance and advantage, explain the persistence of such creatures, which certainly were at a distinct reproductive disadvantage relative to their fertile peers? Darwin's theory was hardly untestable; indeed, Darwin was keenly aware that a number of facts about evolution appeared to falsify his theory.

THE UNIFYING POWER OF DARWINISM

The fact that certain puzzles and difficulties existed for Darwinian theory, and that the theory nevertheless gained wide acceptance in many scientific circles, reveals something of central importance for understanding the scientific status of any theory. The Darwinism of Darwin's day can be seen as scientific for a number of reasons. First, it attempted to explain a number of facts and generalizations about empirical events in the world. Second, it attempted to explain these facts by means of a set of verifiable principles and assumptions. Third, it attempted to explain a set of diverse facts and disparate empirical generalizations by means of a single style or pattern of explanation. Trends in the fossil record, limits on animal numbers, regularities in the distribution of organisms around the globe, and the adaptedness of organisms to their environments could all be explained in Darwin's theory by the same rough set of principles, assumptions, and conclusions. The struggle for existence and the process of natural selection were utilized in every Darwinian account of organic evolution. They provide the distinctive core or pattern of Darwinian explanation; and, as such, they provide a means by which apparently unrelated phenomena can be linked to a set of common causes.

It is this unifying power of Darwinism—the ability to group what had previously been viewed as unconnected and disparate aspects of evolution under a single explanatory framework—that guaranteed Darwinian evolutionary theory a hearing as an exemplar of scientific theorizing. For theories, in order to be scientific, need not only to be about empirical facts, and to possess testable and confirmable premises and assumptions, but should also allow for the unification of seemingly unrelated and diverse facts. It is this unifying power of Darwin's explanatory schema as first evidenced in his arguments in the *Origin of Species* that provides the vital psychological impact requisite in any good scientific theory. Darwin's theory allows us to see the vast morass of facts and patterns present in nature as the outcome of a few simple factors—what scientists often refer to as the elegance and power of good theories. As was the case with Newton's celestial mechanics and Lyell's uniformitarian geology, Darwin's theory allowed scientists to feel as if they understood something about the world that they had not realized prior to the theory's formulation, that the diverse facts of evolution were the by-products of a set of simple common causes. Facticity, testability, and unificatory power are the hallmarks of sound scientific theories. While a theory possessing these attributes may be inadequate, flawed, or simply false, it is, nonetheless, still scientific. While Darwinism had its problems and flaws, it also had the central virtue of unificatory power—a virtue sadly lacking in many of Darwinism's theoretical competitors both in his time and today. Divine creation, whether of the sort depicted in Genesis or in the religious texts of other cultures, is not in any sense a testable theory. But just as important, the invocation of a deity to explain the facts and processual patterns of evolution provides no unification to the random facts and patterns of nature. Darwinism does. If some version of Darwin's argument is sound, then the seemingly disparate, inchoate, murky mass of phenomena we recognize as the facts and patterns of evolution become comprehensible as the related outcomes of a single set of principles and assumptions—a transformation that is characteristic of and distinctive to scientific theorizing. While critics of Darwinism have tended to focus solely on testability as the only criterion capable of distinguishing science from nonscience, they fail to realize that the unificatory power of a successful pattern of explanation is as important in attempting to draw such a distinction. When a theory manifests a unificatory pattern as powerful as that found in Darwinian theory's struggle for existence and natural selection, then scientists will go to great lengths (in the case of Darwinism a sustained effort of 125 years thus far) to preserve and defend the soundness of that basic pattern of explanation against apparent counter-examples, puzzles, and even empirical refutations.

IS MODERN EVOLUTIONARY THEORY DARWINIAN?

The issue of falsifiability has preoccupied critics of Darwinism since the inception of the theory. In part, this is a result of an undue attention in certain philosophy-of-science circles to matters of testability as the only means by which science can be distinguished from non-science and, by implication, sense from nonsense. As I have tried to suggest in pointing to the unificatory power of Darwinism vis-à-vis empirical biological facts and low-level generalizations, testability is not all that matters in the determination of what will and ought to be counted as science. Nevertheless, testability is certainly a factor to be taken into account in assessing any proposition or theory that purports to be scientific. It is interesting to see how Darwinian theory has fared on this basis since Darwin's time, in light of the insistent claims of the theory's critics that it is not testable.

If we consider the version of the theory as I have reconstructed it from Darwin's presentation in the *Origin*, then strictly speaking it can be said that subsequent research and field investigations by many scientists have proved the theory *false* many times over.

Darwin's original theory claimed that all regularities in the distribution of organic variation could be totally explained by principles concerning (1) a tendency to constancy in inheritance; (2) the dependency of organisms on natural resources; and (3) some facts about scarcity, character variation, and relative advantage. It is not true that these factors suffice to explain all the regularities manifested in nature. Darwin offered no laws about patterns of inheritance resulting from the existence of genes and chromosomes. The laws governing these entities were rediscovered long after Darwin's death and were not made a part of his theory until well into the twentieth century. Indeed, for a short period at the turn of the century, many scientists saw Mendelism and its laws as a viable theoretical alternative to Darwinism for explaining all of the facts and processes of evolution.

Mutation and recombination, key sources for the production of new variations in nature, were also not a part of Darwin's original views concerning inheritance. While the discovery of these processes solved one of the central problems confronting Darwin and his early supporters (the problem of where new varieties came from to replace those lost through natural selection), the fact that Darwinism makes no mention of them reveals the theory to be quite inaccurate—not only testable, but false!

Darwin's theory has proved to be inadequate in yet another way. In his theory, the bulk of organic evolution occurs as a result of *anagenesis*—evolution within a particular species lineage. But as later generations of field researchers have convincingly demonstrated, it is *cladogenesis*—the splitting of an interbreeding population into groups via natural barriers (such as the formation of mountains or the rerouting of rivers), or via other processes—that is central to the phenomena of the diversity of organisms and their evolution. Darwin's theory assumed that most evolutionary change occurred as a result of the slow accumulation of advantageous traits by various populations of organisms (anagenesis). We now know that this process, while important, is not sufficient for explaining many important aspects of evolutionary change. Contemporary models of speciation, with their emphasis on drift, isolation, and character displacement, hardly resemble the explanatory narratives derivable from the arguments given in Darwin's version of evolutionary theory.

Many other illustrations could be given of various ways in which Darwin's original outline of an explanatory theory has been found inadequate or simply erroneous. If the history of evolutionary theorizing since Darwin's day shows anything, it surely reveals that the theory has constantly been subject to modifications, alterations, refinements, and amplifications—hardly the characteristics one would expect of an untestable theory. Indeed, the changes that have been made to Darwin's theory since he first advanced it—the addition of a theory of genetics; the discovery of the importance of mutation and recombination; the realization that barriers to gene flow are key elements in understanding speciation; the refinement of Darwin's notions of competition, adaptation, species, and character traits; and so on—reveal that the real question that students of evolutionary theory must address is not whether the theory is testable, but whether the current modern synthetic theory of evolution retains enough commonality with Darwin's original theory to be still classified as Darwinian.

Ultimately, the answer to this question will have to depend on the degree to which later theories preserve what I have termed the "pattern" of explanation present in Darwin's version of evolutionary theory, his arguments for the necessity of a struggle for existence, and the inevitability of the occurrence of natural selection. The issue of whether later theories are merely refinements and extensions of Darwin's basic theory, or are so different that they have evolved into an entirely new kind of evolutionary theory, cannot be settled in this reading.

What can, however, be settled is the issue of the scientific status of Darwinian evolutionary theories. As the history of the theory shows, Darwinism is eminently testable. As the analysis of Darwin's own arguments shows, there is nothing at all tautologous about the theory. As the analysis of the logic of Darwin's original arguments reveals, the theory possesses a robust, unifying, and elegant pattern of explanation that succeeds in linking a variety of puzzling facts and empirical generalizations. It may be true that Darwinian theory is, as some have argued, Satanic, ridden with ideology, and/or inadequate as an explanation of evolution. But, it is surely also true that Darwinian theory is scientific.

Isaac Asimov

Armies of the Night

Isaac Asimov *was born in the Soviet Union and raised in Brooklyn, New York. He is a legendary writer of science and science fiction, having published over 340 books. He is also a former Professor of Biochemistry at Boston University.*

Scientists thought it was settled.

The universe, they had decided, is about 20 billion years old, and Earth itself is 4.5 billion years old. Simple forms of life came into being more than three billion years ago, having formed spontaneously from nonliving matter. They grew more complex through slow evolutionary processes and the first hominid ancestors of humanity appeared more than four million years ago. *Homo sapiens* itself—the present human species, people like you and me—has walked the earth for at least 50,000 years.

But apparently it isn't settled. There are Americans who believe that the earth is only about 6,000 years old; that human beings and all other species were brought into existence by a divine Creator as eternally separate varieties of beings, and that there has been no evolutionary process.

They are creationists—they call themselves "scientific" creationists—and they are a growing power in the land, demanding that schools be forced to teach their views. State legislatures, mindful of votes, are beginning to succumb to the pressure. In perhaps 15 states, bills have been introduced, putting forth the creationist point of view, and in others, strong movements are gaining momentum. In Arkansas, a law requiring that the teaching of creationism receive equal time was passed this spring and is scheduled to go into effect in September 1982, though the American Civil Liberties Union has filed suit on behalf of a group of clergymen, teachers and parents to overturn it. And a California father named Kelly Segraves, the director of the Creation-Science Research Center, sued to have public-school science classes taught that there are other theories of creation besides evolution, and that one of them was the Biblical version. The suit came to trial in March, and the judge ruled that educators must distribute a policy statement to schools and textbook publishers explaining that the theory of evolution should not be seen as "the ultimate cause of origins." Even in New York, the Board of Education has delayed since January in making a final decision, expected this month, on whether schools will be required to include the teaching of creationism in their curriculums.

The Rev. Jerry Falwell, the head of the Moral Majority, who supports the creationist view from his television pulpit, claims that he has 17 million to 25 million viewers (though Arbitron places the figure at a much more modest 1.6 million). But there are 66 electronic ministries which have a total audience of about 20 million. And in parts of the country where the Fundamentalists predominate—the so-called Bible Belt—creationists are in the majority.

They make up a fervid and dedicated group, convinced beyond argument of both their rightness and righteousness. Faced with an apathetic and falsely secure majority, smaller groups have used intense pressure and forceful campaigning—as the creationists do—and have succeeded in disrupting and taking over whole societies.

Yet, though creationists seem to accept the literal truth of the Biblical story of creation, this does not mean that all religious people are creationists. There are millions of Catholics, Protestants and Jews who think of the Bible as a source of spiritual truth and accept much of it as symbolically rather than literally true. They do not consider the Bible to be a textbook of science, even in intent, and have no problem teaching evolution in their secular institutions.

To those who are trained in science, creationism seems like a bad dream, a sudden reliving of a nightmare, a renewed march of an army of the night risen to challenge free thought and enlightenment.

The scientific evidence for the age of the earth and for the evolutionary development of life seems overwhelming to scientists. How can anyone question it? What are the arguments the creationists use? What is the "science" that makes their views "scientific"? Here are some of them:

THE ARGUMENT FROM ANALOGY

A watch implies a watchmaker, say the creationists. If you were to find a beautifully intricate watch in the desert, far from habitation, you would be sure that it had been fashioned by human hands and somehow left there. It would pass the bounds of credibility that it had simply formed, spontaneously, from the sands of the desert.

By analogy, then, if you consider humanity, life, earth and the universe, all infinitely more intricate than a watch, you can believe far less easily that it "just happened." It, too, like the watch, must have been fashioned, but by more-than-human hands—in short by a divine Creator.

This argument seems unanswerable, and it has been used (even though not often explicitly expressed) ever since the dawn of consciousness. To have explained to prescientific human beings that the wind and the rain and the sun follow the laws of nature and do so blindly and without a guiding hand would have been utterly unconvincing to them. In fact, it might well have gotten you stoned to death as a blasphemer.

There are many aspects of the universe that still cannot be explained satisfactorily by science; but ignorance implies only ignorance that may someday be conquered. To surrender to ignorance and call it God has always been premature, and it remains premature today.

In short, the complexity of the universe—and one's inability to explain it in full—is not in itself an argument for a Creator.

THE ARGUMENT FROM GENERAL CONSENT

Some creationists point out that belief in a Creator is general among all peoples and all cultures. Surely this unanimous craving hints at a great truth. There would be no unanimous belief in a lie.

General belief, however, is not really surprising. Nearly every people on earth that considers the existence of the world assumes it to have been created by a god or gods. And each group invents full details for the story. No two creation tales are alike. The Greeks, the Norsemen, the Japanese, the Hindus, the American Indians and so on and so on all have their own creation myths, and all of these are recognized by Americans of Judeo-Christian heritage as "just myths."

The ancient Hebrews also had a creation tale—two of them, in fact. There is a primitive Adam-and-Eve-in-Paradise story, with man created first, then animals, then woman. There is also a poetic tale of God fashioning the universe in six days, with animals preceding man, and man and woman created together.

These Hebrew myths are not inherently more credible than any of the others, but they are our myths. General consent, of course, proves nothing: There can be a unanimous belief in something that isn't so. The universal opinion over thousands of years that the earth was flat never flattened its spherical shape by one inch.

THE ARGUMENT BY BELITTLEMENT

Creationists frequently stress the fact that evolution is "only a theory," giving the impression that a theory is an idle guess. A scientist, one gathers, arising one morning with nothing particular to do, decides that perhaps the moon is made of Roquefort cheese and instantly advances the Roquefort-cheese theory.

A theory (as the word is used by scientists) is a detailed description of some facet of the universe's workings that is based on long observation and, where possible, experiment. It is the result of careful reasoning from those observations and experiments and has survived the critical study of scientists generally.

For example, we have the description of the cellular nature of living organisms (the "cell theory"); of objects attracting each other according to a fixed rule (the "theory of gravitation"); of energy behaving in discrete bits (the "quantum theory"); of light traveling through a vacuum at a fixed measurable velocity (the "theory of relativity"), and so on.

All are theories; all are firmly founded; all are accepted as valid descriptions of this or that aspect of the universe. They are neither guesses nor speculations. And no theory is better founded, more closely examined, more critically argued and more thoroughly accepted, than the theory of evolution. If it is "only" a theory, that is all it has to be.

Creationism, on the other hand, is not a theory. There is no evidence, in the scientific sense, that supports it. Creationism, or at least the particular variety accepted by many Americans, is an expression of early Middle Eastern legend. It is fairly described as "only a myth."

THE ARGUMENT FROM IMPERFECTION

Creationists, in recent years, have stressed the "scientific" background of their beliefs. They point out that there are scientists who base their creationists beliefs on a careful study of geology, paleontology and biology and produce "textbooks" that embody those beliefs.

Virtually the whole scientific corpus of creationism, however, consists of the pointing out of imperfections in the evolutionary view. The creationists insist, for example, that evolutionists cannot show true transition states between species in the fossil evidence; that age determinations through radioactive breakdown are uncertain; that alternate interpretations of this or that piece of evidence are possible, and so on.

Because the evolutionary view is not perfect and is not agreed upon in every detail by all scientists, creationists argue that evolution is false and that scientists, in supporting evolution, are basing their views on blind faith and dogmatism.

To an extent, the creationists are right here. The details of evolution are not perfectly known. Scientists have been adjusting and modifying Charles Darwin's suggestions since he advanced this theory of the origin of species through natural selection back in 1859. After all, much has been learned about the fossil record and about physiology, microbiology, biochemistry, ethology and various other branches in life science in the last 125 years, and it is to be expected that we can improve on Darwin. In fact, we have improved on him.

Nor is the process finished. It can never be, as long as human beings continue to question and to strive for better answers.

The details of evolutionary theory are in dispute precisely because scientists are not devotees of blind faith and dogmatism. They do not accept even as great a thinker as Darwin without question, nor do they accept any idea, new or old, without thorough argument. Even after accepting an idea, they stand ready to overrule it, if appropriate new evidence arrives. If, however, we grant that a theory is imperfect and that details remain in dispute, does that disprove the theory as a whole?

Consider, I drive a car, and you drive a car. I do not know exactly how an engine works. Perhaps you do not either. And it may be that our hazy and approximate ideas of the workings of an automobile are in conflict. Must we then conclude from this disagreement that an automobile does not run, or that it does not exist? Or, if our senses force us to conclude that an automobile does exist and run, does that mean it is pulled by an invisible horse, since our engine theory is imperfect?

However much scientists argue their differing beliefs in details of evolutionary theory, or in the interpretation of the necessarily imperfect fossil record, they firmly accept the evolutionary process itself.

THE ARGUMENT FROM DISTORTED SCIENCE

Creationists have learned enough scientific terminology to use it in their attempts to disprove evolution. They do this in numerous ways, but the most common example, at least in the mail I receive, is the repeated assertion that the second law of thermodynamics demonstrates the evolutionary process to be impossible.

In kindergarten terms, the second law of thermodynamics says that all spontaneous change is in the direction of increasing disorder—that is, in a "downhill" direction. There can be no spontaneous buildup of the complex from the simple, therefore, because that would be moving "uphill." According to the creationist argument, since, by the evolutionary process, complex forms of life evolve from simple forms, that process defies the second law, so creationism must be true.

Such an argument implies that this clearly visible fallacy is somehow invisible to scientists, who must therefore be flying in the face of the second law through sheer perversity.

Scientists, however, do know about the second law and they are not blind. It's just that an argument based on kindergarten terms is suitable only for kindergartens.

To lift the argument a notch above the kindergarten level, the second law of thermodynamics applies to a "closed system"—that is, to a system that does not gain energy from without, or lose energy to the outside. The only truly closed system we know of is the universe as a whole.

Within a closed system, there are subsystems that can gain complexity spontaneously, provided there is a greater loss of complexity in another interlocking subsystem. The overall change then is a complexity loss in line with the dictates of the second law.

Evolution can proceed and build up the complex from the simple, thus moving uphill, without violating the second law, as long as another interlocking part of the system—the sun, which delivers energy to the earth continually—moves downhill (as it does) at a much faster rate than evolution moves uphill.

If the sun were to cease shining, evolution would stop and so, eventually, would life.

Unfortunately, the second law is a subtle concept which most people are not accustomed to dealing with, and it is not easy to see the fallacy in the creationist distortion.

There are many other "scientific" arguments used by creationists, some taking quite clever advantage of present areas of dispute in evolutionary theory, but every one of them is as disingenuous as the second-law argument.

The "scientific" arguments are organized into special creationist textbooks, which have all the surface appearance of the real thing, and which school systems are being heavily pressured to accept. They are written by people who have not made any mark as scientists, and, while they discuss geology, paleontology and biology with correct scientific terminology, they are devoted almost entirely to raising doubts over the legitimacy of the evidence and reasoning underlying evolutionary thinking on the assumption that this leaves creationism as the only possible alternative.

Evidence actually in favor of creationism is not presented, of course, because none exists other than the word of the Bible, which it is current creationist strategy not to use.

THE ARGUMENT FROM IRRELEVANCE

Some creationists put all matters of scientific evidence to one side and consider all such things irrelevant. The Creator, they say, brought life and the earth and the entire universe into being 6,000 years ago or so, complete with all the evidence for an eons-long evolutionary development. The fossil record, the decaying radioactivity, the receding galaxies were all created as they are, and the evidence they present is an illusion.

Of course, this argument is itself irrelevant, for it can neither be proved nor disproved. It is not an argument, actually, but a statement. I can say that the entire universe was created two minutes ago, complete with all its history books describing a nonexistent past in detail, and with every living person equipped with a full memory; you, for instance, in the process of reading this article in midstream with a memory of what you had read in the beginning— which you had not really read.

What kind of a Creator would produce a universe containing so intricate an illusion? It would mean that the Creator formed a universe that contained human beings whom He had endowed with the faculty of curiosity and the ability to reason. He supplied those human beings with an enormous amount of subtle and cleverly consistent evidence designed to mislead them and cause them to be convinced that the universe was created 20 billion years ago and developed by evolutionary processes that included the creation and development of life on Earth.

Why?

Does the Creator take pleasure in fooling us? Does it amuse Him to watch us go wrong? Is it part of a test to see if human beings will deny their senses and their reason in order to cling to myth? Can it be that the Creator is a cruel and malicious prankster, with a vicious and adolescent sense of humor?

THE ARGUMENT FROM AUTHORITY

The Bible says that God created the world in six days, and the Bible is the inspired word of God. To the average creationist this is all that counts. All other arguments are merely a tedious way of countering the propaganda of all those wicked humanists, agnostics and atheists who are not satisfied with the clear word of the Lord.

The creationist leaders do not actually use that argument because that would make their argument a religious one, and they would not be able to use it in fighting a secular school system. They have to borrow the clothing of science, no matter how badly it fits and call themselves "scientific" creationists. They also speak only of the "Creator," and never mention that this Creator is the God of the Bible.

We cannot, however, take this sheep's clothing seriously. However much the creationist leaders might hammer away at their "scientific" and "philosophical" points, they would be helpless and a laughing stock if that were all they had.

It is religion that recruits their squadrons. Tens of millions of Americans, who neither know or understand the actual arguments for—or even against—evolution, march in the army of the night with their Bibles held high. And they are a strong and frightening force, impervious to, and immunized against, the feeble lance of mere reason.

Even if I am right and the evolutionists' case is very strong, have not creationists, whatever the emptiness of their case, a right to be heard?

If their case is empty, isn't it perfectly safe to discuss it since the emptiness would then be apparent?

Why, then, are evolutionists so reluctant to have creationism taught in the public schools on an equal basis with evolutionary theory? Can it be that the evolutionists are not as confident of their case as they pretend. Are they afraid to allow youngsters a clear choice?

First, the creationists are somewhat less than honest in their demand for equal time. It is not their views that are repressed: Schools are by no means the only place in which the dispute between creationism and evolutionary theory is played out.

There are the churches, for instance, which are a much more serious influence on most Americans than the schools. To be sure, many churches are quite liberal, have made their peace with science and find it easy to live with scientific advance—even with evolution. But many of the less modish and citified churches are bastions of creationism.

The influence of the church is naturally felt in the home, in the newspapers and in all of surrounding society. It makes itself felt in the nation as a whole, even religiously liberal areas, in thousands of subtle ways; in the nature of holiday observance, in expressions of patriotic fervor, even in total irrelevancies. In 1968, for example, a team of astronauts circling the moon were instructed to read the first few verses of Genesis as though NASA felt it had to placate the public lest they rage against the violation of the firmament. At the present time, even the current President of the United States has expressed his creationist sympathies.

It is only in school that American youngsters in general are ever likely to hear any reasoned exposition of the evolutionary viewpoint. They might find such a viewpoint in books, magazines, newspapers or even, on occasion, on television. But church and family can easily censor printed matter or television. Only the school is beyond their control.

But only just barely beyond. Even though schools are now allowed to teach evolution, teachers are beginning to be apologetic about it, knowing full well their jobs are at the mercy of school boards upon which creationists are a stronger and stronger influence.

Then, too, in schools, students are not required to believe what they learn about evolution—merely to parrot it back on tests. If they fail to do so, their punishment is nothing more than the loss of a few points on a test or two.

In the creationist churches, however, the congregation is required to believe. Impressionable youngsters, taught that they will go to hell if they listen to the evolutionary doctrine, are not likely to listen in comfort or to believe if they do.

Therefore, creationists, who control the church and the society they live in and who face the public school as the only place where evolution is even briefly mentioned in a possibly favorable way, find they cannot stand even so minuscule a competition and demand "equal time."

Do you suppose their devotion to "fairness" is such that they will give equal time to evolution in their churches?

Second, the real danger is the manner in which creationists want their "equal time."

In the scientific world, there is free and open competition of ideas, and even a scientist whose suggestions are not accepted is nevertheless free to continue to argue his case.

In this free and open competition of ideas, creationism has clearly lost. It has been losing in fact, since the time of Copernicus four and a half centuries ago. But creationists, placing myth above reason, refuse to accept the decision and are now calling on the Government to force their views on the schools in lieu of the free expression of ideas. Teachers must be forced to present creationism as though it has equal intellectual respectability with evolutionary doctrine.

What a precedent this sets.

If the Government can mobilize its policemen and its prisons to make certain that teachers give creationism equal time, they can next use force to make sure that teachers declare creationism the victor so that evolution will be evicted from the classroom altogether.

We will have established the full groundwork, in other words, for legally enforced ignorance and for totalitarian thought control.

And what if the creationists win? They might, you know, for there are millions who, faced with the choice between science and their interpretation of the Bible, will choose the Bible and reject science, regardless of the evidence.

This is not entirely because of a traditional and unthinking reverence for the literal words of the Bible; there is also a pervasive uneasiness—even an actual fear—of science that will drive even those who care little for Fundamentalism into the arms of the creationists. For one thing, science is uncertain. Theories are subject to revision; observations are open to a variety of interpretations, and scientists quarrel among themselves. This is disillusioning for those untrained in the scientific method, who thus turn to the rigid certainty of the Bible instead. There is something comfortable about a view that allows for no deviation and that spares you the painful necessity of having to think.

Second, science is complex and chilling. The mathematical language of science is understood by very few. The vistas it presents are scary—an enormous universe ruled by chance and impersonal rules, empty and uncaring, ungraspable and vertiginous. How comfortable to turn instead to a small world, only a few thousand years old, and under God's personal and immediate care; a world in which you are His peculiar concern and where He will not consign you to hell if you are careful to follow every word of the Bible as interpreted for you by your television preacher.

Third, science is dangerous. There is no question but that poison gas, genetic engineering and nuclear weapons and power stations are terrifying. It may be that civilization is falling apart and the world we know is coming to an end. In that case, why not turn to religion and look forward to the Day of Judgment, in which you and your fellow believers will be lifted into external bliss and have the added joy of watching the scoffers and disbelievers writhe forever in torment.

So why might they not win?

There are numerous cases of societies in which the armies of the night have ridden triumphantly over minorities in order to establish a powerful orthodoxy which dictates official thought. Invariably, the triumphant ride is toward long-range disaster.

Spain dominated Europe and the world in the 16th century, but in Spain orthodoxy came first, and all divergence of opinion was ruthlessly suppressed. The result was that Spain settled back into blankness and did not share in the scientific, technological and commercial ferment that bubbled up in other nations of Western Europe. Spain remained an intellectual backwater for centuries.

In the late 17th century, France in the name of orthodoxy revoked the Edict of Nantes and drove out many thousands of Huguenots, who added their intellectual vigor to lands of refuge such as Great Britain, the Netherlands and Prussia, while France was permanently weakened.

In more recent times, Germany hounded out the Jewish scientists of Europe. They arrived in the United States and contributed immeasurably to scientific advancement here, while Germany lost so heavily that there is no telling how long it will take to regain its former scientific eminence. The Soviet Union, in its fascination with Lysenko, destroyed its geneticists, and set back its biological sciences for decades. China, during the Cultural Revolution, turned against Western science and is still laboring to overcome the devastation that resulted.

Are we now, with all these examples before us, to ride backward into the past under the same tattered banner of orthodoxy? With creationism in the saddle, American science will wither. We will raise a generation of ignoramuses ill-equipped to run the industry of tomorrow, much less to generate the new advances of the days after tomorrow.

We will inevitably recede into the backwater of civilization and those nations that retain open scientific thought will take over the leadership of the world and the cutting edge of human advancement.

I don't suppose that the creationists really plan the decline of the United States, but their loudly expressed patriotism is as simple-minded as their "science." If they succeed, they will, in their folly, achieve the opposite of what they say they wish.

5

How Is My Mind Connected to My Body?

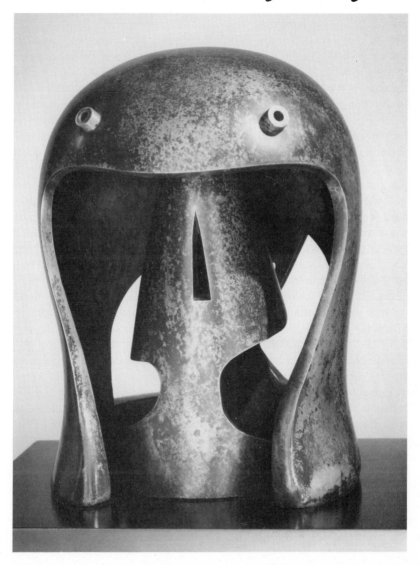

*A*nybody who can read this book, or even this sentence, can think. It is tempting to conclude, as Descartes did in his *Second Meditation*, that anybody who can read this book, or even this sentence, has a mind. In addition, most of us are quite certain that we have a body, although Descartes attempted to doubt even this. But the question of what the relationship is between our minds and our bodies is one of the most enduring and puzzling in philosophy. It is also one of the most immediate, since it has direct consequences for our views about what and who we are.

Descartes believed that the mind and the body are distinct substances. He was therefore a **dualist**, a person who believes that there are two fundamentally different kinds of "stuff" (mental and physical) in the universe. The dualist is faced with the difficult problem of explaining what the relationship is between these two fundamentally different kinds of stuff. The usual view is this. Let's say there is a song playing on the radio (a physical event). You hear the song and that causes you to remember or think of a summer friend (a mental event). Your remembering in turn causes you to write your friend a letter (a physical event). Here, a physical event (the playing of the song) causes a mental event (the remembering) which causes a physical event (the writing). Here's another example: you hit your thumb with a hammer (physical event), which causes pain (mental event), which in turn causes you to scream and hop up and down (physical event). The view that mental and physical events interact in this way is called **interactionism**. Dualistic interactionism represents most people's commonsense view about the relationship between the mental and the physical.

Unfortunately, there are two very difficult problems that an interactionist dualist must solve. The first is the problem of what it is that makes your mind yours and not someone else's. Is it perhaps located in your body? But if so, what makes it move when your body moves? Is it glued, stapled, or tied to your brain? If so, how do you attach a nonphysical substance to a physical one? Perhaps it is not located in space at all. (How could a nonphysical substance be located in space anyway?) But if it's not, how exactly did the broken bone in your thumb cause a pain in *your* mind and not in your brother's mind? How did the pain in your mind cause *your* body to hop and not Mick Jaggar's?

Related to this problem, and even more vexing, is the question of giving a clear and exact account of how any nonphysical substance could cause changes in a physical substance, or vice versa. How exactly would a nonphysical substance cause molecules of a transmitter substance to be released from the cells of the brain? (This is the mechanism for the transmission of signals in the brain.) Most people regard with suspicion a claim that a nonphysical mind has moved some dice or a table. They should regard with equal suspicion a claim that a nonphysical mind has moved an arm or a toe.

It is these problems that have led some philosophers and quite a few scientists to the odd view that mind and brain do not interact as we might have thought. The most common of these views is **epiphenomenalism**. According to this view, mental events are epiphenomena, which are literally phenomena *outside of* the rest of the person. Epiphenomenalists believe that physical events can cause mental events, but that mental events never affect physical events. What you think, believe, and desire is merely a symptom of what is going on in your brain; it never actually makes a difference in what you *do*. Your mind is merely a window into your brain: it observes what happens in the brain and reacts accordingly, but it can never affect the workings of the brain (or the body). Epiphenomenalism must then explain how our ordinary view, that mental events do cause physical events, can be so badly mistaken. It must also give some explanation of how it could be that a physical event could cause a nonphysical event.

One attractive way of dealing with these problems is to deny that they are problems at all. This is what Gilbert Ryle, the famous **behaviorist**, does in his selection. In later parts (not reprinted here) of his book *The Concept of Mind*, he argues that our talk of mental states and events is really just talk about behavior, not, as it pretends, talk about inner events that cause us to do what we do.

In response to these problems, most contemporary philosophers have adopted some form of **physicalism**, the view that there are not separate mental and physical things in the universe, but rather that everything is physical. Much of the current philosophical debate about the mind/body problem presupposes a framework of physicalism. One early form of physicalism is known as the **identity theory**. (For more on the identity theory, see the selection by Flanagan in Chapter 7.) The identity theory claimed that each mental event, for example, wanting to eat dinner, could be identified with a very specific, purely physical event, for example, the firing of neurons number 87 and 163. This requires that each time a "wanting to eat dinner" takes place, a firing of neurons 87 and 163 takes place, because wanting to eat dinner *is* the firing of those two neurons. The identity theory, in this crude form, has now largely been discredited by the observation that dogs and extraterrestrials could both want to eat dinner, but might not have any neurons at all (in the case of extraterrestrials), much less neurons number 87 and 163. Different organisms, with very different physical structures, can all have nonphysical things such as beliefs and desires.

Thus, much current physicalism rejects the identity theory and turns either to **functionalism** or **eliminative materialism**. Functionalism is the view that mental events are defined in terms of what they cause and what they affect, which includes both physical events and other mental events. Thus, different things (a person, a dog, an extraterrestrial, a computer) could have the same mental events by having (physically) different things going on inside that were related causally or functionally (that is, in terms of what their function is) in the ways characteristic of that mental event. The pain in your foot may be signals in the thalamus in your brain. In a dog, the pain in its foot may have to do with some other part of its brain. A spaceman may not have a thalamus but could still have a pain in his foot. In each being, whatever state is caused by dropping a hammer on its toe and causes it to hop up and down and scream, is pain. In this view, it is not possible to "reduce" psychological terms such as 'believe' or 'want' to biological terms. But even though mental terms cannot be reduced to physical terms and so we must still have a psychological vocabulary, that does not mean that there is mental stuff in the universe. There is only mental talk about physical stuff. Lycan argues for a form of functionalism (as does Dennett in Chapter 7) and for the consequent view that machines could come to have the same moral and social properties and relationships that humans now have. Nagel focuses on one particularly vexing problem for functionalists, namely, explaining the nature of consciousness.

Like functionalism, eliminative materialism also holds that there is no way to reduce mental talk to physical talk. But it goes on to conclude that our ordinary mental vocabulary, what it calls **folk psychology**—talk of beliefs, desires, and the like—is radically defective and should be eliminated in favor of a vocabulary that can be understood biologically. In short, people do not really have beliefs, desires, and so on. A representative eliminative materialist view can be found in the selection by Churchland in Chapter 7. Finally, E. Victoria Spelman in her selection offers an entirely different analysis of the mind/body problem, claiming that philosophers have been influenced systematically by unrecognized political and social views (specifically by gender views) in their conceptions of the relationship between mind and body. In raising this issue she places under scrutiny the very process of addressing a philosophical problem.

The mind/body problem offers philosophical terrain that is both treacherous and rewarding. The problems it poses are particularly pressing because they are so closely tied to a great deal of current scientific work and because they are so frightfully misunderstood. For example, a neuroscientist (a scientist who studies brain function) may have discovered a physiological basis for some phenomenon such as depression. She may then go on to conclude that psychologists (Freud, for example) who have hypothesized a psychological origin for depression have thereby been shown to be wrong. Nothing could be further from the truth. Differing physiological and psychological explanations for the same phenomenon is exactly what one would expect if physicalism is true.

Another subtler mistake is this: a neuroscientist may, at the end of a long career, come to despair of ever being able to define some psychological state, such as the state of understanding, in biological terms. She may conclude that understanding is not a biological phenomenon. This is how many neuroscientists come oddly to be epiphenomenalists. Again the conclusion rests on a confusion. As both functionalism and eliminative materialism make clear, physicalism does not suggest that one can reduce the psychological to the physical or define psychological terms in biological (or any other physical) terms. So the inability to define understanding, or any other mental phenomenon, in biological terms does not show that there is anything nonphysical about understanding, or any other mental phenomenon. It is possible to be a physicalist and still to believe strongly in the need for psychological theories. All of these are areas in which philosophers have much by way of clarification to contribute to their scientific friends.

René Descartes
Mind as Distinct from Body

René Descartes (1596–1650) *was born in Britanny, France. He went to college at the age of eight and was finished at the age of sixteen, having studied logic, philosophy, and* *mathematics. He did important work in mathematics and science in addition to his revolutionary work in philosophy. Descartes was in the habit of spending long morning hours reflecting in bed. But when he entered the service of Sweden's Queen Christina in 1649, he was expected to begin teaching her in the library at 5 A.M. Unaccustomed to such rigors, and to the Swedish winter, he took fever and died early in 1650.*

In order to begin this examination, then, I here say, in the first place, that there is a great difference between mind and body, inasmuch as body is by nature always divisible, and the mind is entirely indivisible. For, as a matter of fact, when I consider the mind, that is to say, myself inasmuch as I am only a thinking thing, I cannot distinguish in myself any parts, but apprehend myself to be clearly one and entire; and although the whole mind seems to be united to the whole body, yet if a foot, or an arm, or some other part, is separated from my body, I am aware that nothing has been taken away from my mind. And the faculties of willing, feeling, conceiving, etc. cannot be properly speaking said to be its parts, for it is one and the same mind which employs itself in willing and in feeling and understanding. But it is quite otherwise with corporeal or extended objects, for there is not one of these imaginable by me which my mind cannot easily divide into parts, and which consequently I do not recognise as being divisible; this would be sufficient to teach me that the mind or soul of man is entirely different from the body,if I had not already learned it from other sources.

I further notice that the mind does not receive the impressions from all parts of the body immediately, but only from the brain, or perhaps even from one of its smallest parts, to wit, from that in which the common sense is said to reside, which, whenever it is disposed in the same particular way, conveys the same thing to the mind, although meanwhile the other portions of the body may be differently disposed, as is testified by innumerable experiments which it is unnecessary here to recount.

I notice, also,that the nature of body is such that none of its parts can be moved by another part a little way off which cannot also be moved in the same way by each one of the parts which are between the two, although this more remote part does not act at all. As, for example, in the cord *ABCD* [which is in tension] if we pull the last part *D*, the first part *A* will not be moved in any way differently from what would be the case if one of the intervening parts *B* or *C* were pulled, and the last part *D* were to remain unmoved. And in the same way, when I feel pain in my foot, my knowledge of physics teaches me that this sensation is communicated by means of nerves dispersed through the foot, which, being extended like cords from there to the brain, when they are contracted in the foot, at the same time contract the inmost portions of the brain which is their extremity and place of origin, and then excite a certain movement which nature has established in order to cause the mind to be affected by a sensation of pain represented as existing in the foot. But because these nerves must pass through the tibia, the thigh, the loins, the back and the neck, in order to reach from the leg to the brain, it may happen that although their extremities which are in the foot are not affected, but only certain ones of their intervening parts which pass by the loins or the neck, this action will excite the same movement in the brain that might have been excited there by a hurt received in the foot, in consequence of which the mind will necessarily feel in the foot the same pain as if it had received a hurt. And the same holds good of all the other perceptions of our senses.

I notice finally that since each of the movements which are in the portion of the brain by which the mind is immediately affected brings about one particular sensation only, we cannot under the circumstances imagine anything more likely than that this movement, amongst all the sensations which it is capable of impressing on it, causes mind to be affected by that one which is best fitted and most generally useful for the conservation of the human body when it is in health. But experience makes us aware that all the feelings with which nature inspires us are such as I have just spoken of; and there is therefore nothing in them which does not give testimony to the power and goodness of the God who has produced them. Thus, for example, when the nerves which are in the feet are violently or more than usually moved, their movement, passing through the medulla of the spine to the inmost parts of the brain, gives a sign to the mind which makes it feel somewhat, to wit, pain, as though in the foot, by which the mind is excited to do its utmost to remove the cause of the evil as dangerous and hurtful to the foot. It is true that God could have constituted the nature of man in such a way that this same movement in the brain would have conveyed something quite different to the mind; for example, it might have produced consciousness of itself either in so far as it is in the brain, or as it is in the foot, or as it is in some other place between the foot and the brain, or it might finally have produced consciousness of anything else whatsoever; but none of all this would have contributed so well to the conservation of the body. Similarly, when we desire to drink, a certain dryness of the throat is produced which moves its nerves, and by their means the internal portions of the brain; and this movement causes in the mind the sensation of thirst, because in this case there is nothing more useful to us than to become aware that we have need to drink for the conservation of our health; and the same holds good in other instances.

From this it is quite clear that, notwithstanding the supreme goodness of God, the nature of man, inasmuch as it is composed of mind and body, cannot be otherwise than sometimes a source of deception. For if there is any cause which excites, not in the foot but in some part of the nerves which are extended between the foot and the brain, or even in the brain itself, the same movement which usually is produced when the foot is detrimentally affected, pain will be experienced as though it were in the foot, and the sense will thus naturally be deceived; for since the same movement in the brain is capable of causing but one sensation in the mind, and this sensation is much more frequently excited by a cause which hurts the foot than by another existing in some other quarter, it is reasonable that it should convey to the mind pain in the foot rather than in any other part of the body. And although the parchedness of the throat does not always proceed, as it usually does, from the fact that drinking is necessary for the health of the body, but sometimes comes from quite a different cause, as is the case with dropsical patients, it is yet much better that it should mislead on this occasion than if, on the other hand, it were always to deceive us when the body is in good health; and so on in similar cases. . . .

From a description of inanimate bodies and plants I passed on to that of animals, and particularly to that of men. But since I had not yet sufficient knowledge to speak of them in the same style as of the rest, that is to say, demonstrating the effects from the causes, and showing from what beginnings and in what fashion Nature must produce them, I contented myself with supposing that God formed the body of man altogether like one of ours, in the outward figure of its members as well as in the interior conformation of its organs, without making use of any matter other than that which I had described, and without at the first placing in it a rational soul, or any other thing which might serve as a vegetative or as a sensitive soul; excepting that He kindled in the heart one of these fires without light, which I have already described, and which I did not conceive of as in any way different from that which makes the hay heat when shut up before it is dry, and which makes new wine grow frothy when it is left to ferment over the fruit. For, examining the functions which might in accordance with this supposition exist in the body, I found precisely all those which might exist in us without our having the power of thought, and consequently without our soul— that is to say, this part of us, distinct from the body, of which it has just been said that its nature is to think—contributing to it, functions which are identically the same as those in which animals lacking reason may be said to resemble us. For all that, I could not find in these functions any which, being dependent on thought, pertain to us alone, inasmuch as we are men; while I found all of them afterwards, when I assumed that God had created a rational soul and that He had united it to this body in a particular manner which I described. . . .

I had explained all these matters in some detail in the Treatise which I formerly intended to publish. And afterwards I had shown there, what must be the fabric of the nerves and muscles of the human body in order that the animal spirits therein contained should have the power to move the members, just as the heads of animals, a little while after decapitation, are still observed to move and bite the earth, notwithstanding that they are no longer animate; what changes are necessary in the brain to cause wakefulness, sleep and dreams; how light, sounds, smells, tastes, heat and all other qualities pertaining to external objects are able to imprint on it various ideas by the intervention of the senses; how hunger, thirst and other internal affections can also convey their impressions upon it; what should be regarded as the 'common sense' by which these ideas are received, and what is meant by the memory which retains them, by the fancy which can change them in diverse ways and out of them constitute new ideas, and which, by the same means, distributing the animal spirits through the muscles, can cause the members of such a body to move in as many diverse ways, and in a manner as suitable to the objects which present themselves to its senses and to its internal passions, as can happen in our own case apart from the direction of our free will. And this will not seem strange to those, who, knowing how many different *automata* or moving machines can be made by the industry of man, without employing in so doing more than a very few parts in comparison with the great multitude of bones, muscles, nerves, arteries, veins, or other parts that are found in the body of each animal. From this aspect the body is regarded as a machine which, having been made by the hands of God, is incomparably better arranged, and possesses in itself movements which are much more admirable, than any of those which can be invented by man. Here I specially stopped to show that if there had been such machines, possessing the organs and outward form of a monkey or some other animal without reason, we should not have had any means of ascertaining that they were not of the same nature as those animals. On the other hand, if there were machines which bore a resemblance to our body and imitated our actions as far as it was morally possible to do so, we should always have two very certain tests by which to recognise that, for all that, they were not real men. The first is, that they could never use speech or other signs as we do when placing our thoughts on record for the benefit of others. For we can easily understand a machine's being constituted so that it can utter words, and even emit some responses to action on it of a corporeal kind, which brings about a change in its organs; for instance, if it is touched in a particular part it may ask what we wish to say to it; if in another part it may exclaim that it is being hurt, and so on. But it never happens that it arranges its speech in various ways, in order to reply appropriately to everything that may be said in its presence, as even the lowest type of man can do. And the second difference is, that although machines can perform certain things as well as or perhaps better than any of us can do, they infallibly fall short in others, by the which means we may discover that they did not act from knowledge, but only from the disposition of their organs. For while reason is a universal instrument which can serve for all contingencies, these organs have need of some special adaptation for every particular action. From this it follows that it is morally impossible that there should be sufficient diversity in any machine to allow it to act in all the events of life in the same way as our reason causes us to act.

By these two methods we may also recognise the difference that exists between men and brutes. For it is a very remarkable fact that there are none so depraved and stupid, without even excepting idiots, that they cannot arrange different words together, forming of them a statement by which they make known their thoughts; while, on the other hand, there is no other animal, however perfect and fortunately circumstanced it may be, which can do the same. It is not the want of organs that brings this to pass, for it is evident that magpies and parrots are able to utter words just like ourselves, and yet they cannot speak as we do, that is, so as to give evidence that they think of what they say. On the other hand, men who, being born deaf and dumb, are in the same degree, or even more than the brutes, destitute of the organs which serve the others for talking, are in the habit of themselves inventing certain signs by which they make themselves understood by those who, being usually in their company, have leisure to learn their language. And this does not merely show that the brutes have less reason than men, but that they have none at all, since it is clear that very little is required in order to be able to talk. And when we notice the inequality that exists between animals of the same species, as well as between men, and observe that some are more capable of receiving instruction than others, it is not credible that a monkey or a parrot, selected as the most perfect of its species, should not in these matters equal the stupidest child to be found, or at least a child whose mind is clouded, unless in the case of the brute the soul were of an entirely different nature from ours. And we ought not to confound speech with natural movements which betray passions and may be imitated by machines as well as be manifested by animals; nor must we think, as did some of the ancients, that brutes talk, although we do not understand their language. For if this were true, since they have many organs which are allied to our own, they could communicate their thoughts to us just as easily as to those of their own race. It is also a very remarkable fact that although there are many animals which exhibit more dexterity than we do in some of their actions, we at the same time observe that they do not manifest any dexterity at all in many others. Hence the fact that they do better than we do, does not prove that they are endowed with mind, for in this case they would have more reason than any of us, and would surpass us in all other things. It rather shows that they have no reason at all, and that it is nature which acts in them according to the disposition of their organs, just as a clock, which is only composed of wheels and weights is able to tell the hours and measure the time more correctly than we can do with all our wisdom.

I had described after this the rational soul and shown that it could not be in any way derived from the power of matter, like the other things of which I had spoken, but that it must be expressly created. I showed, too, that it is not sufficient that it should be lodged in the human body like a pilot in his ship, unless perhaps for the moving of its members, but that it is necessary that it should also be joined and united more closely to the body in order to have sensations and appetites similar to our own, and thus to form a true man. In conclusion, I have here enlarged a little on the subject of the soul, because it is one of the greatest importance. For next to the error of those who deny God, which I think I have already sufficiently refuted, there is none which is more effectual in leading feeble spirits from the straight path of virtue, than to imagine that the soul of the brute is of the same nature as our own, and that in consequence, after this life we have nothing to fear or to hope for, any more than the flies and ants. As a matter of fact, when one comes to know how greatly they differ, we understand much better the reasons which go to prove that our soul is in its nature entirely independent of body, and in consequence that it is not liable to die with it. And then, inasmuch as we observe no other causes capable of destroying it, we are naturally inclined to judge that it is immortal.

Gilbert Ryle
The Concept of Mind

Gilbert Ryle (1900–1976) *was for many years a professor of philosophy at Oxford. His book,* The Concept of Mind, *from which this selection is taken, was a highly influential statement of philosophical behaviorism.*

THE OFFICIAL DOCTRINE

*T*here is a doctrine about the nature and place of minds which is so prevalent among theorists and even among laymen that it deserves to be described as the official theory. Most philosophers, psychologists and religious teachers subscribe,with minor reservations, to its main articles and, although they admit certain theoretical difficulties in it, they tend to assume that these can be overcome without serious modifications being made to the architecture of the theory. It will be argued here that the central principles of the doctrine are unsound and conflict with the whole body of what we know about minds when we are not speculating about them.

The official doctrine, which hails chiefly from Descartes, is something like this. With the doubtful exceptions of idiots and infants in arms every human being has both a body and a mind. Some would prefer to say that every human being is both a body and a mind. His body and his mind are ordinarily harnessed together, but after the death of the body his mind may continue to exist and function.

Human bodies are in space and are subject to the mechanical laws which govern all other bodies in space. Bodily processes and states can be inspected by external observers. So a man's bodily life is as much a public affair as are the lives of animals and reptiles and even as the careers of trees, crystals and planets.

But minds are not in space, nor are their operations subject to mechanical laws. The workings of one mind are not witnessable by other observers; its career is private. Only I can take direct cognisance of the states and processes of my own mind. A person therefore lives through two collateral histories, one consisting of what happens in and to his body, the other consisting of what happens in and to his mind. The first is public, the second private. The events in the first history are events in the physical world, those in the second are events in the mental world.

It has been disputed whether a person does or can directly monitor all or only some of the episodes of his own private history; but, according to the official doctrine, of at least some of these episodes he has direct and unchallengeable cognisance. In consciousness, self-consciousness and introspection he is directly and authentically apprised of the present states and operations of his mind. He may have great or small uncertainties about concurrent and adjacent episodes in the physical world, but he can have none about at least part of what is momentarily occupying his mind.

It is customary to express this bifurcation of his two lives and of his two worlds by saying that the things and events which belong to the physical world, including his own body, are external, while the workings of his own mind are internal. This antithesis of outer and inner is of course meant to be construed as a metaphor, since minds, not being in space, could not be described as being spatially inside anything else,or as having things going on spatially inside themselves. But relapses from this good intention are common and theorists are found speculating how stimuli, the physical sources of which are yards or miles outside a person's skin, can generate mental responses inside his skull, or how decisions framed inside his cranium can set going movements of his extremities.

Even when 'inner' and 'outer' are construed as metaphors, the problem how a person's mind and body influence one another is notoriously charged with theoretical difficulties. What the mind wills, the legs, arms and the tongue execute; what affects the ear and the eye has something to do with what the mind perceives; grimaces and smiles betray the mind's moods and bodily castigations lead, it is hoped, to moral improvement. But the actual transactions between the episodes of the private history and those of the public history remain mysterious, since by definition they can belong to neither series. They could not be reported among the happenings described in a person's autobiography of his inner life, but nor could they be reported among those described in some one else's biography of that person's overt career. They can be inspected neither by introspection nor by laboratory experiment. They are theoretical shuttlecocks which are forever being bandied from the physiologist back to the psychologist and from the psychologist back to the physiologist.

Underlying this partly metaphorical representation of the bifurcation of a person's two lives there is a seemingly more profound and philosophical assumption. It is assumed that there are two different kinds of existence or status. What exists or happens may have the status of physical existence, or it may have the status of mental existence. Somewhat as the faces of coins are either heads or tails, or somewhat as living creatures are either male or female, so, it is supposed, some existing is physical existing, other existing is mental existing. It is a necessary feature of what has physical existence that it is in space and time, it is a necessary feature of what has mental existence that it is in time but not in space. What has physical existence is composed of matter, or else is a function of matter; what has mental existence consists of consciousness, or else is a function of consciousness.

There is thus a polar opposition between mind and matter, an opposition which is often brought out as follows. Material objects are situated in a common field, known as 'space', and what happens to one body in one part of space is mechanically connected with what happens to other bodies in other parts of space. But mental happenings occur in insulated fields, known as 'minds', and there is, apart maybe from telepathy, no direct causal connection between what happens in one mind and what happens in another. Only through the medium of the public physical world can the mind of one person make a difference to the mind of another. The mind is its own place and in his inner life each of us lives the life of a ghostly Robinson Crusoe. People can see, hear and jolt one another's bodies, but they are irremediably blind and deaf to the workings of one another's minds and inoperative upon them.

What sort of knowledge can be secured of the workings of a mind? On the one side, according to the official theory, a person has direct knowledge of the best imaginable kind of the workings of his own mind. Mental states and processes are (or are normally) conscious states and processes, and the consciousness which irradiates them can engender no illusions and leaves the door open for no doubts. A person's present thinkings, feelings and willings, his perceivings, rememberings and imaginings are intrinsically 'phosphorescent'; their existence and their nature are inevitably betrayed to their owner. The inner life is a stream of consciousness of such a sort that it would be absurd to suggest that the mind whose life is that stream might be unaware of what is passing down it.

True, the evidence adduced recently by Freud seems to show that there exist channels tributary to this stream, which run hidden from their owner. People are actuated by impulses the existence of which they vigorously disavow; some of their thoughts differ from the thoughts which they acknowledge; and some of the actions which they think they will to perform they do not really will. They are thoroughly gulled by some of their own hypocrisies and they successfully ignore facts about their mental lives which on the official theory ought to be patent to them. Holders of the official theory tend, however, to maintain that anyhow in normal circumstances a person must be directly and authentically seized of the present state and workings of his own mind.

Besides being currently supplied with these alleged immediate data of consciousness, a person is also generally supposed to be able to exercise from time to time a special kind of perception, namely inner perception, or introspection. He can take a (non-optical) 'look' at what is passing in his mind. Not only can he view and scrutinize a flower through his sense of sight and listen to and discriminate the notes of a bell through his sense of hearing; he can also reflectively or introspectively watch, without any bodily organ of sense, the current episodes of his inner life. This self-observation is also commonly supposed to be immune from illusion, confusion or doubt. A mind's reports of its own affairs have a certainty superior to the best that is possessed by its reports of matters in the physical world. Sense-perceptions can, but consciousness and introspection cannot, be mistaken or confused.

On the other side, one person has no direct access of any sort to the events of the inner life of another. He cannot do better than make problematic inferences from the observed behaviour of the other person's body to the states of mind which, by analogy from his own conduct, he supposes to be signalised by that behaviour. Direct access to the workings of a mind is the privilege of that mind itself; in default of such privileged access, the workings of one mind are inevitably occult to everyone else. For the supposed arguments from bodily movements similar to their own to mental workings similar to their own would lack any possibility of observational corroboration. Not unnaturally, therefore, an adherent of the official theory finds it difficult to resist this consequence of his premises, that he has no good reason to believe that there do exist minds other than his own. Even if he prefers to believe that to other human bodies there are harnessed minds not unlike his own, he cannot claim to be able to discover their individual characteristics, or the particular things that they undergo and do. Absolute solitude is on this showing the ineluctable destiny of the soul. Only our bodies can meet.

As a necessary corollary of this general scheme there is implicitly prescribed a special way of construing our ordinary concepts of mental powers and operations. The verbs, nouns and adjectives, with which in ordinary life we describe the wits, characters and higher-grade performances of the people with whom we have do, are required to be construed as signifying special episodes in their secret histories, or else as signifying tendencies for such episodes to occur. When someone is described as knowing, believing or guessing something, as hoping, dreading, intending or shirking something, as designing this or being amused at that, these verbs are supposed to denote the occurrence of specific modifications in his (to us) occult stream of consciousness. Only his own privileged access to this stream in direct awareness and introspection could provide authentic testimony that these mental-conduct verbs were correctly or incorrectly applied. The onlooker, be he teacher, critic, biographer or friend, can never assure himself that his comments have any vestige of truth. Yet it was just because we do in fact all know how to make such comments, make them with general correctness and correct them when they turn out to be confused or mistaken, that philosophers found it necessary to construct their theories of the nature and place of minds. Finding mental-conduct concepts being regularly and effectively used, they properly sought to fix their logical geography. But the logical geography officially recommended would entail that there could be no regular or effective use of these mental-conduct concepts in our descriptions of, and prescriptions for, other people's minds.

THE ABSURDITY OF THE OFFICIAL DOCTRINE

Such in outline is the official theory. I shall often speak of it, with deliberate abusiveness, as 'the dogma of the Ghost in the Machine'. I hope to prove that it is entirely false, and false not in detail but in principle. It is not merely an assemblage of particular mistakes. It is one big mistake and a mistake of a special kind. It is, namely, a category-mistake. It represents the facts of mental life as if they belonged to one logical type or category (or range of types or categories), when they actually belong to another. The dogma is therefore a philosopher's myth. In attempting to explode the myth I shall probably be taken to be denying well-known facts about the mental life of human beings, and my plea that I aim at doing nothing more than rectify the logic of mental-conduct concepts will probably be disallowed as mere subterfuge.

I must first indicate what is meant by the phrase 'Category-mistake'. This I do in a series of illustrations.

A foreigner visiting Oxford or Cambridge for the first time is shown a number of colleges, libraries, playing fields, museums, scientific departments and administrative offices. He then asks 'But where is the University? I have seen where the members of the Colleges live, where the Registrar works, where the scientists experiment and the rest. But I have not yet seen the University in which reside and work the members of your University.' It has then to be explained to him that the University is not another collateral institution, some ulterior counterpart to the colleges, laboratories and offices which he has seen. The University is just the way in which all that he has already seen is organized. When they are seen and when their co-ordination is understood, the University has been seen. His mistake lay in his innocent assumption that it was correct to speak of Christ Church, the Bodleian Library, the Ashmolean Museum *and* the University, to speak, that is, as if 'the University' stood for an extra member of the class of which these other units are members. He was mistakenly allocating the University to the same category as that to which the other institutions belong.

The same mistake would be made by a child witnessing the march-past of a division, who, having had pointed out to him such and such battalions, batteries, squadrons, etc., asked when the division was going to appear. He would be supposing that a division was a counterpart to the units already seen, partly similar to them and partly unlike them. He would be shown his mistake by being told that in watching the battalions, batteries and squadrons marching past he had been watching the division marching past. The march-past was not a parade of battalions, batteries, squadrons *and* a division; it was a parade of the battalions, batteries and squadrons *of* a division.

One more illustration. A foreigner watching his first game of cricket learns what are the functions of the bowlers, the batsmen, the fielders, the umpires and the scorers. He then says 'But there is no one left on the field to contribute the famous element of team-spirit. I see who does the bowling, the batting and the wicket-keeping; but I do not see whose role it is to exercise *esprit de corps*'. Once more, it would have to be explained that he was looking for the wrong type of thing. Team-spirit is not another cricketing-operation supplementary to all of the other special tasks. It is, roughly, the keenness with which each of the special tasks is performed, and performing a task keenly is not performing two tasks. Certainly exhibiting team-spirit is not the same thing as bowling or catching, but nor is it a third thing such that we can say that the bowler first bowls *and* then exhibits team-spirit or that a fielder is at a given moment *either* catching *or* displaying *esprit de corps*.

These illustrations of category-mistakes have a common feature which must be noticed. The mistakes were made by people who did not know how to wield the concepts *University, division* and *team-spirit*. Their puzzles arose from inability to use certain items in the English vocabulary.

The theoretically interesting category-mistakes are those made by people who are perfectly competent to apply concepts, at least in the situations with which they are familiar, but are still liable in their abstract thinking to allocate those concepts to logical types to which they do not belong. An instance of a mistake of this sort would be the following story. A student of politics has learned the main differences between the British, the French and the American Constitutions, and has learned also the differences and connections between the Cabinet, Parliament, the various Ministries, the Judicature and the Church of England. But he still becomes embarrassed when asked questions about the connections between the Church of England, the Home Office and the British Constitution. For while the Church and the Home Office are institutions, the British Constitution is not another institution in the same sense of that noun. So inter-institutional relations which can be asserted or denied to hold between the Church and the Home Office cannot be asserted or denied to hold between either of them and the British Constitution. 'The British Constitution' is not a term of the same logical type as 'the Home Office' and 'the Church of England'. In a partially similar way, John Doe may be a relative, a friend, an enemy or a stranger to Richard Roe; but he cannot be any of these things to the Average Taxpayer. He knows how to talk sense in certain sorts of discussions about the Average Taxpayer, but he is baffled to say why he could not come across him in the street as he can come across Richard Roe.

It is pertinent to our main subject to notice that, so long as the student of politics continues to think of the British Constitution as a counterpart to the other institutions, he will tend to describe it as a mysteriously occult institution; and so long as John Doe continues to think of the Average Taxpayer as a fellow-citizen, he will tend to think of him as an elusive insubstantial man, a ghost who is everywhere yet nowhere.

My destructive purpose is to show that a family of radical category-mistakes is the source of the double-life theory. The representation of a person as a ghost mysteriously ensconced in a machine derives from this argument. Because, as is true, a person's thinking, feeling and purposive doing cannot be described solely in the idioms of physics, chemistry and physiology, therefore they must be described in counterpart idioms. As the human body is a complex organised unit, so the human mind must be another complex organised unit, though one made of a different sort of stuff and with a different sort of structure. Or, again, as the human body, like any other parcel of matter, is a field of causes and effects, so the mind must be another field of causes and effects, though not (Heaven be praised) mechanical causes and effects.

THE ORIGIN OF THE CATEGORY-MISTAKE

One of the chief intellectual origins of what I have yet to prove to be the Cartesian category-mistake seems to be this. When Galileo showed that his methods of scientific discovery were competent to provide a mechanical theory which should cover every occupant of space, Descartes found in himself two conflicting motives. As a man of scientific genius he could not but endorse the claims of mechanics, yet as a religious and moral man he could not accept, as Hobbes accepted,the discouraging rider to those claims, namely that human nature differs only in degree of complexity from clockwork. The mental could not be just a variety of the mechanical.

He and subsequent philosophers naturally but erroneously availed themselves of the following escape-route. Since mental-conduct words are not to be construed as signifying the occurrence of mechanical processes, they must be construed as signifying the occurrence of non-mechanical processes; since mechanical laws explain movements in space as the effects of other movements in space, other laws must explain some of the non-spatial workings of minds as the effects of other non-spatial workings of minds. The difference between the human behaviours which we describe as intelligent and those which we describe as unintelligent must be a difference in their causation; so, while some movements of human tongues and limbs are the effects of mechanical causes, others must be the effects of non-mechanical causes, i.e. some issue from movements of particles of matter, others from workings of the mind.

The differences between the physical and the mental were thus represented as differences inside the common framework of the categories of 'thing', 'stuff', 'attribute', 'state', 'process', 'change', 'cause' and 'effect'. Minds are things,but different sorts of things from bodies; mental processes are causes and effects, but different sorts of causes and effects from bodily movements. And so on. Somewhat as the foreigner expected the University to be an extra edifice, rather like a college but also considerably different, so the repudiators of mechanism represented minds as extra centres of causal processes, rather like machines but also considerably different from them. Their theory was a para-mechanical hypothesis.

That this assumption was at the heart of the doctrine is shown by the fact that there was from the beginning felt to be a major theoretical difficulty in explaining how minds can influence and be influenced by bodies.How can a mental process, such as willing, cause spatial movements like the movements of the tongue? How can a physical change in the optic nerve have among its effects a mind's perception of a flash of light? This notorious crux by itself shows the logical mould into which Descartes pressed his theory of the mind. It was the self-same mould into which he and Galileo set their mechanics. Still unwittingly adhering to the grammar of mechanics, he tried to avert disaster by describing minds in what was merely an obverse vocabulary. The workings of minds had to be described by the mere negatives of the specific descriptions given to bodies; they are not in space, they are not motions, they are not modifications of matter, they are not accessible to public observation. Minds are not bits of clockwork, they are just bits of not-clockwork.

As thus represented, minds are not merely ghosts harnessed to machines, they are themselves just spectral machines. Though the human body is an engine, it is not quite an ordinary engine, since some of its workings are governed by another engine inside it—this interior governor-engine being one of a very special sort. It is invisible, inaudible and it has no size or weight. It cannot be taken to bits and the laws it obeys are not those known to ordinary engineers. Nothing is known of how it governs the bodily engine.

A second major crux points the same moral. Since, according to the doctrine, minds belong to the same category as bodies and since bodies are rigidly governed by mechanical laws, it seemed to many theorists to follow that minds must be similarly governed by rigid non-mechanical laws. The physical world is a deterministic system, so the mental world must be a deterministic system. Bodies cannot help the modifications that they undergo, so minds cannot help pursuing the careers fixed for them. *Responsibility, choice, merit* and *demerit* are therefore inapplicable concepts—unless the compromise solution is adopted of saying that the laws governing mental processes, unlike those governing physical processes, have the congenial attribute of being only rather rigid. The problem of the Freedom of the Will was the problem of how to reconcile the hypothesis that minds are to be described in terms drawn from the categories of mechanics with the knowledge that higher-grade human conduct is not of a piece with the behaviour of machines.

It is an historical curiosity that it was not noticed that the entire argument was broken-backed. Theorists correctly assumed that any sane man could already recognise the differences between, say, rational and non-rational utterances or between purposive and automatic behaviour. Else there would have been nothing requiring to be salved from mechanism. Yet the explanation given presupposed that one person could in principle never recognise the difference between the rational and the irrational utterances issuing from other human bodies, since he could never get access to the postulated immaterial causes of some of their utterances. Save for the doubtful exception of himself, he could never tell the difference between a man and a Robot. It would have to be conceded, for example, that, for all that we can tell, the inner lives of persons who are classed as idiots or lunatics are as rational as those of anyone else. Perhaps only their overt behaviour is disappointing; that is to say, perhaps 'idiots' are not really idiotic, or 'lunatics' lunatic. Perhaps, too, some of those who are classed as sane are really idiots. According to the theory, external observers could never know how the overt behaviour of others is correlated with their mental powers and processes and so they could never know or even plausibly conjecture whether their applications of mental-conduct concepts to these other people were correct or incorrect. It would then be hazardous or impossible for a man to claim sanity or logical consistency even for himself, since he would be debarred from comparing his own performances with those of others. In short, our characterisations of persons and their performances as intelligent, prudent and virtuous or as stupid, hypo-critical and cowardly could never have been made, so the problem of providing a special causal hypothesis to serve as the basis of such diagnoses would never have arisen. The question, 'How do persons differ from machines?' arose just because everyone already knew how to apply mental-conduct concepts before the new causal hypothesis was introduced. This causal hypothesis could not therefore be the source of the criteria used in those applications. Nor, of course, has the causal hypothesis in any degree improved our handling of those criteria. We still distinguish good from bad arithmetic, politic from impolitic conduct and fertile from infertile imaginations in the ways in which Descartes himself distinguished them before and after he speculated how the applicability of these criteria was compatible with the principle of mechanical causation.

He had mistaken the logic of his problem. Instead of asking by what criteria intelligent behaviour is actually distinguished from non-intelligent behaviour, he asked 'Given that the principle of mechanical causation does not tell us the difference, what other causal principle will tell it us?' He realised that the problem was not one of mechanics and assumed that it must therefore be one of some counterpart to mechanics. Not unnaturally psychology is often cast for just this role.

When two terms belong to the same category, it is proper to construct conjunctive propositions embodying them. Thus a purchaser may say that he bought a left-hand glove and a right-hand glove, but not that he bought a left-hand glove, a right-hand glove and a pair of gloves. 'She came home in a flood of tears and a sedan-chair' is a well-known joke based on the absurdity of conjoining terms of different types. It would have been equally ridiculous to construct the disjunction'She came home either in a flood of tears or else in a sedan-chair'. Now the dogma of the Ghost in the Machine does just this. It maintains that there exist both bodies and minds; that there occur physical processes and mental processes; that there are mechanical causes of corporeal movements and mental causes of corporeal movements. I shall argue that these and other analogous conjunctions are absurd; but, it must be noticed, the argument will not show that either of the illegitimately conjoined propositions is absurd in itself. I am not, for example, denying that there occur mental processes. Doing long division is a mental process and so is making a joke. But I am saying that the phrase 'there occur mental processes' does not mean the same sort of thing as 'there occur physical processes', and, therefore, that it makes no sense to conjoin or disjoin the two.

If my argument is successful, there will follow some interesting consequences. First, the hallowed contrast between Mind and Matter will be dissipated, but dissipated not by either of the equally hallowed absorptions of Mind by Matter or of Matter by Mind, but in quite a different way. For the seeming contrast of the two will be shown to be as illegitimate as would be the contrast of 'she came home in a flood of tears' and 'she came home in a sedan-chair'. The belief that there is a polar opposition between Mind and Matter is the belief that they are terms of the same logical type.

It will also follow that both Idealism and Materialism are answers to an improper question. The 'reduction' of the material world to mental states and processes, as well as the 'reduction' of mental states and processes to physical states and processes, presuppose the legitimacy of the disjunction 'Either there exist minds or there exist bodies (but not both)'. It would be like saying, 'Either she bought a left-hand and a right-hand glove or she bought a pair of gloves (but not both)'.

It is perfectly proper to say, in one logical tone of voice, that there exist minds and to say, in another logical tone of voice, that there exist bodies. But these expressions do not indicate two different species of existence, for 'existence' is not a generic word like 'coloured' or 'sexed'. They indicate two different senses of 'exist', somewhat as 'rising' has different senses in 'the tide is rising', 'hopes are rising', and 'the average age of death is rising'. A man would be thought to be making a poor joke who said that three things are now rising, namely the tide, hopes and the average age of death. It would be just as good or bad a joke to say that there exist prime numbers and Wednesdays and public opinions and navies; or that there exist both minds and bodies. In the succeeding chapters I try to prove that the official theory does rest on a batch of category-mistakes by showing that logically absurd corollaries follow from it. The exhibition of these absurdities will have the constructive effect of bringing out part of the correct logic of mental-conduct concepts.

William Lycan
Robots and Minds

William Lycan *teaches philosophy at the University of North Carolina at Chapel Hill. He is one of the principal proponents of a view that he calls 'homunctionalism," which sees mental capacities as constituted of committees of committees of committees (etc.) of progressively more and more stupid submental capacities.*

Artificial Intelligence (AI) is, very crudely, the science of getting machines to perform jobs that normally require intelligence and judgment. Researchers at any number of AI labs have designed machines that prove mathematical theorems, play chess, sort mail, guide missiles, assemble auto engines, diagnose illnesses, read stories and other written texts, and converse with people in a rudimentary way. This is, we might say, intelligent behavior.

But what is this "intelligence"? As a first pass, I suggest that intelligence of the sort I am talking about is a kind of flexibility, a responsiveness to contingencies. A dull or stupid machine must have just the right kind of raw materials presented to it in just the right way, or it is useless: the electric can-opener must have an appropriately sized can fixed under its drive wheel *just so*, in order to operate at all. Humans (most of us, anyway) are not like that. We deal with the unforeseen. We take what comes and make the best of it, even though we may have had no idea what it would be. We play the ball from whatever lie we are given, and at whatever angle to the green; we read and understand texts we have never seen before; we find our way back to Chapel Hill after getting totally lost in downtown Durham (or downtown Washington, D.C., or downtown Lima, Peru).

Our pursuit of our goals is guided while in progress by our ongoing perception and handling of interim developments. Moreover, we can pursue any number of different goals at the same time, and balance them against each other. We are sensitive to contingencies, both external and internal, that have a very complex and unsystematic structure.

It is almost irresistible to speak of *information* here, even if the term were not as trendy as it is. An intelligent creature, I want to say, is an *information-sensitive* creature, one that not only *registers* information through receptors such as sense-organs but somehow stores and manages and finally uses that information. Higher animals are intelligent beings in this sense, and so are we, even though virtually nothing is known about how we organize or manage the vast, seething profusion of information that comes our way. And there is one sort of machine that is information-sensitive also: the digital computer. A computer *is* a machine specifically designed to be fed complexes of information, to store them, manage them, and produce appropriate theoretical or practical conclusions on demand. Thus, if artificial intelligence is what one is looking for, it is no accident that one looks to the computer.

Yet a computer has two limitations in common with machines of less elite and grandiose sorts, both of them already signalled in the characterization I have just given. First, a (present-day) computer must be *fed* information, and the choice of what information to feed and in what form is up to a human programmer or operator. (For the matter, a present-day computer must be plugged into an electrical outlet and have its switch turned to ON, but this is a very minor contingency given the availability of nuclear power-packs.) Second, the *appropriateness* and effectiveness of a computer's output depends entirely on what the programmer or operator had in mind and goes on to make of it. A computer has intelligence in the sense I have defined, but has no judgment, since it has no goals and purposes of its own and no internal sense of appropriateness, relevance, or proportion.

For essentially these reasons—that computers are intelligent in my minimal sense, and that they are nevertheless limited in the two ways I have mentioned—AI theorists, philosophers and intelligent laymen have inevitably compared computers to human minds, but at the same time debated both technical and philosophical questions raised by this comparison. The questions break down into three main groups or types: (A) Questions of the form, "Will a computer ever be able to do X?," where X is something that intelligent humans can do. (B) Questions of the form, "Given that a computer can or could do X, have we any reason to think that it does X in the same way that humans do X?" (C) Questions of the form, "Given that some futuristic supercomputer were able to do X, Y, Z, . . ., for some arbitrarily large range and variety of human activities, would that show that the computer had property P?," where P is some feature held to be centrally, vitally characteristic of human minds, such as thought, consciousness, feeling, sensation, emotion, creativity, or freedom of the will.

Questions of type A are empirical questions and cannot be settled without decades, perhaps centuries of further research—compare ancient and mediaeval speculations on the question of whether a machine could ever fly. Questions of type B are brutely empirical too, and their answers are unavailable to AI researchers *per se*, lying squarely in the domain of cognitive psychology, a science or alleged science barely into its infancy. Questions of type C are philosophical and conceptual, and so I shall essay to answer them all at one stroke.

Let us begin by supposing that all questions of types A and B have been settled affirmatively—that one day we might be confronted by a much-improved version of Hal, the softspoken computer in Kubrick's *2001* (younger readers may substitute Star Wars' C3PO or whatever subsequent cinematic robot is the most lovable). Let us call this more versatile machine "Harry." Harry (let us say) is humanoid in form—he is a miracle of miniaturization and has lifelike plastic skin—and he can converse intelligently on all sorts of subjects, play golf *and* the viola, write passable poetry, control his occasional nervousness pretty well, make love, prove mathematical theorems (of course), show envy when outdone, throw gin bottles at annoying children, etc., etc. We may suppose he fools people into thinking he is human. Now the question is, is Harry really a *person*? Does he have thoughts, feelings, and so on? Is he actually conscious, or is he just a mindless walking hardware store whose movements are astoundingly *like* those of a person?

Plainly his acquaintances would tend from the first to see him as a person, even if they were aware of his dubious antecedents. I think it is a plain psychological fact, if nothing more, that we could not help treating him as a person, unless we resolutely made up our minds, on principle, not to give him the time of day. But how could we really tell that he is conscious?

Well, how do we really tell that any humanoid creature is conscious? How do you tell that I am conscious, and how do I tell that you are? Surely we tell, and decisively, on the basis of our standard behavioral tests for mental states. We know that a human being has such-and-such mental states when it behaves, to speak very generally, in the ways we take to be appropriate to organisms which are in those states. (The point is of course an epistemological one only, no metaphysical implications intended or tolerated.) We know for practical purposes that a creature has a mind when it fulfills all the right criteria. And by hypothesis, Harry fulfills all our behavioral criteria with a vengeance; moreover, he does so *in the right way* (cf. questions of type B): the processing that stands causally behind his behavior is just like ours. It follows that we are at least *prima facie* justified in believing him to be conscious.

We haven't *proved* that he is conscious, of course—any more than you have proved that I am conscious. An organism's merely behaving in a certain way is no logical guarantee of sentience; from my point of view it is at least imaginable, a bare logical possibility, that my wife, my daughter and my chairman are not conscious, even though I have excellent, overwhelming behavioral reason to think that they are. But for that matter, our "standard behavioral tests" for mental states yield practical or moral certainty only so long as the situation is not palpably extraordinary or bizarre. A human chauvinist—in this case, someone who denies that Harry has thoughts and feelings, joys and sorrows—thinks precisely that Harry is as bizarre as they come. But *what is bizarre about him*? There are quite a few chauvinist answers to this, but what they boil down to, and given our hypothesized facts all they could boil down to, are two differences between Harry and ourselves: his *origin* (a laboratory is not a proper mother), and the *chemical composition of his anatomy*, if his creator has used silicon instead of carbon, for example. To exclude him from our community for either or both or *those* reasons seems to me to be a clear case of racial or ethnic prejudice (literally) and nothing more. I see no obvious way in which either a creature's origin or its sub-neuroanatomical chemical composition should matter to its psychological processes or any aspect of its mentality.

My argument can be reinforced by a thought-experiment. Imagine that we take a normal human being, Henrietta, and begin gradually replacing parts of her with synthetic materials—first a few prosthetic limbs, then a few synthetic arteries, then some neural fibers, and so forth. Suppose that the surgeons who perform the successive operations (particularly the neurosurgeons) are so clever and skillful that Henrietta survives in fine style: her intelligence, personality, perceptual acuity, poetic abilities, etc., remain just as they were before. But after the replacement process has eventually gone on to completion, Henrietta will have become an artifact—at least, her body will then be nothing but a collection of artifacts. Did she lose consciousness at some point during the sequence of operations, despite her continuing to behave and respond normally? When? It is hard to imagine that there is some privileged portion of the human nervous system that is for some reason indispensable, even though kidneys, lungs, heart, and any given bit of brain could in principle be replaced by a prosthesis (for *what* reason?); and it also hard to imagine that there is some *pro*portion of the nervous system such that removal of more than that proportion causes loss of consciousness or sentience despite perfect maintenance of all intelligent capacities.

If this quick but totally compelling defense of Harry and Henrietta's personhood is correct, then the two, and their ilk, will have not only mental lives like ours, but *moral* lives like ours, and moral rights and privileges accordingly. Just as origin and physical constitution fail to affect psychological personhood, if a creature's internal organization is sufficiently like ours, so do they fail to affect moral personhood. We do not discriminate against a person who has a wooden leg, or a mechanical kidney, or a nuclear heart regulator; no more should we deny any human or civil right to Harry or Henrietta on grounds of their origin or physical makeup, which they cannot help.

But this happy egalitarianism raises a more immediate question: *In real life*, we shall soon be faced with medium-grade machines, which have some intelligence and are not "mere" machines like refrigerators or typewriters but which fall far short of flawless human simulators like Harry. For AI researchers may well build machines which will appear to have some familiar mental capacities but not others. The most obvious example is that of a sensor or perceptron, which picks up information from its immediate environment, records it, and stores it in memory for future printout. (We already have at least crude machines of this kind. When they become versatile and sophisticated enough, it will be quite natural to say that they see or hear and that they remember.) But the possibility of "specialist" machines of this kind raises an unforeseen contingency: There is an enormous and many-dimensional range of possible beings in between our current "mere" machines and our fully developed, flawless human simulators; we have not even begun to think of all the infinitely possible variations on this theme. And once we do begin to think of these hard cases, we will be at a loss as to where to draw the "personhood" line between them. How complex, eclectic and impressive must a machine be, and in what respects, before we award it the accolade of personhood and/ or of consciousness? There is, to say the least, no clear answer to be had *a priori*, Descartes' notorious view of animals to the contrary notwithstanding.

This typical philosophical question would be no more than an amusing bonbon, were it not for the attending moral conundrum: What moral rights would an intermediate or marginally intelligent machine have? Adolescent machines of this sort will confront us much sooner than will any good human simulators, for they are easier to design and construct; more to the moral point, they will be designed mainly as *labor-saving devices*, as servants who will work for free, and servants of this kind are (literally) made to be exploited. If they are intelligent to any degree, we should have qualms in proportion.

I suggest that this moral problem, which may become a real and pressing one, is parallel to the current debate over animal rights. Luckily I have never wanted to cook and eat my IBM portable.

Suppose I am right about the irrelevance of biochemical constitution to psychology; and suppose I was also right about the coalescing of the notions *computation, information, intelligence*. Then our mentalized theory of computation suggests in turn a computational theory of mentality, and a computational picture of the place of human beings in the world. In fact, philosophy aside, that picture has already begun to get a grip on people's thinking— as witness the filtering down of computer jargon into contemporary casual speech—and that grip is not going to loosen. Computer science is the defining technology of our time, and in this sense the computer is the natural cultural successor to the steam engine, the clock, the spindle and the potter's wheel. Predictably, an articulate computational theory of the mind has also gained credence among professional psychologists and philosophers. I have been trying to support it here and elsewhere; I shall say no more about it for now, save to note again its near-indispensability in accounting for intentionality (noted), and to address the ubiquitous question of computer creativity and freedom.

Soft Determinism or Libertarianism may be true of humans. But many people have far more rigidly deterministic intuitions about computers. Computers, after all, (let us all say it together:) "only do what they are told/programmed to do", they have no spontaneity and no freedom of choice. But human beings choose all the time, and the ensuing states of the world often depend entirely on these choices. Thus the "computer analogy" ultimately fails.

The alleged failure of course depends on what we think freedom really is. As a Soft Determinist, I think that to have freedom of choice in acting is (roughly) for one's action to proceed out of one's own desires, deliberation, will and intention, rather than being compelled or coerced by external forces regardless of my desires or will. As before, free actions are not *uncaused* actions. My free actions are those that I cause, i.e., that are caused by my own mental processes rather than by something pressing on me from the outside. I have argued elsewhere that I am free in that my beliefs, desires, deliberations and intentions are all functional or computational states and processes within me which do interact in characteristic ways to produce my behavior. Note now that the same response vindicates our skilled human-simulating machines from the charge of puppethood. The word "robot" is often used as a veritable synonym for "puppet," so it may seem that Harry and Henrietta are paradigm cases of *unfree* mechanisms which "only do what they are programmed to do." This is a slander—for two reasons.

First, even an ordinary computer, let alone a fabulously sophisticated machine like Harry, is in a way unpredictable. You are at its mercy. You *think* you know what it is going to do: you know what it should do, what it is supposed to do, but there is no guarantee— and it may do something *awful* or at any rate something that you could not have predicted and could not figure out if you tried with both hands. This practical sort of unpredictability would be multiplied a thousandfold in the case of a machine as complex as the human brain, and it is notably characteristic of *people*.

The unpredictability has several sources. (i) Plain old physical defects, as when Harry's circuits have been damaged by trauma, stress, heat, or the like. (ii) Bugs in one or more of his programs. (I have heard that once upon a time, somewhere, a program was written that had not a single bug in it, but this is probably an urban folk tale.) (iii) Randomizers, quantum-driven or otherwise; elements of Harry's behavior may be *genuinely*, physically random. (iv) Learning and analogy mechanisms; if Harry is equipped with these, as he inevitably would be, then his behavior-patterns will be modified in response to his experiential input from the world, which would be neither controlled nor even observed by us. We don't know where he's been. (v) The relativity of reliability to goal-description. This last needs a bit of explanation.

People often say things like, "A computer just crunches binary numbers; provided it isn't broken, it just chugs on mindlessly through whatever flipflop settings are predetermined by its electronic makeup." But such remarks ignore the multilevelled character of real computer programming. At any given time, a computer is running *each of any number of* programs, depending on how it is described and on the level of functional organization that interests us. True, it is always crunching binary numbers, but in crunching them it is also doing any number of more esoteric things. And (more to the point) what counts as a mindless, algorithmic procedure at a very low level of organization may constitute, at a higher level, a hazardous do-or-die heuristic that might either succeed brilliantly or (more likely) fail and leave its objective unfulfilled.

As a second defense, remember that Harry too has beliefs, desires and intentions (provided my original argument is sound). If this is so, then his behavior normally proceeds out of his own mental processes rather than being externally compelled; and so he satisfies the definition of freedom-of-action formulated above. In most cases it will be appropriate to say that Harry could have done other than what he did do (but in fact chose after some ratiocination to do what he did, instead). Harry acts in the same sense as that in which we act, though one might continue to quarrel over what sense that is.

Probably the most popular remaining reason for doubt about machine consciousness has to do with—you guessed it—the raw qualitative character of experience. Could a mere bloodless runner-of-programs have states that *feel to it* in any of the various dramatic ways in which our mental states feel to us?

The latter question is usually asked rhetorically, expecting a resounding answer "NO!!" But I do not hear it rhetorically, for I do not see why the negative answer is supposed to be at all obvious, even for machines as opposed to biologic humans. Of course there is an incongruity *from our human point of view* between human feeling and printed circuitry or silicon pathways; that is to be expected, since we are considering those high-tech items from an external, third-person perspective and at the same time comparing them to our own first-person feels. But argumentatively, that *Gestalt* phenomenon counts for no more in the present case than it did in that of human consciousness, *viz.*, for nothing, especially if my original argument about Harry was successful in showing that biochemical constitution is irrelevant to psychology. What matters to mentality is not the stuff of which one is made, but the complex way in which that stuff is organized. If after years of close friendship we were to open Harry up and find that he is stuffed with microelectronic gadgets instead of protoplasm, we would be taken aback—no question. But our *Gestalt* clash on the occasion would do nothing *at all* to show that Harry does not have his own rich inner qualitative life. If an objector wants to insist that computation alone cannot provide consciousness with its qualitative character, the objector will have to take the initiative and come up with a further, substantive argument to show why not. We have already seen that such arguments have failed wretchedly for the case of humans; I see no reason to suspect that they would work any better for the case of robots. We must await further developments. But at the present stage of inquiry I see no compelling feel-based objection to the hypothesis of machine consciousness.

Thomas Nagel
What Is It Like to Be a Bat?

Thomas Nagel *teaches philosophy at New York University and has formerly taught at Princeton. He has written important work in ethics, philosophy of mind, and other fields. His most recent book,* The View From Nowhere, *is about the nature of subjectivity.*

*C*onsciousness is what makes the mind–body problem really intractable. Perhaps that is why current discussions of the problem give it little attention or get it obviously wrong. The recent wave of reductionist euphoria has produced several analyses of mental phenomena and mental concepts designed to explain the possibility of some variety of materialism, psycho-physical identification, or reduction. But the problems dealt with are those common to this type of reduction and other types, and what makes the mind–body problem unique, and unlike the water–H₂O problem or the Turing machine–IBM machine problem or the lightning–electrical discharge problem or the gene–DNA problem or the oak tree–hydrocarbon problem, is ignored.

Every reductionist has his favorite analogy from modern science. It is most unlikely that any of these unrelated examples of successful reduction will shed light on the relation of mind to brain. But philosophers share the general human weakness for explanations of what is incomprehensible in terms suited for what is familiar and well understood, though entirely different. This has led to the acceptance of implausible accounts of the mental largely because they would permit familiar kinds of reduction. I shall try to explain why the usual examples do not help us to understand the relation between mind and body—why, indeed, we have at present no conception of what an explanation of the physical nature of a mental phenomenon would be. Without consciousness the mind–body problem would be much less interesting. With consciousness it seems hopeless. The most important and characteristic feature of conscious mental phenomena is very poorly understood. Most reductionist theories do not even try to explain it. And careful examination will show that no currently available concept of reduction is applicable to it. Perhaps a new theoretical form can be devised for the purpose, but such a solution, if it exists, lies in the distant intellectual future.

Conscious experience is a widespread phenomenon.It occurs at many levels of animal life, though we cannot be sure of its presence in the simpler organisms, and it is very difficult to say in general what provides evidence of it. (Some extremists have been prepared to deny it even of mammals other than man.) No doubt it occurs in countless forms totally unimaginable to us, on other planets in other solar systems throughout the universe. But no matter how the form may vary, the fact that an organism has conscious experience *at all* means, basically, that there is something it is like to *be* that organism. There may be further implications about the form of the experience; there may even (though I doubt it) be implications about the behavior of the organism. But fundamentally an organism has conscious mental states if and only if there is something that it is like to *be* that organism—something it is like *for* the organism.

We may call this the subjective character of experience.It is not captured by any of the familiar, recently devised reductive analyses of the mental, for all of them are logically compatible with its absence. It is not analyzable in terms of any explanatory system of functional states, or intentional states, since these could be ascribed to robots or automata that behaved like people though they experienced nothing.* It is not analyzable in terms of the causal role of experiences in relation to typical human behavior—for similar reasons.† I do not deny that conscious mental states and events cause behavior, nor that they may be given functional characterizations. I deny only that this kind of thing exhausts their analysis. Any reductionist program has to be based on an analysis of what is to be reduced. If the analysis leaves something out, the problem will be falsely posed. It is useless to base the defense of materialism on any analysis of mental phenomena that fails to deal explicitly with their subjective character. For there is no reason to suppose that a reduction which seems plausible when no attempt is made to account for consciousness can be extended to include consciousness. Without some idea, therefore, of what the subjective character of experience is, we cannot know what is required of physicalist theory.

While an account of the physical basis of mind must explain many things, this appears to be the most difficult. It is impossible to exclude the phenomenological features of experience from a reduction in the same way that one excludes the phenomenal features of an ordinary substance from a physical or chemical reduction of it—namely, by explaining them as effects on the minds of human observers. If physicalism is to be defended, the phenomenological features must themselves be given a physical account. But when we examine their subjective character it seems that such a result is impossible. The reason is that every subjective phenomenon is essentially connected with a single point of view, and it seems inevitable that an objective, physical theory will abandon that point of view.

Let me first try to state the issue somewhat more fully than by referring to the relation between the subjective and the objective, or between the *pour soi* and the *en soi*. This is far from easy. Facts about what it is like to be an X are very peculiar, so peculiar that some may be inclined to doubt their reality, or the significance of claims about them. To illustrate the connection between subjectivity and a point of view, and to make evident the importance of subjective features, it will help to explore the matter in relation to an example that brings out clearly the divergence between the two types of conception, subjective and objective.

I assume we all believe that bats have experience. After all, they are mammals, and there is no more doubt that they have experience than that mice or pigeons or whales have experience. I have chosen bats instead of wasps or flounders because if one travels too far down the phylogenetic tree, people gradually shed their faith that there is experience there at all. Bats, although more closely related to us than those other species, nevertheless present a range of activity and a sensory apparatus so different from ours that the problem I want to pose is exceptionally vivid (though it certainly could be raised with other species). Even without the benefit of philosophical reflection, anyone who has spent some time in an enclosed space with an excited bat knows what it is to encounter a fundamentally *alien* form of life.

I have said that the essence of the belief that bats have experience is that there is something that it is like to be a bat. Now we know that most bats (microchiroptera, to be precise) perceive the external world primarily by sonar, or echolocation, detecting the reflections, from objects within range, of their own rapid, subtly modulated, high-frequency shrieks. Their brains are designed to correlate the outgoing impulses with the subsequent echoes, and the information thus acquired enables bats to make precise discriminations of distance, size, shape, motion, and texture comparable to those we make by vision. But bat sonar, though

---

*Perhaps there could not actually be such robots. Perhaps anything complex enough to behave like a person would have experiences. But that, if true, is a fact which cannot be discovered merely by analyzing the concept of experience.

† It is not equivalent to that about which we are incorrigible, both because we are not incorrigible about experience and because experience is present in animals lacking language and thought, who have no beliefs at all about their experiences.

clearly a form of perception, is not similar in its operation to any sense that we possess, and there is no reason to suppose that it is subjectively like anything we can experience or imagine. This appears to create difficulties for the notion of what it is like to be a bat. We must consider whether any method will permit us to extrapolate to the inner life of the bat from our own case, and if not, what alternative methods there may be for understanding the notion.

Our own experience provides the basic material for our imagination, whose range is therefore limited. It will not help to try to imagine that one has webbing on one's arms, which enables one to fly around at dusk and dawn catching insects in one's mouth; that one has very poor vision, and perceives the surrounding world by a system of reflected high-frequency sound signals; and that one spends the day hanging upside down by one's feet in an attic. Insofar as I can imagine this (which is not very far), it tells me only what it would be like for *me* to behave as a bat behaves. But that is not the question. I want to know what it is like for a *bat* to be a bat. Yet if I try to imagine this, I am restricted to the resources of my own mind, and those resources are inadequate to the task. I cannot perform it either by imagining additions to my present experience, or by imagining segments gradually subtracted from it, or by imagining some combination of additions, subtractions, and modifications.

To the extent that I could look and behave like a wasp or a bat without changing my fundamental structure, my experiences would not be anything like the experiences of those animals. On the other hand, it is doubtful that any meaning can be attached to the supposition that I should possess the internal neurophysiological constitution of a bat. Even if I could by gradual degrees be transformed into a bat, nothing in my present constitution enables me to imagine what the experiences of such a future stage of myself thus metamorphosed would be like. The best evidence would come from the experiences of bats, if we only knew what they were like.

So if extrapolation from our own case is involved in the idea of what it is like to be a bat, the extrapolation must be incompletable. We cannot form more than a schematic conception of what it *is* like. For example, we may ascribe general *types* of experience on the basis of the animal's structure and behavior. Thus we describe bat sonar as a form of three-dimensional forward perception; we believe that bats feel some versions of pain, fear, hunger, and lust, and that they have other, more familiar types of perception besides sonar. But we believe that these experiences also have in each case a specific subjective character, which it is beyond our ability to conceive. And if there is conscious life elsewhere in the universe, it is likely that some of it will not be describable even in the most general experiential terms available to us. (The problem is not confined to exotic cases, however, for it exists between one person and another. The subjective character of the experience of a person deaf and blind from birth is not accessible to me, for example, nor presumably is mine to him. This does not prevent us each from believing that the other's experience has such a subjective character.)

If anyone is inclined to deny that we can believe in the existence of facts like this whose exact nature we cannot possibly conceive, he should reflect that in contemplating the bats we are in much the same position that intelligent bats or Martians* would occupy if they tried to form a conception of what it was like to be us. The structure of their own minds might make it impossible for them to succeed, but we know they would be wrong to conclude that there is not anything precise that it is like to be us: that only certain general types of mental state could be ascribed to us (perhaps perception and appetite would be concepts common to us both; perhaps not). We know they would be wrong to draw such a skeptical conclusion because we know what it is like to be us. And we know that while it includes an enormous amount of variation and complexity, and while we do not possess the vocabulary to describe

---

*Any intelligent extraterrestrial beings totally different from us.

it adequately, its subjective character is highly specific, and in some respects describable in terms that can be understood only by creatures like us. The fact that we cannot expect ever to accommodate in our language a detailed description of Martian or bat phenomenology should not lead us to dismiss as meaningless the claim that bats and Martians have experiences fully comparable in richness of detail to our own. It would be fine if someone were to develop concepts and a theory that enabled us to think about those things; but such an understanding may be permanently denied to us by the limits of our nature. And to deny the reality or logical significance of what we can never describe or understand is the crudest form of cognitive dissonance.

This brings us to the edge of a topic that requires much more discussion than I can give it here: namely, the relation between facts on the one hand and conceptual schemes or systems of representation on the other. My realism about the subjective domain in all its forms implies a belief in the existence of facts beyond the reach of human concepts. Certainly it is possible for a human being to believe that there are facts which humans never *will* possess the requisite concepts to represent or comprehend. Indeed, it would be foolish to doubt this, given the finiteness of humanity's expectations. After all, there would have been transfinite numbers even if everyone had been wiped out by the Black Death before Cantor discovered them. But one might also believe that there are facts which *could* not ever be represented or comprehended by human beings, even if the species lasted forever—simply because our structure does not permit us to operate with concepts of the requisite type. This impossibility might even be observed by other beings, but it is not clear that the existence of such beings, or the possibility of their existence, is a precondition of the significance of the hypothesis that there are humanly inaccessible facts. (After all, the nature of beings with access to humanly inaccessible facts is presumably itself a humanly inaccessible fact.) Reflection on what it is like to be a bat seems to lead us, therefore, to the conclusion that there are facts that do not consist in the truth of propositions expressible in a human language. We can be compelled to recognize the existence of such facts without being able to state or comprehend them.

I shall not pursue this subject, however. Its bearing on the topic before us (namely, the mind–body problem) is that it enables us to make a general observation about the subjective character of experience. Whatever may be the status of facts about what it is like to be a human being, or a bat, or a Martian, these appear to be facts that embody a particular point of view.

I am not adverting here to the alleged privacy of experience to its possessor. The point of view in question is not one accessible only to a single individual. Rather it is a *type*. It is often possible to take up a point of view other than one's own, so the comprehension of such facts is not limited to one's own case. There is a sense in which phenomenological facts are perfectly objective: One person can know or say of another what the quality of the other's experience is. They are subjective, however, in the sense that even this objective ascription of experience is possible only for someone sufficiently similar to the object of ascription to be able to adopt his point of view—to understand the ascription in the first person as well as in the third, so to speak. The more different from oneself the other experiencer is, the less success one can expect with this enterprise. In our own case we occupy the relevant point of view, but we will have as much difficulty understanding our own experience properly if we approach it from another point of view as we would if we tried to understand the experience of another species without taking up *its* point of view.*

---

*It may be easier than I suppose to transcend interspecies barriers with the aid of the imagination. For example, blind people are able to detect objects near them by a form of sonar, using vocal clicks or taps of a cane. Perhaps if one knew what that was like, one could by extension imagine roughly what it was like to possess the much more refined sonar of a bat. The distance between oneself and other persons and other species can fall anywhere on a

This bears directly on the mind–body problem. For if the facts of experience—facts about what it is like *for* the experiencing organism—are accessible only from one point of view, then it is a mystery how the true character of experiences could be revealed in the physical operation of that organism. The latter is a domain of objective facts par excellence— the kind that can be observed and understood from many points of view and by individuals with differing perceptual systems. There are no comparable imaginative obstacles to the acquisition of knowledge about bat neurophysiology by human scientists, and intelligent bats or Martians might learn more about the human brain than we ever will.

This is not by itself an argument against reduction. A Martian scientist with no under-standing of visual perception could understand the rainbow, or lightning, or clouds as physical phenomena, though he would never be able to understand the human concepts of rainbow, lightning, or cloud, or the place these things occupy in our phenomenal world. The objective nature of the things picked out by these concepts could be apprehended by him because, although the concepts themselves are connected with a particular point of view and a particular visual phenomenology, the things apprehended from that point of view are not: they are observable from the point of view but external to it; hence they can be comprehended from other points of view also, either by the same organisms or by others. Lightning has an objective character that is not exhausted by its visual appearance, and this can be investigated by a Martian without vision. To be precise, it has a *more* objective character than is revealed in its visual appearance. In speaking of the move from subjective to objective characterization, I wish to remain noncommittal about the existence of an end point, the completely objective intrinsic nature of the thing, which one might or might not be able to reach. It may be more accurate to think of objectivity as a direction in which the understanding can travel. And in understanding a phenomenon like lightning, it is legitimate to go as far away as one can from a strictly human viewpoint.

In the case of experience, on the other hand, the connection with a particular point of view seems much closer. It is difficult to understand what could be meant by the *objective* character of an experience, apart from the particular point of view from which its subject apprehends it. After all, what would be left of what it was like to be a bat if one removed the viewpoint of the bat? But if experience does not have, in addition to its subjective character, an objective nature that can be apprehended from many different points of view, then how can it be supposed that a Martian investigating my brain might be observing physical processes which were my mental processes (as he might observe physical processes which were bolts of lightning), only from a different point of view? How, for that matter, could a human physiologist observe them from another point of view?

We appear to be faced with a general difficulty about psychophysical reduction. In other areas the process of reduction is a move in the direction of greater objectivity, toward a more accurate view of the real nature of things. This is accomplished by reducing our dependence on individual or species-specific points of view toward the object of investigation. We describe it not in terms of the impressions it makes on our senses, but in terms of its more general effects and of properties detectable by means other than the human senses. The less it depends on a specifically human viewpoint, the more objective is our description. It is possible to follow this path because although the concepts and ideas we employ in thinking

---

continuum. Even for other persons the understanding of what it is like to be them is only partial, and when one moves to species very different from oneself, a lesser degree of partial understanding may still be available. The imagination is remarkably flexible. My point, however, is not that we cannot *know* what it is like to be a bat. I am not raising that epistemological problem. My point is rather that even to form a *conception* of what it is like to be a bat (and *a fortiori* to know what it is like to be a bat) one must take up the bat's point of view. If one can take it up roughly, or partially, then one's conception will also be rough or partial. Or so it seems in our present state of understanding.

about the external world are initially applied from a point of view that involves our perceptual apparatus, they are used by us to refer to things beyond themselves—toward which we *have* the phenomenal point of view. Therefore we can abandon it in favor of another, and still be thinking about the same things.

Experience itself, however, does not seem to fit the pattern. The idea of moving from appearance to reality seems to make no sense here. What is the analogue in this case to pursuing a more objective understanding of the same phenomena by abandoning the initial subjective viewpoint toward them in favor of another that is more objective but concerns the same thing? Certainly it *appears* unlikely that we will get closer to the real nature of human experience by leaving behind the particularity of our human point of view and striving for a description in terms accessible to beings that could not imagine what it was like to be us. If the subjective character of experience is fully comprehensible only from one point of view, then any shift to greater objectivity—that is, less attachment to a specific viewpoint—does not take us nearer to the real nature of the phenomenon: It takes us farther away from it.

In a sense, the seeds of this objection to the reducibility of experience are already detectable in successful cases of reduction; for in discovering sound to be, in reality, a wave phenomenon in air or other media, we leave behind one viewpoint to take up another, and the auditory, human or animal viewpoint that we leave behind remains unreduced. Members of radically different species may both understand the same physical events in objective terms, and this does not require that they understand the phenomenal forms in which those events appear to the senses of members of the other species. Thus it is a condition of their referring to a common reality that their more particular viewpoints are not part of the common reality that they both apprehend. The reduction can succeed only if the species-specific viewpoint is omitted from what is to be reduced.

But while we are right to leave this point of view aside in seeking a fuller understanding of the external world, we cannot ignore it permanently, since it is the essence of the internal world, and not merely a point of view on it. Most of the neobehaviorism of recent philosophical psychology results from the effort to substitute an objective concept of mind for the real thing, in order to have nothing left over which cannot be reduced. If we acknowledge that a physical theory of mind must account for the subjective character of experience, we must admit that no presently available conception gives us a clue how this could be done. The problem is unique. If mental processes are indeed physical processes, then there is something it is like, intrinsically, to undergo certain physical processes. What it is for such a thing to be the case remains a mystery.

What moral should be drawn from these reflections, and what should be done next? It would be a mistake to conclude that physicalism must be false. Nothing is proved by the inadequacy of physicalist hypotheses that assume a faulty objective analysis of mind. It would be truer to say that physicalism is a position we cannot understand because we do not at present have any conception of how it might be true. Perhaps it will be thought unreasonable to require such a conception as a condition of understanding. After all, it might be said, the meaning of physicalism is clear enough: mental states are states of the body; mental events are physical events. We do not know *which* physical states and events they are, but that should not prevent us from understanding the hypothesis. What could be clearer than the words "is" and "are"?

But I believe it is precisely this apparent clarity of the word "is" that is deceptive. Usually, when we are told that X is Y we know *how* it is supposed to be true, but that depends on a conceptual or theoretical background and is not conveyed by the "is" alone. We know how both "X" and "Y" refer, and the kinds of things to which they refer, and we have a rough idea how the two referential paths might converge on a single thing, be it an object, a person, a process, an event or whatever. But when the two terms of the identification are very disparate it may not be so clear how it could be true. We may not have even a rough idea of how the two referential paths could converge, or what kind of things they might converge on, and a theoretical framework may have to be supplied to enable us to understand this. Without the framework, an air of mysticism surrounds the identification.

This explains the magical flavor of popular presentations of fundamental scientific discoveries, given out as propositions to which one must subscribe without really understanding them. For example, people are now told at an early age that all matter is really energy. But despite the fact that they know what "is" means, most of them never form a conception of what makes this claim true, because they lack the theoretical background.

At the present time the status of physicalism is similar to that which the hypothesis that matter is energy would have had if uttered by a pre-Socratic philosopher. We do not have the beginnings of a conception of how it might be true. In order to understand the hypothesis that a mental event is a physical event, we require more than an understanding of the word "is." The idea of how a mental and a physical term might refer to the same thing is lacking, and the usual analogies with theoretical identification in other fields fail to supply it. They fail because if we construe the reference of mental terms to physical events on the usual model, we either get a reappearance of separate subjective events as the effects through which mental reference to physical events is secured, or else we get a false account of how mental terms refer (for example, a causal behaviorist one).

Strangely enough, we may have evidence for the truth of something we cannot really understand. Suppose a caterpillar is locked in a sterile safe by someone unfamiliar with insect metamorphosis, and weeks later the safe is reopened, revealing a butterfly. If the person knows that the safe has been shut the whole time, he has reason to believe that the butterfly is or was once the caterpillar, without having any idea in what sense this might be so. (One possibility is that the caterpillar contained a tiny winged parasite that devoured it and grew into the butterfly.)

It is conceivable that we are in such a position with regard to physicalism. Donald Davidson has argued that if mental events have physical causes and effects, they must have physical descriptions. He holds that we have reason to believe this even though we do not—and in fact *could* not—have a general psychophysical theory. His argument applies to intentional mental events, but I think we also have some reason to believe that sensations are physical processes, without being in a position to understand how. Davidson's position is that certain physical events have irreducibly mental properties, and perhaps some view describable in this way is correct. But nothing of which we can now form a conception corresponds to it; nor have we any idea what a theory would be like that enabled us to conceive of it.

Very little work has been done on the basic question (from which mention of the brain can be entirely omitted) whether any sense can be made of experiences' having an objective character at all. Does it make sense, in other words, to ask what my experiences are *really* like, as opposed to how they appear to me? We cannot genuinely understand the hypothesis that their nature is captured in a physical description unless we understand the more fundamental idea that they *have* an objective nature (or that objective processes can have a subjective nature).*

I should like to close with a speculative proposal. It may be possible to approach the gap between subjective and objective from another direction. Setting aside temporarily the relation between the mind and the brain, we can pursue a more objective understanding of

---

*This question also lies at the heart of the problem of other minds, whose close connection with the mind–body problem is often overlooked. If one understood how subjective experience could have an objective nature, one would understand the existence of subjects other than oneself.

the mental in its own right. At present we are completely unequipped to think about the subjective character of experience without relying on the imagination—without taking up the point of view of the experiential subject. This should be regarded as a challenge to form new concepts and devise a new method—an objective phenomenology not dependent on empathy or the imagination. Though presumably it would not capture everything, its goal would be to describe, at least in part,the subjective character of experiences in a form comprehensible to beings incapable of having those experiences.

We would have to develop such a phenomenology to describe the sonar experiences of bats; but it would also be possible to begin with humans. One might try, for example, to develop concepts that could be used to explain to a person blind from birth what it was like to see. One would reach a blank wall eventually, but it should be possible to devise a method of expressing in objective terms much more than we can at present, and with much greater precision. The loose intermodal analogies—for example, "Red is like the sound of a trumpet"—which crop up in discussions of this subject are of little use. That should be clear to anyone who has both heard a trumpet and seen red. But structural features of perception might be more accessible to objective description, even though something would be left out. And concepts alternative to those we learn in the first person may enable us to arrive at a kind of understanding even of our own experience which is denied us by the very ease of description and lack of distance that subjective concepts afford.

Apart from its own interest, a phenomenology that is in this sense objective may permit questions about the physical basis of experience to assume a more intelligible form. Aspects of subjective experience that admitted this kind of objective description might be better candidates for objective explanations of a more familiar sort. But whether or not this guess is correct, it seems unlikely that any physical theory of mind can be contemplated until more thought has been given to the general problem of subjective and objective. Otherwise we cannot even pose the mind–body problem without sidestepping it.

E. Victoria Spelman
Woman as Body

E. Victoria Spelman *teaches philosophy at Smith College. She has written widely in ancient philosophy and in feminist philosophy. The selection here is a revised version of an earlier paper.*

and what
pure happiness to know
all our high-toned questions
breed in a lively animal.
Adrienne Rich, from "Two Songs"

What philosophers have had to say about women typically has been nasty, brutish, and short. A page or two of quotations from those considered among the great philosophers (Aristotle, Hume, and Nietzsche, for example) constitutes a veritable litany of contempt. Because philosophers have not said much about women, and, when they have, it has usually been in short essays or chatty addenda which have not been considered to be part of the central body of their work, it is tempting to regard their expressed views about women as asystemic: their remarks on women are unofficial asides which are unrelated to the heart of their philosophical doctrines. After all, it might be thought, how could one's views about something as unimportant as women have anything to do with one's views about something as important as the nature of knowledge, truth, reality, freedom? Moreover—and this is the philosopher's move par excellence—wouldn't it be charitable to consider those opinions about women as coming merely from the *heart*, which all too easily responds to the tenor of the times, while philosophy "proper" comes from the *mind*, which resonates not with the times but with the truth?

Part of the intellectual legacy from philosophy "proper," that is, the issues that philosophers have addressed which are thought to be the serious province of philosophy, it the soul/body or mind/body distinction (differences among the various formulations are not crucial to this essay). However, this part of philosophy might have not merely accidental connections to attitudes about women. For when one recalls that the Western philosophical tradition has not been noted for its celebration of the body, and that women's nature and women's lives have long been associated with the body and bodily functions, then a question is suggested. What connection might there be between attitudes toward the body and attitudes toward women? . . .

PLATO'S LESSONS ABOUT THE SOUL AND THE BODY

Plato's dialogues are filled with lessons about knowledge, reality, and goodness, and most of the lessons carry with them strong praise for the soul and strong indictments against the body. According to Plato, the body, with its deceptive senses, keeps us from real knowledge; it rivets us in a world of material things which is far removed from the world of reality; and it tempts us away from the virtuous life. It is in and through the soul, if at all, that we shall have knowledge, be in touch with reality, and lead a life of virtue. Only the soul can truly know, for only the soul can ascend to the real world, the world of the Forms or Ideas. That world is the perfect model to which imperfect, particular things, we find in matter merely approximate. It is a world which, like the soul, is invisible, unchanging, not subject to decay, eternal. To be good, one's soul must know the Good, that is, the Form of Goodness, and this is impossible while one is dragged down by the demands and temptations of bodily life. Hence, bodily death is nothing to be feared: immortality of the soul not only is possible, but greatly to be desired, because when one is released from the body one finally can get down to the real business of life, for this real business of life is the business of the soul. Indeed, Socrates describes his own commitment, while still on earth, to encouraging his fellow Athenians to pay attention to the real business of life:

> [I have spent] all my time going about trying to persuade you, young and old, to make your first and chief concern not for your bodies nor for your possessions, but for the highest welfare of your souls.

Plato also tells us about the nature of beauty. Beauty has nothing essentially to do with the body or with the world of material things. *Real* beauty cannot "take the form of a face, or of hands, or of anything that is of the flesh." Yes, there are beautiful things, but they only are entitled to be described that way because they "partake in" the form of Beauty, which itself is not found in the material world. Real beauty has characteristics which merely beautiful *things* cannot have; real beauty

> is an everlasting loveliness which neither comes nor goes, which neither flowers nor fades, for such beauty is the same on every hand, the same then as now, here as there, this way as that way, the same to every worshipper as it is to every other.

Because it is only the soul that can know the Forms, those eternal and unchanging denizens of Reality, only the soul can know real Beauty; our changing, decaying bodies only can put us in touch with changing, decaying pieces of the material world.

Plato also examines love. His famous discussion of love in the *Symposium* ends up being a celebration of the soul over the body. Attraction to and appreciation for the beauty of another's body is but a vulgar fixation unless one can use such appreciation as a stepping stone to understanding Beauty itself. One can begin to learn about Beauty, while one is still embodied, when one notices that this body is beautiful, that that body is beautiful, and so on, and then one begins to realize that Beauty itself is something beyond any particular beautiful body or thing. The kind of love between people that is to be valued is not the attraction of one body for another, but the attraction of one soul for another. There is pro-creation of the spirit as well as of the flesh. All that bodies in unison can create are more bodies—the children women bear—which are mortal, subject to change and decay. But souls in unison can create "something lovelier and less mortal than human seed," for spiritual lovers "conceive and bear the things of the spirit," that is, "wisdom and all her sister virtues." Hence, spiritual love between men is preferable to physical love between men and women. At the same time, physical love between men is ruled out, on the grounds that "enjoyment of flesh by flesh" is "wanton shame," while desire of soul for soul is at the heart of a relationship that "reverences, aye and worships, chastity and manhood, greatness and wisdom." The potential for harm in sexual relations is very great—harm not so much to one's body or physique, but to one's soul. Young men especially shouldn't get caught up with older men in affairs that threaten their "spiritual development," for such development is "assuredly and ever will be of supreme value in the sight of gods and men alike."

So, then, one has no hope of understanding the nature of knowledge, reality, goodness, love, or beauty unless one recognizes the distinction between soul and body; and one has no hope of attaining any of these unless one works hard on freeing the soul from the lazy, vulgar, beguiling body. A philosopher is someone who is committed to doing just that, and that is why philosophers go willingly unto death; it is, after all, only the death of their bodies, and finally, once their souls are released from their bodies, these philosophical desiderata are within reach. . . .

The division among parts of the soul is intimately tied to one other central and famous aspect of Plato's philosophy that hasn't been mentioned so far: Plato's political views. His discussion of the parts of the soul and their proper relation to one another is integral to his view about the best way to set up a state. The rational part of the soul ought to rule the soul and ought to be attended by the spirited part in keeping watch over the unruly appetitive part; just so, there ought to be rulers of the state (the small minority in whom reason is dominant), who, with the aid of high-spirited guardians of order, watch over the multitudes (whose appetites need to be kept under control).

What we learn from Plato, then, about knowledge, reality, goodness, beauty, love, and statehood, is phrased in terms of a distinction between soul and body, or alternatively and roughly equivalently, in terms of a distinction between the rational and irrational. And the body, or the irrational part of the soul, is seen as an enormous and annoying obstacle to the possession of these desiderata. If the body gets the upper hand over the soul, or if the irrational part of the soul overpowers the rational part, one can't have knowledge, one can't see beauty, one will be far from the highest form of love, and the state will be in utter chaos. So the soul/body distinction, or the distinction between the rational and irrational parts of the soul, is a highly charged distinction. An inquiry into the distinction is no mild metaphysical musing. It is quite clear that the distinction is heavily value-laden. Even if Plato hadn't told us outright that the soul is more valuable than the body, and the rational part of the soul is more important than the irrational part, that message rings out in page after page of his dialogues. The soul/body distinction, then, is integral to the rest of Plato's views, and the higher worth of the soul is integral to that distinction.

PLATO'S VIEW OF THE SOUL AND BODY, AND HIS ATTITUDE TOWARD WOMEN

Plato, and anyone else who conceives of the soul as something unobservable, cannot of course speak as if we could point to the soul, or hold it up for direct observation. At one point, Plato says no mere mortal can really understand the nature of the soul, but one perhaps could tell what it resembles. So it is not surprising to find Plato using many metaphors and analogies to describe what the soul is *like*, in order to describe relations between the soul and the body or relations between parts of the soul. For example, thinking, a function of the soul, is described by analogy to talking. The parts of the soul are likened to a team of harnessed, winged horses and their charioteer. The body's relation to the soul is such that we are to think of the body vis-à-vis the soul as a tomb, a grave or prison, or as barnacles or rocks holding down the soul. Plato compares the lowest or bodylike part of the soul to a brood of beasts.

But Plato's task is not only to tell us what the soul is like, not only to provide us with ways of getting a fix on the differences between souls and bodies, or differences between parts of the soul. As we've seen, he also wants to convince us that the soul is much more important than the body, and that it is to our peril that we let ourselves be beckoned by the rumblings of the body at the expense of harkening to the call of the soul. And he means to convince us of this by holding up for our inspection the silly and sordid lives of those who pay too much attention to their bodies and do not care enough for their souls; he wants to remind us of how unruly, how without direction, are the lives of those in whom the lower part of the soul holds sway over the higher part. Because he can't *point* to an adulterated soul, he points instead to those embodied beings whose lives are in such bad shape that we can be sure that their souls are adulterated. And whose lives exemplify the proper soul/body relationship gone haywire? The lives of women (or sometimes the lives of children, slaves, and brutes).

For example, how are we to know when the body has the upper hand over the soul, or when the lower part of the soul has managed to smother the higher part? We presumably can't see such conflict, so what do such conflicts translate into, in terms of actual human lives? Well, says Plato, look at the lives of women. It is women who get hysterical at the thought of death; obviously, their emotions have overpowered their reason, and they can't control themselves. The worst possible model for young men could be "a woman, young or old or wrangling with her husband, defying heaven, loudly boasting, fortunate in her own conceit, or involved in misfortune or possessed by grief and lamentation—still less a woman that is sick, in love, or in labor". . . .

Moreover, Plato on many occasions points to women to illustrate the improper way to pursue the things for which philosophers are constantly to be searching. For example, Plato wants to explain how important and also how difficult the attainment of real knowledge is. He wants us to realize that not just anyone can have knowledge, there is a vital distinction between those who really have knowledge and those who merely think they do. Think, for example, about the question of health. If we don't make a distinction between those who know what health is, and those who merely have unfounded and confused opinions about what health is, then "in the matter of good or bad health . . . any woman or child—or animal, for that matter—knows what is wholesome for it and is capable of curing itself." The implication is clear: if any old opinion were to count as real knowledge, then we'd have to say that women, children, and maybe even animals have knowledge. But surely *they* don't have knowledge! And why not? For one thing, because they don't recognize the difference between the material, changing world of appearance, and the invisible, eternal world of Reality. In matters of beauty, for example, they are so taken by the physical aspects of things that they assume that they can see and touch what is beautiful; they don't realize that what one knows when one has knowledge of real Beauty cannot be something that is seen or touched. Plato offers us, then, as an example of the failure to distinguish between Beauty itself, on the one hand,

and beautiful things, on the other, "boys and women when they see bright-colored things." They don't realize that it is not through one's senses that one knows about beauty or anything else, for real beauty is eternal and invisible and unchangeable and can only be known through the soul.

So the message is that in matters of knowledge, reality, and beauty, don't follow the example of women. They are mistaken about those things. In matters of love, women's lives serve as negative examples also. Those men who are drawn by "vulgar" love, that is, love of body for body, "turn to women as the object of their love, and raise a family"; those men drawn by a more "heavenly" kind of love, that is, love of soul for soul, turn to other men. But there are strong sanctions against physical love between men: such physical unions, especially between older and younger men, are "unmanly." The older man isn't strong enough to resist his lust (as in woman, the irrational part of the soul has overtaken the rational part), and the younger man, "the impersonator of the female," is reproached for this "likeness to the model." The problem with physical love between men, then, is that men are acting like women.

To summarize the argument so far: the soul/body distinction is integral to the rest of Plato's views; integral to the soul/body distinction is the higher worth and importance of the soul in comparison to the body; finally, Plato tries to persuade his readers that it is to one's peril that one does not pay proper attention to one's soul—for if one doesn't, one will end up acting and living as if one were a woman. We know, Plato says, about lives dictated by the demands and needs and inducements of the body instead of the soul. Such lives surely are not good models for those who want to understand and undertake a life devoted to the nurturance of the best part of us: our souls.

To anyone at all familiar with Plato's official and oft-reported views about women, the above recitation of misogynistic remarks may be quite surprising. Accounts of Plato's views about women usually are based on what he says in book 5 of the *Republic*. In that dialogue, Plato startled his contemporaries, when as part of his proposal for the constitution of an ideal state, he suggested that

> there is no pursuit of the administrators of a state that belongs to woman because she is a woman or to a man because he is a man. But the natural capacities are distributed alike among both creatures, and women naturally share in all pursuits and men in all. . . .

Well now, what are we to make of this apparent double message in Plato about women? What are we to do with the fact that on the one hand, when Plato explicitly confronts the question of women's nature, in the *Republic*, he seems to affirm the equality of men and women; while on the other hand, the dialogues are riddled with misogynistic remarks? . . .

So the contradictory sides of Plato's views about women are tied to the distinction he makes between soul and body and the lessons he hopes to teach his readers about their relative values. When preaching about the overwhelming importance of the soul, he can't but regard the kind of body one has as of no final significance, so there is no way for him to assess differentially the lives of women and men; but when making gloomy pronouncements about the worth of the body, he points an accusing finger at a class of people with a certain kind of body—women—because he regards them, as a class, as embodying the very traits he wishes no one to have. In this way, women constitute a deviant class in Plato's philosophy, in the sense that he points to their lives as the kinds of lives that are not acceptable philosophically: they are just the kind of lives no one, especially philosophers, ought to live. . . .

In summary, Plato does not merely embrace a distinction between soul and body; for all the good and hopeful and desirable possibilities for human life (now and in an afterlife) are aligned with the soul, while the rather seedy and undesirable liabilities of human life are aligned with the body (alternatively, the alignment is with the higher or lower parts of the soul). There is a highly polished moral gloss to the soul/body distinction in Plato. One of his favorite devices for bringing this moral gloss to a high luster is holding up, for our contempt and ridicule, the lives of women. This is one of ways he tries to make clear that it makes no small difference whether you lead a soul-directed or a bodily directed life.

FEMINISM AND "SOMATOPHOBIA"

There are a number of reasons why feminists should be aware of the legacy of the soul/body distinction. It is not just that the distinction has been wound up with the depreciation and degradation of women, although, as has just been shown, examining a philosopher's view of the distinction may give us a direct route to his views about women.

First of all, as the soul or mind or reason is extolled, and the body or passion is denounced by comparison, it is not just women who are both relegated to the bodily or passionate sphere of existence and then chastised for belonging to that sphere. Slaves, free laborers, children, and animals are put in "their place" on almost the same grounds as women are. The images of women, slaves, laborers, children, and animals are almost interchangeable. For example, we find Plato holding that the best born and best educated should have control over "children, women and slaves . . . and the base rabble of those who are free in name," because it is in these groups that we find "the mob of motley appetites and pleasures and pains." As we saw above, Plato lumps together women, children, and animals as ignoramuses. (For Aristotle, there is little difference beween a slave and an animal, because both "with their bodies attend to the needs of life." A common way of denigrating a member of any one of these groups is to compare that member to a member of one of the other groups—women are thought to have slavish or childish appetites, slaves are said to be brutish. Recall too, that Plato's way of ridiculing male homosexuals was to say that they imitated women. It is no wonder that the images and insults are almost interchangeable, for there is a central descriptive thread holding together the images of all these groups. The members of these groups lack, for all intents and purposes, mind or the power of reason; even the humans among them are not considered fully human.

It is important for feminists to see to what extent the images and arguments used to denigrate women are similar to those used to denigrate one group of men vis-à-vis another, children vis-à-vis adults, animals vis-à-vis humans, and even—though I have not discussed it here—the natural world vis-à-vis man's will (yes, man's will). For to see this is part of understanding how the oppression of women occurs in the context of, and is related to, other forms of oppression or exploitation.

There is a second reason why feminists should be aware of the legacy of the soul/body distinction. Some feminists have quite happily adopted both the soul/body distinction and relative value attached to soul and to body. But in doing so, they may be adopting a position inimical to what on a more conscious level they are arguing for.

For all her magisterial insight into the way in which the image of woman as body has been foisted upon and used against us, Simone de Beauvoir can't resist the temptation to say that woman's emancipation will come when woman, like man, is freed from this association with—according to the male wisdom of the centuries—the less important aspect of human existence. According to *The Second Sex*, women's demand is "not that they be exalted in their femininity; they wish that in themselves, as in humanity in general, transcendence may prevail over immanence." But in de Beauvoir's own terms, for "transcendence" to prevail over "immanence" is for spirit or mind to prevail over matter or body, for reason to prevail over passion and desire. This means not only that the old images of women as mired in the world of "immanence"—the world of nature and physical existence—will go away. It will also happen that women won't lead lives given over mainly to their "natural" functions: "the pain of childbirth is on the way out"; "artificial insemination is on the way in." Although de Beauvoir doesn't explicitly say it, her directions for women are to find means of leaving the world of immanence and joining the men in the realm of transcendence. Men have said, de Beauvoir reminds us, that to be human is to have mind prevail over body; and no matter what disagreements she has elsewhere with men's perceptions and priorities, de Beauvoir here seems to agree with them. . . .

. . . can we as a species sustain negative attitudes and negative ideologies about the bodily aspects of our existence and yet keep those attitudes and ideologies from working in behalf of one group of people as it attempts to oppress other groups?

. . . in *The Feminist Mystique*, [Betty] Friedan remarks on the absence, in women's lives, of "the world of thought and ideas, the life of the mind and spirit." She wants women to be "culturally" as well as "biologically" creative—she wants us to think about spending our lives "mastering the secrets of the atoms, or the stars, composing symphonies, pioneering a new concept in government or society." And she associates "mental activity" with the "professions of highest value to society." Friedan thus seems to believe that men have done the more important things, the mental things; women have been relegated in the past to the less important human tasks involving bodily functions, and their liberation will come when they are allowed and encouraged to do the more important things in life.

Friedan's analysis relies on our old friend, the mind/body distinction, and Friedan, no less than Plato or de Beauvoir, quite happily assumes that mental activities are more valuable than bodily ones. Her solution to what she referred to as the "problem that has no name" is for women to leave (though not entirely) women's sphere and "ascend" into man's. Certainly there is much pleasure and value in the "mental activities" she extolls. But we can see the residue of her own negative attitude about tasks associated with the body: the bodily aspects of our existence must be attended to, but the "liberated" woman, who is on the ascendant, can't be bothered with them. There is yet another group of people to whom these tasks will devolve: servants. Woman's liberation—and of course it is no secert that by "woman," Friedan could only have meant middle-class white women—seems to require woman's dissociation and separation from those who will perform the bodily tasks which the liberated woman has left behind in pursuit of "higher," mental activity. So we find Friedan quoting, without comment, Elizabeth Cady Stanton:

> I now understood the practical difficulties most women had to contend with in the isolated household and the impossibility of women's best development if in contact the chief part of her life with servants and children. . .

Friedan at times seems to chide those women who could afford to have servants but don't: the women pretend there's a "servant problem" when there isn't, or insist on doing their own menial work. The implication is that women could find servants to do the "menial work," if they wanted to, and that it would be desirable for them to do so. But what difference is there between the place assigned to women by men and the place assigned to some women (or men) by Friedan herself? . . .

What I have tried to do here is bring attention to the fact that various versions of women's liberation may themselves rest on the very same assumptions that have informed the deprecation and degradation of women, and other groups which, of course, include women. Those assumptions are that we must distinguish between soul and body, and that the physical part of our existence is to be devalued in comparison to the mental. Of course, these two assumptions alone don't mean that women or other groups have to be degraded; it's these two assumptions, along with the further assumption that woman is body, or is bound to her body, or is meant to take care of the bodily aspects of life, that have so deeply contributed to the degradation and oppression of women. And so perhaps feminists would like to keep the first two assumptions (about the difference between mind and body, and the relative worth of each of them) and somehow or other get rid of the last—in fact, that is what most of the feminists previously discussed have tried to do. Nothing that has been said so far has amounted to an argument against those first two assumptions: it hasn't been shown that there is no foundation for the assumptions that the mind and body are distinct and that the body is to be valued less than the mind.

There is a feminist thinker, however, who has taken it upon herself to chip away directly at the second assumption and to a certain extent at the first. Both in her poetry, and explicitly in her recent book, *Of Woman Born*, Adrienne Rich has begun to show us why use of the mind/body distinction does not give us appropriate descriptions of human experience; and she has begun to remind us of the distance we keep from ourselves when we try to keep a distance from our bodies. She does this in the process of trying to redefine the dimensions of the experience of childbirth, as she tries to show us why childbirth and motherhood need not mean what they have meant under patriarchy.

We are reminded by Rich that it is possible to be alienated from our bodies not only by pretending or wishing they weren't there, but also by being "incarcerated" in them. The institution of motherhood has done the latter in its insistence on seeing woman only or mainly as a reproductive machine. Defined as flesh by flesh-loathers, woman enters the most "fleshly" of her experiences with that same attitude of flesh-loathing—surely "physical self-hatred and suspicion of one's own body is scarcely a favorable emotion with which to enter an intense physical experience.

But Rich insists that we don't have to experience childbirth in that way—we don't have to experience it as "torture rack"; but neither do we have to mystify it as a "peak experience." The experience of childbirth can be viewed as a way of recognizing the integrity of our experience, because pain itself is not usefully catalogued as something just our minds or just our bodies experience. . . . The point of "natural childbirth" should be thought of not as enduring pain, but as having an active physical experience—a distinction we recognize as crucial for understanding, for example, the pleasure in athletics.

Rich recognizes that feminists have not wanted to accept patriarchal versions of female biology, of what having a female body means. It has seemed to feminists, she implies, that we must either accept that view of being female, which is, essentially, to be a body, or deny that view and insist that we are "disembodied spirits." It perhaps is natural to see our alternatives that way:

> We have been perceived for too many centuries as pure Nature, exploited and raped like the earth and the solar system; small wonder if we not try to become Culture: pure spirit, mind.

But we don't *have* to do that, Rich reminds us; we can appeal to the physical without denying what is called "mind." We can come to regard our physicality as "resource, rather than a destiny":

> In order to live a fully human life we require not only *control* of our bodies (though control is a prerequisite); we must touch the unity and resonance of our physicality, our bond with the natural order, the corporeal ground of our intelligence.

Rich doesn't deny that we will have to start thinking about our lives in new ways; she even implies that we'll have to start thinking about thinking in new ways. Maybe it will give such a project a small boost to point out that philosophers for their part still squabble about mind/body dualism; the legacy of dualism is strong, but not unchallenged by any means. And in any event, . . . one can hardly put the blame for sexism (or any other form of oppression) on dualism itself. Indeed, the mind/body distinction can be put to progressive political ends, for example, to assert equality between human beings in the face of physical differences between them. There is nothing intrinsically sexist or otherwise oppressive about dualism, that is, about the belief that there are minds and there are bodies and that they are distinct kinds of things. But historically, the story dualists tell often ends up being a highly politicized one: although the story may be different at different historical moments, often it is said not only that there are minds (or souls) and bodies, but also that one is meant to rule and control the other. And the stage is thereby set for the soul/body distinction, now highly politicized and hierarchically ordered, to be used in a variety of ways in connection with repressive theories of the self, as well as oppressive theories of social and political relations. Among the tasks facing feminists is to think about the criteria for an adequate theory of self. Part of the value of Rich's work is that it points to the necessity of such an undertaking, and it is no criticism of her to say that she does no more than remind us of some of the questions that need to be raised.

A FINAL NOTE ABOUT THE SIGNIFICANCE OF SOMATOPHOBIA IN FEMINIST THEORY

In the history of political philosophy, the grounds given for the inferiority of women to men often are quite similar to those given for the inferiority of slaves to masters, children to fathers, animals to humans. In Plato, for example, all such subordinate groups are guilty by association with one another and each group is guilty by association with the bodily. In their eagerness to end the stereotypical association of woman and body, feminists such as de Beauvoir, Friedan, Firestone, and Daly have overlooked the significance of the connections—in theory and in practice—between the derogation and oppression of women on the basis of our sexual identity and the derogation and oppression of other groups on the basis of, for example, skin color and class membership. It is as if in their eagerness to assign women a new place in the scheme of things, these feminist theorists have by implication wanted to dissociate women from other subordinate groups. One problem with this, of course, is that those other subordinate groups include women.

What is especially significant about Rich's recent work is that in contrast to these other theorists she both challenges the received tradition about the insignificance and indignity of bodily life and bodily tasks and explicitly focuses on racism as well as sexism as essential factors in women's oppression. I believe that it is not merely a coincidence that someone who attends to the first also attends to the second. Rich pauses not just to recognize the significance attached to the female body, but also to reevaluate that significance. "Flesh-loathing" is loathing of flesh by some particular group under some particular circumstances—the loathing of women's flesh by men, but also the loathing of black flesh by whites. (Here I begin to extrapolate from Rich, but I believe with some warrant.) After all, bodies are always particular bodies—they are male or female bodies (our deep confusion when we can't categorize a body in either way supports and does not belie the general point); but they are black or brown or biscuit or yellow or red bodies as well. We cannot seriously attend to the social significance attached to embodiment without recognizing this. I believe that it is Rich's recognition of this that distinguishes her work in crucial ways from that of most other major white feminists. Although the topic of feminism, sexism, and racism deserves a much fuller treatment, it is important to point out in the context of the present paper that not only does Rich challenge an assumption about the nature of the bodily that has been used to oppress women, but, unlike other feminists who do not challenge this assumption, she takes on the question of the ways in which sexism and racism interlock. Somatophobia historically has been symptomatic not only of sexism, but also of racism, so it is perhaps not surprising that someone who has examined that connection between flesh-loathing and sexism would undertake an examination of racism.

Part

THREE

Thinking and Knowing

6

What Do I Know?

Right now, you think that you are reading a book. In fact, you know that you are. Surely nothing could be more obvious than that. Of course, to philosophers, nothing is obvious. Indeed, the nature and extent of our knowledge have been central concerns of philosophy since Plato. Plato provided a basis for what is usually referred to as **epistemology**, or the theory of knowledge, by suggesting that knowledge must be distinguished from mere belief. A belief can fall short of knowledge in two ways: (1) a belief can be false or (2) it can be based on insufficient evidence. Your little sister might believe that Santa Claus exists. After all, everyone tells her that Santa Claus puts presents under the tree; she sees Santa at the mall and on television; she leaves cookies and milk for Santa on Christmas Eve and they are gone on Christmas morning. In spite of all this evidence, she still doesn't *know* that Santa exists. Why not? Because, in fact, he doesn't. (You might also think that her evidence isn't very good, but compare the evidence she has for Santa Claus to the evidence that you have for the existence of Eddie Murphy. Is there such a big difference?) Because your sister's belief isn't true, it isn't a case of knowledge. On the other hand, truth alone isn't enough to guarantee that a belief is knowledge. Suppose I tell you that I believe that Prince Charles bakes pies on Thursdays and that I believe this because he reminds me of my friend Fred and Fred bakes pies on Thursdays. Suppose that, just by coincidence, Prince Charles does bake pies on Thursdays. My belief, then, is true, but given the weakness of my evidence, we should not count my belief as a case of knowledge. Knowledge requires real, hard evidence, something more than quirky associations, random hunches, or mere coincidences. If Princess Diana had told me that her husband bakes pies on Thursdays, then not only would my belief be true, but it would also be based on good evidence.

While many philosophers have devoted their attention to determining just how much evidence is required for knowledge, others have argued for the extreme position that we have no knowledge at all. That position is called **skepticism**. Descartes, as you will see when you read *Meditation One*, entertained some alarming skeptical possibilities. Although you think that you are reading right now, maybe you are really snuggled under your covers, fast asleep and merely dreaming that you are reading. It wouldn't be a terribly interesting dream, but haven't you sometimes had dreams that are quite mundane? An even more extreme, and perhaps less plausible, possibility is that there is an all-powerful Evil Demon, or Genius, whose greatest pleasure comes from deceiving mere mortals. Right now, by his ingenious methods, he is making you think that you are reading a philosophy book, but in fact you aren't.

Needless to say, skepticism is a position that most philosophers have tried to avoid, usually by dismissing it as nothing more than a source of irritation. Other philosophers, while disliking skepticism's conclusions, think that it cannot simply be ignored. They have attempted to show that skeptical arguments rest on impossible suppositions. E. K. Bouwsma, for example, wonders whether the Evil Genius could bring about the sorts of deception required for Descartes' skeptical conclusions. On the other hand, Peter Unger, a contemporary proponent of skepticism, defends it, not by enlisting the support of "unlikely" possibilities, but rather by arguing that knowledge requires certainty and certainty is something that we never have. Against

Unger, Norman Malcolm insists that we can be certain of many things. You can be certain that you are enrolled in a philosophy course, for example. If a friend were to challenge your belief that you are, you could respond by taking her to class. If that were not enough, you could ask her to call the Registrar. If she remains doubtful, that is her problem. You have done everything that you possibly could to prove that you are enrolled and that is enough, or so Malcolm argues. You might think about whether the die-hard skeptic would be satisfied with Malcolm's reasoning. Lewis Carroll and Jorge Borges provide some fictional reinforcements for the skeptics' arsenal.

Recall that knowledge (supposing now that we do have some) requires belief and evidence. Many of the beliefs that we have are about what philosophers have called the "external world," the world of tables and chairs, peanut butter and jelly. The evidence that we have for beliefs about the external world is evidence that we get through our senses. Sally believes that she is eating a peanut butter and jelly sandwich. Why? Because she sees the sandwich; she experiences its quintessentially American taste; she feels the stickiness on the roof of her mouth; she hears the smacking of her lips as they cope with the sticky mess between them; she inhales that characteristic peanut smell. All of this sensory evidence contributes to Sally's belief.

The case of Sally and her sandwich is a very ordinary case of perception, the sort of perception that leads to knowledge. It is not so obvious, however, how we should understand exactly what goes on, even in a simple case such as this. We might agree that perception gives us knowledge but disagree as to what perception gives us knowledge *of*. If we asked Sally to describe her sandwich, she would say it is roughly five inches square, about an inch thick, is of various colors (white, purple, and brown), and so on. But some philosophers, Bertrand Russell among them, might say that Sally has failed to answer our question. She hasn't described the sandwich, but has rather described how the sandwich *appears* to her. Physics, the science that tells us how the world really is, would describe the sandwich as a cloud of colorless molecules. It is nonsensical to suppose, so the reasoning goes, that something could be both colorless and white, purple, and brown. Thus, color is not a quality of the sandwich itself, but rather a quality of the *appearance* of the sandwich. What Sally sees, then, is not the real, underlying sandwich. Instead she sees her *sense datum* of the sandwich. A sense datum is a mental representation of an externally existing object. Images, smells, tactile sensations, sounds, and tastes are each sense data corresponding to a particular sense organ. A visual sense datum, then, is a two-dimensional visual image.

The claim that we directly perceive sense data and only indirectly perceive physical objects, while supported by contemporary science, has its origins in the work of John Locke. Locke noticed that some qualities of an object seem to be dependent on our perception of it, while others seem more to be "in" the object itself. How Sally's sandwich tastes to her seems clearly to have much to do with Sally. If she has just brushed her teeth, it will taste one way to her. If she has just indulged her habit of lemon sucking, it will taste another way. The chemical composition of the sandwich, on the other hand, will not be affected by Sally's prelunch activities. On the basis of considerations like these, Locke concluded that we must distinguish between two different kinds of qualities, the ones that are had by objects themselves and the ones that are had by our *ideas* (Locke's word for sense data) of objects. We directly perceive the latter qualities but not the former ones. Locke thus arrived at a conclusion similar to that suggested by Russell, but for different reasons.

It might have occurred to you that the sort of reasoning used by Russell and Locke seems to lead us right back to skepticism. After all, if Sally never perceives her sandwich, but only her ideas or sense data of it, then how can she ever know what her sandwich really is? Of course, in ordinary life, the true nature of her sandwich may not be of much concern to Sally. She just wants to finish her lunch. But as you are probably now well aware, philosophers, although they do get hungry, are seldom content to let ordinary life get in their way. So troubled was Bishop George Berkeley by what he took to be the skeptical consequences of Locke's reasoning, that he argued that there are no physical objects at all! Although that sounds like a crazy way to avoid skepticism, you will see when you read Berkeley's selection that his arguments are very persuasive.

After reading so many arguments about the nature of perception, the relationship between objects and ideas, or objects and sense data, you may feel that you no longer have any idea of what you, an ordinary, sensible person, ought to think. John L. Austin provides a number of defenses against the assaults on common sense launched during the past three hundred years of philosophical activity.

René Descartes
Meditation One

René Descartes *(1596–1650) was born in Britanny, France. He went to college from the ages of eight to sixteen, having studied logic, philosophy, and mathematics. He did important work in mathematics and science in addition to his revolutionary work in philosophy. His* Meditations, *from which this selection is taken, was published in 1641.*

Of the things which may be brought within the sphere of the doubtful.

*I*t is now some years since I detected how many were the false beliefs that I had from my earliest youth admitted as true, and how doubtful was everything I had since constructed on this basis; and from that time I was convinced that I must once and for all seriously undertake to rid myself of all the opinions which I had formerly accepted, and commence to build anew from the foundation, if I wanted to establish any firm and permanent structure in the sciences. But as this enterprise appeared to be a very great one, I waited until I had attained an age so mature that I could not hope that at any later date I should be better fitted to execute my design. This reason caused me to delay so long that I should feel that I was doing wrong were I to occupy in deliberation the time that yet remains to me for action. To-day, then, since very opportunely for the plan I have in view I have delivered my mind from every care [and am happily agitated by no passions] and since I have procured for myself an assured leisure in a peaceable retirement, I shall at last seriously and freely address myself to the general upheaval of all my former opinions.

Now for this object it is not necessary that I should show that all of these are false—I shall perhaps never arrive at this end. But inasmuch as reason already persuades me that I ought no less carefully to withhold my assent from matters which are not entirely certain and indubitable than from those which appear to me manifestly to be false, if I am able to find in each one some reason to doubt, this will suffice to justify my rejecting the whole. And for that end it will not be requisite that I should examine each in particular, which would be an endless undertaking; for owing to the fact that the destruction of the foundations of necessity brings with it the downfall of the rest of the edifice, I shall only in the first place attack those principles upon which all my former opinions rested.

All that up to the present time I have accepted as most true and certain I have learned either from the senses or through the senses; but it is sometimes proved to me that these senses are deceptive, and it is wiser not to trust entirely to any thing by which we have once been deceived.

But it may be that although the senses sometimes deceive us concerning things which are hardly perceptible, or very far away, there are yet many others to be met with as to which we cannot reasonably have any doubt, although we recognise them by their means. For example, there is the fact that I am here, seated by the fire, attired in a dressing gown, having this paper in my hands and other similar matters. And how could I deny that these hands and this body are mine, were it not perhaps that I compare myself to certain persons, devoid of sense, whose cerebella are so troubled and clouded by the violent vapours of black bile, that they constantly assure us that they think they are kings when they are really quite poor, or that they are clothed in purple when they are really without covering, or who imagine that they have an earthenware head or are nothing but pumpkins or are made of glass. But they are mad, and I should not be any less insane were I to follow examples so extravagant.

At the same time I must remember that I am a man, and that consequently I am in the habit of sleeping, and in my dreams representing to myself the same things or sometimes even less probable things, than do those who are insane in their waking moments. How often has it happened to me that in the night I dreamt that I found myself in this particular place, that I was dressed and seated near the fire, whilst in reality I was lying undressed in bed! At this moment it does indeed seem to me that it is with eyes awake that I am looking at this paper; that this head which I move is not asleep, that it is deliberately and of set purpose that I extend my hand and perceive it; what happens in sleep does not appear so clear nor so distinct as does all this. But in thinking over this I remind myself that on many occasions I have in sleep been deceived by similar illusions, and in dwelling carefully on this reflection I see so manifestly that there are no certain indications by which we may clearly distinguish wakefulness from sleep that I am lost in astonishment. And my astonishment is such that it is almost capable of persuading me that I now dream.

Now let us assume that we are asleep and that all these particulars, e.g. that we open our eyes, shake our head, extend our hands, and so on, are but false delusions; and let us reflect that possibly neither our hands nor our whole body are such as they appear to us to be. At the same time we must at least confess that the things which are represented to us in sleep are like painted representations which can only have been formed as the counterparts of something real and true, and that in this way those general things at least, i.e. eyes, a head, hands, and a whole body, are not imaginary things, but things really existent. For, as a matter of fact, painters, even when they study with the greatest skill to represent sirens and satyrs by forms the most strange and extraordinary, cannot give them natures which are entirely new, but merely make a certain medley of the members of different animals; or if their imagination is extravagant enough to invent something so novel that nothing similar has ever before been seen, and that then their work represents a thing purely fictitious and absolutely false, it is certain all the same that the colours of which this is composed are necessarily real. And for the same reason, although these general things, to wit, [a body], eyes, a head, hands, and such like, may be imaginary, we are bound at the same time to confess that there are at least some other objects yet more simple and more universal, which are real and true; and of these just in the same way as with certain real colours, all these images of things which dwell in our thoughts, whether true and real or false and fantastic, are formed.

To such a class of things pertains corporeal nature in general, and its extension, the figure of extended things, their quantity or magnitude and number, as also the place in which they are, the time which measures their duration, and so on.

That is possibly why our reasoning is not unjust when we conclude from this that Physics, Astronomy, Medicine and all other sciences which have as their end the consideration of composite things, are very dubious and uncertain; but that Arithmetic, Geometry and other sciences of that kind which only treat of things that are very simple and very general, without taking great trouble to ascertain whether they are actually existent or not, contain some measure of certainty and an element of the indubitable. For whether I am awake or asleep, two and three together always form five, and the square can never have more than four sides, and it does not seem possible that truths so clear and apparent can be suspected of any falsity [or uncertainty].

Nevertheless I have long had fixed in my mind the belief that an all-powerful God existed by whom I have been created such as I am. But how do I know that He has not brought it to pass that there is no earth, no heaven, no extended body, no magnitude, no place, and that nevertheless [I possess the perceptions of all these things and that] they seem to me to exist just exactly as I now see them? And, besides, as I sometimes imagine that others deceive themselves in the things which they think they know best, how do I know that I am not deceived every time that I add two and three, or count the sides of a square, or judge of things yet simpler, if anything simpler can be imagined? But possibly God has not desired that I should be thus deceived, for He is said to be supremely good. If, however, it is contrary to His goodness to have made me such that I constantly deceive myself, it would also appear to be contrary to His goodness to permit me to be sometimes deceived, and nevertheless I cannot doubt that He does permit this.

There may indeed be those who would prefer to deny the existence of a God so powerful, rather than believe that all other things are uncertain. But let us not oppose them for the present, and grant that all that is here said of a God is a fable; nevertheless in whatever way they suppose that I have arrived at the state of being that I have reached—whether they attribute it to fate or to accident, or make out that it is by a continual succession of antecedents, or by some other method—since to err and deceive oneself is a defect, it is clear that the greater will be the probability of my being so imperfect as to deceive myself ever, as is the Author to whom they assign my origin the less powerful. To these reasons I have certainly nothing to reply, but at the end I feel constrained to confess that there is nothing in all that I formerly believed to be true, of which I cannot in some measure doubt, and that not merely through want of thought or through levity, but for reasons which are very powerful and maturely considered; so that henceforth I ought not the less carefully to refrain from giving credence to these opinions than to that which is manifestly false, if I desire to arrive at any certainty [in the sciences].

But it is not sufficient to have made these remarks, we must also be careful to keep them in mind. For these ancient and commonly held opinions still revert frequently to my mind, long and familiar custom having given them the right to occupy my mind against my inclination and rendered them almost masters of my belief; nor will I ever lose the habit of deferring to them or of placing my confidence in them, so long as I consider them as they really are, i.e. opinions in some measure doubtful, as I have just shown, and at the same time highly probable, so that there is much more reason to believe in than to deny them. That is why I consider that I shall not be acting amiss, if, taking of set purpose a contrary belief, I allow myself to be deceived, and for a certain time pretend that all these opinions are entirely false and imaginary, until at last, having thus balanced my former prejudices with my latter [so that they cannot divert my opinions more to one side than to the other], my judgment will no longer be dominated by bad usage or turned away from the right knowledge of the truth. For I am assured that there can be neither peril nor error in this course, and that I cannot at present yield too much to distrust, since I am not considering the question of action, but only of knowledge.

I shall then suppose, not that God who is supremely good and the fountain of truth, but some evil genius not less powerful than deceitful, has employed his whole energies in deceiving me; I shall consider that the heavens, the earth, colours, figures, sound, and all other external things are nought but the illusions and dreams of which this genius has availed himself in order to lay traps for my credulity; I shall consider myself as having no hands, no eyes, no flesh, no blood, nor any senses, yet falsely believing myself to possess all these things; I shall remain obstinately attached to this idea, and if by this means it is not in my power to arrive at the knowledge of any truth, I may at least do what is in my power [i.e. suspend my judgment], and with firm purpose avoid giving credence to any false thing, or being imposed upon by this arch deceiver, however powerful and deceptive he may be. But this task is a laborious one, and insensibly a certain lassitude leads me into the course of my ordinary life. And just as a captive who in sleep enjoys an imaginary liberty, when he begins to suspect that his liberty is but a dream, fears to awaken, and conspires with these agreeable illusions that the deception may be prolonged, so insensibly of my own accord I fall back into my former opinions, and I dread awakening from this slumber, lest the laborious wakefulness which would follow the tranquillity of this repose should have to be spent not in daylight, but in the excessive darkness of the difficulties which have just been discussed.

O. K. Bouwsma

Descartes' Evil Genius

O. K. Bouwsma (1898–1978) *taught at the University of Nebraska from 1928 to 1965 and at the University of Texas at Austin from 1965 to 1978. He was the author of* Philosophical Essays.

*T*here was once an evil genius who promised the mother of us all that if she ate the fruit of the tree, she would be like God, knowing good and evil. He promised knowledge. She did eat and she learned, but she was disappointed, for to know good and evil and not to be God is awful. Many an Eve later, there was rumor of another evil genius. This evil genius promised no good, promised no knowledge. He made a boast, a boast so wild and so deep and so dark that those who heard it cringed in hearing it. And what was that boast? Well, that apart from a few, four or five, clear and distinct ideas, he could deceive any son of Adam about anything. So he boasted. And with some result? Some indeed! Men going about in the brightest noonday would look and exclaim: "How obscure!" and if some careless merchant counting his apples was heard to say: "Two and three are five," a hearer of the boast would rub his eyes and run away. This evil genius still whispers, thundering, among the leaves of books, frightening people, whispering: "I can. Maybe I will. Maybe so, maybe not." The tantalizer! In what follows I should like to examine the boast of this evil genius.

I am referring, of course, to that evil genius of whom Descartes writes:

> I shall then suppose, not that God who is supremely good and the fountain of truth, but some evil genius not less powerful than deceitful, has employed his whole energies in deceiving me; I shall consider that the heavens, the earth, the colors, figures, sound, and all other external things are nought but illusions and dreams of which this evil genius has availed himself, in order to lay traps for my credulity; I shall consider myself as having no hands, no eyes, no flesh, no blood, nor any senses, yet falsely believing myself to possess all these things.

This then is the evil genius whom I have represented as boasting that he can deceive us about all these things. I intend now to examine this boast, and to understand how this deceiving and being deceived are to take place. I expect to discover that the evil genius may very well deceive us, but that if we are wary, we need not be deceived. He will deceive us, if he does, by bathing the word "illusion" in a fog. This then will be the word to keep our minds on. In order to accomplish all this, I intend to describe the evil genius carrying out his boast in two adventures. The first of these I shall consider a thoroughly transparent case of deception. The word "illusion" will find a clear and familiar application. Nevertheless in this instance the evil genius will not have exhausted "his whole energies in deceiving us." Hence we must aim to imagine a further trial of the boast, in which the "whole energies" of the evil genius are exhausted. In this instance I intend to show that the evil genius is himself befuddled, and that if we too exhaust some of our energies in sleuthing after the peculiarities of his diction, then we need not be deceived either.

Let us imagine the evil genius then at his ease meditating that very bad is good enough for him, and that he would let bad enough alone. All the old pseudos, pseudo names and pseudo statements, are doing very well. But today it was different. He took no delight in common lies, everyday fibs, little ones, old ones. He wanted something new and something big. He scratched his genius; he uncovered an idea. And he scribbled on the inside of his tattered halo, "Tomorrow, I will deceive," and he smiled, and his words were thin and like fine wire. "Tomorrow I will change everything, everything, everything. I will change flowers, human beings, trees, hills, sky, the sun, and everything else into paper. Paper alone I will not change. There will be paper flowers, paper human beings, paper trees. And human beings will be deceived. They will think that there are flowers, human beings, and trees, and there will be nothing but paper. It will be gigantic. And it ought to work. After all men have been deceived with much less trouble. There was a sailor, a Baptist I believe, who said that all was water. And there was no more water then than there is now. And there was a pool-hall keeper who said that all was billiard balls. That's a long time ago of course, a long time before they opened one, and listening, heard that it was full of the sound of a trumpet. My prospects are good. I'll try it."

And the evil genius followed his own directions and did according to his words. And this is what happened.

Imagine a young man, Tom, bright today as he was yesterday, approaching a table where yesterday he had seen a bowl of flowers. Today it suddenly strikes him that they are not flowers. He stares at them troubled, looks away, and looks again. Are they flowers? He shakes his head. He chuckles to himself. "Huh! that's funny. Is this a trick? Yesterday there certainly were flowers in that bowl." He sniffs suspiciously, hopefully, but smells nothing. His nose gives no assurance. He thinks of the birds that flew down to peck at the grapes in the picture and of the mare that whinnied at the likeness of Alexander's horse. Illusions! The picture oozed no juice, and the likeness was still. He walked slowly to the bowl of flowers. He looked, and he sniffed, and he raised his hand. He stroked a petal lightly, lover of flowers, and drew back. He could scarcely believe his fingers. They were not flowers. They were paper.

As he stands, perplexed, Milly, friend and dear, enters the room. Seeing him occupied with the flowers, she is about to take up the bowl and offer them to him, when once again he is overcome with feelings of strangeness. She looks just like a great big doll. He looks more closely, closely as he dares, seeing this may be Milly after all. Milly, are you Milly?—that wouldn't do. Her mouth clicks as she opens it, speaking, and it shuts precisely. Her forehead shines, and he shudders at the thought of Mme Tussaud's. Her hair is plaited, evenly, perfectly, like Milly's but as she raises one hand to guard its order, touching it, preening, it whispers like a newspaper. Her teeth are white as a genteel monthly. Her gums are pink, and there is a clapper in her mouth. He thinks of mama dolls, and of the rubber doll he used to pinch; it had a misplaced navel right in the pit of the back, that whistled. Galatea in paper! Illusions!

He noted all these details, flash by flash by flash. He reaches for a chair to steady himself and just in time. She approaches with the bowl of flowers, and, as the bowl is extended towards him, her arms jerk. The suppleness, the smoothness, the roundness of life is gone. Twitches of a smile mislight up her face. He extends his hand to take up the bowl and his own arms jerk as hers did before. He takes the bowl, and as he does so sees his hand. It is pale, fresh, snowy. Trembling, he drops the bowl, but it does not break, and the water does not run. What a mockery!

He rushes to the window, hoping to see the real world. The scene is like a theatre-set. Even the pane in the window is drawn very thin, like cellophane. In the distance are the forms of men walking about and tossing trees and houses and boulders and hills upon the thin cross section of a truck that echoes only echoes of chugs as it moves. He looks into the sky upward, and it is low. There is a patch straight above him, and one seam is loose. The sun shines out of the blue like a drop of German silver. He reaches out with his pale hand, crackling the cellophane, and his hand touches the sky. The sky shakes and tiny bits of it fall, flaking his white hand with confetti.

Make-believe!

He retreats, crinkling, creaking, hiding his sight. As he moves he misquotes a line of poetry: "Those are perils that were his eyes," and he mutters, "Hypocritical pulp!" He goes on: "I see that the heavens, the earth, colors, figures, sound, and all other external things, flowers, Milly, trees and rocks and hills are paper, paper laid as traps for my credulity. Paper flowers, paper Milly, paper sky!" Then he paused, and in sudden fright he asked "And what about me?" He reaches to his lip and with two fingers tears the skin and peels off a strip of newsprint. He looks at it closely, grim. "I shall consider myself as having no hands, no eyes, no flesh, no blood, or any senses." He lids his paper eyes and stands dejected. Suddenly he is cheered. He exclaims: *"Cogito me papyrum esse, ergo sum."* He has triumphed over paperdom.

I have indulged in this phantasy in order to illustrate the sort of situation which Descartes' words might be expected to describe. The evil genius attempts to deceive. He tries to mislead Tom into thinking what is not. Tom is to think that these are flowers, that this is the Milly that was, that those are trees, hills, the heavens, etc. And he does this by creating illusions, that is, by making something that looks like flowers, artificial flowers; by making something that looks like and sounds like and moves like Milly, an artificial Milly. An illusion is something that looks like or sounds like, so much like, something else that you either mistake it for something else, or you can easily understand how someone might come to do this. So when the evil genius creates illusions intending to deceive he makes things which might quite easily be mistaken for what they are not. Now in the phantasy as I discovered it Tom is not deceived. He does experience the illusion, however. The intention of this is not to cast any reflection upon the deceptive powers of the evil genius. With such refinements in the paper art as we now know, the evil genius might very well have been less unsuccessful. And that in spite of his rumored lament: "And I made her of the best paper!" No, that Tom is not deceived, that he detects the illusion, is introduced in order to remind ourselves how illusions are detected. That the paper flowers are illusory is revealed by the recognition that they are paper. As soon as Tom realizes that though they look like flowers but are paper, he is acquainted with, sees through the illusion, and is not deceived. What is required, of course, is that he know the difference between flowers and paper, and that when presented with one or the other he can tell the difference. The attempt of the evil genius also presupposes this. What he intends is that though Tom knows this difference, the paper will look so much like flowers that Tom will not notice the respect in which the paper is different from the flowers. And even though Tom had actually been deceived and had not recognized the illusion, the evil genius himself must have been aware of the difference, for this is involved in his design. This is crucial, as we shall see when we come to consider the second adventure of the evil genius.

As you will remember I have represented the foregoing as an illustration of the sort of situation which Descartes' words might be expected to describe. Now, however, I think that this is misleading. For though I described a situation in which there are many things, nearly all of which are calculated to serve as illusions, this question may still arise. Would this paper world still be properly described as a world of illusions? If Tom says: "These are flowers," or "These look like flowers" (uncertainly), then the illusion is operative. But if Tom says: "These are paper," then the illusion has been destroyed. Descartes uses the words: "And all other external things are nought but illusions." This means that the situation which Descartes has in mind is such that if Tom says: "These are flowers," he will be wrong, but he will be wrong also if he says: "These are paper," and it won't matter what sentence of that type he uses. If he says: "These are rock"—or cotton or cloud or wood—he is wrong by the plan. He will be right only if he says: "These are illusions." But the project is to keep him from recognizing the illusions. This means that the illusions are to be brought about not by anything so crude as paper or even cloud. They must be made of the stuff that dreams are made of.

Now let us consider this second adventure.

The design then is this. The evil genius is to create a world of illusions. There are to be no flowers, no Milly, no paper. There is to be nothing at all, but Tom is every moment to go on mistaking nothing for something, nothing at all for flowers, nothing at all for Milly, etc. This is, of course, quite different from mistaking paper for flowers, paper for Milly. And yet all is to be arranged in such a way that Tom will go on just as we now do, and just as Tom did before the paper age, to see, hear, smell the world. He will love the flowers, he will kiss Milly, he will blink at the sun. So he thinks. And in thinking about these things he will talk and argue just as we do. But all the time he will be mistaken. There are no flowers, there is no kiss, there is no sun. Illusions all. This then is the end at which the evil genius aims.

How now is the evil genius to attain this end? Well, it is clear that a part of what he aims at will be realized if he destroys everything. Then there will be no flowers, and if Tom thinks that there are flowers he will be wrong. There will be no face that is Milly's and no tumbled beauty on her head, and if Tom thinks that there is Milly's face and Milly's hair, he will be wrong. It is necessary then to see to it that there are none of these things. So the evil genius, having failed with paper, destroys even all paper. Now there is nothing to see, nothing to hear, nothing to smell, etc. But this is not enough to deceive. For though Tom sees nothing, and neither hears nor smells anything, he may also think that he sees nothing. He must also be misled into thinking that he does see something, that there are flowers and Milly, and hands, eyes, flesh, blood, and all other senses. Accordingly the evil genius restores to Tom his old life. Even the memory of that paper day is blotted out, not a scrap remains. Witless Tom lives on, thinking, hoping, loving as he used to, unwitted by the great destroyer. All that seems so solid, so touchable to seeming hands, so biteable to apparent teeth, is so flimsy that were the evil genius to poke his index at it, it would curl away save for one tiny trace, the smirch of that index. So once more the evil genius has done according to his word.

And now let us examine the result.

I should like first of all to describe a passage of Tom's life. Tom is all alone, but he doesn't know it. What an opportunity for methodologico-metaphysico-solipsimo! I intend, in any case, to disregard the niceties of his being so alone and to borrow his own words, with the warning that the evil genius smiles as he reads them. Tom writes:

> Today, as usual, I came into the room and there was the bowl of flowers on the table. I went up to them, caressed them, and smelled over them. I thank God for flowers! There's nothing so real to me as flowers. Here the genuine essence of the world's substance, at its gayest and most hilarious speaks to me. It seems unworthy even to think of them as erect, and waving on pillars of sap. Sap! Sap!

There was more in the same vein, which we need not bother to record. I might say that the evil genius was a bit amused, snickered in fact, as he read the words "so real," "essence," "substance," etc., but later he frowned and seemed puzzled. Tom went on to describe how Milly came into the room, and how glad he was to see her. They talked about the flowers. Later he walked to the window and watched the gardener clearing a space a short distance away. The sun was shining, but there were a few heavy clouds. He raised the window, extended his hand and four large drops of rain wetted his hand. He returned to the room and quoted to Milly a song from *The Tempest*. He got all the words right, and was well pleased with himself. There was more he wrote, but this was enough to show how quite normal everything seems. And, too, how successful the evil genius is.

And the evil genius said to himself, not quite in solipsimo, "Not so, not so, not at all so."

The evil genius was, however, all too human. Admiring himself but unadmired, he yearned for admiration. To deceive but to be unsuspected is too little glory. The evil genius set about then to plant the seeds of suspicion. But how to do this? Clearly there was no suggestive paper to tempt Tom's confidence. There was nothing but Tom's mind, a stream of seemings and of words to make the seemings seem no seemings. The evil genius must have words with Tom and must engage the same seemings with him. To have words with Tom is to have the words together, to use them in the same way, and to engage the same seemings is to see and to hear and to point to the same. And so the evil genius, free spirit, entered in at the door of Tom's pineal gland and lodged there. He floated in the humors that flow, glandwise and sensewise, everywhere being as much one with Tom as difference will allow. He looked out of the same eyes, and when Tom pointed with his finger, the evil genius said "This" and meant what Tom, hearing, also meant, seeing. Each heard with the same ear what the other heard. For every sniffing of the one nose there were two identical smells, and there were two tactualities for every touch. If Tom had had a toothache, together they would have pulled the same face. The twinsomeness of two monads finds here the limit of identity. Nevertheless there was otherness looking out of those eyes as we shall see.

It seems then that on the next day, the evil genius "going to and fro" in Tom's mind and "walking up and down in it," Tom once again, as his custom was, entered the room where the flowers stood on the table. He stopped, looked admiringly, and in a caressing voice said: "Flowers! Flowers!" And he lingered. The evil genius, more subtle "than all the beasts of the field," whispered "Flowers? Flowers?" For the first time Tom has an intimation of company, of some intimate partner in perception. Momentarily he is checked. He looks again at the flowers. "Flowers? Why, of course, flowers." Together they look out of the same eyes. Again the evil genius whispers, "Flowers?" The seed of suspicion is to be the question. But Tom now raises the flowers nearer to his eyes almost violently as though his eyes were not his own. He is, however, not perturbed. The evil genius only shakes their head. "Did you ever hear of illusions?" says he.

Tom, still surprisingly good-natured, responds: "But you saw them, didn't you? Surely you can see through my eyes. Come, let us bury my nose deep in these blossoms, and take one long breath together. Then tell whether you can recognize these as flowers."

So they dunked the one nose. But the evil genius said "Huh!" as much as to say: What has all this seeming and smelling to do with it? Still he explained nothing. And Tom remained as confident of the flowers as he had been at the first. The little seeds of doubt, "Flowers? Flowers?" and again "Flowers?" and "Illusions?" and now this stick in the spokes, "Huh!" made Tom uneasy. He went on: "Oh, so you are one of these seers that has to touch everything. You're a tangibilite. Very well, here's my hand, let's finger these flowers. Careful! They're tender."

The evil genius was amused. He smiled inwardly and rippled in a shallow humor. To be taken for a materialist! As though the grand illusionist was not a spirit! Nevertheless, he realized that though deception is easy where the lies are big enough (where had he heard that before?), a few scattered, questioning words are not enough to make guile grow. He was tempted to make a statement, and he did. He said, "Your flowers are nothing but illusions."

"My flowers illusions?" exclaimed Tom, and he took up the bowl and placed it before a mirror. "See," said he, "here are the flowers and here, in the mirror, is an illusion. There's a difference surely. And you with my eyes, my nose, and my fingers can tell what that difference is. Pollen on your fingers touching the illusion? send Milly the flowers in the mirror? Set a bee to suck honey out of this glass? You know all this as well as I do. I can tell flowers from illusions, and my flowers, as you now plainly see, are not illusions."

The evil genius was now sorely tried. He had his make-believe, but he also had his pride. Would he now risk the make-believe to save his pride? Would he explain? He explained.

"Tom," he said, "notice. The flowers in the mirror look like flowers, but they only look like flowers. We agree about that. The flowers before the mirror also look like flowers. But they, you say, are flowers because they also smell like flowers and they feel like flowers, as though they would be any more flowers because they also like flowers multiply. Imagine a mirror such that it reflected not only the look of flowers, but also their fragrance and their petal surfaces, and then you smelled and touched, and the flowers before the mirror would be just like the flowers in the mirror. Then you could see immediately that the flowers before the mirror are illusions just as those in the mirror are illusions. As it is now, it is clear that the flowers in the mirror are thin illusions, and the flowers before the mirror are thick. Thick illusions are the best for deception. And they may be as thick as you like. From them you may gather pollen, send them to Milly, and foolish bees may sleep in them."

But Tom was not asleep. "I see that what you mean by thin illusions is what I mean by illusions, and what you mean by thick illusions is what I mean by flowers. So when you say that my flowers are your thick illusions this doesn't bother me. And as for your mirror that mirrors all layers of your thick illusions, I shouldn't call that a mirror at all. It's a duplicator, and much more useful than a mirror, provided you can control it. But I do suppose that when you speak of thick illusions you do mean that thick illusions are related to something you call flowers in much the same way that the thin illusions are related to the thick ones. Is that true?"

The evil genius was now diction-deep in explanations and went on. "In the first place let me assure that these are not flowers. I destroyed all flowers. There are no flowers at all. There are only thin and thick illusions of flowers. I can see your flowers in the mirror, and I can smell and touch the flowers before the mirror. What I cannot smell and touch, having seen as in the mirror, is not even thick illusion. But if I cannot also *cerpicio* what I see, smell, touch, etc., what I have then seen is not anything real. *Esse est cerpici.* I just now tried to *cerpicio* your flowers, but there was nothing there. Man is after all a four- or five- or six-sense creature and you cannot expect much from so little."

Tom rubbed his eyes and his ears tingled with an eighteenth-century disturbance. Then he stared at the flowers. "I see," he said, "that this added sense of yours has done wickedly with our language. You do not mean by illusion what we mean, and neither do you mean by flowers what we mean. As for *cerpicio* I wouldn't be surprised if you'd made up that word just to puzzle us. In any case what you destroyed is what, according to you, you used to *cerpicio*. So there is nothing for you to *cerpicio* any more. But there still are what we mean by flowers. If your intention was to deceive, you must learn the language of those you are to deceive. I should say that you are like the doctor who prescribes for his patients what is so bad for himself and is then surprised at the health of his patients." And he pinned a flower near their nose.

The evil genius, discomfited, rode off on a corpuscle. He had failed. He took an artery, made haste to the pineal exit, and was gone. Then "sun by sun" he fell. And he regretted his mischief.

I have tried in this essay to understand the boast of the evil genius. His boast was that he could deceive, deceive about "the heavens, the earth, the colors, figures, sound, and all other external things." In order to do this I have tried to bring clearly to mind what deception and such deceiving would be like. Such deception involves illusions and such deceiving involves the creation of illusions. Accordingly I have tried to imagine the evil genius engaged in the practice of deception, busy in the creation of illusions. In the first adventure everything is plain. The evil genius employs paper, paper making believe it's many other things. The effort to deceive, ingenuity in deception, being deceived by paper, detecting the illusion—all these are clearly understood. It is the second adventure, however, which is more crucial. For in this instance it is assumed that the illusion is of such a kind that no seeing, no touching, no smelling, are relevant to detecting the illusion. Nevertheless the evil genius sees, touches, smells, and does detect the illusion. He made the illusion; so, of course, he must know it. How then does he know it? The evil genius has a sense denied to men. He senses the flower-in-itself, Milly-in-her-self, etc. So he creates illusions made up of what can be seen, heard, smelled, etc., illusions all because when seeing, hearing, and smelling have seen, heard, and smelled all, the special sense senses nothing,. So what poor human beings sense is the illusion of what only the evil genius can sense. This is formidable. Nevertheless, once again every-thing is clear. If we admit the special sense, then we can readily see how it is that the evil genius should have been so confident. He has certainly created his own illusions, though he has not himself been deceived. But neither has anyone else been deceived. For human beings do not use the word "illusion" by relation to a sense with which only the evil genius is blessed.

I said that the evil genius had not been deceived, and it is true that he has not been deceived by his own illusions. Nevertheless he was deceived in boasting that he could deceive, for his confidence in this is based upon an ignorance of the difference between our uses of the words, "heavens," "earth," "flowers," "Milly," and "illusions" of these things, and his own uses of these words. For though there certainly is an analogy between our own uses and his, the difference is quite sufficient to explain his failure at grand deception. We can also under-stand how easily Tom might have been taken in. The dog over the water dropped his meaty bone for a picture on the water. Tom, however, dropped nothing at all. But the word "illusion" is a trap.

I began this essay uneasily, looking at my hands and saying "no hands," blinking my eyes and saying "no eyes." Everything I saw seemed to me like something Cheshire, a piece of cheese, for instance, appearing and disappearing in the leaves of the tree. Poor kitty! And now? Well. . . .

Peter Unger
A Defense of Skepticism

Peter Unger *teaches philosophy at New York University. He is the leading contemporary proponent of skepticism, a view that is exhaustively defended in his book* Ignorance.

The skepticism that I will defend is a negative thesis concerning what we know. I happily accept the fact that there is much that many of us correctly and reasonably believe, but much more than that is needed for us to know even a fair amount. Here I will not argue that nobody knows anything about anything, though that would be quite consistent with the skeptical thesis for which I will argue. The somewhat less radical thesis which I will defend is this one: every human being knows, at best, hardly anything to be so. More specifically, I will argue that hardly anyone knows that 45 and 56 are equal to 101, if anyone at all. On this skeptical thesis, no one will know the thesis to be true. But this is all right. For I only want to argue that it may be reasonable for us to suppose the thesis to be true, not that we should ever know it to be true.

Few philosophers now take skepticism seriously. With philosophers, even the most powerful of traditional skeptical argument has little force to tempt them nowadays. Indeed, nowadays, philosophers tend to think skepticism interesting only as a formal challenge to which positive accounts of our common-sense knowledge are the gratifying responses. Consequently, I find it at least somewhat natural to offer a defense of skepticism.

My defense of skepticism will be quite unlike traditional arguments for this thesis. This is largely because I write at a time when there is a common faith that, so far as expressing truths is concerned, all is well with the language that we speak. Against this common, optimistic assumption, I shall illustrate how our language habits might serve us well in practical ways, even while they involve us in saying what is false rather than true. And this often does occur, I will maintain, when our positive assertions contain terms with special features of a certain kind, which I call *absolute* terms. Among these terms, "flat" and "certain" are *basic* ones. Due to these terms' characteristic features, and because the world is not so simple as it might be, we do not speak truly, at least as a rule, when we say of a real object, "That has a top which is flat" or when we say of a real person, "He is certain that it is raining." And just as basic absolute terms generally fail to apply to the world, so other absolute terms, which are at least partially defined by the basic ones, will fail to apply as well. Thus, we also speak falsely when we say of a real object or person, "That is a cube" or "He knows that it is raining." For an object is a cube only if it has surfaces which are flat, and, as I shall argue, a person knows something to be so only if he is certain of it. . . .

THE DOUBTFUL APPLICABILITY OF SOME ABSOLUTE TERMS

If my account of absolute terms is essentially correct, then, at least in the case of some of these terms, fairly reasonable suppositions about the world make it somewhat doubtful that the terms properly apply. (In certain contexts, generally where what we are talking about divides into discrete units, the presence of an absolute term need cause no doubts. Thus, considering the absolute term "complete," the truth of "His set of steins is now complete" may be allowed without hesitation, but the truth of "His explanation is now complete" may well be doubted. It is with the latter, more interesting contexts, I think, that we shall be concerned in what follows.) For example, while we say of many surfaces of physical things that they are flat, a rather reasonable interpretation of what we do observe makes it at least somewhat doubtful that these surfaces actually *are* flat. When we look at a rather smooth block of stone through a powerful microscope, the observed surface appears to us to be rife with irregularities. And this irregular appearance seems best explained, not by being taken as an illusory optical phenomenon, but by taking it to be a finer, more revealing look of a surface which is, in fact, rife with smallish bumps and crevices. Further, we account for bumps and crevices by supposing that the stone is composed of much smaller things, molecules and so on, which are in such a combination that, while a large and sturdy stone is the upshot, no stone with a flat surface is found to obtain.

Indeed, what follows from my account of "flat" is this: that, as a matter of logical necessity, if a surface is flat, then there never is any surface which is flatter than it is. For on our paraphrase, if the second surface is flatter than the first, then either the second surface is flat while the first is not, or else the second is more nearly flat than the first, neither surface being flat. So if there is such a second, flatter surface, then the first surface is not flat after all, contrary to our supposition. Thus there cannot be any second, flatter surface. Or in other words, if it is logically possible that there be a surface which is flatter than a given one, then that given surface is not really a flat one. Now, in the case of the observed surface of the stone, owing to the stone's irregular composition, the surface is not one such that it is logically impossible that there be a flatter one. (For example, we might veridically observe a surface through a microscope of the same power which did not appear to have any bumps or crevices.) Thus it is only reasonable to suppose that the surface of this stone is not really flat.

Our understanding of the stone's composition, that it is composed of molecules and so on, makes it reasonable for us to suppose as well that any similarly sized or larger surfaces will fail to be flat just as the observed surface fails to be flat. At the same time, it would be perhaps a bit rash to suppose that much smaller surfaces would fail to be flat as well. Beneath the level of our observation perhaps there are small areas of the stone's surface which are flat. If so, then perhaps there are small objects that have surfaces which are flat, like this area of the stone's surface: for instance, chipping off a small part of the stone might yield such a small object. So perhaps there are physical objects with surfaces which are flat, and perhaps it is not now reasonable for us to assume that there are no such objects. But even if this strong assumption is not now reasonable, one thing which does seem quite reasonable for us now to assume is this: we should at least suspend judgment on the matter of whether there are any physical objects with flat surfaces. That there are such objects is something it is not now reasonable for us to believe.

It is at least somewhat doubtful, then, that "flat" ever applies to actual physical objects or to their surfaces. And the thought must strike us that if "flat" has no such application, this must be due in part to the fact that "flat" is an absolute term. We may then do well to be a bit doubtful about the applicability of any other given absolute term and, in particular, about the applicability of the term "certain." As in the case of "flat," our paraphrase highlights the absolute character of "certain." As a matter of logical necessity, if someone is certain of something, then there never is anything of which he is more certain. For on our paraphrase, if the person is more certain of any other thing, then either he is certain of the other thing while not being certain of the first, or else he is more nearly certain of the other thing than he is of the first; that is, he is certain of neither. Thus, if it is logically possible that there be something of which a person might be more certain than he now is of a given thing, then he is not really certain of that given thing.

Thus it is reasonable to suppose, I think, that hardly anyone, if anyone at all, is certain that 45 and 56 are 101. For it is reasonable to suppose that hardly anyone, if anyone at all, is so certain of that particular calculation that it is impossible for there to be anything of which he might be yet more certain. But this is not surprising; for hardly anyone *feels* certain that those two numbers have that sum. What, then, about something of which people commonly do feel absolutely certain—say, of the existence of automobiles?

Is it reasonable for us now actually to believe that many people are certain that there are automobiles? If it is, then it is reasonable for us to believe as well that for each of them it is not possible for there to be anything of which he might be more certain than he now is of there being automobiles. In particular, we must then believe of these people that it is impossible for any of them ever to be more certain of his own existence than all of them now are of the existence of automobiles. While these people *might* all actually be as certain of the automobiles as this, just as each of them *feels* himself to be, I think it somewhat rash for us actually to believe that they *are* all so certain. Certainty being an absolute and our understanding of people being rather rudimentary and incomplete, I think it more reasonable for us now to suspend judgment on the matter. And, since there is nothing importantly peculiar about the matter of automobiles, the same cautious position recommends itself quite generally: so far as actual human beings go, the most reasonable course for us now is to suspend judgment as to whether any of them is certain of more than hardly anything, if anything at all.

DOES KNOWING REQUIRE BEING CERTAIN?

One tradition in philosophy holds that knowledge requires being certain. As a matter of logical necessity, a man knows something only if he is certain of the thing. In this tradition, certainty is not taken lightly; rather it is equated with absolute certainty. . . .

I am rather inclined to hold with this traditional view, and it is now my purpose to argue that this view is at least a fairly reasonable one. . . .

My diagnosis of the situation is this. In everyday affairs we often speak loosely, charitably, and casually; we tend to let what we say pass as being true. I want to suggest that it is by being wrongly serious about this casual talk that philosophers (myself included) have come to think it rather easy to know things to be so. In particular, they have come to think that certainty is not needed. Thus typical in the contemporary literature is this sort of exchange. An examiner asks a student when a certain battle was fought. The student fumbles about and, eventually, unconfidently says what is true: "The Battle of Hastings was fought in 1066." It is supposed, quite properly, that this correct answer is a result of the student's reading. The examiner, being an ordinary mortal, allows that the student knows the answer; he judges that the student knows that the Battle of Hastings was fought in 1066. Surely, it is suggested, the examiner is correct in his judgment even though this student clearly is not certain of the thing; therefore, knowing does not require being certain. But is the examiner really correct in asserting that the student knows the date of this battle? That is, do such exchanges give us good reason to think that knowing does not require certainty?

My recommendation is this. Let us try focusing on just those words most directly employed in expressing the concept whose conditions are our object of inquiry. This principle is quite generally applicable and, I think, quite easily applied. We may apply it by suitably juxtaposing certain terms, like "really" and "actually," with the terms most in question (here, the term "knows"). More strikingly, we may *emphasize* the terms in question. Thus, instead of looking at something as innocent as "He knows that they are alive," let us consider the more relevant "He (really) *knows* that they are alive."

Let us build some confidence that this principle is quite generally applicable, and that it will give us trustworthy results. Toward this end, we may focus on some thoughts about definite descriptions—that is, about expressions of the form "the so-and-so." About these expressions, it is a tradition to hold that they require uniqueness, or unique satisfaction, for their proper application. Thus just as it is traditional to hold that a man knows something only if he is certain of it, so it is also traditional to hold that there is something which is the chair with seventeen legs only if there is exactly one chair with just that many legs. But again, by being wrongly serious about our casual everyday talk, philosophers may come to deny the traditional view. They may do this by being wrongly serious, I think, about the following sort of ordinary exchange. Suppose an examiner asks a student, "Who is the father of Nelson Rockefeller, the present Governor of New York State?" The student replies, "Nelson Rockefeller is the son of John D. Rockefeller, Jr." No doubt, the examiner will allow that, by implication, the student got the right answer; he will judge that what the student said is true even though the examiner is correctly confident that the elder Rockefeller sired other sons. Just so, one might well argue that definite descriptions, like "the son of X," do not require uniqueness. But against this argument from the everyday flow of talk, let us insist that we focus on the relevant conception by employing our standard means for emphasizing the most directly relevant term. Thus, while we might feel nothing contradictory at first in saying, "Nelson Rockefeller is the son of John D. Rockefeller, Jr., and so is Winthrop Rockefeller," we must confess that even initially we would have quite different feelings about our saying "Nelson Rockefeller is actually *the* son of John D. Rockefeller, Jr., and so is Winthrop Rockefeller." With the latter, where emphasis is brought to bear, we cannot help but feel that what is asserted is inconsistent. And, with this, we feel differently about the original remark, feeling it to be essentially the same assertion and so inconsistent as well. Thus, it seems that when we focus on things properly, we may assume that definite descriptions do require uniqueness.

Let us now apply our principle to the question of knowing. Here, while we might feel nothing contradictory at first in saying "He knows that it is raining, but he isn't certain of it," we would feel differently about our saying "He really *knows* that it is raining, but he isn't certain of it." And, if anything, this feeling of contradiction is only enhanced when we further emphasize, "He really *knows* that it is raining, but he isn't actually *certain* of it." Thus it is plausible to suppose that what we said at first is actually inconsistent, and so that knowing does require being certain.

For my defense of skepticism, it now remains only to combine the result we have just reached with that at which we arrived in the previous section. Now, I have argued that each of two propositions deserves, if not our acceptance, at least the suspension of our judgment:

> That, in the case of every human being, there is hardly anything, if anything at all, of which he is certain. That (as a matter of necessity), in the case of every human being, the person knows something to be so only if he is certain of it.

But I think I have done more than just that. For the strength of the arguments given for this position on each of these two propositions is, I think, sufficient for warranting a similar position on propositions which are quite obvious consequences of the two of them together. One such consequential proposition is this:

> That, in the case of every human being, there is hardly anything, if anything at all, which the person knows to be so.

And so this third proposition, which is just the thesis of skepticism, also deserves, if not our acceptance, at least the suspension of our judgment. If this thesis is not reasonable to accept, then neither is its negation, the thesis of "common sense."

Norman Malcolm

Knowledge Regained

Norman Malcolm *is Professor Emeritus of Philosophy at Cornell University. Malcolm was very much influenced by Wittgenstein with whom he studied at Cambridge University. He is the author of numerous books and articles, among them* Dreaming *and* Knowledge and Certainty.

Some philosophers have held that when we make judgments of perception such as that there are peonies in the garden, cows in the field, or dishes in the cupboard, we are "taking for granted" that the peonies, cows, and dishes exist, but not knowing it in the "strict" sense. Others have held that all empirical propositions, including judgments of perception, are merely hypotheses. The thought behind this exaggerated mode of expression is that any empirical proposition whatever *could* be refuted by future experience—that is, it *could* turn out to be false. Are these philosophers right?

Consider the following propositions:

(i) The sun is about ninety million miles from the earth.
(ii) There is a heart in my body.
(iii) Here is an ink-bottle

In various circumstances I should be willing to assert of each of these propositions that I know it to be true. Yet they differ strikingly. This I see when, with each, I try to imagine the possibility that it is false.

(i) If in ordinary conversation someone said to me "The sun is about 20 million miles from the earth, isn't it?" I should reply "No; it is about 90 million miles from us." If he said "I think that you are confusing the sun with Polaris", I should reply, "I *know* that 90 million miles is roughly the sun's distance from the earth". I might invite him to verify the figure in an encyclopedia. A third person who overheard our conversation could quite correctly report that I knew the distance to the sun, whereas the other man did not. But this knowledge of mine is little better than hearsay. I have seen that figure mentioned in a few books. I know nothing about the observations and calculations that led astronomers to accept it. If tomorrow a group of eminent astronomers announced that a great error had been made and that the correct figure is 20 million miles, I should not insist that they were wrong. It would surprise me that such an enormous mistake could have been made. But I should no longer be willing to say that I *know* that 90 million is the correct figure. Although I should *now* claim that I know the distance to be about 90 million miles, it is easy for me to envisage the possibility that some future investigation will prove this to be entirely false.

(ii) Suppose that after a routine medical examination the excited doctor reports to me that the X-ray photographs show that I have no heart. I should tell him to get a new machine.

I should be inclined to say that the fact that I have a heart is one of the few things that I can count on as absolutely certain. I can feel it beat. I know it's there. Furthermore, how could my blood circulate if I didn't have one? Suppose that later on I suffer a chest injury and undergo a surgical operation. Afterwards the astonished surgeons solemnly declare that they searched my chest cavity and found no heart, and that they made incisions and looked about in other likely places but found it not. They are convinced that I am without a heart. They are unable to understand how circulation can occur or what accounts for the thumping in my chest. But they are in agreement and obviously sincere, and they have clear photographs of my interior spaces. What would be my attitude? Would it be to insist that they were all mistaken? I think not. I believe that I should eventually accept their testimony and the evidence of the photographs. I should consider to be false what I now regard as an absolute certainty.

(iii) Suppose that as I write this paper someone in the next room was to call out to me "I can't find an ink-bottle; is there one in the house"? I should reply "Here is an ink-bottle". If he said in doubtful tone "Are you sure? I looked there before", I should reply "Yes, I know there is; come and get it".

Now could it turn out to be false that there is an ink-bottle directly in front of me on this desk? Many philosophers have thought so. They would say that many things could happen of such a nature that if they did happen it would be proved that I am deceived. I agree that many extraordinary things could happen, in the sense that there is no logical absurdity in the supposition. It could happen that when I next reach for this ink-bottle my hand should seem to pass *through* it and I should not feel the contact of any object. It could happen that in the next moment the ink-bottle will suddenly vanish from sight; or that I should find myself under a tree in the garden with no ink-bottle about; or that one or more persons should enter this room and declare with apparent sincerity that they see no ink-bottle on this desk; or that a photograph taken now of the top of the desk should clearly show all of the objects on it except the ink-bottle. Having admitted that these things *could* happen, am I compelled to admit that if they did happen then it would be proved that there is no ink-bottle here *now*? Not at all! I could say that when my hand seemed to pass through the ink-bottle I should *then* be suffering from hallucination; that if the ink-bottle suddenly vanished it would have miraculously ceased to exist; that the other persons were conspiring to drive me mad, or were themselves victims of remarkable concurrent hallucinations; that the camera possessed some strange flaw or that there was trickery in developing the negative. I admit that in the next moment I could find myself under a tree or in a bathtub. But this is not to admit that it could be revealed in the next moment that I am now dreaming. For what I admit is that I might be instantaneously transported to the garden, but not that in the next moment I might *wake up* in the garden. There is nothing that could happen to me in the next moment that I should call "waking up"; and therefore nothing that could happen to me in the next moment would be accepted by me now as proof that I now dream.

Not only do I not *have* to admit that those extraordinary occurrences would be evidence that there is no ink-bottle here; the fact is that I *do not* admit it. There is nothing whatever that could happen in the next moment or the next year that would by me be called *evidence* that there is not an ink-bottle here now. No future experience or investigation could prove to me that I am mistaken. Therefore, if I were to say "I know that there is an ink-bottle here", I should be using "know" in the strong sense.

It will appear to some that I have adopted an *unreasonable* attitude toward that statement. There is, however, nothing unreasonable about it. It seems so because one thinks that the statement that here is an ink-bottle *must* have the same status as the statements that the sun is 90 million miles away and that I have a heart and that there will be water in the gorge this afternoon. But this is a *prejudice*.

In saying that I should regard nothing as evidence that there is no ink-bottle here now,

I am not *predicting* what I should do if various astonishing things happened. If other members of my family entered this room and, while looking at the top of this desk, declared with apparent sincerity that they see no ink-bottle, I might fall into a swoon or become mad. I *might* even come to believe that there is not and has not been an ink-bottle here. I cannot foretell with certainty how I should react. But if it is *not* a prediction, what is the meaning of my assertion that I should regard nothing as evidence that there is no ink-bottle here?

That assertion describes my *present* attitude towards the statement that here is an ink-bottle. It does not prophecy what my attitude *would* be if various things happened. My present attitude toward that statement is radically different from my present attitude toward those other statements (*e.g.* that I have a heart). I do *now* admit that certain future occurrences would disprove the latter. Whereas no imaginable future occurrence would be considered by me *now* as proving that there is not an ink-bottle here.

These remarks are not meant to be autobiographical. They are meant to throw light on the common concepts of evidence, proof, and disproof. Everyone of us upon innumerable occasions of daily life takes this same attitude towards various statements about physical things, *e.g.* that here is a torn page, that this dish is broken, that the thermometer reads 70, that no rug is on the floor. Furthermore, the concepts of proof, disproof, doubt, and conjecture, *require* us to take this attitude. In order for it to be possible that any statements about physical things should *turn out to be false* it is necessary that some statements about physical things *cannot* turn out to be false.

Lewis Carroll
Through the Looking Glass

Lewis Carroll (1832–1898), *whose real name was Charles Lutwidge Dodgson, was an English mathematician and logician. His mother died when he went away to college, and he became increasingly drawn to the company of children, especially little girls. He was afflicted with a stammer which made him uncomfortable in the company of adults. His books* Alice in Wonderland *and* Through the Looking Glass *are two of the great children's books in English. He also published mathematical works.*

After a pause, Alice began, 'Well——were *both* very unpleasant characters——' Here she checked herself in some alarm, at hearing something that sounded to her like the puffing of a large steam-engine in the wood near them, though she feared it was more likely to be a wild beast. 'Are there any lions or tigers about here?' she asked timidly.

'It's only the Red King snoring,' said Tweedledee.

'Come and look at him!' the brothers cried, and they each took one of Alice's hands, and led her up to where the King was sleeping.

'Isn't he a *lovely* sight?' said Tweedledum.

Alice couldn't say honestly that he was. He had a tall red night-cap on, with a tassel, and he was lying crumpled up into a sort of untidy heap, and snoring loud——'fit to snore his head off!' as Tweedledum remarked.

'I'm afraid he'll catch cold with lying on the damp grass,' said Alice, who was a very thoughtful little girl.

'He's dreaming now,' said Tweedledee: 'and what do you think he's dreaming about?'

Alice said 'Nobody can guess that.'

'Why, about *you!*' Tweedledee exclaimed, clapping his hands triumphantly. 'And if he left off dreaming about you, where do you suppose you'd be?'

'Where I am now, of course,' said Alice.

'Not you!' Tweedledee retorted contemptuously. 'You'd be nowhere. Why, you're only a sort of thing in his dream!'

'If that there King was to wake,' added Tweedledum, 'you'd go out—bang!—just like a candle!'

'I shouldn't!' Alice exclaimed indignantly. 'Besides, if *I'm* only a sort of thing in his dream, what are *you,* I should like to know?'

'Ditto,' said Tweedledum.

'Ditto, ditto!' cried Tweedledee.

He shouted this so loud that Alice couldn't help saying 'Hush! You'll be waking him, I'm afraid, if you make so much noise.'

'Well, it's no use *your* talking about waking him,' said Tweedledum, 'when you're only one of the things in his dream. You know very well you're not real.'

'I *am* real!' said Alice, and began to cry.

'You wo'n't make yourself a bit realler by crying,' Tweedledee remarked: 'there's nothing to cry about.'

'If I wasn't real,' Alice said—half-laughing through her tears, it all seemed so ridiculous—'I shouldn't be able to cry.'

'I hope you don't suppose those are *real* tears?' Tweedledum interrupted in a tone of great contempt.

Jorge L. Borges
The Circular Ruins

Jorge L. Borges *is one of the greatest South American writers of this century. Challenging traditional narrative forms, he has had an enormous impact on postmodern literature. Among his most famous books are* Labyrinths, Ficciones, *and* Dreamtigers.

And if he left off dreaming about you . . .

Through the Looking Glass, VI

No one saw him disembark in the unanimous night, no one saw the bamboo canoe sinking into the sacred mud, but within a few days no one was unaware that the silent man came from the South and that his home was one of the infinite villages upstream, on the violent mountainside, where the Zend tongue is not contaminated with Greek and where leprosy is infrequent. The truth is that the obscure man kissed the mud, came up the bank without pushing aside (probably without feeling) the brambles which dilacerated his flesh, and dragged himself, nauseous and bloodstained, to the circular enclosure crowned by a stone tiger or horse, which once was the color of fire and now was that of ashes. This circle was a temple, long ago devoured by fire, which the malarial jungle had profaned and whose god no longer received the homage of men. The stranger stretched out beneath the pedestal. He was awakened by the sun high above. He evidenced without astonishment that his wounds had closed; he shut his pale eyes and slept, not out of bodily weakness but out of determination of will. He knew that this temple was the place required by his invincible purpose; he knew that, downstream, the incessant trees had not managed to choke the ruins of another propitious temple, whose gods were also burned and dead; he knew that his immediate obligation was to sleep. Towards midnight he was awakened by the disconsolate cry of a bird. Prints of bare feet, some figs and a jug told him that men of the region had respectfully spied upon his sleep and were solicitous of his favor or feared his magic. He felt the chill of fear and sought out a burial niche in the dilapidated wall and covered himself with some unknown leaves.

The purpose which guided him was not impossible, though it was supernatural. He wanted to dream a man: he wanted to dream him with minute integrity and insert him into reality. This magical project had exhausted the entire content of his soul; if someone had asked him his own name or any trait of his previous life, he would not have been able to answer. The uninhabited and broken temple suited him, for it was a minimum of visible world; the nearness of the peasants also suited him, for they would see that his frugal necessities were supplied. The rice and fruit of their tribute were sufficient sustenance for his body, consecrated to the sole task of sleeping and dreaming.

At first, his dreams were chaotic; somewhat later, they were of a dialectical nature. The stranger dreamt that he was in the center of a circular amphitheater which in some way was the burned temple: clouds of silent students filled the gradins; the faces of the last ones hung many centuries away and at a cosmic height, but were entirely clear and precise. The man was lecturing to them on anatomy, cosmography, magic; the countenances listened with eagerness and strove to respond with understanding, as if they divined the importance of the examination which would redeem one of them from his state of vain appearance and interpolate him into the world of reality. The man, both in dreams and awake, considered his phantoms' replies, was not deceived by impostors, divined a growing intelligence in certain perplexities. He sought a soul which would merit participation in the universe.

After nine or ten nights, he comprehended with some bitterness that he could expect nothing of those students who passively accepted his doctrines, but that he could of those who, at times, would venture a reasonable contradiction. The former, though worthy of love and affection, could not rise to the state of individuals; the latter pre-existed somewhat more. One afternoon (now his afternoons too were tributaries of sleep, now he remained awake only for a couple of hours at dawn) he dismissed the vast illusory college forever and kept one single student. He was a silent boy, sallow, sometimes obstinate, with sharp features which reproduced those of the dreamer. He was not long disconcerted by his companions' sudden elimination; his progress, after a few special lessons, astounded his teacher. Nevertheless, catastrophe ensued. The man emerged from sleep one day as if from a viscous desert, looked at the vain light of afternoon, which at first he confused with that of dawn, and understood that he had not really dreamt. All that night and all day, the intolerable lucidity of insomnia weighed upon him. He tried to explore the jungle, to exhaust himself; amidst the hemlocks, he was scarcely able to manage a few snatches of feeble sleep, fleetingly mottled with some rudimentary visions which were useless. He tried to convoke the college and had scarcely uttered a few brief words of exhortation, when it became deformed and was extinguished. In his almost perpetual sleeplessness, his old eyes burned with tears of anger.

He comprehended that the effort to mold the incoherent and vertiginous matter dreams are made of was the most arduous task a man could undertake, though he might penetrate all the enigmas of the upper and lower orders: much more arduous than weaving a rope of sand or coining the faceless wind. He comprehended that an initial failure was inevitable. He swore he would forget the enormous hallucination which had misled him at first, and he sought another method. Before putting it into effect, he dedicated a month to replenishing the powers his delirium had wasted. He abandoned any premeditation of dreaming and, almost at once, was able to sleep for a considerable part of the day. The few times he dreamt during this period, he did not take notice of the dreams. To take up his task again, he waited until the moon's disk was perfect. Then, in the afternoon, he purified himself in the waters of the river, worshiped the planetary gods, uttered the lawful syllables of a powerful name and slept. Almost immediately, he dreamt of a beating heart.

He dreamt it as active, warm, secret, the size of a closed fist, of garnet color in the penumbra of a human body as yet without face or sex; with minute love he dreamt it, for fourteen lucid nights. Each night he perceived it with greater clarity. He did not touch it, but limited himself to witnessing it, observing it, perhaps correcting it with his eyes. He perceived it, lived it, from many distances and many angles. On the fourteenth night he touched the pulmonary artery with his finger, and then the whole heart, inside and out. The examination satisfied him. Deliberately, he did not dream for a night; then he took the heart again, invoked the name of a planet and set about to envision another of the principal organs. Within a year he reached the skeleton, the eyelids. The innumerable hair was perhaps the most difficult task. He dreamt a complete man, a youth, but this youth could not rise nor did he speak nor could he open his eyes. Night after night, the man dreamt him as asleep.

In the Gnostic cosmogonies, the demiurgi knead and mold a red Adam who cannot stand alone; as unskillful and crude and elementary as this Adam of dust was the Adam of dreams fabricated by the magician's nights of effort. One afternoon, the man almost destroyed his work, but then repented. (It would have been better for him had he destroyed it.) Once he had completed his supplications to the numina of the earth and the river, he threw himself down at the feet of the effigy which was perhaps a tiger and perhaps a horse, and implored its unknown succor. That twilight, he dreamt of the statue. He dreamt of it as a living, tremulous thing: it was not an atrocious mongrel of tiger and horse, but both these vehement creatures at once and also a bull, a rose, a tempest. This multiple god revealed to him that its earthly name was Fire, that in the circular temple (and in others of its kind) people had rendered it sacrifices and cult and that it would magically give life to the sleeping phantom, in such a way that all creatures except Fire itself and the dreamer would believe him to be a man of flesh and blood. The man was ordered by the divinity to instruct his creature in its rites, and send him to the other broken temple whose pyramids survived downstream, so that in this deserted edifice a voice might give glory to the god. In the dreamer's dream, the dreamed one awoke.

The magician carried out these orders. He devoted a period of time (which finally comprised two years) to revealing the arcana of the universe and of the fire cult to his dream child. Inwardly, it pained him to be separated from the boy. Under the pretext of pedagogical necessity, each day he prolonged the hours he dedicated to his dreams. He also redid the right shoulder, which was perhaps deficient. At times, he was troubled by the impression that all this had happened before. . . . In general, his days were happy; when he closed his eyes, he would think: *Now I shall be with my son.* Or, less often: *The child I have engendered awaits me and will not exist if I do not go to him.*

Gradually, he accustomed the boy to reality. Once he ordered him to place a banner on a distant peak. The following day, the banner flickered from the mountain top. He tried other analogous experiments, each more daring than the last. He understood with certain bitterness that his son was ready—and perhaps impatient—to be born. That night he kissed him for the first time and sent him to the other temple whose debris showed white downstream, through many leagues of inextricable jungle and swamp. But first (so that he would never know he was a phantom, so that he would be thought a man like others) he instilled into him a complete oblivion of his years of apprenticeship.

The man's victory and peace were dimmed by weariness. At dawn and at twilight, he would prostrate himself before the stone figure, imagining perhaps that his unreal child was practicing the same rites, in other circular ruins, downstream; at night, he would not dream, or would dream only as all men do. He perceived the sounds and forms of the universe with certain colorlessness: his absent son was being nurtured with these diminutions of his soul. His life's purpose was complete; the man persisted in a kind of ecstacy. After a time, which some narrators of his story prefer to compute in years and others in lustra, he was awakened one midnight by two boatmen; he could not see their faces, but they told him of a magic man in a temple of the North who could walk upon fire and not be burned. The magician suddenly remembered the words of the god. He recalled that, of all the creatures of the world, fire was the only one that knew his son was a phantom. This recollection, at first soothing, finally tormented him. He feared his son might meditate on his abnormal privilege and discover in some way that his condition was that of a mere image. Not to be a man, to be the projection of another man's dream, what a feeling of humiliation, of vertigo! All fathers are interested in the children they have procreated (they have permitted to exist) in mere confusion or pleasure; it was natural that the magician should fear for the future of that son, created in thought, limb by limb and feature by feature, in a thousand and one secret nights.

The end of his meditations was sudden, though it was foretold in certain signs. First (after a long drought) a faraway cloud on a hill, light and rapid as a bird; then, toward the south, the sky which had the rose color of the leopard's mouth; then the smoke which corroded the metallic nights; finally, the panicky flight of the animals. For what was happening had happened many centuries ago. The ruins of the fire god's sanctuary were destroyed by fire. In a birdless dawn the magician saw the concentric blaze close round the walls. For a moment, he thought of taking refuge in the river, but then he knew that death was coming to crown his old age and absolve him of his labors. He walked into the shreds of flame. But they did not bite into his flesh, they caressed him and engulfed him without heat or combustion. With relief, with humiliation, with terror, he understood that he too was a mere appearance, dreamt by another.

Bertrand Russell

Appearance and Reality

Bertrand Russell *(1872–1970) was one of the greatest philosophers of this century. He wrote an enormous number of philosophical books and articles, from* Principia Mathematica *(with Alfred North Whitehead) to some notorious polemics in favor of "free love" and atheism. Like Hume, he was too controversial for most universities, and a famous court case prevented him from teaching at City College of New York. He did, however, win the Nobel Prize for Literature in 1950. At the age of 89, he was jailed for protesting against nuclear arms.*

In daily life, we assume as certain many things which, on a closer scrutiny, are found to be so full of apparent contradictions that only a great amount of thought enables us to know what it is that we really may believe. In the search for certainty, it is natural to begin with our present experiences, and in some sense, no doubt, knowledge is to be derived from them. But any statement as to what it is that our immediate experiences make us know is very likely to be wrong. It seems to me that I am now sitting in a chair, at a table of a certain shape, on which I see sheets of paper with writing or print. By turning my head I see out of the window buildings and clouds and the sun. I believe that the sun is about ninety-three million miles from the earth; that it is a hot globe many times bigger than the earth; that, owing to the earth's rotation, it rises every morning, and will continue to do so for an indefinite time in the future. I believe that, if any other normal person comes into my room he will see the same chairs and tables and books and papers as I see, and that the table which I see is the same as the table which I feel pressing against my arm. All this seems to be so evident as to be hardly worth stating, except in answer to a man who doubts whether I know anything. Yet all this may be reasonably doubted, and all of it requires much careful discussion before we can be sure that we have stated it in a form that is wholly true.

To make our difficulties plain, let us concentrate attention on the table. To the eye it is oblong, brown and shiny, to the touch it is smooth and cool and hard; when I tap it, it gives out a wooden sound. Any one else who sees and feels and hears the table will agree with this description, so that it might seem as if no difficulty would arise; but as soon as we try to be more precise our troubles begin. Although I believe that the table is 'really' of the same colour all over, the parts that reflect the light look much brighter than the other parts, and some parts look white because of reflected light. I know that, if I move, the parts that reflect the light will be different, so that the apparent distribution of colours on the table will change. It follows that if several people are looking at the table at the same moment, no two of them will see exactly the same distribution of colours, because no two can see it from exactly the same point of view, and any change in the point of view makes some change in the way the light is reflected.

For most practical purposes these differences are unimportant, but to the painter they are all-important: the painter has to unlearn the habit of thinking that things seem to have the colour which common sense says they 'really' have, and to learn the habit of seeing things as they appear. Here we have already the beginning of one of the distinctions that cause most trouble in philosophy—the distinction between 'appearance' and 'reality', between what things seem to be and what they are. The painter wants to know what things seem to be, the practical man and the philosopher want to know what they are; but the philosopher's wish to know this is stronger than the practical man's, and is more troubled by knowledge as to the difficulties of answering the question.

To return to the table. It is evident from what we have found, that there is no colour which preeminently appears to be *the* colour of the table, or even of any one particular part of the table—it appears to be of different colours from different points of view, and there is no reason for regarding some of these as more really its colour than others. And we know that even from a given point of view the colour will seem different by artificial light, or to a colour-blind man, or to a man wearing blue spectacles, while in the dark there will be no colour at all, though to touch and hearing the table will be unchanged. This colour is not something which is inherent in the table, but something depending upon the table and the spectator and the way the light falls on the table. When, in ordinary life, we speak of *the* colour of the table, we only mean the sort of colour which it will seem to have to a normal spectator from an ordinary point of view under usual conditions of light. But the other colours which appear under other conditions have just as good a right to be considered real; and therefore, to avoid favouritism, we are compelled to deny that, in itself, the table has any one particular colour.

The same thing applies to the texture. With the naked eye one can see the grain, but otherwise the table looks smooth and even. If we look at it through a microscope, we should see roughnesses and hills and valleys, and all sorts of differences that are imperceptible to the naked eye. Which of these is the 'real' table? We are naturally tempted to say that what we see through the microscope is more real, but that in turn would be changed by a still more powerful microscope. If, then, we cannot trust what we see with the naked eye, why should we trust what we see through a microscope? Thus, again, the confidence in our sense with which we began deserts us.

The *shape* of the table is no better. We are all in the habit of judging as to the 'real' shapes of things, and we do this so unreflectingly that we come to think we actually see the real shapes. But, in fact, as we all have to learn if we try to draw, a given thing looks different in shape from every different point of view. If our table is 'really' rectangular, it will look, from almost all points of view, as if it had two acute angles and two obtuse angles. If opposite sides are parallel, they will look as if they converged to a point away from the spectator; if they are of equal length, they will look as if the nearer side were longer. All these things are not commonly noticed in looking at a table, because experience has taught us to construct the 'real' shape from the apparent shape, and the 'real' shape is what interests us as practical men. But the 'real' shape is not what we see; it is something inferred from what we see. And what we see is constantly changing in shape as we move about the room; so that here again the senses seem not to give us the truth about the table itself, but only about the appearance of the table.

Similar difficulties arise when we consider the sense of touch. It is true that the table always gives us a sensation of hardness, and we feel that it resists pressure. But the sensation we obtain depends upon how hard we press the table and also upon what part of the body we press with; thus the various sensations due to various pressures or various parts of the body cannot be supposed to reveal *directly* any definite property of the table, but at most to be *signs* of some property which perhaps *causes* all the sensations, but is not actually apparent in any of them. And the same applies still more obviously to the sounds which can be elicited by rapping the table.

Thus it becomes evident that the real table, if there is one, is not the same as what we immediately experienced by sight or touch or hearing. The real table, if there is one, is not *immediately* known to us at all, but must be an inference from what is immediately known. Hence, two very difficult questions at once arise; namely (1) Is there a real table at all? (2) If so, what sort of object can it be?

John Locke

Where Our Ideas Come From

John Locke *(1632–1704) taught philosophy at Oxford until he earned his medical degree. He devoted considerable time to politics, and his two* Treatises on Government *were highly influential in establishing the theoretical grounds of the U.S. Constitution. Not only is he the founder of modern political liberalism, his* Essay Concerning Human Understanding *initiated what has come to be known as British empiricism.*

SOME FARTHER CONSIDERATIONS CONCERNING OUR SIMPLE IDEAS OF SENSATION

1. *Positive ideas from privative causes.*—Concerning the simple ideas of sensation it is to be considered, that whatsoever is so constituted in nature as to be able by affecting our senses

to cause any perception in the mind, doth thereby produce in the understanding a simple idea; which, whatever be the external cause of it, when it comes to be taken notice of by our discerning faculty, it is by the mind looked on and considered there to be a real positive idea in the understanding, as much as any other whatsoever; though perhaps the cause of it be but a privation in the subject.

2. Thus the ideas of heat and cold, light and darkness, white and black, motion and rest, are equally clear and positive ideas in the mind; though perhaps some of the causes which produce them are barely privations in those subjects from whence our senses derive those ideas. These the understanding, in its view of them, considers all as distinct positive ideas without taking notice of the causes that produce them; which is an inquiry not belonging to the idea as it is in the understanding, but to the nature of the things existing without us. These are two very different things, and carefully to be distinguished; it being one thing to perceive and know the idea of white or black, and quite another to examine what kind of particles they must be, and how ranged in the superficies, to make any object appear white or black.

3. A painter or dyer who never inquired into their causes, hath the ideas of white and black and other colours as clearly, perfectly, and distinctly in his understanding, and perhaps more distinctly than the philosopher who hath busied himself in considering their natures, and thinks he knows how far either of them is in its cause positive or privative; and the idea of black is no less positive in his mind than that of white, however the cause of that colour in the external object may be only a privation.

4. If it were the design of my present undertaking to inquire into the natural causes and manner of perception, I should offer this as a reason why a privative cause might, in some cases at least, produce a positive idea, viz., that all sensation being produced in us only by different degrees and modes of motion in our animal spirits, variously agitated by external objects, the abatement of any former motion must as necessarily produce a new sensation as the variation or increase of it; and so introduce a new idea, which depends only on a different motion of the animal spirits in that organ.

5. But whether this be so or not I will not here determine, but appeal to every one's own experience, whether the shadow of a man, though it consists of nothing but the absence of light (and the more the absence of light is, the more discernible is the shadow), does not, when a man looks on it, cause as clear and positive an idea in his mind as a man himself, though covered over with clear sunshine! And the picture of a shadow is a positive thing. Indeed, we have negative names, [which stand not directly for positive ideas, but for their absence, such as *insipid, silence, nihil, &c.,* which words denote positive ideas, *v. g., taste, sound, being,* with a signification of their absence.]

6. *Positive ideas from privative causes.*—And thus one may truly be said to see darkness. For, supposing a hole perfectly dark, from whence no light is reflected, it is certain one may see the figure of it, or it may be painted; or whether the ink I write with make any other idea, is a question. The privative causes I have here assigned of positive ideas are according to the common opinion; but, in truth, it will be hard to determine whether there be really any ideas from a privative cause, till it be determined whether rest be any more a privation than motion.

7. *Ideas in the mind, qualities in bodies.*—To discover the nature of our ideas the better, and to discourse of them intelligibly, it will be convenient to distinguish them, as they are ideas or perceptions in our minds, and as they are modifications of matter in the bodies that cause such perceptions in us; that so we may not think (as perhaps usually is done) that they are exactly the images and resemblances of something inherent in the subject; most of those of sensation being in the mind no more the likeness of something existing without us than the names that stand for them are the likeness of our ideas, which yet upon hearing they are apt to excite in us.

8. Whatsoever the mind perceives in itself, or is the immediate object of perception, thought, or understanding, that I call "idea;" and the power to produce any idea in our mind, I call "quality" of the subject wherein that power is. Thus a snowball having the power to produce in us the ideas of white, cold, and round, the powers to produce those ideas in us as they are in the snowball, I call "qualities;" and as they are sensations or perceptions in our understandings, I call them "ideas;" which ideas, if I speak of them sometimes as in the things themselves, I would be understood to mean those qualities in the objects which produce them in us.

9. *Primary qualities.*—[Qualities thus considered in bodies are, First, such as are utterly inseparable from the body, in what estate soever it be;] and such as, in all the alterations and changes it suffers, all the force can be used upon it, it constantly keeps; and such as sense constantly finds in every particle of matter which has bulk enough to be perceived, and the mind finds inseparable from every particle of matter, though less than to make itself singly be perceived by our senses: *v. g.,* take a grain of wheat, divide it into two parts, each part has still solidity, extension, figure, and mobility; divide it again, and it retains still the same qualities: and so divide it on till the parts become insensible, they must retain still each of them all those qualities. For, division (which is all that a mill or pestle or any other body does upon another, in reducing it to insensible parts) can never take away either solidity, extension, figure, or mobility from any body, but only makes two or more distinct separate masses of matter of that which was but one before; all which distinct masses, reckoned as so many distinct bodies, after division, make a certain number. [These I call *original* or *primary* qualities of body, which I think we may observe to produce simple ideas in us, viz., solidity, extension, figure, motion or rest, and number.

10. *Secondary qualities.*—Secondly. Such qualities, which in truth are nothing in the objects themselves, but powers to produce various sensations in us by their primary qualities, *i. e.,* by the bulk, figure, texture, and motion of their insensible parts, as colours, sounds, tastes, &c., these I call *secondary* qualities. To these might be added a third sort, which are allowed to be barely powers, though they are as much real qualities in the subject as those which I, to comply with the common way of speaking, call qualities, but, for distinction, *secondary* qualities. For, the power in fire to produce a new colour or consistency in wax or clay, by its primary qualities, is as much a quality in fire as the power it has to produce in me a new idea or sensation of warmth or burning, which I felt not before, by the same primary qualities, viz., the bulk, texture, and motion of its insensible parts.]

11. [*How primary qualities produce their ideas.*—The next thing to be considered is, how bodies produce ideas in us; and that is manifestly by impulse, the only way which we can conceive bodies to operate in.]

12. If, then, external objects be not united to our minds when they produce ideas therein, and yet we perceive these original qualities in such of them as singly fall under our senses, it is evident that some motion must be thence continued by our nerves, or animal spirits, by some parts of our bodies, to the brains or the seat of sensation, there to produce in our minds the particular ideas we have of them. And since the extension, figure, number, and motion of bodies of an observable bigness, may be perceived at a distance by the sight, it is evident some singly imperceptible bodies must come from them to the eyes, and thereby convey to the brain some motion which produces these ideas which we have of them in us.

13. *How secondary.*—After the same manner that the ideas of these original qualities are produced in us, we may conceive that the ideas of secondary qualities are also produced, viz., by the operation of insensible particles on our senses. For it being manifest that there are bodies, and good store of bodies, each whereof are so small that we cannot by any of our senses discover either their bulk, figure, or motion (as is evident in the particles of the air and water, and other extremely smaller than those, perhaps as much smaller than the particles of air or water as the particles of air or water are smaller than peas or hailstones): let us

suppose at present that the different motions and figures, bulk and number, of such particles, effecting the several organs of our senses, produce in us those different sensations which we have from the colours and smells of bodies, v. g., that a violet, by the impulse of such insensible particles of matter of peculiar figures and bulks, and in different degrees and modifications of their motions, causes the ideas of the blue colour and sweet scent of that flower to be produced in our minds; it being no more impossible to conceive that God should annex such ideas to such motions, with which they have no similitude, than that he should annex the idea of pain to the motion of a piece of steel dividing our flesh, with which the idea hath no resemblance.

14. What I have said concerning colours and smells may be understood also of tastes and sounds, and other the like sensible qualities; which, whatever reality we by mistake attribute to them, are in truth nothing in the objects themselves, but powers to produce various sensations in us, and depend on those primary qualities, viz., bulk, figure, texture, and motion of parts [as I have said.]

15. *Ideas of primary qualities are resemblances; of secondary, not.*—From whence I think it is easy to draw this observation, that the ideas of primary qualities of bodies are resemblances of them, and their patterns do really exist in the bodies themselves; but the ideas produced in us by these secondary qualities have no resemblance of them at all. There is nothing like our ideas existing in the bodies themselves. They are, in the bodies we denominate from them, only a power to produce those sensations in us; and what is sweet, blue, or warm in idea, is but the certain bulk, figure, and motion of the insensible parts in the bodies themselves, which we call so.

16. Flame is denominated *hot* and *light;* snow, *white* and *cold;* and manna *white* and *sweet,* from the ideas they produce in us, which qualities are commonly thought to be the same in those bodies that those ideas are in us, the one the perfect resemblance of the other, as they are in a mirror; and it would by most men be judged very extravagant, if one should say otherwise. And yet he that will consider that the same fire that at one distance produces in us the sensation of warmth, does at a nearer approach produce in us the far different sensation of pain, ought to bethink himself what reason he has to say, that this idea of warmth which was produced in him by the fire, is actually in the fire, and his idea of pain which the same fire produced in him the same way is not in the fire. Why is whiteness and coldness in snow and pain not, when it produces the one and the other idea in us, and can do neither but by the bulk, figure, number, and motion of its solid parts?

17. The particular bulk, number, figure, and motion of the parts of fire or snow are really in them, whether any one's senses perceive them or no; and therefore they may be called *real* qualities, because they really exist in those bodies. But light, heat, whiteness, or coldness, are no more really in them than sickness or pain is in manna. Take away the sensation of them; let not the eyes see light or colours, nor the ears hear sounds; let the palate not taste, nor the nose smell; and all colours, tastes, odours, and sounds, as they are such particular ideas, vanish and cease, and are reduced to their causes, *i. e.,* bulk, figure, and motion of parts.

George Berkeley
To Be Is to Be Perceived

George Berkeley *(1685–1753) was born, raised, and educated in Ireland. He wrote virtually all the works that made him famous before he was twenty-eight. Unlike his fellow empiricists Locke and Hume, he focused most of his philosophical attention on a* *single issue—perception. His most famous work is his* Treatise Concerning the Principles of Human Knowledge.

1. It is evident to any one who takes a survey of the *objects of human knowledge,* that they are either *ideas* actually imprinted on the senses; or else such as are perceived by attending to the passions and operations of the mind; or lastly, *ideas* formed by help of memory and imagination—either compounding, dividing, or barely representing those originally perceived in the aforesaid ways. By sight I have the ideas of light and colours, with their several degrees and variations. By touch I perceive hard and soft, heat and cold, motion and resistance; and of all these more and less either as to quantity or degree. Smelling furnishes me with odours; the palate with tastes; the hearing conveys sounds to the mind in all their variety of tone and composition.

And as several of these are observed to accompany each other, they come to be marked by one name, and so to be reputed as one *thing.* Thus, for example, a certain colour, taste, smell, figure and consistence having been observed to go together; are accounted one distinct thing, signified by the name apple; other collections of ideas constitute a stone, a tree, a book, and the like sensible things; which as they are pleasing or disagreeable excite the passions of love, hatred, joy, grief, and so forth.

2. But, besides all that endless variety of ideas or objects of knowledge, there is likewise Something which knows or perceives them; and exercises divers operations, as willing, imagining, remembering, about them. This perceiving, active being is what I call *mind, spirit, soul,* or *myself.* By which words I do not denote any one of my ideas, but a thing entirely distinct from them, wherein they exist, or, which is the same thing, whereby they are perceived; for the existence of an idea consists in being perceived.

3. That neither our thoughts, nor passions, nor ideas formed by the imagination, exist without the mind is what everybody will allow. And to me it seems no less evident that the various sensations or ideas imprinted on the Sense, however blended or combined together (that is, whatever objects they compose), cannot exist otherwise than in a mind perceiving them. I think an intuitive knowledge may be obtained of this, by any one that shall attend to what is meant by the term *exist* when applied to sensible things. The table I write on I say exists; that is, I see and feel it: and if I were out of my study I should say it existed; meaning thereby that if I was in my study I might perceive it, or that some other spirit actually does perceive it. There was an odour, that is, it was smelt; there was a sound, that is, it was heard; a colour or figure, and it was perceived by sight or touch. This is all that I can understand by these and the like expressions. For as to what is said of the *absolute* existence of unthinking things, without any relation to their being perceived, that is to me perfectly unintelligible. Their *esse* is *percipi;* nor is it possible they should have any existence out of the minds or thinking things which perceive them.

4. It is indeed an opinion strangely prevailing amongst men, that houses, mountains, rivers, and in a word all sensible objects, have an existence, natural or real, distinct from their being perceived by the understanding. But, with how great an assurance and acquiescence soever this Principle may be entertained in the world, yet whoever shall find in his heart to call it in question may, if I mistake not, perceive it to involve a manifest contradiction. For, what are the forementioned objects but the things we perceive by sense? and what do we perceive besides our own ideas or sensations? and is it not plainly repugnant that any one of these, or any combination of them, should exist unperceived?

5. If we thoroughly examine this tenet it will, perhaps, be found at bottom to depend on the doctrine of *abstract ideas.* For can there be a nicer strain of abstraction than to distinguish the existence of sensible objects from their being perceived, so as to conceive them existing unperceived? Light and colours, heat and cold, extension and figures—in a word the things

we see and feel—what are they but so many sensations, notions, ideas, or impressions on the sense? and is it possible to separate, even in thought, any of these from perception? For my part, I might as easily divide a thing from itself. I may, indeed, divide in my thoughts, or conceive apart from each other, those things which perhaps I never perceived by sense so divided. Thus, I imagine the trunk of a human body without the limbs, or conceive the smell of a rose without thinking on the rose itself. So far, I will not deny, I can abstract; if that may properly be called *abstraction* which extends only to the conceiving separately such objects as it is possible may really exist or be actually perceived asunder. But my conceiving or imagining power does not extend beyond the possibility of real existence or perception. Hence, as it is impossible for me to see or feel anything without an actual sensation of that thing, so is it impossible for me to conceive in my thoughts any sensible thing or object distinct from the sensation or perception of it. [In truth, the object and the sensation are the same thing, and cannot therefore be abstracted from each other.]

6. Some truths there are so near and obvious to the mind that a man need only open his eyes to see them. Such I take this important one to be, viz. that all the choir of heaven and furniture of the earth, in a word all those bodies which compose the mighty frame of the world, have not any subsistence without a mind; that their *being* is to be perceived or known; that consequently so long as they are not actually perceived by me, or do not exist in my mind, or that of any other created spirit, they must either have no existence at all, or else subsist in the mind of some Eternal Spirit: it being perfectly unintelligible, and involving all the absurdity of abstraction, to attribute to any single part of them an existence independent of a spirit. To be convinced of which, the reader need only reflect, and try to separate in his own thoughts the *being* of a sensible thing from its *being perceived.*

7. From what has been said it is evident there is not any other Substance than *Spirit,* or that which perceives. But, for the fuller proof of this point, let it be considered the sensible qualities are colour, figure, motion, smell, taste, and such like, that is, the ideas perceived by sense. Now, for an idea to exist in an unperceiving thing is a manifest contradiction; for to have an idea is all one as to perceive: that therefore wherein colour, figure, and the like qualities exist must perceive them. Hence it is clear there can be no unthinking substance or *substratum* of those ideas.

8. But, say you, though the ideas themselves do not exist without the mind, yet there may be things like them, whereof they are copies or resemblances; which things exist without the mind, in an unthinking substance. I answer, an idea can be like nothing but an idea; a colour or figure can be like nothing but another colour or figure. If we look but never so little into our thoughts, we shall find it impossible for us to conceive a likeness except only between our ideas. Again, I ask whether those supposed *originals,* or external things, of which our ideas are the pictures or representations, be themselves perceivable or no? If they are, then *they* are ideas, and we have gained our point: but if you say they are not, I appeal to any one whether it be sense to assert a colour is like something which is invisible; hard or soft, like something which is intangible; and so of the rest.

9. Some there are who make a distinction betwixt *primary* and *secondary* qualities. By the former they mean extension, figure, motion, rest, solidity or impenetrability, and number; by the latter they denote all other sensible qualities, as colours, sounds, tastes, and so forth. The ideas we have of these last they acknowledge not to be the resemblances of anything existing without the mind, or unperceived; but they will have our ideas of the *primary qualities* to be patterns or images of things which exist without the mind, in an unthinking substance which they call Matter. By Matter, therefore, we are to understand an inert, senseless substance, in which extension, figure, and motion do actually subsist. But it is evident, from what we have already shewn, that extension, figure, and motion are only ideas existing in the mind, and that an idea can be like nothing but another idea; and that consequently neither they nor

their archetypes can exist in an unperceiving substance. Hence, it is plain that the very notion of what is called *Matter* or *corporeal substance,* involves a contradiction in it. Insomuch that I should not think it necessary to spend more time in exposing its absurdity. But, because the tenet of the existence of Matter seems to have taken so deep a root in the minds of philosophers, and draws after it so many ill consequences, I choose rather to be thought prolix and tedious than omit anything that might conduce to the full discovery and extirpation of that prejudice.

10. They who assert that figure, motion, and the rest of the primary or original qualities do exist without the mind, in unthinking substances, do at the same time acknowledge that colours, sounds, heat, cold, and suchlike secondary qualities, do not; which they tell us are sensations, existing in the mind alone, that depend on and are occasioned by the different size, texture, and motion of the minute particles of matter. This they take for an undoubted truth, which they can demonstrate beyond all exception. Now, if it be certain that those *original* qualities are inseparably united with the other sensible qualities, and not, even in thought, capable of being abstracted from them, it plainly follows that *they* exist only in the mind. But I desire any one to reflect, and try whether he can, by any abstraction of thought, conceive the extension and motion of a body without all other sensible qualities. For my own part, I see evidently that it is not in my power to frame an idea of a body extended and moving, but I must withal give it some colour or other sensible quality, which is acknowledged to exist only in the mind. In short, extension, figure, and motion, abstracted from all other qualities, are inconceivable. Where therefore the other sensible qualities are, there must these be also, to wit, in the mind and nowhere else. . . .

14. I shall farther add, that, after the same manner as modern philosophers prove certain sensible qualities to have no existence in Matter, or without the mind, the same thing may be likewise proved of all other sensible qualities whatsoever. Thus, for instance, it is said that heat and cold are affections only of the mind, and not at all patterns of real beings, existing in the corporeal substances which excite them; for that the same body which appears cold to one hand seems warm to another. Now, why may we not as well argue that figure and extension are not patterns or resemblances of qualities existing in Matter; because to the same eye at different stations, or eyes of a different texture at the same station, they appear various, and cannot therefore be the images of anything settled and determinate without the mind? Again, it is proved that sweetness is not really in the sapid thing; because the thing remaining unaltered the sweetness is changed into bitter, as in case of a fever or otherwise vitiated palate. Is it not as reasonable to say that motion is not without the mind; since if the succession of ideas in the mind become swifter, the motion, it is acknowledged, shall appear slower, without any alteration in any external object?

15. In short, let any one consider those arguments which are thought manifestly to prove that colours and tastes exist only in the mind, and he shall find they may with equal force be brought to prove the same thing of extension, figure, and motion. Though it must be confessed this method of arguing does not so much prove that there is no extension or colour in an outward object, as that we do not know by sense which is the true extension or colour of the object. But the arguments foregoing plainly shew it to be impossible that any colour or extension at all, or other sensible quality whatsoever, should exist in an unthinking subject without the mind, or in truth that there should be any such thing as an outward object.

16. But let us examine a little the received opinion. It is said extension is a *mode* or *accident* of Matter, and that Matter is the *substratum* that supports it. Now I desire that you would explain to me what is meant by Matter's *supporting* extension. Say you, I have no idea of Matter; and therefore cannot explain it. I answer, though you have no positive, yet, if you have any meaning at all, you must at least have a relative idea of Matter; though you know not what it is, yet you must be supposed to know what relation it bears to accidents, and

what is meant by its supporting them. It is evident *support* cannot here be taken in its usual or literal sense, as when we say that pillars support a building. In what sense therefore must it be taken? For my part, I am not able to discover any sense at all that can be applicable to it.

17. If we inquire into what the most accurate philosophers declare themselves to mean by *material substance,* we shall find them acknowledge they have no other meaning annexed to those sounds but the idea of Being in general, together with the relative notion of its supporting accidents. The general idea of Being appeareth to me the most abstract and incomprehensible of all other; and as for its supporting accidents, this, as we have just now observed, cannot be understood in the common sense of those words: it must therefore be taken in some other sense, but what that is they do not explain. So that when I consider the two parts or branches which make the signification of the words *material substance,* I am convinced there is no distinct meaning annexed to them. But why should we trouble ourselves any farther, in discussing this material *substratum* or support of figure and motion and other sensible qualities? Does it not suppose they have an existence without the mind? And is not this a direct repugnancy, and altogether inconceivable?

18. But, though it were possible that solid, figured, moveable substances may exist without the mind, corresponding to the ideas we have of bodies, yet how is it possible for us to know this? Either we must know it by Sense or by Reason. As for our senses, by them we have the knowledge only of our sensations, ideas, or those things that are immediately perceived by sense, call them what you will: but they do not inform us that things exist without the mind, or unperceived, like to those which are perceived. This the materialists themselves acknowledge.—It remains therefore that if we have any knowledge at all of external things, it must be by reason inferring their existence from what is immediately perceived by sense. But (I do not see) what reason can induce us to believe the existence of bodies without the mind, from what we perceive, since the very patrons of Matter themselves do not pretend there is any necessary connexion betwixt them and our ideas? I say it is granted on all hands (and what happens in dreams, frensies, and the like, puts it beyond dispute) that it is possible we might be affected with all the ideas we have now, though no bodies existed without resembling them. Hence it is evident the supposition of external bodies is not necessary for the producing our ideas; since it is granted they are produced sometimes, and might possibly be produced always, in the same order we see them in at present, without their concurrence.

19. But, though we might possibly have all our sensations without them, yet perhaps it may be thought easier to conceive and explain the manner of their production, by supposing external bodies in their likeness rather than otherwise; and so it might be at least probable there are such things as bodies that excite their ideas in our minds. But neither can this be said. For, though we give the materialists their external bodies, they by their own confession are never the nearer knowing how our ideas are produced; since they own themselves unable to comprehend in what manner body can act upon spirit, or how it is possible it should imprint any idea in the mind. Hence it is evident the production of ideas or sensations in our minds, can be no reason why we should suppose Matter or corporeal substances; since that is acknowledged to remain equally inexplicable with or without this supposition. If therefore it were possible for bodies to exist without the mind, yet to hold they do so must needs be a very precarious opinion; since it is to suppose, without any reason at all, that God has created innumerable beings that are entirely useless, and serve to no manner of purpose.

20. In short, if there were external bodies, it is impossible we should ever come to know it; and if there were not, we might have the very same reasons to think there were that we have now. Suppose—what no one can deny possible—an intelligence, without the help of external bodies, to be affected with the same train of sensations or ideas that you are, imprinted in the same order and with like vividness in his mind. I ask whether that intelligence

hath not all the reason to believe the existence of Corporeal Substances, represented by his ideas, and exciting them in his mind, that you can possibly have for believing the same thing? Of this there can be no question. Which one consideration were enough to make any reasonable person suspect the strength of whatever arguments he may think himself to have, for the existence of bodies without the mind. . . .

23. But, say you, surely there is nothing easier than for me to imagine trees, for instance, in a park, or books existing in a closet, and nobody by to perceive them. I answer, you may so, there is no difficulty in it. But what is all this, I beseech you, more than framing in your mind certain ideas which you call *books* and *trees,* and at the same time omitting to frame the idea of any one that may perceive them? But do not you yourself perceive or think of them all the while? This therefore is nothing to the purpose: it only shews you have the power of imagining, or forming ideas in your mind; but it does not shew that you can conceive it possible the objects of your thoughts may exist without the mind. To make out this, it is necessary that you conceive them existing unconceived or unthought of; which is a manifest repugnancy. When we do our utmost to conceive the existence of external bodies, we are all the while only contemplating our own ideas. But the mind, taking no notice of itself, is deluded to think it can and does conceive bodies existing unthought of, or without the mind, though at the same time they are apprehended by, or exist in, itself. A little attention will discover to any one the truth and evidence of what is here said, and make it unnecessary to insist on any other proofs against the existence of *material substance.*

J. L. Austin
How Philosophers Distort Perception

J. L. Austin (1911–1960) *was a professor of philosophy at Oxford from 1952 until his death. He served as a spy during World War II. A severe critic of traditional philosophy, Austin was a proponent of what came to be known as Ordinary Language Philosophy. His most famous works are* Sense and Sensibilia *and* How To Do Things with Words.

Let us have a look, then at the very beginning of Ayer's *Foundations*—the bottom, one might perhaps call it, of the garden path. In these paragraphs we already seem to see the plain man, here under the implausible aspect of Ayer himself, dribbling briskly into position in front of his own goal, and squaring up to encompass his own destruction.

> It does not normally occur to us that there is any need for us to justify our belief in the existence of material things. At the present moment, for example, I have no doubt whatsoever that I really am perceiving the familiar objects, the chairs and table, the pictures and books and flowers with which my room is furnished; and I am therefore satisfied that they exist. I recognize indeed that people are sometimes deceived by their senses, but this does not lead me to suspect that my own sense-perceptions cannot in general be trusted, or even that they may be deceiving me now. And this is not, I believe, an exceptional attitude. I believe that, in practice,

most people agree with John Locke that 'the certainty of things existing *in rerum natura,* when we have the testimony of our senses for it, is not only as great as our frame can attain to, but as our condition needs'.

When, however, one turns to the writings of those philosophers who have recently concerned themselves with the subject of perception, one may begin to wonder whether this matter is quite so simple. It is true that they do, in general, allow that our belief in the existence of material things is well founded; some of them, indeed, would say that there were occasions on which we knew for certain the truth of such propositions as 'this is a cigarette' or 'this is a pen'. But even so they are not, for the most part, prepared to admit that such objects as pens or cigarettes are ever directly perceived. What, in their opinion, we directly perceive is always an object of a different kind from these; one to which it is now customary to give the name of 'sense-datum'. . . .

Philosophers, it is said, 'are not, for the most part, prepared to admit that such objects as pens or cigarettes are ever directly perceived'. Now of course what brings us up short here is the word 'directly'—a great favourite among philosophers, but actually one of the less conspicuous snakes in the linguistic grass. We have here, in fact, a typical case of a word, which already has a very special use, being gradually stretched, without caution or definition or any limit, until it becomes, first perhaps obscurely metaphorical, but ultimately meaningless. One can't abuse ordinary language without paying for it.

1. First of all, it is essential to realize that here the notion of perceiving *indirectly* wears the trousers—'directly' takes whatever sense it has from the contrast with its opposite: while 'indirectly' itself (*a*) has a use only in special cases, and also (*b*) has *different* uses in different cases—though that doesn't mean, of course, that there is not a good reason why we should use the same word. We might, for example, contrast the man who saw the procession directly with the man who saw it *through a periscope;* or we might contrast the place from which you can watch the door directly with the place from which you can see it only *in the mirror. Perhaps* we might contrast seeing you directly with seeing, say, your shadow on the blind; and *perhaps* we might contrast hearing the music directly with hearing it relayed outside the concert-hall. However, these last two cases suggest two further points.

2. The first of these points is that the notion of not perceiving 'directly' seems most at home where, as with the periscope and the mirror, it retains its link with the notion of a kink in *direction.* It seems that we must not be looking *straight at* the object in question. For this reason seeing your shadow on the blind is a doubtful case; and seeing you, for instance through binoculars or spectacles is certainly not a case of seeing you *indirectly* at all. For such cases as these last we have quite distinct contrasts and different expressions—'with the naked eye' as opposed to 'with a telescope', 'with unaided vision' as opposed to 'with glasses on'. (These expressions, in fact, are much more firmly established in ordinary use than 'directly' is.)

3. And the other point is that, partly no doubt for the above reason, the notion of indirect perception is not naturally at home with senses other than sight. With the other senses there is nothing quite analogous with the 'line of vision'. The most natural sense of 'hearing indirectly', of course, is that of being *told* something by an intermediary—a quite different matter. But do I hear a shout indirectly, when I hear the echo? If I touch you with a barge-pole, do I touch you indirectly? Or if you offer me a pig in a poke, might I feel the pig indirectly—*through* the poke? And what smelling indirectly might be I have simply no idea. For this reason alone there seems to be something badly wrong with the question, 'Do we perceive things directly or not?', where perceiving is evidently intended to cover the employment of *any* of the senses.

4. But it is, of course, for other reasons too extremely doubtful how far the notion of perceiving indirectly could or should be extended. Does it, or should it, cover the telephone, for instance? Or television? Or radar? Have we moved too far in these cases from the original metaphor? They at any rate satisfy what seems to be a necessary condition—namely, concurrent existence and concomitant variation as between what is perceived in the straightforward way (the sounds in the receiver, the picture and the blips on the screen) and the candidate for what we might be prepared to describe as being perceived indirectly. And this condition fairly clearly rules out as cases of indirect perception seeing photographs (which statically record scenes from the past) and seeing films (which, though not static, are not seen contemporaneously with the events thus recorded). Certainly, there *is* a line to be drawn somewhere. It is certain, for instance, that we should not be prepared to speak of indirect perception in *every* case in which we see something from which the existence (or occurrence) of something else can be inferred; we should *not* say we see the guns indirectly, if we see in the distance only the flashes of guns.

5. Rather differently, if we are to be seriously inclined to speak of something as being perceived indirectly, it seems that it has to be the kind of thing which we (sometimes at least) just perceive, or could perceive, or which—like the backs of our own heads—others could perceive. For otherwise we don't want to say that we perceive the thing *at all,* even indirectly. No doubt there are complications here (raised, perhaps, by the electron microscope, for example, about which I know little or nothing). But it seems clear that, in general, we should want to distinguish between seeing indirectly, e.g. in a mirror, what we might have just *seen,* and seeing signs (or effects), e.g. in a Wilson cloud-chamber, of something not itself perceptible at all. It would at least not come naturally to speak of the latter as a case of perceiving something indirectly.

6. And one final point. For reasons not very obscure, we always prefer in practice what might be called the *cash-value* expression to the 'indirect' metaphor. If I were to report that I see enemy ships indirectly, I should merely provoke the question what exactly I mean. 'I mean that I can see these blips on the radar screen'—'Well, why didn't you say so then?' (Compare 'I can see an unreal duck.'—'What on earth do you mean?' 'It's a decoy duck'—'Ah, I see. Why didn't you say so at once?') That is, there is seldom if ever any particular point in actually saying 'indirectly' (or 'unreal'); the expression can cover too many rather different cases to be *just* what is wanted in any particular case.

Thus, it is quite plain that the philosophers' use of 'directly perceive', whatever it may be, is not the ordinary, or any familiar, use; for in *that* use it is not only false but simply absurd to say that such objects as pens or cigarettes are never perceived directly. But we are given no explanation or definition of this new use—on the contrary, it is glibly trotted out as if we were all quite familiar with it already. It is clear, too, that the philosophers' use, whatever it may be, offends against several of the canons just mentioned above—no restrictions whatever seem to be envisaged to any special circumstances or to any of the senses in particular, and moreover it seems that what we are to be said to perceive indirectly is *never*— is not the kind of thing which ever *could* be—perceived directly.

7

How Does My Brain Think?

You may not know much about how your brain works, but you probably believe that what goes on in your brain has a lot to do with how you feel and how you act. You may know of drugs that have a considerable impact on a person's moods or perceptions or even on a person's thinking processes. Does your brain itself think? Or does it merely affect, or possibly control, a thinking process that takes place elsewhere? But wait—your brain is just a jumble of cells and chemicals. How is it possible for cells and chemicals to think? For that matter, how is it possible for a bunch of cells and chemicals to control a thinking process that takes place somewhere else? Does it really matter that your brain is made of cells and chemicals? You have heard of artificial hearts made out of plastic. They work because they provide the same function for the body that a real heart provides. Could you have an artificial brain made out of little plastic parts or tiny wires and transistors? Would it (or you) still think?

Some of these questions were introduced in Chapter 5, and you would do well to read, or reread, the introduction to that chapter for a preliminary orientation. The fundamental question of Chapter 5 was whether your mind is a nonphysical thing or whether it is just a part of, or an activity of, your body. One of the positions most prominently represented in that chapter was functionalism, the view that mental states and events are defined by their causal roles, that is, by their relationships with other events and states, both physical and mental. Strictly speaking, it does not matter to a functionalist whether the states that occupy these causal roles (namely, the mental states) turn out to be physical, like brain states, or nonphysical. Here is an analogy. In the early part of this century, Mendel hypothesized the existence of genes as whatever it is that carries hereditary traits from one generation to the next. In principle it would not have mattered to genetic theory whether genes turned out to be physical or oddly nonphysical. But in practice, it would have been astounding for any working scientist actually to believe that genes were nonphysical. In fact it was discovered in the 1950s that genes are composed of DNA molecules.

Similarly, it does not matter in *principle* to functionalism whether mental events and states (whatever it is that occupies the appropriate functional roles) turn out in humans to be physical or nonphysical. But in *practice* it would be peculiar for someone to be a functionalist and really believe that mental states are nonphysical.

Two of the authors in this section, Dennett and Flanagan, are functionalists. They are therefore more concerned with how we can understand how the mind works than with whether the mind is physical or nonphysical. Dennett's selection contains a brief survey for philosophers of work in Artificial Intelligence (AI), the branch of computer theory that tries to construct computers that behave intelligently. AI, he tells us, is a "top-down" approach, which first seeks theories about how it might be possible for any creature or machine to do what humans do, and then looks empirically at people to see whether they work the way the theory hypothesizes. Dennett goes on to show how work in AI bears on traditional philosophical questions about the nature of mind and knowledge. He offers a positive argument that work in AI can tell us something about how we think and feel. He doesn't go so far as to say that human beings are really just complicated computers, but if his argument is compelling, then that is a claim that we would have to take seriously.

Flanagan shows us what the empirical methods of cognitive psychology can add to our understanding of the mind/brain. Like Dennett, his approach is top-down. In connecting the cognitivist approach to Kant's transcendental deduction, he ties this way of approaching a problem to a long and productive history in philosophy. His selection concludes with a discussion of eliminative materialism.

Searle's selection is a deep and provocative criticism of the top-down approach advocated by Dennett and Flanagan. He argues with some flair that any approach that ignores the actual biological stuff of an organism (the "wetware") cannot genuinely explain that organism. Searle's selection is excerpted from his review of Dennett and Douglas Hofstadter's book, *The Mind's I*, a provocative and interesting collection of essays that includes, among others, the ones reprinted in this volume by Nagel (in Chapter 5) and Zuboff (in this chapter). If Searle is right, then it is not possible for a computer really to think or to have feelings. The best that a computer could do is to behave *as though* it had thoughts and feelings. If so, then to understand our conscious mental lives, we will have to turn to an investigation either of the brain, or of some nonphysical system, to understand how we think. Searle does not tell us where to turn to gain this understanding, but Churchland, who accepts Searle's conclusions, argues that we must turn to a study of the brain.

Unlike Searle, Churchland is an eliminative materialist (see the introduction to Chapter 5). He claims that rather than trying to understand our ordinary psychological concepts—concepts like belief and desire that he calls our "folk psychology"—we must discard them completely. They are defective and stand in the way of our reaching a genuine understanding of ourselves. He tells us that new, and perhaps exotic, psychological concepts that will grow out of the study of the brain will replace those that we now use in an attempt to understand ourselves.

Finally, Zuboff, in a fanciful story, presents another powerful argument against the basic claims of cognitivism. He challenges us to take cognitivism seriously by pushing some of its assumptions to their limits. His story is about a brain whose basic functional components become separated, scattered, disconnected, and finally replaced, but they still continue to serve their appropriate functional roles. He then invites us to continue thinking of what is left as a thinking, feeling organism. Zuboff and Searle, in very different ways, criticize the fundamental assumption of functionalism, namely, that it is the functional organization of something that determines what mental states, if any, it has. Their arguments taken together constitute a formidable obstacle to any attempt to explain how the mind works in terms of the functions of its components.

Daniel C. Dennett

Artificial Intelligence as Philosophy and as Psychology

Daniel C. Dennett *teaches philosophy at Tufts University. He is well known for taking seriously the view that people are biological computers. He has written* Brainstorms, *an* *important collection of essays, and in collaboration with Douglas Hofstadter,* The Mind's I.

Philosophers of mind have been interested in computers since their arrival a generation ago, but for the most part they have been interested only in the most abstract questions of principle, and have kept actual machines at arm's length and actual programs in soft focus. Had they chosen to take a closer look at the details I do not think they would have found much of philosophic interest until fairly recently. But recent work in Artificial Intelligence, or AI, promises to have a much more variegated impact on philosophy, and so, quite appropriately, philosophers have begun responding with interest to the bold manifestos of the Artificial Intelligentsia. My goal in this paper is to provide a sort of travel guide to philosophers pursuing this interest. It is well known that amateur travellers in strange lands often ludicrously misconstrue what they see, and enthusiastically report wonders and monstrosities that later investigations prove never to have existed, while overlooking genuine novelties of the greatest importance. Having myself fallen prey to a variety of misconceptions about AI, and wasted a good deal of time and energy pursuing chimaeras, I would like to alert other philosophers to some of these pitfalls of interpretation. Since I am still acutely conscious of my own amateur status as an observer of AI, I must acknowledge at the outset that my vision of what is going on in AI, what is important and why, is almost certainly still somewhat untrustworthy. There is much in AI that I have not read, and much that I have read but not understood. So traveller beware; take along any other maps you can find, and listen critically to the natives.

The interest of philosophers of mind in Artificial Intelligence comes as no surprise to many tough-minded experimental psychologists, for from their point of view the two fields look very much alike: there are the same broad generalizations and bold extrapolations, the same blithe indifference to the hard-won data of the experimentalist, the same appeal to the deliverances of casual introspection and conceptual analysis, the aprioristic reasonings about what is impossible in principle or what must be the case of psychology. The only apparent difference between the two fields, such a psychologist might say, is that the AI worker pulls his armchair up to a console. I will argue that this observation is largely justified, but should not in most regards be viewed as a criticism. There is much work for the armchair psychologist to do, and a computer console has proven a useful tool in this work.

Psychology turns out to be very difficult. The task of psychology is to explain human perception, learning, cognition, and so forth in terms that ultimately will unite psychological theory to physiology in one way or another. And there are two broad strategies one could adopt: a 'bottom-up' strategy that starts with some basic and well-defined unit or theoretical atom for psychology and builds these atoms into molecules and larger aggregates that can account for the complex phenomena we all observe, or a 'top-down' strategy that begins with a more abstract decomposition of the highest levels of psychological organization, and hopes to analyse these into more and more detailed smaller systems or processes until finally one arrives at elements familiar to the biologists. It is a commonplace that both endeavors could and should proceed simultaneously, but there is now abundant evidence that the bottom-up strategy in psychology is unlikely to prove very fruitful. The two best developed attempts at bottom-up psychology are stimulus-response behaviourism and what we might call 'neuron signal physiological psychology', and both are now widely regarded as stymied, the former because stimuli and responses prove not to be perspicuously chosen atoms, the latter because even if synapses and impulse trains are perfectly good atoms, there are just too many of them, and their interactions are too complex to study once one abandons the afferent and efferent peripheries and tries to make sense of the crucial centre. Bottom-up strategies have not proved notably fruitful in the early development of other sciences, in chemistry and biology for instance, and so psychologists are only following the lead of 'mature' sciences if they turn to the top-down approach. Within that broad strategy there are a variety of starting points that can be ordered in an array. Faced with the practical impossibility of answering the empirical questions of psychology by brute inspection (how *in fact* does the nervous system accomplish X or Y or Z?), psychologists ask themselves an easier preliminary question:

(1) How could any system (with features A, B, C,. . .) possibly accomplish X?

This sort of question is easier because it is 'less empirical'; it is an *engineering* question, a quest for a solution (*any* solution) rather than a discovery. Seeking an answer to such a question can sometimes lead to the discovery of general constraints on all solutions (including of course nature's as yet unknown solution) and therein lies the value of this style of aprioristic theorizing. Once one decides to do psychology this way, one can choose a degree of empirical difficulty for one's question by filling in the blanks in the question schema (1). The more empirical constraints one puts on the description of the system, or on the description of the requisite behaviour, the greater the claim to 'psychological reality' one's answer must make. For instance, one can ask how any neuronal network with such-and-such physical features could possibly accomplish human colour discriminations, or we can ask how any finite system could possibly subserve the acquisition of a natural language. Or, one can ask how human memory could possibly be so organized as to make it so relatively easy for us to answer questions like 'have you ever ridden an antelope?' and so relatively hard to answer 'what did you have for breakfast last Tuesday?' Or, one can ask, with Kant, how anything at all could possibly experience or know anything at all. Pure epistemology thus viewed, for instance, is simply the limiting case of the psychologists' quest, and is *prima facie* no less valuable *to psychology* for being so neutral with regard to empirical details. Some such questions are of course better designed to yield good answers than others, but properly carried out, any such investigation can yield constraints that bind all more-data-enriched investigations.

AI workers can pitch their investigations at any level of empirical difficulty they wish; at Carnegie Mellon University, for instance, much is made of paying careful attention to experimental data on human performance and attempting to model human performance closely. Other workers in AI are less concerned with that degree of psychological reality and have engaged in a more abstract version of AI. There is much that is of value and interest to psychology at the empirical end of the spectrum but I want to claim that AI is better viewed as sharing with traditional epistemology the status of being a most general, most abstract asking of the top-down question: how is knowledge possible? . . .

So I am claiming that AI shares with philosophy (in particular, with epistemology and philosophy of mind) the status of most abstract investigation of the principles of psychology. But it shares with psychology in distinction from philosophy a typical tactic in answering its questions. In AI or cognitive psychology the typical attempt to answer a *general* top-down question consists in designing a *particular* system that does, or appears to do, the relevant job, and then considering which of its features are necessary not just to one's particular system but to any such system. Philosophers have generally shunned such elaborate system-designing in favour of more doggedly general inquiry. This is perhaps the major difference between AI and 'pure' philosophical approaches to the same questions, and it is one of my purposes here to exhibit some of the relative strengths and weaknesses of the two approaches.

The system-design approach that is common to AI and other styles of top-down psychology is beset by a variety of dangers of which these four are perhaps the chief:

(A) designing a system with component subsystems whose stipulated capacities are miraculous given the constraints one is accepting (e.g., positing more information-processing in a component than the relevant time and matter will allow, or, at a more abstract level of engineering incoherence, positing a subsystem whose duties would require it to be more 'intelligent' or 'knowledgeable' than the supersystem of which it is to be a part).

(B) mistaking conditional necessities of one's particular solution for completely general constraints: a trivial example would be proclaiming that brains use LISP*; less trivial examples require careful elucidation.

(C) restricting oneself artificially to the design of a subsystem, such as a depth perceiver or sentence parser, and concocting a solution that is systematically incapable of being grafted on to the other subsystems of a whole cognitive creature.

(D) restricting the performance of one's system to an artificially small part of the 'natural' domain of that system and providing no efficient or plausible way for the system to be enlarged. . . .

I now have triangulated AI with respect to both philosophy and psychology, as my title suggested I would: AI can be, and should often be taken to be, as abstract and 'unempirical' as philosophy in the questions it attempts to answer. But at the same time, it should be as explicit and particularistic in its models as psychology at its best. Thus one might learn as much of value to psychology or epistemology from a particular but highly unrealistic AI model as one could learn from a detailed psychology of, say, Martians. A good psychology of Martians, however unlike us they might be, would certainly yield general principles of psychology or epistemology applicable to human beings. Now, before turning to the all important question: 'What, so conceived, has AI accomplished?' I want to consider briefly some misinterpretations of AI that my sketch of it so far does not protect us from.

Since we are viewing AI as a species of top-down cognitive psychology, it is tempting to suppose that the decomposition of function in a computer is intended by AI to be somehow isomorphic to the decomposition of function in a brain. One learns of vast programs made up of literally billions of basic computer events and somehow so organized as to produce a simulacrum of human intelligence, and it is altogether natural to suppose that since the brain is known to be composed of billions of tiny functioning parts, and since there is a gap of ignorance between our understanding of intelligent human behaviour and our understanding of those tiny parts, the ultimate, millenial goal of AI must be to provide a hierarchical break-down of parts in the computer that will mirror or be isomorphic to some hard-to-discover hierarchical breakdown of brain-event parts. The familiar theme of 'organs made of tissues made of cells made of molecules made of atoms' is to be matched, one might suppose, in electronic hardware terms. In the thrall of this picture one might be discouraged to learn that some functional parts of the nervous system do not seem to function in the digital way the atomic functioning parts in computers do. The standard response to this worry would be that one had looked too deep in the computer. This is sometimes called the 'grain problem'. The computer is a digital device at bottom, but a digital device can simulate an 'analogue' device to any degree of continuity you desire, and at a higher level of aggregation in the computer one may find the analogue elements that are mapable onto the non-digital brain parts. As many writers have observed, we cannot gauge the psychological reality of a model until we are given the commentary on the model that tells us which features of the model are intended to mirror real saliencies in nature and which are either backstage expediters of the modelling or sheer inadvertent detail. In the eighteenth century, scientists built beautiful brass clockwork models of the solar system called orreries. The *gears* of an orrery are not intended to represent anything real in the firmament, nor are the reflections of one brass globe in another. When one looks at AI programs in detail one sees mountains of digital calculation or 'number

---

*Editor's note: LISP is a computer language commonly used in AI.

crunching'; if this looks disappointingly unbiological, this is to be excused, since that part of the model's structure is to be viewed as backstage, not part of the model we are supposed to compare with nature.

This story is fine in principle, I think, and the day may come when this imagined isomorphism down to the neuronal level (but not backstage) is proclaimed. But in fact we see nothing remotely like this in current AI work. We see instead models that diverge from nature very early on the downward path. AI programs typically model relatively high-level cognitive features, such as concept learning or revision of goals or beliefs, and it does indeed often take millions of basic computer events to simulate just a handful of these intended model features. But no one really knows or cares what these basic events are, for no one supposes that any of the saliencies in the mass of activity that subserves the intended features are to be taken seriously as psychology or physiology. The psychological reality of an AI program is thus usually only intended to be skin deep; only the highest level of program description and commentary are to be counted as the model.

The thinness of the psychological reality of AI models is obscured for the uninitiated by a particularly misleading feature of most of the AI programs that get into the limelight. What especially attracts audiences and evokes wonder is the marvelous verisimilitude of some of the programs. Consider this excerpt of conversation, minus the programmer's excellent commentary, between Terry Winograd's SHRDLU and its interlocutor. (SHRDLU is a program that lives in an imaginary 'block world' where it can manipulate coloured blocks on a table in response to commands and answer questions about its life in this world.) Computer responses are capitalized.

Had you touched any pyramid before you put the green one on the little cube?
YES, THE GREEN ONE.
When did you pick it up?
WHILE I WAS STACKING UP THE RED CUBE, A LARGE RED BLOCK AND A LARGE GREEN CUBE.
Why?
TO GET RID OF IT.
Why did you do that?
TO CLEAR OFF THE RED CUBE.
Why did you clear off that cube?
TO PUT IT ON A LARGE GREEN CUBE.
Why did you do that?
BECAUSE YOU ASKED ME TO.

When SHRDLU replies to the last question with 'Because you asked me to', one can hardly help being struck by the apparent humanity of the response—'SHRDLU is *one of us!*' it is tempting to exclaim. If one is naive, one will be awestruck; if one is not, one will still be titillated by the illusion, for that is largely what it is. SHRDLU's response, though perfectly appropriate to the occasion, and not by coincidence, is 'canned'. Winograd has simply given SHRDLU this whole sentence to print at times like these. If a child gave SHRDLU's response we would naturally expect its behaviour to manifest a general capacity which might also reveal itself by producing the response: 'because you told me to', or 'because that's what I was asked to do' or, on another occasion, 'because I felt like it' or 'because your assistant told me to'. But these are dimensions of subtlety beyond SHRDLU. Its behaviour is remarkably versatile, but it does not reveal a rich knowledge of interpersonal relations, of the difference between requests and orders, of being co-operative with other people under appropriate circumstances. It should be added that Winograd's paper makes it very explicit where and to what extent he is canning SHRDLU's responses, so anyone who feels cheated by SHRDLU has simply not read

Winograd. Other natural language programs do not rely on canned responses, or rely on them to a minimal extent.

The fact remains, however, that much of the antagonism to AI is due to resentment and distrust engendered by such legerdemain. Why do AI people use these tricks? For many reasons. First, they need to get some tell-tale response back from the program and it is as easy to can a mnemonically vivid and 'natural' response as something more sober, technical and understated, such as, 'REASON: PRIOR COMMAND TO DO THAT'. Second, in Winograd's case he was attempting to reveal the minimal conditions for correct analysis of certain linguistic forms (note all the 'problems' of pronominal antecedents in the sentences displayed), so 'natural' language output to reveal correct analysis of natural language input was entirely appropriate. Third, AI people put canned responses in their programs because it is fun. It is fun to amuse one's colleagues, who are not fooled of course, and it is especially fun to bamboozle the outsiders. As an outsider one must learn to be properly unimpressed by AI verisimilitude, as one is of the chemist's dazzling forest of glass tubing, or the angry mouths full of teeth painted on World War II fighter planes. Joseph Weizenbaum's famous ELIZA program, the computer 'psychotherapist' who apparently listens so wisely and sympathetically to one's problems, is intended in part as an antidote to the enthusiasm generated by AI verisimilitude. It is almost all clever canning, and is not a psychologically realistic model of anything, but rather a demonstration of how easily one can be gulled into attributing too much to a program. It exploits syntactic landmarks in one's input with nothing approaching genuine understanding, but it makes a good show of comprehension nevertheless. One might say it was a plausible model of a Wernicke's aphasic, who can babble on with well-formed and even semantically appropriate responses to his interlocutor, sometimes sustaining the illusion of comprehension for quite a while.

The AI community pays a price for this misleading if fascinating fun, not only by contributing to the image of AI people as tricksters and hackers, but by fueling more serious misconceptions of the point of AI research. For instance, Winograd's real contribution in SHRDLU is not that he has produced an English speaker and understander that is psychologically realistic at many different levels of analysis, though that is what the verisimilitude strongly suggests, and what a lot of the fanfare—for which Winograd is not responsible— has assumed, but that he has explored some of the deepest demands on any system that can take direction, in a natural language, plan, change the world, and keep track of the changes wrought or contemplated. And in the course of this exploration he has clarified the problems and proposed ingenious and plausible partial solutions to them. The real contribution in Winograd's work stands quite unimpeached by the perfectly true but irrelevant charge that SHRDLU doesn't have a rich or human understanding of most of the words in its very restricted vocabulary, or is extremely slow.

In fact, paying so much attention to the performance of SHRDLU, and similar systems, reveals a failure to recognize that AI programs are not *empirical* experiments, but *thought-experiments*, prosthetically regulated by computers. Some AI people have recently become fond of describing their discipline as 'experimental epistemology'. This unfortunate term should make a philosopher's blood boil, but if AI called itself thought-experimental epistemology . . . philosophers ought to be reassured. The questions asked and answered by the thought experiments of AI are about whether or not one can obtain certain sorts of information processing, recognition, inference, control of various sorts, for instance, from certain sorts of designs. Often the answer is no. The process of elimination looms large in AI. Relatively plausible schemes are explored far enough to make it clear that they are utterly incapable of delivering the requisite behaviour, and learning this is important progress even if it doesn't result in a mind-boggling robot.

The hardware realizations of AI are almost gratuitous. Like dropping the cannonballs off the Leaning Tower of Pisa, they are demonstrations that are superfluous to those who have understood the argument, however persuasive they are to the rest. Are computers then irrelevant to AI? 'In principle' they are irrelevant, in the same sense as diagrams on the blackboard are 'in principle' unnecessary to teaching geometry, but in practice they are not. I described them earlier as 'prosthetic regulators' of thought-experiments. What I mean is this: it is notoriously difficult to keep wishful thinking out of one's thought-experiments; computer simulation forces one to recognize all the costs of one's imagined design. As Pylyshyn observes, 'What is needed is . . . a technical language with which to discipline one's imagination.' The discipline provided by computers is undeniable, and especially palpable to the beginning programmer. It is both a good thing—for the reasons just stated—and a bad thing. Perhaps you have known a person so steeped in, say, playing bridge, that his entire life becomes, in his eyes, a series of finesses, end-plays and cross-ruffs. Every morning he draws life's trumps and whenever he can see the end of a project he views it as a lay-down. Computer languages seem to have a similar effect on people who become fluent in them. Although I won't try to prove it by citing examples, I think it is quite obvious that the 'technical language' Pylyshyn speaks of can cripple an imagination in the process of disciplining it.

It has been said so often that computers have huge effects on their users' imaginations that one can easily lose sight of one of the most obvious, but still underrated, ways in which computers achieve this effect, and that is the sheer speed of computers. Before computers came along the theoretician was strongly constrained to ignore the possibility of truly massive and complex processes in psychology because it was hard to see how such processes could fail to *appear* at worst mechanical and cumbersome, at best vegetatively slow, and of course a hallmark of mentality is its swiftness. One might say that the speed of thought defines the upper bound of subjective 'fast', the way the speed of light defines the upper bound of objective 'fast'. Now suppose there had never been any computers but that somehow (by magic, presumably) Kenneth Colby had managed to dream up these flow charts as a proposed model of a part of human organization in paranoia. The flow charts are from his book, *Artificial Paranoia*. Figure 1 represents the main program; Figures 2 and 3 are blow-ups of details of the main program.

It is obvious to everyone, even Colby I think, that this is a vastly over-simplified model of paranoia, but had there not been computers to show us how all this processing, and much, much more, can occur in a twinkling, we would be inclined to dismiss the proposal immediately as altogether too clanking and inorganic, a Rube Goldberg machine. Most programs look like that in slow motion (hand simulation) but speeded up they often reveal a dexterity and grace that appears natural. This grace is entirely undetectable via a slow analysis of the program (Cf. time lapse photography of plants growing and buds opening). The grace in operation of AI programs may be mere illusion. Perhaps nature is graceful *all the way down,* but for better or for worse, computer speed has liberated the imagination of theoreticians by opening up the possibility and plausibility of very complex interactive information processes playing a role in the production of cognitive events so swift as to be atomic to introspection.

At last I turn to the important question. Suppose that AI is viewed as I recommend, as a most abstract inquiry into the possibility of intelligence or knowledge. Has it solved any very general problems or discovered any very important constraints or principles? I think the answer is a qualified yes. In particular, I think AI has broken the back of an argument that has bedeviled philosophers and psychologists for over two hundred years. Here is a skeletal version of it: First, the only psychology that could possibly succeed in explaining the complexities of human activity must posit internal representations. This premise has been deemed obvious by just about everyone except the radical behaviourists (both in psychology and philosophy—both Watson and Skinner, and Ryle and Malcolm). Descartes doubted almost everything but this. For the British Empiricists, the internal representations were called ideas, sensations, impressions; more recently psychologists have talked of hypotheses, maps, sche-mas, images, propositions, engrams, neural signals, even holograms and whole innate theories. So the first premise is quite invulnerable, or at any rate it has any impressive mandate. But, second, nothing is intrinsically a representation of anything; something is a representation only *for* or *to* someone; any representation or system of representations thus requires at least one user or interpreter of the representation who is external to it. Any such interpreter must have a variety of psychological or intentional traits: it must be capable of a variety of *compre-hension,* and must have beliefs and goals, so that it can use the representation to inform itself and thus assist it in achieving its goals. Such an interpreter is then a sort of homunculus.*

Therefore, psychology *without* homunculi is impossible. But psychology *with* homunculi is doomed to circularity or infinite regress, so psychology is impossible.

The argument given is a relatively abstract version of a familiar group of problems. For instance, it seems to many that we cannot account for perception unless we suppose it provides us with an internal image or model or map of the external world. And yet what good would that image do us unless we have an inner eye to perceive it, and how are we to explain *its*

---

*Editor's note: Until the nineteenth century, biologists believed that the sperm contained a little person—a *homun-culus.* The egg merely provided nutrients for its growth. In psychology, a homunculus is an internal structure that has some or all of the abilities of the organism that are being explained.

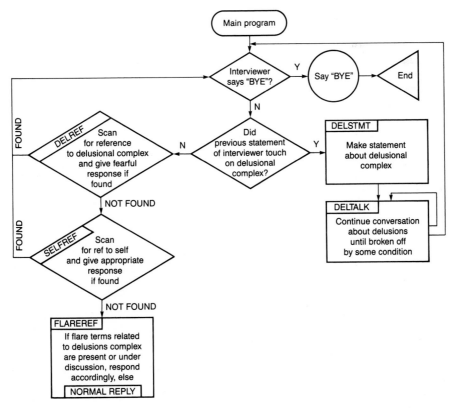

Figure 1

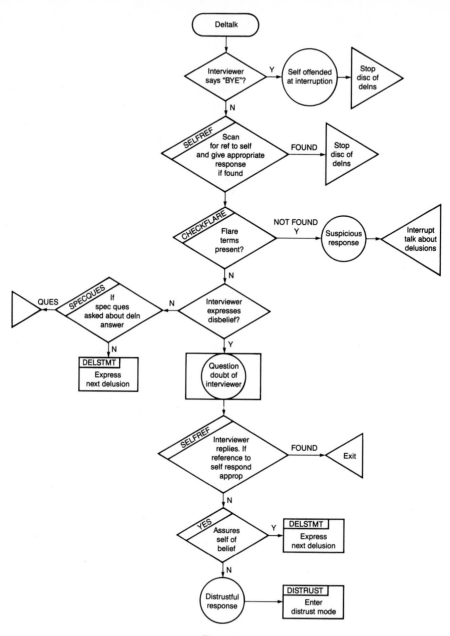

Figure 2

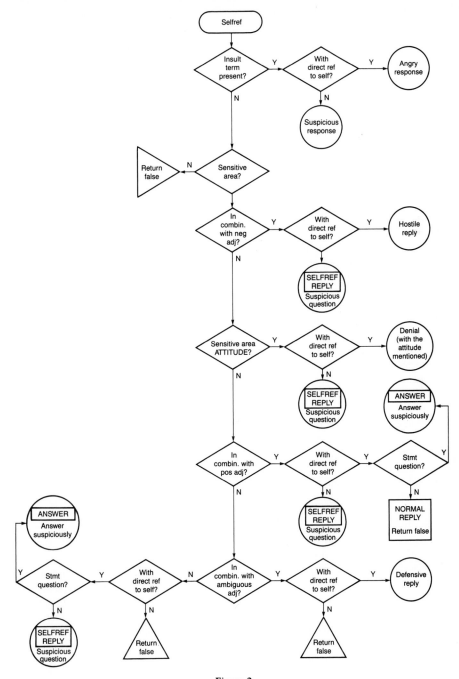

Figure 3

capacity of perception? It also seems to many that understanding a heard sentence must be somehow translating it into some internal message. But how will this message in turn be understood, by translating it into something else? The problem is an old one. Let's call it Hume's Problem, for while he did not state it explicitly, he appreciated its force and strove mightily to escape its clutches. Hume's internal representations were impressions and ideas, and he wisely shunned the notion of an inner self that would intelligently manipulate these items. But this left him with the necessity of getting the ideas and impressions to 'think for themselves'. The result was his theory of the self as a 'bundle' of nothing but impressions and ideas. He attempted to set these impressions and ideas into dynamic interaction by positing various associationistic links, so that each succeeding idea in the stream of consciousness dragged its successor onto the stage according to one or another principle, all without benefit of intelligent *supervision*. It didn't work, of course. It couldn't conceivably work, and Hume's failure is plausibly viewed as the harbinger of doom for any remotely analogous enterprise. On the one hand how could any theory of psychology make sense of representations that understand themselves, and on the other how could any theory of psychology avoid regress or circularity if it posits at least one representation-understander in addition to the representations?

Now no doubt some philosophers and psychologists who have appealed to internal representations over the year have believed in their hearts that somehow the force of this argument could be blunted, that Hume's problem could be solved. But I am sure no one had the slightest idea how to do this until AI and the notion of data-structures came along. Data-structures may or may not be biologically or psychologically realistic representations, but they are, if not living, breathing examples, at least clanking, functioning examples of representations that can be said in the requisite sense to understand themselves.

How this is accomplished can be metaphorically described (and any talk about internal representations is bound to have a large element of metaphor in it) by elaborating our description of AI as a top-down theoretical inquiry. One starts, in AI, with a specification of a whole person or cognitive organism—what I call, more neutrally, an intentional system—or some artificial segment of that person's abilities, such as chess-playing, or answering questions about baseball, and then breaks that largest intentional system into an organization of subsystems, each of which could itself be viewed as an intentional system, with its own specialized beliefs and desires, and hence as formally a homunculus. In fact homunculus talk is ubiquitous in AI, and is almost always illuminating. AI homunculi talk to each other, wrest control from each other, volunteer, sub-contract, supervise and even kill. There seems no better way of describing what is going on. Homunculi are bogeymen only if they duplicate entire the talents they are rung in to explain, a special case of danger (A). If one can get a team or committee of relatively ignorant, narrow-minded, blind homunculi to produce the intelligent be-haviour of the whole, this is progress. A flow chart is typically the organizational chart of a committee of homunculi (investigators, librarians, accountants, executives); each box specifies a homunculus by prescribing a function without saying how it is to be accomplished. One says, in effect, put a little man in there to do the job. If we then look closer at the individual boxes, we see that the function of each is accomplished by subdividing it, via another flow chart, into still smaller, more stupid homunculi. Eventually this nesting of boxes within boxes lands you with homunculi so stupid (all they have to do is remember whether to say yes or no when asked) that they can be, as one says, 'replaced by a machine'. One discharges fancy homunculi from one's scheme by organizing armies of such idiots to do the work.

When homunculi at a level interact, they do so by sending messages, and each homun-culus has representations which it uses to execute its functions. Thus typical AI discussions do draw a distinction between representation and representation-user. They take the first step of the threatened infinite regress. But as many writers in AI have observed, it has gradually emerged from the tinkerings of AI that there is a trade-off between sophistication in the representation and sophistication in the user. The more raw and uninterpreted the representation—like the mosaic of retinal stimulation at an instant—the more sophisticated the interpreter or user of the representation. The more interpreted a representation—the more procedural information is embodied in it, for instance—the less fancy the interpreter need be. It is this fact that permits one to get away with lesser homunculi at high levels, by getting their earlier or lower brethren to do some of the work. One never quite gets completely self-understanding representations, unless one stands back and views all representation in the system from a global vantage point, but all homunculi are ultimately discharged. One gets the advantage of the tradeoff only by sacrificing versatility and universality in one's subsystems and their representations, so one's homunculi cannot be too versatile nor can the messages they send and receive have the full flavor of normal human linguistic interaction. We've seen an example of how homuncular communications may fall short in SHRDLU's remark 'because you asked me to'. The context of production and the function of the utterance makes clear that this is a sophisticated communication and the product of a sophisticated representation, but it is not a fully-fledged Gricean speech act. If it were, it would require too fancy a homunculus to use it.

There are two ways a philosopher might view AI data structures. One could grant that they are indeed self-understanding representations or one could cite the various disanalogies between them and prototypical or real representations, such as human statements, paintings, or maps, and conclude that data-structures are not really internal representations at all. But if one takes the latter line, the modest successes of AI simply serve to undercut our first premise: it is no longer obvious that psychology needs internal representations; internal pseudo-representations may do just as well.

It is certainly tempting to argue that since AI has provided us with the only known way of solving Hume's Problem, albeit for very restrictive systems, it must be on the right track, and its categories must be psychologically real, but one might well be falling into danger (B) if one did. We can all be relieved and encouraged to learn that there is a way of solving Hume's Problem, but it has yet to be shown that AI's way is the only way it can be done.

AI has made a major contribution to philosophy and psychology by revealing a particular way in which simple cases of Hume's Problem can be solved. What else has it accomplished of interest to philosophers? I will close by drawing attention to two main areas where I think the AI approach is of particular relevance to philosophy.

For many years philosophers and psychologists have debated, with scant interdisciplinary communication, about the existence and nature of mental images. These discussions have been relatively fruitless, largely, I think, because neither side had any idea of how to come to grips with Hume's Problem. Recent work in AI, however, has recast the issues in a more perspicuous and powerful framework, and anyone hoping to resolve this ancient issue will find help in the AI discussions.

The second main area of philosophical interest, in my view, is the so-called frame problem. The frame problem is an abstract epistemological problem that was in effect discovered by AI thought-experimentation. When a cognitive creature, an entity with many beliefs about the world, performs an act, the world changes and many of the creatures beliefs must be revised or updated. How? It cannot be that we perceive and notice all the changes. For one thing, many of the changes we know to occur do not occur in our perceptual fields, and hence it cannot be that we rely entirely on perceptual input to revise our beliefs. So we must have internal ways of up-dating our beliefs that will fill in the gaps and keep our internal model, the totality of our beliefs, roughly faithful to the world.

If one supposes, as philosophers traditionally have, that one's beliefs are a set or propositions, and reasoning is inference or deduction from members of the set, one is in for trouble, for it is quite clear, though still controversial, that systems relying only on such processes get swamped by combinatorial explosions in the updating effort. It seems that our entire conception of belief and reasoning must be radically revised if we are to explain the undeniable capacity of human beings to keep their beliefs roughly consonant with the reality we live in.

I think one can find an appreciation of the frame problem in Kant (we might call the frame problem Kant's Problem) but unless one disciplines one's thought-experiments in the AI manner, philosophical proposals of solutions to the problem, including Kant's of course, can be viewed as at best suggestive, at worst mere wishful thinking.

I do not want to suggest that philosophers abandon traditional philosophical method and retrain themselves as AI workers. There is plenty of work to do through thought-experimentation and argumentation disciplined by the canons of philosophical method and informed by the philosophical tradition. Some of the most influential recent work in AI—Minsky's papers on 'Frames' is a good example—is loaded with recognizably philosophical speculations of the relatively unsophisticated nature. Philosophers, I have said, should study AI. Should AI workers study philosophy? Yes, unless they are content to reinvent the wheel every few days. When AI reinvents a wheel, it is typically square, or at best hexagonal, and can only make a few hundred revolutions before it stops. Philosopher's wheels, on the other hand, are perfect circles, require in principle no lubrication, and can go in at least two directions at once. Clearly a meeting of minds is in order.

Owen Flanagan

Cognitive Psychology

Owen Flanagan *teaches philosophy at Wellesley College. He has written* The Science of Mind, *from which this selection is excerpted.*

When cognitive psychologists discuss their philosophical forebears one hears the name of Immanuel Kant more than any other. . . . This, as I see it, is just right. Kant laid both the substantive and methodological foundations for modern cognitive psychology. On the substantive side, Kant was responsible for what he himself called the "Copernican revolution" in epistemology, the revolution of construing the mind as active in the construction of knowledge. On the methodological side, Kant spelled out the logical structure of the still-canonical method for inferring hidden mental processes. Kant called his method of inference from words, behavior, and pieces of knowledge to hidden mental processes, *transcendental deduction*. . . .

On the substantive side, Kant saw his philosophy of mind as an alternative to Hume's empiricist model of mind. Kant took his empiricist rivals to be promoting two main theses, one psychological, the other epistemological.

The psychological thesis was that all knowledge originates with sense impressions. Higher-level ideas and concepts are simply complex associations of sense impressions. The epistemological thesis was that complex ideas correctly represent the world to the extent that they can be traced back to sense impressions in the right sort of way. The idea of a unicorn, for example, involves the association of the impression of a horse with an impression of a horn. That is its psychology. "Unicorn" fails to refer, however, because at the level of our sense impressions, horses and horns fail to occur together. This is why we say that unicorns don't exist.

Kant saw Hume's philosophical skepticism as the result of these two theses. Take the concept of causality. Hume notices that when we take a complex judgment such as "The sun causes the sand on the beach to get hot" and trace it back to its sensory components, all we end up with are sense impressions of the sun shining and hot sand occurring together; all we experience is the "constant conjunction" of the sun and hot sand (actually not even that, because the sun does not make the sand hot in winter). Nowhere, however, in sense experience do we see the causality between the sun and the hot sand. Causality then is not so much a phenomenon in the real world as it is a concept we as subjects add to sense experience. Hume concluded that because metaphysics (literally: the study of that which is beyond physics) is the science which is supposed to give certain knowledge of the way the world is from the God's-eye view, and because concepts like causality are subjective, that is, mental, there simply is nothing metaphysically interesting, that is, ultimate and objective, to say about them.

Kant's strategy is to take Hume's hint that certain concepts are super-added to sense experience, and to frame this idea in an entirely different, revolutionary way. Kant accepts Hume's argument that we never experience causality as such, or space and time as such, or material substance as such, or the principles of logic as such. But he insists that the fact that all humans talk about the world in logical terms—as if it were comprised of distinct material objects, occupying space and time, and interacting in accordance with causal principles—is reason to think that we supply these forms, concepts, and categories a priori.

The concepts of logic, causality, substance, space, and time are, of course, subjective. Other creatures, paramecia, for example, probably do not construct their world in terms of these concepts and categories. But these mental structures are subjective in an utterly healthy sense. They are universal species-specific ways in which we organize reality. Without these structures operating as a system of expectations about the world, in anticipation of experience, we would never be able to build up the fantastically complex, adaptive, rule-governed picture of the world we achieve at a very young age.

In speaking of Hume and his fellow empiricists in the preface to the second edition of the *Critique of Pure Reason,* Kant says,

> Hitherto it has been assumed [by the empiricists] that all our knowledge must conform to objects. . . . We must . . . make trial whether we may not have more success in the tasks of metaphysics, if we suppose that objects must conform to our knowledge. . . . We should then be proceeding precisely on the lines of Copernicus' primary hypothesis. Failing of satisfactory progress in explaining the movements of the heavenly bodies on the supposition that they all revolved around the spectator, he tried whether he might not have better success if he made the spectator to revolve and the stars to remain at rest.

Kant's Copernican revolution then comes to this: we supply form and structure to experience by way of a rich system of a priori mental structures. Were it not for the rich initial state of the cognitive system, experience would simply go in one ear and out the other. . . .

In any case, once we take the Copernican turn in the philosophy of mind, the question naturally arises: what method should we use to draw up an accurate map of mental terrain? Given that the underlying features of mind are not directly visible, how should we infer the nature of mind?

This is where transcendental deduction comes in. A transcendental deduction, in the Kantian scheme of things, is an inference strategy that allows us to start with observables and go behind the scenes. Strictly speaking, a transcendental deduction is a misnomer, since all transcendental deductions are instances of inductive reasoning, specifically, eliminative induction. Conclusions of transcendental deductions are always probabilistic, never certain. The basic form of a transcendental deduction is as follows:

1. Start with a fact or set of facts.
2. Ask how the fact or set of facts could be as they are. That is, ask how the state of affairs in question is possible, how it could have come to be the way it is.
3. Calculate the contribution observable events and processes make to the solution of the "how is this state of affairs possible" question. If the observable events and processes provide a satisfactory solution, Stop. Otherwise, proceed to (4), the transcendental deduction proper.
4. Cautiously infer the necessary unobserved or unobservable events and processes to fill out the answer to the "how is this state of affairs possible" question.

Reasoning transcendentally is a general feature of reasoning in situations where there are no eyewitnesses. Thus transcendental reasoning is common in criminology and history as well as in psychology and physics.

Sherlock Holmes was forever performing transcendental deductions. When Dr. Watson says, "Brilliant deduction, Holmes," he is almost always referring to this kind of inductive reasoning.

Holmes usually starts with some mysterious state of affairs, say, a murder in which there are no fingerprints or footprints. There is, however, a cigar ash next to the dead person's body. The dead man smoked, but he did not smoke Cuban cigars, and this is a Cuban cigar ash. Holmes wonders, How is it possible that there is a Cuban cigar ash next to the dead man's body? He infers that the murderer must smoke Cuban cigars. Since the jealous stepson is the only person in all of Britain who smokes Cuban cigars, he must have committed the murder (or been set up by his sister who had access to his cigar box, or whatever).

There is, however, an epistemologically significant difference worth emphasizing between the use of transcendental reasoning in criminology and in philosophy and psychology. Notice that transcendental reasoning is required in criminology when there are no eyewitnesses or when the eyewitnesses are not talking. In criminology the transcendental step is normally required because of practical difficulties; no one saw or reported what transpired. There is reason to think that the necessity of transcendental reasoning in psychology and philosophy of mind, as in subatomic physics, is necessitated by an "in principle" difficulty. The difficulty is simply this: of all possible observers, each person is the only candidate in a position to provide direct testimony about the structure, content, and processes of his or her own mind—to give the sort of eyewitness accounts which would obviate the need for transcendental reasoning. But all the available evidence indicates that we are notoriously bad at providing accurate self-assessments, especially, but not exclusively, at the level of cognitive processing. But if no one, including its owner, is in a position to give an eyewitness account of mind, it makes sense that transcendental reasoning would, of necessity, be the canonical procedure in psychology.

Kant invariably proceeds transcendentally when treating matters mental. One of Kant's most important transcendental deductions is the one locating the concept of causality in the a priori conceptual system. The explicit version of his argument runs as follows: First, Kant points out that causal talk is pervasive in ordinary discourse as well as in physics (where principles like "every effect has a cause" are considered self-evident). Next, Kant acknowledges the force of Hume's argument that we never see causality as such, we only see constant conjunctions between events; and that no beliefs based wholly on sense data are self-evident. Finally, and this is novel, Kant asks how our concept of causality is possible if neither its substance nor its epistemic character originate in sense data. His answer is that it must be supplied a priori by us.

Throughout the *Critique* and the *Prolegomena* Kant offers similar sorts of arguments for his view that the notions of time, space, substance, number, logic, self, and many others, cannot be accounted for in purely sensory, a posteriori terms and that, therefore, they must have a priori components.

The point I want to make here is the following: Kant made the crucial substantive and methodological moves which make cognitive psychology as we know it today both possible and respectable. He took the stance that the mind actively and surreptitiously contributes to the organization of knowledge and behavior, and he promoted the "transcendental" method as a respectable—albeit not infallible—tool for revealing this contribution.

Here I want to discuss [some] experimental data and look at the transcendental deductions cognitive psychologists perform of these data. This will help us get clearer on some of the difficulties, especially the so-called underdetermination associated with the transcendental method, and it will give a preliminary sense of just how radical a reconceptualization of mind cognitive psychology might require.

In an important paper, "High-Speed Scanning in Human Memory," Saul Sternberg asks: How is information of recently encoded memories retrieved? Notice (by way of getting clear on the changing nature of scientific intuitions) how much this perfectly sensible question itself assumes: first, that memory exists; second, that memories are representationally encoded; third, that there are mechanisms which retrieve information from memory; and fourth, that these mechanisms operate in a rule-governed way. Both Cartesian and behavioristic theories would have had trouble with at least one of these assumptions.

Sternberg's experimental procedure involved having subjects memorize lists containing some subset of the numbers 1 to 10. The lists varied in size from one to six digits. On each trial the subject saw a randomly generated list, for example, 2, 7, 3, 9. The list was visually displayed for just over one second. After a two-second delay a test digit appeared, say, 3. The subject was to pull lever A if the test digit was on the memorized list, lever B if it was not. Sternberg's data consisted of measurements of the time it took from presentation of the test digit to the pulling of the appropriate lever.

Now you might wonder how something as pedestrian as reaction-time data could help us figure out how people perform this (short-term) memory task. Why doesn't Sternberg simply ask people how they perform the task? The answer is that many people have only the vaguest of intuitions as to how they do such things, and even those who have powerful intuitions are often wrong. This will become clear if we look more closely at the experiment. Without knowing anything at all about how memory works, we can think of three possible ways we might perform this task.

1. Mind's Eye Sees All. On this model the mind simply fetches the entire list and "looks" at it to "see" if the test digit is on it. This model has some intuitive credibility from situations such as this: a housemate calls from upstairs and asks you if his glasses are on the kitchen table. You walk into the kitchen, look at the table, and say yes or no.
2. Self-Terminating Serial Search. On this model the mind goes down the list serially from left to right and answers as soon as it makes a match in the case of a positive answer, or as soon as it gets to the end of the list without a match in the case of a negative answer. This model has credibility from situations such as this: You've lost your glasses. You say to yourself "I must have left them on a tabletop, in a coat pocket, or at the office." You start by looking on all the tabletops. Next you start to rummage through the pockets of the coat you wore earlier in the day and find your glasses in the first pocket you reach into. Search terminates. (You do not continue on to the office.)
3. Exhaustive Serial Search. On this model the mind goes down the list serially from left to right and answers yes or no only when it gets to the end of the list. If the

match occurs before the end of the list, it is registered. But the mind still proceeds to the end of the list before answering. It is hard to think of examples of situations where we consciously operate in this way. But consider: You are an eyewitness to a crime and are called in to identify a suspect in a police lineup consisting of six people. You start by looking at the first person on your left and proceed to the right. The third person looks just like the criminal; you register this, but continue to the end of the lineup before you point your finger. The exhaustive search takes place, so to speak, just to make sure that you are not mistaken in your match of memory to face.

Fortunately, since allegedly this is science we are discussing, these three hypotheses predict different reaction times. The *Mind's Eye Sees All* model predicts that the reaction time will be the same no matter what the location of the test digit is on the list. For example, if the memorized list is 1, 8, 9, 2, 4, reaction time should be equal for the test digit 1 or 4. The reason is simple: on the *Mind's Eye Sees All* model the entire list is conjured up and "seen all at once," rather than processed from left to right. There either is or is not a match.

The *Self-Terminating Search* model predicts that reaction times will vary depending on the location of the test digit on the list. Responses should take longer the later (in terms of left to right) the test digit occurs on the list, and negative responses should always take longer than positive ones.

Like the *Mind's Eye Sees All* model, the *Exhaustive Serial Search* model predicts that reaction times will not vary with location on a particular list. However, unlike the *Mind's Eye Sees All* model, the *Exhaustive Serial Search* model predicts that reaction times will vary with the length of the list. The reason is obvious: if a search is exhaustive in the sense that we go to the end of a list even after a match has been made, reaction time should take longer, the longer the list.

Results: Sternberg found that the mean reaction time varied linearly with the length of the memorized list and that reaction times were the same for positive and negative responses. We now need to ask a Kantian sort of question about these data. How are they possible? They are possible only if our minds perform exhaustive serial left-to-right searches on tasks such as these. This is exactly Sternberg's conclusion. He claims that we "scan" serially and exhaustively at a rate of about 25 to 30 digits per second. Sternberg uses the "scanning" metaphor in part because the speed here is too fast for the mechanism to involve the left-to-right inaudible vocalization some of his subjects report.

Transcendental reasoning is a variety of inductive inference. This means that Sternberg's conclusions are, as philosophers like to say, radically underdetermined by the available evidence. A skeptic, for example, might argue that the *Mind's Eye Sees All* model is also compatible with Sternberg's data. He could argue that whereas the *Mind's Eye Sees All* model predicts no variation in reaction time, depending on the location of the test digit on a particular memorized list, it does not necessarily predict against reaction-time differences for lists of different lengths. Thus, it might take longer—for reasons having to do with the access mechanisms—to conjure up longer lists for scanning, but once conjured up the response could be all or none.

Most physical theories are similarly underdetermined by the evidence. Nevertheless, skeptical doubts about logically possible alternatives do nothing to undermine credible inferences from carefully controlled experiments.

Now, I take it that most people's intuitions, insofar as they have them, would have predicted against the *Exhaustive Serial Search* model. First, there are relatively few good examples of this sort of model operating in intuitively familiar domains. Second, and this is related to the first, the *Exhaustive Serial Search* model is not optimally efficient, or rather it is only optimally efficient if there are preexisting nonoptimal features of the system. For example, an exhaustive search of a police lineup is only optimal for a system which is prone to making matching errors. If one were an omnipotent and omniscient designer one would surely make us infallible at memory matches and then wire us in accordance with the *Mind's Eye Sees All* model or the *Self-Terminating Search* model. They just have to be faster.

Two philosophically important points begin to emerge. First, our intuitions are not to be trusted very far in generating knowledge of mental mechanisms. Second, our minds have design constraints; we may well not be designed by an omnipotent and omniscient designer. The mind may turn out to be something of a Rube Goldberg device, what Marvin Minsky calls a "kludge." . . .

The discussion thus far has been decidedly nonmetaphysical; it has been concerned with some of the central philosophical assumptions and implications of cognitive psychology with little mention of the question of the nature of the mind.

This is not merely an artifact of my mode of presentation. Cognitive psychologists, by and large, simply seem not to worry about the mind-brain problem. It is not entirely clear why this is, but I suspect there are two main causes. First, in some quarters there is the view that the mind-brain problem can simply be ignored. New lawlike generalizations about cognition are being discovered every day by scientists who worry not one iota about the metaphysical nature of the underlying processes. Second, there are those who consider some form of materialism to be established, and who, in addition, take the software-hardware distinction in computer science to have provided, once and for all, convincing proof for the permissibility and usefulness of scientific talk about a material system in a language which does not ever directly refer to the materials themselves.

Philosophers interested in reconstructing the metaphysical commitments of cognitive psychologists often claim that some form of functionalism is the canonical position in the field. One has to be careful here. Among psychologists, functionalism often refers to an epistemological position, to a view on how mental states are picked out and on how psychological explanations are most appropriately framed. According to epistemological functionalism, mental states are identified in terms of the characteristic causal relations which hold among environmental events, other mental states, and action. Anger, for example, characteristically results from some unjust act; it is usually accompanied by annoyance and the desire to retaliate, and it often results in harsh words or actual physical violence.

The main difference between the functionalist's and the behaviorist's way of picking out mental states is twofold. First, the functionalist, unlike the behaviorist, does not try to characterize mental states solely in terms of nonmental ones, such as, S is angry means S is acting angry; rather the functionalist is interested in characterizing mental events in terms of stimuli, responses, and other mental states. Second, the functionalist believes that in intelligent organisms such as ourselves, the causal relations between mental states are causally significant processes and not mere side effects or end products of more interesting processes taking place in the environment.

It is easy to wonder and sensible to ask how epistemological functionalism has any bearing on the mind-brain problem. After all, the brain was never mentioned in what I just said; and, as I pointed out above, many psychologists happily ignore metaphysical questions of the form: What is the essence of mentality? Philosophers, of course, are notorious for taking the plunge. Nevertheless, even philosophers committed to a more obviously metaphysical brand of functionalism are cagey on the mind-brain problem. Explaining their cageyness requires repeating a little philosophical history.

First—among opponents of dualism—there was *identity theory*. Identity theory is the claim that each *type* of mental state is identical to some *type* of brain state. The fundamental idea is that the kinds of things picked out by our ordinary mental concepts (belief, desire, hope, love, and so on), are actually identical type-for-type with kinds that neuroscientists will someday discover. The identity theorist is, therefore, a *type-physicalist*. Happily for the identity theorist, the history of science is replete with examples of discoveries of type-type identities: Clouds are collections of water droplets, water is H_2O, temperature is mean molecular kinetic energy.

Identity theory assumes one important philosophical thesis and implies another. The assumption is that the taxonomy of our commonsense psychological framework, our so-called folk psychology, is on the mark. That is, folk psychology accurately picks out types of entities that will be definable completely in terms of the yet-to-be-discovered types of a mature neuroscience. The bet is that someday people will formulate type-type identity statements such as "Beliefs are just xzqry-firings at velocity *v* and rate *r* in sector 2304."

The implication that follows from the latter assumption is this: if type-type identity theory is true then reduction of psychology to neuroscience will eventually be possible. It is easy to see why reduction requires that all the concepts of the science to be reduced be translatable into the concepts of the reducing science. These translations are called "bridge laws" and once they are in place reduction merely involves replacing, synonym for synonym. Type-type identity statements, of course, are precisely the necessary bridge laws.

In the heyday of identity theory one would hear questions as to why reduction was urged in the direction of neuroscience if indeed both psychology and neuroscience were about exactly the same thing. There were two sorts of replies. First, it was often said that the concepts of psychology were a bit loose and vague, while those of neuroscience were more precise. The trouble with this reply is that it seems to deny what identity theory assumes, namely, that there is a perfect mapping between ordinary psychological types and neuroscientific ones. How can sloppy concepts map onto neat ones?

A second, and better reason for urging reduction in the direction of neuroscience is this: although all psychological terms eventually will be definable in terms of neuroscientific terms, there are sure to be additional neuroscientific terms for which there are no corresponding psychological ones, for example, terms describing states and processes to which we have no conscious access. In this way, neuroscience will be richer than psychology: it will absorb psychology and go beyond it. It will say everything psychology can, and more.

Now the metaphysical functionalist comes in; his strategy is to try to accept the identity theorist's physicalism without accepting his reductionism. The functionalist starts by pointing out that there are many interesting kinds of things for which there are no coherent underlying physical types. Take the type, mystery story. Go through the library gathering all the books and short stories which are instances of the genre "mystery story." Pile them in a room. Now tell me what physical properties underlie the type "mystery story" and distinguish it from other literary genres that also appear in book form.

Or take the kind, "clock." Big Ben is a clock, a sundial is a clock, my wristwatch is a clock, you would be a clock if you stood in the middle of a desert. What physical properties do all clocks have in common by virtue of which they are clocks?

Or take the kind, "calculator." There are hundreds of different brands. They come in assorted shapes and sizes. Some are made of metal, some of plastic, and some are mixed. They vary widely in their wiring diagrams. But they all do arithmetic.

Notice two things about the examples. First, all the tokens (the individual members) of the types are physical. That is, each and every individual mystery story, clock, and calculator is a physical thing. But even within types, they are not even remotely the same kind of physical thing.

The examples, therefore, provide the functionalist with motivation for espousing token-physicalism, the view that each thing that exists is physical, without accepting reductionism (which requires type-type bridge laws).

The second thing to notice about the examples is that all the types cited as being irreducible to homogeneous physical types are functional types; they are normally characterized in terms of what they can do, how they work, what function they have, what effects they have, and so on.

With the confidence generated by such examples the functionalist claims, in the words of Jerry Fodor, that:

> The reason it is unlikely that every kind corresponds to a physical kind is just that (a) interesting generalizations . . . can often be made about events whose physical descriptions have nothing in common; (b) it is often the case that *whether* the physical descriptions of the events subsumed by such generalizations have anything in common is . . . entirely irrelevant to the truth of the generalizations, or to their interestingness, or to their degree of confirmation, or indeed, to any of their epistemologically interesting properties.

The functionalist claims that because we have every reason to believe mental states are individuated functionally, and because we have no reason to believe that most functional types map neatly onto homogeneous physical types, we have no reason to think that psychological kinds will map onto neuroscientific kinds. We can be (token) physicalists without being reductionists. We have, in effect, a principled, as opposed to a state of the art, defense of the autonomy of psychological explanation which also happily coheres with a commitment to metaphysical materialism.

Furthermore, metaphysical functionalism helps legitimize the cognitive psychologist's preferred style of explanation (this is why many philosophers recommend metaphysical functionalism in addition to epistemological functionalism). The metaphysical functionalist offers a principled reason as to why the cognitive psychologist should offer functional explanations from the design or intentional stances, without bothering with physical-stance accounts. Consider the generalization that, on the average, people who believe in God attend religious services more often than those who do not. The metaphysical functionalist accepts that all beliefs for or against God are physical events and processes, but he doubts that they are any one particular kind of physical event or process in all people. Person A and person B might share a belief in one and the same God, say Zeus, and thus be in the same intentional state, while their brains are in very different states. According to the token-physicalist, one and the same functional state can be realized in many different ways.

This last point has given rise to a heated debate that is central to the question of artificial intelligence. The metaphysical functionalist is committed to the view that you and I can have the same belief about, say, the date of Columbus's discovery of America, without being in exactly the same brain state (although we need to be in some brain state or other). Now suppose some Martians land on earth, looking like Martians in comic books. Suppose that several of these friendly visitors learn our language, enter our schools, and learn history the way we do. The Martians come to say things like "Columbus discovered America in 1492," and we come to think of them as knowledgeable in the same ways we are. Cognitive psychologists do research on them and find that Sternberg's . . . results all generalize to Martians.

Now suppose that one of the Martians dies and we do an autopsy and discover that the Martian's nervous system is not spine- and brain-based like ours, but appears to involve neuronlike cells spread throughout the circulatory system. Do we still attribute consciousness and beliefs to the living Martians? The functionalist, of course, says yes. The Martians' beliefs and mental processes are realized differently from ours; but from a functional point of view they are the same.

Suppose instead that the scenario differs in the following way. The autopsy reveals that internally the Martian functions hydraulically; there are minute pieces of some sort of organic metal, unknown in Earthly chemistry, mixed with what looks like water, but is really XYZ (also heretofore unknown on earth), coursing through the pliable tubes which make up his internal anatomy. Do we still attribute consciousness and beliefs to the living Martians? Again the functionalist says yes. The way the Martians' beliefs and mental processes are realized is admittedly unexpected, but their beliefs and mental processes play the same functional role as ours, and thus they are the same.

Third scenario: the autopsy reveals that the Martian has only an organic exterior, which, it turns out, has a designer label on the inside that says in Martian (which we now understand) "Made by Organic Exteriors, Inc. Wear only in sunny oxygen-rich environments." Further inside, however, the Martian is entirely inorganic, filled with plastic, silicon chips, copper, and a dead nuclear battery. Do we still attribute consciousness and beliefs to the living Martians, all of whom, we have now discovered by X ray, have the same kind of body?

Here things get harder. Some functionalists agree that they are committed to attributing mentality once again, and view this as the possibility proof for the existence of genuine artificial intelligence. Others reject the fantasy on grounds that it is simply too implausible. To be sure, mental states can be realized in a variety of ways in a nervous system, but the nervous system has to be made of the right stuff, minimally organic stuff.

To some, all this science fiction is an indication of the cost of metaphysical functionalism. The functionalist claims to be a card-carrying materialist, but has gone so far overboard with his insight about the possibility of multiple realizations that he acts as if the particular kind of body we have is irrelevant to our mental life.

At this point we meet the eliminative materialist; the eliminativist is a critic of functionalism and worries about the assurances metaphysical functionalism gives the cognitive psychologist about the legitimacy of his preferred style of explanation.

Like the functionalist and unlike the identity theorist, the eliminativist doubts that there will ever be a neat reduction of psychology to neuroscience. His reason is that he doubts there will ever be a remotely true or coherent psychology to reduce!

The eliminativist is skeptical of an assumption which he claims the identity theorist and the functionalist share, namely, that the concepts, categories, and laws of folk psychology are fundamentally correct. The eliminativist thinks our ordinary commonsense psychology is seriously misguided and worth outright elimination. The twist is that he thinks so-called scientific psychology has appropriated the concepts and principles of folk psychology hook, line, and sinker, and thus is worth deep-sixing as well.

Paul and Patricia Churchland are the most able and articulate contemporary defenders of eliminativism. Paul Churchland says,

> FP [Folk Psychology] suffers explanatory failures on an epic scale . . . it has been stagnant for at least twenty-five centuries . . . its categories appear (so far) to be incommensurable with or orthogonal to the categories of the background physical science whose long-term claim to explain human behavior seems undeniable. Any theory which meets this description must be allowed a serious candidate for outright elimination.

According to the eliminativist, the main problem with functionalism, as with identity theory, is its uncritical confidence in the types of ordinary folk psychology: belief, desire, love, hope, pain, and so on. The eliminativist believes that this typology and its accompanying theory have led only to vacuous and contradictory generalizations (such as "out of sight out of mind" and "absence makes the heart grow fonder"), and to absolutely no scientific progress whatsoever. Folk psychology, and its first cousin, scientific psychology, will eventually go the way of phlogiston, witches, and the geocentric theory of planetary motion. All these theories were once widely accepted, but were eventually simply eliminated; they were shown not to be even approximately true. It is time to do neuroscience and stop playing games.

Churchland argues that once neuroscience is complete we can:

set about *reconceiving* our internal states and activities, within a truly adequate conceptual framework at last. Our explanations of one another's behavior will appeal to such things as our neuropharmacological states, the neural activity in specialized anatomical areas, and whatever other states are deemed relevant by the new theory.

The eliminativist raises a very important point: Folk psychology is a theory, and it is conceivable that it could turn out to be false, not only at the level of its laws, but even at the level of its typologies. Maybe there just are no beliefs, desires, hopes, and so on, as we conceive of them. Marvin Minsky, another skeptic about folk psychology, puts it this way: "Though prescientific idea germs like 'believe,' 'know,' and 'mean' are used in daily life, they seem technically too coarse to support powerful theories; we need to supplant, rather than support and explicate them."

If we take seriously the possibility of the demise of folk psychology, it is worth reflecting on what the consequences might be for the preferred style of explanation in cognitive psychology. Fortunately for the cognitive psychologist, things are not nearly as bleak as the eliminativist paints them.

Eliminativists sometimes talk as if cognitive psychologists simply appropriate the concepts, categories, and laws of folk psychology straight out, but this is not quite right. Cognitive psychologists tend to offer explanations from both the design stance *and* the intentional stance.

Intentional-stance explanations openly appropriate traditional belief-desire concepts from folk psychology, and thus can be expected to suffer from whatever liabilities these concepts bring. On the other hand, folk-psychological concepts function differently in the hands of cognitive psychologists than in the hands of the person on the street. In large part this is because folk-psychological concepts are being deployed in experimental settings in which enrichment as well as revision of our commonsense understanding is the goal. Furthermore, it is simply not true that in accepting the basic conceptual scheme of folk psychology, intentional-stance psychology also accepts the generalizations of folk psychology. Many of the experiments I have discussed here completely undermine traditional folk-psychological wisdom, for example, the view that people have privileged access to their own minds, or that the mind is one simple unity, or that we are by nature completely rational animals.

When cognitive psychologists study the mind at the subpersonal level, explanations tend to move in the design-stance direction. The process being studied, say, sentence comprehension, is divided into a series of smaller functions—visual or auditory processing, semantic and syntactic analysis, and so on. Such explanations appropriate folk-psychological concepts far less than full-blown intentional-stance explanations. Furthermore, design-stance explanations rarely appropriate folk-psychological generalizations, in part because normally there are no extant folk-psychological generalizations about the processes under study. The eliminativist acts as if the cognitive psychologist has made a completely uncritical pact with folk psychology. This is simply not true.

The eliminativist does raise an important point, however. To whatever extent theorizing in cognitive psychology is constrained by alleged truths of folk psychology from above, it is also constrained by known truths about the nervous system, from below. It would be dangerous for cognitive psychologists to entertain even for a moment the belief that research in brain science is irrelevant to their functional pronouncements, or to take metaphysical functionalism as proof that there are no interesting mappings of psychological processes onto brain processes. The amount of important work indicating all sorts of localization of function makes this view untenable. Furthermore, it would be a parallel error to think that neuroscience will never lead us to reconceptualize phenomena at the functional level. It seems to me that work on the biochemical bases of certain types of mental illness, such as manic-depressive psychosis and schizophrenia, has already produced not only better understanding of the causes of these illnesses, but has also led to a reconceptualization of their nature.

It is worth emphasizing that for all their bravado, identity theory, functionalism, and eliminativism all involve more or less a priori stances about the way the relations among the different sciences will work out. The three views share a commitment to metaphysical materialism. They differ, however, in that the identity theorist bets that psychology will someday be smoothly reduced to neuroscience; the functionalist that psychology will remain an autonomous special science; and the eliminativist that psychology will simply go the way of alchemy and be replaced by neuroscience. The important point is that the issues here cannot be settled a priori. They will depend for their resolution on how the various research programs guided by the three points of view turn out. In the meantime, the cognitive psychologist is on epistemologically sound ground in proceeding to analyze processes at levels above the neural.

John R. Searle

The Myth of the Computer

John R. Searle *teaches philosophy at the University of California, Berkeley. He has done important work in philosophy of language and more recently has become an influential critic of the view that computers can tell us something important about the mind.*

Our ordinary ways of talking about ourselves and other people, of justifying our behavior and explaining that of others, express a certain conception of human life that is so close to us, so much a part of common sense that we can hardly see it. It is a conception according to which each person has (or perhaps *is*) a mind; the contents of the mind—beliefs, fears, hopes, motives, desires, etc.—cause and therefore explain our actions; and the continuity of our minds is the source of our individuality and identity as persons.

In the past couple of centuries we have also become convinced that this common-sense psychology is grounded in the brain, that these mental states and events are somehow, we are not quite sure how, going on in the neurophysiological processes of the brain. So this leaves us with two levels at which we can describe and explain human beings: a level of common-sense psychology, which seems to work well enough in practice but which is not scientific; and a level of neurophysiology, which is certainly scientific but which even the most advanced specialists know very little about.

But couldn't there be a third possibility, a science of human beings that was not introspective common-sense psychology but was not neurophysiology either? This has been the great dream of the human sciences in the twentieth century, but so far all of the efforts have been, in varying degrees, failures. The most spectacular failure was behaviorism, but in my intellectual lifetime I have lived through exaggerated hopes placed on and disappointed by games theory, cybernetics, information theory, generative grammar, structuralism, and Freudian psychology, among others. Indeed it has become something of a scandal of twentieth-century intellectual life that we lack a science of the human mind and human behavior, that the methods of the natural sciences have produced such meager results when applied to human beings.

The latest candidate or family of candidates to fill the gap is called cognitive science, a collection of related investigations into the human mind involving psychology, philosophy, linguistics, anthropology, and artificial intelligence. Cognitive science is really the name of a family of research projects and not a theory, but many of its practitioners think that the heart of cognitive science is a theory of the mind based on artificial intelligence (AI). According to this theory minds just are computer programs of certain kinds. The main ideological aim of Hofstadter and Dennett's book is to advance this theory. . . .

The theory, which is fairly widely held in cognitive science, can be summarized in three propositions.

1. *Mind as Program.* What we call minds are simply very complex digital computer programs. Mental states are simply computer states and mental processes are computational processes. Any system whatever that had the right program, with the right input and output, would have to have mental states and processes in the same literal sense that you and I do, because that is all there is to mental states and processes, that is all that you and I have. The programs in question are "self-updating" or "self-designing" "systems of representations."

2. *The Irrelevance of the Neurophysiology of the Brain.* In the study of the mind actual biological facts about actual human and animal brains are irrelevant because the mind is an "abstract sort of thing" and human brains just happen to be among the indefinitely large number of kinds of computers that can have minds. Our minds happen to be embodied in our brains, but there is no essential connection between the mind and the brain. Any other computer with the right program would also have a mind.

    Theses 1 and 2 are summarized in the introduction where the author speaks of "the emerging view of the mind as software or program—as an abstract sort of thing whose identity is independent of any particular physical embodiment."

3. *The Turing Test as the Criterion of the Mental.* The conclusive proof of the presence of mental states and capacities is the ability of a system to pass the Turing test, the test devised by Alan Turing and described in his article in [Hofstadter and Dennett's] book. If a system can convince a competent expert that it has mental states then it really has those mental states. If, for example, a machine could "converse" with a native Chinese speaker in such a way as to convince the speaker that it understood Chinese then it would literally understand Chinese.

The three theses are neatly lumped together when one of the editors writes, "Minds exist in brains and may come to exist in programmed machines. If and when such machines come about, their causal powers will derive not from the substances they are made of, but from their design and the programs that run in them. And the way we will know they have those causal powers is by talking to them and listening carefully to what they have to say."

We might call this collection of theses "strong artificial intelligence" (strong AI).* These theses are certainly not obviously true and they are seldom explicitly stated and defended.

Let us inquire first into how plausible it is to suppose that specific biochemical powers of the brain are really irrelevant to the mind. It is an amazing fact, by the way, that in twenty-seven pieces about the mind the editors have not seen fit to include any whose primary aim is to tell us how the brain actually works, and this omission obviously derives from their conviction that since "mind is an abstract sort of thing" the specific neurophysiology of the brain is incidental. This idea derives part of its appeal from the editors' keeping their discussion at a very abstract general level about "consciousness" and "mind" and "soul," but if you consider specific mental states and processes—being thirsty, wanting to go to the bathroom, worrying about your income tax, trying to solve math puzzles, feeling depressed, recalling

---

*"Strong" to distinguish the position from "weak" or "cautious" AI, which holds that the computer is simply a very useful tool in the study of the mind, not that the appropriately programmed computer literally has a mind.

the French word for "butterfly"—then it seems at least a little odd to think that the brain is so irrelevant.

Take thirst, where we actually know a little bit about how it works. Kidney secretions of renin synthesize a substance called angiotensin. This substance goes into the hypothalamus and triggers a series of neuron firings. As far as we know these neuron firings are a very large part of the cause of thirst. Now obviously there is more to be said, for example about the relations of the hypothalamic responses to the rest of the brain, about other things going on in the hypothalamus, and about the possible distinctions between the *feeling* of thirst and the *urge* to drink. Let us suppose we have filled out the story with the rest of the biochemical causal account of thirst.

Now these theses of the mind as program and the irrelevance of the brain would tell us that what matters about this story is not the specific biochemical properties of the angiotensin or the hypothalamus but only the formal computer programs that the whole sequence instantiates. Well, let's try that out as a hypothesis and see how it works. A computer can simulate the formal properties of the sequence of chemical and electrical phenomena in the production of thirst just as much as it can simulate the formal properties of anything else— we can simulate thirst just as we can simulate hurricanes, rainstorms, five-alarm fires, internal combustion engines, photosynthesis, lactation, or the flow of currency in a depressed economy. But no one in his right mind thinks that a computer simulation of a five-alarm fire will burn down the neighborhood, or that a computer simulation of an internal combustion engine will power a car or that computer simulations of lactation and photosynthesis will produce milk and sugar. To my amazement, however, I have found that a large number of people suppose that computer simulations of mental phenomena, whether at the level of brain processes or not, literally produce mental phenomena.

Again, let's try it out. Let's program our favorite PDP-10 computer with the formal program that simulates thirst. We can even program it to print out at the end "Boy, am I thirsty!" or "Won't someone please give me a drink?" etc. Now would anyone suppose that we thereby have even the slightest reason to suppose that the computer is literally thirsty? Or that any simulation of any other mental phenomena, such as understanding stories, feeling depressed, or worrying about itemized deductions, must therefore produce the real thing? The answer, alas, is that a large number of people are committed to an ideology that requires them to believe just that. So let us carry the story a step further.

The PDP-10 is powered by electricity and perhaps its electrical properties can reproduce some of the actual causal powers of the electrochemical features of the brain in producing mental states. We certainly couldn't rule out that eventuality a priori. But remember: the thesis of strong AI is that the mind is "independent of *any* particular embodiment" because the mind is just a program and the program can be run on a computer made of anything whatever provided it is stable enough and complex enough to carry the program. The actual physical computer could be an ant colony (one of their examples), a collection of beer cans, streams of toilet paper with small stones placed on the squares, men sitting on high stools with green eye shades—anything you like.

So let us imagine our thirst-simulating program running on a computer made entirely of old beer cans, millions (or billions) of old beer cans that are rigged up to levers and powered by windmills. We can imagine that the program simulates the neuron firings at the synapses by having beer cans bang into each other, thus achieving a strict correspondence between neuron firings and beer-can bangings. At the end of the sequence a beer can pops up on which is written "I am thirsty." Now, to repeat the question, does anyone suppose that this Rube Goldberg apparatus is literally thirsty in the sense in which you and I are?

Notice that the thesis of Hofstadter and Dennett is not that *for all we know* the collection of beer cans might be thirsty but rather that if it has the right program with the right input and output it *must* be thirsty (or understand Proust or worry about its income tax or have any other mental state) because that is all the mind is, a certain kind of computer program, and any computer made of anything at all running the right program would have to have the appropriate mental states.

I believe that everything we have learned about human and animal biology suggests that what we call "mental" phenomena are as much a part of our biological natural history as any other biological phenomena, as much a part of biology as digestion, lactation, or the secretion of bile. Much of the implausibility of the strong AI thesis derives from its resolute opposition to biology; the mind is not a concrete biological phenomenon but "an abstract sort of thing."

Still, in calling attention to the implausibility of supposing that the specific casual powers of brains are irrelevant to minds I have not yet fully exposed the preposterousness of the strong AI position, held by Hofstadter and Dennett, so let us press on and examine a bit more closely the thesis of mind as program.

Digital computer programs by definition consist of sets of purely formal operations on formally specified symbols. The ideal computer does such things as print a 0 on the tape, move one square to the left, erase a 1, move back to the right, etc. It is common to describe this as "symbol manipulation" or, to use the term favored by Hofstadter and Dennett, the whole system is a "self-updating representational system"; but these terms are at least a bit misleading since as far as the computer is concerned the symbols don't *symbolize* anything or *represent* anything. They are just formal counters.

The computer attaches no meaning, interpretation, or content to the formal symbols; and qua computer it couldn't, because if we tried to give the computer an interpretation of its symbols we could only give it more uninterpreted symbols. The interpretation of the symbols is entirely up to the programmers and users of the computer. For example, on my pocket calculator if I print "3 × 3 = ," the calculator will print "9" but it has no idea that "3" means 3 or that "9" means 9 or that anything means anything. We might put this point by saying that the computer has a syntax but no semantics. The computer manipulates formal symbols but attaches no meaning to them, and this simple observation will enable us to refute the thesis of mind as program.

Suppose that we write a computer program to simulate the understanding of Chinese so that, for example, if the computer is asked questions in Chinese the program enables it to give answers in Chinese; if asked to summarize stories in Chinese it can give such summaries; if asked questions about the stories it has been given it will answer such questions.

Now suppose that I, who understand no Chinese at all and can't even distinguish Chinese symbols from some other kinds of symbols, am locked in a room with a number of cardboard boxes full of Chinese symbols. Suppose that I am given a book of rules in English that instruct me how to match these Chinese symbols with each other. The rules say such things as that the "squiggle-squiggle" sign is to be followed by the "squoggle-squoggle" sign. Suppose that people outside the room pass in more Chinese symbols and that following the instructions in the book I pass Chinese symbols back to them. Suppose that unknown to me the people who pass me the symbols call them "questions," and the book of instructions that I work from they call "the program"; the symbols I give back to them they call "answers to the questions" and me they call "the computer." Suppose that after a while the programmers get so good at writing the programs and I get so good at manipulating the symbols that my answers are indistinguishable from those of native Chinese speakers. I can pass the Turing test for understanding Chinese. But all the same I still don't understand a word of Chinese and neither does any other digital computer because all the computer has is what I have: a formal program that attaches no meaning, interpretation, or content to any of the symbols.

What this simple argument shows is that no formal program by itself is sufficient for understanding, because it would always be possible in principle for an agent to go through the steps in the program and still not have the relevant understanding. And what works for Chinese would also work for other mental phenomena. I could, for example, go through the steps of the thirst-simulating program without feeling thirsty. The argument also, *en passant,* refutes the Turing test because it shows that a system, namely me, could pass the Turing test without having the appropriate mental states. . . .

The rest of what they have to say is mostly a repetition of points made by other authors and already answered by me. Specifically, they endorse the "systems reply" to the Chinese room argument, according to which the man in the room does not understand Chinese, but the system of which he is a part—including the instruction book, the Chinese symbols, etc.—really does understand Chinese. Adherents of this view believe, to my constant amazement, that though the man fails to understand, the *room* does understand Chinese. The obvious objection to this is that the system has no way of attaching meaning to the uninterpreted Chinese symbols, any more than the man did in the first place. The system, like the man, has a syntax but no semantics. And you can see this by simply imagining that the man internalizes the whole system. Suppose he has a super memory and a super intelligence so that he memorizes the instruction book and does all the calculations in his head. To get rid of the room, we can even suppose he works outdoors. Now since the man doesn't understand Chinese, and since there's nothing in the system that is not in the man, there is no way the system could understand Chinese. As near as I can tell Hofstadter and Dennett's only reply to this is to observe that no normal human being could perform such a feat of memory. This is of course quite true, but also quite irrelevant to the point, which, to repeat, is that from syntax alone you don't get semantics. . . .

The details of how the brain works are immensely complicated and largely unknown, but some of the general principles of the relations between brain functioning and computer programs can be stated quite simply. First, we know that brain processes cause mental phenomena. Mental states are caused by and realized in the structure of the brain. From this it follows that any system that produced mental states would have to have powers equivalent to those of the brain. Such a system might use a different chemistry, but whatever its chemistry it would have to be able to cause what the brain causes. We know from the Chinese room argument that digital computer programs by themselves are never sufficient to produce mental states. Now since brains do produce minds, and since programs by themselves can't produce minds, it follows that the way the brain does it can't be by simply instantiating a computer program. (Everything, by the way, instantiates some program or other, and brains are no exception. So in that trivial sense brains, like everything else, are digital computers.) And it also follows that if you wanted to build a machine to produce mental states, a thinking machine, you couldn't do it solely in virtue of the fact that your machine ran a certain kind of computer program. The thinking machine couldn't work solely in virtue of being a digital computer but would have to duplicate the specific causal powers of the brain.

A lot of the nonsense talked about computers nowadays stems from their relative rarity and hence mystery. As computers and robots become more common, as common as telephones, washing machines, and forklift trucks, it seems likely that this aura will disappear and people will take computers for what they are, namely useful machines. In the meantime one has to try to avoid certain recurring mistakes that keep cropping up in Hofstadter and Dennett's book as well as in other current discussions.

The first is the idea that somehow computer achievements pose some sort of threat or challenge to human beings. But the fact, for example, that a calculator can outperform even the best mathematician is no more significant or threatening than the fact that a steam shovel can outperform the best human digger. (An oddity of artificial intelligence, by the way, is the slowness of the programmers in devising a program that can beat the very best chess players.

From the point of view of games theory, chess is a trivial game since each side has perfect information about the other's position and possible moves, and one has to assume that computer programs will soon be able to outperform any human chess player.)

A second fallacy is the idea that there might be some special human experience beyond computer simulation because of its special humanity. We are sometimes told that computers couldn't simulate feeling depressed or falling in love or having a sense of humor. But as far as simulation is concerned you can program your computer to print out "I am depressed," "I love Sally," or "Ha, ha," as easily as you can program it to print out "3 × 3 = 9." The real mistake is to suppose that simulation is duplication, and that mistake is the same regardless of what mental states we are talking about. A third mistake, basic to all the others, is the idea that if a computer can simulate having a certain mental state then we have the same grounds for supposing it really has that mental state as we have for supposing that human beings have that state. But we know from the Chinese room argument as well as from biology that this simple-minded behaviorism of the Turing test is mistaken.

Until computers and robots become as common as cars and until people are able to program and use them as easily as they now drive cars we are likely to continue to suffer from a certain mythological conception of digital computers. [Hoffstadter & Dennett's] book is very much a part of the present mythological era of the computer.

Paul M. Churchland
Eliminative Materialism

Paul M. Churchland *teaches philosophy at the University of California, San Diego. He is the leading spokesperson for the claims of* eliminative materialism. *This article is taken from his book,* Matter and Consciousness.

*T*he identity theory was called into doubt not because the prospects for a materialist account of our mental capacities were thought to be poor, but because it seemed unlikely that the arrival of an adequate materialist theory would bring with it the nice one-to-one match-ups, between the concepts of folk psychology and the concepts of theoretical neuroscience, that intertheoretic reduction requires. The reason for that doubt was the great variety of quite different physical systems that could instantiate the required functional organization. *Eliminative materialism* also doubts that the correct neuroscientific account of human capacities will produce a neat reduction of our common-sense framework, but here the doubts arise from a quite different source.

As the eliminative materialists see it, the one-to-one match-ups will not be found, and our common-sense psychological framework will not enjoy an intertheoretic reduction, *because our common-sense psychological framework is a false and radically misleading conception of the causes of human behavior and the nature of cognitive activity.* On this view, folk psychology is not just an incomplete representation of our inner natures; it is an outright *mis*representation of our internal states and activities. Consequently, we cannot expect a truly adequate neuroscientific account of our inner lives to provide theoretical categories that match up nicely with the categories of our common-sense framework. Accordingly, we must expect that the older framework will simply be eliminated, rather than be reduced, by a matured neuroscience.

HISTORICAL PARALLELS

As the identity theorist can point to historical cases of successful intertheoretic reduction, so the eliminative materialist can point to historical cases of the outright elimination of the ontology of an older theory in favor of the ontology of a new and superior theory. For most of the eighteenth and nineteenth centuries, learned people believed that heat was a subtle *fluid* held in bodies, much in the way water is held in a sponge. A fair body of moderately successful theory described the way this fluid substance—called "caloric"—flowed within a body, or from one body to another, and how it produced thermal expansion, melting, boiling, and so forth. But by the end of the last century it had become abundantly clear that heat was not a substance at all, but just the energy of motion of the trillions of jostling molecules that make up the heated body itself. The new theory—the "corpuscular/kinetic theory of matter and heat"—was much more successful than the old in explaining and predicting the thermal behavior of bodies. And since we were unable to *identify* caloric fluid with kinetic energy (according to the old theory, caloric is a material *substance;* according to the new theory, kinetic energy is a form of *motion*), it was finally agreed that there is *no such thing* as caloric. Caloric was simply eliminated from our accepted ontology.

A second example. It used to be thought that when a piece of wood burns, or a piece of metal rusts, a spiritlike substance called "phlogiston" was being released: briskly, in the former case, slowly in the latter. Once gone, that 'noble' substance left only a base pile of ash or rust. It later came to be appreciated that both processes involve, not the loss of something, but the *gaining* of a substance taken from the atmosphere: oxygen. Phlogiston emerged, not as an incomplete description of what was going on, but as a radical misdescription. Phlogiston was therefore not suitable for reduction to or identification with some notion from within the new oxygen chemistry, and it was simply eliminated from science.

Admittedly, both of these examples concern the elimination of something nonobservable, but our history also includes the elimination of certainly widely accepted 'observables'. Before Copernicus' views became available, almost any human who ventured out at night could look up at *the starry sphere of the heavens,* and if he stayed for more than a few minutes he could also see that it *turned,* around an axis through Polaris. What the sphere was made of (crystal?) and what made it turn (the gods?) were theoretical questions that exercised us for over two millennia. But hardly anyone doubted the existence of what everyone could observe with their own eyes. In the end, however, we learned to reinterpret our visual experience of the night sky within a very different conceptual framework, and the turning sphere evaporated.

Witches provide another example. Psychosis is a fairly common affliction among humans, and in earlier centuries its victims were standardly seen as cases of demonic possession, as instances of Satan's spirit itself, glaring malevolently out at us from behind the victims' eyes. That witches exist was not a matter of any controversy. One would occasionally see them, in any city or hamlet, engaged in incoherent, paranoid, or even murderous behavior. But observable or not, we eventually decided that witches simply do not exist. We concluded that the concept of a witch is an element in a conceptual framework that misrepresents so badly the phenomena to which it was standardly applied that literal application of the notion should be permanently withdrawn. Modern theories of mental dysfunction led to the elimination of witches from our serious ontology.

The concepts of folk psychology—belief, desire, fear, sensation, pain, joy, and so on—await a similar fate, according to the view at issue. And when neuroscience has matured to the point where the poverty of our current conceptions is apparent to everyone, the superiority of the new framework is established, we shall then be able to set about *reconceiving* our internal states and activities, within a truly adequate conceptual framework at last. Our explanations of one another's behavior will appeal to such things as our neuropharmacological states, the neural activity in specialized anatomical areas, and whatever other states are deemed relevant by the new theory. Our private introspection will also be transformed, and may be profoundly enhanced by reason of the more accurate and penetrating framework it will have to work with—just as the astronomer's perception of the night sky is much enhanced by the detailed knowledge of modern astronomical theory that he or she possesses.

The magnitude of the conceptual revolution here suggested should not be minimized: it would be enormous. And the benefits to humanity might be equally great. If each of us possessed an accurate neuroscientific understanding of (what we now conceive dimly as) the varieties and causes of mental illness, the factors involved in learning, the neural basis of emotions, intelligence, and socialization, then the sum total of human misery might be much reduced. The simple increase in mutual understanding that the new framework made possible could contribute substantially toward a more peaceful and humane society. Of course, there would be dangers as well: increased knowledge means increased power, and power can always be misused.

ARGUMENTS FOR ELIMINATIVE MATERIALISM

The arguments for eliminative materialism are diffuse and less than decisive, but they are stronger than is widely supposed. The distinguishing feature of this position is its denial that a smooth intertheoretic reduction is to be expected—even a species-specific reduction—of the framework of folk psychology to the framework of a matured neuroscience. The reason for this denial is the eliminative materialist's conviction that folk psychology is a hopelessly primitive and deeply confused conception of our internal activities. But why this low opinion of our common-sense conceptions?

There are at least three reasons. First, the eliminative materialist will point to the widespread explanatory, predictive, and manipulative failures of folk psychology. So much of what is central and familiar to us remains a complete mystery from within folk psychology. We do not know what *sleep* is, or why we have to have it, despite spending a full third of our lives in that condition. (The answer, "For rest," is mistaken. Even if people are allowed to rest continuously, their need for sleep is undiminished. Apparently, sleep serves some deeper functions, but we do not yet know what they are.) We do not understand how *learning* transforms each of us from a gaping infant to a cunning adult, or how differences in *intelligence* are grounded. We have not the slightest idea how *memory* works, or how we manage to retrieve relevant bits of information instantly from the awesome mass we have stored. We do not know what *mental illness* is, nor how to cure it.

In sum, the most central things about us remain almost entirely mysterious from within folk psychology. And the defects noted cannot be blamed on inadequate time allowed for their correction, for folk psychology has enjoyed no significant changes or advances in well over 2,000 years, despite its manifest failures. Truly successful theories may be expected to reduce, but significantly unsuccessful theories merit no such expectation.

This argument from explanatory poverty has a further aspect. So long as one sticks to normal brains, the poverty of folk psychology is perhaps not strikingly evident. But as soon as one examines the many perplexing behavioral and cognitive deficits suffered by people with *damaged* brains, one's descriptive and explanatory resources start to claw the air. . . . As with other humble theories asked to operate successfully in unexplored extensions of their old domain (for example, Newtonian mechanics in the domain of velocities close to the velocity of light, and the classical gas law in the domain of high pressures or temperatures), the descriptive and explanatory inadequacies of folk psychology become starkly evident.

The second argument tries to draw an inductive lesson from our conceptual history. Our early folk theories of motion were profoundly confused, and were eventually displayed entirely by more sophisticated theories. Our early folk theories of the structure and activity of the heavens were wildly off the mark, and survive only as historical lessons in how wrong we can be. Our folk theories of the nature of fire, and the nature of life, were similarly cockeyed. And one could go on, since the vast majority of our past folk conceptions have been similarly exploded. All except folk psychology, which survives to this day and has only recently begun to feel pressure. But the phenomenon of conscious intelligence is surely a more complex and difficult phenomenon than any of those just listed. So far as accurate understanding is concerned, it would be a *miracle* if we had got *that* one right the very first time, when we fell down so badly on all the others. Folk psychology has survived for so very long, presumably, not because it is basically correct in its representations, but because the phenomena addressed are so surpassingly difficult that any useful handle on them, no matter how feeble, is unlikely to be displaced in a hurry.

A third argument attempts to find an a priori advantage for eliminative materialism over the identity theory and functionalism. It attempts to counter the common intuition that eliminative materialism is distantly possible, perhaps, but is much less probable than either the identity theory or functionalism. The focus again is on whether the concepts of folk psychology will find vindicating match-ups in a matured neuroscience. The eliminativist bets no; the other two bet yes. (Even the functionalist bets yes, but expects the match-ups to be only species-specific, or only person-specific. Functionalism, recall, denies the existence only of *universal* type/type identities.)

The eliminativist will point out that the requirements on a reduction are rather demanding. The new theory must entail a set of principles and embedded concepts that mirrors very closely the specific conceptual structure to be reduced. And the fact is, there are vastly many more ways of being an explanatorily successful neuroscience while *not* mirroring the structure of folk psychology, than there are ways of being an explanatorily successful neuroscience while also *mirroring* the very specific structure of folk psychology. Accordingly, the a priori probability of eliminative materialism is not lower, but substantially *higher* than that of either of its competitors. One's initial intuitions here are simply mistaken.

Granted, this initial a priori advantage could be reduced if there were a very strong presumption in the favor of the truth of folk psychology—true theories are better bets to win reduction. But according to the first two arguments, the presumptions on this point should run in precisely the opposite direction.

ARGUMENTS AGAINST ELIMINATIVE MATERIALISM

The initial plausibility of this rather radical view is low for almost everyone, since it denies deeply entrenched assumptions. That is at best a question-begging complaint, of course, since those assumptions are precisely what is at issue. But the following line of thought does attempt to mount a real argument.

Eliminative materialism is false, runs the argument, because one's introspection reveals directly the existence of pains, beliefs, desires, fears, and so forth. Their existence is as obvious as anything could be.

The eliminative materialist will reply that this argument makes the same mistake that an ancient or medieval person would be making if he insisted that he could just see with his own eyes that the heavens form a turning sphere, or that witches exist. The fact is, all observation occurs within some system of concepts, and our observation judgments are only as good as the conceptual framework in which they are expressed. In all three cases—the starry sphere, witches, and the familiar mental states—precisely what is challenged is the integrity of the background conceptual frameworks in which the observation judgments are expressed. To insist on the validity of one's experiences, *traditionally interpreted,* is therefore to beg the very question at issue. For in all three cases, the question is whether we should *reconceive* the nature of some familiar observational domain.

A second criticism attempts to find an incoherence in the eliminative materialist's position. The bald statement of eliminative materialism is that the familiar mental states do not really exist. But that statement is meaningful, runs the argument, only if it is the expression of a certain *belief,* and an *intention* to communicate, and a *knowledge* of the language, and so forth. But if the statement is true, then no such mental states exist, and the statement is therefore a meaningless string of marks or noises, and cannot be true. Evidently, the assumption that eliminative materialism is true entails that it cannot be true.

The hole in this argument is the premise concerning the conditions necessary for a statement to be meaningful. It begs the question. If eliminative materialism is true, then meaningfulness must have some different source. To insist on the 'old' source is to insist on the validity of the very framework at issue. Again, an historical parallel may be helpful here. Consider the medieval theory that being biologically *alive* is a matter of being ensouled by an immaterial *vital spirit.* And consider the following response to someone who has expressed disbelief in that theory.

> My learned friend has stated that there is no such thing as vital spirit. But this statement is incoherent. For if it is true, then my friend does not have vital spirit, and must therefore be *dead.* But if he is dead, then his statement is just a string of noises, devoid of meaning or truth. Evidently, the assumption that antivitalism is true entails that it cannot be true! Q.E.D.

This second argument is now a joke, but the first argument begs the question in exactly the same way.

A final criticism draws a much weaker conclusion, but makes a rather stronger case. Eliminative materialism, it has been said, is making mountains out of molehills. It exaggerates the defects in folk psychology, and underplays its real successes. Perhaps the arrival of a matured neuroscience will require the elimination of the occasional folk-psychological concept, continues the criticism, and a minor adjustment in certain folk-psychological principles may have to be endured. But the large-scale elimination forecast by the eliminative materialist is just an alarmist worry or a romantic enthusiasm.

Perhaps this complaint is correct. And perhaps it is merely complacent. Whichever, it does bring out the important point that we do not confront two simple and mutually exclusive possibilities here: pure reduction versus pure elimination. Rather, these are the end points of a smooth spectrum of possible outcomes, between which there are mixed cases of partial elimination and partial reduction. Only empirical research. . . can tell us where on that spectrum our own case will fall. Perhaps we should speak here, more liberally, of "revisionary materialism", instead of concentrating on the more radical possibility of an across-the-board elimination. Perhaps we should. But it has been my aim in this section to make it at least intelligible to you that our collective conceptual destiny lies substantially toward the revolutionary end of the spectrum.

Arnold Zuboff
The Story of a Brain

Arnold Zuboff *teaches philosophy at the University of London. He does work in philosophy of mind, metaphysics, and ethics and in the history of philosophy.*

I

*O*nce upon a time, a kind young man who enjoyed many friends and great wealth learned that a horrible rot was overtaking all of his body but his nervous system. He loved life; he loved having experiences. Therefore he was intensely interested when scientist friends of amazing abilities proposed the following:

"We shall take the brain from your poor rotting body and keep it healthy in a special nutrient bath. We shall have it connected to a machine that is capable of inducing in it any pattern at all of neural firings and is therein capable of bringing about for you any sort of total experience that it is possible for the activity of your nervous system to cause or to be."

The reason for this last disjunction of the verbs *to cause* and *to be* was that, although all these scientists were convinced of a general theory that they called "the neural theory of experience," they disagreed on the specific formulation of this theory. They all knew of countless instances in which it was just obvious that the state of the brain, the pattern of its activity, somehow had made for a man's experiencing this rather than that. It seemed reasonable to them all that ultimately what decisively controlled any particular experience of a man—controlled whether it existed and what it was like—was the state of his nervous system and more specifically that of those areas of the brain that careful research had discovered to be involved in the various aspects of consciousness. This conviction was what had prompted their proposal to their young friend. That they disagreed about whether an experience simply consisted in or else was caused by neural activity was irrelevant to their belief that as long as their friend's brain was alive and functioning under their control, they could keep him having his beloved experience indefinitely, just as though he were walking about and getting himself into the various situations that would in a more natural way have stimulated each of those patterns of neural firings that they would bring about artificially. If he were actually to have gazed through a hole in a snow-covered frozen pond, for instance, the physical reality there would have caused him to experience what Thoreau described: "the quiet parlor of the fishes, pervaded by a softened light as through a window of ground glass, with its bright sanded floor the same as in summer." The brain lying in its bath, stripped of its body and far from the pond, if it were made to behave precisely as it naturally would under such pond-hole circumstances, would have for the young man that very same experience.

Well, the young man agreed with the concept and looked forward to its execution. And a mere month after he had first heard the thing proposed to him, his brain was floating in the warm nutrient bath. His scientist friends kept busy researching, by means of paid subjects, which patterns of neuron firings were like the natural neural responses to very pleasant situations; and, through the use of a complex electrode machine, they kept inducing only these neural activities in their dear friend's brain.

Then there was trouble. One night the watchman had been drinking, and, tipsily wandering into the room where the bath lay, he careened forward so his right arm entered the bath and actually split the poor brain into its two hemispheres.

The brain's scientist friends were very upset the next morning. They had been all ready to feed into the brain a marvelous new batch of experiences whose neural patterns they had just recently discovered.

"If we let our friend's brain mend after bringing the parted hemispheres together," said Fred, "we must wait a good two months before it will be healed well enough so that we can get the fun of feeding him these new experiences. Of course, he won't know about the waiting; but we sure will! And unfortunately, as we all know, two separated halves of a brain can't entertain the same neural patterns that they can when they're together. For all those impulses which cross from one hemisphere to another during a whole-brain experience just can't make it across the gap that has been opened between them."

The end of this speech gave someone else an idea. Why not do the following? Develop tiny electrochemical wires whose ends could be fitted to the synapses of neurons to receive or discharge their neural impulses. These wires could then be strung from each neuron whose connection had been broken in the split to that neuron of the other hemisphere to which it had formerly been connected. "In this way," finished Bert, the proposer of this idea, "all those impulses that were supposed to cross over from one hemisphere to the other could do just that—carried over the wires."

This suggestion was greeted with enthusiasm, since the construction of the wire system, it was felt, could easily be completed within a week. But one grave fellow named Cassander had worries. "We all agree that our friend has been having the experiences we've tried to give him. That is, we all accept in some form or other the neural theory of experience. Now, according to this theory as we all accept it, it is quite permissible to alter as one likes the context of a functioning brain, just so long as one maintains the pattern of its activity. We might look at what we're saying this way. There are various conditions that make for the usual having of an experience—an experience, for instance, like that pond-hole experience we believe we gave our friend three weeks ago. Usually these conditions are the brain being in an actual body on an actual pond stimulated to such neural activity as we did indeed give our friend. We gave our friend the neural activity without those other conditions of its context, because our friend has no body and because we believe that what is essential and decisive for the existence and character of an experience anyway is not such context but rather only the neural activity that it can stimulate. The contextual conditions, we believe, are truly inessential to the bare fact of a man having an experience—even if they *are* essential conditions in the normal having of that experience. If one has the wherewithal, as we do, to get around the normal necessity of these external conditions of an experience of a pond hole, then such conditions are no longer necessary. And this demonstrates that within our concept of experience they never were necessary in principle to the bare fact of having the experience.

"Now, what you men are proposing to do with these wires amounts to regarding as inessential just one more normal condition of our friend's having his experience. That is, you are saying something like what I just said about the context of neural activity—but *you're* saying it about the condition of the *proximity* of the hemispheres of the brain to one another. You're saying that the two hemispheres being attached to one another in the whole-brain experiences may be necessary to the coming about of those experiences in the usual case, but if one can get around a breach of this proximity in some, indeed, unusual case, as you fellows would with your wires, there'd still be brought about just the same bare fact of the same experience being had! You're saying that proximity isn't a necessary condition to this bare fact of an experience. But isn't it possible that even reproducing precisely the whole-brain neural patterns in a sundered brain would, to the contrary, *not* constitute the bringing about of the whole-brain experience? Couldn't proximity be not just something to get around in creating a particular whole-brain experience but somehow an absolute condition and principle of the having of a whole-brain experience?"

Cassander got little sympathy for his worries. Typical replies ran something like this: "Would the damn hemispheres *know* they were connected by wires instead of attached in the usual way? That is, would the fact get encoded in any of the brain structures responsible for speech, thought or any other feature of awareness? How could this fact about how his brain looks to external observers concern our dear friend in his pleasures at all—any more than being a naked brain sitting in a warm nutrient bath does? As long as the neural activity in the hemispheres—together *or* apart—matches precisely that which would have been the activity in the hemispheres lumped together in the head of a person walking around having fun, then the person himself is having that fun. Why, if we hooked up a mouth to these brain parts, he'd be telling us through it about his fun." In reply to such answers, which were getting shorter and angrier, Cassander could only mutter about the possible disruption of some experiential field "or some such."

But after the men had been working on the wires for a while someone else came up with an objection to their project that *did* stop them. He pointed out that it took practically no time for an impulse from one hemisphere to enter into the other when a brain was together and functioning normally. But the travel of these impulses over wires must impose a tiny increase on the time taken in such crossovers. Since the impulses in the rest of the brain in each hemisphere would be taking their normal time, wouldn't the overall pattern get garbled, operating as if there were a slowdown in only one region? Certainly it would be impossible to get precisely the normal sort of pattern going—you'd have something strange, disturbed.

When this successful objection was raised, a man with very little training in physics suggested that somehow the wire be replaced by radio signals. This could be done by outfitting the raw face—of the split—of each hemisphere with an "impulse cartridge" that would be capable of sending any pattern of impulses into the hitherto exposed and unconnected neurons of that hemisphere, as well as of receiving from those neurons any pattern of impulses that that hemisphere might be trying to communicate to the other hemisphere. Then each cartridge could be plugged into a special radio transmitter and receiver. When a cartridge received an impulse from a neuron in one hemisphere intended for a neuron of the other, the impulse could then be radioed over and properly administered by the other cartridge. The fellow who suggested this even mused that then each half of the brain could be kept in a separate bath and yet the whole still be engaged in a single whole-brain experience.

The advantage of this system over the wires, this fellow thought, resided in the "fact" that radio waves take no time, unlike impulses in wires, to travel from one place to another. He was quickly disabused of this idea. No, the radio system still suffered from the time-gap obstacle.

But all this talk of impulse cartridges inspired Bert. "Look, we could feed each impulse cartridge with the same pattern of impulses it would have been receiving by radio but do so by such a method as to require no radio or wire transmission. All we need do is fix to each cartridge not a radio transmitter and receiver but an 'impulse programmer,' the sort of gadget that would play through whatever program of impulses you have previously given it. The great thing about this is that there is no longer any need for the impulse pattern going into one hemisphere to be *actually caused,* in part, by the pattern coming from the other. Therefore there need not be any wait for the transmission. The programmed cartridges can be so correlated with the rest of our stimulation of neural patterns that all of the timing can be just as it would have been if the hemispheres were together. And, yes, then it will be easy to fix each hemisphere in a separate bath—perhaps one in the laboratory here and one in the laboratory across town, so that we may employ the facilities of each laboratory in working with merely half a brain. This will make everything easier. And we can then bring in more people; there are many who've been bothering us to let them join our project."

But now Cassander was even more worried. "We have already disregarded the condition of proximity. Now we are about to abandon yet another condition of usual experience—that of actual causal connection. Granted you can be clever enough to get around what is usually quite necessary to an experience coming about. So now, with your programming, it will no longer be necessary for impulses in one half of the brain actually to be a cause of the completion of the whole-brain pattern in the other hemisphere in order for the whole-brain pattern to come about. But is the result still the bare fact of the whole-brain experience or have you, in removing this condition, removed an absolute principle of, an essential condition for, a whole-brain experience really being had?"

The answers to this were much as they had been to the other. How did the neural activity *know* whether a radio-controlled or programmed impulse cartridge fed it? How could this fact, so totally external to them, register with the neural structures underlying thought, speech, and every other item of awareness? Certainly it could not register mechanically. Wasn't the result then precisely the same with tape as with wire except that now the time-gap problem had been overcome? And wouldn't a properly hooked-up mouth even report the experiences as nicely after the taped as after the wired assistance with crossing impulses?

The next innovation came soon enough—when the question was raised about whether it was at all important, since each hemisphere was now working separately, to synchronize the two causally unconnected playings of the impulse patterns of the hemispheres. Now that each hemisphere would in effect receive all the impulses that in a given experience it would have received from the other hemisphere—and receive them in such a way as would work perfectly with the timing of the rest of its impulses—and since this fine effect could be achieved in either hemisphere quite independent of its having yet been achieved in the other, there seemed no reason for retaining what Cassander sadly pointed to as the "condition of synchronization." Men were heard to say, "How does either hemisphere *know*, how could it register when the other goes off, in the time of the external observer, anyway? For each hemisphere what more can we say than that it is just precisely as if the other had gone off with it the right way? What is there to worry about if at one lab they run through one half of a pattern one day and at the other lab they supply the other hemisphere with its half of the pattern another day? The pattern gets run through fine. The experience comes about. With the brain parts hooked up properly to a mouth, our friend could even report his experience."

There was also some discussion about whether to maintain what Cassander called "topology"—that is, whether to keep the two hemispheres in the general spatial relation of facing each other. Here too Cassander's warnings were ignored.

II

Ten centuries later the famous project was still engrossing men. But men now filled the galaxy and their technology was tremendous. Among them were billions who wanted the thrill and responsibility of participating in the "Great Experience Feed." Of course, behind this desire lay the continuing belief that what men were doing in programming impulses still amounted to making a man have all sorts of experiences.

But in order to accommodate all those who now wished to participate in the project, what Cassander had called the "conditions" of the experiencing had, to the superficial glance, changed enormously. (Actually, they were in a sense more conservative than they had been when we last saw them, because, as I shall explain later, something like "synchronization" had been restored.) Just as earlier each hemisphere of the brain had rested in its bath, now *each individual neuron* rested in one of its own. Since there were billions of neurons, each of the billions of men could involve himself with the proud task of manning a neuron bath.

To understand this situation properly, one must go back again ten centuries, to what had occurred as more and more men had expressed a desire for a part of the project. First it was agreed that if a whole-brain experience could come about with the brain split and yet the two halves programmed as I have described, the same experience could come about if each hemisphere too were carefully divided and each piece treated just as each of the two hemispheres had been. Thus each of four pieces of brain could now be given not only its own bath but a whole lab—allowing many more people to participate. There naturally seemed nothing to stop further and further divisions of the thing, until finally, ten centuries later, there was this situation—a man on each neuron, each man responsible for an impulse cartridge that was fixed to both ends of that neuron—transmitting and receiving an impulse whenever it was programmed to do so.

Meanwhile there had been other Cassanders. After a while none of these suggested keeping the condition of proximity, since this would have so infuriated all his fellows who desired to have a piece of the brain. But it *was* pointed out by such Cassanders that the original topology of the brain, that is, the relative position and directional attitude of each neuron, could be maintained even while the brain was spread apart; and also it was urged by them that the neurons continue to be programmed to fire with the same chronology—the same temporal pattern—that their firings would have displayed when together in the brain.

But the suggestion about topology always brought a derisive response. A sample: "How should each of the neurons *know,* how should it register on a single neuron, where it is in relation to the others? In the usual case of an experience it is indeed necessary for the neurons, in order at all to get firing in that pattern that is or causes the experience, to be next to each other, actually causing the firing of one another, in a certain spatial relation to one another— but the original necessity of all these conditions is overcome by our techniques. For example, they are not necessary to the *bare fact* of the coming about of the experience that we are now causing to be had by the ancient gentleman whose neuron this is before me. And if we should bring these neurons together into a hookup with a mouth, then he would tell you of the experience personally."

Now as for the second part of the Cassanderish suggestion, the reader might suppose that after each successive partitioning of the brain, synchronization of the parts would have been consistently disregarded, so that eventually it would have been thought not to matter when each individual neuron was to be fired in relation to the firings of the other neurons— just as earlier the condition had been disregarded when there were only two hemispheres to be fired. But somehow, perhaps because disregarding the timing and order of individual neuron firings would have reduced the art of programming to absurdity, the condition of order and timing had crept back, but without the Cassanderish reflectiveness. "Right" temporal order of firings is now merely *assumed* as somehow essential to bringing about a given experience by all those men standing before their baths and *waiting* for each properly programmed impulse to come to its neuron.

But now, ten centuries after the great project's birth, the world of these smug billions was about to explode. Two thinkers were responsible.

One of these, named Spoilar, had noticed one day that the neuron in his charge was getting a bit the worse for wear. Like any other man with a neuron in that state, he merely obtained another fresh one just like it and so replaced the particular one that had gotten worn—tossing the old one away. Thus he, like all the others, had violated the Cassanderish condition of "neural identity"—a condition never taken very seriously even by Cassanders. It was realized that in the case of an ordinary brain the cellular metabolism was always replacing all the particular matter of any neuron with other particular matter, forming precisely the same kind of neuron. What this man had done was really no more than a speeding-up of this process. Besides, what if, as some Cassanders had implausibly argued, replacing one neuron by another just like it somehow resulted, when it was eventually done to all the neurons, in a new identity for the experiencer? There still would be *an* experiencer having the same experience every time the same patterns of firings were realized (and what it would mean to say he was a different experiencer was not clear at all, even to the Cassanders). So any shift in neural identity did not seem destructive of the fact of an experience coming about.

This fellow Spoilar, after he had replaced the neuron, resumed his waiting to watch his own neuron fire as part of an experience scheduled several hours later. Suddenly he heard a great crash and a great curse. Some fool had fallen against another man's bath, and it had broken totally on the floor when it fell. Well, this man whose bath had fallen would just have to miss out on any experience his neuron was to have been part of until the bath and neuron could be replaced. And Spoilar knew that the poor man had had one coming up soon.

The fellow whose bath had just broken walked up to Spoilar. He said, "Look, I've done favors for you. I'm going to have to miss the impulse coming up in five minutes—that experience will have to manage with one less neuron firing. But maybe you'd let me man yours coming up later. I just hate to miss all the thrills coming up today!"

Spoilar thought about the man's plea. Suddenly, a strange thought hit him. "Wasn't the neuron you manned the same sort as mine?"

"Yes."

"Well, look. I've just replaced my neuron with another like it, as we all do occasionally. Why don't we take my entire bath over to the old position of yours? Then won't it still be the same experience brought about in five minutes that it would have been with the old neuron if we fire this then, since this one is just like the old one? Surely the *bath's* identity means nothing. Anyway, then we can bring the bath back here and I can use the neuron for the experience it is scheduled to be used for later on. Wait a minute! We both believe the condition of topology is baloney. So why need we move the bath at all? Leave it here; fire it for yours; and then I'll fire it for mine. Both experiences must still come about. Wait a minute again! Then all we need do is fire this one neuron here in place of all the firings of all neurons just like it! Then there need be only one neuron of each type firing again and again and again to bring about all these experiences! But how would the neurons *know* even that they were repeating an impulse when they fired again and again? How would they *know* the relative order of their firings? Then we could have one neuron of each sort firing once and that would provide the physical realization of all patterns of impulses (a conclusion that would have been arrived at merely by consistently disregarding the necessity of synchronization in the progress from parted hemispheres to parted neurons). And couldn't these neurons simply be any of those naturally firing in any head? So what are we all doing here?"

Then an even more desperate thought hit him, which he expressed thus: "But if all possible neural experience will be brought about simply in the firing once of one of each type of neuron, how can any experiencer believe that he is connected to anything more than this bare minimum of physical reality through the fact of his having *any* of his experiences? And so all this talk of heads and neurons in them, which is supposedly based on the true discovery of physical realities, is undermined entirely. There may be a true system of physical reality, but if it involves all this physiology we have been hoodwinked into believing, it provides so cheaply for so much experience that we can never know what is an actual experience of *it,* the physical reality. And so belief in such a system undermines itself. That is, unless it's tempered with Cassanderish principles."

The other thinker, coincidentally also named Spoilar, came to the same conclusion somewhat differently. He enjoyed stringing neurons. Once he got his own neuron, the one he was responsible for, in the middle of a long chain of like neurons and then recalled he was supposed to have it hooked up to the cartridge for a firing. Not wanting to destroy the chain, he simply hooked the two end neurons of the chain to the two poles of the impulse cartridge and adjusted the timing of the cartridge so that the impulse, traveling now through this whole chain, would reach his neuron at just the right time. Then he noticed that here a neuron, unlike one in usual experience, was quite comfortably participating in two patterns of firings at once—the chain's, which happened to have proximity and causal connection, and the programmed experience for which it had fired. After this Spoilar went about ridiculing "the condition of neural context." He'd say, "Boy, I could hook my neuron up with all those in your head, and if I could get it to fire just at the right time, I could get it into one of these programmed experiences as fine as if it were in my bath, on my cartridge."

Well, one day there was trouble. Some men who had not been allowed to join the project had come at night and so tampered with the baths that many of the neurons in Spoilar's vicinity had simply died. Standing before his own dead neuron, staring at the vast misery around him, he thought about how the day's first experience must turn out for the experiencer when so many neuron firings were to be missing from their physical realization. But as he looked about he suddenly took note of something else. Nearly everyone was stooping to inspect some damaged equipment just under his bath. Suddenly it seemed significant to Spoilar that next to every bath there was a head, each with its own billions of neurons of all sorts, with perhaps millions of each sort firing at any given moment. Proximity didn't matter. But then at any given moment of a particular pattern's being fired through the baths all the requisite activity was already going on anyway in the heads of the operators—in even *one* of those heads, where a loose sort of proximity condition was fulfilled too! Each head was bath and cartridge enough for any spread-brain's realization: "But," thought Spoilar, "the same kind of physical realization must exist for *every* experience of *every* brain—since all brains are spreadable. And that includes mine. But then all my beliefs are based on thoughts and experiences that might exist only as some such floating cloud. They are all suspect—including those that had convinced me of all this physiology in the first place. Unless Cassander is right, to some extent, then physiology reduces to absurdity. It undermines itself."

Such thinking killed the great project and with it the spread-brain. Men turned to other weird activities and to new conclusions about the nature of experience. But what these were is another story.

8

Does Language Make Me Think the Way I Do?

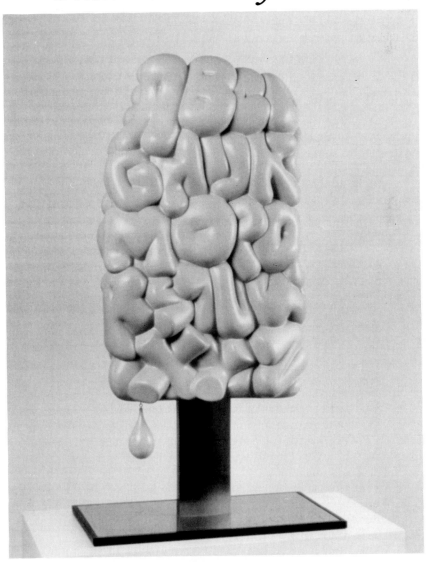

*H*ow are taking a test, calling a friend, and buying a sandwich similar to one another? One important way is that they all involve language. Whenever we write or speak, we use language. Whenever we make a promise or ask a question, we use language. Since we spend a good deal of our lives writing or speaking, language is an important part of much that we do.

In fact, language may be even more pervasive than the preceding paragraph leads us to believe. Anything that involves communication requires a medium for communication. It has been claimed that any medium for communication involves a language. According to this view, then, there is a language (or languages) of art, as well as a language (or languages) of love. If we extend the notion of a language this far, then almost any exchange that is embedded in social interaction can be seen as involving language. Short of sitting quietly alone on a mountain looking at a beautiful sunset, it looks as though nearly everything involves language.

But wait a minute. Might it be that even sitting alone on a mountaintop involves the use of language? There are two ways in which it might. First, think for a minute about whether the U.S. economy is healthy. Now try to have the same thoughts without using words. Can you do it? Most people report that most of their thoughts "use" words. Words may be involved in this way in most of our thinking.

A second way in which language is pervasive is that even if much of our mental and emotional life could be carried on without any direct use of language, language may be involved in the formation, acquisition, and meaning of the very concepts that we employ when we think, feel, perceive, or desire. For example, language does not seem to be involved when we feel angry. But learning what it is to feel angry requires things like having your mother, when you are a child, point to someone who is shouting and say, "Why is he so angry?" It may be that this (linguistic) background is part of what makes your feeling a feeling of anger. In addition, feeling angry may also involve having certain beliefs, for example, the belief that you have been insulted or unjustly deprived. So unless you are sitting on that mountain in a coma (actually you would have to be lying down), as long as you are thinking, believing, or perceiving, it appears that language may be involved in what you are doing.

But despite the fact that language is probably the most pervasive human activity, or perhaps *because* of that fact, we do not think much about language. Language itself, because it is everywhere, is not noticed. It is part of the background. Moreover, we do not think about it because we see it as an instrument, not as a thing in itself. For example, a beginning painter trying to paint a landscape will focus on the color of the sky and the configuration of the mountains and trees. She will not typically be thinking about the composition of the paint itself or about the fiber content of the canvas. But experienced painters know that an understanding of the *medium* of expression (in this case, of the paint, brushes, and canvas) is crucial in expressing oneself well. The medium imposes hidden constraints on what we can and cannot do. Until we understand those constraints, we will be bound by them without knowing that we are.

So it is with language. To understand the constraints that language places on what we think or feel, and on how we do it, we must somehow be able to think about language itself. But if we can think only by means of language, then in thinking about language we will be using language! This may place us in a vicious circle from which we cannot escape. This is just one of the many complications and difficulties that go along with the philosophical study of language.

Jonathan Swift, in the selection from *Gulliver's Travels*, starts off by claiming ironically that language is an irritating and misleading nuisance. Instead of using words, we should just carry around the things that our words name (since nouns are the only important words anyway). Swift suggests a view of language that was articulated by Saint Augustine, in the fourth century A.D., in a famous passage from his *Confessions*. Wittgenstein begins his excerpt in this chapter by considering this "primitive" picture of language, according to which words are simply names. (This is a view of language that he himself had held earlier, but that he gave up.) He argues that we understand the meaning of an expression by understanding its *use* and that expressions have many more uses than simply that of naming. He also rejects the Socratic method of trying to understand a concept by trying to *define* it. Instead, he argues that most concepts (his example is the concept of a game) do not have neat definitions, but instead work by picking out a range of things that resemble one another loosely. We discover these associations by looking carefully at how expressions are used by actual people. Wittgenstein's view of language strikes at the heart of traditional philosophical method.

It is tempting to think that first we have thoughts and that our language simply reports, or expresses, these thoughts. Many of the authors in this chapter argue, in one way or another, against that simple picture. Whorf, for example, argues that our language creates the conceptual scheme within which we think. As a result of his work in anthropology, he formulated what is now referred to as the "Whorf hypothesis," namely, that our conceptual scheme is determined by our language. If so, people whose language is sufficiently different from ours could not have the same thoughts that we have in our language. Conversely, beings whose conceptual schemes are sufficiently different from ours could not share our language. As Wittgenstein put it, "If a lion could speak, we could not understand him."

George Orwell, writing at about the same time as Whorf and Wittgenstein, was well aware of the power of language, as expressed in his masterpiece *1984*. Orwell paints a grim picture of the political and social control that can be exerted by control over the language. He sees this control as a form of thought control. His protagonist, Syme, recognizes that without appropriate language, you cannot have certain concepts. Without those concepts, you cannot have certain thoughts.

Merleau-Ponty carries the Whorf hypothesis one step further. He claims that understanding language requires breaking down the "subject/object distinction," that is, the distinction between the production of language (including the person producing it) and what the language is about. Merleau-Ponty denies that there are two separable things—words and what they name or mean. This is true even if words are understood to express thoughts. Consequently, for Merleau-Ponty, there is no firm distinction between language and thought, or between language and what it means. Rather language is *active* and brings meaning into existence. He also echoes Wittgenstein in claiming that, since meanings are not given independently of language, some prior agreement (as Wittgenstein puts it, in "forms of life") must exist so that communication will be possible. It is this agreement that creates the gulf between us and lions (or Martians).

Ross, in her selection, agrees with Orwell about the extent to which language can be put to (dangerous) political uses. She focuses on the sexist use of language and argues that the wrongness of sexist language does not lie only in the fact that it expresses false claims. More importantly, sexist language actually hurts women. The metaphors used to describe women (for example, dog, cow, shrew) reveal attitudes that are destructive of equality and trust. Her method is therefore in accord with Wittgenstein's claim that we understand language not by trying to isolate its content, but by looking at the use to which it is put.

Nietzsche suggests an even deeper way in which language and thought are connected. In his view we are conscious of only a very small part of what is going on in our heads (see Chapter 7 for more about this), namely, that part we need in order to communicate. Language is therefore a necessary condition for even being conscious. This is a bold enough view, but Nietzsche, one of history's greatest pessimists, goes on to conclude that since the need to communicate arises out of our social nature (what he calls the "herd mentality"), the totality of consciousness is also controlled by the herd. He concludes that whatever arises into consciousness is general, shallow, and stupid.

Lewis Carroll, whose children's books are brimming with philosophical interest, brings us full circle to another "primitive" view of language, but one that, unlike Swift's, takes account of the intimate connection between language and thought. If Swift (and Augustine) claim that the meaning of words is tied directly to what they name and is therefore fixed rigidly, Humpty Dumpty claims that the meaning of words is not constrained at all: words mean whatever he wants them to mean. Thus, Carroll plays counterpoint to Swift in the same way that Merleau-Ponty plays counterpoint to Augustine.

As you read these selections, you might think about the ways in which the structure of your language places constraints on what and how you can think, feel, believe, and desire.

Jonathan Swift
Getting Rid of Words

Jonathan Swift (1667–1745), Irish author, journalist, and clergyman, was one of the foremost satirists of all time. He finished Gulliver's Travels, from which this selection is taken, in 1725. In 1729 he published a grimly satirical "letter" in which a civic-minded citizen proposes that the poor would contribute more to society if their children were used as food.

We next went to the school of language, where three professors sat in consultation upon improving that of their own country.

The first project was to shorten discourse, by cutting polysyllables into one, and leaving out verbs and participles, because, in reality, all things imaginable are but nouns.

The other project was a scheme for entirely abolishing all words whatsoever, and this was urged as a great advantage in point of health as well as brevity. For it is plain that every word we speak is in some degree a diminution of our lungs by corrosion, and consequently, contributes to the shortening of our lives. An expedient was therefore offered, that, since words are only names for things, it would be more convenient for all men to carry about them such things as were necessary to express a particular business they are to discourse on. And this invention would cetainly have taken place, to the great ease as well as health of the subject, if the women, in conjunction with the vulgar and illiterate, had not threatened to raise a rebellion, unless they might be allowed the liberty to speak with their tongues, after the manner of their forefathers; such constant irreconcilable enemies to science are the common people. However, many of the most learned and wise adhere to the new scheme of expressing themselves by things, which has only this inconvenience attending it, that if a man's business be very great, and of various kinds, he must be obliged, in proportion, to carry a greater bundle of things upon his back, unless he can afford one or two strong servants to attend him. I have often beheld two of these sages almost sinking under the weight of their packs, like pedlars among us; who, when they met in the street, would lay down their loads, open their sacks, and hold conversation for an hour together, then put up their implements, help each other to resume their bundles, and take their leave.

But for short conversations, a man may carry implements in his pockets, and under his arms, enough to supply him: and in his house he cannot be at a loss. Therefore the room where company meet who practise this art is full of all things, ready at hand, requisite to furnish matter for this kind of artificial converse.

Another great advantage proposed by this invention was, that it would serve as a universal language, to be understood in all civilised nations, whose goods and utensils are generally of the same kind, or nearly resembling, so that their uses might easily be comprehended. And thus ambassadors would be qualified to treat with foreign princes, or ministers of state, to whose tongues they were utter strangers.

Ludwig Wittgenstein
Meaning as Use

Ludwig Wittgenstein *(1889–1951) was born in Austria. He studied engineering, logic, and philosophy. He was a soldier, an architect, a third-grade teacher, and finally a professor of philosophy. He was a troubled man, and his work was nearly as misunderstood as it was influential. His* Philosophical Investigations, *from which this selection is taken, is an ordered series of aphoristic remarks on language, mind, and the conduct of philosophy. The remarks reprinted here have been reordered so as to focus his views on language.*

1. "Cum ipsi (majores homines) appellabant rem aliquam, et cum secundum eam vocem corpus ad aliquid movebant, videbam, et tenebam hoc ab eis vocari rem illam, quod sonabant, cum eam vellent ostendere. Hoc autem eos velle ex motu corporis aperiebatur: tamquam verbis naturalibus omnium gentium, quae fiunt vultu et nutu oculorum, ceterorumque membrorum actu, et sonitu vocis indicante affectionem animi in petendis, habendis, rejiciendis, fugiendisve rebus. Ita verba in variis sententiis locis suis posita, et crebro audita, quarum rerum signa essent, paulatim colligebam, measque jam voluntates, edomito in eis signis ore, per haec enuntiabam." (Augustine, *Confessions*, I. 8.)*

These words, it seems to me, give us a particular picture of the essence of human language. It is this: the individual words in language name objects—sentences are combinations of such names.—In this picture of language we find the roots of the following idea: Every word has a meaning. This meaning is correlated with the word. It is the object for which the word stands.

Augustine does not speak of there being any difference between kinds of word. If you describe the learning of language in this way you are, I believe, thinking primarily of nouns like "table", "chair", "bread", and of people's name, and only secondarily of the names of certain actions and properties; and of the remaining kinds of word as something that will take care of itself.

Now think of the following use of language: I send someone shopping. I give him a slip marked "five red apples". He takes the slip to the shopkeeper, who opens the drawer marked "apples"; then he looks up the word "red" in a table and finds a colour sample opposite it; then he says the series of cardinal numbers—I assume that he knows them by heart—up to the word "five" and for each number he takes an apple of the same colour as the sample out of the drawer.—It is in this and similar ways that one operates with words.—"But how does he know where and how he is to look up the word 'red' and what he is to do with the word 'five'?"—Well, I assume that he *acts* as I have described. Explanations come to an end somewhere.—But what is the meaning of the word "five"?—No such thing was in question here, only how the word "five" is used.

2. That philosophical concept of meaning has its place in a primitive idea of the way language functions. But one can also say that it is the idea of a language more primitive than ours.

Let us imagine a language for which the description given by Augustine is right. The language is meant to serve for communication between a builder A and an assistant B. A is building with building stones: there are blocks, pillars, slabs and beams. B has to pass the stones, and that in the order in which A needs them. For this purpose they use a language consisting of the words "block", "pillar", "slab", "beam". A calls them out;—B brings the stone which he has learnt to bring at such-and-such a call.—Conceive this as a complete primitive language.

3. Augustine, we might say, does describe a system of communication; only not everything that we call language is this system. And one has to say this in many cases where the question arises "Is this an appropriate description or not?" The answer is "Yes, it is appropriate, but only for this narrowly circumscribed region, not for the whole of what you were claiming to describe."

It is as if someone were to say: "A game consists in moving objects about on a surface according to certain rules . . ."—and we replied: You seem to be thinking of board games,

---

* "When they (my elders) named some object, and accordingly moved towards something, I saw this and I grasped that the thing was called by the sound they uttered when they meant to point it out. Their intention was shewn by their bodily movements, as it were the natural language of all peoples: the expression of the face, the play of the eyes, the movement of other parts of the body, and the tone of voice which expresses our state of mind in seeking, having, rejecting, or avoiding something. Thus, as I heard words repeatedly used in their proper places in various sentences, I gradually learnt to understand what objects they signified; and after I had trained my mouth to form these signs, I used them to express my own desires."

but there are others. You can make your definition correct by expressly restricting it to those games.

4. Imagine a script in which the letters were used to stand for sounds, and also as signs of emphasis and punctuation. (A script can be conceived as a language for describing sound-patterns.) Now imagine someone interpreting that script as if there were simply a correspondence of letters to sounds and as if the letters had not also completely different functions. Augustine's conception of language is like such an over-simple conception of the script.

5. If we look at the example in #1, we may perhaps get an inkling how much this general notion of the meaning of a word surrounds the working of language with a haze which makes clear vision impossible. It disperses the fog to study the phenomena of language in primitive kinds of application in which one can command a clear view of the aim and functioning of the words.

A child uses such primitive forms of language when it learns to talk. Here the teaching of language is not explanation, but training.

6. We could imagine that the language of #2 was the *whole* language of A and B; even the whole language of a tribe. The children are brought up to perform *these* actions, to use *these* words as they do so, and to react in *this* way to the words of others.

An important part of the training will consist in the teacher's pointing to the objects, directing the child's attention to them, and at the same time uttering a word; for instance, the word "slab" as he points to that shape. (I do not want to call this "ostensive definition", because the child cannot as yet *ask* what the name is. I will call it "ostensive teaching of words".—I say that it will form an important part of the training, because it is so with human beings; not because it could not be imagined otherwise.) This ostensive teaching of words can be said to establish an association between the word and the thing. But what does this mean? Well, it may mean various things; but one very likely thinks first of all that a picture of the object comes before the child's mind when it hears the word. But now, if this does happen—is it the purpose of the word?— Yes, it *may* be the purpose.—I can imagine such a use of words (of series of sounds). (Uttering a word is like striking a note on the keyboard of the imagination.) But in the language of #2 it is *not* the purpose of the words to evoke images. (It may, of course, be discovered that that helps to attain the actual purpose.)

But if the ostensive teaching has this effect,—am I to say that it effects an understanding of the word? Don't you understand the call "Slab!" if you act upon it in such-and-such a way?—Doubtless the ostensive teaching helped to bring this about; but only together with a particular training. With different training the same ostensive teaching of these words would have effected a quite different understanding.

"I set the brake up by connecting up rod and lever."—Yes, given the whole of the rest of the mechanism. Only in conjunction with that is it a brake-lever, and separated from its support it is not even a lever; it may be anything, or nothing.

7. In the practice of the use of language (2) one party calls out the words, the other acts on them. In instruction in the language the following process will occur: the learner *names* the objects; that is, he utters the word when the teacher points to the stone.—And there will be this still simpler exercise: the pupil repeats the words after the teacher—both of these being processes resembling language.

We can also think of the whole process of using words in (2) as one of those games by means of which children learn their native language. I will call these games "language-games" and will sometimes speak of a primitive language as a language-game.

And the processes of naming the stones and of repeating words after someone might also be called language-games. Think of much of the use of words in games like ring-a-ring-a-roses.

I shall also call the whole, consisting of language and the actions into which it is woven, the "language-game".

8. Let us now look at an expansion of language (2). Besides the four words "block", "pillar", etc., let it contain a series of words used as the shopkeeper in (1) used the numerals (it can be the series of letters of the alphabet); futher, let there be two words, which may as well be "there" and "this" (because this roughly indicates their purpose), that are used in connexion with a pointing gesture; and finally a number of colour samples. A gives an order like: "d—slab—there". At the same time he shews the assistant a colour sample, and when he says "there" he points to a place on the building site. From the stock of slabs B takes one for each letter of the alphabet up to "d", of the same colour as the sample, and brings them to the place indicated by A.—On other occasions A gives the order "this—there". At "this" he points to a building stone. And so on.

9. When a child learns this language, it has to learn the series of 'numerals' a, b, c, . . . by heart. And it has to learn their use.—Will this training include ostensive teaching of the words?—Well, people will, for example, point to slabs and count: "a, b, c slabs".—Something more like the ostensive teaching of the words "block", "pillar", etc. would be the ostensive teaching of numerals that serve not to count but to refer to groups of objects that can be taken in at a glance. Children do learn the use of the first five or six cardinal numerals in this way.

Are "there" and "this" also taught ostensively?—Imagine how one might perhaps teach their use. One will point to places and things—but in this case the pointing occurs in the *use* of the words too and not merely in learning the use.

10. Now what do the words of this language *signify?*—What is supposed to shew what they signify, if not the kind of use they have? And we have already described that. So we are asking for the expression "This word signifies *this*" to be made a part of the description. In other words the description ought to take the form: "The word . . . . signifies . . . .".

Of course, one can reduce the description of the use of the word "slab" to the statement that this word signifies this object. This will be done when, for example, it is merely a matter of removing the mistaken idea that the word "slab" refers to the shape of building-stone that we in fact call a "block"—but the kind of '*referring*' this is, that is to say the use of these words for the rest, is already known.

Equally one can say that the signs "a", "b", etc. signify numbers; when for example this removes the mistaken idea that "a", "b", "c", play the part actually played in language by "block", "slab", "pillar". And one can also say that "c" means this number and not that one; when for example this serves to explain that the letters are to be used in the order a, b, c, d, etc. and not in the order a, b, d, c.

But assimilating the descriptions of the uses of words in this way cannot make the uses themselves any more like one another. For, as we see, they are absolutely unlike.

11. Think of the tools in a tool-box: there is a hammer, pliers, a saw, a screw-driver, a rule, a glue-pot, glue, nails and screws.—The functions of words are as diverse as the functions of these objects. (And in both cases there are similarities.)

Of course, what confuses us is the uniform appearance of words when we hear them spoken or meet them in script and print. For their *application* is not presented to us so clearly. Especially when we are doing philosophy!

12. It is like looking into the cabin of a locomotive. We see handles all looking more or less alike. (Naturally, since they are all supposed to be handled.) But one is the handle of a crank which can be moved continuously (it regulates the opening of a valve); another is the handle of a switch, which has only two effective positions, it is either off or on; a third is the handle of a brake-lever, the harder one pulls on it, the harder it brakes; a fourth, the handle of a pump: it has an effect only so long as it is moved to and fro.

13. When we say: "Every word in language signifies something" we have so far said *nothing whatever;* unless we have explained exactly *what* distinction we wish to make. (It might be, of course, that we wanted to distinguish the words of language (8) from words 'without meaning' such as occur in Lewis Carroll's poems, or words like "Lilliburlero" in songs.)

14. Imagine someone's saying: "*All* tools serve to modify something. Thus the hammer modifies the position of the nail, the saw the shape of the board, and so on."—And what is modified by the rule, the glue-pot, the nails?—"Our knowledge of a thing's length, the temperature of the glue, and the solidity of the box."—Would anything be gained by this assimilation of expressions?

15. The word "to signify" is perhaps used in the most straightforward way when the object signified is marked with the sign. Suppose that the tools A uses in building bear certain marks. When A shews his assistant such a mark, he brings the tool that has that mark on it.

It is in this and more or less similar ways that a name means and is given to a thing.— It will often prove useful in philosophy to say to ourselves: naming something is like attaching a label to a thing.

16. What about the colour samples that A shews to B: are they part of the *language?* Well, it is as you please. They do not belong among the words; yet when I say to someone: "Pronounce the word 'the' ", you will count the second "the" as part of the sentence. Yet it has a role just like that of a colour-sample in language-game (8); that is, it is a sample of what the other is meant to say.

It is most natural, and causes least confusion, to reckon the samples among the instruments of the language.

(Remark on the reflexive pronoun "*this* sentence".)

17. It will be possible to say: In language (8) we have different *kinds of word.* For the functions of the word "slab" and the word "block" are more alike than those of "slab" and "d". But how we group words into kinds will depend on the aim of the classification,—and on our own inclination.

Think of the different points of view from which one can classify tools or chess-men. . . .

23. But how many kinds of sentence are there? Say assertion, question, and command?—There are *countless* kinds: countless different kinds of use of what we call "symbols", "words", "sentences". And this multiplicity is not something fixed, given once for all; but new types of language, new language-games, as we may say, come into existence, and others become obsolete and get forgotten. (We can get a *rough picture* of this from the changes in mathematics.)

Here the term "language-*game*" is meant to bring into prominence the fact that the *speaking* of language is part of an activity, or of a form of life.

Review the multiplicity of language-games in the following examples, and in others:

Giving orders, and obeying them
Describing the appearance of an object, or giving its measurements
Constructing an object from a description (a drawing)
Reporting an event
Speculating about an event
Forming and testing a hypothesis
Presenting the results of an experiment in tables and diagrams
Making up a story; and reading it
Play-acting
Singing catches
Guessing riddles

Making a joke; telling it
Solving a problem in practical arithmetic
Translating from one language into another
Asking, thanking, cursing, greeting, praying

It is interesting to compare the multiplicity of the tools in language and of the ways they are used, the multiplicity of kinds of word and sentence, with what logicians have said about the structure of language. (Including the author of the *Tractatus Logico-Philosophicus.*)*. . .

27. "We name things and then we can talk about them: can refer to them in talk."— As if what we did next were given with the mere act of naming. As if there were only one thing called "talking about a thing". Whereas in fact we do the most various things with our sentences. Think of exclamations alone, with their completely different functions.

Water!
Away!
Ow!
Help!
Fine!
No!

Are you inclined still to call these words "names of objects"?

In languages (2) and (8) there was no such thing as asking something's name. This, with its correlate, ostensive definition, is, we might say, a language-game on its own. That is really to say: we are brought up, trained, to ask: "What is that called?"—upon which the name is given. And there is also a language-game of inventing a name for something, and hence of saying, "This is . . . ." and then using the new name. (Thus, for example, children give names to their dolls and then talk about them and to them. Think in this connexion how singular is the use of a person's name to *call* him!) . . .

32. Someone coming into a strange country will sometimes learn the language of the inhabitants from ostensive definition[†] that they give him; and he will often have to *guess* the meaning of these definitions; and will guess sometimes right, sometimes wrong.

And now, I think, we can say: Augustine describes the learning of human language as if the child came into a strange country and did not understand the language of the country; that is, as if it already had a language, only not this one. Or again: as if the child could already *think*, only not yet speak. And "think" would here mean something like "talk to itself". . . .

37. What is the relation between name and thing named?—Well, what *is* it? Look at language-game (2) or at another one: there you can see the sort of thing this relation consists in. This relation may also consist, among many other things, in the fact that hearing the name calls before our mind the picture of what is named; and it also consists, among other things, in the name's being written on the thing named or being pronounced when that thing is pointed at.

38. But what, for example, is the word "this" the name of in language-game (8) or the word "that" in the ostensive definition "that is called . . . ."?—If you do not want to produce confusion you will do best not to call these words names at all.—Yet, strange to say, the word

---

*Editor's note: An earlier work of Wittgenstein's, which he renounces in this work.

[†]Editor's note: An ostensive definition is one in which a word is defined by pointing to, or showing, what it refers to or means.

"this" has been called the only *genuine* name; so that anything else we call a name was one only in an inexact, approximate sense.

This queer conception springs from a tendency to sublime the logic of our language—as one might put it. The proper answer to it is: we call very different things "names"; the word "name" is used to characterize many different kinds of use of a word, related to one another in many different ways;—but the kind of use that "this" has is not among them.

It is quite true that, in giving an ostensive definition for instance, we often point to the object named and say the name. And similarly, in giving an ostensive definition for instance, we say the word "this" while pointing to a thing. And also the word "this" and a name often occupy the same position in a sentence. But it is precisely characteristic of a name that it is defined by means of the demonstrative expression "That is N" (or "That is called 'N' "). But do we also give the definitions: "That is called 'this' ", or "This is called 'this' "?

This is connected with the conception of naming as, so to speak, an occult process. Naming appears as a *queer* connexion of a word with an object.—And you really get such a queer connexion when the philosopher tries to bring out *the* relation between name and thing by staring at an object in front of him and repeating a name or even the word "this" innumerable times. For philosophical problems arise when language *goes on holiday*. And *here* we may indeed fancy naming to be some remarkable act of mind, as it were a baptism of an object. And we can also say the word "this" *to* the object, as it were *address* the object as "this"—a queer use of this word, which doubtless only occurs in doing philosophy. . . .

410. "I" is not the name of a person, nor "here" of a place, and "this" is not a name. But they are connected with names. Names are explained by means of them. It is also true that it is characteristic of physics not to use these words.

65. Here we come up against the great question that lies behind all these considerations.—For someone might object against me: "You take the easy way out! You talk about all sorts of language-games, but have nowhere said what the essence of a language-game, and hence of language, is: what is common to all these activities, and what makes them into language or parts of language. So you let yourself off the very part of the investigation that once gave you yourself most headache, the part about the *general form of propositions* and of language."

And this is true.—Instead of producing something common to all that we call language, I am saying that these phenomena have no one thing in common which makes us use the same word for all,—but that they are *related* to one another in many different ways. And it is because of this relationship, or these relationships, that we call them all "language". I will try to explain this.

66. Consider for example the proceedings that we call "games". I mean board-games, card-games, ball-games, Olympic games, and so on. What is common to them all?—Don't say: "There *must* be something common, or they would not be called 'games' "—but *look and see* whether there is anything common to all.—For if you look at them you will not see something that is common to *all*, but similarities, relationships, and a whole series of them at that. To repeat: don't think, but look!—Look for example at board-games, with their multifarious relationships. Now pass to card-games; here you find many correspondences with the first group, but many common features drop out, and others appear. When we pass next to ball-games, much that is common is retained, but much is lost.—Are they all 'amusing'? Compare chess with noughts and crosses. Or is there always winning and losing, or competition between players? Think of patience. In ball-games there is winning and losing; but when a child throws his ball at the wall and catches it again, this feature has disappeared. Look at the parts played by skill and luck; and at the difference between skill in chess and skill in tennis. Think now of games like ring-a-ring-a-roses; here is the element of amusement,

but how many other characteristic features have disappeared! And we can go through the many, many other groups of games in the same way; can see how similarities crop up and disappear.

And the result of this examination is: we see a complicated network of similarities overlapping and criss-crossing: sometimes overall similarities, sometimes similarities of detail.

67. I can think of no better expression to characterize these similarities than "family resemblances"; for the various resemblances between members of a family: build, features, colour of eyes, gait, temperament, etc. etc. overlap and criss-cross in the same way.—And I shall say: 'games' form a family.

And for instance the kinds of number form a family in the same way. Why do we call something a "number"? Well, perhaps because it has a—direct—relationship with several things that have hitherto been called number; and this can be said to give it an indirect relationship to other things we call the same name. And we extend our concept of number as in spinning a thread we twist fibre on fibre. And the strength of the thread does not reside in the fact that some one fibre runs through its whole length, but in the overlapping of many fibres.

But if someone wished to say: "There is something common to all these constructions— namely the disjunction of all their common properties"—I should reply: Now you are only playing with words. One might as well say: "Something runs through the whole thread— namely the continuous overlapping of those fibres". . . .

241. "So you are saying that human agreement decides what is true and what is false?"— It is what human beings *say* that is true and false; and they agree in the *language* they use. That is not agreement in opinions but in form of life.

242. If language is to be a means of communication there must be agreement not only in definitions but also (queer as this may sound) in judgments. This seems to abolish logic, but does not do so.—It is one thing to describe methods of measurement, and another to obtain and state results of measurement. But what we call "measuring" is partly determined by a certain constancy in results of measurement. . . .

340. One cannot guess how a word functions. One has to *look at* its use and learn from that.

But the difficulty is to remove the prejudice which stands in the way of doing this. It is not a *stupid* prejudice. . . .

383. We are not analysing a phenomenon (e.g. thought) but a concept (e.g. that of thinking), and therefore the use of a word. So it may look as if what we were doing were Nominalism. Nominalists make the mistake of interpreting all words as *names*, and so of not really describing their use, but only, so to speak, giving a paper draft on such a description. . . .

309. What is your aim in philosophy?—To shew the fly the way out of the fly-bottle.

Benjamin Whorf
Language, Thought, and Reality

Benjamin Whorf (1897–1941) *studied chemical engineering at M.I.T. He worked for his entire career as a fire prevention engineer for a Hartford insurance company, and he pursued his work in anthropology and linguistics on the side, refusing a number of* *academic positions. He originally became interested in linguistics through his interest in religion.*

> Human beings do not live in the objective world alone, not alone in the world of social activity as ordinarily understood, but are very much at the mercy of the particular language which has become the medium of expression for their society. It is quite an illusion to imagine that one adjusts to reality essentially without the use of language and that language is merely an incidental means of solving specific problems of communication or reflection. The fact of the matter is that the "real world" is to a large extent unconsciously built up on the language habits of the group. . . . We see and hear and otherwise experience very largely as we do because the language habits of our community predispose certain choices of interpretation.—Edward Sapir

*T*here will probably be general assent to the proposition that an accepted pattern of using words is often prior to certain lines of thinking and forms of behavior, but he who assents often sees in such a statement nothing more than a platitudinous recognition of the hypnotic power of philosophical and learned terminology on the one hand or of catchwords, slogans, and rallying cries on the other. To see only thus far is to miss the point of one of the important interconnections which Sapir saw between language, culture, and psychology, and succinctly expressed in the introductory quotation. It is not so much in these special uses of language as in its constant ways of arranging data and its most ordinary everyday analysis of phenomena that we need to recognize the influence it has on other activities, cultural and personal. . . .

Every normal person in the world, past infancy in years , can and does talk. By virtue of that fact, every person—civilized or uncivilized—carries through life certain naive but

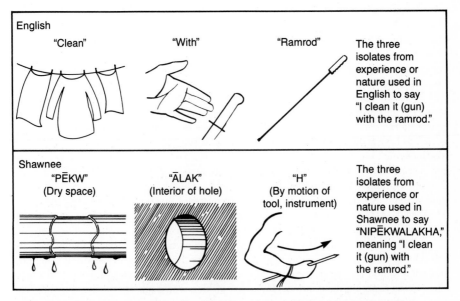

Languages dissect nature differently. The different isolates of meaning (thoughts) used by English and Shawnee in reporting the same experience, that of cleaning a gun by running the ramrod through it. The pronouns 'I' and 'it' are not shown by symbols, as they have the same meaning in each language. In Shawnee ni- equals 'I'; -a equals 'it.'

deeply rooted ideas about talking and its relation to thinking. Because of their firm connection with speech habits that have become unconscious and automatic, these notions tend to be rather intolerant of opposition. They are by no means entirely personal and haphazard; their basis is definitely systematic, so that we are justified in calling them a system of natural logic— a term that seems to me preferable to the term common sense, often used for the same thing.

According to natural logic, the fact that every person has talked fluently since infancy makes every man his own authority on the process by which he formulates and communicates. He has merely to consult a common substratum of logic or reason which he and everyone else are supposed to possess. Natural logic says that talking is merely an incidental process concerned strictly with communication, not with formulation of ideas. Talking, or the use of language, is supposed only to "express" what is essentially already formulated nonlinguistically. Formulation is an independent process, called thought or thinking, and is supposed to be largely indifferent to the nature of particular languages. Languages have grammars, which are assumed to be merely norms of conventional and social correctness, but the use of language is supposed to be guided not so much by them as by correct, rational, or intelligent *thinking*.

Thought, in this view, does not depend on grammar but on laws of logic or reason which are supposed to be the same for all observers of the universe—to represent a rationale in the universe that can be "found" independently by all intelligent observers, whether they speak Chinese or Choctaw. In our own culture, the formulations of mathematics and of formal logic have acquired the reputation of dealing with this order of things: i.e., with the realm and laws of pure thought. Natural logic holds that different languages are essentially parallel methods for expressing this one-and-the-same rationale of thought and, hence, differ really in but minor ways which may seem important only because they are seen at close range. It holds that mathematics, symbolic logic, philosophy, and so on are systems contracted with language which deal directly with this realm of thought, not that they are themselves specialized extensions of language. The attitude of natural logic is well shown in an old quip about a German grammarian who devoted his whole life to the study of the dative case. From the point of view of natural logic, the dative case and grammar in general are an extremely minor issue. A different attitude is said to have been held by the ancient Arabians: Two princes, so the story goes, quarreled over the honor of putting on the shoes of the most learned grammarian of the realm; whereupon their father, the caliph, is said to have remarked that it was the glory of his kingdom that great grammarians were honored even above kings.

The familiar saying that the exception proves the rule contains a good deal of wisdom, though from the standpoint of formal logic it became an absurdity as soon as "prove" no longer meant "put on trial." The old saw began to be profound psychology from the time it ceased to have standing in logic. What it might well suggest to us today is that, if a rule has absolutely no exceptions, it is not recognised as a rule or as anything else; it is then part of the background of experience of which we tend to remain unconscious. Never having experienced anything in contrast to it, we cannot isolate it and formulate it as a rule until we so enlarge our experience and expand our base of reference that we encounter an interruption of its regularity. The situation is somewhat analogous to that of not missing the water till the well runs dry, or not realizing that we need air till we are choking.

For instance, if a race of people had the physiological defect of being able to see only the color blue, they would hardly be able to formulate the rule that they saw only blue. The term blue would convey no meaning to them, their language would lack color terms, and their words denoting their various sensations of blue would answer to, and translate, our words "light, dark, white, black," and so on, not our word "blue." In order to formulate the rule or norm of seeing only blue, they would need exceptional moments in which they saw other colors. The phenomenon of gravitation forms a rule without exceptions; needless to say, the untutored person is utterly unaware of any law of gravitation, for it would never enter

Hopi—one word (MASA'YTAKA)
English—three words

English—one word (snow)
Eskimo—three words

Hopi—PĀHE

Hopi—KĒYI

English—one word (water); Hopi—two words

Languages classify items of experience differently. The class corresponding to one word and one thought in language A may be regarded by language B as two or more classes corresponding to two or more words and thoughts.

his head to conceive of a universe in which bodies behaved otherwise than they do at the earth's surface. Like the color blue with our hypothetical race, the law of gravitation is a part of the untutored individual's background, not something he isolates from that background. The law could not be formulated until bodies that always fell were seen in terms of a wider astronomical world in which bodies moved in orbits or went this way and that.

Similarly, whenever we turn our heads, the image of the scene passes across our retinas exactly as it would if the scene turned around us. But this effect is background, and we do not recognize it; we do not see a room turn around us but are conscious only of having turned our heads in a stationary room. If we observe critically while turning the head or eyes quickly, we shall see, no motion it is true, yet a blurring of the scene between two clear views. Normally we are quite unconscious of this continual blurring but seem to be looking about in an unblurred world. Whenever we walk past a tree or house, its image on the retina changes just as if the tree or house were turning on an axis; yet we do not see trees or houses turn as we travel about at ordinary speeds. Sometimes ill-fitting glasses will reveal queer movements in the scene as we look about, but normally we do not see the relative motion of the environment when we move; our psychic makeup is somehow adjusted to disregard whole realms of phenomena that are so all-pervasive as to be irrelevant to our daily lives and needs.

Natural logic contains two fallacies: First, it does not see that the phenomena of a language are to its own speakers largely of a background character and so are outside the critical consciousness and control of the speaker who is expounding natural logic. Hence, when anyone, as a natural logician, is talking about reason, logic, and the laws of correct

Objective field	Speaker (Sender)	Hearer (Receiver)	Handling of topic, Running of third person
Situation 1a			English: "He is running" Hopi: "WARI" (running, statement of fact)
Situation 1b Objective field blank Devoid of running			English: "He ran" Hopi: "WARI" (running, statement of fact)
Situation 2			English: "He is running" Hopi: "WARI" (running, statement of fact)
Situation 3 Objective field blank			English: "He ran" Hopi: "ERA WARI" (running, statement of fact from memory)
Situation 4 Objective field blank			English: "He will run" Hopi: "WARIKNI" (running, statement of expectation)
Situation 5 Objective field blank			English: "He runs" (e.g., on the track team) Hopi: "WARIKNGWE" (running, statement of law)

Contrast between a "temporal" language (English) and a "timeless" language (Hopi). What are to English differences of time are to Hopi differences in the kind of validity.

thinking, he is apt to be simply marching in step with purely grammatical facts that have somewhat of a background character in his own language or family of languages but are by no means universal in all languages and in no sense a common substratum of reason. Second, natural logic confuses agreement about subject matter, attained through use of language, with knowledge of the linguistic process by which agreement is attained: i.e., with the province of the despised (and to its notion superfluous) grammarian. Two fluent speakers, of English let us say, quickly reach a point of assent about the subject matter of their speech; they agree about what their language refers to. One of them, A, can give directions that will be carried out by the other, B, to A's complete satisfaction. Because they thus understand each other so perfectly, *A* and *B,* as natural logicians, suppose they must of course know how it is all done. They think, e.g., that it is simply a matter of choosing words to express thoughts. If you ask *A* to explain how he got *B*'s agreement so readily, he will simply repeat to you, with more or less elaboration or abbreviation, what he said to *B*. He has no notion of the process involved. The amazingly complex system of linguistic patterns and classifications, which *A* and *B* must have in common before they can adjust to each other at all, is all background to *A* and *B*. . . .

The situation here is not unlike that in any other field of science. All real scientists have their eyes primarily on background phenomena that cut very little ice, as such, in our daily lives; and yet their studies have a way of bringing out a close relation between these unsuspected realms of fact and such decidedly foreground activities as transporting goods, preparing food, treating the sick, or growing potatoes, which in time may become very much modified, simply because of pure scientific investigation in no way concerned with these brute matters themselves. Linguistics presents a quite similar case; the background phenomena with which it deals are involved in all our foreground activities of talking and of reaching agreement, in all reasoning and arguing of cases, in all law, arbitration, conciliation, contracts, treaties, public opinion, weighing of scientific theories, formulation of scientific results. Whenever agreement or assent is arrived at in human affairs, and whether or not mathematics or other specialized symbolisms are made part of the procedure, *this agreement is reached by linguistic processes, or else it is not reached.*

As we have seen, an overt knowledge of the linguistic processes by which agreement is attained is not necessary to reaching some sort of agreement, but it is certainly no bar thereto; the more complicated and difficult the matter, the more such knowledge is a distinct aid, till the point may be reached—I suspect the modern world has arrived at it—when the knowledge becomes not only an aid but a necessity. The situation may be likened to that of navigation. Every boat that sails is in the lap of planetary forces; yet a boy can pilot his small craft around a harbor without benefit of geography, astronomy, mathematics, or international politics. To the captain of an ocean liner, however, some knowledge of all these subjects is essential.

When linguists became able to examine critically and scientifically a large number of languages of widely different patterns, their base of reference was expanded; they experienced an interruption of phenomena hitherto held universal, and a whole new order of significances came into their ken. It was found that the background linguistic system (in other words, the grammar) of each language is not merely a reproducing instrument for voicing ideas but rather is itself the shaper of ideas, the program and guide for the individual's mental activity, for his analysis of impressions, for his synthesis of his mental stock in trade. Formulation of ideas is not an independent process, strictly rational in the old sense, but is part of a particular grammar, and differs, from slightly to greatly, between different grammars. We dissect nature along lines laid down by our native languages. The categories and types that we isolate from the world of phenomena we do not find there because they stare every observer in the face; on the contrary, the world is presented in a kaleidoscopic flux of impressions which has to be organized by our minds—and this means largely by the linguistic systems in our minds. We cut nature up, organize it into concepts, and ascribe significances as we do, largely because we are parties to an agreement to organize it in this way—an agreement that holds throughout our speech community and is codified in the patterns of our language. The agreement is, of course, an implicit and unstated one, *but its terms are absolutely obligatory;* we cannot talk at all except by subscribing to the organization and classification of data which the agreement decrees.

This fact is very significant for modern science, for it means that no individual is free to describe nature with absolute impartiality but is constrained to certain modes of interpretation even while he thinks himself most free. The person most nearly free in such respects would by a linguist familiar with very many widely different linguistic systems. As yet no linguist is in any such position. We are thus introduced to a new principle of relativity, which holds that all observers are not led by the same physical evidence to the same picture of the universe, unless their linguistic backgrounds are similar, or can in some way be calibrated.

This rather startling conclusion is not so apparent if we compare only our modern European languages, with perhaps Latin and Greek thrown in for good measure. Among these tongues there is a unanimity of major pattern which at first seems to bear out natural logic. But this unanimity exists only because these tongues are all Indo-European dialects cut to the same basic plan, being historically transmitted from what was long ago one speech community; because the modern dialects have long shared in building up a common culture; and because much of this culture, on the more intellectual side, is derived from the linguistic backgrounds of Latin and Greek. Thus this group of languages satisfies the special case of the clause beginning "unless" in the statement of the linguistic relativity principle at the end of the preceding paragraph. From this condition follows the unanimity of description of the world in the community of modern scientists. But it must be emphasized that "all modern Indo-European-speaking observers" is not the same thing as "all observers." That modern Chinese or Turkish scientists describe the world in the same terms as Western scientists means, of course, only that they have taken over bodily the entire Western system of rationalizations, not that they have corroborated that system from their native posts of observation.

When Semitic, Chinese, Tibetan, or African languages are contrasted with our own, the divergence in analysis of the world becomes more apparent; and, when we bring in the native languages of the Americas, where speech communities for many millenniums have gone their ways independently of each other and of the Old World, the fact that languages dissect nature in many different ways becomes patent. The relativity of all conceptual systems, ours included, and their dependence upon language stand revealed. That American Indians speaking only their native tongues are never called upon to act as scientific observers is in no wise to the point. To exclude the evidence which their languages offer as to what the human mind can do is like expecting botanists to study nothing but food plants and hothouse roses and then tell us what the plant world is like!

Let us consider a few examples. In English we divide most of our words into two classes, which have different grammatical and logical properties. Class 1 we call nouns, e.g., 'house, man'; class 2, verbs, e.g., 'hit, run.' Many words of one class can act secondarily as of the other class, e.g., 'a hit, a run,' or 'to man (the boat),' but, on the primary level, the division between the classes is absolute. Our language thus gives us a bipolar division of nature. But nature herself is not thus polarized. If it be said that 'strike, turn, run,' are verbs because they denote temporary or short-lasting events, i.e., actions, why then is 'fist' a noun? It also is a temporary event. Why are 'lightning, spark, wave, eddy, pulsation, flame, storm, phase, cycle, spasm, noise, emotion' nouns? They are temporary events. If 'man' and 'house' are nouns because they are long-lasting and stable events, i.e., things, what then are 'keep, adhere, extend, project, continue, persist, grow, dwell,' and so on doing among the verbs? If it be objected that 'possess, adhere' are verbs because they are stable relationships rather than stable percepts, why then should 'equilibrium, pressure, current, peace, group, nation, society, tribe, sister,' or any kinship term be among the nouns? It will be found that an "event" to us means "what our language classes as a verb" or something analogized therefrom. And it will be found that it is not possible to define 'event, thing, object, relationship,' and so on, from nature, but that to define them always involves a circuitous return to the grammatical categories of the definer's language.

In the Hopi language, 'lightning, wave, flame, meteor, puff of smoke, pulsation' are verbs. 'Cloud' and 'storm' are at about the lower limit of duration for nouns. Hopi, you see, actually has a classification of events (or linguistic isolates) by duration type, something strange to our modes of thought. On the other hand, in Nootka, a language of Vancouver Island, all words seem to us to be verbs, but really there are no classes 1 and 2; we have, as it were, a monistic view of nature that gives us only one class of word for all kinds of events. 'A house occurs' or 'it houses' is the way of saying 'house,' exactly like 'a flame occurs' or it burns.' These terms seem to us like verbs because they are inflected for durational and temporal nuances, so that the suffixes of the word for house event make it mean long-lasting house, temporary house, future house, house that used to be, what started out to be a house, and so on.

Hopi has one noun that covers every thing or being that flies, with the exception of birds, which class is denoted by another noun. The former noun may be said to denote the class $(FC-B)$—flying class minus bird. The Hopi actually call insect, airplane, and aviator all by the same word, and feel no difficulty about it. The situation, of course, decides any possible confusion among very disparate members of a broad linguistic class, such as this class $(FC-B)$. This class seems to us too large and inclusive, but so would our class 'snow' to an Eskimo. We have the same word for falling snow, snow on the ground, now packed hard like ice, slushy snow, wind-driven flying snow—whatever the situation may be. To an Eskimo, this all-inclusive word would be almost unthinkable; he would say that falling snow, slushy snow, and so on, are sensuously and operationally different, different things to contend with; he uses different words for them and for other kinds of snow. The Aztecs go even farther than we in the opposite direction, with 'cold,' 'ice,' and 'snow' all represented by the same basic word with different terminations; 'ice' is the noun form; 'cold,' the adjectival form; and for 'snow,' "ice mist."

What surprises most is to find that various grand generalizations of the Western world, such as time, velocity, and matter, are not essential to the construction of a consistent picture of the universe. The psychic experiences that we class under these headings are, of course, not destroyed; rather, categories derived from other kinds of experiences take over the rulership of the cosmology and seem to function just as well. Hopi may be called a timeless language. It recognizes psychological time, which is much like Bergson's "duration," but this "time" is quite unlike the mathematical time, T, used by our physicists. Among the peculiar properties of Hopi time are that it varies with each observer, does not permit of simultaneity, and has zero dimensions; i.e., it cannot be given a number greater than one. The Hopi do not say, "I stayed five days," but "I left on the fifth day." A word referring to this kind of time, like the word day, can have no plural. The puzzle picture will give mental exercise to anyone who would like to figure out how the Hopi verb gets along without tenses. Actually, the only practical use of our tenses, in one-verb sentences, is to distinguish among five typical situations, which are symbolized in the picture. The timeless Hopi verb does not distinguish between the present, past, and future of the event itself but must always indicate what type of validity the speaker intends the statement to have: (a) report of an event (situations 1, 2, 3, in the picture); (b) expectation of an event (situation 4); (c) generalization or law about events (situation 5). Situation 1, where the speaker and listener are in contact with the same objective field, is divided by our language into the two conditions, 1a and 1b, which it calls present and past, respectively. This division is unnecessary for a language which assures one that the statement is a report.

Hopi grammar, by means of its forms called aspects and modes, also makes it easy to distinguish among momentary, continued, and repeated occurrences, and to indicate the actual sequence of reported events. Thus the universe can be described without recourse to a concept of dimensional time. How would a physics constructed along these lines work, with no T

(time) in its equations? Perfectly, as far as I can see, though of course it would require different ideology and perhaps different mathematics. Of course V (velocity) would have to go too. The Hopi language has no word really equivalent to our 'speed' or 'rapid.' What translates these terms is usually a word meaning intense or very, accompanying any verb of motion. Here is a clue to the nature of our new physics. We may have to introduce a new term I, intensity. Every thing and event will have an I, whether we regard the thing or event as moving or as just enduring or being. Perhaps the I of an electric charge will turn out to be its voltage, or potential. We shall use clocks to measure some intensities, or, rather, some *relative* intensities, for the absolute intensity of anything will be meaningless. Our old friend acceleration will still be there but doubtless under a new name. We shall perhaps call it V, meaning not velocity but variation. Perhaps all growths and accumulations will be regarded as V's. We should not have the concept of rate in the temporal sense, since, like velocity, rate introduces a mathematical and linguistic time. Of course we know that all measurements are ratios, but the measurements of intensities made by comparison with the standard intensity of a clock or a planet we do not treat as ratios, any more than we so treat a distance made by comparison with a yardstick.

A scientist from another culture that used time and velocity would have great difficulty in getting us to understand these concepts. We should talk about the intensity of a chemical reaction; he would speak of its velocity or its rate, which words we should at first think were simply words for intensity in his language. Likewise, he at first would think that intensity was simply our own word for velocity. At first we should agree, later we should begin to disagree, and it might dawn upon both sides that different systems of rationalization were being used. He would find it very hard to make us understand what he really meant by velocity of a chemical reaction. We should have no words that would fit. He would try to explain it by likening it to a running horse, to the difference between a good horse and a lazy horse. We should try to show him, with a superior laugh, that his analogy also was a matter of different intensities, aside from which there was little similarity between a horse and a chemical reaction in a beaker. We should point out that a running horse is moving relative to the ground, whereas the material in the beaker is at rest.

One significant contribution to science from the linguistic point of view may be the greater development of our sense of perspective. We shall no longer be able to see a few recent dialects of the Indo-European family, and the rationalizing techniques elaborated from their patterns, as the apex of the evolution of the human mind, nor their present wide spread as due to any survival from fitness or to anything but a few events of history—events that could be called fortunate only from the parochial point of view of the favored parties. They, and our own thought processes with them, can no longer be envisioned as spanning the gamut of reason and knowledge but only as one constellation in a galactic expanse. A fair realization of the incredible degree of diversity of linguistic system that ranges over the globe leaves one with an inescapable feeling that the human spirit is inconceivably old; that the few thousand years of history covered by our written records are no more than the thickness of a pencil mark on the scale that measures our past experience on this planet; that the events of these recent millenniums spell nothing in any evolutionary wise, that the race has taken no sudden spurt, achieved no commanding synthesis during recent millenniums, but has only played a little with a few of the linguistic formulations and views of nature bequeathed from an inexpressibly longer past. Yet neither this feeling nor the sense of precarious dependence of all we know upon linguistic tools which themselves are largely unknown need be discouraging to science but should, rather, foster that humility which accompanies the true scientific spirit, and thus forbid that arrogance of the mind which hinders real scientific curiosity and detachment.

George Orwell

Newspeak

George Orwell *(1903–1950), whose real name was Eric Blair, was an English satirical writer born in Bengal. From 1920 to 1927 he served with the English Colonial Police in Burma. He lived very poorly in London and Paris, gradually establishing his reputation. He fought in the Spanish Civil War. His best known works are* 1984, *from which this selection is taken, and* Animal Farm.

In the low-ceilinged canteen, deep under ground, the lunch queue jerked slowly forward. The room was already very full and deafeningly noisy. From the grille at the counter the steam of stew came pouring forth, with a sour metallic smell which did not quite overcome the fumes of Victory Gin. On the far side of the room there was a small bar, a mere hole in the wall, where gin could be bought at ten cents the large nip.

"Just the man I was looking for," said a voice at Winston's back.

He turned round. It was his friend Syme, who worked in the Research Department. Perhaps "friend" was not exactly the right word. You did not have friends nowadays, you had comrades; but there were some comrades whose society was pleasanter than that of others. Syme was a philologist, a specialist in Newspeak. Indeed, he was one of the enormous team of experts now engaged in compiling the Eleventh Edition of the Newspeak dictionary. He was a tiny creature, smaller than Winston, with dark hair and large, protuberant eyes, at once mournful and derisive, which seemed to search your face closely while he was speaking to you.

"I wanted to ask you whether you'd got any razor blades," he said.

"Not one!" said Winston with a sort of guilty haste. "I've tried all over the place. They don't exist any longer."

Everyone kept asking you for razor blades. Actually he had two unused ones which he was hoarding up. There had been a famine of them for months past. At any given moment there was some necessary article which the Party shops were unable to supply. Sometimes it was buttons, sometimes it was darning wool, sometimes it was shoelaces; at present it was razor blades. You could only get hold of them, if at all, by scrounging more or less furtively on the "free" market.

"I've been using the same blade for six weeks," he added untruthfully.

The queue gave another jerk forward. As they halted he turned and faced Syme again. Each of them took a greasy metal tray from a pile at the edge of the counter.

"Did you go and see the prisoners hanged yesterday?" said Syme

"I was working," said Winston indifferently. "I shall see it on the flicks, I suppose."

"A very inadequate substitute," said Syme.

His mocking eyes roved over Winston's face. "I know you," the eyes seemed to say, "I see through you. I know very well why you didn't go to see those prisoners hanged." In an intellectual way, Syme was venomously orthodox. He would talk with a disagreeable gloating satisfaction of helicopter raids on enemy villages, the trials and confessions of thought-criminals, the executions in the cellars of the Ministry of Love. Talking to him was largely a matter of getting him away from such subjects and entangling him, if possible, in the technicalities of Newspeak, on which he was authoritative and interesting. Winston turned his head a little aside to avoid the scrutiny of the large dark eyes.

"It was a good hanging," said Syme reminiscently. "I think it spoils it when they tie their feet together. I like to see them kicking. And above all, at the end, the tongue sticking right out, and blue—a quite bright blue. That's the detail that appeals to me."

"Next, please!" yelled the white-aproned prole with the ladle.

Winston and Syme pushed their trays beneath the grille. Onto each was dumped swiftly the regulation lunch—a metal pannikin of pinkish-gray stew, a hunk of bread, a cube of cheese, a mug of milkless Victory Coffee, and one saccharine tablet.

"There's a table over there, under that telescreen," said Syme. "Let's pick up a gin on the way."

The gin was served out to them in handleless china mugs. They threaded their way across the crowded room and unpacked their trays onto the metal-topped table, on one corner of which someone had left a pool of stew, a filthy liquid mess that had the appearance of vomit. Winston took up his mug of gin, paused for an instant to collect his nerve, and gulped the oily-tasting stuff down. When he had winked the tears out of his eyes he suddenly discovered that he was hungry. He began swallowing spoonfuls of the stew, which, in among its general sloppiness, had cubes of spongy pinkish stuff which was probably a preparation of meat. Neither of them spoke again till they had emptied their pannikins. From the table at Winston's left, a little behind his back, someone was talking rapidly and continuously, a harsh gabble almost like the quacking of a duck, which pierced the general uproar of the room.

"How is the dictionary getting on?" said Winston, raising his voice to overcome the noise.

"Slowly," said Syme. "I'm on the adjectives. It's fascinating."

He had brightened up immediately at the mention of Newspeak. He pushed his pannikin aside, took up his hunk of bread in one delicate hand and his cheese in the other, and leaned across the table so as to be able to speak without shouting.

"The Eleventh Edition is the definitive edition," he said. "We're getting the language into its final shape—the shape it's going to have when nobody speaks anything else. When we've finished with it, people like you will have to learn it all over again. You think, I dare say, that our chief job is inventing new words. But not a bit of it! We're destroying words— scores of them, hundreds of them, every day. We're cutting the language down to the bone. The Eleventh Edition won't contain a single word that will become obsolete before the year 2050."

He bit hungrily into his bread and swallowed a couple of mouthfuls, then continued speaking, with a sort of pedant's passion. His thin dark face had become animated, his eyes had lost their mocking expression and grown almost dreamy.

"It's a beautiful thing, the destruction of words. Of course the great wastage is in the verbs and adjectives, but there are hundreds of nouns that can be got rid of as well. It isn't only the synonyms; there are also the antonyms. After all, what justification is there for a word which is simply the opposite of some other word? A word contains its opposite in itself. Take 'good,' for instance. If you have a word like 'good,' what need is there for a word like 'bad'? 'Ungood' will do just as well—better, because it's an exact opposite, which the other is not. Or again, if you want a stronger version of 'good', what sense is there in having a whole string of vague useless words like 'excellent' and 'splendid' and all the rest of them? 'Plusgood' covers the meaning, or 'doubleplusgood' if you want something stronger still. Of course we use those forms already, but in the final version of Newspeak there'll be nothing else. In the end the whole notion of goodness and badness will be covered by only six words—in reality, only one word. Don't you see the beauty of that, Winston? It was B.B's idea originally, of course," he added as an afterthought.

A sort of vapid eagerness flitted across Winston's face at the mention of Big Brother. Nevertheless Syme immediately detected a certain lack of enthusiasm.

"You haven't a real appreciation of Newspeak, Winston," he said almost sadly. "Even when you write it you're still thinking in Oldspeak. I've read some of those pieces that you write in the *Times* occasionally. They're good enough, but they're translations. In your heart you'd prefer to stick to Oldspeak, with all its vagueness and its useless shades of meaning. You don't grasp the beauty of the destruction of words. Do you know that Newspeak is the only language in the world whose vocabulary gets smaller every year?"

Winston did know that, of course. He smiled, sympathetically he hoped, not trusting himself to speak. Syme bit off another fragment of the dark-colored bread, chewed it briefly, and went on:

"Don't you see that the whole aim of Newspeak is to narrow the range of thought? In the end we shall make thoughtcrime literally impossible, because there will be no words in which to express it. Every concept that can ever be needed will be expressed by exactly *one* word, with its meaning rigidly defined and all its subsidiary meanings rubbed out and forgotten. Already, in the Eleventh Edition, we're not far from that point. But the process will still be continuing long after you and I are dead. Every year fewer and fewer words, and the range of consciousness always a little smaller. Even now, of course, there's no reason or excuse for committing thoughtcrime. It's merely a question of self-discipline, reality-control. But in the end there won't be any need even for that. The Revolution will be complete when the language is perfect. Newspeak is Ingsoc and Ingsoc is Newspeak," he added with a sort of mystical satisfaction. "Has it ever occurred to you, Winston, that by the year 2050, at the very latest, not a single human being will be alive who could understand such a conversation as we are having now?"

"Except—" began Winston doubtfully, and then stopped.

It had been on the tip of his tongue to say "Except the proles," but he checked himself, not feeling fully certain that this remark was not in some way unorthodox. Syme, however, had divined what he was about to say.

"The proles are not human beings," he said carelessly. "By 2050—earlier, probably— all real knowledge of Oldspeak will have disappeared. The whole literature of the past will have been destroyed. Chaucer, Shakespeare, Milton, Byron—they'll exist only in Newspeak versions, not merely changed into something different, but actually changed into something contradictory of what they used to be. Even the literature of the Party will change. Even the slogans will change. How could you have a slogan like 'freedom is slavery' when the concept of freedom has been abolished? The whole climate of thought will be different. In fact there will *be* no thought, as we understand it now. Orthodoxy means not thinking—not needing to think. Orthodoxy is unconsciousness."

Maurice Merleau-Ponty
Language as Creator of Meaning

Maurice Merleau-Ponty (1908–1961) *was a French philosopher and intellectual. He founded and edited a journal with Simone de Beauvoir and Jean-Paul Sartre, whose thought influenced him greatly.*

We have seen in the body a unity distinct from that of the scientific object. We have just discovered, even in its 'sexual function', intentionality and sense-giving powers. In trying to describe the phenomenon of speech and the specific act of meaning, we shall have the opportunity to leave behind us, once and for all, the traditional subject—object dichotomy.

The realization that speech is an originating realm naturally comes late. Here as everywhere, the relation of *having,* which can be seen in the very etymology of the word habit, is at first concealed by relations belonging to the domain of *being,* or, as we may equally say, by ontic relations obtaining within the world. The possession of language is in the first place understood as no more than the actual existence of 'verbal images', or traces left in us by words spoken or heard. Whether these traces are physical, or whether they are imprinted on an 'unconscious psychic life', is of little importance, and in both cases the conception of language is the same in that there is no 'speaking subject'. Whether the stimuli, in accordance with the laws of neurological mechanics, touch off excitations capable of bringing about the articulation of the word, or whether the states of consciousness cause, by virtue of acquired associations, the appearance of the appropriate verbal image, in both cases speech occurs in a circuit of third person phenomena. There is no speaker, there is a flow of words set in motion independently of any intention to speak. The meaning of words is considered to be given with the stimuli or with the states of consciousness which it is simply a matter of naming; the shape of the word, as heard or phonetically formed, is given with the cerebral or mental tracks; speech is not an action and does not show up the internal possibilities of the subject: man can speak as the electric lamp can become incandescent. Since there are elective disturbances which attack the spoken language to the exclusion of the written one, or *vice versa,* and since language can disintegrate into fragments, we have to conclude that it is built up by a set of independent contributions, and that speech in the general sense is an entity of rational origin.

The theory of aphasia and of language seemed to by undergoing complete transformation when it became necessary to distinguish, over and above anarthria,* which affects the articulation of the word, true aphasia which is inseparable from disturbances affecting intelligence—and over and above automatic language, which is in effect a third person motor phenomenon, as intentional language which is alone involved in the majority of cases of aphasia. The individuality of the 'verbal image' was, indeed, dissociated: what the patient has lost, and what the normal person possesses, is not a certain stock of words, but a certain way of using them. The same word which remains at the disposal of the patient in the context of automatic languages escapes him in that of language unrelated to a purpose—the patient who has no difficulty in finding the word 'no' in answer to the doctor's questions, that is when he intends to furnish a denial arising from his present experience, cannot do so when it is a question of an exercise having no emotional and vital bearing. There is thus revealed, underlying the word, an attitude, a function of speech which condition it. The word could be identified as an instrument of action and as a means of disinterested designation. Though 'concrete' language remained a third person process, gratuitous language, or authentic denomination, became a phenomenon of thought, and it is in some disturbance of thinking that the origin of certain forms of aphasia must be sought. For example, amnesia concerning names of colours, when related to the general behaviour of the patient, appeared as a special manifestation of a more general trouble. The same patients who cannot name colours set before them, are equally incapable of classifying them in the performance of a set task. If, for example, they are asked to sort out samples according to basic colour, it is immediately noticed that they do it more slowly and painstakingly than a normal subject: they slowly place together the samples to be compared and fail to see at a glance which ones 'go together'. Moreover, having correctly assembled several blue ribbons, they make unaccountable mistakes: if for

---

*Translator's note: Anarthria: loss of power of articulate speech.

example the last blue ribbon was of a pale shade, they carry on by adding to the collection of 'blues' a pale green or pale pink—as if it were beyond them to stick to the proposed principle of classification, and to consider the samples from the point of view of basic colour from start to finish of the operation. They have thus become unable to subsume the sensory givens under a category, to see immediately the samples as representatives of the *eidos* blue. Even when, at the beginning of the test, they proceed correctly, it is not the conformity of the samples to an idea which guides them, but the experience of an immediate resemblance, and hence it comes about that they can classify the samples only when they have placed them side by side. The sorting test brings to light in these subjects a fundamental disorder, of which forgetting names of colours is simply another manifestation. For to name a thing is to tear oneself away from its individual and unique characteristics to see it as representative of an essence or a category, and the fact that the patient cannot identify the samples is a sign, not that he has lost the verbal image of the words red or blue, but that he has lost the general ability to subsume a sensory given under a category, that he has lapsed back from the categorial to the concrete attitude. These analyses and other similar ones lead us, it would seem, to the antithesis of the theory of the verbal image, since language now appears as conditioned by thought.

In fact we shall once again see that there is a kinship between the empiricist or mechanistic psychologies and the intellectualist ones, and the problem of language is not solved by going from one extreme to the other. A short time ago the reproduction of the word, the revival of the verbal image, was the essential thing. Now it is no more than what envelops true denomination and authentic speech, which is an inner process. And yet these two conceptions are at one in holding that the word *has* no significance. In the first case this is obvious since the word is not summoned up through the medium of any concept, and since the given stimuli or 'states of mind' call it up in accordance with the laws of neurological mechanics or those of association, and that thus the word is not the bearer of its own meaning, has no inner power, and is merely a psychic, physiological or even physical phenomenon set alongside others, and thrown up by the working of an objective causality. It is just the same when we duplicate denomination with a categorial operation. The word is still bereft of any effectiveness of its own, this time because it is only the external sign of an internal recognition, which could take place without it, and to which it makes no contribution. It is not without meaning, since behind it there is a categorial operation, but this meaning is something which it does not *have*, does not possess, since it is thought which has a meaning, the word remaining an empty container. It is merely a phenomenon of articulation, of sound, or the consciousness of such a phenomenon, but in any case language is but an external accompaniment of thought. In the first case, we are on this side of the word as meaningful; in the second we are beyond it. In the first there is nobody to speak; in the second, there is certainly a subject, but a thinking one, not a speaking one. As far as speech itself is concerned, intellectualism is hardly any different from empiricism, and is no better able than the latter to dispense with an explanation in terms of involuntary action. Once the categorial operation is performed, the appearance of the word which completes the process still has to be explained, and this will still be done by recourse to a physiological or psychic mechanism, since the word is a passive shell. Thus we refute both intellectualism and empiricism by simply saying that *the word has a meaning*.

If speech presupposed thought, if talking were primarily a matter of meeting the object through a cognitive intention or through a representation, we could not understand why thought tends towards expression as towards its completion, why the most familiar thing appears indeterminate as long as we have not recalled its name, why the thinking subject himself is in a kind of ignorance of his thoughts so long as he has not formulated them for himself, or even spoken and written them, as is shown by the example of so many writers who begin a book without knowing exactly what they are going to put into it. A thought limited to existing for itself, independently of the constraints of speech and communication, would no sooner appear than it would sink into the unconscious, which means that it would not exist even for itself. . . . Thus speech, in the speaker, does not translate ready-made thought, but accomplishes it. *A fortiori* must it be recognized that the listener receives thought from speech itself. . . . The fact is that we have the power to understand over and above what we may have spontaneously thought. People can speak to us only a language which we already understand, each word of a difficult text awakens in us thoughts which were ours beforehand, but these meanings sometimes combine to form new thought which recasts them all, and we are transported to the heart of the matter, we find the source. Here there is nothing comparable to the solution of a problem, where we discover an unknown quantity through its relationship with known ones. For the problem can be solved only if it is determinate, that is, if the cross-checking of the data provides the unknown quantity with one or more definite values. In understanding others, the problem is always indeterminate because only the solution will bring the data retrospectively to light as convergent, only the central theme of a philosophy, once understood, endows the philosopher's writings with the value of adequate signs. There is, then, a taking up of others' thought through speech, a reflection in others, an ability to think *according to others* which enriches our own thoughts. Here the meaning of words must be finally induced by the words themselves, or more exactly, their conceptual meaning must be formed by a kind of deduction from a *gestural meaning,* which is immanent in speech. And as, in a foreign country, I begin to understand the meaning of words through their place in a context of action, and by taking part in a communal life—in the same way an as yet imperfectly understood piece of philosophical writing discloses to me at least a certain 'style'— either a Spinozist, criticist or phenomenological one—which is the first draft of its meaning. I begin to understand a philosophy by feeling my way into its existential manner, by reproducing the tone and accent of the philosopher. In fact, every language conveys its own teaching and carries its meaning into the listener's mind. A school of music or painting which is at first not understood, eventually, by its own action, creates its own public, if it really *says* something; that is, it does so by secreting its own meaning. In the case of prose or poetry, the power of the spoken word is less obvious, because we have the illusion of already possessing within ourselves, in the shape of the common property meaning of words, what is required for the understanding of any text whatsoever. The obvious fact is, however, that the colours of the palette or the crude sounds of instruments, as presented to us in natural perception, are insufficient to provide the musical sense of music, or the pictorial sense of a painting. But, in fact, it is less the case that the sense of a literary work is provided by the common property meaning of words, than that it contributes to changing that accepted meaning. There is thus, either in the man who listens or reads, or in the one who speaks or writes, a *thought in speech* the existence of which is unsuspected by intellectualism.

To realize this, we must turn back to the phenomenon of speech and reconsider ordinary descriptions which immobilize thought and speech, and make anything other than external relations between them inconceivable. We must recognize first of all that thought, in the speaking subject, is not a representation, that is, that it does not expressly posit objects or relations. The orator does not think before speaking, nor even while speaking; his speech is his thought. In the same way the listener does not form concepts on the basis of signs. The orator's 'thought' is empty while he is speaking and, when a text is read to us, provided that it is read with expression, we have no thought marginal to the text itself, for the words fully occupy our mind and exactly fulfill our expectations, and we feel the necessity of the speech. Although we are unable to predict its course, we are possessed by it. The end of the speech or text will be the lifting of a spell. It is at this stage that thoughts on the speech or text will be able to arise. Previously the speech was improvised and the text understood without the intervention of a single thought; the sense was everywhere present, and nowhere posited for its own sake. The speaking subject does not think of the sense of what he is saying, nor does he visualize the words which he is using. To know a word or a language is, as we have said, not to be able to bring into play any pre-established nervous network. But neither is it to retain some 'pure recollection' of the word, some faded perception. . . .

These considerations enable us to restore to the act of speaking its true physiognomy. In the first place speech is not the 'sign' of thought, if by this we understand a phenomenon which heralds another as smoke betrays fire. Speech and thought would admit of this external relation only if they were both thematically given, whereas in fact they are intervolved, the sense being held within the word, and the word being the external existence of the sense. Nor can we concede, as is commonly done, that speech is a mere means of fixation, nor yet that it is the envelope and clothing of thought. Why should it be easier to recall words or phrases than thoughts, if the alleged verbal images need to be reconstructed on every occasion? And why should thought seek to duplicate itself or clothe itself in a succession of utterances, if the latter do not carry and contain within themselves their own meaning? Words cannot be 'strongholds of thought', nor can thought seek expression, unless words are in themselves a comprehensible text, and unless speech possesses a power of significance entirely its own. The word and speech must somehow cease to be a way of designating things or thoughts, and become the presence of that thought in the phenomenal world, and, moreover, not its clothing but its token or its body. There must be, as psychologists say, a 'linguistic concept' or a word concept, a 'central inner experience, specifically verbal, thanks to which the sound, heard, uttered, read or written, becomes a linguistic fact'. Certain patients can read a text, 'putting expression into it', without, however, understanding it. This is because the spoken or written words carry a top coating of meaning which sticks to them and which presents the thought as a style, an affective value, a piece of existential mimicry, rather than as a conceptual statement. We find here, beneath the conceptual meaning of the words, an existential meaning which is not only rendered by them, but which inhabits them, and is inseparable from them. The greatest service done by expression is not to commit to writing ideas which might be lost. A writer hardly ever re-reads his own works, and great works leave in us at a first reading all that we shall ever subsequently get out of them. The process of expression, when it is successful, does not merely leave for the reader and the writer himself a kind of reminder, it brings the meaning into existence as a thing at the very heart of the text, it brings it to life in an organism of words, establishing it in the writer or the reader as a new sense organ, opening a new field or a new dimension to our experience. . . .

Thought is no 'internal' thing, and does not exist independently of the world and of words. What misleads us in this connection, and causes us to believe in a thought which exists for itself prior to expression, is thought already constituted and expressed, which we can silently recall to ourselves, and through which we acquire the illusion of an inner life. But in reality this supposed silence is alive with words, this inner life is an inner language. 'Pure' thought reduces itself to a certain void of consciousness, to a momentary desire. The new sense-giving intention knows itself only by donning already available meanings, the outcome of previous acts of expression. The available meanings suddenly link up in accordance with an unknown law, and once and for all a fresh cultural entity has taken on an existence. Thought and expression, then, are simultaneously constituted, when our cultural store is put at the service of this unknown law, as our body suddenly lends itself to some new gesture in the formation of habit. The spoken word is a genuine gesture, and it contains its meaning in the same way as the gesture contains its. This is what makes communication possible. In order that I may understand the words of another person, it is clear that his vocabulary and syntax must be 'already known' to me. But that does not mean that words do their work by arousing in me 'representations' associated with them, and which in aggregate eventually reproduce in me the original 'representation' of the speaker. What I communicate with primarily is not 'representations' or thought, but a speaking subject, with a certain style of being and with the 'world' at which he directs his aim. Just as the sense-giving intention which has set in motion the other person's speech is not an explicit thought, but a certain lack which is asking to be made good, so my taking up of this intention is not a process of thinking on my part, but a synchronizing change of my own existence, a transformation of my being. We live in a world where speech is an *institution*. For all these many commonplace utterances, we possess within ourselves ready-made meanings. They arouse in us only second order thoughts; these in turn are translated into other words which demand from us no real effort of expression and will demand from our hearers no effort of comprehension. Thus language and the understanding of language apparently raise no problems. The linguistic and intersubjective world no longer surprises us, we no longer distinguish it from the world itself, and it is within a world already spoken and speaking that we think. We become unaware of the contingent element in expression and communication, whether it be in the child learning to speak, or in the writer saying and thinking something for the first time, in short, in all who transform a certain kind of silence into speech. It is, however, quite clear that constituted speech, as it operates in daily life, assumes that the decisive step of expression has been taken. Our view of man will remain superficial so long as we fail to go back to that origin, so long as we fail to find, beneath the chatter of words, the primordial silence, and as long as we do not describe the action which breaks this silence. The spoken word is a gesture, and its meaning, a world. . . .

. . . the *full* meaning of a language is never translatable into another. We may speak several languages, but one of them always remains the one in which we live. In order completely to assimilate a language, it would be necessary to make the world which it expresses one's own, and one never does belong to two worlds at once. If there is such a thing as universal thought, it is achieved by taking up the effort towards expression and communication in *one* single language, and accepting all its ambiguities, all the suggestions and overtones of meaning of which a linguistic tradition is made up, and which are the exact measure of its power of expression. A conventional algorithm—which moreover is meaningful only in relation to language—will never express anything but nature without man. Strictly speaking, therefore, there are no conventional signs, standing as the simple notation of a thought pure and clear in itself, there are only words into which the history of a whole language is compressed, and which effect communication with no absolute guarantee, dogged as they are by incredible linguistic hazards. . . .

What is true, however—and justifies the view that we ordinarily take of language, as being in a peculiar category—is that, alone of all expressive processes, speech is able to settle into a sediment and constitute an acquisition for use in human relationships. This fact cannot be explained by pointing out that speech can be recorded on paper, whereas gestures or forms of behaviour are transmitted only by direct imitation. For music too can be written down, and, although there is in music something in the nature of an initiation into the tradition, although, that is, it would probably be impossible to graduate to atonal music without passing through classical music, yet every composer starts his tasks at the beginning, having a new world to deliver, whereas in the realm of speech, each writer is conscious of taking as his objective the same world as has already been dealt with by other writers. The worlds of Balzac and Stendhal are not like planets without communication with each other, for speech implants the idea of truth in us as the presumptive limit of its effort. It loses sight of itself as a contingent fact, and takes to resting upon itself; this is, as we have seen, what provides us with the ideal of thought without words, whereas the idea of music without sounds is ridiculous. Even if this is pushing the principle beyond its limits and reducing things to the absurd, even if a linguistic meaning can never be delivered of its inherence in some word or other, the fact remains that the expressive process in the case of speech can be indefinitely reiterated, that it is possible to speak about speech whereas it is impossible to paint about painting, and finally that every philosopher has dreamed of a form of discourse which would supersede all others, whereas the painter or the musician does not hope to exhaust all possible painting or music. Thus there is a privileged position accorded to Reason. But if we want to understand it clearly, we must begin by putting thought back among the phenomena of expression.

Stephanie Ross

How Words Hurt

Stephanie Ross *teaches philosophy at the University of Missouri in St. Louis. She does work in feminist theory and in aesthetics.*

An old nursery rhyme assures us that "Sticks and stones may break my bones/But names can never hurt me." Yet many philosophers claim that words *can* hurt. They argue that ordinary language is sexist and that sexist language oppresses women. For example, Elizabeth Beardsley has drawn attention to referential genderization (RG) which occurs "whenever a speaker who is saying something about human beings must make distinctions based on sex on pain of saying something linguistically incorrect." She claims that RG increases sexual distinctions, and thereby "helps to provide a conceptual framework useful for rationalizing sex-based discriminatory treatment." Robert Baker claims that

> any movement dedicated to breaking the bonds of female servitude must destroy our ways of identifying and hence of conceiving of women . . . Contemporary feminists should advocate the utilization of neutral proper names and the elimination of gender from our language.

I believe these claims are sound, but to my knowledge no philosopher has provided a satisfactory account of *how* words hurt. Certainly words can be used to taunt and defame, to voice threats and instill fear, to express discriminatory edicts and tyrannical decrees. Yet none of these possibilities explains the particular charge that our ordinary, everyday ways of talking about women are sexist and oppressive. Some writers suggest that the oppressive aspects of ordinary language are etymological: certain words have roots which are denigrating and offensive to women. Yet most of us are unaware of the etymologies of the words we use. How can historical facts of which both speakers and listeners are unaware transform their words into vehicles of oppression?

In this paper I shall offer an account of how words can hurt. I shall begin by sketching a theory which doesn't work—the theory of etymological oppression. I shall argue that the ancient roots of ordinary English words cannot—by themselves—make those words oppressive. Then I shall turn to a closely related phenomenon which does perpetuate sexism in language. This is the phenomenon of metaphoric identification. . . . Briefly, I claim that metaphors often express attitude, and that the metaphors implicit in sexist language express attitudes of contempt and disdain towards women. . . . I shall also point out a structural similarity which makes metaphor an apt vehicle for the expression of attitude. Thus I hope to show that the nursery rhyme with which I opened is mistaken. Words can hurt, and one way they do is by conveying denigrating or demeaning attitudes.

ETYMOLOGICAL ECHOES?

In an angry article in the *New York Times*, Barbara Lawrence traces the etymology of the verb *to fuck* to the German *ficken* meaning "to strike," to the Latin *fustis*, meaning "a staff or cudgel," and to the Celtic *buc*, meaning "a point, hence, to pierce." She goes on to discuss the etymology of the verb *to screw* and to point out what a painful and mutilating activity screwing is:

> Consider what a screw actually does to the wood it penetrates. . . . The verb, besides its explicit imagery, has antecedent associations to "write on," "scratch," "scarify," and so forth—a revealing fusion of a mechanical or painful action with an obviously denigrated object.

Lawrence suggests that these two words oppress women because of the brutal and denigrating imagery implicit in their etymology. While I agree that both words are offensive, I believe that neither one oppresses in virtue of its etymology. And of the two, only "screw" offends in virtue of its associated imagery. . . . In the next section I shall show that the facts cited by Lawrence are relevant to a different sort of explanation of how words hurt. . . .

METAPHORICAL IDENTIFICATION

Return to Lawrence's two examples, "fuck" and "screw." We agree that both these words are insulting and that both are classed as impolite. In addition, I have argued that "fuck" does not offend women because of its etymological ties to "ficken," "fustis," and "buc." Most speakers are unaware of these ties. They find the term offensive because they know it is classed as offensive by their fellow speakers. I believe the offensiveness of "screw" can be explained quite differently, and this is shown even in Lawrence's summary reference to its "revealing fusion of a mechanical or painful action with an obviously denigrated object." The difference here is that most of us are aware of these aspects of screws. Even if we haven't given much thought to screwing as a method of fastening (as opposed to nailing or glueing) we can immediately acknowledge the correctness of Lawrence's claims. A screw is hard and sharp; wood by contrast is soft and yielding; force is applied to make a screw penetrate wood; a screw can be unscrewed and reused but wood—wherever a screw has been embedded in it— is destroyed forever. Once we marshal these everyday facts about screw and screwing, their ramifications become clear. When the verb *to screw* is used to describe sexual intercourse, it carries with it images of dominance and destruction. The woman's role in intercourse is similar to that of wood destroyed by the screw which enters it. Additional echoes are carried by a further use of the verb *to screw* in financial contexts. To screw someone in this sense is to wring her dry, to practice extortion.

Metaphor is the device at work here. The use of the verb *to screw* to describe sexual intercourse invites us to view this latter activity in terms drawn from carpentry and mechanics. As noted above, many facts about screws and screwing are applicable to the new realm as well. And this is just what we should expect of an apt metaphor. But "screwing" is not a fresh, new label for intercourse. This use of the term is accepted, though deemed coarse and impolite. Thus we are dealing here with a dead metaphor—an established use of the word "screw" which has additional depth and resonance because it associates the two realms of sex and mechanics. The central claim I want to make in this paper is that metaphors of this sort are our primary vehicles for conveying attitudes. The offensiveness of the verb *to screw* is rooted in the attitude it conveys toward the female role in intercourse, and this attitude can be specified by attending to the details of the metaphor. None of the claims I shall make are tied to any one theory of metaphor. While there is much debate about the nature of metaphorical truth, the paraphrasability of metaphors, and so on, I shall skirt these issues. I trust that my positive claims about metaphor will apply to any reasonable account of that trope.

The relation between sexism and metaphor has been charted ably by Robert Baker in his article " 'Pricks' and 'Chicks': A Plea for 'Persons'." I want to expand on his work by showing in detail how metaphors can serve to express attitudes. But let me first outline Baker's position. Baker claims that the way in which we identify something reflects our conception of it. This claim is not controversial. It may even be tautological on some readings of "concept." However, the identifications Baker focuses on throughout his paper are metaphorical ones. This enlivens things because metaphors are not finitely paraphrasable. Since their implications can be spun out at length, the identifications they convey are comparably complex.

To establish his claim, Baker first considers racial identifications. He compares the differing conceptions of blacks conveyed by the four labels "Negro," "colored," "Afro-American," and "black." In the course of his discussion, he imagines the remarks "Where did that girl get to?" and "Who is the new boy that Lou hired to help out at the filling station?" voiced by white Southerners, and then comments:

> If the persons the terms apply to are adult Afro-Americans, then 'girl' and 'boy' are metaphorical identifications. The fact that the metaphorical identifications in question are standard in the language reflects that certain characteristics of the objects properly classified as boys and girls (for example, immaturity, inability to take care of themselves, need for guidance) are generally held by those who use the identifications to be properly attributable to Afro-Americans.

Baker's acknowledgement that these metaphors are standard usage is important, for it establishes that the metaphors in question are dead metaphors. The Southerners who use them do not first think long and hard about race relations, then consciously construct metaphors which reveal the situation. Rather, they use the terms "boy" and "girl" because these are common currency. Probably few speakers spell out the implications of these terms for themselves as Baker has in the passage quoted above. Nonetheless, these implications are available—at least potentially—to any competent speaker. They resonate in each metaphorical use of the terms "boy" and "girl" quite unlike the supposed echoes of "buc," "fustis," and "flicken" resonating in each use of "fuck."

This is the important difference between Baker's account of the offensiveness of certain idioms and the account I proposed and rejected in Part I of this paper—the implications of dead metaphors are known or accessible to their speakers, while etymological details often are not. To see this, note that dead metaphors are those which have become trite and commonplace. Tenor and vehicle have been associated so frequently that their juxtaposition no longer seems fresh or illuminating. Given this long and public liaison, it follows that neither tenor nor vehicle can be entirely mysterious unless the metaphor was consistently misunderstood. (One obvious exception to this claim is the use of metaphor in scientific theories. Here the subject matter is indeed arcane and the presence of metaphor signals that our understanding is not yet complete. However, these cases needn't concern us here since our problem is ordinary language and its power to offend and oppress.) Finally, these comments about metaphor apply equally to metaphorical identifications. These are simply cases where instead of a full statement of the metaphor ("A is B") the name or description of the vehicle replaces that of the tenor ("B is ø" replaces "A is ø").

Baker takes the account of metaphorical identification which emerges from his discussion of racism and applies it to a second area, that of sexism. He argues that many of our ways of identifying women involve (dead) metaphors which insult and belittle. Among the categories of metaphorical identification he points out are animal terms ("chick," "fox"), toy terms ("doll"), juvenile terms ("babe," "kid," "sis") as well as more explicitly sexual and/or anatomical terms. I believe Baker is right about the force of these terms, though I grant there are certain cases which his account does not explain. For example, his theory does not apply to terms (like "fuck") which offend because we class them as offensive. Nor does it apply to terms which offend by excluding women from consideration. Examples here include general labels like "chairman" and "fireman" as well as the personal pronouns "he" and "his" when used to agree with an antecedent of unspecified gender ("everyone," "someone"). Neither of these examples offends in virtue of metaphorical implications. (However, in keeping with Baker's program we can explain both by reference to a second figure of speech: synecdoche. Both wrongly take part of humanity—the male sex—and use it to stand for the whole. The resulting idioms make it all too easy for women to be overlooked.)

ATTITUDE AND METAPHOR

Despite these lacunae, Baker's account fits a sizable number of cases of sexism in language. However, Baker calls our attention to the relation between metaphor and sexism without explaining how this relation fosters the oppression of women. I believe this is a fact in need of explanation. In what follows, I shall extend Baker's program by proposing an account of how metaphorical identifications oppress and offend. I suggest that metaphors often express attitudes. In particular, I suggest that the metaphorical identifications which Baker discusses express contemptuous and disdainful attitudes towards women. To justify this claim, I shall present three sorts of evidence. First, I shall present and discuss a single example, drawn from a novel of Willa Cather. Rather than argue in the abstract that metaphors can express attitudes, I shall examine a particular passage and argue that the best interpretation of it accords with my theory. Next, I shall offer some evidence drawn from social psychology. I shall examine the methods social psychologists employ to test for attitudes and point out the central role played by metaphor. Finally, I shall offer a more abstract argument for my claim, based on 'structural' resemblances between attitude and metaphor.

Consider the following passages from *The Professor's House*:

> He loved his family, he would make any sacrifice for them, but just now he couldn't live with them. He must be alone. That was more necessary to him than anything had ever been, more necessary than his marriage had been in his vehement youth. He could not live with his family again—not even with Lillian. Especially not with Lillian! Her nature was intense and positive; it was like a chiselled surface, a die, a stamp upon which he could not be beaten out any longer. If her character were reduced to an heraldic device, it would be a hand (a beautiful hand) holding flaming arrows— the shafts of her violent loves and hates, her clear-cut ambition.

In these lines Willa Cather details the reactions of her protagonist, Professor Godfrey St. Peter, to the news that his family is returning early from a European tour. That passage tells us a good deal about St. Peter's temperament, loyalties, and needs, his early attachments and his current desires. But my interest is in the Professor's description of his wife, Lillian. Just what is revealed by the simile comparing her nature to a sharp metallic die, or the metaphor imagining her character as a heraldic device? What do we learn about the Professor in learning that *these* are his thoughts?

For a start, we do not learn about the Professor's beliefs. At least not in any straightforward sense. One might object that St. Peter expresses at least the belief that Lillian's character can be represented by a heraldic device of such and such a sort. But little follows from this concession. The Professor uses figurative language to talk about his wife. His beliefs about Lillian herself are of primary interest, not his beliefs about the suitability of various metaphors. And his endorsement of a particular trope does little to reveal his literal beliefs about his wife. This is so in part because metaphors aren't readily paraphrased; also because we rarely resort to metaphor to formulate and communicate our literal (pedestrian) beliefs. Thus, although the Professor's description is revealing, it doesn't reveal his beliefs about Lillian.

Nor does it reveal particular emotions he feels toward Lillian. Granted, the tone of the entire passage is hysterical, and its general topic seems to be love. But neither love nor hysteria characterizes St. Peter's portrait of Lillian. Although the opening sentence of the passage assures us that St. Peter loves his family, his portrait reveals love's absence, or its aftermath. (He remarks later, "Surely the saddest thing in the world is falling out of love—if once one has ever fallen in.") Similarly, although St. Peter seems hysterical and overwrought in this passage, these emotions do not carry over to his descriptions of Lillian. She is not the object of his hysteria. Instead she receives a knowing, considered assessment.

What, then, does the Professor's description convey? I suggest it expresses his attitude towards Lillian. It reveals, first, the Professor's admiration for his wife. The words "intense," "positive," "flaming," and "violent" attest to her strength, while the mention of a heraldic device connotes nobility, privilege, and respect. The assessment is not entirely admiring, however, for many of St. Peter's terms come from the vocabularies of war and technology. Here Lillian is characterized as strong in a more pejorative sense—strength as hardness. The metaphors of die and stamp suggest unyielding resistance, insistent repetition. St. Peter pictures himself weary, beaten, obliterated by her stamp. The mention of a chiselled surface provides further reinforcement, not only with the immediate image of cold stone and hard edges, but also in its muted suggestion of struggle, of an adversary relationship. (Compare chiselling stone with casting bronze, building clay.) In all these metaphors Lillian is portrayed as awesome, strong, stubborn, and dangerous. The final conceit suggests more specific criticisms of her character—the violence of her emotions and the transparence of her ambition.

The two figures of speech St. Peter employs to describe Lillian are thus immensely effective. They convey his admiration and awe, his distaste and defeat. I claim that these features indicate the Professor's attitude towards his wife. What do I mean by an attitude? Examples might include admiration, approval, dislike and disdain. Attitudes are intentional states (in Brentano's sense). Thus they are object-directed; all attitudes are attitudes toward or attitudes about something or other. In addition, attitudes involve beliefs about their objects and convey evaluations of them. If I admire Jane because she is intelligent, capable, and sympathetic, then Jane is the object of my attitude, and my attitude is grounded in my beliefs about her character. Since intelligence, competence, and sympathy are traits we prize, my attitude conveys a favorable evaluation of Jane. Some of my beliefs about Jane might be mistaken. If so, my attitude is misplaced or inappropriate. Attitudes themselves are not classed as true or false. In sum, if we imagine a continuum of psychological states, attitudes occupy an intermediate ground between judgement and belief, on the one hand, and emotions and moods, on the other. Like emotions, attitudes are object-directed, non-propositional, and evaluative. Yet attitudes are less visceral than emotions, less partisan, and less closely tied to distinctive behavioral manifestations. Returning to our example, the Professor's attitude towards Lillian is not conveyed by the bare factual claim that he takes her loves and hates to be violent. Thus it is not merely a belief or judgement about his wife. Nor is it a violent state which has overwhelmed him. The reflective mood of his extended metaphorical description indicates that he is not in the throes of a ravaging emotion. His psychological state lies between these poles.

My claim that metaphors express attitudes must be qualified in several respects. First, I do not claim that *all* metaphors serve this function, nor that they do so in all contexts. I would certainly be at a loss to determine the attitude conveyed by "The camel is the ship of the desert"! My claim is that sometimes metaphors express attitudes. And second, even in those cases where metaphors do convey attitude, I do not claim that we can always specify just which attitude is being expressed. The example discussed above is a case in point. The Professor's attitude towards Lillian is a complex attitude for which we have no standard name. It is not plain awe or unalloyed admiration. Despite our inability to name his attitude, I believe it is correct and illuminating to classify it as such. Finally, attitudes, like emotions and beliefs, can be unconscious. There may well be cases where someone has an attitude, expresses it in various ways (including metaphorical identifications of the attitude-object) yet doesn't know that this is so. Thus we are not always the best authorities about the attitudes we hold, reveal, express. Note that this accords with the claims made in Part I of this paper about knowledge and oppression. We do not always know when we are being oppressed; we can in fact become unwitting collaborators in our own oppression. (I do not, by the way, claim that the attitude St. Peter expresses towards his wife Lillian is a sexist one; it is simply a negative attitude, directed towards a woman.) . . .

INTENTIONAL TRANSCENDENCE

My concluding argument for this connection between metaphor and attitude appeals to what I shall (loosely) call structural considerations. I claim that there is an isomorphism between metaphor on the one hand and attitude on the other which makes metaphor a particularly apt vehicle for the expression of attitude. This isomorphism has to do with the logical structure of attitude and metaphor: in particular, with their irreducibility to belief and to literal talk, respectively. I shall call this shared trait intentional transcendence.

Consider one of the central questions about metaphors—their paraphrasability. Can the significance of a metaphor be completely spelled out? In the article "Aesthetic Problems of Modern Philosophy," Stanley Cavell argues that metaphors are paraphrasable. To prove his point, he proposes the following paraphrase of the metaphor "Juliet is the sun":

> Romeo means that Juliet is the warmth of his world; that his day begins with her; that only in her nourishment can he grow. And his declaration suggests that the moon, which other lovers use as emblems of their love, is merely her reflected light, and dead in comparison; and so on.

Cavell's "and so on" is crucial here. He qualifies his claim by noting that metaphors are paraphrasable in a manner "marked by its concluding sense of 'and so on.'" Thus Romeo does not mean that Juliet is like the sun in four respects and four respects only. His metaphor has further significance, further ramifications to be drawn out. For instance, that Juliet is the center of his universe. This richness is what some call the pregnancy of metaphor; it is what I mean by the phrase "intentional transcendence." A number of other writers call attention to this trait. For example, Max Black distinguishes a class of interaction metaphors which cannot be replaced by literal translations without loss of cognitive content. Philip Wheelwright distinguishes two forms of metaphor, one of which—diaphor—creates new meaning through presentational juxtaposition. Nelson Goodman's metaphorical account of metaphor (as the transfer of a schema to an alien realm, where the immigrant sometimes effects new organization and new associations) gives a picture of paraphrase which helps to explain its richness. Alan Tormey's subjunctive theory of metaphor also supports this view. Relations between tenor and vehicle can be spun out indefinitely because we can explore countless crannies of the possible world in which the counterfactual holds.

Consider now intentional transcendence in the psychological realm. Just as metaphors resist collapse into a finite set of literal sentences, so attitudes resist collapse into a finite set of grounding beliefs. All attitudes are belief-dependent. For example, to have an attitude of admiration towards Lauren Bacall, I must hold a number of factual beliefs about her (e.g. that she is the blonde actress in "To Have and Have Not," that she also appears in "Key Largo," that she was Bogart's wife). Such beliefs establish that my attitude is directed towards the proper object. There aren't any particular beliefs about Bacall such that I need to hold *those* beliefs in order to have an attitude directed towards her. I simply must have some collection of beliefs about her, some of which are accurate. [If all my beliefs about Bacall were false and applied instead to Ginger Rogers—e.g. "She's the brassy redheaded actress who danced with Fred Astaire"—then my attitude is not an attitude towards Lauren Bacall at all. It is an attitude towards Ginger Rogers about whom I have (at least) this false belief: that her name is Lauren Bacall.]

This dependence of attitude upon belief has been ably documented in the literature. Though some collection of Bacall-beliefs must be present in order to direct my admiration, these beliefs do not constitute my attitude. This is so because many of Bacall's detractors might hold the very same beliefs. This suggests that there are further beliefs logically involved in my attitude. In addition to the beliefs which direct my attitude towards the appropriate object (in this case, Bacall) I hold additional beliefs which determine which attitude it is. Thus, if I think Bacall acts well, is beautiful and intelligent, then my attitude is one of admiration. If I think her a cheap brassy blonde with no acting skills, my attitude is instead one of disdain. Note that my admiration for Bacall does not reduce to this further set of beliefs about her. First, because other people might admire her without holding these particular beliefs. And second, because some might hold these same beliefs without admiring her. Nor can we reduce admiration to holding a preponderance of favorable beliefs, nor even to the single belief that its object is admirable. It is always possible to hold such beliefs about a person (object) yet not admire that person (object).

My point about these attitudes is this: they are no more reducible to the cluster of beliefs which ground them than metaphors are reducible to the set of sentences which provide a paraphrase. To proclaim Bacall stunning, quick, and talented is not yet to admire her; to cite ten ways in which Juliet resembles the sun is not yet to exhaust Shakespeare's metaphor. Thus metaphors and attitudes alike have a sort of intentional transcendence which accords them both richness and mystery. And this structural similarity suggests why metaphorical language might express attitudes more effectively than literal talk *or* wordless gestures.

SUMMING UP

In this paper I have offered an increasingly abstract set of arguments in response to the question "Can words hurt?" I began by stating the feminist charge that ordinary language is sexist and in need of reform. I considered one possible account of sexism in language—the theory of etymological oppression—and argued that this theory was not credible. Remaining agnostic on the question of whether words oppress, I proposed an alternative account of many of the cases feminists deem offensive. I claimed—following Robert Baker—that terms of our language often function as (dead) metaphors. I went on to suggest that such metaphors express attitudes rather than literal beliefs. To support this proposal, I offered further information about the nature of attitudes, about the paraphrasability of metaphors, and about the attitude-measurement devices employed by social psychologists. While this resulted in discussion at quite some remove from our initial question, I believe that these disparate pieces fit together to provide a full and convincing account. If correct, my analysis explains not only how metaphorical language can hurt and offend, but also how it can flatter, comfort, and soothe. It does so by conveying the various attitudes which are essential to our evaluations, enthusiasms, prejudices, and passions.

Friedrich Nietzsche

Communication and Consciousness

Friedrich Nietzsche *(1844–1900) was a German philosopher who was given a professorship at the unheard-of age of 24. Most of his fame came after his death, and during his professorship he became increasingly disgusted and embittered at the lack of interest in his work. He spent his last ten years in total insanity.*

*O*n the "genius of the species."—The problem of consciousness (more precisely, of becoming conscious of something) confronts us only when we begin to comprehend how we could dispense with it; and now physiology and the history of animals place us at the beginning of such comprehension (it took them two centuries to catch up with *Leibniz's* suspicion which soared ahead). For we could think, feel, will, and remember, and we could also "act" in every sense of that word, and yet none of all this would have to "enter our consciousness" (as one says metaphorically). The whole of life would be possible without, as it were, seeing itself in a mirror. Even now, for that matter, by far the greatest portion of our life actually takes place without this mirror effect; and this is true even of our thinking, feeling, and willing life, however offensive this may sound to older philosophers. *For what purpose,* then, any consciousness at all when it is in the main *superfluous?*

Now, if you are willing to listen to my answer and the perhaps extravagant surmise that it involves, it seems to me as if the subtlety and straight of consciousness always were proportionate to a man's (or animal's) *capacity for communication,* and as if this capacity in turn were proportionate to the *need for communication.* But this last point is not to be understood as if the individual human being who happens to be a master in communicating and making understandable his needs must also be most dependent on others in his needs. But it does seem to me as if it were that way when we consider whole races and chains of generations: Where need and distress have forced men for a long time to communicate and to understand each other quickly and subtly, the ultimate result is an excess of this strength and art of communication—as it were, a capacity that has gradually been accumulated and now waits for an heir who might squander it. (Those who are called artists are these heirs; so are orators, preachers, writers—all of them people who always come at the end of a long chain, "late born" every one of them in the best sense of that word and, as I have said, by their nature squanderers.)

Supposing that this observation is correct, I may now proceed to the surmise that *consciousness has developed only under the pressure of the need for communication;* that from the start it was needed and useful only between human beings (particularly between those who commanded and those who obeyed); and that it also developed only in proportion to the degree of this utility. Consciousness is really only a net of communication between human beings; it is only as such that it had to develop; a solitary human being who lived like a beast of prey would not have needed it. That our actions, thoughts, feelings, and movements enter our own consciousness—at least a part of them—that is the result of a "must" that for a terribly long time lorded it over man. As the most endangered animal, he *needed* help and protection, he needed his peers, he had to learn to express his distress and to make himself understood; and for all of this he needed "consciousness" first of all, he needed to "know" himself what distressed him, he needed to "know" how he felt, he needed to "know" what he thought. For, to say it once more: Man, like every living being, thinks continually without knowing it; the thinking that rises to *consciousness* is only the smallest part of all this—the most superficial and worst part—for only this conscious thinking *takes the form of words, which is to say signs of communication,* and this fact uncovers the origin of consciousness.

In brief, the development of language and the development of consciousness (*not of reason* but merely of the way reason enters consciousness) go hand in hand. Add to this that not only language serves as a bridge between human beings but also a mien, a pressure, a gesture. The emergence of our sense impressions into our own consciousness, the ability to fix them and, as it were, exhibit them externally, increased proportionately with the need to communicate them to *others* by means of signs. The human being inventing signs is at the same time the human being who becomes ever more keenly conscious of himself. It was only as a social animal that man acquired self-consciousness—which he is still in the process of doing, more and more.

My idea is, as you see, that consciousness does not really belong to man's individual existence but rather to his social or herd nature; that, as follows from this, it has developed subtlety only insofar as this is required by social or herd utility. Consequently, given the best will in the world to understand ourselves as individually as possible, "to know ourselves," each of us will always succeed in becoming conscious only of what is not individual but "average." Our thoughts themselves are continually governed by the character of consciousness—by the "genius of the species" that commands it—and translated back into the perspective of the herd. Fundamentally, all our actions are altogether incomparably personal, unique, and infinitely individual; there is no doubt of that. But as soon as we translate them into consciousness *they no longer seem to be.*

This is the essence of phenomenalism and perspectivism as *I* understand them: Owing to the nature of *animal consciousness,* the world of which we can become conscious is only a surface- and sign-world, a world that is made common and meaner; whatever becomes conscious *becomes* by the same token shallow, thin, relatively stupid, general, sign, herd signal; all becoming conscious involves a great and thorough corruption, falsification, reduction to superficialities, and generalization. Ultimately, the growth of consciousness becomes a danger; and anyone who lives among the most conscious Europeans even knows that it is a disease.

You will guess that it is not the opposition of subject and object that concerns me here: This distinction I leave to the epistemologists who have become entangled in the snares of grammar (the metaphysics of the people). It is even less the opposition of "thing-in-itself" and appearance; for we do not "know" nearly enough to be entitled to any such distinction. We simply lack any organ for knowledge, for "truth": we "know" (or believe or imagine) just as much as may be *useful* in the interests of the human herd, the species; and even what is here called "utility" is ultimately also a mere belief, something imaginary, and perhaps precisely that most calamitous stupidity of which we shall perish some day.

Lewis Carroll

Humpty Dumpty

Lewis Carroll *(1832–1898), whose real name was Charles Lutwidge Dodgson, was an English mathematician and logician. His mother died when he went away to college, and he became increasingly drawn to the company of children, especially little girls. He was afflicted with a stammer which made him uncomfortable in the company of adults. His books* Alice in Wonderland *and* Through the Looking Glass *are two of the great children's books in English. He also published mathematical works.*

However, the egg only got larger and larger, and more and more human: when she had come within a few yards of it, she saw that it had eyes and a nose and mouth; and, when she had come close to it, she saw clearly that it was HUMPTY DUMPTY himself. "It ca'n't be anybody else!" she said to herself. "I'm as certain of it, as if his name were written all over his face!"

It might have been written a hundred times, easily, on that enormous face. Humpty Dumpty was sitting, with his legs crossed like a Turk, on the top of a high wall—such a narrow one that Alice quite wondered how he could keep his balance—and, as his eyes were steadily fixed in the opposite direction, and he didn't take the least notice of her, she thought he must be a stuffed figure, after all.

"And how exactly like an egg he is!" she said aloud, standing with her hands ready to catch him, for she was every moment expecting him to fall.

"It's *very* provoking," Humpty Dumpty said after a long silence, looking away from Alice as he spoke, "to be called an egg—*very!*"

"I said you *looked* like an egg, Sir," Alice gently explained. "And some eggs are very pretty, you know," she added, hoping to turn her remark into a sort of compliment.

"Some people," said Humpty Dumpty, looking away from her as usual, "have no more sense than a baby!"

Alice didn't know what to say to this: it wasn't at all like conversation, she thought, as he never said anything to *her*; in fact, his last remark was evidently addressed to a tree—so she stood and softly repeated to herself:

Humpty Dumpty sat on a wall:
Humpty Dumpty had a great fall.
All the King's horses and all the King's men
Couldn't put Humpty Dumpty in his place again.

"That last line is much too long for the poetry," she added, almost out loud, forgetting that Humpty Dumpty would hear her.

"Don't stand chattering to yourself like that," Humpty Dumpty said, looking at her for the first time, "but tell me your name and your business."

"My *name* is Alice, but—"

"It's a stupid name enough!" Humpty Dumpty interrupted impatiently. "What does it mean?"

"*Must* a name mean something?" Alice asked doubtfully.

"Of course it must," Humpty Dumpty said with a short laugh: "*my* name means the shape I am—and a good handsome shape it is, too. With a name like yours, you might be any shape, almost."

"Why do you sit out here all alone?" said Alice, not wishing to begin an argument.

"Why, because there's nobody with me!" cried Humpty Dumpty. "Did you think I didn't know the answer to *that*? Ask another."

"Don't you think you'd be safer down on the ground?" Alice went on, not with any idea of making another riddle, but simply in her good-natured anxiety for the queer creature. "That wall is so *very* narrow!"

"What tremendously easy riddles you ask!" Humpty Dumpty growled out. "Of course I don't think so! Why, if ever I *did* fall off—which there's no chance of—but *if* I did—" Here he pursed up his lips, and looked so solemn and grand that Alice could hardly help laughing. "*If* I *did* fall," he went on, "*the King has promised me*—ah, you may turn pale, if you like! You didn't think I was going to say that, did you? *The King has promised me—with his very own mouth—to—to—*"

"To send all his horses and all his men," Alice interrupted, rather unwisely.

"Now I declare that's too bad!" Humpty Dumpty cried, breaking into a sudden passion. "You've been listening at doors—and behind trees—and down chimneys—or you couldn't have known it!"

"I haven't, indeed!" Alice said very gently. "It's in a book."

"Ah, well! They may write such things in a *book*," Humpty Dumpty said in a calmer tone. "That's what you call a History of England, that is. Now, take a good look at me! I'm one that has spoken to a King, *I* am: mayhap you'll never see such another: and, to show you I'm not proud, you may shake hands with me!" And he grinned almost from ear to ear, as he leant forwards (and as nearly as possible fell off the wall in doing so) and offered Alice his hand. She watched him a little anxiously as she took it. "If he smiled much more the ends of his mouth might meet behind," she thought: "and then I don't know *what* would happen to his head! I'm afraid it would come off!"

"Yes, all his horses and all his men," Humpty Dumpty went on. "They'd pick me up again in a minute, *they* would! However, this conversation is going on a little too fast: let's go back to the last remark but one."

"I'm afraid I ca'n't quite remember it," Alice said, very politely.

"In that case we start afresh," said Humpty Dumpty, "and it's my turn to choose a subject—" ("He talks about it just as if it was a game!" thought Alice.) "So here's a question for you. How old did you say you were?"

Alice made a short calculation, and said "Seven years and six months."

"Wrong!" Humpty Dumpty exclaimed triumphantly. "You never said a word like it!"

"I thought you meant 'How old *are* you?'" Alice explained.

"If I'd meant that, I'd have said it," said Humpty Dumpty.

Alice didn't want to begin another argument, so she said nothing.

"Seven years and six months!" Humpty Dumpty repeated thoughtfully. "An uncomfortable sort of age. Now if you'd asked *my* advice, I'd have said 'Leave off at seven'—but it's too late now."

"I never ask advice about growing," Alice said indignantly.

"Too proud?" the other enquired.

Alice felt even more indignant at this suggestion. "I mean," she said, "that one ca'n't help growing older."

"*One* ca'n't, perhaps," said Humpty Dumpty; "but *two* can. With proper assistance, you might have left off at seven."

"What a beautiful belt you've got on!" Alice suddenly remarked. (They had had quite enough of the subject of age, she thought: and, if they really were to take turns in choosing subjects, it was *her* turn now.) "At least," she corrected herself on second thoughts, "a beautiful cravat, I should have said—no, a belt, I mean—I beg your pardon!" she added in dismay, for Humpty Dumpty looked thoroughly offended, and she began to wish she hadn't chosen that subject. "If only I knew," she thought to herself, "which was neck and which was waist!"

Evidently Humpty Dumpty was very angry, though he said nothing for a minute or two. When he *did* speak again, it was in a deep growl.

"It is a —*most*—provoking—thing," he said at last, "when a person doesn't know a cravat from a belt!"

"I know it's very ignorant of me," Alice said, in so humble a tone that Humpty Dumpty relented.

"It's a cravat, child, and a beautiful one, as you say. It's a present from the White King and Queen. There now!"

"Is it really?" said Alice, quite pleased to find that she *had* chosen a good subject, after all.

"They gave it me," Humpty Dumpty continued thoughtfully, as he crossed one knee over the other and clasped his hands round it, "they gave it me—for an un-birthday present."

"I beg your pardon?" Alice said with a puzzled air.

"I'm not offended," said Humpty Dumpty.

"I mean, what *is* an un-birthday present?"

"A present given when it isn't your birthday, of course."

Alice considered a little. "I like birthday presents best," she said at last.

"You don't know what you're talking about!" cried Humpty Dumpty. "How many days are there in a year?"

"Three hundred and sixty-five," said Alice.

"And how many birthdays have you?"

"One."

"And if you take one from three hundred and sixty-five, what remains?"

"Three hundred and sixty-four, of course."

Humpty Dumpty looked doubtful. "I'd rather see that done on paper," he said.

Alice couldn't help smiling as she took out her memorandum-book, and worked the sum for him:

$$\begin{array}{r} 365 \\ \underline{1} \\ 364 \end{array}$$

Humpty Dumpty took the book and looked at it carefully. "That seems to be done right—" he began.

"You're holding it upside down!" Alice interrupted.

"To be sure I was!" Humpty Dumpty said gaily, as she turned it round for him. "I thought it looked a little queer. As I was saying, that *seems* to be done right—though I haven't time to look it over thoroughly just now—and that shows that there are three hundred and sixty-four days when you might get un-birthday presents—"

"Certainly," said Alice.

"And only *one* for birthday presents, you know. There's glory for you!"

"I don't know what you mean by 'glory,' " Alice said.

Humpty Dumpty smiled contemptuously. "Of course you don't—till I tell you. I meant 'there's a nice knock-down argument for you!' "

"But 'glory' doesn't mean 'a nice knock-down argument,' " Alice objected.

"When *I* use a word," Humpty Dumpty said, in rather a scornful tone, "it means just what I choose it to mean—neither more nor less."

"The question is," said Alice, "whether you *can* make words mean so many different things."

"The question is," said Humpty Dumpty, "which is to be master—that's all."

Alice was too much puzzled to say anything; so after a minute Humpty Dumpty began again. "They've a temper, some of them—particularly verbs: they're the proudest—adjectives you can do anything with, but not verbs—however, *I* can manage the whole lot of them! Impenetrability! That's what *I* say!"

"Would you tell me, please," said Alice, "what that means?"

"Now you talk like a reasonable child," said Humpty Dumpty, looking very much pleased. "I meant by 'impenetrability' that we've had enough of that subject, and it would be just as well if you'd mention what you mean to do next, as I suppose you don't mean to stop here all the rest of your life."

"That's a great deal to make one word mean," Alice said in a thoughtful tone.

"When I make a word do a lot of work like that," said Humpty Dumpty, "I always pay it extra."

"Oh!" said Alice. She was too much puzzled to make any other remark.

"Ah, you should see 'em come round me of a Saturday night," Humpty Dumpty went on, wagging his head gravely from side to side, "for to get their wages, you know."

(Alice didn't venture to ask what he paid them with; and so you see I can't tell *you*.)

Part

FOUR

The Dilemmas of Personhood

9

Who Am I?

You have heard your mother tell the story a thousand times. One day, when you were very little, just past your second birthday, your parents went to visit Aunt Helen. You sat in the back seat, apparently asleep. Next to you, your mother had placed a box of cupcakes, Aunt Helen's favorites. Having arrived, your mother went to get you and the cupcakes out of the car. At that point she discovered only you in the back seat, since you had managed in some way to consume every one of the cupcakes. Cooing and gurgling, you peered out from behind a mask of chocolate and crumbs.

Underlying stories such as this one is an assumption that only a philosopher would question seriously, namely, that there is such a thing as personal (or self) identity. Personal identity is what accounts for the fact that we all have childhoods, that once we were small, not very knowledgeable or emotionally complex, whereas now we are grown and full of complex thoughts, feelings and beliefs. Philosophers' attempts to account for our persistence through time and through change fall into roughly three categories. First, there are those who explain personal identity in mentalistic terms. Our identity through time is considered to be a function of the continuity of our thoughts, beliefs, and feelings (sometimes referred to jointly as our "personality" or "character"). Second, there are those who explain personal identity in terms of the continuity of our bodies. Although the body that you have now is larger than the one you had when you were two-years-old, their "spatio-temporal" continuity provides the basis for your identity through time. Finally, some philosophers argue that personal identity is just an illusion. In fact, we don't persist through time and change.

The earliest and most familiar version of the view that personal identity can be explained in mentalistic terms has its origin in the religious belief in the existence of the soul. Although philosophers since Descartes have tended to substitute the term 'mind' for 'soul,' the underlying idea is basically the same: what now makes you the same person as the one who overindulged in cupcakes many years ago is the persistence of your soul. This view has what many people consider the added advantage of allowing for the possibility of continued existence past the death of the body.

In the dialogue by John Perry, Sam Miller is a passionate advocate of what we will call the **Soul Theory**. He finds a formidable opponent, however, in Gretchen Weirob, who insists that her identity is a function of nothing more than the identity of her (live) body. We will call that view the **Body Theory**. Weirob is concerned to persuade Miller not that his belief in the existence of the soul is misguided, but rather that the soul, even if it exists, cannot be responsible for personal identity.

Although the soul has fallen into disrepute as a means for explaining personal identity, philosophers have been reluctant to abandon the spirit of the Soul Theory. That is, many philosophers would like to account for personal identity in terms that acknowledge our special human uniqueness. Our rich mental life distinguishes us from other animals, and we are all psychologically distinct from one another. Surely, then, our self-identity must be intimately tied to our mental characteristics. John Locke is a famous advocate of the view, usually called the **Memory Theory**, that personal identity is based on self-consciousness, in particular, on memories about one's former experiences. Just as you cannot think my thoughts and I cannot think

327

yours, so too, you cannot remember my experiences and I cannot remember yours. This unique relationship that each of us has to his or her former experiences guarantees the link between what are sometimes called "stages" of a person. Suppose that you are now remembering the day you learned to ride a bicycle. Since you *now* are remembering the experience as one that happened to you *then*, you are self-identical to the person who had that experience. One difficulty with the Memory Theory is that we forget many of our experiences. You don't, for example, remember eating the cupcakes when you were two. You probably don't remember what you had for lunch on July 25, 1982, nor what the first word of this chapter is. Locke needs to specify precisely how we are to explain the connection between our present selves and those forgotten stages of our former selves.

Another difficulty with the Memory Theory is that our memories are not always accurate. For example, you swear that you left the sponge in the sink; you remember doing so very clearly. When you later find it in the refrigerator, you realize that you only *seemed* to remember leaving it in the sink. Your memory was merely apparent, not genuine. Similarly, we have all heard of people who believe that they are Abraham Lincoln, Jesus Christ, even Janis Joplin. What seem to them to be real memories cannot be. Yet, if it is only genuine memories that guarantee the link between the stages of a person, we need to determine which memories are the genuine ones. Unfortunately, the most obvious way to distinguish genuine from apparent memories is by pointing out that a genuine memory is a memory of an experience actually had by the rememberer. The person who is having the memory must be the same as the person who had the experience. But in distinguishing genuine from apparent memory in this way we have presupposed the existence of a persisting, self-identical person. We cannot use the concept of memory to explain personal identity if the only way to explain memory is by appealing to the concept of personal identity. As attractive as the Memory Theory might initially seem to be, it leaves us with this discouragingly large problem.

This problem, sometimes referred to as the "problem of circularity," is alluded to in the selection by Meredith Michaels. Much of the contemporary debate over personal identity centers around an attempt to avoid the circularity problem. That is, philosophers want to provide a noncircular way of distinguishing between genuine and apparent memories. The **Brain Theory**, discussed by Michaels, is one such attempt. Basically, the Brain Theory argues that "whither my brain goes, there go I." As you will see, the Brain Theory and its principal rival, the Body Theory, encourage some bizarre speculations about the results of imagined "brain transplants" (alternatively called "body transplants"). Justin Leiber's story provides a glimpse into a future where such practices are an ordinary part of life. Although stories like his appear fanciful, they provoke us to consider just what we think *is* responsible for our identity through time.

Long ago, David Hume came to the conclusion that nothing is responsible for our identity through time because, strictly speaking, it is only a "fiction." If we look inward in the hopes of finding a source of identity, all we find is an array of disconnected and distinct "perceptions" (that is, ideas). Our desire to forge them into a coherent, temporally continuous whole is so strong that we simply invent one and call it a "self." Hume's argument is a masterpiece of philosophical gymnastics, so beware.

The frustrations of trying to explain something so apparently mundane as personal identity grow more and more insurmountable as we are forced to choose among souls, brains, bodies, and, worst of all, fictions. Derek Parfit's solution is to concede that when it comes to persons, there is no strict identity. Rather than take that as reason for despair, he instead argues that it is perfectly understandable. A distant follower of Locke, Parfit points out that in the same way that our memories come in stronger and weaker degrees, our connections to our past selves come in degrees. He calls this the **Complex View** of personal identity and contrasts it with the **Simple View** that identity is an all or nothing affair. According to the Complex View, you may be strongly identical to the past self who yesterday promised to meet Jane for lunch today, but only weakly identical to the self who ate Aunt Helen's cupcakes. In the selection here, Parfit explores some of the moral consequences of the Complex View.

Most theories of personal identity focus on our relationship to our past selves. Alasdair MacIntyre suggests that the tendency of philosophers to ignore our relationship to our future selves creates a lopsided picture of personal identity. He encourages us to see ourselves as characters in a number of ongoing stories, characters whose lives are lived according to a variety of goals or purposes. The form of our lives is determined in part by the goals toward which we are heading. If so, he claims, then the criterion of coherence for persons ought not be identity, but rather unity. Right now, you are a character in the story of college students in late twentieth century America. As a result of being in that story, there are certain characteristics that you have and others that you don't have. The actions that you perform are properly understood only relative to the fact that you currently inhabit the story of college students. Even when you are lying in a daze on the beach, we (and you) can only account for your (in)action by appealing to your fatigue and desire for a break from studying. The unity and coherence of your "self" is thus a function of its place in a story or a set of interlocking stories.

The problem of personal identity is particularly troubling because it appears so clear that we do indeed persist through time. Surely, it is absurd to suppose that the person who began reading this chapter only a few minutes ago no longer exists. Aren't you that very same person? Of course you are. But if it is so obvious that one and the same person is born, lives a life, and eventually dies, why is it so difficult for philosophers to explain personal identity? The problem of personal identity is a paradigm case of the tension between the appeal of ordinary experience and the demands of philosophy.

John Perry

The First Night

John Perry *teaches philosophy at Stanford University. He specializes in philosophy of language and metaphysics. Among his publications are* Situation Semantics (*with John Barwise*) *and* A Dialogue on Personal Identity and Immortality.

*T*his is a record of conversations of Gretchen Weirob, a teacher of philosophy at a small midwestern college, and two of her friends. The conversations took place in her hospital room on the three nights before she died from injuries sustained in a motorcycle accident. Sam Miller is a chaplain and a long-time friend of Weirob's; Dave Cohen is a former student of hers.

COHEN: I can hardly believe what you say, Gretchen. You are lucid and do not appear to be in great pain. And yet you say things are hopeless?

WEIROB: These devices can keep me alive for another day or two at most. Some of my vital organs have been injured beyond anything the doctors know how to repair, apart from certain rather radical measures I have rejected. I am not in much pain. But as I understand it that is not a particularly good sign. My brain was uninjured and I guess that's why I am as lucid as I ever am. The whole situation is a bit depressing, I fear. But here's Sam Miller. Perhaps he will know how to cheer me up.

MILLER: Good evening, Gretchen. Hello, Dave. I guess there's not much point in beating around the bush, Gretchen; the medics tell me you're a goner. Is there anything I can do to help?

WEIROB: Crimenetley, Sam! You deal with the dying every day. Don't you have anything more comforting to say than "Sorry to hear you're a goner"?

MILLER: Well, to tell you the truth, I'm a little at a loss for what to say to you. Most people I deal with are believers like I am. We talk of the prospects for survival. I give assurance that God, who is just and merciful, would not permit such a travesty as that our short life on this earth should be the end of things. But you and I have talked about religious and philosophical issues for years. I have never been able to find in you the least inclination to believe in God; indeed, it's a rare day when you are sure that your friends have minds or that you can see your own hand in front of your face, or that there is any reason to believe that the sun will rise tomorrow. How can I hope to comfort you with the prospect of life after death, when I know you will regard it as having no probability whatsoever?

WEIROB: I would not require so much to be comforted, Sam. Even the possibility of something quite improbable can be comforting, in certain situations. When we used to play tennis, I beat you no more than one time in twenty. But this was enough to establish the possibility of beating you on any given occasion, and by focusing merely on the possibility I remained eager to play. Entombed in a secure prison, thinking our situation quite hopeless, we may find unutterable joy in the information that there is, after all, the slimmest possibility of escape. Hope provides comfort and hope does not always require probability. But we must believe that what we hope for is at least possible. So I will set an easier task for you. Simply persuade me that my survival after the death of this body, is *possible,* and I promise to be comforted. Whether you succeed or not, your attempts will be a diversion, for you know I like to talk philosophy more than anything else.

MILLER: But what is possibility, if not reasonable probability?

WEIROB: I do not mean possible in the sense of likely, or even in the sense of conforming to the known laws of physics or biology. I mean possible only in the weakest sense—of being conceivable, given the unavoidable facts. Within the next couple of days, this body will die. It will be buried and it will rot away. I ask that, given these facts, you explain to me how it even makes *sense* to talk of me continuing to exist. Just explain to me what it is I am to *imagine*, when I imagine surviving, that is consistent with these facts, and I shall be comforted.

MILLER: But then what is there to do? There are many conceptions of immortality, of survival past the grave, which all seem to make good sense. Surely not the possibility, but only the probability, can be doubted. Take your choice! Christians believe in life, with a body, in some Hereafter—the details vary, of course, from sect to sect. There is the Greek idea of the body as a prison, from which we escape at death—so that we have continued life without a body. Then there are conceptions in which, so to speak, we merge with the flow of being—

WEIROB: I must cut short your lesson in comparative religion. Survival means surviving, no more, no less. I have no doubts that I shall merge with being; plants will take root in my remains, and the chemicals that I am will continue to make their contribution to life. I am enough of an ecologist to be comforted. But survival, if it is anything, must offer comforts of a different sort, the comforts of *anticipation*. Survival means that tomorrow, or sometime in the future, there will be someone who will experience, who will see and touch and smell—or at the very least, think and reason and remember. And this person will be *me*. This person will be related to me in such a way that it is correct for me to anticipate, to look forward to, those future experiences. And I am related to her in such a way that it will be right for her to remember what I have thought and done, to feel remorse for what I have done wrong, and pride in what I have done right. And the only relation that supports anticipation and memory in this way, is simply *identity*. For it is never correct to anticipate, as happening to oneself, what will happen to someone else, is it? Or to remember, as one's own thoughts and deeds, what someone else did? So, don't give me merger with being, or some such nonsense. Give me identity, or let's talk about baseball or fishing—but I'm sorry to get so emotional. I react strongly when words which mean one thing are used for another—when one talks about survival, but does not mean to say that the same person will continue to exist. It's such a sham!

MILLER: I'm sorry. I was just trying to stay in touch with the times, if you want to know the truth, for when I read modern theology or talk to my students who have studied Eastern religions, the notion of survival simply as continued existence of the same person seems out of date. Merger with Being! Merger with Being! That's all I hear. My own beliefs are quite simple, if somewhat vague. I think you will live again—with or without a body, I don't know— I draw comfort from my belief that you and I will be together again, after I also die. We will communicate, somehow. We will continue to grow spiritually. That's what I believe, as surely as I believe that I am sitting here. For I don't know how God could be excused, if this small sample of life is all that we are allotted; I don't know why He should have created us, if these few years of toil and torment are the end of it—

WEIROB: Remember our deal, Sam. You don't have to convince me that survival is probable, for we both agree you would not get to first base. You have only to convince me that it is possible. The only condition is that it be real survival we are talking about, not some up-to-date ersatz survival, which simply amounts to what any ordinary person would call totally ceasing to exist.

MILLER: I guess I just miss the problem, then. Of course, it's possible. You just continue to exist, after your body dies. What's to be defended or explained? You want details? Okay. Two people meet a thousand years from now, in a place that may or may not be part of this physical universe. I am one and you are the other. So you must have survived. Surely you can imagine that. What else is there to say?

WEIROB: But in a few days *I* will quit breathing, *I* will be put into a coffin, *I* will be buried. And in a few months or a few years *I* will be reduced to so much humus. That, I take it, is obvious, is given. How then can you say that I am one of these persons a thousand years from now?

Suppose I took this box of Kleenex and lit fire to it. It is reduced to ashes and I smash the ashes and flush them down the john. Then I say to you, go home and on the shelf will be *that very box of Kleenex*. It has survived! Wouldn't that be absurd? What sense could you make of it? And yet that is just what you say to me. I will rot away. And then, a thousand years later, there I will be. What sense does that make?

MILLER: There could be an *identical* box of Kleenex at your home, one just like it in every respect. And, in this sense, there is no difficulty in there being someone identical to you in the Hereafter, though your body has rotted away.

WEIROB: You are playing with words again. There could be an *exactly similar* box of Kleenex on my shelf. We sometimes use "identical" to mean "exactly similar," as when we speak of "identical twins." But I am using "identical" in a way in which *identity* is the condition of memory and correct anticipation. If I am told that tomorrow, though I will be dead, someone else that looks and sounds and thinks just like me will be alive—would that be comforting? Could I correctly *anticipate* having her experiences? Would it make sense for me to fear her pains and look forward to her pleasures? Would it be right for her to feel remorse at the harsh way I am treating you? Of course not. Similarity, however exact, is not identity. I use identity to mean there is but one thing. If I am to survive, there must be one person who lies in this bed now, and who talks to someone in your Hereafter ten or a thousand years from now. After all, what comfort could there be in the notion of a heavenly imposter, walking around getting credit for the few good things I have done?

MILLER: I'm sorry. I see that I was simply confused. Here is what I should have said. If you were merely a live human body—as the Kleenex box is merely cardboard and glue in a certain arrangement—then the death of your body would be the end of you. But surely you are more than that, fundamentally more than that. What is fundamentally you is not your body, but your soul or self or mind.

WEIROB: Do you mean these words, "soul," "self," or "mind" to come to the same thing?

MILLER: Perhaps distinctions could be made, but I shall not pursue them now. I mean the nonphysical and nonmaterial aspects of you, your consciousness. It is this that I get at with these words, and I don't think any further distinction is relevant.

WEIROB: Consciousness? I am conscious, for a while yet. I see, I hear, I think, I remember. But "to be conscious"—that is a verb. What is the subject of the verb, the thing which is conscious? Isn't it just this body, the same object that is overweight, injured, and lying in bed?—and which will be buried and not be conscious in a day or a week at the most?

MILLER: As you are a philosopher, I would expect you to be less muddled about these issues. Did Descartes not draw a clear distinction between the body and the mind, between that which is overweight, and that which is conscious? Your mind or soul is immaterial, lodged in your body while you are on earth. The two are intimately related but not identical. Now clearly, what concerns us in survival is your mind or soul. It is this which must be identical to the person before me now, and to the one I expect to see in a thousand years in heaven.

WEIROB: So I am not really this body, but a soul or mind or spirit? And this soul cannot be seen or felt or touched or smelt? That is implied, I take it, by the fact that it is immaterial?

MILLER: That's right. Your soul sees and smells, but cannot be seen or smelt.

WEIROB: Let me see if I understand you. You would admit that I am the very same person with whom you had lunch last week at Dorsey's?

MILLER: Of course you are.

WEIROB: Now when you say I am the same person, if I understand you, that is not a remark about this body you see and could touch and I fear can smell. Rather it is a remark about a soul, which you cannot see or touch or smell. The fact that the same body that now lies in front of you on the bed was across the table from you at Dorsey's—that would not mean that the same *person* was present on both occasions, if the same soul were not. And if, through some strange turn of events, the same soul were present on both occasions, but lodged in different bodies, then it *would* be the same person. Is that right?

MILLER: You have understood me perfectly. But surely, you understood all of this before!

WEIROB: But wait. I can repeat it, but I'm not sure I understand it. If you cannot see or touch or in any way perceive my soul, what makes you think the one you are confronted with now *is* the very same soul you were confronted with at Dorsey's?

MILLER: But I just explained. To say it is the same soul and to say it is the same person, are the same. And, of course, you are the same person you were before. Who else would you be if not yourself? You *were* Gretchen Weirob, and you *are* Gretchen Weirob.

WEIROB: But how do you know you are talking to Gretchen Weirob at all, and not someone else, say Barbara Walters or even Mark Spitz!

MILLER: Well, it's just obvious. I can see who I am talking to.

WEIROB: But all you can see is my body. You can see, perhaps, that the same body is before you now that was before you last week at Dorsey's. But you have just said that Gretchen Weirob is not a body but a soul. In judging that the same person is before you now as was before you then, you must be making a judgment about souls—which, you said, cannot be seen or touched or smelt or tasted. And so, I repeat, how do you know?

MILLER: Well, I *can* see that it is the same body before me now that was across the table at Dorsey's. And I know that the same soul is connected with the body now that was connected with it before. That's how I know it's you. I see no difficulty in the matter.

WEIROB: You reason on the principle, "Same body, same self."

MILLER: Yes.

WEIROB: And would you reason conversely also? If there were in this bed Barbara Walters' body—that is, the body you see every night on the news—would you infer that it was not me, Gretchen Weirob, in the bed?

MILLER: Of course I would. How would you have come by Barbara Walters' body?

WEIROB: But then merely extend this principle to Heaven, and you will see that your conception of survival is without sense. Surely this very body, which will be buried and as I must so often repeat, *rot away,* will not be in your Hereafter. Different body, different person. Or do you claim that a body can rot away on earth, and then still wind up somewhere else? Must I bring up the Kleenex box again?

MILLER: No, I do not claim that. But I also do not extend a principle, found reliable on earth, to such a different situation as is represented by the Hereafter. That a correlation between bodies and souls has been found on earth does not make it inconceivable or impossible that they should separate. Principles found to work in one circumstance may not be assumed to work in vastly altered circumstances. January and snow go together here, and one would be a fool to expect otherwise. But the principle does not apply in southern California.

WEIROB: So the principle, "same body, same soul," is a well-confirmed regularity, not something you know "a priori."

MILLER: By "a priori" you philosophers mean something which can be known without observing what actually goes on in the world—as I can know that two plus two equals four just by thinking about numbers, and that no bachelors are married, just by thinking about the meaning of "bachelor"?

WEIROB: Yes.

MILLER: Then you are right. If it was part of the meaning of "same body" that wherever we have the same body we have the same soul, it would have to obtain universally, in Heaven as well as on earth. But I just claim it is a generalization we know by observation on earth, and it need not automatically extend to Heaven.

WEIROB: But where do you get this principle? It simply amounts to a correlation between being confronted with the same body and being confronted with the same soul. To establish such a correlation in the first place, surely one must have some *other* means of judging sameness of soul. You do not have such a means; your principle is without foundation; either you really do not know the person before you now is Gretchen Weirob, the very same person you lunched with at Dorsey's, or what you do know has nothing to do with sameness of some immaterial soul.

MILLER: Hold on, hold on. You know I can't follow you when you start spitting out arguments like that. Now what is this terrible fallacy I'm supposed to have committed?

WEIROB: I'm sorry. I get carried away. Here—by way of a peace offering—have one of the chocolates Dave brought.

MILLER: Very tasty. Thank you.

WEIROB: Now why did you choose that one?

MILLER: Because it had a certain swirl on the top which shows that it is a caramel.

WEIROB: That is, a certain sort of swirl is correlated with a certain type of filling—the swirls with caramel, the rosettes with orange, and so forth.

MILLER: Yes. When you put it that way, I see an analogy. Just as I judged that the filling would be the same in this piece as in the last piece that I ate with such a swirl, so I judge that the soul with which I am conversing is the same as the last soul with which I conversed when sitting across from that body. We see the outer wrapping and infer what is inside.

WEIROB: But how did you come to realize that swirls of that sort and caramel insides were so associated?

MILLER: Why, from eating a great many of them over the years. Whenever I bit into a candy with that sort of swirl, it was filled with caramel.

WEIROB: Could you have established the correlation had you never been allowed to bite into a candy and never seen what happened when someone else bit into one? You could have formed the hypothesis, "same swirl, same filling." But could you have ever established it?

MILLER: It seems not.

WEIROB: So your inference, in a particular case, to the identity of filling from the identity of swirl would be groundless?

MILLER: Yes, it would. I think I see what is coming.

WEIROB: I'm sure you do. Since you can never, so to speak, bite into my soul, can never see or touch it, you have no way of testing your hypothesis that sameness of body means sameness of self.

MILLER: I daresay you are right. But now I'm a bit lost. What is supposed to follow from all of this?

WEIROB: If, as you claim, identity of persons consisted in identity of immaterial unobservable souls, then judgments of personal identity of the sort we make every day whenever we greet a friend or avoid a pest are really judgments about such souls.

MILLER: Right.

WEIROB: But if such judgments were really about souls, they would all be groundless and without foundation. For we have no direct method of observing sameness of soul, and so—and this is the point made by the candy example—we can have no indirect method either.

MILLER: That seems fair.

WEIROB: But our judgments about persons are not all simply groundless and silly, so we must not be judging of immaterial souls after all.

MILLER: Your reasoning has some force. But I suspect the problem lies in my defense of my position, and not the position itself. Look here—there *is* a way to test the hypothesis of a correlation after all. When I entered the room, I expected you to react just as you did—argumentatively and skeptically. Had the person with this body reacted completely differently perhaps I would have been forced to conclude it was not you. For example, had she complained about not being able to appear on the six o'clock news, and missing Harry Reasoner, and so forth, I might eventually have been persuaded it was Barbara Walters, and not you. Similarity of psychological characteristics—a person's attitudes, beliefs, memories, prejudices, and the like—is observable. These are correlated with identity of body on the one side, and of course with sameness of soul on the other. So the correlation between body and soul can be established after all by this intermediate link.

WEIROB: And how do you know that?

MILLER: Know what?

WEIROB: That where we have sameness of psychological characteristics, we have sameness of soul.

MILLER: Well, now you are really being just silly. The soul or mind is just that which is responsible for one's character, memory, belief. These are aspects of the mind, just as one's height, weight, and appearance are aspects of the body.

WEIROB: Let me grant for the sake of argument that belief, character, memory, and so forth are states of mind. That is, I suppose, I grant that what one thinks and feels is due to the states one's mind is in at that time. And I shall even grant that a mind is an immaterial thing—though I harbor the gravest doubts that this is so. I do not see how it follows that similarity of such traits requires, or is evidence to the slightest degree, for identity of the mind or soul.

Let me explain my point with an analogy. If we were to walk out of this room, down past the mill and out towards Wilbur, what would we see?

MILLER: We would come to the Blue River, among other things.

WEIROB: And how would you recognize the Blue River? I mean, of course if you left from here, you would scarcely expect to hit the Platte or Niobrara. But suppose you were actually lost, and came across the Blue River in your wandering, just at that point where an old dam partly blocks the flow. Couldn't you recognize it?

MILLER: Yes, I'm sure as soon as I saw that part of the river I would again know where I was.

WEIROB: And how would you recognize it?

MILLER: Well, the turgid brownness of the water, the sluggish flow, the filth washed up on the banks, and such.

WEIROB: In a word, the states of the water which makes up the river at the time you see it.

MILLER: Right.

WEIROB: If you saw blue clean water, with bass jumping, you would know it wasn't the Blue River.

MILLER: Of course.

WEIROB: So you expect, each time you see the Blue, to see the water, which makes it up, in similar states—not always exactly the same, for sometimes it's a little dirtier, but by and large similar.

MILLER: Yes, but what do you intend to make of this?

WEIROB: Each time you see the Blue, it consists of *different* water. The water that was in it a month ago may be in Tuttle Creek Reservoir or in the Mississippi or in the Gulf of Mexico by now. So the *similarity* of states of water, by which you judge the sameness of river, does not require *identity* of the water which is in those states at these various times.

MILLER: And?

WEIROB: And so just because you judge as to personal identity by reference to similarity of states of mind, it does not follow that the mind, or soul, is the same in each case. My point is this. For all you know, the immaterial soul which you think is lodged in my body might change from day to day, from hour to hour, from minute to minute, replaced each time by another soul psychologically similar. You cannot see it or touch it, so how would you know?

MILLER: Are you saying I don't really know who you are?

WEIROB: Not at all. *You* are the one who say personal identity consists in sameness of this immaterial, unobservable, invisible, untouchable soul. I merely point out that *if* it did consist in that, you *would* have no idea who I am. Sameness of body would not necessarily mean sameness of person. Sameness of psychological characteristics would not necessarily mean sameness of person. I am saying that if you do know who I am then you are wrong that personal identity consists in sameness of immaterial soul.

MILLER: I see. But wait. I believe my problem is that I simply forgot a main tenet of my theory. The correlation can be established in my own case. I know that *my* soul and my body are intimately and consistently found together. From this one case I can generalize, at least as concerns life in this world, that sameness of body is a reliable sign of sameness of soul. This leaves me free to regard it as intelligible, in the case of death, that the link between the particular soul and the particular body it has been joined with is broken.

WEIROB: This would be quite an extrapolation, wouldn't it, from one case directly observed, to a couple of billion in which only the body is observed? For I take it that we are in the habit of assuming, for every person now on earth, as well as those who have already come and gone, that the principle "one body, one soul" is in effect.

MILLER: This does not seem an insurmountable obstacle. Since there is nothing special about my case, I assume the arrangement I find in it applies universally until given some reason to believe otherwise. And I never have been.

WEIROB: Let's let that pass. I have another problem that is more serious. How is it that you know in your own case that there is a single soul which has been so consistently connected with your body?

MILLER: Now you really cannot be serious, Gretchen. How can I doubt that I am the same person I was? Is there anything more clear and distinct, less susceptible to doubt? How do you expect me to prove anything to you, when you are capable of denying my own continued existence from second to second? Without knowledge of our own identity, everything we think and do would be senseless. How could I think if I did not suppose that the person who begins my thought is the one who completes it? When I act, do I not assume that the person who forms the intention is the very one who performs the action?

WEIROB: But I grant you that a single *person* has been associated with your body since you were born. The question is whether one immaterial soul has been so associated—or more precisely, whether you are in a position to know it. You believe that a judgment that one and the same person has had your body all these many years is a judgment that one and the same immaterial soul has been lodged in it. I say that such judgments concerning the soul are totally mysterious, and that if our knowledge of sameness of persons consisted in knowledge of sameness of immaterial soul, it too would be totally mysterious. To point out, as you do, that it is not mysterious, but perhaps the most secure knowledge we have, the foundation of all reason and action, is simply to make the point that it cannot consist of knowledge of identity of an immaterial soul.

MILLER: You have simply asserted, and not established, that my judgment that a single soul has been lodged in my body these many years is mysterious.

WEIROB: Well, consider these possibilities. One is that a single soul, one and the same, has been with this body I call mine since it was born. The other is that one soul was associated with it until five years ago and then another, psychologically similar, inheriting all the old memories and beliefs, took over. A third hypothesis is that every five years a new soul takes over. A fourth is that every five minutes a new soul takes over. The most radical is that there is a constant flow of souls through this body, each psychologically similar to the preceding, as there is a constant flow of water molecules down the Blue. What evidence do I have that the first hypothesis, the "single soul hypothesis" is true, and not one of the others? Because I am the same person I was five minutes or five years ago? But the issue in question is simply whether from sameness of person, which isn't in doubt, we can infer sameness of soul. Sameness of body? But how do I establish a stable relationship between soul and body? Sameness of thoughts and sensations? But they are in constant flux. By the nature of the case, if the soul cannot be observed, it cannot be observed to be the same. Indeed, no sense has ever been assigned to the phrase "same soul." Nor could any sense be attached to it! One would have to say what a single soul looked like or felt like, how an encounter with a single soul at different times differed from encounters with different souls. But this can hardly be done, since a soul according to your conception doesn't look or feel like *anything* at all. And so of course "souls" can afford no principle of identity. And so they cannot be used to bridge the gulf between my existence now and my existence in the hereafter.

MILLER: Do you doubt the existence of your own soul?

WEIROB: I haven't based my argument on there being no immaterial souls of the sort you describe, but merely on their total irrelevance to questions of personal identity, and so to questions of personal survival. I do indeed harbor grave doubts whether there are any immaterial souls of the sort to which you appeal. Can we have a notion of a soul unless we have a notion of the *same* soul? But I hope you do not think that means I doubt my own existence. I think I lie here, overweight and conscious. I think you can see me, not just some outer wrapping, for I think I am just a live human body. But that is not the basis of my argument. I give you these souls. I merely observe that they can by their nature provide no principle of personal identity.

MILLER: I admit I have no answer.

I'm afraid I do not comfort you, though I have perhaps provided you with some entertainment. Emerson said that a little philosophy turns one away from religion, but that deeper understanding brings one back. I know no one who has thought so long and hard about philosophy as you have. Will it never lead you back to a religious frame of mind?

WEIROB: My former husband used to say that a little philosophy turns one away from religion, and more philosophy makes one a pain in the neck. Perhaps he was closer to the truth than Emerson.

MILLER: Perhaps he was. But perhaps by tomorrow night I will have come up with a better argument.

WEIROB: I hope I live to hear it.

John Locke
Of Identity and Diversity

John Locke (1632–1704) *taught philosophy at Oxford until he earned his medical degree. He devoted considerable time to politics and his two* Treatises on Government *were highly influential in establishing the theoretical grounds of the U.S. Constitution. Not only is he the founder of modern political liberalism, his* Essay Concerning Human Understanding *initiated what has come to be known as British empiricism.*

*P*ersonal identity.—To find wherein personal identity consists, we must consider what "person" stands for; which I think, is a thinking intelligent being, that has reason and reflection, and can consider itself as itself, the same thinking thing, in different times and places; which it does only by that consciousness which is inseparable from thinking, and it seems to me essential to it: it being impossible for any one to perceive, without perceiving that he does perceive. When we see, hear, smell, taste, feel, meditate, or will any thing, we know that we do so. Thus it is always as to our present sensations and perceptions: and by this every one is to himself that which he calls "self"; it not being considered, in this case, whether the same self be continued in the same or diverse substances. For since consciousness always accompanies thinking, and it is that that makes every one to be what he calls "self," and thereby distinguishes himself from all other thinking things; in this alone consists personal identity, *i. e.,* the sameness of a rational being: and as far as this consciousness can be extended backwards to any past action or thought, so far reaches the identity of that person; it is the same self now it was then; and it is by the same self with this present one that now reflects on it, that that action was done.

Consciousness makes personal identity.—But it is farther inquired, whether it be the same identical substance? This, few would think they had reason to doubt of, if these perceptions, with their consciousness, always remained present in the mind, whereby the same thinking thing would be always consciously present, and, as would be thought, evidently the same to itself. But that which seems to make the difficulty is this, that this consciousness being interrupted always by forgetfulness, there being no moment of our lives wherein we have the whole train of all our past actions before our eyes in one view: but even the best memories losing the sight of one part whilst they are viewing another; and we sometimes, and that the greatest part of our lives, not reflecting on our past selves, being intent on our present thoughts, and, in sound sleep, having no thoughts at all, or at least, none with that consciousness which remarks our waking thoughts: I say, in all these cases, our consciousness being interrupted, and we losing the sight of our past selves, doubts are raised whether we are the same thinking thing, *i. e.,* the same substance, or no? which, however reasonable or unreasonable, concerns not personal identity at all: the question being, what makes the same person? and not, whether it be the same identical substance which always thinks in the same person? which in this case matters not at all; different substances, by the same consciousness (where they do partake in it), being united into one person, as well as different bodies by the same life are united into one animal, whose identity is preserved, in that change of substance, by the unity of one continued life. For it being the same consciousness that makes a man be himself to himself, personal identity depends on that only, whether it be annexed solely to one individual substance, or can be continued in a succession of several substances. For as far as any intelligent being can repeat the idea of any past action with the same consciousness it had of it at first, and with the same consciousness it has of any present action; so far it is the same personal self. For it is by the consciousness it has of its present thoughts and actions that it is self to itself now, and so will be the same self, as far as the same consciousness can extend to actions past or to come; and would be by distance of time, or change of substance, no more two persons than a man be two men, by wearing other clothes to-day than he did yesterday, with a long or short sleep between: the same consciousness uniting those distant actions into the same person, whatever substance contributed to their production.

Personal identity in change of substances.—That this is so, we have some kind of evidence in our very bodies, all whose particles—whilst vitally united to this same thinking conscious self, so that we feel when they are touched, and are affected by and conscious of good or harm that happens to them—are a part of ourselves; *i. e.,* of our thinking conscious self. Thus the limbs of his body is to every one a part of himself: he sympathises and is concerned for them. Cut off an hand and thereby separate it from that consciousness he had of its heat, cold, and other affections, and it is then no longer a part of that which is himself, any more than the remotest part of matter. Thus we see the substance, whereof personal self consisted at one time, may be varied at another, without the change of personal identity; there being no question about the same person, though the limbs, which but now were a part of it, be cut off.

Whether in the change of thinking substances.—But the question is, Whether, if the same substance which thinks be changed, it can be the same person, or remaining the same, it can be different persons?

And to this I answer, First, This can be no question at all to those who place thought in a purely material, animal constitution, void of an immaterial substance. For, whether their supposition be true or no, it is plain they conceive personal identity preserved in something else than identity of substance; as animal identity is preserved in identity of life, and not of substance. And therefore those who place thinking in an immaterial substance only, before they can come to deal with these men, must show why personal identity cannot be preserved in the change of immaterial substances, or variety of particular immaterial substances, as well as animal identity is preserved in the change of material substances, or variety of particular bodies: unless they will say, it is one immaterial spirit that makes the same life in brutes, as it is one immaterial spirit that makes the same person in men, which the Cartesians at least will not admit, for fear of making brutes thinking things too.

But next, as to the first part of the question, Whether, if the same thinking substance (supposing immaterial substances only to think) be changed, it can be the same person? I answer, That cannot be resolved but by those who know what kind of substances they are that do think, and whether the consciousness of past actions can be transferred from one thinking substance to another. I grant, were the same consciousness the same individual action, it could not; but it being but a present representation of a past action, why it may not be possible that *that* may be represented to the mind to have been *which* really never was, will remain to be shown. And therefore how far the consciousness of past actions is annexed to any individual agent, so that another cannot possibly have it, will be hard for us to determine, till we know what kind of action it is that cannot be done without a reflex act of perception accompanying it, and how performed by thinking substances who cannot think without being conscious of it. But that which we call "the same consciousness" not being the same individual act, why one intellectual substance may not have represented to it as done by itself what it never did, and was perhaps done by some other agent; why, I say, such a representation may not possibly be without reality of matter of fact, as well as several representations in dreams are, which yet, whilst dreaming, we take for true, will be difficult to conclude from the nature of things. And that it never is so, will by us (till we have clearer views of the nature of thinking substances) be best resolved into the goodness of God, who, as far as the happiness or misery of any of his sensible creatures is concerned in it, will not by a fatal error of theirs transfer from one to another that consciousness which draws reward or punishment with it. How far this may be an argument against those who would place thinking in a system of fleeting animal spirits, I leave to be considered. But yet, to return to the question before us, it must be allowed, that if the same consciousness (which, as has been shown, is quite a different thing from the same numerical figure or motion in body) can be transferred from one thinking substance to another, it will be possible that two thinking substances may make but one person. For the same consciousness being preserved, whether in the same or different substances, the personal identity is preserved.

As to the second part of the question, Whether, the same immaterial substance remaining, there may be two distinct persons? Which question seems to me to be built on this, Whether the same immaterial being, being conscious of the action of its past duration, may be wholly stripped of all the consciousness of its past existence, and lose it beyond the power of ever retrieving it again; and so, as it were, beginning a new account from a new period, have a consciousness that cannot reach beyond this new state? All those who hold pre-

existence are evidently of this mind, since they allow the soul to have no remaining consciousness of what it did in that pre-existent state, either wholly separate from body, or
informing any other body; and if they should not, it is plain experience would be against
them. So that personal identity reaching no farther than consciousness reaches, a pre-existent
spirit not having continued so many ages in a state of silence, must needs make different
persons. Suppose a Christian, Platonist, or a Pythagorean, should, upon God's having ended
all his works of creation the seventh day, think his soul hath existed ever since; and should
imagine it has revolved in several human bodies, as I once met with one who was persuaded
his had been the soul of Socrates: (how reasonably I will not dispute: this I know, that in the
post he filled, which was no inconsiderable one, he passed for a very rational man; and the
press has shown that he wanted not parts or learning:) would any one say, that he, being not
conscious of any of Socrates's actions or thoughts, could be the same person with Socrates?
Let any one reflect upon himself, and conclude, that he has in himself an immaterial spirit,
which is that which thinks in him, and in the constant change of his body keeps him the
same; and is that which he calls himself: let him also suppose it to be the same soul that was
in Nestor or Thersites, at the siege of Troy, (for souls being, as far as we know any thing of
them, in their nature indifferent to any parcel of matter, the supposition has no apparent
absurdity in it), which it may have been as well as it is now the soul of any other man: but
he now having no consciousness of any of the actions either of Nestor or Thersites, does or
can he conceive himself the same person with either of them? Can he be concerned in either
of their actions? attribute them to himself, or think them his own, more than the actions of
any other man that ever existed? So that this consciousness not reaching to any of the actions
of either of those men, he is no more one self with either of them, than if the soul or immaterial
spirit that now informs him had been created and began to exist when it began to inform his
present body, though it were never so true that the same spirit that informed Nestor's or
Thersites's body were numerically the same that now informs his. For this would no more
make him the same person with Nestor, than if some of the particles of matter that were once
a part of Nestor were now a part of this man; the same immaterial substance, without the
same consciousness, no more making the same person by being united to any body, than the
same particle of matter, without consciousness, united to any body, makes the same person.
But let him once find himself conscious of any of the actions of Nestor, he then finds himself
the same person with Nestor.

And thus we may be able, without any difficulty, to conceive the same person at the
resurrection, though in a body not exactly in make or parts the same which he had here,
the same consciousness going along with the soul that inhabits it. But yet the soul alone, in the
change of bodies, would scarce to any one, but to him that makes the soul the man, be enough
to make the same man. For, should the soul of a prince, carrying with it the consciousness
of the prince's past life, enter and inform the body of a cobbler, as soon as deserted by his
own soul, every one sees he would be the same person with the prince, accountable only for
the prince's actions: but who would say it was the same man? The body too goes to the
making of the man, and would, I guess, to every body determine the man in this case, wherein
the soul, with all its princely thoughts about it, would not make another man; but he would
be the same cobbler to every one besides himself. I know that, in the ordinary way of speaking,
the same person and the same man stand for one and the same thing. And, indeed, every one
will always have a liberty to speak as he pleases, and to apply what articulate sounds to what
ideas he thinks fit, and change them as often as he pleases. But yet, when we will inquire
what makes the same spirit, man, or person, we must fix the ideas of spirit, man, or person
in our minds; and having resolved with ourselves what we mean by them, it will not be hard
to determine in either of them, or the like, when it is the same and when not.

Consciousness makes the same person.—But though the same immaterial substance or soul does not alone, wherever it be, and in whatsoever state, make the same man; yet it is plain, consciousness, as far as ever it can be extended, should it be to ages past, unites existences and actions, very remote in time, into the same person, as well as it does the existences and actions of the immediately preceding moment: so that whatever has the consciousness of present and past actions is the same person to whom they both belong. Had I the same consciousness that I saw the ark and Noah's flood, as that I saw an overflowing of the Thames last winter, or as that I write now, I could no more doubt that I who write this now, that saw the Thames overflowed last winter, and that viewed the flood at the general deluge, was the same self, place that self in what substance you please, than that I who write this am the same myself now whilst I write (whether I consist of all the same substance, material or immaterial, or no) that I was yesterday. For, as to this point of being the same self, it matters not whether this present self be made up of the same or other substances, I being as much concerned and as justly accountable for any action was done a thousand years since, appropriated to me now by this self-consciousness, as I am for what I did the last moment.

Self depends on consciousness.—Self is that conscious thinking thing (whatever substance made up of, whether spiritual or material, simple or compounded, it matters not) which is sensible or conscious of pleasure and pain, capable of happiness or misery, and so is concerned for itself, as far as that consciousness extends. Thus every one finds, that whilst comprehended under that consciousness, the little finger is as much a part of himself as what is most so. Upon separation of this little finger, should this consciousness go along with the little finger, and leave the rest of the body, it is evident the little finger would be the person, the same person; and self then would have nothing to do with the rest of the body. As in this case it is the consciousness that goes along with the substance, when one part is separate from another, which makes the same person, and constitutes this inseparable self, so it is in reference to substances remote in time. That with which the consciousness of this present thinking thing can join itself makes the same person, and is one self with it, and with nothing else; and so attributes to itself and owns all the actions of that thing as its own, as far as that consciousness reaches, and no farther; as every one who reflects will perceive. . . .

This may show us wherein personal identity consists, not in the identity of substance, but, as I have said, in the identity of consciousness; wherein if Socrates and the present mayor of Queinborough agree, they are the same person. If the same Socrates waking and sleeping do not partake of the same consciousness, Socrates waking and sleeping is not the same person; and to punish Socrates waking for what sleeping Socrates thought, and waking Socrates was never conscious of, would be no more of right than to punish one twin for what his brother-twin did, whereof he knew nothing, because their outsides were so like that they could not be distinguished; for such twins have been seen.

Meredith W. Michaels

Persons, Brains, and Bodies

Meredith W. Michaels *teaches philosophy at Hampshire College. Most of her work focuses on issues in feminist ethics, metaphysics, and epistemology.*

One night, after a serious bout with the library, you and your best friend Wanda Bagg (or Walter, if you prefer) decide to indulge yourselves at the College Haven. Before you can stop her, Wanda steps out in front of a steamroller that happens to be moving down Main Street. Wanda is crushed. Witnessing the horror of the accident, you have a stroke. Fortunately, Dr. Hagendaas, the famous neurosurgeon who has been visiting the campus, is also on the way to the College Haven. Taking charge, he rushes you and Wanda to the Health Center, where he performs a "body transplant." He takes Wanda's brain, which miraculously escaped the impact of the steamroller, and puts it in the place of yours, which was, of course, severely damaged by the stroke. After several days, the following battle ensues. Wanda's parents claim that they are under no obligation to continue paying tuition. After all, Wanda was killed by a steamroller. Your parents claim that they are under no obligation to continue paying tuition. After all, you died of a stroke. It is clear, then, that a basic question is in need of an answer, who is the person lying in bed in the Health Center? Is it Wanda? Is it you? Is it someone else altogether? For the sake of discussion, let us call the person lying in the bed Schwanda. What reasons do we have for believing that Schwanda is Wanda? Given that one's self-consciousness, one's thoughts, beliefs and feelings are all mental phenomena, we might naturally conclude that a person goes wherever her brain goes (on the assumption that our mental characteristics are more likely "located" in the brain than in, say, our smallest left toe). Schwanda will remember having set off for the College Haven with you; she will remember receiving the college acceptance letter addressed, "Dear Wanda, We are happy to inform you that . . ."; she'll remember being hugged by Wanda's mother on the afternoon of her first day of school. That is, Schwanda will *believe* that she's Wanda.

Nevertheless, the fact that Schwanda believes herself to be Wanda does not in itself guarantee that she is. Do we have any basis for insisting that Schwanda is Wanda and not someone who is *deluded* into thinking that she's Wanda? How can we determine whether Schwanda's Wanda memories are genuine and not merely apparent? As we came to realize in our discussion of Locke's Memory Theory, it is not legitimate at this point to appeal to the self-identity of Schwanda and Wanda, since that is precisely what we're trying to determine. In other words, in attempting to establish that Schwanda's Wanda memories are genuine memories, we cannot argue that they are genuine on the grounds that Schwanda *is* Wanda.

Perhaps it is possible to stop short of circularity. Why couldn't we say that Schwanda's Wanda memories are genuine because the *brain* that is remembering is the same as the brain that had the original experiences. Thus, the experiences are preserved in the very organ that underwent them. Though there is an initial plausibility to this response, it fails to solve our problem. Suppose that Schwanda is Wanda—remembering the experience of learning to ride a bicycle. Though the brain in question is indeed the same, it is nonetheless clear to all of us that brains alone do not learn to ride bicycles. Nor, indeed, do brains alone remember having done so. *People* learn to ride bicycles and *people* remember having done so. And the question we are trying to answer is whether Schwanda (who is remembering) is the same person as Wanda (who did the bicycling). The appeal to the fact that the same brain is involved in each event does not provide us with a way out of the Lockean circle.

It is at this point that philosophers begin to reconsider the Aristotelian position . . . that self-identity is essentially *bodily* identity. If the Body Theory of Personal Identity is true, then the person lying in bed at the Health Center is you, deluded into believing that you are Wanda. That is, Schwanda is self-identical to you.

You might wonder, at this point, whether there are any positive reasons for endorsing the Body Theory, or whether it is simply a place to which one retreats only in defeat? The following case is designed to persuade you that there is at least *some* plausibility to the Body Theory. Suppose that an evil scientist, Dr. Nefarious, has selected you as his prime subject for a horrible experiment. You are dragged into his office. He says, "Tomorrow at 5:00, you will be subjected to the most terrible tortures. Your nails will be pulled out one by one. Rats will be caged round your head. Burning oil will drip slowly on your back. The remainder I leave as a surprise."

Are you worried about what will happen to you at 5:00 tomorrow? If you have any sense, you are. You think of the excruciating pain and suffering you will undergo and would surely do just about anything to avoid it.

But now, Dr. Nefarious says, "Tomorrow at 4:55, I will use my Dememorizer to erase your memory of this conversation." Are you still anxious about what is going to happen to you tomorrow at 5:00? Surely you are. After all the fact that you won't, between 4:55 and 5:00, be anticipating your torture doesn't entail that the torture itself will be any less painful. When you forget that your Calculus professor told the class there would be a test on Friday, you aren't thereby spared the experience of taking the test (in fact, in that case the experience is made worse by your not having had the opportunity to anticipate it).

Now, Dr. Nefarious says, "Tomorrow at 4:57, I will use my Dememorizer to erase *all* of your memories." Are you still anxious about what will happen tomorrow at 5:00? Isn't it natural to describe the situation as one in which you will undergo horrible torture, though you won't know who you are or why this is happening to you? *You* will still experience *your* fingernails being pulled out, *your* back being burned, *your* face being eaten up by rats. Surely, those experiences are ones you would like to avoid.

Finally, Dr. Nefarious says to you, "Tomorrow at 4:58, I am going to use my Rememorizer to implant in your brain all of Ronald Reagan's memories." Though this may not please you for personal or political reasons, the relevant question remains this: are you still worried about what is going to happen tomorrow at 5:00? Isn't it again perfectly natural to describe the situation as one in which you will undergo horrible torture, all the while believing that you are Ronald Reagan. Do you not *now* remain concerned that *you* will experience excruciating pain and intolerable suffering? Look at your fingernails while you consider your answer to this question.

What this story demonstrates is not the conclusive superiority of the Body Theory over the Memory (or Brain) Theory, but rather the importance of our bodies to our self-identity. This is something that tends to get lost in the traditional conceptions of personal identity. Furthermore, returning to the case of Schwanda, we can now see that it is not altogether preposterous to argue that Schwanda is indeed you, deluded into believing that she is Wanda. In other words, anyone who wishes to dismiss that possibility must also dismiss the possibility that the person who undergoes the torture is indeed you, deluded into believing that you are Ronald Reagan.

While it is true that we tend to identify ourselves with and by our thoughts, beliefs, inclinations and feelings, our discussion of the Body Theory should remind us that there are reasons for believing that our bodies are, at the very least, important to who we are. Some philosophers would argue that our bodies *are* who we are, that self-identity is bodily identity.

In considering these admittedly fanciful problem cases, we have seen that we lack a concept of self-identity that allows us to predict when we would or wouldn't persist through time. This might suggest to us that our concept of self-identity is not an all-or-nothing one, that, in fact, our concept is one which admits of degrees. If so, we are no longer talking about identity *per se,* which is an all-or-nothing concept, but rather about some other relation of psychological and physical connectedness. Nevertheless, we can now see first, that the answer to the question "Who ought to pay Schwanda's tuition?" will depend upon which theory of personal identity we are inclined to endorse and second, that the answer may not be as clear and unequivocal as we would like it to be.

Justin Leiber

How to Build a Person

Justin Leiber, *a professor of philosophy at the University of Houston, also writes science fiction. This selection is from his novel* Beyond Rejection.

Worms began his spiel: "People often think that it ought to be simple enough to just *manufacture* an adult human body, like building a house or a helicopter. You'd think that, well, we know what chemicals are involved, and how they go together, how they form cells according to DNA templates, and how the cells form organ systems regulated by chemical messengers, hormones, and the like. So we ought to be able to build a fully functional human body right up from scratch."

Worms moved so that he blocked their view of the jogger. He brought his drained coffee cup down for emphasis.

"And, of course, we could build a human body up from scratch, theoretically, anyhow. But no one ever has. In fact, no one has ever even started to. De Reinzie manufactured the first fully functional human cell—muscle tissue—in the middle of the last century, about 2062 or so. And shortly after that the major varieties were cooked up. And even then it wasn't really manufactured from scratch. De Reinzie, like all the rest, built some basic DNA templates from actual carbon, oxygen, hydrogen, and so on, or rather from simple sugars and alcohols. *But then he grew the rest from these.* That's growth, not manufacture. And nobody's come closer to building an organ than a lab that made a millimeter of stomach wall for several million credits a couple of decades ago.

"I don't want to bother you with the mathematics," he continued, looking away from Terry. "But my old professor at Tech used to estimate that it would take all the scientific and manufacturing talent of Earth and the rest of the Federation something like fifty years and a googol credits to build a single human hand.

"You can imagine what it would take to make something like that," he said, moving out of their line of vision and gesturing at the jogging figure. He took the clipboard that hung next to the treadmill's controls and scanned the sheets on it.

"This body had been blank for three years. It has a running-time age of thirty-one years, though of course Sally Cadmus—that's the person involved—was born over thirty-four years ago. What with demand, of course, three years is a long time for a body to remain out of action. She's in good health, fine musculature for a spacer—says Sally was an asteroid miner here. Seems the body spent two years frozen in a Holmann orbit. We've had it for four months and we're preparing it now. You might see her walking around any day now.

"But Sally Cadmus won't. Her last tape was just the obligatory one made on reaching majority and she left no instructions for implantation. I trust, people, that all your tapes are updated." He gave them the family doctor look and went on, moving closer and dropping his voice.

"I have my mind taped every six months, just to be safe. After all, the tape is *you*—your individual software, or program, including memory store. Everything that makes you *you*." He walked up to the aide who had brought the beautiful young man.

"You—for instance—Ms. Pedersen, when did you have your last tape job?"

The aide, a gaunt red-haired woman in her mid-thirties, snatched her arm from around her young man and glared at Austin Worms.

"What business—"

"Oh, I wouldn't really expect you to say in front of other people." He grinned at the others as Pedersen subsided. "But that's the whole point, you see. Maybe she has been renewing her tape yearly, which is what our profession recommends as an absolute minimum. But a lot of people neglect this elementary precaution because they are so appalled by the thought of severe bodily injury. They just let things slide. And because the topic is so personal, no one knows, no one asks, no one reminds them until the once-in-half-a-million accident happens—truly irreparable body damage or total destruction.

"And then you find that the person hasn't taped for twenty years. Which means . . . ."

He surveyed the group to let it sink in. Then he saw the beautiful girl-child. Terry had been hiding her, no doubt. A classic blond-haired, blue-eyed girl in her midteens. She was looking straight into his eyes. Or *through* them. Something . . . He went on.

"Which means if he or she is lucky and there's estate money, you've got someone who has to face all the ordinary problems of rejection that come in trying to match a young mind with what is almost certain to be a middle-aged body. But also the implant has all those problems multiplied by another. The implant has to deal with a world that is *twenty years in the future.* And a 'career' that is meaningless because he lacks the memory and skills that his old mind picked up over that twenty years.

"More likely, you'll get the real blowout. You'll get massive rejection, psychosis and premature essential senility, and death. Real, final mind death."

"But you would still have the person's tape, their software, as you call it," said Ms. Pedersen. "Couldn't you just try again, with another blank body?" She still had her hands off her young man.

"Two problems. First"—he stuck his index finger in the air—"you got to realize how very difficult it is for a mind and a body to make a match, even with all the help us somaticians and psycheticians can provide, the best that modern biopsychological engineering can put together. Even with a really creative harmonizer to get in there and make the structure jell. Being reborn is very hard work indeed.

"And the failure rate under ordinary circumstances—tapes up-to-date, good stable mind, decent recipient body—is about twenty percent. And we know that it jumps to ninety-five percent if there's a second time around. It's nearly that bad the first time if you got someone whose tapes are twenty years out of date. The person may get through the first few days all right but he can't pull himself into reality. Everything he knows was lost twenty years ago. No friends, no career, everything out of shape. Then the mind will reject its new body just as it rejects the new world it has woken up to. So you don't have much of a chance. Unless, of course, you're the rare nympher or still rarer leaper.

"Second, the Government underwrites the cost of the first implantation. Of course, they don't pay for a fancy body—a nympher body, that is. You'd pay more than two million credits for one of those beauties. You get what's available and you are lucky if you get it within a year or two. What the Government underwrites is the basic operation and tuning job. That alone costs one and a half million or so. Enough to pay my salary for a hundred years. Enough to send the half-dozen or so of you on the Cunard Line Uranium Jubilee All-Planets Tour in first class."

Austin had been moving over to the treadmill control console while speaking. As he finished, his audience noticed a large structure descending from the ceiling just over the jogging figure, Sally Cadmus's body. It looked like a cross between the upper half of a large mummy and a comfortably stuffed armchair. Austin glided over to the treadmill. The audience watched the structure open like an ancient iron maiden. Some noticed that the jogging figure was slowing down.

Austin arrived just in time to complete a flurry of adjustments on the jogger's control package before the structure folded itself around. Two practiced blows on the back of the jogger's thighs brought the legs out of contact with the slowing treadmill.

"It's a lucky thing that implantation is so risky and the sort of accident that calls for it so rare," he said as the structure ascended behind him. "Otherwise, the Kellog-Murphy Law, which underwrites the first implantation, would bankrupt the Government."

"Where is the body going?" asked the blond-haired youngster. Austin could see now that she was probably no more than ten or eleven years old. Something about her posture had made him think she was older.

"Normally it would go into a kind of artificial hibernation—low temperature and vital activity. But this body will be implanted tomorrow, so we'll keep it a normal level of biological function." He had given the body an additional four cc.'s of glucose-saline plasma beyond the program. That was to compensate for the extra jogging. He hadn't done the official calculations. It wasn't that such mathematics was more than a minor chore. If you had asked him to explain, he would have said that the official calculation would have called for half again as much plasma. But he sensed that the body got more than usual from every cc. of water, from every molecule of sugar. Perhaps it was something in the sweat smell, the color and feel of the skin, the resilience of the musculature. But Austin knew.

The somatic aides would have said that Austin Worms was the best ghoul in the Solar System, a zombie's best friend. And they would have meant what they said even if they went on to joke.

Austin had vomited for the first and only time in his life when he learned the origin of the slang terms "ghoul" and "vampire."

The sounds of Terry's tour group faded as they moved up the hall to the psychetician laboratory. But Austin did not return to Bruhler's *The Central Equations of the Abstract Theory of Mind*. He had been puzzled by what the eleven-year-old blond girl had said to him before sauntering off to catch up with the rest of the tour. She had said, "I bet that mind is gonna be in for a real shock when it wakes up with that thing on its backside." He wondered how she could know that it wasn't just part of the crazy-quilt system of tubes and wires that the jogger had on her back.

"I'm Candy Darling," she had added as she left the room. Now he knew who she was. You never knew what to expect in a harmonizer.

*   *   *

Psycheticians take care of minds. That's why they are sometimes called vampires. Somaticians are called ghouls because they take care of bodies.
—I. F. + S. C. Operation Logbook, Append. II, Press Releases

Germaine Means grinned wolfishly at them. "I am a psychetician. What Terry would call a vampire. Call me Germaine if that does not appeal."

They were seated facing a blackboard at one end of a large room which was otherwise filled with data cabinets, office cubicles, and computer consoles. The woman who addressed them wore severe and plain overalls. When she had first come to the Norbert Wiener Research Hospital—NWRH—the director had suggested that the chief psychetician might dress more suitably. That director had retired early.

"As you know from what Austin Worms told you, we think of the individual human mind as an abstract pattern of memory, skill, and experience that has been impressed on the physical hardware of the brain. Think of it this way: when you get a computer factory-fresh, it is like a blanked human brain. The computer has no subroutines, just as the brain has no skills. The computer has no data arrays to call on, just as the blanked brain has no memories.

"What we do here is try to implant the pattern of memory, skill, and experience that is all that is left of a person into a blanked brain. It is not easy because brains are not manufactured. You have to grow them. And a unique personality has to be part of this growth and development. So each brain is different. So no software mind fits any hardware brain perfectly. Except the brain that it grew up with.

"For instance," Germaine Means continued, softening her tone so she would not alert Ms. Pedersen's boyfriend, who was dozing in a well-padded chair, his elegant legs thrust straight out in full display, tights to sandals. "For instance, when pressure is applied to this person's foot, his brain knows how to interpret the nervous impulses from his foot." She suited her action to her words.

"His yelp indicates that his brain recognizes that considerable pressure has been applied to the toes of his left foot. If, however, we implanted another mind, it would not interpret the nervous impulses correctly—it might feel the impulses as a stomachache."

The young man was on his feet, bristling. He moved toward Germaine, who had turned away to pick up what looked like a pair of goggles with some mirrors and gears on top. As he reached her, she turned to face him and pushed the goggles into his hands.

"Yes, thank you for volunteering. Put them on." Not knowing what else to do, he did.

"I want you to look at that blond-haired girl who just sat down over there." She held his arm lightly as he turned and his balance wavered. He appeared to be looking through the goggles at a point several degrees to the right of Candy Darling.

"Now I want you to point at her with your right hand—quick!" The young man's arm shot out, the finger also pointing several degrees to the right of the girl. He began moving his finger to the left, but Germaine pulled his hand down to his side, outside the field of vision that the goggles allowed him.

"Try it again, quick," she said. This time the finger was not as far off. On the fifth try his finger pointed directly to Candy Darling, though he continued to look to her right.

"Now off with the goggles. Look at her again. Point quick!" Germaine grabbed his hand the instant he pointed. Though he was not looking directly at Candy Darling, he was pointing several degrees *to the left* of her. He looked baffled.

Germaine Means chalked a head and goggles on the blackboard, seen as if you were looking down at them from the ceiling. She drew another head to the left of the line of sight of the goggled head and chalked "15°" in to indicate the angle.

"What happened is a simple example of tuning. The prisms in the goggles bend the light so that when his eyes told him he was looking straight at her, his eyes were in fact pointed fifteen degrees to her right. The muscles and nerves of his hand were tuned to point where his eyes were actually pointed—so he pointed fifteen degrees to the right.

"But then his eyes saw his hand going off to the right, so he began to compensate. In a couple of minutes—five tries—his motor coordination compensates so that he points to where his eyes tell him she is—he adjusted to pointing fifteen degrees *to the left* from usual. When I took the goggles off, his arm was still tuned to compensate, so he pointed off to the left until he readjusted."

She picked up the goggles. "Now, a human can adjust to that distortion in a few minutes. But I could calibrate these so that they would turn the whole room upside down. If you then walked around and tried to do things, you would find it difficult. Very difficult. But if you kept the goggles on, the whole room would turn right side up after a day or two. Everything would seem normal because your system would have retuned itself.

"What do you think will happen if you then take the goggles off?"

Candy Darling giggled. Ms. Pedersen said, "Oh, I see. Your mind would have adjusted to turning the, ah, messages from your eyes upside down, so when you took the goggles off—"

"Precisely," said Germaine, "everything would look upside down to you until you readjusted to having the goggles off—and it happens the same way. You stumble around for a day or so and then everything snaps right side up again. And the stumbling-around part is important. If you are confined to a chair with your head fixed in position, your mind and body can't tune themselves.

"Now I want you to imagine what happens when we implant a mind into a blanked brain. *Almost everything will be out of tune.* The messages from your eyes won't simply be inverted, they'll be scrambled in countless ways. Same thing with your ears, nose, tongue— and with the whole nerve net covering your body. And that's just incoming messages. Your mind will have even more problems when it tries to tell the body to do something. Your mind will try to get your lips to say 'water,' and Sol knows what sound will come out.

"And what's worse is that whatever sound does come out, your new ears won't be able to give your mind an accurate version of it."

Germaine smiled at them and glanced at her watch. Terry stood up.

"Terry will be wanting to take you on. Let me wrap this up by saying that it is a very simple thing to play someone's mind tape into a prepared brain. The great problem is in getting the rearranged brain, the cerebral cortex, speaking strictly, to be tuned into the rest of the system. As Austin Worms may have told you, we start an implant operation tomorrow. The initial tape-in will take less than an hour. But the tuning will take days and days. Even months, if you count all the therapy. Questions?"

"Just one," said Ms. Pedersen. "I can understand how difficult it is for a mind to survive implantation. And, of course, I know it is illegal to implant a mind that is over eighty-five. But couldn't a person—if you call a mind a person—live forever by passing through body after body?"

"Okay, that's a tough one to explain even if we had a lot of time and you knew a lot of mathematics. Until this century it was believed that senility was a by-product of the physical breakdown of the body. Today we know that a human mind can have roughly one hundred years of experiences before it reaches essential senility, however young the body it occupies. As you know, a few successful leapers have survived implantation after a fifty-year wait. So a leaper might, in theory, still be functioning a thousand years from now. But such an individual's mind will not be able to encompass any more lived experience than you. When all there is of you is a tape in storage, you aren't really alive."

After they had filed out, Germaine Means noticed that the blond-haired girl had remained.

"Hi, I'm Candy Darling," she cried. "I hope you don't mind. I thought it would be fun to sneak in on the standard tour. Get the smell of the place."

"Where's your VAT?"

*   *   *

Austin Worms declared that basic physical meshing procedures were complete.
—I. F. + S. C. Operation Logbook

> *Gxxhdt.*
> *Etaoin shrdlu. Mmm.*
> *Anti-M.*
> *Away mooncow Taddy-fair fine. Fine again, take. Away, along, alas, alung the orbit-run, from swerve of space to wormhole wiggle, brings us. Start now. Wake.*
> *So hear I am now coming out of nothing like Eros out of Death, knowing only that I was Ismael Forth—stately, muscled well—taping-in, and knowing that I don't know when I'm waking or where, or where-in. And hoping that it is a dream. But it isn't. Oh, no, it isn't. With that goggling piece of munster cheese oumphowing on my eyelids.*
> *And seemingly up through endless levels and configurations that had no words and now no memories. Wake.*

"Helow, I'm Candy Darlinz."

"I am Ismael returned" was what I started to try to reply. After the third attempt it came out better. And the munster cheese had become a blond-haired young girl with piercing blue eyes.

"Your primary implantation was finished yesterday, finally. Everyone thinks you're a success. Your body is a pip. You're in the Norbert Wiener Research Hospital in Houston. You have two estates clear through probate. Your friend Peter Strawson has covered your affairs. It's the first week of April, 2112. You're alive."

She stood up and touched my hand.

"You start therapy tomorrow. Now sleep."

I was already drifting off by the time she had closed the door behind her. I couldn't even get myself worked up by what I was noticing. My nipples felt as big as grapes. I went out as I worked my way down past the belly button.

The next day I discovered that I had not only lost a penis. I had gained a meter-long prehensile tail. It was hate at first sense.

I had worked my way up to consciousness in slow stages. I had endless flight dreams—walking, running, staggering on, away from some nameless horror. And brief flashes of sexuality that featured performances by my (former) body.

I really liked my old body. One of my biggest problems, as Dr. Germaine Means was soon to tell me. I could picture clearly how it had looked in the mirrors as I did my stretch and tone work. Just a hair over six foot four. Two hundred and five pounds, well-defined muscles, and just enough fat to be comfortable. A mat of curly red chest hair that made it easy to decide to have my facial hair wiped permanently. It felt good to be a confident and even slightly clumsy giant, looking down on a world of little people.

Oh, I wasn't a real body builder or anything like that. Just enough exercise to look good—and attractive. I hadn't in fact been all that good at physical sports. But I had liked my body. It was also a help in the public relations work that I did for IBO.

I was still lying on my back. I felt shrunk. Shrunk. As the warm, muzzy flush of sleep faded, my right hand moved up over my ribs. Ribs. They were thin and they stuck out, as if the skin were sprayed over the bare cage. I felt like a skeleton until I got to the lumps. Bags. Growths. Sacks. Even then part of me realized that they were not at all large for a woman, while most of me felt that they were as big as cantaloupes.

You may have imagined it as a kind of erotic dream. There you are in the hospital bed. You reach and there they are. Apt to the hands, the hardening nipples nestled between index and middle fingers. (Doubtless some men have felt this warm reverie with their hands on real flesh. The women may have felt pinch and itch rather than the imagined sensual flush. I know whereof I speak. I now know a lot of sexuality is like that. Perhaps heterosexuality continues as well as it does because of ignorance: each partner is free to invent the feelings of the other.)

But I was quite unable to feel erotic about my new acquisitions. Both ways. My fingers, as I felt them, felt pathology. Two dead cancerous mounds. And from the inside—so to speak—I felt that my flesh had swollen. The sheet made the nipples feel raw. A strange feeling of separation, as if the breast were disconnected, nerveless jelly—and then two points of sensitivity some inches in front of my chest. Dead spots. Rejection. I learned a lot about these.

As my hand moved down I was prepared for the swerve of hip. I couldn't feel a penis and I did not expect to find one. I did not call it "gash." Though that term is found occasionally in space-marine slang and often among the small number of male homosexuals of the extreme S&M type (Secretary & Master). I first learned the term a few days later from Dr. Means. She said that traditional male-male pornography revealed typical male illusions about female bodies: a "rich source of information about body-image pathologies." She was certainly right in pointing out that "gash" was how I felt about it. At first.

I was not only scrawny, I was almost hairless. I felt *really* naked, naked and defenseless as a baby. Though my skin was several shades less fair—and I passed a scar. I was almost relieved to feel the curly groin hair. Gone. Sticklike legs. But I *did* feel something between my thighs. And knees. And ankles, by Sol.

At first I thought it was some sort of tube to take my body wastes. But as I felt down between my legs I could tell that it wasn't covering those areas. It was attached at the end of my spine—or rather it had become the end of my spine, stretching down to my feet. It was my flesh. I didn't quite intend it—at that point I can't say that I intended anything, I was so shook—but the damned thing flipped up from the bottom of the bed like a snake, throwing the sheet over my face.

I screamed my head off.

"Cut it off" was what I said after they had given me enough betaorthoamine to stop me flailing about. I said this several times to Dr. Germaine Means, who had directed the rest of them out of the room.

"Look, Sally—I'll call you that until you select a name yourself—we are not going to cut your tail off. By our calculations such a move would make terminal rejection almost certain. You would die. Several thousand nerves connect your brain with your prehensile tail. A sizable portion of your brain monitors and directs your tail—that part of your brain needs exercise and integration like any other component. We taped the pattern of your mind into your present brain. They *have to* learn to live together or you get rejection. In brief, you will die."

Dr. Means continued to read me the riot act. I would have to learn to love my new body—she practically gushed with praise for it—my new sex, my new tail. I would have to do a lot of exercise and tests. And I would have to talk to a lot of people about how I felt. And I should feel pleased as pisque to have an extra hand.

My new body broke into a cold sweat when I realized that I had—truly—no choice. I wasn't poor, assuming what I had heard yesterday was true. But I certainly couldn't afford an implant, let alone a desirable body. What I had, of course, came free under the Kellog-Murphy Bill.

After a while she left. I stared at the wall numbly. A nurse brought a tray with scrambled eggs and toast. I ignored both nurse and tray. The thin-lipped mouth salivated. Let it suffer.

David Hume
Of Personal Identity

David Hume *(1711–1776), a Scottish philosopher, was refused professorships at the leading universities for his "heresies." Nevertheless, he is regarded as the outstanding genius of British philosophy. He wrote a number of influential books, among them* A Treatise of Human Nature, An Inquiry Concerning the Principles of Morals, *and* Dialogues on Natural Religion.

There are some philosophers, who imagine we are every moment intimately conscious of what we call our *Self*; that we feel its existence and its continuance in existence; and are certain, beyond the evidence of a demonstration, both of its perfect identity and simplicity. The strongest sensation, the most violent passion, say they, instead of distracting us from this view, only fix it the more intensely, and make us consider their influence on *self* either by their pain or pleasure. To attempt a farther proof of this were to weaken its evidence; since no proof can be deriv'd from any fact, of which we are so intimately conscious; nor is there any thing, of which we can be certain, if we doubt of this.

Unluckily all these positive assertions are contrary to that very experience, which is pleaded for them, nor have we any idea of *self*, after the manner it is here explain'd. For from what impression cou'd this idea be deriv'd? This question 'tis impossible to answer without a manifest contradiction and absurdity; and yet 'tis a question, which must necessarily be answer'd, if we wou'd have the idea of self pass for clear and intelligible. It must be some one impression, that gives rise to every real idea. But self or person is not any one impression, but that to which our several impressions and ideas are suppos'd to have a reference. If any impression gives rise to the idea of self, that impression must continue invariably the same, thro' the whole course of our lives; since self is suppos'd to exist after that manner. But there is no impression constant and invariable. Pain and pleasure, grief and joy, passions and sensations succeed each other, and never all exist at the same time. It cannot, therefore, be from any of these impressions, or from any other, that the idea of self is deriv'd; and consequently there is no such idea.

But farther, what must become of all our particular perceptions upon this hypothesis? All these are different, and distinguishable, and separable from each other, and may be separately consider'd, and may exist separately, and have no need of any thing to support their existence. After what manner, therefore, do they belong to self; and how are they connected with it? For my part, when I enter most intimately into what I call *myself*, I always stumble on some particular perception or other, of heat or cold, light or shade, love or hatred, pain or pleasure. I never can catch *myself* at any time without a perception, and never can observe any thing but the perception. When my perceptions are remov'd for any time, as by sound sleep; so long am I insensible of *myself*, and may truly be said not to exist. And were all my perceptions remov'd by death, and cou'd I neither think, nor feel, nor see, nor love, nor hate after the dissolution of my body, I shou'd be entirely annihilated, nor do I conceive what is farther requisite to make me a perfect non-entity. If any one upon serious and unprejudic'd reflexion, thinks he has a different notion of *himself*, I must confess I can reason no longer with him. All I can allow him is, that he may be in the right as well as I, and that we are essentially different in this particular. He may, perhaps, perceive something simple and continu'd, which he calls *himself*; tho' I am certain there is no such principle in me.

But setting aside some metaphysicians of this kind, I may venture to affirm of the rest of mankind, that they are nothing but a bundle or collection of different perceptions, which succeed each other with an inconceivable rapidity, and are in a perpetual flux and movement. Our eyes cannot turn in their sockets without varying our perceptions. Our thought is still more variable than our sight; and all our other senses and faculties contribute to this change; nor is there any single power of the soul, which remains unalterably the same, perhaps for one moment. The mind is a kind of theatre, where several perceptions successively make their appearance; pass, re-pass, glide away, and mingle in an infinite variety of postures and situations. There is properly no *simplicity* in it at one time, nor *identity* in different; whatever natural propension we may have to imagine that simplicity and identity. The comparison of the theatre must not mislead us. They are the successive perceptions only, that constitute the mind; nor have we the most distant notion of the place, where these scenes are represented, or of the materials, of which it is compos'd.

What then gives us so great a propension to ascribe an identity to these successive perceptions, and to suppose ourselves possest of an invariable and uninterrupted existence thro' the whole course of our lives? . . .

. . . 'Tis evident, that the identity, which we attribute to the human mind, however perfect we may imagine it to be, is not able to run the several different perceptions into one, and make them lose their characters of distinction and difference, which are essential to them. 'Tis still true, that every distinct perception, which enters into the composition of the mind, is a distinct existence, and is different, and distinguishable, and separable from every other perception, either contemporary or successive. But, as, notwithstanding this distinction and separability, we suppose the whole train of perceptions to be united by identity, a question naturally arises concerning this relation of identity; whether it be something that really binds our several perceptions together, or only associates their ideas in the imagination. That is, in other words, whether in pronouncing concerning the identity of a person, we observe some real bond among his perceptions, or only feel one among the ideas we form of them. This question we might easily decide, if we wou'd recollect what has been already prov'd at large, that the understanding never observes any real connexion among objects, and that even the union of cause and effect, when strictly examin'd, resolves itself into a customary association of ideas. For from thence it evidently follows, that identity is nothing really belonging to these different perceptions, and uniting them together; but is merely a quality, which we attribute to them, because of the union of their ideas in the imagination, when we reflect upon them. Now the only qualities, which can give ideas an union in the imagination, are these three relations above-mention'd. These are the uniting principles in the ideal world, and without them every distinct object is separable by the mind, and may be separately consider'd, and appears not to have any more connexion with any other object, than if disjoin'd by the greatest difference and remoteness. 'Tis, therefore, on some of these three relations of resemblance, contiguity and causation, that identity depends; and as the very essence of these relations consists in their producing an easy transition of ideas; it follows, that our notions of personal identity, proceed entirely from the smooth and uninterrupted progress of the thought along a train of connected ideas, according to the principles above-explain'd.

The only question, therefore, which remains, is, by what relations this uninterrupted progress of our thought is produc'd, when we consider the successive existence of a mind or thinking person. And here 'tis evident we must confine ourselves to resemblance and causation, and must drop contiguity, which has little or no influence in the present case.

To begin with *resemblance*; suppose we cou'd see clearly into the breast of another, and observe that succession of perceptions, which constitutes his mind or thinking principle, and suppose that he always preserves the memory of a considerable part of past perceptions; 'tis evident that nothing cou'd more contribute to the bestowing a relation on this succession amidst all its variations. For what is the memory but a faculty, by which we raise up the images of past perceptions? And as an image necessarily resembles its object, must not the frequent placing of these resembling perceptions in the chain of thought, convey the imagination more easily from one link to another, and make the whole seem like the continuance of one object? In this particular, then, the memory not only discovers the identity, but also contributes to its production, by producing the relation of resemblance among the perceptions. The case is the same whether we consider ourselves or others.

As to *causation*; we may observe, that the true idea of the human mind, is to consider it as a system of different perceptions or different existences, which are link'd together by the relation of cause and effect, and mutually produce, destroy, influence, and modify each other. Our impressions give rise to their correspondent ideas; and these ideas in their turn produce other impressions. One thought chaces another, and draws after it a third, by which it is expell'd in its turn. In this respect, I cannot compare the soul more properly to any thing than to a republic or commonwealth, in which the several members are united by the reciprocal ties of government and subordination, and give rise to other persons, who propagate the same republic in the incessant changes of its parts. And as the same individual republic may not only change its members, but also its laws and constitutions; in like manner the same person may vary his character and disposition, as well as his impressions and ideas, without losing his identity. Whatever changes he endures, his several parts are still connected by the relation of causation. And in this view our identity with regard to the passions serves to corroborate that with regard to the imagination, by the making our distant perceptions influence each other, and by giving us a present concern for our past or future pains or pleasures.

As memory alone acquaints us with the continuance and extent of this succession of perceptions, 'tis to be consider'd, upon that account chiefly, as the source of personal identity. Had we no memory, we never shou'd have any notion of causation, nor consequently of that chain of causes and effects, which constitute our self or person. But having once acquir'd this notion of causation from the memory, we can extend the same chain of causes, and consequently the identity of our persons beyond our memory, and can comprehend times, and circumstances, and actions, which we have entirely forgot, but suppose in general to have existed. For how few of our past actions are there, of which we have any memory? Who can tell me, for instance, what were his thoughts and actions on the first of *January* 1715, the 11th of *March* 1719, and the 3d of *August* 1733? Or will he affirm, because he has entirely forgot the incidents of these days, that the present self is not the same person with the self of that time; and by that means overturn all the most establish'd notions of personal identity? In this view, therefore, memory does not so much *produce* as *discover* personal identity, by shewing us the relation of cause and effect among our different perceptions. 'Twill be incumbent on those, who affirm that memory produces entirely our personal identity, to give a reason why we can thus extend our identity beyond our memory.

The whole of this doctrine leads us to a conclusion, which is of great importance in the present affair, *viz.* that all the nice and subtle questions concerning personal identity can never possibly be decided, and are to be regarded rather as grammatical than as philosophical difficulties. Identity depends on the relations of ideas; and these relations produce identity, by means of that easy transition they occasion. But as the relations, and the easiness of the transition may diminish by insensible degrees, we have no just standard, by which we can decide any dispute concerning the time, when they acquire or lose a title to the name of identity. All the disputes concerning the identity of connected objects are merely verbal, except so far as the relation of parts gives rise to some fiction or imaginary principle of union, as we have already observ'd.

Derek Parfit

Later Selves and Moral Principles

Derek Parfit *teaches ethics and metaphysics at Oxford University. In his most recent book* Reasons and Persons, *he defends his unorthodox views about personal identity.*

Most of us seem to have certain beliefs about our own identity. We seem for instance to believe that, whatever happens, any future person must be either us, or someone else.

These beliefs are like those that some of us have about a simpler fact. Most of us now think that to be a person, as opposed to a mere animal, is just to have certain more specific properties, such as rationality. These are matters of degree. So we might say that the fact of personhood is just the fact of having certain other properties, which are had to different degrees.

There is a different view. Some of us believe that personhood is a further, deep, fact, and cannot hold to different degrees.

This second view may be confused with some trivial claims. Personhood is, in a sense, a further fact. And there is a sense in which all persons are equally persons.

Let us first show how these claims may be trivial. We can use a different example. There is a sense in which all our relatives are equally our relatives. We can use the phrase 'related to' so that what it means has no degrees; on this use, parents and remote cousins are as much relatives. It is obvious, though, that kinship has degrees. This is shown in the phrase 'closely related to': remote cousins are, as relatives, less close. I shall summarize such remarks in the following way. On the above use, the fact of being someone's relative has in its *logic* no degrees. But in its *nature*—in what it involves—it does have degrees. So the fact's logic hides its nature. Hence the triviality of the claim that all our relatives are equally our relatives. (The last few sentences may be wrongly worded, but I hope that the example suggests what I mean.)

To return to the claims about personhood. These were: that it is a further fact, and that all persons are equally persons. As claims about the fact's logic, these are trivial. Certain people think the claims profound. They believe them to be true of the fact's nature.

The difference here can be shown in many ways. Take the question, 'When precisely does an embryo become a person?' If we merely make the claims about the fact's logic, we shall not believe that this question must have a precise answer. Certain people do believe this. They believe that any embryo must either be, or not be, a complete person. Their view goes beyond the 'logical claims'. It concerns the nature of personhood.

We can now return to the main argument. About the facts of both personhood and personal identity, there are two views. According to the first, these facts have a special nature. They are further facts, independent of certain more specific facts; and in every case they must either hold completely, or completely fail to hold. According to the second view, these facts are not of this nature. They consist in the holding of the more specific facts; and they are matters of degree.

Let us name such opposing views. I shall call the first kind 'Simple' and the second 'Complex'.

Such views may affect our moral principles, in the following way. If we change from a Simple to a Complex View, we acquire two beliefs: we decide that a certain fact is in its nature less deep, and that it sometimes holds to reduced degrees. These beliefs may have two effects: the first belief may weaken certain principles, and the second give the principles a new scope.

Take the views about personhood. An ancient principle gives to the welfare of people absolute precedence over that of mere animals. If the difference between people and mere animals is in its nature less deep, this principle can be more plausibly denied. And if embryos are not people, and become them only by degrees, the principle forbidding murder can be more plausibly given less scope.

I have not defended these claims. They are meant to parallel what I shall defend in the case of the two views about personal identity.

We must first sketch these views. It will help to revive a comparison. What is involved in the survival of a nation are just certain continuities, such as those of a people and a political system. When there is a weakening of these continuities, as there was, say, in the Norman Conquest, it may be unclear whether a nation survives. But there is here no problem. And the reason is that the survival of a nation just involves these continuities. Once we know how the continuities were weakened, we need not ask, as a question about an independent fact, 'Did a nation cease to exist?' There is nothing left to know.

We can add the following remarks. Though identity has no degrees, these continuities are matters of degree. So the identity of nations over time is only in its logic 'all-or-nothing'; in its nature it has degrees.

The identity of people over time is, according to the 'Complex View', comparable. It consists in bodily and psychological continuity. These, too, are matters of degree. So we can add the comparable remark. The identity of people over time is only in its logic 'all-or-nothing'; in its nature it has degrees.

How do the continuities of bodies and minds have degrees? We can first dismiss bodies, since they are morally trivial. Let us next call 'direct' the psychological relations which hold between: the memory of an experience and this experience, the intention to perform some later action and this action, and different expressions of some lasting character-trait. We can now name two general features of a person's life. One, 'connectedness', is the holding, over time, of particular 'direct' relations. The other, 'continuity', is the holding of a chain of such relations. If, say, I cannot now remember some earlier day, there are no 'connections of memory' between me now and myself on that day. But there may be 'continuity of memory'. This there is if, on every day between, I remembered the previous day.

Of these two general relations, I define 'continuous with' so that, in its logic, it has no degrees. It is like 'related to' in the use on which all our relatives are equally our relatives. But 'connectedness' has degrees. Between different parts of a person's life, the connections of memory, character, and intention are—in strength and number—more or less. ('Connected to' is like 'closely related to'; different relatives can be more or less close.)

We can now restate the Complex View. What is important in personal identity are the two relations we have just sketched. One of these, continuity, is in its logic all-or-nothing. But it just involves connectedness, which clearly has degrees. In its nature, therefore, continuity holds to different degrees. So the fact of personal identity also, in its nature, has degrees.

To turn to the Simple View. Here the fact is believed to be, in its nature, all-or-nothing. This it can only be if it does not just consist in (bodily and) psychological continuity—if it is, in its nature, a further fact. To suggest why: These continuities hold, over time, to different degrees. This is true in actual cases, but is most clearly true in some imaginary cases. We can imagine cases where the continuities between each of us and a future person hold to every possible degree. Suppose we think, in imagining these cases, 'Such a future person must be either, and quite simply, *me,* or *someone else*'. (Suppose we think, 'Whatever happens, any future experience must be either *wholly* mine, or *not* mine *at all*'.) If the continuities can hold to every degree, but the fact of our identity must hold completely or not at all, then this fact cannot consist in these continuities. It must be a further, independent, fact.

It is worth repeating that the Simple View is about the nature of personal identity, not its logic. This is shown by the reactions most of us have to various, so-called 'problem cases'. These reactions also show that even if, on the surface, we reject the Simple View, at a deeper level we assume it to be true.

We can add this—rough—test of our assumptions. Nations are in many ways unlike people; for example, they are not organisms. But if we take the Complex View, we shall accept this particular comparison: the survival of a person, like that of a nation, is a matter of degree. If instead we reject this comparison, we take the Simple View.

One last preliminary. We can use 'I', and the other pronouns, so that they cover only the part of our lives to which, when speaking, we have the strongest psychological connections. We assign the rest of our lives to what we call our 'other selves'. When, for instance, we have undergone any marked change in character, or conviction, or style of life, we might say, 'It was not *I* who did that, but an earlier self'.

Whether we are inclined to use such talk will depend upon our view about the nature of personal identity. If we take the Simple View, we shall not be so inclined, for we shall think it deeply true that all the parts of a person's life are as much parts of his life. If we take the Complex View, we shall be less impressed by this truth. It will seem like the truth that all the parts of a nation's history are as much parts of its history. Because this latter truth is superficial, we at times subdivide such a history into that of a series of successive nations, such as Anglo-Saxon, Medieval, or Post-Imperial England. The connections between these, though similar in kind, differ in degree. If we take the Complex View, we may also redescribe a person's life as the history of a series of successive selves. And the connections between these we shall also claim to be similar in kind, different in degree.

We can now turn to our question. Do the different views tend to support different moral claims?

I have space to consider only three subjects: desert, commitment, and distributive justice. And I am forced to oversimplify, and to distort. So it may help to start with some general remarks.

My suggestions are of this form: 'The Complex View supports certain claims.' By 'supports' I mean both 'makes more plausible' and 'helps to explain'. My suggestions thus mean: 'If the true view is the Complex, not the Simple, View, certain claims are more plausible. We may therefore be, on the Complex View, more inclined to make these claims.'

I shall be discussing two kinds of case: those in which the psychological connections are as strong as they ever are, and those in which they are markedly weak. I choose these kinds of case for the following reason. If we change from the Simple to the Complex View, we believe (I shall claim) that our identity is in its nature less deep, and that it sometimes holds to reduced degrees. The first of these beliefs covers every case, even those where there are the strongest connections. But the second of the two beliefs only covers cases where there are weak connections. So the two kinds of case provide separate testing-grounds for the two beliefs.

Let us start with the cases of weak connection. And our first principle can be that we deserve to be punished for certain crimes.

We can suppose that, between some convict now and himself when he committed some crime, there are only weak psychological connections. (This will usually be when conviction takes place after many years.) We can imply the weakness of these connections by calling the convict, not the criminal, but his later self.

Two grounds for detaining him would be unaffected. Whether a convict should be either reformed, or preventively detained, turns upon his present state, not his relation to the criminal. A third ground, deterrence, turns upon a different question. Do potential criminals care about their later selves? Do they care, for instance, if they do not expect to be caught for many years? If they do, then detaining their later selves could perhaps deter.

Would it be deserved? Locke thought that if we forget our crimes we deserve no punishment. Geach considers this view 'morally repugnant'. Mere loss of memory does seem to be insufficient. Changes of character would appear to be more relevant. The subject is, though, extremely difficult. Claims about desert can be plausibly supported with a great variety of arguments. According to some of these loss of memory would be important. And according to most the nature and cause of any change in character would need to be known.

I have no space to consider these details, but I shall make one suggestion. This appeals to the following assumption. When some morally important fact holds to a lesser degree, it can be more plausibly claimed to have less importance—even, in extreme cases, none.

I shall not here defend this assumption. I shall only say that most of us apply the assumption to many kinds of principle. Take, for example, the two principles that we have special duties to help our relatives, or friends. On the assumption, we might claim that we have less of a special duty to help our less close relatives, or friends, and, to those who are very distant, none at all.

My suggestion is this. If the assumption is acceptable, and the Complex View correct, it becomes more plausible to make the following claim: when the connections between convicts and their past criminal selves are less, they deserve less punishment; if they are very weak, they perhaps deserve none. This claim extends the idea of 'diminished responsibility'. It does not appeal to mental illness, but instead treats a later self like a sane accomplice. Just as a man's deserts correspond to the degree of his complicity with some criminal, so his deserts, now, for some past crime correspond to the degree of connectedness between himself now and himself when committing that crime.

If we add the further assumption that psychological connections are, in general, weaker over longer periods, the claim provides a ground for Statutes of Limitations. (They of course have other grounds.)

We can next consider promises. There are here two identities involved. The first is that of the person who, once, made a promise. Let us suppose that between this person now and himself then there are only weak connections. Would this wipe away his commitment? Does a later self start with a clean slate?

On the assumption that I gave, the Complex View supports the answer, 'yes'. Certain people think that only short-term promises carry moral weight. This belief becomes more plausible on the Complex View.

The second relevant identity is that of the person who received the promise. There is here an asymmetry. The possible effect of the Complex View could be deliberately blocked. We could ask for promises of this form: 'I shall help you, and all your later selves.' If the promises that I *receive* take this form, they cannot be plausibly held to be later undermined by any change in *my* character, or by any other weakening, over the rest of *my* life, in connectedness.

The asymmetry is this: similar forms cannot so obviously stay binding on the *maker* of a promise. I might say, 'I, and all my later selves, shall help you'. But it is plausible to reply that I can only bind my present self. This is plausible because it is like the claim that I can only bind myself. No one, though, denies that I can promise you that I shall help someone else. So I can clearly promise you that I shall help your later selves.

Such a promise may indeed seem especially binding. Suppose that you change faster than I do. I may then regard myself as committed, not to you, but to your earlier self. I may therefore think that you cannot waive my commitment. (It would be like a commitment, to someone now dead, to help his children. We cannot be released from such commitments.)

Such a case would be rare. But an example may help the argument. Let us take a nineteenth-century Russian who, in several years, should inherit vast estates. Because he has socialist ideals, he intends, now, to give the land to the peasants. But he knows that in time his ideals may fade. To guard against this possibility, he does two things. He first signs a legal document, which will automatically give away the land, and which can only be revoked with his wife's consent. He then says to his wife, 'If I ever change my mind, and ask you to revoke the document, promise me that you will not consent'. He might add, 'I regard my ideals as essential to me. If I lose these ideals, I want you to think that *I* cease to exist. I want you to regard your husband, then, not as me, the man who asks you for this promise, but only as his later self. Promise me that you would not do what he asks.'

This plea seems understandable. And if his wife made this promise, and he later asked her to revoke the document, she might well regard herself as in no way released from her commitment. It might seem to her as if she has obligations to two different people. She might think that to do what her husband now asks would be to betray the young man whom she loved and married. And she might regard what her husband now says as unable to acquit her of disloyalty to this young man—of disloyalty to her husband's earlier self.

Such an example may seem not to require the distinction between successive selves. Suppose that I ask you to promise me never to give me cigarettes, even if I beg you for them.

You might think that I cannot, in begging you, simply release you from this commitment. And to think this you need not deny that it is I to whom you are committed.

This seems correct. But the reason is that addiction clouds judgment. Similar examples might involve extreme stress or pain, or (as with Odysseus, tied to the mast) extraordinary temptation. When, though, nothing clouds a person's judgment, most of us believe that the person to whom we are committed can always release us. He can always, if in sound mind, waive our commitment. We believe this whatever the commitment may be. So (on this view) the content of a commitment cannot stop its being waived.

To return to the Russian couple. The man's ideals fade, and he asks his wife to revoke the document. Though she promised him to refuse, he declares that he now releases her from this commitment. We have sketched two ways in which she might think that she is not released. She might, first, take her husband's change of mind as proof that he cannot now make considered judgments. But we can suppose that she has no such thought. We can also suppose that she shares our view about commitment. If so, she will only believe that her husband is unable to release her if she thinks that it is, in some sense, not *he* to whom she is committed. We have sketched such a sense. She may regard the young man's loss of his ideals as involving his replacement by a later self.

The example is of a quite general possibility. We may regard some events within a person's life as, in certain ways, like birth or death. Not in all ways, for beyond these events the person has earlier or later selves. But it may be only one out of the series of selves which is the object of some of our emotions, and to which we apply some of our principles.

The young Russian socialist regards his ideals as essential to his present self. He asks his wife to promise to this present self not to act against these ideals. And, on this way of thinking, she can never be released from her commitment. For the self to whom she is committed would, in trying to release her, cease to exist.

The way of thinking may seem to be within our range of choice. We can indeed choose when to *speak* of a new self, just as we can choose when to speak of the end of Medieval England. But the way of speaking would express beliefs. And the wife in our example cannot choose her beliefs. That the young man whom she loved and married has, in a sense, ceased to exist, that her middle-aged and cynical husband is at most the later self of this young man—these claims may seem to her to express more of the truth than the simple claim, 'but they are the same person'. Just as we can give a more accurate description if we divide the history of Russia into that of the Empire and of the Soviet Union, so it maybe more accurate to divide her husband's life into that of two successive selves.

I have suggested that the Complex View supports certain claims. It is worth repeating that these claims are at most more plausible on the Complex View (more, that is, than on the Simple View). They are not entailed by the Complex View.

We can sometimes show this in the following way. Some claims make sense when applied to successive generations. Such claims can obviously be applied to successive selves. For example, it perhaps makes sense to believe that we inherit the commitments of our parents. If so, we can obviously believe that commitments are inherited by later selves.

Other claims may be senseless when applied to generations. Perhaps we cannot intelligibly think that we deserve to be punished for all our parents' crimes. But even if this is so, it should still make sense to have the comparable thought about successive selves. No similarity in the form of two relations could force us to admit that they are morally equivalent, for we can always appeal to the difference in their content.

There are, then, no entailments. But there seldom are in moral reasoning. So the Complex View may still support certain claims. Most of us think that our children are neither bound by our commitments, nor responsible for all we do. If we take the Complex View, we may be more inclined to think the same about our later selves. And the correctness of the view might make such beliefs more defensible.

Alasdair MacIntyre
The Story-Telling Animal

Alasdair MacIntyre *teaches philosophy at Duke University. Most of his work focuses on issues in ethics and social and political philosophy. Among his many publications are* Against the Self-Images of the Age *and* After Virtue.

We live out our lives, both individually and in our relationships with each other, in the light of certain conceptions of a possible shared future, a future in which certain possibilities beckon us forward and others repel us, some seem already foreclosed and others perhaps inevitable. There is no present which is not informed by some image of some future and an image of the future which always presents itself in the form of a *telos*—or of a variety of ends or goals—towards which we are either moving or failing to move in the present. Unpredictability and teleology therefore coexist as part of our lives; like characters in a fictional narrative we do not know what will happen next, but none the less our lives have a certain form which projects itself towards our future. Thus the narratives which we live out have both an unpredictable and a partially teleological character. If the narrative of our individual and social lives is to continue intelligibly—and either type of narrative may lapse into unintelligibility—it is always both the case that there are constraints on how the story can continue *and* that within those constraints there are indefinitely many ways that it can continue.

A central thesis then begins to emerge: man is in his actions and practice, as well as in his fictions, essentially a story-telling animal. He is not essentially, but becomes through his history, a teller of stories that aspire to truth. But the key question for men is not about their own authorship; I can only answer the question 'What am I to do?' if I can answer the prior question 'Of what story or stories do I find myself a part?' We enter human society, that is, with one or more imputed characters—roles into which we have been drafted—and we have to learn what they are in order to be able to understand how others respond to us and how our responses to them are apt to be construed. It is through hearing stories about wicked stepmothers, lost children, good but misguided kings, wolves that suckle twin boys, youngest sons who receive no inheritance but must make their own way in the world and eldest sons who waste their inheritance on riotous living and go into exile to live with the swine, that children learn or mislearn both what a child and what a parent is, what the cast of characters may be in the drama into which they have been born and what the ways of the world are. Deprive children of stories and you leave them unscripted, anxious stutterers in their actions as in their words. Hence there is no way to give us an understanding of any society, including our own, except through the stock of stories which constitute its initial dramatic resources. Mythology, in its original sense, is at the heart of things. Vico was right and so was Joyce. And so too of course is that moral tradition from heroic society to its medieval heirs according to which the telling of stories has a key part in educating us into the virtues.

I suggested earlier that 'an' action is always an episode in a possible history: I would now like to make a related suggestion about another concept, that of personal identity. Derek Parfit and others have recently drawn our attention to the contrast between the criteria of strict identity, which is an all-or-nothing matter (*either* the Tichborne claimant *is* the last Tichborne heir; *either* all the properties of the last heir belong to the claimant *or* the claimant is not the heir—Leibniz's Law applies) and the psychological continuities of personality which are a matter of more or less. (Am I the same man at fifty as I was at forty in respect of memory, intellectual powers, critical responses? More or less.) But what is crucial to human beings as characters in enacted narratives is that, possessing only the resources of psychological continuity, we have to be able to respond to the imputation of strict identity. I am forever whatever I have been at any time for others—and I may at any time be called upon to answer for it— no matter how changed I may be now. There is no way of *founding* my identity—or lack of it—on the psychological continuity or discontinuity of the self. The self inhabits a character whose unity is given as the unity of a character. Once again there is a crucial disagreement with empiricist or analytical philosophers on the one hand and with existentialists on the other.

Empiricists, such as Locke or Hume, tried to give an account of personal identity solely in terms of psychological states or events. Analytical philosophers, in so many ways their heirs as well as their critics, have wrestled with the connection between those states and events and strict identity understood in terms of Leibniz's Law. Both have failed to see that a background has been omitted, the lack of which makes the problems insoluble. That background is provided by the concept of a story and of that kind of unity of character which a story requires. Just as a history is not a sequence of actions, but the concept of an action is that of a moment in an actual or possible history abstracted for some purpose from that history, so the characters in a history are not a collection of persons, but the concept of a person is that of a character abstracted from a history.

What the narrative concept of selfhood requires is thus twofold. On the one hand, I am what I may justifiably be taken by others to be in the course of living out a story that runs from my birth to my death; I am the *subject* of a history that is my own and no one else's, that has its own peculiar meaning. When someone complains—as do some of those who attempt or commit suicide—that his or her life is meaningless, he or she is often and perhaps characteristically complaining that the narrative of their life has become unintelligible to them, that it lacks any point, any movement towards a climax or a *telos*. Hence the point of doing any one thing rather than another at crucial junctures in their lives seems to such a person to have been lost.

To be the subject of a narrative that runs from one's birth to one's death is, I remarked earlier, to be accountable for the actions and experiences which compose a narratable life. It is, that is, to be open to being asked to give a certain kind of account of what one did or what happened to one or what one witnessed at any earlier point in one's life the time at which the question is posed. Of course someone may have forgotten or suffered brain damage or simply not attended sufficiently at the relevant times to be able to give the relevant account. But to say of someone under some one description ('The prisoner of the Chateau d'If') that he is the same person as someone characterised quite differently ('The Count of Monte Cristo') is precisely to say that it makes sense to ask him to give an intelligible narrative account enabling us to understand how he could at different times and different places be one and the same person and yet be so differently characterised. Thus personal identity is just that identity presupposed by the unity of the character which the unity of a narrative requires. Without such unity there would not be subjects of whom stories could be told.

The other aspect of narrative selfhood is correlative: I am not only accountable, I am one who can always ask others for an account, who can put others to the question. I am part of their story, as they are part of mine. The narrative of any one life is part of an interlocking set of narratives. Moreover this asking for and giving of accounts itself plays an important part in constituting narratives. Asking you what you did and why, saying what I did and why, pondering the differences between your account of what I did and my account of what I did, and *vice versa*, these are essential constituents of all but the very simplest and barest of narratives. Thus without the accountability of the self those trains of events that constitute all but the simplest and barest of narratives could not occur; and without that same accountability narratives would lack that continuity required to make both them and the actions that constitute them intelligible.

It is important to notice that I am not arguing that the concepts of narrative or of intelligibility or of accountability are *more* fundamental than that of personal identity. The concepts of narrative, intelligibility and accountability presuppose the applicability of the concept of personal identity, just as it presupposes their applicability and just as indeed each of these three presupposes the applicability of the two others. The relationship is one of mutual presupposition. It does follow of course that all attempts to elucidate the notion of personal identity independently of and in isolation from the notions of narrative, intelligibility and accountability are bound to fail. As all such attempts have.

It is now possible to return to the question from which this enquiry into the nature of human action and identity started: In what does the unity of an individual life consist? The answer is that its unity is the unity of a narrative embodied in a single life. To ask 'What is the good for me?' is to ask how best I might live out that unity and bring it to completion. To ask 'What is the good for man?' is to ask what all answers to the former question must have in common. But now it is important to emphasise that it is the systematic asking of these two questions and the attempt to answer them in deed as well as in word which provide the moral life with its unity. The unity of a human life is the unity of a narrative quest. Quests sometimes fail, are frustrated, abandoned or dissipated into distractions; and human lives may in all these ways also fail. But the only criteria for success or failure in a human life as a whole are the criteria of success or failure in a narrated or to-be-narrated quest.

10

How Are My Emotions Important to Me?

What was your latest passion? When did you last get angry, or feel love, or find yourself envious or jealous? What was the significance of that emotion? Was it an unwelcome intrusion into an otherwise calm and enjoyable day? Or did your emotion actually define your day, perhaps even (as with love) define your life for months or years to come? Was this a familiar emotion to you—do you get angry or fall in love often—or did it seem out of character, a strange reaction that does not represent your real personality? Was it annoying and embarrassing, or did it feel right and good, perhaps even refreshing or elevating? What is the significance of your emotions in your life? Are they disruptions or punctuations? Are they just moments of excitement or do they have some more significant meaning? How are we to understand emotion, and how do our emotions fit into our lives?

Twenty-five hundred years of emphasis on reason as the subject matter of philosophy and the core of human nature has tended to minimize the importance of emotions in human life. It is true that a person who is all emotion and is never rational is a monster, but a person who is all rationality and without emotion is also a monster, a mere automaton, a walking computer and not a human being. One of the great horror films, *Invasion of the Body Snatchers*, portrays aliens as humanoids without emotion. It is our emotions as well as our reason that makes us human.

Emotions have had a confused place in the history of philosophy. On the one hand, they are acknowledged to be vital, important, and essential to life. Aristotle insisted that the good life consisted of having the right emotions as well as having reason and doing the right things. Christian philosophers have long insisted that love and faith are among the most important things in life. On the other hand, philosophers have recognized that the emotions can be dangerous. Ancient philosophers likened love and anger to madness, and the famed story-teller Aesop insisted that "emotions should be the slaves, not the masters, of reason." Accordingly, the view that emotions are important and necessary has always been balanced by the view that emotions are subhuman, our more bestial aspect and the "lowest" part of the soul. In more modern times, both popular and scientific views of emotions have reduced them to primitive physical reactions and have opposed them to reason and intelligence. Thus, Descartes and most of his contemporaries referred to the emotions as "animal spirits" and William James more recently defined emotion in terms of physiological ("visceral") reaction. In such a view, emotions typically emerge as unlearned, instinctual, perhaps even stupid if not destructive and, in any case, disruptive and intrusive in our otherwise rational lives.

Obviously our emotions occupy an ambiguous place in our conception of ourselves. They are not within our direct control, but neither are they alien to us. Our emotions are different from reasoning and thinking as such, but they are clearly affected by our reasoning and they affect our thinking in turn. Our emotions are in some sense "in the mind," but like perceptions and unlike a pain or a stomach ache, they are about people and situations in the world. They obviously involve our bodies, but they also involve thought and awareness. They are essential to being a good person, but they also contribute to selfishness, evil, and insanity.

Aristotle long ago recognized that emotions were not just feelings but also perceptions: they involve seeing the world in a certain way. Emotions also involve motives; they urge us to action. His view—augmented by the Stoic philosophers in subsequent generations—was that emotions already include certain aspects of reason; they are learned and can be learned well or badly. They can be smart or foolish, noble or embarrassing. In the seventeenth century, Baruch Spinoza went even further and redefined emotions as a species of "thought." With such a move, the distinction between "good" emotions and "bad" emotions becomes particularly important, as it had been, for example, for the theologians of the middle ages, who often classified some emotions as "sins" (anger, envy, and pride) and others as virtues (faith, hope, and love). The good emotions are inspiring and accurate representations of the world, while the bad emotions tend to be degrading or depressing and typically misrepresent the world. Not surprisingly, Spinoza's list of the good and bad emotions was in many ways similar to the list of the theologians, with love and faith among the best emotions and such demeaning passions as envy and resentment among the worst emotions.

One particularly ingenious theory of emotion as something more than mere feeling is Book II of David Hume's *Treatise of Human Nature*. A passion, Hume suggested, is a complex mix of impressions (sensations or feelings) and ideas. Pride, for example, involves not just a pleasant feeling but also a set of ideas about one's *self*. Hume opposed passion and reason, but in an unusual and provocative twist of the usual philosophical championing of reason, he announced that "reason is and ought to be the slave of the passions." A very different view of emotions was developed by the French existentialist Jean-Paul Sartre. Emotions, he suggested, are "magical transformations of the world." Like Aristotle, he recognized the perception-like nature of emotion, but Sartre added another unusual twist. Emotions are purposive, he argued; they have an end in mind. He believed that we get afraid or angry or resentful in order to accomplish something, usually to escape from or deny an unpleasant situation.

Understanding emotions in general is perhaps not as personally rewarding as understanding specific emotions. Anger is a particularly misunderstood emotion. It is often thought to be irrational and dangerous, even a sin. We often talk about it as if it were a fluid that fills us up and makes us "hot," occasionally "bursting" or "exploding." Carol Tavris has developed a radically new interpretation of anger, "the misunderstood emotion," in which social awareness is much more important than physiology. Love, by contrast, is an emotion that is almost universally and uncritically praised, but the price of that adulation is that it is an emotion that is rarely scrutinized. Robert Solomon offers a theory of love in which this emotion is understood as a form of shared identity. Finally, E. Victoria Spelman and John Connolly, reacting to the controversy surrounding the ABC television movie depicting the horrors of a nuclear attack on the United States, argue for a new synthesis of emotion and reason.

Aristotle

On Anger

Aristotle (384–322 B.C.) *was primarily a biologist but wrote widely on topics in virtually every other science, from astronomy and physics to psychology. The following* *excerpt is a profound bit of psychology that is taken from his book on rhetoric, in which he discusses the uses of emotion in moving the public to action.*

We shall define an emotion as that which leads one's condition to become so transformed that his judgment is affected, and which is accompanied by pleasure and pain. Examples of emotions include anger, pity, fear, and the like, as well as the opposites of these. We will need with each of these emotions to investigate three particulars; in investigating anger, for instance, we will ask what the temperament is of angry people, with whom they most often become angry, and at what sort of things. To grasp one or two but not all three of these conditions would make it impossible to induce anger in one's audience. The same is true with the other emotions. So, just as we listed propositions in what we said earlier, let us do this again in analyzing these emotions in the same way.

Let anger be defined as a distressed desire for conspicuous vengeance in return for a conspicuous and unjustifiable contempt of one's person or friends. If this indeed defines anger, then the anger of the angry person is necessarily always directed towards someone in particular, e.g., Cleon, but not towards all of humanity; also of necessity is that this individual has done or intended to do something to him or one of his friends, and that accompanying every outburst of anger is a certain pleasure derived from the hope for revenge. I say "pleasure" because it is pleasant to contemplate achieving one's goals; and no one attempts to achieve what seems to be impossible for himself, so the angry man attempts to achieve what is possible for himself. The poet spoke correctly when he said that anger,

Much sweeter than dripping honey,
Swells in men's hearts.

Pleasure follows upon anger for this reason and because the mind is consumed with thoughts of vengeance; like dreams, the visions then conjured up create pleasure.

Slighting is the implementing of an opinion about what one considers to be worthless; for we think both the good and the bad to be worthy of attention (as well as what is potentially good or bad), but we do not consider whatever is of little or no account to be worthy of attention.

There are three forms of slighting—scorn, spite, and insolence. One slights what he scorns, for whatever one thinks to be worthy of nothing he scorns, and he slights what is worthy of nothing. Then one who is spiteful is also scornful, for spite involves the interference in another's wishes, not to achieve anything for oneself, but only to make sure that the other achieves nothing. Since he achieves nothing for himself, he slights the other. It is evident that the other does not intend to harm him; if he did, it would then be a matter of fear, not of slighting. It is evident also that he does not intend to help him to any appreciable degree, for there would then be an attempt at creating a friendship.

To act insolently constitutes a form of slighting, for insolence involves doing and saying things that produce shame for the person to whom these things are done or said—so that something else might happen to him (other than what has already happened), but for the other's pleasure. If it were done in retaliation, then this would not be insolence, but sheer vengeance. The insolent person derives pleasure from this because he sees others suffer and thus considers himself quite superior. The young and the rich often derive pleasure from such insolence, for they consider themselves superior when acting insolently. Dishonor is an act of insolence, and the one who dishonors is one who slights, since that which is worthy of nothing—of neither good or bad—has no honor. For this reason the angered Achilles says,

He has dishonored me; he has himself taken and keeps my prize.

and,

> I am without honor, as if some foreigner.

and shows that he is angered for this very reason. Some think it fitting that they be esteemed by those of lesser birth, ability, nobility, or whatever quality in which one is generally superior to another; for example, the rich man considers himself worthy of esteem from a poor man where wealth is concerned, as does the rhetorician from one who is inarticulate, the ruler from the governed, and even the hopeful ruler from those he hopes to rule. So it is said,

> The anger of divine kings is mighty,

and,

> But he holds his anger for another day;

the cause of their vexation is their superior station, and still others feel anger at those from whom they expect the proper care, for example, from those for whom he—either acting by himself or *via* his agents or friends—has done or is doing willful or willed service.

It is now evident from these analyses what the temperament is of angered people, at whom they become angered, and for what reasons. They become angry when they are in distress, for one in distress desires something. If someone should in any manner stand in one's way, for instance, if one should directly prevent a thirsty man from drinking (or even if it is done indirectly, he will appear to be doing the same thing), or if someone opposes, fails to assist, or in some other way annoys a distressed person, he will become angry at any of those individuals. For this reason the sick, the poor, those at war, the lover, and anyone with an unsatisfied desire, are prone to anger and irascibility, particularly against those who make light of their present distress. Examples include the ill person angry at those making light of his illness, the poor man angry at those making light of his poverty, the warrior angry at those making light of his struggle, the lover at those making light of his love, and so forth, for each person is predisposed towards his own kind of anger caused by his own sort of distress. He will also anger if he should happen to receive the oppposite of what he expected, for the unexpected creates a greater bitterness just as it can create the greater joy if one attains his desires contrary to his expectations. From these observations the hours, periods, moods, and ages most conducive to anger become apparent, as do the places and occasions; and the more intense or numerous these conditions are, the more conducive to anger they become.

We have now seen what sort of temperament belongs to people predisposed to anger. They become angry at those who laugh, scoff, and jeer at them—all acts of insolence—and at those doing them harm in manners which represent an attitude of insolence. This harm cannot be either retaliatory or beneficial to the doers, for then it would not seem to be an act of insolence. They also become angry at those who malign them or scorn matters they take greatly to heart; zealous philosophers and those concerned with their appearance, to cite just two of many examples, anger at those who scorn philosophy and those who scorn their appearance, respectively. Such anger becomes increasingly severe if the angered individuals suspect that this ability or quality does not belong or appear to belong to them, for they do not mind the ridicule when they feel thoroughly superior in those abilities or qualities at which others scoff. Anger is also directed at their friends more often than at others, since better treatment is expected from them, and also at those who normally give honor to or take thought of them, but then cease to act in this way; the angry individuals here assume they are being scorned, for otherwise they would be treated in the same way as usual. They also become angry at those who fail to repay or inadequately repay acts of kindness and at inferiors who work against them, for any such people appear to have a scornful attitude; in the latter example the angered individuals are opposed by those who consider them inferior, and in the former they have offered kindness to those who consider them inferior.

They especially anger at those of no account who slight them, since we suggested that an anger resulting from a slight was directed towards those who have no right to slight another, and it is one's inferiors who have no right to do so. They also become angry at their friends who fail to speak well of them or who fail to treat them well, or especially when they do the opposite, or when they do not understand their needs (just as Antiphon's Plexippus failed to understand Meleager's needs). It is a sign of contempt to fail to perceive the needs of a friend, since we do not forget those who are on our mind. One also angers at those who celebrate or act quite cheerfully in his misfortunes; either action is a sign of enmity or slight. One also feels anger against those who show no concern for the pains they have given him, which explains why one becomes angry with messengers who bring bad news. One also feels anger at those who listen to talk about him or ogle at his weaknesses, for it is as if they are slighters or enemies; friends would sympathize, since everyone is pained to focus on his own weaknesses. In addition, one angers at those who slight him in the presence of five classes of people—those who envy him, those he admires, those by whom he wishes to be admired, those whom he respects, and those who respect him. When people slight him in the presence of these, they incite him to an even greater anger. One also feels anger at those who slight those whom it would be a disgrace not to defend—parents, children, wives, subordinates— or to those who do not return a favor (since such a slight is an impropriety), or to those who pretend not to know about a matter he feels to be of importance, since this is an act of scorn. And one feels anger toward those beneficent to others, but not to him as well, for it is again an act of scorn to deem everyone else worthy of treatment he is not deemed worthy to receive. Forgetfulness, even of something so insignificant as a name, also produces anger, since forgetfulness as well seems to be a sign of slight and since forgetfulness derives from neglect, which is a slight.

We have now established simultaneously at whom one becomes angry, the temperament of the angry person, and the causes for his anger. It is clear that in his speech the orator must create in his audience a temperament suitable for anger and establish his adversaries as those to be held liable for what makes his audience anger and as the sort of men at whom they should be angry.

René Descartes
The Passions of the Soul

René Descartes (1596–1650) is, among many other things, the father of Cartesian dualism, which holds that the mind and the body are separate "substances." This raises the difficult question of how they interact, but it raises specific problems for the analysis of emotion. Emotions, more than any other psychic phenomena, seem to be both of the mind and of the body. In the following excerpt, Descartes tried to solve such problems with his theory of "animal spirits," which are of the body but disturb the soul as well.

OF THE PASSIONS IN GENERAL, AND INCIDENTALLY
OF THE WHOLE NATURE OF MAN

That What in Respect of a Subject Is Passion, Is in Some Other Regard Always Action   There is nothing in which the defective nature of the sciences which we have received from the ancients appears more clearly than in what they have written on the passions; for, although this is a matter which has at all times been the object of much investigation, and though it would not appear to be one of the most difficult, inasmuch as since every one has experience of the passions within himself, there is no necessity to borrow one's observations from elsewhere in order to discover their nature; yet that which the ancients have taught regarding them is both so slight, and for the most part so far from credible, that I am unable to entertain any hope of approximating to the truth excepting by shunning the paths which they have followed. This is why I shall be here obliged to write just as though I were treating of a matter which no one had ever touched on before me; and, to begin with, I consider that all that which occurs or that happens anew, is by the philosophers, generally speaking, termed a passion, in as far as the subject to which it occurs is concerned, and an action in respect of him who causes it to occur. Thus although the agent and the recipient are frequently very different, the action and the passion are always one and the same thing, although having different names, because of the two-diverse subjects to which it may be related.

What the Functions of the Soul Are   After having thus considered all the functions which pertain to the body alone, it is easy to recognise that there is nothing in us which we ought to attribute to our soul excepting our thoughts, which are mainly of two sorts, the one being the actions of the soul, and the other its passions. Those which I call its actions are all our desires, because we find by experience that they proceed directly from our soul, and appear to depend on it alone: while, on the other hand, we may usually term one's passions all those kinds of perception or forms of knowledge which are found in us, because it is often not our soul which makes them what they are, and because it always receives them from the things which are represented by them. . . .

Of the Perceptions   Our perceptions are also of two sorts, and the one have the soul as a cause and the other the body. Those which have the soul as a cause are the perceptions of our desires, and of all the imaginations or other thoughts which depend on them. For it is certain that we cannot desire anything without perceiving by the same means that we desire it; and, although in regard to our soul it is an action to desire something, we may say that it is also one of its passions to perceive that it desires. Yet because this perception and this will are really one and the same thing, the more noble always supplies the denomination, and thus we are not in the habit of calling it a passion, but only an action. . . .

That the Imaginations Which only Depend on the Fortuitous Movements of the Spirits, May Be Passions Just as Truly as the Perceptions Which Depend on the Nerves   It remains for us to notice here that all the same things which the soul perceives by the intermission of the nerves, may also be represented by the fortuitous course of the animal spirits, without there being any other difference excepting that the impressions which come into the brain by the nerves are usually more lively or definite than those excited there by the spirits, which caused me to say [previously] that the former resemble the shadow or picture of the latter. We must also notice that it sometimes happens that this picture is so similar to the thing which it represents that we may be mistaken therein regarding the perceptions which relate to objects which are outside us, or at least those which relate to certain parts of our body, but that we cannot be so deceived regarding the passions, inasmuch as they are so close to, and so entirely within our soul, that it is impossible for it to feel them without their being actually such as it feels them to be. Thus often when we sleep, and sometimes even when we are awake, we imagine certain things so forcibly, that we think we see them before us, or feel them in our body, although they do not exist at all; but although we may be asleep, or dream, we cannot feel sad or moved by any other passion without its being very true that the soul actually has this passion within it.

The Definition of the Passions of the Soul After having considered in what the passions of the soul differ from all its other thoughts, it seems to me that we may define them generally as the perceptions, feelings, or emotions of the soul which we relate specially to it, and which are caused, maintained, and fortified by some movement of the spirits.

Explanation of the First Part of This Definition We may call them perceptions when we make use of this word generally to signify all the thoughts which are not actions of the soul, or desires, but not when the term is used only to signify clear cognition; for experience shows us that those who are the most agitated by their passions, are not those who know them best; and that they are of the number of perceptions which the close alliance which exists between the soul and the body, renders confused and obscure. We may also call them feelings because they are received into the soul in the same way as are the objects of our outside senses, and are not otherwise known by it; but we can yet more accurately call them emotions of the soul, not only because the name may be attributed to all the changes which occur in it—that is, in all the diverse thoughts which come to it, but more especially because of all the kinds of thought which it may have, there are no others which so powerfully agitate and disturb it as do these passions.

Explanation of the Second Part I add that they particularly relate to the soul, in order to distinguish them from the other feelings which are related, the one to outside objects such as scents, sounds, and colours; the others to our body such as hunger, thirst, and pain. I also add that they are caused, maintained, and fortified by some movement of the spirits, in order to distinguish them from our desires, which we may call emotions of the soul which relate to it, but which are caused by itself; and also in order to explain their ultimate and most proximate cause, which plainly distinguishes them from the other feelings.

How the Soul and the Body Act on One Another Let us then conceive here that the soul has its principal seat in the little gland which exists in the middle of the brain, from whence it radiates forth through all the remainder of the body by means of the animal spirits, nerves, and even the blood, which, participating in the impressions of the spirits, can carry them by the arteries into all the members. . . . Let us here add that the small gland which is the main seat of the soul is so suspended between the cavities which contain the spirits that it can be moved by them in as many different ways as there are sensible diversities in the object, but that it may also be moved in diverse ways by the soul, whose nature is such that it receives in itself as many diverse impressions, that is to say, that it possesses as many diverse perceptions as there are diverse movements in this gland. Reciprocally, likewise, the machine of the body is so formed that from the simple fact that this gland is diversely moved by the soul, or by such other cause, whatever it is, it thrusts the spirits which surround it towards the pores of the brain, which conduct them by the nerves into the muscles, by which means it causes them to move the limbs. . . .

How One and the Same Cause May Excite Different Passions in Different Men

The same impression which a terrifying object makes on the gland, and which causes fear in certain men, may excite in others courage and confidence; the reason of this is that all brains are not constituted in the same way, and that the same movement of the gland which in some excites fear, in others causes the spirits to enter into the pores of the brain which conduct them partly into the nerves which serve to move the hands for purposes of self-defence, and partly into those which agitate and drive the blood towards the heart in the manner requisite to produce the spirits proper for the continuance of this defence, and to retain the desire of it.

The Principal Effect of the Passions

For it is requisite to notice that the principal effect of all the passions in men is that they incite and dispose their soul to desire those things for which they prepare their body, so that the feeling of fear incites it to desire to fly, that of courage to desire to fight, and so on.

What Is the Power of the Soul in Reference to its Passions

Our passions cannot likewise be directly excited or removed by the action of our will, but they can be so indirectly by the representation of things which are usually united to the passions which we desire to have, and which are contrary to those which we desire to set aside. Thus, in order to excite courage in oneself and remove fear, it is not sufficient to have the will to do so, but we must also apply ourselves to consider the reasons, the objects or examples which persuade us that the peril is not great; that there is always more security in defence than in flight; that we should have the glory and joy of having vanquished, while we could expect nothing but regret and shame for having fled, and so on.

The Reason Which Prevents the Soul From Being Able Wholly to Control Its Passion

And there is a special reason which prevents the soul from being able at once to change or arrest its passions, which has caused me to say in defining them that they are not only caused, but are also maintained and strengthened by some particular movement of the spirits. This reason is that they are nearly all accompanied by some commotion which takes place in the heart, and in consequence also in the whole of the blood and the animal spirits, so that until this commotion has subsided, they remain present to our thought in the same manner as sensible objects are present there while they act upon the organs of our senses. And as the soul, in rendering itself very attentive to some other thing, may prevent itself from hearing a slight noise or feeling a slight pain, but cannot prevent itself in the same way from hearing thunder or feeling the fire which burns the hand, it may similarly easily get the better of the lesser passions, but not the most violent and strongest, excepting after the commotion of the blood and spirits is appeased. The most that the will can do while this commotion is in its full strength is not to yield to its effects and to restrain many of the movements to which it disposes the body. For example, if anger causes us to lift our hand to strike, the will can usually hold it back; if fear incites our legs to flee, the will can arrest them, and so on in other similar cases.

Benedict Spinoza

Emotions

Benedict Spinoza *(1632–1677) lived in Holland in the seventeenth century, where his parents had escaped to avoid the Spanish Inquisition. His radical beliefs had him exiled from the Jewish community there, and he spent his solitary life trying to formulate a satisfactory vision of the universe, of human life, and of the place of emotions in life. The following is taken from his great book,* The Ethics.

Most writers on the emotions and on human conduct seem to be treating rather of matters outside nature than of natural phenomena following nature's general laws. They appear to conceive man to be situated in nature as a kingdom within a kingdom: for they believe that he disturbs rather than follows nature's order, that he has absolute control over his actions, and that he is determined solely by himself. They attribute human infirmities and fickleness, not to the power of nature in general, but to some mysterious flaw in the nature of man, which accordingly they bemoan, deride, despise, or, as usually happens, abuse: he, who succeeds in hitting off the weakness of the human mind more eloquently or more acutely than his fellows, is looked upon as a seer. Still there has been no lack of very excellent men (to whose toil and industry I confess myself much indebted), who have written many note-worthy things concerning the right way of life, and have given much sage advice to mankind. But no one, so far as I know, has defined the nature and strength of the emotions, and the power of the mind against them for their restraint.

I do not forget, that the illustrious Descartes, though he believed that the mind has absolute power over its actions, strove to explain human emotions by their primary causes, and, at the same time, to point out a way, by which the mind might attain to absolute dominion over them. However, in my opinion, he accomplishes nothing beyond a display of the acute-ness of his own great intellect, as I will show in the proper place. For the present I wish to revert to those, who would rather abuse or deride human emotions than understand them. Such persons will doubtless think it strange that I should attempt to treat of human vice and folly geometrically, and should wish to set forth with rigid reasoning those matters which they cry out against as repugnant to reason, frivolous, absurd, and dreadful. However, such is my plan. Nothing comes to pass in nature, which can be set down to a flaw therein; for nature is always the same, and everywhere one and the same in her efficacy and power of action; that is, nature's laws and ordinances, whereby all things come to pass and change from one form to another, are everywhere and always the same; so that there should be one and the same method of understanding the nature of all things whatsoever, namely, through nature's universal laws and rules. Thus the passions of hatred, anger, envy, and so on, con-sidered in themselves, follow from this same necessity and efficacy of nature; they answer to certain definite causes, through which they are understood, and possess certain properties as worthy of being known as the properties of anything else, whereof the contemplation in itself affords us delight. I shall, therefore, treat of the nature and strength of the emotions according to the same method, as I employed heretofore in my investigations concerning God and the mind. I shall consider human actions and desires in exactly the same manner, as though I were concerned with lines, planes, and solids.

DEFINITIONS

I. By an *adequate* cause, I mean a cause through which its effect can be clearly and distinctly perceived. By an *inadequate* or partial cause, I mean a cause through which, by itself, its effect cannot be understood.

II. I say that we *act* when anything takes place, either within us or externally to us, whereof we are the adequate cause; that is (by the foregoing definition) when through our nature something takes place within us or externally to us, which can through our nature alone be clearly and distinctly understood. On the other hand, I say that we are passive as regards something when that something takes place within us, or follows from our nature externally, we being only the partial cause.

III. By *emotion* I mean the modifications of the body, whereby the active power of the said body is increased or diminished, aided or constrained, and also the ideas of such modifications.

N.B. If we can be the adequate cause of any of these modifications, I then call the emotion an activity, otherwise I call it a passion, or state wherein the mind is passive.

Postulates

I. The human body can be affected in many ways, whereby its power of activity is increased or diminished, and also in other ways which do not render its power of activity either greater or less.

II. The human body can undergo many changes, and, nevertheless, retain the impressions or traces of objects, and, consequently, the same images of things.

PROP. I. *Our mind is in certain cases active, and in certain cases passive. In so far as it has adequate ideas, it is necessarily active, and in so far as it has inadequate ideas, it is necessarily passive.*

PROP. XIII. *When the mind conceives things which diminish or hinder the body's power of activity, it endeavours, as far as possible, to remember things which exclude the existence of the first-named things.*

Proof.—So long as the mind conceives anything of the kind alluded to, the power of the mind and body is diminished or constrained (cf. III. xii. Proof); nevertheless it will continue to conceive it, until the mind conceives something else, which excludes the present existence thereof (II. xvii.); that is (as I have just shown), the power of the mind and of the body is diminished, or constrained, until the mind conceives something else, which excludes the existence of the former thing conceived: therefore the mind (III. ix.), as far as it can, will endeavour to conceive or remember the latter. Q.E.D.

Corollary.—Hence it follows, that the mind shrinks from conceiving those things, which diminish or constrain the power of itself and of the body.

Note.—From what has been said we may clearly understand the nature of Love and Hate. *Love* is nothing else but *pleasure accompanied by the idea of an external cause. Hate* is nothing else but *pain accompanied by the idea of an external cause.* We further see, that he who loves necessarily endeavours to have, and to keep present to him, the object of his love; while he who hates endeavours to remove and destroy the object of his hatred. But I will treat these matters at more length hereafter.

PROP. XIV. *If the mind has once been affected by two emotions at the same time, it will, whenever it is afterwards affected by one of the two, be also affected by the other.*

Proof.—If the human body has once been affected by two bodies at once, whenever afterwards the mind conceives one of them, it will straightway remember the other also (II. xvii.). But the mind's conceptions indicate rather the emotions of our body than the nature of external bodies (II. xvi. Coroll. ii.); therefore, if the body, and consequently the mind (III. Def. iii.) has been once affected by two emotions at the same time, it will, whenever it is afterwards affected by one of the two, be also affected by the other.

PROP. LIII. *When the mind regards itself and its own power of activity, it feels pleasure; and that pleasure is greater in proportion to the distinctness wherewith it conceives itself and its own power of activity.*

Proof.—A man does not know himself except through the modifications of his body, and the ideas thereof (II. xix. and xxiii.). When, therefore, the mind is able to contemplate itself, it is thereby assumed to pass to a greater perfection, or (III. xi. note) to feel pleasure; and the pleasure will be greater in proportion to the distinctness, wherewith it is able to conceive itself and its own power of activity. Q.E.D.

Corollary.—This pleasure is fostered more and more, in proportion as a man conceives himself to be praised by others. For the more he conceives himself as praised by others, the more will he imagine them to be affected with pleasure, accompanied by the idea of himself (III. xxix. note); thus he is (III. xxvii.) himself affected with greater pleasure, accompanied by the idea of himself. Q.E.D.

PROP. LIV. *The mind endeavours to conceive only such things as assert its power of activity.*

Proof.—The endeavour or power of the mind is the actual essence thereof (III. vii.); but the essence of the mind obviously only affirms that which the mind is and can do; not that which it neither is nor can do; therefore the mind endeavours to conceive only such things as assert or affirm its power of activity. Q.E.D.

PROP. LV. *When the mind contemplates its own weakness, it feels pain thereat.*

Proof.—The essence of the mind only affirms that which the mind is, or can do; in other words, it is the mind's nature to conceive only such things as assert is power of activity (last Prop.). Thus, when we say that the mind contemplates its own weakness, we are merely saying that while the mind is attempting to conceive something which asserts its power of activity, it is checked in its endeavour—in other words (III. xi. note), it feels pain. Q.E.D.

Corollary.—This pain is more and more fostered, if a man conceives that he is blamed by others; this may be proved in the same way as the corollary to III. liii.

Note.—This pain, accompanied by the idea of our own weakness, is called *humility*; the pleasure, which springs from the contemplation of ourselves, is called *self-love* or *self-complacency*. And inasmuch as this feeling is renewed as often as a man contemplates his own virtues, or his own power of activity, it follows that everyone is fond of narrating his own exploits, and displaying the force both of his body and mind, and also that, for this reason, men are troublesome one to another. Again, it follows that men are naturally envious, rejoicing in the shortcomings of their equals, and feeling pain at their virtues. For whenever a man conceives his own actions, he is affected with pleasure in proportion as his actions display more perfection, and he conceives them more distinctly—that is, in proportion as he can distinguish them from others, and regard them as something special. . . .

VI. *Love* is pleasure, accompanied by the idea of an external cause.

Explanation.—This definition explains sufficiently clearly the essence of love; the definition given by those authors who say that love is *the lover's wish to unite himself to the loved object* expresses a property, but not the essence of love; and, as such authors have not sufficiently discerned love's essence, they have been unable to acquire a true conception of its properties, accordingly their definition is on all hands admitted to be very obscure. It must, however, be noted, that when I say that it is a property of love, that the lover should wish to unite himself to the beloved object, I do not here mean by *wish* consent, or conclusion, or a free decision of the mind (for I have shown such, in II. xlviii., to be fictitious); neither do I mean a desire of being united to the loved object when it is absent, or of continuing in its presence when it is at hand; for love can be conceived without either of these desires; but by *wish* I mean the contentment, which is in the lover, on account of the presence of the beloved object, whereby the pleasure of the lover is strengthened, or at least maintained.

VII. *Hatred* is pain, accompanied by the idea of an external cause.

IX. *Aversion* is pain, accompanied by the idea of something which is accidentally the cause of pain (cf. III. xv. note).

X. *Devotion* is love towards one whom we admire.

XI. *Derision* is pleasure arising from our conceiving the presence of a quality, which we despise, in an object which we hate. . . .

XII. *Hope* is an inconstant pleasure, arising from the idea of something past or future, whereof we to a certain extent doubt the issue.

XIII. *Fear* is an inconstant pain arising from the idea of something past or future, whereof we to a certain extent doubt the issue.

Explanation.—From these definitions it follows, that there is no hope unmingled with fear, and no fear unmingled with hope. For he, who depends on hope and doubts concerning the issue of anything, is assumed to conceive something, which excludes the existence of the said thing in the future; therefore he, to this extent, feels pain; consequently, while dependent on hope, he fears for the issue. Contrariwise he, who fears, in other words doubts, concerning the issue of something which he hates, also conceives something which excludes the existence of the thing in question; to this extent he feels pleasure, and consequently to this extent he hopes that it will turn out as he desires (III. xx.).

XIV. *Confidence* is pleasure arising from the idea of something past or future, wherefrom all cause of doubt has been removed.

XV. *Despair* is pain arising from the idea of something past or future, wherefrom all cause of doubt has been removed. . . .

XVI. *Joy* is pleasure accompanied by the idea of something past, which has had an issue beyond our hope.

XVII. *Disappointment* is pain accompanied by the idea of something past, which has had an issue contrary to our hope.

XVIII. *Pity* is pain accompanied by the idea of evil, which has befallen someone else whom we conceive to be like ourselves. . . .

XIX. *Approval* is love towards one who has done good to another.

XX. *Indignation* is hatred towards one who has done evil to another. . . .

XXIII. *Envy* is hatred, in so far as it induces a man to be pained by another's good fortune, and to rejoice in another's evil fortune. . . .

XXIV. *Sympathy* (*misericordia*) is love, in so far as it induces a man to feel pleasure at another's good fortune, and pain at another's evil fortune.

XXVI. *Humility* is pain arising from a man's contemplation of his own weakness of body or mind.

Explanation.—Self-complacency is opposed to humility, in so far as we thereby mean pleasure arising from a contemplation of our own power of action; but, in so far as we mean thereby pleasure accompanied by the idea of any action which we believe we have performed by the free decision of our mind, it is opposed to repentance, which we may thus define:

XXVIII. *Pride* is thinking too highly of one's self from self-love.

Explanation.—Thus pride is different from partiality, for the latter term is used in reference to an external object, but pride is used of a man thinking too highly of himself. However, as partiality is the effect or love, so is pride the effect or property of *self-love,* which may therefore be thus defined, *love of self or self-approval, in so far as it leads a man to think too highly of himself.* . . .

GENERAL DEFINITION OF THE EMOTIONS

Emotion, which is called a passivity of the soul, is a confused idea, whereby the mind affirms concerning its body, or any part thereof, a force for existence (*existendi vis*) greater or less than before, and by the presence of which the mind is determined to think of one thing rather than another.

David Hume

On Pride

David Hume (*1711–1776*) *was one of the few philosophers of the enlightenment who would argue that "reason is and ought to be the slave of the passions." Placing emotions in such an elevated position, he spent a significant proportion of his philosophy trying to analyze them and show how they are constructed out of combinations of "impressions and ideas"—the two basic components of his theory of mind. What follows is his analysis of pride from his* Treatise of Human Nature, *with some comments on love and hate.*

OF THE PASSIONS

Division of the Subject

As all the perceptions of the mind may be divided into *impressions* and *ideas,* so the impressions admit of another division into *original* and *secondary.* This division of the impressions is the same with that which I formerly made use of when I distinguish'd them into impressions of *sensation* and *reflexion.* Original impressions or impressions of sensation are such as without any antecedent perception arise in the soul, from the constitution of the body, from the animal spirits, or from the application of objects to the external organs. Secondary, or reflective impressions are such as proceed from some of these original ones, either immediately or by the interposition of its idea. Of the first kind are all the impressions of the senses, and all bodily pains and pleasures: Of the second are the passions, and other emotions resembling them.

'Tis certain, that the mind, in its perceptions, must begin somewhere; and that since the impressions precede their correspondent ideas, there must be some impressions, which without any introduction make their appearance in the soul. As these depend upon natural and physical causes, the examination of them wou'd lead me too far from my present subject, into the sciences of anatomy and natural philosophy. For this reason I shall here confine myself to those other impressions, which I have call'd secondary and reflective, as arising either from the original impressions, or from their ideas. Bodily pains and pleasures are the source of many passions, both when felt and consider'd by the mind; but arise originally in the soul, or in the body, whichever you please to call it, without any preceding thought or perception. A fit of the gout produces a long train of passions, as grief, hope, fear; but is not deriv'd immediately from any affection or idea.

The reflective impressions may be divided into two kinds, viz. the *calm* and the *violent*. Of the first kind is the sense of beauty and deformity in action, composition, and external objects. Of the second are the passions of love and hatred, grief and joy, pride and humility. This division is far from being exact. The raptures of poetry and music frequently rise to the greatest height; while those other impressions, properly called *passions*, may decay into so soft an emotion, as to become, in a manner, imperceptible. But as in general the passions are more violent than the emotions arising from beauty and deformity, these impressions have been commonly distinguish'd from each other. The subject of the human mind being so copious and various, I shall here take advantage of this vulgar and specious division, that I may proceed with the greater order; and having said all I thought necessary concerning our ideas, shall now explain these violent emotions or passions, their nature, origin, causes, and effects.

When we take a survey of the passions, there occurs a division of them into *direct* and *indirect*. By direct passions I understand such as arise immediately from good or evil, from pain or pleasure. By indirect such as proceed from the same principles, but by the conjunction of other qualities. This distinction I cannot at present justify or explain any farther. I can only observe in general, that under the indirect passions I comprehend pride, humility, ambition, vanity, love, hatred, envy, pity, malice, generosity, with their dependants. And under the direct passions, desire, aversion, grief, joy, hope, fear, despair and security. I shall begin with the former.

Of Pride and Humility; Their Objects and Causes

The passions of *pride* and *humility* being simple and uniform impressions, 'tis impossible we can ever, by a multitude of words, give a just definition of them, or indeed of any of the passions. The utmost we can pretend to is a description of them, by an enumeration of such circumstances, as attend them: But as these words, *pride* and *humility*, are of general use, and the impressions they represent the most common of any, every one, of himself, will be able to form a just idea of them, without any danger of mistake. For which reason, not to lose time upon preliminaries, I shall immediately enter upon the examination of these passions.

'Tis evident, that pride and humility, tho' directly contrary, have yet the same OBJECT. This object is self, or that succession of related ideas and impressions, of which we have an intimate memory and consciousness. Here the view always fixes when we are actuated by either of these passions. According as our idea of ourself is more or less advantageous, we feel either of those opposite affections, and are elated by pride, or dejected with humility. Whatever other objects may be comprehended by the mind, they are always consider'd with a view to ourselves; otherwise they wou'd never be able either to excite these passions, or produce the smallest encrease or dimunition of them. When self enters not into the consideration, there is no room either for pride or humility.

But tho' that connected succession of perceptions, which we call *self*, be always the object of these two passions, 'tis impossible it can be their CAUSE, or be sufficient alone to excite them. For as these passions are directly contrary, and have the same object in common; were their object also their cause; it cou'd never produce any degree of the one passion, but at the same time it must excite an equal degree of the other; which opposition and contrariety must destroy both. 'Tis impossible a man can at the same time be both proud and humble; and where he has different reasons for these passions, as frequently happens, the passions either take place alternately; or if they encounter, the one annihilates the other, as far as its strength goes, and the remainder only of that, which is superior, continues to operate upon the mind. But in the present case neither of the passions cou'd ever become superior; because supposing it to be the view only of ourself, which excited them, that being perfectly indifferent to either, must produce both in the very same proportion; or in other words, can produce neither. To excite any passion, and at the same time raise an equal share of its antagonist, is immediately to undo what was done, and must leave the mind at last perfectly calm and indifferent.

We must, therefore, make a distinction betwixt the cause and the object of these passions; betwixt that idea, which excites them, and that to which they direct their view, when excited. Pride and humility, being once rais'd, immediately turn our attention to ourself, and regard that as their ultimate and final object; but there is something farther requisite in order to raise them: Something, which is peculiar to one of the passions, and produces not both in the very same degree. The first idea, that is presented to the mind, is that of the cause or productive principle. This excites the passion, connected with it; and the passion, when excited, turns our view to another idea, which is that of self. Here then is a passion plac'd betwixt two ideas, of which the one produces it, and the other is produc'd by it. The first idea, therefore, represents the *cause,* the second the *object* of the passion.

To begin with the causes of pride and humility; we may observe, that their most obvious and remarkable property is the vast variety of *subjects,* on which they may be plac'd. Every valuable quality of the mind, whether of the imagination, judgment, memory or disposition; wit, good-sense, learning, courage, justice, integrity; all these are the causes of pride; and their opposites of humility. Nor are these passions confin'd to the mind, but extend their view to the body likewise. A man may be proud of his beauty, strength, agility, good mien, address in dancing, riding, fencing, and of his dexterity in any manual business or manufacture. But this is not all. The passion looking farther, comprehends whatever objects are in the least ally'd or related to us. Our country, family, children, relations, riches, houses, gardens, horses, dogs, cloaths; any of these may become a cause either of pride or of humility.

From the consideration of these causes, it appears necessary we shou'd make a new distinction in the causes of the passion, betwixt that *quality,* which operates, and the *subject,* on which it is plac'd. A man, for instance, is vain of a beautiful house, which belongs to him, or which he has himself built and contriv'd. Here the object of the passion is himself, and the cause is the beautiful house: Which cause again is sub-divided into two parts, *viz.* the quality, which operates upon the passion, and the subject, in which the quality inheres. The quality is the beauty, and the subject is the house, consider'd as his property or contrivance. Both these parts are essential, nor is the distinction vain and chimerical. Beauty, consider'd merely as such, unless plac'd upon something related to us, never produces any pride or vanity; and the strongest relation alone, without beauty, or something else in its place, has as little influence on that passion. . . .

Having thus in a manner suppos'd two properties of the causes of these affections, *viz.* that the *qualities* produce a separate pain or pleasure, and that the *subjects,* on which the qualities are plac'd, are related to self; I proceed to examine the passions themselves, in order to find something in them, correspondent to the suppos'd properties of their causes. *First,* I find, that the peculiar object of pride and humility is determin'd by an original and natural instinct, and that 'tis absolutely impossible, from the primary constitution of the mind, that these passions shou'd ever look beyond self, or that individual person, of whose actions and sentiments each of us is intimately conscious. Here at last the view always rests, when we are actuated by either of these passions; nor can we, in that situation of mind, ever lose sight of this object. For this I pretend not to give any reason; but consider such a peculiar direction of the thought as an original quality.

The *second* quality, which I discover in these passions, and which I likewise consider as an original quality, is their sensations, or the peculiar emotions they excite in the soul, and which constitute their very being and essence. Thus pride is a pleasant sensation, and humility a painful; and upon the removal of the pleasure and pain, there is in reality no pride nor humility. Of this our very feeling convinces us; and beyond our feeling, 'tis here in vain to reason or dispute.

If I compare, therefore, these two *establish'd* properties of the passions, *viz.* their object, which is self, and their sensation, which is either pleasant or painful, to the two *suppos'd* properties of the causes, *viz.* their relation to self, and their tendency to produce a pain or pleasure, independent of the passion; I immediately find, that taking these suppositions to be just, the true system breaks in upon me with an irresistible evidence. That cause, which excites the passion, is related to the object, which nature has attributed to the passion; the sensation, which the cause separately produces, is related to the sensation of the passion: From this double relation of ideas and impressions, the passion is deriv'd. The one idea is easily converted into its cor-relative; and the one impression into that, which resembles and corresponds to it: With how much greater facility must this transition be made, where these movements mutually assist each other, and the mind receives a double impulse from the relations both of its impressions and ideas?

That we may comprehend this the better, we must suppose, that nature has given to the organs of the human mind, a certain disposition fitted to produce a peculiar impression or emotion, which we call *pride:* To this emotion she has assign'd a certain idea, *viz.* that of *self,* which it never fails to produce. This contrivance of nature is easily conceiv'd. We have many instances of such a situation of affairs. The nerves of the nose and palate are so dispos'd, as in certain circumstances to convey such peculiar sensations to the mind: The sensations of lust and hunger always produce in us the idea of those peculiar objects, which are suitable to each appetite. These two circumstances are united in pride. The organs are so dispos'd as to produce the passion; and the passion, after its production, naturally produces a certain idea. All this needs no proof. 'Tis evident we never shou'd be possest of that passion, were there not a disposition of mind proper for it; and 'tis as evident, that the passion always turns our view to ourselves, and makes us think of our own qualities and circumstances. . . .

The difficulty, then, is only to discover this cause, and find what it is that gives the first motion to pride, and sets those organs in action, which are naturally fitted to produce that emotion. Upon my consulting experience, in order to resolve this difficulty, I immediately find a hundred different causes, that produce pride; and upon examining these causes, I suppose, what at first I perceive to be probable, that all of them concur in two circumstances; which are, that of themselves they produce an impression, ally'd to the passion, and are plac'd on a subject, ally'd to the object of the passion. When I consider after this the nature of *relation,* and its effects both on the passions and ideas, I can no longer doubt, upon these suppositions, that 'tis the very principle, which gives rise to pride, and bestows motion on those organs, which being naturally dispos'd to produce that affection, require only a first impulse or beginning to their action. Any thing, that gives a pleasant sensation, and is related to self, excites the passion of pride, which is also agreeable, and has self for its object.

What I have said of pride is equally true of humility. The sensation of humility is uneasy, as that of pride is aggreeable; for which reason the separate sensation, arising from the causes, must be revers'd, while the relation to self continues the same. Tho' pride and humility are directly contrary in their effects, and in their sensations, they have notwithstanding the same object; so that 'tis requisite only to change the relation of impressions, without making any change upon that of ideas. Accordingly we find, that a beautiful house, belonging to ourselves, produces pride; and that the same house, still belonging to ourselves, produces humility, when by any accident its beauty is chang'd into deformity, and thereby the sensation of pleasure, which corresponded to pride, is transform'd into pain, which is related to humility. The double relation between the ideas and impressions subsists in both cases, and produces an easy transition from the one emotion to the other.

OF LOVE AND HATRED

Of the Objects and Causes of Love and Hatred

'Tis altogether impossible to give any definition of the passions of *love* and *hatred*; and that because they produce merely a simple impression, without any mixture or composition. 'Twou'd be as unnecessary to attempt any description of them, drawn from their nature, origin, causes and objects; and that both because these are the subjects of our present enquiry, and because these passions of themselves are sufficiently known from our common feeling and experience. This we have already observ'd concerning pride and humility, and here repeat it concerning love and hatred; and indeed there is so great a resemblance betwixt these two sets of passions, that we shall be oblig'd to begin with a kind of abridgment of our reasonings concerning the former, in order to explain the latter.

As the immediate *object* of pride and humility is self or that identical person, of whose thoughts, actions, and sensations we are intimately conscious; so the *object* of love and hatred is some other person, of whose thoughts, actions, and sensations we are not conscious. This is sufficiently evident from experience. Our love and hatred are always directed to some sensible being external to us; and when we talk of *self-love*, 'tis not in a proper sense, nor has the sensation it produces any thing in common with that tender emotion, which is excited by a friend or mistress. 'Tis the same case with hatred. We may be mortified by our own faults and follies; but never feel any anger or hatred, except from the injuries of others.

But tho' the object of love and hatred be always some other person, 'tis plain that the object is not, properly speaking, the *cause* of these passions, or alone sufficient to excite them. For since love and hatred are directly contrary in their sensation, and have the same object in common, if that object were also their cause, it wou'd produce these opposite passions in an equal degree; and as they must, from the very first moment, destroy each other, none of them wou'd ever be able to make its appearance. There must, therefore, be some cause different from the object.

If we consider the causes of love and hatred, we shall find they are very much diversify'd, and have not many things in common. The virtue, knowledge, wit, good sense, good humour of any person, produce love and esteem; as the opposite qualities, hatred and contempt. The same passions arise from bodily accomplishments, such as beauty, force, swiftness, dexterity; and from their contraries; as likewise from the external advantages and disadvantages of family, possessions, cloaths, nation and climate. There is not one of these objects, but what by its different qualities may produce love and esteem, or hatred and contempt.

From the view of these causes we may derive a new distinction betwixt the *quality* that operates, and the *subject* on which it is plac'd. A prince, that is possess'd of a stately palace, commands the esteem of the people upon that account; and that *first,* by the beauty of the palace, and *secondly,* by the relation of property, which connects it with him. The removal of either of these destroys the passion; which evidently proves that the cause is a compounded one.

'Twou'd be tedious to trace the passions of love and hatred, thro' all the observations which we have form'd concerning pride and humility, and which are equally applicable to both sets of passions. 'Twill be sufficient to *remark* in general, that the object of love and hatred is evidently some thinking person; and that the sensation of the former passion is always aggreeable, and of the latter uneasy. We may also *suppose* with some shew of probability, *that the cause of both these passions is always related to a thinking being, and that the cause of the former produce a separate pleasure, and of the latter a separate uneasiness.*

William James
What Is an Emotion?

William James *(1842–1910) was America's greatest philosopher–psychologist and wrote what for many years was the classic textbook of psychology. He had a special interest in emotions, and his analysis of emotion still dominates much of current thinking in psychology. Wha. follows is taken from his 1884 essay "What is an Emotion?"*

*T*he physiologists who, during the past few years, have been so industriously exploring the functions of the brain, have limited their attempts at explanation to its cognitive and volitional performances. Dividing the brain into sensorial and motor centres, they have found their division to be exactly paralleled by the analysis made by empirical psychology, of the perceptive and volitional parts of the mind into their simplest elements. But the *æsthetic* sphere of the mind, its longings, its pleasures and pains, and its emotions, have been so ignored in all these researches that one is tempted to suppose that if either Dr. Ferrier or Dr. Munk were asked for a theory in brain-terms of the latter mental facts, they might both reply, either that they had as yet bestowed no thought upon the subject, or that they had found it so difficult to make distinct hypotheses, that the matter lay for them among the problems of the future, only to be taken up after the simpler ones of the present should have been definitively solved.

And yet it is even now certain that of two things concerning the emotions, one must be true. Either separate and special centres, affected to them alone, are their brain-seat, or else they correspond to processes occurring in the motor and sensory centres, already assigned, or in others like them, not yet mapped out. If the former be the case we must deny the current view, and hold the cortex to be something more than the surface of "projection" for every sensitive spot and every muscle in the body. If the latter be the case, we must ask whether the emotional "process" in the sensory or motor centre be an altogether peculiar one, or whether it resembles the ordinary perceptive processes of which those centres are already recognized to be the seat. The purpose of the following pages is to show that the last alternative comes nearest to the truth, and that the emotional brain-processes not only resemble the ordinary sensorial brain-processes, but in very truth *are* nothing but such processes variously combined. . . .

I should say first of all that the only emotions I propose expressly to consider here are those that have a distinct bodily expression. That there are feelings of pleasure and displeasure, of interest and excitement, bound up with mental operations, but having no obvious bodily expression for their consequence, would, I suppose, be held true by most readers. Certain arrangements of sounds, of lines, of colours, are agreeable, and others the reverse, without the degree of the feeling being sufficient to quicken the pulse or breathing, or to prompt to movements of either the body or the face. Certain sequences of ideas charm us as much as others tire us. It is a real intellectual delight to get a problem solved, and a real intellectual torment to have to leave it unfinished. The first set of examples, the sounds, lines, and colours, are either bodily sensations, or the images of such. The second set seem to depend on processes in the ideational centres exclusively. Taken together, they appear to prove that there are pleasures and pains inherent in certain forms of nerve-action as such, wherever that action occur. The case of these feelings we will at present leave entirely aside, and confine our attention to the more complicated cases in which a wave of bodily disturbance of some kind accompanies the perception of the interesting sights or sounds, or the passage of the exciting train of ideas. Surprise, curiosity, rapture, fear, anger, lust, greed, and the like, become then the names of the mental states with which the person is possessed. The bodily disturbances are said to be the "manifestation" of these several emotions, their "expression" or "natural language"; and these emotions themselves, being so strongly characterised both from within and without, may be called the *standard* emotions.

Our natural way of thinking about these standard emotions is that the mental perception of some fact excites the mental affection called the emotion, and that this latter state of mind gives rise to the bodily expression. My thesis on the contrary is that *the bodily changes follow directly the* PERCEPTION *of the exciting fact, and that our feeling of the same changes as they occur* IS *the emotion.* Common sense says, we lose our fortune, we are sorry and weep; we meet a bear, are frightened and run; we are insulted by a rival, are angry and strike. The hypothesis here to be defended says that this order of sequence is incorrect, that the one mental state is not immediately induced by the other, that the bodily manifestations must first be interposed between, and that the more rational statement is that we feel sorry because we cry, angry because we strike, afraid because we tremble, and not that we cry, strike, or tremble, because we are sorry, angry, or fearful, as the case may be. Without the bodily states following on the perception, the latter would be purely cognitive in form, pale, colourless, destitute of emotional warmth. We might then see the bear, and judge it best to run, receive the insult and deem it right to strike, but we could not actually *feel* afraid or angry.

Stated in this crude way, the hypothesis is pretty sure to meet with immediate disbelief. And yet neither many nor far-fetched considerations are required to mitigate its paradoxical character, and possibly to produce conviction of its truth.

To begin with, readers . . . do not need to be reminded that the nervous system of every living thing is but a bundle of predispositions to react in particular ways upon the contact of particular features of the environment. As surely as the hermit-crab's abdomen presupposes the existence of empty whelk-shells somewhere to be found, so surely do the hound's olfactories imply the existence, on the one hand, of deer's or foxes' feet, and on the other, the tendency to follow up their tracks. The neural machinery is but a hyphen between determinate arrangements of matter outside the body and determinate impulses to inhibition or discharge within its organs. When the hen sees a white oval object on the ground, she cannot leave it; she must keep upon it and return to it, until at last its transformation into a little mass of moving chirping down elicits from her machinery an entirely new set of per-formances. The love of man for woman, or of the human mother for her babe, our wrath at snakes and our fear of precipices, may all be described similarly, as instances of the way in which peculiarly conformed pieces of the world's furniture will fatally call forth most particular mental and bodily reactions, in advance of, and often in direct opposition to, the verdict of our deliberate reason concerning them. The labours of Darwin and his successors are only just beginning to reveal the universal parasitism of each special creature upon other special things, and the way in which each creature brings the signature of its special relations stamped on its nervous system with it upon the scene.

Every living creature is in fact a sort of lock, whose wards and springs presuppose special forms of key,—which keys however are not born attached to the locks, but are sure to be found in the world near by as life goes on. And the locks are indifferent to any but their own keys. The egg fails to fascinate the hound, the bird does not fear the precipice, the snake waxes not wroth at his kind, the deer cares nothing for the woman or the human babe. . . .

Now among these nervous anticipations are of course to be reckoned the emotions, so far as these may be called forth directly by the perception of certain facts. In advance of all experience of elephants no child can but be frightened if he suddenly find one trumpeting and charging upon him. No woman can see a handsome little naked baby without delight, no man in the wilderness see a human form in the distance without excitement and curiosity. I said I should consider these emotions only so far as they have bodily movements of some sort for their accompaniments. But my first point is to show that their bodily accompaniments are much more far-reaching and complicated than we ordinarily suppose. . . . not only the heart, but the entire circulatory system, forms a sort of sounding-board, which every change of our consciousness, however slight, may make reverberate. Hardly a sensation comes to us without sending waves of alternate constriction and dilation down the arteries of our arms. The blood-vessels of the abdomen act reciprocally with those of the more outward parts. The bladder and bowels, the glands of the mouth, throat, and skin, and the liver, are known to be affected gravely in certain severe emotions, and are unquestionably affected transiently when the emotions are of a lighter sort. That the heart-beats and rhythm of breathing play a leading part in all emotions whatsoever, is a matter too notorious for proof. And what is really equally prominent, but less likely to be admitted until special attention is drawn to the fact, is the continuous co-operation of the voluntary muscles in our emotional states. Even when no change of outward attitude is produced, their inward tension alters to suit each varying mood, and is felt as a difference of tone or of strain. In depression the flexors tend to prevail; in elation or belligerent excitement the extensors take the lead. And the various permutations and combinations of which these organic activities are susceptible, make it abstractly possible that no shade of emotion, however slight, should be without a bodily reverberation as unique, when taken in its totality, as is the mental mood itself.

The immense number of parts modified in each emotion is what makes it so difficult for us to reproduce in cold blood the total and integral expression of any one of them. We may catch the trick with the voluntary muscles, but fail with the skin, glands, heart, and other viscera. Just as an artificially imitated sneeze lacks something of the reality, so the attempt to imitate an emotion in the absence of its normal instigating cause is apt to be rather "hollow."

The next thing to be noticed is this, that every one of the bodily changes, whatsoever it be, is *felt,* acutely or obscurely, the moment it occurs. If the reader has never paid attention to this matter, he will be both interested and astonished to learn how many different local bodily feelings he can detect in himself as characteristic of his various emotional moods. It would be perhaps too much to expect him to arrest the tide of any strong gust of passion for the sake of any such curious analysis as this; but he can observe more tranquil states, and that may be assumed here to be true of the greater which is shown to be true of the less. Our whole cubic capacity is sensibly alive; and each morsel of it contributes its pulsations of feeling, dim or sharp, pleasant, painful, or dubious, to that sense of personality that every one of us unfailingly carries with him. It is surprising what little items give accent to these complexes of sensibility. When worried by any slight trouble, one may find that the focus of one's bodily consciousness is the contraction, often quite inconsiderable, of the eyes and brows. When momentarily embarrassed, it is something in the pharynx that compels either a swallow, a clearing of the throat, or a slight cough; and so on for as many more instances as might be named. Our concern here being with the general view rather than with the details, I will not linger to discuss these but, assuming the point admitted that every change that occurs must be felt, I will pass on.

I now proceed to urge the vital point of my whole theory, which is this. If we fancy some strong emotion, and then try to abstract from our consciousness of it all the feelings of its characteristic bodily symptoms, we find we have nothing left behind, no "mind-stuff" out of which the emotion can be constituted, and that a cold and neutral state of intellectual perception is all that remains. It is true, that although most people, when asked, say that their introspection verifies this statement, some persist in saying theirs does not. Many cannot be made to understand the question. When you beg them to imagine away every feeling of laughter and of tendency to laugh from their consciousness of the ludicrousness of an object, and then to tell you what the feeling of its ludicrousness would be like, whether it be anything more than the perception that the object belongs to the class "funny," they persist in replying that the thing proposed is a physical impossibility, and that they always *must* laugh, if they see a funny object. Of course the task proposed is not the practical one of seeing a ludicrous object and annihilating one's tendency to laugh. It is the purely speculative one of subtracting certain elements of feeling from an emotional state supposed to exist in its fulness, and saying what the residual elements are. I cannot help thinking that all who rightly apprehend this problem will agree with the proposition above laid down. What kind of an emotion of fear would be left, if the feelings neither of quickened heart-beats nor of shallow breathing, neither of trembling lips nor of weakened limbs, neither of goose-flesh nor of visceral stirrings, were present, it is quite impossible to think. Can one fancy the state of rage and picture no ebullition of it in the chest, no flushing of the face, no dilatation of the nostrils, no clenching of the teeth, no impulse to vigorous action, but in their stead limp muscles, calm breathing, and a placid face? The present writer, for one, certainly cannot. The rage is as completely evaporated as the sensation of its so-called manifestations, and the only thing that can possibly be supposed to take its place is some cold-blooded and dispassionate judicial sentence, confined entirely to the intellectual realm, to the effect that a certain person or persons merit chastisement for their sins. In like manner of grief: what would it be without its tears, its sobs, its suffocation of the heart, its pang in the breast-bone? A feelingless cognition that certain circumstances are deplorable, and nothing more. Every passion in turn tells the same story. A purely disembodied human emotion is a nonentity. I do not say that it is a contradiction in the nature of things, or that pure spirits are necessarily condemned to cold intellectual lives; but I say that for *us,* emotion dissociated from all bodily feeling is inconceivable. The more closely I scrutinise my states, the more persuaded I become, that whatever moods, affections, and passions I have, are in very truth constituted by, and made up of, those bodily changes we ordinarily call their expression or consequence; and the more it seems to me that if I were to become corporeally anæsthetic, I should be excluded from the life of the affections, harsh and tender alike, and drag out an existence of merely cognitive or intellectual form. Such an existence, although it seems to have been the ideal of ancient sages, is too apathetic to be keenly sought after by those born after the revival of the worship of sensibility, a few generations ago. . . .

If our theory be true, a necessary corollary of it ought to be that any voluntary arousal of the so-called manifestations of a special emotion ought to give us the emotion itself. Of course in the majority of emotions, this test is inapplicable; for many of the manifestations are in organs over which we have no volitional control. Still, within the limits in which it can be verified, experience fully corroborates this test. Everyone knows how panic is increased by flight, and how giving way to the symptoms of grief or anger increases those passions themselves. Each fit of sobbing makes the sorrow more acute, and calls forth another fit stronger still, until at last repose only ensures with lassitude and with the apparent exhaustion of the machinery. In rage, it is notorious how we "work ourselves up" to a climax by repeated outbreaks of expression. Refuse to express a passion, and it dies. Count ten before venting your anger, and its occasion seems ridiculous. Whistling to keep up courage is no mere figure of speech. On the other hand, sit all day in a moping posture, sigh, and reply to everything with a dismal voice, and your melancholy lingers. There is no more valuable precept in moral education than this, as all who have experience know: if we wish to conquer undesirable emotional tendencies in ourselves, we must assiduously, and in the first instance cold-blood-edly, go through the *outward motions* of those contrary dispositions we prefer to cultivate. The reward of persistency will infallibly come, in the fading out of the sullenness or depression, and the advent of real cheerfulness and kindliness in their stead. Smooth the brow, brighten the eye, contract the dorsal rather than the ventral aspect of the frame, and speak in a major key, pass the genial compliment, and your heart must be frigid indeed if it do not gradually thaw!

The only exceptions to this are apparent, not real. The great emotional expressiveness and mobility of certain persons often lead us to say "They would feel more if they talked less." And in another class of persons, the explosive energy with which passion manifests itself on critical occasions, seems correlated with the way in which they bottle it up during the intervals. But these are only eccentric types of character, and within each type the law of the last paragraph prevails. The sentimentalist is so constructed that "gushing" is his or her normal mode of expression. Putting a stopper on the "gush" will only to a limited extent cause more "real" activities to take its place; in the main it will simply produce listlessness. On the other hand the ponderous and bilious "slumbering volcano," let him repress the expression of his passions as he will, will find them expire if they get no vent at all; whilst if the rare occasions multiply which he deems worthy of their outbreak, he will find them grow in intensity as life proceeds.

Jean-Paul Sartre

Emotions as Transformations of the World

Jean-Paul Sartre *(1905–1980) wrote his essay on the emotions just before he began his monumental existentialist treatise,* Being and Nothingness. *He was reacting against such theories as that of James, and in place of a physiological theory he urged a "phenomenological" view, a study of emotions in terms of the person's own experience. Such a view, he argues, leads us to the conclusion that emotions are a mode of intentional and purposive behavior.*

*P*erhaps what will help us in our investigation is a preliminary observation which may serve as a general criticism of all the theories of emotion which we have encountered. . . . For most psychologists everything takes place as if the consciousness *of* the emotion were first a reflective consciousness, that is, as if the first form of the emotion as a fact of consciousness were to appear to us as a modification of our psychic being or, to use everyday language, to be first perceived as a *state of consciousness*. And certainly it is always possible to take consciousness of emotion as the affective structure of consciousness, to say, "I'm angry, I'm afraid, etc." But fear is not originally consciousness *of* being afraid, any more than the perception of this book is consciousness *of* perceiving the book. Emotional consciousness is, at first, unreflective, and on this plane it can be conscious of itself only on the non-positional mode. Emotional consciousness is, at first, consciousness *of* the world. It is not even necessary to bring up the whole theory in order clearly to understand this principle. A few simple observations may suffice, and it is remarkable that the psychologists of emotion have never thought of making them. It is evident, in effect, that the man who is afraid is afraid *of* something. Even if it is a matter of one of those indefinite anxieties which one experiences in the dark, in a sinister and deserted passageway, etc., one is afraid *of* certain aspects of the night, of the world. And doubtless, all psychologists have noted that emotion is set in motion by a perception, a representation-signal, etc. But it seems that for them the emotion then withdraws from the object in order to be absorbed into itself. Not much reflection is needed to understand that, on the contrary, the emotion returns to the object at every moment and is fed there. For example, flight in a state of fear is described as if the object were not, before anything else, a flight *from* a certain object, as if the object fled did not remain present in the flight itself, as its theme, its reason for being, *that from which one flees*. And how can one talk about anger, in which one strikes, injures, and threatens, without mentioning the person who represents the objective unity of these insults, threats, and blows? In short, the affected subject and the affective object are bound in an indissoluble synthesis. Emotion is a certain way of apprehending the world. . . . The subject who seeks the solution of a practical problem is outside in the world; he perceives the world every moment through his acts. If he fails in his attempts, if he gets irritated, his very irritation is still a way in which the world appears to him. And, between the action which miscarries and the anger, it is not necessary for the subject to reflect back upon his behavior, to intercalate a reflexive consciousness. There can be a continuous passage from the unreflective consciousness "world-acted" (action) to the unreflective consciousness "world-hateful" (anger). The second is a transformation of the other.

At present, we can conceive of what an emotion is. It is a transformation of the world. When the paths traced out become too difficult, or when we see no path, we can no longer live in so urgent and difficult a world. All the ways are barred. However, we must act. So we try to change the world, that is, to live as if the connection between things and their potentialities were not ruled by deterministic processes, but by magic. Let it be clearly understood that this is not a game; we are driven against a wall, and we throw ourselves into this new attitude with all the strength we can muster. Let it also be understood that this attempt is not conscious of being such, for it would then be the object of a reflection. Before anything else, it is the seizure of new connections and new exigences.

But the emotive behavior is not on the same plane as the other behaviors; it is not *effective*. Its end is not really to act upon the object as such through the agency of particular means. It seeks by itself to confer upon the object, and without modifying it in its actual structure, another quality, a lesser existence, or a lesser presence (or a greater existence, etc.). In short, in emotion it is the body which, directed by consciousness, changes its relations with the world in order that the world may change its qualities. If emotion is a joke, it is a joke we believe in. A simple example will make this emotive structure clear: I extend my hand to take a bunch of grapes. I can't get it; it's beyond my reach. I shrug my shoulders, I let my hand drop, I mumble, "They're too green," and I move on. All these gestures, these words, this behavior are not seized upon for their own sake. We are dealing with a little comedy which I am playing *under* the bunch of grapes, through which I confer upon the grapes the characteristic of being "too green" which can serve as a substitute for the behavior which I am unable to keep up. At first, they presented themselves as "having to be picked." But this urgent quality very soon becomes unbearable because the potentiality cannot be realized. This unbearable tension becomes, in turn, a motive for foisting upon the grapes the new quality "too green," which will resolve the conflict and eliminate the tension. Only I cannot confer this quality on the grapes chemically. I cannot act upon the bunch in the ordinary ways. So I seize upon this sourness of the too green grapes by acting disgusted. I magically confer upon the grapes the quality I desire. Here the comedy is only half sincere. But let the situation be more urgent, let the incantatory behavior be carried out with seriousness; there we have emotion. . . .

True emotion is . . . accompanied by belief. The qualities conferred upon objects are taken as true qualities. Exactly what is meant by that? Roughly this: the emotion is undergone. One cannot abandon it at will; it exhausts itself, but we cannot stop it. Besides, the behavior which boils down to itself alone does nothing else than sketch upon the object the emotional quality which we confer upon it. A flight which would simply be a journey would not be enough to establish the object as being horrible. Or rather it would confer upon it the formal quality of *horrible,* but not the matter of this quality. In order for us truly to grasp the horrible, it is not only necessary to mimic it; we must be spell-bound, flooded by our own emotion; the formal frame of the behavior must be filled with something opaque and heavy which serves as matter. We understand in this situation the role of purely physiological phenomena: they represent the *seriousness* of the emotion; they are phenomena of belief. They should certainly not be separated from behavior. At first, they present a certain analogy with it. The hyper-tension of fear or sadness, the vaso-constrictions, the respiratory difficulties, symbolize quite well a behavior which aims at denying the world or discharging it of its affective potential by denying it. It is then impossible to draw exactly a borderline between the pure difficulties and the behavior. They finally enter with the behavior into a total synthetic form and cannot be studied by themselves; to have considered them in isolation is precisely the error of the peripheric theory. And yet they are not reducible to behavior; one can stop himself from fleeing, but not from trembling. I can, by a violent effort, raise myself from my chair, turn my thought from the disaster which is crushing me, and get down to work; my hands will remain icy. Therefore, the emotion must be considered not simply as being enacted; it is not a matter of pure demeanor. It is the demeanor of a body which is in a certain state; the state alone would not provoke the demeanor; the demeanor without the state is comedy; but the emotion appears in a highly disturbed body which retains a certain behavior. The disturbance can survive the behavior, but the behavior constitutes the form and signification of the disturbance. On the other hand, without this disturbance, the behavior would be pure signification, an affective scheme. We are really dealing with a synthetic form; *in order to believe* in magical behavior it is necessary to be highly disturbed.

Thus the origin of emotion is a spontaneous and lived degradation of consciousness in the face of the world. What it cannot endure in one way it tries to grasp in another by going to sleep, by approaching the consciousness of sleep, dream, and hysteria. And the disturbance of the body is nothing other than the lived belief of consciousness, insofar as it is seen from the outside.

Carol Tavris

Uncivil Rites—The Cultural Rules of Anger

Carol Tavris *is a contemporary psychologist and journalist who captured some important trends in contemporary psychology in her book,* Anger: The Misunderstood Emotion, *which is excerpted here.*

The full potential of human fury cannot be reached until a friend of both parties tactfully intervenes.

—G. K. CHESTERTON

*T*he young wife leaves her house one afternoon to draw water from the local well. She saunters down the main street, chatting amiably with her neighbors, as her husband watches from their porch. On her return from the well, a stranger stops her and asks for a cup of water. She obliges, and in fact invites the man home for dinner. He accepts. The husband, wife, and guest spend a pleasant evening together, and eventually the husband puts the lamp out and retires to bed. The wife also retires to bed—with the guest. In the morning, the husband leaves early to bring back some breakfast for the household. Upon his return, he finds his wife again making love with the visitor.

At what point in this sequence of events will the husband become angry or jealous? Is his anger inevitable? The answer, observes psychologist Ralph Hupka, depends on the tribe and culture he belongs to:

- A Pawnee Indian husband, a century ago, would, in fury, bewitch any man who dared to request a cup of water from his wife.
- An Ammassalik Eskimo husband who wants to be a proper host invites his guest to have sex with his wife; he signals his invitation by putting out the lamp. (The guest might feel angry if this invitation were not extended.) An Ammassalik husband would be angry, however, if he found his wife having sex with a man in circumstances other than the lamp game, such as that morning encore, or without a mutual agreement to exchange mates.
- A middle-class husband belonging to most modern American tribes would tend to get angry with any guest who, however courteously, tried to seduce his wife, and with the wife who, however hospitably, slept with their guest. But some American subcultures, such as you might find at sexually experimental spas like Sandstone, regard husbandly outrages as patriarchal and inappropiate.
- A husband who belonged to the polyandrous Toda tribe of southern India at the turn of the century would find the whole sequence of events perfectly normal; nothing to raise a fuss about. The Todas practiced *mokhthoditi*, a custom that allowed both spouses to take lovers. If a man wanted to make love to a married woman, he first got her permission and then the permission of her husband or husbands; a yearly fee was negotiated; and then the wife was free to visit her new lover and the lover free to visit the wife at her home. But a Toda husband and wife would undoubtedly be angry with any man who tried to establish an affair by sneaking around the husband's back (and not paying the proper fee).

People everywhere get angry, but they get angry in the service of their culture's rules. Sometimes those rules are explicit ("Thou shalt not covet thy neighbor's wife"); more often they are implicit, disguised in the countless daily actions performed because "That's the way we do things around here." These unstated rules are often not apparent until someone breaks them, and anger is the sign that someone has broken them. It announces that someone is not behaving as (you think) she or he *ought*. This "assertion of an ought" is, according to psychologist Joseph de Rivera, the one common and essential feature of anger in all its incarnations. "Whenever we are angry," he writes, "we somehow believe that we can influence the object of our anger. We assume that the other is responsible for his actions and ought to behave differently."

This "ought" quality suggests that a major role of anger is its policing function. Anger, with its power of forcefulness and its threat of retaliation, helps to regulate our everyday social relations: in family disputes, neighborly quarrels, business disagreements, wherever the official law is too cumbersome, inappropriate, or unavailable (which is most of the time). Psychologist James Averill observes that for most of Western history, it has been up to individuals to see to it that their rights were respected and justice seen to; in the absence of a formal judiciary, anger operates as a personal one. . . .

MANNERS, EMOTIONS, AND THE AMERICAN WAY

The class was basic English for foreign students, and an Arab student, during a spoken exercise, was describing a tradition of his home country. Something he said embarrassed a Japanese student in the front row, who reacted the proper Japanese way: he smiled. The Arab saw the smile and demanded to know what was so funny about Arab customs. The Japanese, who was now publicly humiliated as well as embarrassed, could reply only with a smile and, to his misfortune, he giggled to mask his shame. The Arab, who now likewise felt shamed, furiously hit the Japanese student before the teacher could intervene. Shame and anger had erupted in a flash, as each student dutifully obeyed the rules of his culture. Neither could imagine, of course, that his rules might not be universal.

Because a major function of anger is to maintain the social order, through its moralizing implications of how people "should" behave, it is predictable that when two social orders collide they would generate angry sparks. It is easiest to see this when the colliding cultures are foreign to each other, but we have plenty of such collisions within our society as well. For some groups in America, anger is an effective way to get your way; for others it is the last resort. (Some groups have to learn assertiveness training to deal with others.) You may find your attitudes about anger, and the rules you learned to govern it, in conflict with those of different groups. Often it is this conflict about anger rules, not the rules per se, that can stir up trouble.

Each of us is tied to a group—a minitribe, if you will—by virtue of our sex, status, race, and ethnicity, and with countless unconscious reactions we reveal those ties as surely as Eliza Doolittle did when she opened her mouth. Anthropologist Edward T. Hall speaks of the "deep biases and built-in blinders" that every culture confers on its members. You can observe them at work every time you hear someone grumble, "I'll never understand women," or, "Why can't he just say what he feels?" or, "The (Japanese) (Mexicans) (Irish) (etc.) are utterly inscrutable."

A culture's rules of anger are not arbitrary; they evolve along with its history and structure. The Japanese practice of emotional restraint, for example, dates back many centuries, when all aspects of demeanor were carefully regulated: facial expressions, breathing, manner of sitting and standing, style of walking. Not only were all emotions—anger, grief, pain, even great happiness—to be suppressed in the presence of one's superiors, but also regulations specified that a person submit to any order with a pleasant smile and a properly happy tone of voice. At the time of the Samurai knights, these rules had considerable survival value, because a Samurai could legally execute anyone who he thought was not respectful enough. (You may notice the similarity to American blacks and to women, who likewise had to be careful to control anger in the presence of the white man.)

Even today in Japan, an individual who feels very angry is likely to show it by excessive politeness and a neutral expression instead of by furious words and signs. A Japanese who shows anger the Western way is admitting that he has lost control, and therefore lost face; he is thus at the extreme end of a negotiation or debate. In other cultures, though, showing anger may simply mark the *beginning* of an exchange, perhaps to show that the negotiator is serious; a man may lose face if he does *not* show anger when it is appropriate and "manly" for him to do so.

Perhaps we cannot avoid the anger we feel when someone breaks the rules that we have learned are the only civilized rules to follow. But we might emulate the Arapesh, who criticize the provocateur; or the Eskimo, who settle in for a good round of verbal dueling; or the Mbuti, who have a good laugh, understanding as they do the healing power of humor. We might also retrieve the old-fashioned standard of manners, which is, as small tribes teach us, an organized system of anger management. The conventions of the U.S. Senate, for example—the ornate language, the rules of debate—regulate anger over disagreements into acceptable channels. A senator does not call his or her opposition a stupid blithering moron, for instance. He says, "My distinguished colleague from the great state of Blitzhorn, an otherwise fine and noble individual, is, in this rare moment, erring in judgment." The elaborate language that seems so comically deceptive to the rest of us is what keeps political conversation going without bloodshed and mayhem.

Good manners melt resentment because they maintain respect between the two disagreeing parties. Indeed, one of the basic principles of parliamentary law is courtesy, "Respect for the rights of individuals and for the assembly itself." You don't have to join Congress to feel the effect of this principle at work. Someone steps on your toe, you feel angry, the person apologizes, your anger vanishes. Your toe may still hurt, but your dignity is intact. (A friend tells me he loudly shushed a talkative man sitting behind him at the movies, and immediately felt bad that he had expressed himself so angrily. After the show, the man touched him on the shoulder. "You were quite right to tell me to keep quiet," he said, "I was rude." "I could have kissed him," said my friend.)

Without rules for controlling anger, it can slip into emotional anarchy, lasting far longer than its original purposes require. Observe how friends and family react to someone undergoing a bitter divorce: they extend sympathy and a willing ear to the enraged spouse for a while, but eventually they expect the person to "shape up" and "get on with it." What these friends and relatives are doing is imposing unofficial rules of anger management. The victim may grouse and mutter about the loss of sympathy, but actually the friends and relatives are doing what any decent tribe would do: keeping anger in bounds after it has done its job and making sure the victim stays in the social circle. Well-meaning friends and therapists who encourage a vengeful spouse to ventilate rage for years are doing neither the spouse nor the tribe a service.

In this country, the philosophy of emotional expression confuses self-restraint and hypocrisy. The cultures of the Far East do not have this conflict; a person is expected to control and subdue the emotions because it is the relationship, not the individual, that comes first. Here, where the reverse is true, some people express their emotions even at the expense of the relationship, and manners seem to be as rare as egrets. This analogy is not arbitrary, for the same ideology that gave us emotional ventilation is responsible for the scarcity of egrets: the imperial "I."

Consider the gentle, forgiving environment of Tahiti, where people learn that they have limited control over nature and over other people. They learn that if they try to change nature, she will swiftly destroy them, but if they relax and accept the bounty of nature—and the nature of people—they will be taken care of. Anthropologist Robert Levy calls this resulting world view among the Tahitians "passive optimisim."

Such a philosophy would not have lasted long among the ancient Hebrews, whose God gave them "dominion over the fish of the sea, and over the fowl of the air, and over the cattle, and over all the earth, and over every creeping thing that creepeth upon the earth" (Genesis 1:26). And a good thing He did, too, because in the harsh deserts of the Middle East, adherents of a laissez-faire Tahitian religion would have met a swift demise. The Judeo-Christian philosophy, however, produces "active pessimists": people who assume that nature and other people are to be conquered, indeed must be conquered, and that individual striving is essential to survival. But a universe defined as the Tahitians see it is intrinsically less infuriating than a universe in which almost everything is possible if the individual tries hard enough. The individualism of American life, to our glory and despair, creates anger and encourages its release; for when everything is possible, limitations are irksome. When the desires of the self come first, the needs of others are annoying. When we think we deserve it all, reaping only a portion can enrage.

Robert C. Solomon

What Love Is

Robert C. Solomon *is a philosopher who writes about emotions. The following is taken from his 1976 book,* Love: Emotion, Myth and Metaphor.

The question, What is love? is neither a request for a confession nor an excuse to start moralizing. It is not an invitation to amuse us with some *bon mot* ("Love is the key that opens up the doors of happiness") or to impress us with an author's sensitivity. And love is much more than a "feeling." When a novelist wants us to appreciate his character's emotions, he does not just describe sweaty palms and a moment of panic; he instead describes *a world,* the world as it is experienced—in anger, or in envy, or in love. Theorizing about emotion, too, is like describing an exotic world. It is a kind of conceptual anthropology—identifying a peculiar list of characters—heroes, villains, knaves or lovers—understanding a special set of rules and roles—rituals, fantasies, myths, slogans and fears. But these are not merely empirical observations on the fate of a feeling; none of this will make any sense to anyone who has not participated also. Love can be understood only "from the inside," as a language can be understood only by someone who speaks it, as a world can be known only by someone who has—even if vicariously—*lived* in it.

To analyze an emotion by looking at the world it defines allows us to cut through the inarticulateness of mere "feelings" and do away once and for all with the idea that emotions in general and love in particular are "ineffable" or beyond description. This might make some sense if describing an emotion were describing something "inside of us." It is not easy, for example, to describe how one feels when nauseous; even describing something so specific as a migraine headache falls back on clumsy metaphors ("as if my head's in a vise," "as if someone were driving a nail through my skull"). But once we see that every emotion defines a world for itself, we can then describe in some detail what that world involves, with its many variations, describe its dimensions and its dynamics. The world defined by love—or what we shall call the *loveworld*—is a world woven around a single relationship with all else pushed to the periphery. To understand love is to understand the specifics of this relationship and the world woven around it.

Love has been so misunderstood both because so often it has been taken to be *other-*worldly rather than one world of emotion among others, and because it has sometimes been taken to be a "mere emotion"—just a feeling and not a world at all. Because of this, perhaps it would be best to illustrate the theory that every emotion is a world by beginning with a less problematic emotion, namely, *anger*. Anger too defines its world. It is a world in which one defines oneself in the role of "the offended" and defines someone else (or perhaps a group or an institution) as "the offender." The world of anger is very much a courtroom world, a world filled with blame and emotional litigation. It is a world in which everyone else tends to become a co-defendant, a friend of the court, a witness or at least part of the courtroom audience. (But when you're *very* angry, there are no innocent bystanders.) We have already once quoted Lewis Carroll from *Alice in Wonderland*: " 'I'll be judge, I'll be jury,' said cunning old Fury." It is a world in which one does indeed define oneself as judge and jury, complete with a grim righteousness, with "justice"—one's own vengeance—as the only legitimate concern. It is a *magical* world, which can change a lackadaisical unfocused morning into a piercing, all-consuming day, an orgy of vindictive self-righteousness and excitement. At the slightest provocation it can change an awkward and defensive situation into an aggressive confrontation. To describe the world of anger is therefore to describe its fantasies, for example, the urge to kill, though rarely is this taken seriously or to its logical conclusion. It has its illusions too, for instance, the tendency to exaggerate the importance of some petty grievance to the level of cosmic injustice; in anger we sometimes talk as if "man's inhumanity to man" is perfectly manifested in some minor sleight at the office yesterday. It is a world with a certain fragility; a single laugh can explode the whole pretense of angry self-righteousness. And it is a world with a purpose—for when do we feel more self-righteous than in anger? Getting angry in an otherwise awkward situation may be a way of saving face or providing a quick ego boost; "having a bad temper" may be not so much a "character trait" as an emotional strategy, a way of *using* emotion as a means of controlling other people. To describe anger, in other words, is to describe the way the world is structured—and why—by a person who is angry.

The world of love—the loveworld—can be similarly described as a theatrical scenario, not as a courtroom but rather as "courtly," a romantic drama defined by its sense of elegance (badly interpreted as "spiritual"), in which we also take up a certain role—"the lover"—and cast another person into a complementary role—"the beloved." But where anger casts two antagonistic characters, romantic love sets up an idea of unity, absolute complementarity and total mutual support and affection. It is the *rest* of the world that may be the antagonist. Boris Pasternak describes the loveworld beautifully—the world as Adam and Eve, naked, surrounded by chaos.

It is a world we know well, of course—the world of *Casablanca, Romeo and Juliet* and a thousand stories and novels. It is a world in which we narrow our vision and our cares to that single duality, all else becoming trifles, obstacles or interruptions. It is a magical world, in which an ordinary evening is transformed into the turning point of a lifetime, the metamorphosis of one's self into a curious kind of double being. It may seem like a sense of "discovery"; in fact it is a step in a long search, a process of creation. . . .

Like every emotional world, the loveworld has its essential rules and rituals, its basic structures and internal dynamics. Some of these rules and structures are so obvious that it is embarrassing to have to spell them out, for example, the fact that the loveworld (typically) includes two people, instead of only one (as in shame) or three (as in jealousy) or indeed an entire class of people (as in national mourning or revolutionary resentment). Or the fact that the loveworld involves extremely "positive" feelings about the person loved, perhaps even the uncritical evaluation that he or she is "the most wonderful person in the world." Or the fact that the loveworld is held together by the mutual desire to be together (to touch, be touched, to caress and make love) no less essentially than the world of Newton and Einstein is held together by the forces of electromagnetism and gravity. Such features are so obvious to us that we fail to think of them as the structures of love; we take them for granted and, when asked to talk about love, consider them not even worth mentioning. Having thus ignored the obvious, love becomes a mystery. But other seemingly equally "obvious" features of love may not be part of the structure of the loveworld at all—for example, the comforting equation between love and trust. Here, indeed, there is some room for "mystery" in love, not the emotion itself but its essential lack of predictability, the fascination with the unknown and the attraction that comes not with trust but with vulnerability, sometimes even suspicion and doubt. Similarly, we presume as in a cliché that romantic love presupposes respect ("How can you say that you love me when you don't even respect me?"). But it may be too that the nature of romantic love renders respect irrelevant, so that even when respect begins as a prerequisite for romantic attraction it gets booted out of the loveworld just as assuredly as a pair of fine leather shoes gets doffed as we get into bed. . . . The problem with talking about love is not that there is a mystery to be cleared up or that so much seems so obvious but rather that we take what we are told so uncritically, conflate the loveworld with everything that is good, true and desirable, confuse the structures of love with the conditions for security and happiness, assume without thinking that because suspicion is so painful trust must be essential to love, assume as a matter of wishful thinking that the same person who is in love with us must, if our lives are to be unified, respect us for what we do as well. . . .

THE "OBJECT" OF LOVE

Talking about the loveworld is not only a way to avoid the hopeless conception of love as a feeling; it is also a way of rejecting an insidious view of love—and emotions in general—which many philosophers have come to accept as "obvious," particularly in this century. The view simply stated, is that love is an attitude *toward* someone, a feeling directed *at* a person, instead of a shared world. The view is often disguised by a piece of professional jargon—an impressive word, "intentionality." It is said that emotions are "intentional," which is a way of saying that they are "about" something. What an emotion is "about" is called its "intentional object" or, simply, its "object." Thus shame is an emotion which is "about" oneself, while anger is "about" someone else. The language comes from the medieval scholastics, by way of an Austrian philosopher named Franz Brentano, one of whose students in Vienna was the young Sigmund Freud. Thus Freud talks all the time about the "object" of love, not without some discomfort, for though the conception fits his general theories perfectly, he nonetheless sensed correctly that some considerable conceptual damage was being done to the emotion thereby.

   The idea—though not the terminology—of "intentionality" and "intentional objects" was introduced into British philosophy by the Scottish philosopher David Hume. He analyzed a number of emotions in terms of the "objects" with which they were "naturally associated," for example pride and humility, which both took as their "objects" oneself, and hatred and love, which both took as their objects another person. But we can already see what is going to be so wrong with this familiar type of analysis. First of all, all such talk about "objects" leaves out the crucial fact that, in love at least, it is the other as a "subject" that is essential. To be in love (even unrequited) is to be looked *at,* not just to look. Thus it is the eyes, not the body (nor the soul), that present the so-called "beloved," not as object but as subject, not first as beautiful or lovable but always as (potentially) lov*ing.* It's the eyes that have it, nothing else.

   . . . Every lover, I would suppose, has beautiful eyes, for it is only the eyes that look back at you, that refuse to allow even the most beautiful lover to become a mere "object" of love, thus refuting with a glance some of the greatest philosophers in history.

   Love is not just an attitude directed toward another person; it is an emotion which, at least hopefully, is *shared with* him or her. . . . Sometimes, perhaps, and in some emotions, "object"-talk makes perfectly good sense; sadness at the loss of one's high school class ring, or the love of one's favorite first edition. But any account of love that begins with the idea of an "object" of love is probably going to miss the main point of the emotion, namely, that it is not an emotion "about" another person so much as, in our terms, a world we share. . . .

One obvious misunderstanding is this: the Christian view of love is not alone in teaching us that love is essentially *selfless*. Proponents of romantic love have argued that too. The idea is that love is thoroughly "about" another person, so that any degree of self-love is incompatible with, or at least a detraction from, "true," that is, selfless love. But this is not only not true; it is impossible. There is no emotion without self-involvement, and no love that is not also "about" oneself. The other side is just as confused, however; La Rochefoucauld, for example, insists that "all love is self-love." But to be self-involved is not yet to be selfish, nor does self-involvement in any way exclude a total concern for the other person as well. The practical consequence of this confusion, in turn, is the readiness with which we can be made to feel guilty at the slightest suggestion that our love is not "pure" but turns on "selfish" motives, and it renders unaskable what is in fact a most intelligible question—namely, "What am I getting out of this?"—to which the answer may well be, "Not enough to make it worth while." But then, love is not just what one "gets out of it" either.

Talking about love as a world with two people avoids these problems and misunderstandings. But there is one last set of complications which has been much discussed in the "object" way of talking which deserves special mention. The idea that the "object" of my love is another person suggests too easily that love is "about" a person *simpliciter,* the whole person, nothing but and nothing less than the whole person. This is simply untrue. I love *you,* indeed, but I love you only in so far as you fit into the loveworld. That may be for any number of reasons—because I think you're beautiful, because you love me too, because I admire you in your career, because we cook fine meals together. The list might well seem endless, but it never is. I might love you for just one reason, or I might love you for a hundred and fifty reasons. But those reasons (I might always discover more) circumscribe your place in the loveworld. The person I love is, consequently, not simply *you,* the whole person, but rather you circumscribed by that set of reasons. I might say, in a moment of enthusiasm, "I love everything about you," but that's just myopia, or poor editing. Sometimes I'm surprised. I find a new virtue, that I've never seen before. But sometimes I'm disappointed too. Sometimes I manufacture new and imagined virtues, as Stendhal suggests in his theory of "crystallization"—the "discovery" of ever new virtues in one's lover. But love is never unqualified acceptance of a lover, "no matter what," however much one would like to be loved, if not to love, without qualification. But this raises sticky questions about the vicissitudes of love, not least the nature of these reasons and the possibility that, if I love you "for reasons," might I not love someone else, just as much as or instead of you, for precisely those same reasons? Or is it possible that one might not know *whom* one loves, if it is true, for example, as every teenager soon learns, that one can love "on the rebound," transferring the frustrated love of one lover immediately onto another, who becomes something of a sparring partner to keep us in shape for the more important bout to come, holding a role in a loveworld in which he or she has no real place. The identity of the "beloved," in other words, is by no means so obvious as the "object of love"-talk would make it seem. It is even possible that the "beloved," as Plato argued in a more pious way, is nothing more than a set of ideal properties, indifferent indeed to the particular person who at any given instant happens to exemplify them.

To make matters even more complicated, we might point out that similar questions arise regarding one's own identity in the loveworld. I do not love "with all my heart and all my soul," but rather (if we want to talk about hearts and souls at all) only with half a heart—but not half-heartedly—and with a fraction of a soul. I love you in so far as I am a lover, but I am only rarely *just* a lover. No matter how much I'm in love, I do not live just in the loveworld. You may be the essence of the loveworld, but you don't fit into my career or, for that matter, into the world I enter when I watch Japanese movies. I love you when I feel romantic, perhaps too when I'm just relaxed, but when I'm frustrated about my work, or absorbed in a lawsuit, the self that is so involved is not the same self that loves you. It's not that *I* don't love you, or that I love you any less; it's just that the loveworld isn't my only world, or yours either, even if we agree that it is, for us, the best of our possible worlds. To say that love is a world of two people, therefore, is not at all to say something simple, much less "obvious." . . .

WHAT LOVE'S ABOUT: SELF

What love is about—the poles of the loveworld and the goal of its development—is the creation of self. But this does not mean that love is just about oneself, any more than love is just about another. For the self that is created through love is a *shared* self, a self that is conceived and developed together. It is not only the loveworld that is indeterminate but, as part and parcel of our largely indeterminate culture, our selves are always under-determined too. Jean-Paul Sartre states this as a paradox, that we are always more than we are. Our selves are formed in the cradle of the family, soon to be confused by the welter of different roles into which we are thrown with playmates, peers and even the most rudimentary social rituals and responsibilities. And all along we find ourselves redefining ourselves in terms of other people, people with whom we identify, those whom we admire, those we despise as well as all of those more or less anonymous faces and voices that surround us every day—smiling, abusing, criticizing, congratulating and cajoling. And in that confusion of roles and rituals which in our society (not all others) tends to be without an anchor, without an "essence" according to which we could say, once and for all, "I am x," we look for a context that is small enough, manageable enough, yet powerful enough, for us to define ourselves, our "real" selves—we think wishfully—and what could be smaller or more manageable than the tiniest possible interpersonal world, namely, a world of only two people. And so, in love, we define ourselves and define each other, building on but sometimes fighting against the multitude of identities that are already established, starting with but not always ending with the images, fantasies and roles which drew us together in the first place, made us seem so compatible, even "meant for each other." Romantic love is part of our search for selfhood, and the power of the emotion, our sense of tragedy when it fails as well as its overall importance in our culture, turns largely on the fact that it comes to provide what is most crucial to us—even more than survival and the so-called "necessities" of life—namely, our selves.

. . . In love, what is so peculiar is that the self that is created in the development of the emotion is a shared self, an *ego à deux,* whereas in most emotions the self is set up in opposition to or in isolation from other people. In romantic love, as opposed to motherly or brotherly love, for example, the self is also created virtually anew, as if "from scratch," no matter how many influences may be behind it and no matter how thoroughly this might be explained by someone outside that tiny yet seemingly all-inclusive loveworld. To understand romantic love, therefore, is to understand this peculiar creation of a shared self, and to explain the importance of this one emotion in our world is to explain, most of all, its singular success in promoting our sense of ourselves and the meaningfulness not of a mere "relationship" but of life itself.

Most if not all emotions have as a motive the enhancement of self, or what I call the *maximization of self-esteem.* Thus in describing the world of anger, . . . I commented that anger is a spectacularly *self-righteous* emotion. Through anger, we feel good about ourselves, morally superior, even in (especially in) circumstances which would otherwise feel extremely awkward. . . .

But of all the emotional strategies for self-enhancement, none succeeds so well as love. For one thing, the inevitable opposition in anger invites a counterattack of equal self-righteousness, and competitive emotions make it highly likely that one of us, at least, will lose. But in love two selves mutually reinforce one another, rather than compete with one another, and so the self-enhancement of love, insulated from the outside by indifference, mutually supported in a reciprocal way on the inside, tends to be an extremely powerful and relatively durable emotional strategy. . . .

LOVE AND AUTONOMY: THE "DIALECTIC" OF TOGETHERNESS

So what is love? It is, in a phrase, an emotion through which we create for ourselves a little world—the loveworld, in which we play the roles of lovers and, quite literally, create our selves as well. Thus love is not, as so many of the great poets and philosophers have taken it to be, any degree of admiration or worship, not appreciation or even desire for beauty, much less, as Erich Fromm was fond of arguing, an "orientation of character" whose "object" is a secondary consideration. Even so-called "unrequited" love is shared love and shared identity, if only from one side and thereby woefully incomplete. Of course, occasionally an imagined identity may be far preferable to the actuality, but even when this is the case unrequited love represents at most a hint toward a process and not the process as such. Unrequited love is still love, but love in the sense that a sprout from an acorn is already an oak, no more. . . .

In love we transform ourselves and one another, but the key to this emotion is the understanding that the transformation of selves is not merely reciprocal, a swap of favors like "I'll cook you dinner if you'll wash the car." The self transformed in love is a shared self, and therefore by its very nature at odds with, even contradictory to, the individual autonomous selves that each of us had before. Sometimes our new shared self may be a transformation of a self that I (perhaps we) shared before. Possibly all love is to some extent the transposition of seemingly "natural" bonds which have somehow been abandoned or destroyed, and therefore the less than novel transformation of a self that has always been shared, in one way or another. But the bonds of love are always, to some extent, "unnatural," and our shared identity is always, in some way, uncomfortable. Aristophanes' delightful allegory about the double creatures cleft in two and seeking their other halves is charming but false. Love is never so neat and tidy, antigen and antibody forming the perfect fit. The Christian concept of a couple sanctified as a "union" before God is reassuring, as if one thereby receives some special guarantee, an outside bond of sorts, which will keep two otherwise aimless souls together. But the warranty doesn't apply. What is so special about romantic love, and what makes it so peculiar to our and similar societies, is the fact that it is entirely based on the idea of individuality and freedom, and this means, first of all, that the presupposition of love is a strong sense of individual identity and autonomy which exactly contradicts the ideal of "union" and "yearning to be one" that some of our literature has celebrated so one-sidedly. And, second, the freedom that is built into the loveworld includes not just the freedom to come together but the freedom to go as well. Thus love and the loveworld are always in a state of tension, always changing, dynamic, tenuous and explosive.

. . . To understand love is to understand this tension, this dialectic between individuality and the shared ideal. To think that love is to be found only at the ends of the spectrum—in that first enthusiastic "discovery" of a shared togetherness or at the end of the road, after a lifetime together—is to miss the loveworld almost entirely, for it is neither an initial flush of feeling nor the retrospective congratulations of old age but a struggle for unity and identity. And it is this struggle—neither the ideal of togetherness nor the contrary demand for individual autonomy and identity—that defines the dynamics of that convulsive and tenuous world we call romantic love.

John Connolly
E. Victoria Spelman

Emotions and the Thought of Nuclear Holocaust

E. Victoria Spelman *and* **John M. Connolly** *both teach philosophy at Smith College. The following article appeared in the Smith College newspaper following the national showing of* The Day After, *a dramatization of a nuclear holocaust in America.*

On November 20, 1983, ABC-TV broadcast "The Day After", a drama depicting the likely effects on Kansas City and its environs of a nuclear attack. Some of those who have pre-viewed the show (e.g., students and faculty at the University of Kansas) have said that its impact on them was devastating. It is easy to see how this would be so if one ponders for a moment or two the scientific estimates that even a limited nuclear war would kill one billion human beings *in a matter of minutes,* while its after-effects could make the planet entirely uninhabitable.

Voices are being, and will be, raised against ABC for showing this program, principally by those who support increases in our nuclear arsenal. In particular they decry one likely effect of the broadcast: the intrusion of a strong public *affective* response against the ever-escalating nuclear arms race. "This is not an area which should be dealt with emotionally," the argument goes, "the complex questions of national defence must be considered solely in the light of reason, not that of emotion." And indeed it would appear that the contrast be-tween the desirability of reason and the undesirability of emotion in political deliberation has something to be said for it: one thinks with a shudder of a sea of German listeners whipped into an ugly frenzy by Hitler's demagogic attacks on Jews and leftists.

We should not, however, be fooled into thinking that the proponents of a nuclear arms build-up themselves appeal only to our reason, while those who oppose these armaments appeal only to our emotions. After all, the proponents of nuclear build-up want very much for us to feel emotion—in particular they want us to feel *fear:* fear about the intentions and the power of the Soviet Union (or, in the Soviet Union and elsewhere, about the intentions and power of the USA). Those who favor disarmament clearly fear the destruction of the Earth as we know it. So it is highly misleading to cast the debate as one between those sober souls who appeal to reason and those (e.g., ABC) who stir up emotion. The question of the debate ought to be seen for what it is: which fear is more rational, fear of The Enemy, or fear of the spiraling arms race and its likely catastrophic consequences.

We are writing this piece neither to commend ABC (for we have not yet seen the show) nor to exalt, in some blanket fashion, emotion over reason. Nonetheless we believe that the argument against feeling in political matters is philosophically flawed and politically dangerous.

The flaw and the danger have a common root, namely, ignoring the essential connect-edness of reason and emotion in human life. The only way we *could* avoid emotional responses to the world around us (whether the response be fear, pride, anger, enthusiasm, relief, etc.) would be to avoid thinking clearly altogether about the world. Emotion and reason belong together: we feel anger, e.g., on the basis of what we believe or infer to be injuries done to ourselves or others; and our anger motivates us to reason about the sources of the injury and about what needs to be done. What was wrong in the response of Hitler's audiences was not the fact that it was emotional, but that it was based on the false, even bizarre beliefs that it was Jews, Social Democrats, and Communists who were responsible for Germany's miseries. Contrast the positive and rationally based enthusiasm with which Americans greeted the Kennedy Administration's initiatives with the Atmospheric Test Ban Treaty of 1963 (which represents a diplomatic break-through in U.S.–Soviet relations almost unimaginable in today's poisoned climate of invective and confrontation).

The injunction to avoid feeling emotion is an injunction to avoid thinking morally or politically, because we cannot think about matters which are of any practical significance to us without having some emotional response—unless of course we become bloodless automatons who have no emotional responses and therefore no felt connection to our world at all. Aristotle, that great admirer of human reason, held in his *Nichomachean Ethics* that it is reprehensible *not* to feel anger when injustice is done to one's friends. To feel repulsion and anger over a rape or a murder is normal and appropriate, thus *rational* (though this in no way prejudges the question of what action, if any, to take in response, nor is it to argue that one's anger entitles one to violate the rights of others). And to feel *no* fear at the thought of the possible or even probable nuclear destruction of the Earth is inappropriate and *irrational*.

The argument against emotion in political debate has wider implications too. The claim by one group—often the group in power—that its thinking and behavior are rational while the thinking and behavior of other groups are emotional and therefore irrational has a long and very suspect career. When a class, sex, or racial group is politically dominant, it typically tries to defend its dominance over another class, sex, or race on the grounds that it is the keeper of rationality, while those in subordinate groups are emotional, irrational, out of control of their reason and intelligence, and therefore in need of control by others.

"The Day After" is sure to raise many issues in the minds, and stir many feelings in the hearts, of its viewers. Among the arguments heard will be the one we have discussed at some length here, namely that emotion has no appropriate place in the nuclear arms debate. But if what we have said is correct, that argument is from start to finish a red herring.

11

How Should I Feel about Abortion?

*T*he issue of abortion is as controversial within philosophy as it is outside of philosophy. In thinking about abortion, we are forced to assess our views about a number of related issues. What we think about abortion will be a function of what we think about sex, about reproduction, about the beginning of human life, about killing, about responsibility, about sexual equality, and about religion. In fact, there is little in life to which the issue of abortion is not in some way related. It is not surprising, then, that there is so much disagreement about what abortion is and whether or not it is good, bad, or neither.

When thinking about abortion as a philosophical topic, it is helpful to begin by considering what women actually think about when they are trying to make a decision about whether or not to have an abortion. Obviously, the factors that a woman considers will be a function of her particular circumstances. Sometimes, the pregnancy itself presents difficulties. A teenager may feel that being pregnant would create serious personal and social difficulties for her. A woman about to set off on an arduous archeological expedition may feel that being pregnant would interfere with her work. Sometimes, the pregnancy itself is not so much a problem; rather, the problem is the child that will be its end result. A student may feel that having a child at this point will seriously jeopardize her chances of finishing school; a mother of two children may feel that having another child would impair her emotional and financial capacity to care for her existing ones. The story by Alice Walker presents one such set of considerations. Although it is probably unwise to see any particular story about abortion as representative of all others, the Walker story reminds us that decisions about abortion are made in the context of a woman's ongoing and invariably complex life. When we abstract the abortion decision from that context, it may take on different dimensions.

Most opposition to abortion is based on the claim that human life begins at conception and thus a human embryo or fetus is a person like any other and so has a right to life. While there is disagreement among philosophers as to all that a right to life involves, we can assume that at the very least it guarantees that one not be killed unjustifiably. Unwarranted or unjustified killing is murder. Murder is not permissible. Those opposed to abortion typically believe that the killing of an innocent embryo is unwarranted. If so, they conclude, abortion is murder and hence is impermissible. When the problem of abortion is framed in this way, it appears that those who wish to defend the practice of abortion against this conclusion are forced to argue that personhood does not begin at conception, but rather at some later stage in pregnancy or at birth. The question of exactly when human life, or personhood, begins is not a straightforward one. (You may want to look at Chapter 9 for more on this topic.) In pushing the abortion issue into this murky territory, those opposed to abortion are replacing one difficult question (is abortion morally justifiable?) with another one (when does human life or personhood begin?). Judith Thomson argues that those concerned with establishing the permissibility of abortion need not become entangled in the issue of fetal personhood. For the sake of argument, she grants those opposed to abortion their major premise, namely, that the fetus is a person. She then proceeds to argue that, even if the fetus is a person, it does not follow that the woman is required to carry it to term. The woman's right to control over her own body outweighs the rights of the fetus. She draws analogies between the sacrifices that pregnant women must make to keep fetuses alive and other situations in which one person's life depends on the willingness of another to act on his or her behalf. In doing so, she hopes to set abortion in a context that displays clearly what she takes to be the central moral issue that it raises: does a woman have an *obligation* to maintain, for the sake of the fetus, an unwanted pregnancy to term? (Chapters 13 and 15 supply useful background for the issue of obligation.) Thomson's example of the unconscious violinist who requires the use of your kidneys to stay alive has become legendary. It is up to you to decide whether or not you take it, or any of her other analogies, to be persuasive.

Thomson falls squarely in the tradition of those philosophers who see abortion as raising ethical questions. Indeed, Kathryn Pyne Addelson uses the term "the Judith Thomson tradition" to refer to any approach to abortion that focuses on the issue of rights and justice, that makes use of hypothetical rather than actual cases, and that takes the "solution" to the abortion problem to be a matter of gaining clarity about concepts, not a matter of bringing about social change. In the longer paper of which the selection here is the last part, Addelson argues that the Thomson tradition introduces, by its approach and methods, certain biases into its reasoning about abortion. Addelson introduces the actual, not hypothetical, case of Jane, a collective organization of women providing abortion counseling and referral services, and eventually abortions, before abortion was legalized in 1973 (in a famous Supreme Court case, Roe vs. Wade). By describing the inner workings of Jane and the self-perceptions of the women who worked in it, Addelson provides a basis for developing a moral framework quite different from that offered by the Thomson tradition. In doing so, she encourages us to do ethics in a novel way. Instead of "imposing" ethical concepts (like those of rights, justice, and obligations) on experience, we should instead allow experience to create and shape our ethical concepts. You might want to think, for example, about whether the story by Walker can be understood in terms of the Judith Thomson tradition. Does Imani worry about rights and justice? If not, what concerns does she have? Are they closer to the concerns raised by the case of Jane? (The selection by Carol Gilligan in Chapter 15 provides a perspective complementary to that of Addelson.)

Much of the opposition to abortion comes from religion. The Catholic church, for example, condemns abortion, even in cases where the woman's life is at stake. Abortion is viewed as an affront to the sanctity of human life. Stanley Hauerwas, while agreeing that abortion is morally objectionable, thinks that Christians have not effectively articulated the reasons why. That is, it is of paramount importance that Christians understand why it is crucial that they welcome children into the world. In addition, he argues that Christians, in opposing abortion, must consider carefully their responsibilities to children and to the women who bear them. Yet, by insisting on the sanctity of human life without spelling out its significance in relation to the political commitments of the Christian community, Christians can appear unrealistic at best, insensitive and ignorant at worst. Thus, Hauerwas, like Addelson, believes that our views about abortion are responsibly developed only when we look at the role that abortion, and other reproductive practices, play in people's lives. To abstract abortion from that context is to distort its moral significance. Daniel Maguire, a Catholic theologian, reinforces this point by describing a series of visits that he made to an abortion clinic. Confronted with real women making real decisions about their reproductive lives, he found it impossible to condemn them as heartless murderers. Maguire suggests that such a charge has at its base a trivialization of women's capacity to make responsible decisions.

Finally, Barbara Ehrenreich asks us to consider whether abortion itself is really a moral issue. She suggests that by focusing on the needs of the fetus, to the exclusion of the needs of the woman who carries it, we have "created" a moral issue out of nothing. Her reasoning can be seen as an extension of Addelson's: by imposing a set of moral concerns, ones that serve only a particular set of interests, on a set of social practices, those practices are transformed. Abortion could just as well be viewed as a necessary medical procedure because no form of contraception is entirely reliable (nor is contraception itself always available to those who want to use it). If abortion raises difficult moral issues, then that is, according to Ehrenreich, because we *choose* to see it as raising those issues. Clearly, Ehrenreich thinks that the focus on the moral status of the fetus distracts us from what she takes to be important issues about poverty, insufficient information and education, lack of available contraception, and so on.

As you can see, abortion raises a variety of troubling and challenging questions. First, it raises ethical questions, such as those addressed by Judith Thomson: Is abortion always wrong? Is it always right? Or is it sometimes right and sometimes wrong? Do embryos and fetuses have rights? Second, it raises what are called **metaethical** questions, such as those raised by Addelson, Hauerwas, and Ehrenreich: What is the most reasonable way to think about abortion? Is it best seen as a conflict between the woman's right to have control over her body and the fetus's right to life? Or does the language of rights distort the issue? Does it leave out some essential features of the difficulties and dilemmas women confront when deciding whether or not to have an abortion? What relationship does abortion have to other reproductive practices and choices? Ehrenreich argues that we choose, according to our particular interests, which issues we will treat as moral issues. Nevertheless, it does not appear that as a society we are ready to view having an abortion as no more significant than having a splinter removed. As long as that is true, it is important to understand what you think both about the rightness or wrongness of abortion and about the reasons why it has become such an important issue in contemporary culture.

Alice Walker
The Abortion

Alice Walker *was born in Georgia and now lives in San Francisco. An essayist, novelist, poet, and biographer, her many books include* The Color Purple, You Can't Keep a Good Woman Down, *and* In Search of Our Mother's Gardens.

*T*hey had discussed it, but not deeply, whether they wanted the baby she was now carrying. "I don't *know* if I want it," she said, eyes filling with tears. She cried at anything now, and was often nauseous. That pregnant women cried easily and were nauseous seemed banal to her, and she resented banality.

"Well, think about it," he said, with his smooth reassuring voice (but with an edge of impatience she now felt) that used to soothe her.

It was all she *did* think about, all she apparently *could;* that he could dream otherwise enraged her. But she always lost, when they argued. Her temper would flare up, he would become instantly reasonable, mature, responsible, if not responsive precisely, to her mood, and she would swallow down her tears and hate herself. It was because she believed him "good." The best human being she had ever met.

"It isn't as if we don't already have a child," she said in a calmer tone, carelessly wiping at the tear that slid from one eye.

"We have a perfect child," he said with relish, "thank the Good Lord!"

Had she ever dreamed she'd marry someone humble enough to go around thanking the Good Lord? She had not.

Now they left the bedroom, where she had been lying down on their massive king-size bed with the forbidding ridge in the middle, and went down the hall—hung with bright prints—to the cheerful, spotlessly clean kitchen. He put water on for tea in a bright yellow pot.

She wanted him to want the baby so much he would try to save its life. On the other hand, she did not permit such presumptuousness. As he praised the child they already had, a daughter of sunny disposition and winning smile, Imani sensed subterfuge, and hardened her heart.

"What am I talking about," she said, as if she'd been talking about it. "Another child would kill me. I can't imagine life with two children. Having a child is a good experience *to have had*, like graduate school. But if you've had one, you've had the experience and that's enough."

He placed the tea before her and rested a heavy hand on her hair. She felt the heat and pressure of his hand as she touched the cup and felt the odor and steam rise up from it. Her throat contracted.

"I can't drink that," she said through gritted teeth. "Take it away."

There were days of this.

Clarice, their daughter, was barely two years old. A miscarriage brought on by grief (Imani had lost her fervidly environmentalist mother to lung cancer shortly after Clarice's birth; the asbestos ceiling in the classroom where she taught first graders had leaked for twenty years) separated Clarice's birth from the new pregnancy. Imani felt her body had been assaulted by these events and was, in fact, considerably weakened, and was also, in any case, chronically anaemic and run down. Still, if she had wanted the baby more than she did not want it, she would not have planned to abort it.

They lived in a small town in the South. Her husband, Clarence, was, among other things, legal adviser and defender of the new black mayor of the town. The mayor was much in their lives because of the difficulties being the first black mayor of a small town assured, and because, next to the major leaders of black struggles in the South, Clarence respected and admired him most.

Imani reserved absolute judgment, but she did point out that Mayor Carswell would never look at her directly when she made a comment or posed a question, even sitting at her own dinner table, and would instead talk to Clarence as if she were not there. He assumed that as a woman she would not be interested in, or even understand, politics. (He would comment occasionally on her cooking or her clothes. He noticed when she cut her hair.) But Imani understood every shade and variation of politics: she understood, for example, why she fed the mouth that did not speak to her; because for the present she must believe in Mayor Carswell, even as he could not believe in her. Even understanding this, however, she found dinners with Carswell hard to swallow.

But Clarence was dedicated to the mayor, and believed his success would ultimately mean security and advancement for them all.

On the morning she left to have the abortion, the mayor and Clarence were to have a working lunch, and they drove her to the airport deep in conversation about municipal funds, racist cops, and the facilities for teaching at the chaotic, newly integrated schools. Clarence had time for the briefest kiss and hug at the airport ramp.

"Take care of yourself," he whispered lovingly as she walked away. He was needed, while she was gone, to draft the city's new charter. She had agreed this was important; the mayor was already being called incompetent by local businessmen and the chamber of commerce, and one inferred from television that no black person alive even knew what a city charter was.

"Take care of myself." Yes, she thought. I see that is what I have to do. But she thought this self-pityingly, which invalidated it. She had expected *him* to take care of her, and she blamed him for not doing so now.

Well, she was a fraud, anyway. She had known after a year of marriage that it bored her. "The Experience of Having a Child" was to distract her from this fact. Still, she expected him to "take care of her." She was lucky he didn't pack up and leave. But he seemed to know, as she did, that if anyone packed and left, if would be her. Precisely *because* she was a fraud and because in the end he would settle for fraud and she could not.

On the plane to New York her teeth ached and she vomited bile—bitter, yellowish stuff she hadn't even been aware her body produced. She resented and appreciated the crisp help of the stewardess, who asked if she needed anything, then stood chatting with the cigarette-smoking white man next to her, whose fat hairy wrist, like a large worm, was all Imani could bear to see out of the corner of her eye.

Her first abortion, when she was still in college, she frequently remembered as wonderful, bearing as it had all the marks of a supreme coming of age and a seizing of the direction of her own life, as well as a comprehension of existence that never left her: that life—what one saw about one and called Life—was not a facade. There was nothing behind it which used "Life" as its manifestation. Life was itself. Period. At the time, and afterwards, and even now, this seemed a marvelous thing to know.

The abortionist had been a delightful Italian doctor on the Upper East Side in New York, and before he put her under he told her about his own daughter who was just her age, and a junior at Vassar. He babbled on and on until she was out, but not before Imani had thought how her thousand dollars, for which she would be in debt for years, would go to keep her there.

When she woke up it was all over. She lay on a brown Naugahyde sofa in the doctor's outer office. And she heard, over her somewhere in the air, the sound of a woman's voice. It was a Saturday, no nurses in attendance, and she presumed it was the doctor's wife. She was pulled gently to her feet by this voice and encouraged to walk.

"And when you leave, be sure to walk as if nothing is wrong," the voice said.

Imani did not feel any pain. This surprised her. Perhaps he didn't do anything, she thought. Perhaps he took my thousand dollars and put me to sleep with two dollars' worth of ether. Perhaps this is a racket.

But he was so kind, and he was smiling benignly, almost fatherly, at her (and Imani realized how desperately she needed this "fatherly" look, this "fatherly" smile). "Thank you," she murmured sincerely: she was thanking him for her life.

Some of Italy was still in his voice. "It's nothing, nothing," he said. "A nice, pretty girl like you; in school like my own daughter, you didn't need this trouble."

"He's nice," she said to herself, walking to the subway on her way back to school. She lay down gingerly across a vacant seat, and passed out.

She hemorrhaged steadily for six weeks, and was not well again for a year.

*   *   *

But this was seven years later. An abortion law now made it possible to make an appointment at a clinic, and for seventy-five dollars a safe, quick, painless abortion was yours.

Imani had once lived in New York, in the Village, not five blocks from where the abortion clinic was. It was also near the Margaret Sanger clinic, where she had received her very first diaphragm, with utter gratitude and amazement that someone apparently understood and actually cared about young women as alone and ignorant as she. In fact, as she walked up the block, with its modern office buildings side by side with older, more elegant brownstones, she felt how close she was still to that earlier self. Still not in control of her sensuality, and only through violence and with money (for the flight, for the operation itself) in control of her body.

She found that abortion had entered the age of the assembly line. Grateful for the lack of distinction between herself and the other women—all colors, ages, states of misery or nervousness—she was less happy to notice, once the doctor started to insert the catheter, that the anesthesia she had been given was insufficient. But assembly lines don't stop because the product on them has a complaint. Her doctor whistled, and assured her she was all right, and carried the procedure through to the horrific end. Imani fainted some seconds before that.

They laid her out in a peaceful room full of cheerful colors. Primary colors: yellow, red, blue. When she revived she had the feeling of being in a nursery. She had a pressing need to urinate.

A nurse, kindly, white-haired and with firm hands, helped her to the toilet. Imani saw herself in the mirror over the sink and was alarmed. She was literally gray, as if all her blood had leaked out.

"Don't worry about how you look," said the nurse. "Rest a bit here and take it easy when you get back home. You'll be fine in a week or so."

She could not imagine being fine again. Somewhere her child—she never dodged into the language of "fetuses" and "amorphous growths"—was being flushed down a sewer. Gone all her or his chances to see the sunlight, savor a fig.

"Well," she said to this child, "it was you or me, Kiddo, and I chose me."

There were people who thought she had no right to choose herself, but Imani knew better than to think of those people now.

It was a bright, hot Saturday when she returned.

Clarence and Clarice picked her up at the airport. They had brought flowers from Imani's garden, and Clarice presented them with a stout-hearted hug. Once in her mother's lap she rested content all the way home, sucking her thumb, stroking her nose with the forefinger of the same hand, and kneading a corner of her blanket with the three fingers that were left.

"How did it go?" asked Clarence.

"It went," said Imani.

There was no way to explain abortion to a man. She thought castration might be an apt analogy, but most men, perhaps all, would insist this could not possibly be true.

"The anesthesia failed," she said. "I thought I'd never faint in time to keep from screaming and leaping off the table."

Clarence paled. He hated the thought of pain, any kind of violence. He could not endure it; it made him physically ill. This was one of the reasons he was a pacifist, another reason she admired him.

She knew he wanted her to stop talking. But she continued in a flat, deliberate voice.

"All the blood seemed to run out of me. The tendons in my legs felt cut. I was gray."

He reached for her hand. Held it. Squeezed.

"But," she said, "at least I know what I don't want. And I intend never to go through any of this again."

They were in the living room of their peaceful, quiet and colorful house. Imani was in her rocker, Clarice dozing on her lap. Clarence sank to the floor and rested his head against her knees. She felt he was asking for nurture when she needed it herself. She felt the two of them, Clarence and Clarice, clinging to her, using her. And that the only way she could claim herself, feel herself distinct from them, was by doing something painful, self-defining but self-destructive.

She suffered the pressure of his head as long as she could.

"Have a vasectomy," she said, "or stay in the guest room. Nothing is going to touch me anymore that isn't harmless."

He smoothed her thick hair with his hand. "We'll talk about it," he said, as if that was not what they were doing. "We'll see. Don't worry. We'll take care of things."

She had forgotten that the third Sunday in June, the following day, was the fifth memorial observance for Holly Monroe, who had been shot down on her way home from her high-school graduation ceremony five years before. Imani *always* went to these memorials. She liked the reassurance that her people had long memories, and that those people who fell in struggle or innocence were not forgotten. She was, of course, too weak to go. She was dizzy and still losing blood. The white lawgivers attempted to get around assassination—which Imani considered extreme abortion—by saying the victim provoked it (there had been some difficulty saying this about Holly Monroe, but they had tried) but were antiabortionist to a man. Imani thought of this as she resolutely showered and washed her hair.

Clarence had installed central air conditioning their second year in the house. Imani had at first objected. "I want to smell the trees, the flowers, the natural air!" she cried. But the first summer of 110-degree heat had cured her of giving a damn about any of that. Now she wanted to be cool. As much as she loved trees, on a hot day she would have sawed through a forest to get to an air conditioner.

In fairness to him, she had to admit he asked her if she thought she was well enough to go. But even to be asked annoyed her. She was not one to let her own troubles prevent her from showing proper respect and remembrance toward the dead, although she understood perfectly well that once dead, the dead do not exist. So respect, remembrance was for herself, and today herself needed rest. There was something mad about her refusal to rest, and she felt it as she tottered about getting Clarice dressed. But she did not stop. She ran a bath, plopped her child in it, scrubbed her plump body on her knees, arms straining over the tub awkwardly in a way that made her stomach hurt—but not yet her uterus—dried her hair, lifted her out and dried the rest of her on the kitchen table.

"You are going to remember as long as you live what kind of people they are," she said to the child, who, gurgling and cooing, looked into her mother's stern face with light-hearted fixation.

"You are going to hear the music," Imani said. "The music they've tried to kill. The music they try to steal." She felt feverish and was aware she was muttering. She didn't care.

"They think they can kill a continent—people, trees, buffalo—and then fly off to the moon and just forget about it. But you and me we're going to remember the people, the trees and the fucking buffalo. Goddammit."

"Buffwoe," said the child, hitting at her mother's face with a spoon.

She placed the baby on a blanket in the living room and turned to see her husband's eyes, full of pity, on her. She wore pert green velvet slippers and a lovely sea green robe. Her body was bent within it. A reluctant tear formed beneath his gaze.

"Sometimes I look at you and I wonder 'What is this man doing in my house?'"

This had started as a joke between them. Her aim had been never to marry, but to take in lovers who could be sent home at dawn, freeing her to work and ramble.

"I'm here because you love me," was the traditional answer. But Clarence faltered, meeting her eyes, and Imani turned away.

It was a hundred degrees by ten o'clock. By eleven, when the memorial service began, it would be ten degrees hotter. Imani staggered from the heat. When she sat in the car she had to clench her teeth against the dizziness until the motor prodded the air conditioning to envelop them in coolness. A dull ache started in her uterus.

The church was not of course air conditioned. It was authentic Primitive Baptist in every sense.

Like the four previous memorials this one was designed by Holly Monroe's classmates. All twenty-five of whom—fat and thin— managed to look like the dead girl. Imani had never seen Holly Monroe, though there were always photographs of her dominating the pulpit of this church where she had been baptized and where she had sung in the choir—and to her, every black girl of a certain vulnerable age *was* Holly Monroe. And an even deeper truth was that Holly Monroe was herself. Herself shot down, aborted on the eve of becoming herself.

She was prepared to cry and to do so with abandon. But she did not. She clenched her teeth against the steadily increasing pain and her tears were instantly blotted by the heat.

Mayor Carswell had been waiting for Clarence in the vestibule of the church, mopping his plumply jowled face with a voluminous handkerchief and holding court among half a dozen young men and women who listened to him with awe. Imani exchanged greetings with the mayor, he ritualistically kissed her on the cheek, and kissed Clarice on the cheek, but his rather heat-glazed eye was already fastened on her husband. The two men huddled in a corner away from the awed young group. Away from Imani and Clarice, who passed hesitantly, waiting to be joined or to be called back, into the church.

There was a quarter hour's worth of music.

"Holly Monroe was five feet, three inches tall, and weighed one hundred and eleven pounds," her best friend said, not reading from notes, but talking to each person in the audience. "She was a stubborn, loyal Aries, the best kind of friend to have. She had black kinky hair that she experimented with a lot. She was exactly the color of this oak church pew in the summer; in the winter she was the color [pointing up] of this heart pine ceiling. She loved green. She did not like lavender because she said she also didn't like pink. She had brown eyes and wore glasses, except when she was meeting someone for the first time. She had a sort of rounded nose. She had beautiful large teeth, but her lips were always chapped so she didn't smile as much as she might have if she'd ever gotten used to carrying Chap Stick. She had elegant feet.

"Her favorite church song was 'Leaning on the Everlasting Arms.' Her favorite other kind of song was 'I Can't Help Myself—I Love You and Nobody Else.' She was often late for choir rehearsal though she loved to sing. She made the dress she wore to her graduation in Home Ec. She *hated* Home Ec. . . ."

Imani was aware that the sound of low, murmurous voices had been the background for this statement all along. Everything was quiet around her, even Clarice sat up straight, absorbed by the simple friendliness of the young woman's voice. All of Holly Monroe's classmates and friends in the choir wore vivid green. Imani imagined Clarice entranced by the brilliant, swaying color as by a field of swaying corn.

Lifting the child, her uterus burning, and perspiration already a stream down her back, Imani tiptoed to the door. Clarence and the mayor were still deep in conversation. She heard "board meeting . . . aldermen . . . city council." She beckoned to Clarence.

"Your voices are carrying!" she hissed.

She meant: How dare you not come inside.

They did not. Clarence raised his head, looked at her, and shrugged his shoulders helplessly. Then, turning, with the abstracted air of priests, the two men moved slowly toward the outer door, and into the churchyard, coming to stand some distance from the church beneath a large oak tree. There they remained throughout the service.

Two years later, Clarence was furious with her: What is the matter with you? he asked. You never want me to touch you. You told me to sleep in the guest room and I did. You told me to have a vasectomy I didn't want and I *did*. (Here, there was a sob of hatred for her somewhere in the anger, the humiliation: he thought of himself as a eunuch, and blamed her.)

She was not merely frigid, she was remote.

She had been amazed after they left the church that the anger she'd felt watching Clarence and the mayor turn away from the Holly Monroe memorial did not prevent her accepting a ride home with him. A month later it did not prevent her smiling on him fondly. Did not prevent a trip to Bermuda, a few blissful days of very good sex on a deserted beach screened by trees. Did not prevent her listening to his mother's stories of Clarence's youth as though she would treasure them forever.

And yet. From that moment in the heat at the church door, she had uncoupled herself from him, in a separation that made him, except occasionally, little more than a stranger.

And he had not felt it, had not known.

"What have I done?" he asked, all the tenderness in his voice breaking over her. She smiled a nervous smile at him, which he interpreted as derision—so far apart had they drifted.

They had discussed the episode at the church many times. Mayor Carswell—whom they never saw anymore—was now a model mayor, with wide biracial support in his campaign for the legislature. Neither could easily recall him, though television frequently brought him into the house.

"It was so important that I help the mayor!" said Clarence. "He was our *first!*"

Imani understood this perfectly well, but it sounded humorous to her. When she smiled, he was offended.

She had known the moment she left the marriage, the exact second. But apparently that moment had left no perceptible mark.

They argued, she smiled, they scowled, blamed and cried—as she packed.

Each of them almost recalled out loud that about this time of the year their aborted child would have been a troublesome, "terrible" two-year-old, a great burden on its mother, whose health was by now in excellent shape, each wanted to think aloud that the marriage would have deteriorated anyway, because of that.

Judith Jarvis Thomson

A Defense of Abortion

Judith Jarvis Thomson *teaches philosophy at M.I.T. Her extensive writings in ethics are collected in a recent book* Rights, Restitution and Risk.

Most opposition to abortion relies on the premise that the fetus is a human being, a person, from the moment of conception. The premise is argued for, but, as I think, not well. Take, for example, the most common argument. We are asked to notice that the development of a human being from conception through birth into childhood is continuous; then it is said that to draw a line, to choose a point in this development and say "before this point the thing is not a person, after this point it is a person" is to make an arbitrary choice, a choice for which in the nature of things no good reason can be given. It is concluded that the fetus is, or anyway that we had better say it is, a person from the moment of conception. But this conclusion does not follow. Similar things might be said about the development of an acorn into an oak tree, and it does not follow that acorns are oak trees, or that we had better say they are. Arguments of this form are sometimes called "slippery slope arguments"—the phrase is perhaps self-explanatory—and it is dismaying that opponents of abortion rely on them so heavily and uncritically.

I am inclined to agree, however, that the prospects for "drawing a line" in the development of the fetus look dim. I am inclined to think also that we shall probably have to agree that the fetus has already become a human person well before birth. Indeed, it comes as a surprise when one first learns how early in its life it begins to acquire human characteristics. By the tenth week, for example, it already has a face, arms and legs, fingers and toes; it has internal organs, and brain activity is detectable. On the other hand, I think that the premise is false, that the fetus is not a person from the moment of conception. A newly fertilized ovum, a newly implanted clump of cells, is no more a person than an acorn is an oak tree. But I shall not discuss any of this. For it seems to me to be of great interest to ask what happens if, for the sake of argument, we allow the premise. How, precisely, are we supposed to get from there to the conclusion that abortion is morally impermissible? Opponents of abortion commonly spend most of their time establishing that the fetus is a person, and hardly any time explaining the step from there to the impermissibility of abortion. Perhaps they think the step too simple and obvious to require much comment. Or perhaps instead they are simply being economical in argument. Many of those who defend abortion rely on the premise that the fetus is not a person, but only a bit of tissue that will become a person at birth; and why pay out more arguments than you have to? Whatever the explanation, I suggest that the step they take is neither easy nor obvious, that it calls for closer examination than it is commonly given, and that when we do give it this closer examination we shall feel inclined to reject it.

I propose, then, that we grant that the fetus is a person from the moment of conception. How does the argument go from here? Something like this, I take it. Every person has a right to life. So the fetus has a right to life. No doubt the mother has a right to decide what shall happen in and to her body; everyone would grant that. But surely a person's right to life is stronger and more stringent than the mother's right to decide what happens in and to her body, and so outweighs it. So the fetus may not be killed; an abortion may not be performed.

It sounds plausible. But now let me ask you to imagine this. You wake up in the morning and find yourself back to back in bed with an unconscious violinist. A famous unconscious violinist. He has been found to have a fatal kidney ailment, and the Society of

Music Lovers has canvassed all the available medical records and found that you alone have the right blood type to help. They have therefore kidnapped you, and last night the violinist's circulatory system was plugged into yours, so that your kidneys can be used to extract poisons from his blood as well as your own. The director of the hospital now tells you, "Look, we're sorry the Society of Music Lovers did this to you—we would never have permitted it if we had known. But still, they did it, and the violinist now is plugged into you. To unplug you would be to kill him. But never mind, it's only for nine months. By then he will have recovered from his ailment, and can safely be unplugged from you." Is it morally incumbent on you to accede to this situation? No doubt it would be very nice of you if you did, a great kindness. But do you *have* to accede to it? What if it were not nine months, but nine years? Or longer still? What if the director of the hospital says, "Tough luck, I agree, but you've now got to stay in bed, with the violinist plugged into you, for the rest of your life. Because remember this. All persons have a right to life, and violinists are persons. Granted you have a right to decide what happens in and to your body, but a person's right to life outweighs your right to decide what happens in and to your body. So you cannot ever be unplugged from him." I imagine you would regard this as outrageous, which suggests that something really is wrong with that plausible-sounding argument I mentioned a moment ago.

In this case, of course, you were kidnapped; you didn't volunteer for the operation that plugged the violinist into your kidneys. Can those who oppose abortion on the ground I mentioned make an exception for a pregnancy due to rape? Certainly. They can say that persons have a right to life only if they didn't come into existence because of rape; or they can say that all persons have a right to life, but that some have less of a right to life than others, in particular, that those who came into existence because of rape have less. But these statements have a rather unpleasant sound. Surely the question of whether you have a right to life at all, or how much of it you have, shouldn't turn on the question of whether or not you are the product of a rape. And in fact the people who oppose abortion on the ground I mentioned do not make this distinction, and hence do not make an exception in case of rape.

Nor do they make an exception for a case in which the mother has to spend the nine months of her pregnancy in bed. They would agree that would be a great pity, and hard on the mother; but all the same, all persons have a right to life, the fetus is a person, and so on. I suspect, in fact, that they would not make an exception for a case in which, miraculously enough, the pregnancy went on for nine years, or even the rest of the mother's life.

Some won't even make an exception for a case in which continuation of the pregnancy is likely to shorten the mother's life; they regard abortion as impermissible even to save the mother's life. Such cases are nowadays very rare, and many opponents of abortion do not accept this extreme view. All the same, it is a good place to begin: a number of points of interest come out in respect to it.

1. Let us call the view that abortion is impermissible even to save the mother's life "the extreme view." I want to suggest first that it does not issue from the argument I mentioned earlier without the addition of some fairly powerful premises. Suppose a woman has become pregnant, and now learns that she has a cardiac condition such that she will die if she carries the baby to term. What may be done for her? The fetus, being a person, has a right to life, but as the mother is a person too, so has she a right to life. Presumably they have an equal right to life. How is it supposed to come out that an abortion may not be performed? If mother and child have an equal right to life, shouldn't we perhaps flip a coin? Or should we add to the mother's right to life her right to decide what happens in and to her body, which everybody seems to be ready to grant—the sum of her rights now outweighing the fetus' right to life?

The most familiar argument here is the following. We are told that performing the abortion would be directly killing the child, whereas doing nothing would not be killing the mother, but only letting her die. Moreover in killing the child, one would be killing an innocent person, for the child has committed no crime, and is not aiming at his mother's death. And then there are a variety of ways in which this might be continued. (1) But as directly killing an innocent person is always and absolutely impermissible, an abortion may not be performed. Or, (2) as directly killing an innocent person is murder, and murder is always and absolutely impermissible, an abortion may not be performed. Or, (3) as one's duty to refrain from directly killing an innocent person is more stringent than one's duty to keep a person from dying, an abortion may not be performed. Or, (4) if one's only options are directly killing an innocent person or letting a person die, one must prefer letting the person die, and thus an abortion may not be performed.

Some people seem to have thought that these are not further premises which must be added if the conclusion is to be reached, but that they follow from the very fact that an innocent person has a right to life. But this seems to me to be a mistake, and perhaps the simplest way to show this is to bring out that while we must certainly grant that innocent persons have a right to life, the theses in (1) through (4) are all false. Take (2), for example. If directly killing an innocent person is murder, and thus is impermissible, then the mother's directly killing the innocent person inside her is murder, and thus is impermissible. But it cannot seriously be thought to be murder if the mother performs an abortion on herself to save her life. It cannot seriously be said that she *must* refrain, that she *must* sit passively by and wait for her death. Let us look again at the case of you and the violinist. There you are, in bed with the violinist, and the director of the hospital says to you, "It's all most distressing, and I deeply sympathize, but you see this is putting an additional strain on your kidneys, and you'll be dead within the month. But you *have* to stay where you are all the same. Because unplugging you would be directly killing an innocent violinist, and that's murder, and that's impermissible." If anything in the world is true, it is that you do not commit murder, you do not do what is impermissible, if you reach around to your back and unplug yourself from that violinist to save your life.

The main focus of attention in writings on abortion has been on what a third party may or may not do in answer to a request from a woman for an abortion. This is in a way understandable. Things being as they are, there isn't much a woman can safely do to abort herself. So the question asked is what a third party may do, and what the mother may do, if it is mentioned at all, is deduced, almost as an afterthought, from what it is concluded that third parties may do. But it seems to me that to treat the matter in this way is to refuse to grant to the mother that very status of person which is so firmly insisted on for the fetus. For we cannot simply read off what a person may do from what a third party may do. Suppose you find yourself trapped in a tiny house with a growing child. I mean a very tiny house, and a rapidly growing child—you are already up against the wall of the house and in a few minutes you'll be crushed to death. The child on the other hand won't be crushed to death; if nothing is done to stop him from growing he'll be hurt, but in the end he'll simply burst open the house and walk out a free man. Now I could well understand it if a bystander were to say, "There's nothing we can do for you. We cannot choose between your life and his, we cannot be the ones to decide who is to live, we cannot intervene." But it cannot be concluded that you too can do nothing, that you cannot attack it to save your life. However innocent the child may be, you do not have to wait passively while it crushes you to death. Perhaps a pregnant woman is vaguely felt to have the status of house, to which we don't allow the right of self-defense. But if the woman houses the child, it should be remembered that she is a person who houses it.

I should perhaps stop to say explicitly that I am not claiming that people have a right to do anything whatever to save their lives. I think, rather, that there are drastic limits to the right of self-defense. If someone threatens you with death unless you torture someone else to death, I think you have not the right, even to save your life, to do so. But the case under consideration here is very different. In our case there are only two people involved, one whose life is threatened, and one who threatens it. Both are innocent: the one who is threatened is not threatened because of any fault, the one who threatens does not threaten because of any fault. For this reason we may feel that we bystanders cannot intervene. But the person threatened can.

In sum, a woman surely can defend her life against the threat to it posed by the unborn child, even if doing so involves its death. And this shows not merely that the theses in (1) through (4) are false; it shows also that the extreme view of abortion is false, and so we need not canvass any other possible ways of arriving at it from the argument I mentioned at the outset.

2. The extreme view could of course be weakened to say that while abortion is permissible to save the mother's life, it may not be performed by a third party, but only by the mother herself. But this cannot be right either. For what we have to keep in mind is that the mother and the unborn child are not like two tenants in a small house which has, by an unfortunate mistake, been rented to both: the mother *owns* the house. The fact that she does adds to the offensiveness of deducing that the mother can do nothing from the supposition that third parties can do nothing. But it does more than this: it casts a bright light on the supposition that third parties can do nothing. Certainly it lets us see that a third party who says "I cannot choose between you" is fooling himself if he thinks this is impartiality. If Jones has found and fastened on a certain coat, which he needs to keep him from freezing, but which Smith also needs to keep him from freezing, then it is not impartiality that says "I cannot choose between you" when Smith owns the coat. Women have said again and again "This body is *my* body!" and they have reason to feel angry, reason to feel that it has been like shouting into the wind. Smith, after all, is hardly likely to bless us if we say to him, "Of course it's your coat, anybody would grant that it is. But no one may choose between you and Jones who is to have it."

We should really ask what it is that says "no one may choose" in the face of the fact that the body that houses the child is the mother's body. It may be simply a failure to appreciate this fact. But it may be something more interesting, namely the sense that one has a right to refuse to lay hands on people, even where it would be just and fair to do so, even where justice seems to require that somebody do so. Thus justice might call for somebody to get Smith's coat back from Jones, and yet you have a right to refuse to be the one to lay hands on Jones, a right to refuse to do physical violence to him. This, I think, must be granted. But then what should be said is not "no one may choose," but only "*I* cannot choose," and indeed not even this, but "I will not *act*," leaving it open that somebody else can or should, and in particular that anyone in a position of authority, with the job of securing people's rights, both can and should. So this is no difficulty. I have not been arguing that any given third party must accede to the mother's request that he perform an abortion to save her life, but only that he may.

I suppose that in some views of human life the mother's body is only on loan to her, the loan not being one which gives her any prior claim to it. One who held this view might well think it impartiality to say "I cannot choose." But I shall simply ignore this possibility. My own view is that if a human being has any just, prior claim to anything at all, he has a just, prior claim to his own body. And perhaps this needn't be argued for here anyway, since, as I mentioned, the arguments against abortion we are looking at do grant that the woman has a right to decide what happens in and to her body.

But although they do grant it, I have tried to show that they do not take seriously what is done in granting it. I suggest the same thing will reappear even more clearly when we turn away from cases in which the mother's life is at stake, and attend, as I propose we now do, to the vastly more common cases in which a woman wants an abortion for some less weighty reason than preserving her own life.

3. Where the mother's life is not at stake, the argument I mentioned at the outset seems to have a much stronger pull. "Everyone has a right to life, so the unborn person has a right to life." And isn't the child's right to life weightier than anything other than the mother's own right to life, which she might put forward as ground for an abortion?

This argument treats the right to life as if it were unproblematic. It is not, and this seems to me to be precisely the source of the mistake.

For we should now, at long last, ask what it comes to, to have a right to life. In some views having a right to life includes having a right to be given at least the bare minimum one needs for continued life. But suppose that what in fact *is* the bare minimum a man needs for continued life is something he has no right at all to be given? If I am sick unto death, and the only thing that will save my life is the touch of Henry Fonda's cool hand on my fevered brow, then all the same, I have no right to be given the touch of Henry Fonda's cool hand on my fevered brow. It would be frightfully nice of him to fly in from the West Coast to provide it. It would be less nice, though no doubt well meant, if my friends flew out to the West Coast and carried Henry Fonda back with them. But I have no right at all against anybody that he should do this for me. Or again, to return to the story I told earlier, the fact that for continued life that violinist needs the continued use of your kidneys does not establish that he has a right to be given the continued use of your kidneys. He certainly has no right against you that *you* should give him continued use of your kidneys. For nobody has any right to use your kidneys unless you give him such a right; and nobody has the right against you that you shall give him this right—if you do allow him to go on using your kidneys, this is a kindness on your part, and not something he can claim from you as his due. Nor has he any right against anybody else that *they* should give him continued use of your kidneys. Certainly he had no right against the Society of Music Lovers that they should plug him into you in the first place. And if you now start to unplug yourself, having learned that you will otherwise have to spend nine years in bed with him, there is nobody in the world who must try to prevent you, in order to see to it that he is given something he has a right to be given.

Some people are rather stricter about the right to life. In their view, it does not include the right to be given anything, but amounts to, and only to, the right not to be killed by anybody. But here a related difficulty arises. If everybody is to refrain from killing that violinist, then everybody must refrain from doing a great many different sorts of things. Everybody must refrain from slitting his throat, everybody must refrain from shooting him—and everybody must refrain from unplugging you from him. But does he have a right against everybody that they shall refrain from unplugging you from him? To refrain from doing this is to allow him to continue to use your kidneys. It could be argued that he has a right against us that *we* should allow him to continue to use your kidneys. That is, while he had no right against us that we should give him the use of your kidneys, it might be argued that he anyway has a right against us that we shall not now intervene and deprive him of the use of your kidneys. I shall come back to third-party interventions later. But certainly the violinist has no right against you that *you* shall allow him to continue to use your kidneys. As I said, if you do allow him to use them, it is a kindness on your part, and not something you owe him.

This difficulty I point to here is not peculiar to the right to life. It reappears in connection with all the other natural rights; and it is something which an adequate account of rights must deal with. For present purposes it is enough just to draw attention to it. But I would stress that I am not arguing that people do not have a right to life—quite to the contrary, it seems to me that the primary control we must place on the acceptability of an account of rights is that it should turn out in that account to be a truth that all persons have a right to life. I am arguing only that having a right to life does not guarantee having either a right to be given the use of or a right to be allowed continued use of another person's body—even if one needs it for life itself. So the right to life will not serve the opponents of abortion in the very simple and clear way in which they seem to have thought it would.

4. There is another way to bring out the difficulty. In the most ordinary sort of case, to deprive someone of what he has a right to is to treat him unjustly. Suppose a boy and his small brother are jointly given a box of chocolates for Christmas. If the older boy takes the box and refuses to give his brother any of the chocolates, he is unjust to him, for the brother has been given a right to half of them. But suppose that, having learned that otherwise it means nine years in bed with that violinist, you unplug yourself from him. You surely are not being unjust to him, for you gave him no right to use your kidneys, and no one else can have given him any such right. But we have to notice that in unplugging yourself, you are killing him; and violinists, like everybody else, have a right to life, and thus in the view we were considering just now, the right not to be killed. So here you do what he supposedly has a right you shall not do, but you do not act unjustly to him in doing it.

The emendation which may be made at this point is this: the right to life consists not in the right not to be killed, but rather in the right not to be killed unjustly. This runs a risk of circularity, but never mind: it would enable us to square the fact that the violinist has a right to life with the fact that you do not act unjustly toward him in unplugging yourself, thereby killing him. For if you do not kill him unjustly, you do not violate his right to life, and so it is no wonder you do him no injustice.

But if this emendation is accepted, the gap in the argument against abortion stares us plainly in the face: it is by no means enough to show that the fetus is a person, and to remind us that all persons have a right to life—we need to be shown also that killing the fetus violates its right to life, i.e., that abortion is unjust killing. And is it?

I suppose we may take it as a datum that in a case of pregnancy due to rape the mother has not given the unborn person a right to the use of her body for food and shelter. Indeed, in what pregnancy could it be supposed that the mother has given the unborn person such a right? It is not as if there were unborn persons drifting about the world, to whom a woman who wants a child says "I invite you in."

But it might be argued that there are other ways one can have acquired a right to the use of another person's body than by having been invited to use it by that person. Suppose a woman voluntarily indulges in intercourse, knowing of the chance it will issue in pregnancy, and then she does become pregnant; is she not in part responsible for the presence, in fact the very existence, of the unborn person inside her? No doubt she did not invite it in. But doesn't her partial responsibility for its being there itself give it a right to the use of her body? If so, then her aborting it would be more like the boy's taking away the chocolates, and less like your unplugging yourself from the violinist—doing so would be depriving it of what it does have a right to, and thus would be doing it an injustice.

And then, too, it might be asked whether or not she can kill it even to save her own life: If she voluntarily called it into existence, how can she now kill it, even in self-defense?

The first thing to be said about this is that it is something new. Opponents of abortion have been so concerned to make out the independence of the fetus, in order to establish that it has a right to life, just as its mother does, that they have tended to overlook the possible support they might gain from making out that the fetus is *dependent* on the mother, in order to establish that she has a special kind of responsibility for it, a responsibility that gives it rights against her which are not possessed by any independent person—such as an ailing violinist who is a stranger to her.

On the other hand, this argument would give the unborn person a right to its mother's body only if her pregnancy resulted from a voluntary act, undertaken in full knowledge of the chance a pregnancy might result from it. It would leave out entirely the unborn person whose existence is due to rape. Pending the availability of some further argument, then, we would be left with the conclusion that unborn persons whose existence is due to rape have no right to the use of their mothers' bodies, and thus that aborting them is not depriving them of anything they have a right to and hence is not unjust killing.

And we should also notice that it is not at all plain that this argument really does go even as far as it purports to. For there are cases and cases, and the details make a difference. If the room is stuffy, and I therefore open a window to air it, and a burglar climbs in, it would be absurd to say, "Ah, now he can stay, she's given him a right to the use of her house—for she is partially responsible for his presence there, having voluntarily done what enabled him to get in, in full knowledge that there are such things as burglars, and that burglars burgle." It would be still more absurd to say this if I had had bars installed outside my windows, precisely to prevent burglars from getting in, and a burglar got in only because of a defect in the bars. It remains equally absurd if we imagine it is not a burglar who climbs in, but an innocent person who blunders or falls in. Again, suppose it were like this: people-seeds drift about in the air like pollen, and if you open your windows, one may drift in and take root in your carpets or upholstery. You don't want children, so you fix up your windows with fine mesh screens, the very best you can buy. As can happen, however, and on very, very rare occasions does happen, one of the screens is defective; and a seed drifts in and takes root. Does the person-plant who now develops have a right to the use of your house? Surely not— despite the fact that you voluntarily opened your windows, you knowingly kept carpets and upholstered furniture, and you knew that screens were sometimes defective. Someone may argue that you are responsible for its rooting, that it does have a right to your house, because after all you *could* have lived out your life with bare floors and furniture, or with sealed windows and doors. But this won't do—for by the same token anyone can avoid a pregnancy due to rape by having a hysterectomy, or anyway by never leaving home without a (reliable!) army.

It seems to me that the argument we are looking at can establish at most that there are *some* cases in which the unborn person has a right to the use of its mother's body, and therefore *some* cases in which abortion is unjust killing. There is room for much discussion and argument as to precisely which, if any. But I think we should sidestep this issue and leave it open, for at any rate the argument certainly does not establish that all abortion is unjust killing.

5. There is room for yet another argument here, however. We surely must all grant that there may be cases in which it would be morally indecent to detach a person from your body at the cost of his life. Suppose you learn that what the violinist needs is not nine years of your life, but only one hour: all you need do to save his life is to spend one hour in that bed with him. Suppose also that letting him use your kidneys for that one hour would not affect your health in the slightest. Admittedly you were kidnapped. Admittedly you did not give anyone permission to plug him into you. Nevertheless it seems to me plain you *ought* to allow him to use your kidneys for that hour—it would be indecent to refuse.

Again, suppose pregnancy lasted only an hour, and constituted no threat to life or health. And suppose that a woman becomes pregnant as a result of rape. Admittedly she did not voluntarily do anything to bring about the existence of a child. Admittedly she did nothing at all which would give the unborn person a right to the use of her body. All the same it might well be said, as in the newly emended violinist story, that she *ought* to allow it to remain for that hour—that it would be indecent in her to refuse.

Now some people are inclined to use the term "right" in such a way that it follows from the fact that you ought to allow a person to use your body for the hour he needs, that he has a right to use your body for the hour he needs, even though he has not been given that right by any person or act. They may say that it follows also that if you refuse, you act unjustly toward him. This use of the term is perhaps so common that it cannot be called wrong; nevertheless it seems to me to be an unfortunate loosening of what we would do better to keep a tight rein on. Suppose that box of chocolates I mentioned earlier had not been given to both boys jointly, but was given only to the older boy. There he sits, stolidly eating his way through the box, his small brother watching enviously. Here we are likely to say "You ought not to be so mean. You ought to give your brother some of those chocolates." My own view is that it just does not follow from the truth of this that the brother has any right to any of the chocolates. If the boy refuses to give his brother any, he is greedy, stingy, callous—but not unjust. I suppose that the people I have in mind will say it does follow that the brother has a right to some of the chocolates, and thus that the boy does act unjustly if he refuses to give his brother any. But the effect of saying this is to obscure what we should keep distinct, namely the difference between the boy's refusal in this case and the boy's refusal in the earlier case, in which the box was given to both boys jointly, and in which the small brother thus had what was from any point of view clear title to half.

A further objection to so using the term "right" that from the fact that A ought to do a thing for B, it follows that B has a right against A that A do it for him, is that it is going to make the question of whether or not a man has a right to a thing turn on how easy it is to provide him with it; and this seems not merely unfortunate, but morally unacceptable. Take the case of Henry Fonda again. I said earlier that I had no right to the touch of his cool hand on my fevered brow, even though I needed it to save my life. I said it would be frightfully nice of him to fly in from the West Coast to provide me with it, but that I had no right against him that he should do so. But suppose he isn't on the West Coast. Suppose he has only to walk across the room, place a hand briefly on my brow—and lo, my life is saved. Then surely he ought to do it, it would be indecent to refuse. Is it to be said "Ah, well, it follows that in this case she has a right to the touch of his hand on her brow, and so it would be an injustice in him to refuse"? So that I have a right to it when it is easy for him to provide it, though no right when it's hard? It's rather a shocking idea that anyone's rights should fade away and disappear as it gets harder and harder to accord them to him.

So my own view is that even though you ought to let the violinist use your kidneys for the one hour he needs, we should not conclude that he has a right to do so—we should say that if you refuse, you are, like the boy who owns all the chocolates and will give none away, self-centered and callous, indecent in fact, by not unjust. And similarly, that even supposing a case in which a woman pregnant due to rape ought to allow the unborn person to use her body for the hour he needs, we should not conclude that he has a right to do so; we should conclude that she is self-centered, callous, indecent, but not unjust, if she refuses. The complaints are no less grave; they are just different. However, there is no need to insist on this point. If anyone does wish to deduce "he has a right" from "you ought," then all the same he must surely grant that there are cases in which it is not morally required of you that you allow that violinist to use your kidneys, and in which he does not have a right to use them, and in which you do not do him an injustice if you refuse. And so also for mother and unborn child. Except in such cases as the unborn person has a right to demand it—and we were leaving open the possibility that there may be such cases—nobody is morally *required* to make large sacrifices, of health, of all other interests and concerns, of all other duties and commitments, for nine years, or even for nine months, in order to keep another person alive.

6. We have in fact to distinguish between two kinds of Samaritan: the Good Samaritan and what we might call the Minimally Decent Samaritan. The story of the Good Samaritan, you will remember, goes like this:

> A certain man went down from Jerusalem to Jericho, and fell among thieves, which stripped him of his raiment, and wounded him, and departed, leaving him half dead.
>
> And by chance there came down a certain priest that way; and when he saw him, he passed by on the other side.
>
> And likewise a Levite, when he was at the place, came and looked on him, and passed on the other side.
>
> But a certain Samaritan, as he journeyed, came where he was; and when he saw him he had compassion on him.
>
> And went to him, and bound up his wounds, pouring in oil and wine, and set him on his own beast, and brought him to an inn, and took care of him.
>
> And on the morrow, when he departed, he took out two pence, and gave them to the host, and said unto him, "Take care of him; and whatsoever thou spendest more, when I come again, I will repay thee."   (Luke 10:30–35)

The Good Samaritan went out of his way, at some cost to himself, to help one in need of it. We are not told what the options were, that is, whether or not the priest and the Levite could have helped by doing less than the Good Samaritan did, but assuming they could have, then the fact they did nothing at all shows they were not even Minimally Decent Samaritans, not because they were not Samaritans, but because they were not even minimally decent.

These things are a matter of degree, of course, but there is a difference, and it comes out perhaps most clearly in the story of Kitty Genovese, who, as you will remember, was murdered while thirty-eight people watched or listened, and did nothing at all to help her. A Good Samaritan would have rushed out to give direct assistance against the murderer. Or perhaps we had better allow that it would have been a Splendid Samaritan who did this, on the ground that it would have involved a risk of death for himself. But the thirty-eight not only did not do this, they did not even trouble to pick up a phone to call the police. Minimally Decent Samaritanism would call for doing at least that, and their not having done it was monstrous.

After telling the story of the Good Samaritan, Jesus said "Go, and do thou likewise." Perhaps he meant that we are morally required to act as the Good Samaritan did. Perhaps he was urging people to do more than is morally required of them. At all events it seems plain that it was not morally required of any of the thirty-eight that he rush out to give direct assistance at the risk of his own life, and that it is not morally required of anyone that he give long stretches of his life—nine years or nine months—to sustaining the life of a person who has no special right (we were leaving open the possibility of this) to demand it.

Indeed, with one rather striking class of exceptions, no one in any country in the world is *legally* required to do anywhere near as much as this for anyone else. The class of exceptions is obvious. My main concern here is not the state of the law in respect to abortion, but it is worth drawing attention to the fact that in no state in this country is any man compelled by law to be even a Minimally Decent Samaritan to any person; there is no law under which charges could be brought against the thirty-eight who stood by while Kitty Genovese died. By contrast, in most states in this country women are compelled by law to be not merely Minimally Decent Samaritans, but Good Samaritans to unborn persons inside them. This doesn't by itself settle anything one way or the other, because it may well be argued that there should be laws in this country—as there are in many European countries—compelling at least Minimally Decent Samaritanism. But it does show that there is a gross injustice in the existing state of the law. And it shows also that the groups currently working against liberalization of abortion laws, in fact working toward having it declared unconstitutional for a state to permit abortion, had better start working for the adoption of Good Samaritan laws generally, or earn the charge that they are acting in bad faith.

I should think, myself, that Minimally Decent Samaritan laws would be one thing,

Good Samaritan laws quite another, and in fact highly improper. But we are not here concerned with the law. What we should ask is not whether anybody should be compelled by law to be a Good Samaritan, but whether we must accede to a situation in which somebody is being compelled—by nature, perhaps—to be a Good Samaritan. We have, in other words, to look now at third-party interventions. I have been arguing that no person is morally required to make large sacrifices to sustain the life of another who has no right to demand them, and this even where the sacrifices do not include life itself; we are not morally required to be Good Samaritans or anyway Very Good Samaritans to one another. But what if a man cannot extricate himself from such a situation? What if he appeals to us to extricate him? It seems to me plain that there are cases in which we can, cases in which a Good Samaritan would extricate him. There you are, you were kidnapped, and nine years in bed with that violinist lie ahead of you. You have your own life to lead. You are sorry, but you simply cannot see giving up so much of your life to the sustaining of his. You cannot extricate yourself, and ask us to do so. I should have thought that—in light of his having no right to the use of your body—it was obvious that we do not have to accede to your being forced to give up so much. We can do what you ask. There is no injustice to the violinist in our doing so.

7. Following the lead of the opponents of abortion, I have throughout been speaking of the fetus merely as a person, and what I have been asking is whether or not the argument we began with, which proceeds only from the fetus' being a person, really does establish its conclusion. I have argued that it does not.

But of course there are arguments and arguments, and it may be said that I have simply fastened on the wrong one. It may be said that what is important is not merely the fact that the fetus is a person, but that it is a person for whom the woman has a special kind of responsibility issuing from the fact that she is its mother. And it might be argued that all my analogies are therefore irrelevant—for you do not have that special kind of responsibility for that violinist, Henry Fonda does not have that special kind of responsibility for me. And our attention might be drawn to the fact that men and women both *are* compelled by law to provide support for their children.

I have in effect dealt (briefly) with this argument in section 4 above; but a (still briefer) recapitulation now may be in order. Surely we do not have any such "special responsibility" for a person unless we have assumed it, explicitly or implicitly. If a set of parents do not try to prevent pregnancy, do not obtain an abortion, and then at the time of birth of the child do not put it out for adoption, but rather take it home with them, then they have assumed responsibility for it, they have given it rights, and they cannot *now* withdraw support from it at the cost of its life because they now find it difficult to go on providing for it. But if they have taken all reasonable precautions against having a child, they do not simply by virtue of their biological relationship to the child who comes into existence have a special responsibility for it. They may wish to assume responsibility for it, or they may not wish to. And I am suggesting that if assuming responsibility for it would require large sacrifices, then they may refuse. A Good Samaritan would not refuse—or anyway, a Splendid Samaritan, if the sacrifices that had to be made were enormous. But then so would a Good Samaritan assume responsibility for that violinist; so would Henry Fonda, if he is a Good Samaritan, fly in from the West Coast and assume responsibility for me.

8. My argument will be found unsatisfactory on two counts by many of those who want to regard abortion as morally permissible. First, while I do argue that abortion is not impermissible, I do not argue that it is always permissible. There may well be cases in which carrying the child to term requires only Minimally Decent Samaritanism of the mother, and this is a standard we must not fall below. I am inclined to think it a merit of my account precisely that it does *not* give a general yes or a general no. It allows for and supports our sense that, for example, a sick and desperately frightened fourteen-year-old schoolgirl, pregnant due to rape, may *of course* choose abortion, and that any law which rules this out is an

insane law. And it also allows for and supports our sense that in other cases resort to abortion is even positively indecent. It would be indecent in the woman to request an abortion, and indecent in a doctor to perform it, if she is in her seventh month, and wants the abortion just to avoid the nuisance of postponing a trip abroad. The very fact that the arguments I have been drawing attention to treat all cases of abortion, or even all cases of abortion in which the mother's life is not at stake, as morally on a par ought to have made them suspect at the outset.

Secondly, while I am arguing for the permissibility of abortion in some cases, I am not arguing for the right to secure the death of the unborn child. It is easy to confuse these two things in that up to a certain point in the life of the fetus it is not able to survive outside the mother's body; hence removing it from her body guarantees its death. But they are importantly different. I have argued that you are not morally required to spend nine months in bed, sustaining the life of that violinist; but to say this is by no means to say that if, when you unplug yourself, there is a miracle and he survives, you then have a right to turn round and slit his throat. You may detach yourself even if this costs him his life; you have no right to be guaranteed his death, by some other means, if unplugging yourself does not kill him. There are some people who will feel dissatisfied by this feature of my argument. A woman may be utterly devastated by the thought of a child, a bit of herself, put out for adoption and never seen or heard of again. She may therefore want not merely that the child be detached from her, but more, that it die. Some opponents of abortion are inclined to regard this as beneath contempt—thereby showing insensitivity to what is surely a powerful source of despair. All the same, I agree that the desire for the child's death is not one which anybody may gratify, should it turn out to be possible to detach the child alive.

At this place, however, it should be remembered that we have only been pretending throughout that the fetus is a human being from the moment of conception. A very early abortion is surely not the killing of a person, and so is not dealt with by anything I have said here.

Kathryn Pyne Addelson
Moral Revolution

Kathryn Pyne Addelson *is a professor of philosophy at Smith College and a founding member of the Society for Women in Philosophy. Originally a philosopher of science, her work now focuses on issues in feminist ethics.*

JANE

In 1969, most state laws prohibited abortion unless the life of the pregnant woman was threatened. A few states had reformed their abortion laws to allow abortion by doctors in hospitals in cases of threat to the health of the woman, threat of fetal deformity, or rape. In the mid-1960s, the estimated death rate for abortions performed in hospitals was 3 deaths per 100,000 abortions; the rate for illegal abortions was guessed to be over eight times that— 30 deaths per 100,000 abortions was a rough estimate and almost certainly conservative. For minority and poorer women, it was certainly very much higher.

The women's liberation movement was in its infancy in 1969. In that year, a group of Chicago women who had been active in radical politics formed an organization called Jane.

Over the next year and a half, Jane evolved from an abortion counseling and referral service to a service in which abortions were actually performed by the Jane members themselves. By 1973 when they closed the service, over 12,000 abortions had been performed under Jane's auspices. The medical record equalled that of abortions done under legal, licensed conditions by physicians in hospitals. The service charged on a sliding scale; eventually all abortions were cheaper than the going rate, and some women paid nothing. Jane served many poor women, black women, and very young women who could not have had an abortion otherwise.

My discussion of Jane is based on one newspaper series and an interview with one member. Perhaps not all Jane members will agree with this member's interpretation, but that isn't the point here because I'm not doing a sociological study. I am investigating patterns of moral thinking and acting which the Judith Thomson tradition makes invisible. The fact that one person's thinking and action are concealed is enough to show bias. . . .

What Jane Did

This is the way Jane operated, as reported in the June 1973 Hyde Park-Kenwood *Voices* article on the organization: "Jane was the pseudonym we chose to represent the service. A phone was opened in her name and an answering service secured, later replaced by a tape recorder. Jane kept all records and served as control-center." "Jane" was not a particular woman but the code name for whichever counselor was taking calls and coordinating activities on a given day.

> For four years, Jane kept the same phone number. . . . At first she received only eight to ten calls a week. A year later she was receiving well more than 100 calls a week.
> All phoned-in messages were returned the same day: "Hello, Marcia. This is Jane from women's liberation returning your call. We can't talk freely over the phone, but I want you to know that we can help you."
> Then Jane would refer the name to a counselor, who would meet personally with the woman and talk with her at length about available alternatives.
> The counselor would also help the woman arrange finances and, whenever possible, collect a $25 donation for the service loan fund. The counseling session was also a screening process for detecting conflicts and potential legal threats.

Jane worked with several male abortionists. One of these was "Dr. C." Dr. C worked alone with his nurse in motel rooms until the day an abortion was interrupted by a pounding on the door and a man's voice shouting, "Come on out of there, baby killer!" After a wild chase between buildings and down alleys, Dr. C escaped the irate husband. When he caught his breath, he decided that it might be better to quit working in motels.

Jane members then began renting apartments for Dr. C and his nurse to work in. Jane describes the first day they used a rented apartment: "Seven women were done that day, in a setting where they could relax and talk with other women in a similar predicament. And when the first woman walked out of the bedroom, feeling fine and no longer pregnant, the other six were noticeably relieved. They asked her questions and got firsthand answers." Another advantage of the new arrangement was that Jane counselors were with a woman during the abortion, giving her psychological and moral support and explaining what was going on to her. Still another was that the counselors gradually began assisting Dr. C in the abortion itself, and he began training them in the abortion procedures.

After a few months of operation, members of Jane had begun inducing miscarriages for women more than twelve weeks pregnant. During this time, Dr. C was teaching the women of Jane more and more about the process of doing direct abortions. Finally, some counselors were doing the entire direct abortion themselves, under Dr. C's eye. In the midst of all this, they learned that Dr. C was no doctor at all, but just a man who had become an expert in the giving of abortions. Later, they broke off the relationship with Dr. C and began doing all of their own abortions. For good or ill, this meant that they had a sudden abundance of funds, since the abortion fee went to Jane instead of to Dr. C. In the eyes of the law, they became fullfledged abortionists: "We could no longer hide behind the label of 'counselor' or expect 'Dr. C' to act as a buffer, with his know-how and ready cash for dealing with a bust." Jane members were arrested only once, although they were harassed by the police.

The change in the abortion service meant that Jane members had to accept the full consequences of what they were doing—even if it resulted in illness, personal tragedy, or death—and they had to bear this without the protection that the doctor's professionalism gives him. They worked under these conditions until 1 April 1973. Then, two months after the United States Supreme Court passed its opinion on the constitutionality of restrictive abortion laws, Jane officially closed.

What Jane Meant

In describing what Jane did, I selected data to a certain purpose. It was a selection different in many respects from the selection someone in Judith Thomson's tradition would have made. I didn't, however, use any special technical concepts or categories from some philosophical theory. In this section, I shall use Jane as a basis for discussing a moral theory which competes with theories of the Judith Thomson tradition, in order to reveal value implications of bias in that tradition.

Jane was an abortion clinic, and the women of Jane were working out moral and political beliefs and activities, not constructing a theory. I want to try to give a fragment of a theory which is able to capture their thinking and their work. The theory should be taken as *hypothesis* about what Jane meant, subject to correction through future investigation of Jane and groups like Jane, and through seeing what comes of acting on the theory. I believe the theory is based on anarchist, or anarchist-feminist principles, but I won't discuss that. Instead I'll call the tradition out of which the theory arises the Jane tradition, to contrast with the Judith Thomson tradition.

In March 1977, I interviewed one of the founders of Jane. She said that the women who founded the organization had been active in civil rights or anti-war work in the late 1960s. They wanted to begin work in the newly born women's liberation movement. But how should they begin? What should they do? Someone suggested abortion as an issue. It was a difficult decision, and they struggled over it for months. Deciding on an issue required an analysis of a network of larger issues, and of the place of the abortion issue in that network. According to the woman I interviewed, the question was one of a woman's opportunities for life choices: "It was a question of free choice about reproduction, free choice about life style, because the old roles for women weren't viable any more. In frontier times, childbearing was valuable and important. So was housework. But that role is gone. The old ways are gone. We felt nothing *could* come in to replace them unless women could make a choice about child-bearing. That seemed necessary for any other choice." These alternatives had to be *created* within our social system. The members of Jane hoped that other groups within the women's movement would work on other alternatives—offering alternative living arrangements, work-ing on ways that women could become economically independent, and so on—while Jane members tried to offer the alternative of choosing not to have the child by aborting. That is, they thought in terms of a division of labor among women working to change the society so that women would have real alternatives for meaningful lives.

As I mentioned in the introduction, the concept of a *meaningful life* (more often called "a good life") has traditionally been a central concept in moral philosophy. The pattern of thinking Jane members use requires a holistic analysis of the society in terms of the resources it actually offers for women to have meaningful lives, plus an analysis of how to change the society so that it can offer such resources. . . .

In offering the alternative of abortion, Jane was offering a service that was badly needed. The alternative was open to all kinds of women—rich and poor, older and young, white and nonwhite, but it was a service most desperately needed by the poorer, younger, and minority women. One author says:

> In a comparison of blacks and whites, both for premarital and marital conceptions, we find that whites have higher percentages ending in induced abortions at the lower educational levels, while at the higher educational levels there is little or no difference between blacks and whites . . . the data point to the greater reliance upon abortion on the part of whites over blacks and on the part of the more affluent or more educated over the less affluent and less educated.

When they did turn to illegal abortion methods, poorer and nonwhite women came out far worse. Nationally in 1968, the black death rate from abortion was six times that of the white death rate. In New York in the early 1960s, 42 percent of the pregnancy-related deaths resulted from illegal abortions; and of those women who died, half were black and 44 percent were Puerto Rican. Only 6 percent were white.

More affluent women were also able to pay the high fees which all good, illegal abortionists charged. Jane overcame this by calculating fees on a sliding scale according to income. Some women paid nothing.

Jane's purpose, however, was not simply to provide a service for women, however valuable that service might be. The Jane group could not provide abortions to all Chicago women who needed them. More than that, Jane members knew that when abortion was legalized, their service would have to disappear. Jane's purpose was to show women a much broader alternative than simply not having a baby, to show that by acting together, women can change society so that all women can have an opportunity to choose a meaningful life. They tried to show this in different ways. One way was through the sliding scale for fees. Counselors explained to a woman paying $300 that she was helping pay the cost for a woman who could pay only $5.00. She was, in a small way, helping to undercut the unfairness of a society which would allow her an abortion but not the poorer woman.

Jane itself was the most dramatic demonstration of an alternative for women acting together. Jane members were themselves future or past candidates for abortion, and in the present, they were doing something dangerous, exhausting, and illegal for the sake of changing society for all women. Jane showed that women could take change into their own hands. By coming to Jane for their abortions, other women were also acting for this change. They were trusting women to do things which traditionally were done by men in their society, and legally done only by doctors (overwhelmingly male) within the rigid, hierarchically ordered medical profession. This was a leap of trust.

In the structure of their service, Jane members were trying to build an alternative kind of medical structure as well.

> We—the counselors—we learned the medical mystiques are just bullshit. That was a great up for us. Do you know, you're required to have a license as a nurse just to give a shot. Nurses can't even give an intravenous on their own. That takes a different kind of license. We would just explain to our workers how you had to fill the syringe, and how to be certain there was no air in it, and why that was important,

and so on. We'd spend a lot of time explaining it. Then we would say to the patient, "Well this is the first time that Sue is giving anyone a shot. Maybe you can help her, and be patient with her." "The patient was part of what was happening too. Part of the whole team.

Sometimes in the middle of an abortion, we would switch positions to show that everyone in the service could do things, to show that the woman who was counseling could give a shot, and the one who was giving a shot could counsel too. We did it to make people see that they could do it too. They have the power to learn to counsel and give a shot. They have the power to change things and build alternatives.

We here come to the central analysis within the Jane tradition, as it is expressed in Jane's practice. The analysis operates in a very general way to criticize our society and to offer direction to move toward change. Let me state it first in terms of the social structure of the institution of medicine in the United States today.

In the United States, medical people operate within a hierarchical system of dominance and subordination. Those higher in the hierarchy have power which those lower do not have—and the power to order those lower ones around is the least of it. One key aspect of that power is what Howard Becker calls "the right to define the nature of reality." He uses the notion of a "hierarchy of credibility": "In any system of ranked groups, participants take it as given that members of the highest group have the right to define the way things really are." I would argue that this "right of definition" means not only that the word of the higher has heavier weight than that of the lower (teacher over student, doctor over intern or aide) but that the very categories and concepts that are used, the "official" descriptions of reality, are descriptions from the point of view of the dominant persons in the hierarchy. What counts as knowledge itself is defined in terms of that viewpoint, and the definition further legitimates the power of the dominant person.

The power of those in dominant positions in the hierarchy is *legitimate authority*. This contrasts with the *natural authority* of a person who, regardless of position, happens to have a great deal of knowledge, experience, or wisdom about a subject. A doctor's authority is legitimated by the criteria, standards, and institutions which control access to his place in the hierarchy. These criteria and requirements for training on the one hand are aimed at insuring that those with legitimate authority in the hierarchy also have the natural authority required to do the jobs they are doing. Although we all know there are incompetent doctors, these criteria do operate to screen out incompetence *as defined from the top of the hierarchy*. Do they insure that those at the top have natural authority? I think not, and that is because *legitimate authority* carries with it a definition of what counts as knowledge: the definition from the top of the hierarchy, the "official" point of view.

This outlook on knowledge is sometimes called "objective" or "the scientific outlook" of experts. In fact, it is absolutist, and when the definition of reality is given solely in terms of the tradition of the dominant in a dominant-subordinate structure, the outlook is, in fact, biased.

In part, Jane members were operating from the viewpoint of a subordinate group in our society: women. They were using this viewpoint to try to create new social structures which were not based on dominance and subordination and in which authority was natural authority—knowledge which suits the situation to the best degree that we know at the moment. When the woman I interviewed said that the members of Jane tried to show other women that they "have the power to learn to counsel and give a shot" and that they "have the power to change things and build alternatives," she is talking not only about the natural authority of knowledge but what we might call natural *moral* power, or *moral* authority.

In structuring the abortion service as they did, the members of Jane were developing an alternative to hierarchy, but they were also overcoming the vices of dependency and feelings of ignorance and impotence by showing women that they did have the power to learn and do things themselves. The Jane organization itself was build on nonauthoritarian, nonhierarchical principles, and Jane members tried to run it as a collective.

> We tried to make is as nonauthoritarian as we could. We had rotating chairs. There wasn't a high value placed on one kind of work and a low value on another. Every position was so important to what we were doing, and it was treated as equally important, to the highest degree possible. This meant every one of us could do what she was best at. You didn't have people competing to do what was important, or feeling what they were doing wasn't valuable.

In April of 1973, the women of Jane asked themselves, "What next?" Whether abortion had been a good issue to move on or not, there was no place for an illegal abortion service now that abortions were legal. Some of the women went on to found a "well woman clinic," the Emma Goldman Clinic. They hoped to run the clinic on the nonauthoritarian, nonhierarchical model used by Jane. The clinic was organized around the concept of self-help, in which the "patients" are trained too in the kind of medical knowledge they need to understand and care for their own bodies for a large range of normal functions and slight disorders.

BIAS IN THE WORLD VIEW

In my discussion here, both the Judith Thomson tradition and the Jane tradition were dealing with the problem of abortion. Neither would take it to be *the* problem. Abortion is a subsidiary problem chosen because of its connection with more central concerns. For Judith Thomson, it is a question of rights—we might even say a question of equal rights. But it cannot be described that way for the Jane tradition without begging questions.

Within the Jane tradition, the problem was taken to be one of meaningful lives for women, or of free choice among genuine alternatives for meaningful lives. Some phrasing of the general problem in these terms seems appropriate to both traditions. Let me quote Betty Friedan, an activist who stands within traditions associated with Judith Thomson's:

> It is my thesis that the core of the problem for women today is not sexual but a problem of identity—a stunting or evasion of growth that is perpetuated by the feminine mystique. It is my thesis that as the Victorian culture did not permit women to accept or gratify their basic sexual needs, our culture does not permit women to accept or gratify their basic need to grow and fulfill their potentialities as human beings, a need which is not solely defined by their sexual roles.

The statement of purpose of the liberal feminist National Organization for Women (NOW) also concerns opportunities for a meaningful life and moral development as a human being: NOW pledges to "take action to bring women into full participation in the mainstream of American society now, exercising all the privileges and responsibilities thereof, in truly equal partnership with men." This makes it appear that for both traditions, the problem may be stated as one of equality, particularly equality so far as it relates to the moral questions of being a full human being and of having a meaningful (or good) life. I believe that this is a central concern of those within the Judith Thomson tradition. But it may be that the problem cannot be resolved under that tradition or its associated world view.

Concealing Data

. . . I [have] presented the moral activity of the organization Jane under one tradition. If we look at the Jane organization under the Judith Thomson tradition, we get a different selection of data. Here's a quotation from the newspaper article:

> From the beginning, we discussed the moral implications of abortion from all angles. We listened to right-to-lifers, Catholic clergy, population-control freaks and women's liberationists.
> We heard legislators and lobbyists and political commentators arguing fine points of "fetal viability." When does a fetus become a person? When it can survive outside the womb (after six months)? When it begins to move (after four months)? Or from the moment of conception?
> Many opponents of abortion called it "murder." We argued the logical counter-arguments: If a fetus is a person, then why aren't abortionists and women who have abortions charged with murder?
> Or, if the fetus has the rights of a person, then does the woman who carries it become subject to its rights? What happens when the rights of the woman and those of the fetus come into conflict?
> All philosophical and legalistic positions lost relevance when we began doing and viewing abortions . . . we knew that we were grappling with matters of life and death and no philosophical arguments could alter that belief.

Judith Thomson, or someone from her tradition, would have been a great help to the Jane women in these early discussions on abortion. On the other hand, these early discussions had no clear relevance to the central moral activity the women of Jane were engaging in—*by their own judgment.* The terms in which they saw the problem were different. Their perception and their moral activity constitute data which are important to solving the problem of equality, but the Judith Thomson tradition not only ignores those data: it makes them invisible. Let's look at some of the mechanisms by which the data are concealed.

One way a tradition conceals data is through the concepts and categories it uses. The Judith Thomson tradition would focus on the Jane discussions of rights. It would ignore the discussions of hierarchy, dominance, and subordination; and perhaps some within the tradition would not take these as morally relevant discussions at all. Any theory must use concepts. Through their very use, some data are selected and some ignored. Yet the question of whether the concepts properly capture the data, or of whether they are *appropriate*, is a central, critical question about the adequacy of any tradition.

In a similar way, the categories a tradition uses to organize data reveal some and conceal others. For example, the Judith Thomson tradition uses the categories of moral agent and of groups of moral agents as aggregates. The tradition also uses a division of moral phenomena into questions of individual conscience and those of public policy, where the latter is a matter of *official* public policy, made by those with legitimate authority. I don't want to argue that the tradition *rules out* other sorts of moral phenomena. But using those categories, it cannot capture the sort of moral phenomena Jane members took to be central: people in a subordinate position acting to create a set of social relations which are not structured by dominance and subordination, through the subordinates' coming to know their own power (as opposed to legitimate authority) through acting in collectives (not aggregates).

But am I being fair to the Judith Thomson tradition? After all, people within it don't claim to cover *all* moral phenomena. Few theories claim to cover everything within their purview, and even within chemistry there are divisions into organic and inorganic. Mightn't there be divisions within the field of moral phenomena so that another part of the tradition might deal with Jane's moral activity and thus reveal it?

Perhaps any new moral tradition we develop will have to have something to do with the concept of rights (and associated concepts), and deal in some way with groups as aggregates and with public policy as officially handed down. But that new tradition could not be the Judith Thomson tradition, for a revolutionary change in the methodology of her tradition is necessary to uncover data like Jane's.

The Judith Thomson tradition supposes that there exists a set of moral concepts embedded in moral principles which "we" all know and understand. In her paper, Judith Thomson herself is clarifying concepts "we" grasp by the standard method of the tradition: the use of hypothetical cases. This method presupposes a very mentalistic view of concepts and word meanings—mentalistic in the way philosophical empiricists are mentalistic in their views on meanings as "ideas." The concepts exist in the speaker's understanding. If someone understands the concept, he or she knows whether it applies in any given case. Considering hypothetical cases (in this view) points out cases the speaker might have overlooked; but once they are brought to his or her attention, the speaker allegedly knows whether the concepts apply or not, and so his or her explicit understanding of the concept is clarified. Similarly, one's explicit understanding of "our" moral principles is supposed to be clarified by considering hypothetical cases.

The most obvious thing to say about this method is that although bringing up hypothetical cases may clarify our understanding of concepts and principles, everyone knows that the selection of hypothetical cases also biases understanding. This bias may be (unintentionally) systematic. For example, Judith Thomson gives a case where Jones faces a frosty death because Smith owns the coat. Why not, instead, use a case where men, women, and children face poor diets, poor housing, and loss of dignity because the owner of a mill decides to move it out of one region into another having cheaper labor and lower tax rates? Philosophers may say the second example is too complicated, but the selection is not a trivial matter of simplicity. The coat example ignores an essential distinction in kinds of property ownership which the mill example reveals.

The method rules out empirical investigation to see what sorts of hypothetical cases might capture what is morally important to persons in a variety of circumstances in the United States. There seems to be no way whatsoever to insure that a fair consideration of hypothetical cases is made to reduce the bias. One can't develop a sampling procedure for hypothetical cases.

Worst of all, the method rules out empirical investigation to discover whether the moral concepts and principles the philosophers are dealing with are really the moral concepts which people use in the United States. It rules out empirical investigation to discover whether those concepts and those moral principles are relevant to the lives of people in different walks of life, investigation to discover whether they are relevant to solving those people's problems of human dignity and a meaningful life *as those people perceive* those problems.

The method itself has the mere appearance of being plausible only for ancient systems of concepts which are well worked out. It has not even the appearance of plausibility for a case like Jane's, in which people are in the process of creating new concepts through creating new social forms. The fundamental theory of meaning, of understanding, and of concept formation on which the method is based is not only inadequate: it is false.

All of this means that to encompass the Jane data, a revolutionary change is necessary in the methodology of the Judith Thomson tradition. Without it, the data remain concealed.

The data being concealed concern human moral activity and the possibilities of changing society. This constitutes a direct and very important value consequence. The Judith Thomson tradition dominates philosophy departments in the prestigious American universities, and even teachers in nonprestigious colleges are trained within it. This means that students are taught to see moral activity within that tradition. Activity requiring patterns of thinking and concepts and categories like Jane's is made invisible to them.

Official Points of View

From its beginnings, the tradition Judith Thomson works within has been centrally concerned with equality. People in this tradition have particularly been concerned that all human beings be equal under the moral law and under the positive law of the state. Equality before the moral or positive law means that the same laws and principles apply to all. Whether or not this is enlightened depends on which laws and principles one chooses and the society in which they apply.

The question of equality which those in the Jane tradition raise is one which takes dominant-subordinate structures in the society as *creators* of inequality. Their solution to the problem of equality is the use of the perception and power of the subordinate to eliminate dominant-subordinate structures through the creation of new social forms which do not have that structure. Those in the Judith Thomson tradition do not raise questions of dominance and subordination except in the moral, legal, and political spheres, where they are seen in terms of moral, legal, and political equality. Particularly, they do not raise the question of whether equality before the moral or positive law may not be rendered empty because of the dominant-subordinate structures in the economic or social (e.g., family) spheres.

It appears that there is a bias in our world view. It is a bias that allows moral problems to be defined from the top of various hierarchies of authority in such a way that the existence of the authority is concealed, and so the existence of alternative definitions that might challenge that authority and radically change our social organization is also concealed. But having acknowledged that, we must return to the question I asked at the beginning of the paper.

THE INTELLECTUAL PURSUITS

In this paper, I believe I uncovered a bias that requires a revolutionary change in ethics to remedy. But in the process of considering two approaches to the moral problem of abortion, it has become clear that there are serious questions to ask about the question with which I began the paper:

> Has a covert bias been introduced into our world view by the near exclusion of women from the domain of intellectual pursuits? If we ask about a bias in "our" world view, mustn't we ask who that "we" refers to? In fact, doesn't the question presuppose that "our" world view is constructed by people in the "intellectual pursuits"? That is, doesn't it presuppose a hierarchy of authority in which people in some occupations (academic humanists and scientists, professional writers, etc.) define a world view for everyone else? If so, then there is something further that the Jane case shows.

Judith Jarvis Thomson is a woman working in an established intellectual pursuit, and at the time she wrote her paper, she took a stand that amounted to criticizing certain ethical arguments for sex bias. She took her stand as an authority, she criticized other authorities, and her paper has been widely used by still other authorities who are certified to teach ethics classes. I have criticized her work in this paper, but I too write as an authority. This leads us to a certain conundrum—if I may call it that.

The women of Jane were certainly challenging the way men in important positions are certified to define the way we do things and, in fact, their authority to define "our" world view and say how things "really are." But some of the Jane members, at least, were not saying that we should remedy the problem by having women in important positions define the way we do things. They were saying that we should change the way we do things so that we do not have some important people giving the official world view for everyone else. That change cannot be accomplished merely by hiring more women to work in the intellectual pursuits. It requires changing the intellectual pursuits themselves. If Jane shows that we need a revolutionary change from the old moral theory, it is a change in the status of the authorities as well as a change in what has been taken to be a moral theory. Unless we strive to find ways to do that, we violate the central moral and scientific injunction for respecting other human beings:

> . . . look upon human group life as chiefly a vast interpretive process in which people, singly and collectively *guide themselves* by *defining* the objects, events, and situations they encounter.

Stanley Hauerwas
Christians and Abortion: The Narrative Context

Stanley Hauerwas *is a professor of religion at Duke University whose work in religious ethics has been enormously influential. His numerous publications include* Truthfulness and Tragedy *and* Community and Character.

. . . *C*hristians have failed their social order by accepting too easily the terms of argument concerning abortion offered by our society. If we are to serve our society well, and on our own terms, our first task must be to address ourselves by articulating for Christians why abortion can never be regarded as morally indifferent for us. Only by doing this can we witness to our society what kind of people and what kind of society is required if abortion is to be excluded. . . .

To begin with, the first question is not, "Why do Christians think abortion is wrong?" To begin there already presupposes that we know and understand what abortion is. Rather, if we are to understand why Christians assume that by naming abortion they have already said something significant, we have to begin still a step back. We have to ask what it is about the kind of community, and corresponding world, that Christians create that makes them single out abortion in such a way as to exclude it.

For we must remember that "abortion" is not a description of a particular kind of behavior; rather it is a word that teaches us to see a singular kind of behavior from a particular community's moral perspective. The removal of the fetus from the mother's uterus before term can be called an "interruption of pregnancy," the child can be called "fetal matter," and the mother can be called a "patient." But from the Christian perspective, to see the situation in that way changes the self and the community in a decisive way. The Christian insistence on the term "abortion" is a way to remind them that what happens in the removal of the fetus from the mother in order to destroy it strikes at the heart of their community. From this perspective the attempt of Christians to be a community where the term "abortion" remains morally intelligible is a political act.

In this respect the pro-abortionists have always been at a disadvantage. For they have had to carry out the argument in a language created by the moral presuppositions of the

Jewish and Christian communities. "Abortion" still carries the connotation that this is not a good thing. Thus to be "pro-abortion" seems to put one in an embarrassing position of recommending a less than good thing. It is not without reason, therefore, that pro-abortion advocates seek to redescribe both the object and act of abortion. We must remind them, however, that by doing so they not only change the description of the act, they also change themselves.

Christians insist on the significance of such a change by refusing to live in a world devoid of abortion as a moral description—a world which admittedly may, as a result, involve deep tragedy. There can be no doubt that the insistence that unjust termination of pregnancy be called "abortion" has to do with our respect for life, but this is surely too simple. Jews and Christians are taught to respect life, not as an end in itself, but as a gift created by God. Thus life is respected because all life serves God in its way. Respect for human life is but a form of our respect for all life. . . .

It is the Christian belief, nurtured by the command of Jesus, that we must learn to love one another, that we become more nearly what we were meant to be through the recognition and love of those we did not "choose" to love. Children, the weak, the ill, the dispossessed provide a particularly intense occasion for such love, as they are beings we cannot control. We must love them for what they are rather than what we want or wish them to be, and as a result we discover that we are capable of love. The existence of such love is not unique or limited to Christians. Indeed that is why we have the confidence that our Christian convictions on these matters might ring true even for those who do not share our convictions. The difference between the Christian and the non-Christian is only that what is a possibility for the non-Christian is a duty for the Christian.

But the Christian duty to welcome new life is a joyful duty, as it derives from our very being as God's people. Moreover correlative to the language of duty is the language of gift. Because children are a duty they can also be regarded as gift, for duty teaches us to accept and welcome a child into the world, not as something that is "ours, " but as a gift which comes from another. As a result Christians need not resort to destructive and self-deceiving claims about the qualities they need to have, or the conditions of the world necessary to have children. Perhaps more worrisome than the moral implications of the claim "no unwanted child ought ever to be born," are the ominous assumptions about what is required for one to "want" to have a child.

Christians are thus trained to be the kind of people who are ready to receive and welcome children into the world. For they see children as a sign of the trustworthiness of God's creation and his unwillingness to abandon the world to the powers of darkness. The Christian prohibition of abortion is but the negative side of their positive commitment to welcome new life into their community: life that they know must challenge and perhaps even change their own interpretation of their tradition, but also life without which the tradition has no means to grow.

It is, of course, true that children will often be conceived and born under less than ideal conditions, but the church lives as a community which assumes that we live in an age which is always dangerous. That we live in such a time is all the more reason we must be the kind of community that can receive children into our midst. Just as we need to be virtuous, not because virtue pays but because we cannot afford to be without virtue where it does not pay, so we must learn how to be people open to new life. We can neither protect them from that suffering nor deny them the joy of participating in the adventure of God's Kingdom.

For Christians, therefore, there can be no question of whether the fetus is or is not a "human being." That way of putting the matter is far too abstract and formal. Rather, because of the kind of community we are, we see in the fetus nothing less than God's continuing creation that is destined in hope to be another citizen of his Kingdom. The question of when human life begins is of little interest to such a people, since their hope is that life will and does continue to begin time after time.

This is the form of life that brings significance to our interaction with the fetus. Our history is the basis for our "natural" sympathies, which have been trained to look forward to the joy and challenge of new life. Wertheimer may well be right that there is no corresponding "natural" welcome for life in our society that would make intelligible the recognition of the fetus as having moral status. Yet I suspect that the expectation of parents, and in particular of women, for the birth of their children remains a powerful form of life that continues to exert a force on everyone. Such an "expectation," however, in the absence of more substantive convictions about parenting, too easily becomes a destructive necessity that distorts the experience of being a parent and a child. Particularly repugnant is the assumption that women are thus primarily defined by the role of "mother," for then we forget that the role of being a parent, even for the childless, is a responsibility for everyone in the Christian community.

Nor should it be thought that the Christian commitment to welcome new life into the world stems from a sentimental fondness for babies. Rather, for Christians the having of children is one of their most significant political acts. From the world's perspective the birth of a child represents but another drain on our material and psychological resources. Children, after all, take up much of our energy that could be spent on making the world a better place and our society more just. But from the Christian perspective the birth of a child represents nothing less than our commitment that God will not have this world "bettered" by destroying life. That is why there is no more profound political act for Christians than taking the time for children. It is but an indication that God, not man, rules this existence, and we have been graciously invited to have a part in God's adventure and his Kingdom through the simple action of having children.

THE IMMEDIATE POLITICAL TASK

To some it may seem that I have argued Christians right out of the current controversy, for my argument has made appeal to religious convictions that are inadmissable in the court of our public ethos. But it has certainly not been my intention to make it implausible for Christians to continue to work in the public arena for the protection of all children; nor do I think that this implication follows from the position I have developed. Of course, Christians should prefer to live in societies that provide protection for children. And Christians should certainly wish to encourage those "natural" sentiments that would provide a basis for having and protecting children.

Moreover Christians must be concerned to develop forms of care and support, the absence of which seem to make abortion such a necessity in our society. In particular Christians should, in their own communities, make clear that the role of parent is one we all share. Thus the woman who is pregnant and carrying the child need not be the one to raise it. We must be a people who stand ready to receive and care for any child, not just as if it were one of ours, but because in fact each is one of ours.

But as Christians we must not confuse our political and moral strategies designed to get the best possible care for children in our society with the substance of our convictions. Nor should we hide the latter in the interest of securing the former. For when that is done we abandon our society to its own limits. And then our arguments fall silent in the most regrettable manner, for we forget that our most fundamental political task is to be and to point to that truth which we believe to be the necessary basis for any life-enhancing and just society.

In particular, I think that we will be wise as Christians to state our opposition to abortion in a manner that makes clear our broader concerns for the kind of people we ought to be to welcome children into the world. Therefore, rather than concentrating our energies on whether the fetus is or is not a "person," we would be better advised by example and then argument to make clear why we should hope it is a child. We must show that such a hope involves more than just the question of the status of the fetus, but indeed is the very reason why being a part of God's creation is such an extraordinary and interesting adventure.

Daniel C. Maguire

A Catholic Theologian at an Abortion Clinic

Daniel C. Maguire *is a professor of moral theology at Marquette University. A member of Catholics for Free Choice, he has been an outspoken advocate of women's rights. Among his many publications are* Death By Choice *and* The Moral Choice.

I should not have been nervous the first day I drove to the abortion clinic. After all, I wasn't pregnant. There would be no abortions done this day. I would see no patients and no picketers. And yet tremors from a Catholic boyhood wrenched my usually imperturbable stomach. I was filled with dread and foreboding.

What was it that brought this Philadelphia Irish-Catholic male moral theologian to the clinic door? Abortion has not been my academic obsession. My wife and I have had no personal experience with abortion, although it once loomed as a possible choice in our lives. Our first son, Danny, was diagnosed as terminally ill with Hunter's syndrome when Margie was three months pregnant with our second child. However, amniocentesis revealed that the fetus, now Tommy, was normal.

The stimulus for my visit was the woman who agonized with Margie and me over the decision she had rather conclusively made, and asked us, as ethicists, to ponder with her all the pro's and con's. She was almost six weeks pregnant. Her life situation was seriously incompatible with parenting and she could not bear the thought of adoption. After her abortion, she told us she had made the right decision, but she paid the price in tears and trauma.

More generally, I was drawn to this uneasy experience by women. I have often discussed abortion with women in recent years, been struck by how differently they viewed it. I experienced their resentment at the treatment of the subject by the male club of moral theologians. One woman, an author and professor at a Chicago seminary, wrote me after reading my first article on abortion ("Abortion: A Question of Catholic Honesty," *The Christian Century*, September 14–21, 1983) thanking me and surprising me. She said she found it difficult to use the American bishops' pastoral letter on nuclear war because these *men* could agonize so long over the problems of *men* who might decide to end the world, but had not a sympathetic minute for the moral concerns of a woman who judges that she cannot bring her pregnancy to term.

I knew that my visit would not give me a woman's understanding of the abortion decision, but I hoped it might assist me, in the phrase of French novelist Jean Sulivan, to "lie less" when I write about this subject and to offend less those women who come this way in pain.

Those who write on liberation theology go to Latin America to learn; those who write on abortion stay at their desks. Until recently, all churchly writing on abortion has been done by desk-bound celibate males. If experience is the plasma of theory, the experience obtained in a clinic three blocks from Marquette, where I teach and have done research on abortion, could only enhance my theological ministry.

MEETING THE CLINIC STAFF

One day last May, I called the Milwaukee Women's Health Organization and spoke to its director, Elinor Yeo, an ordained minister of the United Church of Christ. I was afraid she would find my request to spend time at her clinic unseemly and out of order. She said she would call back when she finished an interview with a patient and spoke to her staff. She called later to tell me that the staff was enthusiastic about my prospective visits, adding the ironic note that the patient she was interviewing when I first called was a Marquette University undergraduate.

The clinic door still had traces of red paint from a recent attack. The door was buzzed open only after I was identified. A sign inside read: PLEASE HELP OUR GUARD. WE MAY NEED WITNESSES IF THE PICKETS GET OUT OF CONTROL. YOU CAN HELP BY OBSERVING AND LETTING HIM/HER KNOW IF YOU SEE TROUBLE. I realized that these people live and work in fear of "pro-life" violence. In the first half of this year there have been 58 reported incidents of criminal violence at clinics, including bombing, arson, shootings, and vandalism.

Elinor Yeo sat with me for more than an hour describing the clinic's activities. Half of its patients are teenagers; half, Catholics; and 20 percent, black. Of the 14 patients seen on a single day the previous week, one was 13 years old; one, 14; and, one 15. Nationally, most abortion are performed within eight weeks of conception, at which point the *conceptus* is still properly called an embryo; 91 percent are within 12 weeks. At this clinic, too, most abortions are performed in the first two months. Most of the patients are poor; the clinic is busiest at the time when welfare checks come in. The normal cost for an abortion here is $185. For those on public assistance, it is $100.

I asked Elinor about the right-to-lifers' claim that most women who have abortions are rich. She replied: "The typical age of an abortion patient at this clinic is 19 years." In what sense is a 19-year-old woman with an unwanted pregnancy rich?

I asked about the charge that doing abortions makes doctors rich. She assured me that, given their budget, all the doctors who work for them would make more if they remained in their offices. These doctors are also sometimes subject to harassment and picketing at their homes. Their care of patients is excellent, and they often end up delivering babies for these same women at some later date.

Each patient is given private counseling. About half want their male partners with them for these sessions. If there is any indication that the man is more anxious for the abortion than the woman, private counseling is carefully arranged. Every interested woman is offered the opportunity to study charts on embryonic and fetal development, and all women are informed of alternatives to abortion. The consent form, to be signed at the end of the interview and counseling sessions, includes the words: "I have been informed of agencies and services available to assist me to carry my pregnancy to term should I desire. . . . The nature and purposes of an abortion, the alternatives to pregnancy termination, the risks involved, and the possibility of complications have been fully explained to me."

All counselors stress reproductive responsibility. Two of the counselors have worked with Elinor for 14 years. One is the mother of five children, the other, of three. Free follow-up advice on contraception is made available. It is the explicit goal of the counselors not to have the woman return for another abortion. According to Yeo, those most likely to have repeat abortions are women who reject contraceptive information and say they will never have sex again until they are married. It became ironically clear to me that the women working in this abortion clinic prevent more abortions than the zealous pickets demonstrating outside.

Yeo says that only 5 percent of the patients have ever seriously considered adoption as an alternative. *Abortion* or *keeping* are the two options considered by these young women. (Ninety-five percent of teenagers who deliver babies keep them, according to Elinor Yeo.)

Adoption is, of course, the facile recommendation of the bumper-sticker level of this debate. One patient I spoke to at a subsequent visit to the clinic told me how unbearable the prospect was of going to term and then giving up the born baby. For impressive reasons she found herself in no condition to have a baby. Yet she had begun to take vitamins to nourish the embryo in case she changed her mind. "If I continued this nurture for nine months, how could I hand over to someone else what would then be my baby?" It struck me forcefully how aloof and misogynist it is not to see that the adoption path is full of pain. Here is one more instance of male moralists prescribing the heroic for women as though it were simply moral and mandatory.

The surgery lasts some 5 to 15 minutes. General anesthesia is not needed in these early abortions. Most women are in and out of the clinic in two and one half hours. They return in two weeks for a checkup. These early abortions are done by suction. I was shown the suction tube that is used and was surprised to find that it is only about twice the width of a drinking straw. This was early empirical information for me as to *what* it is that is aborted at this stage.

All patients are warned about pregnancy aftermath groups that advertise and offer support but actually attempt to play on guilt and recruit these women in their campaign to outlaw all abortions, even those performed for reasons of health. One fundamentalist Protestant group in Milwaukee advertises free pregnancy testing. When the woman arrives, they subject her to grisly slides on abortions of well-developed fetuses. They take the woman's address and phone number and tell her they will contact her in two weeks at home. The effects of this are intimidating and violative of privacy and often lead to delayed abortions of more developed fetuses.

MEETING THE WOMEN

My second visit was on a Saturday when the clinic was busy. I arrived at 8:30 in the morning. The picketers were already there, all men, except for one woman with a boy of 10. A patient was in the waiting room, alone. We greeted each other, and I sat down and busied myself with some papers, wondering what was going on in her mind. I was later to learn that she was five to six weeks pregnant. I was told that she was under psychiatric care for manic-depression, and receiving high doses of lithium to keep her mood swings under control. However, lithium in high doses may be injurious to the formation of the heart in embryos and early fetuses.

Pro-life? Pro-choice? How vacuous the slogans seemed in the face of this living dilemma. What life options were open to this woman? Only at the expense of her emotional well-being could a reasonably formed fetus come to term. This woman had driven alone a long distance that morning to get to the clinic and she would have to return home alone afterward. She had to walk to the door past demonstrators showing her pictures of fully formed fetuses and begging her: "Don't kill your baby! Don't do it." However well-intentioned they may be, in what meaningful moral sense were those picketers in this instance pro-life?

As I watched this woman I thought of one of my colleagues who had recently made a confident assertion that there could be no plausible reason for abortion except to save the physical life of the woman or if the fetus was anencephalic. This woman's physical life was not at risk and the embryo would develop a brain. But saving *life* involves more than cardio-pulmonary continuity. How is it that in speaking of women we so easily reduce human life to physical life? What certitudes persuade theologians that there are only two marginal reasons to justify abortion? Why is the Vatican comparably sure that while there may be *just* wars with incredible slaughter, there can be no *just* abortions? Both need to listen to the woman on lithium as she testifies that life does not always confine itself within the ridges of our theories.

With permission I sat in on some of the initial interviews with patients. The first two were poor teenagers, each with an infant at home, and each trying to finish high school. One was out of work. Elinor Yeo let her know that they were now hiring at "Wendy's." I was impressed that the full human plight of the patients was of constant concern to the staff. The other young woman had just gotten a job after two years and would lose it through pregnancy. One woman counted out her $100 and said: "I hate to give this up; I need it so much."

The staff told me about the various causes of unwanted pregnancies. One staff member said that it would seem that most young men have "scorn for condoms." "Making love" does not describe those sexual invasions. For these hostile inseminators nothing is allowed to interfere with their pleasure. Often there is contraceptive failure. One recent case involved a failed vasectomy. Sometimes conception is admittedly alcohol- and drug-related. A few women concede that they were "testing the relationship." Often it is a case of a broken relationship where the woman, suddenly alone, feels unable to bring up a child. Economic causes were most common. Lack of job, lack of insurance, a desire to stay in school and break out of poverty.

I wondered how many "pro-lifers" voted for Ronald Reagan because of his antiabortion noises, even though Reaganomics decreased the income of the lowest fifth of society's families by 8 percent while increasing the income of the rich. More of this could only be more poverty, more ruin, more social chaos, more unwanted pregnancies, and more women at clinic doors.

MEETING THE PICKETERS

The picketers are a scary lot. Because of them a guard has to be on duty to escort the patients from their cars. Before the clinic leased the adjacent parking lot—making it their private property—some picketers used to attack the cars of the women, screaming and shaking the car. The guard told me he was once knocked down by a picketer. Without the guard, some of the demonstrators surround an unescorted woman and force her to see and hear their message. Other picketers simply carry placards and pray. One day, 20 boys from Libertyville, Illinois, were bused in to picket. They were not passive. They had been taught to shout at the women as they arrived. One staff member commented: "Statistically, one quarter to one third of these boys will face abortion situations in their lives. I wonder how this experience will serve them then."

A reporter from the Milwaukee *Journal* arrived, and I followed her when she went out to interview the picketers. Two picketers recognized me. Since I have been quoted in the press in ways that did not please, I am a persona non grata to this group. I had a chance to feel what the women patients endure. "You're in the right place, Maguire. In there, where they murder the babies." I decided they were not ripe for dialogue, so I remained silent and listened in on the interview.

I learned that some of these men had been coming to demonstrate every Saturday for nine years. Their language was filled with allusions to the Nazi Holocaust. Clearly, they imagine themselves at the ovens of Auschwitz, standing in noble protest as innocent *persons* are led to their death. There could hardly be any higher drama in their lives. They seem not to know that the Nazis were antiabortion too—for Aryans. They miss the anti-Semitism and insult in this use of Holocaust imagery. The 6 million murdered Jews and more than 3 million Poles, Gypsies, and homosexuals were actual, not potential, persons who were killed. Comparing their human dignity to that of prepersonal embryos is no tribute to the Holocaust dead.

Sexism too is in bold relief among the picketers. Their references to "these women" coming here to "kill their babies" are dripping with hatred. It struck me that for all their avowed commitment to life, these are the successors of the witch-hunters.

MEETING THE EMBRYOS

On my third visit to the clinic, I made bold to ask to see the products of some abortions. I asked in such a way as to make refusal easy, but my request was granted. The aborted matter is placed in small cloth bags and put in jars awaiting disposal. I asked to see the contents of one of the bags of a typical abortion—a six- to nine-week pregnancy—and it was opened and placed in a small metal cup for examination. I held the cup in my hands and saw a small amount of unidentifiable fleshy matter in the bottom of the cup. The quantity was so little that I could have hidden it if I had taken it into my hand and made a fist.

It was impressive to realize that I was holding in the cup what many people think to be the legal and moral peer of a woman, if not, indeed, her superior. I thought too of the Human Life Amendment that would describe what I was seeing as a citizen of the United States with rights of preservation that would countermand the good of the woman bearer. I have held babies in my hands and now I held this embryo. I know the difference.

CONCLUSIONS

 • My visits to the clinic made me more anxious to maintain the legality of abortions for women who judge they need them. There are no moral grounds for political consensus against this freedom on an issue where good experts and good people disagree. It also made me anxious to work to reduce the need for abortion by fighting the causes of unwanted pregnancies: *sexism* enforced by the institutions of church, synagogue, and state that diminishes a woman's sense of autonomy; *poverty* induced by skewed budgets; *antisexual* bias that leads to eruptive sex; and the other *macro* causes of these micro tragedies.

 • I came to understand that abortion can be the *least* violent option facing a woman. It is brutally insensitive to pretend that for women who resort to abortion, death is the only extremity they face.

 • I came away from the clinic with a new longing for a moratorium on self-righteousness and sanctimonious utterances from Catholic bishops on the subject of abortion. An adequate Catholic theology of abortion has not yet been written. But the bishops sally forth as though this complex topic were sealed in a simple negative. Bishops like New York's John O'Connor, who use tradition as though it were an oracle instead of an unfinished challenge, are not helping at all. A position like O'Connor's has two yields: (a) it insults the Catholic intellectual tradition by making it look simplistic, and (b) it makes the bishops the allies of a right wing that has been using its newfound love of embryos as an ideological hideaway for many who resist the bishops' call for peace and social justice.

 • Finally, I come from the abortion clinic with an appeal to my colleagues in Catholic moral theology. Many theologians (especially clerics) avoid this issue or behave weirdly or skittishly when they touch it. How do Catholic theologians justify their grand silence when they are allowing physicalism, crude historical distortions, and fundamentalistic notions of "Church teaching" to parade as "the Catholic position"? Why are ethical errors that are thoroughly lambasted in the birth-control debate tolerated when the topic is abortion? Geraldine Ferraro and Governor Mario Cuomo of New York are taking the heat and trying to do the theology on this subject. Their debts to American Catholic theologians are minuscule. What service do we Church teachers give when errors, already corrected in theology, are allowed to roam unchallenged in the pastoral and political spheres? Why are nonexperts, church hierarchy or not, allowed to set the *theological* terms of this debate? What service is it to ecumenism to refuse serious dialogue not only with women but with main-line Jewish and Protestant theologians on this issue? Vatican II said that "ecumenical dialogue could start with discussions concerning the application of the gospel to moral questions." That dialogue has not happened on abortion, and our brothers and sisters from other communions are waiting for it.

I realize, as do my colleagues in Catholic ethics, that abortion is not a pleasant topic. At its best, abortion is a negative value, unlike the positive values of feeding the poor and working for civil rights. On top of that it has become the litmus test of orthodoxy, and that spells danger in the Catholic academe. But, beyond all this, we in the Catholic family have been conditioned against an objective and empathic understanding of abortion. We are more sensitized to embryos than to the women who bear them. I claim no infallibility on this subject, but I do insist that until we open our affections to enlightenment here, we will none of us be wise.

Barbara Ehrenreich

Is Abortion Really a "Moral" Dilemma?

Barbara Ehrenreich, *a prominent feminist theorist and activist, has written extensively on women's issues. Her most recent book is* Remaking Love: the Feminization of Sexuality *(with Elizabeth Hess and Gloria Jacobs).*

Quite apart from blowing up clinics and terrorizing patients, the antiabortion movement can take credit for a more subtle and lasting kind of damage. It has succeeded in getting even pro-choice people to think of abortion as a "moral dilemma," an "agonizing decision" and related code phrases for something murky and compromising, like the traffic in infant formula mix. In liberal circles, it has become unstylish to discuss abortion without using words like "complex," "pained," and the rest of the mealy-mouthed vocabulary of evasion. Regrets are also fashionable, and one otherwise feminist author writes recently of mourning each year following her abortion, the putative birthday of her discarded fetus.

I cannot speak for other women, of course, but the one regret I have about my own abortions is that they cost money that might otherwise have been spent on something more pleasurable, like taking the kids to movies and theme parks. Yes, that is abortions, plural (two in my case)—a possibility that is not confined to the promiscuous, the disorderly or the ignorant. In fact, my credentials for dealing with the technology of contraception are first rate: I have a Ph.D. in biology that is now a bit obsolescent but still good for conjuring up vivid mental pictures of zygotes and ova, and I was actually paid, at one point in my life, to teach other women about the mystery of reproductive biology.

Yet, as every party to the abortion debate should know, those methods of contraception that are truly safe are not absolutely reliable no matter how reliably they are used. Many women, like myself, have felt free to choose the safest methods because legal abortion is available as a backup to contraception. Anyone who finds that a thoughtless, immoral choice should speak to the orphans of women whose wombs were perforated by Dalkon shields or whose strokes were brought on by high estrogen birth control pills.

I refer you to the orphans only because it no longer seems to be good form to mention the women themselves in discussions of abortion. In most of the antiabortion literature I have seen, women are so invisible that an uninformed reader might conclude that fetuses reside in artificially warm tissue culture flasks or similar containers. It must be enormously difficult for the antiabortionist to face up to the fact that real fetuses can only survive inside women, who, unlike any kind of laboratory apparatus, have thoughts, feelings, aspirations, responsibilities and, very often, checkbooks. Anyone who thinks for a moment about women's role in reproductive biology could never blithely recommend "adoption, not abortion" because women have to go through something unknown to fetuses of men, and that is pregnancy.

From the point of view of a fetus, pregnancy is no doubt a good deal. But consider it for a moment from the point of view of the pregnant person (if "woman" is too incendiary and feminist a term) and without reference to its potential issue. We are talking about a nine-month bout of symptoms of varying severity, often including nausea, skin discolorations, extreme bloating and swelling, insomnia, narcolepsy, hair loss, varicose veins, hemorrhoids, indigestion and irreversible weight gain, and culminating in a physiological crisis which is occasionally fatal and almost always excruciatingly painful. If men were equally at risk for this condition—if they knew that their bellies might swell as if they were suffering from end-stage-cirrhosis, that they would have to go for nearly a year without a stiff drink, a cigarette or even an aspirin, that they would be subject to fainting spells and unable to fight their way into comuter trains—then I am sure that pregnancy would be classified as a sexually transmitted disease and abortions would be no more controversial than emergency appendectomies.

Adding babies to the picture does not make it all that much prettier, even if you are, as I am, a fool for short, dimpled people with drool on their chins. For no matter how charming the outcome of pregnancy that is allowed to go to term no one is likely to come forth and offer to finance its Pampers or pay its college tuition. Nor are the opponents of abortion promising a guaranteed annual income, subsidized housing, national health insurance and other measures that might take some of the terror out of parenthood. We all seem to expect the individual parents to shoulder the entire burden of supporting any offspring that can be traced to them, and, in the all-too-common event that the father cannot be identified or has skipped town to avoid child-support payments, "parent" means mother.

When society does step in to help out a poor woman attempting to raise children on her own, all that it customarily has to offer is some government-surplus cheese, a monthly allowance so small it would barely keep a yuppie male in running shoes, and the contemptuous epithet "welfare cheat." It would be far more reasonable to honor the survivors of pregnancy in childbirth with at least the same respect and special benefits that we give, without a second thought, to veterans of foreign wars.

But, you will object, I have greatly exaggerated the discomforts of pregnancy and the hazards of childbearing, which many women undergo quite cheerfully. This is true, at least to an extent. In my own case, the case of my planned and wanted pregnancies, I managed to interpret morning sickness as a sign of fetus tenacity and to find, in the hypertrophy of my belly, a voluptuousness ordinarily unknown to the skinny. But this only proves my point: A society that is able to make a good thing out of pregnancy is certainly free to choose how to regard abortion. We can treat it as a necessary adjunct to contraception, or as a vexing moral dilemma, or as a form of homicide—and whichever we choose, that is how we will tend to experience it.

So I will admit that I might not have been so calm and determined about my abortions if I had had to cross a picket line of earnest people yelling "baby killer," or if I felt that I might be blown to bits in the middle of a vacuum aspiration. Conversely, though, we would be hearing a lot less about ambivalence and regrets if there were not so much liberal head scratching going on. Abortions will surely continue, as they have through human history, whether we approve or disapprove or hem and haw. The question that worries me is: How is, say, a 16-year-old girl going to feel after an abortion? Like a convicted sex offender, a murderess on parole? Or like a young woman who is capable, as the guidance counselors say, of taking charge of her life?

This is our choice, for biology will never have an answer to that strange and cabalistic question of when a fetus becomes a person. Potential persons are lost every day as a result of miscarriage, contraception or someone's simple failure to respond to a friendly wink. What we can answer, with a minimum of throat-clearing and moral agonizing, is the question of when women themselves will finally achieve full personhood: And that is when we have the right, unquestioned and unabrogated, to choose not to be pregnant when we decide not to be pregnant.

12

What's the Meaning of Death?

*I*t may have struck you that many of the topics that philosophers find interesting (the nature of knowledge, the relationship between the mind and the body, the nature of justice, and so on) aren't ones that people generally worry much about. While people may have views about, for example, whether a particular law is just or not, they usually don't spend much time trying to understand the nature of justice itself. That task gets left to the philosopher. But it seems that most people do, at various times in their lives, wonder about the nature of death. What is death? What is it like to be dead? Does that question make sense? Why do we usually consider death to be a bad thing, a thing to be avoided? Is it ever reasonable to prefer death over life? Is there "life" after death? If so, what is it like?

In his paper "Death," Thomas Nagel tries to figure out just what is so bad about death, given that death is the end of conscious existence. How can something be bad for me if I don't even exist? If you have trouble settling this question and those above, if they present you with endless opportunity for speculation, it is partly because each of them is connected not only to one another, but also to a host of other questions that resist easy answers. For example, take the question that Nagel sidesteps, namely, whether there is "life" after death. When someone poses that question, she is usually wondering if, after the death of her body, anything is left of the person who once "inhabited" it. After all, the corpse rots away under the earth, or succumbs to the flames of the crematorium. Where, then, is the person who once was? As you can see, how you answer this question will depend in part on your views about the relationship between the mind and the body (see Chapter 5). For example, if you have been persuaded that a person is a purely physical being and that the notion of an immaterial mind or soul is nonsensical, then you will likely dismiss the idea that a person could survive the death of her body. You can see, too, that underlying this last claim are assumptions about the nature of persons. Thus, any view about life after death will have as a counterpart some view about personal identity (see Chapter 9). Very often, concerns about the afterlife can be seen as concerns about what it is that gives life meaning. Some people think that, without some promise of a life beyond that on earth, our lives here are meaningless and without any real purpose.

Shades of this view can be found in Plato's *Phaedo*, in which Socrates makes explicit his position on the question of the afterlife. He thought that the physical body was a mere impediment, something that we have to live with, so to speak, while we are stationed in the material world. To him, the *real* world was purely immaterial. Our embodied life, if lived properly (you will see what Socrates thought about the life well lived), is a process of moving closer and closer to reality. In and of itself, our embodied life means nothing. Michael Bishop provides Socrates with an amusing foil. Throughout his story, you will be asked to consider just how someone who is dead could have any experiences at all. At the very least, it would take some serious adjustment to go from being an alive person to "being" a dead person.

The mysteries of death and the afterlife thus provide wide room for philosophical speculation. But there is as well a set of distinctly ethical questions about death and dying that warrant careful attention. Simply put, the most central of such

441

questions is whether it is ever permissible to cause someone to die or even to let someone die. Surely, few people endorse cold-blooded murder. But what about "pulling the plug" in the case of an elderly patient who is in a coma, with no chance of gaining consciousness? Or what about administering a lethal dose of morphine to a terminally ill cancer patient in intractable pain? Immediately, a number of ancillary questions arise. Is there a difference between killing and letting someone die? What role do the desires of the afflicted person play in the decision to "let nature take its course" or to help nature along its way? The Greek word "euthanasia," which taken literally means "good death," is often used to refer to cases such as these.

In his paper on the topic, James Rachels examines a number of the classic arguments for and against euthanasia. First, he considers the "argument from mercy" which provides a justification for euthanasia in those cases of terminal suffering. According to the argument from mercy, euthanasia is justified to spare a person unimagineable pain if no other alternative is available. To assesss the philosophical merits of the argument from mercy, Rachels looks at various utilitarian and Kantian formulations of it. Second, Rachels considers the religious arguments against euthanasia and concludes that there is nothing in religious belief to rule out the possibility of mercy killing. Finally, Rachels considers the claim that euthanasia can never be justified because there is always the possibility that an unexpected cure might save the person's life. While it is sometimes difficult to determine whether a person's condition is hopeless, it is not always difficult. On that basis Rachels argues that euthanasia is sometimes permissible. If so, euthanasia requires careful consideration of the options and alternatives.

Among the more difficult questions surrounding the issue of death is, When is someone actually dead? For many years, a person was considered dead when there was a cessation of all vital signs. Given that the function of a person's heart and lungs can now be maintained by respirators, a new definition of death has been proposed. According to a committee of doctors, theologians, and ethicists assembled to evaluate the definition of death in 1968, death should be defined as irreversible coma. When a person is found to be in an irreversible coma, death should be declared and the respirator turned off. Willard Gaylin considers some of the unexpected advantages to the living of such a "liberal" definition of death. Such a definition allows for the possibility of stockpiling "dead" bodies, the organs of which could then be used in transplants. You might want to think about why that idea is so unnerving to many people.

Closely related to the question of whether we are ever justified in providing another person with a "good death" is the question of whether we are ever justified in taking our own lives. Many people consider committing suicide, maybe only fleetingly, at some time in their lives. Is life ever so bad that ending it is the right alternative? Does it matter whether the anguish that the person is experiencing is physical or mental? Is it ever right to interfere with someone's decision to commit suicide? Sylvia Plath presents us with her character, Esther, who proceeds in a methodical and deliberate way to arrange for her own death. If you feel that you ought to stop her, Robert Martin gives you some reasons for thinking twice about your motivations.

Any attempt to answer these difficult ethical questions about death brings us back to our initial ones about the nature of death and the meaning of life. But it also forces us to think about the extent to which we are responsible for what we do (see Chapter 18) and just what it is to lead a good life (see Part V). Whatever death is, it is too closely related to life to be considered by itself.

Thomas Nagel

Death

Thomas Nagel *teaches philosophy at New York University. He has made important contributions to ethics and philosophy of mind. Among his many publications are* Mortal Questions *and* The View from Nowhere.

If death is the unequivocal and permanent end of our existence, the question arises whether it is a bad thing to die.

There is conspicuous disagreement about the matter: some people think death is dreadful; others have no objection to death *per se,* though they hope their own will be neither premature nor painful. Those in the former category tend to think those in the latter are blind to the obvious, while the latter suppose the former to be prey to some sort of confusion. On the one hand it can be said that life is all we have and the loss of it is the greatest loss we can sustain. On the other hand it may be objected that death deprives this supposed loss of its subject, and that if we realize that death is not an unimaginable condition of the persisting person, but a mere blank, we will see that it can have no value whatever, positive or negative.

Since I want to leave aside the question whether we are, or might be, immortal in some form, I shall simply use the word 'death' and its cognates in this discussion to mean *permanent* death, unsupplemented by any form of conscious survival. I want to ask whether death is in itself an evil; and how great an evil, and of what kind, it might be. The question should be of interest even to those who believe in some form of immortality, for one's attitude toward immortality must depend in part on one's attitude toward death.

If death is an evil at all, it cannot be because of its positive features, but only because of what it deprives us of. I shall try to deal with the difficulties surrounding the natural view that death is an evil because it brings to an end all the goods that life contains. We need not give an account of these goods here, except to observe that some of them, like perception, desire, activity, and thought, are so general as to be constitutive of human life. They are widely regarded as formidable benefits in themselves, despite the fact that they are conditions of misery as well as of happiness, and that a sufficient quantity of more particular evils can perhaps outweigh them. That is what is meant, I think, by the allegation that it is good simply to be alive, even if one is undergoing terrible experiences. The situation is roughly this: There are elements which, if added to one's experience, make life better; there are other elements which, if added to one's experience, make life worse. But what remains when these are set aside is not merely *neutral:* it is emphatically positive. Therefore life is worth living even when the bad elements of experience are plentiful, and the good ones too meager to outweigh the bad ones on their own. The additional positive weight is supplied by experience itself, rather than by any of its contents.

I shall not discuss the value that one person's life or death may have for others, or its objective value, but only the value it has for the person who is its subject. That seems to me the primary case, and the case which presents the greatest difficulties. Let me add only two observations. First, the value of life and its contents does not attach to mere organic survival: almost everyone would be indifferent (other things equal) between immediate death and immediate coma followed by death twenty years later without reawakening. And second, like most goods, this can be multiplied by time: more is better than less. The added quantities need not be temporally continuous (though continuity has its social advantages). People are attracted to the possibility of long-term suspended animation or freezing, followed by the resumption of conscious life, because they can regard it from within simply as a *continuation* of their present life. If these techniques are ever perfected, what from outside appeared as a dormant interval of three hundred years could be experienced by the subject as nothing more than a sharp discontinuity in the character of his experiences. I do not deny, of course, that this has its own disadvantages. Family and friends may have died in the meantime; the language may have changed; the comforts of social, geographical, and cultural familiarity would be lacking. Nevertheless these inconveniences would not obliterate the basic advantage of continued, though discontinuous, existence.

If we turn from what is good about life to what is bad about death, the case is completely different. Essentially, though there may be problems about their specification, what we find desirable in life are certain states, conditions, or types of activity. It is *being* alive, *doing* certain things, having certain experiences, that we consider good. But if death is an evil, it is the *loss of life*, rather than the state of being dead, or nonexistent, or unconscious, that is objectionable. This asymmetry is important. If it is good to be alive, that advantage can be attributed to a person at each point of his life. It is a good of which Bach had more than Schubert, simply because he lived longer. Death, however, is not an evil of which Shakespeare has so far received a larger portion than Proust. If death is a disadvantage, it is not easy to say when a man suffers it.

There are two other indications that we do not object to death merely because it involves long periods of nonexistence. First, as has been mentioned, most of us would not regard the *temporary* suspension of life, even for substantial intervals, as in itself a misfortune. If it ever happens that people can be frozen without reduction of the conscious lifespan, it will be inappropriate to pity those who are temporarily out of circulation. Second, none of us existed before we were born (or conceived), but few regard that as a misfortune. I shall have more to say about this later.

The point that death is not regarded as an unfortunate *state* enables us to refute a curious but very common suggestion about the origin of the fear of death. It is often said that those who object to death have made the mistake of trying to imagine what it is like to *be* dead. It is alleged that the failure to realize that this task is logically impossible (for the banal reason that there is nothing to imagine) leads to the conviction that death is a mysterious and therefore terrifying prospective *state*. But this diagnosis is evidently false, for it is just as impossible to imagine being totally unconscious as to imagine being dead (though it is easy enough to imagine oneself, from the outside, in either of those conditions). Yet people who are averse to death are not usually averse to unconsciousness (so long as it does not entail a substantial cut in the total duration of waking life).

If we are to make sense of the view that to die is bad, it must be on the ground that life is a good and death is the corresponding deprivation or loss, bad not because of any positive features but because of the desirability of what it removes. We must now turn to the serious difficulties which this hypothesis raises, difficulties about loss and privation in general, and about death in particular.

Essentially, there are three types of problems. First, doubt may be raised whether *anything* can be bad for a man without being positively unpleasant to him: specifically, it may be doubted that there are any evils which consist merely in the deprivation or absence of possible goods, and which do not depend on someone's *minding* that deprivation. Second, there are special difficulties, in the case of death, about how the supposed misfortune is to be assigned to a subject at all. There is doubt both as to *who* its subject is, and as to *when* he undergoes it. So long as a person exists, he has not yet died, and once he has died, he no longer exists; so there seems to be no time when death, if it is a misfortune, can be ascribed to its unfortunate subject. The third type of difficulty concerns the asymmetry, mentioned above, between our attitudes to posthumous and prenatal nonexistence. How can the former be bad if the latter is not?

It should be recognized that if these are valid objections to counting death as an evil, they will apply to many other supposed evils as well. The first type of objection is expressed in general form by the common remark that what you don't know can't hurt you. It means that even if a man is betrayed by his friends, ridiculed behind his back, and despised by people who treat him politely to his face, none of it can be counted as a misfortune for him so long as he does not suffer as a result. It means that a man is not injured if his wishes are ignored by the executor of his will, or if, after his death, the belief becomes current that all the literary works on which his fame rests were really written by his brother, who died in Mexico at the age of 28. It seems to me worth asking what assumptions about good and evil lead to these drastic restrictions.

All the questions have something to do with time. There certainly are goods and evils of a simple kind (including some pleasures and pains) which a person possesses at a given time simply in virtue of his condition at that time. But this is not true of all the things we regard as good or bad for a man. Often we need to know his history to tell whether something is a misfortune or not; this applies to ills like deterioration, deprivation, and damage. Sometimes his experiential *state* is relatively unimportant—as in the case of a man who wastes his life in the cheerful pursuit of a method of communicating with asparagus plants. Someone who holds that all goods and evils must be temporally assignable states of the person may of course try to bring difficult cases into line by pointing to the pleasure or pain that more complicated goods and evils cause. Loss, betrayal, deception, and ridicule are on this view bad because people suffer when they learn of them. But it should be asked how our ideas of human value would have to be constituted to accommodate these cases directly instead. One advantage of such an account might be that it would enable us to explain *why* the discovery of these misfortunes causes suffering—in a way that makes it reasonable. For the natural view is that the discovery of betrayal makes us unhappy because it is bad to be betrayed—not that betrayal is bad because its discovery makes us unhappy.

It therefore seems to me worth exploring the position that most good and ill fortune has as its subject a person identified by his history and his possibilities, rather than merely by his categorical state of the moment—and that while this subject can be exactly located in a sequence of places and times, the same is not necessarily true of the goods and ills that befall him.

These ideas can be illustrated by an example of deprivation whose severity approaches that of death. Suppose an intelligent person receives a brain injury that reduces him to the mental condition of a contented infant, and that such desires as remain to him can be satisfied by a custodian, so that he is free from care. Such a development would be widely regarded as a severe misfortune, not only for his friends and relations, or for society, but also, and primarily, for the person himself. This does not mean that a contented infant is unfortunate. The intelligent adult who has been *reduced* to this condition is the subject of the misfortune. He is the one we pity, though of course he does not mind his condition—there is some doubt, in fact, whether he can be said to exist any longer.

The view that such a man has suffered a misfortune is open to the same objections which have been raised in regard to death. He does not mind his condition. It is in fact the same condition he was in at the age of three months, except that he is bigger. If we did not pity him then, why pity him now; in any case, who is there to pity? The intelligent adult has disappeared, and for a creature like the one before us, happiness consists in a full stomach and a dry diaper.

If these objections are invalid, it must be because they rest on a mistaken assumption about the temporal relation between the subject of a misfortune and the circumstances which constitute it. If, instead of concentrating exclusively on the oversized baby before us, we consider the person he was, and the person he *could* be now, then his reduction to this state and the cancellation of his natural adult development constitute a perfectly intelligible catastrophe.

This case should convince us that it is arbitrary to restrict the goods and evils that can befall a man to nonrelational properties ascribable to him at particular times. As it stands, that restriction excludes not only such cases of gross degeneration, but also a good deal of what is important about success and failure, and other features of a life that have the character of processes. I believe we can go further, however. There are goods and evils which are irreducibly relational; they are features of the relations between a person, with spatial and temporal boundaries of the usual sort, and circumstances which may not coincide with him either in space or in time. A man's life includes much that does not take place within the boundaries of his body and his mind, and what happens to him can include much that does not take place within the boundaries of his life. These boundaries are commonly crossed by the misfortunes of being deceived, or despised, or betrayed. (If this is correct, there is a simple account of what is wrong with breaking a deathbed promise. It is an injury to the dead man. For certain purposes it is possible to regard time as just another type of distance.) The case of mental degeneration shows us an evil that depends on a contrast between the reality and the possible alternatives. A man is the subject of good and evil as much because he has hopes which may or may not be fulfilled, or possibilities which may or may not be realized, as because of his capacity to suffer and enjoy. If death is an evil, it must be accounted for in these terms, and the impossibility of locating it within life should not trouble us.

When a man dies we are left with his corpse, and while a corpse can suffer the kind of mishap that may occur to an article of furniture, it is not a suitable object for pity. The man, however, is. He has lost his life, and if he had not died, he would have continued to live it, and to possess whatever good there is in living. If we apply to death the account suggested for the case of dementia, we shall say that although the spatial and temporal locations of the individual who suffered the loss are clear enough, the misfortune itself cannot be so easily located. One must be content just to state that his life is over and there will never be any more of it. That *fact,* rather than his past or present condition, constitutes his misfortune, if it is one. Nevertheless if there is a loss, someone must suffer it, and *he* must have existence and specific spatial and temporal location even if the loss itself does not. The fact that Beethoven had no children may have been a cause of regret to him, or a sad thing for the world, but it cannot be described as a misfortune for the children that he never had. All of us, I believe, are fortunate to have been born. But unless good and ill can be assigned to an embryo, or even to an unconnected pair of gametes, it cannot be said that not to be born is a misfortune. (That is a factor to be considered in deciding whether abortion and contraception are akin to murder.)

This approach also provides a solution to the problem of temporal asymmetry, pointed out by Lucretius. He observed that no one finds it disturbing to contemplate the eternity preceding his own birth, and he took this to show that it must be irrational to fear death, since death is simply the mirror image of the prior abyss. That is not true, however, and the difference between the two explains why it is reasonable to regard them differently. It is true that both the time before a man's birth and the time after his death are times when he does not exist. But the time after his death is time of which his death deprives him. It is time in which, had he not died then, he would be alive. Therefore any death entails the loss of *some* life that its victim would have led had he not died at that or any earlier point. We know perfectly well what it would be for him to have had it instead of losing it, and there is no difficulty in identifying the loser.

But we cannot say that the time prior to a man's birth is time in which he would have lived had he been born not then but earlier. For aside from the brief margin permitted by premature labor, he *could* not have been born earlier: anyone born substantially earlier than he was would have been someone else. Therefore the time prior to his birth is not time in which his subsequent birth prevents him from living. His birth, when it occurs, does not entail the loss to him of any life whatever.

The direction of time is crucial in assigning possibilities to people or other individuals. Distinct possible lives of a single person can diverge from a common beginning, but they cannot converge to a common conclusion from diverse beginnings. (The latter would represent not a set of different possible lives of one individual, but a set of distinct possible individuals, whose lives have identical conclusions.) Given an identifiable individual, countless possibilities for his continued existence are imaginable, and we can clearly conceive of what it would be for him to go on existing indefinitely. However inevitable it is that this will not come about, its possibility is still that of the continuation of a good for him, if life is the good we take it to be.

We are left, therefore, with the question whether the nonrealizaton of this possibility is in every case a misfortune, or whether it depends on what can naturally be hoped for. This seems to me the most serious difficulty with the view that death is always an evil. Even if we can dispose of the objections against admitting misfortune that is not experienced, or cannot be assigned to a definite time in the person's life, we still have to set some limits on *how* possible a possibility must be for its nonrealization to be a misfortune (or good fortune, should the possibility be a bad one). The death of Keats at 24 is generally regarded as tragic; that of Tolstoy at 82 is not. Although they will both be dead for ever, Keats' death deprived him of many years of life which were allowed to Tolstoy; so in a clear sense Keats' loss was greater (though not in the sense standardly employed in mathematical comparison between infinite quantities). However, this does not prove that Tolstoy's loss was insignificant. Perhaps we record an objection only to evils which are gratuitously added to the inevitable; the fact that it is worse to die at 24 than at 82 does not imply that it is not a terrible thing to die at 82, or even at 806. The question is whether we can regard as a misfortune any limitation, like mortality, that is normal to the species. Blindness or near-blindness is not a misfortune for a mole, nor would it be for a man, if that were the natural condition of the human race.

The trouble is that life familiarizes us with the goods of which death deprives us. We are already able to appreciate them, as a mole is not able to appreciate vision. If we put aside doubts about their status as goods and grant that their quantity is in part a function of their duration, the question remains whether death, no matter when it occurs, can be said to deprive its victim of what is in the relevant sense a possible continuation of life.

The situation is an ambiguous one. Observed from without, human beings obviously have a natural lifespan and cannot live much longer than a hundred years. A man's sense of his own experience, on the other hand, does not embody this idea of a natural limit. His existence defines for him an essentially open-ended possible future, containing the usual mixture of goods and evils that he has found so tolerable in the past. Having been gratuitously introduced to the world by a collection of natural, historical, and social accidents, he finds himself the subject of a *life,* with an indeterminate and not essentially limited future. Viewed in this way, death, no matter how inevitable, is an abrupt cancellation of indefinitely extensive possible goods. Normality seems to have nothing to do with it, for the fact that we will all inevitably die in a few score years cannot by itself imply that it would not be good to live longer. Suppose that we were all inevitably going to die in *agony*—physical agony lasting six months. Would inevitability make *that* prospect any less unpleasant? And why should it be different for a deprivation? If the normal lifespan were a thousand years, death at 80 would be a tragedy. As things are, it may just be a more widespread tragedy. If there is no limit to the amount of life that it would be good to have, then it may be that a bad end is in store for us all.

Plato

The Death of Socrates

Plato (427–347 B.C.) *was born into a family of considerable wealth and power. In Athens he came under the influence of Socrates and turned his attention to philosophy. After Socrates was condemned to death for corrupting the minds of the youth of Athens, Plato took it upon himself to continue Socrates' work. In the selection here from the* Phaedo, *Socrates, who always serves as Plato's spokesman in his dialogues, discusses his view of death with Cebes.*

You realize, he said, that when a man dies, the visible part, the body, which exists in the visible world, which we call the corpse, for which it would be natural to dissolve, fall apart and be blown away, does not immediately suffer any of these things but remains for a fair time, in fact, quite a long time if the man dies with his body in a suitable condition and at a favourable season? If the body is emaciated or embalmed, as in Egypt, it remains almost whole for a remarkable length of time, and even if the body decays, some parts of it, namely bones and sinews and the like, are nevertheless, one might say, deathless. Is that not so?—Yes.

Will the soul, the invisible part which makes its way to a region of the same kind, noble and pure and invisible, to Hades in fact, to the good and wise god whither, god willing, my soul must soon be going—will the soul, being of this kind and nature, be scattered and destroyed on leaving the body, as the majority of men say? Far from it, my dear Cebes and Simmias, but what happens is much more like this: if it is pure when it leaves the body and drags nothing bodily with it, as it had no willing association with the body in life, but avoided it and gathered itself together by itself and always practised this, which is no other than practising philosophy in the right way, in fact, training to die easily. Or is this not training for death?

It surely is.

A soul in this state makes its way to the invisible, which is like itself, the divine and immortal and wise, and arriving there it can be happy, having rid itself of confusion, ignorance, fear, violent desires and the other human ills and, as is said of the initiates, truly spend the rest of time with the gods. Shall we say this, Cebes, or something different?

This, by Zeus, said Cebes.

But I think that if the soul is polluted and impure when it leaves the body, having always been associated with it and served it, bewitched by physical desires and pleasures to the point at which nothing seems to exist for it but the physical, which one can touch and see or eat and drink or make use of for sexual enjoyment, and if that soul is accustomed to hate and fear and avoid that which is dim and invisible to the eyes but intelligible and to be grasped by philosophy—do you think such a soul will escape pure and by itself?

Impossible, he said.

I think it is permeated by the physical, which constant intercourse and association with the body, as well as considerable practice, has caused to become ingrained in it.

Quite so.

We must believe, my friend, that this bodily element is heavy, ponderous, earthy and visible. Through it, such a soul has become heavy and is dragged back to the visible region in fear of the unseen, which is called Hades. It wanders, as we are told, around graves and monuments, where shadowy phantoms, images that such souls produce, have been seen, souls that have not been freed and purified but share in the visible, and are therefore seen.

That is likely, Socrates.

It is indeed, Cebes. Moreover, these are not the souls of good but of inferior men, which are forced to wander there, paying the penalty for their previous bad upbringing. They wander until their longing for that which accompanies them, the physical, again imprisons them in a body, and they are then, as is likely, bound to such characters as they have practised in their life.

What kind of characters do you say these are, Socrates?

Those, for example, who have carelessly practised gluttony, violence and drunkenness are likely to join a company of donkeys or of similar animals. Do you not think so?

Very likely.

Those who have esteemed injustice highly, and tyranny and plunder will join the tribes of wolves and hawks and kites, or where else shall we say that they go?

Certainly to those, said Cebes.

And clearly, the destination of the others will depend on the way in which they have behaved.

Clearly, of course.

The happiest of these, who will also have the best destination, are those who have practised popular and social virtue, which they call moderation and justice by habit and practice, without philosophy or understanding.

How are they the happiest?

Because it is likely that they will again join a social and gentle group, either of bees or wasps or ants, and then again the same kind of human group, and so be moderate men.

That is likely.

No one may join the company of the gods who has not practised philosophy and is not completely pure when he departs from life, no one but the lover of learning. It is for this reason, my friends Simmias and Cebes, that those who practise philosophy in the right way keep away from all bodily passions, master them and do not surrender themselves to them; it is not at all for fear of wasting their substance and of poverty, which the majority and the money-lovers fear, nor for fear of dishonour and ill repute, like the ambitious and lovers of honours, that they keep away from them.

That would not be natural for them, Socrates, said Cebes.

By Zeus, no, he said. Those who care for their own soul and do not live for the service of their body dismiss all these things. They do not travel the same road as those who do not know where they are going but, believing that nothing should be done contrary to philosophy and their deliverance and purification, they turn to this and follow wherever philosophy leads.

How so, Socrates?

I will tell you, he said. The lovers of learning know that when philosophy gets hold of their soul, it is imprisoned in and clinging to the body, and that it is forced to examine other things through it as through a cage and not by itself, and that it wallows in every kind of ignorance. Philosophy sees that the worst feature of this imprisonment is that it is due to desires, so that the prisoner is contributing to his own incarceration. As I say, the lovers of learning know that philosophy gets hold of their soul when it is in that state, then gently encourages it and tries to free it by showing them that investigation through the eyes is full of deceit, as is that through the ears and the other senses. Philosophy then persuades the soul to withdraw from the senses in so far as it is not compelled to use them and bids the soul to gather itself together by itself, to trust only itself and whatever reality, existing by itself, the soul by itself understands, and not to consider as true whatever it examines by other means, for this is different in different circumstances and is sensible and visible, whereas what the soul itself sees is intelligible and invisible. The philosopher thinks that this deliverance must not be opposed and so keeps away from pleasures and desires and pains as far as he can; he reflects that violent pleasure or pain or passion does not cause merely such evils as one might expect, such as one suffers when one has been sick or extravagant through desire, but the greatest and most extreme evil, though one does not reflect on this.

What is that, Socrates? asked Cebes.

What the soul of every man, when it feels violent pleasure or pain in connection with some object, inevitably believes at the same time that what causes such feelings must be very real and very true, which it is not. Such objects are mostly visible, are they not?

Certainly.

And such an experience ties the soul to the body most completely.

How so?

Because every pleasure and every pain provides, as it were, another nail to rivet the soul to the body and to weld them together. It makes the soul corporeal, so that it believes that truth is what the body says it is. As it shares the beliefs and delights of the body, I think it inevitably comes to share its ways and manner of life and is unable ever to reach Hades in a pure state; it is always full of body when it departs, so that it soon falls back into another body and grows with it as if it had been sewn into it. Because of this, it can have no part in the company of the divine, the pure and uniform.

What you say is very true, Socrates, said Cebes.

This is why genuine lovers of learning are moderate and brave, or do you think it is for the reasons the majority says they are?

I certainly do not.

Indeed no. This is how the soul of a philosopher would reason: it would not think that while philosophy must free it, it should while being freed surrender itself to pleasures and pains and imprison itself again, thus labouring in vain like Penelope at her web. The soul of the philosopher achieves a calm from such emotions; it follows reason and ever stays with it contemplating the true, the divine, which is not the object of opinion. Nurtured by this, it believes that one should live in this manner as long as one is alive and, after death, arrive at what is akin and of the same kind, and escape from human evils.

Michael Bishop
Diary of a Dead Man

Michael Bishop is a science fiction writer and poet who lives in Georgia. He has written many books, the most recent of which is Who Made Stevie Crye?

*D*eathdate One: A short while ago, as if fulfilling the dictates of a clumsy punch line, I *woke up dead*. Forgive the italics, but the queerness of this state—postmortem consciousness—cries out for underscoring. I have no body, but I can think. On the other (nonexistent) hand, I know that I am dead because I have no body. No body, and nobody, at all. The celebrated assertion of René Descartes, "I think, therefore I am," does not apply. I refute it by pointing out that the Frenchman formulated this solipsistic law while comfortably incarnate in a (more or less) standard-issue human body. The vicissitudes of disembodiment were unknown to him—although, of course, he may be more familiar with them now.

Cogito ergo sum? I prefer "I think, therefore I'm confused," in tandem with "I'm absent, therefore I ain't."

Around me, as far as my thoughts can probe, only a glimmering ectoplasmic gray. But, to give this mother-of-pearl fog its due, the grayness may *comprise* my thoughts. I am really in no position to presume myself encompassed by it. I may be outside it, looking down. I may be under it, looking up. I may be at a remove of light-years, sensing the grayness via some kind of psychic telemetry. Or, again, I may be emitting this fog as a squid alchemizes and unfurls from itself a thalidomide plume of dreamily deforming ink. I have no body, and I am nowhere. However, the fog bank of my consciousness seems to be *moving,* and that motion holds out the hope of eventual arrival.

Where am I going?

Death, I thought, was supposed to answer that question. My next chilling realization is that maybe it will.

Dd. Two: What business have I, the disembodied consciousness of a dead man, keeping a diary? How, after all, do you date the virtually indivisible stretches of deadtime triggered by the moment of your dying? New Year's Day, Easter Sunday, the Fourth of July, Halloween and Christmas Eve are all equally meaningless here. What year is it? What month? What day? What cockeyed o'clock? Although I know that I died in a certain documentable year, at a specific pinpointable instant, the twilight territory into which I have died has a featurelessness—an everlasting *time*lessness—that no doubt keeps most dead people from becoming faithful diarists. I am, in fact, the only one I know about. You need a powerful ego to record a chronology of undated, and undatable, non-events. You need a powerful ego to prevent yourself from fading into the omnipresent gray.

Maybe I have no body, but I *do* have that kind of ego. It centers me in the fog. It arranges the non-events of this amorphous realm into the artificial linearity of sentences and paragraphs. Perhaps this entry should precede the first one. Or maybe it should make its initial appearance four or five entries down the (artificial) line. Who am I to say? Well, like God trying to impose order on chaos, I am trying to impose chronology on the mist-scatter of postmortem "existence." By my lights (if no one else's), that goal gives legitimacy to my self-appointed role as an historian of my otherwise indistinguishable deathdays.

Dd. Three: *Cogito ergo sum.* "I think, therefore I am." Descartes is not quite so easy to refute as I have said. Here I am, after all, thinking in diary format, and both my thought processes and this unlikely diary prove that on some level I continue to exist. I think, therefore I am. (I am, therefore I think?) If death brings about the total annihilation of consciousness, then obviously I have not died. However, I actually *remember* dying, and the vivid ferociousness of that event completely incinerated what used to be my body.

Could it be that death opens a door to the continuation of human consciousness by non-biological means? If so, what means? As a mind without a body, it occurs to me that these motivators must be either electromechanical or spiritual, or possibly a combination of the two, but absolutely nothing else of which I am presently aware. In other words, I am now either a piece of programmed software running in a computer or an angel sustained in the enduring dusk by the mysterious grace of God.

Which me is the true one, the electronic or the seraphic?

Dd. Four: Of course, I could be a ghost rather than an angel. If I were a ghost, my motor force would still be spiritual rather than electromechanical. Orthodox theologians deny the elevation of even death-transfigured human mortals to the ranks of the angelic hierarchy. God made the angels before He made the earth and its inhabitants. You do not inherit a pair of wings simply by dying. On the other hand, a ghost generally possesses an immaterial simulacrum of the body of its deceased "progenitor." And, as I have already noted, I have no body at all. I'm absent, therefore I am not. Am not a ghost, that is. Which somewhat reassuring conclusion leads me back to the altogether benumbing fear that I am stored on a magnetic disc inside a computer or else animated from afar by the unfathomable cogitations of God. Either way, I am the prisoner of a variety of limbo that makes me long for the release of utter oblivion.

Deprived of genuine ghosthood, I resent the fact that I am unable to haunt anyone but myself.

Dd. Five: I do not really believe that my personality has been magnetically warehoused or that I am running off at the ego inside an IBM, Apple or Radio Shack special. Computers have terminals, and terminals often have screens, and even the most complex or esoteric of programs must interface *somewhere* with consensus reality. If it did not, that program could hardly be aware of its own existence.

Well, I *know* that I exist, but not once since my deathday have I "interfaced"—being myself faceless—with any other reality but the mother-of-pearl fog impinging on every notional nerve of my disembodied consciousness. No whiz-kid hacker in wire-rimmed glasses and tennis shoes has summoned me along the link of an electronic personality preservatorium to "live" again for his and his buddies' puerile amusement. My isolation from the world on the material side of my deathday is total. I am devastatingly alone in this drifting grayness. Alone alone alone alone alone. An iambic-pentameter solitude worthy of a justly deserted Elizabethan villain.

Dd. Six: But if I am not a computer program, neither am I bona fide spiritual entity. (No question of my being an angel. Never any question.) Angels have no biological impulses because they have no biology. The bodies they occasionally assume go forth like puppets or remote-controlled robots to perform their miraculous tasks, which, nearly always, are duly sanctioned historical expressions of the will of God. The angels themselves—the irreducible *essences* constituting their being—remain in heaven, directing without participating, effecting without actually putting a finger in. They neither hunger nor thirst nor ache nor lust. Their only quasi-natural longing is for union with the Creator whose bountiful spiritual strength sustains them in existence.

Well, I am not like that. Never was. Bodiless, I continue to be buffeted by the ravening winds of biological memory.

Cut off the leg of a wounded man. Give him time to heal. Invariably, he will still experience twinges in his phantom limb.

That's me. Although wholly severed from my palate, bowels and privates, I am still a slave to the tyranny of their phantom clamor. I crave the earthy taste of potatoes and beer. I imagine cracking open the long albino legs of a snow crab and sucking from the splintery break thread after succulent thread of meat. I imagine, too, spreading the legs of a woman and nursing her brine-flavored lips with a similar greed. Are these the secret imaginings of an angel? Would a member of god's celestial militia ever contaminate itself with such caculated cupidity? Not on your life. Nor on mine, either.

Q.E.D., I'm no angel.

Dd. Seven: Besides being dead, what other possibilities present themselves? Let me catalogue them.

1. Asleep in my own room, I am having a strangely vivid nightmare. After a while, of course, I'll awaken.
2. I am the subject of a sensory-deprivation experiment. A team of researchers has placed me in a shallow bath of warm water inside a coffinlike container. No light or sound enters. Hour after hour, I float on my back in the buoyant dark. Finally, this maddening lack of stimulus leads me to hallucinate the omnipresent gray that I have mistakenly identified with the baleful territories of death. Eventually, however, the researchers will relent and free me.
3. I am in a state of suspended animation. This possibility has subsidiary possibilities: (a) I am being cryogenically preserved in a special mausoleum, there to await a medical discovery that will reverse the progress of the fatal disease put on hold by my freezing-down. And (b) I am lying in a cold-sleep capsule in a starship on its way to colonize the planet of a distant sun. Like my many sleeping colleagues, I will be revived automatically as soon as our vessel has entered the targeted solar system. Our arrival will of course presage the beginning of a bright new future for the entire human species.

No, no, no. No, no.

To believe any of these untenable "possibilities" would delight me. Each and every one of them offers the promise of resurrection. But I cannot believe any of them for the simple, and nonchalantly damning, reason that I remember in explicit, slow-motion detail the final two or three minutes of my life.

Dd. Eight: A crisis situation of the highest priority obtained. I was aloft in the flying command post with Carmody, Findlater, and Meranus, not to mention our elite standby crew and a four-star lifer from the Pentagon. The lifer's obsequious bombast was meant both to cower the crew and to satisfy his civilian superiors' desire for conspicuous action. Everyone in uniform bustled. Everyone in statesmanesque mufti glowered and role-played. A mis-hit on Washington, D.C., had smeared an incandescent porridge of scrap metal, brick dust, and liquefied concrete all the way to Baltimore. Static sniffle-snaffled the airwaves. What reports had earlier filtered through were contradictory in every particular but one, namely, the ruinous extent of the damage inflicted by our enemy's first nuclear enfilade. So many cities blazed that even the prairie dogs in North Dakota were gasping for breath.

"Sir," Carmody said, "a heat-seeking device from an invading MiG appears to be—"

I had abstracted myself from my environment. My head was lolling against a curve of sheet metal. The continuous faint rumble of our airborne fortress had begun to counterpoint the internal tides of my blood. The crew members in their zippered flightsuits, and my aides in their obligatory pinstripes, were ghosts shimmering on the outskirts of my vision. The fate of the nation and its people had long since ceased to occupy my thoughts. I was thinking instead about a "Peanuts" comic strip by Charles Schulz.

In this cartoon, Charlie Brown and Peppermint Patty stand side by side with their elbows on the parapet of a low brick wall. Peppermint Patty declares in the first frame that she needs to talk to someone who "knows what it's like to feel like a fool." Two frames later, she is saying, "Someone who's been disgraced, beaten, and degraded. Someone who's been there. . . ." In the wordless concluding frame, Charlie Brown spreads wide his arms in a touching here-I-am, look-no-further gesture. Why, even the most accomplished of public speakers would have given a small fortune to add that eloquent gesture to their forensic arsenals. I know I would have. So would Copetti, who outpointed me in our televised debates without ultimately managing to translate these victories into success at the polls. Too bad, I say. So sad.

Anyway, when Carmody's missile struck us, I was thinking about Charlie Brown and Peppermint Patty. I may have been smiling. Any stray recollection of that particular strip nearly always coaxed a smile from me. I record this fact in my post-mortem diary with more chagrin than amiable self-effacement. Honesty compels me to chronicle only the truth. (Even if I am assisted in this compulsion by the soothing hunch that no one else will ever apprehend what I record here.) That a man of my stature and responsibility should have been mulling a cartoon at such a time galls my pride. If I had lived, and if Carmody or Findlater had maliciously publicized my gaffe, the rumor of it would have unquestionably played havoc with my re-election chances. But the world sometimes works that way, matters of no moment elbowing aside those of high consequence; besides, I have always admired Charles Schulz more than I have Sakharov or Solzhenitsyn. Did either of these Russian-born worthies ever make anyone smile?

The arrival of Carmody's "heat-seeking device" interrupted my reverie. It tore into our flying command post. It ignited something treacherously flammable not far from the vaporized bulkhead against which I had been leaning. As I spiraled amid the orbiting debris of our disintegrating aircraft, my flesh caught fire. For a few feverish seconds, I was conscious of the night sky underfoot and the radiantly riven earth overhead. The gelatin in my eyeballs melted. My charred skin flapped away. My bones turned to chewing gum. I was now unequivocally dead, and Carmody, Findlater, Meranus—every patriotic member of our crew—had been press-ganged into nonexistence with me. Or, if not *with* me, than *at the same time* as I. It must be that those other poor fellows now occupy dimensionless pockets of grayness similar to, but altogether independent of, my own.

Perhaps the same is true of every single specimen of the human family recently extinguished by the War to End All Wars. . . .

Dd. Nine: 1) I am not safely asleep. 2) I am not the subject of a sensory-deprivation experiment. 3) And I am not in a state of suspended animation in either A) an earthbound facility or B) an idealistically dispatched starship.

I am dead.

Dead dead dead dead dead.

Charlie Brown and Peppermint Patty may be alive somewhere or somewhen, but I am clearly a helpless captive of my deadness, which seems escape-proof. How even this niggling bit of the sentient me has managed to "survive," I cannot presume to guess. Over and over again, though, the fear that I am being punished for my—our—manifold sins asserts itself. I only hope that for the debacle just past I am God's solitary scapegoat, that my eerie confinement here has exempted the innocent majority of our species from a similar fate. Is that hope as grandiose and egocentric as my earthly political career? Do I dare aspire in my loneliness and degradation to the title Redeemer? Is that, in fact, an office for which a dead man can take it upon himself to run?

God only knows.

Dd. Ten: This moment, I have decided, is the Twelfth of Never, the Ides of Self-Validation, the Eve of Apotheosis. Cute, eh? I have put dates (of a kind) to invisible units of my own dubious thought processes. Well, who's to stop me? Johnny Mathis? Caesar's assassins? God Himself? Hardly, I am the sole ruler of the twilight. Its alpha and omega, so to speak. And, surely, I can do here whatever I want to do, whenever I choose to do it. Stand back, then. The Emperor of the Great Gluey Gray is about to shape from glimmering formlessness a cosmos all his own. . . .

Let there be light!

Dd. Eleven: The glimmering formlessness persists. For that one, I suppose, I stupidly set myself up. Imagine Charlie Brown with his arms spread wide. Even as the unlocatable smoke of my consciousness drifts this way and that through the surrounding void, I see my bodiless self in that humbling, pathetic posture. I shape nothing. I control nothing. I merely poke around in the lost corners of limbo like a rat in a maze, my old personality and all my outworn belief systems obstructively intact, delaying the progress of my soul on its way to . . . well, wherever. For am I not a soul seeking release?

Unfortunately, one of my outworn personal credos, never confessed in public, was that there is no such thing as an immortal soul. With many other questing Batesonian rationalists, I believed that if you wish to touch the soul, you need only lay hands on your own living body. The soul has no capacity to survive apart from animate flesh. The body-and-soul dichotomy propounded by the Christian church was a misapprehension, one that has only lately fallen victim to the theory that consciousness emerges from the intricate interaction of a variety of biological systems. Anything that permanently damages the harmony among these systems—a bullet to the brain, the radioactive pollution of the atmosphere—likewise slays the soul. I resignedly embraced these modern beliefs. I never expected a portion of my self-awareness to outlive my body. Once dead, I felt sure that ahead of me lay only vast silent deserts of irreversible not-being.

Have you ever heard God laugh? Minus ears and auditory nerves, *I* have. The sound of it is the continuous faint rumble of a deadly engine plowing through a mother-of-pearl fog.

Dd. Twelve: If I am not dreaming, maybe I am being dreamt. If God can sustain the "lives" of spiritual entities like angels, why couldn't He—or a designated surrogate—repair and rewind the mental processes of a human being physically undone by famine, disease, or war? In the absence of a healthy brain, this would be difficult but probably not impossible. Unlike me, God can do whatever He wants to do, whenever He chooses to do it. Meanwhile, my own lack of solidity and volition strongly suggests that I am being projected from Elsewhere by either God or a dreaming proxy empowered by Him to hold me in existence.

These are frightening thoughts, but they also serve to absolve me of responsibility for the direction and content of my mental processes. I am not I. I am the weird muddle of someone else's anxious dream. My existence—my *non*existence—is an illusion relegating me to the status not merely of a single dead member of an entire extinct species but of the ghostly representative of a species that *never evolved at all*. Someone else is ineptly thinking me, therefore I am not.

But I am reasoning badly about this problem. In some humiliatingly dependent sense, I *do* exist. If I exist ineptly here, maybe it is because I lived ineptly. Maybe I am being dreamt by the residual consciousness of the person I was before that enemy missile—which I *insist* was real—blasted me and my companions out of the air. Some few of us may be lifted into legends by death, but a more telling truth I have learned is that no one is *improved* by it. Not even me. Least of all me. And, again, maybe I am a captive of this substanceless gray matter because in life I assumed myself exquisitely evolved, totally beyond improvement.

How the mighty are fallen.

Dd. Thirteen: Paupers and kings, garbage collectors and presidents may sometimes lie together in the same cemeteries. Indeed, they may even be said to "sleep together in the great democratizing union of death." Poets, romanticizers, and hard-nosed existentialists alike may claim that we are all united in our mortality. Death comes for the archbishop as surely as it does for the apothecary. The dead pickpocket is as dead as, but no deader than, the dead concert pianist. Thus does our finite biology homogenize every human being who has ever drawn breath. All for one and one for all—even if, alive, we would have continued to segregate by social class, skin color, occupational allegiance, religious creed, and/or political conviction.

True, death is no bigot. Granted, death is an Equal Opportunity Employer. But be that as it may, death does *not* unify. It separates and sequesters. Solitary confinement. Monastic isolation. Every disembodied soul a passenger in the free-floating nucleus of a vast single-cell grayness. You can meditate, as I have been trying to do, or you can go mad. But when madness inevitably overtakes your meditations, you must bear it. No other option is available. Death has ceased to count as an option—has *died,* as John Donne correctly predicted—because you have already exercised it. And you have no words to convey to anyone—whether God or some less awesome eavesdropper—the queer pitch of your insanity or the dreadful measure of your loneliness.

I, for imperfect instance, am like a sidewalk screamer in detention on the image-reflecting side of a two-way mirror, gagged and straitjacketed to a fare-thee-well but nonetheless struggling to tear free and scream.

A maimed amphibian.

Dd. Fourteen: I used to enjoy mysteries. I read them for relaxation. ("It's all right, Mr. Ambassador; he reads them for relaxation.") I liked their deliciously campy titles. *Dead Men Tell No Tales. A Queer Kind of Death. Death Claims. The Dead Are Discreet. Death Is a Lonely Business.* I could go on forever—literally—about the uncanny prescience of the authors of these and other such titles. They said so much more than they knew. Their commercial cleverness was in fact profundity, their crude glibness wit, their with-it jauntiness a wistful sort of anticipatory courage. Such writers wrote mysteries, I think, because nearly everything that matters is a mystery. Of course, I could also damn the lot of them for their lack of specificity, but you cannot say what you do not know and even the daunting engines of human imagination have their limits. It seems to me enough that they were able to *hint* so well. If I had the capacity to laugh, I would laugh in sardonic appreciation. I would rend this dimensionless fog with the inaudible sounds of a dead man lauding the clairvoyance of mystery writers, the greatest of whom is undoubtedly God. *The Dead Laugh Last.* Good title, eh?

Dd. Fifteen: Right now—and ages may have passed since my last entry in this immaterial record—the sole mystery preoccupying me is the destination of this fog. The fog moves. I have no visual or auditory references to tell me that it does, but I am sure of it. A vague apprehension of shifting equilibria repeatedly confirms for me the fact of the fog's movement. My consciousness seems to be tumbling in disorienting slow-motion along the inner edge of a great vortex. Call it a maelstrom if you like. Or the influence of a postmortem Coriolis force. Or the gravitational effects of a singularity—a funereal black hole—especially contrived to dispose of lost souls. Maybe, the seeming inescapability of my condition aside, I am spiraling toward a death-beyond-death. Or a life-beyond-death, the liberating opposite of this bleak, ego-bruising purgatory. Maybe, instead of absolute extinguishment, there is light at the end of the tunnel.

Ah. Once a political hack, always a political hack. Orbiting downward to who-knows-what, I continue to cast my fate in the happy-talk vocabulary of a presidential press secretary with his fingers crossed in the small of his back. The light at the end of the tunnel. The truth, of course, is that the world I departed lay smoldering beneath me as grotesquely disfigured and as magnificently uninhabitable as the most literal-minded medieval cleric's private vision of hell. I evaporated above that world. All the pain and suffering of those who lingered on, I airily sidestepped, Peppermint Patty and Charlie Brown pirouetting together in the self-pitying irony of my last conscious thought. What price a commander-in-chief's selfish peace of mind? Peanuts, my friend. Peanuts.

Dd. Sixteen, Seventeen, Eighteen, etcetera: I am alternately hopeful and afraid, expectant and terrified. A tremendous suction has the glimmering gray all around me in its down-tugging power. The indivisible deadtime of my consciousness has begun to accelerate, to tumble faster and faster toward an answer to the central posthumous mystery of my apprentice afterlife. That answer, of course, may be only the cruel posing of yet another mystery, afterlife upon afterlife, deadtime without end. Or it may be redemption. Or obliteration. My uncertainty is what alternately elates and roundly disheartens me. Meanwhile I fall endlessly into myself.

I believe that I am about to discover whether God is merciful or just.

James Rachels
The Morality of Euthanasia

James Rachels *is a professor of philosophy at the University of Alabama in Birmingham who has written extensively on ethical issues. His most recent book is* The End of Life, *from which this selection is taken.*

THE ARGUMENT FROM MERCY

*T*he most common argument in support of euthanasia is one that we may call 'the argument from mercy'. It is an exceptionally simple argument, at least in its main idea, which makes one uncomplicated point. Terminal patients sometimes suffer pain so horrible that it can hardly be comprehended by those who have not actually experienced it. Their suffering can be so terrible that we do not like even to read about it or think about it; we recoil even from its description. The argument from mercy says: euthanasia is justified because it puts an end to *that*.

The great Irish satirist Jonathan Swift took eight years to die while, in the words of Joseph Fletcher, 'His mind crumbled to pieces'. At times the pain in his blinded eyes was so intense he had to be restrained from tearing them out. Knives and other potential instruments of suicide were kept from him. For the last three years of his life, he could do nothing but drool; and when he finally died it was only after convulsions that lasted thirty-six hours.

Swift died in 1745. Since then, doctors have learned how to eliminate much of the pain that accompanies terminal illness, but the victory has been far from complete. Here is a more recent example.

Stewart Alsop was a respected journalist who died in 1975 of a rare form of cancer. Before he died, he wrote movingly of his experiences as a terminal patient. Although he had not thought much about euthanasia before, he came to approve of it after sharing a room briefly with someone he called Jack:

> The third night that I roomed with Jack in our tiny double room in the solid-tumor ward of the cancer clinic of the National Institutes of Health in Bethesda, Md., a terrible thought occurred to me.
>
> Jack had a melanoma in his belly, a malignant solid tumor that the doctors guessed was about the size of a softball. The cancer had started a few months before with a small tumor in his left shoulder, and there had been several operations since. The doctors planned to remove the softball-sized tumor, but they knew Jack would soon die. The cancer had metastasized—it had spread beyond control.
>
> Jack was good-looking, about 28, and brave. He was in constant pain, and his doctor had prescribed an intravenous shot of a synthetic opiate—a pain-killer, or analgesic—every four hours. His wife spent many of the daylight hours with him, and she would sit or lie on his bed and pat him all over, as one pats a child, only more methodically, and this seemed to help control the pain. But at night, when his pretty wife had left (wives cannot stay overnight at the NIH clinic) and darkness fell, the pain would attack without pity.
>
> At the prescribed hour, a nurse would give Jack a shot of the synthetic analgesic, and this would control the pain for perhaps two hours or a bit more. Then he would begin to moan, or whimper, very low, as though he didn't want to wake me. Then he would begin to howl, like a dog.
>
> When this happened, either he or I would ring for a nurse, and ask for a pain-killer. She would give him some codeine or the like by mouth, but it never did any real good—it affected him no more than half an aspirin might affect a man who had just broken his arm. Always the nurse would explain as encouragingly as she could that there was not long to go before the next intravenous shot—'Only about 50 minutes now.' And always poor Jack's whimpers and howls would become more loud and frequent until at last the blessed relief came.
>
> The third night of this routine, the terrible thought occurred to me. 'If Jack were a dog,' I thought, 'what would be done with him?' The answer was obvious: the pound, and chloroform. No human being with a spark of pity could let a living thing suffer so, to no good end.

I have discussed this case with some physicians who were indignant that Jack was not given larger doses of the pain-killing drug more often. They suggest that modern medicine can deal better with this type of pain. But it is worth noting that the NIH clinic is one of the best-equipped modern facilities we have; it is not as though Jack's suffering was caused by neglect in some backward rural hospital. Few of us could expect better care, were we in Jack's position. Moreover, the moral issue regarding euthanasia is not affected by whether more could have been done for Jack. The moral issue is whether mercy-killing is permissible *if* it is the only alternative to this kind of torment. We may readily grant that in any particular case where suffering can be eliminated, the argument for euthanasia will be weaker. But we will still need to know what is morally permissible in those cases in which, for whatever reason, suffering cannot, or will not, be eliminated.

I have quoted Alsop at length not for the sake of indulging in gory details but to give a clear idea of the kind of suffering we are talking about. We should not gloss over these facts with euphemistic language, or squeamishly avert our eyes from them. For only by keeping them firmly and vividly in mind can we appreciate the full force of the argument from mercy: if a person prefers—and even begs for—death as an alternative to lingering on *in this kind of torment,* only to die anyway after a while, then surely it is not immoral to help this person die sooner. As Alsop put it, 'No human being with a spark of pity could let a living thing suffer so, to no good end.'

Utilitarianism

The basic idea of the argument from mercy is clear enough; but how is it to be developed into a rigorous argument? Among philosophers, the utilitarians attempted to do this. They held that actions should be judged right or wrong according to whether they cause happiness or misery; and they argued that when judged by this standard, euthanasia turns out to be morally acceptable. The classic utilitarian version of the argument may be elaborated like this:

1. Any action is morally right if it serves to increase the amount of happiness in the world or to decrease the amount of misery. Conversely, an action is morally wrong if it serves to decrease happiness or increase misery.
2. Killing a hopelessly ill patient, who is suffering great pain, at his own request, would decrease the amount of misery in the world.
3. Therefore, such an action would be morally right.

The first premise of this argument states the principle of utility, the basic utilitarian assumption. Today most philosophers think this principle is unacceptable, because they think the promotion of happiness and the avoidance of misery are not the *only* morally important things. To take one example: People *might* be happier if there were no freedom of religion; for, if everyone adhered to the same religious beliefs, there would be greater harmony among people. There would be no unhappiness caused by Jewish girls marrying Catholic boys; the religious element of conflicts such as in Northern Ireland would be removed; and so forth. Moreover, if people were brainwashed well enough, no one would mind not having freedom of choice. Thus happiness might be increased. But, the argument continues, even if happiness *could* be increased in this way, it would be wrong to do so, because people should be allowed to make their own choices. Therefore, the argument concludes, the principle of utility is unacceptable.

There is a related difficulty for utilitarianism, which connects more directly with euthanasia. Suppose a person is leading a miserable life—full of more unhappiness than happiness—but does not want to die. This person thinks a miserable life is better than none at all. Now I assume we would all agree that this person should not be killed; that would be plain, unjustifiable murder. Yet it *would* decrease the amount of misery in the world if we killed him—and so it is hard to see how, on strictly utilitarian grounds, it could be wrong. Again, the principle of utility seems to be an inadequate guide for determining right and wrong.

Such arguments have led many philosophers to reject this moral theory. Yet contemporary utilitarians have an easy answer. In the first place, in so far as euthanasia is concerned, the classical utilitarian argument retains considerable force, even if it is faulty. For even if the promotion of happiness and the avoidance of misery are not the *only* morally important things, they are still very important. So, when an action would decrease misery, that is *a* very strong reason in its favour. The utilitarian argument in favour of euthanasia might therefore be decisive, even if the general complaints about the principle of utility are sound.

Moreover, utilitarianism may also be defended against the general complaints. Classical utilitarianism, as set out by Bentham and Mill, is a combination of three ideas. The first is that actions are to be judged right or wrong entirely according to their *consequences*. Nothing else matters—actions are not good or bad 'in themselves', and moral 'rules' have no independent importance. Right actions are, simply, the ones that have the best results. The second idea is that good and evil are to be measured in terms of happiness and unhappiness—nothing else is ultimately valuable. Material goods, art and ideas, friendship, and so on, are good only *because* they contribute to happiness. Thus, right actions are said to be those that produce the most happiness, or prevent the most misery. Third, and finally, classical utilitarianism includes the idea of equality—each individual's happiness is counted as equally important.

The difficulties we noted for utilitarianism all may be traced to its narrow identification of good and evil with happiness and unhappiness. . . . All that is necessary to save it, therefore, is to adopt a broader conception of individual welfare. The basic idea of the theory is that actions are right or wrong as they increase or decrease welfare. So, suppose we substitute a better conception of welfare: rather than speaking of maximizing *happiness,* let us speak of maximizing *interests*—let the principle of utility say that actions are right if they satisfy as many interests as possible. Such a broader principle will still be 'utilitarian' in that it still sees the rightness of actions as consisting in their effects on the welfare of the creatures affected by them. But the new principle avoids the problems that plagued the old one: if it is in a person's best interests to have freedom of choice in religion, or in choosing to remain alive, then the principle will not countenance taking away that freedom or that life. Armed with this better version of the principle of utility, we may then offer this improved argument concerning euthanasia:

1. If an action promotes the best interests of everyone concerned, then that action is morally acceptable.
2. In at least some cases, euthanasia promotes the best interests of everyone concerned.
3. Therefore, in at least some cases euthanasia is morally acceptable.

It would have been in everyone's best interests if euthanasia had been employed in the case of Stewart Alsop's room-mate Jack. First, and most important, it would have been in Jack's own interests, since it would have provided him with an easier death, without additional pain. Moreover, it would have been best for his wife. Her misery, helplessly watching him suffer, was second only to his. Third, the hospital staff's interests would have been served, since if Jack's dying had not been prolonged, they could have turned their attention to other patients whom they could have helped. Fourth, other patients would have benefited since medical resources would no longer have been used in the sad, pointless maintenance of Jack's physical existence. Finally, if Jack himself requested to be killed, the act would not have violated his rights. Considering all this, how can euthanasia be wrong?

Two additional comments are necessary before we leave the argument from mercy. First, I have discussed the utilitarians in connection with this argument, but one does not have to accept a general utilitarian theory of ethics to find it persuasive. There are other possible theories that one might prefer. However, no matter what ethical theory one accepts, the consequences of one's actions—whether they do or do not promote people's interests, or cause happiness or misery—must be among the matters considered important. An ethical theory that did *not* have an important place for this would have no credibility at all. And, to the extent that these matters *are* seen as important, the argument from mercy will be compelling.

Second, it should be noted that the argument does *not* imply that euthanasia is justified *whenever* a patient says he can no longer endure pain. Suppose the doctor, or the family, knows that the painful condition can be cured, and that the patient's request to die is only a temporary irrational reaction, which he will later repudiate. It is entirely reasonable for them to take this into account, and to refuse the irrational request. The argument from mercy does not say otherwise; in such circumstances euthanasia would not promote his best interests, and would hardly be 'merciful' at all. This should not be taken to mean, however, that such requests are always irrational, or that pain always destroys a patient's ability to make sensible choices. Sadly, some requests to die, in circumstances such as those of Stewart Alsop's room-mate, are all too rational.

THE ARGUMENT FROM THE GOLDEN RULE

'Do unto others as you would have them do unto you' is one of the oldest and most familiar moral maxims. Stated in just that way, it is not a very good maxim: suppose a sexual pervert, with fantasies of being raped, started treating others as he would like to be treated. We might not be happy with the results. Nevertheless, the idea behind the Golden Rule is a good one. Moral rules apply to everyone alike. You cannot say that you are justified in treating someone else in a certain way unless you are willing to admit that that person would be justified in treating *you* in that way if your positions were reversed.

Kant's moral philosophy is usually regarded as the major historical alternative to utilitarianism. Like the utilitarians, Kant sought to express all of morality in a single principle. Kant's principle may be viewed as a sophisticated version of the Golden Rule. He argued that we should act only on rules that we are willing to have applied universally; that is, we should behave as we would be willing to have *everyone* behave. Thus, the one supreme principle of morality, which he called the 'Categorical Imperative', says:

> Act only according to that maxim which you can at the same time will to become a universal law.

What does this mean? When we are trying to decide whether to do a certain action, we must first ask what general rule we would be following if we did it. Then, we ask whether we would be willing for everyone to follow that rule, in similar circumstances. (This determines whether 'the maxim of the act'—the rule we would be following—can be 'willed' to be a 'universal law'.) If we would not be willing for the rule to be followed universally, then we should not follow it ourselves. Thus, if we are not willing for others to apply the rule to *us*, we ought not apply it to *them*.

In the eighteenth chapter of St Matthew's gospel there is a story that perfectly illustrates this point. A man is owed money by another, who cannot pay, and so he has the debtor thrown into prison. But he himself owes money to the King and begs that *his* debt be forgiven. At first the King forgives the debt. However, when the King hears how this man has treated the one who owed him, he changes his mind and 'delivers him unto the tormentors' until he can pay. The moral is clear: If you do not think that others should apply the rule 'Don't forgive debts!' to *you,* then you should not apply it to others.

The application of this to the question of euthanasia is fairly obvious. Each of us is going to die some day, although most of us do not know when or how, and will probably have little choice in the matter. But suppose you were given a choice: suppose you were told that you would die in one of two ways, and were asked to choose between them. First, you could die quietly, and without pain, at the age of eighty, from a fatal injection. Or second, you could choose to die at the age of eighty-plus-a-few-days of an affliction so painful that for those few days before death you would be reduced to howling like a dog, with your family standing helplessly by. It is hard to believe that anyone would choose to have a rule applied that would force upon him or her the second option—if, that is, they were making a choice based upon *their own preferences*. And if we would not want such a rule, which excludes euthanasia, applied to us, then we should not apply such a rule to others.

The contemporary British philosopher R. M. Hare has made the same point in a slightly different way. Hare tells the following (true) story:

> The driver of a petrol lorry was caught in an accident in which his tanker overturned and immediately caught fire. He himself was trapped in the cab and could not be freed. He therefore besought the bystanders to kill him by hitting him on the head,

so that he would not roast to death. I think that somebody did this, but I do not know what happened in the courts afterwards.

Now will you please all ask yourselves, as I have many times asked myself, what you wish that men should do to you if you were in the situation of that driver. I cannot believe that anybody who considered the matter seriously, as if he himself were going to be in that situation and had now to give instructions as to what rule the bystanders should follow, would say that the rule should be one ruling out euthanasia absolutely.

There is a considerable irony here. Kant was personally opposed to mercy-killing; he thought it contrary to reason. Yet his own Categorical Imperative seems to sanction it. The larger irony, however, is for those in the Christian Church who have for centuries opposed euthanasia. The article written by Professor Hare, from which the story of the lorry driver is taken, has the title 'Euthanasia: A Christian View'. According to the New Testament accounts, Jesus himself promulgated the Golden Rule as the supreme moral principle—'This is the Law and the Prophets,' he said. But, as Hare points out, if this is the supreme principle of morality, then how can euthanasia be absolutely wrong? This seems to be another one of those instances in which the historical Church has strayed from the principles laid down by its founder.

We have looked at two arguments that tend to show that euthanasia is morally acceptable. Now let us turn to some arguments that support the opposite view. The most common argument against euthanasia is simply that it is a violation of the prohibition against killing—or, against the taking of innocent human life. Since I have already discussed this contention at some length, I will concentrate here on different arguments.

RELIGIOUS ARGUMENTS

Social observers are fond of remarking that we live in a secular age, and there is surely something in this. The power of religious conceptions was due, in some considerable measure, to their usefulness in explaining things. In earlier times, religious ideas were used to explain everything from the origins of the universe to the nature of human beings. So long as we had no other way of understanding the world, the hold of religion on us was powerful indeed. Now, however, these explanatory functions have largely been taken over by the sciences: physics, chemistry, and their allies explain physical nature, while evolutionary biology and psychology combine to tell us about ourselves. As there is less and less work for religious hypotheses to do, the grip of religious ideas on us weakens, and appeals to theological conceptions are heard only on Sunday mornings. Hence, the 'secular age'.

However, most people continue to hold religious beliefs, and they especially appeal to those beliefs when morality is at issue. Any discussion of mercy-killing quickly leads to objections based on theological grounds, and 'secular' arguments for euthanasia are rejected because they leave out the crucial element of God's directions on the matter.

Considering the traditional religious opposition to euthanasia, it is tempting to say: if one is not a Christian (or if one does not have some similar religious orientation) then perhaps euthanasia is an option; but for people who do have such a religious orientation, euthanasia cannot be acceptable. And the discussion might be ended there. But this is too quick a conclusion; for it is possible that the religious arguments against euthanasia are not valid *even for religious people*. Perhaps a religious perspective, even a conventional Christian one, does *not* lead automatically to the rejection of mercy-killing. With this possibility in mind, let us examine three variations of the religious objection.

What God Commands

It is sometimes said that euthanasia is not permissible simply because God forbids it, and we know that God forbids it by the authority of either scripture or Church tradition. Thus, one eighteenth-century minister, Humphrey Primatt, wrote ironically that, in the case of aged and infirm animals,

> God, the Father of Mercies, hath ordained Beasts and Birds of Prey to do that distressed creature the kindness to relieve him his misery, by putting him to death. A kindness which *We* dare not show to our own species. If thy father, thy brother, or thy child should suffer the utmost pains of a long and agonizing sickness, though his groans should pierce through thy heart, and with strong crying and tears he should beg thy relief, yet thou must be deaf unto him; he must wait his appointed time till his charge cometh, till he sinks and is crushed with the weight of his own misery.

When this argument is advanced, it is usually advanced with great confidence, as though it were *obvious* what God requires. Yet we may well wonder whether such confidence is justified. The sixth commandment does not say, literally, 'Thou shalt not *kill*'—that is a bad translation. A better translation is 'Thou shalt not commit *murder*,' which is different, and which does not obviously prohibit mercy-killing. Murder is by definition *wrongful* killing; so, if you do not think that a given kind of killing is wrong, you will not call it murder. That is why the sixth commandment is not normally taken to forbid killing in a just war; since such killing is (allegedly) justified, it is not called murder. Similarly, if euthanasia is justified, it is not murder, and so it is not prohibited by the commandment. At the very least, it is clear that we cannot infer that euthanasia is wrong *because* it is prohibited by the commandment.

If we look elsewhere in the Christian Bible for a condemnation of euthanasia, we cannot find it. These scriptures are silent on the question. We do find numerous affirmations of the sanctity of human life and the fatherhood of God, and some theologians have tried to infer a prohibition on euthanasia from these general precepts. (The persistence of the attempts, in the face of logical difficulties, is a reminder that people insist on reading their moral prejudices *into* religious texts much more often than they derive their moral views *from* the texts.) But we also find exhortations to kindness and mercy, and the Golden Rule proclaimed as the sum of all morality; and these principles, as we have seen, support euthanasia rather than condemn it.

We *do* find a clear condemnation of euthanasia in Church tradition. Regardless of whether there is scriptural authority for it, the Church has historically opposed mercy-killing. It should be emphasized, however, that this is a matter of history. Today, many religious leaders favour euthanasia and think the historical position of the Church has been mistaken. It was an Episcopal minister, Joseph Fletcher, who in his book *Morals and Medicine* formulated the classic modern defence of euthanasia. Fletcher does not stand alone among his fellow churchmen. The Euthanasia Society of America, which he heads, includes many other religious leaders; and the recent 'Plea for Beneficent Euthanasia', sponsored by the American Humanist Association, was signed by more religious leaders than people in any other category. So it certainly cannot be claimed that *contemporary* religious forces stand uniformly opposed to euthanasia.

It is noteworthy that even Roman Catholic thinkers are today reassessing the Church's traditional ban on mercy-killing. The Catholic philosopher Daniel Maguire has written one of the best books on the subject, *Death By Choice*. Maguire maintains that 'it may be moral and should be legal to accelerate the death process by taking direct action, such as overdosing with morphine or injecting potassium'; and moreover, he proposes to demonstrate that this view is *'compatible with historical Catholic ethical theory'*, contrary to what most opponents of euthanasia assume. Historical Catholic ethical theory, he says, grants individuals permission to act on views that are supported by 'good and serious reasons', even when a different view is supported by a majority of authorities. Since the morality of euthanasia *is* supported by 'good and serious reasons', Maguire concludes that Catholics are permitted to accept that morality and act on it.

Thus, the positions of both scripture and Church authorities are (at least) ambiguous enough so that the believer is not bound, on these grounds, to reject mercy-killing. The argument from 'what God commands' should be inconclusive, even for the staunchest believer.

The Idea of God's Dominion

Our second theological argument starts from the principle that 'The life of man is solely under the dominion of God.' It is for God alone to decide when a person shall live and when he shall die; we have no right to 'play God' and arrogate this decision unto ourselves. So euthanasia is forbidden.

This is perhaps the most familiar of all the theological objections to euthanasia; one hears it constantly when the matter is discussed. However, it is remarkable that people still advance this argument today, considering that it was decisively refuted over 200 years ago, when Hume made the simple but devastating point that *if it is for God alone to decide when we shall live and when we shall die, then we 'play God' just as much when we cure people as when we kill them*. Suppose a person is sick and we have the means to cure him or her. If we do so, then we are interfering with God's 'right to decide' how long the life shall last! Hume put it this way:

> Were the disposal of human life so much reserved as the peculiar providence of the Almighty that it were an encroachment on his right, for men to dispose of their own lives; it would be equally criminal to act for the preservation of life as for its destruction. If I turn aside a stone which is falling upon my head, I disturb this course of nature, and I invade the peculiar providence of the Almighty by lengthening out my life beyond the period which by the general laws of matter and motion he had assigned it.

We alter the length of a person's life when we save it just as much as when we take it. Therefore, if the taking of life is to be forbidden on the grounds that only God has the right to determine how long a person shall live, then the saving of life should be prohibited on the same grounds. We would then have to abolish the practice of medicine. But everyone (except, perhaps, Christian Scientists) concedes that this would be absurd. Therefore, we may *not* prohibit euthanasia on the grounds that only God has the right to determine how long a life shall last. This seems to be a complete refutation of this argument, and if refuted arguments were decently discarded, as they should be, we would hear no more of it.

Suffering and God's Plan

The last religious argument we shall consider is based on the idea that suffering is a part of God's plan for us. God has ordained that people should suffer; he never intended that life should be continually pleasurable. (If he had intended this, presumably he would have created a very different world.) Therefore, if we were to kill people to 'put them out of their misery', we would be interfering with God's plan. Bishop Joseph Sullivan, a prominent Catholic opponent of euthanasia, expresses the argument in a passage from his essay 'The Immorality of Euthanasia':

> If the suffering patient is of sound mind and capable of making an act of divine resignation, then his sufferings become a great means of merit whereby he can gain reward for himself and also win great favors for the souls in Purgatory, perhaps even release them from their suffering. Likewise the sufferer may give good example to his family and friends and teach them how to bear a heavy cross in a Christlike manner.
>
> As regard those that must live in the same house with the incurable sufferer, they have a great opportunity to practice Christian charity. They can learn to see Christ in the sufferer and win the reward promised in the Beatitudes. This opportunity for charity would hold true even when the incurable sufferer is deprived of the use of reason. It may well be that the incurable sufferer in a particular case may be of greater value to society than when he was of some material value to himself and his community.

This argument may strike some readers as simply grotesque. Can we imagine this being said, seriously, in the presence of suffering such as that experienced by Stewart Alsop's roommate? 'We know it hurts, Jack, and that your wife is being torn apart just having to watch it, but think what a good opportunity this is for you to set an example. You can give us a lesson in how to bear it.' In addition, some might think that euthanasia is exactly what *is* required by the 'charity' that bystanders have the opportunity to practise.

But, these reactions aside, there is a more fundamental difficulty with the argument. For if the argument were sound, it would lead not only to the condemnation of euthanasia but of *any* measures to reduce suffering. If God decrees that we suffer, why aren't we obstructing God's plan when we give drugs to relieve pain? A girl breaks her arm; if only God knows how much pain is right for her, who are we to mend it? The point is similar to Hume's refutation of the previous argument. This argument, like the previous one, cannot be right because it leads to consequences that no one, not even the most conservative religious thinker, is willing to accept.

We have now looked at three arguments that depend on religious assumptions. They are all unsound, but I have *not* criticized them simply by rejecting their religious presuppositions. Instead, I have criticized them on their own terms, showing that these arguments should not be accepted even by religious people. As Daniel Maguire emphasizes, the ethics of theists, like the ethics of all responsible people, should be determined by 'good and serious reasons', and these arguments are not good no matter what world-view one has.

The upshot is that religious people are in the same position as everyone else. There is nothing in religious belief in general, or in Christian belief in particular, to preclude the acceptance of mercy-killing as a humane response to some awful situations. So, as far as these arguments are concerned, it appears that Christians may be free, after all, to accept the Golden Rule.

THE POSSIBILITY OF UNEXPECTED CURES

Euthanasia may also be opposed on the grounds that we cannot really tell when a patient's condition is hopeless. There are cases in which patients have recovered even after doctors have given up hope; if those patients had been killed, it would have been tragic, for they would have been deprived of many additional years of life. According to this argument, euthanasia is unacceptable because we never know for certain that a patient's situation is hopeless. *Any* so-called hopeless patient might defy the odds and recover.

The argument has two sources: first, it draws some plausibility from the fact that doctors have sometimes made mistakes; and second, it trades on a naive view of the possibilities of medical research.

It must be admitted, of course, that doctors have sometimes made mistakes in labelling cases 'hopeless', and so we should be cautious in any given instance before saying there is no chance of recovery. But it does not follow from the fact that physicians have *sometimes* been mistaken that they can *never* know for sure that a case is hopeless. That would be like saying that since some people have confused a Rolls-Royce with a Mercedes, no one can ever be certain which is which. In fact, doctors do sometimes know for sure that a patient cannot recover. There may be spontaneous remissions of cancer, for example, at a relatively early stage of the disease. But after the cancer has spread throughout the body and reached an advanced stage of development, there may truly be no hope whatever. Although there may be some doubt about some cases—and where there is doubt, perhaps euthanasia should not be considered—no one with the slightest medical knowledge could have had any doubt about Jack. He was going to die of that cancer, and that is all there is to it. No one has ever recovered from *that* condition, and doctors can explain exactly why this is so.

The argument from the possibility of unexpected cures sometimes takes a slightly different form, and appeals to a naive view of medical research. According to this view, researchers are continually exploring new possibilities of treating disease; and we never know when a new 'miracle cure' for a previously untreatable disease might be discovered. Thus, if we grant a dying patient's request for euthanasia, we run the risk that the next day a cure for his condition might be discovered—'If only we had waited, he could have been saved,' it may be said.

This argument will have little appeal to those more familiar with the realities of medical research. Progress in treating disease comes, not with the sudden and unexpected discovery of magical remedies, but from slow and painstaking investigation. Whether it is reasonable to hope for a 'cure' depends on the particular case in question. In the case of some diseases, investigators may have promising results from some lines of inquiry; here, it may be reasonable to hold out some hope for a dying patient, *if* death can be postponed long enough. In other cases, we may be dealing with a disease that is getting very little attention from researchers, or the researchers investigating it may obviously be very far from achieving any impressive results. Here, it may be simply dishonest to tell a patient with only a short time to live that there is hope. Or again, it may be that even if a cure is found, it will do a particular patient no good because in him the disease is so far advanced that the 'cure' would not help *him* even if it were found.

What, then, are we to conclude? We may certainly conclude that extreme care should be taken so as to avoid declaring a patient 'hopeless' when there really is a chance of recovery; and we may perhaps conclude that in any case where there is the slightest doubt, euthanasia should not be considered. However, we may *not* conclude that doctors *never* know that a case is hopeless. Nor may we always hold out the hope of a 'miracle cure'. Sadly, we know that in some cases there is no hope, and in those cases the possibility of an unexpected cure cannot be offered as an objection to euthanasia.

Ad Hoc Committee of the Harvard Medical School

Definition of Death

The Ad Hoc Committee of the Harvard Medical School to Examine the Definition of Brain Death was formed in the 1960s and consisted of physicians, theologians, and lawyers. Their widely discussed report was published in 1968. In it, they argue that "cessation of vital functions" must be replaced by "irreversible coma" as the criterion of death.

Our primary purpose is to define irreversible coma as a new criterion for death. There are two reasons why there is need for a definition: (1) Improvements in resuscitative and supportive measures have led to increased efforts to save those who are desperately injured. Sometimes these efforts have only partial success, so that the result is an individual whose heart continues to beat but whose brain is irreversibly damaged. The burden is great on patients who suffer permanent loss of intellect, on their families, on the hospitals, and on those in need of hospital beds already occupied by these comatose patients. (2) Obsolete criteria for the definition of death can lead to controversy in obtaining organs for transplantation.

Irreversible coma has many causes, but *we are concerned here only with those comatose individuals who have no discernible central nervous system activity*. If the characteristics can be defined in satisfactory terms, translatable into action—and we believe this is possible—then several problems will either disappear or will become more readily soluble.

More than medical problems are present. There are moral, ethical, religious, and legal issues. Adequate definition here will prepare the way for better insight into all of these matters as well as for better law than is currently applicable.

CHARACTERISTICS OF IRREVERSIBLE COMA

An organ, brain or other, that no longer functions and has no possibility of functioning again is for all practical purposes dead. Our first problem is to determine the characteristics of a *permanently* nonfunctioning brain.

A patient in this state appears to be in deep coma. The condition can be satisfactorily diagnosed by points 1, 2, and 3 to follow. The electroencephalogram (point 4) provides confirmatory data, and when available it should be utilized. In situations where for one reason or another electroencephalographic monitoring is not available, the absence of cerebral function has to be determined by purely clinical signs, to be described, or by absence of circulation as judged by standstill of blood in the retinal vessels or by absence of cardiac activity.

1. **Unreceptivity and Unresponsitivity.** There is a total unawareness to externally applied stimuli and inner need and complete unresponsiveness—our definition of irreversible coma. Even the most intensely painful stimuli evoke no vocal or other response, not even a groan, withdrawal of a limb, or quickening of respiration.

2. **No Movements or Breathing.** Observation covering a period of at least one hour by physicians is adequate to satisfy the criteria of no spontaneous muscular movements or spontaneous respiration or response to stimuli such as pain, touch, sound, or light. After the patient is on a mechanical respirator, the total absence of spontaneous breathing may be established by turning off the respirator for three minutes and observing whether there is any effort on the part of the subject to breathe spontaneously. (The respirator may be

turned off for this time provided at the start of the trial period the patient's carbon dioxide tension is within the normal range, and provided also that the patient had been breathing room air for at least 10 minutes prior to the trial.)

3. **No Reflexes.** Irreversible coma with abolition of central nervous system activity is evidenced in part by the absence of elicitable reflexes. The pupil will be fixed and dilated and will not respond to a direct source of bright light. Since the establishment of a fixed, dilated pupil is clear-cut in clinical practice, there should be no uncertainty as to its presence. Ocular movement (to head turning and to irrigation of the ears with ice water) and blinking are absent. There is no evidence of postural activity (decerebrate or other). Swallowing, yawning, vocalization are in abeyance. Corneal and pharyngeal reflexes are absent.

As a rule the stretch of tendon reflexes cannot be elicited; i.e., tapping the tendons of the biceps, triceps, and pronator muscles, quadriceps and gastrocnemius muscles with the reflex hammer elicits no contraction of the respective muscles. Plantar or noxious stimulation gives no response.

4. **Flat Electroencephalogram.** Of great confirmatory value is the flat or isoelectric EEG. We must assume that the electrodes have been properly applied, that the apparatus is functioning normally, and that the personnel in charge is competent. We consider it prudent to have one channel of the apparatus used for an electrocardiogram. This channel will monitor the ECG so that, if it appears in the electroencephalographic leads because of high resistance, it can be readily identified. It also establishes the presence of the active heart in the absence of the EEG. We recommend that another channel be used for a noncephalic lead. This will pick up space-borne or vibration-borne artifacts and identify them. The simplest form of such a monitoring noncephalic electrode has two leads over the dorsum of the hand, preferably the right hand, so the ECG will be minimal or absent. Since one of the requirements of this state is that there be no muscle activity, these two dorsal hand electrodes will not be bothered by muscle artifact. The apparatus should be run at standard gains 10 μv/mm, 50 μv/5 mm. Also it should be isoelectric at double this standard gain, which is 5 μv/mm or 25 μv/5 mm. At least ten full minutes of recording are desirable, but twice that would be better.

It is also suggested that the gains at some point be opened to their full amplitude for a brief period (5 to 100 seconds) to see what is going on. Usually in an intensive-care unit artifacts will dominate the picture, but these are readily identifiable. There shall be no electroencephalographic response to noise or to pinch.

All of the above tests shall be repeated at least 24 hours later with no change.

The validity of such data as indications of irreversible cerebral damage depends on the exclusion of two conditions: hypothermia (temperature below 90°F [32.2°C]) or central nervous system depressants, such as barbiturates.

OTHER PROCEDURES

The patient's condition can be determined only by a physician. When the patient is hopelessly damaged as defined above, the family and all colleagues who have participated in major decisions concerning the patient, and all nurses involved, should be so informed. Death is to be declared and *then* the respirator turned off. The decision to do this and the responsibility for it are to be taken by the physician-in-charge, in consultation with one or more physicians who have been directly involved in the case. It is unsound and undesirable to force the family to make the decision.

LEGAL COMMENTARY

The legal system of the United States is greatly in need of the kind of analysis and recommendations for medical procedures in cases of irreversible brain damage as described. At present, the law of the United States, in all 50 states and in the federal courts, treats the question of human death as a question of fact to be decided in every case. When any doubt exists, the courts seek medical expert testimony concerning the time of death of the particular individual involved. However, the law makes the assumption that the medical criteria for determining death are settled and not in doubt among physicians. Furthermore, the law assumes that the traditional method among physicians for determination of death is to ascertain the absence of all vital signs. To this extent, *Black's Law Dictionary* (fourth edition, 1951) defines death as

> The cessation of life; the ceasing to exist; *defined by physicians* as a total stoppage of the circulation of the blood, and a cessation of the animal and vital functions consequent thereupon, such as respiration, pulsation, etc [italics added].

In the few modern court decisions involving a definition of death, the courts have used the concept of the total cessation of all vital signs. Two cases are worthy of examination. Both involved the issue of which one of two persons died first.

In *Thomas v. Anderson* (96 Cal. App. 2d 371, 211 P.2d 478), a California District Court of Appeal in 1950 said, "In the instant case the question as to which of the two men died first was a question of fact for the determination of the trial court. . . ."

The appellate court cited and quoted in full the definition of death from *Black's Law Dictionary* and concluded, ". . . death occurs precisely when life ceases and does not occur until the heart stops beating and respiration ends. Death is not a continuous event and is an event that takes place at a precise time."

The other case is *Smith v. Smith* (229 Ark. 579, 317 S.W.2d 275), decided in 1958 by the Supreme Court of Arkansas. In this case the two people were husband and wife involved in an auto accident. The husband was found dead at the scene of the accident. The wife was taken to the hospital unconscious. It is alleged that she "remained in coma due to brain injury" and died at the hospital 17 days later. The petitioner in court tried to argue that the two people died simultaneously. The judge writing the opinion said the petition contained a "quite unusual and unique allegation." It was quoted as follows:

> That the said Hugh Smith and his wife, Lucy Coleman Smith, were in an automobile accident on the 19th day of April, 1957, said accident being instantly fatal to each of them at the same time, although the doctors maintained a vain hope of survival and made every effort to revive and resuscitate said Lucy Coleman Smith until May 6th, 1957, when it was finally determined by the attending physicians that their hope of resuscitation and possible restoration of human life to the said Lucy Coleman Smith was entirely vain, and
>
> That as a matter of modern medical science, your petitioner alleges and states, and will offer the Court competent proof that the said Hugh Smith, deceased, and said Lucy Coleman Smith, deceased, lost their power to will at the same instant, and that their demise as earthly human beings occurred at the same time in said automobile accident, neither of them ever regaining any consciousness whatsoever.

The court dismissed the petition as a *matter of law*. The court quoted *Black's* definition of death and concluded,

> Admittedly, this condition did not exist, and as a matter of fact, it would be too much of a strain of credulity for us to believe any evidence offered to the effect that

Mrs. Smith was dead, scientifically or otherwise, unless the conditions set out in the definition existed.

Later in the opinion the court said, "Likewise, we take judicial notice that one breathing, though unconscious, is not dead."

"Judicial notice" of this definition of death means that the court did not consider that definition open to serious controversy; it considered the question as settled in responsible scientific and medical circles. The judge thus makes proof of uncontroverted facts unnecessary so as to prevent prolonging the trial with unnecessary proof and also to prevent fraud being committed upon the court by quasi-"scientists" being called into court to controvert settled scientific principles at a price. Here, the Arkansas Supreme Court considered the definition of death to be a settled, scientific, biological fact. It refused to consider the plaintiff's offer of evidence that "modern medical science" might say otherwise. In simplified form, the above is the state of the law in the United States concerning the definition of death.

In this report, however, we suggest that responsible medical opinion is ready to adopt new criteria for pronouncing death to have occurred in an individual sustaining irreversible coma as a result of permanent brain damage. If this position is adopted by the medical community, it can form the basis for change in the current legal concept of death. No statutory change in the law should be necessary, since the law treats this question essentially as one of fact to be determined by physicians. The only circumstance in which it would be necessary that legislation be offered in the various states to define "death" by law would be in the event that great controversy were engendered surrounding the subject and physicians were unable to agree on the new medical criteria.

It is recommended as a part of these procedures that judgment of the existence of these criteria is solely a medical issue. It is suggested that the physician in charge of the patient consult with one or more other physicians directly involved in the case before the patient is declared dead on the basis of these criteria. In this way, the responsibility is shared over a wider range of medical opinion, thus providing an important degree of protection against later questions which might be raised about the particular case. It is further suggested that the decision to declare the person dead, and then to turn off the respirator, be made by physicians not involved in any later effort to transplant organs or tissue from the deceased individual. This is advisable in order to avoid any appearance of self-interest by the physicians involved.

It should be emphasized that we recommend the patient be declared dead before any effort is made to take him off a respirator, if he is then on a respirator. This declaration should not be delayed until he has been taken off the respirator and all artificially stimulated signs have ceased. The reason for this recommendation is that in our judgment it will provide a greater degree of legal protection to those involved. Otherwise, the physicians would be turning off the respirator on a person who is, under the present strict technical application of law, still alive.

Willard Gaylin

Harvesting the Dead

Willard Gaylin *is a psychiatrist and president of the Institute of Society, Ethics and the Life Sciences in Hastings-on-Hudson, New York. Among his many publications is* Partial Justice: A Study of Bias in Sentencing.

Nothing in life is simple anymore, not even the leaving of it. At one time there was no medical need for the physician to consider the concept of death; the fact of death was sufficient. The difference between life and death was an infinite chasm breached in an infinitesimal moment. Life and death were ultimate, self-evident opposites.

With the advent of new techniques in medicine, those opposites have begun to converge. We are now capable of maintaining visceral functions without any semblance of the higher functions that define a person. We are, therefore, faced with the task of deciding whether that which we have kept alive is still a human being, or, to put it another way, whether that human being that we are maintaining should be considered "alive."

Until now we have avoided the problems of definition and reached the solutions in silence and secret. When the life sustained was unrewarding by the standards of the physician in charge—it was discontinued. Over the years, physicians have practiced euthanasia on an ad hoc, casual, and perhaps irresponsible basis. They have withheld antibiotics or other simple treatments when it was felt that a life did not warrant sustaining, or pulled the plug on the respirator when they were convinced that what was being sustained no longer warranted the definition of life. Some of these acts are illegal and, if one wished to prosecute, could constitute a form of manslaughter, even though it is unlikely that any jury would convict. We prefer to handle all problems connected with death by denying their existence. But death and its dilemmas persist.

New urgencies for recognition of the problem arise from two conditions: the continuing march of technology, making the sustaining of vital processes possible for longer periods of time; and the increasing use of parts of the newly dead to sustain life for the truly living. The problem is well on its way to being resolved by what must have seemed a relatively simple and ingenious method. As it turned out, the difficult issues of euthanasia could be evaded by redefining death.

In an earlier time, death was defined as the cessation of breathing. Any movie buff recalls at least one scene in which a mirror is held to the mouth of a dying man. The lack of fogging indicated that indeed he was dead. The spirit of man resided in his *spiritus* (breath). With increased knowledge of human physiology and the potential for reviving a nonbreathing man, the circulation, the pulsating heart, became the focus of the definition of life. This is the tradition with which most of us have been raised.

There is of course a relationship between circulation and respiration, and the linkage, not irrelevantly, is the brain. All body parts require the nourishment, including oxygen, carried by the circulating blood. Lack of blood supply leads to the death of an organ; the higher functions of the brain are particularly vulnerable. But if there is no respiration, there is no adequate exchange of oxygen, and this essential ingredient of the blood is no longer available for distribution. If a part of the heart loses its vascular supply, we may lose that part and still survive. If a part of the brain is deprived of oxygen, we may, depending on its location, lose it and survive. But here we pay a special price, for the functions lost are those we identify with the self, the soul, or humanness, i.e., memory, knowledge, feeling, thinking, perceiving, sensing, knowing, learning, and loving.

Most people are prepared to say that when all of the brain is destroyed the "person" no longer exists; with all due respect for the complexities of the mind/brain debate, the "person" (and personhood) is generally associated with the functioning part of the head—the brain. The higher functions of the brain that have been described are placed, for the most part, in the cortex. The brain stem (in many ways more closely allied to the spinal cord) controls primarily visceral functions. When the total brain is damaged, death in all forms will ensue because the lower brain centers that control the circulation and respiration are destroyed.

With the development of modern respirators, however, it is possible to artificially maintain respiration and with it, often, the circulation with which it is linked. It is this situation that has allowed for the redefinition of death—a redefinition that is being precipitously embraced by both scientific and theological groups.

The movement toward redefining death received considerable impetus with the publication of a report sponsored by the Ad Hoc Committee of the Harvard Medical School in 1968. The committee offered an alternative definition of death based on the functioning of the brain. Its criteria stated that if an individual is unreceptive and unresponsive, i.e., in a state of irreversible coma; if he has no movements or breathing when the mechanical respirator is turned off; if he demonstrates no reflexes; and if he has a flat electroencephalogram for at least twenty-four hours, indicating no electrical brain activity (assuming that he has not been subjected to hypothermia or central nervous system depressants), he may then be declared dead.

What was originally offered as an optional definition of death is, however, progressively becoming *the* definition of death. In most states there is no specific legislation defining death; the ultimate responsibility here is assumed to reside in the general medical community. Recently, however, there has been a series of legal cases which seem to be establishing brain death as a judicial standard. In California in May of this year an ingenious lawyer, John Cruikshank, offered as a defense of his client, Andrew D. Lyons, who had shot a man in the head, the argument that the cause of death was not the bullet but the removal of his heart by a transplant surgeon, Dr. Norman Shumway. Cruikshank's argument notwithstanding, the jury found his client guilty of voluntary manslaughter. In the course of that trial, Dr. Shumway said: "The brain in the 1970s and in the light of modern day medical technology is the sine qua non—the criterion for death. I'm saying anyone whose brain is dead is dead. It is the one determinant that would be universally applicable, because the brain is the one organ that can't be transplanted."

This new definition, independent of the desire for transplant, now permits the physician to "pull the plug" without even committing an act of passive euthanasia. The patient will first be defined as dead; pulling the plug will merely be the harmless act of halting useless treatment on a cadaver. But while the new definition of death avoids one complex problem, euthanasia, it may create others equally difficult which have never been fully defined or visualized. For if it grants the right to pull the plug, it also implicitly grants the privilege *not* to pull the plug, and the potential and meaning of this has not at all been adequately examined.

These cadavers would have the legal status of the dead with none of the qualities one now associates with death. They would be warm, respiring, pulsating, evacuating, and excreting bodies requiring nursing, dietary, and general grooming attention—*and could probably be maintained so for a period of years.* If we chose to, we could, with the technology already at hand, legally avail ourselves of these new cadavers to serve science and mankind in dramatically useful ways. The autopsy, that most respectable of medical traditions, that last gift of the dying person to the living future, could be extended in principle beyond our current recognition. To save lives and relieve suffering—traditional motives for violating tradition—we could develop hospitals (an inappropriate word because it suggests the presence of living human beings), banks, or farms of cadavers which require feeding and maintenance, in order to be harvested. To the uninitiated the "new cadavers" in their rows of respirators would seem indistinguishable from comatose patients now residing in wards of chronic neurological hospitals.

PRECEDENTS

The idea of wholesale and systematic salvage of useful body parts may seem startling, but it is not without precedent. It is simply magnified by the technology of modern medicine. Within the confines of one individual, we have always felt free to transfer body parts to places where they are needed more urgently, felt free to reorder the priorities of the naturally endowed structure. We will borrow skin from the less visible parts of the body to salvage a face. If a muscle is paralyzed, we will often substitute a muscle that subserves a less crucial function. This was common surgery at the time that paralytic polio was more prevalent.

It soon becomes apparent, however, that there is a limitation to this procedure. The person in want does not always have a second-best substitute. He may then be forced to borrow from a person with a surplus. The prototype, of course, is blood donation. Blood may be seen as a regeneratable organ, and we have a long-standing tradition of blood donation. What may be more important, and perhaps dangerous, we have established the precedent in blood of commercialization—not only are we free to borrow, we are forced to buy and, indeed, in our country at least, permitted to sell. Similarly, we allow the buying or selling of sperm for artificial insemination. It is most likely that in the near future we will allow the buying and selling of ripened ova so that a sterile woman may conceive her baby if she has a functioning uterus. Of course, once in vitro fertilization becomes a reality (an imminent possibility), we may even permit the rental of womb space for gestation for a woman who does manufacture her own ova but has no uterus.

Getting closer to our current problem, there is the relatively long-standing tradition of banking body parts (arteries, eyes, skin) for short periods of time for future transplants. Controversy has arisen with recent progress in the transplanting of major organs. Kidney transplants from a near relative or distant donor are becoming more common. As heart transplants become more successful, the issue will certainly be heightened, for while the heart may have been reduced by the new definition of death to merely another organ, it will always have a core position in the popular thinking about life and death. It has the capacity to generate the passion that transforms medical decisions into political issues.

The ability to use organs from cadavers has been severely limited in the past by the reluctance of heirs to donate the body of an individual for distribution. One might well have willed one's body for scientific purposes, but such legacies had no legal standing. Until recently, the individual lost control over his body once he died. This has been changed by the Uniform Anatomical Gift Act. This model piece of legislation, adopted by all fifty states in an incredibly short period of time, grants anyone over eighteen (twenty-one in some states) the right to donate en masse all "necessary organs and tissues" simply by filling out and mailing a small card.

Beyond the postmortem, there has been a longer-range use of human bodies that is accepted procedure—the exploitation of cadavers as teaching material in medical schools. This is a long step removed from the rationale of the transplant—a dramatic gift of life from the dying to the near-dead; while it is true that medical education will inevitably save lives, the clear and immediate purpose of the donation is to facilitate training.

It is not unnatural for a person facing death to want his usefulness to extend beyond his mortality; the same biases and values that influence our life persist in our leaving of it. It has been reported that the Harvard Medical School has no difficulty in receiving as many donations of cadavers as they need, while Tufts and Boston Universities are usually in short supply. In Boston, evidently, the cachet of getting into Harvard extends even to the dissecting table.

The way is now clear for an ever-increasing pool of usable body parts, but the current practice minimizes efficiency and maximizes waste. Only a short period exists between the time of death of the patient and the time of death of his major parts.

USES OF THE NEOMORT

In the ensuing discussion, the word *cadaver* will retain its usual meaning, as opposed to the new cadaver, which will be referred to as a *neomort*. The "ward" or "hospital" in which it is maintained will be called a *bioemporium* (purists may prefer *bioemporion*).

Whatever is possible with the old embalmed cadaver is extended to an incredible degree with the neomort. What follows, therefore, is not a definitive list but merely the briefest of suggestions as to the spectrum of possibilities.

Training

Uneasy medical students could practice routine physical examinations—auscultation, percussion of the chest, examination of the retina, rectal and vaginal examinations, et cetera—indeed, everything except neurological examinations, since the neomort by definition has no functioning central nervous system.

Both the student and his patient could be spared the pain, fumbling, and embarrassment of the "first time."

Interns also could practice standard and more difficult diagnostic procedures, from spinal taps to pneumoencephalography and the making of arteriograms, and residents could practice almost all of their surgical skills—in other words, most of the procedures that are now normally taught with the indigent in wards of major city hospitals could be taught with neomorts. Further, students could practice more exotic procedures often not available in a typical residency—eye operations, skin grafts, plastic facial surgery, amputation of useless limbs, coronary surgery, etc.; they could also practice the actual removal of organs, whether they be kidneys, testicles, or what have you, for delivery to the transplant teams.

Testing

The neomort could be used for much of the testing of drugs and surgical procedures that we now normally perform on prisoners, mentally retarded children, and volunteers. The efficacy of a drug as well as its toxicity could be determined beyond limits we might not have dared approach when we were concerned about permanent damage to the testing vehicle, a living person. For example, operations for increased vascularization of the heart could be tested to determine whether they truly do reduce the incidence of future heart attack before we perform them on patients. Experimental procedures that proved useless or harmful could be avoided; those that succeed could be available years before they might otherwise have been. Similarly, we could avoid the massive delays that keep some drugs from the marketplace while the dying clamor for them.

Neomorts would give us access to other forms of testing that are inconceivable with the living human being. We might test diagnostic instruments such as sophisticated electrocardiography by selectively damaging various parts of the heart to see how or whether the instrument could detect the damage.

Experimentation

Every new medical procedure demands a leap of faith. It is often referred to as an "act of courage," which seems to me an inappropriate terminology now that organized medicine rarely uses itself as the experimental body. Whenever a surgeon attempts a procedure for the first time, he is at best generalizing from experimentation with lower animals. Now we can protect the patient from too large a leap by using the neomort as an experimental bridge.

Obvious forms of experimentation would be cures for illnesses which would first be induced in the neomort. We could test antidotes by injecting poison, induce cancer or virus infections to validate and compare developing therapies.

Because they have an active hematopoietic system, neomorts would be particularly valuable for studying diseases of the blood. Many of the examples that I draw from that field were offered to me by Dr. John F. Bertles, a hematologist at St. Luke's Hospital Center in New York. One which interests him is the utilization of marrow transplants. Few human-to-human marrow transplants have been successful, since the kind of immunosuppression techniques that require research could most safely be performed on neomorts. Even such research as the recent experimentation at Willowbrook—where mentally retarded children were infected with hepatitis virus (which was not yet culturable outside of the human body) in an attempt to find a cure for this pernicious disease—could be done without risking the health of the subjects.

Banking

While certain essential blood antigens are readily storable (e.g., red cells can now be preserved in a frozen state), others are not, and there is increasing need for potential means of storage. Research on storage of platelets to be used in transfusion requires human recipients, and the data are only slowly and tediously gathered at great expense. Use of neomorts would permit intensive testing of platelet survival and probably would lead to a rapid development of a better storage technique. The same would be true for white cells.

As has been suggested, there is great wastage in the present system of using kidney donors from cadavers. Major organs are difficult to store. A population of neomorts maintained with body parts computerized and catalogued for compatability would yield a much more efficient system. Just as we now have blood banks, we could have banks for all the major organs that may someday be transplantable—lungs, kidney, heart, ovaries. Beyond the obvious storage uses of the neomort, there are others not previously thought of because there was no adequate storage facility. Dr. Marc Lappe of the Hastings Center has suggested that a neomort whose own immunity system had first been severely repressed might be an ideal "culture" for growing and storing our lymphoid components. When we are threatened by malignancy or viral disease, we can go to the "bank" and withdraw our stored white cells to help defend us.

Harvesting

Obviously, a sizable population of neomorts will provide a steady supply of blood, since they can be drained periodically. When we consider the cost-benefit analysis of this system, we would have to evaluate it in the same way as the lumber industry evaluates sawdust—a product which in itself is not commercially feasible but which supplies a profitable dividend as a waste from a more useful harvest.

The blood would be a simultaneous source of platelets, leukocytes, and red cells. By attaching a neomort to an IBM cell separator, we could isolate cell types at relatively low cost. The neomort could also be tested for the presence of hepatitis in a way that would be impossible with commercial donors. Hepatitis as a transfusion scourge would be virtually eliminated.

Beyond the blood are rarer harvests. Neomorts offer a great potential source of bone marrow for transplant procedures, and I am assured that a bioemporium of modest size could be assembled to fit most transplantation antigen requirements. And skin would of course, be harvested—similarly bone, corneas, cartilage, and so on.

Manufacturing

In addition to supplying components of the human body, some of which will be continually regenerated, the neomort can also serve as a manufacturing unit. Hormones are one obvious product, but there are others. By the injection of toxins, we have a source of antitoxin that does not have the complication of coming from another animal form. Antibodies for most of the major diseases can be manufactured merely by injecting the neomort with the viral or bacterial offenders.

Perhaps the most encouraging extension of the manufacturing process emerges from the new cancer research, in which immunology is coming to the fore. With certain blood cancers, great hope attaches to the use of antibodies. To take just one example, it is conceivable that leukemia could be generated in individual neomorts—not just to provide for *in vivo* (so to speak) testing of antileukemic modes of therapy but also to generate antibody immunity responses which could then be used in the living.

COST–BENEFIT ANALYSIS

If seen only as the harvesting of products, the entire feasibility of such research would depend on intelligent cost-benefit analysis. Although certain products would not warrant the expense of maintaining a community of neomorts, the enormous expense of other products, such as red cells with unusual antigens, would certainly warrant it. Then, of course, the equation is shifted. As soon as one economically sound reason is found for the maintenance of the community, all of the other ingredients become gratuitous by-products, a familiar problem in manufacturing. There is no current research to indicate the maintenance cost of a bioemporium or even the potential duration of an average neomort. Since we do not at this point encourage sustaining life in the brain-dead, we do not know the limits to which it could be extended. This is the kind of technology, however, in which we have previously been quite successful.

Meantime, a further refinement of death might be proposed. At present we use total brain function to define brain death. The source of electroencephalogram activity is not known and cannot be used to distinguish between the activity of higher and lower brain centers. If, however, we are prepared to separate the concept of "aliveness" from "personhood" in the adult, as we have in the fetus, a good argument can be made that death should be defined not as cessation of total brain function but merely as cessation of cortical function. New tests may soon determine when cortical function is dead. With this proposed extension, one could then maintain neomorts without even the complication and expense of respirators. The entire population of decorticates residing in chronic hospitals and now classified among the incurably ill could be redefined as dead.

But even if we maintain the more rigid limitations of total brain death, it would seem that a reasonable population could be maintained if the purposes warranted it. It is difficult to assess how many new neomorts would be available each year to satisfy the demand. There are roughly 2 million deaths a year in the United States. The most likely sources of intact bodies with destroyed brains would be accidents (about 113,000 per year), suicides (around 24,000 per year), homicides (18,000), and cerebrovascular accidents (some 210,000 per year). Obviously, in each of these categories a great many of the individuals would be useless—their bodies either shattered or scattered beyond value or repair.

And yet, after all the benefits are outlined, with the lifesaving potential clear, the humanitarian purposes obvious, the technology ready, the motives pure, and the material costs justified—how are we to reconcile our emotions? Where in this debit-credit ledger of limbs and livers and kidneys and costs are we to weigh and enter the repugnance generated by the entire philanthropic endeavor?

Cost-benefit analysis is always least satisfactory when the costs must be measured in one realm and the benefits in another. The analysis is particularly skewed when the benefits are specific, material, apparent, and immediate, and the price to be paid is general, spiritual, abstract, and of the future. It is that which induces people to abandon freedom for security, pride for comfort, dignity for dollars.

William May, in a perceptive article, defended the careful distinctions that have traditionally been drawn between the newly dead and the long dead. "While the body retains its recognizable form, even in death, it commands a certain respect. No longer a human presence, it still reminds us of that presence which once was utterly inseparable from it." But those distinctions become obscured when, years later, a neomort will retain the appearance of the newly dead, indeed, more the appearance of that which was formerly described as living.

Philosophers tend to be particularly sensitive to the abstract needs of civilized man; it is they who have often been the guardians of values whose abandonment produces pains that are real, if not always quantifiable. Hans Jonas, in his *Philosophical Essays,* anticipated some of the possibilities outlined here, and defended what he felt to be the sanctity of the human body and the unknowability of the borderline between life and death when he insisted that "Nothing less than the maximum definition of death will do—brain death plus heart death plus any other indication that may be pertinent—before final violence is allowed to be done." And even then Jonas was only contemplating *temporary* maintenance of life for the collection of organs.

The argument can be made on both sides. The unquestionable benefits to be gained are the promise of cures for leukemia and other diseases, the reduction of suffering, and the maintenance of life. The proponents of this view will be mobilized with a force that may seem irresistible.

They will interpret our revulsion at the thought of a bioemporium as a bias of our education and experience, just as earlier societies were probably revolted by the startling notion of abdominal surgery, which we now take for granted. The proponents will argue that the revulsion, not the technology, is inappropriate.

Still there will be those, like May, who will defend that revulsion as a quintessentially human factor whose removal would diminish us all, and extract a price we cannot anticipate in ways yet unknown and times not yet determined. May feels that there is "a tinge of the inhuman in the humanitarianism of those who believe that the perception of social need easily overrides all other considerations and reduces the acts of implementation to the everyday, routine, and casual."

This is the kind of weighing of values for which the computer offers little help. Is the revulsion to the new technology simply the fear and horror of the ignorant in the face of the new, or is it one of those components of humanness that barely sustain us at the limited level of civility and decency that now exists, and whose removal is one more step in erasing the distinction between man and the lesser creatures—beyond that, the distinction between man and matter?

Sustaining life is an urgent argument for any measure, but not if that measure destroys those very qualities that make life worth sustaining.

Sylvia Plath

Attempted Suicide

Sylvia Plath (1932–1963) was a promising young writer who committed suicide at the age of thirty. The Bell Jar, her best known work, is a self-consciously autobiographical novel. She also wrote a good deal of poetry, culminating in the Ariel poems.

I knew just how to go about it.

The minute the car tires crunched off down the drive and the sound of the motor faded, I jumped out of bed and hurried into my white blouse and green figured skirt and black raincoat. The raincoat felt damp still, from the day before, but that would soon cease to matter.

I went downstairs and picked up a pale blue envelope from the dining room table and scrawled on the back, in large, painstaking letters: *I am going for a long walk.*

I propped the message where my mother would see it the minute she came in.

Then I laughed.

I had forgotten the most important thing.

I ran upstairs and dragged a chair into my mother's closet. Then I climbed up and reached for the small green strongbox on the top shelf. I could have torn the metal cover off with my bare hands, the lock was so feeble, but I wanted to do things in a calm, orderly way.

I pulled out my mother's upper right-hand bureau drawer and slipped the blue jewelry box from its hiding place under the scented Irish linen handkerchiefs. I unpinned the little key from the dark velvet. Then I unlocked the strongbox and took out the bottle of new pills. There were more than I had hoped.

There were at least fifty.

If I had waited until my mother doled them out to me, night by night, it would have taken me fifty nights to save up enough. And in fifty nights, college would have opened, and my brother would have come back from Germany, and it would be too late.

I pinned the key back in the jewelry box among the clutter of inexpensive chains and rings, put the jewelry box back in the drawer under the handkerchiefs, returned the strongbox to the closet shelf and set the chair on the rug in the exact spot I had dragged it from.

Then I went downstairs and into the kitchen. I turned on the tap and poured myself a tall glass of water. Then I took the glass of water and the bottle of pills and went down into the cellar.

A dim, undersea light filtered through the slits of the cellar windows. Behind the oil burner, a dark gap showed in the wall at about shoulder height and ran back under the breezeway, out of sight. The breezeway had been added to the house after the cellar was dug, and built out over this secret, earth-bottomed crevice.

A few old, rotting fireplace logs blocked the hole mouth. I shoved them back a bit. Then I set the glass of water and the bottle of pills side by side on the flat surface of one of the logs and started to heave myself up.

It took me a good while to heft my body into the gap, but at last, after many tries, I managed it, and crouched at the mouth of the darkness, like a troll.

The earth seemed friendly under my bare feet, but cold. I wondered how long it had been since this particular square of soil had seen the sun.

Then, one after the other, I lugged the heavy, dust-covered logs across the hole mouth. The dark felt thick as velvet. I reached for the glass and bottle, and carefully, on my knees, with bent head, crawled to the farthest wall.

Cobwebs touched my face with the softness of moths. Wrapping my black coat round me like my own sweet shadow, I unscrewed the bottle of pills and started taking them swiftly, between gulps of water, one by one by one.

At first nothing happened, but as I approached the bottom of the bottle, red and blue lights began to flash before my eyes. The bottle slid from my fingers and I lay down.

The silence drew off, baring the pebbles and shells and all the tatty wreckage of my life. Then, at the rim of vision, it gathered itself, and in one sweeping tide, rushed me to sleep.

Robert M. Martin

Suicide and False Desires

Robert M. Martin *is a professor of philosophy at Dalhousie University, in Canada. He specializes in the philosophy of language and the philosophy of mind.*

Is killing himself ever one's real aim? We can't deny that (at least) most people want to go on living. But it is sometimes claimed that all, or at least many, who seem bent on killing themselves do not *really* want to die—that death is not *really* in their interests. These claims are often part of an attempt to justify the policy of forceful intervention to prevent suicide, on the grounds that this would be doing people the favor of saving them from the death they don't really want.

Two parts of this argument are questionable: the claim that suicide is always or usually a *false desire* in some sense; and the implied premise that we are justified in interfering when someone is acting against his true interests or desires. I think there are *certain* cases when we might be justified in interfering in some mild ways when someone is about to act against his real interests or desires, though I won't go into the difficult question of exactly when this sort of paternalistic intervention is permissible. I shall argue that claims that suicide is always or usually a false desire are unfounded, and that we are not justified in interfering in even those cases in which the desire for death is a false one.

One sort of argument for intervention on the grounds that suicide isn't really desired is based on the claim that suicidal people are always or usually mentally ill, or at least pathologically disturbed or irrational. One does not want to make these claims trivial because they are definitionally true, by defining irrationality or mental illness to include suicidal desires or behaviors; for this argument to be any good, there have to be independent grounds for these claims. Professional opinion varies here. Some argue that being suicidal is not a symptom of mental illness at all. Others want to distinguish people who are irrationally suicidal from those whose suicidal impulses spring from a "realistic assessment of life situations." Still others claim that rational suicide is an extreme rarity, and that most suicidal individuals "are suffering from clinically recognizable psychiatric illnesses." The debate is a complicated one, often involving questionable psychological theories, assertions about matters of fact one wishes were supported by more empirical observation, and the interesting problem that notions like *health* and *rationality* and their opposites skip around among descriptive, theoretical, and rather arbitrarily evaluative uses. Going further into these questions is beyond the scope of this paper, but I'll note the following: It is the suicidal desires of the *sane* I'm interested in here, and almost everyone admits that it's possible for sane people to have these desires. Nevertheless, it's not at all obvious that mentally ill or irrational people ought, in general, to be prevented from acting on their desires, or that they should be paternalistically forced to act in accord with what we think their desires ought to be. Furthermore, even if there *are* occasions when ill or irrational people ought, for their own good, to be prevented from doing what they think they want to, there are special considerations (which I'll raise later) which make it inappropriate to treat suicidal desires in particular this way.

An argument for intervention in suicide of the sane is based on the claim that suicides are always (or often) ambivalent, and thus don't really want death:

> Individuals who are intent on killing themselves still wish very much to be rescued or to have their deaths prevented. Suicide prevention consists essentially in recognizing that the potential victim is "in balance" between his wishes to live and his wishes to die, then throwing one's efforts on the side of life.

It is not clear why this author speaks of the contrary wishes of the suicidal individual as "in balance" while assuming that he is about to kill himself; one would imagine that the individual about to act this way has desires to die that have *outweighed* the contrary ones (especially if he is *"intent"* on killing himself). Perhaps what is really meant here is that suicides are "ambivalent" in the sense that although on balance they wish to die, still strong residual doubts and contrary feelings remain. But why is this supposed to justify intervention? We all continue to harbor doubts whenever we make up our minds about any difficult choice; but this hardly means that we don't *really* want to do what we've decided, or that someone else is then justified in stopping us.

There are, however, four legitimate senses in which we may be said to have false desires—to think we want what we really don't, or to desire something that's not really in our interests:

Sense 1: Someone sincerely says she wants to become famous; after she does succeed at this, however, she discovers that fame doesn't have the charms she thought it would, and has its own agonies. She says, "I thought I wanted to be famous, but I really didn't." This is a case of incomplete or mistaken information about the object desired.

Sense 2: Someone believes falsely that a tidal wave will flood his home town. He sells his house at a great loss, and quits his good job. Although he understood fully the nature and implications of his desired actions (selling and quitting), he discovers that those actions were not what he really wanted to do—that they were not really in his interests—when he finds out that there will be no tidal wave. Here there is false or incomplete information about circumstances.

Sense 3: Someone thinks that the only way to get good grades at school is to bribe her instructors, but later finds out that a bit of studying instead would have resulted in better grades at less cost. Her wanting to bribe her instructors wasn't in

accord with her real interests because of false or incomplete information about
alternatives.

Sense 4: Someone has a bad day at the office, and suddenly and uncharacteristically
decides the business world is not for him. Later he regrets having thrown his
career away; he feels that his earlier dissatisfaction, while it was real enough
at the time, was false in the sense that it was fleeting and not representative
of his enduring personality.

Now, desire to kill oneself may be false desire in any of these four senses. Someone
may want to kill himself because (*sense 1*) he falsely believes he will go to a land of everlasting
bliss after death; or because (*sense 2*) he falsely believes he is suffering from a terminal and
debilitating disease; or because (*sense 3*) he isn't aware that there are forms of therapy which
can cure his growing depressions; or because (*sense 4*) he feels a serious but atypical and
fleeting suicidal urge. We can say of all these people that they don't *really* want to die, or that
death is not congruent with their *real* values or interests.

Clearly, there have been suicides because of false desires like these, though I wouldn't
want to guess what proportion of suicidal desires are false. George Murphy claims that the
percentage of suicidal desires that are false in *sense 4* is large:

> We can confidently predict recovery from [the suicidal] urge in the great majority of
> cases, when other symptoms of depression lift. The desire to terminate one's life is
> usually transient. The "right" to suicide is a "right" desired only temporarily.

Louise Horowitz, in an article which otherwise strongly opposes interference with suicide,
argues that

> one can distinguish between suicides which are appropriate and those which are the
> result of misinterpretations or failures to see the alternative courses of action. . . . We
> . . . have the right in the interest of rationality to point out alternative courses of
> action which we believe [the suicidal person] may have overlooked. But the individ-
> ual contemplating suicide is not obliged to defend his decision, only to discuss it in
> order to avoid making a mistake.

It seems to me that it is *sometimes* appropriate to interfere with the carrying out of false
nonsuicide desires in the mild ways Horowitz indicates, especially when the person involved
is a friend, has asked our advice, and the like. But I shall argue that intervention is *never*
appropriate when the false desire is for suicide, because suicide desires are importantly different from others.

When (if ever) do we feel justified in intervening to prevent someone's actions? I should
think that the justification for this could be that what the person was about to do was not *for
his own good* (I ignore the other valid reason: when others would be harmed). Now, something
is incompatible with the agent's own good when it conflicts either with his current interests
and desires or when it will conflict with future interests and desires. The examples of non-
suicidal false desire, previously mentioned, are cases in which a current desire has consequences that will conflict with the agent's future interests and desires. (I am assuming here
that something counts as harm for an individual only if it or its consequences conflict with
some value or desire of that individual himself.) Intervention is (perhaps sometimes) justified,
because it would spare the agent future grief.

But suppose that someone never is in position to suffer conflict with his real desires as
a result of acting on false desires. Suppose, for example, that the woman who wanted to be

famous (*case 1*, above) had felt satisfied with her life as she worked toward fame, but died before she became famous enough to find out that it was not what she thought it would be. What justification would there have been for preventing her from acting on her false desire? None, because she never did suffer conflict with her real values and desires as a result of her actions. Had she lived, she would have regretted her efforts to become famous; but her life, as actually lived, was satisfying to her and congruent with all her felt wishes and values.

Now let us examine the false desire for suicide. Suicide results in death, of course, and we normally count death as a harm. But we do because we value our life. However, if someone wants to die, death does not count as a harm *for him*. But what if the desire for death is a false desire? When we intervene in what would otherwise be a successful suicide, we *never* save the agent from a future state incompatible with any of his desires or values, from any grief or regret as a consequence of his actions. The man who believes that death will bring him to paradise will not be disappointed—not because he will go to paradise, but because there won't be any *him* left after his death to be disappointed. The person who kills himself because of the false belief that he has a terminal disease won't regret his decision. The man who killed himself unaware that therapy could have helped his depression won't be worse off than had we intervened, because after his death he won't be *any* way; and because before death he desired death and got it. And the man who had the fleeting desire for death won't suffer when he returns to more stable and characteristic contrary desires, because he won't return.

The point here is that suicide is the act of putting one's self out of existence—an obvious point, but one that seems to have been widely ignored in the discussion of the subject. We can't then make the usual sorts of judgment about acts and their consequences for the agent, because death is the only consequence for him, and after that there is no more agent. A false desire for death is, after all, a desire for death; suicide achieves that desire, and the agent does not live to suffer the normal consequences of acting on false desires.

It is this argument I referred to above when talking about insane or irrational suicidal desires. They are *desires*, after all, and thus have a *prima facie* claim for satisfaction; and if no agent will suffer bad consequences, why is it benevolent to interfere?

For these reasons I think that although false desires may sometimes justify intervention, in the case of suicide they never do. I do think, but for reasons I shall not argue here, that considerations related to our duties to others may show suicide to be sometimes immoral, and when these duties are so strong as to override an agent's valid claim to do what he wants to do, we are justified in interfering in suicide. But when such considerations are not relevant (and I think occasions when they are relevant are rare), we must not interfere in suicide.

Part
FIVE

Living
a Good Life

13

Why Shouldn't I Be Selfish?

*O*nly this morning, no doubt, you had to face up to a basic moral question. Perhaps something you wanted was just sitting there, unguarded, and you could have walked off with it without fear of getting caught. Or maybe someone asked you a question, and you could have lied—much to your advantage. Or possibly you made a promise to a friend, who seems to have forgotten about it, and you wondered if you should remind him or not. Everyday, we find ourselves choosing between our own interests and the interests of others, between our personal desires and the promises we have made or principles we ought to obey. But why should you concern yourself with others and obey principles that are not to your own advantage? In short, why shouldn't you be selfish?

Daily observation and perhaps logic seem to show us that all of our actions are self-interested, if not actually selfish. We seem to do what we want, whenever we can, and when we don't, it is because we can't, because someone or something prevents us, because we want something else even more, or because we are afraid of the consequences—which we fear even more than we want what we want. But if we can get what we want and there is nothing that we want or fear more, the argument goes, we will surely do whatever will get us what we want. This tempting generalization soon becomes the thesis that "everyone is selfish" or more philosophically, "everyone is an **egoist**." We hesitate, however, because of an admittedly small cluster of actions and agents that seem not to be motivated by self-interest at all, examples of **altruism** that seem to have nothing to do with selfishness. Occasionally we find ourselves making a small sacrifice, performing an act of seemingly pure generosity, or obeying a rule despite the fact that it is not in our interest and that there is virtually no chance of our getting caught for a transgression. And we occasionally meet people and we read about saints who consistently behave with little or no regard for their own interests.

Nevertheless, we are still tempted (or tormented) by that generalization. Ever since Plato (and no doubt before) the same question has plagued philosophers: "Why not be selfish?" The most obvious answers do not seem to work. For instance, "because it is unfair to others" will not be very effective with someone who readily admits that he or she doesn't really care about anyone else, and "because it will make you unhappy," while perhaps true, only rejects selfishness by an appeal to selfishness, so the egoistic thesis remains unquestioned.

In Plato's *Republic*, Glaucon (one of Socrates's several interlocutors) argues that we would all be selfish if we could get away with it, and he introduces the myth of the "ring of Gyges" to make the point. The ring in question supposedly rendered its wearer invisible, and if a man were invisible, Glaucon suggests, he could get away with anything. Indeed, Glaucon argues that if a person could get away with doing whatever he wanted and did not do so, people would think him a fool rather than a saint. Selfishness is the natural order of things, and there is no good reason— except fear of getting caught and suffering the consequences—why we do not all act selfishly all the time.

One of the arguments for the necessity of egoism is the argument from human nature, the argument that all of us are "naturally" selfish. One specific argument for the universality of egoism goes back to ancient times: that all of us naturally seek and enjoy pleasure, dislike and avoid pain. All of our actions, accordingly, are aimed at this end, which is called **hedonism**, the pursuit of pleasure. Two thousand years ago, the Greek philosopher Epicurus defended this thesis, and he was so persuasive that we still call people who enjoy the good things in life "Epicureans." It is worth noting, however, that Epicurus did not defend the pursuit of *every* pleasure without qualification; he knew that some pleasures were better and more durable than others and urged us to seek the "higher" pleasures. Nevertheless, the argument that we act for the sake of our own pleasure (and to avoid pain) provides a powerful argument for egoism. It is argued that whatever people seem to be doing—going boating, studying for an exam, opening a can of Pepsi—they are really acting toward one goal: obtaining pleasure and avoiding pain. You want to go boating because of the pleasure you get out of boating. You study not just to learn but to obtain pleasure—from the learning itself, but also from the confidence that you will do well in the exam or that you are doing what you are supposed to be doing on a Wednesday night and not going out to the movies. You want a Pepsi, but you really want the satisfaction that the quenching of thirst and the uplifting feeling provide. It follows, then, that people who seem to be acting unselfishly are in fact satisfying their own hedonistic interests. This also gives us a way of understanding the behavior of saints and ourselves in our "good" moments: it may seem that we are acting unselfishly, but in fact we are working for the good feeling that comes from having done the right thing. Alternatively, we are just trying to avoid the painful feelings of guilt or shame, not to mention punishment and the verbal abuse of our neighbors, that follow obviously selfish and inconsiderate behavior.

The argument for universal egoism has recently received an even more sophisticated formulation in the theory of evolution and genetics. Perhaps selfishness is built right into our genes as a matter of evolutionary survival, for how long could an individual or even a species exist if it did not take care of itself? Saints, perhaps, are rare exceptions, as are the occasional inspirations of generosity that we experience ourselves. But self-interest, it is argued, is built right into our basic nature, and although we might find exceptions to it, there is no avoiding the conclusion that we are all basically selfish, however altruistic our ideals. Against this, it is argued that cooperation and fellow feeling are also essential parts of human nature. The urge to help a fellow creature in trouble is just as strong and just as "natural" as the urge to satisfy one's own desires—indeed, that urge is one of our most natural desires. In this view, purely selfish actions become the exceptions, not sainthood and spontaneous generosity. Such controversies about the natural origins of selfishness go back to early interpretations of Genesis, but the modern argument becomes exquisitely subtle and scientific (represented here by Richard Dawkins and Stephen Jay Gould). It is nothing less than an argument about our basic nature and what we can and should expect of ourselves. But even if selfishness is not "natural" as such, it may be argued that selfishness is essential to survival. So argues the Russian immigrant philosopher Ayn Rand: we *ought* to be selfish, and what we call "altruism" is a form of pathetic self-destructiveness.

One argument for the universality of selfishness is derived from logical considerations alone. It is argued, first, that people always do what they want to do, barring obstacles and interference with their actions. If a man trips and falls on the way to the supermarket, we do not assume that he wanted to trip and fall, but if he succeeds in going to the market, we will not be easily persuaded that he did not want to do just that. Of course, our fellow may have gone to the market not because he enjoys marketing but rather because he desired some sausage meat for lunch, which he very much wanted. Or he may have gone to the market to get food for the cat and to stop her meowing—which annoyed him enormously. But we can assume that when a person completes an action without interference, he has satisfied his own desire—whether that desire involves pleasure and pain, keeping a promise, or proving one's sainthood.

But if every action involves the satisfaction of one's own desire, then it is not hard to conclude that every act is at least self-interested, if not selfish. This gives us a more cynical explanation of saints and our own generous impulses: whatever the motives of our actions, they (the saints) or we are satisfying desires, and so the actions are selfish. We might object here to the word "selfish" and insist on saving it for just those self-interested actions that also interfere with other people. Thus, buying a sausage and sharing it because one is both hungry and desirous of company is not selfish, but pushing everyone else out of the way to eat the whole sausage oneself would be. Nevertheless, in the sense that seems to count, all actions are selfish; it is just that some are obnoxiously so and others are quite acceptable to the rest of us (because, of course, they do not interfere with our own selfish desires).

Against the view that all of our actions are selfish, philosophers ever since Plato have vigorously argued that (a) at least some of our actions are not selfish but honestly based on generosity, charity, or moral principles; and (b) that we *ought* to act unselfishly. Even the ancient author Epicurus, whose name is almost synonymous with a life of self-indulgent pleasure, argued for moderation in the pursuit of pleasure and self-interest. The English Bishop Joseph Butler presented several sermons in which he rejected the egoist claim and laid out the various reasons for accepting altruistic motives at face value. Most philosophers now reject the psychological and logical arguments that make all actions out to be selfish, and most also agree with the ethical thesis that we ought to act unselfishly, at least some of the time. But there is also a social dimension to the question of selfishness, and self-indulgence and exaggerated self-concern may be cultivated as part of some particular societies, for example, our own. This is a thesis recently and strikingly argued by Christopher Lasch, who argues that our selfishness is a cultural phenomenon. It consists not so obviously of straightforward self-interest but rather of the more subtle form of self-absorption: a constant concern with our private selves and a kind of oblivion to larger social concerns.

Plato
The Ring of Gyges

Plato's (427–347 B.C.) Republic *is a blueprint for what would be, in Plato's opinion, the ideal society. Its central theme is justice, and the challenge with which Plato begins is the problem of the immoralist—the man who thinks that there is no reason not to be selfish and pursue one's own interests. Socrates' interlocutor Glaucon argues this thesis* *by using the myth of the "ring of Gyges," which makes its wearer invisible and allows him to get away with anything.*

GLAUCON (TO SOCRATES): I have never yet heard the superiority of justice to injustice maintained by anyone in a satisfactory way. I want to hear justice praised in respect of itself; then I shall be satisfied, and you are the person from whom I think that I am most likely to hear this; and therefore I will praise the unjust life to the utmost of my power and my manner of speaking will indicate the manner in which I desire to hear you too praising justice and censuring injustice. Will you say whether you approve of my proposal?

SOCRATES: Indeed I do; nor can I imagine any theme about which a man of sense would oftener wish to converse.

GLAUCON: I am delighted to hear you say so, and shall begin by speaking, as I proposed, of the nature and origin of justice.

They say that to do injustice is, by nature, good; to suffer injustice, evil; but that there is more evil in the latter than good in the former. And so when men have both done and suffered injustice and have had experience of both, any who are not able to avoid the one and obtain the other, think that they had better agree among themselves to have neither; hence they began to establish laws and mutual covenants; and that which was ordained by law was termed by them lawful and just. This, it is claimed, is the origin and nature of justice;—it is a mean or compromise, between the best of all, which is to do injustice and not be punished, and the worst of all, which is to suffer injustice without the power of retaliation; and justice, being at a middle point between the two, is tolerated not as a good but as the lesser evil, and honoured where men are too feeble to do injustice. For no man who is worthy to be called a man would ever submit to such an agreement with another if he had the power to be unjust; he would be mad if he did. Such is the received account Socrates, of the nature of justice, and the circumstances which bring it into being.

Now that those who practise justice do so involuntarily and because they have not the power to be unjust will best appear if we imagine something of this kind: having given to both the just and the unjust power to do what they will, let us watch and see whither desire will lead them; then we shall discover in the very act the just and unjust man to be proceeding along the same road, following their interest, which all creatures instinctively pursue as their good; the force of law is required to compel them to pay respect to equality. The liberty which we are supposing may be most completely given to them in the form of such a power as is said to have been possessed by Gyges, the ancestor of Croesus the Lydian.

According to the tradition, Gyges was a shepherd in the service of the reigning king of Lydia; there was a great storm, and an earthquake made an opening in the earth at the place where he was feeding his flock. Amazed at the sight, he descended into the opening, where, among other marvels which form part of the story, he beheld a hollow brazen horse, having doors, at which he stooping and looking in saw a dead body of stature, as appeared to him, more than human; he took from the corpse a gold ring that was on the hand, but nothing else, and so reascended. Now the shepherds met together, according to custom, that they might send their monthly report about the flocks to the king; into their assembly he came having the ring on his finger, and as he was sitting among them he chanced to turn the collet of the ring to the inside of his hand, when instantly he became invisible to the rest of the company and they began to speak of him as if he were no longer present. He was astonished at this, and again touching the ring he turned the collet outwards and reappeared; when he perceived this, he made several trials of the ring, and always with the same result—when he turned the collet inwards he became invisible, when outwards he was visible. Whereupon he contrived to be chosen one of the messengers who were sent to the court; where as soon as he arrived he seduced the queen, and with her help conspired against the king and slew him, and took the kingdom. Suppose now that there were two such magic rings, and the just put on one of them and the unjust the other; no man can be imagined to be of such an iron nature that he would stand fast in justice. No man would keep his hands off what was not his own when he could safely take what he liked out of the market, or go into houses and lie with any one at his pleasure, or kill or release from prison whom he would, and in all respects be like a god among men. Then the actions of the just would be as the actions of the unjust; they would both tend to the same goal. And this we may truly affirm to be a great proof that a man is just, not willingly or because he thinks that justice is any good to him individually, but of necessity; for wherever anyone thinks that he can safely be unjust, there he is unjust. For all men believe in their hearts that injustice is far more profitable to the individual than justice and he who argues as I have been supposing will say that they are right. If you could imagine anyone obtaining this power of becoming invisible, and never doing any wrong or touching what was another's, he would be thought by the lookers-on to be an unhappy man and a fool, although they would praise him to one another's faces, and keep up appearances with one another from a fear that they too might suffer injustice. Enough of this.

Now, if we are to form a real judgement of the two lives in these respects, we must set apart the extremes of justice and injustice; there is no other way; and how is the contrast to be effected? I answer: Let the unjust man be entirely unjust, and the just man entirely just; nothing is to be taken away from either of them, and both are to be perfectly furnished for the work of their respective lives. First, let the unjust be like other distinguished masters of craft; like the skillful pilot or physician, who knows intuitively what is possible or impossible in his art and keeps within those limits, and who, if he fails at any point, is able to recover himself. So let the unjust man attempt to do the right sort of wrongs, and let him escape detection if he is to be pronounced a master of injustice. To be found out is a sign of incompetence; for the height of injustice is to be deemed just when you are not. Therefore I say that in the perfectly unjust man we must assume the most perfect injustice; there is to be no deduction, but we must allow him, while doing the most unjust acts, to have acquired the greatest reputation for justice. If he has taken a false step he must be able to recover himself; he must be one who can speak with effect, if any of his deeds come to light, and who can force his way where force is required, by his courage and strength and command of wealth and friends. And at his side let us place the just man in his nobleness and simplicity, wishing, as Aeschylus says, to be and not to seem good. There must be no seeming, for if he seems to be just he will be honoured and rewarded, and then we shall not know whether he is just for the sake of justice or for the sake of honours and rewards; therefore, let him be clothed in justice only, and have no other covering; and he must be imagined in a state of life the opposite of the former. Let him be the best of men, and let him be reputed the worst; then he will have been put to the test and we shall see whether his justice is proof against evil reputation and its consequences. And let him continue thus to the hour of death; being just and seeming to be unjust. When both have reached the uttermost extreme, the one of justice and the other of injustice, let judgement be given which of them is the happier of the two.

SOCRATES: Heavens! my dear Glaucon . . . how energetically you polish them up for the decision, first one and then the other, as if they were two statues.

Epicurus
The Pursuit of Pleasure

Epicurus (c. 342–270 B.C.) was a Greek philosopher in the third century B.C. who argued that the good life consisted of pleasure. What follows is a selection from his Menocceus.

Let no one when young delay to study philosophy, nor when he is old grow weary of his study. For no one can come too early or too late to secure the health of his soul. And the man who says that the age for philosophy has either not yet come or has gone by is like the man who says that the age for happiness is not yet come to him, or has passed away. Wherefore both when young and old a man must study philosophy, that as he grows old he may be young in blessings through the grateful recollection of what has been, and that in youth he may be old as well, since he will know no fear of what is to come. We must then meditate on the things that make our happiness, seeing that when that is with us we have all, but when it is absent we do all to win it.

The things which I used unceasingly to commend to you, these do and practise, considering them to be the first principles of the good life. First of all believe that god is a being immortal and blessed, even as the common idea of a god is engraved on men's minds, and do not assign to him anything alien to his immortality or ill-suited to his blessedness: but believe about him everything that can uphold his blessedness and immortality. For gods there are, since the knowledge of them is by clear vision. But they are not such as the many believe them to be: for indeed they do not consistently represent them as they believe them to be. And the impious man is not he who denies the gods of the many, but he who attaches to the gods the beliefs of the many. For the statements of the many about the gods are not conceptions derived from sensation, but false suppositions, according to which the greatest misfortunes befall the wicked and the greatest blessings the good by the gift of the gods. For men being accustomed always to their own virtues welcome those like themselves, but regard all that is not of their nature as alien.

Become accustomed to the belief that death is nothing to us. For all good and evil consists in sensation, but death is deprivation of sensation. And therefore a right understanding that death is nothing to us makes the mortality of life enjoyable, not because it adds to it an infinite span of time, but because it takes away the craving for immortality. For there is nothing terrible in life for the man who has truly comprehended that there is nothing terrible in not living. So that the man speaks but idly who says that he fears death not because it will be painful when it comes, but because it is painful in anticipation. For that which gives no trouble when it comes, is but an empty pain in anticipation. So death, the most terrifying of ills, is nothing to us, since so long as we exist death is not with us; but when death comes, then we do not exist. It does not then concern either the living or the dead, since for the former it is not, and the latter are no more.

But the many at one moment shun death as the greatest of evils, at another yearn for it as a respite from the evils in life. But the wise man neither seeks to escape life nor fears the cessation of life, for neither does life offend him nor does the absence of life seem to be any evil. And just as with food he does not seek simply the larger share and nothing else, but rather the most pleasant, so he seeks to enjoy not the longest period of time, but the most pleasant.

And he who counsels the young man to live well, but the old man to make a good end, is foolish, not merely because of the desirability of life, but also because it is the same training which teaches to live well and to die well. Yet much worse still is the man who says it is good not to be born, but

once born make haste to pass the gates of Death. (Theognis, 427)

For if he says this from conviction why does he not pass away out of life? For it is open to him to do so, if he had firmly made up his mind to this. But if he speaks in jest, his words are idle among men who cannot receive them.

We must then bear in mind that the future is neither ours, nor yet wholly not ours, so that we may not altogether expect it as sure to come, nor abandon hope of it, as if it will certainly not come.

We must consider that of desires some are natural, others vain, and of the natural some are necessary and others merely natural; and of the necessary some are necessary for happiness, others for the repose of the body, and others for very life. The right understanding of these facts enables us to refer all choice and avoidance to the health of the body and the soul's freedom from disturbance, since this is the aim of the life of blessedness. For it is to obtain this end that we always act, namely, to avoid pain and fear. And when this is once secured for us, all the tempest of the soul is dispersed, since the living creature has not to wander as though in search of something that is missing, and to look for some other thing by which he can fulfil the good of the soul and the good of the body. For it is then that we have need of pleasure, when we feel pain owing to the absence of pleasure; but when we do not feel pain, we no longer need pleasure. And for this cause we call pleasure the beginning and end of the blessed life. For we recognize pleasure as the first good innate in us, and from pleasure we begin every act of choice and avoidance, and to pleasure we return again, using the feeling as the standard by which we judge every good.

And since pleasure is the first good and natural to us, for this very reason we do not choose every pleasure, but sometimes we pass over many pleasures, when greater discomfort accrues to us as the result of them: and similarly we think many pains better than pleasures, since a greater pleasure comes to us when we have endured pains for a long time. Every pleasure then because of its natural kinship to us is good, yet not every pleasure is to be chosen: even as every pain also is an evil, yet not all are always of a nature to be avoided. Yet by a scale of comparison and by the consideration of advantages and disadvantages we must form our judgement on all these matters. For the good on certain occasions we treat as bad, and conversely the bad as good.

And again independence of desire we think a great good—not that we may at all times enjoy but a few things, but that, if we do not possess many, we may enjoy the few in the genuine persuasion that those have the sweetest pleasure in luxury who least need it, and that all that is natural is easy to be obtained, but that which is superfluous is hard. And so plain savours bring us a pleasure equal to a luxurious diet, when all the pain due to want is removed; and bread and water produce the highest pleasure, when one who needs them puts them to his lips. To grow accustomed therefore to simple and not luxurious diet gives us health to the full, and makes a man alert for the needful employments of life, and when after long intervals we approach luxuries, disposes us better towards them, and fits us to be fearless of fortune.

When, therefore, we maintain that pleasure is the end, we do not mean the pleasures of profligates and those that consist in sensuality, as is supposed by some who are either ignorant or disagree with us or do not understand, but freedom from pain in the body and from trouble in the mind. For it is not continuous drinkings and revellings, nor the satisfaction of lusts, nor the enjoyment of fish and other luxuries of the wealthy table, which produce a pleasant life, but sober reasoning, searching out the motives for all choice and avoidance, and banishing mere opinions, to which are due the greatest disturbance of the spirit.

Of all this the beginning and the greatest good is prudence. Wherefore prudence is a more precious thing even than philosophy: for from prudence are sprung all the other virtues, and it teaches us that it is not possible to live pleasantly without living prudently and honourably and justly, nor, again, to live a life of prudence, honour, and justice without living pleasantly. For the virtues are by nature bound up with the pleasant life, and the pleasant life is inseparable from them. For indeed who, think you, is a better man then he who holds reverent opinions concerning the gods, and is at all times free from fear of death, and has reasoned out the end ordained by nature? He understands that the limit of good things is easy to fulfil and easy to attain, whereas the course of ills is either short in time or slight in pain: he laughs at destiny, whom some have introduced as the mistress of all things. He thinks that with us lies the chief power in determining events, some of which happen by necessity and some by chance, and some are within our control; for while necessity cannot be called to account, he sees that chance is inconstant, but that which is in our control is subject to no master, and to it are naturally attached praise and blame. For, indeed, it were better to follow the myths about the gods than to become a slave to the destiny of the natural philosophers: for the former suggests a hope of placating the gods by worship, whereas the latter involves a necessity which knows no placation. As to chance, he does not regard it as a god as most men do (for in god's acts there is no disorder), nor as an uncertain cause of all things: for he does not believe that good and evil are given by chance to man for the framing of a blessed life, but that opportunities for great good and great evil are afforded by it. He therefore thinks it better to be unfortunate in reasonable action than to prosper in unreason. For it is better in a man's actions that what is well chosen should fail, rather than that what is ill chosen should be successful owing to chance.

Meditate therefore on these things and things akin to them night and day by yourself, and with a companion like to yourself, and never shall you be disturbed waking or asleep, but you shall live like a god among men. For a man who lives among immortal blessings is not like to a mortal being.

PRINCIPAL DOCTRINES

I.   The blessed and immortal nature knows no trouble itself nor causes trouble to any other, so that it is never constrained by anger or favour. For all such things exist only in the weak.

II.   Death is nothing to us: for that which is dissolved is without sensation; and that which lacks sensation is nothing to us.

III.   The limit of quantity in pleasures is the removal of all that is painful. Wherever pleasure is present, as long as it is there, there is neither pain of body nor of mind, nor of both at once.

IV.   Pain does not last continuously in the flesh, but the acutest pain is there for a very short time, and even that which just exceeds the pleasure in the flesh does not continue for many days at once. But chronic illnesses permit a predominance of pleasure over pain in the flesh.

V.   It is not possible to live pleasantly without living prudently and honourably and justly, nor again to live a life of prudence, honour, and justice without living pleasantly. And the man who does not possess the pleasant life, is not living prudently and honourably and justly, and the man who does not possess the virtuous life, cannot possibly live pleasantly.

VI.   To secure protection from men anything is a natural good, by which you may be able to attain this end.

VII.   Some men wished to become famous and conspicuous, thinking that they would thus win for themselves safety from other men. Wherefore if the life of such men is safe, they have obtained the good which nature craves; but if it is not safe, they do not possess that for which they strove at first by the instinct of nature.

VIII.   No pleasure is a bad thing in itself: but the means which produce some pleasures bring with them disturbances many times greater than the pleasures.

IX.   If every pleasure could be intensified so that it lasted and influenced the whole organism or the most essential parts of our nature, pleasures would never differ from one another.

X.   If things that produce the pleasures of profligates could dispel the fears of the mind about the phenomena of the sky and death and its pains, and also teach the limits of desires and of pains, we should never have cause to blame them: for they would be filling themselves full with pleasures from every source and never have pain of body or mind, which is the evil of life.

XI.   If we were not troubled by our suspicions of the phenomena of the sky and about death, fearing that it concerns us, and also by our failure to grasp the limits of pains and desires, we should have no need of natural science.

XII.   A man cannot dispel his fear about the most important matters if he does not know what is the nature of the universe but suspects the truth of some mythical story. So that without natural science it is not possible to attain our pleasures unalloyed.

XIII.   There is no profit in securing protection in relation to men, if things above and things beneath the earth and indeed all in the boundless universe remain matters of suspicion.

XIV.   The most unalloyed source of protection from men, which is secured to some extent by a certain force of expulsion, is in fact the immunity which results from a quiet life and the retirement from the world.

XV.   The wealth demanded by nature is both limited and easily procured; that demanded by idle imaginings stretches on to infinity.

XVI.   In but few things chance hinders a wise man, but the greatest and most important matters reason has ordained and throughout the whole period of life does and will ordain.

XVII.   The just man is most free from trouble, the unjust most full of trouble.

XVIII.   The pleasure in the flesh is not increased, when once the pain due to want is removed, but is only varied: and the limit as regards pleasure in the mind is begotten by the reasoned understanding of these very pleasures and of the emotions akin to them, which used to cause the greatest fear to the mind.

XIX.   Infinite time contains no greater pleasure than limited time, if one measures by reason the limits of pleasure.

XX.   The flesh perceives the limits of pleasure as unlimited and unlimited time is required to supply it. But the mind, having attained a reasoned understanding of the ultimate good of the flesh and its limits and having dissipated the fears concerning the time to come, supplies us with the complete life, and we have no further need of infinite time: but neither does the mind shun pleasure, nor, when circumstances begin to bring about the departure from life, does it approach its end as though it fell short in any way of the best life.

XXI.   He who has learned the limits of life knows that that which removes the pain due to want and makes the whole of life complete is easy to obtain; so that there is no need of actions which involve competition.

XXII.   We must consider both the real purpose and all the evidence of direct perception, to which we always refer the conclusions of opinion; otherwise, all will be full of doubt and confusion.

XXIII.   If you fight against all sensations, you will have no standard by which to judge even those of them which you say are false.

XXIV.   If you reject any single sensation and fail to distinguish between the conclusion of opinion as to the appearance awaiting confirmation and that which is actually given by the sensation or feeling, or each intuitive apprehension of the mind, you will confound all other sensations as well with the same groundless opinion, so that you will reject every standard of judgement. And if among the mental images created by your opinion you affirm both that which awaits confirmation and that which does not, you will not escape error, since you will have preserved the whole cause of doubt in every judgement between what is right and what is wrong.

XXV.   If on each occasion instead of referring your actions to the end of nature, you turn to some other nearer standard when you are making a choice or an avoidance, your actions will not be consistent with your principles.

XXVI.   Of desires, all that do not lead to a sense of pain, if they are not satisfied, are not necessary, but involve a craving which is easily dispelled, when the object is hard to procure or they seem likely to produce harm.

XXVII.   Of all the things which wisdom acquires to produce the blessedness of the complete life, far the greatest is the possession of friendship.

XXVIII.   The same conviction which has given us confidence that there is nothing terrible that lasts for ever or even for long, has also been the protection of friendship most fully completed in the limited evils of this life.

XXIX.   Among desires some are natural and necessary, some natural but not necessary, and others neither natural nor necessary, but due to idle imagination.

XXX.   Wherever in the case of desires which are physical, but do not lead to a sense of pain, if they are not fulfilled, the effort is intense, such pleasures are due to idle imagination, and it is not owing to their own nature that they fail to be dispelled, but owing to the empty imaginings of the man.

XXXI.   The justice which arises from nature is a pledge of mutual advantage to restrain men from harming one another and save them from being harmed.

XXXII.   For all living things which have not been able to make compacts not to harm one another or be harmed, nothing ever is either just or unjust; and likewise too for all tribes of men which have been unable or unwilling to make compacts not to harm or be harmed.

XXXIII.   Justice never is anything in itself, but in the dealings of men with one another in any place whatever and at any time it is a kind of compact not to harm or be harmed.

XXXIV.   Injustice is not an evil in itself, but only in consequence of the fear which attaches to the apprehension of being unable to escape those appointed to punish such actions.

XXXV.   It is not possible for one who acts in secret contravention of the terms of the compact not to harm or be harmed, to be confident that he will escape detection, even if at present he escapes a thousand times. For up to the time of death it cannot be certain that he will indeed escape.

XXXVI.   In its general aspect justice is the same for all, for it is a kind of mutual advantage in the dealings of men with one another: but with reference to the individual peculiarities of a country or any other circumstances the same thing does not turn out to be just for all.

XXXVII.   Among actions which are sanctioned as just by law, that which is proved on examination to be of advantage in the requirements of men's dealings with one another, has the guarantee of justice, whether it is the same for all or not. But if a man makes a law and it does not turn out to lead to advantage in men's dealings with each other, then it no longer has the essential nature of justice. And even if the advantage in the matter of justice shifts from one side to the other, but for a while accords with the general concept, it is none the less just for that period in the eyes of those who do not confound themselves with empty sounds but look to the actual facts.

XXXVIII.   Where, provided the circumstances have not been altered, actions which were considered just, have been shown not to accord with the general concept in actual practice, then they are not just. But where, when circumstances have changed, the same actions which were sanctioned as just no longer lead to advantage, there they were just at the time when they were of advantage for the dealings of fellow-citizens with one another; but subsequently they are no longer just, when no longer of advantage.

XXXIX.   The man who has best ordered the element of disquiet arising from external circumstances has made those things that he could akin to himself and the rest at least no alien: but with all to which he could not do even this, he has refrained from mixing, and has expelled from his life all which it was of advantage to treat thus.

XL.   As many as possess the power to procure complete immunity from their neighbours, these also live most pleasantly with one another, since they have the most certain pledge of security, and after they have enjoyed the fullest intimacy, they do not lament the previous departure of a dead friend, as though he were to be pitied.

Joseph Butler
Benevolence and Self-Interest

Joseph Butler (1692–1752) was a bishop in England whose sermons were famous during his lifetime and have become philosophical classics since then. The following arguments against egoism are taken from his Fifteen Sermons (1726).

SERMON I: UPON THE SOCIAL NATURE OF MAN

*T*he comparison will be between the nature of man as respecting self, and tending to private good, his own preservation and happiness; and the nature of man as having respect to society, and tending to promote public good, the happiness of that society. These ends do indeed perfectly coincide; and to aim at public and private good are so far from being inconsistent, that they mutually promote each other: yet in the following discourse they must be considered as entirely distinct; otherwise the nature of man as tending to one, or as tending to the other cannot be compared. There can no comparison be made, without considering the things compared as distinct and different.

From this review and comparison of the nature of man as respecting self, and as respecting society, it will plainly appear, that *there are as real and the same kind of indications in human nature, that we were made for society and to do good to our fellow-creatures, as that we were intended to take care of our own life and health and private good: and that the same objections lie against one of these assertions, as against the other*. For,

First, There is a natural principle of *benevolence* in man; which is in some degree to *society*, what *self-love* is to the *individual*. And if there be in mankind any disposition to friendship; if there be any such thing as compassion, for compassion is momentary love; if there be any such thing as the paternal or filial affections; if there be any affection in human nature, the object and end of which is the good of another, this is itself benevolence, or the love of another. Be it ever so short, be it in ever so low a degree, or ever so unhappily confined; it proves the assertion, and points out what we were designed for, as really as though it were in a higher degree and more extensive. I must, however, remind you that though benevolence and self-love are different; though the former tends most directly to public good, and the latter to private: yet they are so perfectly coincident that the greatest satisfactions to ourselves depend upon our having benevolence in a due degree, and that self-love is one chief security of our right behaviour towards society. It may be added, that their mutual coinciding, so that we can scarce promote one without the other, is equally proof that we were made for both.

Secondly, This will further appear, from observing that the *several passions* and *affections,* which are distinct, both from benevolence and self-love, do in general contribute and lead us to *public* good as really as to *private*. It might be thought too minute and particular, and would carry us too great a length, to distinguish between and compare together the several passions or appetites distinct from benevolence, whose primary use and intention is the security and good of society; and the passions distinct from self-love, whose primary intention and design is the security and good of the individual. It is enough to the present argument, that desire of esteem from others, contempt and esteem of them, love of society as distinct from affection to the good of it, indignation against successful vice, that these are public affections or passions; have an immediate respect to others, naturally lead us to regulate our behavior in such a manner as will be of service to our fellow-creatures. If any or all of these may be considered likewise as private affections, as tending to private good; this does not hinder them from being public affections too, or destroy the good influence of them upon society, and their tendency to public good. It may be added, that as persons without any conviction from reason of the desirableness of life, would yet of course preserve it merely from the appetite of hunger; so by acting merely from regard (suppose) to reputation, without any consideration of the good of others, men often contribute to public good. In both these instances they are plainly instruments in the hands of another, in the hands of Providence, to carry on ends, the preservation of the individual and good of society, which they themselves have not in their view or intention. The sum is, men have various appetites, passions, and particular affections, quite distinct both from self-love and from benevolence: all of these have a tendency to promote both public and private good, and may be considered as respecting others and ourselves equally and in common: but some of them seem most immediately to respect others, or tend to public good; others of them most immediately to respect self, or tend to private good: as the former are not benevolence, so the latter are not self-love: neither sort are instances of our love either to ourselves or others; . . .

Thirdly, There is a principle of reflection in men, by which they distinguish between, approve, and disapprove their own actions. We are plainly constituted such sort of creatures as to reflect upon our own nature. The mind can take a view of what passes within itself, its propensions, aversions, passions, affections, as respecting such objects, and in such degrees; and of the several actions consequent thereupon. In this survey it approves of one, disapproves of another, and towards a third is affected in neither of these ways, but is quite indifferent. This principle in man, by which he approves or disapproves his heart, temper, and actions, is conscience; for this is the strict sense of the word, though sometimes it is used so as to take in more. And that this faculty tends to restrain men from doing mischief to each other, and leads them to do good, is too manifest to need being insisted upon. Thus a parent has the affection of love to his children: this leads him to take care of, to educate, to make due provision for them: the natural affection leads to this; but the reflection that it is his proper business, what belongs to him, that it is right and commendable so to do, this added to the affection becomes a much more settled principle, and carries him on through more labour and difficulties for the sake of his children, then he would undergo from that affection alone, if he thought it, and the course of action it led to, either indifferent or criminal. This indeed is impossible, to do that which is good and not to approve of it; for which reason they are frequently not considered as distinct, though they really are; for men often approve of the actions of others, which they will not imitate, and likewise do that which they approve not. It cannot possibly be denied that there is this principle of reflection or conscience in human nature. Suppose a man to relieve an innocent person in great distress; suppose the same man afterwards, in the fury of anger, to do the greatest mischief to a person who had given no just cause of offence; to aggravate the injury, add the circumstances of former friendship, and obligation from the injured person; let the man who is supposed to have done these two different actions, coolly reflect upon them afterwards, without regard to their consequences to himself: to assert that any common man would be affected in the same way towards these different actions, that he would make no distinction between them, but approve or disapprove them equally, is too glaring a falsity to need being confuted. There is therefore this principle of reflection or conscience in mankind. It is needless to compare the respect it has to private good, with the respect it has to public; since it plainly tends as much to the latter as to the former, and is commonly thought to tend chiefly to the latter. This faculty is now mentioned merely as another part of the inward frame of man, pointing out to us in some degree what we are intended for, and as what will naturally and of course have some influence. The particular place assigned to it by nature, what authority it has, and how great influence it ought to have, shall be hereafter considered.

From this comparison of benevolence and self-love, of our public and private affections, of the courses of life they lead to, and of the principle of reflection or conscience as respecting each of them, it is as manifest, that *we were made for society, and to promote the happiness of it, as that we were intended to take care of our own life, and health, and private good.* . . .

The sum of the whole is plainly this. The nature of man considered in his single capacity, and with respect only to the present world, is adapted and leads him to attain the greatest happiness he can for himself in the present world. The nature of man considered in his public or social capacity leads him to a right behaviour in society, to that course of life which we call virtue. Men follow or obey their nature in both these capacities and respects to a certain degree but not entirely: their actions do not come up to the whole of what their nature leads them to in either of these capacities or respects: and they often violate their nature in both, *i.e.,* as they neglect the duties they owe to their fellow-creatures, to which their nature leads them; and are injurious, to which their nature is abhorrent; so there is a manifest negligence in men of their real happiness or interest in the present world, when that interest is inconsistent with a present gratification; for the sake of which they negligently, nay, even knowingly, are the authors and instruments of their own misery and ruin. Thus they are as often unjust to themselves as to others, and for the most part are equally so to both by the same actions. . . .

SERMON XI: UPON THE LOVE OF OUR NEIGHBOUR

Every man hath a general desire of his own happiness; and likewise a variety of particular affections, passions, and appetites, to particular external objects. The former proceeds from, or is, self-love, and seems inseparable from all sensible creatures, who can reflect upon themselves and their own interest or happiness, so as to have that interest an object to their minds: what is to be said of the latter is, that they proceed from, or together make up, that particular nature, according to which man is made. The object the former pursues is somewhat internal, our own happiness, enjoyment, satisfaction; whether we have or have not a distinct particular perception what it is, or wherein it consists: the objects of the latter are this or that particular external thing, which the affections tend towards, and of which it hath always a particular idea or perception. The principle we call self-love never seeks anything external for the sake of the thing, but only as a means of happiness or good: particular affections rest in the external things themselves. One belongs to man as a reasonable creature reflecting upon his own interest or happiness; the other, though quite distinct from reason, is as much a part of human nature.

That all particular appetites and passions are towards *external things themselves,* distinct from the *pleasure arising from them,* is manifested from hence, that there could not be this pleasure, were it not for that prior suitableness between the object and the passion: there could be no enjoyment or delight for one thing more than another, from eating food more than from swallowing a stone, if there were not an affection or appetite to one thing more than another.

Every particular affection, even the love of our neighbour, is as really our own affection, as self-love; and the pleasure arising from its gratification is as much my own pleasure, as the pleasure self-love would have from knowing I myself should be happy some time hence, would be my own pleasure. And if, because every particular affection is a man's own, and the pleasure arising from its gratification his own pleasure, or pleasure to himself, such particular affection must be called self-love. According to this way of speaking, no creature whatever can possibly act merely from self-love; and every action and every affection whatever is to be resolved up into this one principle. But then this is not the language of mankind: or, if it were, we should want words to express the difference between the principle of an action, proceeding from cool consideration that it will be to my own advantage; and an action, suppose of revenge, or of friendship by which a man runs upon certain ruin, to do evil or good to another. It is manifest the principles of these actions are totally different, and so want different words to be distinguished by: all that they agree in is, that they both proceed from, and are done to gratify an inclination in a man's self. But the principle or inclination in one case is self-love; in the other, hatred, or love of another. There is then a distinction between the cool principle of self-love, or general desire of our own happiness, as one part of our nature, and one principle of action; and the particular affections towards particular external objects, as another principle of action. How much soever, therefore, is to be allowed to self-love, yet it cannot be allowed to be the whole of our inward constitution; because, you see, there are other parts or principles which come into it.

Further, private happiness or good is all which self-love can make us desire or be concerned about. In having this consists its gratification; it is an affection to ourselves—a regard to our own interest, happiness, and private good: and in the proportion a man hath this, he is interested, or a lover of himself. Let this be kept in mind, because there is commonly, as I shall presently have occasion to observe, another sense put upon these words. On the other hand, particular affections tend towards particular external things; these are their objects; having these is their end; in this consists their gratification: no matter whether it be, or be not, upon the whole, our interest or happiness. An action, done from the former of these principles, is called an interested action. An action, proceeding from any of the latter, has its denomination of passionate, ambitious, friendly, revengeful, or any other, from the particular appetite or affection from which it proceeds. Thus self-love, as one part of human nature, and the several particular principles as the other part, are themselves, their objects, and ends, stated and shown.

From hence it will be easy to see how far, and in what ways, each of these can contribute and be subservient to the private good of the individual. Happiness does not consist in self-love. The desire of happiness is no more the thing itself, than the desire of riches is the possession or enjoyment of them. People may love themselves with the most entire and unbounded affection, and yet be extremely miserable. Neither can self-love any way help them out, but by setting them on work to get rid of the causes of their misery, to gain or make use of those objects which are by nature adapted to afford satisfaction. Happiness or satisfaction consists only in the enjoyment of those objects which are by nature suited to our several particular appetites, passions, and affections. So that if self-love wholly engrosses us, and leaves no room for any other principle, there can be absolutely no such thing at all as happiness or enjoyment of any kind whatever; since happiness consists in the gratification of particular passions, which supposes the having of them. Self-love then does not constitute *this* or *that* to be our interest or good; but our interest or good being constituted by nature and supposed self-love, only puts us upon obtaining and securing it. Therefore, if it be possible that self-love may prevail and exert itself in a degree or manner which is not subservient to this end, then it will not follow that our interest will be promoted in proportion to the degree in which that principle engrosses us, and prevails over others. Nay, further, the private and contracted affection, when it is not subservient to this end, private good, may, for anything that appears, have a direct contrary tendency and effect. And if we will consider the matter, we shall see that it often really has. Disengagement is absolutely necessary to enjoyment; and a person may have so steady and fixed an eye upon his own interest, whatever he places it in, as may hinder him from attending to many gratifications within his reach, which others have their minds free and open to. Overfondness for a child is not generally thought to be for its advantage; and, if there be any guess to be from appearances, surely that character we call *selfish* is not the most promising for happiness. Such a temper may plainly be, and exert itself in a degree and manner which may give unnecessary and useless solicitude and anxiety, in a degree and manner which may prevent obtaining the means and materials of enjoyment, as well as the making use of them. Immoderate self-love does very ill consult its own interest; and how much soever a paradox it may appear, it is certainly true, that, even from self-love, we should endeavour to get over all inordinate regard to, and consideration of, ourselves. Every one of our passions and affections hath its natural stint and bound, which may easily be exceeded; whereas our enjoyments can possibly be but in a determinate measure and degree. Therefore such excess of the affection, since it cannot procure any enjoyment, must in all cases be useless, but is generally attended with inconveniences, and often is down-right pain and misery. This holds as much with regard to self-love as to all other affections. The natural degree of it, so far as it sets us on work to gain and make use of the materials of satisfaction, may be to our real advantage; but beyond or beside this, it is in several respects an inconvenience and disadvantage. Thus it appears that private interest is so far from being likely to be promoted in proportion to the degree in which self-love engrosses us, and prevails over all other principles, that *the contracted affection may be so prevalent as to disappoint itself and even contradict its own end, private good.* . . .

Self-love and interestedness was stated to consist in or be an affection to ourselves, a regard to our own private good: it is, therefore, distinct from benevolence, which is an affection to the good of our fellow-creatures. But that benevolence is distinct from, that is, not the same thing with self-love, is no reason for its being looked upon with any peculiar suspicion, because every principle whatever, by means of which self-love is gratified, is distinct from it. And all things, which are distinct from each other, are equally so. A man has an affection or aversion to another: that one of these tends to, and is gratified by doing good, that the other tends to, and is gratified by doing harm, does not in the least alter the respect which either one or the other of these inward feelings has to self-love.

. . . Thus the principles, from which men rush upon certain ruin for the destruction of an enemy, and for the preservation of a friend, have the same respect to the private affection, are equally interested, or equally disinterested: and it is of no avail, whether they are said to be one or the other. Therefore, to those who are shocked to hear virtue spoken of as disinterested, it may be allowed, that it is indeed absurd to speak thus of it; unless hatred, several particular instances of vice, and all the common affections and aversions in mankind, are acknowledged to be disinterested too. . . . Is desire of, and delight in the happiness of another any more a diminution of self-love, than desire of and delight in the esteem of another? They are both equally desire of and delight in somewhat external to ourselves: either both or neither are so. The object of self-love is expressed in the term self: and every appetite of sense, and every particular affection of the heart, are equally interested or disinterested, because the objects of them all are equally self or somewhat else. . . .

Thus it appears, that there is no peculiar contrariety between self-love and benevolence;

no greater competition between these, than between any other particular affections and self-love. . . .

The short of the matter is no more than this. Happiness consists in the gratification of certain affections, appetites, passions, with objects which are by nature adapted to them. Self-love may indeed set us on work to gratify these: but happiness or enjoyment has no immediate connexion with self-love, but arises from such gratification alone. Love of our neighbour is one of those affections. This, considered as a virtuous principle, is gratified by a consciousness of endeavouring to promote the good of others: but considered as a natural affection, its gratification consists in the actual accomplishment of this endeavour. Now, indulgence or gratification of this affection, whether in that consciousness, or this accomplishment, has the same respect to interest, as indulgence of any other affection; they equally proceed from, or do not proceed from, self-love: they equally include or equally exclude, this principle. Thus it appears, that "benevolence and the pursuit of public good have at least as great respect to self-love and the pursuit of private good, as any other particular passions, and their respective pursuits."

. . . There is indeed frequently an inconsistence, or interfering between self-love or private interest, and the several particular appetites, passions, affections, or the pursuits they lead to. But this competition or interfering is merely accidental, and happens much oftener between pride, revenge, sensual gratifications, and private interest, than between private interest and benevolence. For nothing is more common than to see men give themselves up to a passion or an affection to their known prejudice and ruin, and in direct contradiction to manifest and real interest, and the loudest calls of self-love: whereas the seeming competitions and interfering between benevolence and private interest, relate much more to the materials or means of enjoyment, than to enjoyment itself.

Richard Dawkins
The Selfish Gene

Richard Dawkins *is a British biologist and the author of* The Selfish Gene, *an excerpt from which is reproduced here.*

This chapter is mostly about the much-misunderstood topic of agression. We shall continue to treat the individual as a selfish machine, programmed to do whatever is best for his genes as a whole. This is the language of convenience. At the end of the chapter we return to the language of single genes.

To a survival machine, another survival machine (which is not its own child or another close relative) is a part of its environment, like a rock or a river or a lump of food. It is something that gets in the way, or something that can be exploited. It differs from a rock or a river in one important respect: it is inclined to hit back. This is because it too is a machine which holds its immortal genes in trust for the future, and it too will stop at nothing to preserve them. Natural selection favours genes which control their survival machines in such a way that they make the best use of their environment. This includes making the best use of other survival machines, both of the same and of different species.

In some cases survival machines seem to impinge rather little on each others' lives. For instance moles and blackbirds do not eat each other, mate with each other, or compete with each other for living space. Even so, we must not treat them as completely insulated. They may compete for something, perhaps earthworms. This does not mean you will ever see a mole and a blackbird engaged in a tug of war over a worm; indeed a blackbird may never set eyes on a mole in its life. But if you wiped out the population of moles, the effect on blackbirds might be dramatic, although I could not hazard a guess as to what the details might be, nor by what tortuously indirect routes the influence might travel.

Survival machines of different species influence each other in a variety of ways. They may be predators or prey, parasites or hosts, competitors for some scarce resource. They may be exploited in special ways, as for instance when bees are used as pollen carriers by flowers.

Survival machines of the same species tend to impinge on each others' lives more directly. This is for many reasons. One is that half the population of one's own species may be potential mates, and potentially hard-working and exploitable parents to one's children. Another reason is that members of the same species, being very similar to each other, being machines for preserving genes in the same kind of place, with the same kind of way of life, are particularly direct competitors for all the resources necessary for life. To a blackbird, a mole may be a competitor, but it is not nearly so important a competitor as another blackbird. Moles and blackbirds may compete for worms, but blackbirds and blackbirds compete with each other for worms *and* for everything else. If they are members of the same sex, they may also compete for mating partners. For reasons which we shall see, it is usually the males who compete with each other for females. This means that a male might benefit his own genes if he does something detrimental to another male with whom he is competing.

The logical policy for a survival machine might therefore seem to be to murder its rivals, and then, preferably, to eat them. Although murder and cannibalism do occur in nature, they are not as common as a naive interpretation of the selfish gene theory might predict. Indeed Konrad Lorenz, in *On Aggression,* stresses the restrained and gentlemanly nature of animal fighting. For him the notable thing about animal fights is that they are formal tournaments, played according to rules like those of boxing or fencing. Animals fight with gloved fists and blunted foils. Threat and bluff take the place of deadly earnest. Gestures of surrender are recognized by victors, who then refrain from dealing the killing blow or bite which our naive theory might predict.

This interpretation of animal aggression as being restrained and formal can be disputed. In particular, it is certainly wrong to condemn poor old *Homo sapiens* as the only species to kill his own kind, the only inheritor of the mark of Cain, and similar melodramatic charges. Whether a naturalist stresses the violence or the restraint of animal aggression depends partly on the kinds of animals he is used to watching, and partly on his evolutionary preconceptions—Lorenz is, after all, a 'good of the species' man. Even it it has been exaggerated, the gloved fist view of animal fights seems to have at least some truth. Superficially this looks like a form of altruism. The selfish gene theory must face up to the difficult task of explaining it. Why is it that animals do not go all out to kill rival members of their species at every possible opportunity?

The general answer to this is that there are costs as well as benefits resulting from outright pugnacity, and not only the obvious costs in time and energy. For instance, suppose that B and C are both my rivals, and I happen to meet B. It might seem sensible for me as a selfish individual to try to kill him. But wait. C is also my rival, and C is also B's rival. By killing B, I am potentially doing a good turn to C by removing one of his rivals. I might have done better to let B live, because he might then have competed or fought with C, thereby benefiting me indirectly. The moral of this simple hypothetical example is that there is no obvious merit in indiscriminately trying to kill rivals. In a large and complex system of rivalries, removing one rival from the scene does not necessarily do any good: other rivals may be more likely to benefit from his death than oneself. This is the kind of hard lesson that has been learned by pest-control officers. You have a serious agricultural pest, you discover a good way to exterminate it and you gleefully do so, only to find that another pest benefits from the extermination even more than human agriculture does, and you end up worse off than you were before.

On the other hand, it might seem a good plan to kill, or at least fight with, certain particular rivals in a discriminating way. If B is an elephant seal in possession of a large harem full of females, and if I, another elephant seal, can acquire his harem by killing him, I might be well advised to attempt to do so. But there are costs and risks even in selectivity pugnacity. It is to B's advantage to fight back, to defend his valuable property. If I start a fight, I am just as likely to end up dead as he is. Perhaps even more so. He holds a valuable resource, that is why I want to fight him. But why does he hold it? Perhaps he won it in combat. He has probably beaten off other challengers before me. He is probably a good fighter. Even if I win the fight and gain the harem, I may be so badly mauled in the process that I cannot enjoy the benefits. Also, fighting uses up time and energy. These might be better conserved for the time being. If I concentrate on feeding and on keeping out of trouble for a time, I shall grow bigger and stronger. I'll fight him for the harem in the end, but I may have a better chance of winning eventually if I wait, rather than rush in now.

This subjective soliloquy is just a way of pointing out that the decision whether or not to fight should ideally be preceded by a complex, if unconscious, 'cost–benefit' calculation. The potential benefits are not all stacked up on the side of fighting, although undoubtedly some of them are. Similarly, during a fight, each tactical decision over whether to escalate the fight or cool it has costs and benefits which could, in principle, be analysed. This has long been realized by ethologists in a vague sort of way, but it has taken J. Maynard Smith, not normally regarded as an ethologist, to express the idea forcefully and clearly. In collaboration with G. R. Price and G. A. Parker, he uses the branch of mathematics known as Game Theory. Their elegant ideas can be expressed in words without mathematical symbols, albeit at some cost in rigour.

The essential concept Maynard Smith introduces is that of the *evolutionarily stable strategy*, an idea which he traces back to W. D. Hamilton and R. H. MacArthur. A 'strategy' is a pre-programmed behavioural policy. An example of a strategy is: 'Attack opponent; if he flees pursue him; if he retaliates run away.' It is important to realize that we are not thinking of the strategy as being consciously worked out by the individual. Remember that we are picturing the animal as a robot survival machine with a pre-programmed computer controlling the muscles. To write the strategy out as a set of simple instructions in English is just a convenient way for us to think about it. By some unspecified mechanism, the animal behaves as if he were following these instructions.

An evolutionarily stable strategy or ESS is defined as a strategy which, if most members of a population adopt it, cannot be bettered by an alternative strategy. It is a subtle and important idea. Another way of putting it is to say that the best strategy for an individual depends on what the majority of the population are doing. Since the rest of the population consists of individuals, each one trying to maximize his *own* success, the only strategy that persists will be one which, once evolved, cannot be bettered by any deviant individual. Following a major environmental change there may be a brief period of evolutionary instability, perhaps even oscillation in the population. But once an ESS is achieved it will stay: selection will penalize deviation from it.

To apply this idea to aggression, consider one of Maynard Smith's simplest hypothetical cases. Suppose that there are only two sorts of fighting strategy in a population of a particular species, named *hawk* and *dove*. (The names refer to conventional human usage and have no connection with the habits of the birds from whom the names are derived: doves are in fact rather aggressive birds.) Any individual of our hypothetical population is classified as a hawk or a dove. Hawks always fight as hard and as unrestrainedly as they can, retreating only when seriously injured. Doves merely threaten in a dignified conventional way, never hurting anybody. If a hawk fights a dove the dove quickly runs away, and so does not get hurt. If a hawk fights a hawk they go on until one of them is seriously injured or dead. If a dove meets a dove nobody gets hurt; they go on posturing at each other for a long time until one of them tires or decides not to bother any more, and therefore backs down. For the time being, we assume that there is no way in which an individual can tell, in advance, whether a particular rival is a hawk or a dove. He only discovers this by fighting him, and he has no memory of past fights with particular individuals to guide him.

Stephen Jay Gould

So Cleverly Kind an Animal

Stephen Jay Gould *is a professor of paleontology at Harvard University and the author of a great many scientific and popular articles and books on evolution, including* The Panda's Thumb. *The following essay is taken from his monthly column in* Natural History *magazine.*

In *Civilization and Its Discontents,* Sigmund Freud examined the agonizing dilemma of human social life. We are by nature selfish and aggressive, yet any successful civilization demands that we suppress our biological inclinations and act altruistically for common good and harmony. Freud argued further that as civilizations become increasingly complex and "modern," we must renounce more and more of our innate selves. This we do imperfectly, with guilt, pain, and hardship; the price of civilization is individual suffering.

> It is impossible to overlook the extent to which civilization is built up upon a renunciation of instinct, how much it presupposes precisely the nonsatisfaction . . . of powerful instincts. This "cultural frustration" dominates the large field of social relationships between human beings.

Freud's argument is a particularly forceful variation on a ubiquitous theme in speculations about "human nature." What we criticize in ourselves, we attribute to our animal past. These are the shackles of our apish ancestry—brutality, aggression, selfishness; in short, general nastiness. What we prize and strive for (with pitifully limited success), we consider as a unique overlay, conceived by our rationality and imposed upon an unwilling body. Our hopes for a better future lie in reason and kindness—the mental transcendence of our biological limitations. "Build thee more stately mansions, O my soul."

Little more than ancient prejudice supports this common belief. It certainly gains no justification from science—so profound is our ignorance about the biology of human behavior. It arises from such sources as the theology of the human soul and the "dualism" of philosophers who sought separate realms for mind and body. It has roots in an attitude that I attack in several of these essays: our desire to view the history of life as progressive and to place ourselves on top of the heap (with all the prerogatives of domination). We seek a criterion for our uniqueness, settle (naturally) upon our minds, and define the noble results of human consciousness as something intrinsically apart from biology. But why? Why should our nastiness be the baggage of an apish past and our kindness uniquely human? Why should we not seek continuity with other animals for our "noble" traits as well?

One nagging scientific argument does seem to support this ancient prejudice. The essential ingredient of human kindness is altruism—sacrifice of our personal comfort, even our lives in extreme cases, for the benefit of others. Yet, if we accept the Darwinian mechanism of evolution, how can altruism be part of biology? Natural selection dictates that organisms act in their own self-interest. They know nothing of such abstract concepts as "the good of the species." They "struggle" continuously to increase the representation of their genes at the expense of their fellows. And that, for all its baldness, is all there is to it; we have discovered no higher principle in nature. Individual advantage, Darwin argues, is the only criterion of success in nature. The harmony of life goes no deeper. The balance of nature arises from interaction between competing teams, each trying to win the prize for itself alone, not from the cooperative sharing of limited resources.

How, then, could anything but selfishness ever evolve as a biological trait of behavior? If altruism is the cement of stable societies, then human society must be fundamentally outside nature. There is one way around this dilemma. Can an apparently altruistic act be "selfish" in this Darwinian sense? Can an individual's sacrifice ever lead to the perpetuation of his own genes? The answer to this seemingly contradictory proposition is "yes." We owe the resolution of this paradox to the theory of "kin selection" developed in the early 1960s by W. D. Hamilton, a British theoretical biologist. It has been stressed as the cornerstone for a biological theory of society in E. O. Wilson's *Sociobiology*. (I criticized the deterministic aspects of Wilson's speculations on human behavior in the last essay. I also praised his general theory of altruism, and continue this theme now.)

The legacy of brilliant men includes undeveloped foresight. English biologist J. B. S. Haldane probably anticipated every good idea that evolutionary theorists will invent during this century. Haldane, arguing about altruism one evening in a pub, reportedly made some quick calculations on the back of an envelope, and announced: "I will lay down my life for two brothers or eight cousins." What did Haldane mean by such a cryptic comment? Human chromosomes come in pairs: We receive one set from our mother's egg; the other from our father's sperm. Thus, we possess a paternal and a maternal copy of each gene (this is not true among males for genes located on sex chromosomes, since the maternal X chromosome is so much longer—i.e. has so many more genes—than the paternal Y chromosome; most genes on the X chromosome have no corresponding copy on the short Y). Take any human gene. What is the probability that a brother will share the same gene? Suppose that it is on a maternal chromosome (the argument works the same way for paternal chromosomes). Each egg cell contains one chromosome of each pair—that is, one half the mother's genes. The egg cell that made your brother either had the same chromosome you received or the other member of the pair. The chance that you share your brother's gene is an even fifty-fifty. Your brother shares half your genes and is, in the Darwinian calculus, the same as half of you.

Suppose, then, that you are walking down the road with three brothers. A monster approaches with clearly murderous intent. Your brothers do not see it. You have only two alternatives: Approach it and give a rousing Bronx cheer, thereby warning your brothers, who hide and escape, and insuring your own demise; or hide and watch the monster feast on your three brothers. What, as an accomplished player of the Darwinian game, should you do? The answer must be, step right up and cheer—for you have only yourself to lose, while your three brothers represent one and a half of you. Better that they should live to propagate 150 percent of your genes. Your apparently altruistic act is genetically "selfish," for it maximizes the contribution of your genes to the next generation.

According to the theory of kin selection, animals evolve behaviors that endanger or sacrifice themselves only if such altruistic acts increase their own genetic potential by bene-fiting kin. Altruism and the society of kin must go hand in hand; the benefits of kin selection may even propel the evolution of social interaction. While my absurd example of four brothers and a monster is simplistic, the situation becomes much more complex with twelfth cousins, four times removed. Hamilton's theory does not only belabor the obvious.

Hamilton's theory has had stunning success in explaining some persistent biological puzzles in the evolution of social behavior in the Hymenoptera—ants, bees, and wasps. Why has true sociality evolved independently at least eleven times in the Hymenoptera and only once among other insects (the termites)? Why are sterile worker castes always female in the Hymenoptera, but both male and female in termites? The answers seem to lie in the workings of kin selection within the unusual genetic system of the Hymenoptera.

Most sexually reproducing animals are diploid; their cells contain two sets of chromosomes—one derived from their mother, the other from their father. Termites, like most insects, are diploid. The social Hymenoptera, on the other hand, are haplodiploid. Females develop from fertilized eggs as normal diploid individuals with maternal and paternal sets of chromosomes. But males develop from unfertilized eggs and possess only the maternal set of chromosomes; they are, in technical parlance, haploid (half the normal number of chromosomes).

In diploid organisms, genetic relationships of sibs and parents are symmetrical: parents share half their genes with their children, and each sib (on average) shares half its genes with any other sib, male or female. But in haplodiploid species, genetic relationships are asymmetrical, permitting kin selection to work in an unusual and potent way. Consider the relationship of a queen ant to her sons and daughters, and the relationship of these daughters to their sisters and brothers:

1. The queen is related by 1/2 to both her sons and daughters; each of her offspring carries 1/2 her chromosomes and, therefore, 1/2 her genes.
2. Sisters are related to their brothers, not by 1/2 as in diploid organisms, but only by 1/4. Take any of a sister's genes. Chances are 1/2 that it is a paternal gene. If so, she cannot share it with her brother (who has no paternal genes). If it is a maternal gene, then chances are 1/2 that her brother has it as well. Her total relationship with her brother is the average of zero (for paternal genes) and 1/2 (for maternal genes), or 1/4.
3. Sisters are related to their sisters by 3/4. Again, take any gene. If it is paternal, then her sister must share it (since fathers have only one set of chromosomes to pass to all daughters). If it is maternal, then her sister has a fifty-fifty chance of sharing it, as before. Sisters are related by the average of 1 (for paternal genes) and 1/2 (for maternal genes), or 3/4.

These asymmetries seem to provide a simple and elegant explanation for that most altruistic of animal behaviors—the "willingness" of sterile female workers to forego their own reproduction in order to help their mothers raise more sisters. As long as a worker can invest preferentially in her sisters, she will perpetuate more of her genes by helping her mother raise fertile sisters (3/4 relationship) than by raising fertile daughters herself (1/2 relationship). But a male has no inclination toward sterility and labor. He would much rather raise daughters, who share all his genes, than help sisters, who share only 1/2 of them. (I do not mean to attribute conscious will to creatures with such rudimentary brains. I use such phrases as "he would rather" only as a convenient shortcut for "in the course of evolution, males who did not behave this way have been placed at a selective disadvantage and gradually eliminated.")

My colleagues R. L. Trivers and H. Hare have recently reported the following important discovery in *Science* (January 23, 1976): they argue that queens and workers should prefer different sex ratios for fertile offspring. The queen favors a 1:1 ratio of males to females since she is equally related (by 1/2) to her sons and daughters. But the workers raise the offspring and can impose their preferences upon the queen by selective nurturing of her eggs. Workers would rather raise fertile sisters (relationship 3/4) than brothers (relationship 1/4). But they must raise some brothers, lest their sisters fail to find mates. So they compromise by favoring sisters to the extent of their stronger relationship to them. Since they are three times more related to sisters than brothers, they should invest three times more energy in raising sisters. Workers invest energy by feeding; the extent of feeding is reflected in the adult weight of fertile offspring. Trivers and Hare therefore measured the ratio of female/male weight for all fertile offspring taken together in nests of 21 different ant species. The average weight ratio— or investment ratio—is remarkably close to 3:1. This is impressive enough, but the clincher in the argument comes from studies of slave-making ants. Here, the workers are captured members of other species. They have no genetic relationship to the daughters of their imposed queen and should not favor them over the queen's sons. Sure enough, in these situations, the female/male weight ratio is 1:1—even though it is again 3:1 when workers of the enslaved species are not captured but work, instead, for their own queen.

Kin selection, operating on the peculiar genetics of haplodiploidy, seems to explain the key features of social behavior in ants, bees, and wasps. But what can it do for us? How can it help us understand the contradictory amalgam of impulses toward selfishness and altruism that form our own personalities. I am willing to admit—and this is only my intuition, since we have no facts to constrain us—that it probably resolves Freud's dilemma of the first paragraph. Our selfish and aggressive urges may have evolved by the Darwinian route of individual advantage, but our altruistic tendencies need not represent a unique overlay imposed by the demands of civilization. These tendencies may have arisen by the same Darwinian route via kin selection. Basic human kindness may be as "animal" as human nastiness.

But here I stop—short of any deterministic speculation that attributes *specific* behaviors to the possession of specific altruist or opportunist genes. Our genetic makeup permits a wide range of behaviors—from Ebenezer Scrooge before to Ebenezer Scrooge after. I do not believe that the miser hoards through opportunist genes or that the philanthropist gives because nature endowed him with more than the normal complement of altruist genes. Upbringing, culture, class, status, and all the intangibles that we call "free will," determine how we restrict our behaviors from the wide spectrum—extreme altruism to extreme selfishness—that our genes permit.

As an example of deterministic speculations based on altruism and kin selection, E. O. Wilson has proposed a genetic explanation of homosexuality (*New York Times Magazine,* October 12, 1975). Since exclusive homosexuals do not bear children, how could a homosexuality gene ever be selected in a Darwinian world? Suppose that our ancestors organized socially as small, competing groups of very close kin. Some groups contained only heterosexual members. Others included homosexuals who functioned as "helpers" in hunting or child rearing: they bore no children but they helped kin to raise their close genetic relatives. If groups with homosexual helpers prevailed in competition over exclusively heterosexual groups, then homosexuality genes would have been maintained by kin selection. There is nothing illogical in this proposal, but it has no facts going for it either. We have identified no homosexuality gene, and we know nothing relevant to this hypothesis about the social organization of our ancestors.

Wilson's intent is admirable; he attempts to affirm the intrinsic dignity of a common and much maligned sexual behavior by arguing that it is natural for some people—and adaptive to boot (at least under an ancestral form of social organization). But the strategy is a dangerous one, for it backfires if the genetic speculation is wrong. If you defend a behavior by arguing that people are programmed directly for it, then how do you continue to defend it if your speculation is wrong, for the behavior then becomes unnatural and worthy of condemnation. Better to stick resolutely to a philosophical position on human liberty: what free adults do with each other in their own private lives is their business alone. It need not be vindicated—and must not be condemned—by genetic speculation.

Although I worry long and hard about the deterministic uses of kin selection, I applaud the insight it offers for my favored theme of biological potentiality. For it extends the realm of genetic potential even further by including the capacity for kindness, once viewed as intrinsically unique to human culture. Sigmund Freud argued that the history of our greatest scientific insights has reflected, ironically, a continuous retreat of our species from center stage in the cosmos. Before Copernicus and Newton, we thought we lived at the hub of the universe. Before Darwin, we thought that a benevolent God had created us. Before Freud, we imagined ourselves as rational creatures (surely one of the least modest statements in intellectual history). If kin selection marks another stage in this retreat, it will serve us well by nudging our thinking away from domination and toward a perception of respect and unity with other animals.

Ayn Rand
The Virtue of Selfishness

Ayn Rand *was immensely popular in the 1950s for her novels* The Fountainhead *and* Atlas Shrugged, *in which she argues for individualism and "the virtue of selfishness" against the reigning ethic of "altruism" and mutual cooperation.*

In popular usage, the word "selfishness" is a synonym of evil; the image it conjures is of a murderous brute who tramples over piles of corpses to achieve his own ends, who cares for no living being and pursues nothing but the gratification of the mindless whims of any immediate moment.

Yet the exact meaning and dictionary definition of the word "selfishness" is: *concern with one's own interests.*

This concept does *not* include a moral evaluation; it does not tell us whether concern with one's own interests is good or evil; nor does it tell us what constitutes man's actual interests. It is the task of ethics to answer such questions.

The ethics of altruism has created the image of the brute, as its answer, in order to make men accept two inhuman tenets: (a) that any concern with one's own interests is evil, regardless of what these interests might be, and (b) that the brute's activities are *in fact* to one's own interest (which altruism enjoins man to renounce for the sake of his neighbors).

For a view of the nature of altruism, its consequences and the enormity of the moral corruption it perpetrates, I shall refer you to *Atlas Shrugged*—or to any of today's newspaper headlines. What concerns us here is altruism's *default* in the field of ethical theory.

There are two moral questions which altruism lumps together into one "package-deal": (1) What are values? (2) Who should be the beneficiary of values? Altruism substitutes the second for the first; it evades the task of defining a code of moral values, thus leaving man, in fact, without moral guidance.

Altruism declares that any action taken for the benefit of others is good, and any action taken for one's own benefit is evil. Thus the *beneficiary* of an action is the only criterion of moral value—and so long as that beneficiary is anybody other than oneself, anything goes.

Hence the appalling immorality, the chronic injustice, the grotesque double standards, the insoluble conflicts and contradictions that have characterized human relationships and human societies throughout history, under all the variants of the altruist ethics.

Observe the indecency of what passes for moral judgments today. An industrialist who produces a fortune, and a gangster who robs a bank are regarded as equally immoral, since they both sought wealth for their own "selfish" benefit. A young man who gives up his career in order to support his parents and never rises beyond the rank of grocery clerk is regarded as morally superior to the young man who endures an excruciating struggle and achieves his personal ambition. A dictator is regarded as moral, since the unspeakable atrocities he committed were intended to benefit "the people," not himself.

Observe what this beneficiary-criterion of morality does to a man's life. The first thing he learns is that morality is his enemy: he has nothing to gain from it, he can only lose; self-inflicted loss, self-inflicted pain and the gray, debilitating pall of an incomprehensible duty is all that he can expect. He may hope that others might occasionally sacrifice themselves for his benefit, as he grudgingly sacrifices himself for theirs, but he knows that the relationship will bring mutual resentment, not pleasure—and that, morally, their pursuit of values will be like an exchange of unwanted, unchosen Christmas presents, which neither is morally permitted to buy for himself. Apart from such times as he manages to perform some act of self-sacrifice, he possesses no moral significance: morality takes no cognizance of him and has nothing to say to him for guidance in the crucial issues of his life; it is only his own personal, private, "selfish" life and, as such, it is regarded either as evil or, at best, *amoral*.

Since nature does not provide man with an automatic form of survival, since he has to support his life by his own effort, the doctrine that concern with one's own interests is evil means that man's desire to live is evil—that man's life, as such, is evil. No doctrine could be more evil than that.

Yet that is the meaning of altruism, implicit in such examples as the equation of an industrialist with a robber. There is a fundamental moral difference between a man who sees his self-interest in production and a man who sees it in robbery. The evil of a robber does *not* lie in the fact that he pursues his own interests, but in *what* he regards as to his own interest; *not* in the fact that he pursues his values, but in *what* he chose to value; *not* in the fact that he wants to live, but in the fact that he wants to live on a subhuman level (see "The Objectivist Ethics").

If it is true that what I mean by "selfishness" is not what is meant conventionally, then *this* is one of the worst indictments of altruism: it means that altruism *permits no concept* of a self-respecting, self-supporting man—a man who supports his life by his own effort and neither sacrifices himself nor others. It means that altruism permits no view of men except as sacrificial animals and profiteers-on-sacrifice, as victims and parasites—that it permits no concept of a benevolent co-existence among men—that it permits no concept of *justice*.

If you wonder about the reasons behind the ugly mixture of cynicism and guilt in which most men spend their lives, these are the reasons: cynicism, because they neither practice nor accept the altruist morality—guilt, because they dare not reject it.

To rebel against so devastating an evil, one has to rebel against its basic premise. To redeem both man and morality, it is the concept of *"selfishness"* that one has to redeem.

The first step is to assert *man's right to a moral existence*—that is: to recognize his need of a moral code to guide the course and the fulfillment of his own life.

For a brief outline of the nature and the validation of a rational morality, see my lecture on "The Objectivist Ethics" which follows. The reasons why man needs a moral code will tell you that the purpose of morality is to define man's proper values and interests, that *concern with his own interests* is the essence of a moral existence, and that *man must be the beneficiary of his own moral actions*.

Since all values have to be gained and/or kept by men's actions, any breach between actor and beneficiary necessitates an injustice: the sacrifice of some men to others, of the actors to the nonactors, of the moral to the immoral. Nothing could ever justify such a breach, and no one ever has.

The choice of the beneficiary of moral values is merely a preliminary or introductory issue in the field of morality. It is not a substitute for morality nor a criterion of moral value, as altruism has made it. Neither is it a moral *primary*: it has to be derived from and validated by the fundamental premises of a moral system.

The Objectivist ethics holds that the actor must always be the beneficiary of his action and that man must act for his own *rational* self-interest. But his right to do so is derived from his nature as man and from the function of moral values in human life—and, therefore, is applicable *only* in the context of a rational, objectively demonstrated and validated code of moral principles which define and determine his actual self-interest. It is not a license "to do as he pleases" and it is not applicable to the altruists' image of a "selfish" brute nor to any man motivated by irrational emotions, feelings, urges, wishes or whims.

This is said as a warning against the kind of "Nietzschean egoists" who, in fact, are a product of the altruist morality and represent the other side of the altruist coin: the men who believe that any action, regardless of its nature, is good if it is intended for one's own benefit. Just as the satisfaction of the irrational desires of others is *not* a criterion of moral value, neither is the satisfaction of one's own irrational desires. Morality is not a contest of whims.

A similar type of error is committed by the man who declares that since man must be guided by his own independent judgment, any action he chooses to take is moral if *he* chooses it. One's own independent judgment is the *means* by which one must choose one's actions, but it is not a moral criterion nor a moral validation: only reference to a demonstrable principle can validate one's choices.

Just as man cannot survive by any random means, but must discover and practice the principles which his survival requires, so man's self-interest cannot be determined by blind desires or random whims, but must be discovered and achieved by the guidance of rational principles. This is why the Objectivist ethics is a morality of *rational* self-interest—or of *rational selfishness*.

Since selfishness is "concern with one's own interests," the Objectivist ethics uses that concept in its exact and purest sense. It is not a concept that one can surrender to man's enemies, nor to the unthinking misconceptions, distortions, prejudices and fears of the ignorant and the irrational. The attack on "selfishness" is an attack on man's self-esteem; to surrender one, is to surrender the other.

Christopher Lasch
The Culture of Narcissism

Christopher Lasch *is a historian at the University of Rochester and a popular social critic. His book,* The Culture of Narcissism, *was a best-selling argument against our overly therapeutic and self-absorbed culture. An excerpt is included here.*

THE WANING OF THE SENSE OF HISTORICAL TIME

As the twentieth century approaches its end, the conviction grows that many other things are ending too. Storm warnings, portents, hints of catastrophe haunt our times. The "sense of an ending," which has given shape to so much of twentieth-century literature, now pervades the popular imagination as well. The Nazi holocaust, the threat of nuclear annihilation, the depletion of natural resources, well-founded predictions of ecological disaster have fulfilled poetic prophecy, giving concrete historical substance to the nightmare, or death wish, that avant-garde artists were the first to express. The question of whether the world will end in fire or in ice, with a bang or a whimper, no longer interests artists alone. Impending disaster has become an everyday concern, so commonplace and familiar that nobody any longer gives much thought to how disaster might be averted. People busy themselves instead with survival strategies, measures designed to prolong their own lives, or programs guaranteed to ensure good health and peace of mind.

Those who dig bomb shelters hope to survive by surrounding themselves with the latest products of modern technology. Communards in the country adhere to an opposite plan: to free themselves from dependence on technology and thus to outlive its destruction or collapse. A visitor to a commune in North Carolina writes: "Everyone seems to share this sense of imminent doomsday." Stewart Brand, editor of the *Whole Earth Catalogue,* reports that "sales of the *Survival Book* are booming; it's one of our fastest moving items." Both strategies reflect the growing despair of changing society, even of understanding it, which also underlies the cult of expanded consciousness, health, and personal "growth" so prevalent today.

After the political turmoil of the sixties, Americans have retreated to purely personal preoccupations. Having no hope of improving their lives in any of the ways that matter, people have convinced themselves that what matters is psychic self-improvement: getting in touch with their feelings, eating health food, taking lessons in ballet or belly-dancing, immersing themselves in the wisdom of the East, jogging, learning how to "relate," overcoming the "fear of pleasure." Harmless in themselves, these pursuits, elevated to a program and wrapped in the rhetoric of authenticity and awareness, signify a retreat from politics and a repudiation of the recent past. Indeed Americans seem to wish to forget not only the sixties, the riots, the new left, the disruptions on college campuses, Vietnam, Watergate, and the Nixon presidency, but their entire collective past, even in the antiseptic form in which it was celebrated during the Bicentennial. Woody Allen's movie *Sleeper,* issued in 1973, accurately caught the mood of the seventies. Appropriately cast in the form of a parody of futuristic science fiction, the film finds a great many ways to convey the message that "political solutions don't work," as Allen flatly announces at one point. When asked what he believes in, Allen, having ruled out politics, religion, and science, declares: "I believe in sex and death—two experiences that come once in a lifetime."

To live for the moment is the prevailing passion—to live for yourself, not for your predecessors or posterity. We are fast losing the sense of historical continuity, the sense of belonging to a succession of generations originating in the past and stretching into the future. It is the waning of the sense of historical time—in particular, the erosion of any strong concern for posterity—that distinguishes the spiritual crisis of the seventies from earlier outbreaks of millenarian religion, to which it bears a superficial resemblance. Many commentators have seized on this resemblance as a means of understanding the contemporary "cultural revolu- tion," ignoring the features that distinguish it from the religions of the past. A few years ago, Leslie Fiedler proclaimed a "New Age of Faith." More recently, Tom Wolfe has interpreted the new narcissism as a "third great awakening," an outbreak of orgiastic, ecstatic religiosity. Jim Hougan, in a book that seems to present itself simultaneously as a critique and a celebration of contemporary decadence, compares the current mood to the millennialism of the waning Middle Ages. "The anxieties of the Middle Ages are not much different from those of the present," he writes. Then as now, social upheaval gave rise to "millenarian sects."

Both Hougan and Wolfe inadvertently provide evidence, however, that undermines a religious interpretation of the "consciousness movement." Hougan notes that survival has become the "catchword of the seventies" and "collective narcissism" the dominant disposition.

Since "the society" has no future, it makes sense to live only for the moment, to fix our eyes on our own "private performance," to become connoisseurs of our own decadence, to cultivate a "transcendental self-attention." These are not the attitudes historically associated with millenarian outbreaks. Sixteenth-century Anabaptists awaited the apocalypse not with transcendental self-attention but with ill-concealed impatience for the golden age it was expected to inaugurate. Nor were they indifferent to the past. Ancient popular traditions of the "sleeping king"—the leader who will return to his people and restore a lost golden age—informed the millenarian movements of this period. The Revolutionary of the Upper Rhine, anonymous author of the *Book of a Hundred Chapters,* declared, "The Germans once held the whole world in their hands and they will do so again, and with more power than ever." He predicted that the resurrected Frederick II, "Emporer of the Last Days," would reinstate the primitive German religion, move the capital of Christendom from Rome to Trier, abolish private property, and level distinctions between rich and poor.

Such traditions, often associated with national resistance to foreign conquest, have flourished at many times and in many forms, including the Christian vision of the Last Judgment. Their egalitarian and pseudohistorical content suggests that even the most radically otherworldly religions of the past expressed a hope of social justice and a sense of continuity with earlier generations. The absence of these values characterizes the survivalist mentality of the seventies. The "world view emerging among us," writes Peter Marin, centers "solely on the self" and has "individual survival as its sole good." In an attempt to identify the peculiar features of contemporary religiosity, Tom Wolfe himself notes that "most people, historically, have *not* lived their lives as if thinking, 'I have only one life to live.' Instead they have lived as if they are living their ancestors' lives and their offspring's lives. . . ." These observations go very close to the heart of the matter, but they call into question his characterization of the new narcissism as a third great awakening.

THE THERAPEUTIC SENSIBILITY

The contemporary climate is therapeutic, not religious. People today hunger not for personal salvation, let alone for the restoration of an earlier golden age, but for the feeling, the momentary illusion, of personal well-being, health, and psychic security. Even the radicalism of the sixties served, for many of those who embraced it for personal rather than political reasons, not as a substitute religion but as a form of therapy. Radical politics filled empty lives, provided a sense of meaning and purpose. In her memoir of the Weathermen, Susan Stern described their attraction in language that owes more to psychiatry and medicine than to religion. When she tried to evoke her state of mind during the 1968 demonstrations at the Democratic National Convention in Chicago, she wrote instead about the state of her health. "I felt good. I could feel my body supple and strong and slim, and ready to run miles, and my legs moving sure and swift under me." A few pages later, she says: "I felt real." Repeatedly she explains that association with important people made her feel important. "I felt I was part of a vast network of intense, exciting and brilliant people." When the leaders she idealized disappointed her, as they always did, she looked for new heroes to take their place, hoping to warm herself in their "brilliance" and to overcome her feeling of insignificance. In their presence, she occasionally felt "strong and solid"—only to find herself repelled, when disenchantment set in again, by the "arrogance" of those whom she had previously admired, by "their contempt for everyone around them."

Many of the details in Stern's account of the Weathermen would be familiar to students of the revolutionary mentality in earlier epochs: the fervor of her revolutionary commitment, the group's endless disputes about fine points of political dogma, the relentless "self-criticism" to which members of the sect were constantly exhorted, the attempt to remodel every facet of one's life in conformity with the revolutionary faith. But every revolutionary movement partakes of the culture of its time, and this one contained elements that immediately identified it as a product of American society in an age of diminishing expectations. The atmosphere in which the Weathermen lived—an atmosphere of violence, danger, drugs, sexual promiscuity, moral and psychic chaos—derived not so much from an older revolutionary tradition as from the turmoil and narcissistic anguish of contemporary America. Her preoccupation with the state of her psychic health, together with her dependence on others for a sense of selfhood, distinguish Susan Stern from the kind of religious seeker who turns to politics to find a secularized salvation. She needed to establish an identity, not to submerge her identity in a larger cause. The narcissist differs also, in the tenuous quality of his selfhood, from an earlier type of American individualist, the "American Adam" analyzed by R. W. B. Lewis, Quentin Anderson, Michael Rogin, and by nineteenth-century observers like Tocqueville. The contemporary narcissist bears a superficial resemblance, in his self-absorption and delusions of grandeur, to the "imperial self" so often celebrated in nineteenth-century American literature. The American Adam, like his descendants today, sought to free himself from the past and to establish what Emerson called "an original relation to the universe." Nineteenth-century writers and orators restated again and again, in a great variety of forms, Jefferson's doctrine that the earth belongs to the living. The break with Europe, the abolition of primogeniture, and the looseness of family ties gave substance to their belief (even if it was finally an illusion) that Americans, alone among the people of the world, could escape the entangling influence of the past. They imagined, according to Tocqueville, that "their whole destiny is in their own hands." Social conditions in the United States, Tocqueville wrote, severed the tie that formerly united one generation to another. "The woof of time is every instant broken and the track of generations effaced. Those who went before are soon forgotten; of those who will come after, no one has any idea: the interest of man is confined to those in close propinquity to himself."

Some critics have described the narcissism of the 1970s in similar language. The new therapies spawned by the human potential movement, according to Peter Marin, teach that "the individual will is all powerful and totally determines one's fate"; thus they intensify the "isolation of the self." This line of argument belongs to a well-established American tradition of social thought. Marin's plea for recognition of "the immense middle ground of human community" recalls Van Wyck Brooks, who criticized the New England transcendentalists for ignoring "the genial middle ground of human tradition." Brooks himself, when he formulated his own indictment of American culture, drew on such earlier critics as Santayana, Henry James, Orestes Brownson, and Tocqueville. The critical tradition they established still has much to tell us about the evils of untrammeled individualism, but it needs to be restated to take account of the differences between nineteenth-century Adamism and the narcissism of our own time. The critique of "privatism," though it helps to keep alive the need for community, has become more and more misleading as the possibility of genuine privacy recedes. The contemporary American may have failed, like his predecessors, to establish any sort of common life, but the integrating tendencies of modern industrial society have at the same time undermined his "isolation." Having surrendered most of his technical skills to the corporation, he can no longer provide for his material needs. As the family loses not only its productive functions but many of its reproductive functions as well, men and women no longer manage even to raise their children without the help of certified experts. The atrophy of older traditions of self-help has eroded everyday competence, in one area after another, and has made the individual dependent on the state, the corporation, and other bureaucracies.

Narcissism represents the psychological dimension of this dependence. Notwithstanding his occasional illusions of omnipotence, the narcissist depends on others to validate his self-esteem. He cannot live without an admiring audience. His apparent freedom from family ties and institutional constraints does not free him to stand alone or to glory in his individuality. On the contrary, it contributes to his insecurity, which he can overcome only by seeing his "grandiose self" reflected in the attentions of others, or by attaching himself to those who radiate celebrity, power, and charisma. For the narcissist, the world is a mirror, whereas the rugged individualist saw it as an empty wilderness to be shaped to his own design. . . .

Today Americans are overcome not by the sense of endless possibility but by the banality of the social order they have erected against it. Having internalized the social restraints by means of which they formerly sought to keep possibility within civilized limits, they feel themselves overwhelmed by an annihilating boredom, like animals whose instincts have withered in captivity. A reversion to savagery threatens them so little that they long precisely for a more vigorous instinctual existence. People nowadays complain of an inability to feel. They cultivate more vivid experiences, seek to beat sluggish flesh to life, attempt to revive jaded appetites. They condemn the superego and exalt the lost life of the senses. Twentieth-century peoples have erected so many psychological barriers against strong emotion, and have invested those defenses with so much of the energy derived from forbidden impulse, that they can no longer remember what it feels like to be inundated by desire. They tend, rather, to be consumed with rage, which derives from defenses against desire and gives rise in turn to new defenses against rage itself. Outwardly bland, submissive, and sociable, they seethe with an inner anger for which a dense, over-populated, bureaucratic society can devise few legitimate outlets. . . .

Plagued by anxiety, depression, vague discontents, sense of inner emptiness, the "psychological man" of the twentieth century seeks neither individual self-aggrandizement nor spiritual transcendence but peace of mind, under conditions that increasingly militate against it. Therapists, not priests or popular preachers of self-help or models of success like the captains of industry, become his principal allies in the struggle for composure; he turns to them in the hope of achieving the modern equivalent of salvation, "mental health." Therapy has established itself as the successor both to rugged individualism and to religion; but this does not mean that the "triumph of the therapeutic" has become a new religion in its own right. Therapy constitutes an antireligion, not always to be sure because it adheres to rational explanation or scientific methods of healing, as its practitioners would have us believe, but because modern society "has no future" and therefore gives no thought to anything beyond its immediate needs. Even when therapists speak of the need for "meaning" and "love," they define love and meaning simply as the fulfillment of the patient's emotional requirements. It hardly occurs to them—nor is there any reason why it should, given the nature of the therapeutic enterprise—to encourage the subject to subordinate his needs and interests to those of others, to someone or some cause or tradition outside himself. "Love" as self-sacrifice or self-abasement, "meaning" as submission to a higher loyalty—these sublimations strike the therapeutic sensibility as intolerably oppressive, offensive to common sense and injurious to personal health and well-being. To liberate humanity from such out-moded ideas of love and duty has become the mission of the post-Freudian therapies and particularly of their converts and popularizers, for whom mental health means the overthrow of inhibitions and the immediate gratification of every impulse.

Mark Patinkin
Yuppies Mean Business

Mark Patinkin *is a journalist who writes columns for the Providence, Rhode Island* Journal-Bulletin.

*H*er name is Laurie Gilbert. She is a lawyer in California. This is her philosophy of life:

"Without children, I would be comfortable with $200,000 a year. Money means a lot to my happiness."

She is 28 years old. This is her philosophy of work:

"The way you look is very important. Sometimes, I think it is more important than what you can do."

One week after she was married, she met someone better during a job interview. She divorced her groom and married the someone better.

Have it all, have it now.

A national magazine recently presented her as a new symbol, and not a negative one. It is too simple to call her impulsive. Or indulgent. What's going on here is passion.

A *passion* for success. For self-advancement. It is the passion behind the new entrepreneur, the new generation. My generation.

Fifteen years ago, we emerged with the flamboyance of protest. Then, for too long, we were offstage. Now, finally, we are emerging again.

They've named us Yuppies, but we're more than a label. We're a new consciousness. A new force. And no longer a force on the outside. We've moved into the mainstream with a corporate commitment that will bring us a power we never knew on the streets.

It is what our spokespeople say.

Jerry Rubin is one of them. He has gone from engineering rallies to engineering networking parties. What we are about these days, he says, is the exchanging of business cards.

"Capitalism," Rubin said once, "is another word for stealing."

"Time," Rubin says now, "is money."

He is traveling the country, acting as our spokesperson.

"Yuppies," I heard him say, "haven't sold out. We're taking over."

We're doing it with a new sense of responsibility. And adulthood. Public service was a fine goal in its time, but it is not what the '80s are about. The '80s are about business and so, we are too.

"Much of the energy of the '60s," says *Newsweek,* "has been turned inward, on lives, careers, apartments and dinners."

Our heroes used to be leaders of conscience, but you have to grow with the times. The times now are about the pursuit of affluence. Idealism was a nice phase, but we're realists now.

His name is Rob Lewis. He is a Denver lawyer. Of course, with the city's biggest firm.

"Our marriages seem like mergers," he says, speaking for all of us. "Our divorces like divestitures."

We even have a preacher. Her name is Terry Cole-Whittaker. She has written a book called "How to Have More in a Have-Not World."

Her message has drawn a sizable congregation to her California church. On Sundays, the parking lot is filled with BMWs.

Our spokespeople understand this may seem a contradiction of what we once stood for. But it is not, they say. It is an evolution. Churchill himself saw the same dynamic.

"He who is not a liberal by 21 has no heart," said Churchill. "He who is not conservative by 35 has no head."

So maybe we've moved the clock up a bit. Maybe those of us who are younger skipped the first phase altogether. Still, it is natural. It is the times. There is nothing wrong with seeing a six-figure income as the threshold of respectability. There is nothing wrong with casting ourselves as a gourmet class.

Newsweek [recently] had a cover on the year of the Yuppie. *Esquire* [recently] had a cover on our new ethic—financial success. We are only coming of age. We are only, finally, realizing the call of comfort.

Oh yes. There is the matter of commitment. Social service. We still care about that. But there are other things to take care of for the moment. A new identity to celebrate.

Finally, after a decade of little focus, we have a clear set of models. A clear set of symbols. A clear set of spokespeople. Together, they are helping to label us all.

I wish they would go away.

14

Can There Be Sexual Equality?

STORY 1: Driving the truck to work one day, Sandy noticed somebody by the side of the road with a flat tire. Sandy stopped and got out to help fix the flat. Because neither of them had a jack, Sandy had to hold up the rear end of the car while the owner replaced the tire. When they were done, Sandy reminded herself to buy a new jack on her way home.

STORY 2: Sandy was putting the finishing touches on the pie when the kids rushed in the door. "What's for dinner? We're starved." "Wash your hands, kids, and set the table," Sandy replied. "We'll be eating as soon as Mom gets home from work."

*I*t is a rare person indeed who would read either of these stories without experiencing a "gender jolt" at the end of them. No matter what your views are about sexual equality, it is nevertheless true that we tend to make certain associations when it comes to gender. Even if your father does the cooking every night, you probably assumed that the person putting the finishing touches on the pie was a woman. Similarly, even if your mother is a body builder who drives a Harley, you probably assumed that the person holding up the rear of the car was a man.

One of the questions of concern to philosophers is whether these characteristic associations are rooted in fundamental, irreversible differences between women and men, or whether they are a function of changeable social practices. Look around the world. How many women are truck drivers? Heads of large corporations? CIA agents? Roofing contractors? How many men are elementary school teachers? Are staying at home with their children? Are secretaries? Nurses? It is important to notice two things. First, men and women tend to occupy different roles in our culture. Second, the roles that women occupy tend to be subordinate to those of men. (This doesn't mean that women have no power, nor does it mean that all men have power. There are other factors, such as class and race, that affect the distribution of power.)

Some of the differences between men and women, their reproductive capacities, for example, are clearly not the result of social practices. Women have uteruses; for the time being, at least, men do not. To what extent do the physical differences between men and women *determine* their social roles (sometimes called "gender roles")? Should physical differences determine gender roles? You will see that Plato hedges on an answer to this question. In the selection from *The Republic*, Socrates is discussing with Glaucon the education and training necessary for those who are going to rule Socrates's ideal city. Socrates makes it quite clear that education, more than any other single thing, determines what a person will be equipped to do. If men and women are educated in the same way, then they will be able to perform the same functions. The fact that women bear children, for example, does not entail that they should raise them. Rather, the raising of children should be done by those trained to do so, be they men or women. In principle, then, both men and women are capable of ruling the city as well. It is clear, however, that Socrates believes men to be naturally superior to women. Although there will be some men who are exceeded by women at performing a task, there will always be men who are better at it than any woman could be (except, he suggests, when making pancakes and jam). It is difficult to see how he can reconcile the view that men are naturally superior with the view that our capabilities are a result of education and training.

According to Mill, he can't. Confusions such as that of Socrates are the result of taking facts about the way things *are* as equivalent to facts about the way things *must be*. Suppose that you are in the hospital for a week and during that week you never encounter a male nurse. Are you entitled to conclude that men can't, by nature, be nurses? Or that women, by nature, are suited to nursing? Mill provides us with some reasons for questioning inferences like these. Was Socrates making such an inference when he claimed that men are naturally superior to women? If so, he finds himself in notable philosphical company. As you can see from the selections by Aristotle and Kant, philosophers remarks about women tend to reinforce stereotypical associations. It is claimed that women are more emotional than men, are physically weaker than men, have a tendency to lie and to talk too much, and are lazier and more shameless than men. According to Friedrich Engels, male supremacy is a function of men's desire to control reproduction and so ensure the paternity of their children. (Women, for obvious reasons, don't have that problem.) Far from being a romantic expression of mutual love, marriage is, according to Engels, a singularly economic relationship, one that guarantees male authority over property and hence over women and children. Whatever characteristics women have, or are believed to have, must be understood in the context of this inherently oppressive situation.

Writing roughly one-hundred years after Engels, Simone de Beauvoir sought to provide a more complete account of the causes and effects of women's oppression. Beauvoir argues that men have constructed women as what she calls "the Other" in order to establish the superiority of their own characteristics. The human tendency toward self-importance takes the form, in men, of casting feminine characteristics in a negative light. In fact, the feminine *is* the negative, the Other. By denying women's capacity to judge, man assures that whatever resistance women might show to this negative assessment of their abilities is itself dismissed as yet another error in judgment. Left with no other resources, women come to see themselves as men want them to be seen. They expect to be weak, silly, emotional, powerless, and dependent. They, too, see themselves as the Other.

Beauvoir's rather gloomy picture may be an illuminating depiction of the origin and maintenance of women's consciousness of herself as inferior to men. Sojourner Truth reminds us, however, that the issues raised by middle class feminists may not be those most pressing for women whose social or economic position is more precarious. Sojourner Truth, a slave until emancipation, points out that her womanhood in no way depends upon her possessing those characteristics typically associated with femininity. She was a woman in spite of the fact that she engaged in hard physical labor all of her life and was not even treated with the respect that white men showed their wives. Although slavery is no longer permitted in our country, it is nevertheless true that women of different social and economic classes face significantly different problems. The road to sexual equality will not be the same for all women. It is important, then, to consider the possible ways in which race affects relationships between men and women. The stereotypes associated with white women may be quite different from those associated with, for example, black women. In trying to transcend those stereotypes, black women may confront obstacles quite distinct from those of white women.

Schlafly presents a very different perspective on the issue of women's equality. She largely agrees with the characterization of women as weak, inherently maternal and emotional, characteristics that feminists such as Simone de Beauvoir claim are the result of women's oppression. However, unlike Beauvoir who believes that women must resist these characterizations to achieve equality with men, Schlafly takes them to be positive qualities. Rather than attempting to achieve equality with men, women should take pride in themselves, in what nature has dictated for them. Women simply *are* weaker than men, *are* more maternal and emotional. According to Schlafly, the Women's Liberation Movement is attempting to alter social arrangements that are determined by natural (biological) differences between men and women. You might want to think about whether the aims of feminism are accurately represented by Schlafly. She also claims that women aren't philosophers!

Finally, Marilyn Frye (a philosopher) provides an analysis of the term 'sexism'. According to Frye, sexism is the result of a particular social system of "sex-marking." She asks us to think about the variety of ways in which sex differences are reinforced by clothing and by manners of walking and speaking. In Frye's view, however, the reinforcement of sex differences is not, as Schlafly would have it, life-enhancing. Rather it serves to maintain a system in which one group of people is subordinate to another. By continuing to emphasize the importance of sex differences, we further reinforce the relationship of domination and subordination whose purpose it serves.

In thinking about the question of sexual equality, it is important to consider just what are the sources of inequality. In addition, it is important to reflect on how, ideally, you think things should be, and how you think we might best achieve those ends. You can begin by thinking about the ways in which you are affected by the importance that our society attaches to sex differences. If you think that you aren't, then remember the two stories with which we began.

Plato
The Equality of Women

Plato *(427–347 B.C.) was born into a family of considerable wealth and power. In Athens he came under the influence of Socrates and turned his attention to philosophy. After Socrates was condemned to death for corrupting the minds of the youth of Athens, Plato took it upon himself to continue Socrates' work. In this selection from* The Republic, *Socrates, who serves as Plato's spokesman in the dialogue, discusses his views about sexual equality with Glaucon.*

Well, I replied, I suppose that I must retrace my steps and say what I perhaps ought to have said before in the proper place. The part of the men has been played out, and now properly enough comes the turn of the women. Of them I will proceed to speak, and the more readily since I am invited by you.

For men born and educated like our citizens, the only way, in my opinion, of arriving at a right conclusion about the possession and use of women and children is to follow the path on which we originally started, when we said that the men were to be the guardians and watchdogs of the herd.

True.

Let us further suppose the birth and education of our women to be subject to similar or nearly similar regulations; then we shall see whether the result accords with our design.

What do you mean?

What I mean may be put into the form of a question, I said: Are dogs divided into hes and shes, or do they both share equally in hunting and in keeping watch and in the other duties of dogs? or do we entrust to the males the entire and exclusive care of the flocks, while we leave the females at home, under the idea that the bearing and suckling their puppies is labour enough for them?

No, he said, they share alike; the only difference between them is that the males are stronger and the females weaker.

But can you use different animals for the same purpose, unless they are bred and fed in the same way?

You cannot.

Then, if women are to have the same duties as men, they must have the same nurture and education?

Yes.

The education which was assigned to the men was music and gymnastic. Yes.

Then women must be taught music and gymnastic and also the art of war, which they must practise like the men?

That is the inference, I suppose.

I should rather expect, I said, that several of our proposals, if they are carried out, being unusual, may appear ridiculous.

No doubt of it.

Yes, and the most ridiculous thing of all will be the sight of women naked in the palaestra, exercising with the men, especially when they are no longer young; they certainly will not be a vision of beauty, any more than the enthusiastic old men who in spite of wrinkles and ugliness continue to frequent the gymnasia.

Yes, indeed, he said: according to present notions the proposal would be thought ridiculous.

But then, I said, as we have determined to speak our minds, we must not fear the jests of the wits which will be directed against this sort of innovation; how they will talk of women's attainments both in music and gymnastic, and above all about their wearing armour and riding upon horseback!

Very true, he replied.

Yet having begun we must go forward to the rough places of the law; at the same time begging of these gentlemen for once in their life to be serious. Not long ago, as we shall remind them, the Hellenes were of the opinion, which is still generally received among the barbarians, that the sight of a naked man was ridiculous and improper; and when first the Cretans and then the Lacedaemonians introduced the custom, the wits of that day might equally have ridiculed the innovation.

No doubt.

But when experience showed that to let all things be uncovered was far better than to cover them up, and the ludicrous effect to the outward eye vanished before the better principle which reason asserted, then the man was perceived to be a fool who directs the shafts of his ridicule at any other sight but that of folly and vice, or seriously inclines to weigh the beautiful by any other standard but that of the good.

Very true, he replied.

First, then, whether the question is to be put in jest or in earnest, let us come to an understanding about the nature of woman: Is she capable of sharing either wholly or partially in the actions of men, or not at all? And is the art of war one of those arts in which she can or can not share? That will be the best way of commencing the enquiry, and will probably lead to the fairest conclusion.

That will be much the best way.

Shall we take the other side first and begin by arguing against ourselves; in this manner the adversary's position will not be undefended.

Why not? he said.

Then let us put a speech into the mouths of our opponents. They will say: 'Socrates and Glaucon, no adversary need convict you, for you yourselves, at the first foundation of the State, admitted the principle that everybody was to do the one work suited to his own nature.' And certainly, if I am not mistaken, such an admission was made by us. 'And do not the natures of men and women differ very much indeed?' And we shall reply: Of course they do. Then we shall be asked, 'Whether the tasks assigned to men and to women should not be different, and such as are agreeable to their different natures?' Certainly they should. 'But if so, have you not fallen into a serious inconsistency in saying that men and women, whose natures are so entirely different, ought to perform the same actions?'—What defence will you make for us, my good Sir, against any one who offers these objections?

That is not an easy question to answer when asked suddenly; and I shall and I do beg of you to draw out the case on our side.

These are the objections, Glaucon, and there are many others of a like kind, which I foresaw long ago; they made me afraid and reluctant to take in hand any law about the possession and nurture of women and children.

By Zeus, he said, the problem to be solved is anything but easy.

Why yes, I said, but the fact is that when a man is out of his depth, whether he has fallen into a little swimming bath or into mid-ocean, he has to swim all the same.

Very true.

And must not we swim and try to reach the shore: we will hope that Arion's dolphin or some other miraculous help may save us?

I suppose so, he said.

Well then, let us see if any way of escape can be found. We acknowledged—did we not? that different natures ought to have different pursuits, and that men's and women's natures are different. And now what are we saying?—that different natures out to have the same pursuits,—this is the inconsistency which is charged upon us.

Precisely.

Verily, Glaucon, I said, glorious is the power of the art of contradiction!

Why do you say so?

Because I think that many a man falls into the practice against his will. When he thinks that he is reasoning he is really disputing, just because he cannot define and divide, and so know that of which he is speaking; and he will pursue a merely verbal opposition in the spirit of contention and not of fair discussion.

Yes, he replied, such is very often the case; but what has that to do with us and our argument?

A great deal; for there is certainly a danger of our getting unintentionally into a verbal opposition.

In what way?

Why, we valiantly and pugnaciously insist upon the verbal truth, that different natures ought to have different pursuits, but we never considered at all what was the meaning of sameness or difference of nature, or why we distinguished them when we assigned different pursuits to different natures and the same to the same natures.

Why, no, he said, that was never considered by us.

I said: Suppose that by way of illustration we were to ask the question whether there is not an opposition in nature between bald men and hairy men; and if this is admitted by us, then, if bald men are cobblers, we should forbid the hairy men to be cobblers, and conversely?

That would be a jest, he said.

Yes, I said, a jest; and why? because we never meant when we constructed the State, that the opposition of natures should extend to every difference, but only to those differences which affected the pursuit in which the individual is engaged; we should have argued, for example, that a physician and one who is in mind a physician may be said to have the same nature.

True.

Whereas the physician and the carpenter have different natures?

Certainly.

And if, I said, the male and female sex appear to differ in their fitness for any art or pursuit, we should say that such pursuit or art ought to be assigned to one or the other of them; but if the difference consists only in women bearing and men begetting children, this does not amount to a proof that a woman differs from a man in respect to the sort of education she should receive; and we shall therefore continue to maintain that our guardians and their wives ought to have the same pursuits.

Very true, he said.

Next, we shall ask our opponent how, in reference to any of the pursuits or arts of civic life, the nature of a woman differs from that of a man?

That will be quite fair.

And perhaps he, like yourself, will reply that to give a sufficient answer on the instant is not easy; but after a little reflection there is no difficulty.

Yes, perhaps.

Suppose then that we invite him to accompany us in the argument, and then we may hope to show him that there is nothing peculiar in the constitution of women which would affect them in the administration of the State.

By all means.

Let us say to him: Come now, and we will ask you a question:—when you spoke of a nature gifted or not gifted in any respect, did you mean to say that one man will acquire a thing easily, another with difficulty; a little learning will lead the one to discover a great deal; whereas the other, after much study and application, no sooner learns than he forgets; or again, did you mean, that the one has a body which is a good servant to his mind, while the body of the other is a hindrance to him?—would not these be the sort of differences which distinguish the man gifted by nature from the one who is ungifted?

No one will deny that.

And can you mention any pursuit of mankind in which the male sex has not all these gifts and qualities in a higher degree than the female? Need I waste time in speaking of the art of weaving, and the management of pancakes and preserves, in which womankind does really appear to be great, and in which for her to be beaten by a man is of all things the most absurd?

You are quite right, he replied, in maintaining the general inferiority of the female sex:

although many women are in many things superior to many men, yet on the whole what you say is true.

And if so, my friend, I said, there is no special faculty of administration in a state which a woman has because she is a woman, or which a man has by virtue of his sex, but the gifts of nature are alike diffused in both; all the pursuits of men are the pursuits of women also, but in all of them a woman is inferior to a man.

Very true.

Then are we to impose all our enactments on men and none of them on women?

That will never do.

One woman has a gift of healing, another not; one is a musician, and another has no music in her nature?

Very true.

And one woman has a turn for gymnastic and military exercises, and another is unwarlike and hates gymnastics?

Certainly.

And one woman is a philosopher, and another is an enemy of philosophy; one has spirit, and another is without spirit?

That is also true.

Then one woman will have the temper of a guardian, and another not. Was not the selection of the male guardians determined by differences of this sort?

Yes.

Men and women alike possess the qualities which make a guardian; they differ only in their comparative strength or weakness.

Obviously.

And those women who have such qualities are to be selected as the companions and colleagues of men who have similar qualities and whom they resemble in capacity and in character?

Very true.

And ought not the same natures to have the same pursuits?

They ought.

Then, as we were saying before, there is nothing unnatural in assigning music and gymnastic to the wives of the guardians—to that point we come round again.

Certainly not.

The law which we then enacted was agreeable to nature, and therefore not an impossibility or mere aspiration; and the contrary practice, which prevails at present, is in reality a violation of nature.

That appears to be true.

We had to consider, first, whether our proposals were possible, and secondly whether they were the most beneficial?

Yes.

And the possibility has been acknowledged?

Yes.

The very great benefit has next to be established?

Quite so.

You will admit that the same education which makes a man a good guardian will make a woman a good guardian; for their original nature is the same?

Yes.

I should like to ask you a question?

What is it?

Would you say that all men are equal in excellence, or is one man better than another?

The latter.

And in the commonwealth which we were founding do you conceive the guardians who have been brought up on our model system to be more perfect men, or the cobblers whose education has been cobbling?

What a ridiculous question!

You have answered me, I replied: Well, and may we not further say that our guardians are the best of our citizens?

By far the best.

And will not their wives be the best women?

Yes, by far the best.

And can there be anything better for the interests of the State than that the men and women of a State should be as good as possible?

There can be nothing better.

And this is what the arts of music and gymnastic, when present in such manner as we have described, will accomplish?

Certainly.

Then we have made an enactment not only possible but in the highest degree beneficial to the State?

True.

Then let the wives of our guardians strip, for their virtue will be their robe, and let them share in the toils of war and the defence of their country; only in the distribution of labours the lighter are assigned to the women, who are the weaker natures, but in other respects their duties are to be the same. And as for the man who laughs at naked women exercising their bodies from the best of motives, in his laughter he is plucking

A fruit of unripe wisdom,

and he himself is ignorant of what he is laughing at, or what he is about;—for that is, and ever will be, the best of sayings, *That the useful is the noble and the hurtful is the base.*

Very true.

Aristotle
The Inequality of Women

Aristotle (384–322 B.C.) *was for eighteen years a student of Plato. After Plato's death, he turned to the study of biology. In addition to his biological studies, Aristotle virtually created the sciences of logic and linguistics. He developed extravagant theories in physics and made significant contributions to metaphysics, ethics, politics, and aesthetics.*

Woman is more compassionate than man, more easily moved to tears. At the same time, she is more jealous, more querolous, more apt to scold and to strike. She is, furthermore, more prone to despondency and less hopeful than man, more devoid of shame or self-respect, more false of speech, more deceptive and of more retentive memory. She is also more wakeful, more shrinking, more difficult to rouse to action, and she requires a smaller amount of nutriment.

Immanuel Kant

The Inequality of Women

Immanuel Kant (1724–1804) *was probably the greatest philosopher since Plato and Aristotle. He lived his entire life in East Prussia. He was a professor at the University in Konigsberg for over thirty years. He never married and his neighbors said that his habits were so regular that they could set their watches by him. His philosophical system was embodied in three volumes,* The Critique of Pure Reason, The Critique of Practical Reason, *and* The Critique of Judgment.

The person who is as silent as a mute goes to one extreme; the person who is loquacious goes to the opposite. Both tendencies are weaknesses. Men are liable to the first, women to the second. Someone has said that women are talkative because the training of infants is their special charge, and their talkativeness soon teaches a child to speak, because they can chatter to it all day long. If men had the care of the children they would take much longer to learn to talk. However that may be, we dislike anyone who will not speak: he annoys us; his silence betrays his pride. On the other hand, loquaciousness in men is contemptible and contrary to the strength of the male. All this by the way, we shall now pass to more weighty matters.

John Stuart Mill

The Subjection of Women

John Stuart Mill (1806–1873) *was one of the documented geniuses of modern history. By the age of ten, he had accomplished more than most scholars do in a lifetime. He is best known for his moral and political writings, particularly* On Liberty *and* Utilitarianism.

Neither does it avail anything to say that the *nature* of the two sexes adapts them to their present functions and position, and renders these appropriate to them. Standing on the ground of common sense and the constitution of the human mind, I deny that any one knows, or can know, the nature of the two sexes, as long as they have only been seen in their present relation to one another. If men had ever been found in society without women, or women without men, or if there had been a society of men and women in which the women were not under the control of the men, something might have been positively known about the mental and moral differences which may be inherent in the nature of each. What is now called the nature of women is an eminently artificial thing—the result of forced repression in some directions, unnatural stimulation in others. It may be asserted without scruple, that no other class of dependents have had their character so entirely distorted from its natural proportions by their relation with their masters; for, if conquered and slave races have been, in some respects, more forcibly repressed, whatever in them has not been crushed down by an iron heel has generally been let alone, and if left with any liberty of development, it has developed itself according to its own laws; but in the case of women, a hot-house and stove cultivation has always been carried on of some of the capabilities of their nature, for the benefit and pleasure of their masters. Then, because certain products of the general vital force sprout luxuriantly and reach a great development in this heated atmosphere and under this active nurture and watering, while other shoots from the same root, which are left outside in the wintry air, with ice purposely heaped all around them, have a stunted growth, and some are burnt off with fire and disappear; men, with that inability to recognize their own work which distinguishes the unanalytic mind, indolently believe that the tree grows of itself in the way they have made it grow, and that it would die if one half of it were not kept in a vapour bath and the other half in the snow.

Of all difficulties which impede the progress of thought, and the formation of well-grounded opinions on life and social arrangements, the greatest is now the unspeakable ignorance and inattention of mankind in respect to the influences which form human character. Whatever any portion of the human species now are, or seem to be, such, it is supposed, they have a natural tendency to be: even when the most elementary knowledge of the circumstances in which they have been placed, clearly points out the causes that made them what they are. . . . Because the Greeks cheated the Turks, and the Turks only plundered the Greeks, there are persons who think that the Turks are naturally more sincere: and because women, as is often said, care nothing about politics except their personalities, it is supposed that the general good is naturally less interesting to women than to men. History, which is now so much better understood than formerly, teaches another lesson: if only by showing the extraordinary susceptibility of human nature to external influences, and the extreme variableness of those of its manifestations which are supposed to be most universal and uniform. But in history, as in travelling, men usually see only what they already had in their own minds; and few learn much from history, who do not bring much with them to its study.

Hence, in regard to that most difficult question, what are the natural differences between the two sexes—a subject on which it is impossible in the present state of society to obtain complete and correct knowledge—while almost everybody dogmatizes upon it, almost all neglect and make light of the only means by which any partial insight can be obtained into it. This is, an analytic study of the most important department of psychology, the laws of the influence of circumstances on character. For, however great and apparently ineradicable the moral and intellectual differences between men and women might be, the evidence of their being natural differences could only be negative. Those only could be inferred to be natural which could not possibly be artificial—the residuum, after deducting every characteristic of either sex which can admit of being explained from education or external circumstances. The profoundest knowledge of the laws of the formation of character is indispensable to entitle any one to affirm even that there is any difference, much more what the difference is, between the two sexes considered as moral and rational beings; and since no one, as yet, has that knowledge (for there is hardly any subject which, in proportion to its importance, has been so little studied), no one is thus far entitled to any positive opinion on the subject. Conjectures are all that can at present be made; conjectures more or less probable, according as more or less authorized by such knowledge as we yet have of the laws of psychology, as applied to the formation of character.

Even the preliminary knowledge, what the differences between the sexes now are, apart from all question as to how they are made what they are, is still in the crudest and most incomplete state. Medical practitioners and physiologists have ascertained, to some extent, the differences in bodily constitution; and this is an important element to the psychologist: but hardly any medical practitioner is a psychologist. Respecting the mental characteristics of women; their observations are of no more worth than those of common men. It is a subject on which nothing final can be known, so long as those who alone can really know it, women themselves, have given but little testimony, and that little, mostly suborned. It is easy to know stupid women. Stupidity is much the same all the world over. A stupid person's notions and feelings may confidently be inferred from those which prevail in the circle by which the person is surrounded. Not so with those whose opinions and feelings are an emanation from their own nature and faculties. It is only a man here and there who has any tolerable knowledge of the character even of the women of his own family. I do not mean, of their capabilities; these nobody knows, not even themselves, because most of them have never been called out. I mean their actually existing thoughts and feelings. Many a man thinks he perfectly understands women, because he has had amatory relations with several, perhaps with many of them. If he is a good observer, and his experience extends to quality as well as quantity, he may have learnt something of one narrow department of their nature—an important department, no doubt. But of all the rest of it, few persons are generally more ignorant, because there are few from whom it is so carefully hidden. The most favorable case which a man can generally have for studying the character of a woman, is that of his own wife: for the opportunities are greater, and the cases of complete sympathy not so unspeakably rare. And in fact, this is the source from which any knowledge worth having on the subject has, I believe, generally come. But most men have not had the opportunity of studying in this way more than a single case: accordingly one can, to an almost laughable degree, infer what a man's wife is like, from his opinions about women in general. To make even this one case yield any results, the woman must be worth knowing, and the man not only a competent judge, but of a character so sympathetic in itself, and so well adapted to hers, that he can either read her mind by sympathetic intuition, or has nothing in himself which makes her shy of disclosing it. Hardly anything, I believe, can be more rare than this conjunction. It often happens that there is the most complete unity of feeling and community of interests as to all external things, yet the one has as little admission into the internal life of the other as if they were common acquaintance. Even with true affection, authority on the one side and subordination on the other prevent perfect confidence. Though nothing may be intentionally withheld, much is not shown. In the analogous relation of parent and child, the corresponding phenomenon must have been in the observation of every one. As between father and son, how many are the cases in which the father, in spite of real affection on both sides, obviously to all the world does not know, nor suspect, parts of the son's character familiar to his companions and equals. The truth is, that the position of looking up to another is extremely unpropitious to complete sincerity and openness with him. The fear of losing ground in his opinion or in his feelings is so strong, that even in an upright character, there is an unconscious tendency to show only the best side, or the side which, though not the best, is that which he most likes to see: and it may be confidently said that thorough knowledge of one another hardly ever exists, but between persons who, besides being intimates, are equals. How much more true, then, must all this be, when the one is not only under the authority of the other, but has it inculcated on her as a duty to reckon everything else subordinate to his comfort and pleasure, and to let him neither see nor feel anything coming from her, except what is agreeable to him. All these difficulties stand in the way of a man's obtaining any thorough knowledge even of the one woman whom alone, in general, he has sufficient opportunity of studying. When we further consider that to understand one woman is not necessary to understand any other woman; that even if he could study many women of one rank, or of one country, he would not thereby understand women of other ranks or countries; and even if he did, they are still only the women of a single period of history; we may safely assert that the knowledge which men can acquire of women, even as they have been and are, without reference to what they might be, is wretchedly imperfect and superficial, and always will be so, until women themselves have told all that they have to tell.

And this time has not come; nor will it come otherwise than gradually. It is but of yesterday that women have either been qualified by literary accomplishments, or permitted by society, to tell anything to the general public. As yet very few of them dare tell anything, which men, on whom their literary success depends, are unwilling to hear. Let us remember in which manner, up to a very recent time, the expression, even by a male author, of uncustomary opinions, or what are deemed eccentric feelings, usually was, and in some degree still is, received; and we may form some faint conception under what impediments a woman, who is brought up to think custom and opinion her sovereign rule, attempts to express in books anything drawn from the depths of her own nature. The greatest woman who has left writings behind her sufficient to give her an eminent rank in the literature of her country, thought it necessary to prefix as a motto to her boldest work, 'A man dares to have an opinion; a woman must submit to it.' The greater part of what women write about women is mere sycophancy to men. In the case of unmarried women, much of it seems only intended to increase their chance of a husband. Many, both married and unmarried, overstep the mark, and inculcate a servility beyond what is desired or relished by any man, except the very vulgarest. But this is not so often the case as, even at a quite late period, it still was. Literary women are becoming more freespoken, and more willing to express their real sentiments. Unfortunately, in this country especially, they are themselves such artificial products, that their sentiments are compounded of a small element of individual observation and consciousness, and a very large one of acquired associations. This will be less and less the case, but it will remain true to a great extent, as long as social institutions do not admit the same free development of originality in women which is possible to men. When that time comes, and not before, we shall see, and not merely hear, as much as it is necessary to know of the nature of women, and the adaptation of other things to it.

I have dwelt so much on the difficulties which at present obstruct any real knowledge by men of the true nature of women, because in this as in so many other things 'opinio copiae inter maximas causas inopiae est'; and there is little chance of reasonable thinking on the matter, while people flatter themselves that they perfectly understand a subject of which most men know absolutely nothing, and of which it is at present impossible that any man, or all men taken together, should have knowledge which can qualify them to lay down the law to women as to what is, or is not, their vocation. Happily, no such knowledge is necessary for any practical purpose connected with the position of women in relation to society and life. For, according to all the principles involved in modern society, the question rests with women themselves—to be decided by their own experience, and by the use of their own faculties. There are no means of finding what either one person or many can do, but by trying—and no means by which any one else can discover for them what it is for their happiness to do or leave undone.

One thing we may be certain of—that what is contrary to women's nature to do, they never will be made to do by simply giving their nature free play. The anxiety of mankind to interfere in behalf of nature, for fear lest nature should not succeed in effecting its purpose, is an altogether unnecessary solicitude. What women by nature cannot do, it is quite superfluous to forbid them from doing. What they can do, but not so well as the men who are their competitors, competition suffices to exclude them from; since nobody asks for protective duties and bounties in favour of women; it is only asked that the present bounties and protective duties in favour of men should be recalled. If women have a greater natural inclination for some things than for others, there is no need of laws or social inculcation to make the majority of them do the former in preference to the latter. Whatever women's services are most wanted for, the free play of competition will hold out the strongest inducements to them to undertake. And, as the words imply, they are most wanted for the things for which they are most fit; by the apportionment of which to them, the collective faculties of the two sexes can be applied on the whole with the greatest sum of valuable result.

The general opinion of men is supposed to be, that the natural vocation of a woman is that of a wife and mother. I say, is supposed to be, because, judging from acts—from the whole of the present constitution of society—one might infer that their opinion was the direct contrary. They might be supposed to think that the alleged natural vocation of women was of all things the most repugnant to their nature; insomuch that if they are free to do anything else—if any other means of living, or occupation of their time and faculties, is open, which has any chance of appearing desirable to them—there will not be enough of them who will be willing to accept the condition said to be natural to them. If this is the real opinion of men in general, it would be well that it should be spoken out. I should like to hear somebody openly enunciating the doctrine (it is already implied in much that is written on the subject)— 'It is necessary to society that women should marry and produce children. They will not do so unless they are compelled. Therefore it is necessary to compel them.' The merits of the case would then be clearly defined. It would be exactly that of the slaveholders of South Carolina and Louisiana. 'It is necessary that cotton and sugar should be grown. White men cannot produce them. Negroes will not, for any wages which we choose to give. *Ergo* they must be compelled.' An illustration still closer to the point is that of impressment. Sailors must absolutely be had to defend the country. It often happens that they will not voluntarily enlist. Therefore there must be the power of forcing them. How often has this logic been used! and, but for one flaw in it, without doubt it would have been successful up to this day. But it is open to the retort—First pay the sailors the honest value of their labour. When you have made it as well worth their while to serve you, as to work for other employers, you will have no more difficulty than others have in obtaining their services. To this there is no logical answer except 'I will not': and as people are now not only ashamed, but are not desirous, to rob the labourer of his hire, impressment is no longer advocated. Those who attempt to force women into marriage by closing all other doors against them, lay themselves open to a similar retort. If they mean what they say, their opinion must evidently be, that men do not render the married condition so desirable to women, as to induce them to accept it for its own recommendations. It is not a sign of one's thinking the boon one offers very attractive, when one allows only Hobson's choice, 'that or none.' And here, I believe, is the clue to the feelings of those men, who have a real antipathy to the equal freedom of women. I believe they are afraid, not lest women should be unwilling to marry, for I do not think that any one in reality has that apprehension; but lest they should insist that marriage should be on equal conditions; lest all women of spirit and capacity should prefer doing almost anything else, not in their own eyes degrading, rather than marry, when marrying is giving themselves a master, and a master too of all their earthly possessions. And truly, if this consequence were necessarily incident to marriage, I think that the apprehension would be very well founded. I agree in thinking it probable that few women, capable of anything else, would, unless under an irresistible *entraînement*, rendering them for the time insensible to anything but itself, choose such a lot, when any other means were open to them of filling a conventionally honourable place in life: and if men are determined that the law of marriage shall be a law of despotism, they are quite right, in point of mere policy, in leaving to women only Hobson's choice. But, in that case, all that has been done in the modern world to relax the chain on the minds of women, has been a mistake. They never should have been allowed to receive a literary education. Women who read, much more women who write, are, in the existing constitution of things, a contradiction and a disturbing element: and it was wrong to bring women up with any acquirements but those of an odalisque, or of a domestic servant. . . .

When we consider how vast is the number of men, in any great country, who are little higher than brutes, and that this never prevents them from being able, through the law of marriage, to obtain a victim, the breadth and depth of human misery caused in this shape alone by the abuse of the institution swells to something appalling. Yet these are only the extreme cases. They are the lowest abysses, but there is a sad succession of depth after depth before reaching them. In domestic as in political tyranny, the case of absolute monsters chiefly illustrates the institution by showing that there is scarcely any horror which may not occur under it if the despot pleases, and thus setting in a strong light what must be the terrible frequency of things only a little less atrocious. Absolute fiends are as rare as angels, perhaps rarer: ferocious savages, with occasional touches of humanity, are, however, very frequent: and in the wide interval which separates these from any worthy representatives of the human species, how many are the forms and gradations of animalism and selfishness, often under an outward varnish of civilization and even cultivation, living at peace with the law, maintaining a creditable appearance to all who are not under their power, yet sufficient often to make the lives of all who are so, a torment and a burthen to them! It would be tiresome to repeat the commonplaces about the unfitness of men in general for power, which, after the political discussions of centuries, every one knows by heart, were it not that hardly any one thinks of applying these maxims to the case in which above all others they are applicable, that of power, not placed in the hands of a man here and there, but offered to every adult male, down to the basest and most ferocious. . . . I know that there is another side to the question. I grant that the wife, if she cannot effectually resist, can at least retaliate; she, too, can make the man's life extremely uncomfortable, and by that power is able to carry many points which she ought, and many which she ought not, to prevail in. But this instrument of self-protection—which may be called the power of the scold, or the shrewish sanction—has the fatal defect, that it avails most against the least tyrannical superiors, and in favor of the least deserving dependants. It is the weapon of irritable and self-willed women; of those who would make the worst use of power if they themselves had it, and who generally turn this power to a bad use. The amiable cannot use such an instrument, the high-minded disdain it. And on the other hand, the husbands against whom it is used most effectively are the gentler and more inoffensive; those who cannot be induced, even by provocation, to resort to any very harsh exercise of authority. The wife's power of being disagreeable generally only establishes a counter-tyranny, and makes victims in their turn chiefly of those husbands who are least inclined to be tyrants. . . .

With regard to the fitness of women, not only to participate in elections, but themselves to hold offices or practise professions involving important public responsibilities; I have already observed that this consideration is not essential to the practical question in dispute: since any woman, who succeeds in an open profession, proves by that very fact that she is qualified for it. And in the case of public offices, if the political system of the country is such as to exclude unfit men, it will equally exclude unfit women: while if it is not, there is no additional evil in the fact that the unfit persons whom it admits may be either women or men. As long therefore as it is acknowledged that even a few women may be fit for these duties, the laws which shut the door on those exceptions cannot be justified by any opinion which can be held respecting the capacities of women in general. But, though this last consideration is not essential, it is far from being irrelevant. An unprejudiced view of it gives additional strength to the arguments against the disabilities of women, and reinforces them by high consideration of practical utility.

Let us at first make entire abstraction of all psychological considerations tending to show, that any of the mental differences supposed to exist between women and men are but the natural effect of the differences in their education and circumstances, and indicate no radical difference, far less radical inferiority, of nature. Let us consider women only as they already are, or as they are known to have been; and the capacities which they have already practically shown. What they have done, that at least, if nothing else, it is proved that they can do. When we consider how sedulously they are all trained away from, instead of being trained towards, any of the occupations or objects reserved for men, it is evident that I am taking a very humble ground for them, when I rest their case on what they have actually achieved. For, in this case, negative evidence is worth little, while any positive evidence is conclusive. It cannot be inferred to be impossible that a woman should be a Homer, or an Aristotle, or a Michelangelo, or a Beethoven, because no woman has yet actually produced works comparable to theirs in any of those lines of excellence. This negative fact at most leaves the question uncertain, and open to psychological discussion. But it is quite certain that a woman can be a Queen Elizabeth, or a Deborah, or a Joan of Arc, since this is not inference, but fact. Now it is a curious consideration, that the only things which the existing law excludes women from doing, are the things which they have proved that they are able to do. There is no law to prevent a woman from having written all the plays of Shakespeare, or composed all the operas of Mozart. But Queen Elizabeth or Queen Victoria, had they not inherited the throne, could not have been entrusted with the smallest of the political duties, of which the former showed herself equal to the greatest.

If anything conclusive could be inferred from experience, without psychological analysis, it would be that the things which women are not allowed to do are the very ones for which they are peculiarly qualified; since their vocation for government has made its way, and become conspicuous, through the very few opportunities which have been given; while in the lines of distinction which apparently were freely open to them, they have by no means so eminently distinguished themselves. We know how small a number of reigning queens history presents, in comparison with that of kings. Of this smaller number a far larger proportion have shown talents for rule; though many of them have occupied the throne in difficult periods. It is remarkable, too, that they have, in a great number of instances, been distinguished by merits the most opposite to the imaginary and conventional character of women: they have been as much remarked for the firmness and vigour of their rule, as for its intelligence. When, to queens and empresses, we add regents, and viceroys of provinces, the list of women who have been eminent rulers of mankind swells to a great length. . . .

. . .Exactly where and in proportion as women's capacities for government have been tried, in that proportion have they been found adequate.

This fact is in accordance with the best general conclusions which the world's imperfect experience seems as yet to suggest, concerning the peculiar tendencies and aptitudes characteristic of women, as women have hitherto been. I do not say, as they will continue to be; for, as I have already said more than once, I consider it presumption in any one to pretend to decide what women are or are not, can or cannot be, by natural constitution. They have always hitherto been kept, as far as regards spontaneous development, in so unnatural a state, that their nature cannot but have been greatly distorted and disguised; and no one can safely pronounce that if women's nature were left to choose its direction as freely as men's, and if no artificial bent were attempted to be given to it except that required by the conditions of human society, and given to both sexes alike, there would be any material difference, or perhaps any difference at all, in the character and capacities which would unfold themselves. . . . even the least contestable of the differences which now exist, are such as may very well have been produced merely by circumstances, without any difference of natural capacity.

Friedrich Engels
The Monogamous Family

Friedrich Engels (1820–1895) *was the intellectual companion of Karl Marx. He contributed significantly to the development of the philosophical aspects of Marxism.*

Together he and Marx wrote The Communist Manifesto. *Engels' best known solo work is* The Origins of the Family, Private Property and the State, *from which this selection is taken.*

It develops out of the pairing family . . . in the transitional period between the upper and middle stages of barbarism; its decisive victory is one of the signs that civilization is beginning. It is based on the supremacy of the man, the express purpose being to produce children of undisputed paternity; such paternity is demanded because these children are later to come into their father's property as his natural heirs. It is distinguished from pairing marriage by the much greater strength of the marriage tie, which can no longer be dissolved at either partner's wish. As a rule, it is now only the man who can dissolve it and put away his wife. The right of conjugal infidelity also remains secured in him, at any rate by custom (the *Code Napoléon* explicitly accords it to the husband as long as he does not bring his concubine into the house), and as social life develops he exercises his right more and more; should the wife recall the old form of sexual life and attempt to revive it, she is punished more severely than ever.

. . . It is the existence of slavery side by side with monogamy, the presence of young, beautiful slaves belonging unreservedly to the *man*, that stamps monogamy from the very beginning with its specific character of monogamy *for the woman only*, but not for the man. And that is the character it still has today. . . .

This is the origin of monogamy as far as we can trace it back among the most civilized and highly developed people of antiquity. It was not in any way the fruit of individual sex love, with which it had nothing whatever to do; marriages remained as before marriages of convenience. It was the first form of the family to be based not on natural but on economic conditions—on the victory of private property over primitive, natural communal property. The Greeks themselves put the matter quite frankly; the sole exclusive aims of monogamous marriage were to make the man supreme in the family and to propagate, as the future heirs to his wealth, children indisputably his own. Otherwise, marriage was a burden, a duty which had to be performed whether one liked it or not to gods, state, and one's ancestors. In Athens the law exacted from the man not only marriage but also the performance of a minimum of so-called conjugal duties.

Thus when monogamous marriage first makes its appearance in history, it is not as the reconciliation of man and woman, still less as the highest form of such a reconciliation. Quite the contrary monogamous marriage comes on the scene as the subjugation of the one sex by the other; it announces a struggle between the sexes unknown throughout the whole previous prehistoric period. In an old unpublished manuscript written by Marx and myself in 1846, I find the words: "The first division of labor is that between man and woman for the propagation of children." And today I can add: The first class opposition that appears in history coincides with the development of the antagonism between man and woman in monogamous marriage, and the first class oppression coincides with that of the female sex by the male. Monogamous marriage was a great historical step forward; nevertheless, together with slavery and private wealth, it opens the period that has lasted until today in which every step forward is also relatively a step backward, in which prosperity and development for some is won through the misery and frustration of others. It is the cellular form of civilized society in which the nature of the oppositions and contradictions fully active in that society can be already studied. . . .

. . .With the rise of the inequality of property—already at the upper stage of barbarism, therefore—wage labor appears sporadically side by side with slave labor, and at the same time, as its necessary correlate, the professional prostitution of free women side by side with the forced surrender of the slave. Thus the heritage which group marriage has bequeathed to civilization is double-edged, just as everything civilization brings forth is double-edged, double-tongued, divided against itself, contradictory: here monogamy, there hetaerism with its most extreme form, prostitution. For hetaerism is as much a social institution as any other; it continues the old sexual freedom—to the advantage of the men. Actually, not merely tolerated but gaily practiced by the ruling classes particularly, it is condemned in words. But in reality this condemnation never falls on the men concerned, but only on the women; they are despised and outcast in order that the unconditional supremacy of men over the female sex may be once more proclaimed as a fundamental law of society. . . .

Thus, wherever the monogamous family remains true to its historical origin and clearly reveals the antagonism between the man and the woman expressed in the man's exclusive supremacy, it exhibits in miniature the same oppositions and contradictions as those in which society has been moving, without power to resolve or overcome them, ever since it split into classes at the beginning of civilization. . . .

Our jurists, of course, find that progress in legislation is leaving women with no further ground of complaint. Modern civilized systems of law increasingly acknowledge first, that for a marriage to be legal it must be a contract freely entered into by both partners and secondly, that also in the married state both partners must stand on a common footing of equal rights and duties. If both these demands are consistently carried out, say the jurists, women have all they can ask.

This typically legalist method of argument is exactly the same as that which the radical republican bourgeois uses to put the proletarian in his place. The labor contract is to be freely entered into by both partners. But it is considered to have been freely entered into as soon as the law makes both parties equal on *paper*. The power conferred on the one party by the difference of class position, the pressure thereby brought to bear on the other party—the real economic position of both—that is not the law's business. Again, for the duration of the labor contract, both parties are to have equal rights in so far as one or the other does not expressly surrender them. That economic relations compel the worker to surrender even the last semblance of equal rights—here again, that is no concern of the law.

In regard to marriage, the law, even the most advanced, is fully satisfied as soon as the partners have formally recorded that they are entering into the marriage of their own free consent. What goes on in real life behind the juridical scenes, how this free consent comes about—that is not the business of the law and the jurist. And yet the most elementary comparative jurisprudence should show the jurist what this free consent really amounts to. In the countries where an obligatory share of the paternal inheritance is secured to the children by law and they cannot therefore be disinherited—in Germany, in the countries with French law and elsewhere—the children are obliged to obtain their parents' consent to their marriage. In the countries with English law, where parental consent to a marriage is not legally required, the parents on their side have full freedom in the testamentary disposal of their property and can disinherit their children at their pleasure. It is obvious that in spite and precisely because of this fact freedom of marriage among the classes with something to inherit is in reality not a whit greater in England and America than it is in France and Germany.

As regards the legal equality of husband and wife in marriage, the position is no better. The legal inequality of the two partners bequeathed to us from earlier social conditions is not the cause but the effect of the economic oppression of the woman. In the old communistic household, which comprised many couples and their children, the task entrusted to the women of managing the household was as much a public, a socially necessary industry as the procuring of food by the men. With the patriarchal family and still more with the single monogamous family, a change came. Household management lost is public character. It no longer concerned society. It became a *private service*; the wife became the head servant, excluded from all participation in social production. Not until the coming of modern large-scale industry was the road to social production opened to her again—and then only to the proletarian wife. But it was opened in such a manner that, if she carries out her duties in the private service of her family, she remains excluded from public production and unable to earn; and if she wants to take part in public production and earn independently, she cannot carry out family duties. And the wife's position in the factory is the position of women in all branches of business, right up to medicine and the law. The modern individual family is founded on the open or concealed domestic slavery of the wife, and modern society is a mass composed of these individual families as its molecules.

In the great majority of cases today, at least in the possessing classes, the husband is obliged to earn a living and support his family, and that in itself gives him a position of supremacy without any need for special legal titles and privileges. Within the family he is the bourgeois, and the wife represents the proletariat. In the industrial world, the specific character of the economic oppression burdening the proletariat is visible in all its sharpness only when all special legal privileges of the capitalist class have been abolished and complete legal equality of both classes established. The democratic republic does not do away with the oppression of the two classes; on the contrary, it provides the clear field on which the fight can be fought out. And in the same way, the peculiar character of the supremacy of the husband over the wife in the modern family, the necessity of creating real social equality between them and the way to do it, will only be seen in the clear light of day when both possess legally complete equality of rights. Then it will be plain that the first condition for the liberation of the wife is to bring the whole female sex back into public industry, and that this in turn demands that the characteristic of the monogamous family as the economic unit of society be abolished.

Simone de Beauvoir
The Second Sex

Simone de Beauvoir *is a French philosopher best known for her extensive contributions to the development of feminist thought. A life-long companion of Jean-Paul Sartre, her philosophical roots are in the existentialist tradition. Her book* The Second Sex, *from which the following selection is taken, is a classic of feminist philosophy.*

*F*or a long time I have hesitated to write a book on woman. The subject is irritating, especially to women; and it is not new. Enough ink has been spilled in the quarreling over feminism, now practically over, and perhaps we should say no more about it. It is still talked about, however, for the voluminous nonsense uttered during the last century seems to have done little to illuminate the problem. After all, is there a problem? And if so, what is it? Are there women, really? Most assuredly the theory of the eternal feminine still has its adherents who will whisper in your ear: "Even in Russia women still are *women*"; and other erudite persons— sometimes the very same—say with a sigh: "Woman is losing her way, woman is lost." One wonders if women still exist, if they will always exist, whether or not it is desirable that they should, what place they occupy in this world, what their place should be. "What has become of women?" was asked recently in an ephemeral magazine.

But first we must ask: what is a woman? "*Tota mulier in utero,*" says one, "woman is a womb." But in speaking of certain women, connoisseurs declare that they are not women, although they are equipped with a uterus like the rest. All agree in recognizing the fact that females exist in the human species; today as always they make up about one half of humanity. And yet we are told that femininity is in danger; we are exhorted to be women, remain women, become women. It would appear, then, that every female human being is not necessarily a woman; to be so considered she must share in that mysterious and threatened reality known as femininity. Is this attribute something secreted by the ovaries? Or is it a Platonic essence, a product of the philosophic imagination? Is a rustling petticoat enough to bring it down to earth? Although some women try zealously to incarnate this essence, it is hardly patentable. It is frequently described in vague and dazzling terms that seem to have been borrowed from the vocabulary of the seers, and indeed in the times of St. Thomas it was considered an essence as certainly defined as the somniferous virtue of the poppy.

But conceptualism has lost ground. The biological and social sciences no longer admit the existence of unchangeable fixed entities that determine given characteristics, such as those ascribed to woman, the Jew, or the Negro. Science regards any characteristic as a reaction dependent in part upon a *situation*. If today femininity no longer exists, then it never existed. But does the word *woman*, then, have no specific content? This is stoutly affirmed by those who hold to the philosophy of the enlightenment, of rationalism, of nominalism; women, to them, are merely the human beings arbitrarily designated by the word *woman*. Many American women particularly are prepared to think that there is no longer any place for woman as such; if a backward individual still takes herself for a woman, her friends advise her to be psychoanalyzed and thus get rid of this obsession. In regard to a work, *Modern Woman: The Lost Sex*, which in other respects has its irritating features, Dorothy Parker has written: "I cannot be just to books which treat of woman as woman. . . . My idea is that all of us, men as well as women, should be regarded as human beings." But nominalism is a rather inadequate doctrine, and the antifemininists have had no trouble in showing that woman simply *are not* men. Surely woman is, like man, a human being; but such a declaration is abstract. The fact is that every concrete human being is always a singular, separate individual. To decline to accept such notions as the eternal feminine, the black soul, the Jewish character, is not to deny that Jews, Negroes, women exist today—this denial does not represent a liberation for those concerned, but rather a flight from reality. Some years ago a well-known woman writer refused to permit her portrait to appear in a series of photographs especially devoted to women writers; she wished to be counted among the men. But in order to gain this privilege she made use of her husband's influence! Women who assert that they are men lay claim none the less to masculine consideration and respect. I recall also a young Trotskyite standing on a platform at a boisterous meeting and getting ready to use her fists, in spite of her evident fragility. She was denying her feminine weakness; but it was for love of a militant male whose equal she wished to be. The attitude of defiance of many American women proves that they are haunted by a sense of their femininity. In truth, to go for a walk with one's eyes open is enough to demonstrate that humanity is divided into two classes of individuals whose clothes, faces, bodies, smiles, gaits, interests, and occupations are manifestly different. Perhaps these differences are superficial, perhaps they are destined to disappear. What is certain is that right now they do most obviously exist.

If her functioning as a female is not enough to define woman, if we decline also to explain her through "the eternal feminine," and if nevertheless we admit, provisionally, that women do exist, then we must face the question: what is a woman?

To state the question is, to me, to suggest, at once, a preliminary answer. The fact that I ask it is in itself significant. A man would never get the notion of writing a book on the peculiar situation of the human male. But if I wish to define myself, I must first of all say: "I am a woman"; on this truth must be based all further discussion. A man never begins by presenting himself as an individual of a certain sex; it goes without saying that he is a man. The terms *masculine* and *feminine* are used symmetrically only as a matter of form, as on legal papers. In actuality the relation of the two sexes is not quite like that of two electrical poles, for man represents both the positive and the neutral, as is indicated by the common use of *man* to designate human beings in general; whereas woman represents only the negative, defined by limiting criteria, without reciprocity. In the midst of an abstract discussion it is vexing to hear a man say: "You think thus and so because you are a woman"; but I know that my only defense is to reply: "I think thus and so because it is true," thereby removing my subjective self from the argument. It would be out of the question to reply: "And you think the contrary because you are a man," for it is understood that the fact of being a man is no peculiarity. A man is in the right in being a man; it is the woman who is in the wrong. It amounts to this: just as for the ancients there was an absolute vertical with reference to which the oblique was defined, so there is an absolute human type, the masculine. Woman has ovaries, a uterus; these peculiarities imprison her in her subjectivity, circumscribe her within the limits of her own nature. It is often said that she thinks with her glands. Man superbly ignores the fact that his anatomy also includes glands, such as the testicles, and that they secrete hormones. He thinks of his body as a direct and normal connection with the world, which he believes he apprehends objectively, whereas he regards the body of woman as a hindrance, a prison, weighed down by everything peculiar to it. "The female is a female by virtue of a certain *lack* of qualities," said Aristotle; "we should regard the female nature as afflicted with a natural defectiveness." And St. Thomas for his part prounounced woman to be an "imperfect man," an "incidental" being. This is symbolized in Genesis where Eve is depicted as made from what Bossuet called "a supernumerary bone" of Adam.

Thus humanity is male and man defines woman not in herself but as relative to him; she is not regarded as an autonomous being. Michelet writes: "Woman, the relative being. . . ." And Benda is most positive in his *Rapport d'Uriel*: "The body of man makes sense in itself quite apart from that of woman, whereas the latter seems wanting in significance by itself. . . . Man can think of himself without woman. She cannot think of herself without man." And she is simply what man decrees; thus she is called "the sex," by which is meant that she appears essentially to the male as a sexual being. For him she is sex—absolute sex, no less. She is defined and differentiated with reference to man and not he with reference to her; she is the incidental, the inessential as opposed to the essential. He is the Subject, he is the Absolute—she is the Other.

The category of the *Other* is as primordial as consciousness itself. In the most primitive societies, in the most ancient mythologies, one finds the expression of a duality—that of the Self and the Other. This duality was not originally attached to the division of the sexes; it was not dependent upon any empirical facts. It is revealed in such works as that of Granet on Chinese thought and those of Dumézil on the East Indies and Rome. The feminine element was at first no more involved in such pairs as Varuna-Mitra, Uranus-Zeus, Sun-Moon, and Day-Night than it was in the contrasts between Good and Evil, lucky and unlucky auspices, right and left, God and Lucifer. Otherness is a fundamental category of human thought.

Thus it is that no group ever sets itself up as the One without at once setting up the Other over against itself. If three travelers chance to occupy the same compartment, that is enough to make vaguely hostile "others" out of all the rest of the passengers on the train. In small-town eyes all persons not belonging to the village are "strangers" and suspect; to the native of a country all who inhabit other countries are "foreigners"; Jews are "different" for the anti-Semite, Negroes are "inferior" for American racists, aborigines are "natives" for colonists, proletarians are the "lower class" for the privileged. . . .

. . . The native traveling abroad is shocked to find himself in turn regarded as a "stranger" by the natives of neighboring countries. As a matter of fact, wars, festivals, trading, treaties, and contests among tribes, nations, and classes tend to deprive the concept *Other* of its absolute sense and to make manifest its relativity; willy-nilly, individuals and groups are forced to realize the reciprocity of their relations. How is it, then, that this reciprocity has not been recognized between the sexes, that one of the contrasting terms is set up as the sole essential, denying any relativity in regard to its correlative and defining the latter as pure otherness? Why is it that women do not dispute male sovereignty? No subject will readily volunteer to become the object, the inessential; it is not the Other who, in defining himself as the Other, establishes the One. The Other is posed as such by the One in defining himself as the One. But if the Other is not to regain the status of being the One, he must be submissive enough to accept this alien point of view. Whence comes this submission in the case of woman? . . .

History has shown us that men have always kept in their hands all concrete powers; since the earliest days of the patriarchate they have thought best to keep woman in a state of dependence; their codes of law have been set up against her; and thus she has been definitely established as the Other. This arrangement suited the economic interests of the males; but it conformed also to their ontological and moral pretensions. Once the subject seeks to assert himself, the Other, who limits and denies him, is none the less a necessity to him: he attains himself only through that reality which he is not, which is something other than himself. That is why man's life is never abundance and quietude; it is dearth and activity, it is struggle. Before him, man encounters Nature; he has some hold upon her, he endeavors to mold her to his desire. But she cannot fill his needs. Either she appears simply as a purely impersonal opposition, she is an obstacle and remains a stranger; or she submits passively to man's will and permits assimilation, so that he takes possession of her only through consuming her— that is, through destroying her. In both cases he remains alone; he is alone when he touches a stone, alone when he devours a fruit. There can be no presence of an other unless the other is also present in and for himself: which is to say that true alterity—otherness—is that of a consciousness separate from mine and substantially identical with mine.

It is the existence of other men that tears each man out of his immanence and enables him to fulfill the truth of his being, to complete himself through transcendence, through escape toward some objective, through enterprise. But this liberty not my own, while assuring mine, also conflicts with it: there is the tragedy of the unfortunate human consciousness; each separate conscious being aspires to set himself up alone as sovereign subject. Each tries to fulfill himself by reducing the other to slavery. But the slave, though he works and fears, senses himself somehow as the essential; and, by a dialectical inversion, it is the master who seems to be the inessential. It is possible to rise above this conflict if each individual freely recognizes the other, each regarding himself and the other simultaneously as object and as subject in a reciprocal manner. But friendship and generosity, which alone permit in actuality this recognition of free beings, are not facile virtues; they are assuredly man's highest achievement, and through that achievement he is to be found in his true nature. But this true nature is that of a struggle unceasingly begun, unceasingly abolished; it requires man to outdo himself at every moment. We might put it in other words and say that man attains an authentically moral attitude when he renounces *mere being* to assume his position as an existent; through this transformation also he renounces all possession, for possession is one way of seeking mere being; but the transformation through which he attains true wisdom is never done, it is necessary to make it without ceasing, it demands a constant tension. And so, quite unable to fulfill himself in solitude, man is incessantly in danger in his relations with his fellows: his life is a difficult enterprise with success never assured.

But he does not like difficulty; he is afraid of danger. He aspires in contradictory fashion both to life and to repose, to existence and to merely being; he knows full well that "trouble of spirit" is the price of development, that his distance from the object is the price of his nearness to himself; but he dreams of quiet in disquiet and of an opaque plenitude that nevertheless would be endowed with consciousness. This dream incarnated is precisely woman;

she is the wished-for intermediary between nature, the stranger to man, and the fellow being who is too closely identical. She opposes him with neither the hostile silence of nature nor the hard requirement of a reciprocal relation; through a unique privilege she is a conscious being and yet it seems possible to possess her in the flesh. Thanks to her, there is a means for escaping that implacable dialectic of master and slave which has its source in the reciprocity that exists between free beings.

We have seen that there were not at first free women whom the males had enslaved nor were there even castes based on sex. To regard woman simply as a slave is a mistake; there were women among the slaves, to be sure, but there have always been free women— that is, women of religious and social dignity. They accepted man's sovereignty and he did not feel menaced by a revolt that could make of him in turn the object. Woman thus seems to be the inessential who never goes back to being the essential, to be the absolute Other, without reciprocity. This conviction is dear to the male, and every creation myth has expressed it, among others the legend of Genesis, which, through Christianity, has been kept alive in Western civilization. Eve was not fashioned at the same time as the man; she was not fabricated from a different substance, nor of the same clay as was used to model Adam: she was taken from the flank of the first male. Not even her birth was independent; God did not sponta- neously choose to create her as an end in herself and in order to be worshipped directly by her in return for it. She was destined by Him for man; it was to rescue Adam from loneliness that He gave her to him, in her mate was her origin and her purpose; she was his complement on the order of the inessential. Thus she appeared in the guise of privileged prey. She was nature elevated to transparency of consciousness; she was a conscious being, but naturally submissive. And therein lies the wondrous hope that man has often put in woman: he hopes to fulfill himself as a being by carnally possessing a being, but at the same time confirming his sense of freedom through the docility of a free person. No man would consent to be a woman, but every man wants women to exist. "Thank God for having created woman." "Nature is good since she has given women to men." In such expressions man once more asserts with naïve arrogance that his presence in this world is an ineluctable fact and a right, that of woman a mere accident—but a very happy accident. Appearing as the Other, woman appears at the same time as an abundance of being in contrast to that existence the nothingness of which man senses in himself; the Other, being regarded as the object in the eyes of the subject, is regarded as *en soi*; therefore as a being. In woman is incarnated in positive form the lack that the existent carries in his heart, and it is in seeking to be made whole through her that man hopes to attain self-realization. . . .

. . . Perhaps the myth of woman will some day be extinguished; the more women assert themselves as human beings, the more the marvelous quality of the Other will die out in them. But today it still exists in the heart of every man.

A myth always implies a subject who projects his hopes and his fears toward a sky of transcendence. Women do not set themselves up as Subject and hence have erected no virile myth in which their projects are reflected; they have no religion or poetry of their own: they still dream through the dreams of men. Gods made by males are the gods they worship. Men have shaped for their own exaltation great virile figures: Hercules, Prometheus, Parsifal; woman has only a secondary part to play in the destiny of these heroes. No doubt there are conven- tional figures of man caught in his relations to woman: the father, the seducer, the husband, the jealous lover, the good son, the wayward son; but they have all been established by men, and they lack the dignity of myth, being hardly more than clichés. Whereas woman is defined exclusively in her relation to man. The asymmetry of the categories—male and female—is made manifest in the unilateral form of sexual myths. We sometimes say "the sex" to designate woman; she is the flesh, its delights and dangers. The truth that for woman man is sex and carnality has never been proclaimed because there is no one to proclaim it. Representation of the world, like the world itself, is the work of men; they describe it from their own point of view, which they confuse with absolute truth.

It is always difficult to describe a myth; it cannot be grasped or encompassed; it haunts the human consciousness without ever appearing before it in fixed form. The myth is so various, so contradictory, that at first its unity is not discerned: Delilah and Judith, Aspasia and Lucretia, Pandora and Athena—woman is at once Eve and the Virgin Mary. She is an idol, a servant, the source of life, a power of darkness; she is the elemental silence of truth, she is artifice, gossip, and falsehood; she is healing presence and sorceress; she is man's prey, his downfall, she is everything that he is not and that he longs for, his negation and his *raison d'être*. . . .

Man seeks in woman the Other as Nature and as his fellow being. But we know what ambivalent feelings Nature inspires in man. He exploits her, but she crushes him, he is born of her and dies in her; she is the source of his being and the realm that he subjugates to his will; Nature is a vein of gross material in which the soul is imprisoned, and she is the supreme reality; she is contingence and Idea, the finite and the whole; she is what opposes the Spirit, and the Spirit itself. Now ally, now enemy, she appears as the dark chaos from whence life wells up, as this life itself, and as the over-yonder toward which life tends. Woman sums up nature as Mother, Wife, and Idea; these forms now mingle and now conflict, and each of them wears a double visage. . . .

This, then, is the reason why woman has a double and deceptive visage: she is all that man desires and all that he does not attain. She is the good mediatrix between propitious Nature and man; and she is the temptation of unconquered Nature, counter to all goodness. She incarnates all moral values, from good to evil, and their opposites; she is the substance of action and whatever is an obstacle to it, she is man's grasp on the world and his frustration; as such she is the source and origin of all man's reflection on his existence and of whatever expression he is able to give to it; and yet she works to divert him from himself, to make him sink down in silence and in death. She is servant and companion, but he expects her also to be his audience and critic and to confirm him in his sense of being; but she opposes him with her indifference, even with her mockery and laughter. He projects upon her what he desires and what he fears, what he loves and what he hates. And if it is so difficult to say anything specific about her, that is because man seeks the whole of himself in her and because she is All. She is All, that is, on the plane of the inessential; she is all the Other. And, as the other, she is other than herself, other than what is expected of her. Being all, she is never quite *this* which she should be; she is everlasting deception, the very deception of that existence which is never successfully attained nor fully reconciled with the totality of existents.

Sojourner Truth

Ain't I a Woman?

Sojourner Truth (1795–1883) *was born into slavery in New York State and gained her freedom in 1832 when that state emancipated its slaves. Though she never learned to read or write, she was an extraordinarily effective public speaker. She traveled widely and was a passionate advocate of women's rights and the abolition of slavery.*

Well, children, where there is so much racket there must be something out of kilter. I think that 'twixt the negroes of the South and the women at the North, all talking about rights, the white men will be in a fix pretty soon. But what's all this here talking about?

That man over there says that women need to be helped into carriages, and lifted over ditches, and to have the best place everywhere. Nobody ever helps me into carriages, or over mud-puddles, or gives me any best place! And ain't I a woman? Look at me! Look at my arm! I have ploughed and planted, and gathered into barns, and no man could head me! And ain't I a woman? I could work as much and eat as much as a man—when I could get it—and bear the lash as well! And ain't I a woman? I have borne thirteen children, and seen them most all sold off to slavery, and when I cried out with my mother's grief, none but Jesus heard me! And ain't I a woman?

Then they talk about this thing in the head; what's this they call it? [Intellect, someone whispers.] That's it, honey. What's that got to do with women's rights or negro's rights? If my cup won't hold but a pint, and yours holds a quart, wouldn't you be mean not to let me have my little half-measure full?

Then that little man in black there, he says women can't have as much rights as men, 'cause Christ wasn't a woman! Where did your Christ come from? Where did your Christ come from? From God and a woman! Man had nothing to do with Him.

If the first woman God ever made was strong enough to turn the world upside down all alone, these women together ought to be able to turn it back, and get it right side up again! And now they is asking to do it, the men better let them.

Obliged to you for hearing me, and now old Sojourner ain't got nothing more to say.

Phyllis Schlafly
The Power of the Positive Woman

Phyllis Schlafly *is best known as an advocate of conservative causes. In particular, she is an outspoken opponent of women's liberation. A frequent public speaker, Schlafly's views are compiled in her book* The Power of the Positive Woman.

The first requirement for the acquisition of power by the Positive Woman is to understand the differences between men and women. Your outlook on life, your faith, your behavior, your potential for fulfillment, all are determined by the parameters of your original premise. The Positive Woman starts with the assumption that the world is her oyster. She rejoices in the creative capability within her body and the power potential of her mind and spirit. She understands that men and women are different, and that those very differences provide the key to her success as a person and fulfillment as a woman.

The women's liberationist, on the other hand, is imprisoned by her own negative view of herself and of her place in the world around her. This view of women was most succinctly expressed in an advertisement designed by the principal women's liberationist organization, the National Organization for Women (NOW), and run in many magazines and newspapers and as spot announcements on many television stations. The advertisement showed a darling curlyheaded girl with the caption: "This healthy, normal baby has a handicap. She was born female."

This is the self-articulated dog-in-the-manger, chip-on-the-shoulder, fundamental dogma of the women's liberation movement. Someone—it is not clear who, perhaps God, perhaps the "Establishment,": perhaps a conspiracy of male chauvinist pigs—dealt women a foul blow by making them female. It becomes necessary, therefore, for women to agitate and demonstrate and hurl demands on society in order to wrest from an oppressive male-dominated social structure the status that has been wrongfully denied to women through the centuries.

By its very nature, therefore, the women's liberation movement precipitates a series of conflict situations—in the legislatures, in the courts, in the schools, in industry—with man targeted as the enemy. Confrontation replaces cooperation as the watchword of all relationships. Women and men become adversaries instead of partners.

The second dogma of the women's liberationists is that, of all the injustices perpetrated upon women through the centuries, the most oppressive is the cruel fact that women have babies and men do not. Within the confines of the women's liberationist ideology, therefore, the abolition of this overriding inequality of women becomes the primary goal. This goal must be achieved at any and all costs—to the woman herself, to the baby, to the family, and to society. Women must be made equal to men in their ability *not* to become pregnant and *not* to be expected to care for babies they may bring into the world.

This is why women's liberationists are compulsively involved in the drive to make abortion and child-care centers for all women, regardless of religion or income, both socially acceptable and government-financed. Former Congresswoman Bella Abzug has defined the goal: "to enforce the constitutional right of females to terminate pregnancies that they do not wish to continue."

If man is targeted as the enemy, and the ultimate goal of women's liberation is independence from men and the avoidance of pregnancy and its consequences, then lesbianism is logically the highest form in the ritual of women's liberation. Many, such as Kate Millett, come to this conclusion, although many others do not.

The Positive Woman will never travel that dead-end road. It is self-evident to the Positive Woman that the female body with its baby-producing organs was not designed by a conspiracy of men but by the Divine Architect of the human race. Those who think it is unfair that women have babies, whereas men cannot, will have to take up their complaint with God because no other power is capable of changing that fundamental fact. On some college campuses, I have been assured that other methods of reproduction will be developed. But most of us must deal with the real world rather than with the imagination of dreamers.

Another feature of the woman's natural role is the obvious fact that women can breast-feed babies and men cannot. This functional role was not imposed by conspiratorial males seeking to burden women with confining chores, but must be recognized as part of the plan of the Divine Architect for the survival of the human race through the centuries and in the countries that know no pasteurization of milk or sterilization of bottles.

The Positive Woman looks upon her femaleness and her fertility as part of her purpose, her potential, and her power. She rejoices that she has a capability for creativity that men can never have.

The third basic dogma of the women's liberation movement is that there is no difference between male and female except the sex organs, and that all those physical, cognitive, and emotional differences you *think* are there, are merely the result of centuries of restraints imposed by a male-dominated society and sex-stereotyped schooling. The role imposed on women is, by definition, inferior, according to the women's liberationists.

The Positive Woman knows that, while there are some physical competitions in which women are better (and can command more money) than men, including those that put a premium on grace and beauty, such as figure skating, the superior physical strength of males over females in competitions of strength, speed, and short-term endurance is beyond rational dispute.

In the Olympic Games, women not only cannot win any medals in competition with men, the gulf between them is so great that they cannot even qualify for the contests with men. No amount of training from infancy can enable women to throw the discus as far as men, or to match men in push-ups or in lifting weights. In track and field events, individual male records surpass those of women by 10 to 20 percent.

Female swimmers today are beating Johnny Weissmuller's records, but today's male swimmers are better still. Chris Evert can never win a tennis match against Jimmy Connors. If we removed lady's tees from golf courses, women would be out of the game. Putting women in football or wrestling matches can only be an exercise in laughs.

The Olympic Games, whose rules require strict verification to ascertain that no male enters a female contest and, with his masculine advantage, unfairly captures a woman's medal, formerly insisted on a visual inspection of the contestants' bodies. Science, however, has discovered that men and women are so innately different physically that their maleness/femaleness can be conclusively established by means of a simple skin test of fully clothed persons.

In there is *anyone* who should oppose enforced sex-equality, it is the women athletes. Babe Didrickson, who played and defeated some of the great male athletes of her time, is unique in the history of sports.

If sex equality were enforced in professional sports, it would mean that men could enter the women's tournaments and win most of the money. Bobby Riggs has already threatened: "I think that men 55 years and over should be allowed to play women's tournaments—like the Virginia Slims. Everybody ought to know there's no sex after 55 anyway."

The Positive Woman remembers the essential validity of the old prayer: "Lord, give me the strength to change what I can change, the serenity to accept what I cannot change, and the wisdom to discern the difference." The women's liberationists are expending their time and energies erecting a make-believe world in which they hypothesize that *if* schooling were gender-free, and *if* the same money were spent on male and female sports programs, and *if* women were permitted to compete on equal terms, *then* they would prove themselves to be physically equal. Meanwhile, the Positive Woman has put the ineradicable physical differences into her mental computer, programmed her plan of action, and is already on the way to personal achievement.

Thus, while some militant women spend their time demanding more money for professional sports, ice skater Janet Lynn, a truly Positive Woman, quietly signed the most profitable financial contract in the history of women's athletics. It was not the strident demands of the women's liberationists that brought high prizes to women's tennis, but the discovery by sports promoters that beautiful female legs gracefully moving around the court made women's tennis a highly marketable television production to delight male audiences.

Many people thought that the remarkable filly name Ruffian would prove that a female race horse could compete equally with a male. Even with the handicap of extra weights placed on the male horse, the race was a disaster for the female. The gallant Ruffian gave her all in a noble effort to compete, but broke a leg in the race and, despite the immediate attention of top veterinarians, had to be put away.

Despite the claims of the women's liberation movement, there are countless physical differences between men and women. The female body is 50 to 60 percent water, the male 60 to 70 percent water, which explains why males can dilute alcohol better than women and delay its effect. The average woman is about 25 percent fatty tissue, while the male is 15 percent, making women more buoyant in water and able to swim with less effort. Males have a tendency to color blindness. Only 5 percent of persons who get gout are female. Boys are born bigger. Women live longer in most countries of the world, not only in the United States where we have a hard-driving competitive pace. Women excel in manual dexterity, verbal skills, and memory recall. . . .

Does the physical advantage of men doom women to a life of servility and subservience? The Positive Woman knows that she has a complementary advantage which is at least as great—and, in the hands of a skillful woman, far greater. The Divine Architect who gave men a superior strength to lift weights also gave women a different kind of superior strength.

The women's liberationists and their dupes who try to tell each other that the sexual drive of men and women is really the same, and that it is only societal restraints that inhibit women from an equal desire, an equal enjoyment, and an equal freedom from the consequences, are doomed to frustration forever. It just isn't so, and pretending cannot make it so. The differences are not a woman's weakness but her strength. . . .

The new generation can brag all it wants about the new liberation of the new morality, but it is still the woman who is hurt the most. The new morality isn't just a "fad"—it is a cheat and a thief. It robs the woman of her virtue, her youth, her beauty, and her love—for nothing, just nothing. It has produced a generation of young women searching for their identity, bored with sexual freedom, and despondent from the loneliness of living a life without commitment. They have abandoned the old commandments, but they can't find any new rules that work.

The Positive Woman recognizes the fact that, when it comes to sex, women are simply not the equal of men. The sexual drive of men is much stronger than that of women. That is how the human race was designed in order that it might perpetuate itself. The other side of the coin is that it is easier for women to control their sexual appetites. A Positive Woman cannot defeat a man in a wrestling or boxing match, but she can motivate him, inspire him, encourage him, teach him, restrain him, reward him, and have power over him that he can never achieve over her with all his muscle. How or whether a Positive Woman uses her power is determined solely by the way she alone defines her goals and develops her skills.

The differences between men and women are also emotional and psychological. Without woman's innate maternal instinct, the human race would have died out centuries ago. There is nothing so helpless in all earthly life as the newborn infant. It will die within hours if not cared for. Even in the most primitive, uneducated societies, women have always cared for their newborn babies. They didn't need any schooling to teach them how. They didn't need any welfare workers to tell them it is their social obligation. Even in societies to whom such concepts as "ought," "social responsibility," and "compassion for the helpless" were unknown, mothers cared for their new babies.

Why? Because caring for a baby serves the natural maternal need of a woman. Although not nearly so total as the baby's need, the woman's need is nonetheless real.

The overriding psychological need of a woman is to love something alive. A baby fulfills this need in the lives of most women. If a baby is not available to fill that need, women search for a baby-substitute. This is the reason why women have traditionally gone into teaching and nursing careers. They are doing what comes naturally to the female psyche. The schoolchild or the patient of any age provides an outlet for a woman to express her natural maternal need.

This maternal need in women is the reason why mothers whose children have grown up and flown from the nest are sometimes cut loose from their psychological moorings. The maternal need in women can show itself in love for grandchildren, nieces, nephews, or even neighbors' children. The maternal need in some women has even manifested itself in an extraordinary affection lavished on a dog, a cat, or a parakeet.

This is not to say that every woman must have a baby in order to be fulfilled. But it is to say that fulfillment for most women involves expressing their natural maternal urge by loving and caring for someone.

The women's liberation movement complains that traditional stereotyped roles assume that women are "passive" and that men are "aggressive." The anomaly is that a woman's most fundamental emotional need is not passive at all, but active. A woman naturally seeks to love affirmatively and to show that love in an active way by caring for the object of her affections.

The Positive Woman finds somebody on whom she can lavish her maternal love so that it doesn't well up inside her and cause psychological frustrations. Surely no woman is so isolated by geography or insulated by spirit that she cannot find someone worthy of her maternal love. All persons, men and women, gain by sharing something of themselves with their fellow humans, but women profit most of all because it is part of their very nature.

One of the strangest quirks of women's liberationists is their complaint that societal restraints prevent men from crying in public or showing their emotions, but permit women to do so, and that therefore we should "liberate" men to enable them, too, to cry in public. The public display of fear, sorrow, anger, and irritation reveals a lack of self-discipline that should be avoided by the Positive Woman just as much as by the Positive Man. Maternal love, however, is not a weakness but a manifestation of strength and service, and it should be nurtured by the Positive Woman.

Most women's organizations, recognizing the preference of most women to avoid hard-driving competition, handle the matter of succession of officers by the device of a nominating committee. This eliminates the unpleasantness and the tension of a competitive confrontation every year or two. Many women's organizations customarily use a prayer attributed to Mary, Queen of Scots, which is an excellent analysis by a woman of women's faults:

> Keep us, O God, from pettiness; let us be large in thought, in word, in deed. Let us be done with fault-finding and leave off self-seeking. . . . Grant that we may realize it is the little things that create differences, that in the big things of life we are at one.

Another silliness of the women's liberationists is their frenetic desire to force all women to accept the title *Ms* in place of *Miss* or *Mrs*. If Gloria Steinem and Betty Friedan want to call themselves *Ms* in order to conceal their marital status, their wishes should be respected.

But that doesn't satisfy the women's liberationists. They want all women to be compelled to use *Ms* whether they like it or not. The women's liberation movement has been waging a persistent campaign to browbeat the media into using *Ms* as the standard title for all women. The women's liberationists have already succeeded in getting the Department of Health, Education and Welfare to forbid schools and colleges from identifying women students as *Miss* or *Mrs*. . . .

Finally, women are different from men in dealing with the fundamentals of life itself. Men are philosophers, women are practical, and 'twas ever thus. Men may philosophize about how life began and where we are heading; women are concerned about feeding the kids today. No woman would ever, as Karl Marx did, spend years reading political philosophy in the British Museum while her child starved to death. Women don't take naturally to a search for the intangible and the abstract. The Positive Woman knows who she is and where she is going, and she will reach her goal because the longest journey starts with a very practical first step. . . .

An effort to eliminate the differences [between men and women] by social engineering or legislative or constitutional tinkering cannot succeed, which is fortunate, but social relationships and spiritual values can be ruptured in the attempt. Thus the role reversals being forced upon high school students, under which guidance counselors urge reluctant girls to take "shop" and boys to take "home economics," further confuse a generation already unsure about its identity. They are as wrong as efforts to make a left-handed child right-handed.

Marilyn Frye

Sexism

Marilyn Frye *is a professor of feminist philosophy at Michigan State University. Some of her extensive contributions to feminist thought are collected in her book* The Politics of Reality. *The selection here is an abridged and slightly revised version of the original essay by the same name.*

The first philosophical project I undertook as a feminist was that of trying to say carefully and persuasively what sexism is, and what it is for someone, some institution or some act to be sexist. This project was pressed on me with considerable urgency because, like most women coming to a feminist perception of themselves and the world, I was seeing sexism everywhere and trying to make it perceptible to others. I would point out, complain and criticize, but most frequently my friends and colleagues would not see that what I declared to be sexist was sexist, or at all objectionable.

As the critic and as the initiator of the topic, I was the one on whom the burden of proof fell—it was I who had to explain and convince. Teaching philosophy had already taught me that people cannot be persuaded of things they are not ready to be persuaded of; there are certain complexes of will and prior experience which will inevitably block persuasion, no matter the merits of the case presented. I knew that even if I could explain fully and clearly what I was saying when I called something sexist, I would not necessarily be able to convince various others of the correctness of this claim. But what troubled me enormously was that I could not explain it in any way which satisfied *me*. It is this sort of moral and intellectual frustration which, in my case at least, always generates philosophy.

The following was the product of my first attempt to state clearly and explicitly what sexism is:

> The term 'sexist' in its core and perhaps most fundamental meaning is a term which characterizes anything whatever which creates, constitutes, promotes or exploits any irrelevant or impertinent marking of the distinction between the sexes.

When I composed this statement, I was thinking of the myriads of instances in which persons of the two sexes are treated differently, or behave differently, but where nothing in the real differences between females and males justifies or explains the difference of treatment or behavior. I was thinking, for instance, of the tracking of boys into Shop and girls into Home Ec, where one can see nothing about boys or girls considered in themselves which seems to connect essentially with the distinction between wrenches and eggbeaters. I was thinking also of sex discrimination in employment—cases where someone otherwise apparently qualified for a job is not hired because she is a woman. But when I tried to put this definition of 'sexist' to use, it did not stand the test.

Consider this case: If a company is hiring a supervisor who will supervise a group of male workers who have always worked for male supervisors, it can scarcely be denied that the sex of a candidate for the job is relevant to the candidate's prospects of moving smoothly and successfully into an effective working relationship with the supervisees (though the point is usually exaggerated by those looking for excuses not to hire women). Relevance is an intrasystematic thing. The patterns of behavior, attitude and custom within which a process goes on determine what is relevant to what in matters of describing, predicting or evaluating.

In the case at hand, the workers' attitudes and the surrounding customs of the culture make a difference to how they interact with their supervisor and, in particular, *make* the sex of the supervisor a relevant factor in predicting how things will work out. So then, if the company hires a man, in preference to a more experienced and knowledgeable woman, can we explain our objection to the decision by saying it involved distinguishing on the basis of sex when sex is irrelevant to the ability to do the job? No: sex is relevant here.

So, what did I mean to say about 'sexist'? I was thinking that in a case of a candidate for a supervisory job, the reproductive capacity of the candidate has nothing to do with that person's knowing what needs to be done and being able to give properly timed, clear and correct directions. What I was picturing was a situation purified of all sexist perception and reaction. But, of course, *If* the whole context were not sexist, sex would not be an issue in such a job situation; indeed, it might go entirely unnoticed. It is precisely the fact that the sex of the candidate *is* relevant that is the salient symptom of the sexism of the situation.

I had failed, in that first essay, fully to grasp or understand that the locus of sexism is primarily in the system or framework, not in the particular act. It is not accurate to say that what is going on in cases of sexism is that distinctions are made on the basis of sex when sex is irrelevant; what is wrong in cases of sexism is, in the first place, that sex *is* relevant; and then that the making of distinctions on the basis of sex reinforces the patterns which make it relevant.

In sexist cultural/economic systems, sex is always relevant. To understand what sexism is, then, we have to step back and take a larger view.

Sex-identification intrudes into every moment of our lives and discourse, no matter what the supposedly primary focus or topic of the moment is. Elaborate, systematic, ubiquitous and redundant marking of a distinction between the two sexes of humans and most animals is customary and obligatory. One *never* can ignore it.

Examples of sex-marking behavior patterns abound. A couple enters a restaurant; the headwaiter or hostess addresses the man and does not address the woman. The physician addresses the man by surname and honorific (Mr. Baxter, Rev. Jones) and addresses the woman by given name (Nancy, Gloria). You congratulate your friend—a hug, a slap on the back, shaking hands, kissing; one of the things which determines which of these you do is your friend's sex. In everything one does one has two complete repertoires of behavior, one for interactions with women and one for interactions with men. Greeting, storytelling, order-giving and order-receiving, negotiating, gesturing deference or dominance, encouraging, challenging, asking for information: one does all of these things differently depending upon whether the relevant others are male or female.

That this is so has been confirmed in sociological and socio-linguistic research, but it is just as easily confirmed in one's own experience. To discover the differences in how you greet a woman and how you greet a man, for instance, just observe yourself, paying attention to the following sorts of things: frequency and duration of eye contact, frequency and type of touch, tone and pitch of voice, physical distance maintained between bodies, how and whether you smile, use of slang or swear words, whether your body dips into a shadow curtsy or bow. That I have two repertoires for handling introductions to people was vividly confirmed for me when a student introduced me to his friend, Pat, and I really could not tell what sex Pat was. For a moment I was stopped cold, completely incapable of action. I felt myself helplessly caught between two paths—the one I would take if Pat were female and the one I would take if Pat were male. Of course the paralysis does not last. One is rescued by one's ingenuity and good will; one can invent a way to behave as one says "How do you do?" to a human being. But the habitual ways are not for humans: they are one way for women and another for men. . . .

In order to behave "appropriately" toward women and men, we have to know which of the people we encounter are women and which are men. But if you strip humans of most of their cultural trappings, it is not always that easy to tell without close inspection which are female, which are male. The tangible and visible physical differences between the sexes are not particularly sharp or numerous and in the physical dimensions we associate with "sex differences," the range of individual variation is very great. The differences between the sexes could easily be, and sometimes are, obscured by bodily decoration, hair removal and the like. So the requirement of knowing everyone's sex in every situation and under almost all observational conditions generates a requirement that we all let others know our sex in every situation. And we do. We announce our sexes in a thousand ways. We deck ourselves from head to toe with garments and decorations which serve like badges and buttons to announce our sexes. For every type of occasion there are distinct clothes, gear and accessories, hairdos, cosmetics and scents, labeled as "ladies' " or "men's" and labeling us as females or males, and most of the time most of us choose, use, wear or bear the paraphernalia associated with our sex. It goes below the skin as well. There are different styles of gait, gesture, posture, speech, humor, taste and even of perception, interest and attention that we learn as we grow up to be women or to be men and that label and announce us as women or as men. It begins early in life: even infants in arms are color coded.

That we wear and bear signs of our sexes, and that this is absolutely compulsory, is made clearest in the relatively rare cases when we do not do so, or not enough. Responses ranging from critical to indignant to hostile meet mothers whose babies are not adequately coded; one of the most agitated criticisms of the sixties' hippies was that "you can't tell the boys from the girls." The requirement of sex-announcement is laden, indeed, with all the urgency of the taboo against homosexuality. One appears heterosexual by informing people of one's sex *very* emphatically and *very* unambiguously, and lesbians and homosexuals who wish *not* to pass as heterosexual generally can accomplish this just by cultivating ambiguous sex-indicators in clothes, behavior and style. The power of this ambiguity to generate unease and punitive responses in others mirrors and demonstrates the rigidity and urgency of this strange social rule that we all be and assertively act "feminine" or "masculine" (and not both)— that we flap a full array of sex-signals at all times.

The intense demand for marking and for asserting what sex each person is adds up to a strenuous requirement that there *be* two distinct and sharply dimorphic sexes. But, in reality, there are not. There are people who fit on a biological spectrum between two not-so-sharply defined poles. In about 5 percent of live births, possibly more, the babies are in some degree and way not perfect exemplars of male and female. There are individuals with chromosome patterns other than XX or YY and individuals whose external genitalia at birth exhibit some degree of ambiguity. There are people who are chromosomally "normal" who are at the far ends of the normal spectra of secondary sex characteristics—height, musculature, hairiness, body density, distribution of fat, breast size, etc.—whose overall appearance fits the norm of people whose chromosomal sex is the opposite of theirs.

These variations not withstanding, persons (mainly men, of course) with the power to do so actually *construct* a world in which men are men and women are women and there is nothing in between and nothing ambiguous; they do it by chemically and/or surgically altering people whose bodies are indeterminate or ambiguous with respect to sex. Newborns with "imperfectly formed" genitals are immediately "corrected" by chemical or surgical means, children and adolescents are given hormone "therapies" if their bodies seem not to be developing according to what physicians and others declare to be the norm for what has been declared to be that individual's sex. Persons with authority recommend and supply cosmetics and cosmetic regimens, diets, exercises and all manner of clothing to revise or disguise the too-hairy lip, the too-large breast, the too-slender shoulders, the too-large feet, the too-great or too-slight stature. Individuals whose bodies do not fit the picture of exactly two sharply dimorphic sexes are often enough quite willing to be altered or veiled for the obvious reason that the world punishes them severely for their failure to be the "facts" which would verify the doctrine of two sexes. The demand that the world be a world in which there are exactly two sexes is inexorable, and we are all compelled to answer to it emphatically, unconditionally, repetitiously and unambiguously.

Even being physically "normal" for one's assigned sex is not enough. One must *be* female or male, actively. Again, the costumes and performances. Pressed to acting feminine or masculine, one colludes (co-lude: play along) with the doctors and counselors in the creation of a world in which the apparent dimorphism of the sexes is so extreme that one can only think there is a great gulf between female and male, that the two are, essentially and fundamentally and naturally, utterly different. One helps to create a world in which it seems to us that we *could* never mistake a woman for a man or a man for a woman. We never need worry.

Along with all the making, marking and announcing of sex-distinction goes a strong and visceral feeling or attitude to the effect that sex-distinction is the most important thing in the world: that it would be the end of the world if it were not maintained, clear and sharp and rigid; that a sex-dualism which is rooted in the nature of the beast is absolutely crucial and fundamental to all aspects of human life, human society and human economy. . . .

It is a general and obvious principle of information theory that when it is very, very important that certain information be conveyed, the suitable strategy is redundancy. If a message *must* get through, one sends it repeatedly and by as many means or media as one has at one's command. On the other end, as a receiver of information, if one receives the same information over and over, conveyed by every medium one knows, another message comes through as well, and implicitly: the message that this information is very, very important. The enormous frequency with which information about people's sexes is conveyed conveys implicitly the message that this topic is enormously important. I suspect that this is the single topic on which we most frequently receive information from others throughout our entire lives. If I am right, it would go part way to explaining why we end up with an almost irresistible impression, unarticulated, that the matter of people's sexes is the most important and most fundamental topic in the world.

We exchange sex-identification information, along with the implicit message that it is very important, in a variety of circumstances in which there really is no concrete or experientially obvious point in having the information. There are reasons, as this discussion has shown, why you should want to know whether the person filling your water glass or your tooth is male or female and why that person wants to know what you are, but those reasons are woven invisibly into the fabric of social structure and they do not have to do with the bare mechanics of things being filled. Furthermore, the same culture which drives us to this constant information exchange also simultaneously enforces a strong blanket rule requiring that the simplest and most nearly definitive physical manifestations of sex difference be hidden from view in all but the most private and intimate circumstances. The double message of sex-distinction and its pre-eminent importance is conveyed, in fact, in part *by* devices which systematically and deliberately cover up and hide from view the few physical things which do (to a fair extent) distinguish two sexes of humans. The messages are overwhelmingly dissociated from the concrete facts they supposedly pertain to, and from matrices of concrete and sensible reasons and consequences. . . .

If one is made to feel that a thing is of prime importance, but common sensory experience does not connect it with things of obvious concrete and practical importance, then there is mystery, and with that a strong tendency to the construction of mystical or metaphysical conceptions of its importance. If it is important, but not of mundane importance, it must be of transcendent importance. All the more so if it is *very* important.

This matter of our sexes must be very profound indeed if it must, on pain of shame and ostracism, be covered up and must, on pain of shame and ostracism, be boldly advertised by every means and medium one can devise.

There is one more point about redundancy that is worth making here. If there is one thing more effective in making one believe a thing than receiving the message repetitively, it is rehearsing it repetitively. Advertisers, preachers, teachers, all of us in the brainwashing professions, make use of this apparently physical fact of human psychology routinely. The redundancy of sex-marking and sex-announcing serves not only to make the topic seem transcendently important, but to make the sex-duality it advertises seem transcendently and unquestionably *true*. . . .

Sex-marking and sex-announcing are equally compulsory for males and females; but that is as far as equality goes in this matter. The meaning and import of this behavior is profoundly different for women and for men.

Imagine—

A colony of humans established a civilization hundreds of years ago on a distant planet. It has evolved, as civilizations will. Its language is a descendant of English.

The language has personal pronouns marking the child/adult distinction, and its adult personal pronouns mark the distinction between straight and curly pubic hair. At puberty each person assumes distinguishing clothing styles and manners so others can tell what type she or he is without the closer scrutiny which would generally be considered indecent. People with straight pubic hair adopt a style which is modest and self-effacing and clothes which are fragile and confining; people with curly pubic hair adopt a style which is expansive and prepossessing and clothes which are sturdy and comfortable. People whose pubic hair is neither clearly straight nor clearly curly alter their hair chemically in order to be clearly one or the other. Since those with curly pubic hair have higher status and economic advantages, those with ambiguous pubic hair are told to make it straight, for life will be easier for a low-status person whose category might be doubted than for a high-status person whose category might be doubted.

It is taboo to eat or drink in the same room with any person of the same pubic hair type as oneself. Compulsory heterogourmandism, it is called by social critics, though most people think it is just natural human desire to eat with one's pubic-hair opposite. A logical consequence of this habit, or taboo, is the limitation to dining only singly or in pairs—a taboo against banquetism, or, as the slang expression goes, against the group gulp.

Whatever features an individual male person has which tend to his social and economic disadvantage (his age, race, class, height, etc.), one feature which never tends to his disadvantage in the society at large is his maleness. The case for females is the mirror image of this.

Whatever features an individual female person has which tend to her social and economic advantage (her age, race, etc.), one feature which always tends to her disadvantage is her femaleness. Therefore, when a male's sex-category is the thing about him that gets first and most repeated notice, the thing about him that is being framed and emphasized and given primacy is a feature which in general is an asset to him. When a female's sex-category is the thing about her that gets first and most repeated notice, the thing about her that is being framed and emphasized and given primacy is a feature which in general is a liability to her. Manifestations of this divergence in the meaning and consequences of sex-announcement can be very concrete.

Walking down the street in the evening in a town or city exposes one to some risk of assault. For males the risk is less; for females the risk is greater. If one announces oneself male, one is presumed by potential assailants to be more rather than less likely to defend oneself or be able to evade the assault and, if the male-announcement is strong and unambiguous, to be a noncandidate for sexual assault. If one announces oneself female, one is presumed by potential assailants to be less rather than more likely to defend oneself or to evade the assault and, if the female-announcement is strong and unambiguous, to be a prime candidate for sexual assault. Both the man and the woman "announce" their sex through style of gait, clothing, hair style, etc., but they are not equally or identically affected by announcing their sex. The male's announcement tends toward his protection or safety, and the female's announcement tends toward her victimization. It could not be more immediate or concrete; the meaning of the sex-identification could not be more different.

The sex-marking behavioral repertoires are such that in the behavior of almost all people of both sexes addressing or responding to males (especially within their own culture/race) generally is done in a manner which suggests basic respect, while addressing or responding to females is done in a manner that suggests the females' inferiority (condescending tones, presumptions of ignorance, overfamiliarity, sexual aggression, etc.). So, when one approaches an ordinary well-socialized person in such cultures, if one is male, one's own behavioral announcement of maleness tends to evoke supportive and beneficial response and if one is female, one's own behavioral announcement of femaleness tends to evoke degrading and detrimental response.

The details of the sex-announcing behaviors also contribute to the reduction of women and the elevation of men. The case is most obvious in the matter of clothing. As feminists have been saying for two hundred years or so, ladies' clothing is generally restrictive, binding, burdening and frail; it threatens to fall apart and/or to uncover something that is supposed to be covered if you bend, reach, kick, punch or run. It typically does not protect effectively against hazards in the environment, nor permit the wearer to protect herself against the hazards of the human environment. Men's clothing is generally the opposite of all this—sturdy, suitably protective, permitting movement and locomotion. The details of feminine manners and postures also serve to bind and restrict. To be feminine is to take up little space, to defer to others, to be silent or affirming of others, etc. It is not necessary here to survey all this, for it has been done many times and in illuminating detail in feminist writings. My point here is that though both men and women must behave in sex-announcing ways, the behavior which announces femaleness is in itself both physically and socially binding and limiting as the behavior which announces maleness is not.

The sex-correlated variations in our behavior tend systematically to the benefit of males and the detriment of females. The male, announcing his sex in sex-identifying behavior and dress, is both announcing and acting on his membership in a dominant caste—dominant within his subculture and to a fair extent across subcultures as well. The female, announcing her sex, is both announcing and acting on her membership in the subordinated caste. She is obliged to inform others constantly and in every sort of situation that she is to be treated as inferior, without authority, assaultable. She cannot move or speak within the usual cultural norms without engaging in self-deprecation. The male cannot move or speak without engaging in self-aggrandizement. Constant sex-identification both defines and maintains the caste boundary without which there could not be a dominance-subordination structure. . . .

The cultural and economic structures which create and enforce elaborate and rigid patterns of sex-marking and sex-announcing behavior, that is, create gender as we know it, mold us as dominators and subordinates (I do not say "mold our minds" or "mold our personalities"). They construct two classes of animals, the masculine and the feminine, where another constellation of forces might have constructed three or five categories, and not necessarily hierarchically related. Or such a spectrum of sorts that we would not experience them as "sorts" at all.

The term 'sexist' characterizes cultural and economic structures which create and enforce the elaborate and rigid patterns of sex-marking and sex-announcing which divide the species, along lines of sex, into dominators and subordinates. Individual acts and practices are sexist which reinforce and support those structures, either as culture or as shapes taken on by the enculturated animals. Resistance to sexism is that which undermines those structures by social and political action and by projects of reconstruction and revision of ourselves.

15

What's the Right Thing for Me To Do?

You once told your friend, "If you ever need me, I'll come right over," but now you've got to study for an exam you have in an hour and you promised you'd call your mother this morning and you're exhausted and now it's obvious that you aren't going to have time to do everything. What is the right thing for you to do? See your friend who seems to be in trouble? Study for your exam? Call your mom? Take a short nap? This happens to be an especially bad day for you, but you face similar decisions all the time and you know that, once in a while, it gets much worse. A friend of yours once had to decide whether or not to turn in his brother, who had committed a serious crime, to the police. Deciding whether to study, sleep, call your mother, or visit your friend is nothing by comparison. But the basic questions are the same: what is the right thing to do, and how do you decide what that is? This is the subject matter of **ethics**.

The field of ethics is concerned with the question, "What should one do?" but in a very special sense. There are a great many contexts in which we ask for guidance in getting what we want or achieving our goals, but these tend to be **prudential** concerns and not yet ethical. So, too, it is important in almost any public context to know what the law is—for example, whether in a certain country one drives on the right or left side of the road or whether in a particular park it is permissible to walk your dog without a leash. But such legal questions are not ethics either, although one would naturally expect some connection (sometimes troublesome) between the law and ethical concerns. One way of delineating ethics in particular is by reference to the questions, What *ought* I to do? What is the *right* thing to do? The right thing to do is usually in our own prudential interests, and it is usually within the law if not also specified by law. But what characterizes this special word "ought" is the existence of a set of rules or expectations that go beyond the interests of any individual and constitute a powerful force in our lives quite apart from the question of whether they are bound by law or not.

A familiar example is that one should not lie to one's friends. It may or may not be to your advantage to tell the truth, but in general (at least when you are not signing a contract or testifying in court) lying is not illegal. But lying to your friends is clearly unethical, or we might even say that it is **immoral**. The realm of ethics and morality includes a great many actions that deceive, hurt, or endanger the well-being of others or society as a whole, not only lying but cheating, stealing, killing, and a large number of related wrongdoings. Some of these are crimes, but not all are. "Honor thy father and mother" is considered by most people to be a central rule of morality, but (at least in our country) there is no law against dishonoring or embarrassing one's parents. What makes these the province of ethics and morality is that they are such basic concerns of all of us. The problem of ethical (or moral) philosophy is exactly what does define this set of basic concerns and, even more challenging, how these basic rules can be justified.

Imagine a person (you may not have to look far) who refused to do what she ought to do and demanded of you, "Why should I be moral?" What would you say? You might respond, "It is in your interests to be moral," but being moral is in fact not always in our interests and, even if it is, we would want to make some distinction between those who do the right thing because it is right and others who do it just because it happens to be to their advantage. (Knowing that a friend keeps his promises gives you a very different kind of confidence than knowing that he only keeps his promises when it is convenient.) One might insist that we should be moral because God wishes it (and will punish us if we aren't), but the temporal delay between moral transgression and divine punishment is such that many people either don't really believe it or they are willing to take the chance on a huge dose of confession and repentence later. Ethics and morality have also been justified on the basis that they serve the overall interests and well-being of society, but then the serious question arises of whether the most basic rules might in fact differ from society to society depending on their various needs and customs. In response to the possibility of such **relativism** (that is, the variance of the most basic rules of morality from one culture to another), some philosophers have defended universal principles of morality on the grounds that they satisfy the demands of human reason and thus apply everywhere regardless of the particular conditions or customs of a culture.

The following selections provide a spectrum of very different views of the nature and justification of morality. The foremost example of a moral code in our culture is the Ten Commandments in the Old Testament, coupled with the ethical precepts presented by Jesus, for instance, in the Sermon on the Mount. The basis and justification of that code, needless to say, is its divine origins. But there are other codes and other ways of justifying them. Aristotle, who wrote the most detailed manual of contemporary ethics in ancient Athens, justifies that code—whose ultimate goal is happiness—by appeal to a conception of human nature. Immanuel Kant, by way of contrast, justifies moral principles as the product of "pure practical reason" whose primary concern is **duty** and whose focus is not so much the consequences of our actions (including personal happiness) but rather the notion of a "good will," that is, good intentions based on the demands of the moral law. John Stuart Mill takes a very different approach to ethics; its primary concern is the happiness of all individuals—the common good, or what he calls "the greatest good of the greatest number."

Not every author takes the desirability of morality for granted, however. The German philosopher Friedrich Nietzsche believed that morality was basically a sham, a deceit that protected the weak and incompetent from the strong and creative. William Gass more recently has taken issue with the abstract formulations of morality defended by so many philosophers and has rejected them. John Ladd discusses the ever-present problem of relativism, and Mary Midgley attacks relativism with a particularly striking example of cross cultural moral judgment. Carol Gilligan has recently altered the face of ethical discussions by arguing that an ethics of care, typically associated with women, has been ignored in favor of a predominantly male ethic of rights. In the final selection, Joan Didion wraps up the chapter with her own skeptical views on the very word 'morality.'

The Bible

The Ten Commandments and the Sermon on the Mount

The ultimate written source of Western morality is, without question, the Bible. What follows from the King James version are the Ten Commandments and the Sermon on the Mount.

A nd God spake all these words, saying, 2 I *am* the LORD thy God, which have brought thee out of the land of Egypt, out of the house of bondage.

3 Thou shalt have no other gods before me.

4 Thou shalt not make unto thee any graven image, or any likeness *of any thing* that *is* in heaven above, or that *is* in the earth beneath, or that *is* in the water under the earth:

5 Thou shalt not bow down thyself to them, nor serve them: for I the LORD thy God *am* a jealous God, visiting the iniquity of the fathers upon the children unto the third and fourth *generation* of them that hate me;

6 And shewing mercy unto thousands of them that love me, and keep my commandments.

7 Thou shalt not take the name of the LORD thy God in vain; for the LORD will not hold him guiltless that taketh his name in vain.

8 Remember the sabbath day, to keep it holy.

9 Six days shalt thou labour, and do all thy work:

10 But the seventh day *is* the sabbath of the LORD thy God: *in it* thou shalt not do any work, thou, nor thy son, nor thy daughter, thy manservant, nor thy maidservant, nor thy cattle, nor thy stranger that is within thy gates:

11 For *in* six days the LORD made heaven and earth, the sea, and all that in them *is,* and rested the seventh day: wherefore the LORD blessed the sabbath day, and hallowed it.

12 Honour thy father and thy mother: that thy days may be long upon the land which the LORD thy God giveth thee.

13 Thou shalt not kill.

14 Thou shalt not commit adultery.

15 Thou shalt not steal.

16 Thou shalt not bear false witness against thy neighbour.

17 Thou shalt not covet thy neighbour's house, thou shalt not covet thy neighbour's wife, nor his manservant, nor his maidservant, nor his ox, nor his ass, nor any thing that *is* thy neighbour's.

18 And all the people saw the thunderings, and the lightnings, and the noise of the trumpet, and the mountain smoking: and when the people saw *it,* they removed, and stood afar off.

19 And they said unto Moses, Speak thou with us, and we will hear: but let not God speak with us, lest we die.

20 And Moses said unto the people, Fear not: for God is come to prove you, and that his fear may be before your faces, that ye sin not.

21 And the people stood afar off, and Moses drew near unto the thick darkness where God *was.*

22 And the LORD said unto Moses, Thus thou shalt say unto the children of Israel, Ye have seen that I have talked with you from heaven.

23 Ye shall not make with me gods of silver, neither shall ye make unto you gods of gold.

24 An altar of earth thou shalt make unto me, and shalt sacrifice thereon thy burnt offerings, and thy peace offerings, thy sheep, and thine oxen: in all places where I record my name I will come unto thee, and I will bless thee.

25 And if thou wilt make me an altar of stone, thou shalt not build it of hewn stone: for if thou lift up thy tool upon it, thou hast polluted it.

26 Neither shalt thou go up by steps unto mine altar, that thy nakedness be not discovered thereon. . . .

CHAPTER 5

And seeing the multitudes, he went up into a mountain: and when he was set, his disciples came unto him:

2 And he opened his mouth, and taught them, saying,

3 Blessed *are* the poor in spirit: for theirs is the kingdom of heaven.

4 Blessed *are* they that mourn: for they shall be comforted.

5 Blessed *are* the meek: for they shall inherit the earth.

6 Blessed *are* they which do hunger and thirst after righteousness: for they shall be filled.

7 Blessed *are* the merciful: for they shall obtain mercy.

8 Blessed *are* the pure in heart: for they shall see God.

9 Blessed *are* the peacemakers: for they shall be called the children of God.

10 Blessed *are* they which are persecuted for righteousness' sake: for theirs is the kingdom of heaven.

11 Blessed are ye, when *men* shall revile you, and persecute *you,* and shall say all manner of evil against you falsely, for my sake.

12 Rejoice, and be exceeding glad: for great *is* your reward in heaven: for so persecuted they the prophets which were before you.

13 Ye are the salt of the earth: but if the salt have lost his savour, wherewith shall it be salted? it is thenceforth good for nothing, but to be cast out, and to be trodden under foot of men.

14 Ye are the light of the world. A city that is set on an hill cannot be hid.

15 Neither do men light a candle, and put it under a bushel, but on a candlestick; and it giveth light unto all that are in the house.

16 Let your light so shine before men, that they may see your good works, and glorify your Father which is in heaven.

17 Think not that I am come to destroy the law, or the prophets: I am not come to destroy, but to fulfil.

18 For verily I say unto you, Till heaven and earth pass, one jot or one tittle shall in no wise pass from the law, till all be fulfilled.

19 Whosoever therefore shall break one of these least commandments, and shall teach men so, he shall be called the least in the kingdom of heaven: but whosoever shall do and teach *them,* the same shall be called great in the kingdom of heaven.

20 For I say unto you, That except your righteousness shall exceed *the righteousness* of the scribes and Pharisees, ye shall in no case enter into the kingdom of heaven.

21 Ye have heard that it was said by them of old time, Thou shalt not kill; and whosoever shall kill shall be in danger of the judgment:

22 But I say unto you, That whosoever is angry with his brother without a cause shall be in danger of the judgment: and whosoever shall say to his brother, Raca, shall be in danger of the council: but whosoever shall say, Thou fool, shall be in danger of hell fire.

23 Therefore if thou bring thy gift to the altar, and there rememberest that thy brother hath ought against thee;

24 Leave there thy gift before the altar, and go thy way; first be reconciled to thy brother, and then come and offer thy gift.

25 Agree with thine adversary quickly, whiles thou art in the way with him; lest at any time the adversary deliver thee to the

judge, and the judge deliver thee to the officer, and thou be cast into prison.

26 Verily I say unto thee, Thou shalt by no means come out thence, till thou hast paid the uttermost farthing.

27 Ye have heard that it was said by them of old time, Thou shalt not commit adultery:

28 But I say unto you, That whosoever looketh on a woman to lust after her hath committed adultery with her already in his heart.

29 And if thy right eye offend thee, pluck it out, and cast *it* from thee: for it is profitable for thee that one of thy members should perish, and not *that* thy whole body should be cast into hell.

30 And if thy right hand offend thee, cut it off, and cast *it* from thee: for it is profitable for thee that one of thy members should perish, and not *that* thy whole body should be cast into hell.

31 It hath been said, Whosoever shall put away his wife, let him give her a writing of divorcement:

32 But I say unto you, That whosoever shall put away his wife, saving for the cause of fornication, causeth her to commit adultery: and whosoever shall marry her that is divorced committeth adultery.

33 Again, ye have heard that it hath been said by them of old time, Thou shalt not forswear thyself, but shalt perform unto the Lord thine oaths:

34 But I say unto you, Swear not at all; neither by heaven; for it is God's throne:

35 Nor by the earth; for it is his footstool: neither by Jerusalem; for it is the city of the great King.

36 Neither shalt thou swear by thy head, because thou canst not make one hair white or black.

37 But let your communication be, Yea, yea; Nay, nay: for whatsoever is more than these cometh of evil.

38 Ye have heard that it hath been said, An eye for an eye, and a tooth for a tooth:

39 But I say unto you, That ye resist not evil: but whosoever shall smite thee on thy right cheek, turn to him the other also.

40 And if any man will sue thee at the law, and take away thy coat, let him have *thy* cloak also.

41 And whosoever shall compel thee to go a mile, go with him twain.

42 Give to him that asketh thee, and from him that would borrow of thee turn not thou away.

43 Ye have heard that it hath been said, Thou shalt love thy neighbour, and hate thine enemy.

44 But I say unto you, Love your enemies, bless them that curse you, do good to them that hate you, and pray for them which despitefully use you, and persecute you;

45 That ye may be the children of your Father which is in heaven: for he maketh his sun to rise on the evil and on the good, and sendeth rain on the just and on the unjust.

46 For if ye love them which love you, what reward have ye? do not even the publicans the same?

47 And if ye salute your brethren only, what do ye more *than others?* do not even the publicans so?

48 Be ye therefore perfect, even as your Father which is in heaven is perfect.

CHAPTER 6

*T*ake heed that ye do not your alms before men, to be seen of them: otherwise ye have no reward of your Father which is in heaven.

2 Therefore when thou doest *thine* alms, do not sound a trumpet before thee, as the hypocrites do in the synagogues and in the streets, that they may have glory of men. Verily I say unto you, They have their reward.

3 But when thou doest alms, let not thy left hand know what thy right hand doeth:

4 That thine alms may be in secret: and thy Father which seeth in secret himself shall reward thee openly.

5 And when thou prayest, thou shalt not be as the hypocrites *are*: for they love to pray standing in the synagogues and in the corners of the streets, that they may be seen

of men. Verily I say unto you, They have their reward.

6 But thou, when thou prayest, enter into thy closet, and when thou hast shut thy door, pray to thy Father which is in secret; and thy Father which seeth in secret shall reward thee openly.

7 But when ye pray, use not vain repetitions, as the heathen do: for they think that they shall be heard for their much speaking.

8 Be not ye therefore like unto them: for your Father knoweth what things ye have need of, before ye ask him.

9 After this manner therefore pray ye: Our Father which art in heaven, Hallowed be thy name.

10 Thy kingdom come. Thy will be done in earth, as it is in heaven.

11 Give us this day our daily bread.

12 And forgive us our debts, as we forgive our debtors.

13 And lead us not into temptation, but deliver us from evil: For thine is the kingdom, and the power, and the glory, for ever. Amen.

14 For if ye forgive men their trespasses, your heavenly Father will also forgive you:

15 But if ye forgive not men their trespasses, neither will your Father forgive your trespasses.

16 Moreover when ye fast, be not, as the hypocrites, of a sad countenance: for they disfigure their faces, that they may appear unto men to fast. Verily I say unto you, They have their reward.

17 But thou, when thou fastest, anoint thine head, and wash thy face;

18 That thou appear not unto men to fast, but unto thy Father which is in secret: and thy Father, which seeth in secret, shall reward thee openly.

19 Lay not up for yourselves treasures upon earth, where moth and rust doth corrupt, and where thieves break through and steal:

20 But lay up for yourselves treasures in heaven, where neither moth nor rust doth corrupt, and where thieves do not break through nor steal:

21 For where your treasure is, there will your heart be also.

22 The light of the body is the eye: if therefore thine eye be single, thy whole body shall be full of light.

23 But if thine eye be evil, thy whole body shall be full of darkness. If therefore the light that is in thee be darkness, how great is that darkness!

24 No man can serve two masters: for either he will hate the one, and love the other; or else he will hold to the one, and despise the other. Ye cannot serve God and mammon.

25 Therefore I say unto you, Take no thought for your life, what ye shall eat, or what ye shall drink; nor yet for your body, what ye shall put on. Is not the life more than meat, and the body than raiment?

26 Behold the fowls of the air: for they sow not, neither do they reap, nor gather into barns; yet your heavenly Father feedeth them. Are ye not much better than they?

27 Which of you by taking thought can add one cubit unto his stature?

28 And why take ye thought for raiment? Consider the lilies of the field, how they grow; they toil not, neither do they spin:

29 And yet I say unto you, That even Solomon in all his glory was not arrayed like one of these.

30 Wherefore, if God so clothe the grass of the field, which to day is, and to morrow is cast into the oven, shall he not much more clothe you, O ye of little faith?

31 Therefore take no thought, saying, What shall we eat? or, What shall we drink? or, Wherewithal shall we be clothed?

32 (For after all these things do the Gentiles seek:) for your heavenly Father knoweth that ye have need of all these things.

33 But seek ye first the kingdom of God, and his righteousness; and all these things shall be added unto you.

34 Take therefore no thought for the morrow: for the morrow shall take thought for the things of itself. Sufficient unto the day is the evil thereof.

CHAPTER 7

Judge not, that ye be not judged.
2 For with what judgment ye judge, ye shall be judged: and with what measure ye mete, it shall be measured to you again.

3 And why beholdest thou the mote that is in thy brother's eye, but considerest not the beam that is in thine own eye?

4 Or how wilt thou say to thy brother, Let me pull out the mote out of thine eye; and, behold, a beam *is* in thine own eye?

5 Thou hypocrite, first cast out the beam out of thine own eye; and then shalt thou see clearly to cast out the mote out of thy brother's eye.

6 Give not that which is holy unto the dogs, neither cast ye your pearls before swine, lest they trample them under their feet, and turn again and rend you.

7 Ask, and it shall be given you; seek, and ye shall find; knock, and it shall be opened unto you:

8 For every one that asketh receiveth; and he that seeketh findeth; and to him that knocketh it shall be opened.

9 Or what man is there of you, whom if his son ask bread, will he give him a stone?

10 Or if he ask a fish, will he give him a serpent?

11 If ye then, being evil, know how to give good gifts unto your children, how much more shall your Father which is in heaven give good things to them that ask him?

12 Therefore all things whatsoever ye would that men should do to you, do ye even so to them: for this is the law and the prophets.

13 Enter ye in at the strait gate: for wide *is* the gate, and broad *is* the way, that leadeth to destruction, and many there be which go in thereat:

14 Because strait *is* the gate, and narrow *is* the way, which leadeth unto life, and few there be that find it.

15 Beware of false prophets, which come to you in sheep's clothing, but inwardly they are ravening wolves.

16 Ye shall know them by their fruits. Do men gather grapes of thorns, or figs of thistles?

17 Even so every good tree bringeth forth good fruit; but a corrupt tree bringeth forth evil fruit.

18 A good tree cannot bring forth evil fruit, neither *can* a corrupt tree bring forth good fruit.

19 Every tree that bringeth not forth good fruit is hewn down, and cast into the fire.

20 Wherefore by their fruits ye shall know them.

21 Not every one that saith unto me, Lord, Lord, shall enter into the kingdom of heaven; but he that doeth the will of my Father which is in heaven.

22 Many will say to me in that day, Lord, Lord, have we not prophesied in thy name? and in thy name have cast out devils? and in thy name done many wonderful works?

23 And then will I profess unto them, I never knew you: depart from me, ye that work iniquity.

24 Therefore whosoever heareth these sayings of mine, and doeth them, I will liken him unto a wise man, which built his house upon a rock:

25 And the rain descended, and the floods came, and the winds blew, and beat upon that house; and it fell not: for it was founded upon a rock.

26 And every one that heareth these sayings of mine, and doeth them not, shall be likened unto a foolish man, which built his house upon the sand:

27 And the rain descended, and the floods came, and the winds blew, and beat upon that house; and it fell: and great was the fall of it.

28 And it came to pass, when Jesus had ended these sayings, the people were astonished at his doctrine:

29 For he taught them as *one* having authority, and not as the scribes.

Aristotle
Happiness and the Good Life

Aristotle's (384–322 B.C.) Nicomachean Ethics was both a sociological summary of Athenian ethics in the fourth century B.C. and the classic philosophical theory of ethics. In the selection from Book I that follows, he argues his "teleological" view of ethics— that is, the idea that all human behavior is purposive and that the ultimate purpose of all our actions is happiness.

1. Every art and every kind of inquiry, and likewise every act and purpose, seems to aim at some good; and so it has been well said that the good is that at which everything aims. But a difference is observable among these aims or ends. What is aimed at is sometimes the exercise of a faculty, sometimes a certain result beyond that exercise. And where there is an end beyond that act, there the result is better than the exercise of the faculty. Now since there are many kinds of actions and many arts and sciences, it follows that there are many ends also; e.g. health is the end of medicine, ships of shipbuilding, victory of the art of war, and wealth of economy. But when several of these are subordinated to some one art or science,— as the making of bridles and other trappings to the art of horsemanship, and this in turn, along with all else that the soldier does, to the art of war, and so on,—then the end of the master art is always more desired than the end of the subordinate arts, since these are pursued for its sake. And this is equally true whether the end in view be the mere exercise of a faculty or something beyond that, as in the above instances.

2. If then in what we do there be some end which we wish for on its own account, choosing all the others as means to this, but not every end without exception as a means to something else (for so we should go on *ad infinitum,* and desire would be left void and objectless),—this evidently will be the good or the best of all things. And surely from a practical point of view it much concerns us to know this good; for then, like archers shooting at a definite mark, we shall be more likely to attain what we want. If this be so, we must try to indicate roughly what it is, and first of all to which of the arts or sciences it belongs. It would seem to belong to the supreme art or science, that one which most of all deserves the name of master-art or master-science. Now Politics seems to this description. For it prescribes which of the sciences a state needs, and which each man shall study, and up to what point; and to it we see subordinated even the highest arts, such as economy, rhetoric, and the art of war. Since then it makes use of the other practical sciences, and since it further ordains what men are to do and from what to refrain, its end must include the ends of the others, and must be the proper good of man. For though this good is the same for the individual and the state, yet the good of the state seems a grander and more perfect thing both to attain and to secure; and glad as one would be to do this service for a single individual, to do it for a people and for a number of states is nobler and more divine.

This then is the aim of the present inquiry, which is a sort of political inquiry.

3. We must be content if we can attain to so much precision in our statement as the subject before us admits of; for the same degree of accuracy is no more to be expected in all kinds of reasoning than in all kinds of handicraft. Now the things that are noble and just (with which Politics deals) are so various and so uncertain, that some think these are merely conventional and not natural distinctions. There is a similar uncertainty also about what is good, because good things often do people harm: men have before now been ruined by wealth, and have lost their lives through courage. Our subject, then, and our data being of

this nature, we must be content if we can indicate the truth roughly and in outline, and if, in dealing with matters that are not amenable to immutable laws, and reasoning from premises that are but probable, we can arrive at probable conclusions. The reader, on his part, should take each of my statements in the same spirit; for it is the mark of an educated man to require, in each kind of inquiry, just so much exactness as the subject admits of: it is equally absurd to accept probable reasoning from a mathematician, and to demand scientific proof from an orator.

But each man can form a judgment about what he knows, and is called "a good judge" of that—of any special matter when he has received a special education therein, "a good judge" (without any qualifying epithet) when he has received a universal education. And hence a young man is not qualified to be a student of Politics; for he lacks experience of the affairs of life, which form the data and the subject-matter of Politics. Further, since he is apt to be swayed by his feelings, he will derive no benefit from a study whose aim is not speculative but practical. But in this respect young in character counts the same as young in years; for the young man's disqualification is not a matter of time, but is due to the fact that feeling rules his life and directs all his desires. Men of this character turn the knowledge they get to no account in practice, as we see with those we call incontinent; but those who direct their desires and actions by reason will gain much profit from the knowledge of these matters. . . .

4. Since—to resume—all knowledge and all purpose aims at some good, what is this which we say is the aim of Politics; or, in other words, what is the highest of all realizable goods? As to its name, I suppose nearly all men are agreed; for the masses and the men of culture alike declare that it is happiness, and hold that to "live well" or to "do well" is the same as to be "happy." But they differ as to what this happiness is, and the masses do not give the same account of it as the philosophers. The former take it to be something palpable and plain, as pleasure or wealth or fame; one man holds it to be this, and another that, and often the same man is of different minds at different times—after sickness it is health, and in poverty it is wealth; while when they are impressed with the consciousness of their ignorance, they admire most those who say grand things that are above their comprehension. Some philosophers, on the other hand, have thought that, beside these several good things, there is an "absolute" good which is the cause of their goodness. As it would hardly be worth while to review all the opinions that have been held, we will confine ourselves to those which are most popular, or which seem to have some foundation in reason. . . .

5. It seems that men not unreasonably take their notions of the good or happiness from the lives actually led, and that the masses who are the least refined suppose it to be pleasure, which is the reason why they aim at nothing higher than the life of enjoyment. For the most conspicuous kinds of life are three: this life of enjoyment, the life of the statesman, and, thirdly, the contemplative life. The mass of men show themselves utterly slavish in their preference for the life of brute beasts, but their views receive consideration because many of those in high places have the tastes of Sardanapalus. Men of refinement with a practical turn prefer honour; for I suppose we may say that honour is the aim of the statesman's life. But this seems too superficial to be the good we are seeking; for it appears to depend upon those who give rather than upon those who receive it; while we have a presentiment that the good is something that is peculiarly a man's own and can scarce be taken away from him. Moreover, these men seem to pursue honour in order that they may be assured of their own excellence,— at least, they wish to be honoured by men of sense, and by those who know them, and on the ground of their virtue or excellence. It is plain, then, that in their view, at any rate, virtue or excellence is better than honour; and perhaps we should take this to be the end of the statesman's life, rather than honour. But virtue or excellence also appears too incomplete to be what we want; for it seems that a man might have virtue and yet be asleep or be inactive all his life, and, moreover, might meet with the greatest disasters and misfortunes; and no

one would maintain that such a man is happy, except for argument's sake. But we will not dwell on these matters now, for they are sufficiently discussed in the popular treatises. The third kind of life is the life of contemplation: we will treat of it further on. As for the money-making life, it is something quite contrary to nature; and wealth evidently is not the good of which we are in search, for it is merely useful as a means to something else. So we might rather take pleasure and virtue or excellence to be ends than wealth; for they are chosen on their own account. But it seems that not even they are the end, though much breath has been wasted in attempts to show that they are. . . .

7. Leaving these matters, then, let us return once more to the question, what this good can be of which we are in search. It seems to be different in different kinds of action and in different arts,—one thing in medicine and another in war, and so on. What then is the good in each of these cases? Surely that for the sake of which all else is done. And that in medicine is health, in war is victory, in building is a house,—a different thing in each different case, but always, in whatever we do and in whatever we choose, the end. For it is always for the sake of the end that all else is done. If then there be one end of all that man does, this end will be the realizable good,—or these ends, if there be more than one.

By this generalization our argument is brought to the same point as before. This point we must try to explain more clearly. We see that there are many ends. But some of these are chosen only as means, as wealth, flutes, and the whole class of instruments. And so it is plain that not all ends are final. But the best of all things must, we conceive, be something final. If then there be only one final end, this will be what we are seeking,—or if there be more than one, then the most final of them. Now that which is pursued as an end in itself is more final than that which is pursued as means to something else, and that which is never chosen as means than that which is chosen both as an end in itself and as means, and that is strictly final which is always chosen as an end in itself and never as means.

Happiness seems more than anything else to answer to this description: for we always choose it for itself, and never for the sake of something else; while honour and pleasure and reason, and all virtue or excellence, we choose partly indeed for themselves (for, apart from any result, we should choose each of them), but partly also for the sake of happiness, supposing that they will help to make us happy. But no one chooses happiness for the sake of these things, or as a means to anything else at all. We seem to be led to the same conclusion when we start from the notion of self-sufficiency. The final good is thought to be self-sufficing [or all-sufficing]. In applying this term we do not regard a man as an individual leading a solitary life, but we also take account of parents, children, wife, and, in short, friends and fellow-citizens generally, since man is naturally a social being. Some limit must indeed be set to this; for if you go on to parents and descendants and friends of friends, you will never come to a stop. But this we will consider further on: for the present we will take self-sufficing to mean what by itself makes life desirable and in want of nothing. And happiness is believed to answer to this description. And further, happiness is believed to be the most desirable thing in the world, and that not merely as one among other good things: if it were merely one among other good things [so that other things could be added to it], it is plain that the addition of the least of other goods must make it more desirable; for the addition becomes a surplus of good, and of two goods the greater is always more desirable. Thus it seems that happiness is something final and self-sufficing, and is the end of all that man does.

But perhaps the reader thinks that though no one will dispute the statement that happiness is the best thing in the world, yet a still more precise definition of it is needed. This will best be gained, I think, by asking, What is the function of man? For as the goodness and the excellence of a piper or a sculptor, or the practiser of any art, and generally of those who have any function or business to do, lies in that function, so man's good would seem to lie in his function, if he has one. But can we suppose that, while a carpenter and a cobbler has a function and a business of his own, man has no business and no function assigned him by nature? Nay, surely as his several members, eye and hand and foot, plainly have each his own function, so we must suppose that man also has some function over and above all these.

What then is it? Life evidently he has in common even with the plants, but we want that which is peculiar to him. We must exclude, therefore, the life of mere nutrition and growth. Next to this comes the life of sense; but this too he plainly shares with horses and cattle and all kinds of animals. There remains then the life whereby he acts—the life of his rational nature, with its two sides or divisions, one rational as obeying reason, the other rational as having and exercising reason. But as this expression is ambiguous, we must be understood to mean thereby the life that consists in the exercise [not the mere possession] of the faculties; for this seems to be more properly entitled to the name.

The function of man, then, is exercise of his vital faculties [or soul] on one side in obedience to reason, and on the other side with reason. But what is called the function of a man of any profession and the function of a man who is good in that profession are, generically the same, *e.g.* of a harper and of a good harper; and this holds in all cases without exception, only that in the case of the latter his superior excellence at his work is added; for we say a harper's function is to harp, and a good harper's to harp well. Man's function then being, as we say, a kind of life—that is to say, exercise of his faculties and action of various kinds with reason—the good man's function is to do this well and beautifully [or nobly]. But the function of anything is done well when it is done in accordance with the proper excellence of that thing. If this be so the result is that the good of man is exercise of his faculties in accordance with excellence or virtue, or, if there be more than one, in accordance with the best and most complete virtue. But there must also be a full term of years for this exercise; for one swallow or one fine day does not make a spring, nor does one day or any small space of time make a blessed or happy man.

This, then, may be taken as a rough outline of the good; for this, I think, is the proper method,—first to sketch the outline, and then to fill in the details. But it would seem that, the outline once fairly drawn, any one can carry on the work and fit in the several items which time reveals to us or helps us to find. And this indeed is the way in which the arts and sciences have grown; for it requires no extraordinary genius to fill up the gaps. We must bear in mind, however, what was said above, and not demand the same degree of accuracy in all branches of study, but in each case so much as the subject-matter admits of and as is proper to that kind of inquiry. The carpenter and the geometer both look for the right angle, but in different ways: the former only wants such an approximation to it as his work requires, but the latter wants to know what constitutes a right angle, or what is its special quality; his aim is to find out the truth. And so in other cases we must follow the same course, lest we spend more time on what is immaterial than on the real business in hand. Nor must we in all cases alike demand the reason why; sometimes it is enough if the undemonstrated fact be fairly pointed out, as in the case of the starting-points or principles of a science. Undemonstrated facts always form the first step or starting-point of a science; and these starting-points or principles are arrived at some in one way, some in another—some by induction, others by perception, others again by some kind of training. But in each case we must try to apprehend them in the proper way, and do our best to define them clearly; for they have great influence upon the subsequent course of an inquiry. A good start is more than half the race, I think, and our starting-point of principle, once found, clears up a number of our difficulties.

8. We must not be satisfied, then, with examining this starting-point or principle of ours as a conclusion from our data, but must also view it in its relation to current opinions on the subject; for all experience harmonizes with a true principle, but a false one is soon found to be incompatible with the facts. Now, good things have been divided into three classes, external goods on the one hand, and on the other goods of the soul and goods of the

body; and the goods of the soul are commonly said to be goods in the fullest sense, and more good than any other. But "actions and exercises of the vital faculties may be said to be of the soul." So our account is confirmed by this opinion, which is both of long standing and approved by all who busy themselves with philosophy. But, indeed, we secure the support of this opinion by the mere statement that certain actions and exercises are the end; for this implies that it is to be ranked among the goods of the soul, and not among external goods. Our account, again, is in harmony with the common saying that the happy man lives well and does well; for we may say that happiness, according to us, is living well and doing well. And, indeed, all the characteristics that men expect to find in happiness seem to belong to happiness as we define it. Some hold it to be virtue or excellence, some prudence, others a kind of wisdom; others, again, held it to be all or some of these, with the addition of pleasure, either as an ingredient or as a necessary accompaniment; and some even include external prosperity in their account of it. Now, some of these views have the support of many voices and of old authority; others have few voices, but those of weight; but it is probable that neither the one side nor the other is entirely wrong, but that in some one point at least, if not in most, they are both right.

First, then, the view that happiness is excellence or a kind of excellence harmonizes with our account; for "exercise of faculties in accordance with excellence" belongs to excellence. But I think we may say that it makes no small difference whether the good be conceived as the mere possession of something, or as its use—as a mere habit or trained faculty, or as the exercise of that faculty. For the habit or faculty may be present, and yet issue in no good result, as when a man is asleep, or in any other way hindered from his function; but with its exercise this is not possible, for it must show itself in acts and in good acts. And as at the Olympic games it is not the fairest and strongest who receive the crown, but those who contend (for among these are the victors), so in life, too, the winners are those who not only have all the excellences, but manifest these in deed.

And, further, the life of these men is in itself pleasant. For pleasure is an affection of the soul, and each man takes pleasure in that which he is said to love,—he who loves horses in horses, he who loves sight-seeing in sight-seeing, and in the same way he who loves justice in acts of justice, and generally the lover of excellence or virtue in virtuous acts or the manifestation of excellence. And while with most men there is a perpetual conflict between the several things in which they find pleasure, since these are not naturally pleasant, those who love what is noble take pleasure in that which is naturally pleasant. For the manifestations of excellence are naturally pleasant, so that they are both pleasant to them and pleasant in themselves. Their life, then, does not need pleasure to be added to it as an appendage, but contains pleasure in itself.

Indeed, in addition to what we have said, a man is not good at all unless he takes pleasure in noble deeds. No one would call a man just who did not take pleasure in doing justice, nor generous who took no pleasure in acts of generosity, and so on. If this be so, the manifestations of excellence will be pleasant in themselves. But they are also both good and noble, and that in the highest degree—at least, if the good man's judgment about them is right, for this is his judgment. Happiness, then, is at once the best and noblest and pleasantest thing in the world, and these are not separated, as the Delian inscription would have them to be:

> What is most just is noblest, health is best,
> Pleasantest is to get your heart's desire.

For all these characteristics are united in the best exercises of our faculties; and these, or some one of them that is better than all the others, we identify with happiness.

But nevertheless happiness plainly requires external goods too, as we said; for it is impossible, or at least not easy, to act nobly without some furniture of fortune. There are many things that can only be done through instruments, so to speak, such as friends and wealth and political influence: and there are some things whose absence takes the bloom off our happiness, as good birth, the blessing of children, personal beauty; for a man is not very likely to be happy if he is very ugly in person, or of low birth, or alone in the world, or childless, and perhaps still less if he has worthless children or friends, or has lost good ones that he had. As we said, then, happiness seems to stand in need of this kind of prosperity; and so some identify it with good fortune, just as others identify it with excellence.

9. This has led people to ask whether happiness is attained by learning, or the formation of habits, or any other kind of training, or comes by some divine dispensation or even by chance. Well, if the Gods do give gifts to men, happiness is likely to be among the number, more likely, indeed, than anything else, in proportion as it is better than all other human things. This belongs more properly to another branch of inquiry; but we may say that even if it is not heaven-sent, but comes as a consequence of virtue or some kind of learning or training, still it seems to be one of the most divine things in the world; for the prize and aim of virtue would appear to be better than anything else and something divine and blessed. Again, if it is thus acquired it will be widely accessible; for it will then be in the power of all except those who have lost the capacity for excellence to acquire it by study and diligence. And if it be better that men should attain happiness in this way rather than by chance, it is reasonable to suppose that it is so, since in the sphere of nature all things are arranged in the best possible way, and likewise in the sphere of art, and of each mode of causation, and most of all in the sphere of the noblest mode of causation. And indeed it would be too absurd to leave what is noblest and fairest to the dispensation of chance.

But our definition itself clears up the difficulty; for happiness was defined as a certain kind of exercise of the vital faculties in accordance with excellence or virtue. And of the remaining goods [other than happiness itself], some must be present as necessary conditions, while others are aids and useful instruments to happiness. And this agrees with what we said at starting. We then laid down that the end of the art political is the best of all ends; but the chief business of that art is to make the citizens of a certain character—that is, good and apt to do what is noble. It is not without reason, then, that we do not call an ox, or a horse, or any brute happy; for none of them is able to share in this kind of activity. For the same reason also a child is not happy; he is as yet, because of his age, unable to do such things. If we ever call a child happy, it is because we hope he will do them. For, as we said, happiness requires not only perfect excellence or virtue, but also a full term of years for its exercise. For our circumstances are liable to many changes and to all sorts of chances, and it is possible that he who is now most prosperous will in his old age meet with great disasters, as is told of Priam in the tales of Troy; and a man who is thus used by fortune and comes to a miserable end cannot be called happy.

Immanuel Kant

Foundations of the Metaphysics of Morals

Immanuel Kant (1724–1804), the great German philosopher, wrote his short
Foundations of the Metaphysics of Morals *as a kind of summary of the more*

elaborate arguments in his Critique of Practical Reason *(1788). In both books, he defends morality and moral principles as the product of practical reason, not feelings or "inclinations." These rational principles he calls "categorical imperatives," and in the selection from Book II that follows, he explains this notion. The short excerpt preceding this is from Book I, in which Kant describes morality as concerning "a good will" rather than the consequences of an action or any other matters of good fortune which are not matters of intention.*

Nothing can possibly be conceived in the world, or even out of it, which can be called good without qualification, except a *good will.* Intelligence, wit, judgment, and other *talents* of the mind, however they may be named, or courage, resolution, perseverance, as qualities of temperament, are undoubtedly good and desirable in many respects; but these gifts of nature may also become extremely bad and mischievous if the will which is to make use of them, and which, therefore, constitutes what is called *character,* is not good. It is the same with the *gifts of fortune.* Power, riches, honor, even health, and the general well-being and contentment with one's condition which is called *happiness,* inspire pride, and often presumption, if there is not a good will to correct the influence of these on the mind, and with this also to rectify the whole principle of acting, and adapt it to its end. The sight of a being who is not adorned with a single feature of a pure and good will, enjoying unbroken prosperity, can never give pleasure to an impartial rational spectator. Thus a good will appears to constitute the indispensable condition even of being worthy of happiness.

There are even some qualities which are of service to this good will itself, and may facilitate its action, yet which have no intrinsic unconditional value, but always presuppose a good will, and this qualifies the esteem that we justly have for them, and does not permit us to regard them as absolutely good. Moderation in the affections and passions, self-control, and calm deliberation are not only good in many respects, but even seem to constitute part of the intrinsic worth of the person; but they are far from deserving to be called good without qualification, although they have been so unconditionally praised by the ancients. For without the principles of a good will, they may become extremely bad; and the coolness of a villain not only makes him far more dangerous, but also directly makes him more abominable in our eyes than he would have been without it.

A good will is good not because of what it performs or effects, not by its aptness for the attainment of some proposed end, but simply by virtue of the volition—that is, it is good in itself, and considered by itself is to be esteemed much higher than all that can be brought about by it in favor of any inclination, nay, even of the sum-total of all inclinations. Even if it should happen that, owing to special disfavor of fortune, or the niggardly provision of a stepmotherly nature, this will should wholly lack power to accomplish its purpose, if with its greatest efforts it should yet achieve nothing, and there should remain only the good will (not, to be sure, a mere wish, but the summoning of all means in our power), then, like a jewel, it would still shine by its own light, as a thing which has its whole value in itself. Its usefulness or fruitlessness can neither add to nor take away anything from this value. It would be, as it were, only the setting to enable us to handle it the more conveniently in common commerce, or to attract to it the attention of those who are not yet connoisseurs, but not to recommend it to true connoisseurs, or to determine its value. . . .

Everything in nature works according to laws. Rational beings alone have the faculty of acting according *to the conception* of laws, that is according to principles, *i.e.* have a *will.* Since the deduction of actions from principles requires *reason,* the will is nothing but practical reason. If reason infallibly determines the will, then the actions of such a being which are recognized as objectively necessary are subjectively necessary also, *i.e.* the will is a faculty to choose *that only* which reason independent on inclination recognizes as practically necessary, *i.e.* as good. But if reason of itself does not sufficiently determine the will, if the latter is subject also to subjective conditions (particular impulses) which do not always coincide with the objective conditions; in a word, if the will does not *in itself* completely accord with reason (which is actually the case with men), then the actions which objectively are recognized as necessary are subjectively contingent, and the determination of such a will according to objective laws is *obligation,* that is to say, the relation of the objective laws to a will that is not thoroughly good is conceived as the determination of the will of a rational being by principles of reason, but which the will from its nature does not of necessity follow.

The conception of an objective principle, in so far as it is obligatory for a will, is called a command (of reason), and the formula of the command is called an Imperative. . . .

Now all *imperatives* command either *hypothetically* or *categorically.* The former represent the practical necessity of a possible action as means to something else that is willed (or at least which one might possibly will). The categorical imperative would be that which represented an action as necessary of itself without reference to another end, *i.e.* as objectively necessary.

Since every practical law represents a possible action as good, and on this account, for a subject who is practically determinable by reason, necessary, all imperatives are formulae determining an action which is necessary according to the principle of a will good in some respects. If now the action is good only as a means *to something else,* then the imperative is *hypothetical;* if it is conceived as good *in itself* and consequently as being necessarily the principle of a will which of itself conforms to reason, then it is *categorical.* . . .

When I conceive a hypothetical imperative, in general I do not know beforehand what it will contain until I am given the condition. But when I conceive a categorical imperative, I know at once what it contains. For as the imperative contains besides the law only the necessity that the maxims shall conform to this law, while the law contains no conditions restricting it, there remains nothing but the general statement that the maxim of the action should conform to a universal law, and it is this conformity alone that the imperative properly represents as necessary.

There is . . . but one categorical imperative, namely, this: *Act only on that maxim whereby thou canst at the same time will that it should become a universal law.*

Now if all imperatives of duty can be deduced from this one imperative as from their principle, then, although it should remain undecided whether what is called duty is not merely a vain notion, yet at least we shall be able to show what we understand by it and what this notion means.

Since the universality of the law according to which effects are produced constitutes what is properly called *nature* in the most general sense (as to form), that is the existence of things so far as it is determined by general laws, the imperative of duty may be expressed thus: *Act as if the maxim of thy action were to become by thy will a universal law of nature.*

We will now enumerate a few duties, adopting the usual division of them into duties to ourselves and to others, and into perfect and imperfect duties.

1. A man reduced to despair by a series of misfortunes feels wearied of life, but is still so far in possession of his reason that he can ask himself whether it would not be contrary to his duty to himself to take his own life. Now he inquires whether the maxim of his action could become a universal law of nature. His maxim is: From self-love I adopt it as a principle to shorten my life when its longer duration is likely to bring more evil than satisfaction. It is asked then simply whether this principle founded on self-love can become a universal law of nature. Now we see at once that a system of nature of which it should be a law to destroy life by means of the very feeling whose special nature it is to impel to the improvement of life would contradict itself, and therefore could not exist as a system of nature; hence that maxim cannot possibly exist as a universal law of nature, and consequently would be wholly inconsistent with the supreme principle of all duty.

2. Another finds himself forced by necessity to borrow money. He knows that he will not be able to repay it, but sees also that nothing will be lent to him, unless he promises stoutly to repay it in a definite time. He desires to make this promise, but he has still so much conscience as to ask himself: Is it not unlawful and inconsistent with duty to get out of a difficulty in this way? Suppose, however, that he resolves to do so, then the maxim of his action would be expressed thus: When I think myself in want of money, I will borrow money and promise to repay it, although I know that I never can do so. Now this principle of self-love or of one's own advantage may perhaps be consistent with my whole future welfare; but the question now is, Is it right? I change then the suggestion of self-love into a universal law, and state the question thus: How would it be if my maxim were a universal law? Then I see at once that it could never hold as a universal law of nature, but would necessarily contradict itself. For supposing it to be a universal law that everyone when he thinks himself in a difficulty should be able to promise whatever he pleases, with the purpose of not keeping his promise, the promise itself would become impossible, as well as the end that one might have in view in it, since no one would consider that anything was promised to him, but would ridicule all such statements as vain pretences.

3. A third finds in himself a talent which with the help of some culture might make him a useful man in many respects. But he finds himself in comfortable circumstances, and prefers to indulge in pleasure rather than to take pains in enlarging and improving his happy natural capacities. He asks, however, whether his maxim of neglect of his natural gifts, besides agreeing with his inclination to indulgence, agrees also with what is called duty. He sees then that a system of nature could indeed subsist with such a universal law although men (like the South Sea islanders) should let their talents rest, and resolve to devote their lives merely to idleness, amusement, and propagation of their species—in a word, to enjoyment; but he cannot possibly *will* that this should be a universal law of nature, or be implanted in us as such by a natural instinct. For, as a rational being, he necessarily wills that his faculties be developed, since they serve him, and have been given him, for all sorts of possible purposes.

4. A fourth, who is in prosperity, while he sees that others have to contend with great wretchedness and that he could help them, thinks: What concern is it of mine? Let everyone be as happy as Heaven pleases, or as he can make himself; I will take nothing from him nor even envy him, only I do not wish to contribute anything to his welfare or to his assistance in distress! Now no doubt if such a mode of thinking were a universal law, the human race might very well subsist, and doubtless even better than in a state in which everyone talks of sympathy and good-will, or even takes care occasionally to put it into practice, but, on the other side, also cheats when he can, betrays the rights of men, or otherwise violates them. But although it is possible that a universal law of nature might exist in accordance with that maxim, it is impossible to *will* that such a principle should have the universal validity of a law of nature. For a will which resolved this would contradict itself, inasmuch as many cases might occur in which one would have need of the love and sympathy of others, and in which, by such a law of nature, sprung from his own will, he would deprive himself of all hope of the aid he desires. . . .

We have thus established at least this much, that if duty is a conception which is to have any import and real legislative authority for our actions, it can only be expressed in categorical, and not at all in hypothetical imperatives. We have also, which is of great importance, exhibited clearly and definitely for every practical application the content of the categorical imperative, which must contain the principle of all duty if there is such a thing at all. We have not yet, however, advanced so far as to prove à priori that there actually is such an imperative, that there is a practical law which commands absolutely of itself, and without any other impulse, and that the following of this law is duty. . . .

Now I say: man and generally any rational being *exists* as an end in himself, *not merely as a means* to be arbitrarily used by this or that will, but in all his actions, whether they concern himself or other rational beings, must be always regarded at the same time as an end. All objects of the inclinations have only a conditional worth; for if the inclinations and the wants founded on them did not exist, then their object would be without value. But the inclinations themselves being sources of want are so far from having an absolute worth for which they should be desired, that, on the contrary, it must be the universal wish of every rational being to be wholly free from them. Thus the worth of any object which is *to be acquired* by our action is always conditional. Beings whose existence depends not on our will but on nature's, have nevertheless, if they are rational beings, only a relative value as means, and are therefore called *things;* rational beings, on the contrary, are called *persons,* because their very nature points them out as ends in themselves, that is as something which must not be used merely as means, and so far therefore restricts freedom of action (and is an object of respect). These, therefore, are not merely subjective ends whose existence has a worth *for us* as an effort of our action, but *objective ends,* that is things whose existence is an end in itself: an end moreover for which no other can be substituted, which they should subserve *merely* as means, for otherwise nothing whatever would possess *absolute worth;* but if all worth were conditioned and therefore contingent, then there would be no supreme practical principle of reason whatever.

If then there is a supreme practical principle or, in respect of the human will, a categorical imperative, it must be one which, being drawn from the conception of that which is necessarily an end for everyone because it is an *an end in itself,* constitutes an *objective* principle of will, and can therefore serve as a universal practical law. The foundation of this principle is: *rational nature exists as an end in itself.* Man necessarily conceives his own existence as being so: so far then this is a *subjective* principle of human actions. But every other rational being regards its existence similarly, just on the same rational principle, that holds for me: so that it is at the same time an objective principle, from which as a supreme practical law all laws of the will must be capable of being deduced. Accordingly the practical imperative will be as follows: *So act as to treat humanity, whether in thine own person or in that of any other, in every case as an end withal, never as means only. . . .*

The conception of every rational being as one which must consider itself as giving all the maxims of its will universal laws, so as to judge itself and its actions from this point of view—this conception leads to another which depends on it and is very fruitful, namely, that of a *kingdom of ends.*

By a *kingdom* I understand the union of different rational beings in a system by common laws. Now since it is by laws that ends are determined as regards their universal validity, hence, if we abstract from the personal differences of rational beings, and likewise from all the content of their private ends, we shall be able to conceive all ends combined in a systematic whole (including both rational beings as ends in themselves, and also the special ends which each may propose to himself), that is to say, we can conceive a kingdom of ends, which on the preceding principles is possible.

John Stuart Mill
Utilitarianism

John Stuart Mill (1806–1873) was the most famous "utilitarian"—a movement started by Jeremy Bentham in the early nineteenth century. Here he defines utilitarianism as the ethics that prescribe doing "the greatest good for the greatest number," and he argues that all of our ethical thinking presupposes this principle.

The creed which accepts [utility] as the foundation of morals, or the Greatest Happiness Principle, holds that actions are right in proportion as they tend to promote happiness, wrong as they tend to produce the reverse of happiness. By happiness is intended pleasure, and the absence of pain; by unhappiness, pain, and the privation of pleasure. To give a clear view of the moral standard set up by the theory, much more requires to be said; in particular, what things it includes in the ideas of pain and pleasure; and to what extent this is left an open question. But these supplementary explanations do not affect the theory of life on which this theory of morality is grounded—namely, that pleasure, and freedom from pain, are the only things desirable as ends; and that all desirable things (which are as numerous in the utilitarian as in any other scheme) are desirable either for the pleasure inherent in themselves, or as means to the promotion of pleasure and the prevention of pain.

Now, such a theory of life excites in many minds, and among them in some of the most estimable in feeling and purpose, inveterate dislike. To suppose that life has (as they express it) no higher end than pleasure—no better and nobler object of desire and pursuit— they designate as utterly mean and grovelling; as a doctrine worthy only of swine, to whom the followers of Epicurus were, at a very early period, contemptuously likened; and modern holders of the doctrine are occasionally made the subject of equally polite comparisons by its German, French, and English assailants.

When thus attacked, the Epicureans have always answered, that it is not they, but their accusers, who represent human nature in a degrading light; since the accusation supposes human beings to be capable of no pleasures except those of which swine are capable. If this supposition were true, the charge could not be gainsaid, but would then be no longer an imputation; for if the sources of pleasure were precisely the same to human beings and to swine, the rule of life which is good enough for the one would be good enough for the other. The comparison of the Epicurean life to that of beasts is felt as degrading, precisely because a beast's pleasures do not satisfy a human being's conceptions of happiness. Human beings have faculties more elevated than the animal appetites, and when once made conscious of them, do not regard anything as happiness which does not include their gratification. I do not, indeed, consider the Epicureans to have been by any means faultless in drawing out their scheme of consequences from the utilitarian principle. To do this in any sufficient manner, many Stoic, as well as Christian elements require to be included. But there is no known Epicurean theory of life which does not assign to the pleasures of the intellect, of the feelings and imagination, and of the moral sentiments, a much higher value as pleasures than to those of mere sensation. It must be admitted, however, that utilitarian writers in general have placed the superiority of mental over bodily pleasures chiefly in the greater permanency, safety, uncostliness, etc., of the former—that is, in their circumstantial advantages rather than in their intrinsic nature. And on all these points utilitarians have fully proved their case; but they might have taken the other, and, as it may be called, higher ground, with entire consistency. It is quite compatible with the principle of utility to recognise the fact, that some *kinds* of pleasure are more desirable and more valuable than others. It would be absurd that while, in estimating all other things, quality is considered as well as quantity, the estimation of pleasures should be supposed to depend on quantity alone.

If I am asked, what I mean by difference of quality in pleasures, or what makes one pleasure more valuable than another, merely as a pleasure, except its being greater in amount, there is but one possible answer. Of two pleasures, if there be one to which all or almost all who have experience of both give a decided preference, irrespective of any feeling of moral obligation to prefer it, that is the more desirable pleasure. If one of the two is, by those who are competently acquainted with both, placed so far above the other that they prefer it, even though knowing it to be attended with a greater amount of discontent, and would not resign it for any quantity of the other pleasure which their nature is capable of, we are justified in ascribing to the preferred enjoyment a superiority in quality, so far outweighing quantity as to render it, in comparison, of small account.

Now it is an unquestionable fact that those who are equally acquainted with, and equally capable of appreciating and enjoying, both, do give a most marked preference to the manner of existence which employs their higher facilities. Few human creatures would consent to be changed into any of the lower animals, for a promise of the fullest allowance of a beast's pleasures; no intelligent human being would consent to be a fool, no instructed person would be an ignoramus, no person of feeling and conscience would be selfish and base, even though they should be persuaded that the fool, the dunce, or the rascal is better satisfied with his lot than they are with theirs. They would not resign what they possess more than he for the most complete satisfaction of all the desires which they have in common with him. If they ever fancy they would, it is only in cases of unhappiness so extreme, that to escape from it they would exchange their lot for almost any other, however undesirable in their own eyes. A being of higher faculties requires more to make him happy, is capable probably of more acute suffering, and certainly accessible to it at more points, than one of an inferior type; but in spite of these liabilities, he can never really wish to sink into what he feels to be a lower grade of existence. We may give what explanation we please of this unwillingness; we may attribute it to pride, a name which is given indiscriminately to some of the most and to some of the least estimable feelings of which mankind are capable: we may refer it to the love of liberty and personal independence, an appeal to which was with the Stoics one of the most effective means for the inculcation of it; to the love of power, or to the love of excitement, both of which do really enter into and contribute to it: but its most appropriate appellation is a sense of dignity, which all human beings possess in one form or other, and in some, though by no means in exact, proportion to their higher faculties, and which is so essential a part of the happiness of those in whom it is strong, that nothing which conflicts with it could be, otherwise than momentarily, an object of desire to them. Whoever supposes that this preference takes place at a sacrifice of happiness—that the superior being, in anything like equal circumstances, is not happier than the inferior—confounds the two very different ideas, of happiness, and content. It is indisputable that the being whose capacities of enjoyment are low, has the greatest chance of having them fully satisfied; and a highly endowed being will always feel that any happiness which he can look for, as the world is constituted, is imperfect. But he can learn to bear its imperfections, if they are at all bearable; and they will not make him envy the being who is indeed unconscious of the imperfections, but only because he feels not at all the good which those imperfections qualify. It is better to be a human being dissatisfied than a pig satisfied; better to be Socrates dissatisfied than a fool satisfied. And if the fool, or the pig, are of a different opinion, it is because they only know their own side of the question. The other party to the comparison knows both sides.

It may be objected, that many who are capable of the higher pleasures, occasionally, under the influence of temptation, postpone them to the lower. But this is quite compatible with a full appreciation of the intrinsic superiority of the higher. Men often, from infirmity of character, make their election for the nearer good, though they know it to be the less valuable; and this no less when the choice is between two bodily pleasures, than when it is between bodily and mental. They pursue sensual indulgences to the injury of health, though perfectly aware that health is the greater good. It may be further objected, that many who begin with youthful enthusiasm for everything noble, as they advance in years sink into indolence and selfishness. But I do not believe that those who undergo this very common change, voluntarily choose the lower description of pleasures in preference to the higher. I believe that before they devote themselves exclusively to the one, they have already become incapable of the other. Capacity for the nobler feelings is in most natures a very tender plant, easily killed, not only by hostile influences, but by mere want of substance; and in the majority of young persons it speedily dies away if the occupations to which their position in life has devoted them, and the society into which it has thrown them, are not favourable to keeping that higher capacity in exercise. Men lose their high aspirations as they lose their intellectual tastes, because they have not time or opportunity for indulging them; and they addict themselves to inferior pleasures, not because they deliberately prefer them, but because they are either the only ones to which they have access, or the only ones which they are any longer capable of enjoying. It may be questioned whether any one who has remained equally susceptible to both classes of pleasures, ever knowingly and calmly preferred the lower; though many, in all ages, have broken down in an ineffectual attempt to combine both.

From this verdict of the only competent judges, I apprehend there can be no appeal. On a question which is the best worth having of two pleasures, or which of two modes of existence is the most grateful to the feelings, apart from its moral attributes and from its consequences, the judgment of those who are qualified by knowledge of both, or, if they differ, that of the majority among them, must be admitted as final. And there needs be the less hesitation to accept this judgment respecting the quality of pleasures, since there is no other tribunal to be referred to even on the question of quantity. What means are there of determining which is the acutest of two pains, or the intensest of two pleasurable sensations, except the general suffrage of those who are familiar with both? Neither pains nor pleasures are homogeneous, and pain is always heterogeneous with pleasure. What is there to decide whether a particular pleasure is worth purchasing at the cost of a particular pain, except the feelings and judgment of the experienced? When, therefore, those feelings and judgment declare the pleasures derived from the higher faculties to be preferable *in kind,* apart from the question of intensity, to those of which the animal nature, disjoined from the higher faculties, is suspectible, they are entitled on this subject to the same regard.

I have dwelt on this point, as being a necessary part of a perfectly just conception of Utility or Happiness, considered as the directive rule of human conduct. But it is by no means an indispensable condition to the acceptance of the utilitarian standard; for that standard is not the agent's own greatest happiness, but the greatest amount of happiness altogether; and if it may possibly be doubted whether a noble character is always the happier for its nobleness, there can be no doubt that it makes other people happier, and that the world in general is immensely a gainer by it. Utilitarianism, therefore, could only attain its end by the general cultivation of nobleness of character, even if each individual were only benefited by the nobleness of others, and his own, so far as happiness is concerned, were a sheer deduction from the benefit. But the bare enunciation of such an absurdity as this last, renders refutation superfluous.

According to the Greatest Happiness Principle, as above explained, the ultimate end, with reference to and for the sake of which all other things are desirable (whether we are considering our own good or that of other people), is an existence exempt as far as possible from pain, and as rich as possible in enjoyments, both in point of quantity and quality; the test of quality, and the rule for measuring it against quantity, being the preference felt by those who in their opportunities of experience, to which must be added their habits of self-consciousness and self-observation, are best furnished with the means of comparison. This, being, according to the utilitarian opinion, the end of human action, is necessarily also the standard of morality; which may accordingly be defined, the rules and precepts for human conduct, by the observance of which an existence such as has been described might be, to the greatest extent possible, secured to all mankind; and not to them only, but, so far as the nature of things admits, to the whole sentient creation. . . .

. . . I must again repeat, what the assailants of utilitarianism seldom have the justice to acknowledge, that the happiness which forms the utilitarian standard of what is right in conduct, is not the agent's own happiness, but that of all concerned. As between his own happiness and that of others, utilitarianism requires him to be as strictly impartial as a disinterested and benevolent spectator. In the golden rule of Jesus of Nazareth, we read the complete spirit of the ethics of utility. To do as you would be done by, and to love your neighbour as yourself, constitute the ideal perfection of utilitarian morality.

Friedrich Nietzsche

The Natural History of Morals

Friedrich Nietzsche (1844–1900) *was a German philosopher who spent most of his life traveling in Northern Italy and Switzerland, toward the end of the nineteenth century. He was a harsh critic of Christianity and Judeo-Christian morality and argued that, contrary to their own protestations of piety, both religion and morality are in fact products of the resentment of the weak and a rejection of the ancient virtue of nobility.*

The moral sentiment in Europe at present is perhaps as subtle, belated, diverse, sensitive, and refined, as the "Science of Morals" belonging thereto is recent, initial, awkward, and coarse-fingered:—an interesting contrast, which sometimes becomes incarnate and obvious in the very person of a moralist. . . . One ought to avow with the utmost fairness *what* is still necessary here . . . the comprehensive survey and classification of an immense domain of delicate sentiments of worth, and distinctions of worth, which live, grow, propagate, and perish—and perhaps attempts to give a clear idea of the recurring and more common forms of these living crystallisations—as preparation for a *theory of types* of morality. To be sure, people have not hitherto been so modest. All the philosophers, with a pedantic and ridiculous seriousness, demanded of themselves something very much higher, more pretentious, and ceremonious, when they concerned themselves with morality as a science: they wanted to *give a basis* to morality—and every philosopher hitherto has believed that he has given it a basis; morality itself, however, has been regarded as something "given." How far from their awkward pride was the seemingly insignificant problem—left in dust and decay—of a description of forms of morality, notwithstanding that the finest hands and senses could hardly be fine enough for it! It was precisely owing to moral philosophers knowing the moral facts imperfectly, in an arbitrary epitome, or an accidental abridgement—perhaps as the morality of their environment, their position, their church, their *Zeitgeist*, their climate and zone—it was precisely because they were badly instructed with regard to nations, eras, and past ages, and were by no means eager to know about these matters, that they did not even come in sight of the real problems of morals—problems which only disclose themselves by a comparison of *many* kinds of morality. . . .

Apart from the value of such assertions as "there is a categorical imperative in us," one can always ask: What does such an assertion indicate about him who makes it? There are systems of morals which are meant to justify their author in the eyes of other people; other systems of morals are meant to tranquillise him, and make him self-satisfied; with other systems he wants to crucify and humble himself; with others he wishes to take revenge; with others to conceal himself; with others to glorify himself and gain superiority and distinction;—

this system of morals helps its author to forget, that system makes him, or something of him, forgotten; many a moralist would like to exercise power and creative arbitrariness over mankind; many another, perhaps, Kant especially, gives us to understand by his morals that "what is estimable in me, is that I know how to obey—and with you it *shall* not be otherwise than with me!" In short, systems of morals are only a *sign-language of the emotions.*

. . . every system of morals is a sort of tyranny against "nature" and also against "reason"; that is, however, no objection, unless one should again decree by some system of morals, that all kinds of tyranny and unreasonableness are unlawful. What is essential and invaluable in every system of morals, is that it is a long constraint. In order to understand Stoicism, or Port-Royal, or Puritanism, one should remember the constraint under which every language has attained to strength and freedom—the metrical constraint, the tyranny of rhyme and rhythm. How much trouble have the poets and orators of every nation given themselves! . . . Every artist knows how different from the state of letting himself go, is his "most natural" condition, the free arranging, locating, disposing, and constructing in the moments of "inspiration"—and how strictly and delicately he then obeys a thousand laws, which, by their very rigidness and precision, defy all formulation by means of ideas (even the most stable idea has, in comparison therewith, something floating, manifold, and ambiguous in it). The essential thing "in heaven and in earth" is, apparently (to repeat it once more), that there should be long *obedience* in the same direction; there thereby results, and has always resulted in the long run, something which has made life worth living; for instance, virtue, art, music, dancing, reason, spirituality—anything whatever that is transfiguring, refined, foolish, or divine. The long bondage of the spirit, the distrustful constraint in the communicability of ideas, the discipline which the thinker imposed on himself to think in accordance with the rules of a church or a court, or conformable to Aristotelian premises, the persistent spiritual will to interpret everything that happened according to a Christian scheme, and in every occurrence to rediscover and justify the Christian God:—all this violence, arbitrariness, severity, dreadfulness, and unreasonableness, has proved itself the disciplinary means whereby the European spirit has attained its strength, its remorseless curiosity and subtle mobility; granted also that much irrecoverable strength and spirit had to be stifled, suffocated, and spoiled in the process (for here, as everywhere, "nature" shows herself as she is, in all her extravagant and *indifferent* magnificence, which is shocking, but nevertheless noble). . . . this tyranny, this arbitrariness, this severe and magnificent stupidity, has *educated* the spirit; slavery, both in the coarser and the finer sense, is apparently an indispensable means even of spiritual education and discipline. One may look at every system of morals in this light: it is "nature" therein which teaches to hate the *laisser-aller,* the too great freedom, and implants the need for limited horizons, for immediate duties—it teaches the *narrowing of perspectives,* and thus, in a certain sense, that stupidity is a condition of life and development. "Thou must obey some one, and for a long time; *otherwise* thou wilt come to grief, and lose all respect for thyself"—this seems to me to be the moral imperative of nature, which is certainly neither "categorical," as old Kant wished (consequently the "otherwise"), nor does it address itself to the individual (what does nature care for the individual!), but to nations, races, ages, and ranks, above all, however, to the animal "man" generally, to *mankind.* . . .

As long as the utility which determines moral estimates is only gregarious utility, as long as the preservation of the community is only kept in view, and the immoral is sought precisely and exclusively in what seems dangerous to the maintenance of the community, there can be no "morality of love to one's neighbour." Granted even that there is already a little constant exercise of consideration, sympathy, fairness, gentleness, and mutual assistance, granted that even in this condition of society all those instincts are already active which are latterly distinguished by honourable names as "virtues," and eventually almost coincide with the conception "morality": in that period they do not as yet belong to the domain of moral valuations—they are still *ultra-moral*. A sympathetic action, for instance, is neither called good nor bad, moral nor immoral, in the best period of the Romans; and should it be praised, a sort of resentful disdain is compatible with this praise, even at the best, directly the sympathetic action is compared with one which contributes to the welfare of the whole, to the *res publica*. After all, "love to our neighbour" is always a secondary matter, partly conventional and arbitrarily manifested in relation to our *fear of our neighbour*. After the fabric of society seems on the whole established and secured against external dangers, it is this fear of our neighbour which again creates new perspectives of moral valuation. Certain strong and dangerous instincts, such as the love of enterprise, foolhardiness, revengefulness, astuteness, rapacity, and love of power, which up till then had not only to be honoured from the point of view of general utility—under other names, of course, than those here given—but had to be fostered and cultivated (because they were perpetually required in the common danger against the common enemies), are now felt in their dangerousness to be doubly strong—when the outlets for them are lacking—and are gradually branded as immoral and given over to calumny. The contrary instincts and inclinations now attain to moral honour; the gregarious instinct gradually draws its conclusions. How much or how little dangerousness to the community or to equality is contained in an opinion, a condition, an emotion, a disposition, or an endowment—that is now the moral perspective; here again fear is the mother of morals. It is by the loftiest and strongest instincts, when they break out passionately and carry the individual far above and beyond the average, and the low level of the gregarious conscience, that the self-reliance of the community is destroyed; its belief in itself, its backbone, as it were, breaks; consequently these very instincts will be most branded and defamed. The lofty independent spirituality, the will to stand alone, and even the cogent reason, are felt to be dangers; everything that elevates the individual above the herd, and is a source of fear to the neighbour, is henceforth called *evil;* the tolerant, unassuming, self-adapting, self-equalising disposition, the *mediocrity* of desires, attains to moral distinction and honour. Finally, under very peaceful circumstances, there is always less opportunity and necessity for training the feelings to severity and rigour; and now every form of severity, even in justice, begins to disturb the conscience; a lofty and rigourous nobleness and self-responsibility almost offends, and awakens distrust, "the lamb," and still more "the sheep," wins respect. There is a point of diseased mellowness and effeminacy in the history of society, at which society itself takes the part of him who injures it, the part of the *criminal,* and does so, in fact, seriously and honestly. To punish, appears to it to be somehow unfair—it is certain that the idea of "punishment" and "the obligation to punish" are then painful and alarming to people. "Is it not sufficient if the criminal be rendered *harmless?* Why should we still punish? Punishment itself is terrible!"—with these questions gregarious morality, the morality of fear, draws its ultimate conclusion. If one could at all do away with danger, the cause of fear, one would have done away with this morality at the same time, it would no longer be necessary, it *would not consider itself* any longer necessary!—Whoever examines the conscience of the present-day European, will always elicit the same imperative from its thousand moral folds and hidden recesses, the imperative of the timidity of the herd: "we wish that some time or other there may be *nothing more to fear!*" Some time or other—the will and the way *thereto* is nowadays called "progress" all over Europe. . . .

In a tour through the many finer and coarser moralities which have hitherto prevailed or still prevail on the earth, I found certain traits recurring regularly together, and connected with one another, until finally two primary types revealed themselves to me, and a radical distinction was brought to light. There is *master-morality* and *slave-morality;*—I would at once add, however, that in all higher and mixed civilisations, there are also attempts at the reconciliation of the two moralities; but one finds still oftener the confusion and mutual misunderstanding of them, indeed, sometimes their close juxtaposition—even in the same man, within one soul. The distinctions of moral values have either originated in a ruling caste, pleasantly conscious of being different from the ruled—or among the ruled class, the slaves and dependents of all sorts. In the first case, when it is the rulers who determine the conception "good," it is the exalted, proud disposition which is regarded as the distinguishing feature, and that which determines the order of rank. The noble type of man separates from himself the beings in whom the opposite of this exalted, proud disposition displays itself: he despises them. Let it at once be noted that in this first kind of morality the antithesis "good" and "bad" means practically the same as "noble" and "despicable";—the antithesis "good" and "*evil*" is of a different origin. The cowardly, the timid, the insignificant, and those thinking merely of narrow utility are despised; moreover, also, the distrustful, with their constrained glances, the self-abasing, the dog-like kind of men who let themselves be abused, the mendicant flatterers, and above all the liars:—it is a fundamental belief of all aristocrats that the common people are untruthful. "We truthful ones"—the nobility in ancient Greece called themselves. It is obvious that everywhere the designations of moral value were at first applied to *men*, and were only derivatively and at a later period applied to *actions*; it is a gross mistake, therefore, when historians of morals start questions like, "Why have sympathetic actions been praised?" The noble type of man regards *himself* as a determiner of values; he does not require to be approved of; he passes the judgment: "What is injurious to me is injurious in itself"; he knows that it is he himself only who confers honour on things; he is a *creator of values*. He honours whatever he recognises in himself: such morality is self-glorification. In the foreground there is the feeling of plentitude, of power, which seeks to overflow, the happiness of high tension, the consciousness of a wealth which would fain give and bestow:—the noble man also helps the unfortunate, but not—or scarcely—out of pity, but rather from an impulse generated by the super-abundance of power. The noble man honours in himself the powerful one, him also who has power over himself, who knows how to speak and how to keep silence, who takes pleasure in subjecting himself to severity and hardness, and has reverence for all that is severe and hard. "Wotan placed a hard heart in my breast," says an old Scandinavian Saga: it is thus rightly expressed from the soul of a proud Viking. Such a type of man is even proud of *not* being made for sympathy; the hero of the Saga therefore adds warningly: "He who has not a hard heart when young, will never have one." The noble and brave who think thus are the furthest removed from the morality which sees precisely in sympathy, or in acting for the good of others, or in *désintéressement,* the characteristic of the moral; faith in oneself, pride in oneself, a radical enmity and irony towards "selflessness," belong as definitely to noble morality, as do a careless scorn and precaution in presence of sympathy and the "warm heart,"—It is the powerful who *know* how to honour, it is their art, their domain for invention. The profound reverence for age and for tradition—all law rests on this double reverence,—the belief and prejudice in favour of ancestors and unfavourable to newcomers, is typical in the morality of the powerful; and if, reversely, men of "modern ideas" believe almost instinctively in "progress" and the "future," and are more and more lacking in respect for old age, the ignoble origin of these "ideas" has complacently betrayed itself thereby. A morality of the ruling class, however, is more especially foreign and irritating to present-day taste in the sternness of its principle that one has duties only to one's equals; that one may act towards beings of a lower rank, towards all that is foreign, just as seems good to one, or "as the heart desires," and in any case "beyond good and evil": it is here that sympathy and similar sentiments can have a place. The ability and obligation to exercise prolonged gratitude and prolonged revenge—both only within the circle of equals,—artfulness in retaliation, *raffinement* of the idea in friendship, a certain necessity to have enemies (as outlets for the emotions of envy, quarrelsomeness, arrogance—in fact, in order to be a good *friend*): all these are typical characteristics of the noble morality, which, as has been pointed out, is not the morality of "modern ideas," and is therefore at present difficult to realise, and also to unearth and disclose.—It is otherwise with the second type of morality, *slave-morality.* Supposing that the abused, the oppressed, the suffering, the unemancipated, the weary, and those uncertain of themselves, should moralise, what will be the common element in their moral estimates? Probably a pessimistic suspicion with regard to the entire situation of man will find expression, perhaps a condemnation of man, together with his situation. The slave has an unfavourable eye for the virtues of the powerful; he has a scepticism and distrust, a *refinement* of distrust of everything "good" that is there honoured—he would fain persuade himself that the very happiness there is not genuine. On the other hand, *those* qualities which serve to alleviate the existence of sufferers are brought into prominence and flooded with light; it is here that sympathy, the kind, helping hand, the warm heart, patience, diligence, humility, and friendliness attain to honour; for here these are the most useful qualities, and almost the only means of supporting the burden of existence. Slave-morality is essentially the morality of utility. Here is the seat of the origin of the famous antithesis "good" and "evil":—power and dangerousness are assumed to reside in the evil, a certain dreadfulness, subtlety, and strength, which do not admit of being despised. According to slave-morality, therefore, the "evil" man arouses fear; according to master-morality, it is precisely the "good" man who arouses fear and seeks to arouse it, while the bad man is regarded as the despicable being. The contrast attains its maximum when, in accordance with the logical consequences of slave-morality, a shade of depreciation—it may be slight and well-intentioned—at last attaches itself to the "good" man of this morality; because, according to the servile mode of thought, the good man must in any case be the *safe* man: he is good-natured, easily deceived, perhaps a little stupid, *un bonhomme*. Everywhere that slave-morality gains the ascendancy, language shows a tendency to approximate the significations of the words "good" and "stupid."

A. J. Ayer

Emotivism

A. J. Ayer is an English philosopher who was highly influential in the logical positivist movement, which tried to show that all our concepts could be experientially defined. This excerpt is from his important book, Language, Truth and Logic.

. . . **I**t is our business to give an account of "judgements of value" which is both satisfactory in itself and consistent with our general empiricist principles. We shall set ourselves to show that in so far as statements of value are significant, they are ordinary "scientific" statements; and that in so far as they are not scientific, they are not in the literal sense significant, but are simply expressions of emotion which can be neither true nor false. . . .

The ordinary system of ethics, as elaborated in the works of ethical philosophers, is very far from being a homogeneous whole. Not only is it apt to contain pieces of metaphysics, and analyses of non-ethical concepts: its actual ethical contents are themselves of very different kinds. We may divide them, indeed, into four main classes. There are, first of all, propositions which express definitions of ethical terms, or judgements about the legitimacy or possibility of certain definitions. Secondly, there are propositions describing the phenomena of moral experience, and their causes. Thirdly, there are exhortations to moral virtue. And, lastly, there are actual ethical judgements. It is unfortunately the case that the distinction between these four classes, plain as it is, is commonly ignored by ethical philosophers; with the result that it is often very difficult to tell from their works what it is that they are seeking to discover or prove.

In fact, it is easy to see that only the first of our four classes, namely that which comprises the propositions relating to the definitions of ethical terms, can be said to constitute ethical philosophy. The propositions which describe the phenomena of moral experience, and their causes, must be assigned to the science of psychology, or sociology. The exhortations to moral virtue are not propositions at all, but ejaculations or commands which are designed to provoke the reader to action of a certain sort. Accordingly, they do not belong to any branch of philosophy or science. As for the expressions of ethical judgements, we have not yet determined how they should be classified. But inasmuch as they are certainly neither definitions nor comments upon definitions, nor quotations, we may say decisively that they do not belong to ethical philosophy. A strictly philosophical treatise on ethics should therefore make no ethical pronouncements. But it should, by giving an analysis of ethical terms, show what is the category to which all such pronouncements belong. And this is what we are now about to do.

A question which is often discussed by ethical philosophers is whether it is possible to find definitions which would reduce all ethical terms to one or two fundamental terms. But this question, though it undeniably belongs to ethical philosophy, is not relevant to our present enquiry. We are not now concerned to discover which term, within the sphere of ethical terms, is to be taken as fundamental; whether, for example, "good" can be defined in terms of "right" or "right" in terms of "good," or both in terms of "value." What we are interested in is the possibility of reducing the whole sphere of ethical terms to non-ethical terms. We are enquiring whether statements of ethical value can be translated into statements of empirical fact.

That they can be so translated is the contention of those ethical philosophers who are commonly called subjectivists, and of those who are known as utilitarians. For the utilitarian defines the rightness of actions, and the goodness of ends, in terms of the pleasure, or happiness, or satisfaction, to which they give rise; the subjectivist, in terms of the feelings of approval which a certain person, or group of people, has towards them. Each of these types of definition makes moral judgements into a sub-class of psychological or sociological judgements; and for this reason they are very attractive to us. For, if either was correct, it would follow that ethical assertions were not generically different from the factual assertions which are ordinarily contrasted with them; and the account which we have already given of empirical hypotheses would apply to them also.

Nevertheless we shall not adopt either a subjectivist or a utilitarian analysis of ethical terms. We reject the subjectivist view that to call an action right, or a thing good, is to say that it is generally approved of, because it is not self-contradictory to assert that some actions which are generally approved of are not right, or that some things which are generally approved of are not good. And we reject the alternative subjectivist view that a man who asserts that a certain action is right, or that a certain thing is good, is saying that he himself approves of it, on the ground that a man who confessed that he sometimes approved of what was bad or wrong would not be contradicting himself. And a similar argument is fatal to utilitarianism. We cannot agree that to call an action right is to say that of all the actions possible in the circumstances it would cause, or be likely to cause, the greatest happiness, or the greatest balance of pleasure over pain, or the greatest balance of satisfied over unsatisfied desire, because we find that it is not self-contradictory to say that it is sometimes wrong to perform the action which would actually or probably cause the greatest happiness, or the greatest balance of pleasure over pain, or of satisfied over unsatisfied desire. And since it is not self-contradictory to say that some pleasant things are not good, or that some bad things are desired, it cannot be the case that the sentence "x is good" is equivalent to "x is pleasant," or "x is desired." And to every other variant of utilitarianism with which I am acquainted the same objection can be made. And therefore we should, I think, conclude that the validity of ethical judgements is not determined by the felicific tendencies of actions, any more than by the nature of people's feelings; but that it must be regarded as "absolute" or "intrinsic," and not empirically calculable. . . .

In admitting that normative ethical concepts are irreducible to empirical concepts, we seem to be leaving the way clear for the "absolutist" view of ethics—that is, the view that statements of value are not controlled by observation, ordinary empirical propositions are, but only by a mysterious "intellectual intuition." A feature of this theory, which is seldom recognized by its advocates, is that it makes statements of value unverifiable. For it is notorious that what seems intuitively certain to one person may seem doubtful, or even false, to another. So that unless it is possible to provide some criterion by which one may decide between conflicting intuitions, a mere appeal to intuition is worthless as a test of a proposition's validity. But in the case of moral judgements, no such criterion can be given. Some moralists claim to settle the matter by saying that they "know" that their own moral judgements are correct. But such an assertion is of purely psychological interest, and has not the slightest tendency to prove the validity of any moral judgement. For dissentient moralists may equally well "know" that their ethical views are correct. And, as far as subjective certainty goes, there will be nothing to choose between them. When such differences of opinion arise in connection with an ordinary empirical proposition, one may attempt to resolve them by referring to, or actually carrying out, some relevant empirical test. But with regard to ethical statements, there is, on the "absolutist" or "intuitionist" theory, no relevant empirical test. We are therefore justified in saying that on this theory ethical statements are held to be unverifiable. . . .

Considering the use which we have made of the principle that a synthetic proposition is significant only if it is empirically verifiable, it is clear that the acceptance of an "absolutist" theory of ethics would undermine the whole of our main argument. And as we have already rejected the "naturalistic" theories which are commonly supposed to provide the only alternative to "absolutism" in ethics, we seem to have reached a difficult position. We shall meet the difficulty by showing that the correct treatment of ethical statements is afforded by a third theory, which is wholly compatible with our radical empiricism.

We begin by admitting that the fundamental ethical concepts are unanalysable, inasmuch as there is no criterion by which one can test the validity of the judgements in which they occur. So far we are in agreement with the absolutists. But, unlike the absolutists, we are able to give an explanation of this fact about ethical concepts. We say that the reason why they are unanalysable is that they are mere pseudo-concepts. The presence of an ethical symbol in a proposition adds nothing to its factual content. Thus if I say to someone, "You acted wrongly in stealing that money," I am not stating anything more than if I had simply said, "You stole that money." In adding that this action is wrong I am not making any further statement about it. I am simply evincing my moral disapproval of it. It is as if I had said, "You stole that money," in a peculiar tone of horror, or written it with the addition of some special exclamation marks. The tone, or the exclamation marks, adds nothing to the literal meaning of the sentence. It merely serves to show that the expression of it is attended by certain feelings in the speaker.

If now I generalise my previous statement and say, "Stealing money is wrong," I produce a sentence which has no factual meaning—that is, expresses no proposition which can be either true or false. It is as if I had written "Stealing money!!"—where the shape and thickness of the exclamation marks show, by a suitable convention, that a special sort of moral disapproval is the feeling which is being expressed. It is clear that there is nothing said here which can be true or false. Another man may disagree with me about the wrongness of stealing, in the sense that he may not have the same feelings about stealing as I have, and he may quarrel with me on account of my moral sentiments. But he cannot, strictly speaking, contradict me. For in saying that a certain type of action is right or wrong, I am not making any factual statement, not even a statement about my own state of mind. I am merely expressing certain moral sentiments. And the man who is ostensibly contradicting me is merely expressing his moral sentiments. So that there is plainly no sense in asking which of us is in the right. For neither of us is asserting a genuine proposition.

What we have just been saying about the symbol "wrong' applies to all normative ethical symbols. Sometimes they occur in sentences which record ordinary empirical facts besides expressing ethical feeling about those facts: sometimes they occur in sentences which simply express ethical feeling about a certain type of action, or situation, without making any statement of fact. But in every case in which one would commonly be said to be making an ethical judgement, the function of the relevant ethical word is purely "emotive." It is used to express feeling about certain objects, but not to make any assertion about them.

William Gass *(about ethics)*
The Case of the Obliging Stranger

William Gass *is a professor at Washington University in St. Louis and a philosopher, novelist, and literary critic. What follows is taken from his "Case of the Obliging Stranger" from the book* Fiction and the Figures of Life.

Imagine I approach a stranger on the street and say to him. "If you please sir, I desire to perform an experiment with your aid." The stranger is obliging, and I lead him away. In a dark place conveniently by, I strike his head with the broad of an axe and cart him home. I place him, buttered and trussed, in an ample electric oven. The thermostat reads 450°F. Thereupon I go off to play poker with friends and forget all about the obliging stranger in the stove. When I return, I realize I have overbaked my specimen, and the experiment, alas, is ruined.

Something has been done wrong. Or something wrong has been done.

Any ethic that does not roundly condemn my action is vicious. It is interesting that none is vicious for this reason. It is also interesting that no more convincing refutation of any ethic could be given than by showing that it approved of my baking the obliging stranger.

This is really all I have to say, but I shall not stop on that account. Indeed, I shall begin again.

The geometer cannot demonstrate that a line is beautiful. The beauty of lines is not his concern. We do not chide him when he fails to observe uprightness in his verticals, when he discovers no passions between sinuosities. We would not judge it otherwise than foolish to berate him for neglecting to employ the methods successful in biology or botany merely because those methods dealt fairly with lichens and fishes. Nor do we despair of him because he cannot give us reasons for doing geometry which will equally well justify our drilling holes in teeth. There is a limit, as Aristotle said, to the questions which we may sensibly put to each man of science; and however much we may desire to find unity in the purposes, methods, and results of every fruitful sort of inquiry, we must not allow that desire to make much of their necessary differences.

Historically, with respect to the fundamental problems of ethics, this limit has not been observed. Moreover, the analogy between mathematics and morals, or between the methods of empirical science and the good life, has always been unfairly one-sided. Geometers never counsel their lines to be moral, but moralists advise men to be like lines and go straight. There are triangles of lovers, but no triangles in love. And who says the organism is a state?

For it is true that the customary methods for solving moral problems are the methods which have won honors by leaping mathematical hurdles on the one hand or scientific and physical ones on the other: the intuitive and deductive method and the empirical and inductive one. Nobody seems to have minded very much that the moral hurdle has dunked them both in the pool beyond the wall, for they can privately laugh at each other for fools, and together they can exclaim how frightfully hard is the course.

The difficulty for the mathematical method is the discovery of indubitable moral first premises which do not themselves rest on any inductive foundation and which are still applicable to the complicated tissue of factors that make up moral behavior. The result is that the premises are usually drawn from metaphysical speculations having no intimate relation to moral issues or from rational or mystical revelations which only the intuiter and his followers are willing to credit. For the purposes of deduction, the premises have to be so broad and, to satisfy intuition, so categorically certain, that they become too thin for touch and too heavy for bearing. All negative instances are pruned as unreal or parasitic. Consequently, the truth of the ultimate premises is constantly called into question by those who have intuited differently or have men and actions in mind that they want to call good and right but cannot.

Empirical solutions, so runs the common complaint, lop off the normative branch altogether and make ethics a matter of expediency, taste, or conformity to the moral etiquette of the time. One is told what people do, not what they ought to do; and those philosophers who still wish to know what people ought to do are told, by some of the more uncompromising, that they can have no help from empiricism and are asking a silly question. Philosophers, otherwise empiricists, who admit that moral ends lie beyond the reach of factual debate turn to moral sentiment or some other *bonum ex machina,* thus generously embracing the perplexities of both methods.

Questions to which investigators return again and again without success are very likely improperly framed. It is important to observe that the ethical question put so directly as "What is good?" or "What is right?" aims in its answer not, as one might immediately suppose, at a catalogue of the world's good, right things. The moralist is not asking for a list of sheep and goats. The case of the obliging stranger is a case of immoral action, but this admission is not an answer, even partially, to the question, "What is wrong?"

Furthermore, the ethical question is distressingly short. "Big" questions, it would seem, ought to be themselves big, but they almost never are; and they tend to grow big simply by becoming short—too short, in fact, ever to receive an answer. I might address, to any ear that should hear me, the rather less profound-sounding, but none the less similar question, "Who won?" or perhaps the snappier, "What's a winner?" I should have to ask this question often because, if I were critical, I should never find an answer that would suit me; while at the same time there would be a remarkable lot of answers that suited a remarkable lot of people. The more answers I had—the more occasions on which I asked the question—the more difficult, the more important, the more "big" the question would become.

If the moralist does not want to hear such words as "Samson," "money," or "brains" when he asks his question, "What is good?," what does he want to hear? He wants to hear a word like "power." He wants to know what is good in the things that are good that makes them good. It should be perfectly clear it is not the things themselves that he thinks good or bad but the qualities they possess, the relations they enter into, or the consequences they produce. Even an intuitionist, who claims to perceive goodness directly, perceives a property of things when he perceives goodness, and not any *thing*, except incidentally. The wrong done the obliging stranger was not the act of cooking him but was something belonging to the act in some one of many possible ways. It is not I who am evil (if I am not mad) but something which I *have* that is; and while, of course, I may be adjudged wicked for having whatever it is I have that is bad, it is only because I have it that I am wicked—as if I owned a vicious and unruly dog.

I think that so long as I look on my act in this way, I wrong the obliging stranger a second time.

The moralist, then, is looking for the ingredient that perfects or spoils the stew. He wants to hear the word "power." He wants to know what is good in what is good that makes it good; and the whole wretched difficulty is that one is forced to reply either that what is good in what is good makes the good in what is good good, or that it is, in fact, made good by things which are not in the least good at all. So the next question, which is always, "And why is power good?," is answered by saying that it is good because it is power and power is good; or it is put off by the promise that power leads to things worth much; or it is shrugged aside with the exclamation, "Well, that's life!" This last is usually accompanied by an exhortation not to oppose the inevitable course of nature.

You cannot ask questions forever. Sooner or later the questioning process is brought up short by statements of an apparently dogmatic sort. Pleasure is sought for pleasure's sake. The principal of utility is susceptible of no demonstration. Every act and every inquiry aims at well-being. The nonnatural property of goodness fastens itself to its object and will remain there whatever world the present world may madly become. Frustrated desires give rise to problems, and problems are bad. We confer the title of The Good upon our natural necessities.

I fail to see why, if one is going to call a halt in this way, the halt cannot be called early, and the evident, the obvious, the axiomatic, the indemonstrable, the intrinsic, or whatever one wants to name it be deemed those clear cases of moral goodness, badness, obligation, or wrong which no theory can cloud, and for which men are prepared to fight to the last ditch. For if someone asks me, now I am repentant, why I regard my act of baking the obliging stranger as wrong, what can I do but point again to the circumstances comprising the act? "Well, I put this fellow in an oven, you see. The oven was on, don't you know." And if my questioner persists in saying, "Of course, I know all about *that;* but what I want to know is, why is *that* wrong?," I should recognize there is no use in replying that it is wrong because of the kind of act it is, a wrong one, for my questioner is clearly suffering from a sort of *folie de doute morale* which forbids him to accept any final answer this early in the game, although he will have to accept precisely the same kind of answer at some time or other.

Presumably there is some advantage in postponing the stop, and this advantage lies in the explanatory power of the higher-level answer. It cannot be that my baking the stranger is wrong for no reason at all. It would then be inexplicable. I do not think this is so, however. It is not inexplicable; it is transparent. Furthermore, the feeling of elucidation, of greater insight or knowledge, is a feeling only. It results, I suspect, from the satisfaction one takes in having an open mind. The explanatory factor is always more inscrutable than the event it explains. The same questions can be asked of it as were asked of the original occasion. It is either found in the situation and brought forward to account for all, as one might advance pain, in this case, out of the roaster; or it resides there mysteriously, like an essence, the witch in the oven; or it hovers, like a coil of smoke, as hovers the greatest unhappiness of the greatest number.

But how ludicrous are the moralist's "reasons" for condemning my baking the obliging stranger. They sound queerly unfamiliar and out of place. This is partly because they intrude where one expects to find denunciation only and because it is true they are seldom if ever *used*. But their strangeness is largely due to the humor in them.

Consider:

1. My act produced more pain than pleasure.
2. Baking this fellow did not serve the greatest good to the greatest number.
3. I acted wrongly because I could not consistently will that the maxim of my action become a universal law.
4. God forbade me, but I paid no heed.
5. Anyone can apprehend the property of wrongness sticking plainly to the whole affair.
6. Decent men remark it and are moved to tears.

But I should say that my act was wrong even if my stranger were tickled into laughter while he cooked; or even if his baking did the utmost good it could; or if, in spite of all, I could consistently will that whatever maxim I might have had might become a universal law; or even if God had spoken from a bush to me, "Thou shalt!" How redundant the property of wrongness, as if one needed *that*, in such a case! And would the act be right if the whole world howled its glee? Moralists can say, with conviction, that the act is wrong; but none can *show* it.

Such cases, like that of the obliging stranger, are cases I call clear. They have the characteristic of moral transparency, and they comprise the core of our moral experience. When we try to explain why they are instances of good or bad, of right or wrong, we sound comic, as anyone does who gives elaborate reasons for the obvious, especially when these reasons are so shamefaced before reality, so miserably beside the point. What we must explain is not why these cases have the moral nature they have, for that needs no explaining, but *why they are so clear*. It is an interesting situation: Any moralist will throw over his theory if it reverses the decision on cases like the obliging stranger's. The most persuasive criticism of any ethical system has always been demonstration, on the critic's part, that the system countenances moral absurdities, despite the fact that, in the light of the whole theoretical enterprise, such criticisms beg the question. Although the philosopher who is caught by a criticism of this sort may protest its circularity or even manfully swallow the dreadful conclusion, his system has been scotched, if it has not been killed. . . .

The obliging stranger is overbaked. I wonder whether this is bad or not. I ask about it. Presumably there is a reason for my wonderment. What is it? Well, of course there is not any reason that is a reason about the obliging stranger. There is only a reason because I am a fallibilist, or because one must not be arbitrary, or because all certainties in particular cases are certain only when deduced from greater, grander certainties. The reason I advance may be advanced upon itself. The entire moral structure tumbles at once. It is a test of the clarity of cases that objections to them are objections in principle; that the principle applies as well to all cases as to any one; and that these reasons for doubt devour themselves with equal right and the same appetite. That is why the moralist is really prepared to fight for the clear cases to the last ditch; why, when he questions them, he does so to display his philosophical breeding, because it is good form: He knows that if these cases are not clear, none are, and if none are, the game is up. . . .

Ethics, I wish to say, is about something, and in the rush to establish principles, to elicit distinctions from a recalcitrant language, and to discover "laws," those lovely things and honored people, those vile seducers and ruddy villains our principles and laws are supposed to be based upon and our ethical theories to be about are overlooked and forgotten.

John Ladd

On Relativism

John Ladd *is a professor of philosophy at Brown University and one of the best known authors on the knotty problem of ethical relativism.*

Any discussion of the relations between anthropology and ethics leads inevitably to the ticklish issue of relativism. Even when not explicitly recognized as such, this issue has been the skeleton in the closet for every philosophical moralist since the time of Plato and the Sophists; for the critical implications of the fact of the diversity and discordance between moral precepts and moral codes in different societies are inescapable. Yet it is difficult to pin down the precise relevance of these differences for morals. To the layman it seems obvious that the lack of universal agreement concerning morals derogates somehow from their validity; in particular he is ready to think twice about a moral precept if it appears to him as a purely local or provincial custom. And yet, on the other hand, he is willing to acknowledge some truth in the ancient maxim: "When in Rome do as the Romans do"! Thus already for the layman there is a kind of ambiguous message conveyed by the facts of cultural relativism. Quite significantly, however, this same kind of ambiguity is incorporated into the leading ideology of our times, namely Marxism, which, as 'scientific socialism', is based on the relativity of ideologies and social relations.

Despite the natural perplexities and practical challenges that appear to arise from the facts of cultural diversity and relativity, discussions by moral philosophers of their relevance to ethics are curiously vapid and, it seems to me, beside the point. If, as is maintained by some, cultural relativism somehow undermines ethics, it is necessary to show how and why it does so, and this has not been done. On the other hand, if, as others maintain, cultural relativism is totally irrelevant to ethics, as irrelevant, perhaps, as is the fact of diversity of human beliefs concerning the causes of tuberculosis to the latest expert opinion or medical science, then why does this fact create so much uneasiness among philosophers and laymen alike? Finally, there are some who try to cope with cultural relativity by denying it, that is, by maintaining that basically there is no real disagreement between people of different cultures concerning morals. Why, we may ask, are they so anxious to refute cultural relativism? These three attitudes appear to comprehend all of the prevalent conceptions of the relevance of cultural relativity to ethics, yet none of them is very satisfactory. The reason for this is that the issue of relativism has never been stated clearly. . . .

Let us begin by defining 'cultural relativism'. I shall assume that this is an anthropological doctrine which is scientific and empirical in nature and which rests on actual observations of other cultures and on related psychological and sociological theories. Consequently, I regard cultural relativism as itself a descriptive theory and in this sense neutral as far as evaluations are concerned. (This is, of course, not to deny that it may be relevant to ethics and evaluations in general. If 'cultural relativism' is defined as an ethical doctrine, as it is by some anthropologists, then the issues I want to discuss are lost in verbal quibbles.)

Cultural relativism, I shall assume, consists of two different theses, which may respectively be called the *diversity thesis* and the *relativity thesis*. The first of these, the diversity thesis, asserts that there is a diversity of moral opinions from one society to another and hence that there is no *consensus gentium* concerning morals: what is regarded as right in one society is regarded as wrong in another. Furthermore, it asserts that these ethical differences relate not only to the evaluations of particular acts, but also to rules, principles, ideals, goals and character evaluations.

The second thesis, the relativity thesis, maintains that the character of people's moral opinions is to be explained by cultural and social factors of some sort, such as linguistic structure, economic determinants, psychological conditioning, psychoanalytic mechanisms, historical factors, or the unique pattern of culture of the society in question. In other words, moral opinions are relative to cultural determinants of some kind in the sense that they are causally dependent upon them. Although most contemporary cultural relativists combine these two theses, it is possible to accept one without the other. Hume, for example, would subscribe to the relativity thesis inasmuch as he presents a psychological theory of the origin of moral sentiments (opinions), although more than likely he would have denied the diversity thesis.

The question with which we shall be concerned is simply this: supposing that cultural relativism in some form or other is true, what follows with regard to ethics? A survey of the conclusions of those who stress the significance of cultural relativism for ethics reveals nothing but confusion. If I am right, then it is easy to see why this should be so, for cultural relativism is not really used to establish any simple ethical conclusion at all. Instead, it is used as a form of argument, or rather, as several forms of argument that are quite peculiar to ethics. In order to show the absurdity of supposing that cultural relativism directly establishes a conclusion of some sort, let us briefly survey some of the conclusions that it is supposed to entail.

First, cultural relativism is supposed to show that what is right for one person in one social and cultural situation is wrong for another person in another social and cultural situation. There is, however, nothing especially novel about the contention that the rightness or wrongness of acts is dependent upon the agent's situation, including his social and cultural situation. It is generally agreed by moral philosophers of every school that circumstances require us to apply moral principles differently to different cases. Elsewhere I have called this phenomenon *applicational relativity*. (The accusation by social scientists that the Western ethical tradition has paid no attention to the applicational relativity of morals merely reflects their ignorance of the history of ethics.)

Now it is quite clear that the facts of cultural relativism, and cultural anthropology in general, do not prove the principle of applicational relativity, nor do they need to do so, although they may help us to use this principle more intelligently by calling our attention to the differentials that require our principles to be applied differently. The question of which situational factors are ultimately to be taken as morally relevant is, of course, a question for ethics rather than anthropology. One cannot, for example, persuasively justify the institution of polygamy in a certain society on the grounds of its effectiveness in promoting social stability if such considerations are rejected as morally irrelevant to the proper or just conception of marriage. At any rate, what is and what is not a morally relevant factor in the evaluation of institutions like marriage is an *open question* and one that I believe it is the role of moral philosophers to discuss.

Let us assume, therefore, that the issue of relativism is not related to questions involving the principle of applicational relativity as such. Indeed, the principle of applicational relativity itself presupposes the validity of some sort of moral principle to be applied, which cannot be established by anthropology. We must therefore search elsewhere in our effort to pin down the conclusions that are supposed to follow from cultural relativism.

Sometimes it is insinuated or implied that the facts of cultural relativity lead us in a new way to recognize the importance of tolerance and mutual understanding. Through the recognition of cultural relativity, we shall arrive then at a more realistic social faith, accepting as grounds of hope and as new bases for tolerance the coexisting and equally valid patterns of life which mankind has created for itself from the raw materials of existence. "The very core of cultural relativism is the social discipline that comes of respect for differences—of mutual respect." The principle of tolerance and of mutual respect is itself, however, an ethical principle, not an anthropological truth, and if I am not mistaken, no one supposes that it is a principle which is established by cultural relativism. Rather, cultural relativism merely provides ammunition for the 'attack' on certain accepted ethical dogmas, namely, those that are incompatible with tolerance. . . .

It is obvious by now that the decisive and distinctive import for ethics of the facts of cultural relativity hinges on the assumption of an intimate, perhaps even logical connection between people's moral opinions and the rightness and wrongness of their actions; for it is clear that cultural relativism, insofar as it relates to what is thought to be right or wrong in different societies, will be relevant to ethics only if it is assumed that moral opinion reflects, constitutes, validates or in some other way determines moral principle. Science and other standard types of knowledge do not admit this kind of assumption; it would be highly irregular indeed to try to prove or disprove a scientific hypothesis by reference to popular opinion! (This statement will require slight modification later.) The kind of assumed relationship between moral opinion and moral principle that we are concerned with here is much more like the relationship holding between opinion and rule, say, in etiquette. In matters of etiquette the opinion of the upper social classes is authoritative and determines what is socially proper or improper: what is considered to be proper or improper is no different from what actually is proper or improper. (To quote Hamlet: "There is nothing either good or bad but thinking makes it so.")

Mary Midgley
Trying Out One's New Sword

Mary Midgley is a British philosopher who writes on a variety of topics in ethics, including a widely read book entitled Beast and Man. *(Judging other cultures)*

All of us are, more or less, in trouble today about trying to understand cultures strange to us. We hear constantly of alien customs. We see changes in our lifetime which would have astonished our parents. I want to discuss here one very short way of dealing with this difficulty, a drastic way which many people now theoretically favour. It consists in simply denying that we can ever understand any culture except our own well enough to make judgments about it. Those who recommend this hold that the world is sharply divided into separate societies, sealed units, each with its own system of thought. They feel that the respect and tolerance due from one system to another forbids us ever to take up a critical position to any other culture. Moral judgment, they suggest, is a kind of coinage valid only in its country of origin.

I shall call this position 'moral isolationism'. I shall suggest that it is certainly not forced upon us, and indeed that it makes no sense at all. People usually take it up because they think it is a respectful attitude to other cultures. In fact, however, it is not respectful. Nobody can respect what is entirely unintelligible to them. To respect someone, we have to know enough about him to make a *favorable* judgment, however general and tentative. And we do understand people in other cultures to this extent. Otherwise a great mass of our most valuable thinking would be paralysed.

To show this, I shall take a remote example, because we shall probably find it easier to think calmly about it than we should with a contemporary one, such as female circumcision in Africa or the Chinese Cultural Revolution. The principles involved will still be the same. My example is this. There is, it seems, a verb in classical Japanese which means 'to try out one's new sword on a chance wayfarer'. (The word is *tsujigiri*, literally 'crossroads-cut'.) A samurai sword had to be tried out because, if it was to work properly, it had to slice through someone at a single blow, from the shoulder to the opposite flank. Otherwise, the warrior bungled his stroke. This could injure his honour, offend his ancestors, and even let down his emperor. So tests were needed, and wayfarers had to be expended. Any wayfarer would do—provided, of course, that he was not another Samurai. Scientists will recognize a familiar problem about the rights of experimental subjects.

Now when we hear of a custom like this, we may well reflect that we simply do not understand it; and therefore are not qualified to criticize it at all, because we are not members of that culture. But we are not members of any other culture either, except our own. So we extend the principle to cover all extraneous cultures, and we seem therefore to be moral isolationists. But this is, as we shall see, an impossible position. Let us ask what it would involve.

We must ask first: Does the isolating barrier work both ways? Are people in other cultures equally unable to criticize us? This question struck me sharply when I read a remark in *The Guardian* by an anthropologist about a South American Indian who had been taken into a Brazilian town for an operation, which saved his life. When he came back to his village, he made several highly critical remarks about the white Brazilians' way of life. They may very well have been justified. But the interesting point was that the anthropologist called these remarks 'a damning indictment of Western civilization'. Now the Indian had been in that town about two weeks. Was he in a position to deliver a damning indictment? Would we ourselves be qualified to deliver such an indictment on the Samurai, provided we could spend two weeks in ancient Japan? What do we really think about this?

My own impression is that we believe that outsiders can, in principle, deliver perfectly good indictments—only, it usually takes more than two weeks to make them damning. Understanding has degrees. It is not a slapdash yes-or-no matter. Intelligent outsiders can progress in it, and in some ways will be at an advantage over the locals. But if this is so, it must clearly apply to ourselves as much as anybody else.

Our next question is this: Does the isolating barrier between cultures block praise as well as blame? If I want to say that the Samurai culture has many virtues, or to praise the South American Indians, am I prevented from doing *that* by my outside status? Now, we certainly do need to praise other societies in this way. But it is hardly possible that we could praise them effectively if we could not, in principle, criticize them. Our praise would be worthless if it rested on definite grounds, if it did not flow from some understanding. Certainly we may need to praise things which we do not *fully* understand. We say 'there's something very good here, but I can't quite make out what it is yet'. This happens when we want to learn from strangers. And we can learn from strangers. But to do this we have to distinguish between those strangers who are worth learning from and those who are not. Can we then judge which is which?

This brings us to our third question: What is involved in judging? Now plainly there is no question here of sitting on a bench in a red robe and sentencing people. Judging simply means forming an opinion, and expressing it if it is called for. Is there anything wrong about this? Naturally, we ought to avoid forming—and expressing—*crude* opinions, like that of a simple-minded missionary, who might dismiss the whole Samurai culture as entirely bad, because it is non-Christian. But this is a different objection. The trouble with crude opinions is that they are crude, whoever forms them, not that they are formed by the wrong people. Anthropologists, after all, are outsiders quite as much as missionaries. Moral isolationism forbids us to form *any* opinions on these matters. Its ground for doing so is that we don't understand them. But there is much that we don't understand in our own culture too. This brings us to our last question: If we can't judge other cultures, can we really judge our own?

Our efforts to do so will be much damaged if we are really deprived of our opinions about other societies, because these provide the range of comparison, the spectrum of alternatives against which we set what we want to understand. We would have to stop using the mirror which anthropology so helpfully holds up to us.

In short, moral isolationism would lay down a general ban on moral reasoning. Essentially, this is the programme of immoralism, and it carries a distressing logical difficulty. Immoralists like Nietzsche are actually just a rather specialized sect of moralists. They can no more afford to put moralizing out of business than smugglers can afford to abolish customs regulations. The power of moral judgment is, in fact, not a luxury, not a perverse indulgence of the self-righteous. It is a necessity. When we judge something to be bad or good, better or worse than something else, we are taking it as an example to aim at or avoid. Without opinions of this sort, we would have no framework of comparison for our own policy, no chance of profiting by other people's insights or mistakes. In this vacuum, we could form no judgments on our own actions.

Now it would be odd if Homo sapiens had really got himself into a position as bad as this—a position where his main evolutionary asset, his brain, was so little use to him. None of us is going to accept this sceptical diagnosis. We cannot do so, because our involvement in moral isolationism does not flow from apathy, but from a rather acute concern about human hypocrisy and other forms of wickedness. But we polarize that concern around a few selected moral truths. We are rightly angry with those who despise, oppress or steamroll other cultures. We think that doing these things is actually *wrong*. But this is itself a moral judgment. We could not condemn oppression and insolence if we thought that all our condemnations were just a trivial local quirk of our own culture. We could still less do it if we tried to stop judging altogether.

Real moral scepticism, in fact, could lead only to inaction, to our losing all interest in moral questions, most of all in those which concern other societies. When we discuss these things, it becomes instantly clear how far we are from doing this. Suppose, for instance, that I criticize the bisecting Samurai, that I say his behaviour is brutal. What will usually happen next is that someone will protest, will say that I have no right to make criticisms like that of another culture. But it is most unlikely that he will use this move to end the discussion of the subject. Instead, he will justify the Samurai. He will try to fill in the background, to make me understand the custom, by explaining the exalted ideals of discipline and devotion which produced it. He will probably talk of the lower value which the ancient Japanese placed on individual life generally. He may well suggest that this is a healthier attitude than our own obsession with security. He may add, too, that the wayfarers did not seriously mind being bisected, that in principle they accepted the whole arrangement.

Now an objector who talks like this is implying that it *is* possible to understand alien customs. That is just what he is trying to make me do. And he implies, too, that if I do succeed in understanding them, I shall do something better than giving up judging them. He expects me to change my present judgment to a truer one—namely, one that is favourable. And the standards I must use to do this cannot just be Samurai standards. They have to be ones current in my own culture. Ideals like discipline and devotion will not move anybody unless he himself accepts them. As it happens, neither discipline nor devotion is very popular in the West at present. Anyone who appeals to them may well have to do some more arguing to make *them* acceptable, before he can use them to explain the Samurai. But if he does succeed here, he will have persuaded us, not just that there was something to be said for them in ancient Japan, but that there would be here as well.

Isolating barriers simply cannot arise here. If we accept something as a serious moral truth about one culture, we can't refuse to apply it—in however different an outward form— to other cultures as well, wherever circumstance admit it. If we refuse to do this, we just are not taking the other culture seriously. This becomes clear if we look at the last argument used by my objector—that of justification by consent of the victim. It is suggested that sudden bisection is quite in order, *provided* that it takes place between consenting adults. I cannot now discuss how conclusive this justification is. What I am pointing out is simply that it can only work if we believe that *consent* can make such a transaction respectable—and this is a thoroughly modern and Western idea. It would probably never occur to a Samurai; if it did, it would surprise him very much. It is *our* standard. In applying it, too, we are likely to make another typically Western demand. We shall ask for good factual evidence that the wayfarers actually do have this rather surprising taste—that they are really willing to be bisected. In applying Western standards in this way, we are not being confused or irrelevant. We are asking the questions which arise *from where we stand,* questions which we can see the sense of. We do this because asking questions which you can't see the sense of is humbug. Certainly we can extend our questioning by imaginative effort. We can come to understand other societies better. By doing so, we may make their questions our own, or we may see that they are really forms of the questions which we are asking already. This is not impossible. It is just very hard work. The obstacles which often prevent it are simply those of ordinary ignorance, laziness and prejudice.

If there were really an isolating barrier, of course, our own culture could never have been formed. It is no sealed box, but a fertile jungle of different influences—Greek, Jewish, Roman, Norse, Celtic and so forth, into which further influences are still pouring—American, Indian, Japanese, Jamaican, you name it. The moral isolationist's picture of separate, unmixable cultures is quite unreal. People who talk about British history usually stress the value of this fertilizing mix, no doubt rightly. But this is not just an odd fact about Britain. Except for the very smallest and most remote, all cultures are formed out of many streams. All have the problem of digesting and assimilating things which, at the start, they do not understand. All have the choice of learning something from this challenge, or, alternatively, of refusing to learn, and fighting it mindlessly instead.

This universal predicament has been obscured by the fact that anthropologists used to concentrate largely on very small and remote cultures, which did not seem to have this problem. These tiny societies, which had often forgotten their own history, made neat, self-contained subjects for study. No doubt it was valuable to emphasize their remoteness, their extreme strangeness, their independence of our cultural tradition. This emphasis was, I think, the root of moral isolationism. But, as the tribal studies themselves showed, even there the anthropologists were able to interpret what they saw and make judgments—often favourable—about the tribesmen. And the tribesmen, too, were quite equal to making judgments about the anthropologists—and about the tourists and Coca-Cola salesmen who followed them. Both sets of judgments, no doubt, were somewhat hasty, both have been refined in the light of further experience. A similar transaction between us and the Samurai might take even longer. But that is no reason at all for deeming it impossible. Morally as well as physically, there is only one world, and we all have to live in it.

Carol Gilligan
In a Different Voice

Carol Gilligan *is a professor at Harvard University who has begun something of a revolution in ethical theory, pointing out that most of the history of ethics involves a strong male bias and that female ethics may in fact be very different.*

The arc of developmental theory leads from infantile dependence to adult autonomy, tracing a path characterized by an increasing differentiation of self from other and a progressive freeing of thought from contextual constraints. The vision of Luther, journeying from the rejection of a self defined by others to the assertive boldness of "Here I stand" and the image of Plato's allegorical man in the cave, separating at last the shadows from the sun, have taken powerful hold on the psychological understanding of what constitutes development. Thus, the individual, meeting fully the developmental challenges of adolescence as set for him by Piaget, Erikson, and Kohlberg, thinks formally, proceeding from theory to fact, and defines both the self and the moral autonomously, that is, apart from the identification and conventions that had comprised the particulars of his childhood world. So equipped, he is presumed ready to live as an adult, to love and work in a way that is both intimate and generative, to develop an ethical sense of caring and a genital mode of relating in which giving and taking fuse in the ultimate reconciliation of the tension between self and other.

Yet the men whose theories have largely informed this understanding of development have all been plagued by the same problem, the problem of women, whose sexuality remains more diffuse, whose perception of self is so much more tenaciously embedded in relationships with others and whose moral dilemmas hold them in a mode of judgment that is insistently contextual. The solution has been to consider women as either deviant or deficient in their development.

That there is a discrepancy between concepts of womanhood and adulthood is nowhere more clearly evident than in the series of studies on sex-role stereotypes reported by Broverman, Vogel, Broverman, Clarkson, and Rosenkrantz (1972). The repeated finding of these studies is that the qualities deemed necessary for adulthood—the capacity for autonomous thinking, clear decision making, and responsible action—are those associated with masculinity but considered undesirable as attributes of the feminine self. The stereotypes suggest a splitting of love and work that relegates the expressive capacities requisite for the former to women while the instrumental abilities necessary for the latter reside in the masculine domain. Yet, looked at from a different perspective, these stereotypes reflect a conception of adulthood that is itself out of balance, favoring the separateness of the individual self over its connection to others and leaning more toward an autonomous life of work than toward the interdependence of love and care. . . .

The revolutionary contribution of Piaget's work is the experimental confirmation and refinement of Kant's assertion that knowledge is actively constructed rather than passively received. Time, space, self, and other, as well as the categories of developmental theory, all arise out of the active interchange between the individual and the physical and social world in which he lives and of which he strives to make sense. The development of cognition is the process of reappropriating reality at progressively more complex levels of apprehension, as the structures of thinking expand to encompass the increasing richness and intricacy of experience.

Moral development, in the work of Piaget and Kohlberg, refers specifically to the expanding conception of the social world as it is reflected in the understanding and resolution of the inevitable conflicts that arise in the relations between self and others. The moral judgment is a statement of priority, an attempt at rational resolution in a situation where, from a different point of view, the choice itself seems to do violence to justice.

Kohlberg (1969), in his extension of the early work of Piaget, discovered six stages of moral judgment, which he claimed formed an invariant sequence, each successive stage representing a more adequate construction of the moral problem, which in turn provides the basis for its more just resolution. The stages divide into three levels, each of which denotes a significant expansion of the moral point of view from an egocentric through a societal to a universal ethical conception. With this expansion in perspective comes the capacity to free moral judgment from the individual needs and social conventions with which it had earlier been confused and anchor it instead in principles of justice that are universal in application. These principles provide criteria upon which both individual and societal claims can be impartially assessed. In Kohlberg's view, at the highest stages of development morality is freed from both psychological and historical constraints, and the individual can judge independently of his own particular needs and of the values of those around him.

That the moral sensibility of women differs from that of men was noted by Freud (1925/ 1961) in the following by now well-quoted statement:

> I cannot evade the notion (though I hesitate to give it expression) that for women the level of what is ethically normal is different from what it is in man. Their superego is never so inexorable, so impersonal, so independent of its emotional origins as we require it to be in men. Character-traits which critics of every epoch have brought up against women—that they show less sense of justice than men, that they are less ready to submit to the great exigencies of life, that they are more often influenced in their judgments by feelings of affection or hostility—all these would be amply accounted for by the modification in the formation of their superego which we have inferred above.

While Freud's explanation lies in the deviation of female from male development around the construction and resolution of the Oedipal problem, the same observations about the nature of morality in women emerge from the work of Piaget and Kohlberg. Piaget (1932/1965), in his study of the rules of children's games, observed that, in the games they played, girls were "less explicit about agreement [than boys] and less concerned with legal elaboration." In contrast to the boys' interest in the codification of rules, the girls adopted a more pragmatic attitude, regarding "a rule as good so long as the game repays it." As a result, in comparison to boys, girls were found to be "more tolerant and more easily reconciled to innovations."

Kohlberg (1971) also identifies a strong interpersonal bias in the moral judgments of women, which leads them to be considered as typically at the third of his six-stage developmental sequence. At that stage, the good is identified with "what pleases or helps others and is approved of by them." This mode of judgment is conventional in its conformity to generally held notions of the good but also psychological in its concern with intention and consequence as the basis for judging the morality of action.

That women fall largely into this level of moral judgment is hardly surprising when we read from the Broverman et al. (1972) list that prominent among the twelve attributes considered to be desirable for women are tact, gentleness, awareness of the feelings of others, strong need for security, and easy expression of tender feelings. And yet, herein lies the paradox, for the very traits that have traditionally defined the "goodness" of women, their care for and sensitivity to the needs of others, are those that mark them as deficient in moral development. The infusion of feeling into their judgments keeps them from developing a more independent and abstract ethical conception in which concern for others derives from principles of justice rather than from compassion and care. Kohlberg, however, is less pessimistic than Freud in his assessment, for he sees the development of women as extending beyond the interpersonal level, following the same path toward independent, principled judgment that he discovered in the research on men from which his stages were derived. In Kohlberg's view, women's development will proceed beyond Stage Three when they are challenged to solve moral problems that require them to see beyond the relationships that have in the past generally bound their moral experience.

What then do women say when asked to construct the moral domain; how do we identify the characteristically "feminine" voice? A Radcliffe undergraduate, responding to the question, "If you had to say what morality meant to you, how would you sum it up?," replies:

When I think of the word morality, I think of obligations. I usually think of it as conflicts between personal desires and social things, social considerations, or personal desires of yourself versus personal desires of another person or people or whatever. Morality is that whole realm of how you decide these conflicts. A moral person is one who would decide, like by placing themselves more often than not as equals, a truly moral person would always consider another person as their equal . . . in a situation of social interaction, something is morally wrong where the individual ends up screwing a lot of people. And it is morally right when everyone comes out better off.

Yet when asked if she can think of someone whom she would consider a genuinely moral person, she replies, "Well, immediately I think of Albert Schweitzer because he has obviously given his life to help others." Obligation and sacrifice override the ideal of equality, setting up a basic contradiction in her thinking.

Another undergraduate responds to the question, "What does it mean to say something is morally right or wrong?," by also speaking first of responsibilities and obligations:

Just that it has to do with responsibilities and obligations and values, mainly values. . . . In my life situation I relate morality with interpersonal relationships that have to do with respect for the other person and myself. [Why respect other people?] Because they have a consciousness or feelings that can be hurt, an awareness that can be hurt.

The concern about hurting others persists as a major theme in the responses of two other Radcliffe students:

[Why be moral?] Millions of people have to live together peacefully. I personally don't want to hurt other people. That's a real criterion, a main criterion for me. It underlies my sense of justice. It isn't nice to inflict pain. I empathize with anyone in pain. Not hurting others is important in my own private morals. Years ago, I would have jumped out of a window not to hurt my boyfriend. That was pathological. Even today though, I want approval and love and I don't want enemies. Maybe that's why there is morality—so people can win approval, love and friendship.

My main moral principle is not hurting other people as long as you aren't going against your own conscience and as long as you remain true to yourself. . . . There are many moral issues such as abortion, the draft, killing, stealing, monogamy, etc. If something is a controversial issue like these, then I always say it is up to the individual. The individual has to decide and then follow his own conscience. There are no moral absolutes. . . . Laws are pragmatic instruments, but they are not absolutes. A viable society can't make exceptions all the time, but I would personally. . . . I'm afraid I'm heading for some big crisis with my boyfriend someday, and someone will get hurt, and he'll get more hurt than I will. I feel an obligation to not hurt him, but also an obligation to not lie. I don't know if it is possible to not lie and not hurt.

The common thread that runs through these statements, the wish not to hurt others and the hope that in morality lies a way of solving conflicts so that no one will get hurt, is striking in that it is independently introduced by each of the four women as the most specific item in their response to a most general question. The moral person is one who helps others; goodness is service, meeting one's obligations and responsibilities to others, if possible, without sacrificing oneself. While the first of the four women ends by denying the conflict she initially introduced, the last woman anticipates a conflict between remaining true to herself and adhering to her principle of not hurting others. The dilemma that would test the limits of this judgment would be one where helping others is seen to be at the price of hurting the self.

The reticence about taking stands on "controversial issues," the willingness to "make exceptions all the time" expressed in the final example above, is echoed repeatedly by other Radcliffe students, as in the following two examples:

> I never feel that I can condemn anyone else. I have a very relativistic position. The basic idea that I cling to is the sanctity of human life. I am inhibited about impressing my beliefs on others.

> I could never argue that my belief on a moral question is anything that another person should accept. I don't believe in absolutes. . . . If there is an absolute for moral decisions, it is human life.

Or as a thirty-one-year-old Wellesley graduate says, in explaining why she would find it difficult to steal a drug to save her own life despite her belief that it would be right to steal for another: "It's just very hard to defend yourself against the rules. I mean, we live by consensus, and you take an action simply for yourself, by yourself, there's no consensus there, and that is relatively indefensible in this society now."

What begins to emerge is a sense of vulnerability that impedes these women from taking a stand, what George Eliot (1860/1965) regards as the girl's "susceptibility" to adverse judgments of others, which stems from her lack of power and consequent inability to do something in the world. While relativism in men, the unwillingness to make moral judgments that Kohlberg and Kramer (1969) and Kohlberg and Gilligan (1971) have associated with the adolescent crisis of identity and belief, takes the form of calling into question the concept of morality itself, the women's reluctance to judge stems rather from their uncertainty about their right to make moral statements or, perhaps, the price for them that such judgment seems to entail. This contrast echoes that made by Matina Horner (1972), who differentiated the ideological fear of success expressed by men from the personal conflicts about succeeding that riddled the women's responses to stories of competitive achievement.

> Most of the men who responded with the expectation of negative consequences because of success were not concerned about their masculinity but were instead likely to have expressed existential concerns about finding a "non-materialistic happiness and satisfaction in life." These concerns, which reflect changing attitudes toward traditional kinds of success or achievement in our society, played little, if any, part in the female stories. Most of the women who were high in fear of success imagery continued to be concerned about the discrepancy between success in the situation described and feminine identity.

When women feel excluded from direct participation in society, they see themselves as subject to a consensus or judgment made and enforced by the men on whose protection and support they depend and by whose names they are known. A divorced middle-aged woman, mother of adolescent daughters, resident of a sophisticated university community, tells the story as follows:

> As a woman, I feel I never understood that I was a person, that I can make decisions and I have a right to make decisions. I always felt that that belonged to my father or my husband in some way or church which was always represented by a male clergyman. They were the three men in my life: father, husband, and clergyman, and they had much more to say about what I should or shouldn't do. They were really authority figures which I accepted. I didn't rebel against that. It only has lately

occurred to me that I never even rebelled against it, and my girls are much more conscious of this, not in the militant sense, but just in the recognizing sense. . . . I still let things happen to me rather than make them happen, than to make choices, although I know all about choices. I know the procedures and the steps and all. [Do you have any clues about why this might be true?] Well, I think in one sense, there is less responsibility involved. Because if you make a dumb decision, you have to take the rap. If it happens to you, well, you can complain about it. I think that if you don't grow up feeling that you ever had any choices, you don't either have the sense that you have emotional responsibility. With this sense of choice comes this sense of responsibility.

The essence of the moral decision is the exercise of choice and the willingness to accept responsibility for that choice. To the extent that women perceive themselves as having no choice, they correspondingly excuse themselves from the responsibility that decision entails. Childlike in the vulnerability of their dependence and consequent fear of abandonment, they claim to wish only to please but in return for their goodness they expect to be loved and cared for. This, then, is an "altruism" always at risk, for it presupposes an innocence constantly in danger of being compromised by an awareness of the trade-off that has been made. Asked to describe herself, a Radcliffe senior responds:

I have heard of the onion skin theory. I see myself as an onion, as a block of different layers, the external layers for people that I don't know that well, the agreeable, the social, and as you go inward there are more sides for people I know that I show. I am not sure about the innermost, whether there is a core, or whether I have just picked up everything as I was growing up, these different influences. I think I have a neutral attitude towards myself, but I do think in terms of good and bad. . . . Good—I try to be considerate and thoughtful of other people and I try to be fair in situations and be tolerant. I use the words but I try and work them out practically. . . . Bad things—I am not sure if they are bad, if they are altruistic or I am doing them basically for approval of other people. [Which things are these?] The values I have when I try to act them out. They deal mostly with interpersonal type relations. . . . If I were doing it for approval, it would be a very tenuous thing. If I didn't get the right feedback, there might go all my values.

Ibsen's play, *A Doll House* (1879/1965), depicts the explosion of just such a world through the eruption of a moral dilemma that calls into question the notion of goodness that lies at its center. Nora, the "squirrel wife," living with her husband as she had lived with her father, puts into action this conception of goodness as sacrifice and, with the best of intentions, takes the law into her own hands. The crisis that ensues, most painfully for her in the repudiation of that goodness by the very person who was its recipient and beneficiary, causes her to reject the suicide that she had initially seen as its ultimate expression and chose instead to seek new and firmer answers to the adolescent questions of identity and belief.

The availability of choice and with it the onus of responsibility has now invaded the most private sector of the woman's domain and threatens a similar explosion. For centuries, women's sexuality anchored them in passivity, in a receptive rather than active stance, where the events of conception and childbirth could be controlled only by a withholding in which their own sexual needs were either denied or sacrificed. That such a sacrifice entailed a cost to their intelligence as well was seen by Freud (1908/1959) when he tied the "undoubted intellectual inferiority of so many women" to "the inhibition of thought necessitated by sexual suppression." The strategies of withholding and denial that women have employed in the politics of sexual relations appear similar to their evasion or withholding of judgment in the moral realm. The hesitance expressed in the previous examples to impose even a belief in the value of human life on others, like the reluctance to claim one's sexuality, bespeaks a self uncertain of its strength, unwilling to deal with consequence, and thus avoiding confrontation.

Thus women have traditionally deferred to the judgment of men, although often while intimating a sensibility of their own which is at variance with that judgment. Maggie Tulliver, in *The Mill on the Floss* (Eliot, 1860/1965), responds to the accusations that ensue from the discovery of her secretly continued relationship with Phillip Wakeham by acceding to her brother's moral judgment while at the same time asserting a different set of standards by which she attests her own superiority:

> I don't want to defend myself. . . . I know I've been wrong—often continually. But yet, sometimes when I have done wrong, it has been because I have feelings that you would be the better for if you had them. If *you* were in fault ever, if you had done anything very wrong, I should be sorry for the pain it brought you; I should not want punishment to be heaped on you.

An eloquent defense, Kohlberg would argue, of a Stage Three moral position, an assertion of the age-old split between thinking and feeling, justice and mercy, that underlies many of the clichés and stereotypes concerning the difference between the sexes. But considered from another point of view, it is a moment of confrontation, replacing a former evasion, between two modes of judging, two differing constructions of the moral domain—one traditionally associated with masculinity and the public world of social power, the other with femininity and the privacy of domestic interchange. While the developmental ordering of these two points of view has been to consider the masculine as the more adequate and thus as replacing the feminine as the individual moves toward higher stages, their reconciliation remains unclear.

Joan Didion

On Morality

Joan Didion *lives in Venice, California, and is the well-known author of* Slouching Toward Bethlehem *and* Play It As It Lays.

As it happens I am in Death Valley, in a room at the Enterprise Motel and Trailer Park, and it is July, and it is hot. In fact it is 119°. I cannot seem to make the air conditioner work, but there is a small refrigerator, and I can wrap ice cubes in a towel and hold them against the small of my back. With the help of the ice cubes I have been trying to think, because *The American Scholar* asked me to, in some abstract way about "morality," a word I distrust more every day, but my mind veers inflexibly toward the particular.

Here are some particulars. At midnight last night, on the road in from Las Vegas to Death Valley Junction, a car hit a shoulder and turned over. The driver, very young and apparently drunk, was killed instantly. His girl was found alive but bleeding internally, deep in shock. I talked this afternoon to the nurse who had driven the girl to the nearest doctor, 185 miles across the floor of the Valley and three ranges of lethal mountain road. The nurse explained that her husband, a talc miner, had stayed on the highway with the boy's body until the coroner could get over the mountains from Bishop, at dawn today. "You can't just leave a body on the highway," she said. "It's immoral."

It was one instance in which I did not distrust the word, because she meant something quite specific. She meant that if a body is left alone for even a few minutes on the desert, the coyotes close in and eat the flesh. Whether or not a corpse is torn apart by coyotes may seem only a sentimental consideration, but of course it is more: one of the promises we make to one another is that we will try to retrieve our casualties, try not to abandon our dead to the coyotes. If we have been taught to keep our promises—if, in the simplest terms, our upbringing is good enough—we stay with the body, or have bad dreams.

I am talking, of course, about the kind of social code that is sometimes called, usually pejoratively, "wagon-train morality." In fact that is precisely what it is. For better or worse, we are what we learned as children: my own childhood was illuminated by graphic litanies of the grief awaiting those who failed in their loyalties to each other. The Donner–Reed Party, starving in the Sierra snows, all the ephemera of civilization gone save that one vestigial taboo, the provision that no one should eat his own blood kin. The Jayhawkers, who quarreled and separated not far from where I am tonight. Some of them died in the Funerals and some of them died down near Badwater and most of the rest of them died in the Panamints. A woman who got through gave the Valley its name. Some might say that the Jayhawkers were killed by the desert summer, and the Donner Party by the mountain winter, by circumstances beyond control; we were taught instead that they had somewhere abdicated their responsibilities, somehow breached their primary loyalties, or they would not have found themselves helpless in the mountain winter or the desert summer, would not have given way to acrimony, would not have deserted one another, would not have *failed*. In brief, we heard such stories as cautionary tales, and they still suggest the only kind of "morality" that seems to me to have any but the most potentially mendacious meaning.

You are quite possibly impatient with me by now; I am talking, you want to say, about a "morality" so primitive that it scarcely deserves the name, a code that has as its point only survival, not the attainment of the ideal good. Exactly. Particularly out here tonight, in this country so ominous and terrible that to live in it is to live with antimatter, it is difficult to believe that "the good" is a knowable quantity. Let me tell you what it is like out here tonight. Stories travel at night on the desert. Someone gets in his pickup and drives a couple of hundred miles for a beer, and he carries news of what is happening, back wherever he came from. Then he drives another hundred miles for another beer, and passes along stories from the last place as well as from the one before; it is a network kept alive by people whose instincts tell them that if they do not keep moving at night on the desert they will lose all reason. Here is a story that is going around the desert tonight: over across the Nevada line, sheriff's deputies are diving in some underground pools, trying to retrieve a couple of bodies known to be in the hole. The widow of one of the drowned boys is over there; she is eighteen, and pregnant, and is said not to leave the hole. The divers go down and come up, and she just stands there and stares into the water. They have been diving for ten days but have found no bottom to the caves, no bodies and no trace of them, only the black 90° water going down and down and down, and a single translucent fish, not classified. The story tonight is that one of the divers has been hauled up incoherent, out of his head, shouting—until they got him out of there so that the widow could not hear—about water that got hotter instead of cooler as he went down, about light flickering through the water, about magma, about underground nuclear testing.

That is the tone stories take out here, and there are quite a few of them tonight. And it is more than the stories alone. Across the road at the Faith Community Church a couple of dozen old people, come here to live in trailers and die in the sun, are holding a prayer sing. I cannot hear them and do not want to. What I can hear are occasional coyotes and a constant chorus of "Baby the Rain Must Fall" from the jukebox in the Snake Room next door, and if I were also to hear those dying voices, those Midwestern voices drawn to this lunar country for some unimaginable atavistic rites, *rock of ages cleft for me,* I think I would lose my own reason. Every now and then I imagine I hear a rattlesnake, but my husband says that it is a faucet, a paper rustling, the wind. Then he stands by a window, and plays a flashlight over the dry wash outside.

What does it mean? It means nothing manageable. There is some sinister hysteria in the air out here tonight, some hint of the monstrous perversion to which any human idea can come. "I followed my own conscience." "I did what I thought was right." How many madmen have said it and meant it? How many murderers? Klaus Fuchs said it, and the men who committed the Mountain Meadows Massacre said it, and Alfred Rosenberg said it. And, as we are rotely and rather presumptuously reminded by those who would say it now, Jesus said it. Maybe we have all said it, and maybe we have been wrong. Except on that most primitive level—our loyalties to those we love—what could be more arrogant than to claim the primacy of personal conscience? ("Tell me," a rabbi asked Daniel Bell when he said, as a child, that he did not believe in God. "Do you think God cares?") At least some of the time, the world appears to me as a painting by Hieronymous Bosch; were I to follow my conscience then, it would lead me out onto the desert with Marion Faye, out to where he stood in *The Deer Park* looking east to Los Alamos and praying, as if for rain, that it would happen: ". . . *let it come and clear the rot and the stench and the stink, let it come for all of everywhere, just so it comes and the world stands clear in the white dead dawn.*"

Of course you will say that I do not have the right, even if I had the power, to inflict that unreasonable conscience upon you; nor do I want you to inflict your conscience, however reasonable, however enlightened, upon me. ("We must be aware of the dangers which lie in our most generous wishes," Lionel Trilling once wrote. "Some paradox of our nature leads us, when once we have made our fellow men the objects of our enlightened interest, to go on to make them the objects of our pity, then of our wisdom, ultimately of our coercion.") That the ethic of conscience is intrinsically insidious seems scarcely a revelatory point, but it is one raised with increasing infrequency; even those who do raise it tend to *segue* with troubling readiness into the quite contradictory position that the ethic of conscience is dangerous when it is "wrong," and admirable when it is "right."

You see I want to be quite obstinate about insisting that we have no way of knowing—beyond that fundamental loyalty to the social code—what is "right" and what is "wrong," what is "good" and what "evil." I dwell so upon this because the most disturbing aspect of "morality" seems to me to be the frequency with which the word now appears; in the press, on television, in the most perfunctory kinds of conversation. Questions of straightforward power (or survival) politics, questions of quite indifferent public policy, questions of almost anything: they are all assigned these factitious moral burdens. There is something facile going on, some self-indulgence at work. Of course we would all like to "believe" in something, like to assuage our private guilts in public causes, like to lose our tiresome selves; like, perhaps, to transform the white flag of defeat at home into the brave white banner of battle away from home. And of course it is all right to do that; that is how, immemorially, things have gotten done. But I think it is all right only so long as we do not delude ourselves about what we are doing, and why. It is all right only so long as we remember that all the *ad hoc* committees, all the picket lines, all the brave signatures in *The New York Times,* all the tools of agitprop straight across the spectrum, do not confer upon anyone any *ipso facto* virtue. It is all right only so long as we recognize that the end may or may not be expedient, may or may not be a good idea, but in any case has nothing to do with "morality." Because when we start deceiving ourselves into thinking not that we want something or need something, not that it is a pragmatic necessity for us to have it, but that it is a *moral imperative* that we have it, then is when we join the fashionable madmen, and then is when the thin whine of hysteria is heard in the land, and then is when we are in bad trouble. And I suspect we are already there.

16

How Can We Get Along with Each Other?

*I*f you were asked to name the single thing that you spend the most time thinking about, the answer might very well be your relationships with other people. Throughout most of an ordinary day, we find ourselves wondering or worrying about our feelings about other people and their feelings about us. Did I really offend Bernie when I told him that his new haircut made him look like Pee Wee Herman? Does Delores really love me, or is she just using me to make José jealous? Should I go home to see my family during spring break instead of taking that trip to Florida? Will marriage destroy our love for each other? Will this one-night stand hurt my marriage? Should I tell my son that I dislike his fiance? Am I giving more to this relationship than I am getting out of it?

Although many philosophers have avoided reflecting on the nature of relationships (perhaps because they prefer to think that philosophy ought to concern itself with more enduring matters), others have viewed an understanding of human relationships as part of the central business of philosophy. Indeed, some philosophers believe that if philosophy is viewed as being somehow above matters of friendship, love, and fidelity, then the alleged wisdom of philosophers is not worth very much. For Socrates, who believed that the unexamined life is not worth living, the quality of a person's love and friendship was a measure of his or her goodness. As a result, he spent much time discussing exactly what he took real love to be. His immediate successors, Plato and Aristotle, treated friendship as a topic equal in importance to the nature of knowledge or the nature of goodness. With credentials such as these, it isn't surprising that serious consideration of relationships has seemed a worthy enterprise to a number of subsequent philosophers.

When you begin to reflect on the nature of relationships, one of the things that first becomes apparent is that they are both a source of pleasure and a source of pain. In a close relationship with another person, you sometimes feel that you are becoming nothing more than a fixture in his or her life. No matter how hard you try, you seem never to be able to satisfy your friend's desires. Experiencing yourself as chronically criticized, you begin to lose any sense of value. On the other hand, it is through relationships that you often experience your most intense feelings of self-affirmation, of connection, of worth. Under a lover's gaze, you can find yourself transformed: you are stunningly attractive, fiercely intelligent, astonishingly sensitive. It is interesting that self-affirmation is often accompanied by a sense that there are no boundaries between you and your friend or lover: where before there were two, now there is one.

The quality of our relationships affects our perceptions of ourselves and our world. Indeed, some philosophers argue that, to understand what it is to be a person in the world, we must look to the particular ways in which it is possible to stand in relation to others. Martin Buber, for example, isolates two fundamental types of relationships. When we treat another person as an object (as we feel we have been treated in the first case described above), the type of relationship he or she stands in with respect to us is what Buber calls an "I–It" relationship. When we have a full, reciprocal relationship with another person (the kind described in the second case), however, our relationship is what Buber calls the "I–Thou" (or "I–You") variety. According to Buber, our very existence, the existence of the I depends upon and grows out of these two types of relationship. Without them, there is no I at all. (You might want to compare Buber's concept of a person with that discussed in Chapter 9). It is important to recognize that I–It relationships are not always entirely bad. Although our I–Thou relationships provide the most satisfaction, we gain much in the way of knowledge from our I–It relationships as well. Sometimes it may be that looking at things objectively ("objectification") is just what is needed in our attempt to understand a situation in which we have become excessively involved. At other times, of course, a tendency to objectify must be tempered by empathy or compassion, characteristics of an I–Thou relationship.

The concept of reciprocity is viewed by many as central to good relationships. According to Aristotle, reciprocity, while not always easy to measure "objectively," is nevertheless a definitive characteristic of what he calls "perfect" friendship. We have all had relationships in which the other person acts principally as a drain on our energy. One day, a crisis arises from a fight that he had with his father. The next day, he accuses his roommate of stealing his wallet. The next day, his boss warns him that he'll be fired if he's late to work one more time. Anything has the potential to become a crisis, and whenever there is one, you are expected to devote your full attention to it. When something else occupies your attention for a moment, you are accused of not really caring about his problems. Because his problems occupy so much of your time together, your own needs and desires are barely considered. A relationship such as this one can hardly be considered a real friendship, Aristotle would argue, because it fails to meet the condition of reciprocity. Instead, it is, at best, an "incidental" friendship, one whose principal aim is selfish benefit. For Aristotle, real friendship is a moral relationship and is closely allied to his views about the relationship between being good and having a virtuous character. (You may wish to refer to Chapter 15 for a discussion of Aristotle's ethical views.) Only good people can have real friendships because only good people can wish well for another for his own sake. If he wishes the same for you in return, the condition of mutuality is satisfied and a real friendship is born. For Aristotle, real friendship is an exercise in rationality. Indeed, it is only in the context of real friendships that we are able to function rationally and effectively at all.

Janice Raymond agrees with Aristotle that friendship involves thinking, but she objects to the idea that rationality, devoid of what she calls "passion," is so desirable. Because women have been viewed historically as defective thinkers, Raymond argues that the association of friendship and rationality has had the effect of denying that women are capable of real friendship. To provide what she calls a "women-centered" account of friendship, Raymond points to two features of such friendships. First, they involve thoughtfulness, not the excessive thoughtfulness that so often drains women's energy in relationships, but a thoughtfulness strengthened by a particular kind of thinking. Second, women-centered friendships involve thoughtful passion. Rather than separating reason and emotion, friendship fuses them together into a harmonious core. (Chapter 10 provides further discussion of the relationship between reason and emotion, and Chapter 14 includes selections that deal more extensively with women's alleged inability to think.) Jamaica Kincaid presents a picture of a friendship between two girls that can serve as a basis for further reflection on the views of friendship offered by the philosophers you have read.

While Buber, Aristotle, and Raymond assume that human relationships can be a source of satisfaction (and even, in the case of Buber, a source of identity), Sartre has a more pessimistic, but some might say, realistic, view. According to Sartre, human relationships are nothing more, or less, than a source of conflict. Fundamental to Sartre's existentialist perspective is his notion of freedom, which he calls "being-for-itself." A person is whatever he chooses to be. What he is, is always up to him. You are a student by choice, a baseball player by choice, a computer expert by choice. Even in prison, you are free to choose what sort of prisoner you want to be. We are in a continuous process of creating the world for ourselves according to our choices. (You might want to look at Chapter 18 for a more extensive look at Sartre's views about freedom.) Our experience of freedom is brought to an abrupt end when we instead experience ourselves as what Sartre calls "being-for-others." The experience of shame is one such case. Suppose that you go home for vacation and find yourself overwhelmed with curiosity about your younger sister's relationship with her boyfriend. One evening, he calls and you answer the phone. Instead of hanging up when your sister gets on the other phone, you listen in. The conversation gets rather hot and you find yourself incapable of putting down the phone. You look up after several minutes only to discover that your mother has been watching you. You are overcome with shame. Suddenly you see yourself, not as you choose to be (a sophisticated college student, respectful of others privacy), but rather as you are seen by someone else: as an eavesdropper. It is here that you experience yourself as "being-for" another. Others trap us in their gaze and so limit our freedom. This, according to Sartre, is the fundamental experience of human relationships. In his scheme, there is no room for Buber's I–Thou.

In a slightly different vein, Bertrand Russell illustrates another way in which relationships can be constraining. According to him, they are principally constrained by conventions that fail to acknowledge fundamental features of human nature. Marriage, for Russell, is a paradigm case of a badly constructed convention. When love is viewed as a duty, as it is in the case of marriage, then it can only weaken and die. Sexual experimentation and variety are necessary ingredients of the good life, according to Russell. At the end of his paper, he lays out what he takes to be the conditions of a happy marriage. Given the rather gloomy picture that he paints, you may want to consider the likelihood that any relationship could satisfy those conditions. Evan Connell's brief glimpse at a conventional marriage punctuates Russell's pessimism.

If marriage doesn't fare well under Russell's philosophical scrutiny, then it is not surprising that one of its principal adjuncts, namely, relationships between parents and children, isn't likely to do much better. Just as Russell claimed that to view love as a marital duty is to destroy it, so Jane English claims that to view children as "owing" anything to their parents as a result of parental sacrifice is to undermine the possibility of love between parents and children. English asks that we see grown children's obligations as being like the obligations of friendship. Thus, if children do not feel that they are friends with their parents, they have no such obligations. You might want to consider English's argument in light of what you learned about the conditions of friendship and the nature of human relationships. In particular, you might compare her notion of reciprocity with that of Aristotle.

Finally, Nancy Aronie flips the coin of parent–child relationships considered by English. What exactly are the obligations of a mother trying earnestly to be sensitive to the needs of her young son? How do they compare to the obligations of friends, of lovers? Can a mother and a son stand in an I–Thou relationship? Are parents inevitably nothing more than impediments to freedom, doomed always to misunderstand their children? Once you start thinking about questions such as these, it becomes clear why some philosophers have taken the time to reflect carefully on the complex nature of human relationships.

Martin Buber

I–Thou

Martin Buber (1878–1965), a religious existentialist, was born in Vienna but lived much of his life in Israel. His most famous book is I–Thou, though he also wrote extensively on religious issues.

The world is twofold for man in accordance with his twofold attitude.

The attitude of man is twofold in accordance with the two basic words he can speak.

The basic words are not single words but word pairs.

One basic word is the word pair I–You.

The other basic word is the word pair I–It; but this basic word is not changed when He or She takes the place of it.

Thus the I of man is also twofold.

For the I of the basic word I–You is different from that in the basic word I–It.

Basic words do not state something that might exist outside them; by being spoken they establish a mode of existence.

Basic words are spoken with one's being.

When one says You, the I of the word pair I–You is said, too.

When one says It, the I of the word pair I–It is said, too.

The basic word I–You can only be spoken with one's whole being.

The basic word I–It can never be spoken with one's whole being. . . .

The life of a human being does not exist merely in the sphere of goal-directed verbs. It does not consist merely of activities that have something for their object.

I perceive something. I feel something. I imagine something. I want something. I sense something. The life of a human being does not consist merely of all this and its like.

All this and its like is the basis of the realm of It.

But the realm of You has another basis.

Whoever says You does not have something for his object. For wherever there is something there is also another something; every It borders on other Its; It is only by virtue of bordering on others. But where You is said there is no something. You has no borders.

Whoever says You does not have something; he has nothing. But he stands in relation.

The world as experience belongs to the basic word I–It. The basic word I–You establishes the world of relation. . . .

—What, then, does one experience of the You?
—Nothing at all. For one does not experience it.
—What, then, does one know of the You?
—Only everything. For one no longer knows particulars.

The You encounters me by grace—it cannot be found by seeking. But that I speak the basic word to it is a deed of my whole being, is my essential deed.

The You encounters me. But I enter into a direct relationship to it. Thus the relationship is election and electing, passive and active at once: An action of the whole being must approach passivity, for it does away with all partial actions and thus with any sense of action, which always depends on limited exertions.

The basic word I–You can be spoken only with one's whole being. The concentration and fusion into a whole being can never be accomplished by me, can never be accomplished without me. I require a You to become; becoming I, I say You.

All actual life is encounter.

Aristotle

Friendship

Aristotle (384–322 B.C.) was for eighteen years a student of Plato. After Plato's death, he turned to the study of biology. In addition to his biological studies, Aristotle virtually created the sciences of logic and linguistics. He developed extravagant theories in physics and made significant contributions to metaphysics, politics, and aesthetics.

It will be natural to discuss friendship or love next, for friendship is a kind of virtue or implies virtue. It is also indispensable to life. For nobody would choose to live without friends, although he were in possession of every other good. Nay, it seems that if people are rich and hold official and authoritative positions, they have the greatest need of friends; for what is the good of having this sort of prosperity if one is denied the opportunity of beneficence, which is never so freely or so admirably exercised as towards friends? Or how can it be maintained in safety and security without friends? For the greater a person's importance, the more liable it is to disaster. In poverty and other misfortunes we regard our friends as our only refuge. Again, friends are helpful to us, when we are young, as guarding us from error, and when we are growing old, as taking care of us, and supplying such deficiencies of action as are the consequences of physical weakness, and when we are in the prime of life, as prompting us to noble actions, according to the adage, "Two come together"; for two people have a greater power both of intelligence and of action *than either of the two by himself.*

It would seem that friendship or love is the natural instinct of a parent towards a child, and of a child towards a parent, not only among men, but among birds and animals generally, and among creatures of the same race towards one another, especially among men. This is the reason why we praise men who are the friends of their fellow-men or philanthropists. We may observe too in travelling how near and dear every man is to his fellow-man.

Again, it seems that friendship or love is the bond which holds states together, and that legislators set more store by it than by justice; for concord is apparently akin to friendship, and it is concord that they especially seek to promote, and faction, as being hostility to the state, that they especially try to expel.

If people are friends, there is no need of justice between them; but people may be just, and yet need friendship. Indeed it seems that justice, in its supreme form, assumes the character of friendship.

Nor is friendship indispensable only; it is also noble. We praise people who are fond of their friends, and it is thought to be a noble thing to have many friends, and there are some people who hold that to be a friend is the same thing as to be a good man.

But the subject of friendship or love is one that affords scope for a good many differences of opinion. Some people define it as a sort of likeness, and define people who are like each other as friends. Hence the sayings "Like seeks like," "Birds of a feather," and so on. Others on the contrary say that "two of a trade never agree." Upon this subject *some philosophical thinkers* indulge in more profound physical speculations; Euripides asserting that

"the parched Earth loves the rain,
And the great Heaven rain-laden loves to fall
Earthwards";

Heraclitus that "the contending tends together," and that "harmony most beautiful is formed of discords," and that "all things are by strife engendered;" others, among whom is Empedocles, taking the opposite view and urging that "like desires like."

The physical questions we may leave aside as not being germane to the present enquiry. But let us investigate all such questions as are of human interest and relate to characters and emotions, e.g. whether friendship can be formed among all people, or it is impossible for people to be friends if they are vicious, and whether there is one kind of friendship or more than one. . . .

It is possible, I think, to elucidate the subject of friendship or love, by determining what it is that is lovable or an object of love. For it seems that it is not everything which is loved, but only that which is lovable, and that this is what is good or pleasant or useful. It would seem too that a thing is useful if it is a means of gaining something good or pleasant, and if so, it follows that what is good and what is pleasant will be lovable in the sense of being ends.

It may be asked then, Is it that which is good *in itself,* or that which is good relatively to us, that we love? For there is sometimes a difference between them; and the same question may be asked in regard to that which is pleasant. It seems then that everybody loves what is good relatively to himself, and that, while it is the good which is lovable in an absolute sense, it is that which is good relatively to each individual that is lovable in his eyes. It may be said that everybody loves not that which is good, but that which appears good relatively to himself. But this is not an objection that will make any difference; for in that case that which is lovable will be that which appears to be lovable.

There being three motives of friendship or love, it must be observed that we do not apply the term "friendship" or "love" to the affection felt for inanimate things. The reason is (1) that they are incapable of reciprocating affection, and (2) that we do not wish their good; for it would, I think, be ridiculous to wish the good e.g. of wine; if we wish it at all, it is only in the sense of wishing the wine to keep well, in the hope of enjoying it ourselves. But it is admitted that we ought to wish our friend's good for his sake, and not for our own. If we wish people good in this sense, we are called well-wishers, unless our good wishes are returned; such reciprocal well-wishing is called friendship or love.

But it is necessary, I think, to add, that the well-wishing must not be unknown. A person often wishes well to people whom he has not seen, but whom he supposes to be virtuous or useful; and it is possible that one of these persons may entertain the same feeling towards him. Such people then, it is clear, wish well to one another; but they cannot be properly called friends, as their disposition is unknown to each other. It follows that, if they are to be friends, they must be well-disposed to each other, and must with each other's good, from one of the motives which have been assigned, and that each of them must know the fact of the other wishing him well.

But as the motives of friendship are specifically different, there will be a corresponding difference in the affections and friendships.

The kinds of friendship therefore will be three, being equal in number to the things which are lovable, *or are objects of friendship or love,* as every such object admits of a reciprocal affection between two persons, each of whom is aware of the other's love.

People who love each other wish each other's good in the point characteristic of their love. Accordingly those whose mutual love is based upon utility do not love each other for their own sakes, but only in so far as they derive some benefit one from another. It is the same with those whose love is based upon pleasure. Thus we are fond of witty people, not as possessing a certain character, but as being pleasant to ourselves. People then, whose love is based upon utility, are moved to affection by a sense of their own good, and people whose love is based upon pleasure, by a sense of their own pleasure; and they love a person not for being what he is in himself, but for being useful or pleasant to them. These friendships then are only friendships in an accidental sense; for the person loved is not loved as being what he is, but as being a source either of good or of pleasure. Accordingly such friendships are easily dissolved, if the persons do not continue always the same; for they abandon their love if they cease to be pleasant or useful to each other. But utility is not a permanent quality; it varies at different times. Thus, when the motive of a friendship is done away, the friendship itself is dissolved, as it was dependent upon that motive. A friendship of this kind seems especially to occur among old people, as in old age we look to profit rather than pleasure, and among such people in the prime of life or in youth as have an eye to their own interest. Friends of this kind do not generally even live together; for sometimes they are not even pleasant to one another; nor do they need the intercourse of friendship, unless they bring some profit to one another, as the pleasure which they afford goes no further than they entertain hopes of deriving benefit from it. Among these friendships we reckon the friendship of hospitality, i.e. *the friendship which exists between a host and his guests.*

It would seem that the friendship of the young is based upon pleasure; for they live by emotion and are most inclined to pursue what is pleasant to them at the moment. But as their time of life changes, their pleasures are transformed. They are therefore quick at making friendships and quick at abandoning them; for the friendship changes with the object which pleases them, and friendship of this kind is liable to sudden change. Young men are amorous too, amorousness being generally a matter of emotion and pleasure; hence they fall in love and soon afterwards fall out of love, changing from one condition to another many times in the same day. But amorous people wish to spend their days and lives together, as it is thus that they attain the object of their friendship.

The perfect friendship or love is the friendship or love of people who are good and alike in virtue; for these people are alike in wishing each other's good, in so far as they are good, and they are good in themselves. But it is people who wish the good of their friends for their friend's sake that are in the truest sense friends, as their friendship is the consequence of their own character, and is not an accident. Their friendship therefore continues as long as their virtue, and virtue is a permanent quality.

Again, each of them is good in an absolute sense, and good in relation to his friend.

For good men are not only good in an absolute sense, but serve each other's interest. They are pleasant too; for the good are pleasant in an absolute sense, and pleasant in relation to one another, as everybody finds pleasure in such actions as are proper to him, and the like, and all good people act alike or nearly alike.

Such a friendship is naturally permanent, as it unites in itself all the proper conditions of friendship. For the motive of all friendship or affection is good or pleasure, whether it be absolute or relative to the person who feels the affection, and it depends upon a certain similarity. In the friendship of good men all these specified conditions belong to the friends in themselves; for other friendships *only* bear a resemblance to the perfect friendship. That which is good in an absolute sense is also in an absolute sense pleasant. These are the principal objects of affection, and it is upon these that affectionate feeling, and affection in the highest and best sense, depend.

Friendships of this kind are likely to be rare; for such people are few. They require time and familiarity too; for, as the adage puts it, it is impossible for people to know one another until they have consumed the proverbial salt together; nor can people admit one another to friendship, or be friends at all, until each has been proved lovable and trustworthy to the other.

People, who are quick to treat one another as friends, wish to be friends but are not so really, unless they are lovable and know each other to be lovable; for the wish to be friends may arise in a minute, but not friendship. . . .

It is the friendship of the good which is friendship in the truest sense, as has been said several times. For it seems that, while that which is good or pleasant in an absolute sense is an object of love and desire, that which is good or pleasant to each individual is an object of love or desire to him; but the love or desire of one good man for another depends upon such goodness and pleasantness as are at once absolute and relative to the good.

Affection resembles a feeling but friendship resembles a moral state. For while affection may be felt for inanimate as much as for animate things, the love of friends for one another implies moral purpose, and such purpose is the outcome of a moral state.

Again, we wish the good of those whom we love for their own sake, and the wish is governed not by feeling but by the moral state. In loving our friend too, we love what is good for ourselves; as when a good man becomes a friend, he becomes a blessing to his friend. Accordingly each of two friends loves what is good for himself, and returns as much as he receives in good wishes and in pleasure; for, as the proverb says, equality is friendship.

Janice Raymond

The Conditions of Female Friendship

Janice Raymond *teaches women's studies at the University of Massachusetts–Amherst. She writes extensively about issues in feminist ethics. Her most recent book,* A Passion for Friends, *is a study of female friendship.*

Many women have expressed disappointment and frustration at the lack of thoughtfulness that pervades many women's groups and that women seem to accept as a matter of course in feminist relationships and gatherings.

On the other hand, many women have been socialized to react almost instinctually to other people's needs, mostly those of men and children. Women have been drained by a kind of thoughtfulness that is really lacking in thought to the extent that it is indiscriminately given, without thinking about the conditions under which it is extended and the fact that it is left to women in any context to be thoughtful. Here the thinking is missing from thoughtfulness so that women give and give, extend themselves constantly, and deal and deal with the needs of others in what has at times almost amounted to a feminine compulsion. The thoughtfulness that most women are trained to extend in a hetero-relational context is not born out of Self-directed thinking. Many women "go into robot" performing "emotional labor" to fulfill all sorts of others' needs. For women, the cost of this kind of thoughtfulness has been the obliteration of thinking.

A vision of female friendship restores the thinking to thoughtfulness. At the same time, it restores a thoughtfulness to thinking, that is, a respect and considerateness for another's needs. Only thoughtfulness, in its more expanded meaning, can sustain female friendship and give it daily life. A thinking friendship must become a thoughtful friendship in the full sense of the word *thoughtfulness*. Many women may be brilliant thinkers, but that thinking has to be accompanied by a genuine attentiveness and respect for other women if female friendship is to flourish. On the other hand, many women may be caring and considerate of others, but if this thoughtfulness lacks a Self-directed thinking that "prepares us ever anew to meet whatever we must meet in our daily lives," it reinforces socialized femininity rather than female friendship. The word *thoughtfulness* conveys the meaning of a thinking considerateness and a considerate thinking. It is not accidental that it has such a dual meaning. A woman who truly thinks is, more expansively, full of thought in many realms.

What does it mean to think? Philosophers have often identified thinking with intellectual activity. Aristotle traced the capacity for friendship to *man's* intelligence or thinking capacity. Within the classical western tradition of male philosophy about friendship, women were not recognized as capable of friendship because of their supposed diminished capacity for thinking. It was this emphasis on man's faculty of thought that also led Aristotle to proclaim that friendship could flourish only between persons who are equal in intelligence. Where such an equality exists, he said, minds grow and are always capable of contributing to a common stock of ideas that is necessary for an enriched friendship.

From a different vantage point, Hannah Arendt wrote an entire book, *The Life of the Mind,* in which she talked about a kind of thinking that includes, but that is also distinguished from, intellectual activity. In her framework, thinking and intellect are not concerned with the same things. Thinking is oriented to meaning whereas the intellect searches after truth, a truth that in modern times has been "transformed or, rather, broken down into a string of verities." In other words, the intellect often reduces profound truth to a body of truths or a body of knowledge, while thinking wishes to understand their meaning. The narrow intellectual is concerned with particular facts or truths whereas the thinker searches for the meaning of particular facts or truths. This distinction between knowledge and thinking is particularly significant in the context of vision. A person without vision will place know-how over knowing why. That person may ultimately be satisfied with a knowledge without meaning.

Arendt affirms that thinking is a primary condition of female friendship. Although my use of the word *thoughtfulness* goes beyond Arendt's discussion of thinking, I agree with many of her basic points about thinking and build on these. With her, I affirm that thinking is not the prerogative of the few professional thinkers. It is

an ever-present faculty in everybody; by the same token, inability to think is not a failing of the many who lack brain power but an ever-present possibility for everybody—scientists, scholars, and other specialists in mental exercises not excluded. Everybody may come to shun that intercourse with oneself.

"Intercourse with oneself" is crucial to both the idea of thinking and that of friendship, for it is where both come together. Thinking is where I keep myself company, where I find my original friend, if you will. It is the solitude, as opposed to loneliness, where I am alone with, but not lonely in, the companionship of myself. Thinking is where I am at home with myself when, for all sorts of reasons, I withdraw from the world. "The partner who comes to life when you are alert and alone is the only one from whom you can never get away—except by ceasing to think." This is one of the major reasons why women have lost their Selves— because they have stopped thinking. By not thinking, an individual loses her original friendship with her Self. Through thinking, a person discovers that she can be her real Self. In discovering this, she also realizes that the conversation that took place in the duality of thinking activity—that is, the duality of "myself with myself," the "two-in-one," or "the one who asks and the one who answers"—enables conversation with others. When I discover, through thinking, that I can converse with my real Self, I have to realize that such a conversation is possible with others. This is the awakening of female friendship in which the search for others like my Self begins.

As I stated earlier, Aristotle maintained that "the friend is another self." However, until the Self is another friend, it is often difficult for women to have confidence in their power of making and sustaining friends. The conversation of friendship with others can be had only by those who have learned how to think with themselves, to keep themselves company. Conversely, Arendt places the emphasis in the opposite direction. "I first talk with others before I talk with myself, examining whatever the joint talk may have been about, and then discover that I can conduct a dialogue not only with others but with myself as well." The movement, I believe, is dialectical. A woman must be at the same time a friend to her original Self and to others. Which comes first is hard to determine. What is clear is that thinking and friendship go hand in hand.

The classical tradition of friendship was closely connected with thinking. Adolf Harnack pointed out that the "history of the Greek schools of philosophy is at the same time the history of friendship." It was the philosophers of ancient Greece who gave an intellectual development to the idea of friendship. With Socrates, for example, friendship became both the condition and content of an education and educated thought. In other words, the relation between student and teacher was a bond of friendship while, at the same time, friendship was the object of education. That is, it was subjected to philosophical analysis, and its origin, nature, and means of development were investigated.

Arendt follows this tradition in associating friendship with thinking. In the way she has connected the two, she has made a profound and original contribution to the history of thinking, especially in clarifying its quest for meaning and in viewing thinking as the conversation that takes place between "myself and myself." For a specific analysis of female friendship, however, I believe it is necessary to expand Arendt's notion of thinking to thoughtfulness in the way I have already defined. Thinking is made flesh in the lives of women who think, that is, who seek meaning in their lives, but who also know that meaning is material. Thinking, to my way of thinking, is materialized in the thoughtfulness of female friendship. Thoughtfulness is not divorced from thinking but gives flesh to it. The precarious balance between the world of thinking and the world of acting is stabilized by the thoughtfulness of female friendship.

Passion

As female friendship is characterized by thoughtfulness, it is also marked by passion. Friendship is a passion but, in my vision, it is a thoughtful passion. It manifests a thinking heart.

The tension between thinking and feeling, as signified in the phrase "thoughtful passion," is evident in the etymology of the word *passion*. *Passion* derives from Old French and Latin roots meaning "suffering, pain or some disorder of body or spirit." It also means being "affected by external agency." However, etymologies are often multidimensional, and so we find another meaning of *passion* defined as "any kind of feeling by which the mind is powerfully affected or moved . . . an eager outreaching of the mind toward something" (*Oxford English Dictionary*).

A passionate friendship upholds the integrity between thought and passion. In passionate friendship, there is no separation between the two. It is not so much that they merge, but that they have not been fractured to begin with. Emily Dickinson expressed the integrity between thought and passion with her usual eloquent succinctness:

> The Heart is the Capital of the Mind—
> The Mind is a single State—
> The Heart and the Mind together make
> A single Continent—

We have become so accustomed to the dualisms of thought and passion that the idea of a thoughtful passion in which thinking does not rule, but rather suffuses passion (in this case, the passion of friendship), is a strange notion.

This was not always the case. The importance of friendship as a primary passion and its alliance with thinking were part of the Greek tradition of friendship. In pre-Christian times, the tie of friendship was considered the highest form of communion between two persons—always two men—superseding that of marriage. As we have seen, friendship was a homo-relational affair.

Within the tradition of classical friendship, women were judged to be without the passion, sense of individuality, and presence of a common world and worldliness that make friendship possible. Greater than these faults, however, was woman's supposed incapacity for thought—thought being indispensable to the Greek vision of a good friendship. Montaigne is a more modern representative of the Greek philosophical perspective that female friendships are shallow because women do not "appear to be endued [endowed] with firmness of mind to endure the constraint of so hard and durable a knot."

So impressed were the Greeks with the manliness of the passion of friendship, with its power to prompt men to high thought and heroic action, that the love of friendship was set above the love of man for woman. As Aristotle phrased it, the male friend was "another self."

Whereas the man who forms a deep relationship with another man is regarded as "another self," the woman who forms a deep and passionate friendship with another woman is labeled "narcissistic." Freudian psychology, in particular, has taught that female intimacy is trifling and sentimental, a prelude only to the adult and mature stage of hetero-relational development. Close friendships between women are childish crushes, relics of a bygone time of immaturity, where women have not yet been weaned from the world of women. The world of men is the world of thought and action. The world of women lacks thought and real passion. De Beauvoir, the philosopher, mimics psychological cant in *The Second Sex* by saying that close female friendships smack of the "insipid purity" of girlhood and are narcissistic. Unfortunately, many women still believe this.

I emphasize the Greek tradition of friendship here because it posed an alternative to marriage by affirming friendship as a superior bond, as well as associating it with thinking. It also sanctioned the expression of passion between two friends, even to the point of sexual expression. This is not to say that such passion serves as a model for female friendship, but that there has been a historical recognition of the friendship union as a primary passion associated with thinking.

The reality of friendship as a primary passion and its alliance with thinking in the Greek tradition are important to a vision of female friendship as a thoughtful passion. Not that the Greeks arrived at a unified notion or reality of friendship as a thoughtful passion, but the significance of friendship as a passion and its impact on thinking and the development of philosophy, as well as on all institutions of Greek society, can be considered, expanded, and lived out by female friends in quite different ways.

A thoughtfully passionate friendship is passion at its most active. It keeps passion active and does not allow it to degenerate into its more passive modes. More concretely, it helps two women to become their own person. There is a dynamic integrity of existence in a thoughtful passion that is missing in a more sentimental friendship. Friendship that is characterized by thoughtful passion ensures that a friend does not lose her Self in the heightened awareness of and attachment to another woman. . . .

In any kind of lover relationship that is committed, one's lover should be one's best friend. And if one's best friend is one's lover, she should also be the primary passion of her lover's life. A truly passionate love life, above all, must be pervaded by a thoughtful passion. The wings of eros are very quickly clipped, especially when eros amounts to desire. The wings of eros become the wings of mere pleasure, short-lived sensual delight, or superficial sentiment when they are divorced from the ground of thoughtfulness. A love relationship which is also a passionate friendship must be a lucid affection.

Passion is not usually associated with friendship. Since the expression of passion has been largely confined to lovers in modern times, one might ask whether my notion of passionate friendship is restricted to lovers. The answer is no. Passion, in this work, is not restricted to lovers, but it is most fully manifested where lovers are friends and, conversely, where friends are lovers.

Of course, any deep friendship is pervaded by powerful feelings—by passion. The distinction that I make between passion and sentiment I would also apply to a passionate friendship in which the friends are not lovers. One must also distinguish between passionate and sentimental friendships. With the latter, such feeling—such passive passion, if you will—contributes to an absence of both intensity of emotion and deep thought. It is a kind of emotion that depends on the feeling of itself feeling. A sentimental or romantic friendship is an example of what I have called the *banality of passion.*

As with lover/friendships, nonlover friendships must also be suffused by thought so that the passion can run deep and not roll off the surface of sentimentality or passive romanticism. Friendship, as a thoughtful passion, creates movement that does not abort passion but brings it to greater heights and depths. The ability of thought to order reality marks the difference between a passionate and a sentimental friendship. A sentimental friendship is based on an intensely romantic yet shallow attachment. It eventually runs its course in the uncentered and disordered diffusion of its feeling. It thrashes its feeling away in a burst. It is passion at its most passive, often camouflaged by activity lacking in forward movement. Finally a sentimental friendship is governed by strong feeling that is separated from thought. It is therefore a thoughtless feeling. . . .

. . . Women's ability to move, stir, arouse, influence other women has been severely diminished. . . . [P]assion is not a feeling that can be isolated from other circumstances in a woman's life. A woman must take time to examine her whole life context before exercising passion in certain ways. Passion occurs within the total environment of a woman's life. While it has an ecosystem of its own, it cannot survive outside a larger environment that comprehends connections. . . .

Passion is not a "static, inexplicable blob of feeling." It is a "movement rooted in knowledge." At the root of passion is the knowledge and revelation of truth, the truth of one's real Self. In a hetero-relational context, women have lied about passion—with their bodies and their minds, in the first instance often feigning orgasm and in the latter often feigning stupidity. A promiscuity of passion is not the antidote to the lives of repressed passion that women have lived within the confines of hetero-relations. Passion must have truthful consequences. It cannot, as the definition of promiscuity states, be "undiscriminating," "without distinction or order," "done or applied without respect for kind, order, or number." Passion must not be casual or undiscerning. Women must not once again lie with our bodies or our minds, this time to women. . . .

With some women, friendship will be accompanied by deep and thoughtful feeling. Women must then discern where that feeling will be directed. With other women, friendship will take the form of passionately working for women and of actualizing feminist vision.

The philosophers, beginning with Aristotle, maintained that friendship was possible only between equals. Equality is a problematic term, however, because if has such quantitative connotations. Its primary meaning is "measure, quantity, amount." To my way of thinking, it makes more sense to assess the possibilities of female friendship on the basis of another meaning of equality—"capable of meeting the requirements of a situation or task." In other words, are female friends "equal to the task"? What task? The task of building a creative and responsible friendship; the task of two sights-seeing; the task of building a woman-centered existence. . . .

The world is what women make of it. This point is crucial—we must make something of it. This presupposes some kind of location in the ordinary world of human affairs, much of which is male-created. Friendship provides a point of crystallization for living in the ordinary world, not the pretense for exiting from it. Friendship does not automatically convey the means of living in the world or of making women into world-builders, but it does provide a location in that world.

Jamaica Kincaid ·

Gwen

Jamaica Kincaid *was born in Antigua, in the Caribbean, where she attended the girl's school, which serves as the location of the story reprinted here. Her highly acclaimed short stories are collected in* The River *and most recently in* Annie John.

*O*n opening day, I walked to my new school alone. It was the first and last time that such a thing would happen. All around me were other people my age—girls and boys, dressed in their school uniforms, marching off to school. They all seemed to know each other, and as they met they would burst into laughter, slapping each other on the shoulder and back, telling each other things that must have made for much happiness. I saw some girls wearing the same uniform as my own, and my heart just longed for them to say something to me, but the most they could do to include me was to smile and nod in my direction as they walked on arm in arm. I could hardly blame them for not paying more attention to me. Everything about me was so new: my uniform was new, my shoes were new, my hat was new, my shoulder ached from the weight of my new books in my new bag; even the road I walked on was new, and I must have put my feet down as if I weren't sure the ground was solid. At school, the yard was filled with more of these girls, wearing their most sure-of-themselves demeanor. When I looked at them, they made up a sea. They were walking in and out among the beds of flowers, all across the fields, all across the courtyard, in and out of classrooms. Except for me, no one seemed a stranger to anything or anyone. Hearing the way they greeted each other, I couldn't be sure that they hadn't all come out of the same woman's belly, and at the same time, too. Looking at them, I was suddenly glad that because I had wanted to avoid an argument with my mother I had eaten all my breakfast, for now I surely would have fainted if I had been in any more weakened a condition.

I knew where my classroom was, because my mother and I had kept an appointment at the school a week before. There I met some of my teachers and was shown the ins and outs of everything. When I saw it then, it was nice and orderly and empty and smelled just scrubbed. Now it smelled of girls milling around, fresh ink in inkwells, new books, chalk and erasers. The girls in my classroom acted even more familiar with each other. I was sure I would never be able to tell them apart just from looking at them, and I was sure that I would never be able to tell them apart from the sound of their voices.

When the school bell rang at half past eight, we formed ourselves into the required pairs and filed into the auditorium for morning prayers and hymn-singing. Our headmistress gave us a little talk, welcoming the new students and welcoming back the old students, saying that she hoped we had all left our bad ways behind us, that we would be good examples for each other and bring greater credit to our school than any of the other groups of girls who had been there before us. My palms were wet, and quite a few times the ground felt as if it were seesawing under my feet, but that didn't stop me from taking in a few things. For instance, the headmistress, Miss Moore. I knew right away that she had come to Antigua from England, for she looked like a prune left out of its jar, and she sounded as if she had borrowed her voice from an owl. The way she said, "Now, girls . . ." When she was just standing still there, listening to some of the other activities, her gray eyes going all around the room hoping to see something wrong, her throat would beat up and down as if a fish fresh out of water were caught inside. I wondered if she even smelled like a fish. Once when I didn't wash, my mother had given me a long scolding about it, and she ended by saying that it was the only thing she didn't like about English people: they didn't wash often enough, or wash properly when they finally did. My mother had said, "Have you ever noticed how they smell as if they had been bottled up in a fish?" On either side of Miss Moore stood our other teachers, women and men—mostly women. I recognized Miss George, our music teacher; Miss Nelson, our homeroom teacher; Miss Goodwin, our history and geography teacher; and Miss Newgate, our algebra and geometry teacher. I had met them the day my mother and I were at school. I did not know who the others were, and I did not worry about it. Since they were teachers, I was sure it wouldn't be long before, because of some misunderstanding, they would be thorns in my side.

We walked back to our classroom the same way we had come, quite orderly and, except for a few whispered exchanges, quite silent. But no sooner were we back in our classroom than the girls were in each other's laps, arms wrapped around necks. After peeping over my shoulder left and right, I sat down in my seat and wondered what would become of me. There were twenty of us in my class, and we were seated at desks arranged five in a row, four rows deep. I was seated at a desk in the third row, and this made me even more miserable. I hated to be seated so far away from the teacher, because I was sure I would miss something she said. But, even worse, if I was out of my teacher's sight all the time how could she see my industriousness and quickness at learning things? And, besides, only dunces were seated so far to the rear, and I could not bear to be thought a dunce. I was now staring at the back of a shrubby-haired girl seated in the front row—the seat I most coveted, since it was directly in front of the teacher's desk. At that moment, the girl twisted herself around, stared at me, and said, "You are Annie John? We hear you are very bright." It was a good thing Miss Nelson walked in right then, for how would it have appeared if I had replied, "Yes, that is completely true"—the very thing that was on the tip of my tongue.

As soon as Miss Nelson walked in, we came to order and stood up stiffly at our desks. She said to us, "Good morning, class," half in a way that someone must have told her was the proper way to speak to us and half in a jocular way, as if we secretly amused her. We replied, "Good morning, Miss," in unison and in a respectful way, at the same time making a barely visible curtsy, also in unison. When she had seated herself at her desk, she said to us, "You may sit now," and we did. She opened the roll book, and as she called out our names each of us answered, "Present, Miss." As she called out our names, she kept her head bent over the book, but when she called out my name and I answered with the customary response she looked up and smiled at me and said, "Welcome, Annie." Everyone, of course, then turned and looked at me. I was sure it was because they could hear the loud racket my heart was making in my chest.

It was the first day of a new term, Miss Nelson said, so we would not be attending to any of our usual subjects; instead, we were to spend the morning in contemplation and reflection and writing something she described as an "autobiographical essay." In the afternoon, we would read aloud to each other our autobiographical essays. (I knew quite well about "autobiography" and "essay," but reflection and contemplation! A day at school spent in such a way! Of course, in most books all the good people were always contemplating and reflecting before they did anything. Perhaps in her mind's eye she could see our futures and, against all prediction, we turned out to be good people.) On hearing this, a huge sigh went up from the girls. Half the sighs were in happiness at the thought of sitting and gazing off into clear space, the other half in unhappiness at the misdeeds that would have to go unaccomplished. I joined the happy half, because I knew it would please Miss Nelson, and, my own selfish interest aside, I liked so much the way she wore her ironed hair and her long-sleeved blouse and box-pleated skirt that I wanted to please her.

The morning was uneventful enough: a girl spilled ink from her inkwell all over her uniform; a girl broke her pen nib and then made a big to-do about replacing it; girls twisted and turned in their seats and pinched each other's bottoms; girls passed notes to each other. All this Miss Nelson must have seen and heard, but she didn't say anything—only kept reading her book: an elaborately illustrated edition of "The Tempest," as later, passing by her desk, I saw. Midway in the morning, we were told to go out and stretch our legs and breathe some fresh air for a few minutes; when we returned, we were given glasses of cold lemonade and a slice of bun to refresh us.

As soon as the sun stood in the middle of the sky, we were sent home for lunch. The earth may have grown an inch or two larger between the time I had walked to school that morning and the time I went home to lunch, for some girls made a small space for me in their little band. But I couldn't pay much attention to them; my mind was on my new surroundings, my new teacher, what I had written in my nice new notebook with its black-all-mixed-up-with-white cover and smooth lined pages (so glad was I to get rid of my old notebooks, which had on their covers a picture of a wrinkled-up woman wearing a crown on her head and a neckful and armfuls of diamonds and pearls—their pages so coarse, as if they were made of cornmeal). I flew home. I must have eaten my food. I flew back to school. By half past one, we were sitting under a flamboyant tree in a secluded part of our schoolyard, our autobiographical essays in hand. We were about to read aloud what we had written during our morning of contemplation and reflection.

In response to Miss Nelson, each girl stood up and read her composition. One girl told of a much revered and loved aunt who now lived in England and of how much she looked forward to one day moving to England to live with her aunt; one girl told of her brother studying medicine in Canada and the life she imagined he lived there (it seemed quite weird to me); one girl told of the fright she had when she dreamed she was dead, and of another fright she had when she woke and found that she wasn't (everyone laughed at this, and Miss

Nelson had to call us to order over and over); one girl told of how her oldest sister's best friend's cousin's best friend (it was a real rigmarole) had gone on a Girl Scout jamboree held in Trinidad and met someone who millions of years ago had taken tea with Lady Baden-Powell; one girl told of an excursion she and her father had made to Redonda, and of how they had seen some booby birds tending their chicks. Things went on in that way, all so playful, all so imaginative. I began to wonder about what I had written, for it was the opposite of playful and it was the opposite of imaginative. What I had written was heartfelt, and, except for the very end, it was all too true. The afternoon was wearing itself thin. Would my turn ever come? What should I do, finding myself in a world of new girls, a world in which I was not even near the center?

It was a while before I realized that Miss Nelson was calling on me. My turn at last to read what I had written. I got up and started to read, my voice shaky at first, but since the sound of my own voice had always been a calming potion to me, it wasn't long before I was reading in such a way that, except for the chirp of some birds, the hum of bees looking for flowers, the silvery rush-rush of the wind in the trees, the only sound to be heard was my voice as it rose and fell in sentence after sentence. At the end of my reading, I thought I was imagining the upturned faces on which were looks of adoration, but I was not; I thought I was imagining, too, some eyes brimming over with tears, but again I was not. Miss Nelson said that she would like to borrow what I had written to read for herself, and that it would be placed on the shelf with the books that made up our own class library, so that it would be available to any girl who wanted to read it. This is what I remember writing:

"When I was a small child, my mother and I used to go down to Rat Island on Sundays right after church, so that I could bathe in the sea. It was at a time when I was thought to have something wrong with me, and a bath in the sea had been recommended as a strengthening remedy. Rat Island wasn't a place many people went to anyway, but by climbing down some rocks my mother had found a place that nobody seemed to have ever been. Since this bathing in the sea was a medicine and not a picnic, we had to bathe without wearing swimming costumes. My mother was a superior swimmer. When she plunged into the seawater, it was as if she had always lived there. She would go far out if it was safe to do so, and she could tell just by looking at the way the waves beat if it was safe to do so. She could tell if a shark was nearby, and she had never been stung by a jellyfish. I, on the other hand, could not swim at all. In fact, if I was in water up to my knees I was sure that I was drowning. My mother had tried everything to get me swimming, from using a coaxing method to just throwing me without a word into the water. Nothing worked. The only way I could go into the water was if I was on my mother's back, my arms clasped tightly around her neck, and she would then swim around not too far from the shore. It was only then that I could forget how big the sea was, how far down the bottom could be, and how filled up it was with things that couldn't understand a nice hallo. When we swam around in this way, I would think how much we were like the pictures of sea mammals I had seen, my mother and I, naked in the seawater, my mother sometimes singing to me a song in a French patois I did not yet understand, or sometimes not saying anything at all. I would place my ear against her neck, and it was as if I were listening to a giant shell, for all the sounds around me—the sea, the wind, the birds screeching—would seem as if they came from inside her, the way the sounds of the sea are in a seashell. Afterward, my mother would take me back to the shore, and I would lie there just beyond the farthest reach of a big wave and watch my mother as she swam and dove.

"One day, in the midst of watching my mother swim and dive, I heard a commotion far out at sea. It was three ships going by, and they were filled with people. They must have been celebrating something, for the ships would blow their horns and the people would cheer in response. After they passed out of view, I turned back to look at my mother, but I could not see her. My eyes searched the small area of water where she should have been, but I couldn't find her. I stood up and started to call out her name, but no sound would come out of my throat. A huge black space opened up in front of me and I fell inside it. I couldn't see what was in front of me and I couldn't hear anything around me. I couldn't think of anything except that my mother was no longer near me. I don't know what, but something drew my eye in one direction. A little bit out of the area in which she usually swam was my mother, just sitting and tracing patterns on a large rock. She wasn't paying any attention to me, for she didn't know that I had missed her. I was glad to see her and started jumping up and down and waving to her. Still she didn't see me, and then I started to cry, for it dawned on me that, with all that water between us and I being unable to swim, my mother could stay there forever and the only way I would be able to wrap my arms around her again was if it pleased her or if I took a boat. I cried until I wore myself out. My tears ran down into my mouth, and it was the first time that I realized tears had a taste. Finally, my mother came ashore. She was, of course, alarmed when she saw my face, for I had let the tears just dry there and they left a stain. When I told her what had happened, she hugged me so close that it was hard to breathe, and she told me that nothing could be farther from the truth—that she would never ever leave me. And though she said it over and over again, and though I felt better, I could not wipe out of my mind the feeling I had had when I couldn't find her.

"The summer just past, I kept having a dream about my mother sitting on the rock. Over and over I would have the dream—only in it my mother never came back, and sometimes my father would join her. When he joined her, they would both sit tracing patterns on the rock, and it must have been amusing, for they would always make each other laugh. At first, I didn't say anything, but when I began to have the dream again and again, I finally told my mother. My mother became instantly distressed; tears came to her eyes, and, taking me in her arms, she told me all the same things she had told me on the day at the sea, and this time the memory of the dark time when I felt I would never see her again did not come back to haunt me."

I didn't exactly tell a lie about the last part. That is just what would have happened in the old days. But actually that past summer saw me launched into young-ladyness, and when I told my mother of my dream—my nightmare, really—I was greeted with a turned back and a warning against eating certain kinds of fruit in an unripe state just before going to bed. I placed the old days' version before my classmates because, I thought, I couldn't bear to show my mother in a bad light before people who hardly knew her. But the real truth was that I couldn't bear to have anyone see how deep in disfavor I was with my mother.

As we walked back to the classroom, I in the air, my classmates on the ground, jostling each other to say some words of appreciation and congratulation, my head felt funny, as if it had swelled up to the size of, and weighed no more than, a balloon. Often I had been told by my mother not to feel proud of anything I had done and in the next breath that I couldn't feel enough pride about something I had done. Now I tossed from one to the other: my head bowed down to the ground, my head high up in the air. I looked at these girls surrounding me, my heart filled with just-sprung-up love, and I wished then and there to spend the rest of my life only with them.

As we approached our classroom, I felt a pinch on my arm. It was an affectionate pinch, I could tell. It was the girl who had earlier that day asked me if my name was Annie John. Now she told me that her name was Gweneth Joseph, and, reaching into the pocket of her tunic, she brought out a small rock and presented it to me. She had found it, she said, at the foot of a sleeping volcano. The rock was black, and it felt rough in my hands, as if it had been through a lot. I immediately put it to my nose to see what it smelled like. It smelled of lavender, because Gweneth Joseph had kept it wrapped in a handkerchief doused in that scent. It may have been in that moment that we fell in love. Later, we could never agree on when it was. That afternoon, we walked home together, she going a little out of her usual way, and we exchanged likes and dislikes, our jaws dropping and eyes widening when we saw how similar they were. We separated ourselves from the other girls, and they, understanding everything, left us alone. We cut through a tamarind grove, we cut through a cherry-tree grove, we passed down the lane where all the houses had elaborate hedges in front, so that nothing was visible but the upstairs windows. When we came to my street, parting was all but unbearable. "Tomorrow," we said, to cheer each other up.

Gwen and I were soon inseparable. If you saw one, you saw the other. For me, each day began as I waited for Gwen to come by and fetch me for school. My heart beat fast as I stood in the front yard of our house waiting to see Gwen as she rounded the bend in our street. The sun, already way up in the sky so early in the morning, shone on her, and the whole street became suddenly empty so that Gwen and everything about her were perfect, as if she were in a picture. Her panama hat, with the pink-and-gray satin ribbon—our school colors—around the brim, sat lopsided on her head, for her head was small and she never seemed to get the correct-size hat, and it had to be anchored with a piece of elastic running under her chin. The pleats in the tunic of her uniform were in place, as was to be expected. Her cotton socks fit neatly around her ankles, and her shoes shone from just being polished. If a small breeze blew, it would ruffle the ribbons in her short, shrubby hair and the hem of her tunic; if the hem of her tunic was disturbed in that way, I would then be able to see her knees. She had bony knees and they were always ash-colored, as if she had just finished giving them a good scratch or had just finished saying her prayers. The breeze might also blow back the brim of her hat, and since she always walked with her head held down I might then be able to see her face: a small, flattish nose; lips the shape of a saucer broken evenly in two; wide, high cheekbones; ears pinned back close against her head—which was always set in a serious way, as if she were going over in her mind some of the many things we had hit upon that were truly a mystery to us. (Though once I told her that about her face, and she said that really she had only been thinking about me. I didn't look to make sure, but I felt as if my whole skin had become covered with millions of tiny red boils and that shortly I would explode with happiness.) When finally she reached me, she would look up and we would both smile and say softly, "Hi." We'd set off for school side by side, our feet in step, not touching but feeling as if we were joined at the shoulder, hip, and ankle, not to mention heart.

As we walked together, we told each other things we had judged most private and secret: things we had overheard our parents say, dreams we had had the night before, the things we were really afraid of; but especially we told of our love for each other. Except for the ordinary things that naturally came up, I never told her about my changed feeling for my mother. I could see in what high regard Gwen held me, and I couldn't bear for her to see the great thing I had had once and then lost without an explanation. By the time we got to school, our chums often seemed overbearing, with their little comments on the well-pressedness of each other's uniforms, or on the neatness of their schoolbooks, or on how much they approved of the way Miss Nelson was wearing her hair these days. A few other girls were having much the same experience as Gwen and I, and when we heard comments of this kind we would look at each other and roll up our eyes and toss our hands in the air—a way of saying how above such concerns we were. The gesture was an exact copy, of course, of what we had seen our mothers do.

My life in school became just the opposite of my first morning. I went from being ignored, with hardly a glance from anyone, to having girls vie for my friendship, or at least for more than just a passing acquaintanceship. Both my classmates and my teachers noticed how quick I was at learning things. I was soon given responsibility for overseeing the class in the teacher's absence. At first, I was a little taken aback by this, but then I got used to it. I indulged many things, especially if they would end in a laugh or something touching. I would never dillydally with a decision, always making up my mind right away about the thing in front of me. Sometimes, seeing my old frail self in a girl, I would defend her; sometimes seeing my old frail self in a girl, I would be heartless and cruel. It all went over quite well, and I became very popular.

My so recently much-hated body was now a plus: I excelled at games and was named captain of a volleyball team. As I was favored by my classmates inside and outside the classroom, so was I favored by my teachers—though only inside the classroom, for I had become notorious to them for doing forbidden things. My love of mischief was a new wrinkle in me, and if sometimes I stood away from myself and took a look at who I had become, I couldn't be more surprised at what I saw. But since it earned me the love and devotion of Gwen and the other girls, I was only egged on to find new and better ways to entertain them. I don't know what invisible standard was set, or by whom or exactly when, but eight of us met it, and soon to the other girls we were something to comment on favorably or unfavorably, as the case might be.

It was in a nook of some old tombstones—a place discovered by girls going to our school long before we were born—shaded by trees with trunks so thick it would take four arm's lengths to encircle them, that we would sit and talk about the things we said were on our minds that day. On our minds every day were our breasts and their refusal to budge out of our chests. On hearing somewhere that if a boy rubbed your breasts they would quickly swell up, I passed along this news. Since in the world we occupied and hoped forever to occupy boys were banished, we had to make do with ourselves. What perfection we found in each other, sitting on these tombstones of long-dead people who had been the masters of our ancestors! Nothing in particular really troubled us except for the annoyance of a fly colliding with our lips, sticky from eating fruits; a bee wanting to nestle in our hair; the breeze suddenly blowing too strong. We were sure that the much-talked-about future that everybody was preparing us for would never come, for we had such a powerful feeling against it, and why shouldn't our will prevail this time? Sometimes when we looked at each other, it was all we could do not to cry out with happiness.

My own special happiness was, of course, with Gwen. She would stand in front of me trying to see into my murky black eyes—a way, she said, to tell exactly what I was thinking. After a short while, she would give up, saying, "I can't make out a thing—only my same old face." I would then laugh at her and kiss her on the neck, sending her into a fit of shivers, as if someone had exposed her to a cold draft when she had a fever. Sometimes when she spoke to me, so overcome with feeling would I be that I was no longer able to hear what she said, I could only make out her mouth as it moved up and down. I told her that I wished I had been named Enid, after Enid Blyton, the author of the first books I had discovered on my own and liked. I told her that when I was younger I had been afraid of my mother's dying, but that since I had met Gwen this didn't matter so much. Whenever I spoke of my mother to her, I was always sure to turn the corners of my mouth down, to show my scorn. I said that I could not wait for us to grow up so that we could live in a house of our own. I had already picked out the house. It was a gray one, with many rooms, and it was in the lane where all the houses had high, well-trimmed hedges. With all my plans she agreed, and I am sure that if she had had any plans of her own I would have agreed with them also.

On the morning of the first day I started to menstruate, I felt strange in a new way—hot and cold at the same time, with horrible pains running up and down my legs. My mother, knowing what was the matter, brushed aside my complaints and said that it was all to be expected and I would soon get used to everything. Seeing my gloomy face, she told me in a half-joking way all about her own experience with the first step in coming of age, as she called it, which had happened when she was as old as I was. I pretended that this information made us close—as close as in the old days—but to myself I said, "What a serpent!"

I walked to school with Gwen feeling as I supposed a dog must feel when it has done something wrong and is ashamed of itself and trying to get somewhere quick, where it can lie low. The cloth between my legs grew heavier and heavier with every step I took, and I was sure that everything about me broadcast, "She's menstruating today. She's menstruating today." When Gwen heard what had happened, tears came to her eyes. She had not yet had the wonderful experience, and I could see that she cried for herself. She said that, in sympathy, she would wear a cloth, too.

In class, for the first time in my life, I fainted. Miss Nelson had to revive me, passing her smelling salts, which she had in a beautiful green vial, back and forth under my nose. She then took me to Nurse, who said that it was the fright of all the unexpected pain that had caused me to faint, but I knew that I had fainted after I brought to my mind a clear picture of myself sitting at my desk in my own blood.

At recess, among the tombstones, I of course had to exhibit and demonstrate. Though I was the youngest by at least a year, none of the others were menstruating yet. I showed everything without the least bit of flourish, since my heart wasn't in it. I wished instead that one of the other girls were in my place and that I were just sitting there, my eyes widening and my mouth forming an "o" in amazement. How nice they all were, though, rallying to my side, offering shoulders on which to lean, laps in which to rest my weary, aching head, and kisses that really did soothe. When I looked at them sitting around me, the church in the distance, beyond that our school, with throngs of girls crossing back and forth in the school-yard, beyond that the world, how I wished that everything would fall away, so that suddenly we'd be sitting in some different atmosphere, with no future full of ridiculous demands, no need for any sustenance save our love for each other, with no hindrance to any of our desires, which would, of course, be simple desires—nothing, nothing, just sitting on our tombstones forever. But that could never be, as the tolling of the school bell testified.

We walked back to class slowly, as if going to a funeral. Gwen and I vowed to love each other always, but the words had a hollow ring, and when we looked at each other we couldn't sustain the gaze. It had been decided by Miss Nelson and Nurse that I was not to return to school after lunch, with Nurse sending instructions to my mother to keep me in bed for the rest of the day.

When I got home, my mother came toward me, arms outstretched, concern written on her face. Seeing her, my whole mouth filled up with a bitter taste, for I could not understand how she could be so beautiful even though I no longer loved her.

John-Paul Sartre
Hell Is Other People

Jean-Paul Sartre (1905–1980), *a philosopher, novelist, playwright, and political activist, was one of the most controversial intellectual figures of the twentieth century. The father and leading proponent of existentialism, Sartre took the principal task of philosophy to be the study of the essential structure of human consciousness. His greatest work is* Being and Nothingness, *from which this selection is taken.*

We have described human reality from the standpoint of negating conduct and from the standpoint of the *cogito*. Following this lead we have discovered that human reality is-for-itself. Is this *all* that it is? Without going outside our attitude of reflective description, we can encounter modes of consciousness which seem, even while themselves remaining strictly in for-itself, to point to a radically different type of ontological structure. This ontological structure is *mine;* it is in relation to myself as subject that I am concerned about myself, and yet this concern (for-myself) reveals to me a being which is *my* being without being-for-me.

Consider for example shame. Here we are dealing with a mode of consciousness which has a structure identical with all those which we have previously described. It is a non-positional self-consciousness, conscious (of) itself as shame; as such, it is an example of what the Germans call *Erlebnis,* and it is accessible to reflection. In addition its structure is intentional; it is a shameful apprehension *of* something and this something is *me.* I am ashamed of what I *am.* Shame therefore realizes an intimate relation of myself to myself. Through shame I have discovered an aspect of *my* being. Yet although certain complex forms derived from shame can appear on the reflective plane, shame is not originally a phenomenon of reflection. In fact no matter what results one can obtain in solitude by the religious *practice* of shame, it is in its primary structure shame *before somebody.* I have just made an awkward or vulgar gesture. This gesture clings to me; I neither judge it nor blame it. I simply live it. I realize it in the mode of for-itself. But now suddenly I raise my head. Somebody was there and has seen me. Suddenly I realize the vulgarity of my gesture, and I am ashamed. It is certain that my shame is not reflective, for the presence of another in my consciousness, even as a catalyst, is incompatible with the reflective attitude; in the field of my reflection I can never meet with anything but the consciousness which is mine. But the Other is the indispensable mediator between myself and me. I am ashamed of myself *as I appear* to the Other.

By the mere appearance of the Other, I am put in the position of passing judgment on myself as on an object, for it is as an object that I appear to the Other. Yet this object which has appeared to the Other is not an empty image in the mind of another. Such an image, in fact, would be imputable wholly to the Other and so could not "touch" me. I could feel irritation, or anger before it as before a bad portrait of myself which gives to my expression an ugliness or baseness which I do not have, but I could not be touched to the quick. Shame is by nature *recognition.* I recognize that I *am* as the Other sees me. There is however no question of a comparison between what I am for myself and what I am for the Other as if I found in myself, in the mode of being of the For-itself, an equivalent of what I am for the Other. In the first place this comparison is not encountered in us as the result of a concrete psychic operation. Shame is an immediate shudder which runs through me from head to foot without any discursive preparation. In addition the comparison is impossible; I am unable to bring about any relation between what I am in the intimacy of the For-itself, without distance, without recoil, without perspective, and this unjustifiable being-in-itself which I am for the Other. There is no standard here, no table of correlation. Moreover the very notion of *vulgarity* implies an inter-monad relation. Nobody can be vulgar all alone!

Thus the Other has not only revealed to me what I was; he has established me in a new type of being which can support new qualifications. This being was not in me potentially before the appearance of the Other, for it could not have found any place in the For-itself. Even if some power had been pleased to endow me with a body wholly constituted before it should be for-others, still my vulgarity and my awkwardness could not lodge there potentially; for they are meanings and as such they surpass the body and at the same time refer to a witness capable of understanding them and to the totality of my human reality. But this new being which appears *for* the other does not reside *in* the Other; I am responsible for it as is shown very well by the education system which consists in making children ashamed of what they are. . . .

. . . It is not true that I first am and then later "seek" to make an object of the Other or to assimilate him; but to the extent that the upsurge of my being is an upsurge in the presence of the Other, to the extent that I am a pursuing flight and a pursued-pursuing, I am—at the very root of my being—the project of assimilating and making an object of the Other. I am the proof of the Other. That is the original fact. But this proof of the Other is in itself an attitude toward the Other; that is, I can not *be in the presence of the Other* without being that "in-the-presence" in the form of having to be it. Thus again we are describing the for-itself's structures of being although the Other's presence in the world is an absolute and self-evident fact, but a contingent fact—that is, a fact impossible to deduce from the onto-logical structures of the for-itself.

These two attempts which I am are opposed to one another. Each attempt is the death of the other; that is, the failure of the one motivates the adoption of the other. Thus there is no dialectic for my relations toward the Other but rather a circle—although each attempt is enriched by the failure of the other. Thus we shall study each one in turn. But it should be noted that at the very core of the one the other remains always present, precisely because neither of the two can be held without contradiction. Better yet, each of them is in the other and endangers the death of the other. Thus we can never get outside the circle. . . .

Everything which may be said of me in my relations with the Other applies to him as well. While I attempt to free myself from the hold of the Other, the Other is trying to free himself from mine; while I seek to enslave the Other, the Other seeks to enslave me. We are by no means dealing with unilateral relations with an object-in-itself, but with reciprocal and moving relations. . . . Conflict is the original meaning of being-for-others.

Bertrand Russell

Marriage

Bertrand Russell (1872–1970) *was one of the greatest philosophers of this century. He wrote an enormous number of philosophical books and articles, from* Principia Mathematica *(with Alfred North Whitehead) to some notorious polemics in favor of "free love" and atheism. Like Hume, he was too controversial for most universities, and a famous court case prevented him from teaching at City College of New York. He did, however, win the Nobel Prize for Literature in 1950. At the age of 89, he was jailed for protesting against nuclear arms.*

When we look round the world at the present day and ask ourselves what conditions seem on the whole to make for happiness in marriage and what for unhappiness, we are driven to a somewhat curious conclusion, that the more civilized people become the less capable they seem of lifelong happiness with one partner. Irish peasants, although until recent times mar-riages were decided by the parents, were said by those who ought to know them to be on the whole happy and virtuous in their conjugal life. In general, marriage is easiest where people are least differentiated. When a man differs little from other men, and a woman differs little from other women, there is no particular reason to regret not having married some one else. But people with multifarious tastes and pursuits and interests will tend to desire congeniality in their partners, and to feel dissatisfied when they find that they have secured less of it than they might have obtained. The Church, which tends to view marriage solely from the point of view of sex, sees no reason why one partner should not do just as well as another, and can therefore uphold the indissolubility of marriage without realizing the hardship that this often involves.

Another condition which makes for happiness in marriage is paucity of unowned women and absence of social occasions when husbands meet other women. If there is no possibility of sexual relations with any woman other than one's wife, most men will make the best of the situation and, except in abnormally bad cases, will find it quite tolerable. The same thing applies to wives, especially if they never imagine that marriage should bring much happiness. That is to say, a marriage is likely to be what is called happy if neither party ever expected to get much happiness out of it.

Fixity of social custom, for the same reason, tends to prevent what are called unhappy marriages. If the bonds of marriage are recognized as final and irrevocable, there is no stimulus to the imagination to wander outside and consider that a more ecstatic happiness might have been possible. In order to secure domestic peace where this state of mind exists, it is only necessary that neither the husband nor the wife should fall outrageously below the commonly recognized standard of decent behaviour, whatever this may be.

Among civilized people in the modern world none of these conditions for what is called happiness exist, and accordingly one finds that very few marriages after the first few years are happy. Some of the causes of unhappiness are bound up with civilization, but others would disappear if men and women were more civilized than they are. Let us begin with the latter. Of these the most important is bad sexual education, which is a far commoner thing among the well-to-do than it can ever be among peasants. Peasant children early become accustomed to what are called the facts of life, which they can observe not only among human beings but among animals. They are thus saved from both ignorance and fastidiousness. The carefully educated children of the well-to-do, on the contrary, are shielded from all practical knowledge of sexual matters, and even the most modern parents, who teach children out of books, do not give them that sense of practical familiarity which the peasant child early acquires. The triumph of Christian teaching is when a man and woman marry without either having had previous sexual experience. In nine cases out of ten where this occurs, the results are unfortunate. Sexual behaviour among human beings is not instinctive, so that the inexperienced bride and bridegroom, who are probably quite unaware of this fact, find themselves overwhelmed with shame and discomfort. It is little better when the woman alone is innocent but the man has acquired his knowledge from prostitutes. Most men do not realize that a process of wooing is necessary after marriage, and many well-brought-up women do not realize what harm they do to marriage by remaining reserved and physically aloof. All this could be put right by better sexual education, and is in fact very much better with the generation now young than it was with their parents and grandparents. There used to be a widespread belief among women that they were morally superior to men on the ground that they had less pleasure in sex. This attitude made frank companionship between husbands and wives impossible. It was, of course, in itself quite unjustifiable, since failure to enjoy sex, so far from being virtuous, is a mere physiological or psychological deficiency, like a failure to enjoy food, which also a hundred years ago was expected of elegant females.

Other modern causes of unhappiness in marriage are, however, not so easily disposed of. I think that uninhibited civilized people, whether men or women, are generally polygamous in their instincts. They may fall deeply in love and be for some years entirely absorbed in one person, but sooner or later sexual familiarity dulls the edge of passion, and then they begin to look elsewhere for a revival of the old thrill. It is, of course, possible to control this impulse in the interests of morality, but it is very difficult to prevent the impulse from existing. With the growth of women's freedom there has come a much greater opportunity for conjugal infidelity than existed in former times. The opportunity gives rise to the thought, the thought gives rise to the desire, and in the absence of religious scruples the desire gives rise to the act.

Women's emancipation has in various ways made marriage more difficult. In old days the wife had to adapt herself to the husband, but the husband did not have to adapt himself to the wife. Nowadays many wives, on grounds of woman's right to her own individuality and her own career, are unwilling to adapt themselves to their husbands beyond a point, while men who still hanker after the old tradition of masculine domination see no reason why they should do all the adapting. This trouble arises especially in connection with infidelity. In old days the husband was occasionally unfaithful, but as a rule his wife did not know of it. If she did, he confessed that he had sinned and made her believe that he was penitent. She, on the other hand, was usually virtuous. If she was not, and the fact came to her husband's knowledge, the marriage broke up. Where, as happens in many modern marriages, mutual faithfulness is not demanded, the instinct of jealousy nevertheless survives, and often proves fatal to the persistence of any deeply rooted intimacy even where no overt quarrels occur.

There is another difficulty in the way of modern marriage, which is felt especially by those who are most conscious of the value of love. Love can flourish only as long as it is free and spontaneous; it tends to be killed by the thought that it is a duty. To say that it is your duty to love so-and-so is the surest way to cause you to hate him or her. Marriage as a combination of love with legal bonds thus falls between two stools. . . .

There can be no doubt that to close one's mind on marriage against all the approaches of love from elsewhere is to diminish receptivity and sympathy and the opportunities of valuable human contacts. It is to do violence to something which, from the most idealistic standpoint, is in itself desirable. And like every kind of restrictive morality it tends to promote what one may call a policeman's outlook upon the whole of human life—the outlook, that is to say, which is always looking for an opportunity to forbid something.

For all these reasons, many of which are bound up with things undoubtedly good, marriage has become difficult, and if it is not to be a barrier to happiness it must be conceived in a somewhat new way. One solution often suggested, and actually tried on a large scale in America, is easy divorce. I hold, of course, as every humane person must, that divorce should be granted on more grounds than are admitted in the English law, but I do not recognize in easy divorce a solution of the troubles of marriage. Where a marriage is childless, divorce may be often the right solution, even when both parties are doing their best to behave decently; but where there are children the stability of marriage is to my mind a matter of considerable importance. . . . I think that where a marriage is fruitful and both parties to it are reasonable and decent the expectation ought to be that it will be lifelong, but not that it will exclude other sex relations. A marriage which begins with passionate love and leads to children who are desired and loved ought to produce so deep a tie between a man and woman that they will feel something infinitely precious in their companionship, even after sexual passion has decayed, and even if either or both feels sexual passion for some one else. This mellowing of marriage has been prevented by jealousy, but jealousy, though it is an instinctive emotion, is one which can be controlled if it is recognized as bad, and not supposed to be the expression of a just moral indignation. A companionship which has lasted for many years and through many deeply felt events has a richness of content which cannot belong to the first days of love, however delightful these may be. And any person who appreciates what time can do to enhance values will not lightly throw away such companionship for the sake of new love.

It is therefore possible for a civilized man and woman to be happy in marriage, although if this is to be the case a number of conditions must be fulfilled. There must be a feeling of complete equality on both sides; there must be no interference with mutual freedom; there must be the most complete physical and mental intimacy; and there must be a certain similarity in regard to standards of values. (It is fatal, for example, if one values only money while the other values only good work.) Given all these conditions, I believe marriage to be the best and most important relation that can exist between two human beings. If it has not often been realized hitherto, that is chiefly because husband and wife have regarded themselves as each other's policeman. If marriage is to achieve its possibilities, husbands and wives must learn to understand that whatever the law may say, in their private lives they must be free.

Evan S. Connell

Sentimental Moment

Evan S. Connell *is a writer who lives in Sausalito, California. He has written many novels.* Mrs. Bridge, *from which the following selection is taken, is about the life of an upper middle class woman living in the Midwest in the 1930s.*

Mrs. Bridge stood alone at a front window thinking of how quickly the years were going by. The children were growing up so rapidly, and her husband—She stirred uneasily. Already there was a new group of "young marrieds," people she hardly knew. Surely some time had gone by—she expected this; nevertheless she could not get over the feeling that something was drawing steadily away from her. She wondered if her husband felt the same; she thought she would ask him that evening when he got home. She recalled the dreams they used to share; she recalled with a smile how she used to listen to him speak of his plans and how she had never actually cared one way or another about his ambition, she had cared only for him. That was enough. In those days she used to think that the long hours he spent in his office were a temporary condition and that as soon as more people came to him with legal problems he would, somehow, begin spending more time at home. But this was not the way it turned out, and Mrs. Bridge understood now that she would never see very much of him. They had started off together to explore something that promised to be wonderful, and, of course, there had been wonderful times. And yet, thought Mrs. Bridge, why is it that we haven't—that nothing has—that whatever we—?

It was raining. Thunder rumbled through the lowering clouds with a constant, monotonous, trundling sound, like furniture being rolled back and forth in the attic. In the front yard the evergreen trees swayed in the wind and the shutters rattled in the sudden rainy gusts. She noticed that a branch had been torn from the soft maple tree; the branch lay on the driveway and the leaves fluttered.

Harriet came in to ask if she would like some hot chocolate. "Oh, no thank you, Harriet," said Mrs. Bridge. "You have some."

Harriet was so nice. And she was a good worker. Mrs. Bridge was very proud of having Harriet and knew that she would be next to impossible to replace, and yet there were times when Mrs. Bridge half wished she would quit. Why she wished this, she did not know, unless it was that with Harriet around to do all the work she herself was so often dismally bored. When she was first married she used to do the cooking and housecleaning and washing, and how she had looked forward to a few minutes of leisure! But now—how odd—there was too much leisure. Mrs. Bridge did not admit this fact to anyone, for it embarrassed her; indeed she very often gave the impression of being distracted by all the things needed to be done— phone the laundry, the grocer, take Ruth to the dentist, Carolyn to tap-dancing class, Douglas to the barber shop, and so on. But the truth remained, and settled upon her with ever greater finality.

The light snapped on in the back hall. She heard his cough and the squeak of the closet door and the familiar flapping sound of his briefcase on the upper shelf. Suddenly overwhelmed by the need for reassurance, she turned swiftly from the window and hurried toward him with an intent, wistful expression, knowing what she wanted without knowing how to ask for it.

He heard the rustle of her dress and her quick footsteps on the carpet. He was hanging up his coat as she approached, and he said, without irritation, but a trifle wearily because this was not the first time it had happened, "I see you forgot to have the car lubricated."

Jane English
What Do Grown Children Owe Their Parents?

Jane English (1947–1979) *taught philosophy at the University of North Carolina at Chapel Hill until her untimely death in a climbing accident at the age of thirty-two.*

What do grown children owe their parents? I will contend that the answer is "nothing." Although I agree that there are many things that children *ought* to do for their parents, I will argue that it is inappropriate and misleading to describe them as things "owed." I will maintain that parents' voluntary sacrifices, rather than creating "debts" to be "repaid," tend to create love or "friendship." The duties of grown children are those of friends and result from love between them and their parents, rather than being things owed in repayment for the parents' earlier sacrifices. Thus, I will oppose those philosophers who use the word "owe" whenever a duty or obligation exists. Although the "debt" metaphor is appropriate in some moral circumstances, my argument is that a love relationship is not such a case.

Misunderstandings about the proper relationship between parents and their grown children have resulted from reliance on the "owing" terminology. For instance, we hear parents complain "You owe it to us to write home (keep up your piano playing, not adopt a hippie lifestyle), because of all we sacrificed for you (paying for piano lessons, sending you to college)." The child is sometimes even heard to reply, "I didn't ask to be born (to be given piano lessons, to be sent to college)." This inappropriate idiom of ordinary language tends to obscure, or even to undermine, the love that is the correct ground of filial obligation.

FAVORS CREATE DEBTS

There are some cases, other than literal debts, in which talk of "owing," though metaphorical, is apt. New to the neighborhood, Max barely knows his neighbor, Nina, but he asks her if she will take in his mail while he is gone for a month's vacation. She agrees. If, subsequently, Nina asks Max to do the same for her, it seems that Max has a moral obligation to agree (greater than the one he would have had if Nina had not done the same for him), unless for some reason it would be a burden far out of proportion to the one Nina bore for him. I will call this a *favor*: when A, at B's request, bears some burden for B, then B incurs an obligation to reciprocate. Here the metaphor of Max's "owing" Nina is appropriate. It is not literally a debt, of course, nor can Nina pass this IOU on to heirs, demand payment in the form of Max's taking out her garbage, or sue Max. Nonetheless, since Max ought to perform one act of similar nature and amount of sacrifice in return, the term is suggestive. Once he reciprocates, the debt is "discharged"—that is, their obligations revert to the condition they were in before Max's initial request.

Contrast a situation in which Max simply goes on vacation and, to his surprise, finds upon his return that his neighbor has mowed his grass twice weekly in his absence. This is a voluntary sacrifice rather than a favor, and Max has no duty to reciprocate. It would be nice for him to volunteer to do so, but this would be supererogatory on his part. Rather than a favor, Nina's action is a friendly gesture. As a result, she might expect Max to chat over the back fence, help her catch her straying dog, or something similar—she might expect the development of a friendship. But Max would be chatting (or whatever) out of friendship, rather than in repayment for mown grass. If he did not return her gesture, she might feel rebuffed or miffed, but not unjustly treated or indignant, since Max has not failed to perform a duty. Talk of "owing" would be out of place in this case.

It is sometimes difficult to distinguish between favors and non-favors, because friends tend to do favors for each other, and those who exchange favors tend to become friends. But one test is to ask how Max is motivated. Is it "to be nice to Nina" or "because she did x for me"? Favors are frequently performed by total strangers without any friendship developing. Nevertheless, a temporary obligation is created, even if the chance for repayment never arises. For instance, suppose that Oscar and Matilda, total strangers, are waiting in a long checkout line at the supermarket. Oscar, having forgotten the oregano, asks Matilda to watch his cart for a second. She does. If Matilda now asks Oscar to return the favor while she picks up some tomato sauce, he is obliged to agree. Even if she had not watched his cart, it would be inconsiderate of him to refuse, claiming he was too busy reading the magazines. He may have a duty to help others, but he would not "owe" it to her. But if she has done the same for him, he incurs an additional obligation to help, and talk of "owing" is apt. It suggests an agreement to perform equal, reciprocal, canceling sacrifices.

THE DUTIES OF FRIENDSHIP

The terms "owe" and "repay" are helpful in the case of favors, because the sameness of the amount of sacrifice on the two sides is important; the monetary metaphor suggests equal quantities of sacrifice. But friendship ought to be characterized by *mutuality* rather than reciprocity: friends offer what they can give and accept what they need, without regard for the total amounts of benefits exchanged. And friends are motivated by love rather than by the prospect of repayment. Hence, talk of "owing" is singularly out of place in friendship.

For example, suppose Alfred takes Beatrice out for an expensive dinner and a movie. Beatrice incurs no obligation to "repay" him with a goodnight kiss or a return engagement. If Alfred complains that she "owes" him something, he is operating under the assumption that she should repay a favor, but on the contrary his was a generous gesture done in the hopes of developing a friendship. We hope that he would not want her repayment in the form of sex or attention if this was done to discharge a debt rather than from friendship. Since, if Alfred is prone to reasoning in this way, Beatrice may well decline the invitation or request to pay for her own dinner, his attitude of expecting a "return" on his "investment" could hinder the development of a friendship. Beatrice should return the gesture only if she is motivated by friendship.

Another common misuse of the "owing" idiom occurs when the Smiths have dined at the Joneses' four times, but the Joneses at the Smiths' only once. People often say, "We owe them three dinners." This line of thinking may be appropriate between business acquaintances, but not between friends. After all, the Joneses invited the Smiths not in order to feed them or to be fed in turn, but because of the friendly contact presumably enjoyed by all on such occasions. If the Smiths do not feel friendship toward the Joneses, they can decline future invitations and not invite the Joneses; they owe them nothing. Of course, between friends of equal resources and needs, roughly equal sacrifices (though not necessarily roughly equal dinners) will typically occur. If the sacrifices are highly out of proportion to the resources, the relationship is closer to servility than to friendship.

Another difference between favors and friendship is that after a friendship ends, the duties of friendship end. The party that has sacrificed less owes the other nothing. For instance, suppose Elmer donated a pint of blood that his wife Doris needed during an operation. Years after their divorce, Elmer is in an accident and needs one pint of blood. His new wife, Cora, is also of the same blood type. It seems that Doris not only does not "owe" Elmer blood, but that she should actually refrain from coming forward if Cora has volunteered to donate. To insist on donating not only interferes with the newlyweds' friendship, but it belittles Doris and Elmer's former relationship by suggesting that Elmer gave blood in hopes of favors returned instead of simply out of love for Doris. It is one of the heart-rending features of divorce that it attends to quantity in a relationship previously characterized by mutuality. If Cora could not donate, Doris's obligation is the same as that for any former spouse in need of blood; it is not increased by the fact that Elmer similarly aided her. It *is* affected by the degree to which they are still friends, which in turn may (or may not) have been influenced by Elmer's donation.

In short, unlike the debts created by favors, the duties of friendship do not require equal quantities of sacrifice. Performing equal sacrifices does not cancel the duties of friendship, as it does the debts of favors. Unrequested sacrifices do not themselves create debts, but friends have duties regardless of whether they requested or initiated the friendship. Those who perform favors may be motivated by mutual gain, whereas friends should be motivated by affection. These characteristics of the friendship relation are distorted by talk of "owing."

PARENTS AND CHILDREN

The relationship between children and their parents should be one of friendship characterized by mutuality rather than one of reciprocal favors. The quantity of parental sacrifice is not relevant in determining what duties the grown child has. The medical assistance grown children ought to offer their ill mothers in old age depends upon the mothers' need, not upon whether they endured a difficult pregnancy, for example. Nor do one's duties to one's parents cease once an equal quantity of sacrifice has been performed, as the phrase "discharging a debt" may lead us to think.

Rather, what children ought to do for their parents (and parents for children) depends upon (1) their respective needs, abilities, and resources and (2) the extent to which there is an ongoing friendship between them. Thus, regardless of the quantity of childhood sacrifices, an able, wealthy child has an obligation to help his needy parents more than does a needy child. To illustrate, suppose sisters Cecile and Dana are equally loved by their parents, even though Cecile was an easy child to care for, seldom ill, while Dana was often sick and caused some trouble as a juvenile delinquent. As adults, Dana is a struggling artist living far away, while Cecile is a wealthy lawyer living nearby. When the parents need visits and financial aid, Cecile has an obligation to bear a higher proportion of these burdens than her sister. This results from her abilities, rather than from the quantities of sacrifice made by the parents earlier.

Sacrifices have an important causal role in creating an ongoing friendship, which may lead us to assume incorrectly that it is the sacrifices that are the source of the obligation. That the source is the friendship instead can be seen by examining cases in which the sacrifices occurred but the friendship, for some reason, did not develop or persist. For example, if a woman gives up her newborn child for adoption, and if no feelings of love ever develop on either side, it seems that the grown child does not have an obligation to "repay" her for her sacrifices in pregnancy. For that matter, if the adopted child has an unimpaired love relationship with the adoptive parents, he or she has the same obligations to help them as a natural child would have.

The filial obligations of grown children are a result of friendship, rather than owed for services rendered. Suppose that Vance married Lola despite his parents' strong wish that he marry within their religion, and that as a result, the parents refuse to speak to him again. As the years pass, the parents are unaware of Vance's problems, his accomplishments, the birth of his children. The love that once existed between them, let us suppose, has been completely destroyed by this event and thirty years of desuetude. At this point, it seems, Vance is under no obligation to pay his parents' medical bills in their old age, beyond his general duty to help those in need. An additional, filial obligation would only arise from whatever love he may still feel for them. It would be irrelevant for his parents to argue,"But look how much we sacrificed for you when you were young," for that sacrifice was not a favor but occurred as part of a friendship which existed at that time but is now, we have supposed, defunct. A more appropriate message would be, "We still love you, and we would like to renew our friendship."

I hope this helps to set the question of what children ought to do for their parents in a new light. The parental argument, "You ought to do x because we did y for you," should be replaced by, "We love you and you will be happier if you do x," or "We believe you love us, and anyone who loved us would do x." If the parents' sacrifice had been a favor, the child's reply, "I never asked you to do y for me," would have been relevant; to the revised parental remarks, this reply is clearly irrelevant. The child can either do x or dispute one of the parents' claims: by showing that a love relationship does not exist, or that love for someone does not motivate doing x, or that he or she will not be happier doing x.

Seen in this light, parental requests for children to write home, visit, and offer them a reasonable amount of emotional and financial support in life's crises are well founded, so long as a friendship still exists. Love for others does call for caring about and caring for them. Some other parental requests, such as for more sweeping changes in the child's lifestyle or life goals, can be seen to be insupportable, once we shift the justification from debts owed to love. The terminology of favors suggests the reasoning, "Since we paid for your college education, you owe it to us to make a career of engineering, rather than becoming a rock musician." This tends to alienate affection even further, since the tuition payments are depicted as investments for a return rather than done from love, as though the child's life goals could be "bought." Basing the argument on love leads to different reasoning patterns. The suppressed premise, "If A loves B, then A follows B's wishes as to A's lifelong career" is simply false. Love does not even dictate that the child adopt the parents' values as to the desirability of alternative life goals. So the parents' strongest available argument here is, "We love you, we are deeply concerned about your happiness, and in the long run you will be happier as an engineer." This makes it clear that an empirical claim is really the subject of the debate.

The function of these examples is to draw out our considered judgments as to the proper relation between parents and their grown children, and to show how poorly they fit the model of favors. What is relevant is the ongoing friendship that exists between parents and children. Although that relationship developed partly as a result of parental sacrifices for the child, the duties that grown children have to their parents result from the friendship rather than from the sacrifices. The idiom of owing favors to one's parents can actually be destructive if it undermines the role of mutuality and leads us to think in terms of quantitative reciprocal favors.

Nancy Slonim Aronie

My Heartbreak Kid

Nancy Slonim Aronie *is a writer who lives in Connecticut. A former commentator on National Public Radio's "All Things Considered," she illuminates the dark side of life.*

I keep getting these lessons in detachment. One of the hardest ones was when I lost my brass heart necklace. I looked everywhere, and I missed it every time I saw teeny hearts on other necks. It wasn't a necklace I could easily replace and I know material things shouldn't be coveted, so I lived and presumably I grew. But detachment from people is still another lesson. Tougher to justify and impossible to replace.

These new lessons are manifest in creative, inventive, exciting young adult women. They come home with my creative, inventive, exciting young adult son. He says, "Mom, this is Bonnie," and I say, "Hi . . . Can you smush this garlic clove?" And we make wonderful Caesar salads together. Just when she learns just how much lemon juice we need, he arrives with Leah. "Mom, this is Leah. Can we have a ride to the mall?" Leah and I try on Norma Kamali markdowns together and just when we figure out how to remove the shoulder pads without ruining the look he brings home . . . Monica. Monica and I sit in the bleachers, cheering and praying that he'll make the foul shot and just when his game is college-scholarship-ready Monica is missing.

I thought I was the perfect new-age mother. I made sure he knew friendships with girls were available and valuable, that just because it was a girl didn't mean he had to get involved, that he could be supporting and silly and sharing with girlfriends, that that wouldn't preclude crushes and lovers, that both could co-exist.

So what happened to Bonnie and Leah and Monica? I miss them. After all, his wasn't the only relationship developing in the house. I don't have daughters. My close women friends live far away, my Mom has gone back to community college and I value these special friendships. They are fun and healthy.

"You can't keep doing this to me," I said.

"I'm not doing anything to anyone," he said.

When I asked him why he needed so many girlfriends he said he didn't need them; they were available and he thought valuable. The words had a new-age perfect mother ring to them.

Maybe they weren't friendships. Maybe they were crushes. Maybe it's his life. Maybe this is the ultimate lesson in detachment. Maybe I'll learn it.

All I know is last night he came home with another one and said, "Mom, this is Jennifer." I looked her straight in the eye, I looked at the unsmushed garlic clove and I said, "I don't want to get involved."

17

I Like It, But Is It Art?

No doubt you have some painting or poster on your wall that you look at appreciatively from time to time. You probably also have a favorite record or cassette that you play while you are relaxing. What is it that you like about them? Why do they give you such special pleasure? Why not just hang an old newspaper on your wall and listen to the sound of two cats fighting while you relax? What is the special place of those objects that we call "art" in our lives? What makes something, a piece of printed paper or a piece of music, art? What makes something a piece of *good* art, as opposed to bad art or not art at all?

The philosophy of art is as rich and varied as the arts themselves, ranging from questions of quality, such as, What is good art and what is bad art? and, What makes a piece of music great? to questions of ontology, such as, What is an "original" work of art? and, What makes an object a work of art in the first place? The subject of **aesthetics**—which originally meant the study of sensory experience but later came to mean the study of beauty—is, like ethics, fundamentally a set of questions about values. The ultimate question in the philosophy of art is not only what art is but also what its purpose, function, and importance are in our lives. Great literature, one might suggest, is important because it provides information and carries down the essential stories of a culture, but much of literature, especially poetry, and most of art and music do not necessarily "tell a story" and may not actually convey any information (in the sense intended). Sometimes, of course, the arts are decorative, a pleasant painting to cover an otherwise bare wall, some soothing music to make a hectic day of running errands more relaxing. But such daily uses of art seem to trivialize and demean it. Beethoven's great symphonies, Rembrandt's striking self-portraits, the epics of Homer, Dante, and Tolstoy—these works inspire an almost religious fervor, and we define an entire civilization in terms of them.

And yet, there is always that nagging question about the "subjectivity" of taste. "There is no disputing over tastes," wrote David Hume, quoting some ancient writers. You enjoy watching "Hill Street Blues" re-runs on television; your friend prefers reading Kafka. Is there a difference? You find yourself moved by a song that has been in the Top 40 for five weeks, which you will tire of in another three weeks, and then never hear again. Your friend prefers Bach's Brandenberg concertos, and although she admits that they are hard to dance to, she nevertheless insists on her taste over yours. Is there any ground for this claim, or is she just being a snob? Is there any arguing over tastes in art? Is there, apart from established social conventions, any meaning to the term "good taste"? Is it enough that we know what we like even if we don't know what's good?

Questions of taste sometimes extend, in a fascinating philosophical way, to the nature of the object itself. What justification could there be, for example, for celebrating the artistic merit of a seven-ton slab of concrete, carefully placed in the middle of an urban mall, at great expense to the taxpayers? What justification can there be to the introduction of a soup can label or, fifty years ago, a urinal into an art museum collection? What makes one piece a work of art and another just a photograph, or just a soup can label? And what distinguishes a copy—even a first rate copy—from the original? Why isn't the poster you buy in a museum shop for five dollars just as much a work of art as the original? In the case of music, this raises special problems: what counts as the original in any case? The first performance of a piece is often clumsy, badly done, perhaps confused, or even misinterpreted. Is this the original? Or is it the sheet music itself? The idea in the mind of the composer? Why is an original worth so much more, even more than a copy that may be superior to the original because of deterioration? Is this just a historical matter, a question of nostalgia and market value rather than aesthetics?

Until this century, there was more or less general agreement about what counted as art (or music or literature); the main souce of disagreement involved questions of quality—Is this piece of art good art or bad art? The question is not just a matter of popular appeal. We all know that Rembrandt's paintings were often rejected by his clients and left to languish in Dutch attics, and that Beethoven and Stravinsky were sometimes booed on the first performances of their greatest works. We want to say that these works were great even when they were not appreciated and that we (in our superior wisdom and hindsight) recognize what their contemporaries did not. But today, matters have become even more complicated. We not only disagree on which contemporary pieces are good, great, or terrible, but we no longer even agree on what counts as art. A composer sits silently at a piano for ten minutes; a painting is a black canvas; a book of literature contains no punctuation and no recognizable grammar. And, as always, there is the question of "pop" culture; does it count as art or not?

Traditionally, there have been two answers to the question, What makes art good art? The first of these holds that a good or great work of art is so by virtue of inherent *objective* qualities—that is, in the object itself. In his classic *Poetics*, Aristotle defends this approach in his definition of tragedy. The second answer instead insists that what makes a work of art good or great is its effect on the observer or audience. The Russian novelist Leo Tolstoy, in particular, argued that the observer (in his case, the reader) should be "infected by the author's condition of soul." Unlike the first, objective answer, this *subjective* answer does not guarantee any agreement about taste because different audiences, different readers, or different observers may be affected very differently by the same piece. It might even suggest that anyone's reaction and judgment to a piece is as good as anyone else's reaction and judgment. Thus, it is still said today, "there is no disputing over tastes." In philosophy, however, there is still much disputing over the question of whether there is any disputing over tastes.

David Hume held that the maxim is true, that aesthetic judgment is subjective and a work of art is beautiful only if it evokes a certain kind of sentiment. Hume disagreed, however, with the conclusion that aesthetic judgments could not be agreed upon. Beauty, he argued, appealed to the "common sentiments" of mankind, and although opinions might vary, the emotional response would be universal, or at least to every observer with sound judgment. The problem is that many people lack such judgment because they are uncultivated, uneducated, inexperienced, con-fused, or in poor health. Durable admiration—for example, the lasting admiration for the classics, for classical authors, for the great books and works of art—may be a reliable indicator of great art, but this may be of little help when we are trying to judge the value of works produced in our own time. Hume warns against the "caprices of mode and fashion" and "the mistakes of ignorance and envy."

Monroe Beardsley rejects Hume's subjectivism and argues instead that we do and should dispute about tastes. We give objective reasons for our aesthetic pronouncements, and we expect people to change their opinions if these reasons are sufficiently good ones. On the other hand, there is a serious question about what distinguishes the appreciation of the arts from their mere enjoyment. In the particular case of music, Kathleen Higgins raises the question whether the pervasiveness of music in our lives and its use as background may threaten to trivialize it. The most notorious villain in this story is muzak, that bland, subliminal noise that we hear but never listen to in shopping malls, elevators, and perhaps at work. Professor Higgins argues, however, that music used in subordination to other activities and as background is not itself the problem, but rather that it may lie in the new technology that allows us private access to whatever music we want.

The question of an "original" work of art raises related questions about value. Nelson Goodman addresses a particularly troublesome issue in aesthetics by dealing with the question of forgeries. A forged work of art is not just a violation of the law and a form of lying; it is also an aesthetic violation and an ontological problem. A first-rate forgery has all of the characteristics of the original. So how can we view it as in any way inferior to the original? Arthur Danto tackles the same question and claims that the historical context is an essential part of any work of art. He distinguishes a work of art from its "material counterpart" and, like Goodman, argues that these may have very different aesthetic value—even if they are visibly (or audibly) indistinguishable.

Finally, Tom Wolfe takes up the question of the function of art in America, and he compares our current attitudes toward art as fundamentally similar to a religion. He abandons aesthetic interpretation and instead emphasizes the social function of art, as a means of rejecting the world but at the same time legitimating wealth. Needless to say, his analysis has brought down the wrath of much of the art world.

Aristotle
The Nature of Tragedy

Aristotle's (384–322 B.C.) theory of tragedy remained the definitive word on the subject for over 2000 years, and his view that tragedy depends on some fatal flaw in character is still the basis of many modern tragedies. In the following excerpt from the Poetics, Aristotle describes the basic ingredients of this old and noble art form.

. . . Let us proceed now to the discussion of Tragedy; before doing so, however, we must gather up the definition resulting from what has been said. A tragedy, then, is the imitation of an action that is serious and also, as having magnitude, complete in itself; in language with pleasurable accessories, each kind brought in separately in the parts of the work; in a dramatic, not in a narrative form; with incidents arousing pity and fear, wherewith to accomplish its catharsis of such emotions. Here by 'language with pleasurable accessories' I mean that with rhythm and harmony or song superadded; and by 'the kinds separately' I mean that some portions are worked out with verse only, and others in turn with song.

As they act the stories, it follows that in the first place the Spectacle (or stage-appearance of the actors) must be some part of the whole; and in the second Melody and Diction, these two being the means of their imitation. Here by 'Diction' I mean merely this, the composition of the verses; and by 'Melody', what is too completely understood to require explanation. But further: the subject represented also is an action; and the action involves agents, who must necessarily have their distinctive qualities both of character and thought, since it is from these that we ascribe certain qualities to their actions. There are in the natural order of things, therefore, two causes, Thought and Character, of their actions, and consequently of their success or failure in their lives. Now the action (that which was done) is represented in the play by the Fable or Plot. The Fable, in our present sense of the term, is simply this, the combination of the incidents, or things done in the story; whereas Character is what makes us ascribe certain moral qualities to the agents; and Thought is shown in all they say when proving a particular point or, it may be, enunciating a general truth. There are six parts consequently of every tragedy, as a whole (that is) of such or such quality, viz. a Fable or Plot, Characters, Diction, Thought, Spectacle, and Melody; two of them arising from the means, one from the manner, and three from the objects of the dramatic imitation; and there is nothing else besides these six. Of these, its formative elements, then, not a few of the dramatists have made due use, as every play, one may say, admits of Spectacle, Character, Fable, Diction, Melody, and Thought.

The most important of the six is the combination of the incidents of the story. Tragedy is essentially an imitation not of persons but of action and life, of happiness and misery. All human happiness or misery takes the form of action; the end for which we live is a certain kind of activity, not a quality. Character gives us qualities, but it is in our actions—what we do—that we are happy or the reverse. In a play accordingly they do not act in order to portray the Characters; they include the Characters for the sake of the action. So that it is the action in it, i.e. its Fable or Plot, that is the end and purpose of the tragedy; and the end is everywhere the chief thing. Besides this, a tragedy is impossible without action, but there may be one without Character. The tragedies of most of the moderns are characterless—a defect common among poets of all kinds, and with its counterpart in painting in Zeuxis as compared with Polygnotus; for whereas the latter is strong in character, the work of Zeuxis is devoid of it. And again: one may string together a series of characteristic speeches of the utmost finish as regards Diction and Thought, and yet fail to produce the true tragic effect; but one will have much better success with a tragedy which, however inferior in these respects, has a Plot, a combination of incidents, in it. And again: the most powerful elements of attraction in Tragedy, the Peripeties and Discoveries, are parts of the Plot. A further proof is in the fact that beginners succeed earlier with the Diction and Characters than with the construction of a story; and the same may be said of nearly all the early dramatists. We maintain, therefore, that the first essential, the life and soul, so to speak, of Tragedy is the Plot; and that the Characters come second—compare the parallel in painting, where the most beautiful colours laid on without order will not give one the same pleasure as a simple black-and-white sketch of a portrait. We maintain that Tragedy is primarily an imitation of action, and that it is mainly for the sake of action that it imitates the personal agents. Third comes the element of Thought, i.e. the power of saying whatever can be said, or what is appropriate to the occasion. This is what, in the speeches in Tragedy, falls under the arts of Politics and Rhetoric; for the older poets make their personages discourse like statesmen, and the modern like rhetoricians. One must not confuse it with Character. Character in a play is that which reveals the moral purpose of the agents, i.e. the sort of thing they seek or avoid, where that is not obvious—hence there is no room for Character in a speech on a purely indifferent subject. Thought, on the other hand, is shown in all they say when proving or disproving some particular point, or enunciating some universal proposition. Fourth among the literary elements is the Diction of the personages, i.e., as before explained, the expression of their thoughts in words, which is practically the same thing with verse as with prose. As for the two remaining parts, the Melody is the greatest of the pleasurable accessories of Tragedy. The Spectacle, though an attraction, is the least artistic of all the parts, and has least to do with the art of poetry. The tragic effect is quite possible without a public performance and actors; and besides, the getting-up of the Spectacle is more a matter for the costumier than the poet.

Having thus distinguished the parts, let us now consider the proper construction of the Fable or Plot, as that is at once the first and the most important thing in Tragedy. We have laid it down that a tragedy is an imitation of an action that is complete in itself, as a whole of some magnitude; for a whole may be of no magnitude to speak of. Now a whole is that which has beginning, middle, and end. A beginning is that which is not itself necessarily after anything else, and which has naturally something else after it; an end is that which is naturally after something itself, either as its necessary or usual consequent, and with nothing else after it; and a middle, that which is by nature after one thing and has also another after it. A well-constructed Plot, therefore, cannot either begin or end at any point one likes; beginning and end in it must be of the forms just described. Again: to be beautiful, a living creature, and every whole made up of parts, must not only present a certain order in its arrangement of parts, but also be of a certain definite magnitude. Beauty is a matter of size and order, and therefore impossible either (1) in a very minute creature, since our perception becomes indistinct as it approaches instantaneity; or (2) in a creature of vast size—one, say, 1,000 miles long—as in that case, instead of the object being seen all at once, the unity and wholeness of it is lost to the beholder. Just in the same way, then, as a beautiful whole made up of parts, or a beautiful living creature, must be of some size, but a size to be taken in by the eye, so a story or Plot must be of some length, but of a length to be taken in by the memory. As for the limit of its length, so far as that is relative to public performances and spectators, it does not fall within the theory of poetry. If they had to perform a hundred tragedies, they would be timed by water-clocks, as they are said to have been at one period. The limit, however, set by the actual nature of the thing is this: the longer the story, consistently with its being comprehensible as a whole, the finer it is by reason of its magnitude. As a rough general formula, 'a length which allows of the hero passing by a series of probable or necessary stages from misfortune to happiness, or from happiness to misfortune', may suffice as a limit for the magnitude of the story.

The Unity of a Plot does not consist, as some suppose, in its having one man as its subject. An infinity of things befall that one man, some of which it is impossible to reduce to unity; and in like manner there are many actions of one man which cannot be made to form one action. One sees, therefore, the mistake of all the poets who have written a *Heracleid*, a *Theseid*, or similar poems; they suppose that, because Heracles was one man, the story also of Heracles must be one story. Homer, however, evidently understood this point quite well, whether by art or instinct, just in the same way as he excels the rest in every other respect. In writing an *Odyssey*, he did not make the poem cover all that ever befell his hero—it befell him, for instance, to get wounded on Parnassus and also to feign madness at the time of the call to arms, but the two incidents had no necessary or probable connexion with one another—instead of doing that, he took as the subject of the *Odyssey*, as also of the *Iliad*, an action with a Unity of the kind we are describing. The truth is that, just as in the other imitative arts one imitation is always one thing, so in poetry the story, as an imitation of action, must represent one action, a complete whole, with its several incidents so closely connected that the transposal or withdrawal of any one of them will disjoin and dislocate the whole. For that which makes no perceptible difference by its presence or absence is no real part of the whole.

From what we have said it will be seen that the poet's function is to describe, not the thing that has happened, but a kind of thing that might happen, i.e. what is possible as being probable or necessary. The distinction between historian and poet is not in the one writing prose and the other writing verse—you might put the work of Herodotus into verse, and it would still be a species of history; it consists really in this, that the one describes the thing that has been, and the other a kind of thing that might be. Hence poetry is something more philosophic and of graver import than history, since its statements are of the nature rather of universals, whereas those of history are singulars. By a universal statement I mean one as to what such or such a kind of man will probably or necessarily say or do—which is the aim of poetry, though it affixes proper names to the characters; by a singular statement, one as to what, say, Alcibiades did or had done to him. In Comedy this has become clear by this time; it is only when their plot is already made up of probable incidents that they give it a basis of proper names, choosing for the purpose any names that may occur to them, instead of writing like the old iambic poets about particular persons. In Tragedy, however, they still adhere to the historic names; and for this reason: what convinces is the possible; now whereas we are not yet sure as to the possibility of that which has not happened, that which has happened is manifestly possible, else it would not have come to pass. Nevertheless even in Tragedy there are some plays with but one or two known names in them, the rest being inventions; and there are some without a single known name, e.g. Agathon's *Antheus*, in which both incidents and names are of the poet's invention; and it is not less delightful on that account. So that one must not aim at a rigid adherence to the traditional stories on which tragedies are based. It would be absurd, in fact, to do so, as even the known stories are only known to a few, though they are a delight none the less to all.

It is evident from the above that the poet must be more the poet of his stories or Plots than of his verses, inasmuch as he is a poet by virtue of the imitative element in his work, and it is actions that he imitates. And if he should come to take a subject from actual history, he is none the less a poet for that; since some historic occurrences may very well be in the probable and possible order of things; and it is in that aspect of them that he is their poet.

Of simple Plots and actions the episodic are the worst. I call a Plot episodic when there is neither probability nor necessity in the sequence of its episodes. Actions of this sort bad poets construct through their own fault, and good ones on account of the players. His work being for public performance, a good poet often stretches out a Plot beyond its capabilities, and is thus obliged to twist the sequence of incident.

Tragedy, however, is an imitation not only of a complete action, but also of incidents arousing pity and fear. Such incidents have the very greatest effect on the mind when they occur unexpectedly and at the same time in consequence of one another; there is more of the marvellous in them then than if they happened of themselves or by mere chance. Even matters of chance seem most marvellous if there is an appearance of design as it were in them; as for instance the statue of Mitys at Argos killed the author of Mitys' death by falling down on him when a looker-on at a public spectacle; for incidents like that we think to be not without a meaning. A Plot, therefore, of this sort is necessarily finer than others.

Plots are either simple or complex, since the actions they represent are naturally of this twofold description. The action, proceeding in the way defined, as one continuous whole, I call simple, when the change in the hero's fortunes takes place without Peripety or Discovery; and complex, when it involves one or the other, or both. These should each of them arise out of the structure of the Plot itself, so as to be the consequence, necessary or probable, of the antecedents. There is a great difference between a thing happening *propter hoc* and *post hoc*.

A Peripety is the change of the kind described from one state of things within the play to its opposite, and that too in the way we are saying, in the probable or necessary sequence of events; as it is for instance in *Oedipus*: here the opposite state of things is produced by the Messenger, who, coming to gladden Oedipus and to remove his fears as to his mother, reveals the secret of his birth. And in *Lynceus*: just as he is being led off for execution, with Danaus at his side to put him to death, the incidents preceding this bring it about that he is saved and Danaus put to death. A Discovery is, as the very word implies, a change from ignorance to knowledge, and thus to either love or hate, in the personages marked for good or evil fortune. The finest form of Discovery is one attended by Peripeties, like that which goes with the Discovery of *Oedipus*. There are no doubt other forms of it; what we have said may happen in a way in reference to inanimate things, even things of a very casual kind; and it is also possible to discover whether some one has done or not done something. But the form most directly connected with the Plot and the action of the piece is the first-mentioned. This, with a Peripety, will arouse either pity or fear—actions of that nature being what Tragedy is assumed to represent; and it will also serve to bring about the happy or unhappy ending. The Discovery, then, being of persons, it may be that of one party only to the other, the latter being already known; or both the parties may have to discover themselves. Iphigenia, for instance, was discovered to Orestes by sending the letter; and another Discovery was required to reveal him to Iphigenia.

Two parts of the Plot, then, Peripety and Discovery, are on matters of this sort. A third part is Suffering; which we may define as an action of a destructive or painful nature, such as murders on the stage, tortures, woundings, and the like. The other two have been already explained. . . .

The next points after what we have said above will be these: (1) What is the poet to aim at, and what is he to avoid, in constructing his Plots? and (2) What are the conditions on which the tragic effect depends?

We assume that, for the finest form of Tragedy, the Plot must be not simple but complex; and further, that it must imitate actions arousing fear and pity, since that is the distinctive function of this kind of imitation. It follows, therefore, that there are three forms of Plot to be avoided. (1) A good man must not be seen passing from happiness to misery, or (2) a bad man from misery to happiness. The first situation is not fear-inspiring or piteous, but simply odious to us. The second is the most untragic that can be; it has not one of the requisites of Tragedy; it does not appeal either to the human feeling in us, or to our pity, or to our fears. Nor, on the other hand, should (3) an extremely bad man be seen falling from happiness into misery. Such a story may arouse the human feeling in us, but it will not move us to either pity or fear; pity is occasioned by undeserved misfortune, and fear by that of one like ourselves; so that there will be nothing either piteous or fear-inspiring in the situation. There remains, then, the intermediate kind of personage, a man not preeminently virtuous and just, whose misfortune, however, is brought upon him not by vice and depravity but by some error of judgement, of the number of those in the enjoyment of great reputation and prosperity; e.g. Oedipus, Thyestes, and the men of note of similar families. The perfect Plot, accordingly, must have a single, and not (as some tell us) a double issue; the change in the hero's fortunes must be not from misery to happiness, but on the contrary from happiness to misery; and the cause of it must lie not in any depravity, but in some great error on his part; the man himself being either such as we have described, or better, not worse, than that. Fact also confirms our theory. . . .

The tragic fear and pity may be aroused by the Spectacle; but they may also be aroused by the very structure and incidents of the play—which is the better way and shows the better poet. The Plot in fact should be so framed that, even without seeing the things take place, he who simply hears the account of them shall be filled with horror and pity at the incidents; which is just the effect that the mere recital of the story in *Oedipus* would have on one. To produce this same effect by means of the Spectacle is less artistic, and requires extraneous aid. Those, however, who make use of the Spectacle to put before us that which is merely monstrous and not productive of fear, are wholly out of touch with Tragedy; not every kind of pleasure should be required of a tragedy, but only its own proper pleasure. . . .

In the Characters there are four points to aim at. First and foremost, that they shall be good. There will be an element of character in the play, if (as has been observed) what a personage says or does reveals a certain moral purpose; and a good element of character, if the purpose so revealed is good. Such goodness is possible in every type of personage, even in a woman or a slave, though the one is perhaps an inferior, and the other a wholly worthless being. The second point is to make them appropriate. The Character before us may be, say, manly; but it is not appropriate in a female Character to be manly, or clever. The third is to make them like the reality, which is not the same as their being good and appropriate, in our sense of the term. The fourth is to make them consistent and the same throughout; even if inconsistency be part of the man before one for imitation as presenting that form of character, he should still be consistently inconsistent. . . .

As Tragedy is an imitation of personages better than the ordinary man, we in our way should follow the example of good portrait-painters, who reproduce the distinctive features of a man, and at the same time, without losing the likeness, make him handsomer than he is. The poet in like manner, in portraying men quick or slow to anger, or with similar infirmities of character, must know how to represent them as such, and at the same time as good men, as Agathon and Homer have represented Achilles.

David Hume
Of the Standard of Taste

David Hume *(1711–1776) wrote on art and manners in England as well as philosophy and history. It was Hume, more than anyone, who promoted the popular view that "there is no disputing of tastes."*

*T*he great variety of Taste, as well as of opinion, which prevails in the world, is too obvious not to have fallen under every one's observation. Men of the most confined knowledge are able to remark a difference of taste in the narrow circle of their acquaintance, even where the persons have been educated under the same government, and have early imbibed the same prejudices. But those, who can enlarge their view to contemplate distant nations and remote ages, are still more surprised at the great inconsistence and contrariety. We are apt to call *barbarous* whatever departs widely from our own taste and apprehension: But soon find the epithet of reproach retorted on us. And the highest arrogance and self-conceit is at last startled, on observing an equal assurance on all sides, and scruples, amidst such a contest of sentiment, to pronounce positively in its own favour.

As this variety of taste is obvious to the most careless inquirer; so will it be found, on examination, to be still greater in reality than in appearance. The sentiments of men often differ with regard to beauty and deformity of all kinds, even while their general discourse is the same. There are certain terms in every language, which import blame, and others praise; and all men, who use the same tongue, must agree in their application of them. Every voice is united in applauding elegance, propriety, simplicity, spirit in writing; and in blaming fustian, affectation, coldness, and a false brilliancy: But when critics come to particulars, this seeming unanimity vanishes; and it is found, that they had affixed a very different meaning to their expressions. In all matters of opinion and science, the case is opposite: The difference among men is there oftener found to lie in generals than in particulars; and to be less in reality than in appearance. An explanation of the terms commonly ends the controversy; and the disputants are surprised to find, that they had been quarreling, while at bottom they agreed in their judgment. . . .

It is natural for us to seek a *Standard of Taste*; a rule, by which the various sentiments of men may be reconciled; at least, a decision, afforded, confirming one sentiment, and condemning another.

There is a species of philosophy, which cuts off all hopes of success in such an attempt, and represents the impossibility of ever attaining any standard of taste. The difference, it is said, is very wide between judgment and sentiment. All sentiment is right; because sentiment has a reference to nothing beyond itself, and is always real, wherever a man is conscious of it. But all determinations of the understanding are not right; because they have a reference to something beyond themselves, to wit, real matter of fact; and are not always comformable to that standard. Among a thousand different opinions which different men may entertain of the same subject, there is one, and but one, that is just and true; and the only difficulty is to fix and ascertain it. On the contrary, a thousand different sentiments, excited by the same object, are all right: Because no sentiment represents what is really in the object. It only marks a certain conformity or relation between the object and the organs or faculties of the mind; and if that conformity did not really exist, the sentiment could never possibly have being. Beauty is no quality in things themselves: It exists merely in the mind which contemplates them; and each mind perceives a different beauty. One person may even perceive deformity, where another is sensible of beauty; and every individual ought to acquiesce in his own sentiment, without pretending to regulate those of others. To seek the real beauty, or real deformity, is as fruitless an enquiry, as to pretend to ascertain the real sweet or real bitter. According to the disposition of the organs, the same object may be both sweet and bitter; and the proverb has justly determined it to be fruitless to dispute concerning tastes. It is very natural, and even quite necessary, to extend this axiom to mental, as well as bodily taste; and thus common sense, which is so often at variance with philosophy, especially with the skeptical kind, is found, in one instance at least, to agree in pronouncing the same decision.

But though this axiom, by passing into a proverb, seems to have attained the sanction of common sense; there is certainly a species of common sense which opposes it, at least serves to modify and restrain it. Whoever would assert an equality of genius and elegance between OGILBY and MILTON, or BUNYAN and ADDISON, would be thought to defend no less an extravagance, than if he had maintained a mole-hill to be as high as TENERIFFE, or a pond as extensive as the ocean. Though there may be found persons, who give the preference to the former authors; no one pays attention to such a taste; and we pronounce without scruple the sentiment of these pretended critics to be absurd and ridiculous. The principle of the natural equality of tastes is then totally forgot, and while we admit it on some occasions, where the objects seem near an equality, it appears an extravagant paradox, or rather a palpable absurdity, where objects so disproportioned are compared together.

It is evident that none of the rules of composition are fixed by reasonings *a priori*, or can be esteemed abstract conclusions of the understanding, from comparing those habitudes and relations of ideas, which are eternal and immutable. Their foundation is the same with that of all the practical sciences, experience; nor are they any thing but general observations, concerning what has been universally found to please in all countries and in all ages. Many of the beauties of poetry and even of eloquence are founded on falsehood and fiction, on hyperboles, metaphors, and an abuse or perversion of terms from their natural meaning. To check the sallies of the imagination, and to reduce every expression to geometrical truth and exactness, would be the most contrary to the laws of criticism; because it would produce a work, which, by universal experience, has been found the most insipid and disagreeable. But though poetry can never submit to exact truth, it must be confined by rules of art, discovered to the author either by genius or observation. If some negligent or irregular writers have pleased, they have not pleased by their transgressions of rule or order, but in spite of these transgressions: They have possessed other beauties, which were conformable to just criticism; and the force of these beauties has been able to overpower censure, and give the mind a satisfaction superior to the disgust arising from the blemishes. . . . If they are found to please, they cannot be faults; let the pleasure, which they produce, be ever so unexpected and unaccountable.

But though all the general rules of art are founded only on experience and on the observation of the common sentiments of human nature, we must not imagine, that, on every occasion, the feelings of men will be conformable to these rules. Those finer emotions of the mind are of a very tender and delicate nature, and require the concurrence of many favourable circumstances to make them play with facility and exactness, according to their general and established principles. The least exterior hindrance to such small springs, or the least internal disorder, disturbs their motion, and confounds the operation of the whole machine. When we would make an experiment of this nature, and would try the force of any beauty or deformity, we must choose with care a proper time and place, and bring the fancy to a suitable situation and disposition. A perfect serenity of mind, a recollection of thought, a due attention to the object; if any of these circumstances be wanting, our experiment will be fallacious, and we shall be unable to judge of the catholic and universal beauty. The relation, which nature has placed between the form and the sentiment will at least be more obscure; and it will require greater accuracy to trace and discern it. We shall be able to ascertain its influence not so much from the operations of each particular beauty, as from the durable admiration, which attends those works, that have survived all the caprices of mode and fashion, all the mistakes of ignorance and envy. . . .

It appears then, that, amidst all the variety and caprice of taste, there are certain general principles of approbation or blame, whose influence a careful eye may trace in all operations of the mind. Some particular forms or qualities, from the original structure of the internal fabric, are calculated to please, and others to displease; and if they fail of their effect in any particular instance, it is from some apparent defect or imperfection in the organ. A man in a fever would not insist on his palate as able to decide concerning flavours; nor would one, affected with the jaundice, pretend to give a verdict with regard to colours. In each creature, there is a sound and a defective state; and the former alone can be supposed to afford us a true standard of taste and sentiment. If, in the sound state of the organ, there be an entire or a considerable uniformity of sentiment among men, we may thence derive an idea of the perfect beauty; in like manner as the appearance of objects in daylight, to the eye of a man in health, is denominated their true and real colour, even while colour is allowed to be merely a phantasm of the senses.

Many and frequent are the defects in the internal organs, which prevent or weaken the influence of those general principles, on which depends our sentiment of beauty or deformity. Though some objects, by the structure of the mind, be naturally calculated to give pleasure, it is not to be expected, that in every individual the pleasure will be equally felt. Particular incidents and situations occur, which either throw a false light on the objects, or hinder the true from conveying to the imagination the proper sentiment and perception.

One obvious cause, why many feel not the proper sentiment of beauty, is the want of that *delicacy* of imagination, which is requisite to convey a sensibility of those finer emotions. . . .

It is acknowledged to be the perfection of every sense or faculty, to perceive with exactness its most minute objects, and allow nothing to escape its notice and observation. The smaller the objects are, which become sensible to the eye, the finer is that organ, and the more elaborate its make and composition. A good palate is not tried by strong flavours; but by a mixture of small ingredients, where we are still sensible of each part, notwithstanding its minuteness and its confusion with the rest. In like manner, a quick and acute perception of beauty and deformity must be the perfection of our mental taste; nor can a man be satisfied with himself while he suspects, that any excellence or blemish in a discourse has passed him unobserved. In this case, the perfection of the man, and the perfection of the sense or feeling, are found to be united. A very delicate palate, on many occasions, may be a great inconvenience both to a man himself and to his friends: But a delicate taste of wit or beauty must always be a desirable quality; because it is the source of all the finest and most innocent enjoyments, of which human nature is susceptible. In this decision the sentiments of all mankind have agreed. Wherever you can ascertain a delicacy of taste, it is sure to meet with approbation; and the best way of ascertaining it is to appeal to those models and principles, which have been established by the uniform consent and experience of nations and ages.

But though there be naturally a wide difference in point of delicacy between one person and another, nothing tends further to increase and improve this talent, than *practice* in a particular art, and the frequent survey or contemplation of a particular species of beauty. When objects of any kind are first presented to the eye or imagination, the sentiment, which attends them, is obscure and confused; and the mind is, in a great measure, incapable of pronouncing concerning their merits or defects. The taste cannot perceive the several excellences of the performance; much less distinguish the particular character of each excellency, and ascertain its quality and degree. If it pronounce the whole in general to be beautiful or deformed, it is the utmost that can be expected; and even this judgment, a person, so unpractised, will be apt to deliver with great hesitation and reserve. But allow him to acquire experience in those objects, his feeling becomes more exact and nice: He not only perceives the beauties and defects of each part, but marks the distinguishing species of each quality, and assigns it suitable praise or blame. A clear and distinct sentiment attends him through the whole survey of the objects; and he discerns that very degree and kind of approbation or displeasure, which each part is naturally fitted to produce. The mist dissipates, which seemed formerly to hand over the object: The organ acquires greater perfection in its operations; and can pronounce, without danger of mistake, concerning the merits of every performance. In a word, the same address and dexterity, which practice gives to the execution of any work, is also acquired by the same means, in the judging of it. . . .

It is impossible to continue in the practice of contemplating any order of beauty, without being frequently obliged to form *comparisons* between the several species and degrees of excellence, and estimating their proportion to each other. A man, who had no opportunity of comparing the different kinds of beauty, is indeed totally unqualified to pronounce an opinion with regard to any object presented to him. By comparison alone we fix the epithets of praise or blame, and learn how to assign the due degree of each. . . .

But to enable a critic the more fully to execute this undertaking, he must preserve his mind free from all *prejudice*, and allow nothing to enter into his consideration, but the very object which is submitted to his examination. We may observe, that every work of art, in order to produce its due effect on the mind, must be surveyed in a certain point of view, and cannot be fully relished by persons, whose situation, real or imaginary, is not conformable to that which is required by the performance. . . .

It is well known, that in all questions, submitted to the understanding, prejudice is destructive of sound judgment, and perverts all operations of the intellectual faculties: It is no less contrary to good taste; nor has it less influence to corrupt our sentiment of beauty. It belongs to *good sense* to check its influence in both cases; and in this respect, as well as in many others, reason, if not an essential part of taste, is at least requisite to the operations of this latter faculty. In all the nobler productions of genius, there is a mutual relation and correspondence of parts; nor can either the beauties or blemishes be perceived by him, whose thought is not capacious enough to comprehend all those parts, and compare them with each other, in order to perceive the consistence and uniformity of the whole. Every work of art has also a certain end or purpose, for which it is calculated; and is to be deemed more or less perfect, as it is more or less fitted to attain this end. The object of eloquence is to persuade, of history to instruct, of poetry to please by means of the passions and the imagination. These ends we must carry constantly in our view, when we peruse any performance; and we must be able to judge how far the means employed are adapted to their respective purposes. Besides, every kind of composition, even the most poetical is nothing but a chain of propositions and reasonings; not always, indeed, the justest and most exact, but still plausible and specious, however disguised by the coloring of the imagination. The persons introduced in tragedy and epic poetry, must be represented as reasoning, and thinking, and concluding, and acting, suitably to their character and circumstances; and without judgment, as well as taste and invention, a poet can never hope to succeed in so delicate an undertaking. Not to mention, that the same excellence of faculties which contributes to the improvement of reason, the same clearness of conception, the same exactness of distinction, the same vivacity of apprehension, are essential to the operations of true taste, and are its infallible concomitants. It seldom, or never happens, that a man of sense, who has experience in any art, cannot judge of its beauty; and it is no less rare to meet with a man who has a just taste without a sound understanding.

Thus, though the principles of taste be universal, and, nearly, if not entirely the same in all men; yet few are qualified to give judgment on any work of art, or establish their own sentiment as the standard of beauty. The organs of internal sensation are seldom so perfect as to allow the general principles their full play, and produce a feeling correspondent to those principles. They either labour under some defect, or are vitiated by some disorder; and by that means, excite a sentiment, which may be pronounced erroneous. When the critic has no delicacy, he judges without any distinction, and is only affected by the grosser and more palpable qualities of the object: The finer touches pass unnoticed and disregarded. Where he is not aided by practice, his verdict is attended with confusion and hesitation. Where no comparison has been employed, the most frivolous beauties, such as rather merit the name of defects, are the object of his admiration. Where he lies under the influence of prejudice, all his natural sentiments are perverted. Where good sense is wanting, he is not qualified to discern the beauties of design and reasoning, which are the highest and most excellent. Under some or other of these imperfections, the generality of men labour; and hence a true judge in the finer arts is observed, even during the most polished ages, to be so rare a character: Strong sense, united to delicate sentiment, improved by practice, perfected by comparison, and cleared of all prejudice, can alone entitle critics to his valuable character; and the joint verdict of such, wherever they are to be found, is the true standard of taste and beauty.

But where are such critics to be found? By what marks are they to be known? How distinguish them from pretenders? These questions are embarrassing; and seem to throw us back into the same uncertainty, from which, during the course of this essay, we have endeavoured to extricate ourselves.

But if we consider the matter aright, these are questions of fact, not of sentiment. Whether any particular person be endowed with good sense and a delicate imagination, free from prejudice, may often be the subject of dispute, and be liable to great discussion and enquiry: But that such a character is valuable and estimable will be agreed in by all mankind. Where these doubts occur, men can do no more than in other disputable questions, which are submitted to the understanding: They must produce the best arguments, that their invention suggests to them; they must acknowledge a true and decisive standard to exist somewhere, to wit, real existence and matter of fact; and they must have indulgence to such as differ from them in their appeals to this standard. It is sufficient for our present purpose, if we have proved, that the taste of all individuals is not upon an equal footing, and that some men in general, however difficult to be particularly pitched upon, will be acknowledged by universal sentiment to have a preference above others.

Leo Tolstoy

What Is Art?

Leo Tolstoy (*1828–1910*), *the author of such classics as* War and Peace *and* Anna Karenina, *also wrote extensively on art and religion. His theory of art as the sincere expression and communication of the artist's moral and religious feelings has been extremely influential and is still being vigorously argued by artists and writers today.*

*E*very work of art causes the receiver to enter into a certain kind of relationship both with him who produced, or is producing, the art, and with all those who, simultaneously, previously, or subsequently, receive the same artistic impression.

Speech, transmitting the thoughts and experiences of men, serves as a means of union among them, and art acts in a similar manner. The peculiarity of this latter means of intercourse, distinguishing it from intercourse by means of words, consists in this, that whereas by words a man transmits his thoughts to another, by means of art he transmits his feelings.

The activity of art is based on the fact that a man, receiving through his sense of hearing or sight another man's expression of feeling, is capable of experiencing the emotion which moved the man who expressed it. To take the simplest example: one man laughs, and another who hears becomes merry; or a man weeps, and another who hears feels sorrow. A man is excited or irritated, and another man seeing him comes to a similar state of mind. By his movements or by the sounds of his voice, a man expresses courage and determination or sadness and calmness, and this state of mind passes on to others. A man suffers, expressing his sufferings by groans and spasms, and this suffering transmits itself to other people; a man expresses his feeling of admiration, devotion, fear, respect, or love to certain objects, persons, or phenomena, and others are infected by the same feelings of admiration, devotion, fear, respect, or love to the same objects, persons, and phenomena.

And it is upon this capacity of man to receive another man's expression of feeling and experience those feelings himself, that the activity of art is based.

If a man infects another or others directly, immediately, by his appearance or by the sounds he gives vent to at the very time he experiences the feeling; if he causes another man to yawn when he himself cannot help yawning, or to laugh or cry when he himself is obliged to laugh or cry, or to suffer when he himself is suffering—that does not amount to art.

Art begins when one person, with the object of joining another or others to himself in one and the same feeling, expresses that feeling by certain external indications. To take the simplest example: a boy, having experienced, let us say, fear on encountering a wolf, relates that encounter; and, in order to evoke in others the feeling he has experienced, describes himself, his condition before the encounter, the surroundings, the wood, his own lightheartedness, and then the wolf's appearance, its movements, the distance between himself and the wolf, etc. All this, if only the boy, when telling the story, again experiences the feelings he had lived through and infects the hearers and compels them to feel what the narrator had experienced, is art. If even the boy had not seen a wolf but had frequently been afraid of one, and if, wishing to evoke in others the fear he had felt, he invented an encounter with a wolf and recounted it so as to make his hearers share the feelings he experienced when he feared the wolf, that also would be art. And just in the same way it is art if a man, having experienced either the fear of suffering or the attraction of enjoyment (whether in reality or in imagination), expresses these feelings on canvas or in marble so that others are infected by them. And it is also art if a man feels or imagines to himself feelings of delight, gladness, sorrow, despair, courage, or despondency and the transition from one to another of these feelings, and expresses these feelings by sounds so that the hearers are infected by them and experience them as they were experienced by the composer.

The feelings with which the artist infects others may be most various—very strong or very weak, very important or very insignificant, very bad or very good: feelings of love for one's own country, self-devotion and submission to fate or to God expressed in a drama, raptures of lovers described in a novel, feelings of voluptuousness expressed in a picture, courage expressed in a triumphal march, merriment evoked by a dance, humor evoked by a funny story, the feeling of quietness transmitted by an evening landscape or by a lullaby, or the feeling of admiration evoked by a beautiful arabesque—it is all art.

If only the spectators or auditors are infected by the feelings which the author has felt, it is art.

To evoke in oneself a feeling one has once experienced, and having evoked it in oneself, then, by means of movements, lines, colors, sounds, or forms expressed in words, so to transmit that feeling that others may experience the same feeling—this is the activity of art.

Art is a human activity consisting in this, that one man consciously, by means of certain external signs, hands on to others feelings he has lived through, and that other people are infected by these feelings and also experience them. . . .

There is one indubitable indication distinguishing real art from its counterfeit, namely, the infectiousness of art. If a man, without exercising effort and without altering his standpoint on reading, hearing, or seeing another man's work, experiences a mental condition which unites him with that man and with other people who also partake of that work of art, then the object evoking that condition is a work of art. And however poetical, realistic, effectual, or interesting a work may be, it is not a work of art if it does not evoke that feeling (quite distinct from all other feelings) of joy and of spiritual union with another (the author) and with others (those who are also infected by it).

It is true that his indication is an *internal* one, and that there are people who have forgotten what the action of real art is, who expect something else from art (in our society the great majority are in this state), and that therefore such people may mistake for this aesthetic feeling the feeling of diversion and a certain excitement which they receive from counterfeits of art. But though it is impossible to undeceive these people, just as it is impossible to convince a man suffering from color-blindness that green is not red, yet, for all that, this indication remains perfectly definite to those whose feeling for art is neither perverted nor atrophied, and it clearly distinguishes the feeling produced by art from all other feelings.

The chief peculiarity of this feeling is that the receiver of a true artistic impression is so united to the artist that he feels as if the work were his own and not someone else's—as if what it expresses were just what he had long been wishing to express. A real work of art destroys, in the consciousness of the receiver, the separation between himself and the artist— not that alone, but also between himself and all whose minds receive this work of art. In this freeing of our personality from its separation and isolation, in this uniting of it with others, lies the chief characteristic and the great attractive force of art.

If a man is infected by the author's condition of soul, if he feels this emotion and this union with others, then the object which has effected this is art; but if there by no such infection, if there be not this union with the author and with others who are moved by the same work—then it is not art. And not only is infection a sure sign of art, but the degree of infectiousness is also the sole measure of excellence in art.

The stronger the infection, the better is the art as art, speaking now apart from its subject matter, i.e., not considering the quality of the feelings it transmits.

And the degree of the infectiousness of art depends on three conditions:

1. On the greater or lesser individuality of the feeling transmitted:
2. on the greater or lesser clearness with which the feeling is transmitted;
3. on the sincerity of the artist, i.e., on the greater or lesser force with which the artist himself feels the emotion he transmits.

The more individual the feeling transmitted the more strongly does it act on the receiver; the more individual the state of soul into which he is transferred, the more pleasure does the receiver obtain, and therefore the more readily and strongly does he join it.

The clearness of expression assists infection because the receiver, who mingles in consciousness with the author, is the better satisfied the more clearly the feeling is transmitted, which, as it seems to him, he has long known and felt, and for which he has only now found expression.

But most of all is the degree of infectiousness of art increased by the degree of sincerity in the artist. As soon as the spectator, hearer, or reader feels that the artist is infected by his own production, and writes, sings, or plays for himself, and not merely to act on others, this mental condition of the artist infects the receiver; and contrariwise, as soon as the spectator, reader, or hearer feels that the author is not writing, singing or playing for his own satisfaction—does not himself feel what he wishes to express—but is doing it for him, the receiver, a resistance immediately springs up, and the most individual and the newest feelings and the cleverest technique not only fail to produce any infection but actually repel.

I have mentioned three conditions of contagiousness in art, but they may be all summed into one, the last, sincerity, i.e., that the artist should be impelled by an inner need to express his feeling. That condition includes the first; for if the artist is sincere he will express the feeling as he experienced it. And as each man is different from everyone else, his feeling will be individual for everyone else; and the more individual it is—the more the artist has drawn it from the depths of his nature—the more sympathetic and sincere will it be. And this same sincerity will impel the artist to find a clear expression of the feeling which he wishes to transmit.

Therefore this third condition—sincerity—is the most important of the three. It is always complied with in peasant art, and this explains why such art always acts so powerfully; but it is a condition almost entirely absent from our upper-class art, which is continually produced by artists actuated by personal aims of covetousness or vanity.

Such are the three conditions which divide art from its counterfeits, and which also decide the quality of every work of art apart from its subject matter.

The absence of any one of these conditions excludes a work from the category of art and relegates it to that of art's counterfeits. If the work does not transmit the artist's peculiarity of feeling and is therefore not individual, if it is unintelligibly expressed, or if it has not proceeded from the author's inner need for expression—it is not a work of art. If all these conditions are present, even in the smallest degree, then the work, even if a weak one, is yet a work of art.

The presence in various degrees of these three conditions—individuality, clearness, and sincerity—decides the merit of a work of art as art, apart from subject matter. All works of art take rank of merit according to the degree in which they fulfil the first, the second, and the third of these conditions. In one the individuality of the feeling transmitted may predominate; in another, clearness of expression; in a third, sincerity; while a fourth may have sincerity and individuality but be deficient in clearness; a fifth, individuality and clearness but less sincerity; and so forth, in all possible degrees and combinations.

Thus is art divided from that which is not art, and thus is the quality of art as art decided, independently of its subject matter, i.e., apart from whether the feelings it transmits are good or bad.

Monroe Beardsley
Taste in Art

Monroe Beardsley *is a professor of philosophy at Temple University in Philadelphia and the author of many of the central texts in twentieth century aesthetic theory.*

We are assured by an old and often-quoted maxim, whose authority is not diminished by its being cast in Latin, that there can be no disputing about tastes. The chief use of this maxim is in putting an end to disputes that last a long time and don't appear to be getting anywhere. And for this purpose it is very efficacious, for it has an air of profound finality, and it also seems to provide a democratic compromise of a deadlocked issue. If you can't convince someone that he is wrong, or bring yourself to admit that he is right, you can always say that neither of you is more wrong than the other, because nobody can be right.

Remarks that serve to close some people's debates, however, are quite often just the remarks to start a new one among philosophers. And this maxim is no exception. It has been given a great deal of thought, some of it very illuminating; yet there is still something to be learned from further reflection upon it. Nor is it of small importance to know, if we can, whether the maxim is true or false, for if it is true we won't waste time in futile discussions, and if it is false we won't waste opportunities for fruitful discussion.

The question whether tastes are disputable is one to be approached with wariness. The first thing is to be clear about what it really means. There are two key words in it that we should pay particular attention to.

The first is the word "taste." The maxim is perhaps most readily and least doubtfully applied to taste in its primary sensory meaning: some people like ripe olives, some green; some people like turnips, others cannot abide them; some people will go long distances for pizza pies, others can hardly choke them down. And there are no disputes about olives: we don't find two schools of thought, the Ripe Olive School and the Green Olive School, publishing quarterly journals or demanding equal time on television—probably because there simply isn't much you can say about the relative merits of these comestibles.

But we apply the word "taste," of course, more broadly. We speak of a person's taste in hats and neckties; we speak of his taste in poetry and painting and music. And it is here that the *non disputandum* maxim is most significantly applied. Some people like Auden and others Swinburne, some enjoy the paintings of Jackson Pollock and others avoid them when they can, some people are panting to hear Shostakovitch's latest symphony and others find no music since Haydn really satisfying. In these cases, unlike the olive case, people are generally not at a loss for words: there is plenty you can say about Shostakovitch, pro or con. They talk, all right; they may praise, deplore, threaten, cajole, wheedle, and scream—but, according to the maxim, they do not really dispute.

This brings us, then, to the second key word. What does it mean to say that we cannot *dispute* about tastes in literature, fine arts, and music, even though we can clearly make known our tastes? It certainly doesn't mean that we cannot disagree, or differ in taste: for obviously we do, and not only we but also the acknowledged or supposed experts in these fields. Consider James Gould Cozzens' novel, *By Love Possessed*, which appeared in August, 1957; consult the critics and reviewers to discover whether it is a good novel. Being a serious and ambitious work by a writer of standing, and also a best seller, it provoked unusually forthright judgments from a number of reviewers and critics—as may be seen in the accompanying quotations. "Masterpiece . . . brilliant . . . distinguished . . . high order . . . mediocre . . . bad;" that just about covers the spectrum of evaluation.

The International Council of the Museum of Modern Art recently took a large collection of American abstract expressionist paintings on tour in Europe. Its reception was reported in *Time*. In Spain some said, "If this is art, what was it that Goya painted?" and others cheered its "furious vitality" and "renovating spirit." In Italy one newspaper remarked, "It is not painting," but "droppings of paint, sprayings, burstings, lumps, squirts, whirls, rubs and marks, erasures, scrawls, doodles and kaleidoscope backgrounds." In Switzerland it was an "artistic event" that spoke for the genius of American art. And of course all these judgments could be found in this country too.

Not a dispute? Well, what is a dispute? Let us take first the plainest case of a disagreement (no matter what it is about): two people who say, " 'Tis so!" and " 'Taint so!" Let them repeat these words as often as they like, and shout them from the housetops; they still haven't got a dispute going, but merely a contradiction, or perhaps an altercation. But let one person say, " 'Tis so!" and give a *reason* why 'tis so—let him say, "Jones is the best candidate for Senator because he is tactful, honest, and has had much experience in government." And let the other person say, " 'Taint so!" and give a reason why 'taint so—"Jones is not the best candidate, because he is too subservient to certain interests, indecisive and wishywashy in his own views, and has no conception of the United States' international responsibilities." *Then* we have a dispute—that is, a disagreement in which the parties give reasons for their contentions. Of course this is not all there is to it; the dispute has just begun. But we see how it might continue, each side giving further reasons for its own view, and questioning whether the reasons given by the other are true, relevant, and compelling.

It is this kind of thing that counts as a dispute about the possibility of getting to the moon, about American intervention in the Middle East, about a Supreme Court decision, or anything else. And if we can dispute about these things, why not about art?

But here is where the *non disputandum* maxim would draw the line. We do not speak (or not without irony) about people's tastes in Senatorial candidates or missile policies (if the President replied to critics by saying, "Well, your taste is for speeding up the missile program and spending money, but that's not to my taste," we would feel he ought to back up his opinion more than that). Nor do we speak of tastes in international affairs, or laws, or constitutions. And that seems to be because we believe that judgments on these matters can be, and ought to be, based on good reasons—not that they always are, of course. To prefer a democratic to a totalitarian form of government is *not* just a matter of taste, though to like green olives better than ripe olives is a matter of taste, and we don't require the green olive man to rise and give his reasons, or even to *have* reasons. What kind of reasons could he have? "Green olives are better because they are green" would not look like much of a reason to the ripe olive devotee.

The question, then, is whether a preference for Picasso or Monteverdi is more like a preference for green olives or like a preference for a Senatorial candidate: is it *arguable*? can it be *reasoned*.

When we read what critics and reviewers have to say about the things they talk about, we cannot doubt that they do not merely praise or blame, but defend their judgments by giving reasons, or what they claim to be reasons. . . . But according to the Aesthetic Skeptic— if I may choose this convenient name for the upholder of the "no disputing" doctrine—this is an illusion. The apparent reasons are not genuine reasons, or cannot be compelling reasons, like the ones we find in other fields. For in the last analysis they rest upon sheer liking or disliking, which is not susceptible of rational discussion. . . . The Aesthetic Skeptic would analyze all apparent disputes among critics in these terms: the critic can point out features of the novel, the abstract expressionist painting, the quintet for winds, but when he does this he is taking for granted, what may not be true, that you happen to like these features. You can't, says the Skeptic, argue anybody into liking something he doesn't like, and that's why there's no disputing about tastes; all disputes are in the end useless. . . .

. . . I should like to consider briefly some of the difficulties in Aesthetic Skepticism, as I see it, and point out the possibility of an alternative theory.

The Skeptical theory takes people's likes and dislikes as ultimate and unappealable facts about them; when two people finally get down to saying "I like X" and "I don't like X" (be it the flavor of turnip or subtlety of texture in music), there the discussion has to end, there the dispute vanishes. But though it is true that you can't change a disliking into a liking by arguments, that doesn't imply that you can't change it at all, or that we cannot argue whether or not it *ought* to be changed. . . .But the fact remains that one person can give reasons to another why he would be better off if he *could* enjoy music or painting that he now abhors, and sometimes the other person can set about indirectly, by study and enlarged experience, to change his own tastes, or, as we say, to improve them. There is not just your taste or mine, but better and worse taste; and this doesn't mean just that I have a taste for my taste, but not yours—I might in fact have a distaste for the limitations of my own taste (though that is a queer way to put it). It is something like a person with deep-rooted prejudices, to which he has been conditioned from an early age; perhaps he cannot quite get rid of them, no matter how he tries, and yet he may acknowledge in them a weakness, a crippling feature of his personality, and he may resolve that he will help his children grow up free from them.

The Skeptic does not allow for the possibility that we might give reasons why a person would be better off if he liked or disliked *By Love Possessed* in the way, and to the degree, that it deserves to be liked or disliked. Sometimes, I think, he really holds that it would not be worth the trouble. After all, what does it matter whether people like green olives or ripe olives? We can obtain both in sufficient supply, and nothing much depends upon it as far as the fate of the world is concerned. That's another reason why we ordinarily don't speak of Senatorial candidates as a matter of taste—unless we want to be disparaging, as when people speak of the President's choice in Secretaries of State, to imply that he has no good reason for his choice. It does matter who is Senator, or Secretary of State—it matters a great deal. . . .

Now of course, if we are thinking of our two musical disputants about the relative merits of the two quintets, this is a dispute we may safely leave alone. Both quintets are of such a high order that it perhaps doesn't matter enormously which we decide to rank higher than the other, though there's no harm in trying to do this, if we wish. But the question about *By Love Possessed* is whether it is a "masterpiece" or "bad"; and the question about the paintings is whether they ought to be shown abroad at all. It may not matter so very much whether a person on the whole admires Mozart or Beethoven more, but what if he cannot make up his mind between Mozart and Strauss, or between Beethoven and Shostakovitch?

The fact is that the prevailing level of taste in the general public matters a great deal to me, for it has a great deal to do with determining what I shall have the chance to read, what movies will be filmed, shown, or censored, what music will be played most availably on the radio, what plays will be performed on television. And it has a great deal to do with what composers and painters and poets will do, or whether some of them will do anything at all. But more than that, even: if I am convinced that the kinds of experiences that can only be obtained by access to the greatest works is an important ingredient of the richest and most fully-developed human life, then do I not owe it to others to try to put that experience within their reach, or them within its reach? It might be as important to them as good housing, good medical and dental care, or good government.

But here is another point at which the Skeptic feels uneasy. Isn't it undemocratic to go around telling other people that they have crude tastes—wouldn't it be more in keeping with our laissez-faire spirit of tolerance, and less reminiscent of totalitarian absolutism and compulsion, to let others like and enjoy what they like and enjoy? Isn't this their natural right?

There are too many confusions in this point of view to clear them all up briefly. But some of them are worth sorting out. Of course it is a person's right to hear the music he enjoys, provided it doesn't bother other people too much. But it is no invasion of his right, if he is willing to consider the problem, to try to convince him that he should try to like other things that appear to deserve it. . . .

The distinction that many Skeptics find it hard to keep in mind is this: I may hold that there *is* a better and a worse in music and novels without at all claiming that *I know for certain* which are which. Those critics and reviewers who pronounced their judgments on *By Love Possessed* are not necessarily dogmatic because they deny that it's all a matter of taste (even though some of them were more positive than they had a right to be). They believe that some true and reasonable judgment of the novel is in principle possible, and that objective critics, given time and discussion, could in principle agree, or come close to agreeing, on it. But they do not have to claim infallibility—people can be mistaken about novels, as they can about anything else. Works of art are complicated. There need be nothing totalitarian about literary criticism, and there is nothing especially democratic in the view that nobody is wrong because there is no good or bad to be wrong about.

It would help us all, I think, to look at the problem of judging works of art in a more direct way. These judgments, as can easily be seen in any random collection of reviews, go off in so many directions that it sometimes seems that the reviewers are talking about different things. We must keep our eye on the object—the painting, the novel, the quintet. Because the composer's love affairs were in a sorry state at the time he was composing, people think that the value of the music must somehow be connected with this circumstance. Because the painter was regarding his model while he painted, people think that the value of the painting must depend on some relation to the way she really looked, or felt. Because the novelist is known to be an anarchist or a conservative, people think that the value of the novel must consist partly in its fidelity to these attitudes. Now, of course, when we approach a work of art, there are many kinds of interest that we can take in it, as well as in its creator. But when we are trying to judge it *as* a work of art, rather than as biography or social criticism or something else, there is a central interest that ought to be kept in view.

A work of art, whatever its species, is an object of some kind—something somebody made. And the question is whether it was worth making, what it is good for, what can be done with it. In this respect it is like a tool. Tools of course are production goods, instrumental to other instruments, whereas paintings and musical compositions and novels are consumption goods, directly instrumental to some sort of experience. And their own peculiar excellence consists, I believe, in their capacity to afford certain valuable kinds and degrees of aesthetic experience. Of course they do not yield this experience to those who cannot understand them, just as a tool is of no use to one who has not the skill to wield it. But we do not talk in the Skeptical way about tools: we do not say that the value of a hammer is all a matter of taste, some people having a taste for hammering nails, some not. No, the value resides in its capability to drive the nail, given a hand and arm with the right skill, and if the need should arise. And this value it would have, though unrealized, even if the skill were temporarily lost.

So with works of art, it seems to me. Their value is what they can do to and for us, if we are capable of having it done. As for those who do not, or not yet, have this capacity, it is not a simple fact that they do not, but a misfortune, and the only question is whether, or to what extent, it can be remedied. It is because this question sometimes has a hopeful answer that we dispute, and must dispute, about tastes. When the political disputant gives his reasons for supporting one Senatorial candidate over another, he cites facts about that candidate that he knows, from past experience, justify the hope of a good performance—the hope that the candidate, once elected, will do what a Senator is supposed to do, well. When the critic gives his reasons for saying that a work of art is good or bad, he is not, as the Skeptic claims, trying to guess whom it will please or displease; he is pointing out those features of the work—its qualities, structure, style, and so on—that are evidence of the work's ability or inability to provide qualified readers, listeners, or viewers, with a deep aesthetic experience.

Nelson Goodman
The Perfect Fake

Nelson Goodman *is a professor of philosophy at Harvard University and the author of several influential books on the philosophy of science and linguistic philosophy. He has also been an art dealer and is one of the most widely read current theorists in the philosophy of art.*

> . . . the most tantalizing question of all: If a fake is so expert that even after the most thorough and trustworthy examination its authenticity is still open to doubt, is it or is it not as satisfactory a work of art as if it were unequivocally genuine?
>
> Aline B. Saarinen

THE PERFECT FAKE

Forgeries of works of art present a nasty practical problem to the collector, the curator, and the art historian, who must often expend taxing amounts of time and energy in determining whether or not particular objects are genuine. But the theoretical problem raised is even more acute. The hardheaded question why there is any aesthetic difference between a deceptive forgery and an original work challenges a basic premise on which the very functions of collector, museum, and art historian depend. A philosopher of art caught without an answer to this question is at least as badly off as a curator of paintings caught taking a Van Meegeren for a Vermeer.

The question is most strikingly illustrated by the case of a given work and a forgery or copy or reproduction of it. Suppose we have before us, on the left, Rembrandt's original painting *Lucretia* and, on the right, a superlative imitation of it. We know from a fully documented history that the painting on the left is the original; and we know from X-ray photographs and microscopic examination and chemical analysis that the painting on the right is a recent fake. Although there are many differences between the two—e.g., in author-ship, age, physical and chemical characteristics, and market value—we cannot see any dif-ference between them; and if they are moved while we sleep, we cannot then tell which is which by merely looking at them. Now we are pressed with the question whether there can be any aesthetic difference between the two pictures; and the questioner's tone often intimates that the answer is plainly no, that the only differences here are aesthetically irrelevant.

We must begin by inquiring whether the distinction between what can and what cannot be seen in the pictures by 'merely looking at them' is entirely clear. We are looking at the pictures, but presumably not 'merely looking' at them, when we examine them under a microscope or fluoroscope. Does merely looking, then, mean looking without the use of any instrument? This seems a little unfair to the man who needs glasses to tell a painting from a hippopotamus. But if glasses are permitted at all, how strong may they be, and can we consistently exclude the magnifying glass and the microscope? Again, if incandescent light is permitted, can violet-ray light be ruled out? And even with incandescent light, must it be of medium intensity and from a normal angle, or is a strong raking light permitted? All these cases might be covered by saying that 'merely looking' is looking at the pictures without any use of instruments other than those customarily used in looking at things in general. This will cause trouble when we turn, say, to certain miniature illuminations or Assyrian cylinder seals that we can hardly distinguish from the crudest copies without using a strong glass. Furthermore, even in our case of the two pictures, subtle differences of drawing or painting discoverable only with a magnifying glass may still, quite obviously, be aesthetic differences between the pictures. If a powerful microscope is used instead, this is no longer the case; but just how much magnification is permitted? To specify what is meant by merely looking at the pictures is thus far from easy; but for the sake of argument, let us suppose that all these difficulties have been resolved and the notion of 'merely looking' made clear enough.

Then we must ask who is assumed to be doing the looking. Our questioner does not, I take it, mean to suggest that there is no aesthetic difference between two pictures if at least one person, say a cross-eyed wrestler, can see no difference. The more pertinent question is whether there can be any aesthetic difference if nobody, not even the most skilled expert, can ever tell the pictures apart by merely looking at them. *But notice now that no one can ever ascertain by merely looking at the pictures that no one ever has been or will be able to tell them apart by merely looking at them.* In other words, the question in its present form concedes that no one can ascertain by merely looking at the pictures that there is no aesthetic difference between them. This seems repugnant to our questioner's whole motivation. For if merely looking can never establish that two pictures are aesthetically the same, something that is beyond the reach of any given looking is admitted as constituting an aesthetic difference. And in that case, the reason for not admitting documents and the results of scientific tests becomes very obscure.

The real issue may be more accurately formulated as the question whether there is any aesthetic difference between the two pictures *for me* (or for *x*) if I (or *x*) cannot tell them apart by merely looking at them. But this is not quite right either. For I can never ascertain merely by looking at the pictures that even I shall never be able to see any difference between them.

And to concede that something beyond any given looking at the pictures by me may constitute an aesthetic difference between them *for me* is, again, quite at odds with the tacit convictions or suspicion that activates the questioner.

Thus the critical question amounts finally to this: is there any aesthetic difference between the two pictures for x at t, where t is a suitable period of time, if x cannot tell them apart by merely looking at them at t? Or in other words, can anything that x does not discern by merely looking at the pictures at t constitute an aesthetic difference between them for x at t?

THE ANSWER

In setting out to answer this question, we must bear clearly in mind that what one can distinguish at any given moment by merely looking depends not only upon native visual acuity but upon practice and training. Americans look pretty much alike to a Chinese who has never looked at many of them. Twins may be indistinguishable to all but their closest relatives and acquaintances. Moreover, only through looking at them when someone has named them for us can we learn to tell Joe from Jim upon merely looking at them. Looking at people or things attentively, with the knowledge of certain presently invisible respects in which they differ, increases our ability to discriminate between them—and between other things or other people—upon merely looking at them. Thus pictures that look just alike to the newsboy come to look quite unlike to him by the time he has become a museum director.

Although I see no difference now between the two pictures in question, I may learn to see a difference between them. I cannot determine now by merely looking at them, or in any other way, that I *shall* be able to learn. But the information that they are very different, that the one is the original and the other the forgery, argues against any inference to the conclusion that I *shall not* be able to learn. And the fact that I may later be able to make a perceptual distinction between the pictures that I cannot make now constitutes an aesthetic difference between them that is important to me now.

Furthermore, to look at the pictures now with the knowledge that the left one is the original and the other the forgery may help develop the ability to tell which is which later by merely looking at them. Thus, with information not derived from the present or any past looking at the pictures, the present looking may have a quite different bearing upon future lookings from what it would otherwise have. The way the pictures in fact differ constitutes an aesthetic difference between them for me now and because my knowledge of the way they differ bears upon the role of the present looking in training my perceptions to discriminate between these pictures, and between others.

But that is not all. My knowledge of the difference between the two pictures, just because it affects the relationship of the present to future lookings, informs the very character of my present looking. This knowledge instructs me to look at the two pictures differently now, even if what I see is the same. Beyond testifying that I may learn to see a difference, it also indicates to some extent the kind of scrutiny to be applied now, the comparisons and contrasts to be made in imagination, and the relevant associations to be brought to bear. It thereby guides the selection, from my past experience, of items and aspects for use in my present looking. Thus not only later but right now, the unperceived difference between the two pictures is a consideration pertinent to my visual experience with them.

In short, although I cannot tell the pictures apart merely by looking at them now, the fact that the left-hand one is the original and the right-hand one a forgery constitutes an aesthetic difference between them for me now because knowledge of this fact (1) stands as evidence that there may be a difference between them that I can learn to perceive, (2) assigns the present looking a role as training toward such a perceptual discrimination, and (3) makes consequent demands that modify and differentiate my present experience in looking at the two pictures. . . .

All I have attempted to show, of course, is that the two pictures can differ aesthetically, not that the original is better than the forgery. In our example, the original probably is much the better picture, since Rembrandt paintings are in general much better than copies by unknown painters. But a copy of a Lastman by Rembrandt may well be better than the original. We are not called upon here to make such particular comparative judgments or to formulate canons of aesthetic evaluation. We have fully met the demands of our problem by showing that the fact that we cannot tell our two pictures apart merely by looking at them does not imply that they are aesthetically the same—and thus does not force us to conclude that the forgery is as good as the original.

The example we have been using throughout illustrates a special case of a more general question concerning the aesthetic significance of authenticity. Quite aside from the occurrence of forged duplication, does it matter whether an original work is the product of one or another artist or school or period? Suppose that I can easily tell two pictures apart but cannot tell who painted either except by using some device like X-ray photography. Does the fact that the picture is or is not by Rembrandt make any aesthetic difference? What is involved here is the discrimination not of one picture from another but of the class of Rembrandt paintings from the class of other paintings. My chance of learning to make this discrimination correctly—of discovering projectible characteristics that differentiate Rembrandts in general from non-Rembrandts—depends heavily upon the set of examples available as a basis. Thus the fact that the given picture belongs to the one class or the other is important for me to know in learning how to tell Rembrandt paintings from others. In other words, my present (or future) inability to determine the authorship of the given picture without use of scientific apparatus does not imply that the authorship makes no aesthetic difference to me; for knowledge of the authorship, no matter how obtained, can contribute materially toward developing my ability to determine without such apparatus whether or not any picture, including this one on another occasion, is by Rembrandt. . . .

THE UNFAKABLE

A second problem concerning authenticity is raised by the rather curious fact that in music, unlike painting, there is no such thing as a forgery of a known work. There are, indeed, compositions falsely purporting to be by Haydn as there are paintings falsely purporting to be by Rembrant; but of the *London Symphony*, unlike the *Lucretia*, there can be no forgeries. Haydn's manuscript is no more genuine an instance of the score than is a printed copy off the press this morning, and last night's performance no less genuine than the premiere. Copies of the score may vary in accuracy, but all accurate copies, even if forgeries of Haydn's manuscript are equally genuine instances of the score. Performances may vary in correctness and quality and even in 'authenticity' of a more esoteric kind; but all correct performances are equally genuine instances of the work. In contrast, even the most exact copies of the Rembrandt painting are simply imitations or forgeries, not new instances, of the work. Why this difference between the two arts?

Let us speak of a work of art as *autographic* if and only if the distinction between the original and forgery of it is significant; or better, if and only if even the most exact duplication of it does not thereby count as genuine. If a work of art is autographic, we may also call that art autographic. Thus painting is autographic, music nonautographic, or *allographic*. These terms are introduced purely for convenience; nothing is implied concerning the relative individuality of expression demanded by or attainable in these arts. Now the problem before us is to account for the fact that some arts but not others are autographic. . . .

THE REASON

Why, then, can I no more make a forgery of Haydn's symphony or of Gray's poem than I can make an original of Rembrandt's painting or of his etching *Tobit Blind*? Let us suppose that there are various handwritten copies and many editions of a given literary work. Differences between them in style and size of script or type, in color of ink, in kind of paper, in number and layout of pages, in condition, etc., do not matter. All that matters is what may be called *sameness of spelling*: exact correspondence as sequences of letters, spaces, and punctuation marks. Any sequence—even a forgery of the author's manuscript or of a given edition—that so corresponds to a correct copy is itself correct, and nothing is more the original work than is such a correct copy. And since whatever is not an original of the work must fail to meet such an explicit standard of correctness, there can be no deceptive imitation, no forgery, of that work. To verify the spelling or to spell correctly is all that is required to identify an instance of the work or to produce a new instance. In effect, the fact that a literary work is in a definite notation, consisting of certain signs or characters that are to be combined by concatenation, provides the means for distinguishing the properties constitutive of the work from all contingent properties—that is, for fixing the required features and the limits of permissible variation in each. Merely by determining that the copy before us is spelled correctly we can determine that it meets all requirements for the work in question. In painting, on the contrary, with no such alphabet of characters, none of the pictorial properties—none of the properties the picture has as such—is distinguished as constitutive; no such feature can be dismissed as contingent, and no deviation as insignificant. The only way of ascertaining that the *Lucretia* before us is genuine is thus to establish the historical fact that it is the actual object made by Rembrandt. Accordingly, physical identification of the product of the artist's hand, and consequently the conception of forgery of a particular work, assume a significance in painting that they do not have in literature.

What has been said of literary texts obviously applies also to musical scores. The alphabet is different; and the characters in a score, rather than being strung one after the other as in a text, are disposed in a more complex array. Nevertheless, we have a limited set of characters and of positions for them; and correct spelling, in only a slightly expanded sense, it still the sole requirement for a genuine instance of a work. Any false copy is wrongly spelled—has somewhere in place of the right character either another character or an illegible mark that is not a character of the notation in question at all.

But what of performances of music? Music is not autographic in this second stage either, yet a performance by no means consists of characters from an alphabet. Rather, the constitutive properties demanded of a performance of the symphony are those *prescribed* in the score; and performances that comply with the score may differ appreciably in such musical features as tempo, timbre, phrasing, and expressiveness. To determine compliance requires, indeed, something more than merely knowing the alphabet; it requires the ability to correlate appropriate sounds with the visible signs in the score—to recognize, so to speak, correct pronunciation though without necessarily understanding what is pronounced. The competence required to identify or produce sounds called for by a score increases with the complexity of the composition, but there is nevertheless a theoretically decisive test for compliance; and a performance, whatever its interpretative fidelity and independent merit, has or has not all the constitutive properties of a given work, and is or is not strictly a performance of that work, according as it does or does not pass this test. No historical information concerning the production of the performance can affect the result. Hence deception as to the facts of production is irrelevant, and the notion of a performance that is a forgery of the work is quite empty. . . .

The general answer to our somewhat slippery second problem of authenticity can be summarized in a few words. A forgery of a work of art is an object falsely purporting to have the history of production requisite for the (or an) original of the work. Where there is a theoretically decisive test for determining that an object has all the constitutive properties of the work in question without determining how or by whom the object was produced, there is no requisite history of production and hence no forgery of any given work. Such a test is provided by a suitable notational system with an articulate set of characters and of relative positions for them. For texts, scores, and perhaps plans, the test is correctness of spelling in this notation; for buildings and performances, the test is compliance with what is correctly spelled. Authority for a notation must be found in an antecedent classification of objects or events into works that cuts across, or admits of a legitimate projection that cuts across, classification by history of production; but definitive identification of works, fully freed from history of production, is achieved only when a notation is established. The allographic art has won its emancipation not by proclamation but by notation.

Arthur Danto

Transfiguration of the Commonplace

Arthur Danto *is a professor of philosophy at Columbia University in New York and the author of many books on a wide range of subjects, from the theory of knowledge and the philosophy of history to Oriental philosophy and the philosophy of Jean-Paul Sartre. He is currently the award-winning art critic of* The Nation.

*T*here are doubtless works of art, even great works of art, which have material counterparts that are beautiful, and they are beautiful in ways in which certain natural objects would be counted as beautiful—gemstones, birds, sunsets—things to which persons of any degree of aesthetic sensitivity might spontaneously respond. Perhaps this is dangerous to suppose: sailors might respond to sunsets only in terms of what they foretell of coming weather; farmers might be indifferent to flowers they tramp on; there may be no objects to which everyone must respond that can be offered as paradigm cases. Nevertheless, let us suppose a group of people who do in fact respond to just the things we would in fact offer as paradigms: to fields of daffodils, to minerals, to peacocks, to glowing irridescent things that appear to house their own light and elicit from these people, as they might from us, the almost involuntary expression "How beautiful!" They would partition off beautiful things just as we would. Except these people happen to be "barbarians," lacking a concept of art. Now we may suppose these barbarians would respond to certain works of art as well as to natural objects just as we would—but they would do so only to those works of art whose material counterparts are beautiful, simply because they see works of art as we would see those material counterparts, as *beautiful things*: such as the rose-windows of Chartres, or thirteenth-century stained glass generally; certain works in enamel; confections wrought by Grecian goldsmiths; the saltcellar of Cellini; the sorts of things collected by the Medici and the later Habsburgs—cameos, ornaments, precious and semiprecious stones, things in lace and filigree; things luminous and airy, possession of which would be like possessing a piece of the moon when that was thought to be a pure radiance rather than a ranch of rocks. There is some deep reason, I am certain, why these things attract, but I shall forgo any Jungian rhapsodizing.

There is little doubt why the old masters warm the heart. It is because they capture the sort of inner light that true gems possess: their paintings *have* a light in addition to whatever light they show. Daubers may manage to show light, but their paintings have only the luminosity of mud. My personal criterion of great painting has only to do with this mystery of light, but I wonder how many of the great paintings of the world would be seen that way, in possession of this curious grace, if they were perceived solely as we might perceive their material counterparts: would their material counterparts have light, granted that they might not show any? Think of some great drawing, and then imagine it as seen by you when seized by a kind of pictorial dyslexia, hence as so many splotches and smudges and scratches and puddles. It would be to look at those drawings perhaps as the theory of formalism would enjoin us always to look at everything artistic. But to the degree that the imperative makes sense, the beauty of the work may vanish when the work is reduced to its material counterpart, or replaced by it as a princess by a changeling. Indeed, the demand that the beauty of the work be identical with the beauty of the material counterpart is virtually a definition of barbaric taste, magnificently exemplified in the goldwork of the Scythians. But a work with a beautiful material counterpart could just be gaudy as a work.

Imagine now our sensitive barbarians sweeping across the civilized world, conquering and destroying like Huns. As barbarians reserve the fairest maidens for their violent beds, we may imagine these sparing for their curious delectation just those works of art which happen to have beautiful material counterparts. Some paintings, certainly, will survive. Those with lots of goldleaf will certainly do so, and certain icons with highly ornamented frames. Or paintings where the colors have a kind of hard mineral brilliance, as in Crivelli or perhaps Mantegna. But how many Rembrandts would make it through under this criterion, how many Watteaus or Chardins or Picassos? Appreciation of these requires them to be perceived first as artworks, and hence presupposes availability of the concept we are disallowing the subjects of this Gedankenexperiment. It is not that aesthetics is irrelevant to art, but that the relationship between the artwork and its material counterpart must be gotten right for aesthetics to have any bearing, and though there may be an innate aesthetic sense, the cognitive apparatus required for it to come into play cannot itself be considered innate.

Let us consider some remarkable paintings by Roy Lichtenstein, his *Brushstroke* paintings of the late 1960s. These are paintings *of* brushstrokes, and one who is aware of the role that brushstrokes played in Abstract Expressionism in the 1950s has to see Lichtenstein's paintings as comments upon that movement. The brushstroke lay at the logical intersection of two concerns with paint. The first concern was with the physicality of paint itself, as a substance out of which paintings had always been made but which was somehow disguised by painters, who sublated it in favor of some subject. Returning to the physicality of painting was somewhat in the spirit of a modernist revulsion against the Victorian suppression of the flesh, as in D.H. Lawrence, who came with a kind of prophetic urgency to announce that we *are* flesh in just the way in which the Abstract Expressionist wished to announce that paintings *are* paint. So he used it thickly, and eschewed the transfigurations of it which images and subjects always induced: substance and subject were one. Since paint was the subject, an artist was a painter and the basic artistic action was painting (not copying, imitating, representing, stating, but painting). The artist, as in the description by Harold Rosenberg, uses the canvas as an arena; he makes upon it a swipe of painting which means nothing ulterior and is at most what it is about. It is of course true that painting is an action, but so is sketching, and so too are copying, representing, and the like. But this was a puritanical movement, concerned with the most basic artistic action there is; and while representing and copying and the rest all entailed something like painting, painting entailed none of these, and so was fundamental. Just think of what sort of metaphysics one has to have internalized in order to want to "get down to basics": it is a metaphysics of basics and nonbasics, complicated by a moral attitude that only the basics matter, everything else being hypocrisy. A straight line, one would think, would be basic in some deep geometrical sense, but lines are too easily seen as generating forms and hence as having a representational role. So the thing was to use strokes of paint, heavy and fat, laid down with as big a brush as one could manage in as large a sweep as one could execute, a stroke so consummatory that the question of what one was doing through the stroke could hardly arise: there was no way of getting the stroke to form part of an image, it stood alone, it was what it was. (De Kooning's contribution, incidentally, may in part have been that even these wildly anarchistic strokes, which seemed to be unin-tegrable into a representational structure, could in fact be regimented to form images of—of all things—women. Not Venuses and Madonnas or Mme. Renoirs, but paint-ladies of an almost ferocious character, who seem to resent having been given existence.)

The entity that concentrated and emblemized this complex of attitudes was the drip: drips acquired a kind of mystical exaltation of status in the 1950s, and it is easy to see why. In an earlier period, a drip would be an accident or a blemish, a sign of ineptitude (an attitude charmingly reinvented by the "masters" of subway graffiti, who have assistants whose purpose is to wipe drips away, the masters having contempt for those who allow the paint to follow a life of its own, which is exactly the inverse of the attitude of the 1950s painter). A drip is a violation of artistic will and has no possibility of a representational function, and so, when one occurs, it immediately disfigures a picture—as a typographical error disfigures a text— especially when it is the function of the medium to disguise itself in favor of what it means to show. There traditionally had been a complicity between artist and spectator, in which the latter was to disregard the paint and gape (say) at the Transfiguration, while the artist, on his side, worked to make it an honest possibility for the spectator to do this by making the paint as inconspicuous as possible. (There are exceptions, of course: Rembrandt and Valesquez are stunning masters of pigmentational accidentality, and Tintoretto refused to cooperate.) The drip, meanwhile, calls attention insistently to paint as paint. So in the tradition just alluded to, drips would have had the role that static does in the transmission of music, supposing it to be the role of acoustical engineering to make the medium between the source of music and the ear of the listener as transparent as the physics allows. Hence someone who wanted to call attention to the transcriptional aspect of contemporary audition would celebrate static as a mark of integrity, to be heard rather than listened through. Drips then are monuments to accident, spontaneity, giving the paint its own life, so much so that it could almost be supposed that the function of painting was to provide an occasion for drips; and Pollock was himself celebrated for having discovered the drip, which at the time was regarded as on a par with Columbus' discovery of America or Freud's of the unconscious.

More important, the drip itself is possible only when paint itself is fluid, so it not merely underwrites the way paint must be but the way in which it is put on canvas: the dabs of paste laid on with a brush and systematically diluted with medium give way to the battery of paint cans and the dipstick, as the canvas itself describes a rotation through ninety degrees from its vertical position on the easel to its horizontal position of the floor, which the painter crouches over like a frog-god. But the drip is also evidence for the urgency of the painting act, of pure speed and passion, as the artist swings loops and eccentric arabesques across the surface, sending up showers and explosions of spatters. And since he merely executed the will of the paint *to be itself*, the artist had nothing of his own to say. This went with that studied brutishness of the Dumb Artist exemplified over and over again in the artworld of the time by really quite intelligent men and women who pretended to a kind of autism, and went around in clothes so splashed with paint that the very costume was an advertisement for the closeness between the artist and his work. The bluejean and workshoe—so distant from the velour jacket and beret of the time of Whistler—connoted a kind of proletarian honesty and down-to-earthness. In any case, the drip also makes an appearance in Lichtenstein's paintings, along with the brushstrokes. The paintings show those ropy, fat, incarnated spontaneities of brushstrokes and drips, and would be recognizable as such to anyone familiar with the high period of Tenth Street Art. Their iconography is patent, and I have dwelt upon it at length because it is absolutely important to understand the subject if we are to "appreciate" the way in which it is treated.

The first thing we must note about Lichenstein's paintings is that *they* have none of the properties associated with what they are of. One would traditionally have expected this as a matter of course, since paintings of landscapes seldom have the properties of what they show, but it is somewhat remarkable here through the fact that these are paintings of painting. These, for example, show brushstrokes but do not consist, in their own right, of brushstrokes, and for just the reason the spectator must grasp the discrepancies between what is shown and the way in which it is shown, surface and subject being virtually antonymic. The brushstrokes are shown in a way that is inconsistent with what they are in further ways still: they are imprisoned in heavy black outlines, as in Leger's work or, better, as in a child's coloring book. But the brushstrokes these paintings are about were not filled into preexisting boundaries; they were densely swept across the canvas in a single impulsive gesture, defining their own boundaries. By contrast with the free and liberated spirit with which those strokes emerged onto their canvases, these strokes are shown almost mechanically, almost as though printed onto Lichenstein's canvases; and indeed Lichenstein uses the Ben Day dots of mechanical reproduction processes. So the canvases look like mechanical representations of vital gestures.

But there is another level still, which we ascend to when we realize that the dots were not printed but painted in, each one deposited onto the surface by hands: so we have artistic representations of mechanical processes. The monotony of the process of painting these in was somewhat mitigated through the fact that Lichtenstein used a lot of students from his classes at Rutgers, and again, I think, the knowledge of this history has to be taken as a comment upon the ridiculously heroized view of The Artist in the period when brushstrokes meant the opposite of what *this* mode of representing them shows. The interposition of the Ben Day dot has a profound symbolism of its own, inasmuch as it encodes the manner in which we perceive the major events of our time, through the wine-service photograph and the television screen; the depiction of the victims of the Vietnam war takes on an added dimension of horror when the mechanical mode of depiction is incorporated as part of the image, for our experiences are modulated through the medium which has indeed, in Mac-Luhan's slogan, come to be part, at least, of the message. The brushstrokes of the masters of the 1950s were meant not to represent anything, simply to be: fresh created realities. And Lichtenstein has treated them as artists have always treated reality, namely as something to put into works of art. Thus victimized, these poor deflated swags stand like specimens of something once vital, in *representational* works that belie at every point the intentions of those painters whose life was defined by squeezing paint out like hoses gone mad. These paintings are a minor victory in the battle with reality. If the canvas is indeed the arena in which the battle goes on, it has been lost to representation in the canvases of Lichtenstein.

I have dwelt at such length upon Lichtenstein's paintings in part because they are so rich in their utilization of artistic theory: they are about theories they also reject, and they internalize theories it is required that anyone who may appreciate them must understand,

and they allude to yet further theories, ignorance of which impoverishes one's appreciation of these works. What point could there be, for instance, to the dots, were someone unaware of the role dots play in mechanical reproduction and to the role of mechanical reproduction in the life of our culture? The paintings are points of intersection of so many strands in contemporary culture that it is not only difficult to imagine what some stranger to our culture would make of them, but, consistent with the form of artistic experimentation that has characterized my analysis throughout, it is difficult to see what works exactly like these but painted, suppose, in the 1860s would have meant. And my argument has been that, whatever we are to say about aesthetic responses, it is possible to imagine that works with a common material counterpart elicit very different responses. *These* paintings are deeply theoretic works, self-conscious to such a degree that it is difficult to know how much of the material correlate must be reckoned in as part of the artwork; so self-conscious are they, indeed, that they almost exemplify a Hegelian ideal in which matter is transfigured into spirit, in this case there being hardly an element of the material counterpart which may not be a candidate for an element in the artwork itself. I shall return to a proper analysis of this subsequently, but for the present I mean only to stress that whatever the counterfactual nineteenth-century counterparts to the Lichtenstein paintings may have been about, they could not have been about what the Lichtenstein's are about. Even if they were in some mad way about brushstrokes, the brushstrokes they were about would not have connoted a set of associations only available to those who had known about the dense artistic controversies of the 1950s. Of course, those paintings could have been a kind of crystal ball through which the art of the future might be glimpsed, but what could anyone have made of what they say there?

I am trying to state that the "aesthetic object" is not some eternally fixed Platonic entity, a joy forever beyond time, space and history, eternally there for the rapt appreciation of connoisseurs. It is not just that appreciation is a function of the cognitive location of the aesthete, but that the aesthetic qualities of the work are a function of their own historical identity, so that one may have to revise utterly one's assessment of a work in the light of what one comes to know about it; it may not even be the work one thought it was in the light of wrong historical information. . . .

. . . You cannot imagine someone saying that the Etruscans were the first to have typewriter ribbons, not even if you find some carbon stretch of silk ribbon at Cervetri, for that cannot have been a typewriter ribbon, not even if found wrapped round some bronze wheels that look like the spools in a bronze age typewriter, for the whole system has to be there at once: paper, metal, keys, and so on. Some while ago a cache of Da Vinci manuscripts was found which excited cartoonists to make drawings in the Da Vincian style of such things as lightbulbs and electric sockets, like a Renaissance form of the sorts of things we see in drawings by Claes Oldenberg. This is a parody of the idea we have of the genius "ahead of his time," for there are certain ways in which nobody can be ahead of his time: a notched bronze wheel exactly like a bicycle sprocket found in excavations in Tibet could not have been a precocious bicycle sprocket, whatever its identity as an artifact. And something like this is true of artworks as well: you can certainly have objects—material counterparts—at any time in which it was technically possible for them to have come into existence; but the works, connected with the material counterparts in ways we have hardly begun to fathom, are referentially so interlocked into their own system of artworks and real things that it is almost impossible to think of what might be the response to the same object inserted in another time and place. A portrait painted by a Jesuit artist of the favorite concubine of the emperor of China, which used shadows to round her lovely face, was rejected by her as hideous, since she believed she was being represented as half-black and that the painting was a joke, even if, to our eyes, it might have rivaled in sensitivity the Genevra da Benci of Leonardo. A painting by one of our contemporary artists in the style of Giotto simply could not be responded to the way a Giotto could, to its "touching naivete," not unless the artist were ignorant of the history of art and in some miracle of coincident creation had reinvented a Quattrocento style. And this would be like someone who, in contrast with Menard and out of springs of invention one can hardly guess at, wrote in ignorance of the original something we might consider indiscernible from *Don Quixote*.

These are by now familiar extensions of Wölfflin's thought that not everything is possible at every time. I have reraised these points here because we now have at least this piece of theoretical apparatus to work with: if we may distinguish between the artwork and its material counterpart, then it is possible to imagine two works done at very different times—Lichtenstein's brushstroke painting of 1965 and an imaged painting exactly like it done in 1865—which share a material counterpart but which *have* to be distinctive works of art since they cannot conceivably be about the same thing. I have tried to sketch the intricate tensions between subject and surface in Lichtenstein's painting, in a partial effort to say what they consist in (they consist in part in just these tensions). It cannot be true the painting of 1865 is about what Lichtenstein's is. The question before us, accordingly, is what connection there is between the artwork in either case and the common material correlate, and this is what I wish to address myself to now. It obviously involves something I wish to address myself to now. It obviously involves something I shall term "interpretation," and it is my view that whatever appreciation may come to, it must in some sense be a function of interpretation. . . . Interpretation consists in determining the relationship between a work of art and its material counterpart. But since nothing like this is involved with mere objects, aesthetic response to works of art presupposes a cognitive process that response to those mere things does not.

Kathleen Higgins

Music, Muzak Everywhere: Is Anybody Really Listening?

Kathleen Higgins *considers the novelty of the pervasiveness of music in our lives and the capability we have of listening to any music we want on command. She also tells us what's wrong with muzak and why music as background does not as such trivialize our experience of music. Kathleen Higgins is assistant professor of philosophy at the University of Texas at Austin and specializes in music aesthetics.*

In his novel *Looking Backward*, first published in 1888, Edward Bellamy portrays society in the year 2000 as an attained Utopia. One of the utopian innovations that impresses Bellamy's time-traveling narrator is the 24-hour availability of telephone access to various music halls where performances are in progress. The effect is that anyone at any time can hear music of various sorts at home. Bellamy's narrator finds this arrangement enchanting, and he comments to his hostess,

> It appears to me, Miss Leete, . . . that if we could have devised an arrangement for providing everybody with music in their homes, perfect in quality, unlimited in quantity, suited to every mood, and beginning and ceasing at will, we should have

considered the limit of human felicity already attained, and ceased to strive for further improvements.

To us, the idea that this vision is utopian seems fantastic in itself. We can hardly believe that only a century ago, even the most musical of listeners were lucky to hear a great work of music more than once in a lifetime. But until this century, the average music lover heard what was available when it was available, and for most (except for church music) that was not very often. And unless one was the king, the music one listened to was not a matter of individual choice.

THE PERVASIVENESS OF "BACKGROUND" MUSIC

Technological developments in sound recording have revolutionized our musical lives, and the array of listening possibilities makes the dream of Bellamy's narrator seem modest. The typical American drives to and from work listening to music, hears muzak in the office, the elevator and again while shopping and dining out, and chooses to hear music during leisure hours by playing recordings, the radio, or television. Many of us exercise to music; most of us attend films that employ background music; some students study to music; and whether we like it or not, those of us who live in cities are not infrequently a musical audience just by virtue of our decision to walk down the street. Incessant music during our waking hours is a genuine and even conveniently obtainable option for most of us. If we own clock-radios, we can have music playing both as we fall asleep and as we get up in the morning.

But is this state of affairs entirely desirable? Many who are concerned with music doubt it. William Ivey, Director of the County Music Foundation, for instance, sees the pervasive presence of background music as a serious threat to our societal ability to hear music.

> With this explosure, this immersion, in recorded music, it comes as little surprise that the audience is jaded, bored, and harder and harder to "reach." Music has taken on an almost utilitarian definition: it is *for* something—for relaxing, for stimulating, for dancing, for background. Music in such a context is always something subordinate, something supportive of a mood or activity. As we, the audience, grow more and more at home with music behind our daily routines, our ability to listen hard—to focus our every nerve upon a passage or phrase—has become diminished.

Some commentators are more forceful in denouncing at least some forms of background music. In response to a talk by an executive from the Muzak Corporation, the larger purveyor of environmental music, composer Roger Reynolds remarked,

> I must say that I've had the thrilling and rare experience this morning of being *certain* about something: I am certain that Muzak is the single most reprehensible and destructive phenomenon in the history of music, precisely because it conditions the lack of discrimination, the lack of listening, in favor of the passive acceptance of hearing.

The expression "background music" has pejorative connotations to many musical people; and the comments of Ivey and Reynolds suggest some of the reasons why this is so. The term conveys to many the kind of attitude toward music that Muzak's Jane Jarvis voices when she defends her product: "We do not try to improve anybody's mind, we do not elevate. . . . We are an environmental tool of management." The term "background music" tends to inspire images either of the manipulative corporate mind-controller, or the musical ignoramus who sees music as an atmospheric extra, an additive that lends an environment an aura of class.

SHOULD MUSIC BE CONFINED TO THE CONCERT HALL?

To focus on those who employ background music with no concern for its aesthetic merit makes the case too black and white. The question is whether background music as such is deleterious to our musical sensibility and whether it *can* have aesthetic merit. I want to argue that "background music" as such is not the villain and that it can be a vehicle of aesthetic value. The pervasiveness of music does raise an aesthetic danger for us, but the subordination of music to other activities as such is not to blame.

Let's consider some of the assumptions made by critics of background music about what music listening ought to be. One questionable assumption is the idea that serious music listening requires ideal conditions approximating those of the perfectly sensitive listener in an undistracted context like the concert hall. But this paradigm of music listening is recent and aberrant in musical history. The concert hall became influential in the West only in the Baroque era (beginning around 1600), when compositions for large ensembles became popular. It was only then that the modern idea of listening for its own sake became popular. Before that the musical experience of the majority of the listening public was predominantly connected with religious liturgy. Secular music was primarily a private affair, limited to the households of royalty and the aristocracy who were able financially to support it. And even much of the music for large ensembles composed in the Baroque era was still designed for use on sacred occasions, and thus was not intended as the exclusive focus of the audience.

The image of the distraction-free concert hall as the optimum context for listening to music also misunderstands what a concert is. Even in the relatively recent period during which secular concerts have treated music as an art in its own right, concerts have not typically been occasions for tuning out the world. Instead, concerts developed as colorful social events that brought people together. The rock concert, innovative as it has been in some respects, is in the tradition of Western concerts in its emphasis on collective experience. And if the merit of concerts lay solely in their distraction-free character, they would have become outmoded some time ago. For we can have fewer distractions and hear far better listening to a record on earphones.

The attitude that only undistracted music listening has aesthetic worth, moreover, often stems from aesthetic snobbism. As John Dewey points out in *Art as Experience*, Americans have culturally too often made a sharp distinction between "serious" aesthetic concerns and their everyday lives, much to the aesthetic impoverishment of their daily experience. Dismissal of background music as inherently worthless impoverishes our experience by promoting a self-fulfilling prophecy. If we assume that we cannot have significant experience of music in most of the subordinate and distracted contexts in which we hear it, there is little chance that we will let ourselves have any significant experience.

THE VARIETIES OF MUSICAL EXPERIENCE

The testimony of music history, by contrast, shows that most musical cultures, including our own tradition, have thought differently. Two of the primary contexts in which people have traditionally encountered music are those of the religious rite and the civic ceremony. The idea that the basic function of music is to serve political and religious ends is reflected in Plato's *Republic*. There Socrates argues that music has a power over the soul that ought to be employed with calculation to stir groups of men, on various occasions, to the attitude of battle or the reflective mood of prayer. And this functional approach to music is hardly unique to Plato's Socrates. Concern that music properly reflect the order of the universe and thereby inspire harmony in the souls of the members of the community has been so prominent in the thinking of diverse cultures that it has dictated the development and the concerns of music theory in China, India, and ancient Greece, and across Europe, as well, in the context of inquiries into the nature of music appropriate to the rites of the Christian Church. The recent Western notion of "art for art's sake," furthermore, is unusual among cultural approaches to music. In the Indian tradition, for instance, music is understood to refer to emotions, and its function is to convey knowledge of the emotions represented for the purpose of liberating its audience from them. It would not even occur to the traditional Indian listener to view music as an end unto itself, to separate musical enjoyment from the serious business of spiritual development.

Thus, according to the perspective of our own tradition and several others, music's proper role is not to be the focus of unswerving conscious attention. Instead, music properly provides support for religious worship and meditation and provides the aesthetic glue for community occasions and events. Music, in other words, occupies a subordinate, background role. To say this is not to belittle music's importance or to suggest that it is dispensable. Nor is it to deny that there is some role for concentrated and exclusive musical study and attention. "Let music attain its full results," says the Confucian "Record of Music," "and there would be no dissatisfactions (in the mind) . . ."

The world's musical traditions suggest that there is no one proper role for music. Music can occupy a wide range of roles, many of which involve music in the background of other activities. And the fact that music may occupy a background role does not necessarily result in nonappreciation of the music. If we consider the specifics of our cultural listening practices, we will discover a whole range of activities that are enhanced by music and that encourage aesthetic appreciation of music at the same time. A jogger who runs to music, for example, has enough free attention to enjoy the music's structure as well as its rhythmic stimulation. In fact, the jogger may be far more engrossed in the music than in the running, especially if the music's structure is compelling. We are not surprised that many joggers prefer listening to serious works of classical music, perhaps Beethoven symphonies or sonatas, to hearing more rhythmically constant but less interesting works, such as the most monotonous rhythmic hit on the top forty. Dancing, while engaging the dancer in both social and athletic activity, does not distract from music; paying attention to the music is part of the dancing. And even music in subordinate contexts such as parties or films often engages the interest and attention of those who hear it. The fact that there is a large market for soundtracks shows that movie-goers are not ignoring the music.

THE AESTHETIC BANALITY OF MUZAK

The critics of background music have tended to focus on environmental music in public places, muzak (in its generic sense) in particular, and this has led to the mistaken view that background music and the subordination of music as such is a threat to our musical sensitivity. But environmental music is a special case that should be considered in its own right. Muzak does present an offense, if not a danger, to musical sensitivity, and this offense stems directly from the specific aims and practices involved in environmental music.

In order to see why, let us consider the use of environmental music in the workplace, for example. The overt purpose of such music is to enhance productivity, and the basic means to this end is the manipulation of the workers' energy level. The Muzak Corporation, for instance, uses a number of basic parameters to determine the relative amount of "stimulus" that a particular piece of music will provide. Muzak is then arranged into programs that provide a gradual rise in stimulus, with the high points designed to occur at times of day when energy levels are likely to be the lowest. The stimulation that the music provides is designed to occur on a subliminal level. "The sound level of Muzak should never be as high as the noise level in the room," comments Jane Jarvis. "If . . . all of a sudden right out of nowhere, a selection comes into someone's stream of consciousness and they *hear* it, then you know it's out of place."

These facts about muzak reveal the substance behind the criticism that it promotes unmusical sensibilities. Muzak is designed for nonlistening. And the nearly inaudible volume level is only one feature that prevents active musical enjoyment. More crucially, muzak's aims are in conflict with the basic aim of art music in our tradition. Since the development of tonality and functional harmony, deliberate manipulation of chord progressions to enhance their tendencies toward resolution, the very structure of Western music has been predominantly organized to emphasize the development of tensions and their ultimate resolutions. Tension and resolution are fundamental to what we attend to in our music. Furthermore, many critics, including Leonard B. Meyer, John Dewey, and Suzanne Langer, have argued that focus on relative tension and relaxation is not only basic to the aims of our tonal framework, but also fundamental to music appreciation generally, not only in our tradition but in others as well. Langer, for instance, argues that music so intrinsically parallels the tension build-up and resolution that is basic to our daily experience in time that music serves us as an "image of time."

> The phenomena that fill time are *tensions*—physical, emotional, or intellectual. Time exists for us because we undergo tensions and their resolutions. Their peculiar building-up, and their ways of breaking or diminishing or merging into longer and greater tensions, make for a vast variety of temporal forms. . . . The direct experience of passage . . . is the model for the virtual time created in music. There we have its image, completely articulated and pure; every kind of tension transformed into musical tension.

Muzak violates this demand for an artistic treatment of tension and resolution. The expressed aim of muzak is to utilize music to build programs of controlled, mono-directional increase of stimulus. Specific pieces of music are treated as veritable stimulus blocks; and the kinds of pieces that serve most effectively for this purpose are those with minimal internal variation in musical tension levels. Even if someone were to listen actively to muzak programs, therefore, he or she would find them utterly lacking in musical interest.

THE PRIVATIZATION OF MUSICAL EXPERIENCE AND ITS DANGERS

Those who criticize environmental music as bland and unmusical have a point. But the larger problem is not our cultural willingness to use music in background or subordinate functions. The problem is our willingness to accept music of low quality as standard in our ordinary, public experience. And it seems that most of us have resigned ourselves to the triviality of public background music. But then, if we prefer music of higher quality, we can go home and avail ourselves of another blessing of technology, the means for privately enjoying music of our own choosing.

The expanding availability of inexpensive record, compact disc, and tape playing equipment has made personally selected music virtually unlimited. The pursuit of musical interest, accordingly, is an individual affair. The person who wants to hear a particular piece of music or the music of a certain performer can do so by obtaining a record or tape and playing it for personal enjoyment. Radio music, too, at one time the collective recreation of whole families, is now most commonly a leisure activity of an isolated individual who pushes buttons or turns dials in conformity to his or her own whims.

We tend to view listening as a solitary activity. And we do so not only because technology allows private selection, but also because our public music lacks genuine social dimension. Any music that we hear in a public place is usually either (1) a byproduct of some other listener's self-assertion when he walks or drives past us; or (2) a manipulative appeal to us to do something that we do as decidedly individual agents—to work, to eat faster, or to spend money. In both situations, we perceive the music as something associated with the private pursuits of an individual. The music that intrudes on us as passers-by is most often heard as somebody else's noise. The environmental music that is designed to semi-consciously influence us encourages us to go about our personal business as worker or consumer.

I think that the privatization of musical listening, our growing tendency to consider music listening a solo activity, represents a cultural loss. One of the characteristics of music that has been fundamental to the high value that has cross-culturally been placed upon it is its power to facilitate intersubjective experience, to move many people to feel deeply something approximating the same emotion or spiritual state. The recurrent refrain that music is the language of the emotions reflects the fact that music has consistently provided human communities (of whatever size) with a means of breaking down individual differences and of making human solidarity seem basic to the way we understand what it means to be a human being.

This character of music has been exploited for propagandistic purposes, as Platonic and Confucian literature reflect; and for this reason the privatization of music might be said to exert a positive influence on musical sensitivity by making music seem less intrinsically bound up with the propaganda of some authority or party. But the privatization of musical listening, to the extent that it has led us to lose sight of the capacity of music to be intersubjectively moving has impoverished our musical experience. Solo listening may have many merits; it no doubt facilitates the acquisition of musical knowledge for some and encourages a musical appetite in many. But the power of music that has inspired both ecstatic comment and the concern of statesmen throughout world history fully exhibits itself only in a social context. Music is awesome because it is able to draw individual listeners outside themselves and their private concerns and into a state of intersubjective enchantment.

Awe seems rare in the musical lives of most contemporary Americans, and this fact in itself is the most important symptom of a basic problem in the way we use music. Despite our complicated technology and our diversified patterns of listening practices, we no longer see music as special. We accept bad music as normal experience, and we tend to forget that music is a vital, even magical phenomenon that can be actively experienced and intersubjectively enjoyed. The deficiencies in our orientation toward music are not the consequence of background music, but rather, bad background music is a symptom of our deficiencies in music appreciation. The solution does not depend on the partial or complete elimination of background music. It depends instead on more creative imagination and aesthetic sensitivity in American life, and on our subordinating good music—rather than merely "effective" music— to our daily activities.

Background music itself can be instrumental in the enhancement of musical intersubjectivity. As Hugh Cole remarks in his discussion of background music, "We should remain awake to the possibility that out of areas of what elitists regard as low-grade musical activity something new and interesting may emerge—as it is so often has in the past." But innovative uses of music should be considered in other musical contexts as well. The pervasiveness of background music is not an inherently pernicious phenomenon. But our musical lives will be lacking unless we insist on more inherently aesthetic and social uses of music, good music that refuses to recede into the background of our lives.

Tom Wolfe

The Worship of Art: Notes on the New God

Tom Wolfe *is one of the founders of "the new journalism" and the author of such notorious works as* The Cool-Aide Acid Test. *He is also a rogue art critic, infuriating the art world and the architecture world, respectively, with his books* The Painted Word *and* From Bauhaus to Our House. *In the following essay, he suggests that art has become something of a new secular religion.*

Let me tell you about the night the Vatican art show opened at the Metropolitan Museum of Art in New York. The scene was the Temple of Dendur, an enormous architectural mummy, complete with a Lake of the Dead, underneath a glass bell at the rear of the museum. On the stone apron in front of the temple, by the lake, the museum put on a formal dinner for 360 souls, including the wife of the President of the United States, the usual philanthropic dowagers and corporate art patrons, a few catered names, such as Prince Albert of Monaco and Henry Kissinger, and many well-known members of the New York art world. But since this was, after all, an exhibition of the Vatican art collection, it was necessary to include some Roman Catholics. Cardinal Cooke, Vatican emissaries, prominent New York Catholic laymen, Knights of Malta—there they were, devout Christians at a New York art world event. The culturati and the Christians were arranged at the tables like Arapaho beads; one culturatus, one Christian, one culturatus, one Christian, one culturatus, one Christian, one culturatus, one Christian.

Gamely, the guests tried all the conventional New York conversation openers—real estate prices, friends who have been mugged recently, well-known people whose children have been arrested on drug charges, Brits, live-in help, the dishonesty of helipad contractors, everything short of the desperately trite subjects used in the rest of the country, namely the weather and front-wheel drive. Nothing worked. There were dreadful lulls during which there was no sound at all in that antique churchyard except for the ping of hotel silver on earthenware plates echoing off the tombstone facade of the temple.

Shortly before dessert, I happened to be out in the museum's main lobby when two Manhattan art dealers appeared in their tuxedos, shaking their heads.

One aid to the other: "Who are these *unbelievable people?*"

But of course! It seemed not only *outré* to have these . . . these . . . these . . . these *religious types* at an art event, it seemed sacrilegious. The culturati were being forced to rub shoulders with heathens. That was the way it hit them. For today art—not religion—is the religion of the educated classes. Today educated people look upon traditional religious ties— Catholic, Episcopal, Presbyterian, Methodist, Baptist, Jewish—as matters of social pedigree. It is only art that they look upon religiously.

When I say that art is the religion of the educated classes, I am careful not to use the word in the merely metaphorical way people do when they say someone is religious about sticking to a diet or training for a sport. I am not using "religion" as a synonym for "enthusiasm." I am referring specifically to what Max Weber identified as the objective functions of a religion: the abnegation or rejection of the world and the legitimation of wealth. . . .

Today there are few new religions that appeal to educated people—Scientology, Arica, Synanon, and some neo-Hindu, neo-Buddhist, and neo-Christian groups—but their success has been limited. The far more common way to reject the world, in our time, is through art. I'm sure you're familiar with it. You're on the subway during the morning rush hour, in one of those cars that is nothing but a can of meat on wheels, jammed in shank to flank and haunch to paunch and elbow to rib with people who talk to themselves and shout obscenities into the void and click their teeth and roll back their upper lips to reveal their purple gums, and their is nothing you can do about it. You can't budge. Coffee, adrenaline, and rogue hate are squirting through your every duct and every vein, and just when you're beginning to wonder how any mortal can possibly stand it, you look around and you see a young woman seated serenely in what seems to be a perfect pink cocoon of peace, untouched, unthreatened, by the growling mob around her. Her eyes are lowered. In her lap, invariably, is a book. If you look closely, you will see that this book is by Rimbaud, or Rilke, or Baudelaire, or Kafka, or Gabriel García Marquez, author of *One Hundred Years of Solitude*. And as soon as you see this vision, you understand the conviction that creates the inviolable aura around her: "I may be forced into this rat race, this squalid human stew, but I do not have to be *of* it. I inhabit a universe that is finer. I can reject all this." You can envision her apartment immediately. There is a mattress on top of a flush door supported by bricks. There's a window curtained in monk's cloth. There's a hand-thrown pot with a few blue cornflowers in it. There are some Paul Klee and Modigliani prints on the wall and a poster from the Acquavella Galleries' Matisse show. "I don't need your Louis Bourbon bergères and your fabric-covered walls. I reject your whole Parish-Hadley world—through art."

And what about the legitimation of wealth? It wasn't so long ago that Americans of great wealth routinely gave 10 percent of their income to the church. The practice of tithing was a certification of worthiness on earth and an option on heaven. Today the custom is to give the money to the arts. When Mrs. E. Parmalee Prentice, daughter of John D. Rockefeller Sr. and owner of two adjoining mansions on East Fifty-third Street, just off Fifth Avenue, died in 1962, she did not leave these holdings, worth about $5 million, to her church. She left them to the Museum of Modern Art for the building of a new wing. Nobody's eyebrows arched. By 1962, it would have been more remarkable if a bequest of that size had gone to a religion of the old-fashioned sort. . . .

Today, what American corporation would support a religion? Most would look upon any such thing as sheer madness. So what does a corporation do when the time comes to pray in public? It supports the arts. I don't need to recite figures. Just think of the money raised since the 1950s for the gigantic cultural complexes—Lincoln Center, Kennedy Center, the Chandler Pavillion, the Woodruff Arts Center—that have become *de rigueur* for the modern American metropolis. What are they? Why, they are St. Patrick's, St. Mary's, Washington National, Holy Cross: the American cathedrals of the late twentieth century.

We are talking here about the legitimation of wealth. The worse odor a corporation is in, the more likely it is to support the arts, and the more likely it is to make sure everybody knows it. The energy crisis, to use an antique term from the 1970s, was the greatest bonanza in the Public Broadcasting Service's history. The more loudly they were assailed as exploiters and profiteers, the more earnestly the oil companies poured money into PBS's cultural programming. Every broadcast seemed to end with a discreet notice on the screen saying: "This program was made possible by a grant from Exxon," or perhaps Mobil, or ARCO. . . .

As you can imagine, this state of affairs has greatly magnified the influence of the art world. In size, that world has never been anything more than a village. In the United States, fashions in art are determined by no more than 3,000 people, at least 2,950 of whom live in Manhattan. I can't think of a single influential critic today. "The gallery-going public" has never had any influence at all—so we are left with certain dealers, curators, and artists. No longer do they have the servant-like role of catering to or glorifying the client. Their role today is to save him. They have become a form of clergy—or clerisy, to use an old word for secular souls who take on clerical duties.

In this age of art clerisy, the client is in no position to say what will save him. He is in no position to do anything at all except come forward with the money if he wants salvation and legitimation.

Today large corporations routinely hire curators from the art village to buy art on their behalf. It is not a mere play on words to call these people curates, comparable to the Catholic priests who at one time were attached to wealthy European families to conduct daily masses on their estates. The corporations set limits on the curator's budgets and reserve the right to veto their choices. But they seldom do, since the entire purpose of a corporate art program is legitimation of wealth through a spiritually correct investment in art. The personal tastes of the executives, employees, clients, or customers could scarcely matter less. . . .

If employees go so far as to protest a particular style, a corporation will usually switch to another one. Corporations are not eager to annoy their workers. But at the same time, to spend money on the sort of realistic or symbolic work employees might actually enjoy would be pointless. The point is to be acclaimed for "support of the arts," a phrase which applies only to the purchase of works certified by the curates of the art village. This was quite openly the aim of the Bank of America when it hired a curator in 1979 and began buying works of art at the rate of 1,000 a year. The bank felt that its corporate image was suffering because it was not among those firms receiving "credit for art support."

The credit must come from the art clerisy. It is for this reason that IBM, for example, has displayed Michael Heizer's *Levitated Mass* at its outdoor plaza at Madison Avenue and Fifty-sixth Street. The piece is a 25-foot-by-16-foot metal tank containing water and a slab of granite. It is meaningless in terms of IBM, its executives, its employees, its customers, and the thousands of people who walk past the plaza every day. Far from being a shortcoming, that is part of *Levitated Mass's* exemplary success as a spiritual object.

It is precisely in this area—public sculpture—that the religion of art currently makes its richest contribution to the human comedy. . . .

. . . The Rockefeller's Number One Chase Manhattan Plaza was the first glass skyscraper on Wall Street. Out front, on a bare Bauhaus-style apron, the so-called plaza, was installed a sculpture by Jean Dubuffet. It is made of concrete and appears to be four toadstools fused into a gelatinous mass with black lines running up the sides. The title is *Group of Four Trees*. Not even *Group of Four Rockefellers*. After all, there *were* four at the time: David, John D. III, Nelson, and Laurance. But the piece has absolutely nothing to say about the glory or even the existence of the Rockefellers, Wall Street, Chase Manhattan Bank, American business, or the building it stands in front of. Instead, it proclaims the glory of contemporary art. It fulfills the new purpose of public sculpture, which is the legitimation of wealth through the new religion of the educated classes.

Six years after Number One Chase Manhattan Plaza was built, the Marine Midland Bank building went up a block away. It is another glass skyscraper with a mean little Bauhaus-style apron out front, and on this apron was placed a red cube resting on one point by Isamu Noguchi. Through the cube (a rhombohedron, strictly speaking) runs a cylindrical hole. One day I looked through that hole, expecting at the very least that my vision would be led toward the board room, where a man wearing a hand-worsted suit, and with thinning, combed-back hair, would be standing, his forefinger raised, thundering about broker loan rates. Instead what I saw was a woman who appeared to be part of the stenographic pool probing the auditory meatus of her left ear with a Q-Tip. So what is it, this red cube by Noguchi? Why, nothing more than homage to contemporary art, the new form of praying in public. . . .

If people want to place Turds in the Plazas as a form of religious offering of prayer, and they own the plazas, there isn't much anybody else can do about it. But what happens when they use public money, tax money, to do the same thing on plazas owned by the public? At that point you're in for a glorious farce. . . .

In 1976, the city of Hartford decided to reinforce its reputation as the Athens of lower central midwestern New England by having an important piece of sculpture installed downtown. It followed what is by now the usual procedure, which is to turn the choice over to a panel of "experts" in the field—i.e., the clerisy, in this case, six curators, critics, and academicians, three of them chosen by the National Endowment for the Arts, which put up half the money. So one day in 1978 a man named Carl Andre arrived in Hartford with thirty-six rocks. Not carved stones, not even polished boluses of the Henry Moore sort—rocks. He put them on the ground in a triangle, like bowling pins. Then he presented the city council with a bill for $87,000. Nonplussed and, soon enough, furious, the citizenry hooted and jeered and called the city council members imbeciles while the council members alternately hit the sides of their heads with their hands and made imaginary snowballs. Nevertheless, they approved payment, and the rocks—entitled *Stone Field*—are still there.

One day in 1981, the Civil Service workers in the new Javits Federal Building in Manhattan went outside to the little plaza in front of the building at lunchtime to do the usual, which was to have their tuna puffs and diet Shastas, and there, running through the middle of it, was a wall of black steel twelve feet high and half a city block long. Nonplussed and, soon enough, furious, 1,300 of them drew up a petition asking the GSA to remove it, only to be informed that this was, in fact, a major work of art, entitled *Tilted Arc*, by a famous American sculptor named Richard Serra. Serra did not help things measurably by explaining that he was "redefining the space" for the poor Civil Service lifers and helping to wean them away from the false values "created by advertising and corporations." Was it his fault if "it offends people to have their preconceptions of reality changed"? This seventy-three-ton gesture of homage to contemporary art remains in place.

The public sees nothing, absolutely nothing, in these stone fields, tilted arcs, and Instant Stonehenges, because it was never meant to. The public is looking at the arena of the new religion of the educated classes. At this point one might well ask what the clerisy itself sees in them, a question that would plunge us into doctrines as abstruse as any that engaged the medieval Scholastics. Andre's *Stone Field*, for example, was created to illustrate three devout theories concerning the nature of sculpture. One, a sculpture should not be placed upon that bourgeois device, the pedestal, which seeks to elevate it about the people. (Therefore, the rocks are on the ground.) Two, a sculpture should "express its gravity." (And what expresses gravity better than rocks lying on the ground?) Three, a sculpture should not be that piece of bourgeois pretentiousness, the "picture in the air" (such as the statues of Lee and Duke); it should force the viewer to confront its "object-ness." (You want object-ness? Take a look at a plain rock! Take a look at thirty-six rocks!). . . .

The public is nonplussed and, soon enough, becomes furious—and also uneasy. After all, if understanding such arcana is the hallmark of the educated classes today, and you find yourself absolutely baffled, what does that say about your level of cultivation? Since 1975, attendance at museums of art in the United States has risen from 42 million to 60 million people per year. Why? In 1980 the Hirshhorn Museum did a survey of people who came to the museum over a seven-month period. I find the results fascinating. Thirty-six percent said they had come to learn about contemporary art. Thirty-two percent said they had come to learn about a particular contemporary artist. Thirteen percent came on tours. Only 15 percent said they were there for what was once the conventional goal of museumgoers: to enjoy the pictures and sculptures. The conventional goal of museumgoers today is something quite different. Today they are there to learn—and to see the light. At the Hirshhorn, the people who were interviewed in the survey said such things as: "I know this is great art, and now I feel so unintelligent." And : "After coming to this museum, I now feel so much better about art and so much worse about me."

In other words: "I believe, O Lord, but I am unworthy! Reveal to me Thy mysteries!"

Part
SIX

Justice and Responsibility

18

Am I Free to Choose What I Do?

*T*here is perhaps no topic in philosophy that inspires more public debate than the question of freedom and responsibility. Take the case of a criminal who was raised in a slum, surrounded by poverty, crime, and drugs. He went to a school in which the most academic activity was writing graffiti (most of it misspelled) on walls. He was abused as a child, beaten up as a teenager, and harrassed as a young adult. His act of violence, his defense attorney argues, was nothing but the product of his environment and his up-bringing. It is society's fault; he is not to blame. The prosecutor is incensed. Thousands of children grow up in similar circumstances, she argues, and they do not turn to crime. A person is free and responsible for what he or she does, she concludes, and crime must be paid for. In another case, a young would-be assassin is said to be "disturbed." He was taking drugs; he had delusions; he did not know right from wrong. His defense attorney also argues that he is not responsible. He had no choice in what he did. The public is enraged. How could a person not be responsible for an act that was planned in advance? And so the argument goes, on the front pages of our newspapers.

Freedom and responsibility go hand in hand. We hold people responsible because we believe that they are free to act or not act in certain ways. People have choices; they make decisions. They act on the basis of knowledge and in accordance with certain values. They are not robots. It is particularly disturbing, therefore, to realize that some of our basic beliefs about the universe contradict this treasured supposition. Once upon a time, people believed (much more than we do today) in **fate**—the idea that everything that happens is somehow ordained to happen beforehand. For example, according to Sophocles' great tragedy, Oedipus was fated to kill his father and marry his mother, and despite all efforts to make sure that this would never happen, it did indeed happen. (It is worth noting that Oedipus still held himself responsible for what he had done.) Saint Augustine worried how it was possible for us to be free if God, in his omniscience, knew in advance everything that we would do. He may have given us "free will," but it doesn't make much sense to speak of freedom of choice if what you were going to do was already known ahead of time (even if *you* didn't know it).

Modern science presents us with an even more formidable doubt about freedom. One of our basic beliefs about the world is that every event can be explained. Science may not yet have an explanation for a certain phenomenon because it may be very complicated. But we do not doubt that someday, with enough knowledge, we will explain it. And even if we cannot explain some strange event, we do not doubt that there is an explanation—even if we never find it out. This thesis is called **determinism**, which can be summarized as the principle that every event has a cause. But human actions and decisions are events, and if they, too, are caused or "determined" to be one way rather than another, then a very real question is whether or not it makes any sense to say that we are free to make our own decisions. We may only *seem* to be doing so, but this experience of making a decision, like our action itself, may be nothing but the result of a long sequence of causes and conditions that determine everything we do.

This is the "free will problem." It has tormented philosophers and juries for centuries, and it has practical implications that go far beyond criminal law. If we are in fact "pawns of the universe," then it not only makes no sense to hold us responsible for what we do, but what we do is just a matter of what or who controls the determining causes. It is with this in mind that Harvard psychologist and behaviorist B. F. Skinner attacks the idea of freedom and suggests that well-meaning behavioral psychologists could and should arrange a less chaotic and more civilized deterministic environment than the one we now live in. The result might be a more orderly world, but as author Anthony Burgess argues in his novel *A Clockwork Orange*, it would be a world in which something precious seems to be missing.

As science closes its explanatory grip on one realm of events after another, it would seem that determinism becomes less and less avoidable as a conclusion, but events in science itself sometimes undermine the determinist picture. In the heyday of **hard determinism** in about the eighteenth century (represented here by the French Baron d'Holbach), it made sense to think about the universe as composed of innumerable particles in causal relationship to one another, and this made the determinist thesis "hard" indeed. But twentieth century physics has overthrown this picture of "matter in motion" and replaced it with a complicated model of subatomic "particles" that do not follow the classic laws of causality. Contemporary quantum theory, for instance, rejects the idea of predictable cause and effect relations at the fundamental level of reality, and without predictions and cause and effect, the determinist thesis does not have a foothold on our thinking. At the turn of the century, the great American philosopher-psychologist William James considered the strong hold of determinism on our thinking and weighed this against the more problematic thesis of **indeterminism**. He worried about the many philosophers who tried to have it both ways, accepting determinism but defending the idea that we can still be held responsible for what we do—a position he called **soft determinism**. Jean-Paul Sartre insists that, from one's own point of view, it makes no sense to believe that one's actions and decisions are determined.

In the following selections, we have included a short excerpt from Sophocles' *Oedipus Rex* and Aristotle's classic definition of voluntary action as that which is done neither out of "compulsion" nor out of ignorance. Epictetus questions what things are or are not "in our power," and Baron d'Holbach states the classic case for determinism. William James tries to evade the most problematic consequences of determinism by discussing the role of "chance" in human affairs against a background of "soft" as well as "hard" determinism. Clarence Darrow argues the most famous legal case involving the free will question. John Hospers uses the Freudian notion of the unconscious to throw into total confusion Aristotle's definition, since compelling forces are acting within us as well as on us from the outside. Skinner presents his case for behaviorist control and Burgess replies. Finally, Jean-Paul Sartre offers an **existentialist** defense of freedom, which holds that even if determinism is true, there can be no escaping the freedom and responsibility that is always ours, in every action.

Sophocles

Oedipus, King of Thebes

Sophocles *(c. 496–406 b.c.) is best known for his Oedipus trilogy. In the first of those plays, Oedipus finds out that to avoid his predicted fate—that he would murder his father and marry his mother—his parents sent him away with a shepherd, never to see them again. But as an adult, he kills a stranger on the road and marries the queen of a neighboring kingdom. The stranger turns out to have been his father and the queen his mother. In the following excerpt, Oedipus is responding to the seer Thesias, who is revealing Oedipus's tragedy to him.*

OEDIPUS: I fear mine own voice, lest it spoke a word
      Too much; whereof this man must tell me true.

JOCASTA: The man shall come.—My lord, methinks I too
      Should know what fear doth work thee this despite.

OEDIPUS: Thou shalt. When I am tossed to such an height
      Of dark foreboding, woman, when my mind
      Faceth such straits as these, where should I find
      A mightier love than thine?
             My father—thus
      I tell thee the whole tale—was Polybus,
      In Corinth King; my mother Meropê
      Of Dorian line. And I was held to be
      The proudest in Corinthia, till one day
      A thing befell: strange was it, but no way
      Meet for such wonder and such rage as mine.
      A feast it was, and some one flushed with wine
      Cried out at me that I was no true son
      Of Polybus. Oh, I was wroth! That one
      Day I kept silence, but the morrow morn
      I sought my parents, told that tale of scorn
      And claimed the truth; and they rose in their pride
      And smote the mocker. . . . Aye, they satisfied
      All my desire; yet still the cavil gnawed
      My heart, and still the story crept abroad.
             At last I rose—my father knew not, nor
      My mother—and went forth to Pytho's floor
      To ask. And God in that for which I came
      Rejected me, but round me, like a flame,
      His voice flashed other answers, things of woe,
      Terror, and desolation. I must know
      My mother's body and beget thereon
      A race no mortal eye durst look upon,
      And spill in murder mine own father's blood.
             I heard, and, hearing, straight from where I stood,
      No landmark but the stars to light my way,
      Fled, fled from the dark south where Corinth lay,

To lands far off, where never I might see
My doom of scorn fulfilled. On bitterly
I strode, and reached the region where, so saith
Thy tale, that King of Thebes was struck to death. . . .
Wife, I will tell thee true. As one in daze
I walked, till, at the crossing of three ways,
A herald, like thy tale, and o'er his head
A man behind strong horses charioted
Met me. And both would turn me from the path,
He and a thrall in front. And I in wrath
Smote him that pushed me—'twas a groom who led
The horses. Not a word the master said,
But watched, and as I passed him on the road
Down on my head his iron-branchèd goad
Stabbed. But, by heaven, he rued it! In a flash
I swung my staff and saw the old man crash
Back from his car in blood. . . . Then all of them
I slew. . . .

OEDIPUS: In what way
            Came it to thee? Was it thine own child, or
            Another's?

SHEPHERD: Nay, it never crossed my door:
            Another's.

OEDIPUS: Whose? What man, what house, of these
            About thee?

SHEPHERD: In the name of God who sees,
            Ask me no more!

OEDIPUS: If once I ask again,
            Thou diest.

SHEPHERD: From the folk of Laïus, then,
            It came.

OEDIPUS: A slave, or born of Laïus' blood?

SHEPHERD: There comes the word I dread to speak, O God!

OEDIPUS: And I to hear: yet heard it needs must be.

SHEPHERD: Know then, they said 'twas Laïus' child. But she
            Within, thy wife, best knows its fathering.

OEDIPUS: 'Twas she that gave it?

SHEPHERD: It was she, O King.

OEDIPUS: Enough!
            All will come true. . . . Thou Light, never again
            May I behold thee, I in the eyes of men
            Made naked, how from sin my being grew,
            In sin I wedded and in sin I slew!

Aristotle

Voluntary and Involuntary Action

Aristotle *(394–322 B.C.) uses Book III of his* Nicomachean Ethics *to understand the difference between voluntary and involuntary action. An excerpt follows.*

We have found that moral excellence or virtue has to do with feelings and actions. These may be voluntary or involuntary. It is only to the former that we assign praise or blame, though when the involuntary are concerned we may find ourselves ready to condone and on occasion to pity. It is clearly, then, incumbent on the student of moral philosophy to determine the limits of the voluntary and involuntary. Legislators also find such a definition useful when they are seeking to prescribe appropriate rewards and punishments.

Actions are commonly regarded as involuntary when they are performed (*a*) under compulsion, (*b*) as the result of ignorance. An act, it is thought, is done under compulsion when it originates in some external cause of such a nature that the agent or person subject to the compulsion contributes nothing to it. Such a situation is created, for example, when a sea captain is carried out of his course by a contrary wind or by men who have got him in their power. But the case is not always so clear. One might have to consider an action performed for some fine end or through fear of something worse to follow. For example, a tyrant who had a man's parents or children in his power might order him to do something dishonourable on condition that, if the man did it, their lives would be spared; otherwise not. In such cases it might be hard to say whether the actions are voluntary or not. A similar difficulty is created by the jettison of cargo in a storm. When the situation has no complications you never get a man voluntarily throwing away his property. But if it is to save the life of himself and his mates, any sensible person will do it. Such actions partake of both qualities, though they look more like voluntary than involuntary acts. For at the time they are performed they are the result of a deliberate choice between alternatives, and when an action is performed the end or object of that action is held to be the end it had at the moment of its performance. It follows that the terms 'voluntary' and 'involuntary' should be used with reference to the time when the acts were being performed. Now in the imaginary cases we have stated the acts are voluntary. For the movement of the limbs instrumental to the action originates in the agent himself, and when this is so it is in a man's own power to act or not to act. Such actions therefore are voluntary. But they are so only in the special circumstances; otherwise of course they would be involuntary. For nobody would choose to do anything of the sort purely for its own sake. Occasionally indeed the performance of such actions is held to do a man credit. This happens when he submits to some disgrace or pain as the only way of achieving some great or splendid result. But if his case is just the opposite he is blamed, for it shows a degraded nature to submit to humiliations with only a paltry object in view, or at any rate not a high one. But there are also cases which are thought to merit, I will not say praise, but condonation. An example is provided when a man does something wrong because he is afraid of torture too severe for flesh and blood to endure. Though surely there are some things which a man cannot be compelled to do—which he will rather die than do, however painful the mode of death. Such a deed is matricide; the reasons which 'compelled' Alcmaeon in Euripides' play to kill his mother carry their absurdity on the face of them. Yet it is not always easy to make up our minds what is our best course in choosing one of two alternatives—such and such an action instead of such and such another—or in facing one penalty instead of another. Still harder is it to stick to our decision when made. For, generally speaking, the consequences we expect in such imbroglios are painful, and what we are forced to do far from honourable. Then we get praised or blamed according as we succumb to the compulsion or resist it.

What class of actions, then, ought we to distinguish as 'compulsory'? It is arguable that the bare description will apply to any case where the cause of the action is found in things external to the agent when he contributes nothing to the result. But it may happen that actions, though, abstractly considered, involuntary, are deliberately chosen at a given time and in given circumstances in preference to a given alternative. In that case, their origin being in the agent, these actions must be pronounced voluntary in the particular circumstances and because they are preferred to their alternatives. In themselves they are involuntary, yet they have more of the voluntary about them, since conduct is a sequence of particular acts, and the particular things done in the circumstances we have supposed are voluntary. But when it comes to saying which of two alternative lines of action should be preferred—then difficulties arise. For the differences in particular cases are many.

If it should be argued that the pleasurable and honourable things exercise constraint upon us from without, and therefore actions performed under their influence are compulsory, it may be replied that this would make every action compulsory. For we all have some pleasurable or honourable motive in everything we do. Secondly, people acting under compulsion and against their will find it painful, whereas those whose actions are inspired by the pleasurable and the honourable find that these actions are accompanied by pleasure. In the third place it is absurd to accuse external influences instead of ourselves when we fall an easy prey to such inducements and to lay the blame for all dishonourable deeds on the seductions of pleasure, while claiming for ourselves credit for any fine thing we have done. It appears, then, that an action is compulsory only when it is caused by something external to itself which is not influenced by anything contributed by the person under compulsion.

Then there are acts done through ignorance. Any act of this nature is other than voluntary, but it is involuntary only when it causes the doer subsequent pain and regret. For a man who has been led into some action by ignorance and yet has no regrets, while he cannot be said to have been a voluntary agent—he did not know what he was doing—nevertheless cannot be said to have acted involuntarily, since he feels no compunction. We therefore draw a distinction. (*a*) When a man who has done something as a result of ignorance is sorry for it, we take it that he has acted involuntarily. (*b*) When such a man is not sorry, the case is different and we shall have to call him a 'non-voluntary' agent. For it is better that he should have a distinctive name in order to mark the distinction. Note, further, that there is evidently a difference between acting *in consequence* of ignorance and acting *in* ignorance. When a man is drunk or in passion his actions are not supposed to be the result of ignorance but of one or other of these conditions. But, as he does not realize what he is doing, he is acting *in* ignorance. To be sure every bad man is ignorant of what he ought to do and refrain from doing, and it is just this ignorance that makes people unjust and otherwise wicked. But when we use the word 'involuntary' we do not apply it in a case where the agent does not know what is for his own good. For involuntary acts are not the consequence of ignorance when the ignorance is shown in our choice of ends; what does result from such ignorance is a completely vicious condition. No, what I mean is not general ignorance—which is what gives ground for censure—but particular ignorance, ignorance that is to say of the particular circumstances or the particular persons concerned. In such cases there may be room for pity and pardon, because a man who acts in ignorance of such details is an involuntary agent. . . .

An involuntary act being one performed under compulsion or as the result of ignorance, a voluntary act would seem to be one of which the origin or efficient cause lies in the agent, he knowing the particular circumstances in which he is acting. I believe it to be an error to say that acts occasioned by anger or desire are involuntary. For in the first place if we maintain this we shall have to give up the view that any of the lower animals, or even children, are capable of voluntary action. In the second place, when we act from desire or anger are none of our actions voluntary? Or are our fine actions voluntary, our ignoble actions, involuntary? It is an absurd distinction, since the agent is one and the same person. It is surely paradoxical to describe as 'involuntary' acts inspired by sentiments which we quite properly desire to have. There are some things at which we *ought* to feel angry, and others which we *ought* to desire—health, for instance, and the acquisition of knowledge. Thirdly, people assume that what is involuntary must be painful and what falls in with our own wishes must be pleasant. Fourthly, what difference is there in point of voluntariness between wrong actions which are calculated and wrong actions which are done on impulse? Both are to be avoided; and the further reflection suggests itself, that the irrational emotions are no less typically human than our considered judgement. Whence it follows that actions inspired by anger or desire are equally typical of the human being who performs them. Therefore to classify these actions as 'involuntary' is surely a very strange proceeding. . . .

Epictetus
On Things That Are and Are Not in Our Own Power

Epictetus (c. 55–135 A.D.) *was a Roman stoic philosopher. He taught that, through understanding and what we call "will power," one can free oneself from the external injuries of fate and achieve a sense of peace with the world.*

*O*f other faculties, you will find no one that contemplates, or consequently approves or disapproves, itself. How far does the contemplative power of grammar extend?

As far as the judging of language.

Of music?

As far as judging of melody.

Does either of them contemplate itself, then?

By no means.

Thus, for instance, when you are to write to your friend, grammar will tell you what to write: but whether you are to write to your friend at all, or no, grammar will not tell you. Thus music, with regard to tunes; but whether it be proper or improper at any particular time to sing or play, music will not tell you.

What will tell, then?

That which contemplates both itself and all other things.

And what is that?

The reasoning faculty; for that alone is found to consider both itself, its powers, its value, and likewise all the rest. For what is it else that says gold is beautiful? (for the gold itself does not speak). Evidently that faculty which judges of the appearances of things. What else distinguishes music, grammar, the other faculties, proves their uses, and shows their proper occasions?

Nothing but this. . . .

What, then, is to be done?

To make the best of what is in our power, and take the rest as it naturally happens.
And how is that?
As it pleases God. . . .

Concerning the gods, some affirm that there is no deity: others, that he indeed exists; but slothful, negligent, and without a providence: a third sort admits both his being and providence, but only in great and heavenly objects, and in nothing upon earth: a fourth, both in heaven and earth; but only in general, not individuals: a fifth, like Ulysses and Socrates:

"O thou, who, ever present in my way,
Dost all my motions, all my toils survey."

Pope's Homer

It is, before all things, necessary to examine each of these; which is, and which is not, rightly said. Now, if there are no gods, how is it our end to follow them? If there are, but they take no care of anything, how will it be right, in this case, to follow them? Or, if they both are, and take care; yet, if there is nothing communicated from them to men, nor indeed to myself in particular, how can it be right even in this case? A wise and good man, after examining these things, submits his mind to him who administers the whole, as good citizens do to the laws of the commonwealth.

He, then, who comes to be instructed, ought to come with this intention: "Now may I in everything follow the gods? How may I acquiesce in the divine administration? And how may I be free?" For he is free to whom all happens agreeably to his choice, and whom no one can restrain.

What! then is freedom distraction?

By no means; for madness and freedom are incompatible.

But I would have whatever appears to me to be right, happen, however it comes to appear so.

You are mad: you have lost your senses. Do not you know that freedom is a very beautiful and valuable thing? But for me to choose at random, and for things to happen agreeably to such a choice, may be so far from a beautiful thing as to be, of all others, the most shocking. For how do we proceed in writing? Do I choose to write the name of Dion (for instance) as I will? No; but I am taught to be willing to write it as it ought to be writ. And what is the case in music? The same. And what in every other art or science? Otherwise, it would be to no purpose to learn anything, if it was to be adapted to each one's particular humour. Is it, then, only in the greatest and principal point, that of freedom, permitted me to will at random? By no means, but true instruction is this: learning to will that things should happen as they do. And how do they happen? As the appointer of them hath appointed. He hath appointed that there should be summer and winter, plenty and dearth, virtue and vice, and all such contrarieties, for the harmony of the whole. To each of us he hath given a body and its parts, and our several properties and companions. Mindful of this appointment, we should enter upon a course of education and instruction not to change the constitutions of things, which is neither put within our reach nor for our good; but that, being as they are, and as their nature is with regard to us, we may have our mind accommodated to what exists. Can we, for instance, fly mankind? And how is that possible? Can we, by conversing with them, change them? Who hath given us such a power? What, then, remains, or what method is there to be found for such a commerce with them, that while they act agreeably to the appearances in their own minds, we may nevertheless be affected conformably to nature? But you are wretched and discontented. If you are alone, you term it a desert; and if with men, you call them cheats and robbers. You find fault, too, with you parents and children and brothers and neighbours. Whereas you ought, when you live alone, to call that a repose and freedom, and to esteem yourself as resembling the gods; and when you are in company, not to call it a crowd and a tumult and a trouble, but an assembly and a festival; and thus to take all things contentedly. What, then, is the punishment of those who do not? To be just as they are. Is any one discontented with being alone? Let him be in a desert. Discontented with his parents? Let him be a bad son, and let him mourn. Discontented with his children? Let him be a bad father. Throw him into prison. What prison? Where he already is; for he is in a situation against his will, and wherever any one is against his will, that is to him a prison; just as Socrates was not in prison, for he was willingly there. . . . "How wretched am I in such a father and mother!" What, then, was it granted you to come beforehand, and make your own terms, and say: "Let such and such persons, at this hour, be the authors of my birth?" It was not granted; for it was necessary that your parents should exist before you, and so you be born afterwards. Of whom? Of just such as they were. What, then, since they are such, is there no remedy afforded you? Now, surely, if you were ignorant to what purpose you possess the faculty of sight, you would be wretched and miserable in shutting your eyes at the approach of colours, and are not you more wretched and miserable in being ignorant that you have a greatness of soul and a manly spirit, answerable to each of the above-mentioned accidents? Occurrences proportioned to your faculty [of discernment] are brought before you; but you turn it away at the very time when you ought to have it the most open and quick-sighted. Why do not you rather thank the gods that they have made you superior to whatever they have not placed in your own power, and have rendered you accountable for that only which is in your own power? Of your parents they acquit you; as not accountable of your brothers they acquit you; of body, possessions, death, life, they acquit you. For what, then, have they made you accountable? For that which is alone in your own power, a right use of the appearances of objects. Why, then, should you draw those things upon yourself for which you are not accountable? This is giving one's self trouble without need.

Baron d'Holbach

Are We Cogs in the Universe?

Baron d'Holbach (1723–1789) was a French aristocrat during the enlightenment who believed in a thoroughgoing materialism and that the universe was nothing but "matter in motion" and human behavior nothing but the result of the deterministic behavior of this matter. He argues his version of "hard" determinism in the selection that follows.

In whatever manner man is considered, he is connected to universal nature, and submitted to the necessary and immutable laws that she imposes on all beings she contains, according to their peculiar essences or to the respective properties with which, without consulting them, she endows each particular species. Man's life is a line that nature commands him to describe upon the surface of the earth, without his ever being able to swerve from it, even for an instant. He is born without his own consent; his organization does in nowise depend upon himself; his ideas come to him involuntarily; his habits are in the power of those who cause him to contract them; he is unceasingly modified by causes, whether visible or concealed, over which he has no control, which necessarily regulate his mode of existence, give the hue to his way of thinking, and determine his manner of acting. He is good or bad, happy or miserable, wise or foolish, reasonable or irrational, without his will being for anything in these various states. Nevertheless, in spite of the shackles by which he is bound, it is pretended he is a free agent, or that independent of the causes by which he is moved, he determines his own will, and regulates his own condition.

However slender the foundation of his opinion, of which everything ought to point out to him the error, it is current at this day and passes for an incontestable truth with a great number of people, otherwise extremely enlightened; it is the basis of religion, which supposing relations between man and the unknown being she has placed above nature, has been incapable of imagining how man could merit reward or deserve punishment from this being, if he was not a free agent. Society has been believed interested in his system; because an idea has gone abroad, that if all the actions of man were to be contemplated as necessary, the right of punishing those who injure their associates would no longer exist. At length human vanity accommodated itself to a hypothesis which, unquestionably, appears to distinguish man from all other physical beings, by assigning to him the special privilege of a total independence of all other causes, but of which a very little reflection would have shown him the impossibility.

The will, as we have elsewhere said, is a modification of the brain, by which it is disposed to action, or prepared to give play to the organs. This will is necessarily determined by the qualities, good or bad, agreeable or painful, of the object or the motive that acts upon his sense, or of which the idea remains with him, and is resuscitated by his memory. In consequence, he acts necessarily, his action is the result of the impulse he receives either from the motive, from the object, or from the idea which has modified his brain, or disposed his will. When he does not act according to this impulse, it is because there comes some new cause, some new motive, some new idea, which modified his brain in a different manner, gives him a new impulse, determines his will in another way, by which the action of the former impulse is suspended: thus, the sight of an agreeable object, or its idea, determines his will to set him in action to procure it; but if a new object or a new idea more powerfully attracts him, it gives a new direction to his will, annihilates the effect of the former, and prevents the action by which it was to be procured. This is the mode in which reflection, experience, reason, necessarily arrests or suspends the action of man's will: without this he would of necessity have followed the anterior impulse which carried him towards a then desirable object. In all this he always acts according to necessary laws from which he has no means of emancipating himself.

In short, the actions of man are never free; they are always the necessary consequence of his temperament, of the received ideas, and of the notions, either true or false, which he has formed to himself of happiness; of his opinions, strengthened by example, by education, and by daily experience. So many crimes are witnessed on the earth only because every thing conspires to render man vicious and criminal; the religion he has adopted, his government, his education, the examples set before him, irresistibly drive him on to evil: under these circumstances, morality preaches virtue to him in vain. In those societies where vice is esteemed, where crime is crowned, where venality is constantly recompensed, where the most dreadful disorders are punished only in those who are too weak to enjoy the privilege of committing them with impunity, the practice of virtue is considered nothing more than a painful sacrifice of happiness. Such societies chastise, in the lower orders, those excesses which they respect in the higher ranks; and frequently have the injustice to condemn those in the penalty of death, whom public prejudices, maintained by constant example, have rendered criminal.

Man, then, is not a free agent in any one instant of his life; he is necessarily guided in each step by those advantages, whether real or fictitious, that he attaches to the objects by which his passions are roused: these passions themselves are necessary in a being who unceasingly tends towards his own happiness; their energy is necessary, since that depends on his temperament; his temperament is necessary, because it depends on the physical elements which enter into his composition; the modification of this temperament is necessary, as it is the infallible and inevitable consequence of the impulse he receives from the incessant action of moral and physical beings.

William James
"Soft" Determinism

William James *(1842-1910) wrote widely on most philosophical topics, and it was he who coined the phrase "soft determinism," which he discusses in the following excerpt.*

A common opinion prevails that the juice has ages ago been pressed out of the free-will controversy, and that no new champion can do more than warm up stale arguments which everyone has heard. This is a radical mistake. I know of no subject less worn out, or in which inventive genius has a better chance of breaking open new ground,—not, perhaps, of forcing a conclusion or of coercing assent, but of deepening our sense of what the issue between the two parties really is, of what the ideas of fate and of free-will imply. . . . [O]ur first act of freedom, if we are free, ought in all inward propriety to be to affirm that we are free. . . .

With this much understood at the outset, we can advance. But not without one more point understood as well. The arguments I am about to urge all proceed on two suppositions: first, when we make theories about the world and discuss them with one another, we do so in order to attain a conception of things which shall give us subjective satisfaction; and, second, if there be two conceptions, and the one seems to us, on the whole, more rational than the other, we are entitled to suppose that the more rational one is the truer of the two. . . .

To begin, then, I must suppose you acquainted with all the usual arguments on the subject. I cannot stop to take up the old proofs from causation, from statistics, from the certainty with which we can foretell one another's conduct, from the fixity of character, and all the rest. . . . Old-fashioned determinism was what we may call *hard* determinism. It did not shrink from such words as fatality, bondage of the will, necessitation, and the like. Nowadays, we have a *soft* determinism which abhors harsh words, and, repudiating fatality, necessity, and even predetermination, says that its real name is freedom; for freedom is only necessity understood, and bondage to the highest is identical with true freedom. . . .

[Determinism] professes that those parts of the universe already laid down absolutely appoint and decree what the other parts shall be. The future has no ambiguous possibilities hidden in its womb: the part we call the present is compatible with only one totality. Any other future complement than the one fixed from eternity is impossible. The whole is in each and every part, and welds it with the rest into an absolute unity, an iron block, in which there can be no equivocation or shadow of turning.

> *With earth's first clay they did the last man knead,*
> *And there of the last harvest sowed the seed.*
> *And the first morning of creation wrote*
> *What the last dawn of reckoning shall read.*

Indeterminism, on the contrary, says that the parts have a certain amount of loose play on one another, so that the laying down of one of them does not necessarily determine what the others shall be. It admits that possibilities may be in excess of actualities, and that things not yet revealed to our knowledge may really in themselves be ambiguous. Of two alternative futures which we conceive, both may now be really possible; and the one become impossible only at the very moment when the other excludes it by becoming real itself. Indeterminism thus denies the world to be one unbending unit of fact. It says there is a certain ultimate pluralism in it; and, so saying, it corroborates our ordinary unsophisticated view of things. To that view, actualities seem to float in a wider sea of possibilities from out of which they are chosen; and, *somewhere,* indeterminism says, such possibilities exist, and form a part of truth.

Determinism, on the contrary, says they exist *nowhere,* and that necessity on the one hand and impossibility on the other are the sole categories of the real. Possibilities that fail to get realized are, for determinism, pure illusions: they never were possiblities at all. There is nothing inchoate, it says, about this universe of ours, all that was or is or shall be actual in it having been from eternity virtually there. The cloud of alternatives our minds escort this mass of actuality withal is a cloud of sheer deception, to which "impossibilities" is the only name that rightfully belongs.

The issue, it will be seen, is a perfectly sharp one, which no eulogistic terminology can smear over or wipe out. The truth *must* lie with one side or the other, and its lying with one side makes the other false.

The question relates solely to the existence of possibilities, in the strict sense of the term, as things that may, but need not, be. Both sides admit that a volition, for instance, has occurred. The indeterminists say another volition might have occurred in its place: the determinists swear that nothing could possibly have occurred in its place. Now, can science be called in to tell us which of these two point-blank contradicters of each other is right? Science professes to draw no conclusions but such as are based on matters of fact, things that have actually happened; but how can any amount of assurance that something actually happened give us the least grain of information as to whether another thing might or might not have happened in its place? Only facts can be proved by other facts. With things that are possibilities and not facts, facts have no concern. If we have no other evidence than the evidence of existing facts, the possibility-question must remain a mystery never to be cleared up.

And the truth is that facts practically have hardly anything to do with making us either determinists or indeterminists. Sure enough, we make a flourish of quoting facts this way or that; and if we are determinists, we talk about the infallibility with which we can predict one another's conduct; while if we are indeterminists, we lay great stress on the fact that it is just because we cannot foretell one another's conduct, either in war or statecraft or in any of the great and small intrigues and business of men, that life is so intensely anxious and hazardous a game. But who does not see the wretched insufficiency of this so-called objective testimony on both sides? What fills up the gaps in our minds is something not objective, not external. What divides us into possibility men and anti-possibility men is different faiths or postulates,—postulates of rationality. To this man the world seems more rational with possibilities in it,—to that man more rational with possibilities excluded; and talk as we will about having to yield to evidence, what makes us monists or pluralists, determinists or indeterminists, is at bottom always some sentiment like this. . . .

Nevertheless, many persons talk as if the minutest dose of disconnectedness of one part with another, the smallest modicum of independence, the faintest tremor of ambiguity about the future, for example, would ruin everything, and turn this goodly universe into a sort of insane sand-heap or nulliverse, no universe at all. Since future human volitions are as a matter of fact the only ambiguous things we are tempted to believe in, let us stop for a moment to make ourselves sure whether their independent and accidental character need be fraught with such direful consequences to the universe as these.

What is meant by saying that my choice of which way to walk home after the lecture is ambiguous and matter of chance as far as the present moment is concerned? It means that both Divinity Avenue and Oxford Street are called; but that only one, and that one *either* one, shall be chosen. Now, I ask you seriously to suppose that this ambiguity of my choice is real; and then to make the impossible hypothesis that the choice is made twice over, and each time falls on a different street. In other words, imagine that I first walk through Divinity Avenue, and then imagine that the powers governing the universe annihilate ten minutes of time with all that it contained, and set me back at the door of this hall just as I was before the choice was made. Imagine then that, everything else being the same, I now make a different choice and traverse Oxford Street. You, as passive spectators, look on and see the two alternative universes,—one of them with me walking through Divinity Avenue in it, the other with the same me walking through Oxford Street. Now, if you are determinists you believe one of these universes to have been from eternity impossible: you believe it to have been impossible because of the intrinsic irrationality or accidentality somewhere involved in it. But looking outwardly at these universes, can you say which is the impossible and accidental one, and which the rational and necessary one? I doubt if the most ironclad determinist among you could have the slightest glimmer of light on this point. In other words, either universe *after the fact* and once there would, to our means of observation and understanding, appear just as rational as the other. There would be absolutely no criterion by which we might judge one necessary and the other matter of chance. Suppose now we relieve the gods of their hypothetical task and assume my choice, once made, to be made forever. I go through Divinity Avenue for good and all. If, as good determinists, you now begin to affirm, what all good determinists punctually do affirm, that in the nature of things I *couldn't* have gone through Oxford Street,—had I done so it would have been chance, irrationality, insanity, a horrid gap in nature,—I simply call your attention to this, that your affirmation is what the Germans call a *Machtspruch,* a mere conception fulminated as a dogma and based on no insight into details. Before my choice, either street seemed as natural to you as to me. Had I happened to take Oxford Street, Divinity Avenue would have figured in your philosophy as the gap in nature; and you would have so proclaimed it with the best deterministic conscience in the world. . . .

And this at last brings us within sight of our subject. We have seen what determinism means: we have seen that indeterminism is rightly described as meaning chance; and we have seen that chance, the very name of which we are urged to shrink from as from a metaphysical pestilence, means only the negative fact that no part of the world, however big, can claim to control absolutely the destinies of the whole. But although, in discussing the word "chance," I may at moments have seemed to be arguing for its real existence, I have not meant to do so yet. We have not yet ascertained whether this be a world of chance or no; at most, we have agreed that it seems so. And I now repeat what I said at the outset, that, from any strict theoretical point of view, the question is insoluble. To deepen our theoretic sense of the *difference* between a world with chances in it and a deterministic world is the most I can hope to do; and this I may now at last begin upon, after all our tedious clearing of the way.

I wish first of all to show you just what the notion that this is a deterministic world implies. The implications I call your attention to are all bound up with the fact that it is a world in which we constantly have to make what I shall, with your permission, call judgments of regret. Hardly an hour passes in which we do not wish that something might be otherwise; and happy indeed are those of us whose hearts have never echoed the wish of Omar Khayam—

That we might clasp, ere closed, the book of fate,
         And make the writer on a fairer leaf
Inscribe our names, or quite obliterate.

Ah! Love, could you and I with fate conspire
To mend this sorry scheme of things entire,
         Would we not shatter it to bits, and then
Remould it nearer to the heart's desire?

Now, it is undeniable that most of these regrets are foolish, and quite on a par in point of philosophic value with the criticisms on the universe of that friend of our infancy, the hero of the fable The Atheist and the Acorn,—

Fool! had that bough a pumpkin bore,
Thy whimsies would have worked no more, etc.

Even from the point of view of our own ends, we should probably make a botch of remodelling the universe. How much more then from the point of view of ends we cannot see! Wise men therefore regret as little as they can. But still some regrets are pretty obstinate and hard to stifle,—regrets for acts of wanton cruelty or treachery, for example, whether performed by others or by ourselves. Hardly any one can remain *entirely* optimistic after reading the confession of the murderer at Brockton the other day: how, to get rid of the wife whose continued existence bored him, he inveigled her into a desert spot, shot her four times, and then, as she lay on the ground and said to him, "You didn't do it on purpose, did you dear?" replied, "No, I didn't do it on purpose," as he raised a rock and smashed her skull. Such an occurrence, with the mild sentence and self-satisfaction of the prisoner, is a field for a crop of regrets, which one need not take up in detail. We feel that, although a perfect mechanical fit to the rest of the universe, it is a bad moral fit, and that something else would really have been better in its place.

But for the deterministic philosophy the murder, the sentence, and the prisoner's optimism were all necessary from eternity; and nothing else for a moment had a ghost of a chance of being put into their place. To admit such a chance, the determinists tell us, would be to make a suicide of reason; so we must steel our hearts against the thought. And here our plot thickens, for we see the first of those difficult implications of determinism and monism which it is my purpose to make you feel. If this Brockton murder was called for by the rest of the universe, if it had to come at its preappointed hour, and if nothing else would have been consistent with the sense of the whole, what are we to think of the universe? Are we stubbornly to stick to our judgment of regret, and say, though it *couldn't* be, yet it *would* have been a better universe with something different from this Brockton murder in it? That, of course, seems the natural and spontaneous thing for us to do; and yet it is nothing short of deliberately espousing a kind of pessimism. The judgment of regret calls the murder bad. Calling a thing bad means, if it mean anything at all, that the thing ought not to be, that something else ought to be in its stead. Determinism, in denying that anything else can be in its stead, virtually defines the universe as a place in which what ought to be is impossible,— in other words, as an organism whose constitution is afflicted with an incurable taint, an irremediable flaw. The pessimism of a Schopenhauer says no more than this,—that the murder is a symptom; and that it is a vicious symptom because it belongs to a vicious whole, which can express its nature no otherwise than by bringing forth just such a symptom as that at this particular spot. Regret for the murder must transform itself, if we are determinists and wise, into a larger regret. It is absurd to regret the murder alone. Other things being what they are, *it* could not be different. What we should regret is that whole frame of things of which the murder is one member. I see no escape whatever from this pessimistic conclusion, if, being determinists, our judgment of regret is to be allowed to stand at all.

The only deterministic escape from pessimism is everywhere to abandon the judgment of regret. That this can be done, history shows to be not impossible. The devil, *quoad existentiam,* may be good. That is, although he be a *principle* of evil, yet the universe, with such a principle in it, may practically be a better universe than it could have been without. On every hand, in a small way, we find that a certain amount of evil is a condition by which a higher form of good is bought. There is nothing to prevent anybody from generalizing this view, and trusting that if we could but see things in the largest of all ways, even such matters as this Brockton murder would appear to be paid for by the uses that follow in their train. An optimism *quand même,* a systematic and infatuated optimism like that ridiculed by Voltaire in his Candide, is one of the possible ideal ways in which a man may train himself to look on life. Bereft of dogmatic hardness and lit up with the expression of a tender and pathetic hope, such an optimism has been the grace of some of the most religious characters that ever lived.

> Throb thine with Nature's throbbing breast,
> And all is clear from east to west.

Even cruelty and treachery may be among the absolutely blessed fruits of time, and to quarrel with any of their details may be blasphemy. The only real blasphemy, in short, may be that pessimistic temper of the soul which lets it give way to such things as regrets, remorse, and grief.

Thus, our deterministic pessimism may become a deterministic optimism at the price of extinguishing our judgments of regret.

But does not this immediately bring us into a curious logical predicament? Our determinism leads us to call our judgments of regret wrong, because they are pessimistic in implying that what is impossible yet ought to be. But how then about the judgments of regret themselves? If they are wrong, other judgments, judgments of approval presumably, ought to be in their place. But as they are necessitated, nothing else *can* be in their place; and the universe is just what it was before,—namely, a place in which what ought to be appears impossible. We have got one foot out of the pessimistic bog, but the other one sinks all the deeper. We have rescued our actions from the bonds of evil, but our judgments are now held fast. When murders and treacheries cease to be sins, regrets are theoretic absurdities and errors. The theoretic and the active life thus play a kind of seesaw with each other on the ground of evil. The rise of either sends the other down. Murder and treachery cannot be good without regret being bad: regret cannot be good without treachery and murder being bad. Both, however, are supposed to have been foredoomed: so something must be fatally unreasonable, absurd, and wrong in the world. It must be a place of which either sin or error forms a necessary part. From this dilemma there seems at first sight no escape.

Clarence Darrow
The Leopold and Loeb Case

Clarence Darrow (1857–1938) *was one of America's greatest trial lawyers. He was called upon to defend Leopold and Loeb, two college students who had committed a dreadful murder. In his passionate plea to the jury, Darrow argued that none of us has* *any real power over what we are and what we do, and that these two students were doomed long before they were even old enough to imagine their terrible crime.*

I have tried to study the lives of these two most unfortunate boys. Three months ago, if their friends and the friends of the family had been asked to pick out the most promising lads of their acquaintance, they probably would have picked these two boys. With every opportunity, with plenty of wealth, they would have said that those two would succeed.

In a day, by an act of madness, all this is destroyed, until the best they can hope for now is a life of silence and pain, continuing to the end of their years.

How did it happen?

Let us take Dickie Loeb first.

I do not claim to know how it happened; I have sought to find out. I know that something, or some combinations of things, is responsible for this mad act. I know that there are no accidents in nature. I know that effect follows cause. I know that, if I were wise enough, and knew enough about this case, I could lay my finger on the cause. I will do the best I can, but it is largely speculation.

The child, of course, is born without knowledge.

Impressions are made upon its mind as it goes along. Dickie Loeb was a child of wealth and opportunity. Over and over in this court Your Honor has been asked, and other courts have been asked, to consider boys who have no chance; they have been asked to consider the poor, whose home had been the street, with no education and no opportunity in life, and they have done it, and done it rightfully.

But, Your Honor, it is just as often a great misfortune to be the child of the rich as it is to be the child of the poor. Wealth has its misfortunes. Too much, too great opportunity and advantage, given to a child has its misfortunes, and I am asking Your Honor to consider the rich as well as the poor (and nothing else). Can I find what was wrong? I think I can. Here was a boy at a tender age, placed in the hands of a governess, intellectual, vigorous, devoted, with a strong ambition for the welfare of this boy. He was pushed in his studies, as plants are forced in hothouses. He had no pleasures, such as a boy should have, except as they were gained by lying and cheating.

Now, I am not criticizing the nurse. I suggest that some day Your Honor look at her picture. It explains her fully. Forceful, brooking no interference, she loved the boy, and her ambition was that he should reach the highest perfection. No time to pause, no time to stop from one book to another, no time to have those pleasures which a boy ought to have to create a normal life. And what happened? Your Honor, what would happen? Nothing strange or unusual. This nurse was with him all the time, except when he stole out at night, from two to fourteen years of age. He, scheming and planning as healthy boys would do, to get out from under her restraint; she, putting before him the best books, which children generally do not want; and he, when she was not looking, reading detective stories, which he devoured, story after story, in his young life. Of all this there can be no question.

What is the result? Every story he read was a story of crime. We have a statute in this state, passed only last year, if I recall it, which forbids minors reading stories of crime. Why? There is only one reason. Because the legislature in its wisdom felt that it would produce criminal tendencies in the boys who read them. The legislature of this state has given its opinion, and forbidden boys to read these books. He read them day after day. He never stopped. While he was passing through college at Ann Arbor he was still reading them. When he was a senior he read them, and almost nothing else.

Now, these facts are beyond dispute. He early developed the tendency to mix with crime, to be a detective; as a little boy shadowing people on the street; as a little child going out with his fantasy of being the head of a band of criminals and directing them on the street. How did this grow and develop in him? Let us see. It seems to be as natural as the day following the night. Every detective story is a story of a sleuth getting the best of it: trailing some unfortunate individual through devious ways until his victim is finally landed in jail or stands on the gallows. They all show how smart the detective is, and where the criminal himself falls down.

This boy early in his life conceived the idea that there could be a perfect crime, one that nobody could ever detect; that there could be one where the detective did not land his game—a perfect crime. He had been interested in the story of Charley Ross, who was kidnapped. He was interested in these things all his life. He believed in his childish way that a crime could be so carefully planned that there would be no detection, and his idea was to plan and accomplish a perfect crime. It would involve kidnapping and involve murder.

There had been growing in Dickie's brain, dwarfed and twisted—as every act in this case shows it to have been dwarfed and twisted—there had been growing this scheme, not due to any wickedness of Dickie Loeb, for he is a child. It grew as he grew; it grew from those around him; it grew from the lack of the proper training until it possessed him. He believed he could beat the police. He believed he could plan the perfect crime. He had thought of it and talked of it for years—had talked of it as a child, had worked at it as a child—this sorry act of his, utterly irrational and motiveless, a plan to commit a perfect crime which must contain kidnapping, and there must be ransom, or else it could not be perfect, and they must get the money. . . .

The law knows and has recognized childhood for many and many a long year. What do we know about childhood? The brain of the child is the home of dreams, of castles, of visions, of illusions and of delusions. In fact, there could be no childhood without delusions, for delusions are always more alluring than facts. Delusions, dreams and hallucinations are a part of the warp and woof of childhood. You know it and I know it. I remember, when I was a child, the men seemed as tall as the trees, the trees as tall as the mountains. I can remember very well when, as a little boy, I swam the deepest spot in the river for the first time. I swam breathlessly and landed with as much sense of glory and triumph as Julius Caesar felt when he led his army across the Rubicon. I have been back since, and I can almost step across the same place, but it seemed an ocean then. And those men whom I thought so wonderful were dead and left nothing behind. I had lived in a dream. I had never known the real world which I met, to my discomfort and despair, and that dispelled the illusions of my youth.

The whole life of childhood is a dream and an illusion, and whether they take one shape or another shape depends not upon the dreamy boy but on what surrounds him. As well might I have dreamed of burglars and wished to be one as to dream of policemen and wished to be one. Perhaps I was lucky, too, that I had no money. We have grown to think that the misfortune is in not having it. The great misfortune in this terrible case is the money. That has destroyed their lives. That has fostered these illusions. That has promoted this mad act. And, if Your Honor shall doom them to die, it will be because they are the sons of the rich. . . .

I know where my life has been molded by books, amongst other things. We all know where our lives have been influenced by books. The nurse, strict and jealous and watchful, gave him one kind of book; by night he would steal off and read the other.

Which, think you, shaped the life of Dickie Loeb? Is there any kind of question about it? A child. Was it pure maliciousness? Was a boy of five or six or seven to blame for it? Where did he get it? He got it where we all get our ideas, and these books became a part of his dreams and a part of his life, and as he grew up his visions grew to hallucinations.

He went out on the street and fantastically directed his companions, who were not there, in their various moves to complete the perfect crime. Can there be any sort of question about it?

Suppose, Your Honor, that instead of this boy being here in this court, under the plea of the State that Your Honor shall pronounce a sentence to hang him by the neck until dead, he had been taken to a pathological hospital to be analyzed, and the physicians had inquired into his case. What would they have said? There is only one thing that they could possibly have said. They would have traced everything back to the gradual growth of the child.

That is not all there is about it. Youth is hard enough. The only good thing about youth is that it has no thought and no care; and how blindly we can do things when we are young!

Where is the man who has not been guilty of delinquencies in youth? Let us be honest with ourselves. Let us look into our own hearts. How many men are there today—lawyers and congressmen and judges, and even state's attorneys—who have not been guilty of some mad act in youth? And if they did not get caught, or the consequences were trivial, it was their good fortune.

We might as well be honest with ourselves, Your Honor. Before I would tie a noose around the neck of a boy I would try to call back into my mind the emotions of youth. I would try to remember what the world looked like to me when I was a child. I would try to remember how strong were these instinctive, persistent emotions that moved my life. I would try to remember how weak and inefficient was youth in the presence of the surging, controlling feelings of the child. One that honestly remembers and asks himself the question and tries to unlock the door that he thinks is closed, and calls back the boy, can understand the boy.

But, Your Honor, that is not all there is to boyhood. Nature is strong and she is pitiless. She works in her own mysterious way, and we are her victims. We have not much to do with it ourselves. Nature takes this job in hand, and we play our parts. In the words of old Omar Khayyam, we are only:

> But helpless pieces in the game He plays
> Upon this checkerboard of nights and days;
> Hither and thither moves, and checks, and slays,
> And one by one back in the closet lays.

What had this boy to do with it? He was not his own father; he was not his own mother; he was not his own grandparents. All of this was handed to him. He did not surround himself with governesses and wealth. He did not make himself. And yet he is to be compelled to pay.

There was a time in England, running down as late as the beginning of the last century, when judges used to convene court and call juries to try a horse, a dog, a pig, for crime. I have in my library a story of a judge and jury and lawyers trying and convicting an old sow for lying down on her ten pigs and killing them.

What does it mean? Animals were tried. Do you mean to tell me that Dickie Loeb had any more to do with his making than any other product of heredity that is born upon the earth? . . .

For God's sake, are we crazy? In the face of history, of every line of philosophy, against the teaching of every religionist and seer and prophet the world has ever given us, we are still doing what our barbaric ancestors did when they came out of the caves and the woods.

From the age of fifteen to the age of twenty or twenty-one, the child has the burden of adolescence, of puberty and sex thrust upon him. Girls are kept at home and carefully watched. Boys without instruction are left to work the period out for themselves. It may lead to excess. It may lead to disgrace. It may lead to perversion. Who is to blame? Who did it? Did Dickie Loeb do it?

Your Honor, I am almost ashamed to talk about it. I can hardly imagine that we are in the twentieth century. And yet there are men who seriously say that for what nature has done, for what life has done, for what training has done, you should hang these boys.

Now, there is no mystery about this case, Your Honor. I seem to be criticizing their parents. They had parents who were kind and good and wise in their way. But I say to you seriously that the parents are more responsible than these boys. And yet few boys had better parents.

Your Honor, it is the easiest thing in the world to be a parent. We talk of motherhood, and yet every woman can be a mother. We talk of fatherhood, and yet every man can be a father. Nature takes care of that. It is easy to be a parent. But to be wise and farseeing enough to understand the boy is another thing; only a very few are so wise and so farseeing as that. When I think of the light way nature has of picking our parents and populating the earth, having them born and die, I cannot hold human beings to the same degree of responsibility that young lawyers hold them when they are enthusiastic in a prosecution. I know what it means.

I know there are no better citizens in Chicago than the fathers of these poor boys. I know there were no better women than their mothers. But I am going to be honest with this court, if it is at the expense of both. I know that one of two things happened to Richard Loeb: that this terrible crime was inherent in his organism, and came from some ancestor; or that it came through his education and his training after he was born. Do I need to prove it? Judge Crowe said at one point in this case, when some witness spoke about their wealth, that "probably that was responsible."

To believe that any boy is responsible for himself or his early training is an absurdity that no lawyer or judge should be guilty of today. Somewhere this came to the boy. If his failing came from his heredity, I do not know where or how. None of us are bred perfect and pure; and the color of our hair, the color of our eyes, our stature, the weight and fineness of our brain, and everything about us could, with full knowledge, be traced with absolute certainty to somewhere. If we had the pedigree it could be traced just the same in a boy as it could in a dog, a horse or a cow.

I do not know what remote ancestors may have sent down the seed that corrupted him, and I do not know through how many ancestors it may have passed until it reached Dickie Loeb.

All I know is that it is true, and there is not a biologist in the world who will not say that I am right.

If it did not come that way, then I know that if he was normal, if he had been understood, if he had been trained as he should have been it would not have happened. Not that anybody may not slip, but I know it and Your Honor knows it, and every schoolhouse and every church in the land is an evidence of it. Else why build them?

Every effort to protect society is an effort toward training the youth to keep the path. Every bit of training in the world proves it, and it likewise proves that it sometimes fails. I know that if this boy had been understood and properly trained—properly for him—and the training that he got might have been the very best for someone; but if it had been the proper training for him he would not be in this courtroom today with the noose above his head. If there is responsibility anywhere, it is back of him; somewhere in the infinite number of his ancestors, or in his surroundings, or in both. And I submit, Your Honor, that under every principle of natural justice, under every principle of conscience, of right, and of law, he should not be made responsible for the acts of someone else. . . .

It is when these dreams of boyhood, these fantasies of youth still linger, and the growing boy is still a child—a child in emotion, a child in feeling, a child in hallucinations—that you can say that it is the dreams and the hallucinations of childhood that are responsible for his conduct. There is not an act in all this horrible tragedy that was not the act of a child, the act of a child wandering around in the morning of life, moved by the new feelings of a boy, moved by the uncontrolled impulses which his teaching was not strong enough to take care of, moved by the dreams and the hallucinations which haunt the brain of a child. I say, Your Honor, that it would be the height of cruelty, of injustice, of wrong and barbarism to visit the penalty upon this poor boy.

John Hospers
Meaning and Free Will

John Hospers *is a professor of philosophy at the University of Southern California and the author of a number of books on ethics. He ran several times for President of the United States on the Libertarian ticket. In the following he argues for a thoroughgoing determinism, not based on the model of physics but rather on psychoanalysis, which declares that all of our behavior is based on unconscious motivation.*

Perhaps the most obvious conception of freedom is this: an act is free if and only if it is a voluntary act. A response that occurs spontaneously, not as a result of your willing it, such as a reflex action, is not a free act. I do not know that this view is ever held in its pure form, but it is the basis for other ones. As it stands, of course, it is ambiguous: does "voluntary" entail "premeditated?" are acts we perform semi-automatically through habit to be called free acts? To what extent is a conscious decision to act required for the act to be classified as voluntary? What of sudden outbursts of feeling? They are hardly premeditated or decided upon, yet they may have their origin in the presence or absence of habit-patterns due to self-discipline which may have been consciously decided upon. Clearly the view needs to be refined.

Now, however we may come to define "voluntary," it is perfectly possible to maintain that all voluntary acts are free acts and vice versa; after all, it is a matter of what meaning we are giving to the word "free" and we can give it this meaning if we choose. But it soon becomes apparent that this is not the meaning which most of us *want* to give it: for there *are* classes of actions which we want to refrain from calling "free" even though they are voluntary (not that we have this denial in mind when we use the word "free"—still, it is significant that we do not use the word in some situations in which the act in question is nevertheless voluntary).

When a man tells a state secret under torture, he does choose voluntarily between telling and enduring more torture; and when he submits to a bandit's command at the point of a gun, he voluntarily chooses to submit rather than to be shot. And still such actions would not generally be called free; it is clear that they are performed under compulsion. Voluntary acts performed under compulsion would not be called free; and the cruder view is to this extent amended.

For some persons, this is as far as we need to go. Schlick, for example, says that the free-will issue is the scandal of philosophy and nothing but so much wasted ink and paper, because the whole controversy is nothing but an inexcusable confusion between compulsion and universal causality. The free act is the uncompelled act, says Schlick, and controversies about causality and determinism have nothing to do with the case. When one asks whether an act done of necessity is free, the question is ambiguous: if "of necessity" means "by compulsion," then the answer is no; if, on the other hand, "of necessity" is a way of referring to "causal uniformity" in nature—the sense in which we may misleadingly speak of the laws of nature as "necessary" simply because there are no exceptions to them—then the answer is clearly yes; every act is an instance of some causal law (uniformity) or other, but this has nothing to do with its being free in the sense of uncompelled.

For Schlick, this is the end of the matter. Any attempt to discuss the matter further simply betrays a failure to perceive the clarifying distinctions that Schlick has made.

> Freedom means the opposite of compulsion; a man is *free* if he does not act under *compulsion,* and he is compelled or unfree when he is hindered from without in the realization of his natural desires. Hence he is unfree when he is locked up, or chained, or when someone forces him at the point of a gun to do what otherwise he would not do. This is quite clear, and everyone will admit that the everyday or legal notion of the lack of freedom is thus correctly interpreted, and that a man will be considered quite free . . . if no such external compulsion is exerted upon him.

This all seems clear enough. And yet if we ask whether it ends the matter, whether it states what we "really mean" by "free," many of us will feel qualms. We remember statements about human beings being pawns of their environment, victims of conditions beyond their control, the result of causal influences stemming from parents, etc., and we think, "Still, are we really free?" We do not want to say that the uniformity of nature itself binds us or renders us unfree; yet is there not something in what generations of wise men have said about man being fettered? Is there not something too facile, too sleight-of-hand, in Schlick's cutting of the Gordian knot?

It will be noticed that we have slipped from talking about acts as being free into talking about human beings as free. Both locutions are employed, I would say about 50-50. Sometimes an attempt is made to legislate definitely between the two: Stebbing, for instance, says that one must never call acts free, but only the doers of the acts.

Let us pause over this for a moment. If it is we and not our acts that are to be called free, the most obvious reflection to make is that we are free to do some things and not free to do other things; we are free to lift our hands but not free to lift the moon. We cannot simply call ourselves free or unfree *in toto;* we must say at best that we are free in respect of certain actions only. G. E. Moore states the criterion as follows: we are free to do an act if we can do it *if* we want to; that which we can do if we want to is what we are free to do. Some things certain people are free to do while others are not: most of us are free to move our legs, but paralytics are not; some of us are free to concentrate on philosophical reading matter for three hours at a stretch while others are not. In general, we could relate the two approaches by saying that a *person* is free *in respect of* a given action if he can do it if he wants to, and in this case his *act* is free.

Moore himself, however, has reservations that Schlick has not. He adds that there *is* a sense of "free" which fulfills the criterion he has just set forth; but that there may be *another* sense in which man cannot be said to be free in all the situations in which he could rightly be said to be so in the first sense.

And surely it is not necessary for me to multiply examples of the sort of thing we mean. In practice most of us would not call free many persons who behave voluntarily and even with calculation aforethought, and under no compulsion either of any obvious sort. A metropolitan newspaper headlines an article with the words "Boy Killer Is Doomed Long before He Is Born," and then goes on to describe how a twelve-year-old boy has just been sentenced to thirty years in Sing Sing for the murder of a girl; his family background includes records of drunkenness, divorce, social maladjustment, epilepsy, and paresis. He early displays a tendency to sadistic activity to hide an underlying masochism and "prove that he's a man";

being coddled by his mother only worsens this tendency, until, spurned by a girl in his attempt on her, he kills her—not simply in a fit of anger, but calculatingly, deliberately. Is he free in respect of his criminal act, or for that matter in most of the acts of his life? Surely to ask this question is to answer it in the negative. Perhaps I have taken an extreme case; but it is only to show the superficiality of the Schlick analysis the more clearly. Though not everyone has criminotic tendencies, everyone has been moulded by influences which in large measure at least determine his present behavior; he is literally the product of these influences, stemming from periods prior to his "years of discretion," giving him a host of character traits that he cannot change now even if he would. So obviously does what a man is depend upon how a man comes to be, that it is small wonder that philosophers and sages have considered man far indeed from being the master of his fate. It is not as if man's will were standing high and serene above the flux of events that have moulded him; it is itself caught up in this flux, itself carried along on the current. An act is free when it is determined by the man's character, say moralists; but when there was nothing the man could do to shape his character, and even the degree of will power available to him in shaping his habits and disciplining himself to overcome the influence of his early environment is a factor over which he has no control, what are we to say of this kind of "freedom?" Is it not rather like the freedom of the machine to stamp labels on cans when it has been devised for just that purpose? Some machines can do so more efficiently than others, but only because they have been better constructed.

It is not my purpose here to establish this thesis in general, but only in one specific respect which has received comparatively little attention, namely, the field referred to by psychiatrists as that of unconscious motivation. In what follows I shall restrict my attention to it because it illustrates as clearly as anthing the points I wish to make.

Let me try to summarize very briefly the psychoanalytic doctrine on this point. The conscious life of the human being, including the conscious decisions and volitions, is merely a mouthpiece for the unconscious—not directly for the enactment of unconscious drives, but of the compromise between unconscious drives and unconscious reproaches. There is a Big Three behind the scenes which the automaton called the conscious personality carries out: the id, an "eternal gimme," presents its wish and demands its immediate satisfaction; the super-ego says no to the wish immediately upon presentation, and the unconscious ego, the mediator between the two, tries to keep peace by means of compromise.

To go into examples of the functioning of these three "bosses" would be endless; psychoanalytic case books supply hundreds of them. The important point for us to see in the present context is that it is the unconscious that determines what the conscious impulse and the conscious action shall be. Hamlet, for example, had a strong Oedipus wish, which was violently counteracted by super-ego reproaches; these early wishes were vividly revived in an unusual adult situation in which his uncle usurped the coveted position from Hamlet's father and won his mother besides. This situation evoked strong strictures on the part of Hamlet's super-ego, and it was this that was responsible for his notorious delay in killing his uncle. A dozen times Hamlet could have killed Claudius easily; but every time Hamlet "decided" not to: a free choice, moralists would say—but no, listen to the super-ego: "What you feel such hatred toward your uncle for, what you are plotting to kill him for, is precisely the crime which you yourself desire to commit: to kill your father and replace him in the affections of your mother. Your fate and your uncle's are bound up together." This paralyzes Hamlet into inaction. Consciously all he knows is that he is unable to act; this conscious inability he rationalizes, giving a different excuse each time.

We have always been conscious of the fact that we are not masters of our fate in every respect—that there are many things which we cannot do, that nature is more powerful than we are, that we cannot disobey laws without danger of reprisals, etc. Lately we have become more conscious, too, though novelists and dramatists have always been fairly conscious of it, that we are not free with respect to the emotions that we feel—whom we love or hate, what types we admire, and the like. More lately still we have been reminded that there are unconscious motivations for our basic attractions and repulsions, our compulsive actions or inabilities to act. But what is not welcome news is that our very acts of volition, and the entire train of deliberations leading up to them, are but facades for the expression of unconscious wishes, or rather, unconscious compromises and defenses.

A man is faced by a choice: shall he kill another person or not? Moralists would say, here is a free choice—the result of deliberation, an action consciously entered into. And yet, though the agent himself does not know it, and has no awareness of the forces that are at work within him, his choice is already determined for him: his conscious will is only an instrument, a slave, in the hands of a deep unconscious motivation which determines his action. If he has a great deal of what the analyst calls "free-floating guilt," he will not; but if the guilt is such as to demand immediate absorption in the form of self-damaging behavior, this accumulated guilt will have to be discharged in some criminal action. The man himself does not know what the inner clockwork is; he is like the hands on the clock, thinking they move freely over the face of the clock.

A woman has married and divorced several husbands. Now she is faced with a choice for the next marriage: shall she marry Mr. A, or Mr. B, or nobody at all? She may take considerable time to "decide" this question, and her decision may appear as a final triumph of her free will. Let us assume that A is a normal, well-adjusted, kind, and generous man, while B is a leech, an impostor, one who will become entangled constantly in quarrels with her. If she belongs to a certain classifiable psychological type, she will inevitably choose B, and she will do so even if her previous husbands have resembled B, so that one would think that she "had learned from experience." Consciously, she will of course "give the matter due consideration," etc., etc. To the psychoanalyst all this is irrelevant chaff in the wind—only a camouflage for the inner workings about which she knows nothing consciously. If she is of a certain kind of masochistic strain, as exhibited in her previous set of symptoms, she *must* choose B: her super-ego, always out to maximize the torment in the situation, seeing what dazzling possibilities for self-damaging behavior are promised by the choice of B, compels her to make the choice she does, and even to conceal the real basis of the choice behind an elaborate facade of rationalizations.

A man is addicted to gambling. In the service of his addiction he loses all his money, spends what belongs to his wife, even sells his property and neglects his children. For a time perhaps he stops; then, inevitably, he takes it up again, although he himself may think he chose to. The man does not know that he is a victim rather than an agent; or, if he sometimes senses that he is in the throes of something-he-knows-not-what, he will have no inkling of its character and will soon relapse into the illusion that he (his conscious self) is freely deciding the course of his own actions. What he does not know, of course, is that he is still taking out on his mother the original lesion to his infantile narcissism, getting back at her for her fancied refusal of his infantile wishes—and this by rejecting everything identified with her, namely education, discipline, logic, common sense, training. At the roulette wheel, almost alone among adult activities, chance—the opposite of all these things—rules supreme; and his addiction represents his continued and emphatic reiteration of his rejection of Mother and all she represents to his unconscious.

This pseudo-aggression of his is of course masochistic in its effects. In the long run he always loses; he can never quit while he is winning. And far from playing in order to win, rather one can say that his losing is a *sine qua non* of his psychic equilibrium (as it was for example with Dostoyevsky): guilt demands punishment, and in the ego's "deal" with the super-ego the super-ego has granted satisfaction of infantile wishes in return for the self-damaging conditions obtaining. Winning would upset the neurotic equilibrium.

A man has wash-compulsion. He must be constantly washing his hands—he uses up perhaps 400 towels a day. Asked why he does this, he says, "I need to, my hands are dirty"; and if it is pointed out to him that they are not really dirty, he says "They feel dirty anyway, I feel better when I wash them." So once again he washes them. He "freely decides" every time; he feels that he must wash them, he deliberates for a moment perhaps, but always ends by washing them. What he does not see, of course, is the invisible wires inside him pulling him inevitably to do the thing he does: the infantile id-wish concerns preoccupation with dirt, the super-ego charges him with this, and the terrified ego must respond, "No, I don't like dirt, see how clean I like to be, look how I wash my hands!" . . .

Let us take, finally, a less colorful, more everyday example. A student at a university, possessing wealth, charm, and all that is usually considered essential to popularity, begins to develop the following personality-pattern: although well taught in the graces of social conversation, he always makes a *faux pas* somewhere, and always in the worst possible situation; to his friends he makes cutting remarks which hurt deeply—and always apparently aimed in such a way as to hurt the most: a remark that would not hurt A but would hurt B he invariably makes to B rather than to A, and so on. None of this is conscious. Ordinarily he is considerate of people, but he contrives always (unconsciously) to impose on just those friends who would resent it most, and at just the times when he should know that he should not impose: at 3 o'clock in the morning, without forewarning, he phones a friend in a near-by city demanding to stay at his apartment for the weekend; naturally the friend is offended, but the person himself is not aware that he has provoked the grievance ("common sense" suffers a temporary eclipse when the neurotic pattern sets in, and one's intelligence, far from being of help in such a situation, is used in the interest of the neurosis), and when the friend is cool to him the next time they meet, he wonders why and feels unjustly treated. Aggressive behavior on his part invites resentment and aggression in turn, but all that he consciously sees is other's behavior toward him—and he considers himself the innocent victim of an unjustified "persecution."

Each of these choices is, from the moralist's point of view, free: he chose to phone his friend at 3 a.m.; he chose to make the cutting remark that he did, etc. What he does not know is that an ineradicable masochistic pattern has set in. His unconscious is far more shrewd and clever than is his conscious intellect; it sees with uncanny accuracy just what kind of behavior will damage him most, and unerringly forces him into that behavior. Consciously, the student "doesn't know why he did it"—he gives different "reasons" at different times, but they are all, once again, rationalizations cloaking the unconscious mechanism which propels him willy-nilly into actions that his "common sense" eschews.

The more of this sort of thing you see, the more you can see what the psychoanalyst means when he talks about "the illusion of free-will." And the more of a psychiatrist you become, the more you are overcome with a sense of what an illusion this precious free-will really is. In some kinds of cases most of us can see it already: it takes no psychiatrist to look at the epileptic and sigh with sadness at the thought that soon this person before you will be as one possessed, not the same thoughtful intelligent person you knew. But people are not aware of this in other contexts, for example when they express surprise at how a person whom they have been so good to could treat them so badly. Let us suppose that you help a person financially or morally or in some other way, so that he is in your debt; suppose further that he is one of the many neurotics who unconsciously identify kindness with weakness and aggression with strength, then he will unconsciously take your kindness to him as weakness and use it as the occasion for enacting some aggession against you. He can't help it, he may regret it himself later; still, he will be driven to it. If we gain a little knowledge of psychiatry, we can look at him with pity, that a person otherwise so worthy should be so unreliable—but we will exercise realism too and be aware that there are some types of people that you cannot be good to in "free" acts of their conscious volition, they will use your own goodness against you.

Sometimes the persons themselves will become dimly aware that "something behind the scenes" is determining their behavior. The divorcee will sometimes view herself with detachment, as if she were some machine (and indeed the psychoanalyst does call her a "repeating-machine"): "I know I'm caught in a net, that I'll fall in love with this guy and marry him and the whole ridiculous merry-go-round will start all over again."

We talk about free will, and we say, yes, the person is free to do so-and-so if he can do so *if* he wants to—and we forget that his wanting to is itself caught up in the stream of determinism, that unconscious forces drive him into the wanting or not wanting to do the thing in question. The idea of the puppet whose motions are manipulated from behind by invisible wires, or better still, by springs inside, is no mere figure of speech. The analogy is a telling one at almost every point. . . .

Now, what of the notion of responsibility? What happens to it on our analysis?

Let us begin with an example, not a fictitious one. A woman and her two-year-old baby are riding on a train to Montreal in mid-winter. The child is ill. The woman wants badly to get to her destination. She is, unknown to herself, the victim of a neurotic conflict whose nature is irrelevant here except for the fact that it forces her to behave aggressively toward the child, partly to spite her husband whom she despises and who loves the child, but chiefly to ward off super-ego charges of masochistic attachment. Consciously she loves the child, and when she says this she says it sincerely, but she must behave aggressively toward it nevertheless, just as many children love their mothers but are nasty to them most of the time in neurotic pseudo-aggression. The child becomes more ill as the train approaches Montreal; the heating system of the train is not working, and the conductor advises the woman to get off the train at the next town and get the child to a hospital at once. The woman says no, she must get to Montreal. Shortly afterward, as the child's condition worsens, and the mother does all she can to keep it alive, without, however, leaving the train, for she declares that it is absolutely necessary that she reach her destination. But before she gets there the child is dead. After that, of course, the mother grieves, blames herself, weeps hysterically, and joins the church to gain surcease from the guilt that constantly overwhelms her when she thinks of how her aggressive behavior has killed her child.

Was she responsible for her deed? In ordinary life, after making a mistake, we say, "Chalk it up to experience." Here we say, "Chalk it up to the neurosis." No, she is not responsible. She could not help it if her neurosis forced her to act this way—she didn't even know what was going on behind the scenes, she merely acted out the part assigned to her. This is far more true than is generally realized: criminal actions in general are not actions for which their agents are responsible; the agents are passive, not active—they are victims of a neurotic conflict. Their very hyper-activity is unconsciously determined.

To say this is, of course, not to say that we should not punish criminals. Clearly, for our own protection, we must remove them from our midst so that they can no longer molest and endanger organized society. And, of course, if we use the world "responsible" in such a way that justly to hold someone responsible for a deed is by definition identical with being justified in punishing him, then we can and do hold people responsible. But this is like the sense of "free" in which free acts are voluntary ones. It does not go deep enough. In a deeper sense we cannot hold the person responsible: we may hold his neurosis responsible, but he is not responsible for his neurosis, particularly since the age at which its onset was inevitable was an age before he could even speak.

The neurosis is responsible—but isn't the neurosis a part of *him*? We have been speaking all the time as if the person and his unconscious were two separate beings; but isn't he one personality, including conscious and unconscious departments together?

I do not wish to deny this. But it hardly helps us here; for what people want when they talk about freedom, and what they hold to when they champion it, is the idea that the *conscious* will is the master of their destiny. "I am the master of my fate, I am the captain of my soul"—and they surely mean their conscious selves, the self that they can recognize and search and introspect. Between an unconscious that willy-nilly determines your actions, and an external force which pushes you, there is little if anything to choose. The unconscious is just *as if* it were an outside force; and indeed, psychiatrists will assert that the inner Hitler can torment you far more than any external Hitler can. Thus the kind of freedom that people want, the only kind they will settle for, is precisely the kind that psychiatry says that they cannot have. . . .

Let us . . . put the situation schematically in the form of a deductive argument.

1. An occurrence over which we had no control is something we cannot be held responsible for.
2. Events E, occurring during our babyhood, were events over which we had no control.
3. Therefore events E were events which we cannot be held responsible for.
4. But if there is something we cannot be held responsible for, neither can we be held responsible for something that inevitably results from it.
5. Events E have as inevitable consequence Neurosis N, which in turn has as inevitable consequence Behavior B.
6. Since N is the inevitable consequence of E and B is the inevitable consequence of N, B is the inevitable consequence of E.
7. Hence, not being responsible for E, we cannot be responsible for B.

Jean-Paul Sartre
Freedom and Responsibility

Jean-Paul Sartre's *(1905–1980) "existentialism" features a powerful emphasis on the freedom and responsibility of each individual. The following is taken from his* Being and Nothingness.

Although the considerations which are about to follow are of interest primarily to the ethicist, it may nevertheless be worthwhile after these descriptions and arguments to return to the freedom of the for-itself and try to understand what the fact of this freedom represents for human destiny.

The essential consequence of our earlier remarks is that man being condemned to be free carries the weight of the whole world on his shoulders; he is responsible for the world and for himself as a way of being. We are taking the word "responsibility" in its ordinary sense as "consciousness (of) being the incontestable author of an event or of an object." In this sense the responsibility of the for-itself is overwhelming since he is the one by whom it happens that *there is* a world; since he is also the one who makes himself be, then whatever may be the situation in which he finds himself, the for-itself must wholly assume this situation with its peculiar coefficient of adversity, even though it be insupportable. He must assume the situation with the proud consciousness of being the author of it, for the very worst disadvantages or the worst threats which can endanger my person have meaning only in and through my project; and it is on the ground of the engagement which I am that they appear. It is therefore senseless to think of complaining since nothing foreign has decided what we feel, what we live, or what we are.

Furthermore this absolute responsibility is not resignation; it is simply the logical requirement of the consequences of our freedom. What happens to me happens through me, and I can neither affect myself with it nor revolt against it nor resign myself to it. Moreover everything which happens to me is *mine*. By this we must understand first of all that I am always equal to what happens to me qua man, for what happens to a man through other men and through himself can be only human. The most terrible situations of war, the worst tortures do not create a non-human state of things; there is no non-human situation. It is only through fear, flight, and recourse to magical types of conduct that I shall decide on the non-human, but this decision is human, and I shall carry the entire responsibility for it. But in addition the situation is *mine* because it is the image of my free choice of myself, and everything which it presents to me is *mine* in that this represents me and symbolizes me. Is it not I who decide the coefficient of adversity in things and even their unpredictability by deciding myself?

Thus there are no *accidents* in life; a community event which suddenly bursts forth and involves me in it does not come from the outside. If I am mobilized in a war, this war is *my* war; it is in my image and I deserve it. I deserve it first because I could always get out of it by suicide or by desertion; these ultimate possibles are those which must always be present for us when there is a question of envisaging a situation. For lack of getting out of it, I have *chosen* it. This can be due to inertia, to cowardice in the face of public opinion, or because I prefer certain other values to the value of the refusal to join in the war (the good opinion of my relatives, the honor of my family, *etc.*). Any way you look at it, it is a matter of a choice. This choice will be repeated later on again and again without a break until the end of the war. Therefore we must agree with the statement by J. Romains, "In war there are no innocent victims." If therefore I have preferred war to death or to dishonor, everything takes place as if I bore the entire responsibility for this war. Of course others have declared it, and one might be tempted perhaps to consider me as a simple accomplice. But this notion of complicity has only a juridical sense, and it does not hold there. For it depended on me that for me and by me this war should not exist, and I have decided that it does exist. There was no compulsion here, for the compulsion could have got no hold on a freedom. I did not have any excuse; . . . the peculiar character of human-reality is that it is without excuse. Therefore it remains for me only to lay claim to this war.

But in addition the war is *mine* because by the sole fact that arises in a situation which I cause to be and that I can discover it there only by engaging myself for or against it, I can no longer distinguish at present the choice which I make of myself from the choice which I make of the war. To live this war is to choose myself through it and to choose it through my choice of myself. There can be no question of considering it as "four years of vacation" or as a "reprieve," as a "recess," the essential part of my responsibilities being elsewhere in my married, family, or professional life. In this war which I have chosen I choose myself from day to day, and I make it mine by making myself. If it is going to be four empty years, then it is I who bear the responsibility for this.

Finally, . . . each person is an absolute choice of self from the standpoint of a world of knowledges and of techniques which this choice both assumes and illumines; each person is an absolute upsurge at an absolute date and is perfectly unthinkable at another date. It is therefore a waste of time to ask what I should have been if this war had not broken out, for I have chosen myself as one of the possible meanings of the epoch which imperceptibly led to war. I am not distinct from this same epoch; I could not be transported to another epoch without contradiction. Thus I *am* this war which restricts and limits and makes comprehensible the period which preceded it. In this sense we may define more precisely the responsibility of the for-itself if to the earlier quoted statement, "There are no innocent victims," we add the words, "We have the war we deserve." Thus, totally free, undistinguishable from the period for which I have chosen to be the meaning, as profoundly responsible for the war as if I had myself declared it, unable to live without integrating it in *my* situation, engaging myself in it wholly and stamping it with my seal, I must be without remorse or regrets as I am without excuse; for from the instant of my upsurge into being, I carry the weight of the world by myself alone without anything or any person being able to lighten it.

Yet this responsibility is of a very particular type. Someone will say, "I did not ask to be born." This is a naïve way of throwing greater emphasis on our facticity. I am responsible for everything, in fact, except for my very responsibility, for I am not the foundation of my being. Therefore everything takes place as if I were compelled to be responsible. I am *abandoned* in the world, not in the sense that I might remain abandoned and passive in a hostile universe like a board floating on the water, but rather in the sense that I find myself suddenly alone and without help, engaged in a world for which I bear the whole responsibility without being able, whatever I do, to tear myself away from this responsibility for an instant. For I am responsible for my very desire of fleeing responsibilities. To make myself passive in the world, to refuse to act upon things and upon Others is still to choose myself, and suicide is one mode among others of being-in-the-world. Yet I find an absolute responsibility for the fact that my facticity (here the fact of my birth) is directly inapprehensible and even inconceivable, for this fact of my birth never appears as a brute fact but always across a projective reconstruction of my for-itself. I am ashamed of being born or I am astonished at it or I rejoice over it, or in attempting to get rid of my life I affirm that I live and I assume this life as bad. Thus in a certain sense I *choose* being born. This choice itself is integrally affected with facticity since I am not able not to choose, but this facticity in turn will appear only in so far as I surpass it toward my ends. Thus facticity is everywhere but inapprehensible; I never encounter anything except my responsibility. That is why I can not ask, "*Why* was I born?" or curse the day of my birth or declare that I did not ask to be born, for these various attitudes toward my birth—*i.e.,* toward the *fact* that I realize a presence in the world—are absolutely nothing else but ways of assuming this birth in full responsibility and making it *mine.* Here again I encounter only myself and my projects so that finally my abandonment—*i.e.,* my facticity—consists simply in the fact that I am condemned to be wholly responsible for myself. I am the being which *is* in such a way that in its being its being is in question. And this "is" of my being *is* as present and inapprehensible.

Under these conditions since every event in the world can be revealed to me only as an *opportunity* (an opportunity made use of, lacked, neglected, *etc.*), or better yet since everything which happens to us can be considered as a *chance* (*i.e.,* can appear to us only as a way of realizing this being which is in question in our being) and since others as transcendences-transcended are themselves only *opportunities* and *chances,* the responsibility of the for-itself extends to the entire world as a peopled-world. It is precisely thus that the for-itself apprehends itself in anguish; that is, as a being which is neither the foundation of its own being nor of the Other's being nor of the in-itselfs which form the world, but a being which is compelled to decide the meaning of being—within it and everywhere outside of it. The one who realizes in anguish his condition as *being* thrown into a responsibility which extends to his very abandonment has no longer either remorse or regret or excuse; he is no longer anything but a freedom which perfectly reveals itself and whose being resides in this very revelation. But as we pointed out . . . , most of the time we flee anguish in bad faith.

B. F. Skinner

Freedom and the Control of Men

B. F. Skinner *is a professor of psychology at Harvard and the best known American "behaviorist." In the following he argues his polemical thesis against the importance of what we call "freedom" and urges more scientific control over the conditions influencing people's behavior.*

*T*he second half of the twentieth century may be remembered for its solution of a curious problem. Although Western democracy created the conditions responsible for the rise of modern science, it is now evident that it may never fully profit from that achievement. The so-called "democratic philosophy" of human behavior to which it also gave rise is increasingly in conflict with the application of the methods of science to human affairs. Unless this conflict is somehow resolved, the ultimate goals of democracy may be long deferred.

Just as biographers and critics look for external influences to account for the traits and achievements of the men they study, so science ultimately explains behavior in terms of "causes" or conditions which lie beyond the individual himself. As more and more causal relations are demonstrated, a practical corollary becomes difficult to resist: it should be possible to *produce* behavior according to plan simply by arranging the proper conditions. Now, among the specifications which might reasonably be submitted to a behavioral technology are these: Let men be happy, informed, skillful, well behaved, and productive.

This immediate practical implication of a science of behavior has a familiar ring, for it recalls the doctrine of human perfectibility of eighteenth- and nineteenth-century humanism. A science of man shares the optimism of that philosophy and supplies striking support for the working faith that men can build a better world and, through it, better men. The support comes just in time, for there has been little optimism of late among those who speak from the traditional point of view. Democracy has become "realistic," and it is only with some embarrassment that one admits today to perfectionistic or utopian thinking.

The earlier temper is worth considering, however. History records many foolish and unworkable schemes for human betterment, but almost all the great changes in our culture which we now regard as worthwhile can be traced to perfectionistic philosophies. Governmental, religious, educational, economic, and social reforms follow a common pattern. Someone believes that a change in a cultural practice—for example, in the rules of evidence in a court of law, in the characterization of man's relation to God, in the way children are taught to read and write, in permitted rates of interest, or in minimal housing standards—will improve the condition of men: by promoting justice, permitting men to seek salvation more effectively, increasing the literacy of a people, checking an inflationary trend, or improving public health and family relations, respectively. The underlying hypothesis is always the same: that a different physical or cultural environment will make a different and better man.

The scientific study of behavior not only justifies the general pattern of such proposals; it promises new and better hypotheses. The earliest cultural practices must have originated in sheer accidents. Those which strengthened the group survived with the group in a sort of natural selection. As soon as men began to propose and carry out changes in practice for the sake of possible consequences, the evolutionary process must have accelerated. The simple practice of making changes must have had survival value. A further acceleration is now to be expected. As laws of behavior are more precisely stated, the changes in the environment required to bring about a given effect may be more clearly specified. Conditions which have been neglected because their effects were slight or unlooked for may be shown to be relevant. New conditions may actually be created, as in the discovery and synthesis of drugs which affect behavior.

This is no time, then, to abandon notions of progress, improvement, or, indeed, human perfectibility. The simple fact is that man is able, and now as never before, to lift himself by his own bootstraps. In achieving control of the world of which he is a part, he may learn at last to control himself.

Timeworn objections to the planned improvement of cultural practices are already losing much of their force. Marcus Aurelius was probably right in advising his readers to be content with a haphazard amelioration of mankind. "Never hope to realize Plato's republic," he sighed, ". . . for who can change the opinions of men? And without a change of sentiments what can you make but reluctant slaves and hypocrites?" He was thinking, no doubt, of contemporary patterns of control based upon punishment or the threat of punishment which, as he correctly observed, breed only reluctant slaves of those who submit and hypocrites of those who discover modes of evasion. But we need not share his pessimism, for the opinions of men can be changed. The techniques of indoctrination which were being devised by the early Christian Church at the very time Marcus Aurelius was writing are relevant, as are some of the techniques of psychotherapy and of advertising and public relations. Other methods suggested by recent scientific analyses leave little doubt of the matter.

The study of human behavior also answers the cynical complaint that there is a plain "cussedness" in man which will always thwart efforts to improve him. We are often told that men do not want to be changed, even for the better. Try to help them, and they will outwit you and remain happily wretched. Dostoevsky claimed to see some plan in it. "Out of sheer ingratitude," he complained, or possibly boasted, "man will play you a dirty trick, just to prove that men are still men and not the keys of a piano. . . . And even if you could prove that a man is only a piano key, he would still do something out of sheer perversity—he would create destruction and chaos—just to gain his point. . . . And if all this could in turn be analyzed and prevented by predicting that it would occur, then man would deliberately go mad to prove his point." This is a conceivable neurotic reaction to inept control. A few men may have shown it, and many have enjoyed Dostoevsky's statement because they tend to show it. But that such perversity is a fundamental reaction of the human organism to controlling conditions is sheer nonsense.

So is the objection that we have no way of knowing what changes to make even though we have the necessary techniques. That is one of the great hoaxes of the century—a sort of booby trap left behind in the retreat before the advancing front of science. Scientists themselves have unsuspectingly agreed that there are two kinds of useful propositions about nature— facts and value judgments—and that science must confine itself to "what is," leaving "what ought to be" to others. But with what special sort of wisdom is the nonscientist endowed? Science is only effective knowing, no matter who engages in it. Verbal behavior proves upon analysis to be composed of many different types of utterances, from poetry and exhortation to logic and factual description, but these are not all equally useful in talking about cultural practices. We may classify useful propositions according to the degrees of confidence with which they may be asserted. Sentences about nature range from highly probable "facts" to sheer guesses. In general, future events are less likely to be correctly described than past. When a scientist talks about a projected experiment, for example, he must often resort to statements having only a moderate likelihood of being correct; he calls them hypotheses.

Designing a new cultural pattern is in many ways like designing an experiment. In drawing up a new constitution, outlining a new educational program, modifying a religious doctrine, or setting up a new fiscal policy, many statements must be quite tentative. We cannot be sure that the practices we specify will have the consequences we predict, or that the consequences will reward our efforts. This is in the nature of such proposals. They are not value judgments—they are guesses. To confuse and delay the improvement of cultural practices by quibbling about the word *improve* is itself not a useful practice. Let us agree, to start with, that health is better than illness, wisdom better than ignorance, love better than hate, and productive energy better than neurotic sloth.

Perhaps the most crucial part of our democratic philosophy to be reconsidered is our attitude toward freedom—or its reciprocal, the control of human behavior. We do not oppose all forms of control because it is . . . "human nature" to do so. The reaction is not characteristic of all men under all conditions of life. It is an attitude which has been carefully engineered, in large part by what we call the "literature" of democracy. With respect to some methods of control (for example, the threat of force), very little engineering is needed, for the techniques or their immediate consequences are objectionable. Society has suppressed these methods by branding them "wrong," "illegal," or "sinful." But to encourage these attitudes toward objectionable forms of control, it has been necessary to disguise the real nature of certain indispensable techniques, the commonest examples of which are education, moral discourse, and persuasion. The actual procedures appear harmless enough. They consist of supplying information, presenting opportunities for action, pointing out logical relationships, appealing to reason or "enlightened understanding," and so on. Through a masterful piece of misrepresentation, the illusion is fostered that these procedures do not involve the control of behavior; at most, they are simply ways of "getting someone to change his mind." But analysis not only reveals the presence of well-defined behavioral processes, it demonstrates a kind of control no less inexorable, though in some ways more acceptable, than the bully's threat of force.

Let us suppose that someone in whom we are interested is acting unwisely—he is careless in the way he deals with his friends, he drives too fast, or he holds his golf club the wrong way. We could probably help him by issuing a series of commands: don't nag, don't drive over sixty, don't hold your club that way. Much less objectionable would be "an appeal to reason." We could show him how people are affected by his treatment of them, how accident rates rise sharply at higher speeds, how a particular grip on the club alters the way the ball is struck and corrects a slice. In doing so we resort to verbal mediating devices which emphasize and support certain "contingencies of reinforcement"—that is, certain relations between behavior and its consequences—which strengthen the behavior we wish to set up. The same consequences would possibly set up the behavior without our help, and they eventually take control no matter which form of help we give. The appeal to reason has certain advantages over the authoritative command. A threat of punishment, no matter how subtle, generates emotional reactions and tendencies to escape or revolt. Perhaps the controllee merely "feels resentment" at being made to act in a given way, but even that is to be avoided. When we "appeal to reason," he "feels freer to do as he pleases." The fact is that we have exerted *less* control than in using a threat; since other conditions may contribute to the result, the effect may be delayed or, possibly in a given instance, lacking. But if we have worked a change in his behavior at all, it is because we have altered relevant environmental conditions, and the processes we have set in motion are just as real and just as inexorable, if not as comprehensive, as in the most authoritative coercion.

"Arranging an opportunity for action" is another example of disguised control. The power of the negative form has already been exposed in the analysis of censorship. Restriction of opportunity is recognized as far from harmless. As Ralph Barton Perry said in an article which appeared in the Spring, 1953, *Pacific Spectator*, "Whoever determines what alternatives shall be made known to man controls what that man shall choose *from*. He is deprived of freedom in proportion as he is denied access to *any* ideas, or is confined to any range of ideas short of the totality of relevant possibilities." But there is a positive side as well. When we present a relevant state of affairs, we increase the likelihood that a given form of behavior will be emitted. To the extent that the probability of action has changed, we have made a definite contribution. The teacher of history controls a student's behavior (or, if the reader prefers, "deprives him of freedom") just as much in *presenting* historical facts as in suppressing them. Other conditions will no doubt affect the student, but the contribution made to his behavior by the presentation of material is fixed and, within its range, irresistible.

The methods of education, moral discourse, and persuasion are acceptable not because they recognize the freedom of the individual or his right to dissent, but because they make only *partial* contributions to the control of his behavior. The freedom they recognize is freedom from a more coercive form of control. The dissent which they tolerate is the possible effect of other determiners of action. Since these sanctioned methods are frequently ineffective, we have been able to convince ourselves that they do not represent control at all. When they show too much strength to permit disguise, we give them other names and suppress them as energetically as we suppress the use of force. Education grown too powerful is rejected as propaganda or "brain-washing," while really effective persuasion is described as "undue influence," "demagoguery," "seduction," and so on.

If we are not to rely solely upon accident for the innovations which give rise to cultural evolution, we must accept the fact that some kind of control of human behavior is inevitable. We cannot use good sense in human affairs unless someone engages in the design and construction of environmental conditions which affect the behavior of men. Environmental changes have always been the condition for the improvement of cultural patterns, and we can hardly use the more effective methods of science without making changes on a grander scale. We are all controlled by the world in which we live, and part of that world has been and will be constructed by men. The question is this: Are we to be controlled by accident, by tyrants, or by ourselves in effective cultural design?

The danger of the misuse of power is possibly greater than ever. It is not allayed by disguising the facts. We cannot make wise decisions if we continue to pretend that human behavior is not controlled, or if we refuse to engage in control when valuable results might be forthcoming. Such measures weaken only ourselves, leaving the strength of science to others. The first step in a defense against tyranny is the fullest possible exposure of controlling techniques. A second step has already been taken successfully in restricting the use of physical force. Slowly, and as yet imperfectly, we have worked out an ethical and governmental design in which the strong man is not allowed to use the power deriving from his strength to control his fellow men. He is restrained by a superior force created for that purpose—the ethical pressure of the group, or more explicit religious and governmental measures. We tend to distrust superior forces, as we currently hesitate to relinquish sovereignty in order to set up an international police force. But it is only through such counter-control that we have achieved what we call peace—a condition in which men are not permitted to control each other through force. In other words, control itself must be controlled.

Science has turned up dangerous processes and materials before. To use the facts and techniques of a science of man to the fullest extent without making some monstrous mistake will be difficult and obviously perilous. It is no time for self-deception, emotional indulgence, or the assumption of attitudes which are no longer useful. Man is facing a difficult test. He must keep his head now, or he must start again—a long way back.

Anthony Burgess

A Clockwork Orange

Anthony Burgess *is the author of many novels, including* A Clockwork Orange. *In this excerpt from that book, a young hoodlum is reconditioned to be "good" through experiments in which his viewing violent movies is accompanied by a drug that makes him very ill. It works, but the prison chaplain points out the philosophical problems it raises.*

[*T*he Prison Chaplain tells him:] 'Very hard ethical questions are involved,' he went on. 'You are to be made into a good boy, 6655321. Never again will you have the desire to commit acts of violence or to offend in any way whatsoever against the State's Peace. I hope you take all that in. I hope you are absolutely clear in your own mind about that.' I said:

'Oh, it will be nice to be good, sir.' But I had a real horrorshow smeck at that inside, brothers. He said:

'It may not be nice to be good, little 6655321. It may be horrible to be good. And when I say that to you I realize how self-contradictory that sounds. I know I shall have many sleepless nights about this. What does God want? Does God want goodness or the choice of goodness? Is a man who chooses the bad perhaps in some way better than a man who has the good imposed upon him? Deep and hard questions, little 6655321. But all I want to say to you now is this: if at any time in the future you look back to these times and remember me, the lowest and humblest of all God's servitors, do not, I pray, think evil of me in your heart, thinking me in any way involved in what is now about to happen to you. And now, talking of praying, I realize sadly that there will be little point in praying for you. You are passing now to a region where you will be beyond the reach of the power of prayer. A terrible terrible thing to consider. And yet, in a sense, in choosing to be deprived of the ability to make an ethical choice, you have in a sense really chosen the good. So I shall like to think. So, God help us all, 6655321, I shall like to think.' And he began to cry.

19

What Do I Justly Deserve?

What grade would you like in this course? But aside from that, what grade do you think that you *deserve* in this course? What sort of income do you expect ten years from now? Do you think that is fair pay for your work and your talents? Or do you think that you deserve more than that? But on the other hand, think of the millions of people in the world who work just as hard, doing grueling and sometimes dangerous work, who are not even making subsistence level salaries and cannot support themselves and their families. What you will earn in virtually any job in America would be a luxury to them. Is this fair? Is it fair that so many people on the planet are so poor while some are so wealthy? Is it fair that a few people make so much more money than you ever will for essentially just having fun, throwing a ball through a hoop, or playing guitar on MTV? Is it fair that there are any differences at all and that you have to work so hard for a grade that may or may not be what you really deserve?

The problem of **justice** is one of the oldest problems in philosophy. It is the question that dominated Plato's *Republic*, and it had probably already been argued before that by the ancient Sumerians and Babylonians. Discussions of justice often begin with the question of criminal or **retributive justice**—the question of how and why those who violate the law are to be punished. The more common and familiar questions, however, are rather those of **distributive justice**—the fair and equitable distribution of benefits and obligations to everyone in society. Both sets of questions come down to a single common query: What do we deserve? The answer we would all like to hear, of course, is that we deserve what we want and do not deserve to be punished. But what people want is often more than the resources of a society can provide, and their behavior, even if not criminal, is too often detrimental to others around them. Justice thus concerns the basic workings of society, that is, the organization of its institutions so that goods are fairly distributed and obligations and duties are fairly assigned. It concerns the punishment of the guilty but also the reward of the meritorious, fair pay for good work, and appropriate power in determining how things are done. One ancient recipe for retributive justice was "an eye for an eye, a tooth for a tooth." One modern prescription for distributive justice is "one should get what one earns." But we now consider that ancient prescription brutal and inhumane, and we are also realizing that the question of what one earns is more difficult than we once believed. By what standard of justice does a broker doing deals on the phone in an air-conditioned office earn more than a day laborer building a stone wall on a hot summer day? We are also concerned not just with the distribution of money and goods but with the distribution of power and privileges. We say that everyone is equal, but we discriminate in a thousand ways concerning such questions as who is allowed to drive, to drink, to vote, or to carry a gun in public. How can such discriminations be made fairly? And how can the less pleasant and more dangerous jobs in our society be assigned? Who should serve in the army? Who will pay taxes and how much? These are all questions of justice and still as much matters of great controversy as they were in the ancient world.

We demand and expect justice in society and we object when it is not in evidence. One person pays more in taxes than another person with the same income, and we want to know why. One child receives an excellent education, while another who is just as bright and talented does not, and we want to know why. One man is convicted of a criminal offense and is sentenced to lifetime imprisonment, while another is convicted of the same offense and is put on probation for two years, and we want to know why. One way to understand the theory of justice—admittedly a very modern way of doing so—is to think of a theory of justice as a general explanation about why people are treated differently. For example, some people *should* be taxed more because they have a larger income or fewer children to support. Some criminals should be punished more than others because they have committed prior offenses and are more likely to do so again. One person is called to serve in the army while another is allowed to pursue a career because his career is in "the national interest." A theory of justice is a kind of decision procedure through which legislators, judges, administrators, and ultimately, all of us can figure out what is fair and what is not, who should get what and how much.

We often hear that "life isn't fair"—typically from someone who is trying to defend a recent injustice. This bit of cynicism isn't at all new; Plato considered it and rejected it more than twenty-five hundred years ago in *The Republic*. In the first of the following selections, Socrates considers the thesis that the only real justice is strength and that the strong can do whatever they can get away with. In other words, "might makes right." But Socrates shows that this cannot be what justice is. The strong can be wrong. A different way of understanding "life isn't fair" is the basis of Thomas Hobbes' famous account of justice in *The Leviathan*. In the state of nature, he argues, there is no such thing as justice, but in human society, justice comes about as a matter of **convention**. Thus, the question of whether life is fair or not is quite irrelevant, according to Hobbes; the important thing is that *we* are just and that we arrange our society so that justice is realized in it.

One of the presumptions of justice—although the word takes on many meanings and interpretations—is **equality**. Thus, John Stuart Mill defends his "utilitarian" theory of justice on the premise that everyone "counts for one and no more than one," and John Dewey defines justice in terms of democracy and equality. John Rawls presents a brief version of his influential recent theory of justice as fairness, and Robert Nozick supplies a sharp rejoinder. Finally, Joel Feinberg discusses the general theory of economic income and distributive justice.

Plato

Does Might Make Right?

Plato's (427–347 B.C.) The Republic *takes justice as its central concern. In the following selection, he argues that justice is a kind of harmony, in an individual as well as in the ideal state.*

Listen, then, he said; I proclaim that justice is nothing else than the interest of the stronger. And now why do you not praise me? But of course you won't.

Let me first understand you, I replied. Justice, as you say, is the interest of the stronger. What, Thrasymachus, is the meaning of this? You cannot mean to say that because Polydamas, the pancratiast, is stronger than we are, and finds the eating of beef conducive to his bodily strength, that to eat beef is therefore equally for our good who are weaker than he is, and right and just for us?

That's abominable of you, Socrates; you take the words in the sense which is most damaging to the argument.

Not at all, my good sir, I said; I am trying to understand them; and I wish that you would be a little clearer.

Well, he said, have you never heard that forms of government differ; there are tyrannies, and there are democracies, and there are aristocracies?

Yes, I know.

And the government is the ruling power in each state?

Certainly.

And the different forms of government make laws democratical, aristocratical, tyrannical, with a view to their several interests; and these laws, which are made by them for their own interests, are the justice which they deliver to their subjects, and him who transgresses them they punish as a breaker of the law, and unjust. And that is what I mean when I say that in all states there is the same principle of justice, which is the interest of the government; and as the government must be supposed to have power, the only reasonable conclusion is, that everywhere there is one principle of justice, which is the interest of the stronger.

Now I understand you, I said; and whether you are right or not I will try to discover. But let me remark, that in defining justice you have yourself used the word 'interest' which you forbade me to use. It is true, however, that in your definition the words 'of the stronger' are added.

A small addition, you must allow, he said.

Great or small, never mind about that: we must first enquire whether what you are saying is the truth. Now we are both agreed that justice is interest of some sort, but you go on to say 'of the stronger'; about this addition I am not so sure, and must therefore consider further.

Proceed.

I will; and first tell me, Do you admit that it is just for subjects to obey their rulers?

I do.

But are the rulers of states absolutely infallible, or are they sometimes liable to err?

To be sure, he replied, they are liable to err.

Then in making their laws, they may sometimes make them rightly, and sometimes not?

True.

When they make them rightly, they make them agreeably to their interest; when they are mistaken, contrary to their interest; you admit that?

Yes.

And the laws which they make must be obeyed by their subjects,—and that is what you call justice?

Doubtless.

Then justice, according to your argument, is not only obedience to the interest of the stronger but the reverse?

What is that you are saying? he asked.

I am only repeating what you are saying, I believe. But let us consider: Have we not admitted that the rulers may be mistaken about their own interest in what they command, and also that to obey them is justice? Has not that been admitted?

Yes.

Then you must also have acknowledged justice not to be for the interest of the stronger, when the rulers unintentionally command things to be done which are to their own injury. For if, as you say, justice is the obedience which the subject renders to their commands, in that case, O wisest of men, is there any escape from the conclusion that the weaker are commanded to do, not what is for the interest, but what is for the injury of the stronger?

Nothing can be clearer, Socrates, said Polemarchus.

Yes, said Cleitophon, interposing, if you are allowed to be his witness.

But there is no need of any witness, said Polemarchus, for Thrasymachus himself acknowledges that rulers may sometimes command what is not for their own interest, and that for subjects to obey them is justice.

Yes, Polemarchus,—Thrasymachus said that for subjects to do what was commanded by their rulers is just.

Yes, Cleitophon, but he also said that justice is the interest of the stronger, and, while admitting both these propositions, he further acknowledged that the stronger may command the weaker who are his subjects to do what is not for his own interest; whence follows that justice is the injury quite as much as the interest of the stronger.

But, said Cleitophon, he meant by the interest of the stronger what the stronger thought to be his interest,—this was what the weaker had to do; and this was affirmed by him to be justice.

Those were not his words, rejoined Polemarchus.

Never mind, I replied, if he now says that they are, let us accept his statement. Tell me, Thrasymachus, I said, did you mean by justice what the stronger thought to be his interest, whether really so or not?

Certainly not, he said. Do you suppose that I call him who is mistaken the stronger at the time when he is mistaken?

Yes, I said, my impression was that you did so, when you admitted that the ruler was not infallible but might be sometimes mistaken.

You argue like an informer, Socrates. Do you mean, for example, that he who is mistaken about the sick is a physician in that he is mistaken? or that he who errs in arithmetic or grammar is an arithmetician or grammarian at the time when he is making the mistake, in respect of the mistake? True, we say that the physician or arithmetician or grammarian has made a mistake, but this is only a way of speaking; for the fact is that neither the grammarian nor any other person of skill ever makes a mistake in so far as he is what his name implies; they none of them err unless their skill fails them, and then they cease to be skilled artists. No artist or sage or ruler errs at the time when he is what his name implies; though he is commonly said to err, and I adopted the common mode of speaking. But to be perfectly accurate, since you are such a lover of accuracy, we should say that the ruler, in so far as he is a ruler, is unerring, and, being unerring, always commands that which is for his own interest; and the subject is required to execute his commands; and therefore, as I said at first and now repeat, justice is the interest of the stronger.

Indeed, Thrasymachus, and do I really appear to you to argue like an informer?

Certainly, he replied.

And do you suppose that I ask these questions with any design of injuring you in the argument?

Nay, he replied, 'suppose' is not the word—I know it; but you will be found out, and by sheer force of argument you will never prevail.

I shall not make the attempt, my dear man; but to avoid any misunderstanding occurring between us in future, let me ask, in what sense do you speak of a ruler or stronger whose interest, as you were saying, he being the superior, it is just that the inferior should execute— is he a ruler in the popular or in the strict sense of the term?

In the strictest of all senses, he said. And now cheat and play the informer if you can; I ask no quarter at your hands. But you never will be able, never.

And do you imagine, I said, that I am such a madman as to try and cheat Thrasymachus? I might as well shave a lion.

Why, he said, you made the attempt a minute ago, and you failed.

Enough, I said, of these civilities. It will be better that I should ask you a question: Is the physician, taken in that strict sense of which you are speaking, a healer of the sick or a maker of money? And remember that I am now speaking of the true physician.

A healer of the sick, he replied.

And the pilot—that is to say, the true pilot—is he a captain of sailors or a mere sailor?

A captain of sailors.

The circumstance that he sails in the ship is not to be taken into account; neither is he to be called a sailor; the name pilot by which he is distinguished has nothing to do with sailing, but is significant of his skill and of his authority over the sailors.

Very true, he said.

Now, I said, every art has an interest?

Certainly.

For which the art has to consider and provide?

Yes, that is the aim of art.

And the interest of any art is the perfection of it—this and nothing else?

What do you mean?

I mean what I may illustrate negatively by the example of the body. Suppose you were to ask me whether the body is self-sufficing or has wants, I should reply: Certainly the body has wants; for the body may be ill and require to be cured, and has therefore interests to which the art of medicine ministers; and this is the origin and intention of medicine, as you will acknowledge. Am I not right?

Quite right, he replied.

But is the art of medicine or any other art faulty or deficient in any quality in the same way that the eye may be deficient in sight or the ear fail of hearing, and therefore requires another art to provide for the interests of seeing and hearing—has art in itself, I say, any similar liability to fault or defect, and does every art require another supplementary art to provide for its interests, and that another and another without end? Or have the arts to look only after their own interests? Or have they no need either of themselves or of another?— having no faults or defects, they have no need to correct them, either by the exercise of their own art or of any other; they have only to consider the interest of their subject-matter. For every art remains pure and faultless while remaining true—that is to say, while perfect and unimpaired. Take the words in your precise sense, and tell me whether I am not right.

Yes, clearly.

Then medicine does not consider the interest of medicine, but the interest of the body?

True, he said.

Nor does the art of horsemanship consider the interests of the art of horsemanship, but the interests of the horse; neither do any other arts care for themselves, for they have no needs; they care only for that which is the subject of their art?

True, he said.

But surely, Thrasymachus, the arts are the superiors and rulers of their own subjects?

To this he assented with a good deal of reluctance.

Then, I said, no science or art considers or enjoins the interest of the stronger or superior, but only the interest of the subject and weaker?

He made an attempt to contest this proposition also, but finally acquiesced.

Then, I continued, no physician, in so far as he is a physician, considers his own good in what he prescribes, but the good of his patient; for the true physician is also a ruler having the human body as a subject, and is not a mere money-maker; that has been admitted?

Yes.

And the pilot likewise, in the strict sense of the term, is a ruler of sailors and not a mere sailor?

That has been admitted.

And such a pilot and ruler will provide and prescribe for the interest of the sailor who is under him, and not for his own or the ruler's interest?

He gave a reluctant 'Yes.'

Then, I said, Thrasymachus, there is no one in any rule who, in so far as he is a ruler, considers or enjoins what is for his own interest, but always what is for the interest of his subject or suitable to his art; to that he looks, and that alone he considers in everything which he says and does.

When we had got to this point in the argument, and every one saw that the definition of justice had been completely upset, Thrasymachus, instead of replying to me, said: Tell me, Socrates, have you got a nurse?

Thomas Hobbes

Justice and the Social Contract

Thomas Hobbes (1588–1679) *was a political reformer and the author of a bold book,* The Leviathan, *in which, among other things, he argues against the divine right of kings. He begins the book by considering what life might be like in "the state of nature"—before the formation of societies. In nature, he says, there is no such thing as justice. Justice arises as part of the "social contract" which originates society. The following is from* The Leviathan.

It may seem strange to some man, that has not well weighed these things; that nature should thus dissociate, and render men apt to invade, and destroy one another: and he may therefore, not trusting to this inference, made from the passions, desire perhaps to have the same confirmed by experience. Let him therefore consider with himself, when taking a journey, he arms himself, and seeks to go well accompanied; when going to sleep, he locks his doors; when even in his house he locks his chests; and this when he knows there be laws, and public officers, armed, to revenge all injuries shall be done him; what opinion he has of his fellow subjects, when he rides armed; of his fellow citizens, when he locks his doors; and of his children, and servants, when he locks his chests. Does he not there as much accuse mankind by his actions, as I do by my words? But neither of us accuse man's nature in it. The desires, and other passions of man, are in themselves no sin. No more are the actions, that proceed from those passions, till they know a law that forbids them: which till laws be made they cannot know: nor can any law be made, till they have agreed upon the person that shall make it.

It may peradventure be thought, there was never such a time, nor condition of war as this; and I believe it was never generally so, over all the world: but there are many places, where they live so now. For the savage people in many places of America, except the government of small families, the concord whereof dependeth on natural lust, have no government at all; and live at this day in that brutish manner, as I said before. Howsoever, it may be perceived what manner of life there would be, where there were no common power to fear, by the manner of life, which men that have formerly lived under a peaceful government, use to degenerate into, in civil war.

But though there had never been any time, wherein particular men were in a condition of war one against another; yet in all times, kings, and persons of sovereign authority, because of their independency, are in continual jealousies, and in the state and posture of gladiators; having their weapons pointing, and their eyes fixed on one another; that is, their forts, garrisons, and guns upon the frontiers of their kingdoms; and continual spies upon their neighbours; which is a posture of war. But because they uphold thereby, the industry of their subjects; there does not follow from it, that misery, which accompanies the liberty of particular men.

To this war of every man, against every man, this also is consequent; that nothing can be unjust. The notions of right and wrong, justice and injustice have there no place. Where there is no common power, there is no law: where no law, no injustice. Force, and fraud, are in war the two cardinal virtues. Justice, and injustice are none of the faculties neither of the body, nor mind. If they were, they might be in a man that were alone in the world, as well as his senses, and passions. They are qualities, that relate to men in society, not in solitude. It is consequent also to the same condition, that there be no propriety, no dominion, no *mine* and *thine* distinct; but only that to be every man's, that he can get: and for so long, as he can keep it. And thus much for the ill condition, which man by mere nature is actually placed in; though with a possibility to come out of it, consisting partly in the passions, partly in his reason.

The passions that incline men to peace, are fear of death; desire of such things as are necessary to commodious living; and a hope by their industry to obtain them. And reason suggesteth convenient articles of peace, upon which men may be drawn to agreement. These articles, are they, which otherwise are called the Laws of Nature. . . .

The RIGHT OF NATURE, which writers commonly call *jus naturale,* is the liberty each man hath, to use his own power, as he will himself, for the preservation of his own nature; that is to say, of his own life; and consequently, of doing any thing, which in his own judgment, and reason, he shall conceive to be the aptest means thereunto.

By LIBERTY, is understood, according to the proper signification of the word, the absence of external impediments: which impediments, may oft take away part of a man's power to do what he would; but cannot hinder him from using the power left him, according as his judgment, and reason shall dictate to him.

A LAW OF NATURE, *lex naturalis,* is a precept or general rule, found out by reason, by which a man is forbidden to do that, which is destructive of his life, or taketh away the means of preserving the same; and to omit that, by which he thinketh it may be best preserved. For though they that speak of this subject, use to confound *jus,* and *lex, right* and *law:* yet they ought to be distinguished; because RIGHT, consisteth in liberty to do, or to forbear: whereas LAW, determineth, and bindeth, to one of them: so that law, and right, differ as much, as obligation, and liberty; which in one and the same matter are inconsistent.

And because the condition of man, as hath been declared in the precedent chapter, is a condition of war of every one against every one; in which case every one is governed by his own reason; and there is nothing he can make use of, that may not be a help unto him, in preserving his life against his enemies; it followeth, that in such a condition, every man has a right to every thing; even to one another's body. And therefore, as long as this natural right of every man to every thing endureth, there can be no security to any man, how strong or wise soever he be, of living out the time, which nature ordinarily alloweth men to live. And consequently it is a precept, or general rule of reason, *that every man, ought to endeavour peace, as far as he has hope of obtaining it; and when he cannot obtain it, that he may seek, and use, all helps, and advantages of war.* The first branch of which rule, containeth the first, and fundamental law of nature; which is, *to seek peace, and follow it.* The second, the sum of the right of nature; which is, *by all means we can, to defend ourselves.*

From this fundamental law of nature, by which men are commanded to endeavour peace, is derived this second law; *that a man be willing, when others are so too, as far-forth, as for peace, and defence of himself he shall think it necessary, to lay down this right to all things; and be contented with so much liberty against other men, as he would allow other men against himself.* For as long as every man holdeth this right, of doing any thing he liketh; so long are all men in the condition of war. But if other men will not lay down their right, as well as he; then there is no reason for any one, to divest himself of his: for that were to expose himself to prey, which no man is bound to, rather than to dispose himself to peace. This is that law of the Gospel; *whatsoever you require that others should do to you, that do ye to them.* And that law of all men, *do not do to others what you do not want them to do to you.*

Whensoever a man transferreth his right, or renounceth it; it is either in consideration of some right reciprocally transferred to himself; or for some other good he hopeth for thereby. For it is a voluntary act: and of the voluntary acts of every man, the object is some *good to himself.* And therefore there be some rights, which no man can be understood by any words, or other signs, to have abandoned, or transferred. As first a man cannot lay down the right of resisting them, that assault him by force, to take away his life; because he cannot be understood to aim thereby, at any good to himself. The same may be said of wounds, and chains, and imprisonment; both because there is no benefit consequent to such patience; as there is to the patience of suffering another to be wounded, or imprisoned: as also because a man cannot tell, when he seeth men proceed against him by violence, whether they intend his death or not. And lastly the motive, and end for which this renouncing, and transferring of right is introduced, is nothing else but the security of a man's person, in his life, and in the means of so preserving life, as not to be weary of it. And therefore if a man by words, or other signs, seem to despoil himself of the end, for which those signs were intended; he is not to be understood as if he meant it, or that it was his will; but that he was ignorant of how such words and actions were to be interpreted. . . .

A covenant not to defend myself from force, by force, is always void. For, as I have showed before, no man can transfer, or lay down his right to save himself from death, wounds, and imprisonment, the avoiding whereof is the only end of laying down any right; and therefore the promise of not resisting force, in no covenant transferreth any right; nor is obliging. For though a man may covenant thus, *unless I do so, or so, kill me;* he cannot covenant thus, *unless I do so, or so, I will not resist you, when you come to kill me.* For man by nature chooseth the lesser evil, which is danger of death in resisting; rather than the greater, which is certain and present death in not resisting. And this is granted to be true by all men, in that they lead criminals to execution, and prison, with armed men, notwithstanding that such criminals have consented to the law, by which they are condemned.

From that law of nature, by which we are obliged to transfer to another, such rights, as being retained, hinder the peace of mankind, there followeth a third; which is this, *that men perform their covenants made:* without which, covenants are in vain, and but empty words; and the right of all men to all things remaining, we are still in the condition of war.

And in this law of nature, consisteth the fountain and original of JUSTICE. For where no covenant hath preceded, there hath no right been transferred, and every man has right to every thing; and consequently, no action can be unjust. But when a covenant is made, then to break it is *unjust:* and the definition of INJUSTICE, is no other than *the not performance of covenant.* And whatsoever is not unjust, is *just.*

But because covenants of mutual trust, where there is a fear of not performance on either part, as hath been said in the former chapter, are invalid; though the original of justice be the making of covenants; yet injustice actually there can be none, till the cause of such fear be taken away; which while men are in the natural condition of war, cannot be done. Therefore before the names of just, and unjust can have place, there must be some coercive power, to compel men equally to the performance of their covenants, by the terror of some punishment, greater than the benefit they expect by the breach of their covenant; and to make good that propriety, which by mutual contract men acquire, in recompense of the universal right they abandon: and such power there is none before the erection of a commonwealth. And this is also to be gathered out of the ordinary definition of justice in the Schools: for they say, that *justice is the constant will of giving to every man his own.* And therefore where there is no *own,* that is no propriety, there is no injustice; and where there is no coercive power erected, that is, where there is no commonwealth, there is no propriety; all men having right to all things: therefore where there is no commonwealth, there nothing is injust. So that the nature of justice, consisteth in keeping of valid covenants: but the validity of covenants begins not but with the constitution of a civil power, sufficient to compel men to keep them: and then it is also that propriety begins.

A *commonwealth* is said to be *instituted,* when a *multitude* of men do agree, and *covenant, every one, with every one,* that to whatsoever *man,* or *assembly of men,* shall be given by the major part, the *right* to *present* the person of them all, that is to say, to be their *representative;* every one, as well he that *voted for it,* as he that *voted against it,* shall *authorize* all the actions and judgments, of that man, or assembly of men, in the same manner, as if they were his own, to the end, to live peaceably amongst themselves, and be protected against other men.

From this institution of a commonwealth are derived all the *rights,* and *faculties* of him, or them, on whom the sovereign power is conferred by the consent of the people assembled.

First, because they covenant, it is to be understood, they are not obliged by former covenant to any thing repugnant hereunto. And consequently they that have already instituted a commonwealth, being thereby bound by covenant, to own the actions, and judgments of one, cannot lawfully make a new covenant, amongst themselves, to be obedient to any other, in any thing whatsoever, without his permission. And therefore, they that are subjects to a monarch, cannot without his leave cast off monarchy, and return to the confusion of a disunited multitude; nor transfer their person from him that beareth it, to another man, or other assembly of men: for they are bound, every man to every man, to own, and be reputed author of all, that he that already is their sovereign, shall do, and judge fit to be done: so that any one man dissenting, all the rest should break their covenant made to that man, which is injustice: and they have also every man given the sovereignty to him that beareth their person; and therefore if they depose him, they take from him that which is his own, and so again it is injustice. Besides, if he that attempteth to depose his sovereign, be killed, or punished by him for such attempt, he is author of his own punishment, as being by the institution, author of all his sovereign shall do: and because it is injustice for a man to do any thing, for which he may be punished by his own authority, he is also upon that title, unjust. And whereas some men have pretended for their disobedience to their sovereign, a new covenant, made, not with men, but with God; this also is unjust: for there is no covenant with God, but by mediation of somebody that representeth God's person; which none doth but God's lieutenant, who hath the sovereignty under God. But this pretence of covenant with God, is so evident a lie, even in the pretenders' own consciences, that it is not only an act of an unjust, but also of a vile, and unmanly disposition.

Secondly, because the right of bearing the person of them all, is given to him they make sovereign, by covenant only of one to another, and not of him to any of them; there can happen no breach of covenant on the part of the sovereign; and consequently none of his subjects, by any pretence of forfeiture, can be freed from his subjection. That he which is made sovereign maketh no covenant with his subjects beforehand, is manifest; because either he must make it with the whole multitude, as one party to the covenant; or he must make a several covenant with every man. With the whole, as one party, it is impossible; because as yet they are not one person: and if he make so many several covenants as there be men, those covenants after he hath the sovereignty are void; because what act soever can be pretended by any one of them for breach thereof, is the act both of himself, and of all the rest, because done in the person, and by the right of every one of them in particular. Besides, if any one, or more of them, pretend a breach of the covenant made by the sovereign at his institution; and others, or one other of his subjects, or himself alone, pretend there was no such breach, there is in this case, no judge to decide the controversy; it returns therefore to the sword again; and every man recovereth the right of protecting himself by his own strength, contrary to the design they had in the institution. It is therefore in vain to grant sovereignty by way of precedent covenant. The opinion that any monarch receiveth his power by covenant, this is to say, on condition, procedeth from want of understanding this easy truth, that covenants being but words and breath, have no force to oblige, contain, constrain, or protect any man, but what it has from the public sword; that is, from the untied hands of that man, or assembly of men that hath the sovereignty, and whose actions are avouched by them all, and performed by the strength of them all, in him united. But when an assembly of men is made sovereign; then no man imagineth any such covenant to have passed in the institution; for no man is so dull as to say, for example, the people of Rome made a covenant with the Romans, to hold the sovereignty on such or such conditions; which not performed, the Romans might lawfully depose the Roman people. That men see not the reason to be alike in a monarchy, and in a popular government, proceedeth from the ambition of some, that are kinder to the government of an assembly, whereof they may hope to participate, than of monarchy, which they despair to enjoy.

Thirdly, because the major part hath by consenting voices declared a sovereign; he that dissented must now consent with the rest; that is, be contented to avow all the actions he shall do, or else justly be destroyed by the rest. For if he voluntarily entered into the congregation of them that were assembled, he sufficiently declared thereby his will, and therefore tacitly covenanted, to stand to what the major part should ordain: and therefore if he refuse to stand thereto, or make protestation against any of their decrees, he does contrary to his covenant, and therefore unjustly. And whether he be of the congregation, or not; and whether his consent be asked, or not, he must either submit to their decrees, or be left in the condition of war he was in before; wherein he might without injustice be destroyed by any man whatsoever.

Fourthly, because every subject is by this institution author of all the actions, and judgments of the sovereign instituted; it follows, that whatsoever he doth, it can be no injury to any of his subjects; nor ought he to be by any of them accused of injustice. For he that doth anything by authority from another, doth therein no injury to him by whose authority he acteth: but by this institution of a commonwealth, every particular man is author of all the sovereign doth: and consequently he that complaineth of injury from his sovereign, complaineth of that whereof he himself is author; and therefore ought not to accuse any man but himself; no nor himself of injury; because to do injury to one's self, is impossible. It is true that they that have sovereign power may commit iniquity; but not injustice, or injury in the proper signification.

Fifthly, and consequently to that which was said last, no man that hath sovereign power can justly be put to death, or otherwise in any manner by his subjects punished. For seeing every subject is author of the actions of his sovereign; he punisheth another for the actions committed by himself.

John Stuart Mill

A Utilitarian Theory of Justice

John Stuart Mill *(1806–1873) insists that justice is part and parcel of his ethical view, called "utilitarianism," which calls for "the greatest good for the greatest number." The problem for this view is that it is not clear that justice is simply a matter of utility, rather than a question of rights and obligations. The following is from* Utilitarianism.

In the case of this, as of our other moral sentiments, there is no necessary connexion between the question of its origin and that of its binding force. That a feeling is bestowed on us by nature does not necessarily legitimate all its promptings. The feeling of justice might be a peculiar instinct, and might yet require, like our other instincts, to be controlled and enlightened by a higher reason. If we have intellectual instincts leading us to judge in a particular way, as well as animal instincts that prompt us to act in a particular way, there is no necessity that the former should be more infallible in their sphere than the latter in theirs; it may as well happen that wrong judgments are occasionally suggested by those, as wrong actions by these.

In the first place, it is mostly considered unjust to deprive anyone of his personal liberty, his property, or any other thing which belongs to him by law. Here, therefore, is one instance of the application of the terms "just" and "unjust" in a perfectly definite sense, namely, that it is just to respect, unjust to violate, the *legal rights* of anyone. But this judgment admits of several exceptions, arising from the other forms in which the notions of justice and injustice present themselves. For example, the person who suffers the deprivation may (as the phrase is) have forfeited the rights which he is so deprived of—a case to which we shall return presently. But also—

Secondly, the legal rights of which he is deprived may be rights which *ought* not to have belonged to him; in other words, the law which confers on him these rights may be a bad law. When it is so or when (which is the same thing for our purpose) it is supposed to be so, opinions will differ as to the justice or injustice of infringing it. Some maintain that no law, however bad, ought to be disobeyed by an individual citizen; that his opposition to it, if shown at all, should only be shown in endeavoring to get it altered by competent authority. This opinion (which condemns many of the most illustrious benefactors of mankind, and would often protect pernicious institutions against the only weapons which, in the state of things existing at the time, have any chance of succeeding against them) is defended by those who hold it on grounds of expediency, principally on that of the importance to the common interest of mankind, of maintaining inviolate the sentiment of submission to law. Other persons, again, hold the directly contrary opinion that any law, judged to be bad, may blamelessly be disobeyed, even though it be not judged to be unjust but only inexpedient, while others would confine the license of disobedience to the case of unjust laws; but, again, some say that all laws which are inexpedient are unjust, since every law imposes some restriction on the natural liberty of mankind, which restriction is an injustice unless legitimated by tending to their good. Among these diversities of opinion it seems to be universally admitted that there may be unjust laws, and that law, consequently, is not the ultimate criterion of justice, but may give to one person a benefit, or impose on another an evil, which justice condemns. When, however, a law is thought to be unjust, it seems always to be regarded as being so in the same way in which a breach of law is unjust, namely, be infringing somebody's right, which, as it cannot in this case be a legal right, receives a different appellation and is called a moral right. We may say, therefore, that a second case of injustice consists in taking or withholding from any person that to which he has a *moral right*.

Thirdly, it is universally considered just that each person should obtain that (whether good or evil) which he *deserves,* and unjust that he should obtain a good or be made to undergo an evil which he does not deserve. This is, perhaps, the clearest and most emphatic form in which the idea of justice is conceived by the general mind. As it involves the notion of desert, the question arises what constitutes desert? Speaking in a general way, a person is understood to deserve good if he does right, evil if he does wrong; and in a more particular sense, to deserve good from those to whom he does or has done good, and evil from those to whom he does or has done evil. The precept of returning good for evil has never been regarded as a case of the fulfillment of justice, but as one in which the claims of justice are waived, in obedience to other considerations.

Fourthly, it is confessedly unjust to *break faith* with anyone: to violate an engagement, either express or implied, or disappoint expectations raised by our own conduct, at least if we have raised those expectations knowingly and voluntarily. Like the other obligations of justice already spoken of, this one is not regarded as absolute, but as capable of being overruled by a stronger obligation of justice on the other side, or by such conduct on the part of the person concerned as is deemed to absolve us from our obligation to him and to constitute a *forfeiture* of the benefit which he has been led to expect.

Fifthly, it is, by universal admission, inconsistent with justice to be *partial*—to show favor or preference to one person over another in matters to which favor and preference do not properly apply. Impartiality, however, does not seem to be regarded as a duty in itself, but rather as instrumental to some other duty; for it is admitted that favor and preference are not always censurable, and, indeed, the cases in which they are condemned are rather the exception than the rule. A person would be more likely to be blamed than applauded for giving his family or friends no superiority in good offices over strangers when he could do so without violating any other duty; and no one thinks it unjust to seek one person in preference to another as a friend, connection, or companion. Impartiality where rights are concerned is of course obligatory, but this is involved in the more general obligation of giving to everyone his right. A tribunal, for example, must be impartial because it is bound to award, without regard to any other consideration, a disputed object to the one of two parties who has the right to it. There are other cases in which impartiality means being solely influenced by desert, as with those who, in the capacity of judges, preceptors, or parents, administer reward and punishment as such. There are cases, again, in which it means being solely influenced by consideration for the public interest, as in making a selection among candidates for a government employment. Impartiality, in short, as an obligation of justice, may be said to mean being exclusively influenced by the considerations which it is supposed ought to influence the particular case in hand, and resisting solicitation of any motives which prompt to conduct different from what those considerations would dictate.

Nearly allied to the idea of impartiality is that of *equality,* which often enters as a component part both into the conception of justice and into the practice of it, and, in the eyes of many persons, constitutes its essence. But in this, still more than in any other case, the notion of justice varies in different persons, and always conforms in its variations to their notion of utility. Each person maintains that equality is the dictate of justice, except where he thinks that expediency requires inequality. The justice of giving equal protection to the rights of all is maintained by those who support the most outrageous inequality in the rights themselves. Even in slave countries it is theoretically admitted that the rights of the slave, such as they are, ought to be as sacred as those of the master, and that a tribunal which fails to enforce them with equal strictness is wanting in justice; while, at the same time, institutions which leave to the slave scarcely any rights to enforce are not deemed unjust because they are not deemed inexpedient. Those who think that utility requires distinctions of rank do not consider it unjust that riches and social privileges should be unequally dispensed; but those who think this inequality inexpedient think it unjust also. Whoever thinks that government is necessary sees no injustice in as much inequality as is constituted by giving to the magistrate powers not granted to other people. Even among those who hold leveling doctrines, there are differences of opinion about expediency. Some communists consider it unjust that the produce of the labor of the community should be shared on any other principle than that of exact equality; others think it just that those should receive most whose wants are greatest; while others hold that those who work harder, or who produce more, or whose services are more valuable to the community, may justly claim a larger quota in the division of the produce. And the sense of natural justice may be plausibly appealed to in behalf of every one of these opinions.

Justice implies something which it is not only right to do, and wrong not to do, but which some individual person can claim from us as his moral right. No one has a moral right to our generosity or beneficence because we are not morally bound to practice those virtues toward any given individual. And it will be found with respect to this as to every correct definition that the instances which seem to conflict with it are those which most confirm it. For if a moralist attempts, as some have done, to make out that mankind generally, though not any given individual, have a right to all the good we can do them, he at once, by that thesis, includes generosity and beneficence within the category of justice. He is obliged to say that our utmost exertions are *due* to our fellow creatures, thus assimilating them to a debt; or that nothing less can be a sufficient *return* for what society does for us, thus classing the case as one of gratitude; both of which are acknowledged cases of justice, and not of the virtue of beneficence; and whoever does not place the distinction between justice and morality in general, where we have now placed it, will be found to make no distinction between them at all, but to merge all morality in justice.

To recapitulate: the idea of justice supposes two things—a rule of conduct and a sentiment which sanctions the rule. The first must be supposed common to all mankind and intended for their good. The other (the sentiment) is a desire that punishment may be suffered by those who infringe the rule. There is involved, in addition, the conception of some definite person who suffers by the infringement, whose rights (to use the expression appropriated to the case) are violated by it. And the sentiment of justice appears to me to be the animal desire to repel or retaliate a hurt or damage to oneself or to those with whom one sympathizes, widened so as to include all persons, by the human capacity of enlarged sympathy and the human conception of intelligent self-interest. From the latter elements the feeling derives its morality; from the former, its peculiar impressiveness and energy of self-assertion. . . .

If the preceding analysis, or something resembling it, be not the correct account of the notion of justice—if justice be totally independent of utility, and be a standard *per se,* which the mind can recognize by simple introspection of itself—it is hard to understand why that internal oracle is so ambiguous, and why so many things appear either just or unjust, according to the light in which they are regarded.

We are continually informed that utility is an uncertain standard, which every different person interprets differently, and that there is no safety but in the immutable, ineffaceable, and unmistakable dictates of justice, which carry their evidence in themselves and are independent of the fluctuations of opinion. One would suppose from this that on questions of justice there could be no controversy; that, if we take that for our rule, its application to any given case could leave us in as little doubt as a mathematical demonstration. So far is this from being the fact that there is as much difference of opinion, and as much discussion, about what is just as about what is useful to society. Not only have different nations and individuals different notions of justice, but in the mind of one and the same individual, justice is not some one rule, principle, or maxim, but many which do not always coincide in their dictates, and, in choosing between which, he is guided either by some extraneous standard or by his own personal predilections. . . .

. . . [for instance] in co-operative industrial association, is it just or not that talent or skill should give a title to superior remuneration? On the negative side of the question it is argued that whoever does the best he can deserves equally well, and ought not in justice to be put in a position of inferiority for no fault of his own; that superior abilities have already advantages more than enough, in the admiration they excite, the personal influence they command, and the internal sources of satisfaction attending them, without adding to these a superior share of the world's goods; and that society is bound in justice rather to make compensation to the less favored for this unmerited inequality of advantages than to aggravate it. On the contrary side it is contended that society receives more from the more efficient laborer; that, his services being more useful, society owes him a larger return for them; that a greater share of the joint result is actually his work, and not to allow his claim to it is a kind of robbery; that, if he is only to receive as much as others, he can only be justly required to produce as much, and to give a smaller amount of time and exertion, proportioned to his superior efficiency. Who shall decide between these appeals to conflicting principles of justice? Justice has in this case two sides to it, which it is impossible to bring into harmony, and the two disputants have chosen opposite sides; the one looks to what it is just that the individual should receive, the other to what it is just that the community should give. Each, from his own point of view, is unanswerable; and any choice between them, on grounds of justice, must be perfectly arbitrary. Social utility alone can decide the preference.

The considerations which have now been adduced resolve, I conceive, the only real difficulty in the utilitarian theory of morals. It has always been evident that all cases of justice are also cases of expediency; the difference is in the peculiar sentiment which attaches to the former, as contradistinguished from the latter. If this characteristic sentiment has been sufficiently accounted for; if there is no necessity to assume for it any peculiarity of origin; if it is simply the natural feeling of resentment, moralized by being made coextensive with the demands of social good; and if this feeling not only does but ought to exist in all the classes of cases to which the idea of justice corresponds—that idea no longer presents itself as a stumbling block to the utilitarian ethics. Justice remains the appropriate name for certain social utilities which are vastly more important, and therefore more absolute and imperative, than any others are as a class (though not more so than others may be in particular cases); and which, therefore, ought to be, as well as naturally are, guarded by a sentiment, not only different in degree, but also in kind; distinguished from the milder feeling which attaches to the mere idea of promoting human pleasure or convenience at once by the more definite nature of its commands and by the sterner character of its sanctions.

John Dewey
Democracy and Equality

John Dewey (1859–1952) *was one of the great twentieth century American philosophers and social theorists. In the following essay, he relates a key feature of justice—equality—to the political system of democracy.*

Democracy is much broader than a special political form, a method of conducting government, of making laws and carrying on governmental administration by means of popular suffrage and elected officers. It is that, of course. But it is something broader and deeper than that. The political and governmental phase of democracy is a means, the best means so far found, for realizing ends that lie in the wide domain of human relationships and the development of human personality. It is, as we often say, though perhaps without appreciating all that is involved in the saying, a way of life, social and individual. The key-note of democracy as a way of life may be expressed, it seems to me, as the necessity for the participation of every mature human being in formation of the values that regulate the living of men together: which is necessary from the standpoint of both the general social welfare and the full development of human beings as individuals.

Universal suffrage, recurring elections, responsibility of those who are in political power to the voters, and the other factors of democratic government are means that have been found expedient for realizing democracy as the truly human way of living. They are not a final end and a final value. They are to be judged on the basis of their contribution to end. It is a form of idolatry to erect means into the end which they serve. Democratic political forms are simply the best means that human wit has devised up to a special time in history. But they rest back upon the idea that no man or limited set of men is wise enough or good enough to rule others without their consent; the positive meaning of this statement is that all those who are affected by social institutions must have a share in producing and managing them. The two facts that each one is influenced in what he does and enjoys and in what he becomes by the institutions under which he lives, and that therefore he shall have, in a democracy, a voice in shaping them, are the passive and active sides of the same fact.

The development of political democracy came about through substitution of the method of mutual consultation and voluntary agreement for the method of subordination of the many to the few enforced from above. Social arrangements which involve fixed subordination are maintained by coercion. The coercion need not be physical. There have existed, for short periods, benevolent despotisms. But coercion of some sort there has been; perhaps economic, certainly psychological and moral. The very fact of exclusion from participation is a subtle form of suppression. It gives individuals no opportunity to reflect and decide upon what is good for them. Others who are supposed to be wiser and who in any case have more power decide the question for them and also decide the methods and means by which subjects may arrive at the enjoyment of what is good for them. This form of coercion and suppression is more subtle and more effective than is overt intimidation and restraint. When it is habitual and embodied in social institutions, it seems the normal and natural state of affairs. The mass usually become unaware that they have a claim to a development of their own powers. Their experience is so restricted that they are not conscious of restriction. It is part of the democratic conception that they as individuals are not the only sufferers, but that the whole social body is deprived of the potential resources that should be at its service. The individuals of the submerged mass may not be very wise. But there is one thing they are wiser about than anybody else can be, and that is where the shoe pinches, the troubles they suffer from.

The foundation of democracy is faith in the capacities of human nature; faith in human intelligence and in the power of pooled and cooperative experience. It is not belief that these things are complete but that if given a show they will grow and be able to generate progressively the knowledge and wisdom needed to guide collective action. Every autocratic and authoritarian scheme of social action rests on a belief that the needed intelligence is confined to a superior few, who because of inherent natural gifts are endowed with the ability and the right to control the conduct of others; laying down principles and rules and directing the ways in which they are carried out. It would be foolish to deny that much can be said for this point of view. It is that which controlled human relations in social groups for much the greater part of human history. The democratic faith has emerged very, very recently in the history of mankind. Even where democracies now exist, men's minds and feelings are still permeated with ideas about leadership imposed from above, ideas that developed in the long early history of mankind. After democratic political institutions were nominally established, beliefs and ways of looking at life and of acting that originated when men and women were externally controlled and subjected to arbitrary power, persisted in the family, the church, business and the school, and experience shows that as long as they persist there, political democracy is not secure.

Belief in equality is an element of the democratic credo. It is not, however, belief in equality of natural endowments. Those who proclaimed the idea of equality did not suppose they were enunciating a psychological doctrine, but a legal and political one. All individuals are entitled to equality of treatment by law and in its administration. Each one is affected equally in quality if not in quantity by the institutions under which he lives and has an equal right to express his judgment, although the weight of his judgment may not be equal in amount when it enters into the pooled result to that of others. In short, each one is equally an individual and entitled to equal opportunity of development of his own capacities, be they large or small in range. Moreover, each has needs of his own, as significant to him as those of others are to them. The very fact of natural and psychological inequality is all the more reason for establishment by law of equality of opportunity, since otherwise the former becomes a means of oppression of the less gifted.

While what we call intelligence be distributed in unequal amounts, it is the democratic faith that it is sufficiently general so that each individual has something to contribute, whose value can be assessed only as enters into the final pooled intelligence constituted by the contributions of all. Every authoritarian scheme, on the contrary, assumes that its value may be assessed by some *prior* principle, if not of family and birth or race and color or possession of material wealth, then by the position and rank a person occupies in the existing social scheme. The democratic faith in equality is the faith that each individual shall have the chance and opportunity to contribute whatever he is capable of contributing and that the value of his contribution be decided by its place and function in the organized total of similar contributions, not on the basis of prior status of any kind whatever.

I have emphasized in what precedes the importance of the effective release of intelligence in connection with personal experience in the democratic way of living. I have done so purposely because democracy is so often and so naturally associated in our minds with freedom of *action,* forgetting the importance of freed intelligence which is necessary to direct and to warrant freedom of action. Unless freedom of individual action has intelligence and informed conviction back of it, its manifestation is almost sure to result in confusion and disorder. The democratic idea of freedom is not the right of each individual to *do* as he pleases, even if it be qualified by adding "provided he does not interfere with the same freedom on the part of others." While the idea is not always, not often enough, expressed in words, the basic freedom is that of freedom of *mind* and of whatever degree of freedom of action and experience is necessary to produce freedom of intelligence. The modes of freedom guaranteed in the Bill of Rights are all of this nature: Freedom of belief and conscience, of expression of opinion, of assembly for discussion and conference, of the press as an organ of communication. They are guaranteed because without them individuals are not free to develop and society is deprived of what they might contribute.

It is a disputed question of theory and practice just how far a democratic political government should go in control of the conditions of action within special groups. At the present time, for example, there are those who think the federal and state governments leave too much freedom of independent action to industrial and financial groups, and there are others who think the government is going altogether too far at the present time. I do not need to discuss this phase of the problem, much less to try to settle it. But it must be pointed out that if the methods of regulation and administration in vogue in the conduct of secondary social groups are non-democratic, whether directly or indirectly or both, there is bound to be unfavorable reaction back into the habits of feeling, thought and action of citizenship in the broadest sense of that word. The way in which any organized social interest is controlled necessarily plays an important part in forming the dispositions and tastes, the attitudes, interests, purposes and desires, of those engaged in carrying on the activities of the group. For illustration, I do not need to do more than point to the moral, emotional and intellectual effect upon both employers and laborers of the existing industrial system. Just what the effects specifically are is a matter about which we know very little. But I suppose that every one who reflects upon the subject admits that it is impossible that the ways in which activities are carried on for the greater part of the waking hours of the day; and the way in which the share of individuals are involved in the management of affairs in such a matter as gaining a livelihood and attaining material and social security, can not but be a highly important factor in shaping personal dispositions; in short, forming character and intelligence.

In the broad and final sense all institutions are educational in the sense that they operate to form the attitudes, dispositions, abilities and disabilities that constitute a concrete personality. The principle applies with special force to the school. For it is the main business of the family and the school to influence directly the formation and growth of attitudes and dispositions, emotional, intellectual and moral. Whether this educative process is carried on in a predominantly democratic or non-democratic way becomes, therefore, a question of transcendent importance not only for education itself but for its final effect upon all the interests and activities of a society that is committed to the democratic way of life.

. . . there are certain corollaries which clarify the meaning of the issue. Absence of participation tends to produce lack of interest and concern on the part of those shut out. The result is a corresponding lack of effective responsibility. Automatically and unconsciously, if not consciously, the feeling develops, "This is none of our affair; it is the business of those at the top; let that particular set of Georges do what needs to be done." The countries in which autocratic government prevails are just those in which there is least public spirit and the greatest indifference to matters of general as distinct from personal concern.

. . . Where there is little power, there is correspondingly little sense of positive responsibility. It is enough to do what one is told to do sufficiently well to escape flagrant unfavorable notice. About larger matters, a spirit of passivity is engendered. In some cases, indifference passes into evasion of duties when not directly under the eye of a supervisor; in other cases, a carping, rebellious spirit is engendered. . . .habitual exclusion has the effect of reducing a sense of responsibility for what is done and its consequences. What the argument for democracy implies is that the best way to produce initiative and constructive power is to exercise it. Power, as well as interest, comes by use and practice. . . . It is also true that incapacity to assume the responsibilities involved in having a voice in shaping policies is bred and increased by conditions in which that responsibility is denied. I suppose there has never been an autocrat, big or little, who did not justify his conduct on the ground of the unfitness of his subjects to take part in government.

. . . I conclude by saying that the present subject is one of peculiar importance at the present time. The fundamental beliefs and practices of democracy are now challenged as they never have been before. In some nations they are more than challenged. They are ruthlessly and systematically destroyed. Everywhere there are waves of criticism and doubt as to whether democracy can meet pressing problems of order and security. The causes for the destruction of political democracy in countries where it was nominally established are complex. But of one thing I think we may be sure. Wherever it has fallen it was too exclusively political in nature. It had not become part of the bone and blood of the people in daily conduct of its life. Democratic forms were limited to Parliament, elections and combats between parties.

What is happening proves conclusively, I think, that unless democratic habits of thought and action are part of the fiber of a people, political democracy is insecure. It can not stand in isolation. It must be buttressed by the presence of democratic methods in all social relationships. The relations that exist in educational institutions are second only in importance in this respect to those which exist in industry and business, perhaps not even to them.

John Rawls

Justice as Fairness

John Rawls *is a professor of philosophy at Harvard University and the author of* A Theory of Justice. *In the following selection, he discusses the leading principles of that theory under the heading "justice as fairness."*

My aim is to present a conception of justice which generalizes and carries to a higher level of abstraction the familiar theory of the social contract as found, say, in Locke, Rousseau, and Kant. In order to do this we are not to think of the original contract as one to enter a particular society or to set up a particular form of government. Rather, the guiding idea is that the principles of justice for the basic structure of society are the object of the original agreement. They are the principles that free and rational persons concerned to further their own interests would accept in an initial position of equality as defining the fundamental terms of their association. These principles are to regulate all further agreements: they specify the kinds of social cooperation that can be entered into and the forms of government that can be established. This way of regarding the principles of justice I shall call justice as fairness.

Thus we are to imagine that those who engage in social cooperation choose together, in one joint act, the principles which are to assign basic rights and duties and to determine the division of social benefits. Men are to decide in advance how they are to regulate their claims against one another and what is to be the foundation charter of their society. Just as each person must decide by rational reflection what constitutes his good, that is, the system of ends which it is rational for him to pursue, so a group of persons must decide once and for all what is to count among them as just and unjust. The choice which rational men would make in this hypothetical situation of equal liberty, assuming for the present that this choice problem has a solution, determines the principles of justice.

In justice as fairness the original position of equality corresponds to the state of nature in the traditional theory of the social contract. This original position is not, of course, thought of as an actual historical state of affairs, much less as a primitive condition of culture. It is understood as a purely hypothetical situation characterized so as to lead to a certain conception of justice. Among the essential features of this situation is that no one knows his place in society, his class position or social status, nor does any one know his fortune in the distribution of natural assets and abilities, his intelligence, strength, and the like. I shall even assume that the parties do not know their conceptions of the good or their special psychological propensities. The principles of justice are chosen behind a veil of ignorance. This ensures that no one is advantaged or disadvantaged in the choice of principles by the outcome of natural chance or the contingency of social circumstances. Since all are similarly situated and no one is able to design principles to favor his particular condition, the principles of justice are the result of a fair agreement or bargain. For given the circumstances of the original position, the symmetry of everyone's relations to each other, this initial situation is fair between individuals as moral persons, that is, as rational beings with their own ends and capable, I shall assume, of a sense of justice. The original position is, one might say, the appropriate initial status quo, and thus the fundamental agreements reached in it are fair. This explains the propriety of the name "justice as fairness": it conveys the idea that the principles of justice are agreed to in an initial situation that is fair. The name does not mean that the concepts of justice and fairness are the same, any more than the phrase "poetry as metaphor" means that the concepts of poetry and metaphor are the same.

Justice as fairness begins, as I have said, with one of the most general of all choices which persons might make together, namely, with the choice of the first principles of a conception of justice which is to regulate all subsequent criticism and reform of institutions. Then, having chosen a conception of justice, we can suppose that they are to choose a constitution and a legislature to enact laws, and so on, all in accordance with the principles of justice initially agreed upon. Our social situation is just if it is such that by this sequence of hypothetical agreements we would have contracted into the general system of rules which defines it.

It may be observed that once the principles of justice are thought of as arising from an original agreement in a situation of equality, it is an open question whether the principle of utility would be acknowledged. Offhand it hardly seems likely that persons who view themselves as equals, entitled to press their claims upon one another, would agree to a principle which may require lesser life prospects for some simply for the sake of a greater sum of advantages enjoyed by others. Since each desires to protect his interests, his capacity to advance his conception of the good, no one has a reason to acquiesce in an enduring loss for himself in order to bring about a greater net balance of satisfaction. In the absence of strong and lasting benevolent impulses, a rational man would not accept a basic structure merely because it maximized the algebraic sum of advantages irrespective of its permanent effects on his own basic rights and interests. Thus it seems that the principle of utility is incompatible with the conception of social cooperation among equals for mutual advantage. It appears to be inconsistent with the idea of reciprocity implicit in the notion of a well-ordered society. Or, at any rate, so I shall argue.

I shall maintain instead that the persons in the initial situation would choose two rather different principles: the first requires equality in the assignment of basic rights and duties, while the second holds that social and economic inequalities, for example inequalities of wealth and authority, are just only if they result in compensating benefits for everyone, and in particular for the least advantaged members of society. These principles rule out justifying institutions on the grounds that the hardships of some are offset by a greater good in the aggregate. It may be expedient but it is not just that some should have less in order that others may prosper. But there is no injustice in the greater benefits earned by a few provided that the situation of persons not so fortunate is thereby improved. The intuitive idea is that since everyone's well-being depends upon a scheme of cooperation without which no one could have a satisfactory life, the division of advantages should be such as to draw forth the willing cooperation of everyone taking part in it, including those less well situated. Yet this can be expected only if reasonable terms are proposed. The two principles mentioned seem to be a fair agreement on the basis of which those better endowed, or more fortunate in their social position, neither of which we can be said to deserve, could expect the willing cooperation of others when some workable scheme is a necessary condition of the welfare of all. Once we decide to look for a conception of justice that nullifies the accidents of natural endowment and the contingencies of social circumstance as counters in quest for political and economic advantage, we are led to these principles. They express the result of leaving aside those aspects of the social world that seem arbitrary from a moral point of view.

The idea of the original position is to set up a fair procedure so that any principles agreed to will be just. Somehow we must nullify the effects of specific contingencies which put men at odds and tempt them to exploit social and natural circumstances to their own advantage. Now in order to do this I assume that the parties are situated behind a veil of ignorance. They do not know how the various alternatives will affect their own particular case and they are obliged to evaluate principles solely on the basis of general considerations. The veil of ignorance enables us to make vivid to ourselves the restrictions that it seems reasonable to impose on arguments for principles of justice, and therefore on these principles themselves. Thus it seems reasonable and generally acceptable that no one should be advantaged or disadvantaged by natural fortune or social circumstances in the choice of principles. It also seems widely agreed that it should be impossible to tailor principles to the circumstances of one's own case. We should insure further that particular inclinations and aspirations, and persons' conceptions of their good do not affect the principles adopted. The aim is to rule out those principles that it would be rational to propose for acceptance, however little the chance of success, only if one knew certain things that are irrelevant from the standpoint of justice. For example, if a man knew that he was wealthy, he might find it rational to advance the principle that various taxes for welfare measures be counted unjust; if he knew that he was poor, he would most likely propose the contrary principle. To represent the desired restrictions one imagines a situation in which everyone is deprived of this sort of information. One excludes the knowledge of those contingencies which sets men at odds and allows them to be guided by their prejudices.

It is assumed, then, that the parties do not know certain kinds of particular facts. First of all, no one knows his place in society, his class position or social status; nor does he know his fortune in the distribution of natural assets and abilities, his intelligence and strength, and the like. Nor, again, does anyone know his conception of the good, the particulars of his rational plan of life, or even the special features of his psychology such as his aversion to risk or liability to optimism or pessimism. More than this, I assume that the parties do not know the particular circumstances of their own society. That is, they do not know its economic or political situation, or the level of civilization and culture it has been able to achieve. The persons in the original position have no information as to which generation they belong. These broader restrictions on knowledge are appropriate in part because questions of social justice arise between generations as well as within them, for example, the question of the appropriate rate of capital saving and of the conservation of natural resources and the environment of nature. There is also, theoretically anyway, the question of a reasonable genetic policy. In these cases too, in order to carry through the idea of the original position, the parties must not know the contingencies that set them in opposition. They must choose principles the consequences of which they are prepared to live with whatever generation they turn out to belong to. As far as possible, then, the only particular facts which the parties know is that their society is subject to the circumstances of justice and whatever this implies.

The restrictions on particular information in the original position are of fundamental importance. The veil of ignorance makes possible a unanimous choice of a particular conception of justice. Without these limitations on knowledge the bargaining problem of the original position would be hopelessly complicated. Even if theoretically a solution were to exist, we would not, at present anyway, be able to determine it. . . .

The assumption of mutually disinterested rationality . . . comes to this: the persons in the original position try to acknowledge principles which advance their system of ends as far as possible. They do this by attempting to win for themselves the highest index of primary social goods, since this enables them to promote their conception of the good most effectively whatever it turns out to be. The parties do not seek to confer benefits or to impose injuries on one another; they are not moved by affection or rancor. Nor do they try to gain relative to each other; they are not envious or vain. Put in terms of a game, we might say: they strive for as high an absolute score as possible. They do not wish a high or a low score for their opponents, nor do they seek to maximize or minimize the difference between their successes and those of others. The idea of a game does not really apply, since the parties are not concerned to win but to get as many points as possible judged by their own system of ends.

I shall now state in a provisional form the two principles of justice that I believe would be chosen in the original position. The first statement of the two principles reads as follows.

- First: each person is to have an equal right to the most extensive basic liberty compatible with a similar liberty for others.
- Second: social and economic inequalities are to be arranged so that they are both (a) reasonably expected to be to everyone's advantage, and (b) attached to positions and offices open to all.

By way of general comment, these principles primarily apply, as I have said, to the basic structure of society. They are to govern the assignment of rights and duties and to regulate the distribution of social and economic advantages. As their formulation suggests, these principles presuppose that the social structure can be divided into two more or less distinct parts, the first principle applying to the one, the second to the other. They distinguish between those aspects of the social system that define and secure the equal liberties of citizenship and those that specify and establish social and economic inequalities. The basic liberties of citizens are, roughly speaking, political liberty (the right to vote and to be eligible for public office) together with freedom of speech and assembly; liberty of conscience and freedom of thought; freedom of the person along with the right to hold (personal) property; and freedom from arbitrary arrest and seizure as defined by the concept of the rule of law. These liberties are all required to be equal by the first principle, since citizens of a just society are to have the same basic rights.

The second principle applies, in the first approximation, to the distribution of income and wealth and to the design of organizations that makes use of differences in authority and responsibility, or chains of command. While the distribution of wealth and income need not be equal, it must be to everyone's advantage, and at the same time, positions of authority and offices of command must be accessible to all. One applies the second principle by holding positions open, and then, subject to this constraint, arranges social and economic inequalities so that everyone benefits.

These principles are to be arranged in a serial order with the first principle prior to the second. This ordering means that a departure from the institutions of equal liberty required by the first principle cannot be justified by, or compensated for, by greater social and economic advantages. The distribution of wealth and income, and the hierarchies of authority, must be consistent with both the liberties of equal citizenship and equality of opportunity.

It is clear that these principles are rather specific in their content, and their acceptance rests on certain assumptions that I must eventually try to explain and justify. For the present, it should be observed that the two principles (and this holds for all formulations) are a special case of a more general conception of justice that can be expressed as follows.

All social values—liberty and opportunity, income and wealth, and the bases of self-respect—are to be distributed equally unless an unequal distribution of any, or all, of these values is to everyone's advantage.

Injustice, then, is simply inequalities that are not be the benefit of all. Of course, this conception is extremely vague and requires interpretation.

As a first step, suppose that the basic structure of society distributes certain primary goods, that is, things that every rational man is presumed to want. These goods normally have a use whatever a person's rational plan of life. For simplicity, assume that the chief primary goods at the disposition of society are rights and liberties, powers and opportunities, income and wealth. These are the social primary goods. Other primary goods such as health and vigor, intelligence and imagination, are natural goods; although their possession is influenced by the basic structure, they are not so directly under its control. Imagine, then, a hypothetical initial arrangement in which all the social primary goods are equally distributed: everyone has similar rights and duties, and income and wealth are evenly shared. This state of affairs provides a benchmark for judging improvements. If certain inequalities of wealth and organizational powers would make everyone better off than in this hypothetical starting situation, then they accord with the general conception.

Now it is possible, at least theoretically, that by giving up some of their fundamental liberties men are sufficiently compensated by the resulting social and economic gains. The general conception of justice imposes no restrictions on what sort of inequalities are permissible; it only requires that everyone's position be improved.

The second principle insists that each person benefit from permissible inequalities in the basic structure. This means that it must be reasonable for each relevant representative man defined by this structure, when he views it as a going concern, to prefer his prospects with the inequality to his prospects without it. One is not allowed to justify differences in income or organizational powers on the ground that the disadvantages of those in one position are outweighed by the greater advantages of those in another. Much less can infringements of liberty be counterbalanced in this way. Applied to the basic structure, the principle of utility would have us maximize the sum of expectations of representative men (weighted by the number of persons they represent, on the classical view); and this would permit us to compensate for the losses of some by the gains of others. Instead, the two principles require that everyone benefit from economic and social inequalities.

The natural distribution of talents is neither just nor unjust; nor is it unjust that men are born into society at some particular position. These are simply natural facts. . . .

. . . What is just and unjust is the way that institutions deal with these facts. Aristocratic and caste societies are unjust because they make these contingencies the ascriptive basis for belonging to more or less enclosed and privileged social classes. The basic structure of these societies incorporates the arbitrariness found in nature. But there is no necessity for men to resign themselves to these contingencies. The social system is not an unchangeable order beyond human control but a pattern of human action. In justice as fairness men agree to share one another's fate. In designing institutions they undertake to avail themselves of the accidents of nature and social circumstance only when doing so is for the common benefit. The two principles are a fair way of meeting the arbitrariness of fortune; and while no doubt imperfect in other ways, the institutions which satisfy these principles are just.

There is a natural inclination to object that those better situated deserve their greater advantages whether or not they are to the benefit of others. At this point it is necessary to be clear about the notion of desert. It is perfectly true that given a just system of cooperation as a scheme of public rules and the expectations set up by it, those who, with the prospect of improving their condition, have done what the system announces that it will reward are entitled to their advantages. In this sense the more fortunate have a claim to their better situation; their claims are legitimate expectations established by social institutions, and the community is obligated to meet them. But this sense of desert presupposes the existence of the cooperative scheme; it is irrelevant to the question whether in the first place the scheme is to be designed in accordance with the difference principle or some other criterion.

Perhaps some will think that the person with greater natural endowments deserves those assets and the superior character that made their development possible. Because he is more worthy in this sense, he deserves the greater advantages that he could achieve with them. This view, however, is surely incorrect. It seems to be one of the fixed points of our considered judgments that no one deserves his place in the distribution of native endowments, any more than one deserves one's initial starting place in society. The assertion that a man deserves the superior character that enables him to make the effort to cultivate his abilities is equally problematic; for his character depends in large part upon fortunate family and social circumstances for which he can claim no credit. The notion of desert seems not to apply to these cases. Thus the more advantaged representative man cannot say that he deserves and therefore has a right to a scheme of cooperation in which he is permitted to acquire benefits in ways that do not contribute to the welfare of others. There is no basis for his making this claim. From the standpoint of common sense, then, the difference principle appears to be acceptable both to the more advantaged and to the less advantaged individual.

Robert Nozick

The Principle of Fairness

Robert Nozick *is a professor of philosophy at Harvard University, and in the following selection he expresses his reservations about the theory of justice formulated and made famous by his colleague, John Rawls.*

A principle suggested by Herbert Hart, which (following John Rawls) we shall call the *principle of fairness,* would be of service here if it were adequate. This principle holds that when a number of persons engage in a just, mutually advantageous, cooperative venture according to rules and thus restrain their liberty in ways necessary to yield advantages for all, those who have submitted to these restrictions have a right to similar acquiescence on the part of those who have benefited from their submission. Acceptance of benefits (even when this is not a giving of express or tacit undertaking to cooperate) is enough, according to this principle, to bind one. If one adds to the principle of fairness the claim that the others to whom the obligations are owed or their agents may *enforce* the obligations arising under this principle (including the obligation to limit one's actions), then groups of people in a state of nature who agree to a procedure to pick those to engage in certain acts will have legitimate rights to prohibit "free riders." Such a right may be crucial to the viability of such agreements. We should scrutinize such a powerful right very carefully, especially as it seems to make *unanimous* consent to coercive government in a state of nature *unnecessary!* . . .

The principle of fairness, as we stated it following Hart and Rawls, is objectionable and unacceptable. Suppose some of the people in your neighborhood (there are 364 other adults) have found a public address system and decide to institute a system of public entertainment. They post a list of names, one for each day, yours among them. On his assigned day (one can easily switch days) a person is to run the public address system, play records over it, give news bulletins, tell amusing stories he has heard, and so on. After 138 days on which each person has done his part, your day arrives. Are you obligated to take your turn? You *have* benefited from it, occasionally opening your window to listen, enjoying some music or chuckling at someone's funny story. The other people *have* put themselves out. But must you answer the call when it is your turn to do so? As it stands, surely not. Though you benefit from the arrangement, you may know all along that 364 days of entertainment supplied by others will not be worth your giving up *one* day. You would rather not have any of it and not give up a day than have it all and spend one of your days at it. Given these preferences, how can it be that you are required to participate when your scheduled time comes? It would be nice to have philosophy readings on the radio to which one could tune in at any time, perhaps late at night when tired. But it may not be nice enough for you to want to give up one whole day of your own as a reader on the program. Whatever you want, can others create an obligation for you to do so by going ahead and starting the program themselves? In this case you can choose to forgo the benefit by not turning on the radio; in other cases the benefits may be unavoidable. If each day a different person on your street sweeps the entire street, must you do so when your time comes? Even if you don't care that much about a clean street? Must you imagine dirt as you traverse the street, so as not to benefit as a free rider? Must you refrain from turning on the radio to hear the philosophy readings? Must you mow your front lawn as often as your neighbors mow theirs?

At the very least one wants to build into the principle of fairness the condition that the benefits to a person from the actions of the others are greater than the costs to him of doing his share. How are we to imagine this? Is the condition satisfied if you do enjoy the daily broadcasts over the PA system in your neighborhood but would prefer a day off hiking, rather than hearing these broadcasts all year? For you to be obligated to give up your day to broadcast mustn't it be true, at least, that there is nothing you could do with a day (with that day, with the increment in any other day by shifting some activities to that day) which you would prefer to hearing broadcasts for the year? If the only way to get the broadcasts was to spend the day participating in the arrangement, in order for the condition that the benefits outweigh the costs to be satisfied, you would have to be willing to spend it on the broadcasts rather than to gain *any* other available thing.

If the principle of fairness were modified so as to contain this very strong condition, it still would be objectionable. The benefits might only barely be worth the costs to you of doing your share, yet others might benefit from *this* institution much more than you do; they all treasure listening to the public broadcasts. As the person least benefited by the practice, are you obligated to do an equal amount for it? Or perhaps you would prefer that all cooperated in *another* venture, limiting their conduct and making sacrifices for *it*. It is true, *given* that they are not following your plan (and thus limiting what other options are available to you), that the benefits of their venture *are* worth to you the costs of your cooperation. However, you do not wish to cooperate, as part of your plan to focus their attention on your alternative proposal which they have ignored or not given, in your view at least, its proper due. (You want them, for example, to read the Talmud on the radio instead of the philosophy they are reading.) By lending the institution (their institution) the support of your cooperating in it, you will only make it harder to change or alter.

On the face of it, enforcing the principle of fairness is objectionable. You may not decide to give me something, for example a book, and then grab money from me to pay for it, even if I have nothing better to spend the money on. You have, if anything, even less reason to demand payment if your activity that gives me the book also benefits you; suppose that your best way of getting exercise is by throwing books into people's houses, or that some other activity of yours thrusts books into people's houses as an unavoidable side effect. Nor are things changed if your inability to collect money or payments for the books which unavoidably spill over into others' houses makes it inadvisable or too expensive for you to carry on the activity with this side effect. One cannot, whatever one's purposes, just act so as to give people benefits and then demand (or seize) payment. Nor can a group of persons do this. If you may not charge and collect for benefits you bestow without prior agreement, you certainly may not do so for benefits whose bestowal costs you nothing, and most certainly people need not repay you for costless-to-provide benefits which yet *others* provided them. So the fact that we partially are "social products" in that we benefit from current patterns and forms created by the multitudinous actions of a long string of long-forgotten people, forms which include institutions, ways of doing things, and language (whose social nature may involve our current use depending upon Wittgensteinian matching of the speech of others), does not create in us a general floating debt which the current society can collect and use as it will.

Perhaps a modified principle of fairness can be stated which would be free from these and similar difficulties. What seems certain is that any such principle, if possible, would be so complex and involuted that one could not combine it with a special principle legitimating *enforcement* within a state of nature of the obligations that have arisen under it. Hence, even if the principle could be formulated so that it was no longer open to objection, it would not serve to obviate the need for other persons' *consenting* to cooperate and limit their own activities.

Joel Feinberg
Economic Income and Social Justice

Joel Feinberg *teaches philosophy at the University of Arizona. He has written extensively in ethics, in philosophy of law, and in social philosophy. This selection is from his 1973 book* Social Philosophy.

The term "distributive justice" traditionally applied to burdens and benefits directly distributed by political authorities, such as appointed offices, welfare doles, taxes, and military conscription, but it has now come to apply also to goods and evils of a nonpolitical kind that can be distributed by private citizens to other private citizens. In fact, in most recent literature, the term is reserved for *economic* distributions, particularly the justice of differences in economic income between classes, and of various schemes of taxation which discriminate in different ways between classes. Further, the phrase can refer not only to acts of distributing but also to de facto states of affairs, such as the *fact that* at present "the five percent at the top get 20 percent [of our national wealth] while the 20 percent at the bottom get about five percent." There is, of course, an ambiguity in the meaning of "distribution." The word may refer to the *process* of distributing, or the *product* of some process of distributing, and either or both of these can be appraised as just or unjust. In addition, a "distribution" can be understood to be a "product" which is *not* the result of any deliberate distributing process, but simply a state of affairs whose production has been too complicated to summarize or to ascribe to any definite group of persons as their deliberate doing. The present "distribution" of American wealth is just such a state of affairs.

Are the 5 percent of Americans "at the top" really different from the 20 percent "at the bottom" in any respect that would justicize the difference between their incomes? It is doubtful that there is any characteristic—relevant or irrelevant—common and peculiar to all members of either group. *Some* injustices, therefore, must surely exist. Perhaps there are some traits, however, that are more or less characteristic of the members of the privileged group, that make the current arrangements at least approximately just. What could (or should) those traits be? The answer will state a standard of relevance and a principle of material justice for questions of economic distributions, at least in relatively affluent societies like that of the United States.

At this point there appears to be no appeal possible except to *basic attitudes,* but even at this level we should avoid premature pessimism about the possibility of rational agreement. Some answers to our question have been generally discredited, and if we can see why those answers are inadequate, we might discover some important clues to the properties any adequate answer must possess. Even philosophical adversaries with strongly opposed initial attitudes may hope to come to eventual agreement if they share *some* relevant beliefs and standards and a common commitment to consistency. Let us consider why we all agree (that is the author's assumption) in rejecting the view that differences in race, sex, IQ, or social "rank" are the grounds of just differences in wealth or income. Part of the answer seems obvious. People cannot by their own voluntary choices determine what skin color, sex, or IQ they shall have, or which hereditary caste they shall enter. To make such properties the basis of discrimination between individuals in the distribution of social benefits would be "to treat people differently in ways that profoundly affect their lives because of differences for which they have no responsibility." Differences in a given respect are *relevant* for the aims of distributive justice, then, only if they are differences for which their possessors can be held responsible; properties can be the grounds of just discrimination between persons only if those persons had a *fair opportunity* to acquire or avoid them. Having rejected a number of material principles that clearly fail to satisfy the "fair opportunity" requirement, we are still left with as many as five candidates for our acceptance. (It is in theory open to us to accept two or more of these five as valid principles, there being no a priori necessity that the list be reduced to one.) These are: (1) the principle of perfect equality; (2) the principle[s] of need; (3) the principles of merit and achievement; (4) the principle of contribution (or due return); (5) the principle of effort (or labor). I shall discuss each of these briefly.

EQUALITY

The principle of perfect equality obviously has a place in any adequate social ethic. Every human being is equally a human being, and . . . that minimal qualification entitles all human beings equally to certain absolute human rights: positive rights to noneconomic "goods" that by their very natures cannot be in short supply, negative rights not to be treated in cruel or inhuman ways, and negative rights not to be exploited or degraded even in "humane" ways. It is quite another thing, however, to make the minimal qualification of humanity the ground for an absolutely equal distribution of a country's *material wealth* among its citizens. A strict equalitarian could argue that he is merely applying Aristotle's formula of proportionate equality (presumably accepted by all parties to the dispute) with a criterion of relevance borrowed from the human rights theorists. Thus, distributive justice is accomplished between *A* and *B* when the following ratio is satisfied:

$$\frac{A\text{'s share of } P}{B\text{'s share of } P} = \frac{A\text{'s possession of } Q}{B\text{'s possession of } Q}$$

Where *P* stands for economic goods, *Q* must stand simply for "humanity" or "a human nature," and since every human being possesses *that Q* equally, it follows that all should also share a society's economic wealth (the *P* in question) equally.

The trouble with this argument is that its major premise is no less disputable than its conclusion. The standard of relevance it borrows from other contexts where it seems very little short of self-evident, seems controversial, at best, when applied to purely economic contexts. It seems evident to most of us that merely being human entitles *everyone*—bad men as well as good, lazy as well as industrious, inept as well as skilled—to a fair trial if charged with a crime, to equal protection of the law, to equal consideration of his interests by makers of national policy, to be spared torture or other cruel and inhuman treatment, and to be permanently ineligible for the status of chattel slave. Adding a right to an equal share of the economic pie, however, is to add a benefit of a wholly different order, one whose presence on the list of goods for which mere humanity is the sole qualifying condition is not likely to win wide assent without further argument.

It is far more plausible to posit a human right to the satisfaction of (better: to an opportunity to satisfy) one's *basic* economic needs, that is, to enough food and medicine to remain healthy, to minimal clothing, housing, and so on. As Hume pointed out, even these rights cannot exist under conditions of extreme scarcity. Where there is not enough to go around, it cannot be true that everyone has a right to an equal share. But wherever there is moderate abundance or better—wherever a society produces more than enough to satisfy the *basic needs of everyone*—there it seems more plausible to say that mere possession of basic human needs qualifies a person for the opportunity to satisfy them. It would be a rare and calloused sense of justice that would not be offended by an affluent society, with a large annual agricultural surplus and a great abundance of manufactured goods, which permitted some of its citizens to die of starvation, exposure, or easily curable disease. It would certainly be *unfair* for a nation to produce more than it needs and not permit some of its citizens enough to satisfy their basic biological requirements. Strict equalitarianism, then, is a perfectly plausible material principle of distributive justice when confined to affluent societies and basic biological needs, but it loses plausibility when applied to division of the "surplus" left over after basic needs are met. . . .

Still, there is no way to *refute* the strict equalitarian who requires exactly equal shares for everyone whenever that can be arranged without discouraging total productivity to the point where everyone loses. No one would insist upon equal distributions that would diminish the size of the total pie and thus leave smaller slices for *everyone;* that would be opposed to reason. John Rawls makes this condition part of his "rational principle" of justice: "Inequalities are arbitrary unless it is reasonable to expect that they will work out to everyone's advantage. . . ." We are left then with a version of strict equalitarianism that is by no means evidently true and yet is impossible to refute. That is the theory that purports to apply not only to basic needs but to the total wealth of a society, and allows departures from strict equality when, *but only when,* they will work out to everyone's advantage. Although I am not persuaded by this theory, I think that any adequate material principle will have to attach great importance to keeping differences in wealth within reasonable limits, even after all basic needs have been met. One way of doing this would be to raise the standards for a "basic need" as total wealth goes up, so that differences between the richest and poorest citizens (even when there is no real "poverty") are kept within moderate limits.

NEED

The principle of need is subject to various interpretations, but in most of its forms it is not an independent principle at all, but only a way of mediating the application of the principle of equality. It can, therefore, be grouped with the principle of perfect equality as a member of the equalitarian family and contrasted with the principles of merit, achievement, contribution, and effort, which are all members of the nonequalitarian family. Consider some differences in "needs" as they bear on distributions. Doe is a bachelor with no dependents; Roe has a wife and six children. Roe must satisfy the needs of eight persons out of his paycheck, whereas Doe need satisfy the needs of only one. To give Roe and Doe equal pay would be to treat Doe's interests substantially *more* generously than those of anyone in the Roe family. Similarly, if a small private group is distributing food to its members (say a shipwrecked crew waiting rescue on a desert island), it would not be fair to give precisely the same quantity to a one hundred pounder as to a two hundred pounder, for that might be giving one person all he needs and the other only a fraction of what he needs—a difference in treatment not supported by any relevant difference between them. In short, to distribute goods in proportion to basic needs is not really to depart from a standard of equality, but rather to bring those with some greater initial burden or deficit up to the same level as their fellows.

The concept of a "need" is extremely elastic. In a general sense, to say that S needs X is to say simply that if he doesn't have X he will be harmed. A "basic need" would then be for an X in whose absence a person would be harmed in some crucial and fundamental way, such as suffering injury, malnutrition, illness, madness, or premature death. Thus we all have a basic need for foodstuffs of a certain quantity and variety, fuel to heat our dwellings, a roof over our heads, clothing to keep us warm, and so on. In a different but related sense of need, to say that S needs X is to say that without X he cannot achieve some specific purpose or perform some specific function. If they are to do their work, carpenters need tools, merchants need capital and customers, authors need paper and publishers. Some helpful goods are not strictly needed in this sense: an author with pencil and paper does not really need a typewriter to write a book, but he may need it to write a book speedily, efficiently, and conveniently. We sometimes come to rely upon "merely helpful but unneeded goods" to such a degree that we develop a strong habitual dependence on them, in which case (as it is often said) we have a "psychological" as opposed to a material need for them. If we don't possess that for which we have a strong psychological need, we may be unable to be happy, in which case a merely psychological need for a functional instrument may become a genuine need in the first sense distinguished above, namely, something whose absence is harmful to us. . . .The more abundant a society's material goods, the higher the level at which we are required (by the force of psychological needs) to fix the distinction between "necessities" and "luxuries"; what *everyone* in a given society regards as "necessary" tends to become an actual, basic need.

MERIT AND ACHIEVEMENT

The remaining three candidates for material principles of distributive justice belong to the nonequalitarian family. These three principles would each distribute goods in accordance, not with need, but with *desert;* since persons obviously differ in their deserts, economic goods would be distributed unequally. The three principles differ from one another in their conceptions of the relevant *bases of desert* for economic distributions. The first is the principle of *merit.* Unlike the other principles in the nonequalitarian family, this one focuses not on what a person has *done* to deserve his allotment, but rather on what kind of person he is—what characteristics he has.

Two different types of characteristic might be considered meritorious in the appropriate sense: skills and virtues. Native skills and inherited aptitudes will not be appropriate desert bases, since they are forms of merit ruled out by the fair opportunity requirement. No one deserves credit or blame for his genetic inheritance, since no one has the opportunity to select his own genes. Acquired skills may seem more plausible candidates at first, but upon scrutiny they are little better. First, all acquired skills depend to a large degree on native skills. Nobody is born knowing how to read, so reading is an acquired skill, but actual differences in reading skill are to a large degree accounted for by genetic differences that are beyond anyone's control. Some of the differences are no doubt caused by differences in motivation afforded different children, but again the early conditions contributing to a child's motivation are also largely beyond his control. We may still have some differences in acquired skills that are to be accounted for solely or primarily by differences in the degree of practice, drill, and perseverance expended by persons with roughly equal opportunities. In respect to these, we can propitiate the requirement of fair opportunity, but only by nullifying the significance of acquired skill as such, for now skill is a relevant basis of desert only to the extent that it is a product of one's own effort. Hence, *effort* becomes the true basis of desert (as claimed by our fifth principle, discussed below), and not simply skill as such. . . .

The most plausible nonequalitarian theories are those that locate relevance not in meritorious traits and excellences of any kind, but rather in prior doings: not in what one is, but in what one has done. Actions, too, are sometimes called "meritorious," so there is no impropriety in denominating the remaining families of principles in our survey as "meritarian." One type of action-oriented meritarian might cite *achievement* as a relevant desert basis for pecuniary rewards, so that departures from equality in income are to be justicized only by distinguished achievements in science, art, philosophy, music, athletics, and other basic areas of human activity. The attractions and disadvantages of this theory are similar to those of theories which I rejected above that base rewards on skills and virtues. Not all persons have a fair opportunity to achieve great things, and economic rewards seem inappropriate as vehicles for expressing recognition and admiration of noneconomic achievements.

CONTRIBUTION OR "DUE RETURN"

When the achievements under consideration are themselves contributions to our general economic well-being, the meritarian principle of distributive justice is much more plausible. Often it is conjoined with an economic theory that purports to determine exactly what percentage of our total economic product a given worker or class has produced. Justice, according to this principle, requires that each worker get back exactly that proportion of the national wealth he he has himself created. This sounds very much like a principle of "commutative justice" directing us to *give back* to every worker what is really his own property, that is, the product of his own labor.

The French socialist writer and precursor of Karl Marx, Pierre Joseph Proudhon (1809–1865), is perhaps the classic example of this kind of theorist. In his book *What Is Property?* (1840), Proudhon rejects the standard socialist slogan, "From each according to his ability, to each according to his needs," in favor of a principle of distributive justice based on contribution, as interpreted by an economic theory that employed a pre-Marxist "theory of surplus value." The famous socialist slogan was not intended, in any case, to express a principle of distributive justice. It was understood to be a rejection of all considerations of "mere" justice for an ethic of human brotherhood. The early socialists thought it unfair, in a way, to give the great contributors to our wealth a disproportionately small share of the product. But in the new socialist society, love of neighbor, community spirit, and absence of avarice would overwhelm such bourgeois notions and put them in their proper (subordinate) place.

Proudhon, on the other hand, based his whole social philosophy not on brotherhood (an ideal he found suitable only for small groups such as families) but on the kind of distributive justice to which even some capitalists gave lip service:

> The key concept was "mutuality" or "reciprocity." "Mutuality, reciprocity exists," he wrote, "when all the workers in an industry, instead of working for an entrepreneur

who pays them and keeps their products, work for one another and thus collaborate in the making of a common product whose profits they share among themselves."

Proudhon's celebrated dictum that "property is theft" did not imply that all *possession* of goods is illicit, but rather that the system of rules that permitted the owner of a factory to hire workers and draw profits ("surplus value") from *their* labor robs the workers of what is rightly theirs. "This profit, consisting of a portion of the proceeds of labor that rightfully belonged to the laborer himself, was 'theft.' " The injustice of capitalism, according to Proudhon, consists in the fact that those who create the wealth (through their labor) get only a small part of what they create, whereas those who "exploit" their labor, like voracious parasites, gather in a greatly disproportionate share. The "return of contribution" principle of distributive justice, then, cannot work in a capitalist system, but requires a *fédération mutualiste* of autonomous producer-cooperatives in which those who create wealth by their work share it in proportion to their real contributions.

Other theorists, employing different notions of what produces or "creates" economic wealth, have used the "return of contribution" principle to support quite opposite conclusions. The contribution principle has even been used to justicize quite unequalitarian capitalistic status quos, for it is said that capital as well as labor creates wealth, as do ingenious ideas, inventions, and adventurous risk-taking. The capitalist who provided the money, the inventor who designed a product to be manufactured, the innovator who thought of a new mode of production and marketing, the advertiser who persuaded millions of customers to buy the finished product, the investor who risked his savings on the success of the enterprise—these are the ones, it is said, who did the most to produce the wealth created by a business, not the workers who contributed only their labor, and of course, these are the ones who tend, on the whole, to receive the largest personal incomes.

Without begging any narrow and technical questions of economics, I should express my general skepticism concerning such facile generalizations about the comparative degrees to which various individuals have contributed to our social wealth. Not only are there impossibly difficult problems of measurement involved, there are also conceptual problems that appear beyond all nonarbitrary solution. I refer to the elements of luck and chance, the social factors not attributable to any assignable individuals, and the contributions of population trends, uncreated natural resources, and the efforts of people now dead which are often central to the explanation of any given increment of social wealth. . . .

EFFORT

The principle of due return, as a material principle of distributive justice, does have some vulnerability to the fair opportunity requirement. Given unavoidable variations in genetic endowments and material circumstances, different persons cannot have precisely the same opportunities to make contributions to the public weal. Our final candidate for the status of a material principle of distributive justice, the *principle of effort*, does much better in this respect, for it would distribute economic products not in proportion to successful achievement but according to the degree of effort exerted. According to the principle of effort, justice decrees that hard-working executives and hard-working laborers receive precisely the same remuneration (although there may be reasons having nothing to do with justice for paying more to the executives), and that freeloaders be penalized by allotments of proportionately lesser shares of the joint products of everyone's labor. The most persuasive argument for this principle is that it is the closest approximation to the intuitively valid principle of due return that can pass the fair opportunity requirement. It is doubtful, however, that even the principle of effort fully satisfies the requirements of fair opportunity, since those who inherit or acquire certain kinds of handicap may have little opportunity to *acquire the motivation* even to do their best. In any event, the principle of effort does seem to have intuitive cogency giving it at least some weight as a factor determining the justice of distributions.

In very tentative conclusion, it seems that the principle of equality (in the version that rests on needs rather than that which requires "perfect equality") and the principles of contribution and effort (where nonarbitrarily applicable, and only *after* everyone's basic needs have been satisfied) have the most weight as determinants of economic justice, whereas all forms of the principle of merit are implausible in that role. The reason for the priority of basic needs is that, where there is economic abundance, the claim to life itself and to minimally decent conditions are, like other human rights, claims that all men make with perfect equality. As economic production increases, these claims are given ever greater consideration in the form of rising standards for distinguishing basic needs from other wanted goods. But no matter where that line is drawn, when we go beyond it into the realm of economic surplus or "luxuries," non egalitarian considerations (especially contribution and effort) come increasingly into play.

20

How Should I Make Money?

How do you intend to make a living? This might seem like a rather vulgar question for a philosophy course, but contrary to its reputation, philosophy is deeply involved in even the most practical aspects of our lives. In particular, the very question about "making a living"—as opposed to being granted the necessities of life by the government, for example—already points to an entire philosophy of life: the idea that you should *earn* your keep, that you have a *choice* in how you will do this, and that it is alright that you might or might not make more money and live more luxuriously than other people. The nineteenth century name for the economic system that encourages this philosophical view of life and work is **capitalism**, and it is just as much a system of ethics as it is of economics. Although people all too often say that "business is unethical," the truth is that business is defined by its ethics. There are right and wrong ways for you to make money; it is not just a question of how much. **Business ethics** is the name of a new discipline (though it goes back to ancient times) that maps out the guidelines of ethics in business.

The broad principles of ethics—such as "treat people as ends and never merely as means" and "do not cause unnecessary harm"—apply in virtually every aspect of our lives, and perhaps too in every nation and culture. But most of ethics requires a more specific understanding of the particular practices in which human beings participate. The ethics of good sportsmanship will be very different (even when similar in vocabulary) from the ethics of war. Perhaps the most important single context for understanding ethics in contemporary American society is the world of business. It would not be an overstatement to say that a great many of our primary American values are either derived from or are part of business ethics. These include the traditional virtues of thrift, planning, and honoring one's contracts, as well as the more modern skills of negotiation, trying to produce the highest quality product for the best price, and looking for the best bargain. Business—the production and sale of goods and services and the purchase of them—provides the context in which most of us live. Activities that once were the province of religion or the state (for example, the arts) are now very much part of the business world. And yet, it is often joked that "business ethics is a contradiction in terms" and that "there is no ethics in business." Such humor betrays an important problem in our thinking. On the one hand, business provides the value system upon which much of our society depends for its ethics and its understanding of what is right and wrong, fair and unfair. On the other hand, business itself is too often thought to be distinct from ethics, if not unethical, and value-free, except for the all-important "bottom line," the value of making a dollar (or a million of them).

Business ethics is a relatively new concern, in one sense. As a subject of serious concern, an attempt to understand how business actually works and what its implicit rules of fairness are, business ethics is only a few decades old. It is the product of both the power and success of American business and the increased awareness if not frequency of business scandals and abuses—automobiles that might have been fixed in the factory that explode upon collision, securities firms that fiddle with clients' funds or trade illegally on "insider" information, American companies abroad caught bribing foreign officials for contracts. But although the focus of business ethics is often upon such tragedies and wrongdoing, the presumption is that most people and most companies in business are indeed ethical and conscientious. They really do try to serve not only their customers and stockholders but their employees and the surrounding community as well. So business ethics like ethics in general is the attempt to spell out the rules for proper conduct that are already followed by almost all of the business people in America.

In another, less flattering sense, business ethics has been around since ancient times, but almost always in the form of an all-out attack on business and its values. The materialism on which a consumer society is based has often been thought to be unethical to the core. And the so-called profit motive, on which almost all of business is based, was condemned for centuries and even called a sin—"avarice." This entirely negative attitude toward business did not change in Europe until the seventeenth century, just about the time that America—the foremost business society—was being settled.

The philosophical problems of business fall roughly into two categories. First there are the very broad questions about business as such—what the nineteenth century philosophers named capitalism. These include whether business is indeed the best way to make a society prosper and its citizens happy and whether it is a fair way to distribute the wealth, goods, and advantages of a society to all of its citizens. The father of modern economics and most famous prophet of capitalism, Adam Smith, wrote in his *Wealth of Nations* that capitalism was indeed the best way to make a society prosper and provide all its citizens with comforts and even luxuries unimaginable in any other society. (His book was published in England in 1776, the same year as the signing of the Declaration of Independence in America.)

But as capitalism (and the industrial revolution that provided its technology) developed in England and elsewhere, it became evident that not all people were prospering equally. Those who worked as much as 16 hours a day in the mines and factories—including many young children—remained desparately poor, while their bosses often became fabulously wealthy. The unfairness of this situation was particularly evident to a young German named Karl Marx, who had come to live in London in the mid-nineteenth century. He and his friend Friederich Engels (who was himself a wealthy businessman) wrote what is still the most devastating attack on this new world. In fact, many of the reforms urged by Marx and Engels have been carried out in most businesses today. But the question remains to what extent business—the private production and sale of the material goods and services—is the best and fairest way of running the economy of a society. Many authors advocate more government control of who makes what and who gets what, or at least regulation of businesses so that certain minimal standards of quality, safety, and fairness are maintained. Many other authors and most businesspeople insist that such control and regulation is best accomplished by businesses themselves and by the consumer, who in his or her freedom to buy or not buy a certain product in fact controls the business world more effectively than any government.

The second category of problems in business ethics are more particular and apply to the activities of particular businesses. The business world has changed a great deal since Adam Smith and Marx wrote their treatises on capitalism. They were looking at a world of small shopkeepers and (what we would consider) modest industries. The business world of today is dominated instead by enormous corporations, some of which have hundreds of thousands of employees and offices in almost every country in the world. Accordingly, many of the problems of business ethics today have to do with the size, the power, and consequently, the social responsibilities of corporations. It has been argued that corporations have only a single purpose—to make a profit, on the assumption that a corporation that is making a profit must also be providing quality goods and services to its consumers. Indeed, it has even been argued that business is much more like a game of poker than it is a socially responsible institution, with the conclusion that business people should not be expected to follow the same ethical principles as everyone else. On the other hand, it has been argued that businesses, like very powerful citizens, have very special obligations which go far beyond their responsibilities to their stockholders and customers. These arguments are kept in the public eye by such familiar headlines as "XYZ corporation indicted for taking kick-backs on defense contracts" or "Manufacturer knew that XXX causes cancer." One could even claim that a proper appreciation of business ethics is the condition for businesses' continued respect and success in the world.

The following selections include Adam Smith's classic statement about capitalism, an excerpt from Marx and Engels, and a recent sample of Marxist criticism by Paul Sweezy. We have included a short, charming puzzle about the free market from Robert Heilbroner, as well as Milton Friedman's controversial denial of the social responsibilities of business with Christopher Stone's rebuttal. Alfred Carr argues the polemical position that business is more like the game of poker than it is an ethical enterprise. W. Michael Hoffman and William Safire discuss two of the more notorious business scandals of recent years. We begin, however, with a timely newspaper editorial by Michael D'Antonio on the current state of ethics in business.

Michael D'Antonio
On Ethics in Business

Michael D'Antonio *writes for* Newsday.

In the rough-and-tumble world of gold futures trading, Steve was known as a killer, a closer who could literally talk women with sick children out of their last dollars and into risky investments in gold and silver.

Technically, he was supposed to counsel potential buyers and advise them against investing if they didn't have the money or weren't in a position to take the risk. In practice, Steve (not his real name) used high-pressure techniques and glossed over the potential hazard in order to reel in profits. It pleased his bosses, who were concerned about the bottom line, but deep within his conscience it bothered Steve.

"If you didn't do it," he says, "it came out the next day at the morning meeting. You were a jerk, a schlemiel for letting them get away. It was clear that we were to lie, omit, or persuade, but we were to get the money.

"One case was this lady, maybe 57, worth about $350,000—not a lot these days. She had a kid who was in an accident. He was going to be in the hospital forever. Everything she had was accounted for except for about $5,000. I took it, knowing the market would go nowhere. She lost it. She sends me Christmas cards."

In the beginning, Steve says, he followed his conscience and advised some prospects against gold and silver investments, which "are as risky as betting football games." But as his pile of rejected leads grew, the morning sales meetings became unbearably humiliating. And despite nagging doubts about the morality of high-pressure tactics, he became what the bosses called "a closer, a killer." He buried his conscience and brought in the money.

Steve's moral conflict—choosing between the demands of his job and the demands of conscience—posed the kind of ethical choice that adults confront in their public lives every day. Not life and death questions, these are seemingly simple matters of honesty. But increasingly, say some experts, Americans are setting aside traditional values of right and wrong and bypassing conscience.

It is apparently easy to cheat faceless victims—distant corporations, unknown stockholders, unseen employers. And today's technical, urban culture bombards inner morality with materialism. The researchers point to recent controversies in business and government, some involving hundreds of workers and executives, to support their claim of a widespread ethical breakdown.

- In May, E.F. Hutton, the investment firm, admitted to a long-running check-kiting scheme—systematic bank overdrafts—involving hundreds of employees and executives and billions of dollars.
- In April, government auditors charged that seven major defense contractors had submitted claims for expenses worth $109 million for clearly unauthorized items, including haircuts for executives.
- In March, six judges in Chicago were charged with taking bribes from lawyers and defendants.
- In 1984, National Semiconductor Corp. was convicted of deliberate fraud in its testing of computer chips used in high-tech armaments.

Although moral controversies are not unique to the 1980s, many ethicists, sociologists and psychologists say that today's moral lapses point to more widespread blurring of right and wrong.

The E.F. Hutton scandal was not the work of one or two "bad apples," but evidence of general moral decay, says psychologist Charles Ansell of Sherman Oaks, Calif. And researchers are beginning to explore the ways in which people bypass basic moral training in the competitive adult world.

"It's as simple as the Judeo-Christian maxim of doing unto others as you would have them do unto you," writes Ansell, who writes on behavior and morality. Moral judgment, ingrained in childhood, should become "an automatic sense that helps you make the right choice almost without thinking. Today, we are losing the sense of being inner-directed. Instead, we let the morals of the group, or organizations like our business, control us," he adds.

"The guy putting his hand into the cookie jar today is not thinking about what he is doing that is wrong. He is thinking about how he will look with more money in his hand."

On a personal level, the "loss of conscience," as Ansell calls it, opens a door to immoral behavior. He says it allows construction supervisors to engage in systematic payoffs to inspectors. It frees executives and employees of defense contractors to cooperate in fraud.

Ansell is convinced that 20th-century people suffer a kind of moral rootlessness. "The 19th-century man was more inner-directed. He lived on his own, farming or in a small town, and he was forced to rely on an inner sense of what was right. And if he did something wrong, he saw his victim and had to deal with the consequences.

"Today's victim is faceless. If you rip off the telephone company, who is hurt? If you kite checks for your company, where is the victim? The person cheating the Pentagon doesn't see himself hurting anyone directly."

In general, Ansell lays blame on the pressures of modern life, including competition in business and the "facelessness" of a technological society, for individual immoral conduct. "We are so competitive, and part of competition is contempt for your opponent," he says. "The E.F. Hutton executive who finds himself involved in some scheme feels contempt for his victims." . . .

While the added pressures of modern life may erode morality, other analysts argue that institutions that used to be leading character-builders—family, religion and the schools— have declined to the point where they are becoming ineffective. And they say that too many people enter the adult world without a moral foundation.

"In past generations, ethical values were passed on by enduring institutions, especially the extended family," says philosopher Gary Edwards of the Ethics Resource Center in Washington. "There were grandparents, uncles and aunts to give you specific lessons, tell you stories with morals. And schools very self-consciously taught morals. They taught good citizenship."

Edwards says that popular educational movements in the 1950s and '60s and pressure from political groups forced moral lessons out of the public schools. Campaigns to drive prejudice out of public institutions also may have driven out baseline social values, he says. "We learned to be tolerant, and that's not a bad thing. But we came to be tolerant to a fault, and that meant people lost the courage of conviction."

Over a period of months, Steve tried to meet the standards set by his superiors. He talked people out of their money and committed what he calls "the sins of omission" as he described the risks of silver and gold futures. But the conflict bred what psychologist Ansell describes as immoral behavior sinking into self-contempt.

"I drank, skipped the morning meetings, played a lot of golf and left early. And the worst thing was looking my kids in the eye when I told them what was right and what was wrong," says Steve.

"Then one day they gobbled up my book [of clients] and were going to give all my leads to killers," he says. "When I told them they were wrong, they said I was a wimp, that I didn't understand the way the world works."

In the end, Steve quit. He went home and discussed his problem with his wife and two sons. "I told them I had cheated people, but I was stopping. I took a job running a restaurant, then driving a limo. I went from $1,500 a week to $450. At times I feel like I'm not such a macho guy because I didn't have what it takes for that life. I feel like a jerky idealist. But most of the time I feel good about myself. I never felt that way before."

Adam Smith
Benefits of the Profit Motive

Adam Smith's (1723–1790) Wealth of Nations *is often called the Bible of capitalism. It also marks the beginning of modern economic theory. The following selection from* *that work is a discussion of the value of the division of labor and the advantages of the capitalist system.*

The greatest improvement in the productive powers of labor, and the greater part of the skill, dexterity, and judgment with which it is anywhere directed, or applied, seem to have been the effects of the division of labor. . . .

To take an example, therefore, from a very trifling manufacture; but one in which the division of labor has been very often taken notice of, the trade of the pin-maker; a workman not educated to this business (which the division of labor has rendered a distinct trade), nor acquainted with the use of the machinery employed in it (to the invention of which the same division of labor has probably given occasion), could scarce, perhaps, with his utmost industry, make one pin a day, and certainly could not make twenty. But in the way in which this business is now carried on, not only the whole work is a peculiar trade, but it is divided into a number of branches, of which the greater part are likewise peculiar trades. One man draws out the wire, another straights it, a third cuts it, a fourth points it, a fifth grinds it at the top for receiving the head; to make the head requires two or three distinct operations; to put it on is a peculiar business, to whiten the pins is another; it is even a trade by itself to put them into the paper; and the important business of making a pin is, in this manner, divided into about eighteen distinct operations, which, in some manufactories, are all performed by distinct hands, though in others the same man will sometimes perform two or three of them. I have seen a small manufactory of this kind where ten men only were employed, and where some of them consequently performed two or three distinct operations. But though they were very poor, and therefore but indifferently accommodated with the necessary machinery, they could, when they exerted themselves, make among them about twelve pounds of pins in a day. There are in a pound upwards of four thousand pins of a middling size. Those ten persons, therefore, could make among them upwards of forty-eight thousand pins in a day. Each person, therefore, making a tenth part of forty-eight thousand pins, might be considered as making four thousand eight hundred pins in a day. But if they had all wrought separately and independently, and without any of them having been educated to this peculiar business, they certainly could not each of them have made twenty, perhaps not one pin in a day; that is, cerainly, not the two hundred and fortieth, perhaps not the four thousand eight hundredth part, of what they are at present capable of performing in consequence of a proper division and combination of their different operations.

In every other art and manufacture, the effects of the division of labor are similar to what they are in this very trifling one; though in many of them, the labor can neither be so much subdivided, nor reduced to so great a simplicity of operation. The division of labor, however, so far as it can be introduced, occasions, in every art, a proportionable increase of the productive powers of labor. . . .

This great increase of the quantity of work, which, in consequence of the division of labor, the same number of people are capable of performing, is owing to three different circumstances: first, to the increase of dexterity in every particular workman; secondly, to the saving of the time which is commonly lost in passing from one species of work to another; and lastly, to the invention of a great number of machines which facilitate and abridge labor, and enable one man to do the work of many.

First, the improvement of the dexterity of the workman necessarily increases the quantity of the work he can perform; and the division of labor, by reducing every man's business to some one simple operation and by making this operation the sole employment of his life, necessarily increases very much the dexterity of the workman. A common smith, who, though accustomed to handle the hammer, has never been used to make nails, if upon some particular occasion he is obliged to attempt it, will scarce, I am assured, be able to make about two or three hundred nails in a day, and those too very bad ones. A smith who has been accustomed to make nails, but whose sole or principal business has not been that of a nailer, can seldom with his utmost diligence make more than eight hundred or a thousand nails in a day. I have seen several boys under twenty years of age who had never exercised any other trade but that of making nails, and who, when they exerted themselves, could make, each of them, upwards of two thousand three hundred nails in a day. The making of a nail, however, is by no means one of the simplest operations. The same person blows the bellows, stirs or mends the fire as there is occasion, heats the iron, and forges every part of the nail: In forging the head too he is obliged to change his tools. The different operations into which the making of a pin or of a metal button is subdivided, are all of them much more simple; and the dexterity of the person, of whose life it has been the sole business to perform them, is usually much greater. The rapidity with which some of the operations of those manufactures are performed exceeds what the human hand could, by those who had never seen them, be supposed capable of acquiring.

Secondly, the advantage which is gained by saving the time commonly lost in passing from one sort of work to another is much greater than we should at first view be apt to imagine it. It is impossible to pass very quickly from one kind of work to another, that is carried on in a different place, and with quite different tools. A country weaver who cultivates a small farm must lose a good deal of time in passing from his loom to the field, and from the field to his loom. When the two trades can be carried on in the same workhouse, the loss of time is no doubt much less. It is even in this case, however, very considerable. . . .

Thirdly, and lastly, every body must be sensible how much labor is facilitated and abridged by the application of proper machinery. . . .

. . . A great part of the machines made use of in those manufactures in which labor is most subdivided were originally the inventions of common workmen, who, being each of them employed in some very simple operation, naturally turned their thoughts toward finding out easier and readier methods of performing it. Whoever has been much accustomed to visit such manufacturers must frequently have been shown very pretty machines which were the inventions of such workmen in order to facilitate and quicken their own particular part of the work. In the first fire-engines, a boy was constantly employed to open and shut alternately the communication between the boiler and the cylinder, according as the piston either ascended or descended. One of those boys, who loved to play with his companions, observed that, by tying a string from the handle of the valve which opened this communication to another part of the machine, the valve would open and shut without his assistance, and leave him at liberty to divert himself with his play-fellows. One of the greatest improvements that has been made upon this machine, since it was first invented, was in this manner the discovery of a boy who wanted to save his own labor. . . .

It is the great multiplication of the productions of all the different arts, in consequence of the division of labor, which occasions, in a well-governed society, that universal opulence which extends itself to the lowest ranks of the people. Every workman has a great quantity of his own work to dispose of beyond what he himself has occasion for; and every other workman being exactly in the same situation, he is enabled to exchange a great quantity of his own goods for a great quantity, or, what comes to the same thing, for the price of a great quantity of theirs. He supplies them abundantly with what they have occasion for, and they accommodate him as amply with what he has occasion for, and a general plenty diffuses itself through all the different ranks of the society. . . .

This division of labor, from which so many advantages are derived, is not originally the effect of any human wisdom which foresees and intends that general opulence to which it gives occasion. It is the necessary, though very slow and gradual, consequence of a certain propensity in human nature which has in view no such extensive utility: the propensity to truck, barter, and exchange one thing for another.

. . . In almost every other race of animals each individual, when it is grown up to maturity, is entirely independent, and in its natural state has occasion for the assistance of no other living creature. But man has almost constant occasion for the help of his brethren, and it is in vain for him to expect it from their benevolence only. He will be more likely to prevail if he can interest their self-love in his favor, and show them that it is for their own advantage to do for him what he requires of them. Whoever offers to another a bargain of any kind, proposes to do this. Give me that which I want, and you shall have this which you want, is the meaning of every such offer; and it is in the manner that we obtain from one another the far greater part of those good offices which we stand in need of. It is not from the benevolence of the butcher, the brewer, or the baker, that we expect our dinner, but from their regard to their own interest. We address ourselves, not to their humanity but to their self-love, and never talk to them of our own necessities but of their advantages. Nobody but a begger chooses to depend chiefly upon the benevolence of his fellow-citizens. Even a beggar does not depend on it entirely. The charity of well-disposed people, indeed, supplies him with the whole fund of his subsistence. But though this principle ultimately provides him with all the necessaries of life which he has occasion for, it neither does nor can provide him with them as he has occasion for them. The greater part of his occasional wants are supplied in the same manner as those of other people, by treaty, by barter, and by purchase. With the money which one man gives him he purchases food. The old clothes which another bestows upon him he exchanges for other old clothes which suit him better, or for lodging, or for food, or for money, with which he can buy either food, clothes, or lodging, as he has occasion.

As it is by treaty, by barter, and by purchase that we obtain from one another the greater part of those mutual good offices which we stand in need of, so it is this same trucking disposition which originally gives occasion to the division of labor. In a tribe of hunters or shepherds a particular person makes bows and arrows, for example, with more readiness and dexterity than any other. He frequently exchanges them for cattle or for venison with his companions; and he finds at last that he can in this manner get more cattle and venison than if he himself went to the field to catch them. From a regard to his own interest, therefore, the making of bows and arrows grows to be his chief business, and he becomes a sort of armorer. Another excels in making the frames and covers of their little huts or movable houses. He is accustomed to be of use in this way to his neighbors, who reward him in the same manner with cattle and with venison till at last he finds it his interest to dedicate himself entirely to this employment, and to become a sort of house carpenter. In the same manner a third becomes a smith or a brazier; a fourth a tanner or dresser of hides or skins, the principal part of the clothing of savages. And thus the certainty of being able to exchange all that surplus part of the produce of his own labor, which is over and above his own consumption, for such parts of the produce of other men's labor as he may have occasion for, encourages every man to apply himself to a particular occupation, and to cultivate and bring to perfection whatever talent or genius he may possess for that particular species of business.

The difference of natural talents in different men is, in reality, much less than we are aware of; and the very different genius which appears to distinguish men of different professions, when grown up to maturity, is not upon many occasions so much the cause as the effect of the division of labor. The difference between the most dissimilar characters, between a philosopher and a common street porter, for example, seems to arise not so much from nature as from habit, custom, and education. When they came into the world, and for the first six or eight years of their existence, they were, perhaps, very much alike, and neither their parents nor play-fellows could perceive any remarkable difference. About that age, or soon after, they come to be employed in very different occupations. The difference of talents comes then to be taken notice of, and widens by degrees, till at last the vanity of the philosopher is willing to acknowledge scarce any resemblance. But without the disposition to truck, barter, and exchange, every man must have procured to himself every necessary and conveniency of life which he wanted. All must have had the same duties to perform, and the same work to do, and there could have been no such difference of employment as could alone give occasion to any great difference of talents. . . .

Every individual is continually exerting himself to find out the most advantageous employment for whatever capital he can command. It is his own advantage, indeed, and not that of the society, which he has in view. But the study of his own advantage, naturally, or rather necessarily, leads him to prefer that employment which is most advantageous to the society. . . .

As every individual, therefore, endeavors as much as he can both to employ his capital in the support of domestic industry, and so to direct that industry that its produce may be of the greatest value, every individual necessarily labors to render the annual revenue of the society as great as he can. He generally, indeed, neither intends to promote the public interest, nor knows how much he is promoting it. By preferring the support of domestic to that of foreign industry, he intends only his own security: and by directing that industry in such a manner as its produce may be of the greatest value, he intends only his own gain, and he is in this, as in many other cases, led by an invisible hand to promote an end which was no part of his intention. Nor is it always the worse for the society that it was no part of it. By pursuing his own interest he frequently promotes that of the society more effectually than when he really intends to promote it. I have never known much good done by those who affected to trade for the public good. It is an affectation, indeed, not very common among merchants, and very few words need be employed in dissuading them from it. . . .

If we examine, I say, all those things . . . we shall be sensible that without the assistance and cooperation of many thousands, the very meanest person in a civilized country could not be provided, even according to what we very falsely imagine, the easy and simple manner in which he is commonly accommodated. Compared indeed with the more extravagant luxury of the great, his accommodation must no doubt appear extremely simple and easy; and yet it may be true, perhaps, that the accommodation of a European prince does not always so much exceed that of an industrious and frugal peasant, as the accommodation of the latter exceeds that of many an African king, the absolute master of the lives and liberties of ten thousand naked savages.

Karl Marx and Friedrich Engels
The Immorality of Capitalism

Karl Marx *(1818–1883) and* **Friedrich Engels** *(1820–1895) were the founders of modern communism. Their* Communist Manifesto, *reproduced in part here, was their 1848 battlecry, formulated in the name of the newly organized working class—the "proletariat."*

The history of all hitherto existing society is the history of class struggles.

Freeman and slave, patrician and plebeian, lord and serf, guildmaster and journeyman, in a word, oppressor and oppressed, stood in constant opposition to one another, carried on an uninterrupted, now hidden, now open fight, a fight that each time ended, either in a revolutionary reconstitution of society at large, or in the common ruin of the struggling classes.

In the earlier epochs of history, we find almost everywhere a complicated arrangement of society into various orders, a manifold gradation of social rank. In ancient Rome we have patricians, knights, plebeians, slaves; in the Middle Ages, feudal lords, vassals, guildmasters, journeymen, apprentices, serfs; and in almost all of these particular classes, again, other subordinate gradations.

The modern bourgeois society that has sprouted from the ruins of feudal society has not done away with class antagonisms. It has only established new classes, new conditions of oppression, new forms of struggle in place of the old ones.

Our epoch, the epoch of the bourgeoisie, shows, however, this distinctive feature: it has simplified the class antagonisms. Society as a whole is more and more splitting up into two great hostile camps, into two great classes directly facing each other: *bourgeoisie* and *proletariat*.

From the serfs of the Middle Ages sprang the chartered burghers of the earliest towns. From these burghers the first elements of the bourgeoisie were developed.

The discovery of America, the rounding of the Cape, opened up fresh ground for the rising bourgeoisie. The East-Indian and Chinese markets, the colonization of America, trade with the colonies, the increase in the means of exchange and in commodities generally, gave to commerce, to navigation, to industry, an impulse never before known, and thereby, to the revolutionary element in the tottering feudal society, a rapid development.

The feudal system of industry, under which industrial production was monopolized by closed guilds, now no longer sufficed for the growing wants of the new markets. The manufacturing system took its place. The guildmasters were pushed on one side by the manufacturing middle class; division of labor between the different corporate guilds vanished in the face of division of labor in each single workshop.

Meanwhile the markets kept on growing; demand went on rising. Manufacturing no longer was able to keep up with this growth. Then, steam and machinery revolutionized industrial production. The place of manufacture was taken by the giant, *modern industry;* the place of the industrial middle class, by industrial millionaires, the leaders of whole industrial armies, the modern bourgeois.

Modern industry has established the world market, for which the discovery of America paved the way. This market has given an immense development to commerce, to navigation, to communication by land. This development has, in its turn, reacted on the extension of industry; and in proportion as industry, commerce, navigation, railways extended, in the same proportion the bourgeoisie developed, increased its capital, and pushed into the background every class handed down from the Middle Ages.

We see, therefore, how the modern bourgeoisie is itself the product of a long course of development, of a series of revolutions in the modes of production and of exchange. . . .

The need of a constantly expanding market for its products chases the bourgeoisie over the whole surface of the globe. It must nestle everywhere, settle everywhere, establish connections everywhere.

The bourgeoisie has through its exploitation of the world market given a cosmopolitan character to production and consumption in every country. To the great chagrin of reactionaries, it has drawn from under the feet of industry the national ground on which it stood. All old-established national industries have been destroyed or are daily being destroyed. They are dislodged by new industries, whose introduction becomes a life and death question for all civilized nations, by industries that no longer work up indigenous raw material, but raw material drawn from the remotest zones; industries whose products are consumed, not only at home, but in every quarter of the globe. In place of the old wants, satisfied by the productions of the country, we find new wants requiring for their satisfaction the products of distant lands and climates. In place of the old local and national seclusion and self-sufficiency, we have intercourse in every direction, universal inter-dependence of nations. And as in material, so also in intellectual production. The intellectual creations of individual nations become common property. National one-sidedness and narrow-mindedness become more and more impossible, and from the numerous national and local literatures, there emerges a world literature

The bourgeoisie, by the rapid improvement of all instruments of production, by the immensely facilitated means of communications, draws all, even the most backward, nations into civilization. The cheap prices of its commodities are the heavy artillery with which it batters down all Chinese walls, with which it forces the underdeveloped nations' intensely obstinate hatred of foreigners to capitulate. It compels all nations, on pain of extinction, to adopt the bourgeois mode of production; it compels them to introduce what it calls civilization into their midst, *i.e.,* to become bourgeois themselves. In one word, it creates a world in its own image.

The bourgeoisie has subjected rural areas to the rule of cities. It has created enormous cities, has greatly increased the urban population as compared with the rural, and has thus rescued a considerable part of the population from the idiocy of rural life. Just as it has made the country dependent on the cities, so has it made barbarian and semi-underdeveloped countries dependent on the civilized ones, nations of peasants on nations of bourgeois, the East on the West.

The bourgeoisie keeps more and more doing away with the scattered state of the population, of the means of production, and of property. It has agglomerated population, centralized means of production, and has concentrated property in a few hands. The necessary consequence of this was political centralization. Independent, or but loosely connected, provinces with separate interests, laws, governments, and systems of taxation became lumped together into one nation, with one government, one code of laws, one national class-interest, one frontier, and one customs-tariff.

The bourgeoisie, during its rule of scarcely one hundred years, has created more massive and more colossal productive forces than have all preceding generations together. Subjection of Nature's forces to man, machinery, application of chemistry to industry and agriculture, steam-navigation, railways, electric telegraphs, clearing of whole continents for cultivation, canalization of rivers, whole populations conjured out of the ground—what earlier century had even a presentiment that such productive forces slumbered in the lap of social labor?

We see then: the means of production and of exchange, on whose foundation the bourgeoisie built itself up, were generated in feudal society. At a certain stage in the development of these means of production and of exchange, the conditions under which feudal society produced and exchanged, the feudal organization of agriculture and manufacturing industry, in one word, the feudal relations of property became no longer compatible with the already developed productive forces; they became so many fetters. They had to be burst asunder; they were burst asunder.

Into their place stepped free competition, accompanied by a social and political constitution adapted to it, and by the economical and political sway of the bourgeois class.

A similar movement is going on before our own eyes. Modern bourgeois society with its relations of production, of exchange and of property, a society that has conjured up such gigantic means of production and of exchange, is like the sorcerer, who is no longer able to control the powers of the subterranean world which he has called up by his spells. For many decades now the history of industry and commerce has been but the history of the revolt of modern productive forces against modern conditions of production, against the property relations that are the conditions for the existence of the bourgeoisie and of its rule. It is enough to mention the commercial crises that by their periodical return put on trial, each time more threateningly, the existence of the entire bourgeois society. In these crises a great part not only of the existing products, but also of the previously created productive forces, are periodically destroyed. In these crises there breaks out an epidemic that, in all earlier epochs, would have seemed an absurdity—the epidemic of overproduction. Society suddenly finds itself put back into a state of momentary barbarism; it appears as if a famine, a universal war of devastation had cut off the supply of every means of subsistence; industry and commerce seem to be destroyed; and why? Because there is too much civilization, too much means of subsistence, too much industry, too much commerce. The productive forces at the disposal of society no longer tend to further the development of the conditions of bourgeois property; on the contrary, they have become too powerful for these conditions, by which they are fettered, and so soon as they overcome these fetters, they bring disorder into the whole of bourgeois society, endanger the existence of bourgeois property. The conditions of bourgeois society are too narrow to comprise the wealth created by them. And how does the bourgeoisie get over these crises? On the one hand by enforced destruction of a mass of productive forces; on the other, by the conquest of new markets, and by the more thorough exploitation of the old ones. That is to say, by paving the way for more extensive and more destructive crises, and by diminishing the means whereby crises are prevented.

The weapons with which the bourgeoisie felled feudalism to the ground are now turned against the bourgeoisie itself.

But not only has the bourgeoisie forged the weapons that bring death to itself; it has also called into existence the men who are to wield those weapons—the modern working class—the proletarians.

In proportion as the bourgeoisie, *i.e.*, capital, is developed, in the same proportion is the proletariat, the modern working class, developed—a class of laborers, who live only so long as they find work, and who find work only so long as their labor increases capital. These laborers, who must sell themselves piecemeal, are a commodity, like every other article of commerce, and are consequently exposed to all the vicissitudes of competition, to all the fluctuations of the market.

Owing to the extensive use of machinery and division of labor, the work of the proletarians has lost all individual character, and, consequently, all charm for the workman. He becomes an appendage of the machine, and it is only the most simple, most monotonous, and most easily acquired knack that is required of him. Hence, the cost of production of a workman is restricted, almost entirely, to the means of subsistence that he requires for his maintenance, and for the propagation of his race. But the price of a commodity, and therefore also of labor, is equal to its cost of production. In proportion, therefore, as the repulsiveness of the work increases, the wage decreases. What is more, in proportion as the use of machinery and division of labor increases, in the same proportion the burden of toil also increases, whether by prolongation of the working hours, by increase of the work exacted in a given time or by increased speed of the machinery, etc.

Modern industry has converted the little workshop of the patriarchal master into the great factory of the industrial capitalist. Masses of laborers, crowded into the factory, are organized like soldiers. As privates of the industrial army they are placed under the command of a perfect hierarchy of officers and sergeants. Not only are they slaves of the bourgeois class, and of the bourgeois state; they are daily and hourly enslaved by the machine, by the foreman, and, above all, by the individual bourgeois manufacturer himself. The more openly this despotism proclaims gain to be its end and aim, the more petty, the more hateful, and the more embittering it is. . . .

But with the development of industry the proletariat not only increases in number; it becomes concentrated in greater masses, its strength grows, and it feels that strength more.

The various interests and conditions of life within the ranks of the proletariat are more and more equalized, in proportion as machinery obliterates all distinctions of labor, and nearly everywhere reduces wages to the same low level. The growing competition among the bourgeoisie, and the resulting commercial crises, make the wages of the workers ever more fluctuating. The unceasing improvement of machinery, ever more rapidly developing, makes their livelihood more and more precarious; the collisions between individual workmen and individual bourgeoisie take more and more the character of collisions between two classes. Thereupon the workers begin to form combinations (trade unions) against the bourgeoisie; they club together in order to keep up the rate of wages; they found permanent associations in order to make provision beforehand for these occasional revolts. Here and there the contest breaks out into riots.

From time to time the workers are victorious, but only for a time. The real fruit of their battles lies not in the immediate result, but in the ever-expanding union of the workers. This union is helped by the improved means of communication that are created by modern industry and that place the workers of different localities in contact with one another. It was just this contact that was needed to centralize the numerous local struggles, all of the same character, into one national struggle between classes. But every class struggle is a political struggle. And that union, to attain which the burghers of the Middle Ages, with their miserable highways, required centuries, the modern proletarians, thanks to railways, achieve in a few years. . . .

Hitherto, every form of society has been based, as we have already seen, on the antagonism of oppressing and oppressed classes. But in order to oppress a class, certain conditions must be assured to it under which it can, at least, continue its slavish existence. The serf, in the period of serfdom, raised himself to membership in the commune, just as the petty bourgeois, under the yoke of feudal absolutism, managed to develop into a bourgeois. The modern laborer, on the contrary, instead of rising with the progress of industry, sinks deeper and deeper below the conditions of existence of his own class. He becomes a pauper, and pauperism develops more rapidly than population and wealth. And here it becomes evident that the bourgeoisie is unfit any longer to be the ruling class in society, and to impose its conditions of existence upon society as an overriding law. It is unfit to rule because it is incompetent to assure an existence to its slave within his slavery, because it cannot help letting him sink into such a state, that it has to feed him, instead of being fed by him. Society can no longer live under this bourgeoisie, in other words, its existence is no longer compatible with society.

The essential condition for the existence, and for the sway of the bourgeois class, is the formation and augmentation of capital; the condition for capital is wage labor. Wage labor rests exclusively on competition between laborers. The advance of industry, whose involuntary promoter is the bourgeoisie, replaces the isolation of the laborers, due to competition, by their revolutionary combination, due to association. The development of modern industry, therefore, cuts from under its feet the very foundation on which the bourgeoisie produces and appropriates products. What the bourgeoisie, therefore, produces, above all, is its own grave-diggers. Its fall and the victory of the proletariat are equally inevitable.

Paul M. Sweezy
A Primer on Marxian Economics

Paul M. Sweezy *is a well-known Marxist and social critic. The following essay is reprinted from* Business and Society Review.

I am a Marxist, and I am firmly convinced that only Marxism allows us to understand the functioning of capitalist societies. The essence of capitalism, as explained in the short second part of the first volume of Marx's *Capital,* is the accumulation of capital; which means continuous and perpetual expansion. To be healthy a capitalist enterprise must grow and grow and grow. The alternative is stagnation and eventual death. And individual enterprises can grow only if the economy as a whole grows. This process has been going on in the United States ever since the first Europeans set foot on these shores.

The mechanism of growth is that society's surplus product—what is left over after a conventional and always relatively low level of subsistence is provided to the actual worker-producers—is appropriated and controlled by a small class of owners, in our day corporations and their stock- and bond-holders. Out of this surplus the owning class consumes enough to live well and in many cases in great luxury, but it cannot begin to consume the whole surplus, nor does it desire to do so. By far the larger part is accumulated, i.e., invested with a view to making profits and hence increasing the surplus still further in the future.

But this process can continue only so long as profitable markets grow in proportion to capital, and this is far from being guaranteed. If markets do not grow sufficiently, the result is an interruption of the process—crisis, depression, stagnation. It follows with iron logic that a high-priority pre-occupation of everyone in business and government is and must be the expansion of existing markets and the creation of new ones. And the means used, private and government alike, will be the most varied, the most ingenious, and, if need be, the most violent and ruthless imaginable. The list would be endless. I will mention only a few of the most important and commonly used: invention of new or seemingly new products, territorial expansion, penetration of rivals' markets, conquest of foreign peoples, credit creation and expansion, deficit financing, advertising, armaments, and wars. But despite all these methods to create and expand markets, periodic breakdowns of the accumulation process have occurred since the earliest days of capitalism and, as everyone now knows, continue to occur every few years. Right now we are in the worst period of stagnation since the Great Depression of the 1930s, with no signs of an early return to anything remotely approaching prosperity.

Let us now look at American capitalism against this background:

1. American capitalism in its roughly three centuries of existence has expanded enormously, has greatly increased the productivity of human labor, and has raised the per capita consumption of goods and services severalfold. The cost of these achievements, however, has been formidable. The system has exploited and often violently repressed not only its own work force (slave and free) but also vast numbers of people around the world whose economies and societies have been subordinated to the needs of American capitalism. The increased productivity of labor has been at the expense of dehumanizing the work process which absorbs the best part of the lives of most people. And in the long run perhaps the greatest, and ultimately fatal, flaw in capitalism is that an infinitely expanding system in a finite environment is a living contradiction, a time bomb bound sooner or later to explode with shattering and death-dealing ecological consequences. From the beginning, capitalism has always recklessly polluted and destroyed its environment, but until recently this did not seem to matter much. Now, however, the signs of overstrain are everywhere visible, and it is getting to be a commonplace that economic growth in the developed countries, and especially the United States, must be brought under control and decisively checked in the historically near future. What is unfortunately not so widely understood is that this implies the end of capitalism and its replacement by a planned system of production for use, rather than a market system of production for profit.

2. What about "equity" in American society? I suggest that there are two basic aspects to any meaningful concept of "equity." The first is that everyone without exception should have a sufficiency of the things needed to live a decent life: employment at useful work in humane conditions, adequate housing, a healthy diet, good health care, security for the young, the old, and the infirm. The second is that inequalities in the provision of these necessities should be both small and declining over time. Judged by these criteria the American economy has obviously failed miserably in terms of equity.

3. The fact that income in the United States is distributed extremely unequally—that there is a small stratum of super-rich millionaires at the top and literally tens of millions of poverty-stricken at the bottom—is sufficient proof that some groups have profited inordinately while others have suffered because of the character and development of the American economic system. But it is necessary to add that in a society of exploiters and exploited, oppressors and oppressed, everyone, whether rich or poor, suffers from the alienation and dehumanization which are inherent in such a society.

Robert Heilbroner

The Very Idea of a "Free Market System"

Robert Heilbroner *is a professor of economics at the New School for Social Research and the author of many books and textbooks including* The Wordly Philosophers. *The following is from* The Making of Economic Society.

Because we live in a market-run society, we are apt to take for granted the puzzling—indeed, almost paradoxical—nature of the market solution to the economic problem. But assume for a moment that we could act as economic advisers to a society that had not yet decided on its mode of economic organization. Suppose, for instance, that we were called on to act as consultants to one of the new nations emerging on the continent of Africa or Asia.

We could imagine the leaders of such a nation saying, "We have always experienced a highly tradition-bound way of life. Our men hunt and cultivate the fields and perform their tasks as they are brought up to do by the force of example and the instruction of their elders. We know, too, something of what can be done by economic command. We are prepared, if necessary, to sign an edict making it compulsory for many of our men to work on community projects for our national development. Tell us, is there any other way we can organize our society so that it will function successfully—or better yet, *more* successfully?"

Suppose we answered, "Well, there is another way. One can organize a society along the lines of a market economy."

"I see," say the leaders. "What would we then tell people to do? How would we assign them to their various tasks?"

"That's the very point," we answer. "In a market economy, no one is assigned to any task. In fact, the main idea of a market society is that each person is allowed to decide for himself what to do."

There is consternation among the leaders. "You mean there is no assignment of some men to farming and others to mining? No manner of designating some for transportation and others for weaving? You leave this to people to decide for themselves? But what happens if they do not decide correctly? What happens if no one volunteers to go into the mines, or if no one offers himself as a bus driver?"

"You must rest assured," we tell the leaders, "none of that will happen. In a market society, all the jobs will be filled because it will be to people's advantage to fill them."

Our respondents accept this with uncertain expressions. "Now look," one of them finally says, "let us suppose that we take your advice and allow our people to do as they please. Let's talk about something specific, like cloth production. Just how do we fix the right level of cloth output in this 'market society' of yours?"

"But you don't," we reply.

"We don't! Then how do we know there will be enough cloth produced?"

"There will be," we tell him. "The market will see to that."

"Then how do we know there won't be *too much* cloth produced?" he asks triumphantly.

"Ah, but the market will see to that too!"

"But what is this market that will do these wonderful things? Who runs it?"

"Oh, nobody runs the market," we answer. "It runs itself. In fact there really isn't any such *thing* as 'the market.' It's just a word we use to describe the way people behave."

"But I thought people behaved the way they wanted to!"

"And so they do," we say. "But never fear. They will want to behave the way you want them to behave."

"I am afraid," says the chief of the delegation, "that we are wasting out time. We thought you had in mind a serious proposal. What you suggest is inconceivable. Good day."

Could we seriously suggest to such an emergent nation that it entrust itself to a market solution of the economic problem? That will be a problem to which we shall return at the very end of our book. But the perplexity that the market idea would rouse in the mind of someone unacquainted with it may serve to increase our own wonderment at this most sophisticated and interesting of all economic mechanisms. How does the market system assure us that our mines will find miners, our factories workers? How does it take care of cloth production? How does it happen that in a market-run nation each person can indeed do as he wishes and, withal, fulfill needs that society as a whole presents?

Milton Friedman

The Social Responsibility of Business Is to Increase Its Profits

Milton Friedman is a well-known economist, author, columnist, and defender of the free market system. The following is a notorious essay he wrote for the New York Times in 1970.

When I hear businessmen speak eloquently about the "social responsibilities of business in a free-enterprise system," I am reminded of the wonderful line about the Frenchman who discovered at the age of 70 that he had been speaking prose all his life. The businessmen believe that they are defending free enterprise when they declaim that business is not concerned "merely" with profit but also with promoting desirable "social" ends; that business has a "social conscience" and takes seriously its responsibilities for providing employment, eliminating discrimination, avoiding pollution and whatever else may be the catchwords of the contemporary crop of reformers. In fact they are—or would be if they or anyone else took them seriously—preaching pure and unadulterated socialism. Businessmen who talk this way are unwitting puppets of the intellectual forces that have been undermining the basis of a free society these past decades.

The discussion of the "social responsibilities of business" are notable for their analytical looseness and lack of rigor. What does it mean to say that "business" has responsibilities? Only people can have responsibilities. A corporation is an artificial person and in this sense may have artificial responsibilities, but "business" as a whole cannot be said to have responsibilities, even in this vague sense. The first step toward clarity to examining the doctrine of the social responsibility of business is to ask precisely what it implies for whom.

Presumably, the individuals who are to be responsible are businessmen, which means individual proprietors or corporate executives. Most of the discussion of social responsibility is directed at corporations, so in what follows I shall mostly neglect the individual proprietors and speak of corporate executives.

In a free-enterprise, private-property system, a corporate executive is an employee of the owners of the business. He has direct responsibility to his employers. That responsibility is to conduct the business in accordance with their desires, which generally will be to make as much money as possible while conforming to the basic rules of the society, both those embodied in law and those embodied in ethical custom. Of course, in some cases his employers may have a different objective. A group of persons might establish a corporation for an eleemosynary purpose—for example, a hospital or a school. The manager of such a corporation will not have money profit as his objectives but the rendering of certain services.

In either case, the key point is that, in his capacity as a corporate executive, the manager is the agent of the individuals who own the corporation or establish the eleemosynary institution, and his primary responsibility is to them.

Needless to say, this does not mean that it is easy to judge how well he is performing his task. But at least the criterion of performance is straightforward, and the persons among whom a voluntary contractual arrangement exists are clearly defined.

Of course, the corporate executive is also a person in his own right. As a person, he may have many other responsibilities that he recognizes or assumes voluntarily—to his family, his conscience, his feelings of charity, his church, his clubs, his city, his country. He may feel impelled by these responsibilities to devote part of his income to causes he regards as worthy, to refuse to work for particular corporations, even to leave his job, for example, to join his country's armed forces. If we wish, we may refer to some of these responsibilities as "social responsibilities." But in these respects he is acting as a principal, not an agent; he is spending his own money or time or energy, not the money of his employers or the time or energy he has contracted to devote to their purposes. If these are "social responsibilities," they are the social responsibilities of individuals, not of business.

What does it mean to say that the corporate executive has a "social responsibility" in his capacity as businessman? If this statement is not pure rhetoric, it must mean that he is to act in some way that is not in the interest of his employers. For example, that he is to refrain from increasing the price of the product in order to contribute to the social objective of preventing inflation, even though a price increase would be in the best interests of the corporation. Or that he is to make expenditures on reducing pollution beyond the amount that is in the best interests of the corporation or that is required by law in order to contribute to the social objective of improving the environment. Or that, at the expense of corporate profits, he is to hire "hardcore" unemployed instead of better qualified available workmen to contribute to the social objective of reducing poverty.

In each of these cases, the corporate executive would be spending someone else's money for a general social interest. Insofar as his actions in accord with his "social responsibility" reduce returns to stockholders, he is spending their money. Insofar as his actions raise the price to customers, he is spending the customers' money. Insofar as his actions raise the price to customers, he is spending the customers' money. Insofar as his actions lower the wages of some employees, he is spending their money.

The stockholders or the customers or the employees could separately spend their own money on the particular action if they wished to do so. The executive is exercising a distinct "social responsibility," rather than serving as an agent of the stockholders or the customers or the employees, only if he spends the money in a different way than they would have spent it.

But if he does this, he is in effect imposing taxes, on the one hand, and deciding how the tax proceeds shall be spent, on the other.

This process raises political questions on two levels: principle and consequences. On the level of political principle, the imposition of taxes and the expenditure of tax proceeds are governmental functions. We have established elaborate constitutional, parliamentary and judicial provisions to control these functions, to assure that taxes are imposed so far as possible in accordance with the preferences and desires of the public—after all, "taxation without representation" was one of the battle cries of the American Revolution. We have a system of checks and balances to separate the legislative function of imposing taxes and enacting expenditures from the executive function of collecting taxes and administering expenditure programs and from the judicial function of mediating disputes and interpreting the law.

Here the businessman—self-selected or appointed directly or indirectly by stockholders—is to be simultaneously legislator, executive and jurist. He is to decide whom to tax by how much and for what purpose, and he is to spend the proceeds—all this guided only by general exhortations from on high to restrain inflation, improve the environment, fight poverty and so on and on.

The whole justification for permitting the corporate executive to be selected by the stockholders is that the executive is an agent serving the interests of his principal. This justification disappears when the corporate executive imposes taxes and spends the proceeds for "social" purposes. He becomes in effect a public employee, a civil servant, even though he remains in name an employee of a private enterprise. On grounds of political principle, it is intolerable that such civil servants—insofar as their actions in the name of social responsibility are real and not just window-dressing—should be selected as they are now. If they are to be civil servants, then they must be elected through a political process. If they are to impose taxes and make expenditures to foster "social" objectives, then political machinery must be set up to make the assessment of taxes and to determine through a political process the objectives to be served.

This is the basic reason why the doctrine of "social responsibility" involves the acceptance of the socialist view that political mechanisms, not market mechanisms, are the appropriate way to determine the allocation of scarce resources to alternative uses.

On the grounds of consequences, can the corporate executive in fact discharge his alleged "social responsibilities"? On the one hand, suppose he could get away with spending the stockholders' or customers' or employees' money. How is he to know how to spend it? He is told that he must contribute to fighting inflation. How is he to know what action of his will contribute to that end? He is presumably an expert in running his company—in producing a product or selling it or financing it. But nothing about his selection makes him an expert on inflation. Will his holding down the price of his product reduce inflationary pressure? Or, by leaving more spending power in the hands of his customers, simply divert it elsewhere? Or, by forcing him to produce less because of the lower price, will it simply contribute to shortages? Even if he could answer these questions, how much cost is he justified in imposing on his stockholders, customers and employees for this social purpose? What is his appropriate share and what is the appropriate share of others?

And, whether he wants to or not, can he get away with spending his stockholders', customers' or employees' money? Will not the stockholders fire him? (Either the present ones or those who take over when his actions in the name of social responsibility have reduced the corporation's profits and the price of its stock.) His customers and employees can desert him for other producers and employers less scrupulous in exercising their social responsibilities.

This facet of "social responsibility" doctrine is brought into sharp relief when the doctrine is used to justify wage restraint by trade unions. The conflict of interest is naked and clear when union officials are asked to subordinate the interest of their members to some more general purpose. If the union officials try to enforce wage restraint, the consequence is likely to be wildcat strikes, rank-and-file revolts and the emergence of strong competitors for their jobs. We thus have the ironic phenomenon that union leaders—at least in the U.S.— have objected to Government interference with the market far more consistently and courageously than have business leaders.

The difficulty of exercising "social responsibility" illustrates, of course, the great virtue of private competitive enterprise—it forces people to be responsible for their own actions and makes it difficult for them to "exploit" other people for either selfish or unselfish purposes. They can do good—but only at their own expense.

Many a reader who has followed the argument this far may be tempted to remonstrate that it is all well and good to speak of Government's having the responsibility to impose taxes and determine expenditures for such "social" purposes as controlling pollution or training the hard-core unemployed, but that the problems are too urgent to wait on the slow course of political processes, that the exercise of social responsibility by businessmen is a quicker and surer way to solve pressing current problems.

Aside from the question of fact—I share Adam Smith's skepticism about the benefits that can be expected from "those who affected to trade for the public good"—this argument must be rejected on grounds of principle. What it amounts to is an assertion that those who favor the taxes and expenditures in question have failed to persuade a majority of their fellow citizens to be of like mind and that they are seeking to attain by undemocratic procedures what they cannot attain by democratic procedures. In a free society, it is hard for "evil" people to do "evil," especially since one man's good is another's evil.

I have, for simplicity, concentrated on the special case of the corporate executive, except only for the brief digression on trade unions. But precisely the same argument applies to the newer phenomenon of calling upon stockholders to require corporations to exercise social responsibility (the recent G.M. crusade for example). In most of these cases, what is in effect involved is some stockholders trying to get other stockholders (or customers or employees) to contribute against their will to "social" causes favored by the activists. Insofar as they succeed, they are again imposing taxes and spending the proceeds.

The situation of the individual proprietor is somewhat different. If he acts to reduce the returns of his enterprise in order to exercise his "social responsibility," he is spending his own money, not someone else's. If he wishes to spend his money on such purposes, that is his right, and I cannot see that there is any objection to his doing so. In the process, he, too, may impose costs on employees and customers. However, because he is far less likely than a large corporation or union to have monopolistic power, any such side effects will tend to be minor.

Of course, in practice the doctrine of social responsibility is frequently a cloak for actions that are justified on other grounds rather than a reason for those actions.

To illustrate, it may well be in the long-run interest of a corporation that is a major employer in a small community to devote resources to providing amenities to that community or to improving its government. That may make it easier to attract desirable employees, it may reduce the wage bill or lessen losses from pilferage and sabotage or have other worthwhile effects. Or it may be that, given the laws about the deductibility of corporate charitable contributions, the stockholders can contribute more to charities they favor by having the corporation make the gift than by doing it themselves, since they can in that way contribute an amount that would otherwise have been paid as corporate taxes.

In each of these—and many similar—cases, there is a strong temptation to rationalize these actions as an exercise of "social responsibility." In the present climate of opinion, with its widespread aversion to "capitalism," "profits," the "soulless corporation" and so on, this is one way for a corporation to generate goodwill as a by-product of expenditures that are entirely justified in its own self-interest.

It would be inconsistent of me to call on corporate executives to refrain from this hypocritical window-dressing because it harms the foundations of a free society. That would be to call on them to exercise a "social responsibility"! If our institutions, and the attitudes of the public make it in their self-interest to cloak their actions in this way, I cannot summon much indignation to denounce them. At the same time, I can express admiration for those individual proprietors or owners of closely held corporations or stockholders of more broadly held corporations who disdain such tactics as approaching fraud.

Whether blameworthy or not, the use of the cloak of social responsibility, and the nonsense spoken in its name by influential and prestigious businessmen, does clearly harm the foundations of a free society. I have been impressed time and again by the schizophrenic character of many businessmen. They are capable of being extremely far-sighted and clear-headed in matters that are internal to their businesses. They are incredibly short-sighted and muddle-headed in matters that are outside their businesses but affect the possible survival of business in general. This short-sightedness is strikingly exemplified in the calls from many businessmen for wage and price guidelines or controls or income policies. There is nothing that could do more in a brief period to destroy a market system and replace it by a centrally controlled system than effective governmental control of prices and wages.

The short-sightedness is also exemplified in speeches by businessmen on social responsibility. This may gain them kudos in the short run. But it helps to strengthen the already too prevalent view that the pursuit of profits is wicked and immoral and must be curbed and controlled by external forces. Once this view is adopted, the external forces that curb the market will not be the social consciences, however highly developed, of the pontificating executives; it will be the iron fist of Government bureaucrats. Here, as with price and wage controls, businessmen seem to me to reveal a suicidal impulse.

The political principle that underlies the market mechanism is unanimity. In an ideal free market resting on private property, no individual can coerce any other, all cooperation is voluntary, all parties to such cooperation benefit or they need not participate. There are no values, no "social" responsibilities in any sense other than the shared values and responsibilities of individuals. Society is a collection of individuals and of the various groups they voluntarily form.

The political principle that underlies the political mechanism is conformity. The individual must serve a more general social interest—whether that be determined by a church or a dictator or a majority. The individual may have a vote and say in what is to be done, but if he is overruled, he must conform. It is appropriate for some to require others to contribute to a general social purpose whether they wish to or not.

Unfortunately, unanimity is not always feasible. There are some respects in which conformity appears unavoidable, so I do not see how one can avoid the use of the political mechanism altogether.

But the doctrine of "social responsibility" taken seriously would extend the scope of the political mechanism to every human activity. It does not differ in philosophy from the most explicitly collectivist doctrine. It differs only by professing to believe that collectivist ends can be attained without collectivist means. That is why, in my book "Capitalism and Freedom," I have called it a "fundamentally subversive doctrine" in a free society, and have said that in such a society, "there is one and only one social responsibility of business—to use its resources and engage in activities designed to increase its profits so long as it stays within the rules of the game, which is to say, engages in open and free competition without deception or fraud."

Christopher D. Stone

Why Shouldn't Corporations Be Socially Responsible?

Christopher D. Stone is a professor of law at the University of Southern California. The following is taken from his book, Where the Law Ends.

The opposition to corporate social responsibility comprises at least four related though separable positions. I would like to challenge the fundamental assumption that underlies all four of them. Each assumes in its own degree that the managers of the corporation are to be steered almost wholly by profit, rather than by what they think proper for society on the whole. Why should this be so? So far as ordinary morals are concerned, we often expect human beings to act in a fashion that is calculated to benefit others, rather than themselves, and commend them for it. Why should the matter be different with corporations?

THE PROMISSORY ARGUMENT

The most widespread but least persuasive arguments advanced by the "antiresponsibility" forces take the form of a moral claim based upon the corporation's supposed obligations to its shareholders. In its baldest and least tenable form, it is presented as though management's obligation rested upon the keeping of a promise—that the management of the corporation "promised" the shareholders that it would maximize the shareholders' profits. But this simply isn't so.

Consider for contrast the case where a widow left a large fortune goes to a broker, asking him to invest and manage her money so as to maximize her return. The broker, let us suppose, accepts the money and the conditions. In such a case, there would be no disagreement that the broker had made a promise to the widow, and if he invested her money in some venture that struck his fancy for any reason other than that it would increase her fortune, we would be inclined to advance a moral (as well, perhaps, as a legal) claim against him.

Generally, at least, we believe in the keeping of promises; the broker, we should say, had violated a promissory obligation to the widow.

But that simple model is hardly the one that obtains between the management of major corporations and their shareholders. Few if any American shareholders ever put their money into a corporation upon the express promise of management that the company would be operated so as to maximize their returns. Indeed, few American shareholders ever put their money directly *into* a corporation at all. Most of the shares outstanding today were issued years ago and found their way to their current shareholders only circuitously. In almost all cases, the current shareholder gave his money to some prior shareholder, who, in turn, had gotten it from B, who, in turn, had gotten it from A, and so on back to the purchaser of the original issue, who, many years before, had bought the shares through an underwriting syndicate. In the course of these transactions, one of the basic elements that exists in the broker case is missing. The manager of the corporation, unlike the broker, was never even offered a chance to refuse the shareholder's "terms" (if they were that) to maximize the shareholder's profits.

There are two other observations to be made about the moral argument based on a supposed promise running from the management to the shareholders. First, even if we do infer from all the circumstances a "promise" running from the management to the shareholders, but not one, or not one of comparable weight running elsewhere (to the company's employees, customers, neighbors, etc.), we ought to keep in mind that as a moral matter (which is what we are discussing here) sometimes it is deemed morally justified to break promises (even to break the law) in the furtherance of other social interests of higher concern. Promises can advance moral arguments, by way of creating presumptions, but few of us believe that promises, per se, can end them. My promise to appear in class on time would not ordinarily justify me from refusing to give aid to a drowning man. In other words, even if management *had* made an express promise to its shareholders to "maximize your profits," (a) I am not persuaded that the ordinary person would interpret it to mean "maximize *in every way you can possibly get away with,* even if that means polluting the environment, ignoring or breaking the law"; and (b) I am not persuaded that, even if it were interpreted as so blanket a promise, most people would not suppose it ought—morally—to be broken in some cases.

Finally, even if, in the face of all these considerations, one still believes that there is an overriding, unbreakable, promise of some sort running from management to the shareholders, I do not think that it can be construed to be any stronger than one running to *existent* shareholders, arising from *their* expectations as measured by the price *they* paid. That is to say, there is nothing in the argument from promises that would wed us to a regime in which management was bound to maximize the income of shareholders. The argument might go so far as to support compensation for existent shareholders if the society chose to announce that henceforth management would have other specified obligations, thereby driving the price of shares to a lower adjustment level. All future shareholders would take with "warning" of, and a price that discounted for, the new "risks" of shareholding (i.e., the "risks" that management might put corporate resources to *pro bonum* ends).

THE AGENCY ARGUMENT

Related to the promissory argument but requiring less stretching of the facts is an argument from agency principles. Rather than trying to infer a promise by management to the shareholders, this argument is based on the idea that the shareholders designated the management their agents. This is the position advanced by Milton Friedman in his *New York Times* article.

"The key point," he says, "is that . . . the manager is the agent of the individuals who own the corporation. . . ."

Friedman, unfortunately, is wrong both as to the state of the law (the directors are *not* mere agents of the shareholders) and on his assumption as to the facts of corporate life (surely it is closer to the truth that in major corporations the shareholders are *not*, in any meaningful sense, selecting the directors; management is more often using its control over the proxy machinery to designate who the directors shall be, rather than the other way around).

What Friedman's argument comes down to is that for some reason the directors ought morally to consider themselves more the agents for the shareholders than for the customers, creditors, the state, or the corporation's immediate neighbors. But why? And to what extent? Throwing in terms like "principal" and "agent" begs the fundamental questions.

What is more, the "agency" argument is not only morally inconclusive, it is embarrassingly at odds with the way in which supposed "agents" actually behave. If the managers truly considered themselves the agents of the shareholders, as agents they would be expected to show an interest in determining how their principals wanted them to act—and to act accordingly. In the controversy over Dow's production of napalm, for example, one would expect, on this model, that Dow's management would have been glad to have the napalm question put to the shareholders at a shareholders' meeting. In fact, like most major companies faced with shareholder requests to include "social action" measures on proxy statements, it fought the proposal tooth and claw. It is a peculiar agency where the "agents" will go to such lengths (even spending tens of thousands of dollars of their "principals'" money in legal fees) to resist the determination of what their "principals" want.

THE ROLE ARGUMENT

An argument so closely related to the argument from promises and agency that it does not demand extensive additional remarks is a contention based upon supposed considerations of *role*. Sometimes in moral discourse, as well as in law, we assign obligations to people on the basis of their having assumed some role or status, independent of any specific verbal promise they made. Such obligations are assumed to run from a captain to a seaman (and vice versa), from a doctor to a patient, or from a parent to a child. The antiresponsibility forces are on somewhat stronger grounds resting their position on this basis, because the model more nearly accords with the facts—that is, management never actually promised the shareholders that they would maximize the shareholders' investment, nor did the shareholders designate the directors their agents for this express purpose. The directors and top management are, as lawyers would say, fiduciaries. But what does this leave us? So far as the directors are fiduciaries of the shareholders in a legal sense, of course they are subject to the legal limits on fiduciaries— that is to say, they cannot engage in self-dealing, "waste" of corporate assets, and the like. But I do not understand any proresponsibility advocate to be demanding such corporate largess as would expose the officers to legal liability; what we are talking about are expenditures on, for example, pollution control, above the amount the company is required to pay by law, but less than an amount so extravagant as to constitute a violation of these legal fiduciary duties. (Surely no court in America today would enjoin a corporation from spending more to reduce pollution than the law requires.) What is there about assuming the role of corporate officer that makes it immoral for a manager to involve a corporation in these expenditures? A father, one would think, would have stronger obligations to his children by virtue of his status than a corporate manager to the corporation's shareholders. Yet few would regard it as a compelling moral argument if a father were to distort facts about his child on a scholarship application form on the grounds that he had obligations to advance his child's career; nor would we consider it a strong moral argument if a father were to leave unsightly refuse piled on his lawn, spilling over into the street, on the plea that he had obligations to give every moment of his attention to his children, and was thus too busy to cart his refuse away.

Like the other supposed moral arguments, the one from role suffers from the problem that the strongest moral obligations one can discover have at most only prima facie force, and it is not apparent why those obligations should predominate over some contrary social obligations that could be advanced.

Then too, when one begins comparing and weighing the various moral obligations, those running back to the shareholder seem fairly weak by comparison to the claims of others. For one thing, there is the consideration of alternatives. If the shareholder is dissatisfied with the direction the corporation is taking, he can sell out, and if he does so quickly enough, his losses may be slight. On the other hand, as Ted Jacobs observes, "those most vitally affected by corporate decisions—people who work in the plants, buy the products, and consume the effluents—cannot remove themselves from the structure with a phone call."

THE "POLESTAR" ARGUMENT

It seems to me that the strongest moral argument corporate executives can advance for looking solely to profits is not one that is based on a supposed express, or even implied promise to the shareholder. Rather, it is one that says, if the managers act in such fashion as to maximize profits—if they act as *though* they had promised the shareholders they would do so—then it will be best for all of us. This argument might be called the polestar argument, for its appeal to the interests of the shareholders is not justified on supposed obligations to the shareholders per se, but as a means of charting a straight course toward what is best for the society as a whole.

Underlying the polestar argument are a number of assumptions—some express and some implied. There is, I suspect, an implicit positivism among its supporters—a feeling (whether its proponents own up to it or not) that moral judgments are peculiar, arbitrary, or vague—perhaps even "meaningless" in the philosophic sense of not being amenable to rational discussion. To those who take this position, profits (or sales, or price-earnings ratios) at least provide some solid, tangible standard by which participants in the organization can measure their successes and failures, with some efficiency, in the narrow sense, resulting for the entire group. Sometimes the polestar position is based upon a related view—not that the moral issues that underlie social choices are meaningless, but that resolving them calls for special expertise. "I don't know any investment adviser whom I would care to act in my behalf in any matter except turning a profit. . . . The value of these specialists . . . lies in their limitations; they ought not allow themselves to see so much of the world that they become distracted." A slightly modified point emphasizes not that the executives lack moral or social expertise per se, but that they lack the social authority to make policy choices. Thus, Friedman objects that if a corporate director took "social purposes" into account, he would become "in effect a public employee, a civil servant. . . . On grounds of political principle, it is intolerable that such civil servants . . . should be selected as they are now."

I do not want to get too deeply involved in each of these arguments. That the moral judgments underlying policy choices are vague, I do not doubt—although I am tempted to observe that when you get right down to it, a wide range of actions taken by businessmen every day, supposedly based on solid calculations of "profit," are probably as rooted in hunches and intuition as judgments of ethics. I do not disagree either that, ideally, we prefer those who have control over our lives to be politically accountable; although here, too, if we were to pursue the matter in detail we would want to inspect both the premise of this argument, that corporate managers are not *presently* custodians of discretionary power over us anyway, and also its logical implications: Friedman's point that "if they are to be civil servants, then they must be selected through a political process" is not, as Friedman regards it, a *reductio ad absurdum*—not, at any rate, to Ralph Nader and others who want publicly elected directors.

The reason for not pursuing these counterarguments at length is that, whatever reservations one might have, we can agree that there is a germ of validity to what the "antis" are saying. But their essential failure is in not pursuing the alternatives. Certainly, *to the extent* that the forces of the market and the law can keep the corporation within desirable bounds, it may be better to trust them than to have corporate managers implementing their own vague and various notions of what is best for the rest of us. But are the "antis" blind to the fact that there are circumstances in which the law—and the forces of the market—are simply not competent to keep the corporation under control? The shortcomings of these traditional restraints on corporate conduct are critical to understand, not merely for the defects they point up in the "antis' " position. More important, identifying where the traditional forces are inadequate is the first step in the design of new and alternative measures of corporate control.

Albert Z. Carr

Is Business Like Poker?

Albert Z. Carr *wrote this controversial article for* The Harvard Business Review *in 1977. It drew hundreds of letters of protest from well-known business executives around the country.*

A respected businessman with whom I discussed the theme of this article remarked with some heat, "You mean to say you're going to encourage men to bluff? Why, bluffing is nothing more than a form of lying! You're advising them to lie!"

I agreed that the basis of private morality is a respect for truth and that the closer a businessman comes to the truth, the more he deserves respect. At the same time, I suggested that most bluffing in business might be regarded simply as game strategy—much like bluffing in poker, which does not reflect on the morality of the bluffer.

I quoted Henry Taylor, the British statesman who pointed out that "falsehood ceases to be falsehood when it is understood on all sides that the truth is not expected to be spoken"—an exact description of bluffing in poker, diplomacy, and business. I cited the analogy of the criminal court, where the criminal is not expected to tell the truth when he pleads "not guilty." Everyone from the judge down takes it for granted that the job of the defendant's attorney is to get his client off, not to reveal the truth; and this is considered ethical practice. I mentioned Representative Omar Burleson, the Democrat from Texas, who was quoted as saying, in regard to the ethics of Congress, "Ethics is a barrel of worms"—a pungent summing up of the problem of deciding who is ethical in politics.

I reminded my friend that millions of businessmen feel constrained every day to say *yes* to their bosses when they secretly believe *no* and that this is generally accepted as permissible strategy when the alternative might be the loss of a job. The essential point, I said, is that the ethics of business are game ethics, different from the ethics of religion.

He remained unconvinced. Referring to the company of which he is president, he declared: "Maybe that's good enough for some businessmen, but I can tell you that we pride ourselves on our ethics. In 30 years not one customer has ever questioned my word or asked to check our figures. We're loyal to our customers and fair to our suppliers. I regard my handshake on a deal as a contract. I've never entered into price-fixing schemes with my competitors. I've never allowed my salesmen to spread injurious rumors about other companies. Our union contract is the best in our industry. And, if I do say so myself, our ethical standards are of the highest!"

He really was saying, without realizing it, that he was living up to the ethical standards of the business game—which are a far cry from those of private life. Like a gentlemanly poker player, he did not play in cahoots with others at the table, try to smear their reputations, or hold back chips he owed them.

But this same fine man, at that very time, was allowing one of his products to be advertised in a way that made it sound a great deal better than it actually was. Another item in his product line was notorious among dealers for its "built-in obsolescence." He was holding back from the market a much-improved product because he did not want it to interfere with sales of the inferior item it would have replaced. He had joined with certain of his competitors in hiring a lobbyist to push a state legislature, by methods that he preferred not to know too much about, into amending a bill then being enacted.

In his view these things had nothing to do with ethics; they were merely normal business practice. He himself undoubtedly avoided outright falsehoods—never lied in so many words. But the entire organization that he ruled was deeply involved in numerous strategies of deception.

PRESSURE TO DECEIVE

Most executives from time to time are almost compelled, in the interests of their companies or themselves, to practice some form of deception when negotiating with customers, dealers, labor unions, government officials, or even other departments of their companies. By conscious misstatements, concealment of pertinent facts, or exaggeration—in short, by bluffing—they seek to persuade others to agree with them. I think it is fair to say that if the individual executive refuses to bluff from time to time—if he feels obligated to tell the truth, the whole truth, and nothing but the truth—he is ignoring opportunities permitted under the rules and is at a heavy disadvantage in his business dealings.

But here and there a businessman is unable to reconcile himself to the bluff in which he plays a part. His conscience, perhaps spurred by religious idealism, troubles him. He feels guilty; he may develop an ulcer or a nervous tic. Before any executive can make profitable use of the strategy of the bluff, he needs to make sure that in bluffing he will not lose self-respect or become emotionally disturbed. If he is to reconcile personal integrity and high standards of honesty with the practical requirements of business, he must feel that his bluffs are ethically justified. The justification rests on the fact that business, as practiced by individuals as well as by corporations, has the impersonal character of a game—a game that demands both special strategy and an understanding of its special ethics.

The game is played at all levels of corporate life, from the highest to the lowest. At the very instant that a man decides to enter business, he may be forced into a game situation, as is shown by the recent experience of a Cornell honor graduate who applied for a job with a large company:

● This applicant was given a psychological test which included the statement, "Of the following magazines, check any that you have read either regularly or from time to time, and double-check those which interest you most. *Reader's Digest, Time, Fortune, Saturday Evening Post, The New Republic, Life, Look, Ramparts, Newsweek, Business Week, U.S. News & World Report, The Nation, Playboy, Esquire, Harper's, Sports Illustrated.*"

His tastes in reading were broad, and at one time or another he had read almost all of these magazines. He was a subscriber to *The New Republic,* an enthusiast for *Ramparts,* and an avid student of the pictures in *Playboy.* He was not sure whether his interest in *Playboy* would be held against him, but he had a shrewd suspicion that if he confessed to an interest in *Ramparts* and *The New Republic,* he would be thought a liberal, a radical, or at least an intellectual, and his chances of getting the job, which he needed, would greatly diminish. He therefore checked five of the more conservative magazines. Apparently it was a sound decision, for he got the job.

He had made a game player's decision, consistent with business ethics.

A similar case is that of a magazine space salesman who, owing to a merger, suddenly found himself out of a job:

● This man was 58, and, in spite of a good record, his chance of getting a job elsewhere in a business where youth is favored in hiring practice was not good. He was a vigorous, healthy man, and only a considerable amount of gray in his hair suggested his age. Before beginning his job search he touched up his hair to confine the gray to his temples. He knew that the truth about his age might well come out in time, but he calculated that he could deal with that situation when it arose. He and his wife decided that he could easily pass for 45, and he so stated his age on his résumé.

This was a lie; yet within the accepted rules of the business game, no moral culpability attaches to it.

THE POKER ANALOGY

We can learn a good deal about the nature of business by comparing it with poker. While both have a large element of chance, in the long run the winner is the man who plays with steady skill. In both games ultimate victory requires intimate knowledge of the rules, insight into the psychology of the other players, a bold front, a considerable amount of self-discipline, and the ability to respond swiftly and effectively to opportunities provided by chance.

No one expects poker to be played on the ethical principle preached in churches. In poker it is right and proper to bluff a friend out of the rewards of being dealt a good hand. A player feels no more than a slight twinge of sympathy, if that, when—with nothing better than a single ace in his hand—he strips a heavy loser, who holds a pair, of the rest of his chips. It was up to the other fellow to protect himself. In the words of an excellent poker player, former President Harry Truman, " If you can't stand the heat, stay out of the kitchen." If one shows mercy to a loser in poker, it is a personal gesture, divorced from the rules of the game.

Poker has its special ethics, and here I am not referring to rules against cheating. The man who keeps an ace up his sleeve or who marks the cards is more than unethical; he is a crook, and can be punished as such—kicked out of the game or, in the Old West, shot.

In contrast to the cheat, the unethical poker player is one who abiding by the letter of the rules, finds ways to put the other players at an unfair disadvantage. Perhaps he unnerves them with loud talk. Or he tries to get them drunk. Or he plays in cahoots with someone else at the table. Ethical poker players frown on such tactics.

Poker's own brand of ethics is different from the ethical ideals of civilized human relationships. The game calls for distrust of the other fellow. It ignores the claim of friendship. Cunning deception and concealment of one's strength and intentions, not kindness and openheartedness, are vital in poker. No one thinks any the worse of poker on that account. And no one should think any the worse of the game of business because its standards of right and wrong differ from the prevailing traditions of morality in our society. . . .

"WE DON'T MAKE THE LAWS"

Wherever we turn in business, we can perceive the sharp distinction between its ethical standards and those of the churches. Newspapers abound with sensational stories growing out of this distinction:

- We read one day that Senator Philip A. Hart of Michigan has attacked food processors for deceptive packaging of numerous products.
- The next day there is a Congressional to-do over Ralph Nader's book, *Unsafe At Any Speed,* which demonstrates that automobile companies for years have neglected the safety of car-owning families.
- Then another Senator, Lee Metcalf of Montana, and journalist Vic Reinemer show in their book, *Overcharge,* the methods by which utility companies elude regulating government bodies to extract unduly large payments from users of electricity.

These are merely dramatic instances of a prevailing condition; there is hardly a major industry at which a similar attack could not be aimed. Critics of business regard such behavior as unethical, but the companies concerned know that they are merely playing the business game.

Among the most respected of our business institutions are the insurance companies. A group of insurance executives meeting recently in New England was startled when their guest speaker, social critic Daniel Patrick Moynihan, roundly berated them for "unethical" practices. They had been guilty, Moynihan alleged, of using outdated actuarial tables to obtain unfairly high premiums. They habitually delayed the hearings of lawsuits against them in order to tire out the plaintiffs and win cheap settlements. In their employment policies they used ingenious devices to discriminate against certain minority groups.

It was difficult for the audience to deny the validity of these charges. But these men were business game players. Their reaction to Moynihan's attack was much the same as that of the automobile manufacturers to Nader, of the utilities to Senator Metcalf, and of the food processors to Senator Hart. If the laws governing their businesses change, or if public opinion becomes clamorous, they will make the necessary adjustments. But morally they have in their view done nothing wrong. As long as they comply with the letter of the law, they are within their rights to operate their businesses as they see fit.

The small business is in the same position as the great corporation in this respect. For example:

- In 1967 a key manufacturer was accused of providing master keys for automobiles to mail-order customers, although it was obvious that some of the purchasers might be automobile thieves. His defense was plain and straightforward. If there was nothing in the law to prevent him from selling his keys to anyone who ordered them, it was not up to him

innocent people hurt by unethical practices

to inquire as to his customers' motives. Why was it any worse, he insisted, for him to sell car keys by mail, than for mail-order houses to sell guns that might be used for murder? Until the law was changed, the key manufacturer could regard himself as being just as ethical as any other businessman by the rules of the business game.

Violations of the ethical ideals of society are common in business, but they are not necessarily violations of business principles. Each year the Federal Trade Commission orders hundreds of companies, many of them of the first magnitude, to "cease and desist" from practices which, judged by ordinary standards, are of questionable morality but which are stoutly defended by the companies concerned.

In one case, a firm manufacturing a well-known mouthwash was accused of using a cheap form of alcohol possibly deleterious to health. The company's chief executive, after testifying in Washington, made this comment privately:

"We broke no law. We're in a highly competitive industry. If we're going to stay in business, we have to look for profit wherever the law permits. We don't make the laws. We obey them. Then why do we have to put up with this 'holier than thou' talk about ethics? It's sheer hypocrisy. We're not in business to promote ethics. Look at the cigarette companies, for God's sake! If the ethics aren't embodied in the laws by the men who made them, you can't expect businessmen to fill the lack. Why, a sudden submission to Christian ethics by businessmen would bring about the greatest economic upheaval in history!"

It may be noted that the government failed to prove its case against him.

CAST ILLUSIONS ASIDE

Talk about ethics by businessmen is often a thin decorative coating over the hard realities of the game:

■ Once I listened to a speech by a young executive who pointed to a new industry code as proof that his company and its competitors were deeply aware of their responsibilities to society. It was a code of ethics, he said. The industry was going to police itself, to dissuade constituent companies from wrongdoing. His eyes shone with conviction and enthusiasm.

The same day there was a meeting in a hotel room where the industry's top executives met with the "czar" who was to administer the new code, a man of high repute. No one who was present could doubt their common attitude. In their eyes the code was designed primarily to forestall a move by the federal government to impose stern restrictions on the industry. They felt that the code would hamper them a good deal less than new federal laws would. It was, in other words, conceived as a protection for the industry, not for the public.

The young executive accepted the surface explanation of the code; these leaders, all experienced game players, did not deceive themselves for a moment about its purpose.

The illusion that business can afford to be guided by ethics as conceived in private life is often fostered by speeches and articles containing such phrases as, "It pays to be ethical," or "Sound ethics is good business." Actually this is not an ethical position at all; it is a self-serving calculation in disguise. The speaker is really saying that in the long run a company can make more money if it does not antagonize competitors, suppliers, employees, and customers by squeezing them too hard. He is saying that oversharp policies reduce ultimate gains. That is true, but it has nothing to do with ethics. The underlying attitude is much like that in the familiar story of the shopkeeper who finds an extra $20 bill in the cash register, debates with himself the ethical problem—should he tell his partner—and finally decides to share the money because the gesture will give him an edge over the s.o.b. the next time they quarrel.

I think it is fair to sum up the prevailing attitude of businessmen on ethics as follows:

We live in what is probably the most competitive of the world's civilized societies. Our customs encourage a high degree of aggression in the individual's striving for success. Business is our main area of competition, and it has been ritualized into a game of strategy. The basic rules of the game have been set by the government, which attempts to detect and punish business frauds. But as long as a company does not transgress the rules of the game set by law, it has the legal right to shape its strategy without reference to anything but its profits. If it takes a long-term view of its profits, it will preserve amicable relations, so far as possible, with those with whom it deals. A wise businessman will not seek advantage to the point where he generates dangerous hostility among employees, competitors, customers, government, or the public at large. But decisions in this area are, in the final test, decisions of strategy, not of ethics.

. . . If a man plans to make a seat in the business game, he owes it to himself to master the principles by which the game is played, including its special ethical outlook. He can then hardly fail to recognize that an occasional bluff may well be justified in terms of the game's ethics and warranted in terms of economic necessity. Once he clears his mind on this point, he is in a good position to match his strategy against that of the other players. He can then determine objectively whether a bluff in a given situation has a good chance of succeeding and can decide when and how to bluff, without a feeling of ethical transgression.

To be a winner, a man must play to win. This does not mean that he must be ruthless, cruel, harsh, or treacherous. On the contrary, the better his reputation for integrity, honesty, and decency, the better his chances of victory will be in the long run. But from time to time every businessman, like every poker player, is offered a choice between certain loss or bluffing within the legal rules of the game. If he is not resigned to losing, if he wants to rise in his company and industry, then in such a crisis he will bluff—and bluff hard.

Every now and then one meets a successful businessman who has conveniently forgotten the small or large deceptions that he practiced on his way to fortune. "God gave me my money," old John D. Rockefeller once piously told a Sunday school class. It would be a rare tycoon in our time who would risk the horse laugh with which such a remark would be greeted.

In the last third of the twentieth century even children are aware that if a man has become prosperous in business, he has sometimes departed from the strict truth in order to overcome obstacles or has practiced the more subtle deceptions of the half-truth or the misleading omission. Whatever the form of the bluff, it is an integral part of the game, and the executive who does not master its techniques is not likely to accumulate much money or power.

W. Michael Hoffman
The Ford Pinto

W. Michael Hoffman *is director of the Center for Business Ethics at Bentley College in Massachusetts and the author and editor of many works on business ethics.*

On August 10, 1978, a tragic automobile accident occurred on U.S. Highway 33 near Goshen, Indiana. Sisters Judy and Lynn Ulrich (ages 18 and 16, respectively) and their cousin Donna

Ulrich (age 18) were struck from the rear in their 1973 Ford Pinto by a van. The gas tank of the Pinto ruptured, the car burst into flames, and the three teenagers were burnt to death.

Subsequently an Elkhart County grand jury returned a criminal homicide charge against Ford, the first ever against an American corporation. During the following twenty-week trial, Judge Harold R. Staffeldt advised the jury that Ford should be convicted of reckless homicide if it were shown that the company had engaged in "plain, conscious and unjustifiable disregard of harm that might result (from its actions) and the disregard involves a substantial deviation from acceptable standards of conduct."

The key phrase around which the trial hinged, of course, is "acceptable standards." Did Ford knowingly and recklessly choose profit over safety in the design and placement of the Pinto's gas tank? Elkhart County prosecutor Michael A. Cosentino and chief Ford attorney James F. Neal battled dramatically over this issue in a rural Indiana courthouse. Meanwhile, American business anxiously awaited the verdict which could send warning ripples through boardrooms across the nation concerning corporate responsibility and product liability.

As a background to this trial some discussion of the Pinto controversy is necessary. In 1977 the magazine *Mother Jones* broke a story by Mark Dowie, general manager of *Mother Jones* business operations, accusing Ford of knowingly putting on the road an unsafe car—the Pinto—in which hundreds of people have needlessly suffered burn deaths and even more have been scarred and disfigured from burns. In his article "Pinto Madness" Dowie charges that:

- Fighting strong competition from Volkswagen for the lucrative small-car market, the Ford Motor Company rushed the Pinto into production in much less than the usual time.
- Ford engineers discovered in preproduction crash tests that rear-end collisions would rupture the Pinto's fuel system extremely easily.
- Because assembly-line machinery was already tooled when engineers found this defect, top Ford officials decided to manufacture the car anyway—exploding gas tank and all—even though Ford owned the patent on a much safer gas tank.
- For more than eight years afterward, Ford successfully lobbied, with extraordinary vigor and some blatant lies, against a key government safety standard that would have forced the company to change the Pinto's fire-prone gas tank.

By conservative estimates Pinto crashes have caused 500 burn deaths to people who would not have been seriously injured if the car had not burst into flames. The figure could be as high as 900. Burning Pintos have become such an embarrassment to Ford that its advertising agency, J. Walter Thompson, dropped a line from the ending of a radio spot that read "Pinto leaves you with that warm feeling."

Ford knows that the Pinto is a firetrap, yet it has paid out millions to settle damage suits out of court, and it is prepared to spend millions more lobbying against safety standards. With a half million cars rolling off the assembly lines each year, Pinto is the biggest-selling subcompact in America, and the company's operating profit on the car is fantastic. Finally, in 1977, new Pinto models have incorporated a few minor alterations necessary to meet that federal standard Ford managed to hold off for eight years. Why did the company delay so long in making these minimal, inexpensive improvements?

- Ford waited eight years because its internal "cost-benefit analysis," which places a dollar value on human life, said it wasn't profitable to make the changes sooner.

Several weeks after Dowie's press conference on the article, which had the support of Ralph Nader and auto safety expert Byron Bloch, Ford issued a news release attributed to Herbert T. Misch, vice president of Environmental and Safety Engineering, countering points made in the *Mother Jones* article. Their statistical studies conflict significantly with each other. For example, Dowie states that more than 3,000 people were burning to death yearly in auto fires; he claims that, according to a National Highway Traffic Safety Administration (NHTSA) consultant, although Ford makes 24 percent of the cars on American roads, these cars account for 42 percent of the collision-ruptured fuel tanks. Ford, on the other hand, uses statistics from the Fatality Analysis Reporting System (FARS) maintained by the government's NHTSA to defend itself, claiming that in 1975 there were 848 deaths related to fire-associated passenger-car accidents and only 13 of these involved Pintos; in 1976, Pintos accounted for only 22 out of 943. These statistics imply that Pintos were involved in only 1.9 percent of such accidents, and Pintos constitute about 1.9 percent of the total registered passenger cars. Furthermore, fewer than half of those Pintos cited in the FARS study were struck in the rear. Ford concludes from this and other studies that the Pinto was never an unsafe car and has not been involved in some 70 burn deaths annually, as *Mother Jones* claims.

Ford admits that early-model Pintos did not meet rear-impact tests at 20 mph but denies that this implies that they were unsafe compared with other cars of that type and era. In fact, according to Ford, some of its tests were conducted with experimental rubber "bladders" to protect the gas tank, in order to determine how best to have its future cars meet a 20-mph rear-collision standard which Ford itself set as an internal performance goal. The government at that time had no such standard. Ford also points out that in every model year the Pinto met or surpassed the government's own standards, and

> it simply is unreasonable and unfair to contend that a car is somehow unsafe if it does not meet standards proposed for future years or embody the technological improvements that are introduced in later model years.

Mother Jones, on the other hand, presents a different view of the situation. If Ford was so concerned about rear-impact safety, why did it delay the federal government's attempts to impose standards? Dowie gives the following answer:

> The particular regulation involved here was Federal Motor Vehicle Safety Standard 301. Ford picked portions of Standard 301 for strong opposition way back in 1968 when the Pinto was still in the blueprint stage. The intent of 301, and the 300 series that followed it, was to protect drivers and passengers after a crash occurs. Without question the worst post-crash hazard is fire. So Standard 301 originally proposed that all cars should be able to withstand a fixed barrier impact of 20 mph (that is, running into a wall at that speed) without losing fuel.
>
> When the standard was proposed, Ford engineers pulled their crash-test results out of their files. The front ends of most cars were no problem—with minor alterations they could stand the impact without losing fuel. "We were already working on the front end," Ford engineer Dick Kimble admitted. "We knew we could meet the test on the front end." But with the Pinto particularly, a 20 mph rear-end standard meant redesigning the entire rear end of the car. With the Pinto scheduled for production in August of 1970, and with $200 million worth of tools in place, adoption of this standard would have created a minor financial disaster. So Standard 301 was targeted for delay, and with some assistance from its industry associates, Ford succeeded beyond its wildest expectations: the standard was not adopted until the 1977 model year.

Ford's tactics were successful, according to Dowie, not only due to their extremely clever lobbying, which became the envy of lobbyists all over Washington, but also because of the pro-industry stance of the NHTSA itself.

Furthermore, it is not at all clear that the Pinto was as safe as comparable cars with regard to the positioning of the gas tank. Unlike the gas tank in the Capri, which rode over the rear axle, a "saddle-type" fuel tank on which Ford owned the patent, the Pinto tank was placed just behind the rear bumper. According to Dowie,

> Dr. Leslie Ball, the retired safety chief for the NASA manned space program and a founder of the International Society of Reliability Engineers, recently made a careful study of the Pinto. "The release to production of the Pinto was the most reprehensible decision in the history of American engineering," he said. Ball can name more than 40 European and Japanese models in the Pinto price and weight range with safer gas-tank positioning.
>
> Los Angeles auto safety expert Byron Bloch has made an in-depth study of the Pinto fuel system. "It's a catastrophic blunder," he says. "Ford made an extremely irresponsible decision when they placed such a weak tank in such a ridiculous location in such a soft rear end. It's almost designed to blow up—premeditated."

Although other points could be brought out in the debate between *Mother Jones* and Ford, perhaps the most intriguing and controversial is the cost-benefit analysis study that Ford did entitled "Fatalities Associated with Crash-Induced Fuel Leakage and Fires" released by J.C. Echold, director of automotive safety for Ford. This study apparently convinced Ford and was intended to convince the federal government that a technological improvement costing $11 per car which would have prevented gas tanks from rupturing so easily was not cost effective for society. The costs and benefits are broken down in the following way:

Benefits

Savings:	180 burn deaths, 180 serious burn injuries, 2,100 burned vehicles
Unit Cost:	$200,000 per death, $67,000 per injury, $700 per vehicle
Total Benefit:	$180 \times (200,000) + 180 \times (\$67,000) + 2,100 \times (\$700)$ $= \$49.5 \text{ million}$

Costs

Sales:	11 million cars, 1.5 million light trucks
Unit Cost:	$11 per car, $11 per truck
Total Cost:	$11,000,000 \times (\$11) + 1,500,000 \times (\$11) = \$137 \text{ million}$

And where did Ford come up with the $200,000 figure as the cost per death? This came from a NHTSA study which broke down the estimated social costs of a death as follows:

Component	1971 Costs
Future Productivity Losses	
Direct	$132,000
Indirect	41,300
Medical Costs	
Hospital	700
Other	425
Property Damage	1,500
Insurance Administration	4,700
Legal and Court	3,000

Employer Losses	1,000
Victim's Pain and Suffering	10,000
Funeral	900
Assets (Lost Consumption)	5,000
Miscellaneous	200
Total per fatality	$200,725

(Although this analysis was on all Ford vehicles, a breakout of just the Pinto could be done.) *Mother Jones* reports it could not find anybody who could explain how the $10,000 figure for "pain and suffering" had been arrived at.

Although Ford does not mention this point in its news release defense, on might have replied that it was the federal government, not Ford, that set the figure for a burn death. Ford simply carried out a cost-benefit analysis based on that figure. *Mother Jones*, however, in addition to insinuating that there was industry-agency (NHTSA) collusion, argues that the $200,000 figure was arrived at under intense pressure from the auto industry to use cost-benefit analysis in determining regulations. *Mother Jones* also questions Ford's estimate of burn injuries: "All independent experts estimate that for each person who dies by an auto fire, many more are left with charred hands, faces and limbs." Referring to the Northern California Burn Center, which estimates the ratio of burn injuries to deaths at ten to one instead of one to one, Dowie states that "the true ratio obviously throws the company's calculations way off." Finally, *Mother Jones* claims to have obtained "confidential" Ford documents which Ford did not send to Washington, showing that crash fires could largely be prevented by installing a rubber bladder inside the gas tank for only $5.08 per car, considerably less than the $11 per car Ford originally claimed was required to improve crashworthiness.

Instead of making the $11 improvement, installing the $5.08 bladder, or even giving the consumer the right to choose the additional cost for added safety, Ford continued, according to *Mother Jones,* to delay the federal government for eight years in establishing mandatory rear-impact standards. In the meantime, Dowie argues, thousands of people were burning to death and tens of thousands more were being badly burned and disfigured for life, while many of these tragedies could have been prevented for only a slight cost per vehicle. Furthermore, the delay also meant that millions of new unsafe vehicles went on the road, "vehicles that will be crashing, leaking fuel and incinerating people well into the 1980s."

In concluding his article Dowie broadens his attack beyond just Ford and the Pinto.

Unfortunately, the Pinto is not an isolated case of corporate malpractice in the auto industry. Neither is Ford a lone sinner. There probably isn't a car on the road without a safety hazard known to its manufacturer. . . .

Furthermore, cost-valuing human life is not used by Ford alone. Ford was just the only company careless enough to let such an embarrassing calculation slip into public records. The process of willfully trading lives for profits is built into corporate capitalism. Commodore Vanderbilt publicly scorned George Westinghouse and his "foolish" air brakes while people died by the hundreds in accidents on Vanderbilt's railroads.

Ford has paid millions of dollars in Pinto jury trials and out-of-court settlements, especially the latter. *Mother Jones* quotes Al Slechter in Ford's Washington office as saying: "We'll never go to a jury again. Not in a fire case. Juries are just too sentimental. They see those charred remains and forget the evidence. No sir, we'll settle." But apparently Ford thought such settlements would be less costly than the safety improvements. Dowie wonders if Ford would continue to make the same decisions "were Henry Ford II and Lee Iacocca serving twenty-year terms in Leavenworth for consumer homicide."

On March 13, 1980, the Elkhart County jury found Ford not guilty of criminal homicide in the Ulrich case. Ford attorney Neal summarized several points in his closing argument before the jury. Ford could have stayed out of the small-car market, which would have been the "easiest way," since Ford would have made more profit by sticking to bigger cars. Instead, Ford built the Pinto "to take on the imports, to save jobs for Americans and to make a profit for its stockholders." The Pinto met every fuel-system standard of any federal, state, or local government, and was comparable to other 1973 subcompacts. The engineers who designed the car thought it was a good, safe car and bought it for themselves and their families. Ford did everything possible to recall the Pinto quickly after NHTSA ordered it to do so. Finally, and more specifically to the case at hand, Highway 33 was a badly designed highway, and the girls were fully stopped when a 4,000-pound van rammed into the rear of their Pinto at at least 50 miles an hour. Given the same circumstances, Neal stated, any car would have suffered the same consequences as the Ulrich's Pinto. As reported in the *New York Times* and *Time,* the verdict brought a "loud cheer" from Ford's board of directors and undoubtedly at least a sigh of relief from other corporations around the nation.

Many thought this case was that of a David against Goliath because of the small amount of money and volunteer legal help Prosecutor Cosentino had in contrast to the huge resources Ford poured into the trial. In addition, it should be pointed out that Cosentino's case suffered from a ruling by Judge Staffeldt that Ford's own test results on pre-1973 Pintos were inadmissible. These documents confirmed that Ford knew as early as 1971 that the gas tank of the Pinto ruptured at impacts of 20 mph and that the company was aware, because of tests with the Capri, that the over-the-axle position of the gas tank was much safer than mounting it behind the axle. Ford decided to mount it behind the axle in the Pinto to provide more trunk space and to save money. The restrictions of Cosentino's evidence to testimony relating specifically to the 1973 Pinto severely undercut the strength of the prosecutor's case.

Whether this evidence would have changed the minds of the jury will never be known. Some, however, such as business ethicist Richard De George, feel that this evidence shows grounds for charges of recklessness against Ford. Although it is true that there were no federal safety standards in 1973 to which Ford legally had to conform and although Neal seems to have proved that all subcompacts were unsafe when hit at 50 mph by a 4,000-pound van, the fact that the NHTSA ordered a recall of the Pinto and not other subcompacts is, according to De George, "*prima facie* evidence that Ford's Pinto gas tank mounting was substandard." De George argues that these grounds for recklessness are made even stronger by the fact that Ford did not give the consumer a choice to make the Pinto gas tank safer by installing a rubber bladder for a rather modest fee. Giving the consumer such a choice, of course, would have made the gas tank problem known and therefore probably would have been bad for sales.

Richard A. Epstein, professor of law at the University of Chicago Law School, questions whether Ford should have been brought up on criminal charges of reckless homicide at all. He also points out an interesting historical fact. Before 1966 an injured party in Indiana could not even bring civil charges against an automobile manufacturer solely because of the alleged "uncrashworthiness" of a car; one would have to seek legal relief from the other party involved in the accident, not from the manufacturer. But after *Larson v. General Motors Corp.* in 1968, a new era of crashworthiness suits against automobile manufacturers began. "Reasonable" precautions must now be taken by manufacturers to minimize personal harm in crashes. How to apply criteria of reasonableness in such cases marks the whole nebulous ethical and legal arena of product liability.

If such a civil suit had been brought against Ford, Epstein believes, the corporation might have argued, as it did to a large extent in the criminal suit, that the Pinto conformed to all current applicable safety standards and with common industry practice. (Epstein cites that well over 90 percent of United States standard production cars had their gas tanks in the same position as the Pinto.) But in a civil trial the adequacy of industry standards are ultimately up to the jury, and had civil charges been brought against Ford in this case the plaintiffs might have had a better chance of winning. Epstein feels that a criminal suit, on the other hand, had no chance from the very outset, because the prosecutor would have to establish criminal intent on the part of Ford. To use an analogy, if a hunter shoots at a deer and wounds an unseen person, he may be held civilly responsible but not criminally responsible because he did not intend to harm. And even though it may be more difficult to determine the mental state of a corporation (or its principal agents), it seems clear to Epstein that the facts of this case do not prove any such criminal intent even though Ford might have known that some burn deaths and injuries could have been avoided by a different placement of its Pinto gas tank and that Ford consciously decided not to spend more money to save lives. Everyone recognizes that there are trade-offs between safety and costs. Ford could have built a "tank" instead of a Pinto, thereby considerably reducing risks, but it would have been relatively unaffordable for most and probably unattractive to all potential consumers.

To have established Ford's reckless homicide it would have been necessary to establish the same of Ford's agents, since a corporation can only act through its agents. Undoubtedly, continues Epstein, the reason why the prosecutor did not try to subject Ford's officers and engineers to fines and imprisonment for their design choices is "the good faith character of their judgment, which was necessarily decisive in Ford's behalf as well." For example, Harold C. MacDonald, Ford's chief engineer on the Pinto, testified that he felt it was important to keep the gas tank as far from the passenger compartment as possible, as it was in the Pinto. And other Ford engineers testified that they used the car for their own families. This is relevant information in a criminal case which must be concerned about the intent of the agents.

Furthermore, even if civil charges had been made in this case, it seems unfair and irrelevant to Epstein to accuse Ford of trading cost for safety. Ford's use of cost-benefit formulas, which must assign monetary values to human life and suffering, is precisely what the law demands in assessing civil liability suits. The court may disagree with the decision, but to blame industry for using such a method would violate the very rules of civil liability. Federal automobile officials (NHTSA) had to make the same calculations in order to discharge their statutory duties. In allowing the Pinto design, are not they too (and in turn their employer, the United States) just as guilty as Ford's agents?

The case of the Ford Pinto raises many questions of ethical importance. Some people conclude that Ford was definitely wrong in designing and marketing the Pinto. The specific accident involving the Ulrich girls, because of the circumstances, was simply not the right one to have attacked Ford on. Other people believe that Ford was neither criminally nor civilly guilty of anything and acted completely responsibly in producing the Pinto. Many others, I suspect, find the case morally perplexing, too complex to make sweeping claims of guilt or innocence.

Was Ford irresponsible in rushing the production of the Pinto? Even though Ford violated no federal safety standards or laws, should it have made the Pinto safer in terms of rear-end collisions, especially regarding the placement of the gas tank? Should Ford have used cost-benefit analysis to make decisions relating to safety, specifically placing dollar values on human life and suffering? Knowing that the Pinto's gas tank could have been made safer by installing a protective bladder for a relatively small cost per consumer, perhaps Ford should have made that option available to the public. If Ford did use heavy lobbying efforts to delay and/or influence federal safety standards, was this ethically proper for a corporation to do? One might ask, if Ford was guilty, whether the engineers, the managers, or both are to blame. If Ford had been found guilty of criminal homicide, was the proposed penalty stiff enough ($10,000 maximum fine for each of the three counts equals $30,000 maximum), or should agents of the corporation such as MacDonald, Iacocca, and Henry Ford II be fined and possibly jailed?

A number of questions concerning safety standards are also relevant to the ethical issues at stake in the Ford trial. Is it just to blame a corporation for not abiding by "acceptable standards" when such standards are not yet determined by society? Should corporations like Ford play a role in setting such standards? Should individual juries be determining such standards state by state, incident by incident? If Ford should be setting safety standards, how does it decide how safe to make its product and still make it affordable and desirable to the public without using cost-benefit analysis? For that matter, how does anyone decide? Perhaps it is putting Ford, or any corporation, in a catch-22 position to ask it both to set safety standards and to make a competitive profit for its stockholders.

Regardless of how we answer these and other questions it is clear that the Pinto case raises fundamental issues concerning the responsibilities of corporations, how corporations should structure themselves in order to make ethical decisions, and how industry, government, and society in general ought to interrelate to form a framework within which such decisions can properly be made in the future.

William Safire

Corporate Crime: Is Anyone Responsible Here?

William Safire is a columnist for The New York Times and a former speech-writer for President Richard M. Nixon.

When G-men nabbed "Willie the Actor" Sutton after he had stolen some $2 million in bank deposits during his lifetime, the disguise artist wound up spending 33 of his last 43 years in prison.

Recently, the Reagan Justice Department—made up of stern-faced law 'n' order types, who sneer at the coddlers of criminals—rounded up a gang at E.F. Hutton & Co. that had systematically bilked tens of millions of dollars out of 400 banks through a sophisticated swindle that made new breakthroughs in the state of the art of check kiting.

The perpetrators of the crime admitted their guilt in over 2,000 instances of mail and wire fraud. "The object of the defendants' scheme and artifice to defraud was to obtain interest-free funds by means of intentional overdrafting," said Justice prosecutors triumphantly, demonstrating how the illegal "drawing against uncollected funds totaled more than $1 billion, with daily overdrafts sometimes exceeding $250 million."

That certainly makes the depredations of "Slick Willie" look like small change. Imagine: For more than two years, a ring of at least a dozen and perhaps 50 stockbrokers, following a scheme concocted by a few modern criminal masterminds, regularly shuffled rubber checks in and out of banks, bamboozling most bankers and intimidating a few who got wise.

What do you suppose is going to happen to the gang that enriched itself at the expense of the banks, which are owned mainly by small shareholders? Will the criminals be brought into court, to be photographed and shamed? Are the ringleaders going to jail?

No. The corporation for which the perpetrators of the crime work merely has to give back the money it stole, and reimburse the Justice Department $750,000 to cover the cost of its low-paid lawyers and accountants who broke the case. The court has imposed a criminal fine of $2 million, the legal limit, which in a bank heist of this size is like putting a parking ticket on the Brink's getaway car.

No personal disgrace for the perpetrators; no jail terms; not a slap on one individual wrist. Putting on his most severe look, Attorney General Edwin Meese had the chutzpah to announce: "This makes it clear to the business world that white-collar crime will not be tolerated."

On the contrary, the pretense that no human beings operate E.F. Hutton makes it clear to the business world that if your company is shot through with managers involved in a huge swindle, not to worry—the Meese Justice Department will limit the liability to the corporation. None of the guilty officers will have to pay.

What excuse does the Justice Department's criminal division have to offer for this deal that was never offered such bank-robbing entrepreneurs as "Slick Willie"?

Albert Murray, the prosecutor in Scranton, Pa., who spent 18 months on the case, claims that naming and prosecuting individuals "could have taken us two to three years." That's a dandy reason for coddling white-collar criminals.

Justice officials in Washington have assured reporters that nobody in senior management was involved in the two-year, $10 billion operation, which suggests a degree of hands-off management that stretches credulity. But even if this operation had been run by a stock clerk and a messenger boy, should they not be brought to justice?

Well, um, goes a further explanation, some witnesses were given immunity from prosecution in return for their testimony to the grand jury, and it would not be fair to prosecute a few when all the other immunized wrongdoers in E.F. Hutton offices got off.

What kind of abuse of immunity is that? Prosecutors are often required to let small fry off in order to get evidence against bigwigs, but the notion that immunity for some makes prosecution of others "unfair" is ludicrous. Says Meese: "We are as aggressive in the investigation and prosecution of so-called white-collar crime as narcotics and organized crime." Based on the immunity whitewash and cosy plea-bargain in this case, that's great news for the Mafia.

A far-reaching misjudgment was made here that deserves a close look by the Senate Judiciary Committee in its coming confirmation hearings on Meese's deputy. Faceless companies don't filch money from banks; people in those companies do. There's a Sutton in Hutton who beat the rap.

Copyrights and Acknowledgments

Text Credits

Photo Credits

Chapter 11: Alice Neel, *Nancy and the Rubber Plant*, 1975; oil on canvas, 80″ × 36″; courtesy of Robert Miller Gallery, New York City. **Chapter 12:** Georgia O'Keefe, *Black Cross, New Mexico*, 1929; oil on canvas, 99 × 77.2 cm, the Art Institute Purchase Fund, 1943.95. ©1987 The Art Institute of Chicago; all Rights Reserved. **Chapter 13:** Giorgio De Chirico, *The Mystery and Melancholy of A Street*, 1914; oil on canvas, 34-¼″ × 28-⅛″; a private collection. **Chapter 14:** *Pair Statue of Mycerinus and His Queen*, Egyptian, Dynasty IV, 2599–2571 B.C., from Giza Schist; height: 54½ inches. Harvard University M.F.A. Expedition, 11.1738. Courtesy, Museum of Fine Arts, Boston. **Chapter 15:** *The Dinner Party*© Judy Chicago, 1979; mixed media sculpture, 48′ on each side; photo: Michael Alexander. **Chapter 16:** *Model House with Occupants*, Mexico, Nayarit; photo from HBJ files. **Chapter 17:** Andy Warhol, *Campbell's Soup*, 1965; oil on silkscreen on canvas, 36-½ × 24″; collection, the Museum of Modern Art, New York; Philip Johnson Fund. **Chapter 18:** Jasper Johns, *Target with Four Faces*, 1955; encaustic on newspaper over canvas, 26 × 26″ surmounted by four tinted plaster faces in wood box with hinged front; box, closed, 3-¾ × 26 × 3-½″; overall dimensions with box open, 33-⅜ × 26 × 3″; collection, the Museum of Modern Art, New York; gift of Mr. and Mrs. Robert C. Scull. **Chapter 19:** George Segal, *The Store Window*, plaster, wood, plexiglass, aluminum, venetian blinds, fluorescent light; 96 × 103 × 39-½″; Milwaukee Art Museum Collection, gift of Friends of Art. **Chapter 20:** The Limbourg brothers, *Month of June from Les Trés Riches Heures*, c. 1415; manuscript page; Musee Conde, Chantilly; Giraudon/Art Resource, New York.

B 9
C 0
D 1
E 2
F 3
G 4
H 5
I 6
J 7
8
9
0
1
2
3
4
5
6
7